The Open Handbook of Linguistic Data Management

Open Handbook in Linguistics Series

Series Editor: Heidi B. Harley

The Open Handbook of Linguistic Data Management, Andrea L. Berez-Kroeker, Bradley McDonnell, Eve Koller, and Lauren B. Collister

The Open Handbook of Linguistic Data Management

Edited by Andrea L. Berez-Kroeker, Bradley McDonnell, Eve Koller, and Lauren B. Collister
Foreword by Sarah G. Thomason

The MIT Press
Cambridge, Massachusetts
London, England

This book was set in Stone Serif and Stone Sans by Westchester Publishing Services. Printed and bound in the United States of America.

Library of Congress Cataloging-in-Publication Data

Names: Berez-Kroeker, Andrea L., editor. | McDonnell, Bradley James, editor. | Koller, Eve, editor. | Collister, Lauren B., editor.
Title: The open handbook of linguistic data management / edited by Andrea L. Berez-Kroeker, Bradley McDonnell, Eve Koller and Lauren B. Collister.
Description: Cambridge, Massachusetts : The MIT Press, [2021] | Series: Open handbooks in linguistics series | Includes bibliographical references and index.
Identifiers: LCCN 2020044363 | ISBN 9780262045261 (hardcover)
Subjects: LCSH: Computational linguistics. | Natural language processing (Computer science) | Data mining.
Classification: LCC P98 .O64 2021 | DDC 410.285—dc23
LC record available at https://lccn.loc.gov/2020044363

10 9 8 7 6 5 4 3 2 1

To our parents
Ellen and Bill
Bob and Kris
Nancy and Sanford
Greta and Tom
Jon and Chris

and to linguists, present and future.

Contents

Series Foreword

This series is intended to provide a high-quality venue for the publication of linguistics handbooks that is completely open access. These handbooks are edited by leaders in their subfield and contain a collection of articles by experts, presenting essential content on each topic in an accessible way. Each volume offers a comprehensive overview of the relevant subfield, presenting scholars and students with an overview of the main topics of focus in the area. Each article provides an in-depth guide to important issues and consensus results.

The open access publishing model is especially important for handbook volumes for the following reasons:

- Open handbooks represent a significant benefit to scholars around the world with limited or no access to commercial publishers' book products, because they summarize current research in a compact and organized fashion.

- Many linguist-hours are being poured into commercial for-profit handbook volumes, but their focus and direction is being at least partly driven by publishers' goals, rather than by the field's needs.

- Open exchange of ideas is essential to the advancement of science, and open access to our research products is therefore a key priority for our field, as for all scientific work.

We are proud to partner with the MIT Press to offer this resource to linguists all around the world.

Heidi B. Harley, series editor, on behalf of the editorial team

Foreword

Sarah G. Thomason

January 2020

This Handbook will be an invaluable addition to every linguist's toolbox. All linguists who deal with data (that is, all linguists, right?) need to know how to collect, transcribe, annotate, analyze, store, and share data, and we all need to pay close attention to ethical considerations that arise in most areas of data management. Those of us who do fieldwork must understand the importance of working with communities of language users, including issues of data ownership and communication. Those of us whose research connects with neighboring disciplines—psychology, anthropology, computer science, physics, and others—must ensure that our methods of data management are compatible with best practices in those disciplines as well as in linguistics. We all need to know about archiving our own data, and we all need to wrestle with the relatively new issue of citing data sets properly in our publications.

Some linguists are already managing their data in sophisticated ways, as the chapters in part II, "Data Management Use Cases," show. Others—and this is the category I belong to—know about a few of the topics covered here but are unfamiliar with most of them. As a fieldworker on a gravely endangered language, I know how to collect and transcribe data, and my field notes have a certain amount of metadata tagging. But my field notes, although digitized, don't even begin to approach the level of data management in any of the other ways discussed here. Phoneticians, computational linguists, and some fieldworkers, including authors in this Handbook, are way ahead of fieldworkers like me. But although some of us have more to learn than others, all linguists will learn vitally important things about data management from the chapters in this Handbook: about how to achieve the goals of FAIR, for instance, according to which research data should be findable, accessible, interoperable, and reusable; about different options for processing data, including organizing it for analysis; and about data management in single-language projects and data management in crosslinguistic studies.

I imagine the reason I was asked to write this foreword is that I wrestled with one aspect of this Handbook's topic back in 1994, when as the editor of *Language* I wrote an Editor's Department column that emphasized the need to ensure accuracy of the data in articles published in the journal. I consulted other journal editors and a few other colleagues who also felt strongly about accuracy before writing the column, and I found that they all shared my concerns—and that they all had horror stories similar to the ones I'd found in the course of my editing activities, among them misanalyzed data, data miscopied or even attributed to the wrong language, data extracted from a couple of examples and generalized to an entire language, and data drawn from secondary or tertiary sources without checking the original source. In those print-only days, it wasn't yet feasible for journals to publish supplementary materials online, so the author's examples comprised the only available data in a given article. Nowadays, with the possibility of publishing complete or at least extensive data sets online as supplementary materials, readers can check for consistency. With adequate metadata included, readers can also see how the data was collected and identify the original data sources, if relevant. Even this won't achieve the ideal, because (for instance) an author who was the only fieldworker for a particular language might have made mistakes in collecting the data. But it's a start.

Another issue, one that I didn't have to deal with as an editor but that I've certainly dealt with regularly as a teacher, is how to cite data sets. I've always given my students a template for citing my unpublished Montana Salish dictionary files, but readers of this Handbook will get a more informed view of best practices in the citation of published and unpublished data sets. Yet another issue is how to teach administrators the value of both published and unpublished data sets so that they can be taken into account in hiring, tenure, and promotion cases. These and the many other topics covered in the Handbook will contribute much to the enlightenment of all linguists who do data-intensive research.

I   Conceptual Foundations, Principles, and Implementation of Data Management in Linguistics

1 Data, Data Management, and Reproducible Research in Linguistics: On the Need for *The Open Handbook of Linguistic Data Management*

Andrea L. Berez-Kroeker, Bradley McDonnell, Lauren B. Collister, and Eve Koller

> Data have no value or meaning in isolation; they exist within a knowledge infrastructure—an ecology of people, practices, technologies, institutions, material objects, and relationships.
> —Borgman, *Big Data, Little Data, No Data*

1 Introduction: Why a "handbook" on data management in linguistics?

Data, in many forms and from many sources, underlie the discipline of linguistics. We feel it would not be hyperbolic to say that data are the lifeblood of research, and proper management of data collections is essential to the future of our field. From descriptive to theoretical work, from corpus-based to introspection-based inquiry, from quantitative to qualitative analysis, linguists rely on data every day. Although technologies for producing, managing, and analyzing vast amounts of data have developed in recent decades, we must recognize that linguists have long depended on data to develop generalizations and theories about the nature of human language, even since the field's earliest forays into philology. We see the potential of linguistic data to inform the field and inspire future scientific inquiry and innovation into the nature of humanity through language. To unlock this potential, data must be understandable, discoverable, reusable, shareable, remixable, and transformable. All data sets, from inscriptions on stone tablets to introspective grammaticality judgments to terabytes of recordings of sociolinguistic interviews, must be managed conscientiously and carefully. There is no doubt that managing data requires time, effort, and, in many cases, specialized training, and, as long as technology allows us to collect and use ever-increasing amounts of data, it likely always will.

In developing this Handbook, we followed Borgman's (2015:29) definition of *data* as "entities used as evidence of phenomena for the purposes of research or scholarship." This definition is particularly apt for the field of linguistics, with its many and diverse data sources and forms. We also know that data do not exist in a vacuum, as the epigraph to this chapter indicates. Data, especially in linguistics, are a representation of the people who provided them, so we need to take care to manage data in ethical ways that respect the dignity and autonomy of everyone involved. In this way, the same linguistic data can also serve humanistic endeavors.

Data management is far more than just storing data. It entails a broad range of tasks, as data need to also be collected, cataloged, organized, annotated, described, processed, analyzed, preserved, shared, and cited, if linguistics is to be an open and transparent social science. Implementing these procedures on a broad scale ultimately enables *reproducible research*, which the National Academies of Sciences, Engineering, and Medicine define as research that obtains "consistent results using the same input data; computational steps, methods, and code; and conditions of analysis" (National Academies of Sciences, Engineering, and Medicine 2019:6–7). The upshot of taking this approach is providing greater scientific accountability through facilitating access for other researchers to the data upon which research conclusions are based (see, e.g., Buckheit & Donoho 1995; de Leeuw 2001; Donoho 2010; Berez-Kroeker et al. 2018; see also Gawne & Styles, chapter 2, this volume, for more about reproducible research).

Historically, methods for managing data in our field have been developed somewhat in isolation. Different subfields, research labs, and even individual researchers have developed their own practices and expectations regarding proper management of data. Even though everyone who uses data must manage them at some level, the isolated development of data management methods has meant that there has been very little discussion across the discipline concerning any commonalities or shared best practices that might exist.

Furthermore, despite the time and care that goes into proper data management for the service of reproducible research, our field has only cursorily acknowledged the scholarly value of this work, electing instead to prioritize analysis and theory in publications. Reflecting deeply, either in writing or in practice, on one's data management practices as "meta-research" has been relegated to a second class of publication and scholarship, less overtly valued than a new research paper or book, and has not been widely encouraged outside of the development of specifically instructional textbooks. In fact, data management has often been thought of as an afterthought or as "somebody else's job," with the assumption that librarians or data specialists are the ones who will care for this work (Mons 2018:27).[1] While institutional support in maintaining data is crucial for its discovery and long-term survival, the researchers who collect the data are an essential part of the ongoing care and description of data, and their conscious involvement early on make these data sets usable for future scholars (Borgman 2015:275). Data work should be valued as highly as any other aspect of research.

Fortunately, the field is changing. We have begun to acknowledge the time, care, and expertise that go into proper data management in service of reproducible linguistics. Whereas previously the primary outputs of research were publications almost exclusively in the realm of theory and analysis, it is now increasingly common to see the data themselves as an important output, worthy of valuation in hiring, tenure, and promotion (see Alperin et al., chapter 13, this volume). For example, in 2018 the Linguistic Society of America adopted the Statement on the Evaluation of Language Documentation in Hiring, Tenure, and Promotion,[2] which gives suggestions for evaluating data and other non-traditional research outputs. Furthermore, it is not uncommon now to reflect on one's data management practices in writing, thus creating transparency about data sources and research methods.

Linguists are starting to confront data management issues and make visible the need for better data practices. More than 25 years ago, the issue of questionable data management practices compelled Sally Thomason, the then-editor of *Language*, a top journal in the field, to write a five-page column about her observations regarding the data behind articles submitted to the journal (Thomason

1994; see also Thomason, foreword, this volume). In it, she describes her realization that verifying all data for accuracy is too cumbersome a task to fall solely on the shoulders of the journal editor, and how, being human, she needed to "rely on the assumption that the data in accepted papers is generally correct." Nonetheless, she continues,

> Because of the traditionally high standards of *Language* regarding linguistic data, I have tried to identify cases where I may need to pay special attention to the accuracy of data: cases where the referees found problems with the data, where the data seems to be incompletely attested, or where a spot check reveals errors. When I began my term as editor, I expected that there would be cases of this kind from time to time. I did not expect that these cases would occur frequently—so frequently, in fact, that the assumption that the data in accepted papers is reliable began to look questionable. (409)

Thomason further notes that her concerns about data did not resonate particularly loudly. She provides as an example an interaction with an author in whose submission she found numerous small problems with the data (e.g., incorrect morphological parsing, incorrect glossing): "the author's response on being informed of the errors was disturbing. The most serious mistakes, I was told, came from a theoretical article that the author had cited extensively; it was the authors of that article who were responsible for the mistakes, not the author of the *Language* paper" (410).

Clearly, basing linguistic theory on inaccurate data is harmful for theory, especially when the theory builders are willing to look the other way when confronted with problematic data. Thomason compares the author's reaction to a "What's wrong with this picture?" children's puzzle:

> What you see in such a puzzle is a scene that looks perfectly normal at first glance, but that on closer inspection turns out to have impossible features, like a man sitting comfortably in a chair that has only one leg. A linguistic theory that rests on false or inadequate data is like the man in the chair with one leg: the support is illusory. (410)

Thomason then goes on to offer advice to authors regarding proper handling of the data that underlies publications. Even today her advice still rings true and has led to several recent initiatives. Beginning in the mid-2010s, researchers began to examine *transparency* in linguistics research. Transparency involves making details about research practices explicit in publications: some examples are whether data were collected directly by the author or taken from a published or archival source, whether data were collected in a lab or in the field, what hardware and software tools were used to collect and process data, presenting demographic information about language consultants or interviewees. Gawne et al. (2017) surveyed one hundred descriptive grammars for how forthcoming authors were about their data and collection methods; Schembri (2019) and Hochgesang (2019) both surveyed methodological transparency in sign language linguistics; Gawne et al. (2019) examines transparency of authors in gesture studies; Berez-Kroeker, Gawne et al. (2017) look at transparency in articles from nine journals across the discipline over a ten-year span. In all cases, it was found that authors' attention to conveying details about data and data collection to readers was lacking in some respect (see Berez-Kroeker et al. 2018 for a discussion). This includes, in particular, citing excerpts of data (e.g., interlinearized glossed text or other numbered examples) back to their sources in a way that makes them retrievable by a reader, especially when the data come from a source other than a traditional paper publication, such as a book or a journal article.

Also in the mid-2010s, more than forty linguists and data specialists participated in a multiyear project to develop standards and recommendations for one particular aspect of data management, the citation of data sets in linguistics publications.[3] This group produced a position paper identifying barriers to better citation and attribution of data as a part of linguistic research (Berez-Kroeker et al. 2018). Over time the group evolved into the 100+-member Linguistic Data Interest Group,[4] formed as part of the much larger Research Data Alliance,[5] an international organization that at the time of writing has over nine thousand members from 137 countries. Among the outputs of the project and the Research Data Alliance group are a guide to help linguists understand the value of data citation, known as *The Austin Principles of Data Citation in Linguistics* (Berez-Kroeker, Andreassen et al. 2017),[6] and a set of standardized formats for citing data sets in publications, known as the *Tromsø Recommendations for Citation of Research Data in Linguistics* (Andreassen et al., 2019; see Conzett & De Smedt, chapter 11, this volume).

2 About this Handbook

The editors and many authors in this Handbook have been and continue to be active participants in the Research Data Alliance Linguistic Data Interest Group. Our work with this group has made it clear that even 25 years after Thomason's editorial column, the discipline of linguistics still does not have a culture of broad and open discussion about data. Many linguists we have consulted with have lamented the lack of academic reward for data work, and still more have admitted that they simply do not know very much about how to manage their data in a way that ensures they will be citable, accurate, shareable, and sustainable, nor do they know much about their colleagues' practices in these areas. Despite the barriers, however, the reality of linguistic practice today is that most of us use data, most of us wish to use them thoroughly and carefully, many of us share data and code with our colleagues, and most of us have some methods for managing data, whether or not those methods have been codified. Thus, this Handbook grew out of a need to provide a forum in which researchers could share their data management practices with the aim of learning more about the current state of data work across the field. In this way, we hope that the discipline can reflect deeply about the past and present and foster an open conversation about the future of data work in linguistics.

This Handbook is divided into two parts. Each of the full-length chapters in part I delves into prominent issues surrounding data and data management. Part II consists of shorter *data management use cases*, each of which demonstrates a concrete application of the abstract principles of data management in specific studies, some actual and some hypothetical.

2.1 Part I overview

Because of the nature of linguistic study, creating reproducible data involves considerations such as the ethics of working with and for the benefit of human participants, copyright over creative works and expressions, and techniques for transforming data. These considerations come into play throughout the data management process, from the conception of the study to the development of mid-project file-naming conventions to the final steps of archiving, sharing, and tracking the use of data.

Chapters 2–4 provide details on important conceptual foundations of data management for linguistic data. In chapter 2, Lauren Gawne and Suzy Styles discuss the place of linguistics in the broader data movements across the social sciences, in which openness of data and transparency of research methodologies have become a central concern. In chapter 3, Jeff Good provides a comprehensive survey of the diversity of data types that are used within linguistics, including data that directly represent observable linguistic behavior as well as secondary data types used to support linguistic analysis. In chapter 4, Gary Holton, Wesley Y. Leonard, and Peter L. Pulsifer discuss the range of ethical considerations that are necessary when working with linguistic data of all kinds.

Chapters 5 and 6 present important principles in the implementation of data management. In particular, in chapter 5, Eleanor Mattern covers the life cycle of data, emphasizing consistency and a future-minded orientation while outlining best practices for creating sustainable, reusable, long-lasting data. In chapter 6, Na-Rae Han discusses the processes behind transforming raw data into usable data, including transliteration, loss, augmentation, and corruption of information, all while maintaining reversibility through judicious employment of version control.

Chapters 7, 8, and 9 provide helpful guidance to researchers planning to collect, manage, and share their own data. In chapter 7, Helene N. Andreassen gives advice on archiving one's research data, from preparing data for archiving to selecting an appropriate repository that ensures long-term preservation, retrieval, and visibility. In chapter 8, Susan Smythe Kung describes the process of developing a data management plan, a document that allows researchers to clearly articulate plans for data collection, processing, preservation, and sharing; data management plans are often required by funding organizations and can save researchers time, money, and frustration. In chapter 9, Lauren B. Collister provides a foundation for understanding copyright and its interaction with data, sharing practices to implement throughout the data life cycle to reduce legal barriers to the open sharing and publication of linguistic data.

Chapters 10 and 11 are about finding and reusing prepared linguistic data sets. In chapter 10, Laura Buszard-Welcher discusses how we can move human knowledge into the future by preserving linguistic data—both from living languages and from archived data from sleeping languages—for the long term. In chapter 11, Philipp Conzett and Koenraad De Smedt provide concrete guidance on how to properly cite data through bibliographic references and in-text citations.

Finally, chapters 12 and 13 discuss the valuation of the time and effort involved in data management as a research endeavor. In chapter 12, Robin Champieux and Heather L. Coates describe metrics that can reveal the usage of a data set and help tell the story of its impact beyond the initial research study. In chapter 13, Juan Pablo Alperin, Lesley A. Schimanski, Michelle La, Meredith T. Niles, and Erin C. McKiernan follow with an analysis of the role of data in review, promotion, and tenure based on their extensive corpus of documents.

2.2 Part II overview

The second part of the Handbook provides snapshots of current practices in the form of data management use cases. These come from a sampling of subfields and represent only a selection of the many data management practices available in the field. These use cases were selected to include both signed and spoken languages, and collectively they cover vast swaths of linguistic research, including sociolinguistics, discourse and conversation analysis, language documentation and description, language reclamation, historical linguistics and language change, first- and second-language acquisition, computational applications such as forced alignment and speech recognition, corpus linguistics, experimental linguistics, syntax, psycholinguistics, neurolinguistics, phonology, typology, and semantics. Many more use cases could have been included, and in an effort to make our data management practices and research methodologies more transparent, we editors encourage readers to start a practice of writing your own use cases.[7]

2.3 How to use this Handbook

The aim of the Handbook is to provide a snapshot into current practices, some of which are well established, while others are more cutting-edge. As this is, to our knowledge, the first handbook of its kind, it is not meant to serve as a comprehensive manual or textbook. Nonetheless, there are ways to incorporate the principles and practices described herein into one's own practices, research program, and/or career. We expect the Handbook to be valuable to a broad audience, including students, early career and seasoned researchers, and instructors at many levels. The Handbook can be used as a primary resource for classroom courses on linguistic data management, or selected chapters can serve as examples for management methods in courses focused on particular subfields.

Self-study is also possible, and we have developed an online open access companion course for this volume, available to anyone, free of charge, at http:// linguisticdatamanagement.org.[8] The online course contains synopses of each part I chapter, including keywords to learn, activities to reinforce principles of data management, suggestions for implementing better data management in one's career, quizzes to test your understanding, and cross-referenced links to relevant data management use cases.

3 Acknowledgments

We wish to offer our sincere gratitude to many people who made this Handbook possible. First, we thank the more than one hundred authors who willingly shared their knowledge and experience with our readers. Importantly, because this volume has a pan-linguistics scope, we needed to rely on many experts across the discipline to help us understand the "data scene" in different subfields, as well as identify appropriate authors to contribute. These "area advisors" included Claire Bowern, Kathleen Currie Hall, Na-Rae Han, Heidi B. Harley, Kristine Hildebrandt, Julie Hochgesang, Barb Kelly, Tyler Kendall, Emma Marsden, Steven Moran, and Luca Onnis. Emily Bender, Colleen Fitzgerald, Helen Aristar-Dry, and Eric Bakovic provided valuable discussion on the volume. Special thanks to Susan Smythe Kung, Gary Holton, Peter L. Pulsifer, and the participants in the Developing Standards for Data Citation and Attribution for Reproducible Research in Linguistics project.

Much appreciation goes to Heidi B. Harley and the entire editorial board of the Open Handbooks in Linguistics initiative for envisioning the series and giving us the opportunity to develop one of its first publications; we also thank Philip Laughlin, Alex Hoopes, Marc Lowenthal, and Anthony Zannino at MIT Press for their editorial support. Allison Silver Adelman of Silver Academic Editing provided professional assistance with the substantial task of consistently formatting fifty-five chapters and developing the index. Eve Koller, Shirley Gabber, and Dannii Yarbrough together developed the online companion course.

The editors would like to acknowledge the University Library System at the University of Pittsburgh for their support of Lauren B. Collister's editorial work on this volume, as well as their open access journal publishing services, which housed the platform for the management of chapter submission and reviews as part of their Scholarly Exchange service. We would also like to thank the Public Knowledge Project and the many volunteers who work on Open Journal Systems, which made our jobs as editors much easier and better organized. We also acknowledge the support of the Department of Linguistics and the College of Languages, Linguistics, and Literature at the University of Hawai'i at Mānoa and the Faculty of Culture, Language, and Performing Arts at Brigham Young University Hawai'i.

Finally, this material is based on work supported by the National Science Foundation under grants SMA-1649622 and SMA-1745249. Any opinions, findings, and conclusions or recommendations expressed in this material are those of the author(s) and do not necessarily reflect the views of the National Science Foundation.

Notes

1. We would like to emphasize that we reject the dual implication that data work is not part of linguistics research and that the contributions of librarians in describing, cataloging, preserving, and sharing research is somehow less valuable than that of researchers.

2. https://www.linguisticsociety.org/sites/default/files /Evaluation_Lg_Documentation.pdf.

3. This project was called Developing Standards for Data Citation and Attribution for Reproducible Research in Linguistics (NSF SMA-1447886). For details on activities see https://sites .google.com/a/hawaii.edu/data-citation/.

4. https://rd-alliance.org/groups/linguistics-data-ig.

5. https://rd-alliance.org/.

6. The Austin Principles (http://site.uit.no/linguisticsdatacita tion/) are essentially the FORCE11 *Joint Declaration of Data Citation Principles* (Martone 2014), annotated for linguistics.

7. If you would like to share your own linguistic data management use case, please upload it to our collection on Zenodo: https://zenodo.org/communities/ldmuc/.

8. For readers who are reading this in the print version, the Handbook itself is also available online, open access, and free of charge.

References

Andreassen, Helene N., Andrea L. Berez-Kroeker, Lauren Collister, Philipp Conzett, Christopher Cox, Koenraad De Smedt, Bradley McDonnell, and the Research Data Alliance Linguistic Data Interest Group. 2019. Tromsø recommendations for citation of research data in linguistics. *Research Data Alliance*. https://doi.org/10.15497/rda00040.

Berez-Kroeker, Andrea L., Helene N. Andreassen, Lauren Gawne, Gary Holton, Susan Smythe Kung, Peter Pulsifer, Lauren B. Collister, The Data Citation and Attribution in Linguistics Group, and the Linguistics Data Interest Group. 2017. *The Austin Principles of Data Citation in Linguistics*. Version 1.0. http://site.uit.no/linguisticsdatacitation/austinprinciples/. Accessed March 17, 2020.

Berez-Kroeker, Andrea L., Lauren Gawne, Barbara F. Kelly, and Tyler Heston. 2017. A survey of current reproducibility practices in linguistics journals, 2003–2012. https://sites.google.com/a/hawaii.edu/data-citation/survey. Accessed March 17, 2020.

Berez-Kroeker, Andrea L., Lauren Gawne, Susan Kung, Barbara F. Kelly, Tyler Heston, Gary Holton, Peter Pulsifer, et al. 2018. Reproducible research in linguistics: A position statement on data citation and attribution in our field. *Linguistics* 56:1–18. https://doi.org/10.1515/ling-2017-0032.

Borgman, Christine L. 2015. *Big Data, Little Data, No Data: Scholarship in the Networked World*. Cambridge, MA: MIT Press.

Buckheit, Jonathan B., and David L. Donoho. 1995. WaveLab and reproducible research. In *Wavelets and Statistics*, ed. Anestis Antoniadis and Georges Oppenheim, 55–81. New York: Springer.

De Leeuw, Jan. 2001. Reproducible research: The bottom line. *UCLA Department of Statistics Papers*. http://escholarship.org/uc/item/9050x4r4. Accessed March 17, 2020.

Donoho, David L. 2010. An invitation to reproducible computational research. *Biostatistics* 11:385–388.

Gawne, Lauren, Barbara F. Kelly, Andrea L. Berez-Kroeker, and Tyler Heston. 2017. Putting practice into words: The state of data and methods transparency in grammatical descriptions. *Language Documentation and Conservation* 11:157–189.

Gawne, Lauren, Chelsea Krajcik, Helene N. Andreassen, Andrea L. Berez-Kroeker, and Barbara F. Kelly. 2019. Data transparency and citation in *Gesture*. *Gesture*.

Hochgesang, Julie A. 2019. Sign language description: A Deaf retrospective and application of best practices from language documentation. Paper presented at the Signed and Spoken Language Linguistics Conference, Osaka.

Martone, M., ed. 2014. *Data Citation Synthesis Group: Joint Declaration of Data Citation Principles*. San Diego: FORCE11. https://doi.org/10.25490/a97f-egyk, https://www.force11.org/group/joint-declaration-data-citation-principles-final.

Mons, Barend. 2018. *Data Stewardship for Open Science: Implementing FAIR Principles*. New York: Taylor and Francis. https://doi.org/10.1201/9781315380711.

National Academies of Sciences, Engineering, and Medicine. 2019. *Reproducibility and Replicability in Science*. Washington, DC: The National Academies Press. https://www.nap.edu/catalog/25303/reproducibility-and-replicability-in-science.

Schembri, Adam. 2019. Making visual languages visible: Data and methods transparency in sign language linguistics. Paper presented at Theoretical Issues in Sign Language Research Conference, Hamburg, September 26–28.

Thomason, Sarah. 1994. The editor's department. *Language* 70 (2): 409–413.

2   Situating Linguistics in the Social Science Data Movement

Lauren Gawne and Suzy Styles

1   Introduction

Linguists spend a lot of time working with data, but we do not always give much thought to the role that data plays in building the larger research culture in our field. We can learn a lot about good data management in our own discipline by learning from what is happening in related fields, both in terms of innovations and new benchmarks, as well as when things have not gone right. We look at how data have been conceptualized and managed in other areas of the social sciences, particularly social psychology, and how current attitudes are shaping the future of research. The fundamental theme of this discourse is the centrality of openness, both in terms of transparency of methodology and making primary data more accessible to people beyond the original researchers. This move toward open research aims to reduce biases, both for individual researchers and for the discipline, and encourages more considered data collection and presentation.

We understand that these developments can feel challenging, particularly to researchers who have already established their workflow. Researchers can feel very protective of the data they collected, and sometimes this is for very good reasons. As we will see, the discussions around open research in social psychology have, at times, exacerbated tensions and left some researchers feeling singled out. We believe that linguists can learn from social psychology about new movements toward good open data practice, but we can also learn about building an open research culture that is inclusive and encouraging.

Building an open approach to research is the most ethical way to respect the contribution of the individuals who take the time to participate in your work, by making sure their data contribute as much as possible

to global research outcomes. Making data accessible also brings its own rewards, as openness allows linguists to receive credit for their data collections, increases the likelihood of subsequent research on the original data, and provides incentives via increased citations.

In this chapter, we begin by positioning linguistics within the social sciences, to make a clearer case for what lessons other areas of the discipline can offer us (section 2). We then look at research replicability and reproducibility, particularly with regard to how they are conceptualized in social psychology (section 3), and at the data crisis that has dominated methodological discussions in social psychology, focusing on stories that highlight key issues when research does not have an open foundation (section 4). We then address how these lessons from social psychology apply to our own research through answering a series of frequently raised concerns about open data (section 5).

Many of the issues discussed here are by no means unique to social psychology. We have decided to focus on this area for three reasons. The first is that that data social psychologists work with is of similar complexity to that in linguistics, in that it is data about human behavior that is often nuanced and context-dependent. The second is that the public discussions being had by social psychologists, and the changes in research behavior being implemented, are further along than discussions and changes in other fields of social science. The third reason is that coauthor Suzy Styles works across linguistics and social psychology and is in a good position to "translate" the lessons of social psychology for linguists.

We have also seen discussions of issues regarding a lack of transparent research in other social science subfields including education (Makel & Plucker 2014), sports psychology (Schweizer & Furley 2016), and management (Goldfarb & King 2016; Bergh et al. 2017); as well as scientific fields including medicine (Goldacre 2010), neuroscience (Grabitz et al. 2018), and behavioral ecology (Jennions & Møller 2003); as well as in the broader literature on the scientific method (Baker 2016; Ioannidis 2005, 2012; Zwaan et al. 2018). The social sciences are in a unique position to consider these issues, given that our work inherently focuses on the nature of human behavior (Bollen et al. 2015).

We are writing this chapter together as two researchers who both care about the thoughtful use of data in linguistic research, but come from different research traditions and subfields of linguistics. Lauren Gawne's research is in the language documentation and description model, mostly focusing on Tibet-Burman languages of Nepal. Suzy Styles is a psycholinguist, whose work mostly focuses on cross-sensory processing, particularly in infants and children. We have also worked collaboratively on experimental research investigating the cross-sensory processing of lexical tone for speakers of Syuba and English.

2   Linguistics as a social science

Linguists use data to try to understand the nature of language and how it is used. The next chapter in this Handbook will give an illustration of the breadth of data that is included in linguistics. This heterogeneity is a strength of the discipline, but it also means that there is greater imperative to think critically about the role of data within our work.

Loosely defined, the social sciences are those academic disciplines interested in the way people relate to each other and that use empirical data to address their research questions. Linguistics can also be conceived of as a discipline within the humanities, in its exploration of the nature of human society and culture, or as a discipline straddling the humanities and social sciences. In this chapter we frame linguistics as a social science, because it is worth thinking critically about the nature of the materials on which we base our argumentation about language. Placing linguistics within the paradigm of social sciences centers this data and allows us to consider parallels with other disciplines within the social sciences. The social sciences, such as psychology and linguistics, differ from the "hard sciences" in the nature of the data we collect. Because the social sciences deal with people, the data are typically noisy, complex, error-prone, and inconsistent—just like the people they

represent. This makes the task of analyzing human data notoriously complex (Lykken 1991:4). One way to manage this complexity of data is to be transparent about it. This has been happening in the social sciences. Likewise, the field of linguistics is increasingly engaged in a conversation about the nature of linguistic data and how it is managed. Indeed, this Handbook is a testament to how much ground there is to cover in this discussion.

Questions about the transparency of linguistic data have been raised since at least the 1990s: Thomason voiced concerns about the frequency of erroneous data in publications in an editorial for *Language* (1994), and around the same time, Himmelmann (1998) argued that language documentation and description can only be successful if the claims made about a particular language can be verified by others—that is, if readers are allowed access to the data from which conclusions are drawn. The core argument made by both authors was that research is more reliable if the methods and the underlying data are transparent.

Despite the clarity of these arguments twenty years ago, progress in linguistics has been limited. Berez-Kroeker et al. (2017) surveyed 270 articles from nine linguistics journals published between 2003 and 2012 and found that 60% of articles published did not clearly report the source of the underlying data. Of the 40% that did clarify their data sources, 25% relied on already published data, leaving fewer than 15% of articles disclosing the source of primary data. With such a low rate of data citation, it is hard for the readers of a linguistics paper to establish for themselves (a) whether examples cited in the main text contain errors; (b) whether examples cited in the text are representative of the data set as a whole; and (c) whether the sampling conditions of the original data set qualify or constrain their interpretation. Without the ability to check original data sources, it is therefore unclear how a reader should interpret the conclusions drawn by the original author.

With a growing awareness of the importance of data to the transparency of linguistic analysis, a US National Science Foundation project was set up to bring together over forty linguists from across the world to think about the future of linguistic data. The outcome of three years of these meetings was the paper "Reproducible Research in Linguistics: A Position Statement on Data Citation and Attribution in Our Field" (Berez-Kroeker et al. 2018). This position statement argues:

Linguistic data are the very building blocks of our field. Given that linguistic theories need to be borne out through data, we believe that linguistic data are important resources in their own right and represent valuable assets for the field. Therefore, our field needs to accept responsibility for the proper documentation, preservation, attribution, and citation of these assets. (11)

While linguists are beginning to discuss how we manage and share our research and data, this conversation is further along in other fields. The open access movement, which began slowly in the late 1990s, has changed the publishing landscape with open access journals (Joseph 2013) and now has its sights on open data practice (Kitchin 2014; SPARC, n.d.). See Collister (chapter 9, this volume) for more discussion about the legal issues regarding open data. Open science now includes a broad range of practices, including open data infrastructure, accessibility of data, impact of research, and collaboration (Fecher & Friesike 2014).

Along with open data has come an important conversation about ethical use of data. In social psychology, the argument can be made that participants' efforts are not fully respected if transparency around data and analysis is lacking. While we do not talk about ethical issues very directly in this chapter, we acknowledge this conversation always needs to be kept in mind and find a good basic starting point to be the European Commission's H2020 data management plan guidelines that data should be "as open as possible, as closed as necessary" (H2020 Programme 2016). For a more detailed discussion of ethics and data in linguistics see Holton, Leonard, and Pulsifer (chapter 4, this volume).

3 Replicability, reproducibility, and lucky-cowboy research

Here we revisit *reproducibility* and *replicability* (see Berez-Kroeker et al., chapter 1, this volume) and examine the differences between them: Reproducibility is the use of existing materials and methods to check whether the original conclusions are supported by the evidence, and replicability is the application of the original methodology to a new sample. This allows researchers to check whether the conclusions of the original paper hold true for a different set of data or a different group of people. In other words, is the result generalizable to people who were not included in the original study?

To borrow an analogy introduced by Styles (2018), imagine we asked one hundred cowboys to flip a coin one hundred times each (figure 2.1). The coin is normal, evenly weighted, and has a picture of a head on only one side. It's pretty clear that if none of the cowboys are cheating, the typical response will be fifty heads. If we

Figure 2.1
Coin-flipping cowboys.
Source: Illustration by Dannii Yarbrough.

asked all of the cowboys to line up in a barn according to how many heads they got, we'd get a big bunch of cowboys in the middle of the barn (the 50% mark) and fewer and fewer cowboys as they got near the walls. Whenever we sample from human populations, the people we sample could be anywhere along this line of cowboys. They could be typical cowboys near the middle of the barn, or they might be outliers at the fringes of the barn—lucky cowboys—whose experience of coin flipping is quite unusual. In linguistics, the same logic can be applied to the data upon which inferences are drawn—whether it is sentences selected from a corpus of closed-captioned news reports or acoustic analysis of whether different radio show hosts speak with vocal fry. The sentences selected for analysis might be more or less representative of the corpus, and the voices selected for comparison might be more or less representative of radio hosts, or of people in general.

In the social sciences, where conclusions are made on the basis of data, both replicability and reproducibility are important, because they allow us to independently verify the claims made.

3.1 Replicability

Replicating a study is the process of checking whether the data are representative in general (are the cowboys in this barn similar to cowboys in other barns?). Although replication may be seen as a fundamental tool of the research enterprise, it does not occur particularly frequently in the social sciences. Makel, Plucker, and Hegarty (2012) looked at articles published in one hundred journals between 1900 and 2012 and found that only around 1% were replications. Central to this dispreference for replication studies is a focus on novelty of results (Fanelli 2011; Ferguson & Heene 2012). This has driven an interest in *conceptual replications*, which test hypotheses from earlier studies with a different methodological setup (e.g., with a different cohort of participants or different stimuli) (Schmidt 2009:96). In social psychology it is not uncommon for a single paper to include several experiments that are conceptual replications of a core study, with the aim of demonstrating the robustness of the underlying principle. Although we might think that several replications with small modifications would lead to higher likelihood of direct replication, Kunert (2016) demonstrated that papers originally published with multiple conceptual replications did not replicate more frequently

or reliably than other studies. In section 4.1, we discuss the "file drawer problem" as one possible reason for this.

3.2 Reproducibility

Reproducing a study is the process of checking whether mistakes were made (are the cowboys in the barn are standing in the right spot?) and whether the data selected for analysis are representative of the complete data set (were the cowboys representative of everybody the barn?).

Ideally, research should be both reproducible and replicable, but documenting human behavior, particularly context-specific behavior outside of an experimental setting, can make replication unfeasible. Reproducibility is particularly useful for contexts where even having access to the original methodology makes it unlikely you will be able to replicate the original research. Reproducibility requires that the data are made available. This is not always easy. Wicherts et al. (2006) contacted authors of 141 papers published by the American Psychological Association in 2004, requesting access to their data sets for reproduction of the results, as part of a meta-analysis of outliers in research findings. Although the American Psychological Association has a policy all authors sign stating that they will share data for reproduction, Wicherts et al. only received data sets from 27% of authors. Reproducibility needs to be built on proactive sharing of data, as it is demonstrably difficult to obtain data after a study is published.

Although the terminology of replicating and reproducing studies is not commonly used in linguistics, table 2.1 contains examples of each of these types of research, applied to two famous linguistics studies.

In these examples, reproducing a study allowed errors to be detected and corrected, leading to a more detailed data set in the public domain, and replicating a study led to greater clarity in the sociodemographic characterization of New York speech, along with documenting shifts over time. It is important to note that these kinds of follow-ups can only be performed if (a) the source of the data is clearly described; (b) the methods for acquiring the data are clearly described; (c) the original data sources are accessible; (d) details about selection/inclusion/exclusion are clearly described; and (e) statistical or measurement procedures are clearly described. As such, transparent methods and data citation are central to reproducing and replicating research.

Table 2.1

Examples of reproducing and replicating studies in linguistics

	Reproducing a study	Replicating a study
Original study	Peterson and Barney's American English Vowels (1952)	Labov's Fourth Floor Study ([1966] 2006)
What was done in the original study?	Peterson and Barney recorded the voices of 76 speakers of American English reading from standardized word lists. Each speaker read each word twice. Speakers included adult men, adult women, and children (both male and female). They plotted the F1 against the F2 of individual vowels to show the distribution of formants among speakers of the same language—including speakers with different sized vocal tracts.	Labov visited three large department stores in Manhattan, known to be used by people in different income brackets. He asked shop staff to direct him to a department he previously established was on the fourth floor. He pretended not to hear and asked them to repeat. He noted down the number of times each person used a rhotic pronunciation for the /r/ at the end of each word and compared the rate of rhotic use across the three stores. Labov found that staff at the three stores differed in how often they used rhotic "r". The most expensive store used "r" (the prestige variety) the most often, and the least expensive store used the "r" the least.
Follow-ups	Watrous (1991); Boersma and Weenink (2013); Barreda (2016)	Fowler (1986); Mather (2011)
What did they do? What was different?	Two published versions of the key figure contained discrepancies. Watrous (1991) requested original data, which was shared by Mattingly. A corrected figure was produced and published alongside complete data tables for F0, F1, F2, and F3. Subsequently, data tables were integrated into Praat software by Boersma and Weenink (2013) for graphing. Barreda (2016) included the data tables in a graphing tool in the R package phonTools.	Different linguists returned to the same stores in Manhattan twenty and forty years after the original study. Labov's rapid anonymous survey technique was followed precisely. Between studies, the lowest prestige store closed down, so a substitute store servicing the same socioeconomic status (SES) was chosen in each of the replications. Additional demographic characteristics were recorded in the replication samples.
Were the follow-ups successful?	A more accurate version of the figure was produced. Subsequent researchers can create their own figures from the original data sets using two open source software systems or adapt the graphing code for new purposes.	The same general pattern of rhotic use was found in each replication, with more rhotic "r" in the high-prestige store than in the others. The two replications showed higher rates of rhotic use overall, with steady increase between studies.
What was learned?	1. Errors in original publication were minor and did not undermine the core claims made. 2. Values in the follow-up paper are graphed correctly. 3. Full data set was published. 4. Inclusion of F0 and F3 along with F1 and F2 data allow future users to perform novel analyses/graphing.	1. Labov's method is reliable for eliciting SES differences 2. Labov's sample was representative of general patterns in New York, and those patterns persist—albeit with changes. 3. New York has undergone a gradual shift toward the prestige form over time.
What was required for this follow-up?	1. Clear descriptions of original data source 2. Access to original data (numerical) 3. Clear descriptions of inclusion/exclusion process 4. Clear descriptions of the F1/F2 measurement process 5. Clear descriptions of computations/analyses	1. Clear descriptions of the stores and their SESs 2. Clear descriptions of the elicitation method 3. Clear descriptions of inclusion/exclusion process 4. Clear descriptions of counts and statistical analysis 5. Clear descriptions of the participant demographics

We do not want to imply that a lack of openness about methods means the authors are intentionally hiding anything. Brown et al. (2014) found that only around 30% of decisions about data sampling were clearly articulated in a sample of over 1,000 research publications. People are doing good research, but the whole field has to value openness to normalize best practice in data management. It is also worth stating here that openness is not a binary state. It is possible to have very transparent methods, but only share summary data, and conversely, it is possible to share all the primary data generated by research, but provide insufficient detail regarding how those data were collected or how measurements were performed.

Some work focuses on the reproducibility of the methods of a study or the reproducibility of the results. Goodman, Fanelli, and Ioannidis (2016) also discuss *inference reproducibility*, which is perhaps even more elusive. Different researchers can draw different inferences from the results of a single study, meaning it is possible for someone to replicate both the method and results of an original study, but still not agree to replicate the inference of what those results mean.

4   The data crisis in social psychology

In 2011 a paper emerged that shook the foundations of research methods in social psychology and carries a lesson for all of the social sciences. A paper by Bem (2011) appeared to show evidence of precognition—a psychic power that allowed people's decisions to be influenced by a stimulus that was shown to them *after* they had already made their choice. The paper was peer-reviewed, published in a flagship journal, and, to all appearances, conducted using rigorous controls and standard research methods of the day. The data appeared sound, and yet the conclusions they seemed to support couldn't be physically possible. The paper, and several papers published in its immediate aftermath (LeBel & Peters 2011; Wagenmakers et al. 2011; Galak et al. 2012), indicated that something was wrong with the standard methods that were common throughout the field of psychological research. The lack of transparency in reporting the complete research cycle meant a single spurious result (a lucky cowboy) could be presented in isolation from a mountain of contradictory evidence (all of the other cowboys in the barn). In other words, the result that was selected for publication was not representative of all of the tests that were conducted.

In the wake of this paper, some theorists argued that biases in the existing literature mean we should expect the replication process to call the reputation of all research in the field into question (Ioannidis 2012; Johnson et al. 2017). This has come to be known as the replication crisis (Ioannidis 2012; Loken & Gelman 2017; Zwaan et al. 2018; although see Nelson, Simmons, and Simonsohn 2018 for the more optimistic framing of this as a "renaissance"). These discussions are the most recent part of a longer conversation about the shortcomings of research methods and transparency in social psychology, since Elms's discussion about the "crisis of confidence" in social psychology research methods in 1975 (see also Sterling 1959; Cohen 1962; Walster & Cleary 1970; Lykken 1991; as well as Feynman's famous 1974 denouncement of social psychology as "cargo cult science"). For a more detailed, but still very accessible, discussion of the recent period in social psychology, see Chambers (2017) and Nelson, Simmons, and Simonsohn (2018).

Next, we review some of the major themes in the ongoing conversation about data in social psychology. We chose these topics because we believe they are of particular value to linguists. The first is what is known as the file drawer problem (Rosenthal 1979), with unpublished data creating an untold story of the field. The second is selective interpretation of results. In both of these sections we draw parallels for linguists about how we work with data, but we also draw lessons on how to move the field forward in the most positive way. A lot of the discussion around methodology in the field of social psychology has led to cultural clashes and resentment as people feel that their research integrity is called into question (Meyer & Chabris 2014; Fetterman & Sassenberg 2015).

We focus on scenarios where researchers believe themselves to be working in the best interest of advancing research, rather than egregious misuse of data and outright fraud (but see Simonsohn 2013; Chambers 2017: chapter 5 for examples of this). Research transparency can also help reduce cases of fraud, as well as help well-intentioned researchers find errors in their own data (Nuijten et al. 2016).

4.1   File drawer problem and the shoebox of tapes

In the 1970s Rosenthal coined a phrase for the plethora of psychology studies that are conducted but never published: the file drawer problem (Rosenthal 1979). At the time, he was interested in whether statistical methods can be used to estimate (and potentially correct for) gaps in the published literature. But where do these gaps come from? Let's say 20 researchers in different psychology departments conduct an identical study on whether women and men differ on some arbitrary variable—say, time to respond to e-mails. If, simply by chance, one of the researchers finds a significant difference, this constitutes a novel, positive finding, and the researcher might successfully publish that result. The other 19 researchers are simply less likely to publish. The failure to publish is related to explicit biases in high-profile publication outlets where results showing no difference are less desirable than novel findings of significant difference. What this means for the scientific record is that a single published study can represent an outlier (a lucky cowboy) from the total body of research that was conducted, and the scientific literature can become skewed by the absence of alternative accounts.

Historically, page and data storage limits in high-ranking publication outlets have meant that many details of the research cycle had to be omitted from the primary publication. Primary data is one of the parts of the research cycle that is not included in a traditional journal article. When it comes to the types of articles that are published, there is a long tradition of preference for novelty and bias against negative results in publication, from editors (Neuliep & Crandall 1990) and reviewers (Neuliep & Crandall 1993). Researchers are selective in their publication outputs: researchers are less likely to write up research with data that has a null result than research with a strong result (Franco, Malhotra, & Simonovits 2014), or underreport non-significant conditions in multipart research processes (Franco, Malhotra, & Simonovits 2016). In addition, the rise of competitive funding as a metric for success has also left little room for non-novel results and replications (Lilienfeld 2017). Selective reporting can therefore be understood as rational response to a biased incentive system, and valuing null results and replications (Koole & Lakens 2012) can ensure that large volumes of potentially valuable data may see the light of day.

Recent large-scale replication projects have demonstrated that when the literature is biased in this way, less than half of published psychology papers present effects that can be replicated (Open Science Collaboration 2015; Klein et al. 2018), which weakens public confidence in the credibility of social psychology, affecting the entire field. Although the final effect is the nature of what is published, the only way to address this problem is to change research priorities and publication practices including the management and publication of data. By ensuring research has greater transparency for the entire research cycle—from hypothesis generation to methods and materials, through to publication of full and complete data sets—we can make sure that research does not languish in the file drawer.

Many linguists will be familiar with the idea that it is easier to publish work with a certain kind of theoretical "hook" or empirical novelty, and this may bias researchers to focus on linguistic features deemed more "exotic," or languages that were previously undocumented. Publication bias aside, linguists, like other social scientists, often collect far more data than they include in their published articles, be they recorded audio, transcriptions, a collection of sentences extracted from a corpus. The average linguistics paper or grammar contains only a summary of the rich original data—this is, after all the purpose of research, to synthesize information so that insights can be drawn about the nature of language, or the way people use it. However, each data source contains vastly more information than the narrow range of features it was originally evaluated for, and these details may be of interest to generations of future linguists. As the majority of papers fail to disclose the source of their primary data, and those that do rarely make the primary data available, this represents a similar problem to the file drawer of the social sciences—although perhaps better characterized as the shoebox of tapes on the shelf.

In response to these changing priorities, novel solutions have emerged for how the outputs of research can be archived by researchers themselves. Digital archives such as the Dataverse family of institutional repositories allow researchers to upload a variety of digital file formats and create their own metadata records. This means that researchers can archive digital materials from digital documents, to video/audio files, raw text, or numeric data. Free-to-use repositories such as GitHub allow researchers to share the code used to run or analyze their studies. Many of the new generation of repositories are digital object identifier (DOI) granting (meaning that digital documents have a unique digital identifier, and can be cited) with clear time-stamping and transparent version control. Some research archiving hubs, such as the Open Science Framework (OSF) allow in-platform browsing of content, multiuser functionality, and integrated links to other archives.

This generation of user-driven archiving solutions allows researchers to collate content along the entire research pipeline and to control access permissions at different stages of the research cycle. With contemporary tools such as these at their disposal, researchers can clear the content from the file drawer more effectively than ever before, even for data sets that are not reflected in traditional, peer-reviewed journal articles. This means that researchers can get credit for the work of creating the data, where in a traditional model of novelty, it may not have ever been made available.

To give an example from our own research, we used OSF to create an archive of project materials for a study investigating links between the senses in groups of people who use different languages (Styles & Gawne 2017). Despite being based in different countries for the majority of the project, the multiuser interface allowed both authors to upload elements to the archive, create metadata descriptions of the contents, and collate the collection in real time. We archived our test materials during the planning phase of the project. These materials included audio files prepared in the lab, as well as audio files generated in the field, and photographs of the original stimuli used in the study. After collecting data, we uploaded data tables for the individual responses to our task, anonymized to protect the identity of individuals. When we submitted our first manuscript for peer review, we were able to create a private link for anonymous peer review, ensuring that our reviewers could access all of our materials and data during the review process. When our first article was accepted for publication, we updated the status of the repository to "public," and the links that appear in the article allow any reader to access the full set of data and materials. Our OSF repository[1] also contains a second data set that is currently private while we finalize the manuscript for submission, as well as the materials, analysis plan, and a preregistration of hypotheses for a third study that is currently in progress. As

this example demonstrates, self-archiving can support a transparent research process, with full data available for review. Furthermore, the OSF system allows "blind" review links where the data we present are available for checking within the existing double-blind peer-review system (reproducing results, or conducting alternative analysis to see whether the results hold under different circumstances). An added bonus of this workflow is that our research outputs are deposited in such a way that if one of the studies does not result in a traditional publication, the data become research outputs in their own right and will remain public and accessible: We are effectively clearing out the file drawer as we go along. Furthermore, as we create these archives, the DOI-generating repositories allow our documents to be uniquely identified so that future researchers can conduct novel research using our tools, materials, or data, and their engagement in our outputs will be reflected by straightforward citations that link back to the data source.

While not all projects in linguistics will benefit from drawing on all of these features, the development of these tools for social sciences research has broad implications for the field. Some fields of linguistics have embraced broad and accessible data sharing and archiving platforms, including child language acquisition via CHILDES, the Child Language Data Exchange System (MacWhinney 2000); corpus linguistics, including tools such as the International Corpus of English,[2] and researchers in the field of language documentation and description (see Salffner 2015 and Caballero 2017 as examples, although Gawne et al. 2017 and Thieberger 2017 note inconsistency in this field).

Because archiving your data is a kind of publication, this kind of digital filing allows you to acknowledge all of the work that you do. Many researchers in the social sciences have multiple sections in their curriculum vitae to address all of their different outputs, including open data sets, and preprints.

Alongside these developments we also need to advocate for structural solutions to the historic biases that have arisen alongside traditional publication formats. As a community of practice, we can also reward people who value a more transparent and open research environment by citing their outputs and acknowledging the important work they do. In 2018, the Linguistic Society of America adopted its "Statement on Evaluation of Language Documentation for Hiring, Tenure, and Promotion,"[3] which provides a good example of valuing data, although we would argue that it is relevant to all subfields, not just language documentation. When hiring, we can create job descriptions that explicitly value open data principles; we can encourage junior researchers to include more publication types in their curriculum vitae; and if we truly come to value these practices, we can reward those with the best practice in open data with the jobs and promotions that their commitment to evidence deserves.

Get your data out of the file drawer and publish it—your data deserve it, and so do you. Where possible, make these collections open, or at least discoverable to other researchers. Using one of the new digital archiving platforms with DOIs or other stable citation practices means that you can be credited for the work of building the original data. The easier part of the journey is to build archiving into your current and future research.

4.2 Selective interpretation and how we choose data for analysis

In 2016, Brian Wansink, then the head of Cornell's Food and Brand Lab, blogged about "The Grad Student Who Never Said No" in which he commented on the difference between two junior researchers in his team. He had offered them both the chance to work on "a data set from a self-funded, failed study which had null results," claiming, "there's got to be something we can salvage because it's a cool (rich & unique) data set." He praised the doctoral student who agreed to work with the data for her ability to "make hay while the sun shines" (producing five papers in the course of a six-month stint in the lab), while dismissing the attitude of the postdoc who refused, produced a smaller number of papers, and left academia. Early commenters on the blog generously assumed the story was a work of academic satire, a cruel parable designed to highlight a broken reward system in academia. Wansink clarified his position as a serious commentary, leading other researchers to query four "buffet" study papers from the data set (Just, Siğirci, & Wansink 2014, 2015; Siğirci & Wansink 2015; Kniffin, Siğirci, & Wansink 2016), as well as other work from Wansink (see van der Zee, Anaya, & Brown 2017). Because the data looked at consumption of pizza, this scandal is sometimes affectionately known as "Pizza-gate." Cornell's Food and Brand Lab specialized in consumer behavior as a subdiscipline of social psychology. The discussion that has come out of this controversy has touched on practices common across social psychology.

For those familiar with how statistical analyses can be manipulated to provide more desirable outcomes, Wansink's blog post was not about a diligent student making the best of a situation, but a demonstration of data manipulation. Wansink encouraged cherry-picking, or using only selected subsets of data that skew toward the preferred outcome, as well as p-hacking and HARKing (or hypothesizing after results are known). The term *p-hacking* refers to running statistics over a variety of subsets of the data until the desired statistical significance is achieved. Statistical significance is a desired aim in the quest for novelty in quantitative research. It is unclear how common this practice is, but meta-analysis suggests it is likely to be common (Head et al. 2015). HARKing is the practice of retroactively coming up with a hypothesis once a test with statistical significance has been identified (Murphy & Aguinis 2017), for example, stating that the hypothesis was about how much pizza women ate in a restaurant in particular conditions, when the original data included both men and women. These practices are known, but their prevalence is hard to quantify without transparent and open research practices. The difference is that Wansink talked about this publicly.

This has led to further unravelling of Wansink's work in other studies, including at least 17 retractions (Retraction Watch 2018), charges of research misconduct, and eventual dismissal. Some say that Wansink has become a scapegoat for researchers trained in an era when these kinds of research practices were more common. The real problem was that he did not recognize the errors of his research practices and appeared to actively obstruct researchers who were interested in actively reproducing his work to find potential corrections for the published record. Although the case has revealed academic misconduct, the case was exacerbated by problems in record keeping. If Wansink had kept better records about how the data had been handled in each of his papers, further investigations may not have been necessary.

The literature on these data inflation practices (not just Wansink's) are consistent in their recommendations as to how to avoid these practices. Central is the need to educate researchers on good data practice. One key feature of the replication crisis is that good data practice can be difficult if the research environment rewards bad behavior (Guest 2016). Other recommendations include ways to limit the temptation to inflate results for novel outcomes and instead reward good data management. The first of these is giving researchers credit for publishing their data and methods. The second is to give greater value to replication. We have discussed both of these herein. The third is preregistering methods and hypotheses, to prevent the temptation to diverge from the original course of study.

Preregistration is the submission of the methods and tools that are intended to be used, before the data collection is carried out (Mellor & Nosek 2018). This limits "researcher degrees of freedom," by requiring the researcher to commit to a plan of analysis before the work begins (Wicherts et al. 2016). There is still scope for exploratory research, as Nelson, Simmons, and Simonsohn (2018:519) note, "preregistrations do not tie researchers' hands, but merely uncover readers' eyes." Preregistration services such as AsPredicted allow researchers to formalize and lock in hypotheses and/or analysis plans before beginning data collection. Preregistration can be lodged using online systems that freeze and date-stamp the submission, and these can be placed on embargo until the authors have collected the data and are reading to publish. We have used the preregistration tool available through OSF to register our hypothesis and methods for research currently being conducted.

The use of preregistration website services is useful, but some researchers are attempting to bring the practice into the journal publishing process itself, with registered reports (Nosek & Lakens 2014). A registered report contains the hypothesis and methods for a research project and is submitted to a journal and undergoes peer review before the data are collected. If the report is successful in the review process, the journal agrees in principle to publish the final paper, regardless of whether the results are statistically significant. The preregistration of methods prevents researchers from redirecting their research, while also reducing the likelihood of papers with nonsignificant results falling victim to the file drawer (Chambers 2013). Negative results are as valuable as positive ones, as they move us toward a more complete understanding of the phenomena being studied (Matosin et al. 2014). While preregistration is particularly useful in quantitative research, it can also be used to articulate the intended scope and limits of the data and methods in qualitative investigations before they commence. It can also ensure that researchers who make their data open are not "scooped" in their analysis, as there is a time-stamped public record of the intended use of the data.

More transparent presentation of methods and data leads to more opportunity for replication and reproduction of research. Normalizing this practice can take help neutralize what some, such as Wansink, see as the threat of criticisms of their research agenda. A survey by Fetterman and Sassenberg (2015) found that scientists overestimated the negative effect on reputation from a failed replication, and a researcher's reputation was more likely to be harmed if they refused to engage with the findings of replications. While replication is a good aim, to really confirm an effect, multiple replications are needed (Maxwell, Lau, & Howard 2015), as well as more meta-analysis (Stanley & Spence 2014), and replication or reproduction studies also need to be transparent about these methodological features as well (Brandt et al. 2014).

There is also a lesson to be learned here about the need to be open to criticism as part of the research process. Ad hominem attacks on people's character as researchers are never acceptable, but appraisal of data and outcomes, and the methods used to obtain these, should be part of a healthy science of linguistics.

It is important to remember the role you play in interpreting your data for your audience. Being clear about your research methods, both to yourself and your audience, can help mitigate selective interpretation of data. Allowing your readers to access your data can also help ensure that others can also follow your analysis.

5 Discussion

We have outlined some of the issues facing social psychology, which are a broader reflection of the issues facing all researchers in the social sciences, including linguistics. We also mentioned some of the solutions that have been proposed to counter these issues, most of which are centered on building a culture of open data and open research. In this section, we discuss three main themes linguists can take away from the social sciences. The first is that there are benefits that openness can bring; the second is that we can make the most of emerging tools and processes to enact openness; and the third is that we need to foster a positive cultural shift both in our own work and the field more generally. Some of these practices have been long established in some subfields of linguistics, and many are also raised in Berez-Kroeker et al. (2018) and throughout this Handbook.

5.1 Openness brings benefits

Researchers are rightly attached to the data they collect; conducting primary research takes a lot of our time and creative energy and drives the original contributions that we make to the collective understanding of language. Researchers can become caught in the sunk cost fallacy, where they feel that that they've invested so much in this work that it would be a loss for them to share it. However, another way of thinking about the effort of data collection is to ask whether there are more efficient ways to get returns on the investment you have already done. There are benefits to taking a more open approach. Open data also attracts attention to your specialist field—be it an underdocumented language or an uncommon grammatical construction—and ensures that if an individual researcher moves on from working on a particular set of data (increasingly common in a sector where we train far more PhDs than there are future jobs for), their data can continue to benefit the ongoing research process. There is evidence that research publications with open data attract higher citation rates (astronomy, Henneken & Accomazzi 2011; gene data, Piwowar & Vision 2013; social sciences, Pienta, Alter, & Lyle 2010). Open data also shows the greatest respect to your research participants, because their contributions go further than the bounds of your own research project.

It can feel like open data management involves a great deal more work on top of an already demanding set of research expectations. We can also decide how we wish to reward positive open data practices, in our field, but also in our institutions and professional organizations, particularly with regard to hiring and promotion (including tenure), awards, and research funding. The research sector is changing and beginning to acknowledge the publication of non-traditional outputs such as corpora and data sets, and funding bodies and publishers are encouraging open data, such as the European Research Council's Horizon 2020 Open Research Data pilot.[4] In our own work we can acknowledge that data and other documents produced at different stages of the research cycle are legitimate outputs of your research, and they can be counted as publications, including adding data as a specific publication type on academic curriculum vitae. See Alperin et al. (chapter 13, this volume) for discussion of valuation of data and data management as a research endeavor.

5.2 Using new tools and processes makes openness easier

Part of the response to the replication crisis in social psychology has been to develop tools and processes that facilitate good open data practice. Many of these tools are designed to be as easy to use as possible. OSF,[5] which we have been using in our own research practice, was created by the Center for Open Science,[6] the same group that have been running the large-scale replications. OSF benefits the work of Center for Open Science researchers, but is also useful for other disciplines. Linguists can harness these, as well as digital tools already created in our field, and institutional repositories and infrastructure, to facilitate their own open access plans. Many researchers feel uncomfortable about sharing data before they have completed their analysis in case another researcher beats them to publication, and the efforts they put into data collection do not result in the kind of publication they hoped for. However, it is important to realize that open data does not have to be open from the very moment it is created. Many online tools and archives provide the options for embargos, and private data sets allow you to protect your research goals, while making sure that your data also has a permanent home by the time of project completion. This does not mean you should leave the archiving of your data until after the project concludes; structuring data for sharing "as you go" and many repositories facilitate this.

Many newer tools and repositories are designed to be as user-friendly as possible. There are practical limits to how many tasks an individual researcher needs to become an expert in. Fortunately, universities are increasingly aware of the importance of open data, and most university libraries have research librarians and technical specialists who can provide support for archiving your materials, or providing training on the use of user-oriented repositories. The data-handling skills you need to make your work open access are the kind of skills that will make your data easier for you to use in your own research. The very best open data are well-organized, have clear metadata explaining what the data are and how they are structured, and are findable through a general web search. These kinds of information make your data easier to find and will make them easier for you to use in years to come.

5.3   A move to openness is about creating a positive cultural shift

We can have all the useful tools and processes in the world, but none of these will matter unless we foster a cultural shift in the discipline toward openness. There are several dimensions we see as key to this cultural shift, at the beginning of this discussion we briefly discussed incentives and there are others we discuss here: the first is the intergenerational shift; the second is openness even when data cannot be shared; or introspective data are used; and the third is reframing how we discuss data created by others, and how we respond to critique of our own analysis.

Common across many of the stories about the replication crisis in social psychology is the role senior researchers had in encouraging junior researchers to participate in potentially questionable data collection and analysis processes, with Wansink's story being perhaps the most egregious for the way he publicly blogged about it as a positive experience for his junior colleague. In many areas of linguistics, students and junior researchers do not always work so directly with senior colleagues on research projects, but are still greatly influenced by them. Supervisorial relationships are built on unequal power relations, and if you are a student or early career researcher in a research lab or department where there is a culture against data sharing, you may have to wait for another project to begin good practices.

When working as part of a team, or in a supervisor-student relationship, working out who "owns" data and who can decide what happens to them can be a complicated problem—particularly if you are one of the junior members of a team. Check with your team members about whether there are structural reasons why the data can't be shared (for example, you don't have permission from the informants, or from the original creator of the data). In the absence of a structural barrier, it is possible that senior team members may not be aware of the advantages of open data. They may be concerned about you completing your research within a fixed timeline, and that focusing on data will prevent you from focusing on publication. They may be concerned that sharing the raw data will allow another researcher to scoop you and prevent you from publishing your work. Talking through these issues may help you to find some common ground. It is also worth remembering that even senior researchers who you admire can feel threatened

by the changing research landscape with regard to data. There are a number of good resources you can share with colleagues to help in these conversations, including the articles and books we reference in this chapter, the frequently asked questions from the Austin Principles of Data Citation in Linguistics web page[7] and resources shared by the ReproducibiliTea[8] global network of journal clubs (Orben 2019).

There are times where it is not appropriate to share data. The interests of the community you work with always take priority, and you should always be sensitive to those interests. However, you have an obligation to revisit this discussion from time to time, including when there are genres, or derivative data (such as modified transcripts) that people are more willing to share with a wider audience, or a step model of open access, where data are only shared with registered or invited individuals. You have an obligation to clearly express in publications that not sharing data is an expressed wish of that community. This helps other communities and researchers to see that this is a conscious choice by a community, or individuals, and not an omission or withholding of data on behalf of the researcher. See Holton, Leonard, and Pulsifer (chapter 4, this volume) for more on people, ethics, and data.

Several linguistic traditions are built on introspection, or other methods where there is not necessarily a clearly defined data collection process. Introspection is still a form of data collection, and while there may not be a set of recordings or texts, there is still an obligation to be transparent about the nature of introspective data and the precise methods used to generate it. Just as a research experiment requires information about participants, publications about introspection should make clear who provided the introspections, and how they were acquired. The concept of open data means openness about methods as well as the data themselves.

One final dimension of openness, and perhaps the most difficult to put into practice, is openness to discussion of publicly available data. The replication crisis in social psychology has seen a number of ways research has been queried and a variety of different responses from original authors. The move toward open data involves a new level of vulnerability for researchers, as they share an element of the research cycle that was previously not made public. This is not dissimilar to the evolution of the practice of sharing preprints of articles intended for peer review. This practice, which started to become normalized in physics and is now moving into other areas of the physical and social sciences (such as through the SocArXiv[9] platform) requires researchers to rethink the research pipeline. The social cost to the individual of sharing research at the prepublication stage comes with a social benefit when the whole field participates (Tennant et al. 2019). In the same way that the practice around preprints is shifting and stabilizing in new fields, expectations about what constitutes good open data will continue to shift and grow; furthermore, open practices do not completely eliminate problems of fraud or even of honest unintentional misanalysis. Critique of open data cannot immediately be on the same level as that of research practices with longer traditions, such as the peer-reviewed journal article. We also need to ensure that we find a way to talk critically about data that does not come across as ad hominem. On the flipside, we also need to accept that open data mean another phase of our research cycle is open to scrutiny. In the flurry of activity in the social science replication crisis, key researchers whose work could not be replicated responded saying they felt personally attacked. None of this reframing of data is easy for any individual researcher, but as a whole we can approach data in a positive and respectful way, to help drive our discipline forward. We believe this is one of the most important lessons we can learn from the replication crisis in social psychology.

6 Conclusion: It all comes down to transparency

This Handbook is designed to help you make choices about how you manage linguistic data. We hope that when you are making those choices you aim to be as transparent in your methodology and presentation of data as possible, to allow other researchers to engage with that data in a way that can help the field move forward positively. The chapters on archiving (Kung, chapter 8, this volume), developing research data management plans (Andreassen, chapter 7, this volume), and data copyright (Collister, chapter 9, this volume) will help you think in practical terms about how to implement transparency in your own research.

Berez-Kroeker et al. (2018:11) in linguistics and Asendorpf et al. (2013) in social psychology both make clear that good linguistic data management practice is not just the responsibility of individual researchers, but of the field as a whole, including institutions, archives, publishers, and funding organizations. Institutions need to better value the development of corpora of data as a key output of research, with a positive valuation of more transparent data. See Alperin et al. (chapter 13, this volume) for more on the valuation of data and data management as a research endeavor. Individual researchers can also collaborate more, sharing the burden of validating key findings and driving research forward (Silberzahn & Uhlmann 2015). Archives need to continue to ensure they are providing a reliable repository of data, but are not difficult to use for both those depositing data and those accessing them. Publishers are increasingly seeing the value in encouraging or requiring researchers to make the data for a publication accessible (Nosek et al. 2015). Researchers in social psychology who are unwilling to wait for the publishers to drive change have started the Peer Reviewer's Openness Initiative (Morey et al. 2016), where people agree that they will use their role as peer reviewer to request a minimum level of data transparency for all papers they review. Funding organizations have an opportunity to set the agenda for how research is conducted through updates to funding rules. While we are not yet at the point where grant applications are essentially treated as preregistration of research methods (as per Bollen et al.'s recommendation to the National Science Foundation in 2015), greater focus should be given to how data will be managed, both in grant proposals and final reports. All of this requires a transformation in the way we approach research data.

Acknowledgments

Thank you to all of our collaborators who make us think critically about data and how we use and share them. Thank you also to the participants in our work who are so often happy to have their contribution to research be as maximally useful as possible. This work was funded in part by La Trobe University, and The National Science Foundation (NSF SMA-1447886), Nanyang Technological University (NAP-SUG-M4081215 and Nanyang Researcher of the Year award to SJS), and the Singapore National Research Foundation (NRF2016-SOL002–011). Thanks also to Brent Roberts and Dan Simons for making the extensive reading list for their 2018 graduate course on Reproducibility and Replicability publicly available.

Notes

1. http://osf.io/wt95v/.

2. http://ice-corpora.net/ice/.

3. https://www.linguisticsociety.org/resource/statement-evaluation-language-documentation-hiring-tenure-and-promotion.

4. http://erc.europa.eu/funding-and-grants/managing-project/open-access.

5. http://osf.io/.

6. http://cos.io/.

7. http://site.uit.no/linguisticsdatacitation/faq/.

8. http://reproducibilitea.org/.

9. http://socopen.org.

References

Asendorpf, J. B., M. Conner, F. De Fruyt, J. De Houwer, J. J. A. Denissen, K. Fiedler, S. Fiedler, et al. 2013. Recommendations for increasing replicability in psychology. *European Journal of Personality* 27 (2): 108–119.

Baker, M. 2016. Is there a reproducibility crisis? *Nature* 533 (7604): 3–5.

Barreda, S. 2016. Investigating the use of formant frequencies in listener judgments of speaker size. *Journal of Phonetics* 55:1–18.

Bem, D. J. 2011. Feeling the future: Experimental evidence for anomalous retroactive influences on cognition and affect. *Journal of Personality and Social Psychology* 100 (3): 407.

Berez-Kroeker, A. L., L. Gawne, B. F. Kelly, and T. Heston. 2017. Survey of current reproducibility practices in linguistics journals, 2003–2012. http://sites.google.com/a/hawaii.edu/data-citation/survey. Accessed October 5, 2018.

Berez-Kroeker, Andrea L., Lauren Gawne, Susan Smythe Kung, Barbara F. Kelly, Tyler Heston, Gary Holton, Peter Pulsifer, et al. 2018. Reproducible research in linguistics: A position statement on data citation and attribution in our field. *Linguistics* 56 (1): 1–18. http://doi:10.1515/ling-2017-0032.

Bergh, D. D., B. M. Sharp, H. Aguinis, and M. Li. 2017. Is there a credibility crisis in strategic management research? Evidence on the reproducibility of study findings. *Strategic Organization* 15 (3): 423–436.

Boersma, P., and D. Weenink. 2013. Praat: Doing phonetics by computer (Version 5.3.39) (computer program). http://www.praat.org. Accessed December 31, 2018.

Bollen, K., J. T. Cacioppo, R. M. Kaplan, J. A. Krosnick, J. L. Olds, and H. Dean. 2015. *Social, Behavioral, and Economic Sciences Perspectives on Robust and Reliable Science*. Report of the Subcommittee on Replicability in Science Advisory Committee to the National Science Foundation Directorate for Social, Behavioral, and Economic Sciences, 3.

Brandt, M. J., H. IJzerman, A. Dijksterhuis, F. J. Farach, J. Geller, R. Giner-Sorolla, J. A. Grange, et al. 2014. The replication recipe: What makes for a convincing replication? *Journal of Experimental Social Psychology* 50:217–224.

Brown, Sacha D., David Furrow, Daniel F. Hill, Jonathon C. Gable, Liam P. Porter, and W. Jake Jacobs. 2014. A duty to describe: Better the devil you know than the devil you don't. *Perspectives on Psychological Science* 9 (6): 626–640.

Caballero, Gabriela. 2017. Choguita Rarámuri (Tarahumara) language description and documentation: A guide to the deposited collection and associated materials. *Language Documentation and Conservation* 11:224–255.

Chambers, C. D. 2013. Registered reports: A new publishing initiative at Cortex. *Cortex* 49 (3): 609–610.

Chambers, Chris. 2017. *The Seven Deadly Sins of Psychology: A Manifesto for Reforming the Culture of Scientific Practice*. Princeton: Princeton University Press.

Cohen, J. 1962. The statistical power of abnormal-social psychological research: A review. *Journal of Abnormal and Social Psychology* 65:145–153.

Elms, A. C. 1975. The crisis of confidence in social psychology. *American Psychologist* 30:967–976.

Fanelli, D. 2011. Negative results are disappearing from most disciplines and countries. *Scientometrics* 90:891–904.

Fecher, B., and S. Friesike. 2014. Open science: One term, five schools of thought. In *Opening Science: The Evolving Guide on How the Internet Is Changing Research, Collaboration and Scholarly Publishing*, ed. S. Bartling and S. Friesike, 17–47. Springer Open. http://doi.org/10.1007/978-3-319-00026-8.

Ferguson, C. J., and M. Heene. 2012. A vast graveyard of undead theories publication bias and psychological science's aversion to the null. *Perspectives on Psychological Science* 7 (6): 555–561.

Fetterman, A. K., and K. Sassenberg. 2015. The reputational consequences of failed replications and wrongness admission among scientists. *PLoS One* 10 (12): e0143723. http://doi.org/10.1371/journal.pone.0143723.

Feynman, Richard P. 1974. Cargo cult science. *Engineering and Science* 37 (7): 10–13.

Fowler, J. 1986. The social stratification of (r) in New York City department stores, 24 years after Labov. Unpublished manuscript.

Franco, A., N. Malhotra, and G. Simonovits. 2014. Publication bias in the social sciences: Unlocking the file drawer. *Science* 345 (6203): 1502–1505.

Franco, A., N. Malhotra, and G. Simonovits. 2016. Underreporting in psychology experiments: Evidence from a study registry. *Social Psychological and Personality Science* 7:8–12.

Galak, J., R. A. LeBoeuf, L. D. Nelson, and J. P. Simmons. 2012. Correcting the past: Failures to replicate psi. *Journal of Personality and Social Psychology* 103 (6): 933.

Gawne, L., B. F. Kelly, A. L. Berez-Kroeker, and T. Heston. 2017. Putting practice into words: The state of data and methods transparency in grammatical descriptions. *Language Documentation and Conservation* 11:157–189.

Goldacre, Ben. 2010. *Bad Science: Quacks, Hacks, and Big Pharma Flacks*. London: McClelland and Stewart.

Goldfarb, B., and A. A. King. 2016. Scientific apophenia in strategic management research: Significance tests and mistaken inference. *Strategic Management Journal* 37 (1): 167–176.

Goodman, S. N., D. Fanelli, and J. P. Ioannidis. 2016. What does research reproducibility mean? *Science Translational Medicine* 8 (341): 341ps12.

Grabitz, C. R., K. S. Button, M. R. Munafò, D. F. Newbury, C. R. Pernet, P. A. Thompson, and D. V. Bishop. 2018. Logical and methodological issues affecting genetic studies of humans reported in top neuroscience journals. *Journal of Cognitive Neuroscience* 30 (1): 25–41. http://doi.org/10.1162/jocn_a_01192.

Guest, Olivia. 2016. Crisis in what exactly? *The Winnower* 6:e146590. doi:10.15200/winn.146590.01538.

H2020 Programme. 2016. *Guidelines on FAIR Data Management in Horizon 2020*. Version 3.0, July 26, 2016. European Commission Directorate-General for Research and Innovation. http://ec.europa.eu/research/participants/data/ref/h2020/grants_manual/hi/oa_pilot/h2020-hi-oa-data-mgt_en.pdf. Accessed November 1, 2018.

Head, M. L., L. Holman, R. Lanfear, A. T. Kahn, and M. D. Jennions. 2015. The extent and consequences of p-hacking in science. *PLoS Biology* 13 (3): e1002106. http://doi.org/10.1371/journal.pbio.1002106.

Henneken, Edwin A., and Alberto Accomazzi. 2011. Linking to data: Effect on citation rates in astronomy. *arXiv* arXiv:1111.3618.

Himmelmann, Nikolaus P. 1998. Documentary and descriptive linguistics. *Linguistics* 6:161–195.

Ioannidis, J. P. 2005. Why most published research findings are false. *PLoS Med* 2:e124.

Ioannidis, J. P. A. 2012. Why science isn't necessarily self-correcting. *Perspectives on Psychological Science* 7 (6): 645–654. http://doi:10.1177/1745691612464056

Jennions, M. D., and A. P. Møller. 2003. A survey of the statistical power of research in behavioral ecology and animal behavior. *Behavioral Ecology* 14 (3): 438–445.

Johnson, Valen E., Richard D. Payne, Tianying Wang, Alex Asher, and Soutrik Mandal. 2017. On the reproducibility of psychological science. *Journal of the American Statistical Association* 112 (517): 1–10. http://doi:10.1080/01621459.2016.1240079.

Joseph, Heather. 2013. The open access movement grows up: Taking stock of a revolution. *PLoS Biology* 11 (10): e1001686. http://doi:10.1371/journal.pbio.1001686.

Just, D. R., Ö. Siğirci, and B. Wansink. 2014. Lower buffet prices lead to less taste satisfaction. *Journal of Sensory Studies* 29 (5): 362–370.

Just, D. R., Ö. Siğirci, and B. Wansink. 2015. Peak-end pizza: Prices delay evaluations of quality. *Journal of Product and Brand Management* 24 (7): 770–778.

Kitchin, Rob. 2014. *The Data Revolution*. London: Sage.

Klein, R. A., M. Vianello, F. Hasselman, B. G. Adams, R. B. Adams, Jr., S. Alper, M. Aveyard, et al. 2018. Many Labs 2: Investigating variation in replicability across sample and setting. *PsyArXiv* November 19. https://doi.org/10.31234/osf.io/9654g.

Kniffin, K. M., Ö. Siğirci, and B. Wansink. 2016. Eating heavily: Men eat more in the company of women. *Evolutionary Psychological Science* 2 (1): 38–46.

Koole, S. L., and D. Lakens. 2012. Rewarding replications: A sure and simple way to improve psychological science. *Perspectives on Psychological Science* 7 (6): 608–614. doi:10.1177/1745691612462586.

Kunert, R. 2016. Internal conceptual replications do not increase independent replication success. *Psychonomic Bulletin and Review* 23 (5): 1631–1638.

Labov, W. (1966) 2006. *The Social Stratification of English in New York City*. Cambridge: Cambridge University Press.

LeBel, E. P., and K. R. Peters. 2011. Fearing the future of empirical psychology: Bem's (2011) evidence of psi as a case study in deficiencies in modal research practice. *Review of General Psychology* 15:371–379. http://doi10.1037/a0025172.

Lilienfeld, S. O. 2017. Psychology's replication crisis and the grant culture: Righting the ship. *Perspectives on Psychological Science* 12 (4): 660–664.

Loken, E., and A. Gelman. 2017. Measurement error and the replication crisis. *Science* 10:584–585. http://doi:10.1126/science.aal3618.

Lykken, D. T. 1991. What's wrong with psychology anyway? In *Thinking Clearly about Psychology*, ed. D. Ciccetti and W. Grove, 3–39. Minneapolis: University of Minnesota Press.

MacWhinney, B. 2000. *The CHILDES Project: Tools for Analyzing Talk*. 3rd ed. Mahwah, NJ: Lawrence Erlbaum Associates.

Makel, M. C., and J. A. Plucker. 2014. Facts are more important than novelty: Replication in the education sciences. *Educational Researcher* 43 (6): 304–316.

Makel, M. C., J. A. Plucker, and B. Hegarty. 2012. Replications in psychology research: How often do they really occur? *Perspectives on Psychological Science* 7:537–542.

Mather, P. A. 2011. The social stratification of /r/ in New York City: Labov's department store study revisited. *Journal of English Linguistics* 40 (4): 338–356.

Matosin, N. E. Frank, M. Engel, J. S. Lum, and K. A. Newell. 2014. Negativity towards negative results: A discussion of the disconnect between scientific worth and scientific culture. *Disease Models and Mechanisms* 7:171–173. doi:10.1242/dmm.015123.

Maxwell, S. E., M. Y. Lau, and G. S. Howard. 2015. Is psychology suffering from a replication crisis? What does "failure to replicate" really mean? *American Psychologist* 70 (6): 487–498. http://doi.org/10.1037/a0039400.

Mellor, D. T., and B. A. Nosek. 2018. Easy pre-registration will benefit any research. *Nature Human Behavior.* doi:10.1038/s41562-018-0294-7.

Meyer, Michelle N., and Christopher Chabris. 2014. Why psychologists' food fight matters. *Slate.* http://www.slate.com/articles/health_and_science/science/2014/07/replication_controversy_in_psychology_bullying_file_drawer_effect_blog_posts.html. Accessed October 4, 2018.

Morey, R. D., C. D. Chambers, P. J. Etchells, C. R. Harris, R. Hoekstra, D. Lakens, S. Lewandowsky et al. 2016. The peer reviewers' openness initiative: Incentivizing open research practices through peer review. *Royal Society Open Science* 3 (1): 150547.

Murphy, K. R., and H. Aguinis. 2017. HARKing: How badly can cherry-picking and question trolling produce bias in published results? *Journal of Business and Psychology* 34 (1): 1–17.

Nelson, L. D., J. Simmons, and U. Simonsohn. 2018. Psychology's renaissance. *Annual Review of Psychology* 69:511–534.

Neuliep, J. W., and R. Crandall. 1990. Editorial bias against replication research. *Journal of Social Behavior and Personality* 5 (4): 85–90.

Neuliep, J. W., and R. Crandall. 1993. Reviewer bias against replication research. *Journal of Social Behavior and Personality* 8 (6): 21–29.

Nosek, B. A., G. Alter, G. C. Banks, D. Borsboom, S. D. Bowman, S. J. Breckler, S. Buck et al. 2015. Promoting an open research culture. *Science* 348 (6242): 1422–1425.

Nosek, B. A., and D. Lakens. 2014. Registered reports: A method to increase the credibility of published results. *Social Psychology* 45 (3): 137–141.

Nuijten, M. B., C. H. Hartgerink, M. A. van Assen, S. Epskamp, and J. M. Wicherts. 2016. The prevalence of statistical reporting errors in psychology (1985–2013). *Behavior Research Methods* 48 (4): 1205–1226.

Orben, A. 2019. A journal club to fix science: ReproducibiliTea can build up open science without top-down initiatives. *Nature* 573:465. doi:10.1038/d41586-019-02842-8.

Open Science Collaboration. 2015. Estimating the reproducibility of psychological science. *Science* 349 (6251): aac4716.

Peterson, G. E., and H. L. Barney. 1952. Control methods used in a study of the vowels. *Journal of the Acoustical Society of America* 24 (2): 175–184.

Pienta, Amy M., George C. Alter, and Jared A. Lyle. 2010. The enduring value of social science research: The use and reuse of primary research data. Ann Arbor, MI: Inter-university Consortium for Political and Social Research. http://hdl.handle.net/2027.42/78307.

Piwowar, Heather A., and Todd J. Vision. 2013. Data reuse and the open data citation advantage. *PeerJ* 1:e175.

Retraction Watch. 2018. The *Joy of Cooking,* vindicated: Journal retracts two more Brian Wansink papers. http://retractionwatch.com/2018/12/05/the-joy-of-cooking-vindicated-journal-retracts-two-more-brian-wansink-papers. Accessed December 31, 2018.

Rosenthal, Robert. 1979. The file drawer problem and tolerance for null results. *Psychological Bulletin* 86 (3): 638–641.

Salffner, Sophie. 2015. A guide to the Ikaan language and culture documentation. *Language Documentation and Conservation* 9:237–267.

Schmidt, S. 2009. Shall we really do it again? The powerful concept of replication is neglected in the social sciences. *Review of General Psychology* 13 (2): 90–100.

Schweizer, G., and P. Furley. 2016. Reproducible research in sport and exercise psychology: The role of sample sizes. *Psychology of Sport and Exercise* 23:114–122.

Siğirci, Ö., and B. Wansink. 2015. Low prices and high regret: How pricing influences regret at all-you-can-eat buffets [retracted article]. *BMC Nutrition* 1 (1): 36.

Silberzahn, R., and E. L. Uhlmann. 2015. Crowdsourced research: Many hands make tight work. *Nature* 526:189–191. http://www.nature.com/news/crowdsourced-research-many-hands-make-tight-work-1.18508.

Simonsohn, Uri. 2013. Just post it: The lesson from two cases of fabricated data detected by statistics alone. *Psychological Science* 24 (10): 1875–1888.

SPARC. n.d. Open Data Factsheet (11.10–2). http://sparcopen.org/our-work/sparc-fact-sheets/. Accessed October 5, 2018.

Stanley, D. J., and J. R. Spence. 2014. Expectations for replications: Are yours realistic? *Perspectives on Psychological Science* 9 (3): 305–318.

Sterling, T. D. 1959. Publication decisions and their possible effects on inferences drawn from tests of significance—or vice versa. *Journal of the American Statistical Association* 54 (285): 30–34.

Styles, Suzy J. 2018. Coin-flipping cowboys: The wild west of data science, lucky cowboys and picking your team after the rodeo is over. DR-NTU (Data), V1. http://doi.org/10.21979/N9/8Z8CRQ.

Styles, Suzy J., and Lauren Gawne. 2017. When does maluma/takete fail? Two key failures and a meta-analysis suggest that phonology and phonotactics matter. *i-Perception* 8 (4): 2041669517724807. http://doi.org/10.1177/2041669517724807.

Tennant, Jonathan P., Harry Crane, Tom Crick, Jacinto Davila, Asura Enkhbayar, Johanna Havemann, Bianca Kramer, et al. 2019. Ten hot topics around scholarly publishing. *Publications* 7 (2): 34.

Thieberger, N. 2017. LD&C possibilities for the next decade. *Language Documentation and Conservation* 11:1–4.

Thomason, S. 1994. The editor's department. *Language* 70:409–423.

van der Zee, Tim, Jordan Anaya, and Nicholas J. L. Brown. 2017. Statistical heartburn: An attempt to digest four pizza publications from the Cornell Food and Brand Lab. *PeerJ Preprints* 5:e2748v1. doi:10.7287/peerj.preprints.2748v1.

Wagenmakers, E.-J., R. Wetzels, D. Borsboom, D., and H. L. J. van der Maas. 2011. Why psychologists must change the way they analyze their data: The case of psi: Comment on Bem. (2011). *Journal of Personality and Social Psychology* 100 (3): 426–432.

Walster, G. W., and T. A. Cleary. 1970. A proposal for a new editorial policy in the social sciences. *American Statistician* 24 (2): 16–19.

Watrous, R. L. 1991. Current status of Peterson–Barney vowel formant data. *Journal of the Acoustical Society of America* 89:2459–2460.

Wicherts, J. M., D. Borsboom, J. Kats, and D. Molenaar. 2006. The poor availability of psychological research data for reanalysis. *American Psychologist* 61 (7): 726–728.

Wicherts, J. M., C. L. Veldkamp, H. E. Augusteijn, M. Bakker, R. C. Van Aert, and M. A. Van Assen. 2016. Degrees of freedom in planning, running, analyzing, and reporting psychological studies: A checklist to avoid *p*-hacking. *Frontiers in Psychology* 7:1832.

Zwaan, R. A., A. Etz, R. E. Lucas, and M. B. Donnellan. 2018. Making replication mainstream. *Behavior and Brain Sciences* 41:e120. doi:10.1017/S0140525X17001972.

3 The Scope of Linguistic Data

Jeff Good

1 The range of linguistic data

There is tremendous diversity in the kinds of data used in the study of language, which reflects the unusual position of linguistics as a discipline where scholars frequently adopt methods associated with the humanities, social sciences, cognitive sciences, and computer science, among other areas. The goal of this chapter is to discuss an illustrative range of linguistic data types within a general classificatory framework that can, in principle, be extended to kinds of data beyond those directly considered here.[1] This framework is offered in the spirit of starting a broader discussion of how linguists can classify the data on which their scholarship is based, and that, in turn, should allow for more informed consideration of issues surrounding data management. This survey is necessarily incomplete because covering all the kinds of data used in linguistic research would require more space than is available. Due to the nature of my own expertise, this survey is somewhat biased toward linguistic data associated with language documentation and description, though attempts have been made to highlight important kinds of data throughout the discipline, and this survey can be usefully complemented by consideration of the kinds of data described in many of the other chapters in this volume.

The foundation of the study of language is data derived from observable linguistic behavior, broadly construed here to include both naturalistic and elicited data (section 2). Data of this kind can be subjected to a wide range of analyses, and these analyses can produce new kinds of linguistic data that become the subject of further analysis. The resulting analyses can take the form of diverse kinds of annotations, representations of syntagmatic and paradigmatic structure, and representations of lexical information, among other possibilities

(section 3). These can then form the basis of generalizations about specific languages or language in general that serve as data for studies looking at topics such as worldwide patterns of language variation or cognitive linguistic universals (section 4).

Alongside data from specific languages and about language more generally, there are a range of data types of importance to linguistic investigation that go beyond language itself. The most significant of these is data about individuals, which, when aligned with data on their language use, are central to subfields such as sociolinguistics and anthropological linguistics (section 5). Increasing attention has also been placed on metadata in linguistics, in particular to support the archiving and discovery of language resources (section 6).

2 Data from observable linguistic behavior

2.1 Observable linguistic behavior, broadly construed

A core tenet of linguistics is its adoption of a descriptive, rather than prescriptive, approach to the analysis of language. This entails the collection of linguistic data that are directly observable, though the field is divided on what kinds of observable data can be considered valid as the basis of linguistic analysis, roughly along so-called functionalist and formalists lines (see, e.g., Newmeyer 1998). In broad terms, more functionally oriented linguists emphasize the importance of naturalistic instances of language in use as foundational data for linguistic investigation, often under the heading of usage-based approaches (see, e.g., Langacker 1987:46; Diessel 2017). By contrast, more formally oriented linguists see it as appropriate to rely on constructed examples of language that can serve as prompts to collect grammaticality judgments from users of a language. Schütze ([1996] 2016) provides relevant critical consideration of this kind of data.

Here, these two classes of data are covered under the broad category of data derived from observable linguistic behavior to contrast them with data that are based on the analysis of such observations. Data from language use are further discussed in section 2.2, which focuses on language documentation, and section 2.3, on textual corpora. In section 2.4, more specialized kinds of data based on observable behavior are considered, including grammaticality judgments and information collected via technical instruments.

2.2   Documentary linguistic data

While naturalistic data of language use can be used to support almost any kind of linguistic work, they are central to one subfield in particular, documentary linguistics, which is based around "the creation, annotation, preservation, and dissemination of transparent records of a language" (Woodbury 2011:159), in particular in contexts of language endangerment. As such, the documentary linguistics literature contains fairly extensive consideration of different kinds of naturalistic data that can be collected and the methods that can be used to facilitate their collection (see also Cox, chapter 22, this volume; Daniels & Daniels, chapter 26, this volume).

Himmelmann (1998:180), for instance, widely cited as the first work to contrast documentary linguistics with other areas of the field, specifically discusses the notion of a "systematics of communicative events" to help those engaged in the documentation of a language to ensure that the data they collect are not merely naturalistic but also representative of the actual linguistic practices of a community. He further suggests that a parameter of "spontaneity" (178) can help structure data collection to produce a more accurate record of a language. The issue of representativeness is a broad one given that it necessarily encompasses not only different genres but also diversity among members of a linguistic community across dimensions such as age, gender, and other culturally significant social groupings (see, e.g., Childs, Good, & Mitchell 2014 for general discussion).

Alongside considerations of what kinds of events to record, a central concern of documentary linguistics has been the mechanics of data collection, as evidenced by work on data management (e.g., Austin 2006; Good 2011; Thieberger & Berez 2012) or audio and video recording techniques (e.g., Margetts & Margetts 2012). An important recent development in documentary linguistics has been increased attention on the collection of video data (see,

e.g., Dimmendaal 2010; Seyfeddinipur 2012; Seyfeddinipur & Rau 2020). Obviously, for sign languages, proper documentation is inconceivable without video recording (see Schembri 2010:112–116). For spoken languages, audio recording can produce records that can support many kinds of linguistic analysis effectively. However, to the extent that interactional communication, even when primarily being accomplished via speech, typically involves a visual component (e.g., via gesture or gaze), many researchers in documentary linguistics have determined that the visual context of a speech event constitutes a valuable kind of data for linguistic analysis, even if it is only arguably "language" data.

While work that situates itself specifically within documentary linguistics tends to focus on endangered varieties, the kinds of data that it focuses on can be collected for any language and similar approaches have been adopted in other subfields, as evidenced for instance by the data sets assembled as part of the TalkBank project (MacWhinney 2007) or speech data used as the basis for sociolinguistic investigation (Kendall 2008, 2011; see also Sonderegger et al., chapter 15, this volume; Kendall & Farrington, chapter 14, this volume; Fridland & Kendall, chapter 18, this volume). Data of this kind can be considered to be documentary in nature, even if language documentation as a term is typically applied to endangered language contexts.

The notion of documentary linguistic data rests on the idea that it is possible to record linguistic events that can be considered "naturalistic" despite the fact that the act of recording them is not a naturalistic part of the event. This issue has been frequently referred to under the heading of the *observer's paradox* (Labov 1972:209; see also Birch 2014:32–34). However, the range of ways that the act of observation may alter patterns of language use across recording contexts and cultures does not yet appear to have been the subject of general investigation.

2.3   Textual corpora

Another significant category of data derived from observable linguistic behavior is textual data. While such data can, in principle, be drawn from any written text for analysis, they most clearly become linguistic data when assembled into a corpus of some kind (see McCarthy & O'Keeffe 2010 for a historical overview linguistic corpora). The term *corpus* can be used broadly to cover both text corpora and audiovisual corpora (of the sort discussed in section 2.2), but the subfield of corpus linguistics is most strongly oriented toward textual analysis (see, e.g., Bonelli 2010:18–19; Gries & Berez 2017:380–381). Moreover, corpus linguistics is typically based on the analysis of textual data when that data can be considered primary data rather than annotations on primary data, as would be the case, for instance, of a transcription of an audio recording (see section 3.2 for consideration of annotation), though, once a transcription exists, the same analytical methods can be applied to the resulting textual record.[2]

The existence of textual corpora highlights the fact that, in societies characterized by widespread literacy, textual data can be significant sources of observable linguistic data. Data from journalistic sources, in particular, have played an important role in the development of large-scale corpora (Bonelli 2010:16), both because of their availability and because they represents a linguistic genre that is naturally text based. Beal, Corrigan, and Moisl (2007:1–2) make a distinction between conventional and unconventional corpora. The former focus on varieties that are associated with standardized writing systems. Examples include the *British National Corpus* (BNC Consortium 2007) (see also Gries, chapter 38, this volume) or the Corpus of Contemporary American English (Davies 2008–). While there is significant space for variation within conventional corpora, there is much less variation than in unconventional corpora, which are based on more heterogeneous input data sources. The corpora on creole languages described by Sebba and Dray (2007) provide an example of the potential complications. For instance, creole language text may be interspersed with text from a standardized language, such as English, in a novel raising questions of just what should be included in a corpus from such a source (189).

Well-developed corpora are not limited to collections of texts themselves but can also contain annotations of the texts and ancillary resources such as lexicons to assist in their interpretation (see section 3). Strassel and Tracey (2016) discuss these kinds of corpora, describing them using the term "language pack." In contrast to this is the increasing use of more ad hoc corpora derived from texts made available online, in particular via services that regularly aggregate new instances of naturally generated text, such as Twitter (see, e.g., Grieve, Nini, & Guo 2017; Scannell, chapter 41, this volume).

Text corpora highlight the dual role of textual data in linguistics in that they can sometimes serve as primary data, as is the case for typical corpora, while in other instances, the textual representations are seen as secondary representations of some other kind of primary data, as is typically the case in language documentation (see section 2.2). They also highlight the role of curation in the creation of linguistic data. Some text corpora, such as the textual portion of the British National Corpus (British National Corpus 2007), are highly curated so that the resulting corpus can be considered representative of a certain set of linguistic varieties. A resource such as News on the Web (Davies 2013), which is based on a selection of online news resources and continuously updated to reflect newly available content, reflects a more passive curatorial approach.

2.4 Specialized data from observable behavior

The kinds of data discussed to this point can be broadly described as "naturalistic" insofar as they are intended to be reflective of actual language use. By contrast, there is one very prominent kind of linguistic data that comes from observable linguistic behavior, but of a highly specialized nature. This involves language user judgments of the acceptability of a given expression. The most well-known class of judgments of this kind are so-called grammaticality judgments (see, e.g., Schütze [1996] 2016 for critical consideration of this kind of data and Sprouse 2013 for a bibliographic overview).

As discussed by Abrusán (2019), there are various possible reasons why a given expression can be considered unacceptable, and they could be primarily syntactic (or morphosyntactic), semantic, or pragmatic, with the details dependent on the expression in question as well as the context in which the expression is interpreted (see also McCawley 1998:5–6). For certain theoretical approaches to linguistics, in particular generative approaches, language data consisting of sets of sentences associated with judgments of their acceptability play a central role in the analytical process.[3] In terms of presentation, sentences deemed to be inappropriate are generally annotated (see section 3.2) with "stigmata" (see McCawley 1998:3) classifying the nature of their unacceptability. The asterisk (*) is the best known of these stigmata and is typically used as a marker of syntactic ungrammaticality.

While not as theoretically prominent, language user judgments are also used to study non-syntactic domains of grammar, with a well-known example involving judgments as to whether specific sound sequences are considered to be possible words in a language even if those sequences happen not to be associated with a given word. A frequently cited example for English is an opposition between the non-words *blick* and *bnick*. The former is generally judged to consist of a sequence of sounds that could be a word in English, while the latter is judged to not be a possible word due to its initial *bn* sequence (see, e.g., Cohn 2001:180).

These data are clearly of observable linguistic behavior, though of a highly specialized kind of behavior specifically designed to facilitate linguistic research. Rather than proposing a categorical distinction between data of this kind and naturalistic data, it is probably better to see these as different ends of a continuum of control in data collection (see Birch 2014:27–29), with data gathered on acceptability judgments being at the highly controlled end of the continuum. While different theoretical approaches may weigh this data more or less heavily with respect to linguistic analysis, this does not change the status of this kind of data as emanating from language "use," albeit of a very atypical kind.

Additional kinds of specialized data on language use involve the collection of fine-grained aspects of linguistic production or perception via instrumental means. An early instance of this kind of data is the palatogram (Ladefoged 1957), which is a record (e.g., in the form of a photograph) of where a substance that has been placed on the palate has been removed due to the movement of the tongue. Another early instance of this kind of data are spectrograms (Koenig, Dunn, & Lacy 1946), a standard part of the tool kit of phonetic analysis, now widely used even by non-phoneticians due to the availability of tools such as Praat (Boersma & Weenink 2019), which make them easy to generate. There is no single catalog of instrumental data that are used in linguistics, and they can clearly take on quite diverse forms. Phillips and Wagers (2007:747), for instance, list various kinds of instrumental data used in psycholinguistic studies such as eye-tracking in self-paced reading tasks and event-related potentials, which can measure electrical brain activity in response to a linguistic stimulus and are based on electroencephalographic measurements (see Kaan 2007; Beres 2017). A similar kind of instrumental data that is increasingly being used is functional magnetic resonance imaging, also to measure brain activity (see, e.g., Willems & van Gerven 2018).

Specialized kinds of data on language use can be contrasted with data of the kind associated with language documentation (see section 2.2) or data from corpora (see section 2.3) by the fact that they are generally collected with a very specific analytical goal in mind, whether this is the formal analysis of a syntactic pattern, modeling the articulation of a particular sound, or understanding how a given linguistic construction is processed. By contrast, documentary and corpus data are generally likely to be usable to support a wide range of investigations across more than one linguistic subfield, though data of such kinds could also be collected to serve a fairly narrow purpose depending on the research practices adopted.

3   Analytical structures applied to data of language use

3.1   Building analyses onto observable data

Most linguistic investigation is not based directly on representations of observable linguistic behavior, but, rather, on data derived from analyses of these observations. This is probably seen most directly in the field's reliance on written representations of linguistic data, whether in the form of transcription systems or orthographies that are used to approximate spoken or signed forms. These represent one kind of possible annotation that can be made on a linguistic data source; annotation in general will be discussed in section 3.2. Linguistic data can also be arranged in ways that facilitate abstract analysis, and two important kinds of structural analysis, across the syntagmatic and paradigmatic dimensions, are considered in section 3.3. The special case of lexical data is considered in section 3.4.

The topics in this section are somewhat heterogeneous in nature. Annotation, for instance, refers to a way of encoding analyses rather than representing any specific kind of analysis, and annotation can, in principle, be used to encode syntactic, paradigmatic, or lexical analyses, for instance. These topics are grouped together as part of a consideration of the kinds of linguistic data that are generated via the analysis of data based on observable linguistic behavior.

3.2   Linguistic annotation

Linguistic annotation is a kind of linguistic data that "involves the association of descriptive or analytical notations" with other kinds of language data (Ide 2017:2). Annotation can either be made directly on "raw" data (i.e., unannotated language data) (see, e.g., Schultze-Berndt 2006:215; Himmelmann 2012:188) or on other annotations.

To make the discussion more concrete, consider the example in (1) from the language Yeri [glottocode: yapu1240],[4] drawn from Wilson (2017:29). This example represents one of the more commonly encountered kinds of annotated data seen in linguistic analysis, interlinear glossed text.

(1) *hem   ta   m-y-aya   maŋa-Ø?*
     1SG   FUT   1SG-2-give.R   what-SG.R

     "What will I give you (sg. or pl.)?" (120517–001:185.991) RNS, JS

Interlinear glossed text is a data format geared toward the presentation of linguistic data from languages other than the language that is being used to describe the data (e.g., English, French, or Russian). It provides a visually compact means of providing translational equivalents under each word of the language being analyzed, typically referred to as *glosses*. It can potentially include an indication of morpheme boundaries (signified by hyphens in (1)) and the use of abbreviations for grammatical terms in the glosses, often presented using distinctive typography (e.g., small capital letters in (1)).[5] In addition to presenting word-by-word glosses, interlinear glossed text is also typically associated with a free translation of the entire linguistic fragment being analyzed, as is found in the third line of (1). Depending on the presentational needs of a given work, interlinear glossed text may include additional lines, for instance a line including a representation of the relevant linguistic fragment in a distinct script from the one being used to present the analysis (e.g., a Cyrillic orthographic representation in addition to a Roman transliteration) or one line representing the linguistic fragment with morpheme boundaries and another without morpheme boundaries. Further discussion of interlinear glossed text in the context of considerations of annotation can be found in Bow, Hughes, and Bird (2003), Palmer and Erk (2007), and Goodman et al. (2015). The Leipzig Glossing Rules (Bickel, Comrie, & Haspelmath 2008) have emerged as a de facto standard for the presentation of interlinear glossed text.

In addition to presenting information needed to understand the linguistic structure of the Yeri sentence, the example in (1) also includes information identifying its source in its last line. Specifically, it is drawn from a recording with identifier 120517–001, and it begins 185.991 seconds into the recording. The abbreviation RNS found after this provides information on the genre of the collected text, which stands for recorded natural speech, and the sequence JS provides the initials of the speaker, John Sirio (Wilson 2017:28).

The example in (1) can be seen as providing multiple layers of annotation. In its first line, two kinds of annotation are provided: a written representation of the reported utterance paired with a basic morphological analysis, indicated with hyphens and, in one case, a zero-morpheme treated as part of the language's inflectional system. The second line also provides some morphological analysis in its association of each morpheme in the first line with a simple English translation or a morphosyntactic category. The final line contains four discrete annotations: a free translation and three pieces of metadata (see section 6) about the source of the example, the nature of the event from which the data was collected, and the speaker of the fragment. This example, thus, provides some sense of the diversity of possible linguistic annotations.

Interlinear glossed text should be primarily understood as a presentation format for encoding specific kinds of annotations insofar as it is optimized for visual interpretation on a page rather than encoding the data in a machine-readable or archival format (see, e.g., Bird & Simons 2003:565; Simons 2006; Good 2011:227–228; Thieberger & Berez 2012:94–96 for relevant discussions). It can be considered a specific instantiation of a general data class of morphologically analyzed texts, which can take on different forms. It has an especially compact presentation and can be compared, for instance, with the presentation of analyzed texts found in Boas (1911), which contains both interlinear translations at the level of the word, though more along the lines of a free translation rather than a gloss, along with footnotes for each word in the text providing further morphological notes, which are sometimes quite detailed.

Linguistic annotation provides an open-ended means of generating linguistic data on the basis of other linguistic data. It has taken on increasing importance as computational methods play a more central role in linguistic research because the ability of a machine to process linguistic data often relies on the presence of well-structured annotations on that data, and work on the digital encoding of linguistic annotations is where the properties of annotations have been most fully explored (see, e.g., Romary & Witt 2014; Ide 2017). An important distinction to be made in this regard is between the conceptual model underlying a system of annotation and the concrete format that is used to express the content of the model (see Ide et al. 2017; Pustejovksy, Bunt, & Zaenen 2017). (See also Han, chapter 6, this volume, for consideration of issues connected to data transformation, which is often relevant when creating and processing annotations.)

Returning to the example in (1), the underlying conceptual model on which the interlinear glossing is based is largely implicit and also somewhat complex. It relies on the notions of word and morpheme, both of which are central to the presentation of the alignment of the elements in the first and second lines, as well as an analysis of the abstract grammatical categories that are required to understand morphosyntactic patterns in the language. The model additionally incorporates some notion of free translation. These elements are common to interlinear glossed text generally, but this particular example combines a model for linguistic analyses with a separate conceptual model for the metadata found after the free translation. As indicated, this metadata model includes information on how the annotations relate to the data being annotated, the genre of the event from which the data are drawn, and the speaker. These annotations do not constitute anything like a "complete" analysis of the data. The morphosyntactic analysis is elaborated in Wilson's (2017) descriptive grammar, and the metadata for the record are elaborated in an archival deposit (Wilson 2014).[6]

For purposes of illustration, a partial schematization of the conceptual structure underlying the presentation in (1) can be seen in figure 3.1. The recording on which the annotations are based is associated with a metadata record as well as a transcription of a specific time segment, indicated in gray. The transcription is, in turn, associated with a word-level parsing, and each word is associated with a gloss. The transcription is also associated with a free translation. Lines are used to represent annotation relations, where an element found below another element can be interpreted as an annotation on the higher element.

The schematization presented in figure 3.1 begins to represent the complexities involved in the structuring of annotations, though some only implicitly. For instance, the word-level analysis associated with the transcription represents a series of annotations that subdivide the higher-level annotation. Other annotations, such as the association of a word to a gloss represent a one-to-one relation. Both the transcription annotation and the metadata annotation are associated with the recording, but the metadata are associated with the entire recording, while the transcription is associated with a fragment of the recording that can be defined with respect to a particular time span.

In a discussion of the annotation capabilities of the ELAN multimedia annotation tool, Brugman and Russel (2004:2068) discuss a number of types of possible annotations that can be used in the analysis of multimedia data sources. These include (i) an annotation directly linked to a specific time span of a recording, (ii) a time-linked subdivision for a series of annotations that exhaustively divide an annotation linked to a time span without any gaps (e.g., a segmental annotation of a word for phonetic analysis), (iii) a subdivision without links to specific times that exhaustively divides a higher-level annotation (e.g., a word divided into morphemes when it is either difficult or unnecessary to directly link the

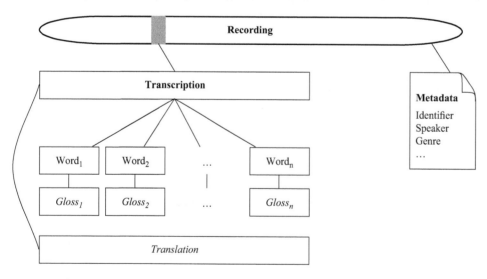

Figure 3.1

Schematization of annotation structure for interlinear glossed text.

morpheme annotations to specific time spans), and (iv) a one-to-one association where a higher-level annotation can be linked only to a single additional annotation for some kind of information (e.g., a part of speech annotation for a word). Another prominent kind of annotation in linguistics involves the association of syntactic tree structures onto textual representations of expressions to create a treebank (see, e.g., Abeillé 2003 for an overview). Detailed discussion of general issues in annotation and numerous case studies, largely from a computational perspective, can be found in Ide and Pustejovksy (2017).

In addition to the issue of the conceptual model underlying an annotation system, there is also the question of the format used to encode an annotation. A high-level distinction centers on an opposition between inline and stand-off annotation (Ide et al. 2017:79–80). The annotation system schematized in figure 3.1 presents an instance of stand-off annotation where the annotations are not included in the primary data file (in that case an audio recording) but, rather, are stored separately. Inline annotation involves embedding the annotations directly with the primary data. An example of this kind of annotation, drawn from Ide et al. (2017:80) is provided in figure 3.2. In this example, annotations are made on the linguistic fragment *Many cultural treasures are, however, not in a representative state. We have to restore them.* Unlike the example in (1), this text fragment should be considered the primary data source rather than being seen as a transcription of some underlying recording (see section 2.3).

The annotations in figure 3.2 are represented using XML (see Gippert 2006:352–361 for an accessible overview). XML is a markup language designed for (among other things) adding annotations to textual data, and this is done via a system of opening and closing tags. In figure 3.2, the opening tags are <S>, for sentence, <FACILITY>, a term being used in this context to refer to a human-made entity serving as a location, and <GROUP>, for a group of people. Closing tags are the

```
<S><FACILITY>Many cultural treasures</FACILITY> are,
however, not in a representative state.
<GROUP>We</GROUP> have to restore
<FACILITY>them</FACILITY>.</S>
```

Figure 3.2
An example of inline XML annotation.

same as opening tags except for the addition a slash before the tag name. This example partially illustrates a tagging system designed for named entity recognition, an information extraction process designed to locate sequences of text specifically referring to entities of various kinds (e.g., people, places, or organizations) (see Nadeau & Sekine 2007).

Annotations both describe existing data and create new kinds of data. For instance, in (1), the written representation of the utterance in the first line can be understood simultaneously as enriching the original recording and creating new written data on the language being described that can serve as the input to further annotation and analysis, as illustrated in the conceptual model in figure 3.1. In addition, many linguistic claims that can be considered data for linguistics, especially generalizations about specific languages (see section 4) that are typically presented in the form of prose could also be reconceptualized (at least partly) as annotations.

Significant work remains on how to do this effectively, and most annotations represent relatively simple kinds of analyses. There has been work, in particular, regarding how the generalizations included in descriptive grammars could be encoded in a machine-readable form using annotations of some kind (see, e.g., Good 2004; Thieberger 2009; Bender et al. 2012; Maxwell 2012; Nordhoff 2012). However, this does not yet seem to have had a significant impact on practices in the field.

3.3 Modeling syntagmatic and paradigmatic structure

Annotations, as described in section 3.2, are a general-purpose method to associate different kinds of information with each other, and their use is not limited to linguistic data. By contrast, the abstract kinds of structural analyses described in this section are central to linguistic investigation and also create important kinds of linguistic data. These are analyses of syntagmatic structure and paradigmatic structure.

As discussed by van Marle (2000:225), syntagmatic relations hold among linguistic elements comprising some kind of linguistic constituent, while paradigmatic relations are based on a vaguer notion of "relatedness" or "connectedness" among linguistic elements within a language. The arrangements of words in a phrase, including head-dependent relationships among its subconstituents, are a well-studied kind of syntagmatic relationship, though syntagmatic relations are not restricted to syntactic structures but can apply to the arrangement of elements within any kind of linguistic constituent (e.g., morphological or prosodic constituents). Well-known kinds of paradigmatic relationships involve inflectional paradigms ranging from the relatively simple singular/plural opposition on English nouns to highly elaborated paradigms found in languages making use of extensive verbal or nominal morphology. However, the notion of a paradigmatic relationship is also broader than this including, for instance, the use of minimal pairs to establish phonemic contrasts in a language or the juxtaposition of two sentences with the same truth conditions (e.g., active and passive variants of a sentence) as a means to establish the syntagmatic relationship of syntactic constituency. Cataloging the entire range of possible syntagmatic and paradigmatic relationships used in linguistic analysis is outside the scope of the present chapter. However, what can be considered is the way that analyses of these relationships become encoded as linguistic data and therefore subject to further analysis.

Two representations of analyses of syntagmatic relations in the sentence *On Wednesday, he told the stories to the children*, drawn from Hayes (1990:86), are presented in (2) and (3). Following common linguistic practice, these relationships are modeled in the form of trees whose nodes are annotated for their linguistic type, thus allowing them to simultaneously encode partonymic (i.e., part-whole) and taxonomic (type-subtype) relations (see Moravcsik 2010 for further discussion). Trees can be understood as a kind of graph, in the technical mathematical use of the term as found in graph theory (see, e.g., Diestel 1997 for an introductory text). A graph, in this sense, is understood as a set of *nodes* (also termed *points* or *vertices*) and *arcs* (also termed *edges* or *lines*) connecting those nodes (see, e.g., Diestel 1997:2). Trees represent a subset of possible graphs and are constrained in a number of ways, for instance by the requirement that they have one and only one root node and that they do not allow "loops"—that is, each node can be dominated by only one other node (see McCawley 1982:91–94, 1998:46–48 for further discussion).

A standard device for representing trees in linguistic work is via tree diagrams of the sort seen in (2) and (3). The tree diagram in (2) presents a possible syntactic constituency analysis for the sentence, and the one in (3) presents a possible analysis of the sentence's prosodic constituency. The labels in (3) stand for the following

prosodic constituent types: W=word, C=clitic group, P= phonological phrase, I=intonational phrase, U=utterance. In both cases, the tree diagrams represent relations among the subconstituents of a given a constituent, thus making them syntagmatic in nature.

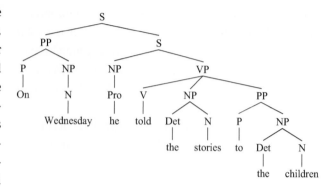

(2)

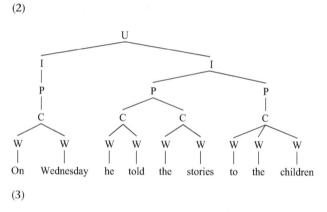

(3)

The use of paradigmatic relationships in linguistic analysis can be illustrated by an examination of the data in table 3.1, illustrating tonal patterns for words in the Mande language Kpelle [glottocode: libe1247]. The forms are adapted from Hyman (2011:207) and based on Welmers (1962:86). The data are arranged to exemplify the range of attested surface tonal patterns in the language and to demonstrate the relatively limited number of tonal melodies found on words.

Tone-bearing units in words can surface with high (H), low (L), mid (M), or falling (F) tones. The table further includes an abstract analysis of these patterns that is facilitated by presenting them in paradigmatic opposition, namely that the surface tonal variation can be reduced to five underlying tonal patterns involving just a two-way high/low tonal opposition if one assumes various rules of tonal association, for instance that a high and low tone appearing on a single tone-bearing unit are realized as a falling tone, as well as a rule simplifying a low-high sequence to a mid-tone (see Hyman 2011:207 for further discussion).

The paradigmatic relationships in the table 3.1 can specifically be found in the arrangement of words in the first column. They have in common that they are words found in the same language. They differ in their surface tonal patterns. For paradigmatic comparison to yield sensible results, the elements being compared must have enough in common to make it possible to provide a linguistic analysis of the source of their differences, though because of the heterogeneous nature of the notion of linguistic relatedness (see van Marle 2000:226), the range of paradigmatic comparisons that are used in linguistic analysis is quite broad. There does not appear to be extensive work surveying the kinds of paradigmatic analyses used in linguistics, though some sense of this can be found in the study of Penton et al. (2004) who propose a general model for the encoding of information found within paradigms, broadly construed to encompass "any kind of rational tabulation of words or phrases to illustrate contrasts and systematic variation" (Bird 1999:33). The paradigms that they consider include not only presentations of morphological and phonological

Table 3.1
Tone patterns in Kpelle

Word	Gloss	Surface	Underlying
pá	'come'	H	H
láá	'lie down'	HH	
ɓóá	'knife'	HH	
pílí	'jump'	HH	
kpòò	'padlock'	LL	L
tɔ̀nɔ̀	'chisel'	LL	
tòlòŋ	'dove'	LL	
kpàkì	'loom'	LL	
yê	'for you'	F	HL
kpôŋ	'door'	F	
tóà	'pygmy antelope'	HL	
kálì	'hoe'	HL	
kpōŋ	'help'	M	LH
sēē	'sit down'	MM	
sūā	'animal'	MM	
kālī	'snake'	MM	
tɛ̄ɛ̂	'black duiker'	MF	LHL
yūɔ̂	'axe'	MF	
kōnâ	'mortar'	MF	
kpānâŋ	'village'	MF	

oppositions but also sociolinguistic variants and historical cognate sets.

Unlike syntagmatic analyses, where there is a relatively standard means to model them in the form of trees, there is no standard means of representing paradigmatic oppositions. Tabular presentations, such as what is seen in table 3.1, are quite commonly employed, but, as shown by Penton et al. (2004), while tabular presentations of paradigmatic data share a presentational similarity, this masks potential complexity in the kinds of information that are presented. To pick an instance of this in table 3.1, the table appears to be structured primarily across two dimensions. The first is the vertical dimension of words with different tonal patterns, and the second is information about those words in the form of an orthographic representation, a gloss, and surface tone melody. However, there is also an implicit third dimension of information relating to a word's underlying tonal category presented both via a tonal underlying form in the fourth column of the table and via horizontal lines separating different blocks of words.

Adopting the relatively broad sense of paradigm employed by Penton et al. and applying it to the analysis of all paradigmatic oppositions provides a framework for understanding the distinction between viewing data from a synchronic and diachronic perspective in linguistic analysis. Synchronic analysis can be viewed as the analysis of data sets that are not paradigmatically opposed across the dimension of time while diachronic analysis would then be viewed as the analysis of data sets that are paradigmatically opposed across time (as well as other possible dimensions of variation). Synchronic analysis could involve the comparative analysis of linguistic varieties attested at different times (e.g., if the Latin case system were considered alongside the Finnish case system as part of a typological study of case). However, what makes a given analysis or set of data "diachronic" is that the dimension of time is considered important to the investigation.

An analytical construct of relevance in this context is the feature structure (see Sag, Wasow, & Bender 2003:50–58 for an accessible introduction; Carpenter 1992 for detailed formal consideration, and Romary & Witt 2014:183–186 for discussion in the context of linguistic annotation). These are sets of feature–value pairings that are grouped together to describe some linguistic element. Depending on the analytical approach being adopted, the value of a feature can be another feature structure, allowing for complex, nested structures. Feature structures have been used as central analytical devices in syntactic frameworks such as head-driven phrase structure grammar (HPSG) (Sag, Wasow, & Bender 2003) and lexical-functional grammar (Bresnan 2001) and represent a flexible and powerful of way encoding both syntagmatic and paradigmatic analyses. A representation of a feature structure used to express the syntactic properties of the name *Kim* in English, drawn from Sag, Wasow, and Bender (2003:474), in HPSG is provided in figure 3.3. This feature structure is represented in the form of an attribute–value matrix where feature names are presented in capital letters and their associated values are presented to the right of the feature name. HPSG feature structures can additionally be associated with a specification of the type of linguistic object being described by the feature structure, indicated with an italicized label in the upper-right corner of an attribute value matrix in figure 3.3.

Full details on how to interpret the attribute–value matrix representation in figure 3.3 can be found in Sag, Wasow, and Bender (2003). In broad terms, it is used to present analysis of *Kim* that includes a specification of its phonological form (PHON), syntax (SYN), argument structure (ARG-ST), and semantics (SEM). The phonological representation of *Kim* is provided using English orthography. The syntactic features assigned to *Kim* are that it is of type *noun* and that it participates in a third singular agreement pattern. Because *Kim* does not take arguments

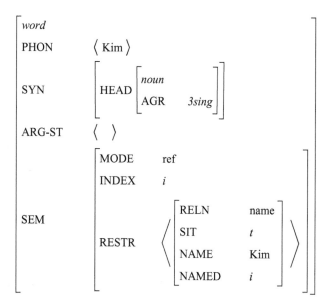

Figure 3.3
Attribute–value matrix representation of a feature structure for the name *Kim*.

(which would normally be expected of verbs rather than nouns), it is listed as having an empty argument structure. The semantic properties of *Kim* indicate that it is used to refer to an entity with that name. What is of note in the present context about this complex feature structure is that it simultaneously encodes syntagmatic information—specifically, in its presentation of a phonological representation of the word and its specification that the word requires no additional arguments to be syntactically realized—and paradigmatic information—for instance, in its specification that the word is associated with the third singular agreement class. This reflects the fact that fully analyzing any syntactic constituent requires knowledge of both its syntagmatic and paradigmatic properties.

As is the case with annotations (see section 3.2), syntagmatic and paradigmatic analyses of linguistic data can themselves become data for further levels of analysis. Perhaps the most prominent case of this in linguistics is the treatment of syntactic trees as the basic units of syntactic theorizing in transformationalist approaches rather than, for instance, strings of segments (see, e.g., McCawley 1982:92). An example from the paradigmatic domain involves the study of syncretism, a phenomenon whose investigation assumes the existence of morphological paradigms and is detected by looking for patterns of formal identity in parts of those paradigms (see, e.g., Baerman, Brown, & Corbett 2005:13).

As indicated, syntagmatic and paradigmatic analyses are abstract in nature. For them to be conveyed, they must be encoded in some way. This could be done informally via prose, for instance, or via formats optimized for presentation on the printed page of the sort seen in (2) and (3) and in table 3.1. They can also be encoded in the form of annotations (see section 3.2). Annotations and structural analyses are not mutually exclusive but rather represent a distinction between a frequently used device to represent analyses (e.g., as annotations) against different conceptual kinds of analyses (e.g., syntagmatic and paradigmatic).

3.4 Lexical data

The final kind of data to be considered in this section are lexical data (see also Beier & Michael, chapter 24, this volume). While it would be logically possible to treat lexical data as a hybrid data class containing some syntagmatic and some paradigmatic information (comparable to what was seen in figure 3.3), in practice lexical data have a special place in linguistic analysis, which is why they are treated separately here. The importance of lexical data (especially when presented in the form of dictionaries) has led to the development of the distinct field of inquiry known as lexicography (see, e.g., Durkin 2016), which is somewhat separate from the field of linguistics as whole. This can be contrasted with the study of the grammars (in the sense of descriptions of languages written by linguists). While there are works on the topic of grammaticography (see, e.g., Mosel 2006), these are quite limited and grammaticography has not developed into a separate field of inquiry in the same way lexicography has.

In part due to the widespread use of lexical resources in computational applications, lexical data have been the subject of especially extensive investigation as a data type, in particular in work on modeling lexical entry structure to facilitate the development of lexical databases. Bell and Bird (2000) present an early consideration of this topic based on an examination of fifty-five dictionaries and lexicons from a broad set of languages (see also Ide, Kilgarriff, & Romary 2000 for another relevant early work). Something similar is done in Trippel (2006:46–92) where a greater diversity of types of lexical resources is considered (see also Trippel 2009).

Building on previous work (e.g., Gibbon 2002), Trippel (2006:40–45) breaks down the structure of lexicons—and, by extension, lexical data—into three components: microstructure, mesostructure, and macrostructure. The *microstructure* encompasses the information typically associated with the core of a lexical entry (e.g., an orthographic representation of a word, part of speech, and description of meaning). The *macrostructure* corresponds roughly to what, in visual terms, one might refer to as the "layout" of a lexical resource, covering, for instance, how entries are ordered (if ordering is relevant, as is the case for print dictionaries but not necessarily lexical databases), which part of an entry will be privileged for operations such as sorting or referring to an entry (most typically in the form of a headword), and how inflectionally related forms are handled in the lexicon structure. The *mesostructure* is the least prominent aspect of lexicon structure, at least from a presentational standpoint, and it encompasses the various ways that entries can be related to each other (e.g., via cross-references), the nature of the categories used in the lexicon (e.g., transcription conventions or how different subcategories of parts of speech relate to each other), and references to relevant external resources such as a corpus. The fact that

lexical data structures show this degree of complexity is a reflection of the fact that analyses of the abstract lexicons associated with languages are themselves complex, requiring reference to a lexicon as a whole, information about individual lexical items, and semantic and formal connections among them.

To make the discussion more concrete, consider the representations of the same lexical information provided in example (4) and figure 3.4, drawn from the TEI Consortium (2019:section 9.3.4).[7] These are partial representations of the information found in a dictionary entry. In (4), a standard presentation format is presented of the sort associated with a print dictionary. In figure 3.4, a partial XML representation, focusing on the etymological content of the entry, is given (see section 3.2 for discussion of XML).[8]

(4) **neume** \n(y)üm\ n [F, fr. ML pneuma, neuma, fr. Gk pneuma breath—more at **pneumatic**]: any of various symbols used in the notation of Gregorian chant . . .

```
<entry>
<!–...–>
 <etym>
  <lang>F</lang> fr. <lang>ML</lang>
  <mentioned>pneuma</mentioned>
  <mentioned>neuma</mentioned> fr. <lang>Gk</lang>
  <mentioned>pneuma</mentioned>
  <gloss>breath</gloss>
  <xr type="etym">more at <ptr target="#pneumatic"/>
  </xr>
 </etym>
 <sense>
  <def>any of various symbols used in the notation of
Gregorian chant
<!–...–>
  </def>
 </sense>
</entry>
<!–...–>
<entry xml:id="pneumatic">
 <etym>
<!–...–>
 </etym>
</entry>
```

Figure 3.4
An XML representation of a lexical entry, including mesostructural data.

The information in example (4) and figure 3.4 most directly relates to lexical microstructure because it is primarily encoding a lexical entry. It also saliently encodes mesostructural information in the explicit reference to another lexical entry with the headword *pneumatic*. The presentation format achieves this via the phrasing *more at*. The XML representation does this via a "pointer" tag (abbreviated as ptr in figure 3.4), which references another entry—whose content is mostly unspecified in the XML—with the identifier *pneumatic*. Macrostructural relations are implicit in these representations and connect to the overall conventions used for entry layout and structure. The fact that the entry identifier for one of the entries encoded in figure 3.4 is *pneumatic* reveals an aspect of the macrostructure of this resource, namely that the primary reference point for an entry is some kind of citation form (as is typical for most dictionaries designed for human readability). These remarks cover only a small part of the information encoded in the lexical entry, and some sense of its complexity can be seen by simply comparing the representation in (4) with the one in figure 3.4, which attempts to make explicit much of the information implicitly encoded in (4).

While the example illustrated by (4) and figure 3.4 is drawn from a traditional dictionary entry, the scope of possible kinds of lexical data is quite vast. A widely used lexical data type in historical and comparative linguistics, the word list, represents one possible extreme. The lexical information contained in a word list is minimal in nature, consisting generally merely of a form connected to a semantic label (see Poornima & Good 2010). At the other extreme, resources such as the Oxford English Dictionary (OED Online 2019) can be almost encyclopedic in the information provided in their entries.

Lexical data can also be organized in a variety of ways. The traditional thesaurus, for instance, is oriented around concepts rather than forms. In a similar fashion, the widely used WordNet database (Fellbaum 1998) provides thesaurus-like information, though with more precise semantic specification, in a machine-readable form.

The wide range of ways that lexical data can be organized, along with the fact that being able to compare and combine the information in multiple lexical resources can serve important functions, especially in the domain of translation, has led to significant work on developing generalized models for resources containing lexical data. This can be seen quite clearly, for instance, in the development of lexical markup framework, which can be understood as a metamodel for the creation of lexical resources (see Calzolari, Monachini, & Soria 2013). In the present context, what makes this work of particular interest is that it is based on the analysis of linguistic data as a kind of data in and of itself rather than as the representation of some "deeper" linguistic reality.

As with syntagmatic and paradigmatic analyses, discussed in section 3.3, lexical analyses are, in principle, abstract in nature and can be expressed in various forms, including via annotations, as evidenced by the presentation in figure 3.4.

4 Generalizations about languages and language

The goal of most linguistic scholarship is to discover and make use of generalizations about specific languages or language in general on the basis of data of the kind discussed in sections 2 and 3. To pick some simplistic examples, on the basis of the annotated sentence found in (1), a syntactician might conclude that Yeri is a language where subjects generally precede verbs, or, on the basis of an examination of the oppositions presented in figure 3.1, a phonologist might conclude that Kpelle is a language with a two-way underlying tonemic distinction.

In the present context, these kinds of generalizations are of interest for two reasons. On the one hand, they show how certain kinds of data (e.g., annotations or transcriptions) can be used as the basis for more general claims about a language. Descriptive and formal linguistic analysis, in fact, relies on this kind of analytical step. On the other hand, generalizations such as these can also become data for other kinds of investigation. This is seen especially clearly in the subfield of linguistic typology, which investigates crosslinguistic patterns of variation and, therefore, makes use of language-specific generalizations as a prerequisite to typological investigation.

In figure 3.5, a map presenting the global distribution of basic clausal word order is presented (Dryer 2013). Accompanying this map, table 3.2 indicates how the different symbols on the map translate to specific word order types (where S = subject, O = object, and V = verb) and the number of languages in the sample analyzed as attesting each of the seven types used in the study.

A study like Dryer's can be used to arrive at various kinds of linguistic generalizations, such as observations that SOV and SVO order are by the most common attested

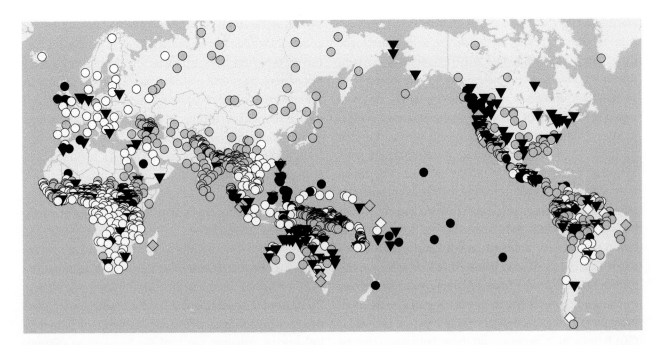

Figure 3.5
The global distribution of different patterns of basic clausal word order.

Table 3.2
Number of languages showing each word order type in a sample of 1,377 languages

Symbol	Basic order	Number
◉	SOV	565
○	SVO	488
●	VSO	95
◆	VOS	25
◇	OVS	11
◆	OSV	4
▼	No dominant order	189

basic clausal word order patterns or that SVO word order predominates in sub-Saharan Africa, Southeast Asia, and Europe. These high-level generalizations can only be made when the lower-level generalizations categorizing each language into a specific type are treated as a kind of data. There is thus a kind of analytical "chain" from making a record of observable linguistic behavior, to adding annotations to that record, to devising a general analysis of the characteristics of a language, to assembling those analyses to arrive at generalizations over large classes of languages or, potentially, language in general. Linguistic analysis at one point in the chain can serve as the underlying data for another kind of analysis at a later point in the chain. There is no obvious end point in this kind of data chaining because each new set of generalizations can be the input to further analysis. Higher levels in these chains frequently involve working with quantitative data derived from data collected from observable behavior, and, depending on the point of view of the researcher, the data created at a higher level may be viewed as a "processed" form of the data at a lower level.

There is nothing specifically linguistic about this stepwise pattern of analysis. However, it nevertheless merits consideration in a linguistic context because the kinds of data that will be involved at each step of the chain are specifically linguistic. Fully assessing the range of such chains of data used in the field is outside of the present work, but this would seem to represent an important problem for fully understanding general requirements for linguistic data management. An especially salient division in linguistics in this respect is when and how observable linguistic data come to be used to arrive at generalizations of how language is used in the world, as depicted in figure 3.5, and when and how it is used to motivate proposals for abstract cognitive models of the grammatical knowledge held by language users of the sort associated with the generative tradition.

Perhaps the most important and underappreciated class of linguistic generalizations that are used as data are the (usually implicit) claims that specific languages exist in the first place. Resources such as Ethnologue (Eberhard, Simons, & Fennig 2019) and Glottolog (Hammarström, Forkel, & Haspelmath 2019) are based on a tremendous amount of data of varying kinds and provide a crucial kind of analytical "infrastructure" for linguistics. Being able to generate a map such as the one in figure 3.5, for instance, presupposes that there is an agreed set of languages in the world and that each can be assigned some location, and typological work generally relies on pre-existing language catalogs and uses their information as data. Resources that aim to be comprehensive on a global scale such as Ethnologue and Glottolog can also be used in studies seeking to understand the state of the world's languages or language families across some significant dimension of variation (e.g., endangerment as in Whalen & Simons 2012). Cysouw and Good (2013) present a proposal on how languages can be defined in terms of the data sets taken to document and describe them, which provides a model for understanding how language catalogs can be created in a way that makes clear the data and analyses that they are based on.

5   Data on language users and situations

Work in sociolinguistics and anthropological linguistics emphasizes the importance of considering data on language use from the perspective of the identity of the participants involved in a given linguistic interaction and the overall context in which the interaction takes place (see, e.g., Hymes [1962] 1971 and Eckert 2012, as well as Poplack, chapter 16, this volume, and Grama, chapter 17, this volume). While detailed sociolinguistic and contextual information is not considered relevant for the interpretation of certain kinds of data (e.g., grammatical acceptability judgments), it is crucial for sociolinguistic investigations and analyses of the relationship between language and culture. Yaeger-Dror and Cieri (2014:467–468) discuss some kinds of identity information that one might need to gather data on to conduct sociolinguistic studies, placing them under the heading of *demographic factors*. These include such things as age, ethnicity, or religion. It may also be important to collect data on the social networks of individuals, and this requires, among other things, collecting identifiers for them (e.g., in the form of a name or a research study code). The precise factors one may want to gather data on are dependent on the study

as well as the social characteristics of the individuals and communities being investigated (see, e.g., Stanford & Preston 2009:6–7 for relevant discussion). Work in the variationist sociolinguistic tradition has tended to emphasize the collection of information on demographic factors due to its interest in exploring correlations between aspects of individual identity and language use.

In addition to data about individuals, sociolinguistic and anthropological linguistic research may also collect data on *situational factors* (Yaeger-Dror & Cieri 2014:468) such as the relationship among the people present during a particular speech event, the nature of the place (e.g., public or private) where the event takes place, or how the event fits into social categories of kinds of social situations (e.g., a religious ceremony or casual interaction). Work in the anthropological linguistic tradition often emphasizes detailed consideration of the role of situational factors for influencing language use, and the best-known example of this is probably the line of research falling under the heading of the ethnography of communication (see, e.g., Hymes [1962] 1971 for a foundational work and Michael 2011:126–128 for overview discussion). To give some sense of the range of situational factors that might need to be considered as well as their potential cultural specificity, the study by Duranti (1981:361–363) of language use in village council meetings within a Samoan village identified the following as significant for understanding the characteristics of turn-taking during these events: the seating arrangement of the participants, the order in which participants are served a ceremonially important drink, the position of a participant's legs while sitting, and whether a participant is wearing clothing on the upper part of their body.

While data about language users and the situations in which speech events take place is not linguistic data in a narrow sense in that they are not strictly about language itself, they are clearly linguistic data in the broader sense that they are collected and used by linguists to come to a better understanding of data derived from observable linguistic behavior.

6   Linguistic metadata, data preservation, and data replicability

While not central to traditional linguistic research, the rise of digital language resources has led to metadata becoming an increasingly important kind of data for linguistics (as well as many other fields). *Metadata* is generally defined along the lines of data about data, though, in the present context, some qualification of this definition is in order. There are some kinds of data about data that are best considered to simply be new data formed on the basis of existing data. This is the case, for instance, with many of the kinds of annotations discussed in section 3.2. The term metadata is generally applied to data about other data when the new data are not seen as directly supporting further analysis. In example (1), the identifier included with the example, 120517–001, which is used to associate the transcription with the recording that it is based on, would normally be considered metadata because an identifier that serves a largely "bookkeeping" function is not treated as new data that support further linguistic analysis.

In some cases, whether a piece of information would be considered metadata or not is dependent on the kind of analysis being conducted. Again, looking at (1), it includes an identifier of the speaker, JS, who produced the utterance. If this example were being used to illustrate a typological feature of the language, then this identifier would be most readily classified as metadata. If this example were being used in a sociolinguistic study to illustrate variation of some kind among different language users, then this identifier would move closer to being data. Strictly speaking, the identifier itself would still be metadata because it is merely an identifier for a person, not the person itself. However, a key difference is that the identity of the speaker could be relevant for understanding variation in a language but would not be relevant if the example is being used to illustrate something understood as a general fact of the language.

If we understand *linguistic* data to be data about languages, then metadata would not, strictly speaking, be linguistic data. If we think of linguistic data as the data needed to effectively conduct linguistic research, then metadata are taking on an increasingly important role in any kind of research that involves the collection of resources that are considered valuable for long-term preservation and of interest beyond the specific project for which they were collected (see also Andreassen, chapter 7, this volume). Resources produced during the course of endangered language documentation (see section 2.2) fall into this class as do resources associated with a project like TalkBank (MacWhinney 2007), which seeks to support data sharing among researchers collecting recordings of conversational interactions.

Broadly speaking, an important division here is between data produced under a paradigm of replicability as opposed to reproducibility (see Berez-Kroeker et al. 2017 for detailed consideration in a linguistic context as well as Gawne & Styles, chapter 2, this volume). Replicable research methods, in principle, allow for equivalent data to be collected at more than one place and time so that results can be verified across multiple studies. Reproducible research methods allow for access to the data on which a study was originally based and provide enough details on the methodology used to analyze that data so that another researcher can verify how the results of the original research were arrived at (Berez-Kroeker et al. 2017:4–5). Linguistic research will never permit the same degree of replicability as is possible in some of the natural sciences. However, some methodological approaches, such as the collection of grammaticality judgments for a given language based on a carefully prepared list of sentences or the phonetic analysis of words collected in a highly controlled way, should allow for replication assuming similar kinds of language users can be found. Other approaches, such as the collection of an oral history from a skilled storyteller of an endangered language or child language data recorded within a household, do not allow for replicability. This division is not necessarily a strict one. Data gathered via the use of a standard prompt across subjects, such as the well-known example of the so-called frog stories where language users are shown a picture-based narrative and asked to recount it orally (see Berman & Slobin 1994), can be expected to be broadly similar across studies if collected across a wide enough pool of language users, but significant individual-level variation would also be considered normal in a way that would be less expected in the case of, for instance, a carefully controlled grammatical judgment elicitation task.

While modern data storage technologies greatly facilitate the preservation of all kinds of linguistic data, long-term archiving has been the highest priority for data that is either difficult or impossible to replicate, whether because there are significant barriers to collecting it more than once (e.g., a recording from one of the last users of an endangered language) or because it requires significant resources to create (e.g., large annotated text corpora). Data of these kinds have been the primary focus for the development of metadata standards for linguistics because of the likelihood that they will be reused. The two sets of metadata standards that are probably most widely discussed within linguistics at present are the Open Language Archives Community (OLAC) standard (Simons & Bird 2008) and the Component Metadata Infrastructure (CMDI) framework (Broeder et al. 2012). The OLAC standard, by design, provides a specification of the baseline metadata that should be associated with a linguistic resource, and this makes it optimized for information exchange about the content of an archive, for example, to support resource discovery. CMDI has a component-based model that allows different projects to create their own metadata standards by using parts of other standards or defining specific sets of metadata fields for their own needs.

Metadata standards developed within the CMDI framework are designed to be as compatible with each other as their different content will allow. The framework was created in recognition of the fact that the specific metadata needs of different subfields are too diverse to be subsumed under a single standard, and its design, in part, represents a response to issues that arose in developing the ISLE Metadata Initiative (IMDI) standard (Broeder et al. 2012:1), which was primarily intended for use with multimedia corpora (Broeder & Van Uytvanck 2014:159).[9] IMDI is much more expansive than OLAC and a comparison of the two gives some sense for the possible scope of linguistic metadata (see also Austin 2006:94 for a list of possible functions for linguistic metadata). OLAC metadata are primarily oriented around creating a basic descriptive record for each linguistic resource in a collection, while IMDI metadata additionally allow for the description of information about the relationships among resources within a collection to be described (e.g., grouping a given set of resources into a corpus corresponding to work done during a specific project), the characteristics of the people involved in the creation of a resource, and the context in which a recording was made, among other kinds of information (see Broeder & Wittenburg 2006:127).

It seems clear that linguistic metadata will increase in importance as a kind of linguistic data as more resources become digitally available and expectations increase for their degree of interoperation, that is, the ability for the information contained within them to be effectively combined for different applications (see Witt et al. 2009 for relevant discussion in a linguistic context and Wilkinson et al. 2016 for more general discussion). Finally, while the discussion in this chapter is largely aimed at the research community, it is worth emphasizing that, in many cases, languages resources will be of interest to language communities as well as the general public, and metadata can play a central role in ensuring that those resources can be discovered and used in a wide range of contexts.

7   The breadth and expanding scope of linguistic data

While "data" play a leading role in analysis across all subdisciplines of linguistics, understanding the full scope of the data made use of by linguists has not been a central concern of the field. Nevertheless, the wide range of data types involved in linguistic analysis would seem to provide an underrecognized opportunity for linguistics to be at the forefront of questions of data management because linguists are familiar with a much wider range of data types than are scholars working in many other disciplines.

In fact, if one understands linguistic data to include data of any kind that are used to support linguistic investigation, this survey has, for reasons of practicality, left out many kinds of data that are not specifically connected to language but are important in interdisciplinary studies. Bostoen et al. (2015), for example, place linguistic data alongside data from biogeography, palynology (the study of particulate samples), and archaeology in making a proposal regarding the dynamics of the Bantu language expansion in sub-Saharan Africa. Similarly, Pakendorf et al. (2017) consider the relationship between linguistic and genetic data as a means of arriving at a better understanding of the historical forces shaping language contact among different language groups in southern Africa. In other domains, Yu, Abrego-Collier, and Sonderegger (2013) combine linguistic data with information from psychological assessment tasks to look at factors that could explain individual differences in language use, and Berez (2015) demonstrates how the integration of linguistic data and geographic information systems data can yield useful insights in the analysis of spatial language. If we include data from allied fields alongside "core" kinds of data about language, then it is clear that the scope of "linguistic" data can extend far beyond what has been discussed here.

As a final note, it seems worth briefly remarking on the interplay between data and the methods used to analyze data. Heggarty, Maguire, and McMahon (2010), for instance, consider one of the most long-standing problems in linguistic analysis—the reconstruction of the historical relationships of languages within a language family—in light of the availability of phylogenetic methods and tools developed within the biological sciences. The use of these methods raises significant questions regarding the curation and coding of lexical data (e.g., whether binary or multistate variables should be used) that were not in focus when more traditional methods were employed.

Time-aligned annotation of the sort discussed in section 3.2 provides another relevant example. The availability of technologies allowing for the creation of digital recordings and tools to annotate those recordings has, in effect, created a new kind of linguistic data that did not exist previously. The field of linguistics is currently seeing rapid changes in the methods used to analyze language, and it seems likely that in the coming years this will result in the scope of linguistic data being similarly expanded to better support the kinds of analyses these methods support.

Notes

1. I would like to thank the editors of this Handbook as well as Philipp Conzett and Koenraad De Smedt for comments on an earlier version of this chapter.

2. "Hybrid" corpora also exist that combine primary text data with data in other formats such as audio and video with accompanying transcription (see, e.g., Anderson, Beavan, & Kay 2007).

3. I use the term acceptable here broadly to encompass sentences that are considered syntactically grammatical, semantically interpretable (rather than anomalous), or pragmatically felicitous.

4. See section 4 for discussion of Glottolog (Hammarström, Forkel, & Haspelmath 2019), which is the source of glottocodes.

5. The abbreviations in the gloss line of the example in (1) are used as follows: 1=first person, 2=second person, F=feminine, R=realis, SG=singular.

6. The full metadata record for the recording associated with the example in (1) can be found at https://hdl.handle.net/1839 /B7031E9D-78CC-44DF-8B2A-889D541E3180.

7. The example in TEI Consortium (2019:section 9.3.4) appears to be adapted from an edition of Merriam-Webster's *New Collegiate Dictionary*. The example uses a markup format developed by the Text Encoding Initiative, which is more widely used in fields outside of linguistics. However, see Romary and Witt (2014) for consideration of the application of the recommendations of this initiative to linguistic resources.

8. The sequence <!— ... —> in the XML representation in figure 3.4 is a so-called comment, meaning that it is to be interpreted as a human-readable remark on the XML structure. In this case, the comment consists of "..." and indicates that some aspects of the data represented in (4) are left out of the XML representation.

9. Detailed discussion of the IMDI standard is found in Broeder and Wittenburg (2006).

References

Abeillé, Anne. 2003. Introduction. In *Treebanks: Building and Using Parsed Corpora*, ed. Anne Abeillé, xiii–xxvi. Dordrecht: Kluwer.

Abrusán, Márta. 2019. Semantic anomaly, pragmatic infelicity, and ungrammaticality. *Annual Review of Linguistics* 5 (1): 329–351.

Anderson, Jean, Dave Beavan, and Christian Kay. 2007. SCOTS: Scottish Corpus of Texts and Speech. In *Creating and Digitizing Language Corpora: Volume 1: Synchronic Databases*, ed. Joan C. Beal, Karen P. Corrigan, and Hermann L. Moisl, 17–34. Basingstoke, UK: Palgrave Macmillan.

Austin, Peter K. 2006. Data and language documentation. In *Essentials of Language Documentation*, ed. Jost Gippert, Nikolaus Himmelmann, and Ulrike Mosel, 87–112. Berlin: Mouton de Gruyter.

Baerman, Matthew, Dunstan Brown, and Greville G. Corbett. 2005. *The Syntax–Morphology Interface: A Study of Syncretism*. Cambridge: Cambridge University Press.

Beal, Joan C., Karen P. Corrigan, and Hermann L. Moisl, eds. 2007. *Creating and Digitizing Language Corpora: Volume 1: Synchronic Databases*. Basingstoke, UK: Palgrave Macmillan.

Bell, John, and Steven Bird. 2000. A preliminary study of the structure of lexicon entries. In *Proceedings from the Workshop on Web-Based Language Documentation and Description*. Philadelphia, December 12–15, 2000. https://web.archive.org/web /20010603214720/https://www.ldc.upenn.edu/exploration /expl2000/papers/bell/bell.html (originally available at http:// www.ldc.upenn.edu/exploration/expl2000/papers/bell/bell.html).

Bender, Emily M., Sumukh Ghodke, Timothy Baldwin, and Rebecca Dridan. 2012. From database to treebank: On enhancing hypertext grammars with grammar engineering and treebank search. *Language Documentation and Conservation* Special Publication 4:179–206. http://hdl.handle.net/10125/4535.

Beres, Anna M. 2017. Time is of the essence: A review of electroencephalography (EEG) and event-related brain potentials (ERPs) in language research. *Applied Psychophysiology and Biofeedback* 42 (4): 246–255. https://doi.org/10.1007/s10484-017-9371-3.

Berez, Andrea L. 2015. Directionals, episodic structure, and geographic information systems: AREA/PUNCTUAL distinctions in Ahtna travel narration. *Linguistics Vanguard* 1 (1): 155–175.

Berez-Kroeker, Andrea L., Lauren Gawne, Susan Smythe Kung, Barbara F. Kelly, Tyler Heston, Gary Holton, Peter Pulsifer, et al. 2017. Reproducible research in linguistics: A position statement on data citation and attribution in our field. *Linguistics* 56 (1): 1–18.

Berman, Ruth A., and Dan Isaac Slobin. 1994. *Relating Events in Narrative: A Cross-linguistic Developmental Study.* Hillsdale, NJ: Lawrence Erlbaum.

Bickel, Balthasar, Bernard Comrie, and Martin Haspelmath. 2008. *The Leipzig Glossing Rules: Conventions for Interlinear Morpheme by Morpheme Glosses.* https://www.eva.mpg.de/lingua/pdf/Glossing-Rules.pdf.

Birch, Bruce. 2014. Data collection. In *The Oxford Handbook of Corpus Phonology*, ed. Jacques Durand, Ulrike Gut, and Gjert Kristoffersen, 27–45. Oxford: Oxford University Press.

Bird, Steven. 1999. Multidimensional exploration of online linguistic field data. In *Proceedings of the 29th Annual Meeting of the Northeast Linguistics Society*, ed. Pius Tamanji, Masako Hirotani, and Nancy Hall, 33–47. Amherst, MA: Graduate Linguistics Student Association.

Bird, Steven, and Gary Simons. 2003. Seven dimensions of portability for language documentation and description. *Language* 79:557–582.

BNC Consortium. 2007. *The British National Corpus,* version 3 (BNC XML edition). Distributed by Bodleian Libraries, University of Oxford, on behalf of the BNC Consortium. http://www.natcorp.ox.ac.uk/.

Boas, Franz. 1911. Linguistics and ethnology. In *Handbook of American Indian languages*, ed. Franz Boas, 59–73. Washington, DC: Government Printing Office.

Boersma, Paul, and David Weenink. 2019. *Praat: Doing Phonetics by Computer* [computer program]. http://www.praat.org/.

Bonelli, Elena Tognini. 2010. Theoretical overview of the evolution of corpus linguistics. In *The Routledge Handbook of Corpus Linguistics*, ed. Anne O'Keeffe and Michael McCarthy, 14–27. Abingdon, UK: Routledge.

Bostoen, Koen, Bernard Clist, Charles Doumenge, Rebecca Grollemund, Jean-Marie Hombert, Joseph Koni Muluwa, and Jean Maley. 2015. Middle to late Holocene paleoclimatic change and the early Bantu expansion in the rain forests of Western Central Africa. *Current Anthropology* 56 (3): 354–384.

Bow, Catherine, Baden Hughes, and Steven Bird. 2003. Towards a general model for interlinear text. In *Proceedings of E-MELD 2003: Digitizing and Annotating Texts and Field Recordings.* East Lansing, Michigan, July 11–13. http://e-meld.org/workshop/2003/bowbadenbird-paper.html.

Bresnan, Joan. 2001. *Lexical-Functional Syntax.* Oxford: Blackwell.

Broeder, Daan, and Dieter Van Uytvanck. 2014. Metadata formats. In *The Oxford Handbook of Corpus Phonology*, ed. Jacques Durand, Ulrike Gut, and Gjert Kristoffersen, 150–165. Oxford: Oxford University Press.

Broeder, Daan, Menzo Windhouwer, Dieter Van Uytvanck, Twan Goosen, and Thorsten Trippel. 2012. CMDI: A component metadata infrastructure. In *Proceedings of the Workshop on Describing LRs with Metadata: Towards Flexibility and Interoperability in the Documentation of LR, LREC 2012*, Istanbul, Turkey, 1–4. http://www.lrec-conf.org/proceedings/lrec2012/workshops/11.LREC2012%20Metadata%20Proceedings.pdf.

Broeder, Daan, and Peter Wittenburg. 2006. The IMDI metadata framework, its current application and future direction. *International Journal of Metadata, Semantics and Ontologies* 1 (2): 119–132.

Brugman, Hennie, and Albert Russel. 2004. Annotating multimedia/multi-modal resources with ELAN. In *Proceedings of the Fourth International Conference on Language Resources and Evaluation (LREC'04)*, 2065–2068. Lisbon: ELRA. http://www.lrec-conf.org/proceedings/lrec2004/pdf/480.pdf.

Calzolari, Nicoletta, Monica Monachini, and Claudia Soria. 2013. LMF: Historical context and perspectives. In *LMF: Lexical Markup Framework*, ed. Gil Francopoulo, 1–18. London: ISTE Ltd and Wiley and Sons.

Carpenter, Bob. 1992. *The Logic of Typed Feature Structures.* Cambridge: Cambridge University Press.

Childs, G. Tucker, Jeff Good, and Alice Mitchell. 2014. Beyond the ancestral code: Towards a model for sociolinguistic language documentation. *Language Documentation and Conservation* 8: 168–191.

Cohn, Abigail. 2001. Phonology. In *The Handbook of Linguistics*, ed. Mark Aronoff and Janie Rees-Miller, 180–212. Oxford: Blackwell.

Cysouw, Michael, and Jeff Good. 2013. Languoid, doculect, and glossonym: Formalizing the notion "language." *Language Documentation and Conservation* 7:331–359.

Davies, Mark. 2008–. *The Corpus of Contemporary American English (COCA): 600 million words, 1990–present.* https://corpus.byu.edu/coca/.

Davies, Mark. 2013. *Corpus of News on the Web (NOW): 3+ billion words from 20 countries, updated every day.* https://corpus.byu.edu/now/.

Diessel, Holger. 2017. Usage-based linguistics. *Oxford Research Encyclopedia of Linguistics.* https://dx.doi.org/10.1093/acrefore/9780199384655.013.363.

Diestel, Reinhard. 1997. *Graph Theory.* New York: Springer.

Dimmendaal, Gerrit J. 2010. Language description and "the new paradigm": What linguists may learn from ethnocinematographers. *Language Documentation and Conservation* 4:152–158.

Dryer, Matthew S. 2013. Order of subject, object and verb. In *The World Atlas of Language Structures Online*, ed. Matthew S.

Dryer and Martin Haspelmath. Leipzig: Max Planck Institute for Evolutionary Anthropology. http://wals.info/chapter/81.

Duranti, Alessandro. 1981. Speechmaking and the organisation of discourse in a Samoan *fono*. *Journal of the Polynesian Society* 90 (3): 357–400.

Durkin, Philip, ed. 2016. *The Oxford Handbook of Lexicography*. Oxford: Oxford University Press.

Eberhard, David M., Gary F. Simons, and Charles D. Fennig, eds. 2019. *Ethnologue: Languages of the World*, 22nd ed. Dallas: SIL International. http://www.ethnologue.com.

Eckert, Penelope. 2012. Three waves of variation study: The emergence of meaning in the study of sociolinguistic variation. *Annual Review of Anthropology* 41 (1): 87–100.

Fellbaum, Christiane, ed. 1998. *WordNet: An Electronic Lexical Database*. Cambridge: MIT Press.

Gibbon, Dafydd. 2002. Prosodic information in an integrated lexicon. In *Speech Prosody 2002*. ISCA Archive. http://www.isca-speech.org/archive/sp2002.

Gippert, Jost. 2006. Linguistic documentation and the encoding of textual materials. In *Essentials of Language Documentation*, ed. Jost Gippert, Nikolaus Himmelmann, and Ulrike Mosel, 337–361. Berlin: Mouton de Gruyter.

Good, Jeff. 2004. The descriptive grammar as a (meta)database. In *Proceedings of E-MELD 2004: Linguistic Databases and Best Practice*. Detroit, Michigan. July 15–18. http://www.e-meld.org/workshop/2004/jcgood-paper.html.

Good, Jeff. 2011. Data and language documentation. In *The Cambridge Handbook of Endangered Languages*, ed. Peter K. Austin and Julia Sallabank, 212–234. Cambridge: Cambridge University Press.

Goodman, Michael Wayne, Joshua Crowgey, Fei Xia, and Emily M. Bender. 2015. Xigt: Extensible interlinear glossed text for natural language processing. *Language Resources and Evaluation* 49 (2): 455–485.

Gries, Stefan Th., and Andrea L. Berez. 2017. Linguistic annotation in/for corpus linguistics. In *Handbook of Linguistic Annotation*, ed. Nancy Ide and James Pustejovsky, 379–409. Dordrecht, the Netherlands: Springer.

Grieve, Jack, Andrea Nini, and Diansheng Guo. 2017. Analyzing lexical emergence in Modern American English online. *English Language and Linguistics* 21 (1): 99–127.

Hammarström, Harald, Robert Forkel, and Martin Haspelmath. 2019. *Glottolog 3.4*. Jena, Germany: Max Planck Institute for the Science of Human History. https://glottolog.org/.

Hayes, Bruce. 1990. Precompiled phrasal phonology. In *The Phonology-Syntax Connection*, ed. Sharon Inkelas and Draga Zec, 85–108. Stanford: CSLI.

Heggarty, Paul, Warren Maguire, and April McMahon. 2010. Splits or waves? Trees or webs? How divergence measures and network analysis can unravel language histories. *Philosophical Transactions of the Royal Society B: Biological Sciences* 365:3829–3843.

Himmelmann, Nikolaus P. 1998. Documentary and descriptive linguistics. *Linguistics* 36:161–195.

Himmelmann, Nikolaus P. 2012. Linguistic data types and the interface between language documentation and description. *Language Documentation and Conservation* 6:187–207.

Hyman, Larry M. 2011. Tone: Is it different? In *The Handbook of Phonological Theory*, 2nd ed., ed. John A. Goldsmith, Jason Riggle, and Alan C. L. Yu, 197–239. Chichester: Wiley-Blackwell.

Hymes, Dell H. (1962) 1971. The ethnography of speaking. In *Anthropology and Human Behavior*, ed. Thomas Gladwin and William C. Sturtevant, 13–53. Washington, DC: The Anthropological Society of Washington.

Ide, Nancy. 2017. Introduction: The handbook of linguistic annotation. In *Handbook of Linguistic Annotation*, ed. Nancy Ide and James Pustejovsky, 1–18. Dordrecht, the Netherlands: Springer.

Ide, Nancy, Christian Chiarcos, Manfred Stede, and Steve Cassidy. 2017. Designing annotation schemes: From model to representation. In *Handbook of Linguistic Annotation*, ed. Nancy Ide and James Pustejovsky, 73–111. Dordrecht, the Netherlands: Springer.

Ide, Nancy, Adam Kilgarriff, and Laurent Romary. 2000. A formal model of dictionary structure and content. In *Proceedings of the Ninth EURALEX International Congress*, ed. Ulrich Heid, Stefan Evert, Egbert Lehmann, and Christian Rohrer, 113–126. Stuttgart, Germany: Institut für Maschinelle Sprachverarbeitung. http://arxiv.org/abs/0707.3270.

Ide, Nancy, and James Pustejovsky, eds. 2017. *Handbook of Linguistic Annotation*. Dordrecht, the Netherlands: Springer.

Kaan, Edith. 2007. Event-related potentials and language processing: A brief overview. *Language and Linguistics Compass* 1 (6): 571–591.

Kendall, Tyler. 2008. On the history and future of sociolinguistic data. *Language and Linguistics Compass* 2 (2): 332–351.

Kendall, Tyler. 2011. Corpora from a sociolinguistic perspective. *Revista Brasileira de Linguística Aplicada* 11:361–389. doi:10.1590/S1984–63982011000200005.

Koenig, W., H. K. Dunn, and L. Y. Lacy. 1946. The sound spectrograph. *Journal of the Acoustical Society of America* 18:19–49. doi:10.1121/1.1916342.

Labov, William. 1972. *Sociolinguistic Patterns*. Philadelphia: University of Pennsylvania Press.

Ladefoged, Peter. 1957. Use of palatography. *Journal of Speech and Hearing Disorders* 22 (5): 764–774.

Langacker, Ronald W. 1987. *Foundations of Cognitive Grammar: Volume I: Theoretical Prerequisites.* Stanford: Stanford University Press.

MacWhinney, Brian. 2007. The TalkBank project. In *Creating and Digitizing Language Corpora: Volume 1: Synchronic Databases,* ed. Joan C. Beal, Karen P. Corrigan, and Hermann L. Moisl, 164–180. Basingstoke, UK: Palgrave Macmillan.

Margetts, Anna, and Andrew Margetts. 2012. Audio and video recording techniques for linguistic research. In *The Oxford Handbook of Linguistic Fieldwork,* ed. Nicholas Thieberger, 13–53. Oxford: Oxford University Press.

Maxwell, Mike. 2012. Electronic grammars and reproducible research. *Language Documentation and Conservation* Special Publication 4:207–234. http://hdl.handle.net/10125/4536.

McCarthy, Michael, and Anne O'Keeffe. 2010. Historical perspective: What are corpora and how have they evolved? In *The Routledge Handbook of Corpus Linguistics,* ed. Anne O'Keeffe and Michael McCarthy, 3–13. Abingdon, UK: Routledge.

McCawley, James D. 1982. Parentheticals and discontinuous constituent structure. *Linguistic Inquiry* 13:91–106.

McCawley, James D. 1998. *The Syntactic Phenomena of English,* 2nd ed. Chicago: University of Chicago Press.

Michael, Lev. 2011. Language and culture. In *The Cambridge Handbook of Endangered Languages,* ed. Peter K. Austin and Julia Sallabank, 120–140. Cambridge: Cambridge University Press.

Moravcsik, Edith A. 2010. Conflict resolution in syntactic theory. *Studies in Language* 34 (3): 636–669.

Mosel, Ulrike. 2006. Grammaticography: The art and craft of writing grammars. In *Catching Language: The Standing Challenge of Grammar Writing,* ed. Felix Ameka, Alan Dench, and Nicholas Evans, 41–68. Berlin: Mouton de Gruyter.

Nadeau, David, and Satoshi Sekine. 2007. A survey of named entity recognition and classification. *Lingvisticæ Investigationes* 30 (1): 3–26.

Newmeyer, Frederick J. 1998. *Language Form and Language Function.* Cambridge: MIT Press.

Nordhoff, Sebastian. 2012. The grammatical description as a collection of form-meaning-pairs. *Language Documentation and Conservation* Special Publication 4:33–62. http://hdl.handle.net/10125/4529.

OED Online. 2019. Oxford: Oxford University Press. http://www.oed.com.

Pakendorf, Brigitte, Hilde Gunnink, Bonny Sands, and Koen Bostoen. 2017. Prehistoric Bantu-Khoisan language contact. *Language Dynamics and Change* 7 (1): 1–46.

Palmer, Alexis, and Katrin Erk. 2007. IGT-XML: An XML format for interlinearized glossed text. In *Proceedings of the Linguistic Annotation Workshop (LAW '07),* 176–183. Stroudsburg, PA: Association for Computational Linguistics. http://dl.acm.org/citation.cfm?id=1642059.1642087.

Penton, David, Catherine Bow, Steven Bird, and Baden Hughes. 2004. Towards a general model for linguistic paradigms. In *Proceedings of E-MELD 2004: Linguistic Databases and Best Practice.* Detroit, Michigan, July 15–18. http://e-meld.org/workshop/2004/bird-paper.pdf.

Phillips, Colin, and Matthew Wagers. 2007. Relating structure and time in linguistics and psycholinguistics. In *The Oxford Handbook of Psycholinguistics,* ed. M. Gareth Gaskell, 739–756. Oxford: Oxford University Press.

Poornima, Shakthi, and Jeff Good. 2010. Modeling and encoding traditional wordlists for machine applications. In *Proceedings of the 2010 Workshop on NLP and Linguistics: Finding the Common Ground (NLPLING '10),* ed. Fei Xia, William Lewis, and Lori Levin, 1–9. Stroudsburg, PA: Association for Computational Linguistics.

Pustejovksy, James, Harry Bunt, and Annie Zaenen. 2017. Designing annotation schemes: From theory to model. In *Handbook of Linguistic Annotation,* ed. Nancy Ide and James Pustejovksy, 21–72. Dordrecht, the Netherlands: Springer.

Romary, Laurent, and Andreas Witt. 2014. Data formats for phonological corpora. In *The Oxford Handbook of Corpus Phonology,* ed. Jacques Durand, Ulrike Gut, and Gjert Kristoffersen, 166–190. Oxford: Oxford University Press.

Sag, Ivan A., Thomas Wasow, and Emily M. Bender. 2003. *Syntactic Theory: A Formal Introduction,* 2nd ed. Stanford: CSLI.

Schembri, Adam. 2010. Documenting sign languages. In *Language Documentation and Description,* vol. 7, ed. Peter K. Austin, 105–143. London: SOAS.

Schultze-Berndt, Eva. 2006. Linguistic annotation. In *Essentials of Language Documentation,* ed. Jost Gippert, Nikolaus Himmelmann, and Ulrike Mosel, 213–251. Berlin: Mouton de Gruyter.

Schütze, Carson T. (1996) 2016. *The Empirical Base of Linguistics: Grammaticality Judgments and Linguistic Methodology.* Berlin: Language Science Press.

Sebba, Mark, and Susan Dray. 2007. Developing and using a corpus of written creole. In *Creating and Digitizing Language Corpora: Volume 1: Synchronic Databases,* ed. Joan C. Beal, Karen P. Corrigan, and Hermann L. Moisl, 181–204. Basingstoke, UK: Palgrave Macmillan.

Seyfeddinipur, Mandana. 2012. Reasons for documenting gesture and suggestions for how to go about it. In *The Oxford Handbook of Linguistic Fieldwork,* ed. Nicholas Thieberger, 147–165. Oxford: Oxford University Press.

Seyfeddinipur, Mandana, and Felix Rau. Keeping it real: Video data in language documentation and language archiving. *Language Documentation and Conservation* 14:503–519.

Simons, Gary F. 2006. *Ensuring That Digital Data Last: The Priority of Archival Form over Working Form and Presentation Form.* Dallas: SIL International. https://web.archive.org/web/20130315021812/http://www-01.sil.org/silewp/2006/003/SILEWP2006-003.htm (originally available at: http://www.sil.org/silewp/2006/003/SILEWP2006-003.htm).

Simons, Gary F., and Steven Bird, eds. 2008. *OLAC Metadata.* http://www.language-archives.org/OLAC/metadata.html.

Sprouse, Jon. 2013. Acceptability judgments. In *Oxford Bibliographies Online: Linguistics.* Oxford: Oxford University Press.

Stanford, James N., and Dennis R. Preston. 2009. The lure of a distant horizon: Variation in Indigenous minority languages. In *Variation in Indigenous Minority Languages*, ed. James N. Stanford and Dennis R. Preston, 1–20. Amsterdam: Benjamins.

Strassel, Stephanie, and Jennifer Tracey. 2016. LORELEI language packs: Data, tools, and resources for technology development in low resource languages. In *Proceedings of the Tenth International Conference on Language Resources and Evaluation (LREC 2016)*, 3273–3280. Paris: ELRA.

TEI Consortium. 2019. Dictionaries. In *TEI P5: Guidelines for Electronic Text Encoding and Interchange [version 3.5.0]*, ed. TEI Consortium, chapter 9. https://www.tei-c.org/release/doc/tei-p5-doc/en/html/DI.html.

Thieberger, Nicholas. 2009. Steps toward a grammar embedded in data. In *New Challenges in Typology: Transcending the Borders and Refining the Distinctions*, ed. Patience Epps and Alexandre Arkhipov, 389–407. Berlin: Mouton de Gruyter.

Thieberger, Nicholas, and Andrea L. Berez. 2012. Linguistic data management. In *The Oxford Handbook of Linguistic Fieldwork*, ed. Nicholas Thieberger, 90–118. Oxford: Oxford University Press.

Trippel, Thorsten. 2006. *The Lexicon Graph Model: A Generic Model for Multimodal Lexicon Development.* Saarbrücken, Germany: AQ-Verlag.

Trippel, Thorsten. 2009. Representation formats and models for lexicons. In *Representation Formats and Models for Lexicons*, ed. Andreas Witt and Dieter Metzing, 165–184. Berlin: Springer.

van Marle, Jaap. 2000. Paradigmatic and syntagmatic relations. In *Morphology: An International Handbook on Inflection and Word-formation*, ed. Geert Booij, Christian Lehmann, and Joachim Mugdan, 225–234. Berlin: De Gruyter.

Welmers, William E. 1962. The phonology of Kpelle. *Journal of African Languages* 1:69–93.

Whalen, D. H., and Gary F. Simons. 2012. Endangered language families. *Language* 88 (1): 155–173.

Wilkinson, Mark D., Michel Dumontier, IJsbrand Jan Aalbersberg, Gabrielle Appleton, Myles Axton, Arie Baak, Niklas Blomberg, et al. 2016. The FAIR guiding principles for scientific data management and stewardship. *Scientific Data* 3 (1): 160018. https://doi.org/10.1038/sdata.2016.18.

Willems, Roel M., and Marcel A. J. van Gerven. 2018. New fMRI methods for the study of language. In *The Oxford Handbook of Psycholinguistics*, ed. Shirley-Ann Rueschemeyer and M. Gareth Gaskell, 975–991. Oxford: Oxford University Press.

Wilson, Jennifer. 2014. Yeri. *The Language Archive.* https://hdl.handle.net/1839/00-0000-0000-001A-E16A-5.

Wilson, Jennifer. 2017. A grammar of Yeri: A Torricelli language of Papua New Guinea. PhD dissertation, University at Buffalo.

Witt, Andreas, Ulrich Heid, Felix Sasaki, and Gilles Sérasset. 2009. Multilingual language resources and interoperability. *Language Resources and Evaluation* 43 (1): 1–14.

Woodbury, Anthony C. 2011. Language documentation. In *The Cambridge Handbook of Endangered Languages*, ed. Peter K. Austin and Julia Sallabank, 159–186. Cambridge: Cambridge University Press.

Yaeger-Dror, Malcah, and Christopher Cieri. 2014. Introduction to the special issue on archiving sociolinguistic data. *Language and Linguistics Compass* 8 (11): 465–471.

Yu, Alan C. L., Carissa Abrego-Collier, and Morgan Sonderegger. 2013. Phonetic imitation from an individual-difference perspective: Subjective attitude, personality and "autistic" traits. *PLOS ONE* 8:e74746.

4 Indigenous Peoples, Ethics, and Linguistic Data

Gary Holton, Wesley Y. Leonard, and Peter L. Pulsifer

1 Introduction: Linguistic data and Indigenous peoples

The world is dominated by just a few large languages that mediate mass communication, social media, education, politics, and many other domains. A study by Kornai (2013) found just sixteen of the world's nearly seven thousand languages to be "digitally thriving," with a firmly established online presence and the tools necessary to live and interact in an increasingly digitally connected world. These sixteen languages are spoken natively by some 2.8 billion people, or nearly 40% of the world's population. These are the languages of Big Data, machine translation, automated speech recognition—the ones that technology companies care most about. For these languages, ethical protocols are largely driven by commercial interests and entail regional legal structures pertaining to data governance.[1] But the vast majority of the world's linguistic diversity is found elsewhere: namely, within the thousands of minority languages, many of which belong to small, often politically and economically marginalized Indigenous groups.[2] Data from these small and often critically endangered languages are key for understanding linguistic diversity—a major focus of linguistic science—but also for maintaining that diversity through language maintenance and reclamation efforts. Linguistic research on Indigenous minority languages takes place against a backdrop of increasing threats to Indigenous language vitality and pressures to shift away from Indigenous languages toward languages of wider communication—often colonial languages (e.g., English, Spanish, Mandarin). We emphasize that language endangerment, along with the response by various stakeholders such as linguists, archivists, and especially the communities these languages come from, is central to the discussion of Indigenous peoples,

ethics, and linguistic data. While the causes of language endangerment are many and complex, social and cultural dislocation due to unequal power relations between minority communities and majority populations have played major roles in facilitating language shift (Grenoble 2011). Traditional models of linguistic research often mirror these unequal power relationships (Leonard 2018), with the result that linguists researching Indigenous languages may be seen as agents of social and cultural dislocation as well. Moreover, Indigenous communities may view linguistic research as out of step with the impending threat of language loss. In particular, communities experiencing rapid language shift and consequent language endangerment may take a more holistic view of language research as being embedded within a process of language reclamation (cf. Leonard 2017) and psychological healing (cf. Meek 2010; Jacob 2013) against a backdrop of numerous ethical violations that underlie language shift. Hence, any discussion of ethics in linguistic data requires a discussion of Indigenous data and must adhere to protocols for working with Indigenous data, as well as to the broader sociopolitical contexts in which language work takes place. However, where formal, legal frameworks do exist governing Indigenous and minority language data, these frameworks tend to be modeled on those developed for large languages rather than the cultural values or political concerns of Indigenous populations. We thus focus in this chapter on ethical issues in relation to Indigenous languages and the communities they come from, for it is in this context that the intersection of people, ethics, and data has been least formalized, despite its significant implications.

1.1 Who defines "linguistic data"?

Some of the limitations in theorizing this intersection reflect that in most scholarly literature the notion of "linguistic data" is not explicitly defined. A working definition might be "data used in the study of language" (Good, chapter 3, this volume), but even this seemingly broad definition assumes a particularly narrow and decontextualized view of the relationship between people and data. Often, what counts as data—and by extension what counts as an ethical response to data collection and management—is in the eye of the beholder, thus opening the door to several possible ethical breaches. For example, a particular string of speech may be viewed as data by a researcher but as a sacred incantation by language users. A more general issue is the tendency for language researchers to equate language with data, and by extension to view language as a mere data point. This reductionist view groups everything produced through research as "data" and thus serves to dehumanize and decontextualize language. Especially through any belief system in which language is defined in relation to its users, the assumption that linguistic data could exist in isolation becomes odd, and such an approach is especially problematic for any discussion of ethics because ethics emerge from people and particular contexts. Hence, any useful definition of linguistic data must avoid divorcing data from their sources, with the particular understanding of what constitutes "data" in a given context clarified.

Although the concept of linguistic data itself may be difficult to define, it is nevertheless useful to distinguish among different types of data. Himmelmann (2012) distinguishes among raw data, primary data, and structural data, based on a cline of decreasing language user involvement. *Raw data* consist of original, unannotated recordings and (non-standardized) writings. *Primary data* consist of the annotations, especially transcriptions and translations, applied to the raw data. *Structural data* consist of structural and typological inferences—the "facts" of language. Inherent in this typology is the notion that at least some types of linguistic data are "manufactured" or "produced" rather than collected. Through this lens, primary and structural data may be construed by some as research products and thus creations of the researcher rather than the language community.

While this typology has some utility within the field of linguistics with respect to theorizing language documentation and language archiving, among other areas, it is insufficient for understanding ethics in relation to linguistic data. In particular, the distinction between raw data (produced by speakers and signers) and primary/structural data (produced by researchers) reflects a Western epistemology of data that potentially disenfranchises language users by removing their agency, while concurrently absolving researchers from acknowledging that they always play roles in representing languages because even basic annotations emerge through particular cultural lenses and conventions. At the extreme, this leads to objectification that obscures the fact that language as a social practice is "embedded in a broader cultural matrix, and it depends critically on that matrix for the activity to be meaningful" (Whaley 2011:344). In contrast, Indigenous approaches to linguistic data tend to reflect a "holistic understanding of language as contextualized language" (Fitzgerald 2017:e291). A linguistic message may be encoded as a string of phonemes built into morphemes and clauses, but this string itself also has meaning, expressing information that may have unique cultural significance attached to the people involved in creating it (which may go beyond actual speakers and signers), the place where it was created, and other factors. From this broader perspective, there is not one set of ethical principles for raw data and another for primary/structural data. Given that all data types ultimately derive from speakers and signers in language communities, all data types must engage equally with ethics.

1.2 Who "owns" linguistic data?

Another complexity to the intersection of people, ethics, and data is the notion of language ownership—by whom and to what extent—and the related notion of whether it is ownership, as opposed to other types of relationships such as connection, kinship, or stewardship, that should guide policies and practices surrounding linguistic data. We adopt *ownership* as a working term, recognizing that this word is used in many existing discussions and policies involving language ethics in Indigenous communities (cf. Guerrettaz 2015). Furthermore, the grammars of most languages permit their users to assert ownership over languages and even individual speech forms. Thus, one can speak of "my language" or "my words" using a possessive form.[3] Nevertheless, we emphasize that understanding particular ethical contexts entails engagement with local understandings of the relationships between languages and communities. Central to this exercise is elucidating local meanings of *language* itself, as the type of relationship and associated nuances of ownership often emerge from this definition. Notably, it is common in Indigenous definitions to link language and peoplehood (Leonard 2017), and some such as the following center the relationships between people, ethics, and language highlighted in this chapter:

> Language is
> our unique relationship to the Creator,
> our attitudes, beliefs, values, and
> fundamental notions of what is truth.
> Our languages are the cornerstone of
> who we are as a People.
> Without our languages,
> our cultures cannot survive.
>
> (quoted in Shaw 2001:39, from *Principles for Revitalization of First Nations Languages, Towards Linguistic Justice for First Nations,* Assembly of First Nations, Education Secretariat, 1990)

Emerging from examples such as this one, but also common in non-Indigenous communities, is recognition that languages are social constructs, codes shared by communities of language users. In this sense, linguistic data are very different from many other forms of data because the knowledge exists at the community level even though discrete productions of language occur by individuals. Linguistic data are also not completely public (as with, e.g., meteorological measurements), but nor are they completely private (as with, e.g., medical or genetic records). Moreover, given the social-intersectional nature of language as a communicative medium, privacy concerns are not always addressed at the time of data collection. Many of the questions of ethics and linguistic data center on issues of ownership and consequent rights of access. In considering these questions, it is important to bear in mind the special and unique place of linguistic data as simultaneously public and private, and how existing legal structures may fail to adequately recognize ownership of linguistic data. For example, within the legal structures of countries such as the United States, creative forms of language are often given legal protections (copyright), while everyday utilitarian language is considered to be in the public domain (Collister, chapter 9, this volume). Indigenous communities may, however, feel that all forms of language—whether deemed "creative" or not—should be legally protected and formally placed under community ownership.

The principle that linguistic data are imbued with ownership, which comes with rights and responsibilities, is embedded within current best practice standards in linguistic research, particularly those that provide guidelines for data citation. The *Austin Principles of Data Citation in Linguistics* note that "citations should facilitate readers retrieving information about who contributed to the data, and how they contributed" (Berez-Kroeker, Andreassen, et al. 2018). Similarly, Bird and Simons (2003:571–572) assert citation as one of seven key values that underlie language documentation efforts: "We value the ability of users of a resource to give credit to its creators, as well as to learn the provenance of the sources on which it is based." However, data citation standards remain in their infancy within linguistics (cf. Berez-Kroeker, Gawne, et al. 2018), and even where such standards have been adopted, there is little consistency as to who should be credited (though see Conzett & De Smedt, chapter 11, this volume, on emerging standards in this area). Is the creator or contributor the person who produced the language artifact, the linguist who recorded it, or both? Omitting these details from source citations has the effect of divorcing linguistic data from their sources and, by extension, from the larger sociopolitical contexts in which ethical concerns must be addressed.

One concept that is useful for the purposes of exploring the complexity of ethical approaches to linguistic data is the notion of "legacy" data, that is, those data "which were created when concerns surrounding intellectual property were less sensitive than they are today" (O'Meara & Good 2010:162), and for which usage restrictions often need to be newly considered or reevaluated. Many communities are confronting situations in which their ancestral languages have not been actively used for years or are remembered by just a few Elders.

Often this shift is a result of a history of colonization that has resulted in a transfer of language knowledge from communities to data repositories housed in non-Indigenous archives, where the materials have been deposited by non-Indigenous researchers (often linguists) and curated around Western norms. For example, language materials may be housed separately from ethnographic materials that from the community of origin's perspective should not be separated from language (but see O'Neal 2015 for a summary of efforts to decolonize archives; see also Linn 2014; Shepard 2016; and Wasson, Holton, & Roth 2016 regarding efforts specific to language archives). Archives and data repositories must recognize and respond to the diverse histories and agendas surrounding legacy data. As noted by Christen

(2011:209), "there is neither a singular call, nor a one-size-fits-all answer to the archival questions indigenous peoples bring to bear on the institutions that hold much of their cultural heritage."

We concur with Christen and others who emphasize the inappropriateness of a one-size-fits-all approach, but also observe the following common themes for language work based on legacy data. First is that the stakes tend to be very high when archival legacy data play a crucial role in language reclamation—and some reclamation efforts begin entirely with archival materials (cf. Spence 2018; Lukaniec, chapter 25, this volume). Second is that the original collection and curation of these data are removed in time and social context from these contemporary language reclamation practices, which are increasingly intertwined with broader decolonial efforts by Indigenous communities. As the ethics of legacy data may be different from the ethics of data being actively created, people working with legacy materials must take special care to ensure that ethical concerns are adequately addressed. Failure to do so can result in unintended consequences such as over- or undersharing of materials: Sensitive materials may (and often do) end up in the public domain, or communities may be barred from accessing materials recorded by ancestral community members. Even where consent was obtained, legacy research protocols may be out of step with modern practices and hence warrant reexamination. For example, some legacy materials may be openly available to researchers without legal restrictions; however, if those materials were originally gathered without explicit, documented consent, then the source community may desire to have a voice in determining access conditions. This may even be the case in situations where consent was given but where cultural norms and expectations have shifted since the time of original consent.

2   Indigenous communities, languages, and ethics in linguistics

The mismatch between the contexts of original creation and contemporary use in the case of legacy data aligns with the evolution of ethical practices in linguistics over the past half century, which we summarize in some detail in this section in recognition of how disciplinary histories and norms inform ideas about ethics and vice versa. Particularly important for the current discussion is linguistic fieldwork, which is the context wherein Indigenous language data are often collected. The traditional "ethical" fieldwork model, dubbed the "linguist-focused" model by Czaykowska-Higgins (2009:22), is concerned with minimizing ill effects to the speakers and signers—often stylized as "informants"—involved in the language work. This is very much in line with ethical concerns as expressed by institutional review boards and other bodies concerned with preventing harm to individual research "subjects." As Hale (2001:76) notes, "linguists are inevitably responsible to the larger human community which its [research] results could affect." But in spite of this reference to community, the traditional model reflects a view in which the individual is the natural unit of analysis for determining ethical issues (Leonard & Haynes 2010). Beyond obtaining consent from individual language users and ensuring that they are protected from physical harm, the traditional model is essentially extractive: "'Good' speakers, whose legitimacy is determined by the researcher . . . produce language that is transformed into 'data', which is conceptualised through a 'language as object' metaphor . . . that tends to emphasise structural properties at the expense of social practices" (Leonard 2017:18). In this model, which remains highly valued in the field, data are manufactured as part of the research process and then explicitly decontextualized.

The renewed focus on language documentation and conservation that has emerged over the past two decades has led to a major reexamination of ethical practices in linguistic research (cf. Rice 2006, 2010; Czaykowska-Higgins 2009; Innes & Debenport 2010; Dobrin & Berson 2011). Rice (2006) observes a transition toward a more empowering and participatory model of linguistic research. The most notable outcome of these discussions has been the emergence of a more community-based notion of ethics that emphasizes the responsibilities of researchers not just to individuals but also to communities. This change is reflected in the *Ethics Statement* adopted by the Linguistic Society of America (2009), which makes explicit reference to community:

> While acknowledging that what constitutes the relevant community is a complex issue, we urge linguists to consider how their research affects not only individual research participants, but also the wider community. In general, linguists should strive to determine what will be constructive for all those involved in a research encounter, taking into account the community's cultural norms and values.[4]

What counts as "constructive" in relation to the Linguistic Society of America *Ethics Statement* may vary from one community to another, but it is likely to include some form of what has come to be known as community-based research, that is, research not only *for, on,* and *with* language communities, but also *by* communities (Czaykowska-Higgins 2009:24). This typically involves a training component that develops research capacity within a community (Genetti & Siemens 2013).

At the same time, the trend toward more community-based models of language research has been accompanied by the emergence of two countervailing trends. First, what might be termed the endangered languages movement (cf. Krauss 1992)—which in many ways has spurred on this new discussion of ethics—has at the same time led to objectification and commodification of languages and their users (Hill 2002; Dobrin 2008; Dobrin, Austin, & Nathan 2009; Whaley 2011). This reductionist view envisions a kind of triage in which language research is prioritized based on typological characteristics and vitality assessments. Languages with rare or unusual sound systems or grammatical structures are viewed as important objects of study. Funding applications are justified based on perceived threats to the language, and by extension draw attention to linguistic data as products that must be collected and archived. Language communities are reduced to numbers of users and ranked according to position on scales of language vitality.

Second, the open data movement has led to a more empirical approach to linguistics, in which claims about language are grounded in data, and research results are expected to be both verifiable and reproducible (Berez-Kroeker, Gawne, et al. 2018). This trend has placed an emphasis on long-term archiving of linguistic data and led to the development of best-practice standards and archiving mandates from both funding agencies and academic institutions (Henke & Berez-Kroeker 2016). Moreover, there is also an increasing expectation that these archives be publicly accessible with few restrictions (Seyfeddinipur et al. 2019). These developments have resulted in an exponential increase in both the number of dedicated language archives and the volume of archival material. However, these repositories are most often located outside the control of the communities from which the archival deposits have been extracted (Shepard 2014), thus running counter to the spirit of community-based language work unless special provisions are made.

Underlying both the endangered languages and the open data movements is the notion of language as an object of study. This notion is in some ways fundamental to the traditional conceptualization of linguistic science, in which "language data are extracted from context of usage, and linguistic experiments are replicable" (Grenoble & Whitecloud 2014:344). Yet, this view is in direct conflict with the idea that these data never exist in isolation. Resolving this tension is central to linguistic ethics.

Countering the objectified view of language research is an emerging collaborative model that engages language communities as full partners and thus helps to highlight and validate Indigenous perspectives on language. For example, building on the notion of community-based language research, Leonard and Haynes (2010) propose a process of *collaborative consultation,* which involves continuous reflection and sharing throughout the research process. Referencing two North American Indigenous communities, Leonard and Haynes illustrate the collaborative consultation approach with the notion of speakerhood. They recognize that within any speech community, language research is inextricably tied with the notion of speakerhood; however, this issue is particularly challenging within endangered language communities, where knowledge of language is by definition in decline. A linguist-focused view of ethics might treat speakerhood, similar to the notion of what counts as data, as an objective "fact" that can be measured and assessed without community input. In contrast, a collaborative consultation model frames such issues not as unilateral decisions but rather as negotiable determinations developed through consultation among the stakeholders in a research project. In other words, this model assumes that language communities are not mere sources of data but instead become research partners from the outset (Leonard & Haynes 2010; Rice 2018). By extension, language communities' ethical norms and concerns guide the research development and implementation at all stages.

We observe that the community-based and collaborative approaches discussed are not only emerging as best practices in linguistic research, but are also increasingly a requirement for language researchers. For example, the Council of Athabascan Tribal Governments' Indigenous Knowledge Policy explicitly requires that researchers engage in collaborative research methodologies (Council of Athabascan Tribal Governments 2018). However, while such collaborative approaches are becoming increasingly common in the academy, they remain heavily marked in the sense that they have to be explained and justified and are rarely the default in academic ethical protocols. For example, university ethical oversight structures continue to largely focus on ethics with respect to protecting *individual* research participants, thus easily overlooking or deemphasizing concerns that occur at the community level. This is insufficient when language ownership occurs at the community level and becomes completely deficient when a proposed research project does not technically meet the criteria for oversight by ethical review boards and thus gets no such review. The latter issue is of special concern for projects that involve legacy data that are legally deemed to already be within the public domain.

The response to such situations often involves incorporating Indigenous knowledges and protocols into the existing (largely Western) models, for example, by adding in some sort of required consultation with community leaders about a research project. We recognize beneficial outcomes to such efforts but suggest that this approach is inadequate because it largely maintains the power structures and research models that have facilitated exploitation of Indigenous peoples and languages. Language researchers are increasingly thinking about future uses of materials, but what about the deeper question of how current power relationships will change? Ethical approaches to linguistic data must consider not only the ethical uses of those data but also the ethics of the relationships underlying the data. Thus, we shift the question to one of how data protocols can begin from Indigenous knowledges and protocols, structurally embedding ethical community-centered concerns into all aspects of data collection, management, and use.

3   Indigenous research methods and data sovereignty

To address this question, we highlight important themes that emerge from Indigenous research methods, which collectively privilege Indigenous knowledge systems and protocols, and often critique the assumptions and ethics of dominant research practices (e.g., Wilson 2008; Kovach 2009; Chilisa 2011; Smith 2012; Lambert 2014; Tuck & Yang 2014; Snow et al. 2016). As noted by the Intercontinental American Indigenous Research Association, central to Indigenous research methods is the notion that knowledge is produced through relationships—"with

people in a specific Place, with the culture of Place as understood through [specific Indigenous] cultures, with the source of the research data, and with the person who knows or tells the story that provides information."[5] By extension, and in strong contrast to the language-as-object approach, linguistic data become meaningful and interpretable through awareness of the social contexts in which they are produced and of the people who produce (and reproduce) them.[6] *People* in this case goes beyond the individuals who originally produced the data, such as individual speakers and signers, to also consider others such as Elders and other community leaders, the researcher's professional networks, and so on—stakeholders whose relationships with each other inform the context. Anchored in the strong focus on relationships and the associated accountability, it is common in discussions of Indigenous research methods to recognize several "R-words" that should guide research—and by extension, inform data ethics. Beyond *relationship*, we expand on the following four *R*-words outlined by Snow et al. (2016:360): *responsibility, respect, reciprocity*, and (conceived of as a single principle) *rights and regulations*.[7] *Responsibility* goes beyond accountability to individual research participants to include communities and their ways of knowing, with an eye toward the sociopolitical contexts in which research occurs and to the power structures that it reflects and affects. *Respect* to communities and to their knowledge systems entails centering both in the collection, management, and use of linguistic data. *Reciprocity* includes what many linguists working in community research contexts describe as "giving back" (e.g., by creating language pedagogical materials), but also entails reciprocal relations with respect to the construction of knowledge in areas such as data interpretation. The principle of *rights and regulations*, which attends to the protocols of participation and ownership that ensue from Indigenous self-determination, is central to the Indigenous Data Sovereignty (IDS) movement, which advocates for the direct involvement of Indigenous stakeholders in the collection, management, and use of data about Indigenous peoples. While the term data sovereignty is used primarily within Indigenous contexts, the movement is part of a broader dialogue and set of policies/laws within broader society that are focused on maintaining control over data about individuals and organizations. IDS includes the recognition of the right of Indigenous peoples and nations to govern collection, ownership, and application of their own data, which are widely recognized as cultural, strategic, and economic assets.[8] Moreover, recent developments in the IDS movement are calling for the observance of core protocol and practices when working with Indigenous peoples and knowledge. These include, but are not limited to:

- recognition that tribes must exercise sovereignty when conducting research and managing data;
- following cultural protocols;
- being flexible;
- extending hospitality;
- ensuring appropriate compensation for expertise;
- understanding that access to knowledge is not a universal right;
- recognizing that responsible stewardship includes the task of learning how to interpret and understand data and research;
- accepting that research must benefit Native people.

(School for Advanced Research 2018; National Congress of American Indians 2018, as cited in Carroll, Rodriguez-Lonebear, & Martinez 2019)

In practice, IDS is being realized at national and regional scales through the development of principles and practices by Indigenous peoples, their representative organizations, and non-Indigenous stakeholders. For example, the First Nations Information Governance Centre (2014) in Canada developed and asserted the "OCAP Principles," which highlight both the relationships (Ownership, Control, Access) between Indigenous peoples and the data and information created by or about them, and the more concrete aspect of physical possession of data and information (Possession). The US Indigenous Data Sovereignty Network has proposed guidelines to facilitate harnessing Indigenous ways of knowing and doing and applying them to the "management and control of a Native nation's data ecosystem" (Rainie, Rodriguez-Lonebear, & Martinez 2017). Inuit Tapiriit Kanatami, the National Inuit Organization in Canada, established the National Inuit Strategy on Research, which has a priority area focused on ensuring Inuit access, ownership, and control over data and information. Although linguistic data are not explicitly addressed, the scope of National Inuit Strategy on Research spans all research activities involving or about Inuit, and an associated implementation plan (Inuit

Tapiriit Kanatami 2018) seeks to eliminate exploitative and colonial approaches to research, as noted by Inuit Tapiriit Kanatami President Natan Obed:

> For far too long, researchers have enjoyed great privilege as they have passed through our communities and homeland, using public or academic funding to answer their own questions about our environment, wildlife, and people. Many of these same researchers then ignore Inuit in creating the outcomes of their work for the advancement of their careers, their research institutions, or their governments. This type of exploitative relationship must end. (3)

Additionally, the Inuit Circumpolar Council-Alaska, through its Alaskan Inuit Food Security Framework aims to establish a model where Indigenous knowledge is considered as part of environmental management and all other relevant activities from the outset. These integrative approaches establish Indigenous knowledge as an essential part of the research process (Inuit Circumpolar Council-Alaska 2015). Ultimately, this involves respect—not only for the data but also for the underlying knowledge systems. To ensure that community needs and knowledge frame all stages of such research and its applications, partnerships and relationships are at the heart of these and other Indigenous research protocols. For example, this is made explicit in the University of Hawai'i *Kūlana Noi'i* (research standards): "The Kūlana Noi'i provide guidance for building and sustaining not just working partnerships but long-term relationships between communities and researchers" (University of Hawai'i Sea Grant 2019). Similarly, in reference to research involving Pacific peoples, the University of Otago's *Pacific Research Protocols* specifically address the issue of balance with research relationships and partnerships. Moreover, the protocols recognize the need to acknowledge the appropriate function of shared knowledge and that the ownership of primary data lies with the people who contribute that knowledge (University of Otago 2011:14).

On an international scale, the International Indigenous Data Sovereignty Interest Group of the Research Data Alliance and the Global Indigenous Data Alliance put forward the CARE Principles for Indigenous Data Governance: **C**ollective benefit, **A**uthority to control, **R**esponsibility, and **E**thics.[9] These CARE principles, which are focused on people and purpose, intersect with the more data-oriented, broadly cited FAIR principles (**F**indable, **A**ccessible, **I**nteroperable, and **R**eusable).[10] While the

CARE principles are arguably the most prominent of the emerging general protocols, a similar focus is found in a number of community-based protocols, such as the San Code of Research Ethics.[11] Centering principles, aspirations, and goals related to IDS, these examples provide a sound foundation for guiding and informing data-related activities, including reflexive and principle-oriented linguistic research and data collection. These laws and policies are partly a response to perceived and identified privacy issues and breaches on major social media platforms and institutional infrastructures (e.g., banks, credit agencies, and insurance companies). Thus, there is a broader societal concern about ethical data management and use that is translating into new social structures (e.g., norms and laws) that have normative and legal implications for linguists. In this way, linguistic data sovereignty is just one part of a larger approach in which Indigenous communities control not just access to linguistic data, but also the production, interpretation, and dissemination of those data.

4   Intersections of linguistic research with the open data movement

As previously indicated in this chapter and elsewhere in this volume, citable, open data is currently the dominant movement in the domain of research data management (Kitchin 2014:49; Nosek et al. 2015; Collister, chapter 9, this volume).[12] As a result, researchers are now much more likely to deposit linguistic data in archives, ensuring that these data are accessible both to the source communities and the broader public. However, if applied universally, open data principles can contradict IDS principles (e.g., understanding that access to knowledge is not a universal right; cf. Rainie et al. 2019). More nuanced, recent statements and declarations on open data management are identifying the need to include exceptions to fully open data. For example, the International Arctic Science Committee Statement of Principles and Practices for Arctic Data Management (International Arctic Science Committee 2013) uses the term "ethically open access" that identifies the following exceptions to this requirement of full, free, and open access:

- where human subjects are involved, confidentiality shall be protected as appropriate and guided by the principles of informed consent;

- where local and traditional knowledge is concerned, rights of the knowledge holders shall not be compromised;
- where data release may cause harm, specific aspects of the data may need to be kept protected (for example, locations of sensitive sites).

These exceptions are well recognized in current language documentation practices. For example, funding agencies do not require that sensitive or otherwise restricted documentation be archived (Seyfeddinipur et al. 2019). However, as linguists increasingly use cloud-based platforms, networked "apps," machine learning and artificial intelligence technologies, and other new tools (cf. Galla 2016), we further caution that there is a need to be aware of the potential ethical implications of using these tools. For example, if linguists use popular platforms such as YouTube or Google Drive in a research workflow that includes linguistic data, they may assign certain rights to the platform provider, whether intended or not. For example, the Google Terms of Service grant Google license to "publish, publicly perform, or publicly display your content, if you've made it visible to others" and to "modify and create derivative works based on your content."[13] And the Zoom video conferencing Terms of Service grant the company the right to store recordings of meetings on its servers.[14] By accepting such terms of service, a linguist may unintentionally contravene (Indigenous) data sovereignty and general ethical principles and policies by licensing content to a third party. The act of providing (uploading, storing) content (e.g., recordings, transcripts) on such a platform without prior, informed consent from the outset may result in an unwitting ethical breach. Thus, while linguistics moves toward open data culture and practice, the related ethical nuances and caveats must always be considered. Establishing protocols for proper consent related to data collection and use, and for data management of Indigenous languages is critically important and urgent. There is a need for research and data management planning to be driven by Indigenous peoples, communities, families, and organizations. There is a need for infrastructure and resources so this can be realized.

5   Conclusion: Linguistic data cannot be divorced from their sources

Ethics are often framed as problems to be worked around. However, that data are intimately tied to their sources need not be seen as a hindrance to overcome, but instead can be a positive step, providing context necessary for interpreting those data. Anchoring data analysis in the relationships and contexts from which the data come can lead to outcomes that would otherwise be missed (cf. Mithun 2001; Rice 2001). Moreover, explicitly acknowledging the links between data and their sources facilitates both reproducible research and applied use.[15] This is true for archival documentation just as much as it is for new data collection: the current ethical context of the use of legacy materials may differ from the ethical context in which the materials were created, but the ties between data and sources remain nonetheless. In essence, the intersection of people, ethics, and data is about relationships—past, present, and future. Reflecting on ethics in language research, Czaykowska-Higgins (2018) characterizes this emphasis on relationships as "rehumanizing linguistics, acknowledging the centrality of relationships and difference in language documentation work, emphasizing accountability to those relationships, and grounding ethical research methodologies in social relations" (116). The actions that language researchers take now in terms of data management decisions will guide how the relationships will evolve.

To return to the principle from which we started this chapter: linguistic data cannot be divorced from their sources. While ethical practices may differ across different research contexts, this principle remains and lies at the heart of ethics in linguistic data. As the various chapters in this volume clearly attest, the field of linguistics is evolving quickly into a more data-driven science. There is ample evidence that recognizing—and indeed celebrating—the relationships between people, ethics, and data will ensure a more robust science of human language in which linguistic communities and associated knowledge systems play a more symmetrical role.

Notes

1. This chapter focuses on ethical issues in relation to Indigenous language data. The discussion of ethical issues in relation to world languages has taken place primarily within the subfields of applied linguistics and sociolinguistics. See Eckert (2013), De Costa (2015), and the various references therein.

2. While we will use the term Indigenous language throughout this chapter, it should be understood that many of the ethical concerns surrounding Indigenous peoples and languages apply equally to other minority language groups such as Cajun

French, which are not typically referred to with the label Indigenous.

3. That said, Hinton (2002:151) questions whether a metaphor of ownership is actually evoked by the so-called possessive construction in English.

4. The emphasis on community is reiterated even more strongly in the 2019 Ethics Statement (Linguistic Society of America 2019).

5. https://www.americanindigenousresearchassociation.org/about-us/. Accessed May 11, 2020.

6. While Indigenous research methods are being increasingly adopted outside Indigenous contexts, these methods are more often construed as applying to the data collection process rather than the data themselves. Data are still typically seen as independent, divorced from their sources. As we argue in this chapter, this view is fundamentally flawed in the context of Indigenous and minority language research.

7. Other R-words include *relevance* to the community as a necessary goal for research, *reverence*, *reflexivity* as a necessary practice by researchers, and *relationality* (the concept that relationships and their associated complex interdependencies form a foundation to everything).

8. This is true not only in the realm of linguistic data but more broadly as well, as evidenced by recent trends toward the monetization of data, and resulting policy changes that grant rights of control over personal data (cf. Marelli & Testa 2018; Choi, Jeon, & Kim 2019). IDS itself, while increasingly well defined in its own specific context, similarly exists within a much broader context that includes discourse around open data, privacy, and the emerging ecosystem of platforms and methods (e.g., machine learning). Both IDS and the broader context have implications for each other—for example, the broader context of privacy control and intellectual property law has implications for IDS; similarly, IDS is having an impact on broader research data dialogues.

9. https://www.gida-global.org/care.

10. https://www.force11.org/group/fairgroup/fairprinciples.

11. https://www.globalcodeofconduct.org/affiliated-codes/.

12. For information about the broader open science movement, see the Organisation for Economic Co-operation and Development's overview: https://www.oecd.org/science/inno/open-science.htm; for an example specific to linguistic data, see https://linguistics.okfn.org.

13. https://policies.google.com/terms. Accessed May 11, 2020.

14. http://zoom.us/terms. Accessed May 17, 2020.

15. Data citation practices that explicitly acknowledge speakers and other contributors can help to maintain this connection between data and source (see Andreassen et al. 2019).

References

Andreassen, Helene N., Andrea L. Berez-Kroeker, Lauren Collister, Philipp Conzett, Christopher Cox, Koenraad De Smedt, Bradley McDonnell, and the Research Data Alliance Linguistic Data Interest Group. 2019. Tromsø recommendations for citation of research data in linguistics (Version 1). *Research Data Alliance*. https://doi.org/10.15497/rda00040.

Berez-Kroeker, Andrea L., Helene N. Andreassen, Lauren Gawne, Gary Holton, Susan Smythe Kung, Peter Pulsifer, Lauren B. Collister, The Data Citation and Attribution in Linguistics Group, and the Linguistics Data Interest Group. 2018. *The Austin Principles of Data Citation in Linguistics*. Version 1.0. http://site.uit.no/linguisticsdatacitation/austinprinciples/.

Berez-Kroeker, Andrea L., Lauren Gawne, Susan Smythe Kung, Barbara F. Kelly, Tyler Heston, Gary Holton, Peter Pulsifer, et al. 2018. Reproducible research in linguistics: A position statement on data citation and attribution in our field. *Linguistics* 57 (1): 1–18. https://doi.org/10.1515/ling-2017-0032.

Bird, Steven, and Gary Simons. 2003. Seven dimensions of portability for language documentation and description. *Language* 79 (3): 557–582.

Carroll, Stephanie Russo, Desi Rodriguez-Lonebear, and Andrew Martinez. 2019. Indigenous data governance: Strategies from United States Native Nations. *Data Science Journal* 18 (1): 31. https://doi.org/10.5334/dsj-2019-031.

Chilisa, Bagele. 2011. *Indigenous Research Methodologies*. London: SAGE Publications.

Choi, Jay Pil, Doh-Shin Jeon, and Byung-Cheol Kim. 2019. Privacy and personal data collection with information externalities. *Journal of Public Economics* 173:113–124. https://doi.org/10.1016/j.jpubeco.2019.02.001.

Christen, Kimberly. 2011. Opening archives: Respectful repatriation. *American Archivist* 74:185–210.

Council of Athabascan Tribal Governments. 2018. *Researching Gwich'in/Upper Koyukon Indigenous Knowledge in the CATG Region*. Fort Yukon, AK: Council of Athabascan Tribal Governments.

Czaykowska-Higgins, Ewa. 2009. Research models, community engagement, and linguistic fieldwork: Reflections on working within Canadian Indigenous communities. *Language Documentation and Conservation* 3 (1): 15–50. http://hdl.handle.net/10125/4423.

Czaykowska-Higgins, Ewa. 2018. Reflections on ethics: Rehumanizing linguistics, building relationships across difference. In *Reflections on Language Documentation 20 Years after Himmelmann 1998*, ed. Bradley McDonnell, Andrea L. Berez-Kroeker, and Gary Holton, 110–121. Honolulu: University of Hawai'i Press. http://hdl.handle.net/10125/24813.

De Costa, Peter I., ed. 2015. *Ethics in Applied Linguistics Research: Language Researcher Narratives*. New York: Routledge.

Dobrin, Lise M. 2008. From linguistic elicitation to eliciting the linguist: Lessons in community empowerment from Melanesia. *Language* 84 (2): 300–324.

Dobrin, Lise M., Peter Austin, and David Nathan. 2009. Dying to be counted: The commodification of endangered languages in documentary linguistics. In *Language Documentation and Description*, vol. 6, ed. Peter K. Austin, 37–52. London: SOAS.

Dobrin, Lise M., and Josh Berson. 2011. Speakers and language documentation. In *The Cambridge Handbook of Endangered Languages*, ed. Peter K. Austin and Julia Sallabank, 187–211. Cambridge: Cambridge University Press.

Eckert, Penelope. 2013. Ethics in linguistics research. In *Research Methods in Linguistics*, ed. Robert J. Podesva and Devyani Sharma, 11–26. Cambridge: Cambridge University Press.

First Nations Information Governance Centre. 2014. *Ownership, Control, Access and Possession (OCAP™): The Path to First Nations Information Governance*. Ottawa, Canada: First Nations Information Governance Centre.

Fitzgerald, Colleen M. 2017. Understanding language vitality and reclamation as resilience: A framework for language endangerment and "loss" (Commentary on Mufwene). *Language* 93 (4): e280–e297.

Galla, Candace Kaleimamoowahinekapu. 2016. Indigenous language revitalization, promotion, and education: Function of digital technology. *Computer Assisted Language Learning* 29 (7): 1137–1151. https://doi.org/10.1080/09588221.2016.1166137.

Genetti, Carol, and Rebekka Siemens. 2013. Training as empowering social action: An ethical response to language endangerment. In *Responses to Language Endangerment: In Honor of Mickey Noonan*, ed. Elena Mihas, Bernard Perley, Gabriel Rei-Doval, and Kathleen Wheatley, 59–77. Amsterdam: John Benjamins.

Grenoble, Lenore A. 2011. Language ecology and endangerment. In *The Cambridge Handbook of Endangered Languages*, ed. Peter K. Austin and Julia Sallabank, 27–44. Cambridge: Cambridge University Press. https://doi.org/10.1017/CBO9780511975981.002.

Grenoble, Lenore A., and Simone S. Whitecloud. 2014. Conflicting goals, ideologies, and beliefs in the field. In *Endangered Languages: Beliefs and Ideologies in Language Documentation and Revitalization*, ed. Peter K. Austin and Julia Sallabank, 337–354. London: British Academy. https://doi.org/10.5871/bacad/9780197265765.003.0016.

Guerrettaz, Anne Marie. 2015. Ownership of language in Yucatec Maya revitalization pedagogy. *Anthropology and Education Quarterly* 46 (2): 167–185. https://doi.org/10.1111/aeq.12097.

Hale, Ken. 2001. Ulwa (Southern Sumu): The beginnings of a language research project. In *Linguistic Fieldwork*, ed. Paul

Newman and Martha Ratliff, 76–101. Cambridge: Cambridge University Press.

Henke, Ryan, and Andrea L. Berez-Kroeker. 2016. A brief history of archiving in language documentation, with an annotated bibliography. *Language Documentation and Conservation* 10:411–457. http://hdl.handle.net/10125/24714.

Hill, Jane H. 2002. "Expert rhetorics" in advocacy for endangered languages: Who is listening, and what do they hear? *Journal of Linguistic Anthropology* 12 (2): 119–133. https://doi.org/10.1525/jlin.2002.12.2.119.

Himmelmann, Nikolaus P. 2012. Linguistic data types and the interface between language documentation and description. *Language Documentation and Conservation* 6:187–207. http://hdl.handle.net/10125/4503.

Hinton, Leanne. 2002. Commentary: Internal and external language advocacy. *Journal of Linguistic Anthropology* 12 (2): 150–156. https://doi.org/10.1525/jlin.2002.12.2.150.

Innes, Pamela, and Erin Debenport, eds. 2010. *Ethical Dimensions of Language Documentation*. Special issue, *Language and Communication* 30 (3).

International Arctic Science Committee. 2013. IASC Data Statement. https://iasc.info/data-observations/iasc-data-statement.

Inuit Circumpolar Council-Alaska. 2015. *Alaskan Inuit Food Security Conceptual Framework: How to Assess the Arctic from an Inuit Perspective*. Anchorage: Inuit Circumpolar Council-Alaska.

Inuit Tapiriit Kanatami. 2018. *National Inuit Strategy on Research*. https://www.itk.ca/wp-content/uploads/2018/04/ITK_NISR-Report_English_low_res.pdf.

Jacob, Michelle M. 2013. *Yakama Rising: Indigenous Cultural Revitalization, Activism, and Healing*. Tucson: University of Arizona Press.

Kitchin, Rob. 2014. *The Data Revolution: Big Data, Open Data, Data Infrastructures and Their Consequences*. London: SAGE Publications.

Kornai, András. 2013. Digital language death. *PLoS ONE* 8 (10): e77056. https://doi.org/10.1371/journal.pone.0077056.

Kovach, Margaret. 2009. *Indigenous Methodologies: Characteristics, Conversations, and Contexts*. Toronto: University of Toronto Press.

Krauss, Michael E. 1992. The world's languages in crisis. *Language* 68 (1): 4–10.

Kukutai, Tahu, and John Taylor. 2016. *Indigenous Data Sovereignty: Toward an Agenda*. Canberra: Australian National University Press.

Lambert, Lori. 2014. *Research for Indigenous Survival: Indigenous Research Methodologies in the Behavioral Sciences*. Lincoln: University of Nebraska Press.

Leonard, Wesley Y. 2017. Producing language reclamation by decolonising "language." *Language Documentation and Description* 14:15–36.

Leonard, Wesley Y. 2018. Reflections on (de)colonialism in language documentation. In *Reflections on Language Documentation 20 Years after Himmelmann 1998*, ed. Bradley McDonnell, Andrea L. Berez-Kroeker, and Gary Holton, 55–65. Honolulu: University of Hawai'i Press. http://hdl.handle.net/10125/24808.

Leonard, Wesley Y., and Erin Haynes. 2010. Making "collaboration" collaborative: An examination of perspectives that frame linguistic field research. *Language Documentation and Conservation* 4:269–293. http://hdl.handle.net/10125/4482.

Linguistic Society of America. 2009. *Ethics Statement*. https://www.linguisticsociety.org/sites/default/files/Ethics_Statement.pdf. Accessed May 17, 2020.

Linguistic Society of America. 2019. *LSA Revised Ethics Statement*, final version (approved July 2019). https://www.linguisticsociety.org/content/lsa-revised-ethics-statement-approved-july-2019. Accessed May 17, 2020.

Linn, Mary S. 2014. Living archives: A community-based language archive model. *Language Documentation and Description* 12:53–67.

Marelli, Luca, and Giuseppe Testa. 2018. Scrutinizing the EU General Data Protection Regulation. *Science* 360 (6388): 496–498. https://doi.org/10.1126/science.aar5419.

Meek, Barbra A. 2010. *We Are Our Language: An Ethnography of Language Revitalization in a Northern Athabaskan Community*. Tucson: University of Arizona Press.

Mithun, Marianne. 2001. Who shapes the record: The speaker and the linguist. In *Linguistic Fieldwork*, ed. Paul Newman and Martha Ratliff, 34–54. Cambridge: Cambridge University Press.

National Congress of American Indians. 2018. Resolution KAN-18–011: Support of US Indigenous Data Sovereignty and Inclusion of Tribes in the Development of Tribal Data Governance Principles. June 4, 2018. http://www.ncai.org/resources/resolutions/support-of-us-indigenous-data-sovereignty-and-inclusion-of-tribes-in-the-development-of-tribal-data.

Nosek, B. A., G. Alter, G. C. Banks, D. Borsboom, S. D. Bowman, S. J. Breckler, S. Buck, et al. 2015. Promoting an open research culture. *Science* 348 (6242): 1422–1425. https://doi.org/10.1126/science.aab2374.

O'Meara, Carolyn, and Jeff Good. 2010. Ethical issues in legacy language resources. *Language and Communication* 30 (3): 162–170. https://doi.org/10.1016/j.langcom.2009.11.008.

O'Neal, Jennifer R. 2015. "The right to know": Decolonizing Native American archives. *Journal of Western Archives* 6 (1): 1–17.

Rainie, Stephanie Carroll, Tahu Kukutai, Maggie Walter, Oscar Luis Figueroa-Rodríguez, Jennifer Walker, and Per Axelsson.

2019. Issues in open data: Indigenous data sovereignty. In *State of Open Data*, ed. Tim Davies, Stephen B. Walker, Mor Rubinstein, and Fernando Perini, 300–319. Cape Town: African Minds. https://doi.org/10.5281/zenodo.2677801.

Rainie, Stephanie Carroll, Desi Rodriguez-Lonebear, and Andrew Martinez. 2017. *Policy Brief: Indigenous Data Sovereignty in the United States*. Tucson: Native Nations Institute, University of Arizona.

Rice, Keren. 2001. Learning as one goes. In *Linguistic Fieldwork*, ed. Paul Newman and Martha Ratliff, 230–249. Cambridge: Cambridge University Press.

Rice, Keren. 2006. Ethical issues in linguistic fieldwork: An overview. *Journal of Academic Ethics* 4 (1): 123–155. https://doi.org/10.1007/s10805-006-9016-2.

Rice, Keren. 2010. The linguist's responsibilities to the community of speakers: Community-based research. In *Language Documentation: Practice and Values*, ed. Lenore A. Grenoble and N. Louanna Furbee, 25–36. Amsterdam: John Benjamins.

Rice, Keren. 2018. Collaborative research: Visions and realities. In *Insights from Practices in Community-based Research: From Theory to Practice around the Globe*, ed. Shannon T. Bischoff and Carmen Jany, 13–37. Berlin: Mouton de Gruyter.

School for Advanced Research. 2018. Community+Museum Guidelines for Collaboration. https://sarweb.org/guidelinesforcollaboration/.

Seyfeddinipur, Mandana, Felix Ameka, Lissant Bolton, Jonathan Blumtritt, Brian Carpenter, Hilaria Cruz, Sebastian Drude, et al. 2019. Public access to research data in language documentation: Challenges and possible strategies. *Language Documentation and Conservation* 13:545–563. http://hdl.handle.net/10125/24901.

Shaw, Patricia A. 2001. Language and identity, language and the land. *BC Studies: The British Columbian Quarterly* 131:39–55.

Shepard, Michael Andrew Alvarez. 2014. "The substance of self-determination": Language, culture, archives and sovereignty. PhD dissertation, University of British Columbia.

Shepard, Michael Alvarez. 2016. The value-added language archive: Increasing cultural compatibility for Native American communities. *Language Documentation and Conservation* 10:458–479. http://hdl.handle.net/10125/24715.

Smith, Linda Tuhiwai. 2012. *Decolonizing Methodologies: Research and Indigenous Peoples,* 2nd ed. London: Zed Books.

Snow, Kevin C., Danica G. Hays, Guia Caliwagan, David J. Ford Jr., Davide Mariotti, Joy Maweu Mwendwa, and Wendy E. Scott. 2016. Guiding principles for indigenous research practices. *Action Research* 14 (4): 357–375. https://doi.org/10.1177/1476750315622542.

Spence, Justin. 2018. Learning languages through archives. In *The Routledge Handbook of Language Revitalization*, ed. Leanne

Hinton, Leena Huss, and Gerald Roche, 179–187. New York: Routledge.

Tuck, Eve, and K. Wayne Yang. 2014. R-words: Refusing research. In *Humanizing Research: Decolonizing Qualitative Inquiry with Youth and Communities*, ed. Django Paris and Maisha T. Winn, 223–247. Los Angeles: SAGE Publications.

University of Hawai'i Sea Grant. 2019. *Kūlana Noi'i*. Honolulu: University of Hawai'i Sea Grant College Program. http://seagrant.soest.hawaii.edu/kulana-noii/.

University of Otago. 2011. *Pacific Research Protocols*. Otago, New Zealand: University of Otago. https://www.otago.ac.nz/research/otago085503.pdf.

Wasson, Christina, Gary Holton, and Heather S. Roth. 2016. Bringing user-centered design to the field of language archives. *Language Documentation and Conservation* 10:641–681. http://hdl.handle.net/10125/24721.

Whaley, Lindsay J. 2011. Some ways to endanger an endangered language project. *Language and Education* 25 (4): 339–348. https://doi.org/10.1080/09500782.2011.577221.

Wilson, Shawn. 2008. *Research Is Ceremony: Indigenous Research Methods*. Black Point, Nova Scotia, Canada: Fernwood Publishing.

5 The Linguistic Data Life Cycle, Sustainability of Data, and Principles of Solid Data Management

Eleanor Mattern

1 Introduction

With the growth of data management requirements from funding agencies and a recognition of the value of reproducibility, replication, and data reuse, there have been efforts by disciplinary communities, administrators of data repositories, and libraries to develop guidance and services to support researchers as they care for and share data. This chapter is not written by a linguist. Instead, it is one library and archives professional's effort to connect discussion, guidance, and research on the management of digital data to the linguistics discipline. Because there are disciplinary differences in the types of data collected and used, varying expectations from funders and journals for data preservation and sharing, and distinct traditions for open research, this chapter takes a high-level view. As a starting point, this chapter considers the data life cycle model as a means for perceiving the persistent and ongoing nature of data management. It reviews guidance and best practices for sustaining data, emphasizing the value of consistency and a future-minded orientation as the core principles that should underlie this work.

2 Life cycle of research data

Archivists and records managers have long employed the metaphor of a records life cycle as a means for conceptualizing distinct stages of an information object: its creation, a period of active use, an inactive phase in which its long-term value is assessed; and the destruction or the long-term preservation of the record in an archival repository (Bantin 1998). Through the records life cycle model, archivists and records managers identified actions (e.g., selection for archiving or destruction) and infrastructure (e.g., an archival repository for

a selected record) required to manage the records and support the longevity of selected records.

With research data, we have seen similar efforts, both from the library and archival communities and from domain-based researchers, to conceptualize the life cycle of digital data. Data service providers such as libraries have employed these visual representations of research and data workflows as a means to communicate the data curation activities that facilitate the sustainability of research data and to identify support services in place to assist researchers with data management. Alex Ball, data librarian at the University of Bath, writes that "the importance of lifecycle models is that they provide a structure for considering the many operations that will need to be performed on a data record throughout its life" (2012:3). For a researcher, mapping their research workflows against a life cycle model can help to encourage data management practices that can facilitate data integrity, value, and persistence (Poole 2016:963).

Life cycle models differ in subject and scope; some visualize the life cycle of research and others provide a more granular representation of the life cycle of research data. They take different shapes, with some representing cyclical processes and others linear sequences of steps. There are life cycle models that depict a multidirectional, recursive process, and others a unidirectional, forward moving one (Cox & Tam 2018). The language of "life cycle" and the cyclical nature of many of the representations, however, suggests an aspiration for data reuse. Cox and Tam write "Circular lifecycles can also be seen as having a strength in improving on the visualisation of research as a chain, by expressing the desire for data reuse, stressing that in some sense the process is to be repeated" (151).

For all their differences, there are common, high-level stages that we find in life cycle models, with the UK Data

Service's model serving as a simple, domain-neutral illustration of these general stages:

- Planning research
- Collecting data
- Processing and analyzing data
- Publishing and sharing data
- Preserving data
- Reusing data[1]

In this chapter, we will look at some good practices for data management that are associated with these stages and that cut across a life cycle model. Figure 5.1 adapts the US Geological Survey Science Data Lifecycle Model. Through the three bottom arrows, this model illustrates the cross-cutting data curation activities that are not confined to one stage. In this particular model, describing data sets, managing the quality of the data, and backing up data are ongoing, continuous data management actions that cut through a research project (Faundeen et al. 2013).

In the UK Data Service's cyclical model and in the linear US Geological Survey model, we see a neat, sequential representation of a data workflow. Research and data life cycle models are simplified representations of researchers' workflows and absent of some of the messier realities that characterize research and data workflows. In the Mattern et al. (2015) study of humanities and social scientists' research workflows, participants sketched their research workflows and annotated their sketches to indicate where they encounter data-related challenges. Their life cycle sketches included research and data stages that are not depicted in the neater models that libraries and research organizations tend to publish. Two participants in this small study, for example, described "confusion"

as a phase in their work. Like the participants in the Mattern et al. study, linguists are unlikely to view their workflows as simple, sequential stages. However, the value of a life cycle model is akin, as Cox and Tam (2018) argue, to the value of a methods textbook: they represent, at a high level, the movement and stages inherent to research and data workflows.

Thieberger and Berez-Kroeker (2012) conceptualize a "workflow for well-formed data" for linguistic fieldwork, which is a step toward a domain and community-specific data life cycle. They write,

> The workflow begins with project planning, which for our purposes includes preparing to use technology in the field and deciding on which file naming and metadata conventions you will use before you make your first recording. . . . After recordings are made and metadata are collected, data must be transcribed and annotated with various software tools, and then used for analysis and in representation of the language via print or multimedia. Note that depositing materials in an archive is carried out at every phase of the procedure. (96–97)

We can draw connections between this discussion of a workflow for linguistics fieldwork data and the stages in the UK Data Service and the US Geological Survey Science Data Lifecycle Model. Thieberger and Berez's model similarly begins with a planning stage. All three describe a data collection and a data analysis stage. Like the US Geological Survey's life cycle, Thieberger and Berez describe data management activities that cut across all phases in a workflow. Unlike most life cycle models that represent data archiving as a final stage, Thieberger and Berez characterize this sharing and preservation work as ongoing during the life of a research project. This is a notable departure but suggestive of a research reality: few projects may have one distinct end point at which

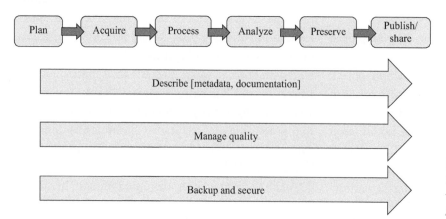

Figure 5.1

Representation of the US Geological Survey Science Data Lifecycle Model.
Source: Faundeen et al. (2013).

time data becomes archival. Indeed, because of the fragility of digital media, archiving and preservation are best addressed throughout research.

Linguists may collect more data, perhaps in the form of large numbers of audio and video recordings, than they ultimately transcribe, annotate, and analyze. This means that different data in a single research project may move through a data life cycle in different ways. Drawing on the UK Data Archives' model, this means that some data, for example, would not reach the processing and analyzing phase or the preserving phase. A researcher may build more robust metadata records for annotated and analyzed data and may ultimately choose to archive a discreet subset of the larger data corpus. For all data, however, a linguist should ensure that a plan is in place.

3 Sustainability of research data

As Lavoie (2012) reminds readers, the term "sustainability" has multiple connotations generally and in the context of research data. He introduces three meanings of sustainability pertinent to digital records such as digital research data sets: (1) economic sustainability, or the resources involved in digital stewardship; (2) social sustainability, or a "shared commitment to preservation among groups of stakeholders with a common interest in long-term access to a particular set of digital materials"; and (3) "sustainability from a technical perspective, in the sense of developing repository architectures, workflows, tools and preservation techniques that are robust, flexible and scalable" (68). These three meanings are worthy of consideration.

Lavoie's chapter focuses primarily on economic sustainability and provides a valuable discussion of the issues, challenges, and approaches of resourcing research data management that is relevant for all disciplines. He argues for the importance of selecting research data for long-term preservation. This is an understood reality in libraries and archives, with archivists referring to this selection process as "appraisal." Because resources are finite, selection of specific materials with evidential or research value (in this case, selected research data sets) for long-term preservation and access is aligned with economic feasibility.

Fran Berman, professor of computer science at Rensselaer Polytechnic Institute and former director of the San Diego Supercomputer Center, offers a second perspective

on sustainability, arguing that there is a role for disciplinary communities to set criteria and methods for selection of research data for long-term preservation. Describing a model of social sustainability, Berman (2008:52) writes, "the need for community appraisal will push academic disciplines beyond individual stewardship, where project leaders decide which data is valuable, which should be preserved, and how long it should be preserved (except where regulation, policy, and/or publication protocols mandate specific stewardship and preservation timeframes)." With this, she calls on linguists and other domain-based researchers to develop selection frameworks. Indeed, we see examples of community-developed appraisal criteria that guide inclusion of data sets in data repositories; the Inter-university Consortium for Political and Social Research (ICPSR), for example, has a published and clearly defined set of collecting priorities (ICPSR 2012). Berman's call for community-based selection criteria is resonant with the second meaning of sustainability that Lavoie introduces: social sustainability, or a community's commitment to research data management. There are a number of efforts in the linguistics scholarly community that point to this commitment, with this volume, the Linguistics Data Consortium,[2] the *Austin Principles of Data Citation in Linguistics* (Berez-Kroeker et al. 2018), and the Research Data Alliance Linguistics Data Interest Group,[3] among them.

Lavoie's third meaning of sustainability—the workflows, infrastructure, and practices that support the longevity of research data—overlies the entirety of the research data life cycle. He writes, "when we speak of 'sustainable research,' it is perhaps more accurate to say we are speaking of sustainable data curation activities" (2012:81). This is the meaning of sustainability that forms the focus of section 4: sustainable practice that supports sustainable research data.

4 Data management practices

This chapter references the data life cycle as a framework for examining key practices for responsible and consistent data management, including actions that cut across all stages of the life cycle. In recent years, there have been a host of useful resources created and published that aim to assist researchers in sustaining their research data.[4] This section draws on these to provide a broad discussion on good habits, frames of mind, and actions.

4.1 Planning

In Theieberger and Berez's (2012) workflow, they explain that they decide on conventions for their file naming and metadata before collecting data in the field and, with this, point to a key practice in responsible data management: planning. Funding agencies, as described in Kung (chapter 8, this volume), are increasingly requiring data management plans (DMPs) as part of a grant application, but even where there is no requirement, investing time in crafting a plan can help to refine existing data practices (Mannheimer 2018:15) and encourage efficiency (Corti et al. 2014; Kung, chapter 8, this volume). DMPs generally include a description of the data that will be collected, the metadata and documentation that will be produced, the ways the data will be stored and backed up, security and privacy protections for relevant data, data access policies during a project, and a long-term plan for data sharing and preservation (Digital Curation Centre 2013; Burnette, Williams, & Imker 2016:2). With this broad coverage, DMPs "typically cover all or portions of the data life cycle" (Michener 2015). An effective plan for a collaborative project will additionally describe the responsibilities for all research partners, to help ensure that all involved understand what their roles are in managing data (Corti et al. 2014:29).

A good practice around DMPs is to treat them as "living documents," reviewing and editing them to reflect changes in data management practices and to address emergent data management needs and challenges (Michener 2015). In a data life cycle model, then, good practice would have researchers returning to the planning stage regularly. While DMPs are often characterized as mechanisms that save researchers time in the long-run, linguists Gawne and Berez-Kroeker (2018) realistically acknowledge that "management and curation of data for archiving is a time-consuming process, even when the documentation workflow is set up to optimize the process" (25).

4.2 Sustainable file formats

The selection of file formats that linguists use to store and preserve their data is a fundamental data management practice that can help to ensure sustainability and reuse of these research outputs. The evaluation and selection of data formats should ideally occur before data collection begins, making it a decision that occurs at the planning stage of a life cycle and that is then implemented throughout later stages.[5]

Much of guidance on data management best practices addresses the distinction between open versus proprietary file formats and the relevance of this distinction to sustainability of research data. *Open file formats* are formats that can be accessed using more than one software program and that are supported by more than one developer; *proprietary formats*, conversely, are supported by one developer and may be dependent on only one software application for use. While there are proprietary commercial software and corresponding file formats that are ubiquitous (for example, Adobe Photoshop and .psd files), where there is dependency on a single software application, there are vulnerability and limitations to access. As Trevor Owens (2018) of the Library of Congress explains, "the more a format depends on a particular piece of hardware, operating system, or software to render, the more susceptible it is to being unrenderable if one of those dependencies fail" (121). If saving data in open formats would result in a loss of functionality or information, retaining data in the proprietary format and making a copy in an open format is a recommended practice, particularly at the preservation and archiving stage of the data life cycle (Van den Eynden et al. 2011:13; Stanford Libraries, n.d.).

There are more immediate implications that the selection of a proprietary or dependent format introduces. If the researchers' goal is to support wide use of data sets that they make available, making the data available in formats that would not require the purchase of commercial software removes a barrier for reuse.

When assessing the sustainability of a digital file format, there is less probable risk associated with widely used file formats. Owens (2018:121) writes, "If you have PDFs, MP3s, JPEGs, or GIFs, you've got every reason to believe that people will be able to open those files. If those formats become risky, their wide use makes it likely that tools and services will be created to help migrate them." Selecting file formats that are widely adopted, in other words, provides some security for the future accessibility of the data records.

There are a number of resources available to help researchers select sustainable file formats for the types of data that they are creating.[6] The UK Data Service's recommended file formats table is a useful starting point. For a tabular data file such as a spreadsheet, the UK Data

Service's recommended formats are comma-separated values (.csv) and tab-delimited file (.tab). The organization also identifies acceptable formats, including the widely used Microsoft Excel formats (.xls/.xlsx), reflecting Owens's commentary on the relationship between file format adoption and sustainability.[7]

For researchers seeking a more detailed assessment of the preservation-friendliness of selected file formats, the Library of Congress's "Sustainability of Digital Formats" web resource provides detailed descriptions for a range of file formats; in addition to information about the degree of adoption and dependencies associated with the format, the Library of Congress considers the level of documentation that exists for the format and whether there is metadata embedded in the file, additional factors supporting format sustainability.[8] The Library of Congress's guidance on sustainable formats additionally points to the importance of selecting 'lossless' formats, or formats that do not lose information when compressed or made smaller; for images, for example, a TIFF file is a lossless format and a JPEG is a 'lossy' one.[9]

Table 5.1 depicts selected data types in linguistics research (Himmelmann 2012; Language Archive 2019) and, using the aforementioned resources and considerations, associated sustainable file format types.

The recommendations in table 5.1 reflect the Library of Congress's overview of formats and sustainability factors, as well as guidance from the US National Archives and Records Administration.[11] However, the table also accounts for the functionalities of linguistics-specific software programs, namely Praat and ELAN. A researcher working with audio files and Praat, for example, should be aware that Praat is unable to open the common audio file type .mp3 files and instead supports the .wav format (Styler 2017). Guidance on Praat, moreover, stresses the lossy nature of the .mp3, stating "friends don't let friends save phonetic data in lossy formats (e.g., .mp3, AAC, .wmv)" (63). For researchers working with spectrograms in Praat, the software allows for export of "Praat Pictures" as PDFs (48). This means the researcher will lose the interactivity with the spectrogram that the software provides, but will be able to generate a static file for preservation and access purposes.

4.3 File names and organizational structures

Anyone who uses a digital camera or a cell phone camera has likely encountered the systematic, yet inscrutable, file naming scheme associated with their images. Load the images onto a computer and one encounters file names that mean little to the creator, a string that begins with IMG and is followed by a number. When there are hundreds or thousands of these similarly named files, locating a desired image can be a challenging task indeed. A solid file-naming convention is one

Table 5.1

Recommended file formats for sustainability

Data type	Recommended format
Audio recordings	• Free Lossless Audio Codec (.flac) • Waveform Audio File Format (.wav)
ELAN files (.eaf EUDICO Annotation Format)[10]	• Tab Delimited Text (.txt). • Timed Text Markup Language (TTML) (for annotations)
Photographs, spectrograms and images (e.g., functional magnetic resonance imaging)	• TIFF (.tif) • PDF/a
Spreadsheets and databases	• XML-based formats • Comma-separated values files (.csv) • SQLite • SIARD (Software Independent Archiving of Relational Databases)
Text files (e.g., transcripts and observational notes, translations with interlinear glossing); annotations	• eXtensible Mark-up Language (.xml) • Plain text format (.txt) (encoding: ASCII, UTI-8, UTF-16) • Rich Text Format (.rtf) • Portable Document Format/Archival (PDF/A)
Tabular data and databases	• XML-based formats • Comma-separated values files (.csv) • SQLite • SIARD (Software Independent Archiving of Relational Databases)

that is meaningful to the researcher and consistently employed. Again, the determination of this convention ideally happens at the start of the research workflow, at the planning stage in our data life cycle and should be documented by the research team. This section will briefly review existing guidance for developing a convention and approaches for managing versioning.

There is no one way to name files and good practice is a memorable and sustainable one for the individual researcher and team. Libraries and the UK Data Service, again useful starting points for guidance, identify a number of elements that a researcher might choose to include in a file name (Corti et al. 2014:67):

- Date: Using a consistently structured date at the beginning of a file name can be helpful for sorting files chronologically, if that is relevant to the nature of the research. The International Standards Organization[12] format for a date, YYYY-MM-DD, facilitates this chronological sorting and will be widely understood as a date by other users (Witmer 2017).

- Project name or acronym

- Researcher name or initials

- Version number

- Ordinal numbering system: Using leading zeros (001, 002, 003, etc.) will assist with sorting. (Smithsonian Library, n.d.)

General guidance on filing naming suggests that brevity, rather than cumbersome and lengthy conventions, will be most sustainable in practice. Moreover, some software applications have difficulty with spaces and many special characters in file names; avoiding spaces and instead separating elements with an underscore, hyphen, or camel case is advisable (Witmer 2017).

With a new project, it is also necessary to develop a strategy for organizing files that is documented and simple enough to consistently follow throughout the life cycle of a project. A hierarchical organization, with all relevant files grouped under a common top-level project directory, is a common and advisable approach (Noble 2009). As with file-naming conventions, the best organizational strategy for subfolders is one that is logical and easy to employ. A simple text file that lives in the top-level folder and that overviews the organizational approach for the project files can function as a useful memory tool for a researcher and a valuable guide for someone approaching the project data for the first time.[13]

4.4   Data storage

This section considers decision making around active storage and the value of a distributed approach to active data storage. In Hart et al. (2016) "Ten Simple Rules for Digital Data Storage," we again encounter the importance of systematizing a data management practice and developing this system early. As strategies and required resources are dependent on the volume of project data, Hart et al.'s guidance for large data sets (terabytes to petabytes) is particularly valuable, offering insight into time-saving solutions for requesting project data stored on commercial cloud solutions. For all researchers, the authors soundly emphasize the necessity of a storage backup scheme and the importance of regularly evaluating whether the scheme is functioning; backups may fail, the authors acknowledge, even when a solid procedure is in place. Specifying at the planning stage how often the backups will be assessed and by whom—and then implementing that plan—can mitigate the risk of loss of the backup.

The National Digital Stewardship Alliance (NDSA), a consortium focused on building digital preservation capacity, has published a set of recommendations for sustaining digital records that, while geared toward organizations, are pertinent to the individual researcher. The NDSA (2013) advises keeping three copies in at least two geographic locations, a standard to which Hart et al. (2016) also subscribe. Hart et al. advise, "Ideally you should have two on-site copies (such as on a computer, an external hard drive, or a tape) and one off-site copy (e.g., cloud storage), with care taken to ensure that the off-site copy is as secure as the on-site copies. Keeping backups in multiple locations additionally protects against data loss due to theft or natural disasters." We regularly encounter this recommendation in library guidance, framed as the 3-2-1 rule (three copies; in two different storage media; with at least one off-site copy).[14] In the linguistics community, Thieberger and Berez (2012) address the importance of backups in research, offering different strategies for creating copies. For linguists doing fieldwork, they suggest that external hard drives, cloud storage, and USB "on-the-go" devices can all be good backup strategies, depending on the circumstances in the field (99–100).

4.5   Metadata and data documentation

This section provides an introduction to the purpose and importance of metadata and data documentation in supporting the sustainability of research data. Funders commonly request that researchers indicate in a DMP what documentation and metadata will describe their data and, as the US Geological Survey's data life cycle (figure 5.1) depicts, the researchers will carry out the associated work throughout a research project.

We encounter metadata regularly in our lives: in a library catalog, in the product descriptions on Amazon, and on the title page and front matter of a book. *Metadata* are information about an object that helps us to understand, find, and use that object. As Miller (2004) explains, metadata help an individual other than the original creator

> to decide whether or not [an information object] is of value to them; to discover where, when and by whom it was created, as well as for what purpose; to know what tools will be needed to manipulate the resource; to determine whether or not they will actually be allowed access to the resource itself and how much this will cost them. Metadata is, in short, a means by which largely meaningless data may be transformed into information, interpretable and reusable by those other than the creator of the data resource. (4)

Thoughtfully created metadata that provide context into the creation and scope of a research data set are not only good practice but also essential to supporting data reuse. As the ICPSR (2012) explains, metadata are "often the only form of communication between the secondary analyst and the data producer, so they must be comprehensive and provide all of the needed information for accurate analysis."

There are a number of forms that metadata take in relation to research data. Structured information, often encoded as XML, is one. To share data in a disciplinary or institutional repository, a researcher will often be expected to provide information about the data set in a specified format, or metadata schema.

When developing a DMP and if planning on archiving their data in a repository, researchers are well advised to look at the metadata requirements in a data repository and to plan accordingly. When a linguist chooses to archive and share their research data, as discussed in Andreassen (chapter 7, this volume), they may encounter either a metadata schema that is disciplinary-agnostic or one that has been built with linguistics research in mind. In the case of a university institutional repository, the linguist would be more likely to encounter a domain-neutral schema. A linguist depositing in the

Data Archive at the Max Planck Institute for Psycholinguistics, on the other hand, will be invited to provide more robust metadata to describe session recordings and annotations; this repository employs the ISLE Meta Data Initiative, "a metadata standard to describe multi-media and multi-modal language resources" (Geerts 2018).

In addition to International Standard for Language Engineering, there are a number of metadata schemas that linguists may adopt for describing their research data sets or that they may encounter when archiving data in a repository. Dublin Core, likely the most well-known metadata schema, is one of these. Made up of fifteen elements (e.g., creator, date, title), Dublin Core is a simple, all-purpose scheme and "has the most mapped element sets among and across domain-specific and community-oriented metadata standards" (Zeng & Qin 2008:16). Among these community-specific metadata schemas built from Dublin Core is the Open Language Archives Community standard. Designed to facilitate sharing of linguistics data, Open Language Archives Community metadata include all fifteen Dublin Core elements and elements that would make "it possible to describe language resources with greater precision" (e.g., discourse type, linguistic field) (Simons & Bird 2008).

The DataCite metadata schema is a domain-neutral set of elements, or fields, developed for structuring information about a data set (DataCite Metadata Working Group 2017, 2018). The standard includes a small number of required metadata elements (e.g., creator, title, resource type) and additional recommended and optional elements (e.g., description, rights, version). Numerous disciplinary metadata schemas have also been developed and the Digital Curation Centre (n.d.) has produced a valuable catalog of these standards. In the social sciences, the Data Documentation Initiative standard "an international XML-based standard for the content, presentation, transport, and preservation of documentation (i.e., metadata)" for data sets is widely accepted and employed.[15] ICPSR (n.d.), for example, uses Data Documentation Initiative as the repository metadata standard.

In addition to structured information that accompanies a data set, metadata may take the form of a readme file or data dictionary. A readme file is a simple text file that helps other users to understand and contextualize the data and to discern the interconnections among project records and data sets. The readme file additionally highlights the methods for data collection and the ways in which the data were processed.[16] Cornell University Libraries offers a comprehensive overview of the information that should be included in a readme file (table 5.2).

Data dictionaries share the purpose of a readme file in that they provide necessary contextual information to support the understandability and clearness of the data set. However, data dictionaries generally focus on content included under the "Data-specific information" in Cornell's readme file template. Often created to support a database or spreadsheet, data dictionaries serve as variable glossary and key and are generally structured in a tabular format.[18] DataONE, a scientific community-led project focused on building researcher capacity for data management and sharing, explains that "a data dictionary provides a detailed description for each element or variable in your data set and data model. Data dictionaries are used to document important and useful information such as a descriptive name, the data type, allowed values, units, and text description."[19] For linguists building databases—for example, of endangered language metadata or for a crosslinguistic typological study—a data dictionary can help ensure data quality, interpretation, and reuse.[20]

Table 5.2
Cornell University: Recommended content for a readme file

General information
- Provide a title for the data set
- Name/institution/address/e-mail information for
  - Principal investigator (or person responsible for collecting the data)
  - Associate or coinvestigators
  - Contact person for questions
- Date of data collection (can be a single date, or a range)
- Information about geographic location of data collection
- Keywords used to describe the data topic
- Language information
- Information about funding sources that supported the collection of the data

Data and file overview
- Short description of what data it contains
- Format of the file if not obvious from the file name
- If the data set includes multiple files that relate to one another, the relationship between the files or a description of the file structure that holds them (possible terminology might include "data set" or "study" or "data package")
- Date that the file was created
- Date(s) that the file(s) was updated (versioned) and the nature of the update(s), if applicable
- Information about related data collected but that is not in the described data set

Sharing and access information
- Licenses or restrictions placed on the data
- Links to publications that cite or use the data
- Links to other publicly accessible locations of the data
- Recommended citation for the data

Methodological information
- Description of methods for data collection or generation (include links or references to publications or other documentation containing experimental design or protocols used)
- Description of methods used for data processing (describe how the data were generated from the raw or collected data)
- Any instrument-specific information needed to understand or interpret the data
- Standards and calibration information, if appropriate
- Describe any quality-assurance procedures performed on the data
- Definitions of codes or symbols used to note or characterize low quality/questionable/outliers that people should be aware of
- People involved with sample collection, processing, analysis and/or submission

Data-specific information
- Count of number of variables, and number of cases or rows
- Variable list, including full names and definitions (spell out abbreviated words) of column headings for tabular data
- Units of measurement
- Definitions for codes or symbols used to record missing data
- Specialized formats or other abbreviations used

Source: Cornell University's "Guide to Writing 'readme' Style Metadata."[17]

5 Conclusion

Section 4 looked at basic practices to support sustainable research data. This concluding section considers broader principles. Lavoie (2012) argues that sustainable research data can be equated to sustainable data curation practices. Sustainable practices are ones that are most compatible to researchers' existing workflows.

Core to effective data management is the creation of a strategy that is compatible to a researcher's existing workflows. If a researcher regularly uses software or applications that can be adopted to strengthen data management practices, this may be the more effective approach than learning an entirely new software system to assist with data management; for example, if a linguist is comfortable with Excel or a relational database system, they might consider using this familiar tool for metadata creation, rather than a distinct metadata creation tool.[21] This is because the best data management strategy is one that the researcher is able to consistently employ throughout the research life cycle.

Perhaps the most important principle to data management is that a future-minded orientation is essential. A consistent, effective data management approach ensures that the data creator is able to make sense of their own data two weeks, three months, or four years from when it was collected. A researcher should assess what would be valuable for their own memory, their own continued access, and their own future use of the data.

Moreover, funders and open data advocates, both major players in advancing the development of data management policy and approaches, have emphasized the value of data for future reuse. In linguistics, it is not difficult to recognize why reusable data is so essential. In the subfield of language documentation, for example, it is critical to future research that there is a reusable record of a language community that has no remaining fluent users or that is endangered. In linguistics subfields more broadly—whether experimental research in phonetics or psycholinguistic studies—there are benefits that come from having sustainable data. Linguists can use data sets for replication and for expanding on previous lessons drawn from the data.

The linguistics research community has made concerted efforts to consider long-term data stewardship, as evidenced by the establishment of language-focused data archives and metadata schemas (see Andreassen, chapter 7, this volume, and Buszard-Welcher, chapter 10, this volume). Ultimately, however, the stewardship of data through its life cycle and oversight of research data sustainability fall primarily to individual linguists. While supporting the longevity of information was once the role of librarians, repository managers, and archives, inaction on the part of researchers will place data at risk for loss and impede the possibility of reuse. Part II of this volume offers specific case studies of how linguists in different subfields and on different projects have approached data management in practice.

Acknowledgments

I am grateful for the thoughtful feedback and valuable recommendations from the reviewers assigned to this chapter and the editors. I am particularly grateful for their assistance in situating this chapter more deeply in the linguistics context.

Notes

1. UK Data Service, "Research data lifecycle," https://www.ukdataservice.ac.uk/manage-data/lifecycle.aspx.

2. Linguistics Data Consortium, https://www.ldc.upenn.edu/.

3. Research Data Alliance, "Linguistics Data IG," https://www.rd-alliance.org/groups/linguistics-data-ig.

4. As a starting point, see Corti et al. (2014). Guides by academic libraries are valuable sources of information about data management practices: University of Minnesota Libraries, "Research Data Services," https://www.lib.umn.edu/datamanagement.

5. Australian National Data Service, "File formats," https://www.ands.org.au/guides/file-formats.

6. Academic library guides are useful sources for a high-level discussion of sustainable formats. See, for example, Stanford Libraries, "Best practices for file formats"; University of Pennsylvania Libraries, "Data management best practices: Sustainable file types," https://guides.library.upenn.edu/datamgmt/fileformats.

7. UK Data Service, "Recommended formats," https://www.ukdataservice.ac.uk/manage-data/format/recommended-formats.aspx.

8. Library of Congress, "The sustainability of digital formats," last updated March 25, 2019, https://www.loc.gov/preservation/digital/formats/index.html.

9. Cornell University Research Data Management Service Group, "File formats," https://data.research.cornell.edu/content/file-formats.

10. Language Archive (2019).

11. National Archives and Records Administration, "Appendix A: Tables of file formats," last updated September 2019, https://www.archives.gov/records-mgmt/policy/transfer-guidance-tables.html.

12. International Standards Organization, "Date and time format—ISO 8601," https://www.iso.org/iso-8601-date-and-time-format.html.

13. Cornell University Research Data Management Service Group, "File management," https://data.research.cornell.edu/content/file-management.

14. University of Virginia Library Research Data Services + Sciences, "Data storage and backups," https://data.library.virginia.edu/data-management/plan/storage/.

15. Stanford Libraries, "Advanced metadata," https://library.stanford.edu/research/data-management-services/data-best-practices/creating-metadata/advanced-metadata.

16. University of Pittsburgh Library System, "Research data management @ Pitt," https://pitt.libguides.com/managedata/.

17. https://data.research.cornell.edu/content/readme; Cornell's guidance is licensed under a Creative Commons Attribution 4.0 International License.

18. Several data dictionary templates exist that can be adapted for a linguistics project. The open government data community has provided templates to guide the creation of data documentation for shared data sets, but these have value beyond this sector. See, for example, NYC OpenData's data dictionary template (accessible under "Resources and guidelines," https://opendata.cityofnewyork.us/open-data-coordinators/) and the US Department of Agriculture's template (https://data.nal.usda.gov/data-dictionary-blank-template).

19. DataONE, "Create a data dictionary," accessed October 2, 2019, https://www.dataone.org/best-practices/create-data-dictionary.

20. Linguistics examples were offered by volume peer reviewer.

21. Stanford Libraries, "Metadata tools," https://library.stanford.edu/research/data-management-services/data-best-practices/creating-metadata/metadata-tools.

References

Ball, Alex. 2012. *Review of Data Management Life cycle Models.* REDm-MED project document. Bath, UK: University of Bath. https://purehost.bath.ac.uk/ws/portalfiles/portal/206543/redm1rep120110ab10.pdf.

Bantin, Philip C. 1998. Strategies for managing electronic records: A new archival paradigm? An affirmation of our archival traditions? *Archival Issues* 23 (1): 17–34.

Berez-Kroeker, Andrea L., Helene N. Andreassen, Lauren Gawne, Gary Holton, Susan Smythe Kung, Peter Pulsifer, Lauren B. Collister, The Data Citation and Attribution in Linguistics Group, and the Linguistics Data Interest Group. 2018. *The Austin Principles of Data Citation in Linguistics*, version 1.0. http://site.uit.no/linguisticsdatacitation/austinprinciples/. Accessed October 24, 2019.

Berman, Francine. 2008. Got data? A guide to data preservation in the information age. *Communications of the ACM* 51 (12): 50–56.

Burnette, Margaret H., Sarah C. Williams, and Heidi J. Imker. 2016. From plan to action: Successful data management plan implementation in a multidisciplinary project. *Journal of EScience Librarianship* 5 (1): 1–12. https://doi.org/10.7191/jeslib.2016.1101.

Corti, Louise, Veerle Van den Eynden, Libby Bishop, and Matthew Woollard. 2014. *Managing and Sharing Research Data: A Guide to Good Practice.* London: Sage Publications Inc.

Cox, Andrew Martin, and Winnie Wan Ting Tam. 2018. A critical analysis of lifecycle models of the research process and research data management. *Aslib Journal of Information Management* 70 (2): 142–157. https://doi.org/10.1108/AJIM-11-2017-0251.

DataCite Metadata Working Group. 2017. *DataCite Metadata Schema for the Publication and Citation of Research Data*, version 4.2. http://doi.org/10.5438/rv0g-av03.

DataCite Metadata Working Group. 2018. *DataCite Metadata Schema Documentation for the Publication and Citation of Research Data*, version 4.2. https://doi.org/10.5438/bmjt-bx77.

Digital Curation Centre. 2013. *Checklist for a Data Management Plan*, version 4.0. Edinburgh: Digital Curation Centre. http://www.dcc.ac.uk/resources/data-management-plans.

Digital Curation Centre. n.d. *Disciplinary Metadata.* http://www.dcc.ac.uk/resources/metadata-standards.

Faundeen, John L., Thomas E. Burley, Jennifer A. Carlino, David L. Govoni, Heather S. Henkel, Sally L. Holl, Vivian B. Hutchison, et al. 2013. *The United States Geological Survey Science Data Lifecycle Model.* Reston, VA: US Geological Survey. http://dx.doi.org/10.3133/ofr20131265.

Gawne, Lauren, and Andrea L. Berez-Kroeker. 2018. Reflections on reproducible research. In *Reflections on Language Documentation 20 Years after Himmelmann 1998*, ed. Bradley McDonnell, Andrea L. Berez-Kroeker, and Gary Holton, 22–32. Honolulu: University of Hawai'i Press. https://scholarspace.manoa.hawaii.edu/bitstream/10125/24805/ldc-sp15-gawne.pdf.

Geerts, Jeroen. 2018. *Deposit Manual*, version 1.1. Nijmegen, the Netherlands: The Language Archive, MPI for Psycholinguistics. https://archive.mpi.nl/deposit-manual.

Hart, Edmund, Pauline Barmby, David LeBauer, François Michonneau, Sarah Mount, Patrick Mulrooney, Timothée Poisot, et al. 2016. Ten simple rules for digital data storage. *PLoS Computational Biology* 12 (10): e1005097. https://doi.org/10.1371/journal.pcbi.1005097.

Himmelmann, Nikolaus P. 2012. Linguistic data types and the interface between language documentation and description. *Language Documentation and Conservation* 6:87–207. http://hdl.handle.net/10125/4503.

Inter-university Consortium for Political and Social Research (ICPSR). 2012. *Guidelines for Effective Data Management Plans.* Ann Arbor, MI: ICPSR. https://www.icpsr.umich.edu/files/datamanagement/DataManagementPlans-All.pdf.

Inter-university Consortium for Political and Social Research (ICPSR). n.d. *Metadata.* https://www.icpsr.umich.edu/icpsrweb/content/datamanagement/lifecycle/metadata.html. Accessed October 24, 2019.

Language Archive. *ELAN—Linguistic Annotator*, version 5.8. Last updated October 8, 2019. https://tla.mpi.nl/tools/tla-tools/elan/.

Lavoie, Brian F. 2012. Sustainable research data. In *Managing Research Data*, ed. Graham Pryor, 67–82. London: Facet Publishing.

Mannheimer, Sara. 2018. Toward a better data management plan: The impact of DMPs on grant funded research practices. *Journal of EScience Librarianship* 7 (3): 1–18. https://doi.org/10.7191/jeslib.2018.1155.

Mattern, Eleanor, Wei Jeng, Liz Lyon, Daqing He, and Aaron Brenner. 2015. Using participatory design and visual narrative inquiry to investigate researchers' data challenges and recommendations for library research data services. *Program: Electronic Library and Information Systems* 49 (4): 408–423. https://doi.org/10.1108/PROG-01-2015-0012.

Michener, William K. 2015. Ten simple rules for creating a good data management plan. *PLoS Computational Biology* 11 (10): e1004525. https://doi.org/10.1371/journal.pcbi.1004525.

Miller, Paul. 2004. Metadata: What it means for memory institutions. In *Metadata Applications and Management*, ed. G. E. Gorman and Daniel G. Dorner, 4–16. Lanham, MD: Scarecrow Press.

National Digital Stewardship Alliance (NDSA). 2013. *Levels of Digital Preservation*, version 1. https://ndsa.org/activities/levels-of-digital-preservation/.

Noble, William Stafford. 2009. A quick guide to organizing computational biology projects. *PLOS Computational Biology* 5 (7): e1000424. https://doi.org/10.1371/journal.pcbi.1000424.

Owens, Trevor. 2018. *The Theory and Craft of Digital Preservation.* Baltimore: Johns Hopkins University Press.

Poole, Alex H. 2016. The conceptual landscape of digital curation. *Journal of Documentation* 72 (5): 961–986.

Simons, Gary, and Steven Bird, eds. 2008. *Recommended Metadata Extensions.* Open Language Archives Community. http://www.language-archives.org/REC/olac-extensions.html.

Smithsonian Library. n.d. *Smithsonian Data Management Best Practices: Naming and Organizing Files.* https://library.si.edu/sites/default/files/tutorial/pdf/filenamingorganizing20180227.pdf.

Stanford Libraries. n.d. Best practices for file formats. https://library.stanford.edu/research/data-management-services/data-best-practices/best-practices-file-formats.

Styler, Will. 2017. *Using Praat for Linguistic Research*, version 1.8. Last updated December 25, 2017. http://wstyler.ucsd.edu/praat/.

Thieberger, Nicholas, and Andrea L. Berez. 2012. Linguistic data management. In *The Oxford Handbook of Linguistic Fieldwork*, ed. Nicholas Thieberger, 90–118. Oxford: Oxford University Press.

Van den Eynden, Veerle, Louise Corti, Matthew Woollard, Libby Bishop, and Laurence Horton. 2011. *Managing and Sharing Data: Best Practices for Researchers*, 3rd ed. Colchester, UK: UK Data Archive. https://data-archive.ac.uk/media/2894/managingsharing.pdf.

Witmer, Scott David. 2017. Personal digital archiving guide part 1: Preservation planning. *Bits and Pieces* (University of Michigan Libraries blog). April 26, 2017. https://www.lib.umich.edu/blogs/bits-and-pieces/personal-digital-archiving-guide-part-1-preservation-planning.

Zeng, Marcia Lei, and Jian Qin. 2008. *Metadata*, 3rd ed. New York: Neal-Schulman Publishers.

6 Transforming Data

Na-Rae Han

1 Introduction

Data rarely come in a readily usable form. From the moment they are sourced to the end point when they are published or archived for long-term storage, they typically undergo many stages of transformation. Throughout the life cycle, it is up to the data practitioners—creators, end users, and anyone who processes data in any manner—to ensure its integrity by tightly controlling the four main outcomes of a transformative operation—*transliteration*, *loss*, *augmentation*, and *corruption* of information—all the while maintaining reversibility through judicious employment of version control. This chapter presents an overview of considerations going into planning and managing data transformation processes as well as recommended tools and best practices. Of the two main forms of linguistic data—textual and audiovisual—the chapter will largely focus on the former.

2 Why transform data

There are several use cases in which the need for data transformation may arise. A research project may begin with a targeted data collection effort—fieldwork, surveys, elicitation, and more; the resultant data will then go through the usual process of organization, cleanup, and transformation in the course of the intended research activity. Further polishing and documentation may also be applied in preparation for its ultimate publication to accompany the research output.[1]

Another frequent scenario starts with a published data set. Adopting such data to use in one's research project will often require conversion or reformatting of data files as the very first step, as each software platform is typically designed to work with certain types of input. Data transformation in this case is conducted primarily with the purpose of producing intermediate forms that can then be passed to a data analysis platform of choice. In this scenario, data transformation is performed for personal use on an as-needed basis.

In this last and increasingly common scenario, proliferation of digital text has enabled linguists to adopt a *data science*[2] approach through which spontaneously occurring instances of language are harvested and repurposed for linguistic research. These data sources' native formats are often ill-suited for the purpose of data exchange and analysis and hence will require conversion. For example, web contents are usually encoded as HTML,[3] and text documents typically exist as word-processed formats such as Microsoft Word or PDF: their proprietary nature and/or heavy presence of stylistic elements mean the linguistic content contained within are not readily processable as *data*. In addition, these types of "data in the wild" are notoriously noisy and will necessitate multiple steps of cleaning and transformation before they can be utilized in scholarly research. With appropriate copyright clearance and redaction of personal information, it may then be published and shared with scholarly communities at large, the original language community, and a wider public (see Collister, chapter 9, this volume).

3 What's transformed: Form vs. information content

Data as stored in their electronic form are binary sequences of 0s and 1s, where there is no distinction between form and content. On a higher level, however, it makes a conceptual sense to draw a principled distinction between transformation's two main targets—*form* and *information content* of data.

The issues surrounding file storage mostly concern the *form* of data. Examples include conversion between DOS-format and Unix-format text files, and character-encoding conversion between, say, ASCII and eight-bit Unicode transformation format (UTF-8). To a limited extent, conversion from a proprietary format such as Microsoft Excel workbook (.xlsx file extension) or Microsoft Word (.docx) into a portable, open standards such as comma-separated values (CSV, .csv file extension) or a plain text file (.txt) can be thought of as a matter of form only. With such form-focused transformation, the intent on information content is, invariably, *preservation*: relevant operations are done in a way that no information content is lost during the process, and any loss of information, if unavoidable, must be minimized, controlled, and remedied. Note that conversion from proprietary formats such as Microsoft Word or Excel is fundamentally not lossless and will incur removal of typesetting references such as paragraph formatting and font sizes. Loss of these data bits, unless they encode linguistically relevant information,[4] is something that is desired and intended as part of a transformation process.

Beyond individual files, a data set involving multiple files and directories may need reorganization, especially during a development cycle. Renaming of files and directories, creation or removal of directory structures, and moving of files are common tasks; furthermore, multiple files may need to be joined into one, or a single file may need splitting. At first these operations may seem to only concern the form of the data, but they in fact tend to be prompted by a need to address deeper, often implicit, central parameters of a given data set, which is to say they hinge crucially on the *metadata* aspect of data content. Consider, for example, how positive and negative movie reviews may be segregated into two folders named "neg" and "pos" and how file names often bear extralinguistic information such as a language user's gender and types of elicitation tasks. File and directory structures are often co-opted this way as the principal means to encode the key dimensions of a data set. When files and directories undergo reorganization, these crucial bits of information will need to be preserved and encoded in some other, improved, way. Undertaking such an overhaul, then, must be preceded by a careful reflection on the purpose and design of the data set at hand. Also important is compliance with best practices and data management principles shared by the research community at large; Corti et al. (2019) and Mattern (chapter 5, this volume) provide in-depth recommendations on this very topic.

Turning now to the effect of data transformation on information content, let us distinguish its four main outcomes: *transliteration*, *loss*, *augmentation*, and *corruption* of information. *Information* in this regard does not narrowly refer to literal symbols, tokens, or values but should be understood broadly as *meaningful distinction* as present in the data.

1. *Transliteration* occurs when the information contained within data is converted to its isomorphic counterpart. The source and the target will have one-to-one mapping, and as a result no information is gained or lost through the process. An important corollary is that the output of transliteration can always be transformed back to its original form. At the file level, certain format conversions can be conducted in this fashion, such as one between CSV and tab-separated values (TSV). Closer to the actual content of data, relabeling a closed set of attributes can be done in an isomorphic manner: converting integer labels "1-2-3" to string-based and more descriptive "low-medium-high" is a simple example. A more complex case might involve, say, converting raw frequency counts of words into a more relative measure such as the per-million frequency count: this process is considered transliteration as long as the total word count that forms the basis of the latter figure stays known, thereby ensuring recoverability of the former, original raw counts.

2. *Loss* refers to loss of immaterial information that was managed in a purposeful manner; it can therefore be thought of as more of "trimming" or "simplification." There are a few reasons why one would implement loss of information. The first is to increase internal *consistency* of information: mapping an open set of attribute values into a closed set will necessarily incur loss of information but hopefully of the spurious kind only, which leads to increased data-internal consistency. The second reason is to increase information *density*: language data pulled directly from authentic communication streams will be saddled with vast amounts of noise and clutter, which then will need to be pruned to bring the main purpose of the data set into a sharper relief. Another is *redaction*: naturally occurring data may contain sensitive and private information that should be purged before publication.

3. *Augmentation* occurs when new information is added into a data set from a secondary data source. The new knowledge can consist of a layer of linguistic interpretation, commonly referred to as annotation: it can be added via manual annotation done by humans, or through the use of automated natural language processing tools. Producing and then incorporating various types of standard measurement is another way; merging in information culled from a static, published data source is yet another. When managed right, augmentation can be an excellent way to increase utility of a data set.

4. *Corruption* occurs with *unintended loss* of *meaningful* information that was present in the original data. A failed attempt at encoding conversion may leave an entire data file unusable; a poorly managed transformation operation may accidentally erase a meaningful distinction contained in the source data. Corruption may also occur in the course of adding *new* information, when such a process leads to introduction of unreliable or even false distinctions that are taken as legitimate or slip in unnoticed as a by-product. In other words, newly added knowledge that is low in fidelity is more of a detriment, even an element of corruption, than an improvement to a data set.

When managing a data transformation project, it is imperative to vigilantly ward off corruption as an unintended consequence while maintaining a clear-eyed approach to the desired outcomes of transliteration, loss, and augmentation. These three modes must also be isolated from each other: a single processing step should identify one of the three as its target outcome and execute it with precision. Versioning likewise should be conducted in-step; data versions that are associated with a clearly delineated set of changes that neatly align with the three modes of transformation will facilitate their management. One key consideration is that these operations must be kept reversible through stages of transformation, for which employment of popular version control systems such as Git becomes paramount.

4 Transformation operations in depth

This section presents an in-depth look at many commonly used transformation operations.

4.1 File format conversion

Electronic documents come in many different formats, which are signaled by file name extensions such as .docx, .xlsx, .pdf, .html, .xml, .json, and so forth (see table 6.1 for detailed specifications). These formats reflect their origin as digital content: for instance, student writings typically come in the Microsoft Word format, and scraped web documents will likely be in HTML. These formats will then need to be converted into those that are more suited to the purpose of data analysis and, further, data exchange (Austin 2006; Bird & Simmons 2003). The first essential consideration in this process is that of proprietary versus open-standard formats. Proprietary formats such as Microsoft Word and Excel are not accessible without a paid software license, and they are not machine-readable through industry-standard computational platforms, which make them particularly ill-suited in a data processing context. Their ownership by private companies also means long-term accessibility is far from guaranteed. It is therefore imperative that such files be converted and saved as formats with wider utility, such as XML, plain text files, or CSV files. Table 6.1 summarizes popular file formats for textual data.

The ultimate choice of a data file's format hinges on the natural organization of the information it carries. In general, CSV is well established as the standard format of choice for tabular data consisting of columns and rows of records; the plain text format with the .txt extension is best for a large number of flat-structured texts that are individually too long to store as a single column value in a tabular structure; hierarchically structured textual data, especially those with annotation, will find a best fit in XML.

Whatever the end choice, it is important to understand that these optimal data-exchange file formats are all essentially plain text files. While truly plain text files, by convention given the .txt extension, are understood to be a piece of continuous text, other formats such as CSV, TSV, XML, and JavaScript Object Notation (JSON) are merely an extension where a predefined set of reserved characters (e.g., "," in CSV and "\t" in TSV acting as column separators) or a sequence of characters (e.g., < ... > in XML that acts as markup tags) are designated as formatting constructs and keywords. Applications specializing in these formats are able to open the files, parse the formatting constructs and contents into appropriate data structures, and present a rendered view, along with functions through which an end user can manipulate the data

Table 6.1

Common file formats and recommended conversions

Extension	File format description	Plain-text format?	Suitable for data exchange?	Recommendation
.doc, .docx	Microsoft Word files	No	No; proprietary file format	Convert to XML or plain text
.xls, .xlsx	Microsoft Excel spreadsheet files	No	No; proprietary file format	Convert to CSV or TSV
.csv	Comma-separated values	Yes	Yes	
.tsv	Tab-separated values	Yes	Yes	
.pdf	Portable Document Format, developed by Adobe	No	No; while not proprietary, contains non-textual elements	Convert to XML or plain text
.xml	Extensible Markup Language with nested data structure	Yes	Yes	
.html, .htm	HyperText Markup Language, web pages	Yes	No; typically contains scripts and many web-related code bits	Clean up scripts and other extras; convert to XML
.md	Markdown, essentially a plain-text file with light formatting	Yes	No; contains formatting information	
.json	JavaScript Object Notation; popular format in social media	Yes	Yes	
.txt	Plain-text file	Yes	Yes	

content. But because these are still plain text files underneath, they can readily be opened and modified as such through simple text editors; in this type of interface, formatting constructs such as "," and "<" lose their special-character status and are treated as literal characters like any other that can be freely edited. This brings the associated risk of accidentally damaging the all-important data structure of a file itself, but the upside is that this affords the end user the ultimate control over the file content.

In dealing with file formats, it is important to understand this duality of format-specific meta-characters. For instance, because the comma "," is a special delimiter character in CSV, *literal* tokens of comma as in "Blood, sweat, and tears" or "10,000,000" in a CSV file will somehow need to be discernable as such. How is this accomplished? There are a few standard approaches. One is to utilize the practice of *escaping*, where a single meta-character is designated with the function of turning literalness on and off. The backslash "\" is the most common such escape character. In CSV, hence, any instances of "," will be understood as a field delimiter except for those prefixed by "\" as in "\,"; whitespace characters such as the newline and the tab characters

are commonly represented in an escaped form, as in the tab character "\t". In such schemes, a literal backslash is produced through self-escaping, that is, as "\\". Another common method is to turn on literalness within a certain scope: in some implementation of CSV, commas are understood to be literal when appearing inside a string sequence enclosed in a pair of double quotes ("..."). Lastly, a literal version of a special character may be expressed as a designated code: in HTML, the literal versions of the less-than ("<") and greater-than (">") characters are written as < and > utilizing & and ; which themselves are special characters in HTML. The ability to correctly recognize these elements and translate them accordingly is at the core of file format converters; however, having an overall understanding of this underlying principle comes in handy in occasional trouble shooting, often through the use of a text editor.

Embracing text editors as a go-to application in one's workflow is a hallmark of experienced data practitioners. Novices will find it tempting to retreat to the familiarity of Microsoft Word and Excel, which after all seem reasonably capable of importing, editing, and exporting back most of these formats. However, one should consider the fact that these consumer-oriented applications are hobbled by their propensity for applying alterations without the user's knowledge (see section 6), with often fatal consequences to data integrity. Text editors, by contrast, take more principled and transparent approaches when it comes to file content manipulation and tend to give the end users explicit and finer control. There are many excellent text editors available, including Notepad++[5] (Windows), Sublime Text[6] (Mac), and Atom[7] (all platforms), that are recommended over the bare-bones text editors that come preinstalled in Windows 10 and the Mac OS operating systems.

Returning to the matter of conversion, how does one go about converting a file from one format to another? When dealing with only a handful of files, the simplest choice is manual export through the format's known native application. For example, Microsoft Word documents can be "saved as" XML or a plain text file; Excel likewise provides an option to save a workbook file as a CSV (.csv) file. Additionally, one may utilize third-party applications specializing in document conversion; Pandoc,[8] in particular, bills itself as a universal document converter and is capable of handling such diverse formats as Microsoft Word, Open Office, HTML, XML, and LaTeX. The sheer number of compatible formats seems impressive enough, but the true power of third-party tools such as Pandoc lies with their command-line capability: most can be called in a command-line interface along with optional parameters for fine-tuning, making it possible to automate conversion of a large number of files. As with any tools, though, conversion tools are not fail-proof and the end result will need careful inspection. We will return to command-line–based automation in section 5.1.

4.2 Text files: Character encoding, line ending

As we have seen, data-exchange file formats are fundamentally plain text files, for which one can identify two central issues—character encoding and line ending. Unicode (Unicode Consortium 2019) is gaining increasingly wide adoption as the universal character encoding standard, yet the reality is that text files still come in many different and often hard-to-detect character encodings. Unlike Linux and the Mac OS which use UTF-8, a subtype of Unicode, as the OS-default character set, Windows adopts non-Unicode character-encoding systems for its various language versions, which is a common

source of encoding conflict. For its English and Western language versions it uses a system called Windows-1252, also known as CP-1252 or ANSI (for American National Standards Institute). For the sake of cross-platform compatibility, text files should be encoded in Unicode whenever possible, in UTF-8 (a subtype of Unicode that uses eight bits as the minimum character width) or UTF-16 (same but uses sixteen bits as the minimum width).

One commonly encountered source of variability within Unicode encoding is what is known as the "byte order mark" or BOM, represented as a non-printing Unicode character code U+FEFF at the beginning of a file. Basically, BOMs work as a signature that specifies the encoding and byte order of a file to an application that reads it in. However, their presence or absence is something that is mandated by an individual application's protocol, which creates complications. The details surrounding BOM usage are highly technical, so let us simply make a note of a few fundamental issues here: (1) use of a BOM may be required at the protocol level adopted by a particular application, and (2) conversion therefore must be done with an application in mind, and finally (3) BOMs should be avoided to the extent possible. For further details, readers should consult the Unicode Consortium's standard document[9] and its frequently asked questions section on BOMs.[10]

The second important aspect of text file encoding is line ending, which again shows OS dependency. Historically Unix and Linux have used LF (line feed, a single "\n" character) to encode the end of a line, which the Mac OS has since adopted; Windows, on the other hand, uses CRLF (carriage return followed by line feed, encoded as a sequence of two characters "\r\n"). This creates a fundamental dissonance between the two groups of operating systems regarding what exactly constitutes a line in a text file; a text file with "\n" line breaks, when opened in a Windows application, may show up as a single continuous line of text without a break. Windows OS however is reportedly on track to increase compatibility with the Unix-style line breaks. Here, too, the recommendation is to adopt Unix-style LF line breaks, irrespective of the OS.

Further complicating the matter is the concept of *locale*, a set of system-wide parameters that defines the default language, country, regions, and other variations. The problem of default character encoding that we have discussed is closely related to locales, which follows from the OS's region and language setting. Importantly, applications depend on the locale setting when opening and interpreting a file, which then means that the same file, opened on different OSs or under different language versions of the same OS, may behave differently. Crucially, applications will also apply locale-specific settings when saving out files, which may lead to unwitting modifications of the fundamental characteristics such as line ending and character encoding. It is therefore imperative, especially in a collaborative environment, to be aware of and look for locale-induced problems.

Converting a text file to use a different character encoding or a different line ending is something that all text editors are equipped to handle. Figure 6.1 is a screenshot of Notepad++; through its "Encoding" menu, the text file currently in ANSI (i.e., Windows-1252) encoding can be converted to UTF-8. The line ending is currently set to Unix (LF) as shown in the bottom status bar, which can be converted via "Edit" → "EOL Conversion" menu (EOL: end-of-line).

Beyond a single file, converting a folder full of text files is best handled through batch processing in a command-line environment. Popular tools specializing in these conversion tasks are Unix-native applications: once considered tools of the trade for those exclusively inhabiting the Unix/Linux world, their general availability has drastically expanded in recent years. These tools now come preinstalled or otherwise easily installable in the Mac OS; on the Windows side, the Git Bash package[11]

comes bundled with most popular Unix command-line tools. To name a few, `dos2unix` and its reverse `unix2dos` are used for line break conversion; `iconv` on the other hand is a venerable tool used for encoding conversion. The example command that follows converts an input file's content from (`-f`) the Windows-1252 encoding to (`-t`) UTF-8, the output stream of which is redirected into (`>`) a new file called `outputfile.txt`.

```
iconv -f windows-1252 -t utf-8 inputfile.txt >
outputfile.txt
```

4.3 File and directory operations

A need for conversion often extends to multiple files, at times hundreds or even thousands of them, at which point automating the process through the command line becomes an absolute necessity. Figure 6.2 illustrates how the same operation using `iconv` is repeated on all text files (ending in .txt extension) in the directory, using the Bash shell's `for` loop syntax and variables. The converted files, bearing the original file name designated through the variable `$file`, are saved in a new directory called `converted`.

This is an example of a relatively simple operation executed on the fly, but more complex tasks can be planned out and executed through the use of a shell script. Section 5.1 lists a few learning resources on the Bash shell and scripting.

More generally, reorganization of the entire file and directory structure of a data set will often involve command-line operations. File format conversion and

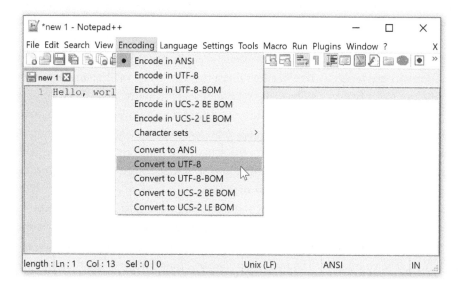

Figure 6.1

Encoding conversion in Notepad++.

```
MINGW64:/c/Users/narae/Documents/state_union                          —    □    ×

narae@T480s MINGW64 ~/Documents/state_union
$ mkdir converted

narae@T480s MINGW64 ~/Documents/state_union
$ ls
1945-Truman.txt        1961-Kennedy.txt   1975-Ford.txt     1989-Bush.txt      converted/
1953-Eisenhower.txt    1963-Johnson.txt   1978-Carter.txt   1993-Clinton.txt   README
1954-Eisenhower.txt    1970-Nixon.txt     1981-Reagan.txt   2001-GWBush-1.txt

narae@T480s MINGW64 ~/Documents/state_union
$ for file in *txt
> do
> iconv -f windows-1252 -t utf-8 $file > converted/$file
> done

narae@T480s MINGW64 ~/Documents/state_union
$ ls converted
1945-Truman.txt        1961-Kennedy.txt   1975-Ford.txt     1989-Bush.txt
1953-Eisenhower.txt    1963-Johnson.txt   1978-Carter.txt   1993-Clinton.txt
1954-Eisenhower.txt    1970-Nixon.txt     1981-Reagan.txt   2001-GWBush-1.txt
```

Figure 6.2

Batch processing on multiple files through command line.

encoding conversion are two particularly common use cases. At other times, files may be joined, split up, grouped into new directories, and renamed. There are Unix tools specializing in such operations, which are typically coupled with a loop syntax available through popular shells such as Bash and Zsh. The Mac OS, based on Unix, supplies the command-line interface and both shells natively through its Terminal app. On the Windows side, the Bash shells and Unix tools are available through Windows Subsystem for Linux[12] and also Git Bash installation. See section 5.1 for details.

As briefly noted in section 3, reorganization of file and directory structure is often prompted by a deeper consideration surrounding the design of a data set. Folders, files, and text lines are largely platform-independent units of information storage and hence the primary device for imposing organization. An optimal setup therefore may see them aligned with discrete categories intrinsically present in a data set, with separate folders provisioned for salient top-level categories, and each text file or line of text corresponding to a single data sample, and so forth. Overhauling this alignment is a leading cause for undertaking file and directory restructuring. An archive of student writing samples that came as a single, long word-processed file is best split into multiple plain text files with a single file corresponding to a single writing sample. On the other hand, language samples from social media tend to be short with rich metadata therefore are best stored as a single file with a tabulated format, with each line corresponding to a row entry.

How this overall alignment is configured has a fundamental impact on the constitution of a data set. The extent to which metadata should be encoded in the file and directory structure is in fact a design-critical issue. A flat directory with tens of thousands of unordered, poorly or inconsistently named files could use folder organization; conversely, excessive depth in directory hierarchy should be avoided, as deeply nested directories can be a hindrance to navigation. File names, on the other hand, are often co-opted to encode central parameters such as demographic information, a practice that can quickly become intractable. Given these considerations, beyond one or possibly two top-tier parameters, it is best to keep directory structures and file names simple and instead record metadata in a separate, tabulated documentation file, where each file name is listed with as many parameter attributes as there are without being bound by space concerns. Again, shuffling around these integral bits of information—extracting them from file and directory names; redirecting them into a new file; renaming, moving, and deleting files and directories—are all tasks that are best automated through command-line operations and, needless to say, with utmost care.

4.4 Data cleaning and normalization

Data, especially if sourced from naturally occurring communication streams, is bound to be messy. It may contain irregularities that necessitate manual or automated correction. It may also contain a mass of irrelevant content that distracts from the intended purpose of the data set. Personal information may be present, which will require redaction and anonymization. Standardization and normalization steps will ensure consistent codification of attribute values. These tasks, especially if done through automated means, require methodical approaches as well as a tight control on quality. Inadequately executed data cleaning and reorganizing operations are a common source of data corruption.

The first type of data cleaning effort concerns culling of extraneous content. When data is first exported from the original source, it will likely contain an excess of extralinguistic information that might not provide much utility. For instance, surveys conducted through popular online platforms typically record entries such as Internet protocol addresses of respondents, time and duration of access, and more; they will then show up as columns when the survey data are exported as a spreadsheet form. When publishing these data alongside the research, it may be beneficial to drop such data fields and categories entirely, which not only addresses the privacy concern but also keeps the data content on point.

This type of categorical removal tends to be fairly straightforward, but more nuanced assessments are called for when deciding on inclusion or removal of data samples. With a set of thousands of essays submitted by students, some may be of questionable value. Should you be dropping writings that solely consist of "asdfasdfasdf"? How about one that simply reads "I don't know, this question is hard" or multiple copies submitted by a single author with only slight variation? Should you be dropping writings by respondents who skipped over a demographic background question? Furthermore, if handling a large data set, it will be impossible to manually inspect all data entries, which means one will then need to decide what criteria and computational means should be employed to precisely spot and filter out undesirable samples.

Additionally, data culling may be motivated by design considerations. For a data set aiming to focus on a few key parameters, dropping of certain samples may be justified if they are not a good fit in those regards. Likewise, if achieving a balance among certain parameter values is part of the design goals, a decision may be made to remove excess samples. In conducting these quota-based removals, care must be taken to ward off selection bias by adopting randomization in the process.

Another chief motivation for data cleaning is normalization. Missing values are part of naturally occurring data and will call for a decision on their treatment: leaving as is, filling in with a default value, filling in through approximation, or dropping of samples are possible choices. Validation of data values is another critical step: what is presumed to be a closed set of values is often not, which will then require correction. For instance, when you have part-of-speech tagged text data, it may be entirely possible for invalid tags to be present; they can only be discovered via a data set–wide validation, which involves rounding up all tags and reducing them into a unique set. User-reported values present yet another challenge. A data column that contains information on a language user's first language, if self-reported, will contain an unruly set of string values ranging from, say, "Sinhalese," "sinhala," "Sinhala language," "Sinhales [sic] and Tamil," which will need to be interpreted and then mapped onto unique, closed-set values, such as the International Organization for Standardization's ISO 639 language code *si* or *sin*, and in the last case possibly *sin;tam*.

In some other instances, contextually dependent data may be converted into related yet more readily usable values. For example, survey data may only include information on respondents' birth year; it may be advantageous to covert the information into their age at the time of data collection and, depending on the purpose of the data, even be necessary to bin the age values into a few key groups. It is also common for a data set to start with certain categorical values encoded in community-internal shorthand, which may benefit from remapping into a more universally interpretable system of representation before publication.

Lastly, anonymization is often a crucial step before publication. Personal names, user identifications and e-mails are all sensitive information that needs to be redacted. User identifications are typically used as a record identifier, which will then need to be replaced across the data set with randomly generated unique identifiers. In-text mentions of personal names and email addresses will need to be identified and then replaced by a designated placeholder. Correctly identifying all instances, however, will be a challenge, because these are typically an open set; such operations are therefore undertaken by use of pattern matching via regular expressions or off-the-shelf natural language processing (NLP) applications capable of named entity recognition.

All in all, data cleaning and normalization are no doubt the most underrated aspects of data-side work: they routinely reveal themselves to be more complex and more time- and effort-intensive than one would initially anticipate. At the same time, the payout of good, quality work tends to remain largely invisible—people rarely take time to appreciate a data set on its cleanliness and thoughtful construction—while the stakes of data corruption and data loss are high. Another related paradox is that the tasks involved are viewed as grunt work, yet executing them right will require considerable experience and high levels of technical sophistication. It is therefore not uncommon to encounter cases of time-strapped faculty members coming to regret tasking undergraduate research assistants with data-cleaning work, because they end up spending more time either teaching the students the processes or tracking down and fixing their mistakes.

Despite these challenges, or perhaps because of them, the importance of getting these steps right cannot be emphasized enough. The creators of a data set, with access to the full context surrounding its origin, are in the best position to apply informed interpretation and bring order to the data in the way that minimizes loss of meaningful distinctions. Publishing insufficiently cleaned or normalized data in turn has many negative consequences: it creates unnecessary duplication of efforts on the part of individual end users; without access to the full context, users run the risk of arriving at an incorrect interpretation; and research founded on disparate postprocessing treatments will be neither readily comparable nor easily reproducible.[13]

Lastly on the tools side, cleaning operations on a handful of data files may be accomplished manually via software platforms that are native to the data format. For example, Microsoft Excel can handle pruning of columns or simple remapping of values in tabular data; text editor programs such as Notepad++ and Atom all come with find-and-replace functions that can even work on user-supplied regular expression patterns. With a larger data set, and with more complex data cleaning tasks, it becomes necessary to bring in more comprehensive computational tools such as command-line scripting, Python, and R. On these platforms, a user can conduct a full range of data inspection—sampling, probing, compiling descriptive statistics, rounding up attribute values—all the while diligently checking for anomalies. Then, custom functions can be defined that will target particular values, patterns, or constructions and produce transformed values, which then can be applied to the underlying data to obtain a transformed output. This sort of bulk transformation however is powerful and is all too frequently a source of data corruption. We will return to this topic in section 6.2.

4.5 Synthesis, merging, text processing

This section covers processes by which new information is added into a data set. There are two main modes: first, pulling from additional data sources and merging in relevant bits of data points, and second, augmenting text content with interpretive knowledge such as word tokens and parts of speech often through the use of popular NLP applications.

Augmenting your data with additional information available from a published source can aid discovery and enhance its value for the research community. For example, if you have collected an archive of geotagged Tweets, correlating the geotags with zip code and further the location's demographic makeup may provide a key insight for sociolinguistic studies. In text data, marking individual words with their frequency ranking from a published corpus will likewise prove useful. These are all instances of merging information from an external source. There are a few important considerations.

First, external data may contain inaccuracies or spurious entries that could then become a permanent part of your data set. In a memorable episode in my own research group, tokens of *also* were found to have *conjurer* listed as the lemma in our augmented data set; an investigation tracked down the source as the single errant line in the popular Someya lemma list[14] seen in figure 6.3.

This anecdote illustrates perils of blindly trusting external data; one must always carefully vet their sources and then scrutinize the end result of incorporation.

Second, merging from external sources is rarely a problem-free, one-step procedure and will require some, often extensive, measure of postprocessing. Examples include cases that are not covered by the external data source, subtle categorical mismatches and inconsistencies, and edge cases. They will need to be resolved in some way with clear documentation. The quality of attention paid in this postprocessing stage often makes

```
2626 conifer -> conifers
2627 conjecture -> conjectures,conjecturing,conjectured
2628 conjunction -> conjunctions
2629 conjure -> conjures,conjuring,conjured
2630 conjurer -> conjurers,also,spelled
2631 conk -> conks,conking,conked
```

Figure 6.3

An illustration of an error lurking in a widely used external data source.

or breaks the usefulness of the knowledge being added. Lastly, if publication of your data set is the ultimate goal, special attention needs to be paid to the copyright and licensing of the external data set, as they may have an implication on the publication of the incorporated data portions (see Collister, chapter 9, this volume).

Beyond merging from a static data resource, adding basic types of linguistic interpretation obtained through the use of text processing applications is another way of augmenting textual data. Sentence-level or word-level tokenization, lemmatization, and part-of-speech tagging are among popular steps (Lu 2014). Certain languages have a fairly well-established tokenization and part-of-speech conventions adopted by scholarly communities, which tend to coincide with the availability of NLP tools that are known to produce highly accurate automated output. The level of accuracy will vary depending on the task at hand: for English, word tokenization is something that is typically done in a deterministic fashion with high regularity and accuracy, while part-of-speech tagging accuracy currently tops out at 97.85%,[15] which some may argue crosses the threshold of being good enough to replace human annotation whose reported interannotator agreement rate is around 97% (Manning 2011).

But are these reported figures truly representative? With the exception of tokenization for certain languages, virtually every modern NLP tool is based on stochastic models trained and evaluated on the same pool of often highly homogeneous text; the reported performance figure is therefore liable to drop, sometimes significantly, when applied to out-of-domain text. Consequently, rather than taking a reported performance figure at face value, researchers would do well to conduct their own evaluation of how an NLP tool actually fares on their own text. This can be achieved by manually inspecting a small sample portion of the processed output. Additionally, conducting an output-wide sweep will help discover data-specific

weak spots that the application is particularly ill-equipped to handle, which then can be fixed through postprocessing. In other words, in augmenting data through the use of NLP applications the same set of considerations apply as before, which is to thoroughly test the resource itself and be prepared to apply rigorous postprocessing and correction. Omitting these steps will invariably lead to noisy output that adds little value, or worse, a layer of interpreted linguistic knowledge whose lack of reliability ends up weakening subsequent linguistic research founded on it.

If these were the stakes, why go to the trouble of creating these new interpreted layers and publishing them? There are many benefits. First of all, certain earlier text processing tasks in the pipeline such as tokenization are viewed as essential: a running piece of raw text is nothing but a sequence of characters, and breaking it down into discrete sentences and/or word tokens is considered a foundational early step on which all later, higher-level linguistic inquiries will rest. A layer of word tokens published along with the original, raw text will therefore not only save time on the part of end users but also ensure all subsequent linguistic analyses build on common ground. All in all, a layer of automatically generated linguistic interpretation can be a true value-add when the output quality is sufficiently high, results are vetted through validation, and anomalies are corrected through postprocessing to the extent possible. One final and critical requirement: the entire process and the evaluation outcome must be clearly documented, so that future users of the data set can make informed decisions.

4.6 Manual annotation

The need for manual annotation arises in a couple of different settings. First, data samples collected for a personal research project may require further linguistic interpretation in the form of categorical judgment. For example, sentence elicitations may need to be supplemented by a judgment on the speech act they encode. This type of annotation effort is referred to as *coding* in some research communities and is typically undertaken on a small scale by the individual researcher who is the creator and end user of the produced linguistic interpretation. A second scenario is more institutional: a manual annotation project is undertaken with an express purpose of building and publishing a large-scale linguistic data set. This type of institutional annotation project typically involves a team of linguists who may take on varying roles, a system of quality-checking in place for interannotator agreement, creation of annotation guidelines, a managed project plan and a budget, and a specialized annotation software platform. In either scenario, the process leads to *creation* of linguistic data, rather than transformation thereof, and therefore is outside of the scope of this chapter. Interested readers should consult Ide and Pustejovsky (2017).

5 Essential tools

This section provides an overview of essential tools that are commonly employed in data transformation projects. Perhaps unsurprisingly, they comprise core computational skill sets as well as the platforms popularized by the recently emerging field of data science.

5.1 Command-line tools

As illustrated throughout this chapter, command-line Unix utilities are essential in facilitating automation of certain transformation tasks, especially those that involve format conversion operations. They are readily available on a Mac OS: the Mac OS is based on Unix and thusly supplies the command-line interface and the Bash shell (lately the Z shell) natively through its Terminal app. On the Windows side, its native command-line environment called Command Prompt is entirely separate from the Unix-based suite of tools. However, recent developments have made Unix tools easily accessible in the Microsoft Windows platform. First, Windows 10 now lets users install and run a copy of Linux natively within Windows via Windows Subsystem for Linux. Second, Git's Windows installation includes Git Bash, a Bash command-line emulation layer, as well as most of the popular Unix command-line tools we have seen previously; this path comes with a minimal overhead

and therefore is highly recommended for beginners and experienced users alike. Additionally, there are a number of non-Unix applications that are nevertheless designed to be used in a command-line environment such as Pandoc and, on the speech file side, SoX.[16]

Making the leap from the familiar graphical user interface into a command-line environment can be disorienting, but there are an ever-increasing number of learning resources online: The Unix Shell by Software Carpentry[17] (Devenyi et al. 2019) is particularly well received. Lu (2014) has an excellent chapter on how to process text in the command-line interface with detailed illustration and use cases tailored specifically for corpus linguistic research. Poser (2018) has been maintaining an extensive list of computational resources useful for linguistic research, which is found online.[18]

5.2 End-to-end processing tools

Operations that reach deep into the content of data, such as data cleaning, merging, and text processing, are best approached by enlisting more versatile computational tools such as Python and R. Python is a general-purpose programming language that has recently become the dominant platform of choice in NLP and, more broadly, artificial intelligence. R on the other hand has been a tool of choice for statistics-oriented research that has gained a wide adoption among linguists. They are capable of directly handling common formats such as HTML/XML, CSV, SQL, JSON, and even PDFs. Each boasts a large user base, active development communities, and open-source libraries for essential text transformation tasks. Python in particular was aided by a prominent library called Natural Language Toolkit (Bird, Loper, & Klein 2009) in emerging as the dominant platform for conducting primary text processing steps such as tokenization and part-of-speech tagging. The recent rise of the Pandas library has reinforced Python's handling of tabular data, traditionally a stronghold of R. Many text processing operations are also available in R through its open-source libraries. Using these programming languages, data transformation can be conducted in a streamlined, end-to-end workflow while maintaining a finer control over the outcome of each processing step.

5.3 Version control and documentation

If there is one cardinal rule in data manipulation, it is that every transformation step must be reversible. Version control systems are indispensable in this regard: they serve as your safeguard for recovery as well as a powerful tool for managing the entire data processing pipeline while keeping a bird's-eye view over the history of a transformation cycle. Initially designed as a system for administering software development, version control systems have since emerged as a principal tool of trade for data practitioners. The most popular platform by far is Git,[19] an open-source project that is seeing universal adoption. In a personal project, it operates as a pure versioning system on a folder and its file content, called *repository*. In a multiuser project, Git additionally acts as a collaboration platform, as it offers solutions for managing file contents contributed by multiple users. Git forces users to structure development of a project into a succession of version commits, while providing tools to navigate and document changes throughout the version history. Becoming a successful user of Git entails breaking from one's old ingrained work habits and adopting an entirely new mindset on managing a project.

Extending Git's core capability is GitHub,[20] a popular repository hosting service. Keeping an online copy of a repository as the master copy serves multiple purposes: first is a data backup, and the second is a venue for publication. Lately, data development efforts as well as their resulting data sets are publicly hosted and distributed on GitHub. Data-focused research is increasingly finding a public-facing project home on GitHub, as do research projects small and large, including those that draw participants from across the globe. One such example is the Universal Dependencies Project[21] (Nivre et al. 2017), whose aim is to construct a data set of massively cross-linguistic syntactic annotation: it has over two hundred contributors producing more than one hundred tree-banks in over seventy languages. In this connected era of the Internet, running a data-focused project out of GitHub is becoming a primary vehicle for keeping up the visibility of its public profile.

6 Guarding against data corruption

When operating on data, it is all too easy for unintended errors to slip in. Instances of data corruption lead to a waste of valuable time and resources required for correction. Worse yet, they may go unnoticed for a long period of time; a belated discovery may threaten to invalidate research findings that have been produced since. Having

a versioning system in place is an absolute minimum that will enable recovery, but this is helpful only in the event when an error gets discovered and does so before its publication. Prevention of corruption in the first place is therefore paramount. This section covers common pitfalls and recommended strategies for combating the threat of corruption and ensuring integrity of data.

6.1 Accidental corruption: Humans and applications

One of the common sources of data corruption has to do with the realities of modern computing: textual data displayed for the human eye within a given software platform is fundamentally a rendered view. What looks like an ordinary stretch of text may be hiding invisible control characters and formatting-related tags, which may then get copied along with the genuine text content when an unsuspecting researcher goes for copy-and-paste. In addition, two characters that look alike to the naked eye may in fact be two entirely different ones, which then introduces a spurious distinction. Case in point: an ill-considered copy-paste job may introduce *co—worker* as a token that will then be interpreted by text processing tools as entirely distinct from *co-worker*.

Another, related, danger comes from the fact that software platforms will invariably apply their own rendering and transformation in the course of opening a file, which then may inadvertently be saved out, overwriting the original. Microsoft Word's conversion of plain ASCII quotation markers (") into *smart* quotes ("or") is a well-known issue; opening a CSV file in Python's Pandas library may convert integer values (e.g., 1, 2, 3) into real-valued ones (e.g., 1.0, 2.0, 3.0) unless proper configuration is specified. Pandas also may apply its own conversion: on the Windows platform, it is known to auto-convert Unix-style line ending "\n" into Windows-style "\r\n" when dealing with textual data types. Your copy of Excel, unless it was patched in recent months, may insert an invisible character "\uFEFF" at the beginning of a CSV file as a BOM. The list goes on.

Human error is another common cause. An errant keystroke slipping into a data file is distressingly easy, so is replacing or deleting a file copy entirely. A vital practice in this regard is establishing an operating procedure for *viewing* file content as entirely separate from one for *editing*. The moment you open up a data file in edit-enabled applications such as Microsoft Word, Excel, and even text editor programs, you risk unintentionally modifying the data. Many text-based data formats such as plain text (.txt extension), CSV, and HTML can be opened through popular browsers such as Chrome and Safari, which limit users to the viewing mode. The command-line interface also offers a good mode of operation for viewing and exploring data content. Interacting with text data in a command-line environment through standard Unix tools such as `less`, `cat`, `grep`, and other input/output piping methods will afford the user an added benefit: the power to sift through large quantities of data on the fly.

6.2 Corruption introduced during transformation operations

The last source of corruption is arguably the most intractable: inadequately managed data transformation efforts conducted on a mass scale. For example, an operation that is meant to anonymize personal names in a corpus may end up overapplying and removing homonymous words such as *April*, *frank*, and *park* across the board. Moreover, insufficiently restricted conversion rules may end up matching strings mid-word, changing, say, "Parking is a problem" into "<ANONYMOUS_NAME>ing is a problem." These are essentially a transformation operation applying where it should not, that is, a case of poor *precision*. These examples may seem contrived, but linguists, many of whom by training tend to focus on salient linguistic exemplars, are liable to underestimate the long tails of edge cases that make up a huge bulk in naturally occurring language data. To make matters worse, the sheer volume of data that likely had necessitated these automations would rule out manual inspection of the output and may ultimately lead to unexpected errors going undiscovered.

If regulating a vast number of positive hits is a difficult task, harder still is keeping tabs on a transformation operation failing to apply where it should, which is a matter of *recall*. When a transformation does not apply across the board to all intended targets, this too can be seen as type of data corruption, as the end result is unevenly applied transformation and therefore increased noise in the data. Going back to the anonymization example, in a vast amount of text data, how does one make sure that all personal names have been correctly detected? There is no easy and sure-fire way to ensure this, especially if the text contains non-standard capitalization and other irregularities.

The only defense against transformation-induced data corruption is a practice of rigorous postevaluation.

The effect of a given transformation operation may not be vetted individually across all instances, but as a principle a methodical probing procedure should be put in place that rounds up frequent transformation cases along with some spot-checks performed on edge cases. An experienced practitioner of data manipulation will know to devise a comprehensive set of test cases that is intended to keep both the precision and recall of the transformation close to 100%, which then should be supplemented by exhaustive testing on the output. In addition, the practice of sustained monitoring through routine exploratory data analysis goes a long way: compiling data set–wide statistics on several key data points and actively monitoring them will help expose any anomalies that were introduced via an earlier processing step.

Lastly but most importantly: documentation is key. All aspects of a transformation task—the application, function, or code that was used; the target and its scope; expected and actual outcomes; quality control steps taken; postprocessing steps taken; and everything else—should be noted and recorded as part of a version control history. This is not only an instrument for troubleshooting any case of corruption discovered down the line but also a way of inculcating sound working habits in the daily workflow of a data practitioner. Eventually, the key details of the transformation operations should accompany the data set at the time of publication.

6.3 Warding off corruption: Summary of strategies

To sum up, this is a list of ground principles for warding off data corruption.

1. A version control system enables recovery and therefore is an absolute necessity.

2. Data corruption instances tend to escape immediate notice; prevention therefore is paramount.

3. Understand that all software platforms apply their own rendering and transformation to data files they open; each additional application in a work pipeline will introduce another risk factor that will have to be managed.

4. Beware of what is visible within an application's view; underlying code representation may be entirely different or hiding extraneous code bits.

5. Stem off accidental modification by separating file viewing methods from editing procedures.

6. Mass transformation operations, especially those based on pattern-matching, should be executed with care, with a tight control on both precision and recall.

7. Every transformation operation should be accompanied by methodical postevaluation as well as spot-checks.

8. Employ exploratory data analysis at regular intervals to ensure integrity of your data as they move through each stage of transformation.

9. Keep meticulous documentation of these processing steps.

7 Conclusion

Transforming data is often necessary and crucial part of a data workflow, either in a personal research context or in a more concerted data set production effort. As data proliferate in our daily lives, linguists have access to ever-growing volumes of text whose transformation must rely on automation and computational tools. Transforming data at these elevated scales brings the risk of data corruption, which can be contained through adoption of rigorous data practices with an emphasis on quality control. All in all, there is an art to transforming data, which comprises specific skill sets as well as work habits and practices that could take years to develop. Fortunately, educational opportunities on computational and data-science methods have become abundant as of late: linguists who set their eyes on data-centric research should not delay their training.

Notes

1. Thieberger and Berez (2012) present a comprehensive overview of linguistic data management from the perspective of documentary linguistics.

2. Wikipedia.org (https://en.wikipedia.org/wiki/Data_science, accessed November 19, 2019) defines *data science* as "a multidisciplinary field that uses scientific methods, processes, algorithms and systems to extract knowledge and insights from structured and unstructured data."

3. Detailed information on these file formats are presented in section 4.1.

4. An example: a lexical resource may utilize italics or boldface to mark a token as the citation form, head word, and so forth. Transformation to plain text will erase all such meaningful distinctions; a markup text format, such as HTML or XML, that can store stylistic information therefore will be a better candidate as the new format.

5. https://notepad-plus-plus.org/.

6. https://www.sublimetext.com/.

7. https://atom.io/.

8. https://pandoc.org/.

9. http://www.unicode.org/versions/Unicode12.0.0/UnicodeStandard-12.0.pdf.

10. https://unicode.org/faq/utf_bom.html#BOM.

11. https://gitforwindows.org/.

12. https://docs.microsoft.com/en-us/windows/wsl/about.

13. Increasingly, concerted efforts are being made in the linguistics community with the aim to promote recognition of data creation and publication work as an important part of scholarship. Alperin et al. (chapter 13, this volume) make a case, as do Champieux and Coates (chapter 12, this volume).

14. Available at https://www.laurenceanthony.net/software/antconc/.

15. Akbik, Blythe, and Vollgraf (2018), according to https://aclweb.org/aclwiki/POS_Tagging_(State_of_the_art).

16. http://sox.sourceforge.net/.

17. https://swcarpentry.github.io/shell-novice/.

18. http://billposer.org/Linguistics/Computation/Resources.html.

19. https://git-scm.com/.

20. https://github.com.

21. https://universaldependencies.org/, GitHub home at https://github.com/UniversalDependencies.

References

Akbik, Alan, Duncan Blythe, and Roland Vollgraf. 2018. Contextual string embeddings for sequence labeling. In *Proceedings of the 27th International Conference on Computational Linguistics*, 1638–1629.

Austin, Peter K. 2006. Data and language documentation. In *Essentials of Language Documentation*, ed. Jost Gippert, Nikolaus Himmelmann, and Ulrike Mosel, 87–112. Berlin: Mouton de Gruyter.

Bird, Steven, Edward Loper, and Ewan Klein. 2009. *Natural Language Processing with Python*. Sebastopol, CA: O'Reilly Media.

Bird, Steven, and Gary Simmons. 2003. Seven dimensions of portability for language documentation and description. *Language* 79:557–582.

Corti, Louise, Veerle Van den Eynden, Libby Bishop, and Matthew Woollard. 2019. *Managing and Sharing Research Data: A Guide to Good Practice*. London: Sage.

Devenyi, Gabriel A., Gerard Capes, Colin Morris, and Will Pitchers, eds. 2019. swcarpentry/shell-novice: Software Carpentry: the UNIX shell, June 2019 (Version v2019.06.1). Zenodo. http://doi.org/10.5281/zenodo.3266823.

Ide, Nancy, and Pustejovsky, James, eds. 2017. *Handbook of Linguistic Annotation*. Houten, the Netherlands: Springer Netherlands. http://doi:10.1007/978-94-024-0881-2.

Lu, Xiaofei. 2014. *Computational Methods for Corpus Annotation and Analysis*. Houten, the Netherlands: Springer Netherlands. http://doi:10.1007/978-94-017-8645-4.

Manning, Christopher. 2011. Part-of-speech tagging from 97% to 100%: Is it time for some linguistics? In *Proceedings of the 12th International Conference on Computational Linguistics and Intelligent Text Processing*, vol. 1, ed. Alexander Gelbukh, 171–189. Berlin: Springer-Verlag.

Nivre, Joakim, Daniel Zeman, Filip Ginter, and Francis Tyers. 2017. Universal dependencies. In *Proceedings of the 15th Conference of the European Chapter of the Association for Computational Linguistics: Tutorial Abstracts*, E17-5001. Stroudsburg, PA: Association for Computational Linguistics.

Poser, Bill. 2018. Computational resources for linguistic research. Accessed version: last revised September 10, 2018. http://billposer.org/Linguistics/Computation/Resources.html.

POS Tagging (State of the art). n.d. The ACL Wiki, the Association for Computational Linguistics (website). Modified March 4, 2019. https://aclweb.org/aclwiki/POS_Tagging_(State_of_the_art).

Thieberger, Nicholas, and Andrea Berez. 2012. Linguistic data management. In *The Oxford Handbook of Linguistic Fieldwork*, ed. Nicholas Thieberger, 90–118. Oxford: Oxford University Press.

Unicode Consortium. 2019. The Unicode® Standard Version 12.1.0–Core Specification. https://unicode.org/versions/Unicode 12.1.0/.

7 Archiving Research Data

Helene N. Andreassen

1 Introduction

Imagine you are a senior researcher in neurolinguistics, and you have recently submitted a paper to an international journal that requires data sets underpinning the analyses to be made openly available to the readers.[1] You get very positive feedback overall from the reviewers, but they ask you to provide more details on some aspects of the data collection methods, which you agree to do. After revision, your paper gets published and your results provoke quite some discussion among the researchers in your field. A fellow neurolinguist, whose work you've read but who you've never met in person, performs a replication study, using the original data set, to test the validity of your findings, and this fortunately proves successful. Moreover, she has ideas about how to take this research further and invites you to collaborate with her team on a future project.

Now imagine you are a PhD research fellow in phonology, and you are deep into the analysis chapter of your dissertation. You read a peer-reviewed paper about relevant phonological processes in a related language, where the authors claim the existence of a given pattern. This is stellar evidence to include in your own argument, but there are no examples in the paper, nor any link to the data. You are unsure whether you can trust this claim without seeing any empirical evidence, but you don't know the authors personally and fear it would be perceived as impolite to contact them and ask for data. You thus end up not incorporating the alleged finding into your chapter.

Finally, imagine you are a language teacher at your tribe's immersion school, and you come across a collection of newly digitized language recordings from a previous generation of speakers. You are able to delve into these recordings and enhance your lesson plans on particular grammatical constructions by providing new examples of

them in use. Or imagine you are a postdoctoral researcher in morphosyntax with funding from the regional center for indigenous research, education, and knowledge production. Because this data collection is published with open access, you are able to compare recordings across generations and get one step further in identifying the context for an ongoing morphological change.

These scenarios together underline the importance of being thorough and transparent in terms of research data management (RDM) and of working toward a culture of sharing knowledge.[2] This is unfortunately not always the case. While Thomason (1994) observes too many instances of sloppy and unreflective practices in authors' treatment and analysis of research data, over twenty years later, Berez-Kroeker et al. (2017) and Gawne et al. (2017) demonstrate that there is still much room for improvement regarding the transparency of methods and location of research data in linguistic publications.[3]

To approach an ideal state of research transparency, Thomason (1994) suggests advice that places responsibility on both the authors and reusers.[4] Authors should provide sufficient details about the sources of data and methodology of data collection to allow for a deeper understanding and evaluation of their research. Reusers, on their part, should consult and cite primary sources when available; *primary source*, as Thomason uses it, refers to the fieldworker linguist's publication, which for practical purposes is the nearest one can get to the language user. It is worth noting that Thomason wrote her editorial note in the pre-Internet era, when there was no technical infrastructure linking publications and supporting research data, nor even any data repositories.[5] Publications were the primary source and the main window to empirical evidence. Today, with the infrastructure in place and an ever-increasing number of high-quality repositories (see Whyte 2015), we should conceive of the primary source as the publication *in combination with the supporting research data.*

In this chapter, I discuss archiving research data: why and how to do it.[6] Although the focus is on archiving open data, the large majority of advice also holds for data with restricted access. In section 2, I present potential benefits of archiving, and in section 3, I turn to some key barriers to data sharing. In section 4, I focus on how to archive research data, including how to select a data repository, and in section 5, I turn to the challenge of archiving data with personal information. Section 6 concludes the chapter.

2 Potential benefits of archiving research data

Data collection is time-consuming, labor-intensive, and costly; sharing these valuable resources with others might not be the first thought that comes to mind when your data set is finalized.[7] Recently, however, there has been increasing focus on open science in academia, where two key arguments are knowledge sharing and research transparency. In what follows, I detail a set of potential benefits of opening up your research via data archiving (see also Tenopir et al. 2011).

First, archiving might be advantageous for the authors of research data. For instance, if reviewers of your manuscript can also access the data, they may be able to provide more complete feedback on your work, which might improve its quality. It is true that the review of data for peer-reviewed publications is currently not standard procedure, but initiatives such as the Peer Reviewers' Openness Initiative (Morey et al. 2016) indicate an increased focus on data access. Moreover, access to well-described data improves the replicability of your research,[8] and replication studies, in turn, may strengthen the credibility of your arguments (Peels 2019), or, conversely, speed up the correction or retraction of your publication (see, e.g., Ijzerman et al. 2015). Furthermore, because data sets can be conceived of as scholarly products in their own right, as suggested, for example, by the San Francisco Declaration on Research Assessment (DORA, n.d.), they deserve intellectual recognition and should be cited with as much care and detail as other sources (see Conzett & De Smedt, chapter 11, this volume). If others adhere to this practice when they consult or reuse your data, you get the credit you deserve. Another potential benefit of archiving your data is the enhanced visibility of your

research, which might boost the chances of your work having a greater impact on future research and innovation. More concretely, visibility may lead to new collaborations or to more people using your research and citing you. Publications containing a link to the data have been found to have increased citation rates compared with publications with no such link (Drachen et al. 2016; Leitner et al. 2016). Finally, an increasing number of funding agencies and publishers require or highly encourage that the data underpinning publications be made openly available, providing there is no legal, ethical, security, or commercial reason not to do so (see, e.g., European Commission 2016). Willingness to share data might thus improve your future chances of getting funding and of being evaluated for publication in desired channels.

Creating knowledge is a joint project (Bender & Good 2010), and archiving data has great potential benefits to the research community. For instance, when you deposit your data in a high-quality repository, you ensure that peers can find and reuse them.[9] This might reduce the risk of duplication of effort and thereby positively affect cost efficiency. The time you allot to data archiving could be evaluated in light of the probability of the reuse of the data, to obtain a certain efficiency gain (Pronk 2019). Archiving linguistic data may be particularly important regardless, because many studies in the field focus on observation of individuals and are therefore not directly replicable (Berez-Kroeker et al. 2018). In addition, the fact that 47.1% of the world's living languages are to some degree endangered (Belew & Simpson 2018:28) underlines the importance of securing future access to existing data. Another potential positive side effect of data sharing is the improvement of scientific methods. Many repositories recommend that authors include—or at least link to—information about the methods used in the data collection and in the data analysis (Pedersen 2008; Wieling, Rawee, & van Noord 2018). With access to both data and methods, your research community is better equipped to discuss and evaluate the methods, which in turn may guide the design of future research. Finally, data archiving may facilitate comparison or aggregation of data sets from different studies. It is true that comparable data are not easily achieved, given that most individual data collections and treatments are carried out with specific research questions in mind. However, if data sets are uploaded to a repository with a generous reuse license, other researchers may recode and reanalyze the data and make them fit into larger data sets (see, e.g., Kendall 2015). In addition, the ongoing discussion of strategies for facilitating the comparison and aggregation of data sets may in time reduce the expected workload (Cieri 2014; see also Bhattacharya et al. 2018).

Even though most linguistic data are collected for research purposes, they may also serve a role in education. This section therefore ends with some thoughts on how data archiving might benefit teachers and students. While instruction in higher education has traditionally focused on transmitting information to students, current awareness of the positive effect of student-centered teaching (Freeman et al. 2014) should encourage teachers of language and linguistics to actively involve students in the learning process. Also trending is the closely related research-based teaching approach, where learning activities center around the research process and research skills, "such as the ability to . . . gather and analyse data" (Huet 2018:728). Many teachers see the learning benefit of students collecting data themselves, but this may be too time-consuming or otherwise impractical, especially if the desired language variety is geographically inaccessible. Data collection might also be too challenging for students if the language users belong to a marginalized group, because this might require a high level of expertise on the part of the data collector (von Benzon & van Blerk 2017). With the increasing availability of open data, teachers can carry out research-based learning activities using real research data, without having to leave the classroom (Atenas, Havemann, & Priego 2015). The exploratory approach of the "three Is"—that is, *illustration* (looking at data), *interaction* (discussing the data), and *induction* (discovering rules)—is one example of data-driven learning that fits nicely with an active learning pedagogy (Johns 1991; McEnery & Xiao 2010), and which is feasible thanks to reusable research data.

This section has presented a number of potential benefits of data archiving, which in principle should encourage researchers to devote time to this in the research process. The next section reflects on a set of barriers that might explain why many researchers nevertheless still refrain from archiving.

3 Barriers to archiving research data

Although there are many potential benefits from archiving research data in a repository, less than 50% of researchers actually practice it (Berghmans et al. 2017; Stuart et al. 2018). At the same time, a higher number of researchers view data sharing favorably, or at least see that they could benefit from having access to other people's data (Tenopir et al. 2011; Berghmans et al. 2017). Why this mismatch between attitude and practice?

Archiving the research data that underpin text publications is fairly new, and many scholars have not acquired the skills needed to organize and document their data according to best practices. Nor do they know which repository to use. While these are legitimate barriers, current measures are in place to support researchers in this work. For instance, doctoral education in many countries is increasingly including RDM training, and there is also a plethora of free, online courses on basic RDM, such as, the FOSTER Open Science Training Courses (FOSTER, n.d.) and the Technische Universiteit (TU) Delft Open Science MOOC (TU Delft, n.d.).[10] Finally, an increasing number of institutions have their own RDM teams, typically located in the library, which offer courses and guidance on how to structure, document, and archive data. Nevertheless, preparing data for archiving takes time, regardless of whether you implement good practices from the beginning or make an all-out effort, and isolating hours to do this amid other commitments is not an easy task. In addition, because the publication of research data currently does not reward any publication points, is generally associated with little prestige, and because there are few immediate consequences if authors don't publish their data, the relatively low percentage of researchers who archive is, to a certain extent, understandable. If it is your intention to archive your data, I suggest writing a data management plan early in the project, which provides a rough overview of what needs to be done to get the data ready for archiving (see Kung, chapter 8, this volume).

A second barrier to data archiving might be the fear of what happens when others get access to the data. Some might be afraid that others will carry out and publish research that the authors of the data could have done themselves. Others might be afraid of having their data scrutinized and of possible criticism from peer reviewers or colleagues. While critique might require that they work on the data more—or, in the worst-case scenario, lead to their paper getting retracted—it might also provoke a fear of not having done the data collection well enough. Again, these are legitimate fears that should be taken seriously by advocates of open data. However, given the current focus on the transparency of science in many fields and institutions, we can hope that RDM gains more focus and prestige in the research community in the foreseeable future, and that data sharing is not seen as a response to institutional or journal requirements, but more as an integrated part of the publication process where authors and peers can constructively communicate with reference to both text and data material.

One final barrier, which pertains to all research involving human beings, is ethical and legal concerns. As considered in sections 4 and 5, there are many complex issues related to data protection, and many researchers are unsure about what they can and cannot archive openly, how to archive protected material, and whom to ask for advice. I haven't come across any data-sharing regulations requiring researchers to openly archive sensitive material, which clearly indicates that, for all stakeholders, data protection trumps data sharing. However, the issue is not black and white. Even research with protected data should be transparent; this can be achieved rather easily with open metadata.[11] We return to this in section 5.

The barriers highlighted here are genuine and do not always come with quick-fix solutions. For this reason, I strongly suggest that you introduce these barriers as topics of discussion in your research group. This way, with many individual researchers expressing the same concerns, the barriers might be put on the agenda in relevant forums and ultimately contribute to positive change. I also would suggest that you seek advice from relevant entities outside your research group that might help you overcome some of these barriers, whether an institutional RDM team, legal team, or data protection officer.

In the next section, I focus on how to archive research data. First, I offer some advice on how to select a repository, before turning to the key actions of the archiving process itself.

4   How to archive research data

If you plan to deposit data in a repository, you must first become familiar with the basic aspects of the RDM life cycle (see Mattern, chapter 5, this volume).[12] The reason is simple: how you plan your project and how you manage your data throughout the project period will determine which data you can archive, and how efficiently you can do it. In this section, which focuses on the publication phase of the RDM life cycle, I use information from two different repositories for support and illustration: while the Archive of the Indigenous Languages of Latin America (AILLA, n.d.; see deposit guide in Kung & Sullivant 2018) focuses on data from a geographically restricted region, and typically contains large collections with restricted access, the Tromsø Repository of Language and Linguistics (TROLLing, n.d.; see deposit guide on DataverseNO, n.d.b) focuses on open, processed data sets, typically replication data for published research papers.

4.1   Selection of repository

When we write research papers, we do not haphazardly select the journal to which we submit. Rather, we examine whether the journal has a peer-review system, whether its readership corresponds to our intended one, and—more and more often, as requirements on open science become stricter—whether it allows open access publication or self-archiving of manuscripts. You should be equally critical when selecting a data repository, in particular if you are preoccupied with the visibility and safeguarding of your research data.

4.1.1 Repository search   Repositories come in different types:[13]

- *Domain-specific* repositories, because they are closely linked to a research community, typically focus on a certain type of data and normally provide extensive curation services.[14] Examples: CHILDES (Child Language Data Exchange System, n.d.) and PARADISEC (Pacific and Regional Archive for Digital Sources in Endangered Cultures, n.d.).

- *General* repositories typically serve a broad range of disciplines, but generally provide few curation services. Examples: Figshare (n.d.) and Zenodo (n.d.).

- *Institutional* repositories, built to document and preserve research produced at an institution, are typically run by libraries. Curation services may vary with resources. Example: DataverseNO (n.d.a).

- *National* repositories may complement institutional repositories, for example, by offering services for large data sets or data with sensitive information. Example: CESSDA Data Catalogue (Consortium of European Social Science Data Archives, n.d.).

- *Project-specific* repositories are tailored to specific data sets and contributor groups. Examples: ESLO (Enquêtes sociolinguistiques à Orléans, n.d.), TGDP (Texas

German Dialect Project, n.d.), and Oahpa (n.d.; online language-learning resources for the Sami languages).

Before embarking on data collection, you should have an idea about which repository to use, as repositories may vary with regard to requirements on content and metadata. It may happen that you discover, later in the research process, that the planned repository is not optimal after all, given the nature of the data you ended up collecting. I therefore suggest that you continually evaluate the match between the data and the preselected repository to make the deposit process the least cumbersome possible.

To find a suitable repository, I encourage you to discuss possibilities with your research group or others with expertise on your research topic and methodology. Another strategy is to examine the repository information in data citations in the bibliographic reference lists of relevant scientific literature. You could also use the Registry of Research Data Repositories (re3data, n.d.), a registry where you can filter for subject (e.g., linguistics), and where you can find information about, for example, the topic and terms of use of each repository. You could further consult the repositories listed in the Open Language Archives Community (OLAC, n.d.) or browse the Common Language Resources and Technology Infrastructure Virtual Language Observatory (CLARIN, n.d.b). In most cases, the repository homepage provides information on whether it is open for deposit by external scholars.

4.1.2 Repository checklist Alter and Gonzalez (2018) recommend using domain-specific repositories, as these are most likely to have domain-specific expertise and curation services that will enhance the value of the data. They further recommend "trusted" repositories, which support archival standards for discovery, documentation, and preservation. However, you should also consider the audience(s) you want to reach with your data, and how you can achieve this. In this section, I detail five aspects to consider when selecting a repository, taken from Whyte (2015):

1. Is the repository reputable?

2. Will the repository take the data you want to deposit?

3. Will the data be safe in legal terms?

4. Will the repository sustain the data value?

5. Will the repository support analysis and track data usage?

Information that may help you answer these questions can normally be found in the repository mission statement, deposit guidelines, or curator guidelines. If you find the terminology to be too cryptic or the information too vague, I recommend asking colleagues who have archiving experience or your local RDM team or contacting the repository directly.

Is the repository reputable? The repository should at least be listed in a repository registry, for example, TROLLing is listed in the Registry of Research Data Repositories and AILLA is listed in OLAC, or be broadly recognized in the research community. You might also want to investigate whether the repository has been endorsed by relevant funders, publishers, or societies. Some repositories are awarded a certificate stating their compliance with specific international standards, such as, CoreTrustSeal (n.d.). However, certification is rather new, and there are many repositories recommended in the research and publisher communities that are not (yet) certified (Husen et al. 2017); therefore, certification should not necessarily be used as the element that tips the scales in one direction or the other.

Will the repository take the data you want to deposit? Different discipline-specific repositories may accept different types of data. You might want to choose a repository that focuses on a specific type of data, such as, TROLLing, which primarily contains processed, open linguistic data and code, or a repository that focuses on linguistic data in general, for example, one of the CLARIN centers (CLARIN, n.d.a). You could search for a thematic repository with a solid international reputation in the domain and which publishes data similar to those you deposit, for example, CHILDES if you work with child language data, or PARADISEC if you work with endangered languages in the Pacific region around Australia. In brief, domain-specific repositories may have more or less strict requirements on data sets pertaining to research topic, methods, degree of processing, and technical specifications that you should investigate before starting to prepare your data for deposit.

Will the data be safe in legal terms? Depending on your type of data, you will need to consider the relevance of various legal terms and conditions. You should ensure that the ownership of the data is not transferred to a third party, but that it remains with the original owner, which is typically your institution, for example, from AILLA (n.d.): "This agreement does not take away any rights from the depositor or any other creator of these materials; all parties to the creation of the materials retain all of their original rights." In addition, you should be able to determine which license to apply to the data[15] and to explicitly confirm that the data were created in accordance with legal and ethical criteria. This is typically done by signing the repository's terms and agreements before depositing data, for example, from TROLLing (n.d.):

> In order to submit a Dataset, you represent that . . . nothing in the Dataset, to the best of your knowledge, infringes on anyone's copyright or other intellectual property rights . . . nothing in the Dataset violates any contract terms (e.g., Nondisclosure Agreement, Material Transfer Agreement, Terms of Use, etc.) . . . nothing in the Dataset contains any private information, confidential information, proprietary information of others, export controlled information, or otherwise protected data or information that should not be publicly shared.

If you have data with personal information, these must be handled with particular care, as these are typically subject to data protection legislation. If your research is subject to the General Data Protection Regulation (GDPR, n.d.), the following requirements are in force. In all cases, you need to make sure that your institution has a data processing agreement with the desired repository and that the repository fulfills any security requirements issued by your institution. You must also check that you retain the right to control access to the data after depositing them. Finally, if you plan to archive the data outside your jurisdiction, keep in mind that the rules protecting them at home still apply, and that there are mechanisms for ensuring legal transfer to a so-called third country (see GDPR, n.d.:articles 44–50).

Will the repository sustain the data value? The FAIR data principles (see Janda, this volume; Wilkinson et al. 2016) constitute a set of guidelines to ensure that research data are *findable, accessible, interoperable,* and *reusable.* An increasing number of repositories support these, but unfortunately, many still don't.[16] If you want your data to be FAIR, you need to pay attention to aspects such as metadata, persistent identifiers, file format requirements, version control, and the possibility of linking to related materials. First, data sets should be discoverable at least through metadata of the title, author/creator, and date for deposit. Most repositories provide metadata fields where other information can be entered, such as

domain, topic, language, type of data, data collection methods, and collection date. Metadata enhance the visibility of your data set and the ease of reuse, which is further facilitated if the repository uses metadata that are compliant with metadata standards in the field, such as, the Dublin Core Metadata Initiative (n.d.) for the humanities—and the OLAC Metadata (2008) extension for language resources specifically—and the Data Documentation Initiative (DDI, n.d.) for the social sciences. These ensure standardized descriptions of the data and facilitate comparison and aggregation of data sets (Cieri 2014). The repository should also provide a digital object identifier (DOI) or another persistent identifier for the data set landing page, which provides a persistent link to its location on the Internet. Some repositories issue persistent identifiers on subset- or data file–level, which can be useful functionality in the case of large data sets. I further recommend that you examine the repository's requirements on file formats, and whether it has a system for detecting non-persistent ones in the deposited data sets. The repository should also offer version control to ensure that all changes made to the data set after publication are tracked and explicitly detailed. Finally, check that there are metadata fields for related material. If the data are replication data for a text publication, the metadata should include a reference to the publication. If the data set is a subset of a larger collection archived elsewhere (or not archived), this should be specified in the metadata. In general, I recommend that you develop an understanding of how the desired repository is run, whether it provides curator services, and if there are long-term preservation strategies.

Will the repository support analysis and track data usage? When you archive your data, you might be interested in making them maximally visible, reused, and cited. If so, you should investigate whether the repository supports the harvesting of metadata by search engines or library discovery services. Moreover, in particular for larger repositories, you should check whether it is possible to retrieve your data set within the repository using keyword filters. Finally, you might want to know whether you can monitor the activity on your data set, for example, the number of views and downloads.

4.1.3 Requirements Funders, institutions, and journals may have requirements regarding the type of repository their researchers use. The US National Science Foundation, for instance, which already requires that research data resulting from their funding must be shared, has expressed ambitions to investigate the repository landscape and to develop repository standards (see National Science Foundation 2015:7). Turning to requirements at the institutional level, these largely vary when it comes to levels of specification. At the more explicit end of the scale, for instance, is the TU Delft Research Data Framework Policy, which requires that institutional data that can be shared are archived in a repository that adheres to the FAIR principles and preserves the data for at least ten years. Their policy also requires that restricted data have archived metadata, and that any publication based on these data state why access is restricted and who can access them (TU Delft 2018:7). For an example of a journal publisher's requirements, I will refer to the research data policy of Springer Nature (n.d.) and in particular the policy of their journal *Natural Language and Linguistic Theory* (n.d.). This journal requires authors to provide sufficient information about the data collection in their manuscript, as well as repository information if the data have been archived. If such information is not given, the manuscript will be returned to the author, prior to review.

4.2   Key actions of data archiving

It is the researcher's responsibility to determine which data can be archived and which data should be archived. When making this decision, keep in mind that you cannot predict the future use of your data (Lindsay 2015), and that you need to think beyond the current specialist research community. Also keep in mind that future reuse of your data might necessitate access to one or more of the following:

- raw data
- processed data
- pilot data
- incomplete data sets
- notes
- negative results
- source code, statistical code
- experimental material

If you are in doubt about what to archive, consult the standard procedures in your subfield or discuss the potential value of the data with your research group (see also Digital Curation Centre 2014). When you have

decided which repository to use, and you have finalized your data files, you can start working on your deposit. You can speed up this process by logging your RDM during the collection and treatment of the data, as much of this information is relevant for the metadata fields and the readme file.[17] Tenopir et al. (2011) observed a lack of awareness among researchers regarding the importance of metadata, and I therefore encourage you to become familiar with types of metadata and develop a strategy for recording them early in the RDM. The repository metadata templates typically contain both required and optional fields, and I recommend that you enter as much information as possible, in particular if one main purpose of archiving your data is reuse by others: keep in mind that the metadata you enter constitute what will be searchable by others. It may also be helpful to imagine yourself in the position of the reuser and reflect on which metadata you would need to trust the data set.

As mentioned in section 3, data archiving is a time-consuming process, and it might be tempting to simply enter a reference to your text publication in the data set metadata, directing the reuser there to find all of the necessary information on the research question and data collection methods. However, it is important to remember that in many cases there are still paywalls preventing researchers from accessing desired text publications.

You also need to evaluate the format of your files to secure future access. Both AILLA and TROLLing require that files come in a persistent format,[18] which means that, for example, the much-used Microsoft Excel and Word files must be converted prior to deposit. If you don't know how to convert your files, and if there is nothing in the deposit guide to help you, seek help online or from your local RDM or information technology team. Furthermore, most repositories come with recommendations about which license to apply to the data, that is, which type of reuse you will allow for your data after publication. There are many types of licenses, for example, Creative Commons (n.d.), and if this is unknown terrain, I encourage you to investigate what the license recommended by the repository actually implies.

A common desire among researchers is to keep their data locked down until publication of their research paper. However, you may want to cite your data in the text manuscript. Because one main component of a data citation is the location of the data (e.g., a DOI), you would need to at least create the landing page of your data set prior to the submission of your manuscript. Repositories vary when it comes to flexibility in this regard. Both AILLA and TROLLing allow a temporary embargo on the data files, meaning that you can create and publish your data set, but only the metadata will be publicly available until the embargo period is over, typically when the paper is published.[19] You might also want the peer reviewers to access and provide feedback on your data set while evaluating your paper. Again, repositories vary, but in TROLLing, for instance, the system can create a private URL to the unpublished and still-modifiable data set, which you can send to the editor alongside the manuscript.

Finally, you may want to modify your data set after its initial publication; a typical change to the metadata would be adding the reference information for the corresponding research paper. More substantial changes may also occur, such as adding new files, either to complement the existing data set or to replace a file containing errors or personal information. Note that many repositories do not allow the deletion of files, but these often have version control, which automatically creates a new version number for the revised data set, where you can enter an explanation of the changes.

More information on how to prepare your data for archiving may be found in Mattern (chapter 5, this volume). In the next section, I turn to challenges associated with archiving data containing personal information.

5   How to archive data with personal information

As mentioned in section 3, an oft-cited concern among researchers is the protection of the language users who have volunteered to contribute valuable empirical material (see Holton, Leonard, & Pulsifer, chapter 4, this volume). With the application of the GDPR on May 25, 2018, affecting all researchers in EU member states, stricter rules are now imposed on projects that involve data with personal information. Among other things, the regulation introduces the principle of accountability, whereby the data controller, the person who "determines the purposes and means of the processing of personal data" (article 4 no. 7), must demonstrate compliance with all aspects of the GDPR, including what happens with the data in the archiving process.[20] In general, institutional and journal policies clearly state that data should not be shared openly if there are ethical or legal reasons not to do so. These data nevertheless should be safeguarded in a suitable repository, except if they are subject to destruction for some reason. Furthermore, the metadata that can be shared should be archived openly to make the data set discoverable; see, for example, Meyerhoff and Schleef (2015). This way, even though access to the data is restricted, the research stays transparent in that the data set is discoverable and in principle accessible (Meyer 2018).

Repositories vary in what they support when it comes to file protection. For instance, while TROLLing requires all data files to be open, possibly after an embargo period, AILLA offers four different access levels. Given the totality of your data set, you need to determine what you can and cannot do. There are at least four possible alternatives:

1. Open: Raw data, processed data, metadata. Restricted: Nothing.

2. Open: Processed data, metadata. Restricted: Raw data.

3. Open: Metadata. Restricted: Raw data, processed data.

4. Open: Nothing. Restricted: Raw data, processed data, metadata.

Many projects will have some data that cannot be openly shared, for example, interviews with sensitive content, and some data that can, for example, annotated intonation curves extracted from interviews. For such projects, you might want to keep all files together in a repository with access control, such as AILLA, or select two different repositories for the different types of data, for example, AILLA for the interview files and TROLLing for the annotated intonation curves, and then link the data sets via metadata. Needless to say, the actual data landscape is more nuanced than what is spelled out here; one example that illustrates this is a project documenting the linguistic and musical diversity of the Warruwi community in Australia (O'Keeffe et al. 2018). The project had a dual purpose—to make the data available for research and make them reusable by the language community. The data collection contained narratives that shouldn't be heard by male language users, and while some female informants felt assured that a label such as "women and girls only" would be respected, others required that the data be archived with access control. We take from this that by collaborating closely with the language community, and by including the language users as informed decision makers in different stages of the research process, researchers can manage the data in a way that also respects cultural differences (see Kirilova & Karcher 2017 for a recent reflection on archiving qualitative research data).

If the golden standard is for data to be "as open as possible, as closed as necessary," to cite the European Commission (2016:4), researchers constantly need to balance the trade-offs between sharing and risk and between ease of access and data protection. Again, writing a data management plan early in the project might help you identify possible challenges that could be overcome by interacting with the language users. When it comes to selecting a repository for data with personal information, Kirilova and Karcher (2017), from the Qualitative Data Repository (n.d.), suggest that you target one with personnel deeply familiar with your scientific domain and methodology, who can guide you on deposit-related aspects even during the research process.

6   Conclusion

This chapter has focused on archiving research data. I have presented some of the potential benefits of archiving as well as some perceived barriers, and I have given advice on the archiving process. I would like to end the chapter with a strong encouragement to not think of archiving as extra work on top of your research, but rather as an integral part of it. Archiving according to best practices is not only meant to respond to requirements and facilitate your research data management, but also, and more importantly, to make your research better and more transparent. If you consider it too time-consuming, with little reward, consider the fact that you as a researcher can contribute to the cultural change that is needed to make sharing worth it. If you're a junior researcher, prepare for the future by already building archiving into your routines. If you're a senior researcher, support and advocate the junior scholars who do a good job of archiving, and otherwise use your experienced voice to highlight the importance of research data and good research data management. Ultimately, if more people archive and share data, the potential benefits presented in this chapter may become more common, which in turn may improve the overall quality of the scientific enterprise.

Notes

1. I would like to thank Per Pippin Aspaas, Laura A. Janda, Ingvild Stock-Jørgensen (University of Tromsø – The Arctic University of Norway [UiT]), Andrea Berez-Kroeker (University of Hawai'i at Mānoa), and two anonymous reviewers for valuable comments on a previous version of this chapter. I would also like to thank the RDM team at the UiT University Library and the RDA Linguistics Data Interest Group for fruitful discussions on this topic over the years.

2. By *transparent*, I mean being explicit about the evidence supporting scientific claims, i.e., the application and implementation of methodology, the collection and analysis of data, and the interpretation of outcomes (Munafò et al. 2017).

3. By *publication*, I mean a scientific text publication.

4. By *reusers*, I mean people who read and cite publications or data sets in their own work, or people who use already published research data for different purposes.

5. By *repository*, I mean "a database or a virtual archive established to collect, disseminate and preserve scientific output . . . [where] the action of depositing material . . . is (self)archiving" (OpenAIRE 2018).

6. By *archiving*, I mean transferring data to a resource provider, e.g., a repository or a data center, all while complying with any documented guidance, policies, or legal requirements.

7. By *data set*, I mean data with content of a particular kind, that are related and treated collectively, and which have a shared and distinctive intended application (Renear, Sacchi, & Wickett 2010).

8. By *replicability*, I mean a "study . . . having certain features such that a replication study of it could be carried out" (Peels 2019:4).

9. See Vines et al. (2014) for a thought-provoking example from biology.

10. MOOC: Massive Online Open Courses. Links to web resources are included in the References.

11. By *metadata*, I mean "descriptive or contextual information which refers to or is associated with another object or resource . . . [which] usually takes the form of a structured set of elements which describe the information resource and assists in the identification, location and retrieval of it by users, while facilitating content and access management" (Higgins 2007; see also Mattern, chapter 5, this volume).

12. The RDM life cycle can be divided into three broad phases: the planning phase, where you prepare your project; the active phase, where you collect data and perform analyses of results; and the publication phase, where you publish your paper and archive your research data.

13. The description of domain-specific, general, and institutional repositories is taken from Alter and Gonzalez (2018).

14. By *curation*, I mean "maintaining, preserving and adding value to digital research data throughout its lifecycle" (Digital Curation Centre n.d.).

15. I refer to Collister (chapter 9, this volume) for details on copyright and licenses.

16. See Abu-Alam (2019) for a thought-provoking example from polar research.

17. By *readme file*, I mean a document that provides an overview and a short description of the data set; see Andreassen and Lyche (2017) and Arkhangelskiy (2019) for examples. This is often required by repositories.

18. See an example of file format guidelines here: https://site .uit.no/dataverseno/deposit/prepare/.

19. By *embargo*, I mean that access to the data files is restricted for a given time period.

20. For more information about the GDPR and language resources, see Kamocki, Ketzan, and Wildgans (2018).

References

Abu-Alam, Tamer S. 2019. Open Arctic Research Index: Final report and recommendations. https://doi.org/10.7557/7.4682.

AILLA (Archive of the Indigenous Languages of Latin America). n.d. https://ailla.utexas.org/. Accessed June 10, 2019.

Alter, George, and Richard Gonzalez. 2018. Responsible practices for data sharing. *American Psychologist* 73 (2): 146–156. https://doi.org/10.1037/amp0000258.

Andreassen, Helene N., and Chantal Lyche. 2017. Readme_ schwa.pdf [data file]. In *Replication Data for: Le rôle de la variation dans le développement phonologique: Acquisition du schwa illustrée par deux corpus d'apprenants norvégiens*. DataverseNO, V1. https://doi.org/10.18710/QULOBC/TAWHYH.

Arkhangelskiy, Timofey. 2019. 00_ReadMe.txt [data file]. In *Replication Data for: Russian verbal borrowings in Udmurt*. DataverseNO, V1. https://doi.org/10.18710/5N34CG/RS5CIZ.

Atenas, Javiera, Leo Havemann, and Ernesto Priego. 2015. Open data as open educational resources: Towards transversal skills and global citizenship. *Open Praxis* 7 (4): 377–389. https://doi.org/10.5944/openpraxis.7.4.233.

Belew, Anna, and Sean Simpson. 2018. The status of the world's endangered languages. In *The Oxford Handbook of Endangered Languages*, ed. Kenneth L. Rehg and Lyle Campbell, 1–36. Oxford: Oxford University Press.

Bender, Emily M., and Jeff Good. 2010. A grand challenge for linguistics: Scaling up and integrating models. https://faculty .washington.edu/ebender/papers/GrandChallenge.pdf.

Berez-Kroeker, Andrea L., Lauren Gawne, Barbara F. Kelly, and Tyler Heston. 2017. A survey of current reproducibility practices in linguistics journals, 2003–2012. https://sites.google .com/a/hawaii.edu/data-citation/survey.

Berez-Kroeker, Andrea L., Lauren Gawne, Susan Smythe Kung, Barbara F. Kelly, Tyler Heston, Gary Holton, Peter Pulsifer, et al. 2018. Reproducible research in linguistics: A position statement on data citation and attribution in our field. *Linguistics* 56 (1): 1–18. https://doi.org/10.1515/ling-2017-0032.

Berghmans, Stephane, Helena Cousijn, Gemma Deakin, Ingeborg Meijer, Adrian Mulligan, Andrew Plume, Alex Rushforth, et al. 2017. Open data: The researcher perspective—Survey and case studies. Mendeley Data, version 1. https://doi.org/10 .17632/bwrnfb4bvh.1.

Bhattacharya, Tanmoy, Nancy Retzlaff, Damián E. Blasi, William Croft, Michael Cysouw, Daniel Hruschka, Ian Maddieson, et al. 2018. Studying language evolution in the age of big data. *Journal of Language Evolution* 3 (2): 94–129. https://doi.org/10 .1093/jole/lzy004.

Child Language Data Exchange System (CHILDES). n.d. https:// childes.talkbank.org/. Accessed June 10, 2019.

Cieri, Christopher. 2014. Challenges and opportunities in sociolinguistic data and metadata sharing. *Language and Linguistics Compass* 8 (11): 472–485. https://doi.org/10.1111/lnc3.12112.

CLARIN (Common Language Resources and Technology Infrastructure). n.d.a. Depositing Services. https://www.clarin.eu /content/depositing-services. Accessed June 10, 2019.

CLARIN (Common Language Resources and Technology Infrastructure). n.d.b. Virtual Language Observatory. https://www .clarin.eu/content/virtual-language-observatory-vlo. Accessed June 10, 2019.

Consortium of European Social Science Data Archives (CESSDA). n.d. CESSDA Data Catalogue. https://datacatalogue .cessda.eu/. Accessed June 10, 2019.

CoreTrustSeal. n.d. https://www.coretrustseal.org/. Accessed June 10, 2019.

Creative Commons. n.d. About CC Licenses. https://creative commons.org/about/cclicenses/. Accessed June 10, 2019.

DataverseNO. n.d.a. https://dataverse.no/. Accessed June 10, 2019.

DataverseNO. n.d.b. Deposit Guide. https://info.dataverse.no/. Accessed June 10, 2019.

DDI (Data Documentation Initiative). n.d. http://www.ddiall iance.org/. Accessed June 10, 2019.

Digital Curation Centre. 2014. Five steps to decide what data to keep: DDC checklist for appraising research data, version 1. Edinburgh: Digital Curation Centre. https://www.dcc.ac.uk /guidance/how-guides/five-steps-decide-what-data-keep.

Digital Curation Centre. n.d. What is digital curation. https://www.dcc.ac.uk/about/digital-curation. Accessed June 10, 2019.

DORA (Declaration on Research Assessment). n.d. https://sfdora.org/. Accessed June 8, 2019.

Drachen, Thea Marie, Ole Ellegaard, Asger Væring Larsen, and Søren Bertil Fabricius Dorch. 2016. Sharing data increases citations. *Liber Quarterly* 26 (2): 67–82. https://doi.org/10.18352/lq.10149.

Dublin Core Metadata Initiative. n.d. http://www.dublincore.org/. Accessed June 10, 2019.

Enquêtes sociolinguistiques à Orléans (ESLO). n.d. http://eslo.huma-num.fr/. Accessed June 10, 2019.

European Commission. 2016. H2020 programme: Guidelines on FAIR data management in Horizon 2020, version 3.0. https://ec.europa.eu/research/participants/data/ref/h2020/grants_manual/hi/oa_pilot/h2020-hi-oa-data-mgt_en.pdf.

Figshare. n.d. https://figshare.com/. Accessed June 10, 2019.

FOSTER (Facilitate Open Science Training for European Research). n.d. Open Science training courses. https://www.fosteropenscience.eu/toolkit. Accessed June 10, 2019.

Freeman, Scott, Sarah L. Eddy, Miles McDonough, Michelle K. Smith, Nnadozie Okoroafor, Hannah Jordt, and Mary Pat Wenderoth. 2014. Active learning increases student performance in science, engineering, and mathematics. *Proceedings of the National Academy of Sciences* 111 (23): 8410–8415. https://doi.org/10.1073/pnas.1319030111.

Gawne, Lauren, Barbara F. Kelly, Andrea L. Berez-Kroeker, and Tyler Heston. 2017. Putting practice into words: The state of data and methods transparency in grammatical descriptions. *Language Documentation and Conservation* 11:157–189. http://hdl.handle.net/10125/24731.

GDPR (General Data Protection Regulation). n.d. https://gdpr-info.eu/. Accessed June 10, 2019.

Higgins, Sarah. 2007. What are metadata standards. Digital Curation Centre. http://www.dcc.ac.uk/. Accessed June 10, 2019.

Huet, Isabel. 2018. Research-based education as a model to change the teaching and learning environment in STEM disciplines. *European Journal of Engineering Education* 43 (5): 725–740. https://doi.org/10.1080/03043797.2017.1415299.

Husen, Sean Edward, Zoë G. de Wilde, Anita de Waard, and Helena Cousijn. 2017. Recommended versus certified repositories: Mind the gap. *Data Science Journal* 16 (42): 1–10. https://doi.org/10.5334/dsj-2017-042.

Ijzerman, Hans, Nina F. E. Regenberg, Justin Saddlemyer, and Sander L. Koole. 2015. Perceptual effects of linguistic category priming: The Stapel and Semin (2007) paradigm revisited in twelve experiments. *Acta Psychologica* 157:23–29. https://doi.org/10.1016/j.actpsy.2015.01.008.

Johns, Tim. 1991. Should you be persuaded—two samples of data-driven learning materials. *English Language Research Journal* 4:1–16.

Kamocki, Pawel, Erik Ketzan, and Julia Wildgans. 2018. Language resources and research under the General Data Protection Regulation. In *CLARIN Legal Issues Committee (CLIC) White Papers Series*. https://www.clarin.eu/.

Kendall, Tyler. 2015. Making old data sources into new data sources: On the aggregation of sociolinguistic data sets and the future of real-time and cross-study analysis. *From Data to Evidence*, Helsinki, Finland, October 19–22. https://www.helsinki.fi/en/researchgroups/varieng/d2e-from-data-to-evidence.

Kirilova, Dessi, and Sebastian Karcher. 2017. Rethinking data sharing and human participant protection in social science research: Applications from the qualitative realm. *Data Science Journal* 16 (43): 1–7. https://doi.org/10.5334/dsj-2017-043.

Kung, Susan, and Ryan Sullivant. 2018. AILLA self-deposit tool training. Archive of the Indigenous Languages of Latin America. https://ailla.utexas.org/.

Leitner, Florian, Concha Bielza, Sean L. Hill, and Pedro Larrañaga. 2016. Data publications correlate with citation impact. *Frontiers in Neuroscience* 10:419. https://doi.org/10.3389/fnins.2016.00419.

Lindsay, Greg. 2015. The latest medical breakthrough in spinal cord injuries was made by a computer program. *Fast Company*, October 14, 2015. https://www.fastcompany.com/3052282/the-latest-medical-breakthrough-in-spinal-cord-injuries-was-made-by-a-computer-program.

McEnery, Tony, and Richard Xiao. 2010. What corpora can offer in language teaching and learning. In *Handbook of Research in Second Language Teaching and Learning*, ed. Eli Hinkel, 364–380. London: Routledge.

Meyer, Michelle N. 2018. Practical tips for ethical data sharing. *Advances in Methods and Practices in Psychological Science* 1 (1): 131–144. https://doi.org/10.1177/2515245917747656.

Meyerhoff, Miriam, and Erik Schleef. 2015. *Sociolinguistics and Immigration: Linguistic Variation among Adolescents in London and Edinburgh* (data set). UK Data Service. https://doi.org/10.5255/UKDA-SN-851797.

Morey, Richard D., Christopher D. Chambers, Peter J. Etchells, Christine R. Harris, Rink Hoekstra, Daniël Lakens, Stephan Lewandowsky, et al. 2016. The Peer Reviewers' Openness Initiative: Incentivizing open research practices through peer review. *Royal Society Open Science* 3:150547. https://doi.org/10.1098/rsos.150547.

Munafò, Marcus R., Brian A. Nosek, Dorothy V. M. Bishop, Katherine S. Button, Christopher D. Chambers, Nathalie Percie du Sert, Uri Simonsohn, et al. 2017. A manifesto for reproducible science. *Nature Human Behaviour* 1:0021. https://doi.org/10.1038/s41562-016-0021.

National Science Foundation. 2015. Today's data, tomorrow's discoveries: Increasing access to the results of research funded by the National Science Foundation. https://www.nsf.gov/pubs /2015/nsf15052/nsf15052.pdf.

Natural Language and Linguistic Theory. n.d. Instructions for authors: Data management. https://www.springer.com/journal /11049/submission-guidelines#Instructions%20for%20Authors . Accessed June 10, 2019.

Oahpa. n.d. http://oahpa.no/index.eng.html. Accessed June 10, 2019.

O'Keeffe, Isabel, Linda Barwick, Carolyn Coleman, David Manmurulu, Jenny Manmurulu, Janet Gardjilart Bumarda Mardbinda, Paul Naragoidj, and Ruth Singer. 2018. Multiple uses for old and new recordings: Perspectives from the multilingual community of Warruwi. In *Communities in Control: Learning Tools and Strategies for Multilingual Endangered Language Communities. Proceedings of FEL XXI Alcanena 2017*, ed. Nicholas Ostler, Vera Ferreira, and Chris Moseley, 140–147. Hungerford, UK: Foundation for Endangered Languages.

OLAC (Open Language Archives Community). n.d. http://www .language-archives.org/archives. Accessed June 10, 2019.

OLAC Metadata. 2008. http://www.language-archives.org/OLAC /metadata.html. Accessed January 15, 2020.

OpenAIRE. 2018. What are repositories? Modified October 11, 2018. https://www.openaire.eu/. Accessed June 7, 2019.

Pacific and Regional Archive for Digital Sources in Endangered Cultures (PARADISEC). n.d. http://www.paradisec.org.au/. Accessed June 10, 2019.

Pedersen, Ted. 2008. Empiricism is not a matter of faith. *Computational Linguistics* 34 (3): 465–470. https://doi.org/10.1162 /coli.2008.34.3.465.

Peels, Rik. 2019. Replicability and replication in the humanities. *Research Integrity and Peer Review* 4 (2): 1–12. https://doi.org /10.1186/s41073-018-0060-4.

Pronk, Tessa E. 2019. The time efficiency gain in sharing and reuse of research data. *Data Science Journal* 18 (10): 1–8. http:// doi.org/10.5334/dsj-2019-010.

Qualitative Data Repository. n.d. https://qdr.syr.edu/. Accessed June 10, 2019.

re3data (Registry of Research Data Repositories). n.d. https:// www.re3data.org/. Accessed June 10, 2019.

Renear, Allen H., Simone Sacchi, and Karen M. Wickett. 2010. Definitions of *dataset* in the scientific and technical literature. In *ASIS&T '10 Proceedings of the 73rd ASIS&T Annual Meeting on Navigating Streams in an Information Ecosystem*, ed. Cathy Marshall, Elaine Toms, and Andrew Grove, 1–4. Silver Springs, MD: American Society for Information Science.

Springer Nature. n.d. Research data policies. https://www .springernature.com/gp/authors/research-data-policy/data -policy-types/12327096. Accessed June 10, 2019.

Stuart, David, Grace Baynes, Iain Hrynaszkiewicz, Katie Allin, Dan Penny, Mithu Lucraft, and Mathias Astell. 2018. Practical challenges for researchers in data sharing (whitepaper). Springer Nature. March 21, 2018. https://doi.org/10.6084/m9 .figshare.5975011.

Tenopir, Carol, Suzie Allard, Kimberly Douglass, Arsev Umur Aydinoglu, Lei Wu, Eleanor Read, Maribeth Manoff, and Mike Frame. 2011. Data sharing by scientists: Practices and perceptions. *PLOS One* 6 (6): e21101. https://doi.org/10.1371/journal .pone.0021101.

Texas German Dialect Project (TGDP). n.d. https://tgdp.org/. Accessed June 10, 2019.

Thomason, Sarah G. 1994. The editor's department. *Language* 70 (2): 409–413. http://www.jstor.org/stable/415877.

TROLLing (Tromsø Repository of Language and Linguistics). n.d. https://trolling.uit.no. Accessed June 10, 2019.

TU Delft. 2018. TU Delft Research Data Framework Policy. https://doi.org/10.5281/zenodo.2573160.

TU Delft. n.d. Open Science: Sharing your research with the world (MOOC). https://online-learning.tudelft.nl/courses /open-science-sharing-your-research-with-the-world/.

Vines, Timothy H., Arianne Y. K. Albert, Rose L. Andrew, Florence Débarre, Dan G. Bock, Michelle T. Franklin, Kimberly J. Gilbert, et al. 2014. The availability of research data declines rapidly with article age. *Current Biology* 24 (1): 94–97. https:// doi.org/10.1016/j.cub.2013.11.014.

von Benzon, Nadia, and Lorraine van Blerk. 2017. Research relationships and responsibilities: 'Doing' research with 'vulnerable' participants: Introduction to the special edition. *Social & Cultural Geography* 18 (7): 895–905. https://doi.org/10.1080 /14649365.2017.1346199.

Whyte, Angus. 2015. Where to keep research data: DCC checklist for evaluating data repositories, version 1. Edinburgh: Digital Curation Centre. http://www.dcc.ac.uk/.

Wieling, Martijn, Josine Rawee, and Gertjan van Noord. 2018. Reproducibility in computational linguistics: Are we willing to share? *Computational Linguistics* 44 (4): 641–649. https://doi.org /10.1162/coli_a_00330.

Wilkinson, Mark D., Michel Dumontier, IJsbrand Jan Aalbersberg, Gabrielle Appleton, Myles Axton, Arie Baak, Niklas Blomberg, et al. 2016. The FAIR Guiding Principles for scientific data management and stewardship. *Scientific Data* 3:160018. https://doi.org/10.1038/sdata.2016.18.

Zenodo. n.d. https://zenodo.org/. Accessed June 10, 2019.

8   Developing a Data Management Plan

Susan Smythe Kung

1   Introduction to DMPs

A data management plan, commonly referred to as a DMP, is a written document that outlines a researcher's long-term and short-term plans for generating, handling, describing, organizing, processing, analyzing, preserving, and sharing the data resulting from a research project.[1] A DMP includes detailed procedures for data collection; all aspects of organization and processing before the data are shared or disseminated; and a plan for how the data will be released so that they can be found and accessed in perpetuity, with proper attention paid to relevant legal and ethical concerns. The DMP is the road map or guidebook for how the data will be handled during every phase of the research life cycle. The very act of writing a DMP can be enormously beneficial to researchers as it requires them to think through the logistics, ethics, and expenses associated with carrying out their proposed research. Though the purpose of writing a DMP is to establish a prescribed program for managing data, researchers should understand that they will need to review their DMPs periodically and revise them as necessary (this will be discussed in more detail in section 3).

While some researchers might never be required to write a DMP (NSF 2018), research data management (RDM)[2] is something that all researchers must do throughout their education and careers. RDM is not something that researchers simply write about and then forget, but rather they must practice it on a daily basis to do good research, keep their data orderly, and produce valid and reproducible results. Thus, for each research project that is undertaken, the researcher should create a comprehensive DMP that covers every aspect of data management during the data life cycle and that can be modified to satisfy the DMP requirements of any given research funder, publisher, or organization.

Creating a DMP will help you budget for all aspects of data management, including activities associated with generating, storing, analyzing, anonymizing, and archiving the data. Many researchers, when they plan their research budgets, include only the costs associated with the activities of data collection, storage, and analysis, and they do not think to include costs associated with things like anonymization or long-term digital preservation (archiving) of their data. You should learn what resources are available to you at your institution regarding RDM services such as storage, computational processing, preservation, archiving, and such.[3] Be practical and make sure that you do not include anything in your DMP that is beyond your resources; be realistic and plan accordingly with the resources that are available to you. It is especially important to get in touch with the archive or repository that you plan to use for the long-term preservation of your data to find out their requirements for format types, file names, documentation and metadata standards, deposit size limits, rights and restrictions, fees, time lines and such (for more information, see Andreassen, chapter 7, this volume). Build these requirements into your DMP from the beginning.

Make the first draft of your DMP as comprehensive as possible and do not worry about a page limit. Although the resulting DMP might be too long and overly detailed to submit to a particular funder or publisher, it will serve as a comprehensive plan for you (and your team) to follow, and it can be modified to make it applicable to any purpose, including tailoring it to the requirements of a particular funder (see section 3 for information on revising and repurposing your DMP).

Many university websites or librarians will point researchers to the DMPTool[4] or other templates that are specific to different funders. Because these tools and templates were designed to satisfy the DMP requirements of various funders, they put more emphasis on the inclusion of funder requirements than on the inclusion of research activities themselves, and they put almost no emphasis on the resources needed to carry out the research activities (Williams, Bagwell, & Nahm Zozus 2017). Nevertheless, these tools are useful for tailoring a more comprehensive DMP into something shorter that will satisfy the requirements of a particular funder. While these tools can help you to create a DMP that meets the requirements of a particular funder, they cannot do the work of planning how you will manage your research data with the resources, budget, personnel, and time that you realistically have at your disposal. Only you can write an accurate and adequate DMP that will chart the course for how you will manage your research data.

Section 2 will guide you through the component topics that you should address in your DMP, including data generation, analysis, and handling (section 2.1); the legalities and ethics of data generation and use (section 2.2); data storage, backup, and security (section 2.3); data documentation and metadata (section 2.4); data dissemination, preservation, and sharing (section 2.5); and your responsibilities and the time line for carrying out your RDM (section 2.6). Section 3 provides guidance on when and how to revise your DMP, as well as how to adapt it to the requirements of funders. Section 4 summarizes the importance of a comprehensive yet flexible DMP and lists additional resources that you can turn to for help.

2   Components of DMPs

The aim of this section is to introduce you to various elements of a comprehensive DMP. Keep in mind that some components might not be relevant to your particular project. At the end of each subsection, there is a list of questions for you to consider with respect to your project; these questions are labeled as figures 8.1–8.6, whose numbers correspond to the associated subsection. You might find it helpful to read the list of questions for each subsection prior to reading the text of that subsection. As you read the text, answer the questions and take notes about the activities, resources, and issues that are relevant to your research circumstances. If you answer the questions as you go, you will have the necessary scaffolding on which you can then build your comprehensive DMP by the time you finish reading this chapter.

2.1   Data generation, analysis, and handling

A key concept that must first be established when writing a DMP is the definition of *data*. Because every subdiscipline of linguistics uses different types of data, and every project within that subdiscipline might use a subset of those types of data, there is no single generic definition that works for all DMPs. Rather, every researcher must explain what they consider to be data for their given research project (see Good, chapter 3, this volume). Furthermore, thinking about the *content* of the data that you plan to collect (e.g., paradigms, conversations, grammaticality judgements) will help you determine the *digital parameters* (file types and formats) of that data. For example, a cognitive linguist might make audio and video recordings of experimental protocols and later code those recorded experiments in spreadsheets; the digital data parameters might include .wav audio files, .mov video files, and .csv spreadsheets. When writing a DMP for a funder, the content of the data should be described in the proposal while the digital parameters should be made explicit in the DMP. However, a comprehensive DMP should include both.

The digital parameters of the data should also be described in terms of the best practices that are used for collecting particular data types. Best practices for data collection can vary depending on the intended use of the data, so they should be clearly articulated in the DMP. Furthermore, best practices are subject to change or revision over time, so it is important to document the best practices that are recognized by your field at the time that you collect your data.

Once you have established the digital parameters of the data you intend to collect or generate, you should next specify any equipment, software, and/or other tools that you will use to both generate and analyze the data (see Han, chapter 6, this volume). For example, you might use a Zoom H6 digital recorder to collect audio recordings of tokens in .wav format that you will later analyze with Praat software for phonetic analysis to create XML files in .TextGrid format, and you might code vowel formants using a spreadsheet in .csv format.

If you plan to create any analog data (non-digital data such as drawings, sketches, diagrams, notes, and so on), describe them, and explain how those data will be handled and analyzed. If they will eventually be digitized, list the resulting digital formats.

Next, consider any data you plan to use that you will obtain from other sources, such as archives, data corpuses, collaborators, among others. What formats will those data be in and what formats will you create as you work with them? If you plan to use any existing data, you should explain the source of these data, as well as their types and formats and any changes that you will make to them. If the data are analog, explain how you will get them into a digital format that you can use for your project.

It is important to note whether any of the data must be kept private, confidential, or restricted in some way. Explain in detail the subset of the data that will be affected and what measures will be undertaken to maintain privacy, confidentiality, or restrictions. This must be done for all data types, no matter the source.

If you plan to create or generate any raw data (e.g., run experiments or make audio and video recordings), you will need to establish a plan for differentiating the raw data from your working files. And no matter what kind of data you are using—raw or working—you need to establish a system for version control. The need for quality assurance and/or quality control procedures varies greatly among (sub)disciplines, projects, and data types, so make sure to describe any procedures that you plan to implement for your project (e.g., training activities, computer visualization, computer or human review).

If you plan to use a research management tool, such as a database, name the tool and describe how you will use it. Research management tools can vary greatly between different disciplines, including different subdisciplines of linguistics, and they might come and go faster than you can plan and carry out a project.[5]

If you will have a team of people working on this project (even a team of two), you should establish the roles, responsibilities, and tasks of each team member with respect to data generation, analysis, handling, and quality assurance. Describe team members in terms of their project titles, responsibilities and tasks, qualifications or training to do these tasks, and allowed access to different data types, particularly with respect to confidential data.

Finally, do not put anything into your DMP that you do not understand. Do your homework and research things such as tools, software, or metadata schema to use and best practices in your field to follow. Do not put something into your DMP just because your colleague or friend did and especially if you do not fully understand what it is. Misunderstood tools, practices, and the like

---

After or as you read section 2.1, "Data generation, analysis, and handling," answer the following questions:

1. What kind of data will your project produce?
   a. What type, format, and amount of digital data will you produce?
   b. Will you be creating any analog data? If so, what kind?
   c. Will the analog data be digitized? When? In what format(s)?
   d. Will you reuse existing data? If so, describe those data and their source(s).
2. What best practices for data collection/generation (relevant to your subdiscipline and the data types) will you follow for collecting the data?
3. What equipment, software, and/or other tools will you use to generate and analyze the data?
4. Will any of the data need to be kept private, confidential, or restricted? If so, explain why and how that will be accomplished.
5. How will you differentiate raw data from working data files?
6. How will you manage file versioning?
7. Will you need to implement any kind of quality assurance or quality control protocols for generating or handling the data? If so, describe them.
8. Will you use any research management tool(s) or software?
9. Will anyone besides you be generating or handling the data? If so,
   a. Who are the team members?
   b. What roles will they play in the research?

Figure 8.1

Questions: Data generation, analysis, and handling.

will be glaringly obvious to the experts who will read your DMP, and those misunderstandings could work against you in the long run.

2.2 Legalities and ethics of data generation and use

Some of the legal and ethical issues associated with carrying out research projects include data ownership of newly generated data, the intellectual property associated with data generated during the project as well as existing data that might be used, and ethical considerations for some or all of the data. This section will not go into great detail regarding the intellectual property law or ethics associated with RDM (see Collister, chapter 9, this volume, and Mattern, chapter 5, this volume, respectively, for more detailed discussions of these topics); rather, it explains what needs to be covered in a DMP.

When planning a research project, many people do not stop to think about who will own the data, or its inherent intellectual property (IP),[6] that they collect or create. Some never even think about ownership, while others assume that they, as the project owner, will also own the data and any associated IP. However, that is not always the case. In actuality, the owner might be the research funder, the university or lab that sponsored the funded research, the researcher(s) who designed the project and got the funding, the researcher(s) who collected the data, the language consultants or project participants who provided the data by sharing their personal histories or cultural knowledge, the communities to which these language users belong, or someone else. In the United States, it is often the case that the research institution or university that sponsored the research owns the data and the inherent IP (Blum 2012, cited in Henderson 2016). This means that while the researcher is allowed to disseminate (publish, present) ideas, theories, and conclusions drawn from that data—and thus own the copyright to those publications—that researcher's university owns the actual data. If you are affiliated with a university, or some other research institution, regardless of your status (faculty or student), you should find out whether this is the case at your institution. If you are a staff member or someone who was hired specifically to work on a sponsored project, then the work you do is likely to be considered *work for hire*, depending on the terms of your employment; if it is, then you might not own the data or the IP, depending on the laws of the country where you work. Because every university or

institution is different, it is in your best interest to investigate the policy of your institution and your country.

If your project is funded by a private funder, then that funder might own the data and the inherent IP. Read the fine print and ask questions so that you will understand your legal rights to use the data for your particular project both while it lasts and after it ends.

Moreover, the details of copyright laws vary from one country to another, so data created in one country might be subject to different IP laws than data created in another country. If you are working in multiple countries, you might want to consult a copyright professional at your institution or the WIPO Lex,[7] an IP database maintained by the World Intellectual Property Organization. Thus, it is important to explain in the DMP—according to country-specific IP law—who will own any data produced by the project.[8]

If you plan to reuse existing data, you must explain in the DMP your legal right to use that data (e.g., a nonexclusive license from the copyright holder, fair dealings or fair use, public domain)[9] or how you will get permission to reuse that data. Bear in mind that there might be costs associated with using certain data sets, such as fees to use a particular database or corpus or a license fee to reproduce a recording. Be sure to consider these fees as part of the costs of RDM. It is your responsibility to investigate the legalities of the ownership and use of the data that you plan to work with. Once you understand who owns the data and its IP, make the details of ownership explicit in your DMP.

Ethical issues can affect how the data are collected and stored, who can access or use the data, how long the data may be kept, and whether the data must be destroyed at the end of the project. Your DMP should address such ethical issues that are covered by institutional review boards (IRBs) or research ethics boards (REBs), such as informed consent, anonymity or deidentification, and privacy, as well as ethical issues that might not be covered, such as the need to protect Traditional Knowledge and long-term data archiving or preservation.

A key area in which the accepted ethics of working with human subjects for a linguistics project differ from other disciplines is in the anonymization of data. Rather than automatically anonymizing linguistic data, it is an accepted practice to give each project participant (i.e., language user) the opportunity to be named in the project metadata so that they will receive proper attribution for their part in the research.[10] They must also give their consent for the project data to be put into a repository or archive without being anonymized. If they do not give their full consent, the data must be anonymized or excluded according to their wishes. This practice of proper and faithful attribution applies to all project members as well, including interviewers and interviewees, transcribers and translators, and annotators and coders of the data. While this practice is especially prevalent for language documentation projects, it is spreading to other subdisciplines in linguistics (Berez-Kroeker et al. 2018).

There are research environments in which you might be required to enter into a contract or memorandum of understanding (a non-legally binding agreement between two friendly parties) to gain access to a research location or population, such as an industry workplace or a tribal reservation. If this is the case, seek legal advice from your institution's legal department or somewhere else.

For some types of projects, such as language documentation or acquisition projects, you might have an ethical responsibility to digitally repatriate (return) some or all of the collected data (Kung 2021). If so, your DMP should explain how and when you will do repatriation activities, and you should take the associated costs into consideration when planning your project budget. It is quite simple to copy files onto external storage media such as a USB drive or share the files via file sharing or storage systems, but these costs need to be planned for and built into the project from the start.

2.3 Data storage, backup, and security

In the DMP, researchers must lay out a clear plan for storing and backing up data, migrating them as necessary, and keeping them secure. This plan should include an estimation of the approximate volume of data to be collected and stored; a plan for how the data will be securely stored and redundantly backed up during all phases of the research project; and an explanation of who will have access to the data, how they will be given access, and how personal information about research participants will be protected.

Most researchers have experienced some sort of data mishap in which they have lost access to an important file or to the latest version of that file. The loss might

---

After or as you read section 2.2, "Legalities and ethics of data generation and use," answer the following questions:

1. What parts of your data are subject to copyright?
2. Who will own the intellectual property (IP) rights to the data that you generate?
   a. Are you working under any contracts or terms and conditions? If so, what are the terms of "ownership"?
   b. Are you working in different countries that might have different IP laws? If so, investigate the IP issues for each country.
3. If you are reusing data, do you need to get permission or a license to do so?
   a. Are there any fees associated with reusing existing data?
4. What are the ethical considerations associated with the data?
   a. What are the requirements of your institution's REB or IRB?
   b. How will you obtain informed consent?
   c. Will you need to anonymize or de-identify the data?
   d. What country-specific privacy laws will apply to the data?
   e. Do the data include Traditional Knowledge that needs to be protected?
5. What ethical or copyright issues might be associated with archiving and sharing the data?
6. Will you have to enter into a contract or memorandum of understanding to engage in research in your field site?
7. Will you need to digitally repatriate the data to the research community or participants? If so, how will you do that?

Figure 8.2
Questions: Legalities and ethics of data generation and use.

have been due to any number of events both in their control (user errors such as failing to save work or accidental deletion) and out of their control (system errors such as a failed automatic backup, loss or theft of a hard drive, unexpected power outages or surges, and so on). Furthermore, different storage media types are subject to different types of issues. External media and laptops can be lost, stolen, dropped, erased, or overwritten. Servers can go down or be inaccessible during maintenance. Cloud storage might not be available or allowed. External storage media (hard drives, USB drives, DVDs) have limited life spans. Storage and backup failures will happen, so it is extremely important to have a backup plan in place at the outset of the project.

There are a few mnemonics in the literature on RDM that are designed to remind us of the importance of storage and backup. *The 3-2-1 rule* (Leopando 2013, cited in Briney 2015) says to keep three copies on (at least) two types of storage media in (at least) one off-site storage location. The 3-2-1 rule would be satisfied by keeping three copies of the data on your lab computer and in cloud storage (i.e., two media types, one off-site).[11] While *LOCKSS* is the name of a digital preservation solution used by some academic libraries, it also refers to a good practice for personal data preservation: lots of copies keep stuff safe.[12] In your DMP, you should lay out your plan for storage and backup: how many copies you will keep, what kind of media you will use, and where your storage media will be located.

If you plan to use information technology (IT)-managed or cloud-based storage,[13] you should name the service provider and discuss the associated backup and security benefits or issues. IT-managed storage should include regular backups or snapshots of the data on a revolving schedule, so note this schedule in the DMP. If your storage service does not include regular backups, explain how you will back up your data and at what intervals. What other storage media will you use, and how will you back them up?

You should always make a copy of your raw data as soon as possible after you collect or generate it, and then keep the raw data separate from the working data, that is, the data that you plan to process, manipulate, analyze, and/or anonymize. Describe how you will keep the raw data separate from the working data.

If you have ever left a file made with a proprietary program untouched for several years and then tried to open it using the latest version of that program, then you know that this can be difficult or problematic to do. Because operating systems and software are constantly updated (and sometimes discontinued), you need to be proactive about migrating your files into the updated versions, including both your working files and your raw data files. Be sure to cover periodic file migration in your DMP, especially if you plan for your project (and your raw data) to last for several years. A way to make file migration easier is to save and store your data in lossless, stable, open (non-proprietary) file formats.

If you plan to collect any analog data (e.g., notebooks, drawings or sketches, physical artifacts or samples), explain how you will store and back these data up. If they will be digitized, explain how and when, as well as where the original, physical artifact will be stored.

In cases in which the data are generated in a fieldwork location where there is no access to IT-managed or cloud-based storage, researchers should describe how the data will be transferred securely from the field to the lab or home office (see Robinson 2006).

One of the hardest aspects of planning for data management is estimating the approximate amount of data that will be compiled; in other words, approximately how much data in giga- or terabytes and how many files do you anticipate will result from this project? For projects that also require audio and video data, estimate the number of recording hours for each format. Estimating the total amount of data is a crucial step, as the number and size of the files that will have to be stored and archived have direct impacts on the cost. If your project will last for multiple years, at what rate will your storage capacity needs increase?

Topics that fall under the heading of data security include all laws and rules that regulate data confidentiality, privacy, and cultural sensitivity. Your IRB/REB will require you to have a plan in place to deal with all but the last of these whenever you do research with human subjects. If you are an independent researcher or affiliated with an organization that does not have an IRB, you must familiarize yourself with the relevant rules and laws that will be applicable to your research.[14]

The definition of confidential data can vary between countries and between universities in the same country. In the United States, all universities consider social security numbers and student grades to be confidential. Medical information in the United States is subject to the Health

Insurance Portability and Accountability Act of 1996.[15] In the European Union, the General Data Protection Regulation[16] that went into effect in May 2018 protects the personal information of all EU citizens; and a similar law, a Lei Geral de Proteção de Dados Pessoais, went into effect in Brazil in September 2020.[17] These laws are intended to protect personal data that are collected, processed, and used by businesses, and they protect data that are transported across international borders. At the time of writing, it is still not clear how these laws will affect research done with human subjects in the relevant countries or through international research collaborations.

Though few countries have national laws that protect Indigenous IP or Cultural or Traditional Knowledge, many tribes or groups have particular protocols (laws, rules, or belief systems) that classify information and regulate how and when it can be accessed and by whom. Make sure that you address these protocols in your DMP and explain how you will protect these sorts of sensitive data and who will have access to the data.

In general, if you are working with a team, explain which team members will have access to any sensitive data and their qualifications for accessing them. Explain the security of your storage media and whether different types of data will be stored in different places. If you use IT-managed storage, will anyone besides your team have access? Regardless of the storage media, how will you prevent data manipulation? Will any of your data have to be encrypted? While encryption might make data more secure, it can also make the data more difficult to backup and impossible to preserve. Consider carefully which, if any, data types need to be encrypted.

2.4 Documentation and metadata

Have you ever opened a folder on your computer, external hard drive, or cloud storage that you have not opened in a long time and realized that you cannot remember what any of the files or subfolders contain or even their relationships to each other? Or have you opened a spreadsheet and been completely baffled by the contents of the rows and columns or the relationship between them? The solution is documentation. *Documentation* explains the context of a research project and how that project is carried out (methodology,

---

After or as you read section 2.3, "Data storage, backup, and security," answer the following questions:

1. How will you store and back up your data during data collection and analysis?
    a. Will you be using a data storage service (e.g., IT-managed storage, cloud storage)?
    b. Who will be responsible for backing up the data? You? A data storage service?
    c. How often will the data be backed up?
2. How will you keep raw data separate from working data?
3. How/when will you migrate your data?
4. How will analog data be stored and backed up?
5. If you will be generating data at a field site, how will you safely and securely transfer it to your office/home?
6. How much data will you need to store?
    a. Estimate of the amount of anticipated data in gigabytes or terabytes.
    b. For projects that also require audio and video data, estimate the number of recording hours for each format.
7. What are the costs associated with storage and backup?
8. How will you keep your data secure?
    a. Who will have access to the data and how will they be given access?
    b. How will personal information about research participants be protected?

Figure 8.3

Questions: Data storage, backup, and security.

protocols, workflows, procedures, manuals, programs, equipment configurations, software settings, and such); how data are organized, managed, stored, and backed up; how data files, points, or sets are related; and how data quality is controlled or ensured (Michener 2015). Good documentation helps to prevent misunderstandings, and well-documented data are easier to find, understand, analyze, share, and reuse (Henderson 2016). Think about the documentation as being the instructions that a future researcher (or your future self) will need to understand your project to be able to reuse the data.

Documentation should be ongoing and updated regularly, and especially when there is a change of any kind to any aspect of the DMP. Two common methods of documentation are *readme* files and *data dictionaries*. *Readme* files (e.g., Readme.txt) are meant to be human-readable forms of documentation present in every digital directory (folder) that contains project data. The top-level directory (main folder) should include a project description that puts the entire project in context. Readme files can be used to document all terms, conventions, codes, abbreviations, units of measure, recording frequencies, software settings, and so on used in the project (also called a "data dictionary"); this document lists everything that someone new to the project will need to know. At lower directory levels, the readme file should explain what the individual files are and how they are related to each other. A data dictionary is a key to a database system; it lists all of the terms, definitions, conventions, codes, abbreviations, units of measure, and such that are used in a project database, and it explains how the different tables (or files) are related to each other (Briney 2015; Henderson 2016).

Documentation should include an explanation for file-naming and version control practices that are to be used for the project. Before picking a file-naming schema, check with the repository that will preserve your data to see whether it has a required file-naming schema or set of conventions that you should follow (Henderson 2016; Kung et al. 2018). Using the repository's file-naming schema or conventions from the start could save you a lot of time and effort later. If your intended archive does not require you to follow a particular file-naming schema or convention, you should nevertheless adhere to some best practices, such as those that follow.

Keep file names as short as possible (fewer than 25 characters, including the extension) and use only letters A to Z, numbers 0 to 9, the hyphen, and the underscore. Avoid special fonts, diacritics, spaces, periods (except to separate the file name from the format extension), and other special characters because these might be problematic for some operating systems or scripts (if not yours, then perhaps those of the repository that will provide your long-term digital preservation). In choosing a file-naming schema, pick two or three things that will help you distinguish or remember the files contents, such as date, location, protocol, or participant identifiers (Henderson 2016; Kung et al. 2018). Avoid using participants' names or initials in file names in case they decide that they want to remain anonymous; remember that they might make this decision years after your research is complete, which would be especially problematic if you (or someone else) have already published a data set containing their name or initials. Dates should be in the international archival standard (International Organization of Standardization's ISO 8601), with or without hyphens, YYYYMMDD or YYYY-MM-DD, but bear in mind that using hyphens will make your file names longer. Use leading zeros for any numbered file names or versions (Henderson 2016; Kung et al. 2018).

File versions should be indicated with either a version number or a date appended to the end of the file name, such as filename_v03.txt, filenameV04.txt, or filename20181025.txt. Special version control software such as Git saves the differences between files rather than duplicates of the entire file (Briney 2015; Kung et al. 2018). Whatever schema you decide to use for file-naming and version control, make sure to document them.

The term *metadata* refers to "structured information about an item" (Henderson 2016:72), and this structured documentation makes your data discoverable and machine readable in systems. Tracking metadata is a crucial component of research documentation. *Descriptive metadata* include information such as author, title, abstract, keywords, publication date, and so on. *Administrative metadata* include the technical information about a file, as well as the rights management (copyright, licenses) and preservation information. *Structural metadata* are information about the relationship between files or other objects in a data set (Henderson 2016; Riley 2017; Thieberger & Berez 2012). Metadata should be documented about each file at the time of creation or as soon as possible afterward. The more comprehensive the metadata, the more useful the data (Michener 2015).

All research sponsors require you to name in your DMP the metadata schema that you will use. There are many different metadata schemas, including Dublin Core, Metadata Object Description Schema, Metadata Authority Description Schema, Schema.org, Web Ontology Language, Data Documentation Initiative, and Preservation Metadata: Implementation Strategies, to name just a few. The metadata that should be collected varies from (sub)discipline to (sub)discipline, so how do you decide on an appropriate metadata schema to use for your project? If you have identified the data repository that you plan to use, you should adopt the metadata schema that is used in that repository. Many humanities and social science repositories (including many language archives) use either Dublin Core or Metadata Object Description Schema, depending on the repository software, and some even use both. However, be aware that many general data repositories do not cater their metadata elements to any specific discipline; thus, it is a good idea to find out the types of metadata fields that are commonly used in your field or discipline and collect those to make your data useful for your discipline.

For research to be reproducible, researchers must be transparent about their methodology for data collection, handling, and analysis, as well as about the sources of their data (Berez-Kroeker et al. 2018). This requires thorough documentation of the methodology and tracking of the metadata, both of which are crucial to properly describe the nature of the data, as well as the context under which the data were generated. The DMP should include explanation of the processes by which documentation and metadata will be captured or created and the standards that will be followed. If you are working with a team, assign documentation tasks to particular project members to increase the chances that the documentation is done consistently. Good documentation is crucial when/if project personnel change.

2.5 Data dissemination, preservation, and sharing

Dissemination of research findings has traditionally included scholarly publications and conference presentations, but now scholars increasingly are expected to disseminate the research data on which their findings are based by means of data preservation, data sharing, and data publication. Original linguistic research data and data sets must be accessible for the research to be reproducible, and reproducibility is a necessary component of verification and accountability of published findings (Berez-Kroeker et al. 2018). Thus, more and more publishers, research funders, universities, and departments require research data to be shared through data archiving and/or publication. Furthermore, many government-sponsored funders maintain the position that if the research data were collected with public funds, then those data should be made available to the public whenever possible (Stebbins 2013; Horizon 2020 Programme 2017). Additional reasons for data preservation and sharing include the following. Archived data sets can be used for new research. Data sets from different sources can be used to create new data sets. Data sets of similar data from different time periods can be longitudinally compared for new research findings. Published or archived data sets can be considering for hiring, tenure, and promotion decisions. Published data sets can be used for public outreach and classroom teaching (kindergarten to twelfth grade and higher education).

After or as you read section 2.4, "Documentation and metadata," answer the following questions:

1. How will you document any relationships between digital files? Between digital files and analog data?
2. What file-naming schema will you use?
3. How will you control versions?
4. What metadata schema will you use?
5. How will you track your metadata?
6. Who will be responsible for maintaining documentation for the duration of the project?

Figure 8.4

Questions: Documentation and metadata.

Archived files are automatically migrated to new formats as technology changes, and individual researchers no longer have to be responsible for this cumbersome task (Henderson 2016; Kung et al. 2018).

While all research data must be stored for the duration of the project, only a subset of the data should be preserved (Henderson 2016; Kung et al. 2018). Most researchers do not realize that there is a difference between *storing* data and *preserving* data. *Data storage* refers to the location where you keep your files, for example, cloud storage, IT-managed storage, or a hard drive, so that you or your team can access them. *Data preservation* goes beyond simply *storing* data to include management and production of all of the activities that must be done to digital files and their metadata to ensure that they can be accessed into the future as software and hardware change (Beagrie & Jones 2008). When you put your data files in cloud storage you are simply storing them; when you deposit data files into a digital repository, you are entrusting them to an organization that is committed to digitally preserving them for an agreed duration of time. Once data files are preserved in a digital repository, they are considered published, and they are both discoverable and accessible online for reuse (provided you have not placed embargoes or other restrictions on them).

However, not all data should be preserved (in their original state). Some data must be deleted or destroyed at the end of a research project if required by the IRB or REB protocol; some data sets that include private or confidential information might need to be anonymized or deidentified; and some data types might need to be restricted or embargoed in some way (Briney 2015; Henderson 2016; Kung et al. 2018). The DMP should include a detailed description of the future of the data to be generated by the project and an explanation of how, when, and where the data will be archived and made available for reuse (i.e., shared). Researchers should explain any modifications to the data that will be needed before they can be submitted to the repository, including anonymization or format conversion. Data should be as open as possible, but as closed as necessary (Horizon 2020 Programme 2017), so you should discuss any access and reuse limitations that will be placed on archived data.

Your choice of data repository might be influenced by the funding source, the publication journal, your home institution, or your discipline. If you need help finding a data repository for your data, consult one or all of the following lists: the Registry of Research Data Repositories (https://www.re3data.org/), the Digital Endangered Languages and Musics Archives Network (http://www.delaman.org/), or the Open Access Directory's Data Repositories list (http://oad.simmons.edu/oadwiki/Data_repositories). Software should be deposited in a software repository like GitHub (https://github.com/) or GitLab (https://about.gitlab.com/). For more tips on how to find an appropriate repository, see Andreassen (chapter 7, this volume).

Before you name a digital repository in your DMP, you should first contact that repository to make sure that it is able to accept your data. You should also familiarize yourself with its policies regarding metadata schema, file format types, file size limits, deposit or collection limits, file names, data delivery procedures, access policies, deposit schedules, fees,[18] and restrictions or embargoes.[19] If you know that you have data that must be restricted or embargoed, search for a repository that allows restricted data sets. If you plan to restrict data indefinitely or control access to the data, you should have an *inheritance plan* in place for what will happen to those data when you are no longer available to control them; this is essentially a will for the data because archived data will likely outlive the data collector (Kung et al. 2018).

Many repositories set limits on the amount of data they will accept from a given researcher or a particular project, so you might have to carefully select the most important data from your project to archive. Moreover, most data repositories and archives require data depositors to curate their own files into organized collections of data sets, so you should include this work in your time line (see section 2.6). It can be challenging to decide exactly which data should go into the repository, and data curation is time-consuming and tedious work that, if left until the end of the project, can prove difficult and overwhelming (Kung et al. 2018). Many researchers who leave their data selection and curation until the very end of their projects fail to budget sufficient time, resulting in poorly organized data sets and collections, insufficient metadata or documentation, missed deadlines for final project reports, and sometimes even rejected final reports. Data curation that is done on a regular basis results in well-organized, well-described, and well-documented data collections that can be easily discovered, accessed, and reused. For instructions on how to appraise, select, and prepare your own data for deposit in a digital repository, see Andreassen (chapter 7, this volume). For information on how to prepare language documentation data for archiving in a language archive, see Kung et al. (2018); although this work is intended as a resource for language documentation collections, much of the content is applicable for all types of linguistic data. Williams, Bagwell, and Nahm Zozus (2017) suggest that the DMP should be archived along with the data that resulted from the research project given that it is an important and comprehensive part of the documentation of the project.

Files submitted to archives or repositories for long-term preservation should be in lossless, standard, open (non-proprietary) formats. Many repositories limit the format types that they will accept to make the work of digital preservation more sustainable. While some repositories will allow you to upload any file format you want (including proprietary formats), this does *not* mean that the repository is promising to migrate that file format as technology and formats change; read the policy pages carefully, ask questions, and then plan to deposit only standard, open formats. Never put encrypted files into a repository because they cannot be migrated to new formats; and use standard character encoding such as eight- or sixteen-bit Unicode transformation format (check with the repository to see what they support).

You must explain in your DMP how you will license your research data when you archive them. Licensing determines how data files can be shared and reused, and there are several different licensing systems, including traditional copyright (all rights reserved), Creative Commons licenses,[20] Open Data Commons licenses,[21] Local Contexts' Traditional Knowledge licenses,[22] and GNU licenses.[23] Before you pick a type of license to use, determine which licenses are used by the repository where you plan to deposit the research data and make sure that you understand the differences between the different licenses and their uses. If you used existing data from some other source in your project, it is likely already licensed; discuss with the repository manager what you should do with those data, then document that discussion and your decision in your DMP.

If you collected data of any kind in a community (Indigenous or not) that does not have access to your chosen data repository (e.g., access is restricted to the affiliates of the university where the repository is located) or to the Internet in general, establish a plan in your DMP for returning a copy of the research data to the community in a form that will be useful for the community members (Kung 2021). Moreover, if any of the data contains Traditional Knowledge that needs to be restricted for cultural heritage reasons, explain these reasons in your DMP, verify that your chosen archive will accept these materials,

---

After or as you read section 2.5, "Data dissemination, preservation, and sharing," answer the following questions:

1. How will you disseminate and share data from your project?
2. What portion of the data must be archived?
3. Will a portion of the data have to be deleted or destroyed?
4. Will a portion of the data need to be anonymized or deidentified?
5. Where will the data (or code) be archived?
   a. Name the digital repository where you plan to archive your data.
   b. Who has access to this digital repository?
6. What are the potential costs associated with the archiving and long-term preservation of your data?
7. Will a portion of the data need to be embargoed or restricted?
8. How will you license the data for reuse?
9. If relevant, how will the data be shared with or repatriated to the speech community?
10. What, if any, special protocols or rules (Indigenous or Traditional Knowledge) will apply to the data?
    a. How will those protocols be implemented in the chosen archive?

Figure 8.5

Questions: Data dissemination, preservation, and sharing.

and establish a plan—both with the Indigenous Community and the repository—for who may access the data and how. If the Indigenous Community has its own protocols or rules of access for particular types of data, note these protocols in your DMP, and determine whether your chosen archive has a way to enforce the community's protocols. There is always the possibility that the data might have to be controlled by a gatekeeper (you or a community member) who is familiar with the protocols and can enforce them. Discuss the possibilities, including an inheritance plan, with the repository and the community before you deposit the data.

2.6 Time line and responsibilities

Every DMP must include a time line for its implementation from start to finish. When writing your DMP, you must explain who is to be responsible for implementing the DMP and for ensuring it is followed, reviewed, and revised according to the time line (even if that person is you). Name every person, department, or organization that will be responsible for carrying out some aspect of your data management; what they/it will be responsible for doing (e.g., data collection, data entry, transcription, translation, annotation, coding, quality assurance or control, metadata creation and documentation, lab or methodology documentation, storage, backup or snapshots, systems administration, data curation, repository submission); and when they will do it. Consider what level of expertise is needed for each role and assign the role appropriately. Be explicit about any resources (including hardware, software, technology, skills, and such) that will be required to carry out the assigned tasks.

The time line should indicate when data will be collected and analyzed, as well as when data will be submitted to the repository, when the repository will process and ingest the data, when the data will be available for public access, and when any access embargos will expire. Be aware that while many of the tasks detailed in your DMP will be in your control to schedule and carry out, this is not necessarily the case when it comes to archiving your data. Be sure to consult the repository that you plan to use to establish a time line for deposits and archiving that will work for you both; this will ensure that the repository will be expecting your data according to your prearranged time line. While you might hope to be able to deposit all of the research data during the last funded month of your project, that most likely will not be possible for the repository. Keep in mind that many university-based repositories have very few full-time, non-student staff, so there might not be sufficient technical staff available to help you with your deposit during the summer and winter breaks.

3 Revising and adapting a DMP

Once the DMP is written, it provides a guide to or road map for the steps that will be followed while carrying out the research. Miksa et al. (2019) describe DMPs as "living documents" and go on to explain that "the amount and granularity of information contained within them evolves over time—from high-level estimates and expectations down to precise descriptions of actions that have actually been taken" (10). Thus, the DMP should be revised any time a change of any sort is made to the project, including the type or amount of data to be collected or the protocols for how the data are collected, analyzed, stored, preserved, and so on. As the DMP is revised, check whether any costs (e.g., storage, archiving) need to be adjusted accordingly. Document the changes to your DMP using version control and noting all changes that were made, who made them, and when (Miksa et al. 2019).

After or as you read section 2.6, "Time line and responsibilities," answer the following questions:

1. Who will be responsible for implementing and overseeing the DMP?
2. What is your time line for this project (from data generation to final archiving and dissemination)?
   a. When will each major task take place on this time line?
   b. Who will be in charge of implementing the tasks according to this time line?

Figure 8.6
Questions: Time line and responsibilities.

Once you have written your comprehensive DMP that covers every aspect of data management relevant to your project and circumstances, you can then edit it to address (only) the specific requirements of particular funders. Williams, Bagwell, and Nahm Zozus (2017) examined DMP requirements of different funders and identified 43 different required DMP topics; however, they found very little overlap in these required topics between funders. While the DMP requirements of many funders focus almost entirely on postcollection or postpublication data management, some funders also require that the DMP cover data management during the data collection and analysis phases of research as well. While there are online tools designed to aid researchers in writing a DMP, in particular the DMPTool[24] and DPMonline,[25] these tools have different DMP templates for different funders. Thus, there is no single template for a DMP that can satisfy the requirements and simultaneously meet the page limits of every possible funding agency. Moreover, Williams, Bagwell, and Nahm Zozus found that most funders that require a DMP put more emphasis on sharing data sets on which publications are based, and less emphasis on research activities and resources that actually "impact data quality, provide traceability or support reproducibility" (130).

Some funders now require researchers to submit both human-readable and machine-actionable DMPs (maDMPs; see Miksa et al. 2019; NSF 2019).[26] Online tools such as the DMPTool and ezDMP[27] can be used to create maDMPs once the researcher has all the necessary information to plug into the template. A comprehensive DMP can easily be used for this purpose, as well.

4 Summary

By now you should have a better understanding of the importance of a comprehensive DMP for your own RDM. It is true that, at the outset of a research project, it is simply not possible to know the exact details of all the possible variables, such as the amount of data that will be generated, all of the possible files types that will be created, all of the software that will be used, or the exact number of collaborators who might contribute to the project. Nevertheless, you need to make a rough plan that estimates these details to help you think through your project and plan your budget. As your project evolves, you should update and revise your DMP to reflect the changes, and as you revise the DMP, make sure to version it according to your plan for versioning the rest of your data. Your goal should be to write a comprehensive—but flexible—DMP that will aid you in planning your research project from start to finish and that can be easily modified for submission to research sponsors, publishers, and repositories. "When conceptualized and operationalized as comprehensive documentation of the data lifecycle for a study, a data management plan is a powerful tool and an integral component of the data management quality system" (Williams, Bagwell, & Nahm Zozus 2017:135).

If you still need guidance in drafting your DMP, your first stop should be your institution's data (management) services department or unit, which is usually affiliated with the university library. If your institution does not provide data management services or you are not affiliated with a university, consult some of the resources that are included in the references such as Berez-Kroeker, Collister, & Kung (2017), Digital Curation Centre (2013), Inter-university Consortium for Political and Social Research (2012), Kung et al. (2018), and Penn State (2019). Finally, sample DMPs can be found in Kung (2019), a data set containing supplementary materials that accompany this chapter. If you use the samples as templates for your own DMP, make sure that you customize the information so that it is relevant to your research project.

Even though writing a comprehensive DMP seems like a lot of work at or prior to the outset of a project, a well-organized plan for data management will pay off in the long run. Burnette, Williams, and Imker (2016) worked with a team of researchers at the University of Illinois to write and implement a DMP. At the end of the project, the principal investigators reported reductions in lost data and time, as well as stress and anxiety levels. Burnette et al. quote an unidentified principal investigator as saying, "It's not good science unless the data is managed well since 'you are only as good as your data'" (8). All investigators involved agreed that though creating and initially implementing the DMP took a lot of work at the outset, having a plan to follow saved them a great deal of time and effort and gave them peace of mind as the project advanced. Thus, writing a DMP is well worth the effort. Not only will you save yourself time and energy later, but you will produce orderly data that is suitable for analyzing, archiving, sharing, and reusing.

Notes

1. This chapter is based on Berez-Kroeker, Collister, and Kung (2017). I would like to acknowledge my two coauthors of that work, Andrea Berez-Kroeker and Lauren Collister, and thank them for trusting me to write this chapter on my own. Any mistakes in this current work are entirely my own. This material is based on work supported by the National Science Foundation under grant numbers SMA-1447886 and BCS-1653380.

2. See Mattern, chapter 5, this volume.

3. Note that these services might change from one year to the next; the services that were available for your last research project might have changed.

4. The DMPTool (https://dmptool.org/) is free for anyone regardless of university affiliation; see the "Quick Start Guide" at https://dmptool.org/help.

5. Two popular tools at the time of writing include the Open Science Framework (OSF, https://osf.io/) and AirTable (https://airtable.com/).

6. *Intellectual property* (IP) is a term that covers copyright, patents, trademarks, and trade secrets. The two types of IP that are the most relevant to research data are copyrights and patents (see Collister, chapter 9, this volume, and Alperin et al., chapter 13, this volume).

7. https://wipolex.wipo.int/en/main/legislation.

8. This is especially important if you expect any patents to result from your research project. See Alperin et al. (chapter 13, this volume) for some discussion of patents resulting from research.

9. See Collister (chapter 9, this volume) for more information about these terms.

10. See Berez-Kroeker et al. (2018) for a discussion for the need for attribution in linguistics.

11. However, note that if the cloud storage syncs to a folder on your hard drive (like Dropbox and Box can do), this counts as only one copy because if you delete a file in one place, it is also deleted from the other (Briney 2015).

12. LOCKSS is an open-source solution for peer-to-peer (distributed) digital preservation and integrity assurance that was founded at Stanford Library (https://www.lockss.org/).

13. IT-managed storage is a storage environment that is managed by a service provider. Most universities or institutions have some sort of storage that is managed by their IT department.

14. There are several online training programs for research ethics and compliance with both national and international foci; the CITI Program (Collaborative Institutional Training Initiative; https://about.citiprogram.org/en/homepage/) is one that is frequently used by organizations and individuals in the United States. Whatever training program you use, make sure

to include the costs associated with research ethics training in your project budget.

15. https://www.hhs.gov/hipaa/for-professionals/security/laws-regulations/index.html.

16. https://gdpr.eu/.

17. http://www.planalto.gov.br/ccivil_03/_Ato2015-2018/2018/Lei/L13709.htm.

18. Long-term digital preservation can be very expensive, so many repositories charge fees. Plan your budget accordingly.

19. An *embargo* is a restriction that is applied for a limited time, for example, five years to finish a degree, two years while research results are published, and so on.

20. Creative Commons licenses (https://creativecommons.org/) are widely used in the humanities and social sciences and by institutional data repositories.

21. Open Data Commons licenses (https://opendatacommons.org/) are frequently used for databases and code.

22. Traditional Knowledge licenses (http://localcontexts.org/tk-licenses/) are intended to be used by Indigenous Peoples to protect and share their Traditional Knowledge.

23. GNU licenses (https://www.gnu.org/licenses/) are for licensing software.

24. For the DMPTool, see note 4.

25. As of February 2018, the US-based DMPTool and the UK-based DMPonline have merged into a single tool (see DMPTool 2018); however the DMPonline tool is still available at https://dmponline.dcc.ac.uk/.

26. Thus far the requirement for maDMPs is limited to certain STEM programs and has not spread to linguistics programs. It will likely take time for all disciplines to catch up to STEM, but it is inevitable that maDMPs will soon become the norm.

27. The ezDMP (https://ezdmp.org/index) tool creates maDMPs specifically for National Science Foundation grants; the user must log in with either a Google or an ORCID (Open Researcher and Contributor ID; https://orcid.org/) account.

References

Beagrie, Neil, and Maggie Jones. 2008. *Preservation Management of Digital Materials: The Handbook*. Glasgow: Digital Preservation Coalition (DPC). https://www.dpconline.org/docs/digital-preservation-handbook/299-digital-preservation-handbook/file.

Berez-Kroeker, Andrea, Lauren Collister, and Susan Smythe Kung. 2017. Workshop on data management plans for linguistic research. LSA Summer Institute, University of Kentucky, July 29–30, 2017. *Archive of the Indigenous Languages of Latin*

America. Access: Open. PID: ailla:254604. https://www.ailla.utexas.org/islandora/object/ailla%3A254604.

Berez-Kroeker, Andrea L., Lauren Gawne, Susan Smythe Kung, Barbara F. Kelly, Tyler Heston, Gary Holton, Peter Pulsifer, et al. 2018. Reproducible research in linguistics: A position statement on data citation and attribution in our field. *Linguistics* 56 (1): 1–18. https://doi.org/10.1515/ling-2017-0032.

Blum, Carol. 2012. *Access to, Sharing and Retention of Research Data: Rights and Responsibilities*. Washington, DC: Council on Governmental Relations. https://www.cogr.edu/sites/default/files/access_to_sharing_and_retention_of_research_data-_rights_&_responsibilities.pdf.

Briney, Kristin. 2015. *Data Management for Researchers*. Exeter, UK: Pelagic Publishing.

Burnette, Margaret H., Sarah C. Williams, and Heidi J. Imker. 2016. From plan to action: Successful data management plan implementation in a multidisciplinary project. *Journal of eScience Librarianship* 5 (1): e1101. https://doi.org/10.7191/jeslib.2016.1101.

Digital Curation Centre (DCC). 2013. *Checklist for a Data Management Plan, v.4.0*. Edinburgh: Digital Curation Centre. http://www.dcc.ac.uk/resources/data-management-plans.

DMPTool. 2018. "New DMPTool launched today!" *DMPTool Blog*. February 27, 2018. https://blog.dmptool.org/tag/enhancements/.

Henderson, Margaret E. 2016. *Data Management: A Practical Guide for Librarians*. Lanham, MD: Rowman and Littlefield, ProQuest Ebook Central.

Horizon 2020 Programme. 2017. Guidelines to the rules on open access to scientific publications and open access to research data in Horizon 2020, version 3.2. European Commission Directorate-General for Research and Innovation, March 21, 2017. http://ec.europa.eu/research/participants/data/ref/h2020/grants_manual/hi/oa_pilot/h2020-hi-oa-pilot-guide_en.pdf.

Inter-university Consortium for Political and Social Research (ICPSR). 2012. *Guide to Social Science Data Preparation and Archiving: Best Practice Throughout the Data Life Cycle*, 6th ed. Ann Arbor, MI: ICPSR. https://www.icpsr.umich.edu/files/deposit/dataprep.pdf.

Kung, Susan Smythe. 2019. Data management plans for linguistic research. *Texas Data Repository Dataverse*. https://doi.org/10.18738/T8/538EEN.

Kung, Susan Smythe. 2021. Data archiving, access, and repatriation. In *The International Encyclopedia of Linguistic Anthropology*, ed. James Stanlaw. Hoboken, NJ: Wiley Publishers.

Kung, Susan Smythe, J. Ryan Sullivant, Vera Ferreira, and Alicia Niwagaba. 2018. How to organize your materials and data for a language archive (CoLang2018_Curation_Workshop_Slides.pdf). Linguistic Data Curation Tutorials. *The Archive of the Indigenous*

Languages of Latin America. Access: Open. PID ailla:257452. https://www.ailla.utexas.org/islandora/object/ailla:257452.

Leopando, Jonathan. 2013. World backup day: The 3-2-1 rule. *Trend Micro*. April 2, 2013. https://blog.trendmicro.com/trendlabs-security-intelligence/world-backup-day-the-3-2-1-rule/.

Michener, William K. 2015. Ten simple rules for creating a good data management plan. *PLoS Computational Biology* 11 (10): e1004525. https://doi.org/10.1371/journal.pcbi.1004525.

Miksa, Tomasz, Stephanie Simms, Daniel Mietchen, and Sarah Jones. 2019. Ten principles for machine-actionable data management plans. *PLOS Computational Biology* 15 (3): e1006750. https://doi.org/10.1371/journal.pcbi.1006750.

National Science Foundation. 2018. Data management for NSF SBE directorate proposals and awards. May 15, 2018. https://www.nsf.gov/news/news_summ.jsp?cntn_id=118038.

National Science Foundation. 2019. NSF 19–069 Dear colleague letter: Effective practices for data. *National Science Foundation* (website). May 20, 2019. https://www.nsf.gov/pubs/2019/nsf19069/nsf19069.jsp?WT.mc_id=USNSF_25&WT.mc_ev=click.

Penn State University Libraries. 2019. *Data Management Toolkit*. https://guides.libraries.psu.edu/dmptoolkit.

Riley, Jenn. 2017. *Understanding Metadata: What Is Metadata, and What Is It For? A Primer*. Baltimore: National International Standards Organization (NISO). https://www.niso.org/publications/understanding-metadata-2017.

Robinson, Laura C. 2006. Archiving directly from the field. In *Sustainable Data from Digital Fieldwork*, ed. Linda Barwick and Nicholas Thieberger, 23–32. Sydney: Sydney University Press. http://hdl.handle.net/2123/1291.

Stebbins, Michael. 2013. Expanding public access to the results of federally funded research. *The White House Blog*. February 22, 2013. https://obamawhitehouse.archives.gov/blog/2013/02/22/expanding-public-access-results-federally-funded-research.

Thieberger, Nicholas, and Andrea Berez. 2012. Linguistic data management. In *The Oxford Handbook of Linguistic Fieldwork*, ed. Nicholas Thieberger, 90–118. Oxford: Oxford University Press. https://doi.org/10.1093/oxfordhb/9780199571888.013.0005.

Williams, Mary, Jacqueline Bagwell, and Meredith Nahm Zozus. 2017. Data management plans: The missing perspective. *Journal of Biomedical Informatics* 71 (July): 130–142. https://doi.org/10.1016/j.jbi.2017.05.004.

9   Copyright and Sharing Linguistic Data

Lauren B. Collister

1   Introduction

A key component underlying many aspects of a data management process is intellectual property rights, specifically copyright. Intellectual property rights are based on the question: who owns the data that are being collected? The follow-up question that scholars need to ask is: how does that ownership impact what a researcher can do with the data when it comes time to publish and share?

Many scholars operate under the assumption that because they are doing the work of collecting and managing the data that means that the data belong to the scholar. This is not always the case, however, both ethically due to cultural principles of ownership of language (see Holton, Leonard, & Pulsifer, chapter 4, this volume) and legally due to the particularities of copyright law. An understanding of copyright and its intersection with the ownership of data can save a headache later in the project; as Newman (2007:29) writes, "the failure of scholars to pay attention to such [copyright] matters has had serious negative consequences." Many scholars have had an experience with an unanticipated copyright question, such as having to prove that they have permission to include an image or figure in a published journal article. These unanticipated questions can be particularly troublesome when they potentially impact an entire data set on which a research project is founded. Many scholars discover the complex intellectual property questions about their data far too late in the process to easily deal with any concerns or complications and find themselves looking for work-arounds or last-minute solutions. These situations often result in the inability of a scholar to share the data that he or she so painstakingly collected. This chapter is intended to help readers get ahead of these questions by providing an overview of intellectual property, specifically copyright, and how these laws apply to linguistic data and how they can enable the sharing of linguistic data.

With the focus on linguistic data, I must mention that the world of intellectual property and scholarship is much bigger than this chapter can cover; where I can, I provide pointers to helpful references and tools to pursue more information. However, this chapter necessarily has some limitations. First, this discussion of copyright and data is situated in a broader context because copyright also applies to other scholarly products, such as journal articles, dissertations, and teaching materials. For a good grounding in copyright issues beyond data, Newman (2007) is essential reading. Second, because linguistic data is so diverse (see Good, chapter 3, this volume), the overview provided by this chapter cannot cover every possibility for all the types of linguistic data that currently exist or that will exist. Finally, this chapter will contain some information about ethics, especially when ethical considerations intersect with copyright, but will not contain an overview of ethics for all of data. Readers are strongly encouraged to review chapter 5 by Holton, Leonard, and Pulsifer in this volume for more information on ethical considerations for data as well as laws, principles, and frameworks that may apply, such the OCAP (Ownership, Control, Access, and Possession) principles from the First Nations Information Governance Centre in Canada (2014) and other principles and guidance resulting from the Indigenous Data Sovereignty Movement.

With the above-mentioned limitations in mind, the intent behind this chapter is to provide foundational knowledge to enable a linguist to ask the right questions about intellectual property with the goal of sharing linguistic data. *Share* is an intentionally broad term that encompasses a wide range of activities from publishing data alongside an article or book to depositing data in a repository to posting a data set on a website; what all of these activities have in common is making data accessible and findable on the internet. While *sharing* data may include person-to-person data exchanges over e-mail or the direct transferring of files, this chapter will be most relevant to those who want to put their data set online in some way.

Sharing data is essential to the goal of reproducible research to avoid the "file drawer problem" discussed by Gawne and Styles (chapter 2, this volume). Houtkoop et al. (2018) have shown that the primary barriers to sharing of data are cultural issues in academic research—namely that it is not the regular practice of people in the field (yet). When scholars *are* interested in sharing their data, they express concern and confusion about intellectual property (especially when it comes to open data), and the lack of established practice in the field means that they do not have examples to look to for guidance. Chapter 8 of this volume covered how to share data as part of a data management plan, including where one might ultimately archive the work (see Andreassen, chapter 7, this volume). The goal of this chapter is to enable scholars, first, to understand how intellectual property affects their work and, second, to ultimately ensure open access (free of barriers to access, re-use, and distribute) to their linguistic data when ethically appropriate. This work to enable access to data can facilitate easier discovery and citation of linguistic data (see Conzett & De Smedt, chapter 11, this volume), which will lead to metrics and tracking of re-use of one's data set (see Champieux & Coates, chapter 12, this volume) and ultimately an essential addition to a research portfolio (e.g., Alperin et al., chapter 13, this volume).

To begin this section of the data journey, I will start with a definition and explanation of copyright, including how and when it applies to data. With this definition in hand, I will next address exceptions to copyright, followed by intersecting concepts that can impact copyright and data. Having identified whether copyright applies to data and how, along with other considerations for determining the copyright status of data, this chapter closes by addressing intellectual property rights and responsibilities when sharing data.

2   What is copyright?

Copyright law is intended to give authors of original works certain rights to those works, including the right to reproduce, distribute, publicly display and perform, and make adaptations of the work in question. While this definition seems simple enough, what counts as an *author* and what counts as an *original work* have important consequences for scholarly work, especially data. When starting a data collection project, it is pertinent to ask whether the data being collected or used are covered by copyright. In this section, I will describe what kinds of data might be covered by copyright, followed by the time limitations and scope of copyright; this section will help linguists understand when and how copyright might apply to their data.

Is copyright the only intellectual property that linguists need to worry about? Copyright is just one type of intellectual property, and other types of intellectual property in the United States include *patents* (a grant of a property right by the government to an inventor to exclude others from making, using or selling an invention) and *trademarks* (a name, symbol, or phrase used in interstate commerce to identify the source of a product or service) (Barnett, Collister, & McAllister-Erickson 2019). It is unlikely that trademarks will intersect with data, and if a data set is a component of a patent then consultation with a lawyer or legal counsel is recommended; both of these are outside of the scope of this discussion. Another type of intellectual property, *sui generis* rights in the European Union and South Korea, may also apply to some data sets, and these will also be covered in section 2.1.

2.1   What copyright covers

Copyright laws typically cover *original* works created by an *author*. In the Copyright Law of the United States, "Copyright protection subsists, in accordance with this title, in original works of authorship" (US Copyright Office 2016:section 102(a)), and in the United Kingdom, "a work should be regarded as original, and exhibit a degree of labour, skill or judgement" (UK Copyright Service 2017:section 4).

An initial question to answer is who counts as an *author* when it comes to the "original works of authorship" covered by copyright. In identifying legal authorship for copyright, an author is typically a person who "makes creative or editorial decisions about how ideas and facts are expressed" (Carroll 2015:4). This legal definition of authorship is not the same as contributions to a scholarly work, which are addressed by initiatives such as the

Contributor Roles Taxonomy (CRediT) from the Consortia Advancing Standards in Research Administration (CASRAI),[1] in which people have assisted a work of scholarship beyond the writing of the text (e.g., data curation, software development, conducting experiments) may be listed either as authors of a work or in an acknowledgment section (Brand et al. 2015). The legal definition of authorship may also not match, or be in direct conflict with, community and cultural ideas about ownership, especially of language (see Holton, Leonard, & Pulsifer, chapter 4, this volume). The author as the legal entity who owns the rights to the work is the person or entity that makes decisions about the work. Typically with academic works, the copyright holders and authors are those listed on the bylines of journal articles and books; with data sets that have many contributors, copyright should be negotiated among the contributors (contracts can be an essential part of this process, and are discussed in section 2.4). More than one person can hold copyright to a work, and each author has the full rights of copyright to the work and can legally (although perhaps not ethically) exercise those rights independently without the permission of the other copyright holder(s).

If a work must be original to be covered by copyright, then it follows that non-original work is not subject to copyright, which applies quite often to data used in scholarly work. Michael Carroll (2015) described copyright's relationship to scholarship well when he wrote that "copyright law is founded on certain science-friendly policies. Copyright imposes no restrictions on the sharing of the basic building blocks of knowledge—facts and ideas—which are part of the public domain. Researchers routinely rely on this freedom to copy in their daily practice" (3). Measurements of and facts about the world do not fall under the protection of copyright. The US Copyright Office explicitly defines some of these exclusions by stating, "In no case does copyright protection for an original work of authorship extend to any idea, procedure, process, system, method of operation, concept, principle, or discovery, regardless of the form in which it is described, explained, illustrated, or embodied in such work" (2016:section 102(b)). Work that is not protected by copyright or any other intellectual property laws (patents and trademarks) is said to be in the public domain, which means that "the public owns these works, not an individual author or artist. Anyone can use a public domain work without

obtaining permission, but no one can ever own it" (Stim 2013). The public domain, in the words of Duke University's Center for the Study of the Public Domain (2011), is "'free' as in 'free speech,' not 'free' as in 'free beer'—because it is unprotected by intellectual property rights, it is free of centralized control as a legal matter, and you can use it without having to get permission." It is important to remember that *public domain* is a legal term with a specific definition—creative work that is not protected by copyright—and does not refer to anything that is freely available to view. Sometimes people use the phrase *public domain* inaccurately to refer to material that is free to view and download online—even though some material may be free to access and view, copyright still applies and re-use, translation, adaptation, or selling of the material would require permission from the copyright holder. It is important not to confuse free to view with legally free to use.

Further complicating matters is the distinction between *data* and a *database*. While the facts and measurements may not be subject to copyright because they are not original, the arrangement or compilation of these facts potentially could be if that arrangement or compilation is sufficiently creative (Sims 2012). Additionally, in the European Union and South Korea, databases created entirely within the borders of these countries that require "substantial investment" to assemble or maintain are protected by a specific set of laws referring to *sui generis* rights. These rights protect against "extraction or reutilization of substantial parts of a protected database as well as frequent extraction of insubstantial parts of a protected database" with exceptions given for non-commercial research (Carroll 2015:5–6). Database rights, including *sui generis* rights and copyright, may impact corpora, lexicons, or other grammars that linguists may use or create as data sets.

It is therefore the case that copyright may not apply to data sets if they are measurements of or facts about the world, but copyright may apply to analyses and representations of those data sets; it may be the case that the researcher may own her written observations about an object, but she may not own the object itself (Borgman 2015:178). This has some simple examples that are often used in the physical or natural sciences: measurements of rainfall, coordinates of locations, recipes, and formulas. In these cases, the researcher would own any text that she wrote about those measurements or the creative visualizations that she created to display those measurements, but the actual measurements themselves would be in the public domain and therefore usable by anybody without permission needed.

In linguistics, because of the nature of the field, the situation can become complicated quickly. Some linguistic data may be subject to copyright because linguists deal in words, phrases, and sentences that may be in themselves creative expression, not measurements or facts about the world. Take, for example, a situation in which a linguist wants to compare the difference between [a] in two language varieties and uses as data recordings of radio interviews done with speakers of the two varieties. The linguist may excerpt all examples of [a] and analyze the formants and frequencies. In this situation, copyright would not apply to those vowel measurements or the method of doing those measurements, but copyright would apply to the recording that was the source material for the measurements. This is because the recording itself almost certainly contains material that could be classified as an *original* work—unless the recording were very dry indeed, such as a speaker reading nothing but a list of measurements or telephone numbers. The question for the linguist becomes then, who owns the copyright to the recordings, and can permission be gained to use the data? Before asking for permission to use the data, two more pieces of knowledge are needed: understanding whether copyright may have expired (and therefore the work is in the public domain), and whether Fair Use (or Fair Dealing) exceptions to copyright may apply and be sufficient for the project at hand.

2.2 When copyright applies

The *when* question of copyright asks both when copyright comes into effect and when it expires. In the United States, copyright is granted to an author of an original work automatically when that work is "fixed in any tangible medium of expression, now known or later developed, from which they can be perceived, reproduced, or otherwise communicated, either directly or with the aid of a machine or device" (US Copyright Office 2016:section 102). In other words, when the work becomes perceivable by another human being, whether or not another human being has actually perceived the work, the author is automatically granted copyright. The author does not need to apply for formal copyright protection or fill out any forms to have copyright over

the work. This situation applies to most of the countries of the world; text in the Berne Convention for the Protection of Literary and Artistic Works, an international treaty signed by 176 countries as of the time of this publication,[2] states that material is protected when it is "fixed in some material form" and requires that authors must not have to comply with any formalities to be granted the rights of copyright (World Intellectual Property Organization 1979:article 2(2)). The "material" or "tangible" form referred to in these laws is intended to provide some proof of the existence of the material that is sufficiently permanent to allow it to be perceived by another person after its creation. Words spoken out loud dissipate and, although they may be heard by another person immediately, merely speaking words is not sufficiently permanent to qualify as "fixed in some material form"; however, these words may be fixed through audio or video recording or by writing the words down on paper or computer. Finally, Tribal lands have their own intellectual property laws that may differ from the countries they border, and for linguists working with Indigenous languages (whether doing new data collection or working with legacy data from an archive), it is important to consult the Tribal laws before making any decisions about copyright and its applicability (see Reed, forthcoming, for a thorough discussion).

If copyright applies when the work is fixed in a material form, when does it expire? This is a much more complicated question and varies not just by country, but by when the work was created and the laws that were in effect at that time. The Berne Convention grants protection for the life of the author plus fifty years, but allows each signatory country to set longer term limits (World Intellectual Property Organization 1979:article 7). In the United States, for example, for new works or those which have been created since 1978, copyright is in effect for the life of the author plus seventy years (US Copyright Office 2016:section 302). In other situations (such as in the United States pre-1978), whether a work was published or unpublished impacts the duration of copyright, and in some cases, the material had to be accompanied by a set copyright statement.

Thinking back to the example of the linguist analyzing [a] in recordings of radio broadcasts, she would be dealing with copyright because the broadcasts were recorded and therefore fixed in a material form. Because copyright status differs according to a number of considerations such as the year of publication, the registration status, and the law at that time, there are a number of tools that have been developed to identify whether an item is covered by copyright or not. Wikimedia Commons has a helpful guide to copyright rules by country that includes length of copyright.[3] Peter Hirtle of Cornell University has developed an extensive chart showing dates and parameters for copyright status in the United States.[4] For Canadian copyright status, the University of Alberta's Copyright Office has an excellent flowchart to determine whether an item is in the public domain.[5] In the European Union, public domain calculators are available for several countries via the Out of Copyright website.[6] Depending on when and where the radio broadcasts occurred for her project, the linguist for this example data set should check the specifics for the recordings in question and whether they might be in the public domain: what year were they made? Where were they done? These tools, or perhaps a local copyright librarian, could help her find out the status of the recordings and whether they are in the public domain or not.

2.3 Exceptions to copyright: Fair Use and Fair Dealing

If copyright still applies to the data set (that is, if the data are not in the public domain), then it still may be used for research purposes without obtaining explicit permission. Copyright law sometimes contains features that allow people to use copyrighted works under certain conditions. Fair Use in the United States is one example of these features, which allows people to use portions of copyrighted material for purposes such as commentary, criticism, scholarship, or parody, as long as the use does not "interfere with the copyright holder's legitimate economic interests" (Newman 2007:35). To make a Fair Use assessment, there are four considerations: the purpose and character of the use, the nature of the work being used, the amount of the original work being used, and the effect of the use on the potential market of the original. There is another consideration that often comes into play, which is whether the use transformed the copyrighted material "by using it for a different purpose than that of the original, rather than just repeating the work for the same intent and value as the original" (International Communication Association 2010:6). To help scholars make these assessments, a number of checklists exist to help users make a Fair Use evaluation; two examples of helpful checklists are the Thinking Through

Fair Use tool from the University of Minnesota Libraries and the Fair Use Checklist from the Columbia University Libraries.[7] Additionally, when dealing with Indigenous cultural materials, linguists are recommended to consult the discussions of Fair Use as cultural appropriation by Trevor Reed (2020, forthcoming).

In the United Kingdom, Canada, Australia, and elsewhere, Fair Dealing is a user's right to use copyrighted works without permission or payment of royalties. Fair Dealing and Fair Use are not the same in all countries; for example, in Canada, "fair dealing for the purpose of research, private study, education, parody or satire does not infringe copyright" and specific requirements for mentioning the source are defined for criticism, review, and news reporting. Canada also has exceptions to copyright for non-commercial user-generated content, reproductions for private purposes, and recording broadcasted programs for later use (Canada, Minister of Justice 1985:C–42, section 29). However, Fair Dealing uses are subject to Moral Rights, which allow for the preservation the integrity of a work or performer (Canada, Minister of Justice 1985:C–42, section 28). For Fair Dealing assessments, the University of Ottawa provides a Fair Dealing decision tree.[8]

Fair Use and Fair Dealing intersect with linguistic data when a researcher wants to use copyrighted works as a source of data. One increasingly common example of this situation is text and data mining of copyrighted material such as books. Fair Use or Fair Dealing may apply to these research works and allow for them, but these provisions do not necessarily allow for the re-sharing of the source data when publishing the work. It might be Fair Use to compile a corpus all of the books by Stephen King to perform text analysis on them, but sharing that corpus openly online would interfere with the economic interests of the copyright holder. Under the "transformative use" component of Fair Use, a data set that contains word frequency counts derived from the corpus could be shared as long as it was not directly and extensively quoting the books in a way that could be a substitute for reading or purchasing the books.[9] For our example linguist with her radio interviews, she might be able to use the recordings as data even though they are under copyright using a Fair Use argument; she may then share vowel measurement data and potentially audio file snippets of individual vowels depending on how extensive the quotation of the original source is. To direct people to the original source for the data, she could choose to share a link to the source recordings if they are available online or a citation where others could find the source data without her re-sharing or re-publishing the original recordings herself. When choosing data sources for projects, it is important to consider both whether copyright and Fair Use/Fair Dealing may allow the source to be used for research as well as whether the final data set will be shareable when the research project is complete.

2.4 Intersections with copyright

In addition to copyright, when working with data specifically, two other important constructs exist that may intersect with copyright questions and need to be considered: contracts and ethics.

Contracts are agreements made between two (or more) parties that address the rights and responsibilities of each party. While copyright is the default status typically assigned automatically when the work is fixed in a tangible form, a contract is an active agreement that can alter or override copyright. Scholars most often encounter contracts when publishing papers or books—these contracts are between a publisher and the copyright holder (the scholar/author) and lay out the rights that the publisher has over the copyrighted material (the article). Sometimes, these contracts are called *copyright transfer agreements*, and in them a scholar signs over all rights under copyright to the publisher to publish the work; in return, the scholar may get royalties, limited re-use rights, or the right to make derivative works. Other times, the contract is a license that states that the scholar keeps copyright and assigns to the publisher a license that permits the publisher to do certain things on behalf of the author, such as the right to be the outlet of first publication and the right to make and distribute copies. Our example linguist using radio interviews for data may encounter these contracts because the radio station or media entity will most likely be the owner of the content, not the speakers in the actual interview, and a contract between the speakers and the media outlet may determine both who owns the rights and what can be done with the content.

For an author, these copyright transfer agreements are important to read, especially when research data are a part of a publication; be careful when transferring the rights to a research publication to a third party, especially when the word *exclusive* is used. When a publisher is the exclusive holder of all rights associated with copyright, a scholar such as our example linguist may find herself in the unenviable position of having to request permission from a publishing company to re-use her own data set if she published it with a journal or other publisher and signed a copyright transfer agreement. In an even worse scenario that came across my desk in 2017, a graduate student was asked by a publisher to pay a licensing fee to use material from their own published article in their dissertation. Publishing contracts are an important agreement that can have long-lasting effects, including on research data, and therefore it is extremely important to pay attention to the agreements and ask for clarity from the publisher when there are any questions. It is also good practice to enlist a librarian to help with this conversation, as publisher ownership of research is of great interest and importance to the work of librarianship.

Another common scenario that scholars may encounter is contracts spelling out the requirements of grant funding. In many countries, government grants may come with a requirement to publish all work done from grant funding in an open access publishing outlet, and many private foundations are enacting similar policies. For example, in the United States, any article that results from a grant that comes from the National Institutes of Health (NIH) must be deposited in PubMed Central, a repository created to facilitate the open sharing of the outcomes of federally funded research. Many EU funders have signed on to Plan S, an agreement to require all publications that result from research funded by public grants to be published in compliant Open Access journals or platforms.[10] Policies on data sharing are expanding from funders as well; the National Science Foundation (NSF) in the United States has a policy that states that grantees are "expected to share with other researchers, at no more than incremental cost and within a reasonable time, the primary data, samples, physical collections and other supporting materials created or gathered in the course of work under NSF grants."[11] When applying for a grant from any organization, governmental or otherwise, look for their requirements for data sharing and ownership of data to fully understand the scope and implications for data created or gathered during the project.

Contracts also appear in the forms of Terms of Service or other license agreements, such as those for a database, website, or media service. This situation may be particularly relevant to scholars working with language corpora, which are often subject to licensing and Terms of Service, and the publishers of the corpora may have specific rules about how to excerpt and cite material. While many people do not read these contracts before clicking "I agree" (and analysis of the language of these contracts has shown that they are "far beyond what a functionally literate adult could be expected to understand" [Luger, Moran, & Rodden 2013:2687] so even those who do read them can hardly be expected to comprehend the terms), it is important when using services such as these for research to read the license agreement. These contracts may stipulate what a user can and cannot do with the material provided by the service, and this can mean that a scholar cannot do some things that they might usually expect to be able to in a research environment (such as sharing their data, or even publishing excerpts of the data in a journal article). These Terms of Service can also change over time, especially when using social media or other online corpora that are subject to rules that change often and supersede previous agreements (Wheeler 2018). When publishing or sharing research data online, Terms of Service may also violate ethical considerations regarding ownership of data or sharing of sensitive or private data (see Holton, Leonard, & Pulsifer, chapter 4, this volume, for some examples).

Contracts also come into play between scholars and both their research subjects and their research assistants. When the data being generated by a subject or consultant of a research project is sufficiently creative—for example when creating a narrative, telling a story, or performing a song or poem—copyright can apply to the material in the scholar's data set. To be able to quote or excerpt the data, the scholar needs a good contract in which the interviewees or research subjects agree to allow the researcher to use their material, and in which the scholar discloses her plan for sharing or disseminating the data. This is typically part of the informed consent process and required for most work with human subjects; it is very important to include the sharing of research data in this consent process and to explain clearly to participants how their data will be re-used and shared, and to make certain that they agree to allow their material to be distributed. A researcher may also employ a translator to work with data collected, make translations or glosses of texts, or to be an intermediary between the researcher and community members. Students may be employed to help annotate, clean up data, or develop visualizations based on data sets. Because some of this work may qualify those people as authors of material and therefore owners of copyright, it is important to have a good contract setting out who owns the work being produced during the project. Typically these contracts fall under the concept of Work for Hire, in which the employee agrees that all material created in the course of her employment is the property of the research project or the researcher. The scholar typically offers compensation (monetary, course credit, or stipend) in return for the employee's work, and additionally may credit their colleagues for their contribution. Contracts are a helpful tool for understanding and communicating these situations and can spell out all of these responsibilities and rights in a clear way so that all parties know who owns what, as well as what will be done with the material being created. It is essential to work directly with the community and within established framework and guidance to create these contracts and to update them when necessary (Holton, Leonard, & Pulsifer, chapter 4, this volume); this is vital work for a scholar to infuse ethical scholarship into the legal aspects of academic work.

Another important consideration is that even though something might be technically legal under copyright law, permissible with a Fair Use argument, or allowed under a contract agreement, this does not mean that the act is ethical. *Ethics* refers to "norms for conduct that distinguish between acceptable and unacceptable behavior" and there are many ethical norms in research and data collection and sharing that are important to consider in conjunction with legal and contractual rights (Resnik 2015). The sharing of personal data is a major component in ethical considerations. In 2016, a group of researchers released to the public a data set of the personal profiles of around 70,000 users obtained from the online dating website OkCupid. The researchers argued that the data were publicly available, although their methodology section does not discuss privacy settings, and that all they were doing was presenting the data "in a more useful form" (Zimmer 2016). Whether or not these profiles were legal and accessible, ethical guidelines about the release of personal data should have been considered in this case. The General Data Protection Regulation in the European Union is one example of law governing the sharing of personal data and it impacts how researchers should process and anonymize personal data (Klavan, Tavast, & Kelli 2018).

Ethics also intersects with culturally sensitive or protected material, which is codified in documents such as the UN Declaration on the Rights of Indigenous People that states that Indigenous people "have the right to maintain, control, protect and develop their intellectual property over such cultural heritage, traditional knowledge, and traditional cultural expressions" (2008:article 31). Principles and practices of cooperative fieldwork (e.g., Dwyer 2006) can help linguists collect data in ways that address and respect ethical concerns. For guidance on how to approach scholarship and data in a people-centered, ethical way, see Holton, Leonard, and Pulsifer (chapter 4, this volume).

3   Copyright and sharing data

Gawne and Styles (chapter 2, this volume) set out an argument for making linguistic data available to facilitate reproducibility and verifiability of research in our field. Once a research project is complete—and sometimes even before it is complete—scholars are able to make their data sets available for others to use (subject to the above-mentioned ownership, ethical, and privacy considerations). This shared data, when done without barriers to access or re-use, is called open data (Dietrich et al. 2009). Copyright status, as well as ethics and contract situations, can impact how data sets can be shared and in what form. In section 2, I set out ways to identify whether copyright applies to data sets during the collection phase. In this section, I will cover the impact of copyright on the act of sharing data.

3.1   Data in the public domain

If copyright does not apply, the data can be legally considered to be in the public domain. This means that, taking into account ethical considerations such as anonymization of personally identifying information and cultural considerations of ownership and access to language, researchers are free to share their data sets in the most open way possible. To be completely open, a researcher may explicitly designate their data set as in the public domain, including the arrangement and description of the data (e.g., a readme file). Typical scholarly practice is to still cite the source of data, and a data set should come with a suggested citation, whether it is provided by a repository or archive or the suggested citation is created by the researcher. Conzett and De Smedt (chapter 11,

this volume) provide an overview of data citation guidance that will be helpful in doing this work.

Even if it is unclear whether data are in the public domain or not, scholars who may have ownership of the data can remove all doubt by dedicating the data set to the public domain. This can be done with a statement such as "this dataset is dedicated to the public domain" (Stim 2013) or with a Creative Commons zero (CC0) license, which is a legal tool for waiving copyright (Creative Commons, n.d.). These are illocutionary acts, specifically a declaration (Searle 1975:366), and by making the statement on the document, the owner changes the status of those documents and makes them available for others to use and re-use freely.

3.2   Data owned by the scholar

If copyright does apply and the scholar or data collector is the author who owns copyright (whether through being the original author creating the material or having rights assigned to the scholar through contracts), then the author can choose what to do with the data set. Because copyright is automatic and defaults to all rights reserved, without any act by the author, the data are not free to be re-used by others unless the author acts to make it so. The author can share the data set without any additional copyright information, but if any other scholar wants to re-use the data, that scholar will have to ask for permission from the data set's author.

To facilitate open data, the author can apply an open license that allows the author to retain their copyright but allows others to re-use the data set with certain conditions. A license is a contract between the owner of the data and the users of data that allows use of the data in certain ways. If a data set is subject to copyright in any way, a license can help others know how to re-use it and how to attribute it properly, and they save the author the time and hassle of granting permission to individual requests.

Creative Commons (CC) licenses are an example of open licenses that can be used by the author of content. These licenses are legal documents that a copyright holder can apply to their work, with the basic stipulation being that if someone re-uses the data set, she is required to attribute the source with a citation of the original data set (this is the BY clause in a CC-BY license). Other parameters of CC licenses include a non-commercial use restriction (NC), a prohibition on changing the content (no derivatives, or ND), and a requirement that all works based on the original must be also openly licensed (share alike, or SA).

Another license that can appear on data sets is the GNU General Public License (GNU GPL, sometimes including the version number and appearing as GPLv3) (Smith 2014). The GNU GPL is a free software license that allows the creator to retain copyright but has very permissive re-use rights, with the only restriction being that any derivative or improved version of the work must also be released under a free software license.

Regardless of which particular license is chosen for a data set, the Research Data Alliance recommends that "access to and re-use of research data should be open and unrestricted as a default rule, or otherwise be granted to users with the fewest limitations possible" (RDA-CODATA Legal Interoperability Interest Group 2016:3). Using the most open possible license encourages the open and easy re-use of data for future projects. A restrictive license imposes conditions on re-use that may make a data set incompatible with another data set, thus limiting a future researcher's ability to combine data sets for a single project.

Many tools exist to help scholars choose a license for their data. If the data come with software or other code, the Choose an Open Source License tool will be helpful.[12] The Public License Selector tool guides scholars through a series of questions that will help determine which license to use.[13] Creative Commons also operates their own license selector specifically for CC licenses.[14]

3.3 Data owned by another party

When using material owned by another party as data for a research project, it is sometimes possible to share the data as part of a research project, but this may require an extra step on the part of the researcher. The question to ask in this case is whether the material contains a permissive license for sharing, and if not, what is the process for obtaining permission to share?

The material may be openly licensed using a CC or other license as described in section 3.2. In this case, sharing, including re-distributing the material online and potentially publishing it in a repository or other outlet, is allowed under certain parameters; as long as the researcher follows those parameters, the data set can be shared. Some Terms of Use or other contracts may set out conditions for sharing of data sets. In these cases, it is important

to follow the requirements closely in accordance with the contract's terms. For scholars who are working with multiple data sets with different licenses, those licenses may contradict each other and reduce interoperability; in this situation, consult the RDA-CODATA *Legal Interoperability of Research Data Principles and Implementation Guidelines* (2016).

When data are not licensed in any way or they contain a license that prohibits re-use or sharing, permission must be granted for the data to be shared. This may happen to the example linguist with the radio interviews that may be owned by a media or broadcast entity. If the linguist wants to share those original interviews, she can write to the data owner (in this case, the media company or radio station) and inform the owner about the research project and her wish to create an open data set including the materials owned by the company. The researcher should disclose where and how the data set will be shared (e.g., in a data repository) and what license she wishes to apply to the data. In some cases, the owner of the material will consent to this open sharing as long as attribution is retained (e.g., the linguist credits the media company with a full citation of the interview recording, air date, and program name). Other times, the owner of the data would not allow for an open license to be placed on their material, but may consent to having it included as part of the materials for the study but retaining their copyright—if this is the case for our example linguist's recordings, it will be her responsibility to label her data set clearly and appropriately, stating that the recordings belong to the media company, and (if she wants to be helpful) including contact information for others to use to obtain permission. This latter case would mean that if another scholar wished to re-use these recordings found in the data set created by our example linguist, that scholar would have to obtain her own permission to use the recordings. In both of these cases, the owner of the content may require a payment for the re-use of their content.

If sharing permission is not granted by the owner, this does not preclude a Fair Use of the data for the research project. While Fair Use or Fair Dealing may allow for the use of copyrighted material owned by another person or entity than the scholar, these do not allow for the sharing of the data set containing that copyrighted material, which may negatively impact future research built on the project as well as impede reproducibility. For the example linguist, she has a potential solution where she can share the transformed data set of her vowel measurements openly and include citation information and a link to the original broadcast recordings for other scholars to find. This allows her to share her analysis based on the facts of the data set and direct people to the source location that exists elsewhere; it requires an extra step for those who are looking to re-use the data or reproduce the study, but still makes clear the data's provenance. For other linguists who have compiled a corpus or other data set that reproduces the original source material wholly, the sharing options may be much more limited, and therefore re-use or replicability may be difficult or impossible. When possible, especially for research use, it is recommended to get permission to share the data early in the project to avoid a situation where sharing of research data becomes impossible.

4 Conclusion

This chapter provided an overview of copyright and intellectual property considerations for data, and how those considerations can impact the open sharing of data sets. Attention to intellectual property questions is important from the outset of a project involving data to facilitate the sharing of data associated with the research project and to avoid difficult situations at the end of a process. With the ultimate goal being sharing data as openly as possible, asking intellectual property questions can facilitate sharing and make the process much easier for the scholar.

Because of the difference in copyright law in different areas of the world and the variety of linguistic data, not every situation can be covered in this short introduction, but this chapter should be a good start. For more help with copyright, scholars can consult with a librarian. Many academic libraries have a staff member dedicated to copyright or intellectual property. This person will likely have a title like Copyright Librarian; additionally, Scholarly Communication Librarians can provide guidance when it comes to intellectual property. In large cities, public libraries may also have a copyright expert who can assist with questions about these issues. Because they are librarians and (usually) not lawyers, while they can help with resources and information, they cannot offer legal advice. When drawing up contracts for participants in a research study, an Institutional Review Board (IRB) should

be able to offer guidance as part of an informed consent process. It is important to inform IRB staff of intent to openly share data so that they can advise on any ethical or legal issues in the data collection period that may need attention specifically for the end goal of sharing data. The General Counsel at a college or university should be the resource for Work for Hire contracts when working with translators, data collectors, or research assistants.

The most important message about copyright and the sharing of data is that these should not be left for the end of a project. Attending to copyright before data collection will put a researcher on solid footing when proceeding to writing and analysis, and sharing of a data set can not only benefit a scholar with more attention to her work, but also benefits the field by making linguistic work more reproducible.

Notes

1. https://www.casrai.org/credit.html.

2. https://www.wipo.int/treaties/en/ShowResults.jsp?&treaty_id=15.

3. https://commons.wikimedia.org/wiki/Commons:Copyright_rules_by_territory.

4. https://copyright.cornell.edu/publicdomain.

5. https://www.ualberta.ca/copyright/resources/tools.

6. http://outofcopyright.eu/.

7. https://www.lib.umn.edu/copyright/fairthoughts; https://copyright.columbia.edu/basics/fair-use/fair-use-checklist.html.

8. https://copyright.uottawa.ca/what-is-copyright/exceptions-copyright/fair-dealing-decision-tree.

9. For an interesting example of this, see the 2008 case *Warner Bros. Entertainment, Inc. v. RDR Books*, 575 Federal Supplement 2d 513 (S.D.N.Y. 2008) where an "unauthorized" lexicon of terms from the Harry Potter book series was found to not be Fair Use because, although the court found that the lexicon itself was transformative, the text of the lexicon quoted extensively from the novels and movies, which outweighed the transformative aspect of the lexicon. https://www.copyright.gov/fair-use/summaries/warnerbros-rdrbooks-sdny2008.pdf.

10. https://www.coalition-s.org/.

11. https://www.nsf.gov/bfa/dias/policy/dmp.jsp.

12. https://choosealicense.com/.

13. https://ufal.github.io/public-license-selector/.

14. https://creativecommons.org/share-your-work/.

References

Barnett, John, Lauren Collister, and Jonah McAllister-Erickson. 2019. Copyright and intellectual property toolkit. *LibGuides, University of Pittsburgh.* https://pitt.libguides.com/copyright.

Borgman, Christine L. 2015. *Big Data, Little Data, No Data: Scholarship in the Networked World.* Cambridge: MIT Press.

Brand, Amy, Liz Allen, Micah Altman, Marjorie Hlava, and Jo Scott. 2015. Beyond authorship: Attribution, contribution, collaboration, and credit. *Learned Publishing* 28 (2): 151–155. https://doi.org/10.1087/20150211.

Canada, Minister of Justice. 1985. *Copyright Act. Consolidated Federal Laws of Canada.* C. C–42. https://laws-lois.justice.gc.ca/eng/acts/C-42/page-9.html#h-26.

Carroll, Michael W. 2015. Sharing research data and intellectual property law: A primer. *PLOS Biology* 13 (8): e1002235. https://doi.org/10.1371/journal.pbio.1002235.

Center for the Study of the Public Domain. 2011. Public domain frequently asked questions. https://law.duke.edu/cspd/publicdomainday/2011/pddfaq.

Creative Commons. n.d. CC0. *Creative Commons.* https://creativecommons.org/share-your-work/public-domain/cc0. Accessed March 27, 2019.

Dietrich, Daniel, Jonathan Gray, Tim McNamara, Antti Poikola, Rufus Pollock, Julian Tait, and Ton Zijlstra. 2009. What is open data? In *The Open Data Handbook.* London: Open Knowledge Foundation. http://opendatahandbook.org/guide/en/what-is-open-data.

Dwyer, Arienne M. 2006. Ethics and practicalities of cooperative fieldwork and analysis. In *Fundamentals of Language Documentation: A Handbook,* ed. Jost Gippert, Nikolaus Himmelmann, and Ulrike Mosel, 31–66. Berlin: Mouton de Gruyter. https://kuscholarworks.ku.edu/handle/1808/7058.

First Nations Information Governance Centre. 2014. *Ownership, Control, Access and Possession (OCAP™): The Path to First Nations Information Governance.* Ottawa: First Nations Information Governance Centre.

Houtkoop, Bobby Lee, Chris Chambers, Malcolm Macleod, Dorothy V. M. Bishop, Thomas E. Nichols, and Eric-Jan Wagenmakers. 2018. Data sharing in psychology: A survey on barriers and preconditions. *Advances in Methods and Practices in Psychological Science* 1 (1): 70–85. https://doi.org/10.1177/2515245917751886.

International Communication Association. 2010. Code of best practices in Fair Use for scholarly research in communication. *The International Communication Association.* http://cmsimpact.org/code/code-best-practices-fair-use-scholarly-research-communication.

Klavan, Jane, Arvi Tavast, and Aleksei Kelli. 2018. The legal aspects of using data from linguistic experiments for creating language resources. In *Human Language Technologies—The Baltic Perspective,* ed. Kadri Muischnek and Kaili Müürisep, 71–78. Frontiers in Artificial Intelligence and Applications 307. Amsterdam, IOS Press. https://doi.org/10.3233/978-1-61499-912-6-71.

Luger, Ewa, Stuart Moran, and Tom Rodden. 2013. Consent for all: Revealing the hidden complexity of terms and conditions. In *CHI '13: Proceedings of the SIGCHI Conference on Human Factors in Computing Systems,* 2687–2696. New York: ACM. https://doi.org/10.1145/2470654.2481371.

Newman, Paul. 2007. Copyright essentials for linguists. *Language Documentation* 1 (1): 28–43. http://hdl.handle.net/10125/1724.

RDA-CODATA Legal Interoperability Interest Group. 2016. *Legal Interoperability of Research Data: Principles and Implementation Guidelines. Research Data Alliance.* https://doi.org/10.5281/zenodo.162241.

Reed, Trevor. 2020. Fair Use as cultural appropriation: Why the "forgotten factor" matters. American Library Association Copyright, Legislation, Education, and Advocacy Network. Video, 1:01:40. Copytalk Webinar Archive. http://www.ala.org/advocacy/copyright/copytalk.

Reed, Trevor. Forthcoming. Creative sovereignties: Should copyright apply on Tribal lands? *Journal for the Copyright Society USA,* Available at SSRN: https://ssrn.com/abstract=3736137.

Reed, Trevor. Forthcoming. Fair use as cultural appropriation. *California Law Review,* Vol. 109, 2021, Available at SSRN: https://ssrn.com/abstract=3456164.

Resnik, David B. 2015. What is ethics in research and why is it important? *National Institute of Environmental Health Sciences* (blog). December 1, 2015. https://www.niehs.nih.gov/research/resources/bioethics/whatis/index.cfm.

Searle, John R. 1975. A taxonomy of illocutionary acts. *Language, Mind, and Knowledge. Minnesota Studies in the Philosophy of Science* 7:344–369. http://conservancy.umn.edu/handle/11299/185220.

Sims, Nancy. 2012. Friday fun: Facts, expression, and illustrations. *Copyright Librarian* (blog). August 3, 2012. http://simsjd.com/copyrightlibn/2012/08/03/facts-and-expression.

Smith, Brett. 2014. A quick guide to GPLv3. *Free Software Foundation.* https://www.gnu.org/licenses/quick-guide-gplv3.html.

Stim, Rich. 2013. Welcome to the public domain. *Stanford Copyright and Fair Use Center* (website). April 3, 2013. https://fairuse.stanford.edu/overview/public-domain/welcome.

UK Copyright Service. 2017. P-01: UK copyright law fact sheet. *The UK Copyright Service.* September 27, 2017. https://www.copyrightservice.co.uk/copyright/p01_uk_copyright_law.

United Nations. 2008. United Nations Declaration on the Rights of Indigenous Peoples. *United Nations*. https://www.un .org/development/desa/indigenouspeoples/declaration-on-the -rights-of-indigenous-peoples.html.

US Copyright Office. 2016. Copyright law of the United States and related laws contained in Title 17 of the United States code. Circular 92. *United States Copyright Office*. https://www .copyright.gov/title17.

Wheeler, Jonathan. 2018. Mining the first 100 days: Human and data ethics in Twitter research. *Journal of Librarianship and Scholarly Communication* 6 (2): eP2235. https://doi.org/10.7710 /2162-3309.2235.

World Intellectual Property Organization. 1979. *Berne Convention for the Protection of Literary and Artistic Works (as amended on September 28, 1979) (Authentic text)*. *WIPO Lex* (database). https://wipolex.wipo.int/en/text/283698.

Zimmer, Michael. 2016. OkCupid study reveals the perils of big-data science. *Wired*. May 14, 2016. https://www.wired.com /2016/05/okcupid-study-reveals-perils-big-data-science.

10   Linguistic Data in the Long View

Laura Buszard-Welcher

1   Introduction

How do we move human knowledge into the future?[1] It seems like this should be a fundamental question for any archival effort, because the intention of transmitting knowledge to future stakeholders is presumably a primary reason to go to the trouble of archiving in the first place. It becomes an especially important question for the creation and archiving of language data, because many of the world's languages are endangered, and this is an aspect of our shared humanity where we are at great risk of losing an expansive amount of human knowledge—of the languages themselves and any knowledge that is dependent on being communicated through them and the culture they are part of and express. Collected and archived endangered language data may be the only record of its kind available to the future,[2] and in the case of critically endangered languages, may be the only record of the language that remains at all.

For those in the trenches working to document against the ticking clock of language endangerment, there are pressing tasks of data collection, analysis, and presentation. For the archivist, there are tasks of ingesting collections, organizing and making them discoverable, migrating them as formats and storage practices change, all while managing the resources needed to maintain the archive and the accessibility of collections indefinitely. So, given the critical path to just getting everything done, perhaps it is not surprising that the question of how we move human knowledge into the future (and whether we are actually accomplishing that) usually remains unasked and unaddressed.

I came to the realization that this is a fundamental problem in archiving as a result of my own work, where I interact with a number of projects that are developing materials and methods—as well as curating content—for very long-term archiving, that is, on the scale of hundreds to even thousands of years. Indeed, I work on one such project myself.[3] If anyone would be working on the problem of how to move knowledge into the future, it seems like it should be this cohort of very long-term archivists. But we generally don't address the question either. We are pursuing emerging technologies, such as storing data in nano-manipulated quartz crystals (SPIE 2016) or the nucleotides of DNA (Church, Gao, & Kosuri 2012) or discovering methods we didn't even know existed such as quantum information storage in the orbital angular momentum of photons (Erhard et al. 2017). We are also exploring new archival environments such as storing data in salt mines (Memory of Mankind, n.d.), or on the moon (Arch Mission Foundation, n.d.), or in geosynchronous orbit (Quast 2018), or transmitting data across interstellar space (Interstellar Beacon, n.d.). These are methods of moving data into the future, but don't specifically address how knowledge will be transmitted to the future.

Partly the problem of how to move knowledge into the future relies on making sure it lasts and remains accessible. Any of these explorations into new archival materials and methods could lead to ways of reliably storing or transmitting data in the very long term, and they could help solve the problem of how to store large amounts of data reliably in the here and now. Yet none of these projects is explicitly focused on the problem of how future archival users will be able to make any sense or gather any meaning out of the data they retrieve, if indeed they can discover and access it.

I suspect that as linguists this problem may sit squarely in our bailiwick because humans encode, express, and transmit knowledge over vast lengths of time through our languages and cultures. I will say at the outset that I don't have a solution to this problem and apparently neither does anyone else. However, I think as linguists—especially linguists who create and archive endangered language documentation data—we should be thinking about this. In what follows, I'll look at a variety of linguistic data archives (broadly construed) and for each, ask what we can learn from them. Where have we succeeded in moving knowledge into the future? Where have our efforts fallen short? What will help our data last and be meaningful in the future?

2 Archives of the past

How long do you think the linguistic data you create will last? Do you expect to be able to access and use it throughout your career? Will other researchers? How about the next generation of scholars? What about in one hundred years? Five hundred? One thousand or more?[4]

I came of age as a researcher at the end of the late paper-record era, before data practices were digital or even digitized. Also, for many people creating language documentation as I was, there weren't obvious destination archives for the data once collected. The main venue for sharing the data was through analysis and publication, and those products tended to include only illustrative examples that proved or disproved a particular theoretical point. The vast majority of collected data for many researchers remained unpublished and inaccessible to the research community.

Therefore, I could tell you how long my data would probably last—it was however long it would take for the paper to molder on my bookshelves. Or less time than that, in the case of my tape cassette recordings. Some of those had become unusable within a matter of a few years. Thankfully we have made great strides toward addressing this problem as a discipline. We are creating a culture of data management and archiving that is built into our data creation practices; there are now many available language archives, and we are expected to identify an archive as the destination for our data before it is even created. There is no longer any good excuse for allowing your data to molder on your computer hard drive or office bookshelves.

However, it is another question how long your data *should* last. The data I generate are primarily endangered language documentation, and I want that data to last as long as possible—for whomever might have need of it,

but especially for the language communities themselves and their descendants, because they have the strongest connection to the information contained within that data, and the greatest stake in its future.

But again, how long is long? My organization, the Long Now Foundation, likes to take what is for most people an absurdly long frame of reference—the last ten thousand years and the next ten thousand—and think about it as a human-actionable time frame. We call this the "Long Now." We even build "artifacts for the future" that are meant to last and be meaningful to humans for millennia.[5] If we adopt this as our frame of agency, can it help us think about problems in the here and now? What would it mean to take responsibility for our data, ensuring it could last and remain meaningful for the next ten thousand years?

Probably few of us would imagine that the data we archive could last or be as important in the future as famous examples that enabled the decipherment and discovery of ancient languages and cultures, such as the Rosetta Stone. At the same time, the archives we are creating could collectively be seen as just as important because they may be the only archival data available about these languages in the future. What can we learn from "accidental" linguistic archives that have held so much value for the future? If the archival data we are creating today were to be viewed from an equally distant future, would any of it remain, and what meaning if any could be derived from it?

The Rosetta Stone was not created as an archival object. It was not even created as a unique object, as copies were housed in temples across Egypt (British Museum, n.d.). It is just the one copy that chanced to survive. "Lots of Copies Keeps Stuff Safe," also known as LOCKSS, turns out to be a useful strategy for long-term archiving and one used in modern digital preservation systems (Stanford University, n.d.).

The Rosetta Stone is made of granodiorite, an igneous rock that today is either crushed and made into roads, or used for ornamental building materials. Indeed, when the Rosetta Stone was found by Napoleon's soldiers, it had been reused as building material in Fort Julien near Rosetta (Rashid) in Egypt. Having reuse value can, surprisingly, occasionally work in the favor of long-term preservation of information. Another noteworthy example of this is the Archimedes Palimpsest, a thirteenth-century prayer book with text that overwrote at least seven Archimedes treatises written in the tenth century, two of which exist nowhere else (Archimedes Palimpsest, n.d.).

Despite the advantages of modern digital data creation and archiving, I should point out there is potential value for data stored in physical formats and in it being analog. If I had a gold coin for every time someone has suggested to me that inscribing information into stone would be the best means of preserving it for the long-term, I'd be a very rich lady. Of course, these suggestions have a valid point, as inscriptions in stone can be very robust and can withstand quite a bit of abuse or neglect as did the Rosetta Stone. Do we have anything in the digital realm that can compare? Or even anything in the digital realm that can compete with information on paper kept in an acid-free environment, which could potentially last five hundred years?[6] Inscribing your field notes onto large slabs of granodiorite isn't very practical or cost-effective, nor are copies, unless you happen to have the resources of Ptolemy V. Related to the longevity of analog formats, note the information on the Rosetta Stone degraded gracefully, rather than catastrophically (except for the part that broke off). It is much more likely that digital data will fail catastrophically, as with a corrupted file.

The Rosetta Stone is also relatively unencumbered by encoding. One has the primary encoding of the message in human language and then the secondary encoding of that language into writing. But the additional layers of encoding required by a digital file or by translating a digital file into other formats such as the nucleotides of DNA could serve as serious barriers to decoding the information in the future. In comparison, all we needed to do to figure out the Rosetta Stone was look at it (the writing was small, but human-eye visible) and then learn how to read it. We should at least be as kind to the future.

Moving from aspects of archival format to content, it is instructive for our primary question here of "how do we move human knowledge into the future" that the textual content of the Rosetta Stone isn't of particular importance today. The value of the artifact isn't in its message (which was a decree) but rather how that message was presented. The nearly same content was written in three different languages and writing systems: Ancient Egyptian hieroglyphs, Demotic (a script used for writing a later stage of Egyptian), and Ancient Greek.

The translations served a symbolic as well as practical purpose at the time the stones were inscribed and erected: hieroglyphs were appropriate for a religious text, Demotic for a decree, and Greek as the language of the people. It was the parallel format of the multilingual text that was key to enabling the decipherment of hieroglyphs.

It turns out that we may be creating some future Rosetta Stone–like data in our modern documentation practices today. An example of parallel data from modern fieldwork practices is interlinear glossed text, where text from the language being described is provided with word and morpheme translations as well as a free translation in another, usually more widespread, audience language. Because the creation of glossed texts is a part of the process of linguistic analysis and the development of lexical and grammatical resources, the practice of developing interlinear glossed text, particularly time-aligned with an audio or video recording, is a core activity of language documentation and description. Besides being very practical in the here and now, it could be that the parallel interlinear glossed text we collect will be key resources for the future, so long as either the source or translation languages remain accessible.

Another type of parallel data that linguists create comes from the practice of collecting a Swadesh vocabulary list. A Swadesh list (as it is commonly known) is a vocabulary elicitation tool created by the linguist Morris Swadesh in the mid-twentieth century. Its intended purpose was to generate data for the study of glottochronology, which aimed to determine the rate of lexical change in language. It was also a tool for lexical comparison between languages to develop hypotheses of language relatedness. Swadesh developed several versions of the list and finally settled on a list of one hundred basic concepts commonly expressed lexically across the world's languages. When the Swadesh list is used in fieldwork today, it is generally in early lexical elicitation. The Swadesh list fell out of use as a research tool for many decades when the theory of glottochronology was deprecated. Over half a century later, however, the theory and use of Swadesh data collections were revived for study using methods of computational analysis (Wichmann et al. 2010).

The Swadesh list is an example of a data type that derives its parallelism by virtue of being collected by many different researchers for many different languages using the same templated structure. For lack of a term, I'll call this *exocentric parallelism*. Data sets built this way are typically the result of a coordinated activity of a group, rather than the product of any one researcher. It represents the intellectual and cultural infrastructure of a field of study.

Another example of parallel data creation is a text translated into many different languages. Short parallel texts of this type are often created for practical purposes, such as ballots and drivers' tests (or in published decrees, like the Rosetta Stone). Religious texts are often translated across languages, and translations of the Bible alone probably constitute the single largest exocentric parallel text collection in the world (Wycliffe Bible Translators, n.d.). In the domain of non-religious texts, translations of the Universal Declaration of Human Rights (interestingly, a modern kind of decree) exist for several hundred languages and are even a showcase project for the Unicode Consortium (Unicode, n.d.).

The *Pear Film* is another example of an elicitation tool intended for translation into many different languages (Chafe, n.d.). It is a short film of about six minutes in length that doesn't have any conversation or narration, rather the characters act out a series of events. The viewer then paraphrases the action of the film in their own language. The *Pear Film* was used to study narrative structure across languages, and while the parallelism is based on a shared target for translation, the translations themselves may vary considerably in structure and lexical choice.

Another good example of parallel text collection is the practice by phoneticians of transcribing the fable "The North Wind and the Sun." This text has been translated and transcribed for many languages, and they are published as illustrations of some of the language descriptions in the *Journal of the International Phonetic Association*.

Aside from very long translations, parallel data sets do not typically contain a great deal of meaningful content in any given language, in and of themselves. A single Swadesh list, for example, will not provide much information about the people who used the language and how they experienced the world. Neither did the Rosetta Stone decree. Rather, it provided the means of decipherment of a much larger corpus of existing texts. And this, in turn, unlocked the experience of an ancient civilization as recorded by them in text form, some part of which is available to us today.

Another famous example of an "accidental" linguistic archive (or historical archive with linguistic import) is the very large corpus of Hittite texts discovered in 1906 by Hugo Winckler at an excavation in Boğazköy, Turkey, being the ancient archives of the Hittites at their capital Hattusas (Sturtevant & Hahn 1951). For linguists who are not experts in Hittite, its discovery represents less an example of epic decipherment (although that in and of itself is truly impressive) and more an example of a linguistic theory that was epically proven when the evidence of Hittite emerged, because it displays certain archaic features of reconstructed Proto-Indo-European that other extant languages had lost.[7]

The texts were written on clay tablets using a Babylonian cuneiform script. Like many forms of written language around the world, writing systems are far more commonly borrowed and adapted than uniquely created.[8] This adaptation both helped and hindered understanding of the spoken language. It helped that the cuneiform writing system was already well understood from its use with many other ancient languages well represented in the archaeological record. It was a hindrance in that the writing system used was (like Ancient Egyptian hieroglyphs and Maya glyphs) a combination of ideograms and a syllabary, and the ideograms often represented non-Hittite Sumerian or Akkadian word signs. The adaptation also illustrates a common problem when a writing system of an unrelated language is adopted to represent another: Hittite had consonant clusters that weren't well suited to a syllabary, and various strategies had to be employed by scribes to make everything work.[9]

The puzzles of decipherment left by these ancient artifacts may seem like a problem of the past, but consider that today our documentation and linguistic analysis is still very much text-dependent, and for glosses and translations, we typically use modern writing systems that represent many of these same issues: English writing is widespread as a language for translation, but already represents a wide gap between its alphabetic spelling and its pronunciation. Japanese is a major world language but represents many of the same compromises as Hittite in adapting Chinese ideographic writing to fit its non-Sinitic grammar and frequent use of loan word vocabulary.

These linguistic records from the deep past show us possible strategies for building long-lasting, long meaningful data collections. One of these strategies is an expansive and varied corpus, and the more in each of these dimensions, the better. As "accidental" linguistic archives, they represent the kind of information that the effort of writing was reserved for: bureaucratic records of trade and proclamations. But occasionally we are rewarded with treasured glimpses into wider culture: recorded rituals, prayers, recipes, poetry, legends, historical accounts, and even fascinating procedural texts.[10] Because we are purposeful creators of corpora, we can think about ways we think the material will be used in the future, and while constraints of time mean we must still pick and choose, we can pay special attention to those areas of culture and language that seem most valuable and unique.[11]

Another important strategy for data longevity is providing tools to decode whatever layers of encoding may exist. In this respect, modern digital archives are far more complex than any of these ancient artifacts. To see this, imagine a scenario from the not-too-distant future where language data are written for storage in DNA (this technology is available now and could be much more widespread in the near future). Say we wanted to encode a simple message such as "The quick brown fox jumps over the lazy dog" in DNA. First, we have the text as written, and/or transcribed in the International Phonetic Alphabet. This glottographic writing is the first layer of encoding we have introduced. Then we need to get it into digital text form. The relationship between analog writing and digital writing is highly complex, especially if you want to be thorough about it—witness the extensive Unicode Standard (printed out, it would be about 1,500 pages long) (Unicode 2017). So, in the transition from analog to digital writing we have introduced another layer of encoding. Then we have to go from the representation of text in binary 1s and 0s and map these onto the nucleotides of DNA (hopefully standard practices for how to do this will emerge by the time the technology becomes widespread).

Now, for fun, imagine you discover such an archive three thousand years from now. Perhaps you found it by sampling the DNA of a de-extincted passenger pigeon genetically modified to have a florescent pink tail feather as a marker of the archival data it contains.[12] Then you'd need to work back through all of the layers of mapped encoding. From the ACGT of DNA to binary 1s and 0s. Then you would need to know that the data string was encoded text, and that the Unicode text was the glottographic rendering of some form of language.[13] Given

how bad humans are at producing, much less reading instruction manuals, the fact that you have gotten this far seems pretty far-fetched.[14] Nevertheless, you succeed and obtain the string "The quick brown fox jumps over the lazy dog." Now, what on postapocalyptic Neo-Earth does it mean?

Let's go further with our scenario and imagine this string is the Rosetta Stone decoding key that unlocks a corpus of ancient texts in the English language (a corpus that also provides attestation for the use of archaic letters X and Q). You even find a Basic English lexicon and grammatical sketch that help provide referents and uses for most of the words in your short text string. You might even use your linguistic sleuthing skills to figure out that the sentence is a pangram. From there, would you guess at its use in ancient typography or its cultural import in students trying to master typewriters and other keyboard text-entry tools? Would you suspect that the sentence had moral import? Or not having any context, would you take it more literally and think that it was just about a fox and a hound?

Without a great deal of other information or access to a native language user, you would be hard-pressed to know for certain. No archival data completely document a language, much less the experiences of a people. To be sure, some languages are much better documented than others, but for most endangered languages, the best of our efforts will still leave a thin, incomplete record, and if the history of these ancient linguistic artifacts is any guide, the record will only become more fragmentary with the passing of time.

3 Archives of the present

Compared with "accidental" archives of the deep past, there is reason to expect that data created by more recent language documentation projects—ones in the last 150 years or so—would be better equipped to move human knowledge as expressed in language into the future. After all, these were efforts to purposefully document and study language in all its variety; many of them done with the awareness that the languages being studied were in danger of falling out of use, and the linguistic record being created might be the only record of them available in the future. Also, archival records of the past 150 years are much closer to our own time and understanding. We have a sense of continuity with them unlike with the records of the deep past where greater gulfs of difference exist.

As a graduate student in linguistics at the University of California, Berkeley, I had the opportunity to work in a language archive, the Survey of California and Other Indian Languages (also known today as the California Language Archive, or "the Survey" by those affiliated with it). This was during the time that the Master-Apprentice and Breath of Life programs were first being developed, and the Survey was very much a part of both, as it provided access to critical source material for those working to revitalize critically endangered languages, or languages that are no longer in active use and the archival record is the only documentation descendants have for the purpose of bringing the languages back as lived languages once again (Advocates for Indigenous California Language Survival, n.d.a,b).

Like other archives of its generation, the Survey came into being first as a place to put the growing collection of field notes created by linguistic researchers working on language documentation. In the case of the Survey, these were the students of Mary Haas, who had set them to the task of documenting as many of the languages of California as they could.[15] They very much realized that the languages were passing out of use and that time for documenting them was critical. When I started graduate school in the 1990s, the Survey collection was housed in an office where several of us had our work desks. As former students retired, or passed away, boxes and boxes of field notes would arrive and we would stack them wherever we could (sometimes even on our work tables) until we could find the time and place to properly catalog and shelve them (a glimpse into our own futures, as now many of my cohort have our own collections of language documentation in the Survey). While archiving was fairly ad hoc for many years, the Survey has gradually been developed into an exemplar of a modern regional language archive, with a fully digitized collection and web-accessible finding aids.

Part of the collection in the Survey contains elicitations and other source material for grammatical sketches of languages across California, and these were often worked up and published as doctoral dissertations. However, a large part of the collection were stacks of shoeboxes full of notecards containing lexical data for the preparation of dictionaries or notebooks full of transcribed texts (some with accompanying audio recordings)

intended to be eventually published as annotated collections of texts. Many of these were expertly collected and carefully kept, but never published. Thus, a tremendous amount of source data and language description in manuscript form remains to this day the primary documentation that exists for many, many languages. Other archives of this type created for regional language documentation are the Alaska Native Languages Center, the Archive of the Indigenous Languages of Latin America, the Pacific and Regional Archive for Digital Sources in Endangered Cultures, the Native American Languages collection at the Sam Noble Museum in Oklahoma, and most recently, the Kaipuleohone Language Archive at the University of Hawai'i.

While these archives all continue to build their collections with language documentation created by new faculty and student research, the bulk of their collections and a great deal of their value is in the collections they house that are now between a half century and a century old. This amount of time provides a good distance for us to evaluate these language documentation collections with our question in mind: Have they been able to move human knowledge forward, and if not, what gaps exist?

I expect it is common for anyone who works with manuscript or other historical language documentation to come away humbled by the experience. It is a stark reminder of how your own data may be viewed or experienced fifty or a hundred years hence. It is also a powerful reminder that when creating endangered language documentation you are providing an essential record for the future, as no other may exist. I provide a few examples from my own experience of being "humbled in the archives" that illustrate different scenarios of data use by future stakeholders: linguists, heritage language community members, and humanity as a whole.

Future linguists. Primary future stakeholders for archived language data are future linguists, and linguistic theories might be advanced or argued against based on archival language data. Having myself worked on the Potawatomi language (Neshnabémwen) for many years, I saw several iterations of morphological theories being worked and reworked based on complex but orderly Potawatomi verbal inflectional morphology. Doubtless, morphologists will continue to test their theories on it into the future, although the full paradigmatic record is fragmentary (Lockwood 2017). I myself was never so persuaded by the explanatory power of an elegant theory applied to data as I was when trying to explain verb stem alternations found in Miwok languages of California to participants of the Breath of Life workshop being held by the Survey. The Miwok languages are some of the best documented languages of California, thanks in large part to the work of linguists Catherine Callaghan and Silvia Broadbent, both students of Mary Haas. However, their grammatical descriptions required complex statements about the relationship of stem class alternations, patterns of consonants and vowels that we today recognize as being non-prosodic templatic morphology, as found in Semitic languages such as Arabic (McCarthy & Prince 1990). Not only has later linguistic theory improved our understanding of Miwok languages, we now have another language group that exemplifies templatic morphology, strengthening the case for its explanatory power.

Heritage language community members. As I mentioned, I worked on the documentation of critically endangered Neshnabémwen for many years, both with native speakers, as well as with a large amount of historical language documentation created by a succession of Jesuit priests and later by the linguist Charles Hockett who worked with fluent speakers in the 1940s. Both, but especially the latter, provided the basis for eliciting complex verbal morphology that is attested for the most part, but not in its entirety, today. Whether this is the result of the extreme contraction of the language-using community within the last century or regular language change is unknown and perhaps at this point unknowable. Attestations of the verbal paradigms provided by fluent elders over the last three decades as part of modern language documentation efforts are being used today for language revitalization activities. Perhaps, in time, new generations of users will go back to the older records of the nineteenth and twentieth centuries to explore and possibly incorporate some of the broader paradigms into their own usage. It is an available option only because those archival records exist.

Another example from the Neshnabémwen archival record relates to the recording and passing on of extra-linguistic knowledge, where I fear a great deal is being lost when languages are no longer used. Linguists today often document ethnobotanical knowledge as part of larger language documentation projects. I never focused on this with Neshnabémwen, partly because I have no talent for it, and also a fluent elder I was working with was very knowledgeable and wrote and published

on it himself (Thunder 1996). I did find an extensive ethnobotany collected by Huron Smith who worked in the 1920s with many of the native tribes of Wisconsin including the Potawatomi (Smith 1933). He would have been working at a time when the language had many more native speakers than there were at the time of my field research, when there were about fifty speakers in total. I showed the work to the fluent elder who was a knowledgeable herbalist and remarked that despite the otherwise copious detail, many of uses of the plants were simply labeled as "medicine" with no further information. We speculated why the Smith record was so vague about information that would seem so beneficial to future generations (at the time of our discussion, many of the plant names and uses recorded by Smith were no longer known). One possible reason, we thought, is that the person who identified the plants considered the knowledge to be too sensitive to commit to publication where readers who had no direct connection might inadvertently misuse the knowledge, potentially causing great harm to themselves or others. It would be irresponsible to disclose the information this way, even if it meant the knowledge would be lost.

This example illustrates the detailed encyclopedic ethnobotanical knowledge of the world's ecosystems contained and communicated through human languages. The loss of this knowledge is only a part of the broader set of knowledge we are losing when languages cease to be used. In the case of Neshnabémwen and other language communities that are striving for language maintenance and revitalization, there is a conduit for the continuity of knowledge through lived communication and practice. In the next example, that conduit was largely severed, and while we may never know the magnitude of the loss to humanity, we have evidence that it was great.

Humanity. One day in the Survey, a group of well-trained linguists sat puzzling over a text. We were a small working group of professors and graduate students attempting to develop an annotated corpus of the texts told by Ishi in his Yahi language to the linguist Edward Sapir in 1915 (Ishi & Luthin 1955; Hinton et al. 2001–2002). The texts were expertly transcribed by Sapir and given running translations in English. We also had access to published resources in the closely related Yana languages including a dictionary (Sapir & Swadesh 1960) and grammatical sketch (Sapir 1922). We found we were able to provide word and morpheme glosses for most of the texts, but sometimes certainty about the meaning of a passage simply eluded us. The story was wonderful, about the original human quest for fire, and there is a similar story told by the Yana (Sapir 1910:23–34). In the passage, the grizzly bear ties his hair into a top knot, and (we think) wafts up in the smoke and ashes of the fire until he reaches a sky hole (we have the unanalyzed string glossed as "penetrated through hole in sky"). He pops through the sky hole and lands (presumably) on the floor of the sky—the next line literally reads "he sat down." There he sits and looks out to the four directions, finally spotting fire in the far South (Ishi & Luthin 1955:237–238). This was as close of a translation as we could get. There were many such passages in the corpus, although this one nearly twenty years later is one that really stands out in my memory. There was no way to learn more. We had all of the records of related Yana languages and used them wherever we could. There was no one to consult to learn more. Ishi was the last surviving speaker of Yahi, other Yana languages subsequently ceased to be spoken, and the records of Yahi made by Edward Sapir are the only ones that exist.

With respect to extralinguistic knowledge, Ishi was an expert archer. There is good evidence that he was a specialist in the making of bows and arrows, and in hunting with them, and one of his stories "Tale of Lizard" is embellished by a loving account of the craft of arrow-making (Ishi & Luthin 1955:2–68). His skill was noted by Saxton Pope, who was Ishi's physician. They developed a friendship, and Pope learned arrow-making and hunting techniques from Ishi, and after Ishi's death became an expert archer himself, carrying on Ishi's legacy. Pope would later write *Hunting with a Bow and Arrow*, now a classic work on archery, and would go on to become a major popularizer of bow hunting in the twentieth century (Pope 2000). If you practice archery today, there is a strong chance you are practicing skills transmitted through a direct line of knowledge and practice that can trace its source to Ishi.[16] We only have a fleeting glimpse of Ishi's mastery of archery in the brief linguistic record we have of his time working with Sapir. What other encyclopedic knowledge have we lost forever? These examples hopefully serve to illustrate the depth of knowledge practiced in cultures around the world and communicated across generations through languages, many of which are highly endangered. And is not this, collectively, the

knowledge we have attained as human beings about how to live—and hopefully thrive—in the myriad environments on planet Earth over the past millennia?

Turning to archives created more recently, it is worth taking a look at another major kind of language archive: those that were created to house the linguistic data from grant-funded endangered language documentation projects. There are only two major such archives in existence (would there were more), and these were developed at the beginning of the twenty-first century with substantial funding from philanthropic sources. This funding not only provided grants for endangered language documentation projects that were and are taking place around the world, but tools and infrastructure (such as archives) to support the research as well.[17] The efforts have been very important and influential in the field. The primary two are the Endangered Languages Archive, which was established in 2002 alongside the Endangered Language Documentation Program funded by the Arcadia Fund (SOAS, n.d.), and the Language Archive, which was created alongside the Dokumentation bedrohter Sprachen program that was funded by the Volkswagen Foundation starting in the year 1999, which has since moved to the Max Planck Institute for Psycholinguistics (Max Planck Institute for Psycholinguistics, n.d.).

Unlike the Survey and similar archives, the materials in these archives were all "born digital." Likewise, the archives were purpose-built to house and serve digital resources rather than physical ones, sidestepping the large task that most regional archives have had of digital conversion. Because they were developing digital infrastructure such as tools for language documentation and had close partnerships with their associated archives, they were able to develop project workflows and metadata schemes that structured digital resources from the point of data creation to eventual archival ingestion. They were drivers of innovation and were central to the broader initiatives that structure archival practices to this day.

One example of this is with the metadata schemes we use to describe language resources. The Dokumentation bedrohter Sprachen project required that its projects use the ISLE Meta Data Initiative scheme, a broad and detailed set of resource descriptors.[18] This metadata scheme is used today by both the Language Archive and Archive of the Indigenous Languages of Latin America. An alternative and simplified set of descriptors was developed by the Open Language Archives Community

(OLAC). As part of the Open Archive Initiative, OLAC sought to make language resources discoverable across otherwise siloed digital language archives. Because the ISLE Meta Data Initiative metadata set can be mapped to OLAC, the initiative was able to create a central metarepository of language resources (OLAC 2011).

The Digital Endangered Languages and Musics Archives Network (DELAMAN) was also established at this time and has created a community and network for the coordinated development of language archive infrastructure (DELAMAN, n.d.). All of the archives discussed here are represented in DELAMAN, and DELAMAN has adopted the OLAC metadata standard to represent all of its member archives. It is therefore likely that DELAMAN will play a key role in the future development of OLAC.

Other projects such as Electronic Metastructure for Endangered Languages Data sought to create tools and refine practices for digital data collection and the stewardship of electronic resources (EMELD 2010). One tool that was developed, the GOLD ontology (General Ontology for Linguistic Description), proposed a taxonomy of morphosyntactic descriptors that could be used to describe the morphosyntactic properties of any of the world's languages. If linguists mapped the morphosyntactic features of the languages they were documenting to the GOLD ontology, a GOLD-driven search function could find instances of the use of any particular feature across the linked data sets.[19] The GOLD ontology has not gained traction as a practice for language documentation research, but it still represents a tantalizing view into a future where linked language data are not siloed in archives but are discoverable and harvestable across them.

4 Archives of the future

If we extrapolate from archives of the present and their current development efforts, we can speculate about their near-term future, say the next ten to one hundred years, and have a reasonable expectation of being accurate, at least in part. Next, I offer a few prognostications centered on what I think will be areas of language archive focus in the future.

Digital focus. One area of speculation relates to the challenge of maintaining digital language resources. The physical archives of the recent past can withstand a bit of benign neglect. Paper can be left in boxes on bookshelves or in attics for decades. While this is not

ideal, it certainly has frequently happened and the paper was later ingested into archives and data recovered from it.[20] We have wax cylinder language recordings from the early twentieth century that could not even be listened to until recently because any playing of them would further degrade the audio quality. Now thanks to new technology that reads them optically they can be remastered without damage (IRENE, n.d.).

However, this is not the case with digital resources, at least not so far in our experience. Digital resources are near-constantly being moved into the future—migrated onto new storage media, or new file formats, or new metadata formats or new content management systems. While the migration of any one digital resource may not be a significant task, it certainly is for an archive to manage the forward migration of all of its digital assets, and funding for most archives is not assured indefinitely. Some of the archives discussed here have experienced significant funding disruptions in the past two decades of their existence. Fortunately, these were of short enough duration that the digital records were preserved. We should all bear in mind though as we commit precious language documentation to a digital future that there is no good "lack-of-funding-model" for digital resources. Language archives must be supported into the future to ensure the digital longevity and future digital access of the data we are creating today.

Community focus. Another area of speculation relates to who the primary users of archived endangered language data will be in the future. I believe that the next stage of archival development will come from a strengthened focus on heritage language communities, and the use of archived language data for the purpose of language revitalization. The regional archives have a head start on this by virtue of their history, and regional archives already typically have a close working relationship with the language communities represented in their region. Activities like the Breath of Life workshop that started at the Survey are now taking place in many regional language archives, and there is even a National Breath of Life in the United States so that participants can access and learn about resources housed in government archives. These kinds of activities foster community across language boundaries and create new centers of shared innovation.

As languages are revitalized and reawakened, we should expect that the digital resources they create should be archived as language resources as well. If an archive has a strong relationship with a language community, the community could have a reasonable expectation that it would be able to archive its resources alongside the historical ones, should that be desired. Otherwise, the existing archives ought to play a supporting role in helping those communities establish their own as part of the larger language archive community, should that be desired. Alternatively, one could imagine a parallel network of revitalized language archives, hopefully that are not siloed from existing language archives or from each other.

Archives such as Endangered Languages Archive and the Language Archive, which were developed as part of grant-funded collection efforts, don't themselves have this same direct relationship with language communities, although their individual language documentation projects do. Grant-created archives, to the extent that they wish to lead in this area, will need to find other ways to build community. One way you could imagine them doing this is by becoming training centers for community-based linguists, who would in turn lead community-based language revitalization efforts.

Legacy data focus. If current trends continue, we expect many more languages will cease to be used in the coming decades. Also, the ability to continue documentation work on them is heavily dependent on funding. As opportunities to document endangered languages wane, I expect there will be a renewed focus on existing legacy collections of language data housed in regional archives. Not just digitizing them, as this has largely already been accomplished, but rather going back to all of those manuscript collections of data and working them up into computationally tractable data sets: rekeying handwritten notes, annotating them, providing them with detailed metadata, and hopefully incorporating them into new research and publications.

Computational focus. As many of the world's languages disappear, archives will become the only repository of a great deal of language data, and theoretical claims as well as hypotheses as to what is possible cross-linguistically will have to be tested against all of it. This means we will need more application programming interface (API) access into collections of data,[21] and we will want to prepare and expose primary data to these APIs so that we can search across archives and collections and conduct research from any location while accessing the entire worldwide corpus of archived language data. This may not happen in the next decade, but I hope to see good progress on it in my remaining lifetime. I expect that most of the work involved will be in making computationally tractable data sets, and this will require the development and accommodation to shared standards—if not the GOLD ontology, then in resources like it.

Related to the creation of computationally tractable data sets from legacy resources, I expect that language archives will become leaders in the creation of corpora and other natural language processing resources to better enable the world's languages to be used in electronically mediated communication. As I have argued elsewhere, there is economic motivation for enabling only a fraction of the world's largest languages in this important new domain of language use in the modern world. To participate, smaller language communities will have to bootstrap themselves by creating corpora and tools for their language using natural language processing (Buszard-Welcher 2018). They will need support to do all of this, and I can't imagine a better partnership to accomplish it than with the language archives of the world.

Training focus. Besides the training and support activities discussed, I believe that language archives will become central for the training of linguists, who will be needed in all of these activities. This requires retooling for many traditional linguistic departments so that linguists will have access to applied specializations alongside theoretical ones. To a certain extent this has already happened with the renewed focus on documenting endangered languages, but more specializations are needed—in archiving and information science, in natural language processing, in corpus linguistics, in programming and building APIs as well as archival software and tools, in language revitalization and community-based linguistics—as well as ways of applying all of these skills to the continued effort of endangered language documentation.

It is worth thinking about the role of linguistic archives, and who we expect to be primary communities of use for linguistic data archives in the future. The answers to these questions will undoubtedly be essential to the continued operation of language archives, and as we have argued, language archives need continued support for the linguistic data we create to continue to exist.

5   Conclusion

Returning to the question posed at the beginning of this chapter, How do we move human knowledge into the future?, I think there are a few aspects to its answer. One aspect is in how thoroughly we will be able to document endangered languages while there is still time to do so, and what that documentation contains by way of representing the knowledge and culture of its users. Another aspect lies in our practices of moving that information forward in time: these are our data creation and management practices, our archival practices, and our practices as a discipline and society in committing to the development and forward migration of archival records in the long term. The third aspect is whether in the future, and perhaps distant future, the users of the data we create will be able to obtain any meaning from them, because the passing on of knowledge is heavily dependent on this.

If a primary goal is to preserve human knowledge as expressed in language, then lived language is the primary "mode" of that knowledge—it is also situated, embodied, and encultured. Any recording of it strips some, or much, of this away to an audio or audio visual signal discontinuous from any lived linguistic event. With the passing of time, it increasingly becomes unsituated, disembodied, and un-encultured. Ideally, we enrich archived information both with annotation and metadata that help ground it in its historical context. But still, even the best of it is a simulacrum.

Both modes—lived language, and extracted and archived language—are potentially archival in the long term. Lived language would seem to be the best way to preserve meaning, but it is also precarious and ephemeral as evidenced by the vast majority of threatened and critically endangered languages around the world today. Archiving the audiovisual signal and annotations has its own precariousness but we are getting much better at it. It does not preserve the richness of meaning that lived language does, but it is an important record of it. And in some cases, with considerable effort, records of a language have enabled languages to be lived and meaningful again (Leonard 2007).

So, if a primary goal of our long-term archiving efforts is preserving human knowledge, and that is best ensured by preserving lived languages, then what is the role of archived linguistic data? Can we enrich our data, or our archives, so they are better repositories of knowledge? Could archives be critical infrastructure for lived languages, so that languages are enriched by their archives, bucking them up, or providing a kind of insurance policy against the forces of attrition and obsolescence? Could we make archives part of lived culture itself? If these ideas seem audacious, bordering on the incredible, the first step needn't be, although I expect it is still controversial: we could start by reframing archived endangered language data as archived human knowledge—knowledge that is part of all our shared heritage and needed for our common future.

Notes

1. The phrase "Long View" is a reference to a classic work of scenario planning by Peter Schwartz (1991).

2. For example, documenting aspects of language use that are changing or falling out of use due to attrition.

3. See the Rosetta Project (n.d.) and its "future artifact" the Rosetta Disk.

4. To help think about this question, see Mattern (chapter 5, this volume) on the linguistic data life cycle and Kung (chapter 8, this volume) on how to develop a data management plan.

5. The Rosetta Disk is one such future artifact (Rosetta Project, n.d.). Another is the 10,000 Year Clock, currently being built inside a mountain in the desert of West Texas (Long Now Foundation, n.d.).

6. For an expert conversation on this subject see the Time and Bits Workshop, held in the year 2000 at the Getty Institute (MacLean & Davis 2000).

7. This theory was originally postulated by de Saussure (1879) as a set of reconstructed "coefficients sonantiques" whose presence accounted for certain alternations found in Proto-Indo-European roots. Later, deciphered Hittite data was shown to have reflexes that correspond to two of these abstract elements (see Kuryłowicz 1927 and also Sturtevant & Hahn 1951:47–49 for a discussion). It has become a canonical example to demonstrate the value of internal historical reconstruction (for example, Hock 1991).

8. See Sampson (1985) for a discussion of the origins of many of the world's writing systems.

9. See Sturtevant and Hahn (1951:14) for a discussion of these strategies.

10. See for example the Hittite texts by Kikkulis of Matanni on the training of race horses, with methods still apparently employed today (Sturtevant 1951).

11. A note about this selection principle—in the mid-twentieth century, language documentation projects frequently focused on "high cultural-value" texts such as myths and legends, or narration, to the exclusion of other forms of language use. See Buszard-Welcher (2003) for an example of this where this practice led to obscuring the basic grammatical patterns in use in everyday language. Linguists are probably not the best curators, and language users and language communities can provide guidance for what they are most interested in documenting.

12. More likely archival data in DNA would be stored in vitro rather than in vivo, but we are imagining here, and so need not be prosaic. Also, there are published experiments of data written in DNA in vivo, into the *Escherichia coli* bacterium (Shipman et al. 2017).

13. Given modern language documentation practice, this could be a variety of media file types for recorded audio or video and their accompanying transcriptions. Still, the de-encoding problems exist no matter the file type.

14. I say this somewhat in jest, but there is a real challenge in the long-term archiving of contextualizing information such as metadata alongside the archiving of data themselves.

15. Mary Haas's own field notes have now been accessioned by the American Philosophical Society (n.d.a).

16. There is evidence today that Ishi's archery techniques were not solely Yahi, and it may be that he learned from a Nomlaki or Wintu relative (Kell 1996).

17. Two other programs worth mentioning here are the Endangered Language Fund (Endangered Language Fund, n.d.) and the Phillips Fund of the American Philosophical Society (American Philosophical Society, n.d.b) with associated archives that house the research products of the language documentation and revitalization activities they support.

18. The ISLE acronym within ISLE Meta Data Initiative stands for the International Standard for Language Engineering (EAGLES 2003).

19. For a demonstration of this see ODIN (2016).

20. J. P. Harrington was notorious for leaving his field notes in the attics of the people he worked with (Laird 1993).

21. For our purposes, an API allows data within a data set to be accessed remotely by using structured queries and would return structured data in response to those queries.

References

Advocates for Indigenous California Language Survival. n.d.a. About the advocates. https://aicls.org/about-the-advocates/. Accessed March 31, 2019.

Advocates for Indigenous California Language Survival. n.d.b. Breath of Life Institute. https://aicls.org/breath-of-life-institute/. Accessed March 31, 2019.

American Philosophical Society. n.d.a. Mary Rosamund Haas papers. https://search.amphilsoc.org/collections/view?docId=ead/Mss.Ms.Coll.94-ead.xml;query=haas;brand=default. Accessed March 31, 2019.

American Philosophical Society. n.d.b. Phillips Fund for Native American Research. https://www.amphilsoc.org/grants/phillips-fund-native-american-research. Accessed on March 31, 2019.

Archimedes Palimpsest. n.d. The Archimedes Palimpsest: About. http://archimedespalimpsest.org/about/. Accessed March 31, 2019.

Arch Mission Foundation. n.d. Humanity's backup plan. http://www.archmission.org. Accessed March 31, 2019.

British Museum. n.d. Everything you always wanted to know about the Rosetta Stone. https://blog.britishmuseum.org/everything-you-ever-wanted-to-know-about-the-rosetta-stone/. Accessed March 31, 2019.

Buszard-Welcher, Laura. 2003. Constructional polysemy and mental spaces in Potawatomi discourse. PhD dissertation, University of California, Berkeley.

Buszard-Welcher, Laura. 2018. New media for endangered languages. In *The Oxford Handbook of Endangered Languages*, ed. Kenneth L. Rehg and Lyle Campbell. New York: Oxford University Press.

Chafe, Wallace. n.d. The *Pear Film*. http://www.linguistics.ucsb.edu/faculty/chafe/pearfilm.htm. Accessed March 31, 2019.

Church, George, Yuan Gao, and Sriram Kosuri. 2012. Next generation digital information storage in DNA. *Science* 337 (610): 1628. doi:10.1126/science.1226355.

DELAMAN (Digital Endangered Languages and Musics Archives Network). n.d. http:www.delaman.org. Accessed December 30, 2018.

EAGLES. 2003. The ISLE metadata standard. https://www.mpi.nl/ISLE/. Accessed March 31, 2019.

EMELD. 2010. Electronic Metastructure for Endangered Languages Data. http://emeld.org/. Accessed March 31, 2019.

Endangered Language Fund. n.d. http://www.endangeredlanguagefund.org/. Accessed March 31, 2019.

Erhard, Manuel, Robert Fickler, Mario Krenn, and Anton Zeilinger. 2017. Twisted photons: New quantum perspectives in high dimensions. *Light: Science and Applications* 7 (3): 17146. doi:10.1038/lsa.2017.146.

Hinton, Leanne, Herb Luthin, Jean Perry, and Kenneth W. Whistler. 2001–2002. Yahi texts, Hinton.015.002. In *Leanne Hinton Papers on Indigenous Languages of the Americas*. Berkeley: Survey of California and Other Indian Languages, University of California, Berkeley. http://cla.berkeley.edu/item/2494.

Hock, Hans Heinrich. 1991. *Principles of Historical Linguistics*. Berlin: Walter de Gruyter.

Interstellar Beacon. n.d. The Interstellar Beacon: Backup humanity. https://www.interstellarbeacon.org/. Accessed March 31, 2019.

IRENE. n.d. Sound reproduction R&D home page. http://irene .lbl.gov/. Accessed March 31, 2019.

Ishi and Herb Luthin. 1955. Yahi texts with interlinear glossing, Luthin.002.001. In *Miscellaneous Papers from the Survey of California and Other Indian Languages*. Berkeley: Survey of California and Other Indian Languages, University of California, Berkeley. http://cla.berkeley.edu/item/1410.

Kell, Gretchen. 1996. Ishi apparently wasn't the last Yahi, according to new evidence from UC Berkeley research archaeologist. Press release, University of California, Berkeley. https:// www.berkeley.edu/news/media/releases/96legacy/releases.96 /14310.html. Accessed March 31, 2019.

Kuryłowicz, Jerzy. 1927. ə indo-européen et ḫ hittite. In *Symbolae grammaticae in honorem Ioannis Rozwadowski*, ed. W. Taszycki and W. Doroszewski, 95–104. Kraków: Gebethner and Wolff.

Laird, Carobeth. 1993. *Encounters with an Angry God*. Albuquerque: University of New Mexico Press.

Leonard, Wesley. 2007. Miami language reclamation in the home: A case study. PhD dissertation, University of California, Berkeley.

Lockwood, Hunter Thompson. 2017. How the Potawatomi language lives: A grammar of Potawatomi. PhD dissertation, University of Wisconsin, Madison.

Long Now Foundation. n.d. The 10,000 year clock. http:// longnow.org/clock/. Accessed March 31, 2019.

MacLean, Margaret, and Ben H. Davis, eds. 2000. *Time and Bits: Managing Digital Continuity*. Los Angeles: Getty Research Institute.

Max Planck Institute for Psycholinguistics. n.d. The language archive. https://tla.mpi.nl/home/history/. Accessed March 31, 2019.

McCarthy, John J., and Alan Prince. 1990. Prosodic morphology and templatic morphology. In *Perspectives on Arabic Linguistics II: Papers from the Second Annual Symposium on Arabic Linguistics* 16. https://scholarworks.umass.edu/linguist_faculty_pubs/16.

Memory of Mankind. n.d. Memory of mankind. https://www .memory-of-mankind.com/. Accessed March 31, 2019.

ODIN. 2016. The ODIN data. http://depts.washington.edu /uwcl/odin/. Accessed March 31, 2019.

OLAC. 2011. OLAC: Open Language Archives Community. http://www.language-archives.org/. Accessed March 31, 2019.

Pope, Saxton. 2000. *Hunting with the Bow and Arrow*. Billings, MT: Sylvan Toxophilite Classics.

Quast, Paul. 2018. Beyond the Earth: Schematics for "Companion Guide for Earth" archival elements residing within geosynchronous orbit. https://www.researchgate.net/publication /327473491_Beyond_the_Earth_Schematics_for_'Companion_ Guide_for_Earth'_archival_elements_residing_within_Geosynchronous_Orbit. Accessed March 31, 2019.

Rosetta Project. n.d. The Rosetta Project: Building an archive of all documented human languages. http://www.rosettaproject .org. Accessed March 31, 2019.

Sampson, Geoffrey. 1985. *Writing Systems*. Stanford, CA: Stanford University Press.

Sapir, Edward. 1910. Yana texts. *University of California Publications in American Archaeology and Ethnology* 9 (1): 1–235.

Sapir, Edward. 1922. The fundamental elements of Northern Yana. *University of California Publications in American Archaeology and Ethnology* 13:215–334.

Sapir, Edward, and Morris Swadesh. 1960. *Yana Dictionary*. Berkeley: University of California Press.

Schwartz, Peter. 1991. *The Art of the Long View: Planning for the Future in an Uncertain World*. New York: Currency Doubleday.

Shipman, Seth L., Jeff Nivala, Jeffrey D. Macklis, and George M. Church. 2017. CRISPR–Cas encoding of a digital movie into the genomes of a population of living bacteria. *Nature* 547 (7663): 345–349.

Smith, Huron. 1933. Ethnobotany of the Forest Potawatomi Indians. *Bulletin of the Public Museum of the City of Milwaukee* 7 (1): 1–130.

SOAS. n.d. Endangered languages archive. https://www.soas.ac .uk/elar/about-elar/. Accessed March 31, 2019.

SPIE. 2016. Peter Kazansky: Nanostructures in glass will store data for billions of years. *SPIE Newsroom*. doi:10.1117/2.3201603.02.

Stanford University. n.d. LOCKSS homepage. https://www .lockss.org/. Accessed March 31, 2019.

Sturtevant, Edgar, and E. Adelaide Hahn. 1951. *A Comparative Grammar of the Hittite Language*, rev ed. New Haven, CT: Yale University Press.

Thunder, Jim. 1996. *Medicines of the Potawatomi*. N.p., WI: Self-published.

Unicode. 2017. The Unicode standard. http://unicode.org /standard/standard.html. Accessed March 31, 2019.

Unicode. n.d. UDHR in Unicode. http://unicode.org/udhr/. Accessed March 31, 2019.

Wichmann, Søren, Eric W. Holman, André Müller, Viveka Velupillai, Johann-Mattis List, Oleg Belyaev, Matthias Urban, and Dik Bakker. 2010. Glottochronology as a heuristic for genealogical language relationships. *Journal of Quantitative Linguistics* 17 (4): 303–316. doi:10.1080/09296174.2010.512166.

Wycliffe Bible Translators. n.d. Wycliffe Bible translators. https:// www.wycliffe.org/. Accessed March 31, 2019.

11 Guidance for Citing Linguistic Data

Philipp Conzett and Koenraad De Smedt

1 Introduction

Linguistic data, in their many forms, are a valuable asset in research and education on language. From the predigital age, the earliest data to reach us are written records carved in stone, wooden sticks, or clay tablets, or penned on papyrus, parchment, and such. Early field linguists recorded samples obtained from informants and other sources in notebooks and card files. Speech was recorded on analog devices such as wax cylinders, phonograph records, and magnetic tape. Consultation of such materials as cited in studies was usually cumbersome, but their citation was often relatively straightforward.

In the early digital age, materials were shipped on digital tape reels or CD-ROM, and citation consisted of references to physical media. Nowadays, most digital materials are made available online. This has clear implications for the practice of citation. Furthermore, the use of digital data in linguistics has greatly expanded in volume and variety. Primary data in the form of large digital corpora of text, audio, and video have become widely available and are often annotated at one or more linguistic levels. Some other types of digital data (in the wide sense of the term) relevant for research on language are lexicons, term banks, word nets, computational grammars, translation memories, survey results, quantitative data from experiments, and so on. Locating specific data that were used in studies would amount to looking for a needle in a haystack were it not for proper citation. Unfortunately, citation practices haven't fully kept pace with new kinds of digital data and their distribution.

In this chapter, we sometimes use the more general term *resource* when referring to different types of digital research products, including, for instance, language models and analyzers (e.g., grammars, parsers), annotation tools, statistical code associated with certain data

sets, and other digital assets. Often, we mention *data* for simplicity but most guidelines for data also hold for other resources. A *data set* is a set of data items that is distributed as a whole, but often we use *data* and *data set* interchangeably.

The guidance given in this chapter is primarily targeted at authors of linguistic publications, while a secondary audience consists of academic publishers and resource providers such as repositories and archives.

2 Why and when to cite linguistic data?

In a recent position paper, a group of linguists have argued that *reproducibility* (or *replicability*)—despite its key role in verification and accountability of research—is currently underrepresented in the field of linguistics (Berez-Kroeker, Gawne, et al. 2018). They have also articulated their expectations for how linguists should manage, cite, and maintained their data for long-term access.

Fortunately, there is increasing awareness of the importance of properly citing research data in scholarly outreach. The rationale for data citation can be summarized as follows: "Data citation improves discovery, credit, and attribution of data" (Borgman 2016). A recent statement dealing with data citation that has become prominent is the Joint Declaration of Data Citation Principles put forward by the FORCE11 Data Citation Synthesis Group (Martone 2014). This declaration summarizes the recommendations of earlier studies and has been endorsed by many scholarly organizations, funders, and publishers (Cousijn et al. 2018:2). Asserting the importance of robust and accessible data as the foundation of reproducible scholarship (cf. Gawne & Styles, chapter 2, this volume), the Joint Declaration of Data Citation Principles offers a set of guiding principles on how to refer to data in scholarly communication.

More recently, the *Austin Principles of Data Citation in Linguistics* provide an interpretation of the Joint Declaration of Data Citation Principles that places it in the context of linguistic data specifically (Berez-Kroeker, Andreassen, et al. 2018). The first three of the Austin principles cover the purpose and function of proper data citation under the headings "Importance," "Credit and attribution," and "Evidence." We quote these principles (in italics) and comment on their relevance for our guidelines.

1. Importance
Linguistic data form not only a record of scholarship, but also of cultural heritage, societal evolution, and human potential. Because of this, the data on which linguistic analyses are based are of fundamental importance to the field and should be treated as such. Linguistic data should be citable and cited, and these citations should be accorded the same importance as citations of other, more recognizable products of linguistic research like publications.

For this reason, we argue and suggest as one of the main recommendations in this guidance that rules for data citation should not without reason differ from common rules for citation of other research outputs, such as publications. Our guidelines will thus whenever reasonable be in line with existing guidelines for citation of publications, and in case our guidelines fall short, we recommend the author to stick to citation rules for publication or if possible adapt them to the field of research data.

2. Credit and attribution
In linguistics, citations should facilitate readers retrieving information about who contributed to the data, and how they contributed, when it is appropriate to do so.

Providing proper attribution information is a way to credit contributors and support citation metrics and thus serves as an incentive for data sharing. Good citation standards and practices feed directly into current initiatives such as the Make Data Count project, which addresses "the significant social as well as technical barriers to widespread incorporation of data-level metrics in the research data management ecosystem."[1]

3. Evidence
Linguists should cite the data upon which scholarly claims are based. In order for data to be citable, it should be stored in an accessible location, preferably a data archive or other trusted repository. Authors should ensure that data collection and processing methods are transparent, either through links to metadata or a direct statement in the text, to make clear the relationship between the data and the scholarly claims based on it.

Citing data naturally presupposes that the cited data is findable, and preferably also accessible, interoperable, and reusable, as formulated in the FAIR principles (Wilkinson et al. 2016), which are Findable, Accessible, Interoperable, and Reusable. It is first of all findability that merits our attention in this chapter. To allow review or replication of research outputs (Berez-Kroeker, Gawne, et al. 2018) or to extend previous research, it must be made known where the data can be obtained and under which conditions it can be reused. In practice this means that it is necessary to find and refer to documentation of the data, ideally in the form of structured *metadata* associated with the data set. This information should also explain how the data is encoded and must be interpreted, and in some cases, which tools are compatible with the data. For a more comprehensive overview of different motivations for data citation, see the review provided by Silvello (2018:8–11).

The Linguistics Data Interest Group in the Research Data Alliance[2] has taken the Austin principles to heart and elaborated them through meetings and online group discussions. A summary of this work has recently been made available as "The Tromsø Recommendations for Citation of Research Data in Linguistics" (Andreassen et al. 2019). The guidelines in this chapter are consistent with these recommendations.

3 General recommendations

3.1 Which rules to follow?
Despite the importance of data citation, standards and best practice recommendations on how to cite research data are still in their infancy. We propose a set of principles and guidelines for linguistic data citation. Based on the desideratum that data citation should not unnecessarily differ from the citation of scholarly text, we suggest the following order of adherence to possible guidelines from different sources:

1. Style sheets and guidelines by the publisher of the text in which the data is cited.

2. Guidelines and suggestions by the provider of the cited data, to the extent that the publisher's guidelines for data citation are unclear or incomplete.

3. Our recommendations for best practice, which we elaborate herein, to the extent that the preceding items are missing, incomplete, or contradictory, and can be refined, clarified or extended.

Ideally, a data set or other resource has *metadata* associated with it, which is structured information about the data. A metadata record typically has fields for data type, format, location, provenance, size, license, and other descriptors. Clearly, citation of data should provide some of the same kinds of information, so it is highly desirable that a citation of data is directly based on the metadata record of the data set or is at least consistent with it.

3.2 Data availability statement

In a study resulting in a given publication, the author(s) may have used or consulted different types of data (e.g., tabular data, sound recordings, and statistical code). Irrespective of the type of data, data may be associated with a publication in three different ways, according to JATS4R[3] (Bos et al. 2018):

1. *Generated data* are data that are included or referenced and that were generated and analyzed for the study. Example: Survey data are collected and analyzed for the study.

2. *Analyzed data* are referenced data that were analyzed for the study but that were not generated for the study. Example: Data are selected and extracted from an existing corpus and analyzed for the study.

3. *Non-analyzed data* are data that were neither generated nor analyzed for the study. Example: Existing data on the topic or related topic(s) were not analyzed for the study but are somehow related and may be relevant to researchers in the field.

Reference to non-analyzed data is generally discouraged by publishers, but may be appropriate in case authors want to acknowledge that similar work has been done by other researchers, although for methodological or other reasons their data have not been analyzed (Bos et al. 2018).

For any referenced data, that is, generated, analyzed, and non-analyzed data, authors should provide full and structured citations according to the recommendations described in this chapter. For generated and analyzed data, some recommend that authors should also provide a so-called *data availability statement* (some publishers use the term *data accessibility statement*) (Bos et al. 2018). A data availability statement provides information about where data supporting the results presented in a publication can be found, including, where applicable, unique identifiers referring to the location where these data are made available (Cousijn et al. 2018:5). Some publishers provide templates for data availability statements. The following examples are partly adapted from the author guidelines of Hindawi, one of the world's largest publishers of peer-reviewed, fully Open Access journals:[4]

> Data Availability Statement: The [DATA TYPE] data used to support the findings of this study are available via the [NAME] repository ([DOI or OTHER PERSISTENT IDENTIFIER]).

Note that a data availability statement should also be provided when the data used to support your findings for any legitimate reason(s) cannot be made available:

> Data Availability Statement: The [DATA TYPE] data used to support the findings of this study have not been made available because [REASON].

or in case you have not used any data to support your study:

> Data Availability Statement: No data were used to support this study.

In all cases, data citation or referencing consists of the same two basic elements as used in citation to publications, namely (1) *bibliographic references*, usually collected at the end of the document, but sometimes placed in footnotes, and (2) *in-text citation*, at the place in the text where the data are mentioned. The exact format of in-text citations (e.g., numbered, author-year, or otherwise) and the placing and formatting of bibliographic references are not discussed here as such elements of style are usually part of the publisher's guidelines for authors and typesetting practices.

For advice on where to archive and publish your own generated and/or analyzed research data, see Andreassen (chapter 7, this volume).

4 Bibliographic references

This section describes how to create full references to linguistic data for inclusion in the references (bibliography) section of a publication or in footnotes. For some examples, see section 7, and for a systematic list of examples, we also suggest you consult the "Tromsø Recommendations for Citation of Research Data in Linguistics" (Andreassen et al. 2019) alongside this chapter.

4.1 Template for bibliographic reference

There is some debate about what elements are necessary to make up a complete data reference. Although most accounts depart from recommendations such as the Joint Declaration of Data Citation Principles (Martone 2014), the suggested or recommended elements vary somewhat from recommendation to recommendation (Ball & Duke 2015; Silvello 2018). Adapting these recommendations to the realm of linguistics, the Tromsø recommendations suggest the following two templates for citation of data sets in the bibliography section of a piece of academic writing.

1. The template for a minimal bibliographic reference to a data set has the following elements;[5] this template is also consistent with emerging recommendations by some publishing houses.[6]

    Author, Date, Title, Publisher, Locator.

2. The template for an expanded bibliographic reference to a data set including conditional elements (i.e., required in certain cases depending on resource characteristics) is as follows:

    Author, *Other Attribution (Roles),* **Date, Title, Publisher, Locator,** *Version, Date accessed.*

Elements rendered in bold are part of the minimal template, in other words, they are always required, while elements rendered in italics are considered to be conditional. Conditional elements are elements whose presence is conditioned by either the characteristics of the resource (e.g., references to versioned data sets should include the version number), or on subfield-specific traditions (e.g., in language documentation, it is common to acknowledge the contributions of language consultants by name). Note that we do not assume any order in which the elements of these templates may occur. Their order and formatting may vary, depending on the bibliography style that is part of a publisher's style guide.

In this section, we briefly define and discuss the different elements in some detail. Some elements may come in different types. For instance, the **Author** field may include the name of a principal investigator, but also the name of a data collector; the **Date** may be specified by date of publication or date of deposit, and so on. In cases where such clarification can be beneficial, we propose that elements be more specifically typed, for which we will propose suitable defaults. When using an element type that is not default, the element type should be specified in parentheses, for instance: *2018 (deposit date); John Smith (data collector).*

If the metadata for the data you are to refer to do not provide information about any or some of the elements listed in the templates and you are not able to get hold of the information from the owner or responsible body for the data source, you should not make up the information. Instead, you should state in the reference the lack of information. For instance, if no date at all is available you should add "n.d." or similar in the **Date** slot of the reference, analogous to usual practice for other publications.

Author. By default, **Author** is one or more entities (persons or organizations) responsible for having developed the resource and deposited it. Specific roles may be indicated, as also practiced in other contexts, for example, with *relator* attributes (Hornik, Murdoch, & Zeileis 2012). Roles will vary with the details of the resource and the terminology of the resource provider, but might include "Project Leader," "Investigator," "Researcher," "Data Collector," "Language User," "Consultant," "Project," and "Contact." By default, only the main responsible authors are listed without mentioning their roles. Other entities might be specified (and even required) by resource provider or publisher guidelines and/or the research community at stake and should be marked by their specific roles. Note that if the bibliographic reference specifies multiple roles, then all roles must be included, for example, "Name (Researcher, Depositor)." Whenever possible, use role names that are in line with standard or recommended vocabularies, such as the OLAC (Open Language Archives Community) Role Vocabulary (Johnson 2006) or the controlled list of contributors in the DataCite Metadata Schema (DataCite Metadata Working Group 2019:31–35). Roles other than the default **Author** are listed as *Other Attribution* in the templates. Finally, it should be pointed out that the **Author** field in a reference is not the only place for providing attribution. It is good practice to fully recognize all contributors in the metadata record of a resource. The metadata record is also the place where contributor identifiers such as an ORCID (Open Researcher and Contributor ID) or international standard name identifier—if applicable—should be added (Ball & Duke 2015:6), or at least contact information about the author.

Other Attribution. See **Author**. *Other Attribution* is like **Author** but must mention roles.

Date. By default, **Date** is the date of publication. If the publication date is not available (i.e., there is no formal publication process), use the deposit date, that is, the date when the resource was transferred to and registered in the facility of the resource provider. If no deposit date is registered, then use the collection or production date, that is, the date when the data were collected or produced; preferably the date indicating when the collection or production was completed; alternatively, the period of collection or production. Whether the **Date** field is specified as a year or as a more precise date depends on the style guide by the publisher and the information provided by the cited resource.

Title. The **Title** is the name of the resource, at the level that comprises all citations in the study; for instance, if several parts of a data set are mentioned in the text, it is recommended to list the data set as a whole in the references, while in-text citations refer to the relevant parts. This is analogous to having a single mention to a multi-volume book work in the bibliography, rather than listing the several volumes separately. If, on the other hand, the text cites a single subset or item of the data, the **Title** field may name that directly, followed by "In . . ." or similar, to refer to the full resource of which the data is a part. The level of granularity of citation will be discussed in more detail in section 4.2.

Publisher. The **Publisher** is the entity responsible for providing access to the resource. In most cases this will be the name of the resource provider (e.g., data repository or organization). If possible, this should be the original source, not a harvester of metadata or copier of the data.

Locator. The **Locator** is a digital identifier pointing to the landing page of the resource if available online. This identifier should preferably be at the level (e.g., subset, item) corresponding to what the **Title** refers to. The **Locator** of a digital object should preferably be a persistent identifier (PID) if the publisher provides one.[7] DataCite, the provider of digital object identifiers (DOIs) for data sets, recommends specifying the PID as a fully expanded resolvable persistent uniform resource locator, so instead of, for example, doi.org/10.18710/X5ZFXZ, use https://doi.org/10.18710/X5ZFXZ (DataCite DOI Display Guidelines, n.d.). If there is no such identifier, include the resource provider's internal identifier for the resource (e.g., record number, deposit identification number), in addition to the URL of the landing page. If no PID for the resource exists, include the URL, but make sure that it is available to readers: "If the URL requires a login or is session specific, meaning it will not resolve for readers, provide the URL of the database or archive home page or login page instead of the URL for the work" (American Psychological Association 2020:299, section 9.34). If no online locator exists, indicate the media type; this applies to both digital media (e.g., CD audio, CD-ROM text file) and analog media (e.g., book, archival file).

Version. The *Version* is an identifier, normally a number that is increased whenever data and/or metadata of a resource are changed, but it could also be a time stamp (e.g., for nightly builds), a Git commit identification number, or similar. The default is that there is only one version and the resource is assumed to be stable. An alternative value for *Version* is "dynamic" meaning that the resource may change without explicit versioning or time stamping; in that case, *Date accessed* is also required.

Date accessed. *Date accessed* is a date. If the resource is dynamic or it is uncertain whether the resource is stable and persistent (e.g., monitor corpora that grow in size or treebanks that are reparsed), an access date must be added to the reference.

If for some reason it is necessary or requested to explicitly distinguish data references from other references by indicating their type, authors may add an indicator (tag) at the end of the reference, often in parentheses or brackets, such as (data set), [code], and so forth. (Cousijn et al. 2018:6).

Publishers and/or resource providers might require or recommend additional elements not listed in our templates or listed only as conditional elements. For instance, some data distributors include an indicator of data fixity in the citation information, such as a Universal Numerical Fingerprint (Altman & King 2007). Finally, some resource providers might require citation of a written publication describing the data. In this case, the written publication should be cited in addition to citing the data themselves.

4.2 Granularity

A cited resource may consist of multiple parts. Thus, the question arises at what level of granularity a citation should be given. The choice of granularity level is not straightforward:

> A dataset may form part of a collection and be made up of several files, each containing several tables, each containing many data points. There are also more abstract subsets that can be used, such as features and parameters. At the other end of the scale, it is not always obvious what would constitute an intellectual whole: it can be argued, for example, that investigations should be the primary units of citation rather than individual datasets. (Ball & Duke 2015:7)

As a pragmatic solution, Ball and Duke suggest citing data at the level of granularity that the resource provider has chosen for assigning *Locators* ("identifiers") and that, where *Locators* are provided at several levels of granularity, references should be given at the finest-grained level that meets the need of the citation (7).

The following template may serve as a model for a fine-grained reference to a part of an assembled resource (including conditional and optional elements). As usual, the order of elements may vary.

> *Author of part, Date, Title of part,* In: *Author of assembled resource, Title of assembled resource, Publisher of assembled resource, Locator of part, Version of part, Date accessed of part. [resource type of part]*

The following fine-grained reference was generated by the Tromsø Repository of Language and Linguistics (TROLLing) for a file included in a data set published in the repository.

> Arkhangelskiy, Timofey, 2019, "01_rnc_borrowed _lemmata.txt", In: *Replication data for: Verbal borrowability and turnover rates,* https://doi.org/10 .18710/JFNESU/LETGNY, DataverseNO, V1 [file]

Another example refers to a recording in an archive. In this example, as in the previous one, the *Locator* points directly to the landing page for the item, not to the main page of the archive.

> Krauss, Michael E. (Interviewer), Jeff Leer (Interviewer) & Anna Nelson Harry (Speaker). 1975. *Interview with Anna Nelson Harry.* In: Krauss Eyak Recordings, item ANLC0082. Alaska Native Language Archive. http://www.uaf.edu/anla/item .xml?id=ANLC0082.

As a main rule, you should choose fine-grained citation if the *Author* of the resource part is not identical with the *Author* of the assembled resource. In that case, the *Author* of the assembled resource should be mentioned, if there is one. This is also common practice in citation of scholarly publications, where reference is made to a specific paper or chapter in an anthology with contributions from different authors. If, on the other hand, there are citations to multiple parts of a resource, especially when these have the same *Author* as the assembled resource, one may wish to avoid a long list of separate references for the parts, as in the following made-up example:

> Smith, John, 2018a, "Data set 1",. . . . [dataset]
>
> Smith, John, 2018b, "file_01.txt", *Data set 1,*. . . . [file]
>
> Smith, John, 2018c, "file_02.txt", *Data set 1,*. . . . [file]
>
> . . .

Instead, the highest common denominator of all the parts should be listed in the references, while each in-text citation refers to a specific part by including a fine-grained element. How to add a more specific *Locator* in the in-text citation is explained in the next section.

5 In-text citation

In-text (or in-line) citations are meant to direct the reader to a bibliographic reference at the end of the published work, and, if relevant, indicate which part of the cited data set is referred to. For a style sheet based on the author-date format, for example, APA (American Psychological Association 2020), the minimal template is as follows.

Template for minimal in-text citation of data:

> *Author, Date*

As mentioned in the section on bibliographic references, we recommend that data references are made at the finest-grained level. If the document refers to a single part of an assembled data set, the in-text citation can simply refer to that item in the references. If citing a part or individual item of a data set listed in the reference, you should provide details on which part of the data you wish to cite, for example, by adding a *Locator*, which can be the name or PID of a collection, file, item

(Ball & Duke 2015:7). In this case, the template is as follows.

> Template for in-text citation of data, including *Locator*:
>
> *Author, Date, Locator*

In certain cases, it may be useful to refer to a particular *Subset* of the data, such as a time span or a range of line numbers. If the subset is a time span, we recommend using the International Organization for Standardization's ISO 8601 time codes in the [hh]:[mm]:[ss] format (ISO 8601 2019).

> Template for in-text citation of data, including *Locator* and *Subset*:
>
> *Author, Date, Locator, Subset*

If the cited subset has relevant contributors that differ from the main authors, these contributors and their roles may be mentioned under *Other Attribution*.

> Template for in-text citation of data, including *Locator*, *Subset*, and *Other Attribution (Roles)*:
>
> *Author (Role), Date, Locator, Subset, Other Attribution (Roles)*

If your publication channel uses a number format rather than author-year format for in-text citation, use footnotes or endnotes to indicate the granularity of the citations, if needed. Footnotes (rather than a reference in the main text) are also recommended for long URLs or PIDs when it is necessary to refer to specific resource items, sections, or other parts of a resource.

Actual examples of in-text citations will be given in section 7.

6 Citing unpublished data

Sometimes one may want to cite research data that are not yet publicly available. An increasing number of publishers encourage or even require authors to provide access to the data underlying manuscripts when they are submitted for review. At that point in time, the data may still be under embargo, in a repository submission process, or for other reasons not publicly available. The rule of thumb for citing unpublished data is to provide as much information as possible, and at least the *Author* and the *Title* of resource (Ball & Duke 2015:7). In the data availability statement, one should explain the full details of the status of the resource, such as whether it is deposited, embargoed, restricted, or openly available (Ball & Duke 2015:7).

When a paper presenting new data is submitted for peer review, authors must make sure that any information given about the cited data, either through citation in the text or in the referenced data themselves, complies with any anonymity requirements of the publisher.

Once your manuscript has been accepted for publication, make sure to revisit references to unpublished data in your manuscript and bring them up to date before the final version of your article or book is published (Ball & Duke 2015:7). Analogously, once your article or book is published you should consider including a reference to the publication in the metadata record of the cited data.

7 Examples

Whereas FORCE11 has formulated very general principles for data citation, these have been adapted to a linguistics context and rationale in the above-mentioned Austin principles, but even these are fairly general and do not provide detailed guidelines for various types of language data in possible citation contexts. Drawing on the Tromsø recommendations (Andreassen et al. 2019), we will provide an overview of some data types and examples of current practice for citing these. Where appropriate, we will comment on the examples and provide supplementary information.

Note that the examples represent different citation formatting styles. As mentioned at the outset of this chapter, you should always make sure your citation follows the citation style required or recommended by the publisher.

For more examples, see the "Tromsø Recommendations for Citation of Research Data in Linguistics" (Andreassen et al. 2019). The examples presented there as well as the examples in this chapter represent a variety of good options for formatting citations.

7.1 Corpora and other collections of language materials

Example 1 illustrates how an item that is part of a language archive can be referred to. It also illustrates how the roles of contributors may be specified:

> Example 1:
>
> Hauk, Bryn (Researcher, Depositor), P'ap'ashvili, Omar (Language User), Orbetishvili, Rezo

(Consultant). 2018. Batsbi (Tsova-Tush) Collection, Item BH2–074. Kaipuleohone University of Hawaii Digital Language Archive, http://hdl.handle.net/10125/58935. Accessed on 2019-03-10.

Furthermore, the *Date accessed* is provided here because the resource provider does not provide any version information. In case there are different citations of the archive, the fine-grained element "Item BH2–074" may be omitted from the bibliographic reference. It should then be included in the in-text citation; you might also include a time code to refer to a specific excerpt, and one or more non-author contributors, if these are particularly relevant. This gives some possible variants of in-text citation for this example:

- (Hauk 2018, BH2–074)
- (Hauk 2018, BH2–074, 00:02:33–00:02:47)
- (Hauk 2018, BH2–074, 00:02:33–00:02:47, Rezo Orbetishvili (Consultant))

Example 2 has a website but no PID:

Example 2:

BNC Consortium. The British National Corpus, version 3 (BNC XML Edition). 2007. Oxford: Bodleian Libraries, University of Oxford. http://www.natcorp.ox.ac.uk/.

The following is an example of a resource on CD-ROM. The LDC catalog number is also given.

Example 3:

Liberman, Mark, et al. Emotional Prosody Speech and Transcripts LDC2002S28. CD-ROM. Philadelphia: Linguistic Data Consortium, 2002.

Examples 3 and 4, as suggested by the LDC, lack direct *Locators*. They require that the reader finds the LDC and looks up the resource number in its catalog.

Example 4:

Huang, Shudong, David Graff and George Doddington. Multiple-Translation Chinese Corpus LDC2002T01. Web download file. Philadelphia: Linguistic Data Consortium, 2002.

In quite a few cases, as illustrated in the following examples, the author of the corpus is a project team, in which case the name of the project may be given. PIDs of the *Handle* type are specified as fully resolvable URLs.

Example 5:

ISWOC, 2016. ISWOC West-Saxon Gospels. Created by Information Structure and Word Order Change in Germanic and Romance Languages (Project). Distributed by the INESS Portal. http://hdl.handle.net/11495/DB24-D542-3616-6.

Example 6:

INESS, 2016. NorGram Newspaper text (30 documents from the years 2006–2009) in Norwegian Bokmål from the Norwegian Newspaper Corpus. Created by: Infrastructure for the Exploration of Syntax and Semantics. Distributed by the INESS Portal: http://hdl.handle.net/11495/DB24-E30D-55EA-1. Dynamic data, accessed April 1, 2019.

An in-text citation of a sentence from the corpus could look like the following, including the footnote.

(INESS, 2019, Sentence #3147[8])

The PID in the footnote points directly to a specific sentence in a specific treebank archived in INESS (Norwegian Infrastructure for the Exploration of Syntax and Semantics) infrastructure. This is convenient for the reader. Such a PID can be generated by clicking on a button next to any sentence stored in INESS. The PID is a stable reference to the sentence but not necessarily to the annotation. If the treebank is a dynamic parsebank that may be reparsed, as in this example, the *Date accessed* is also required.

7.2 Databases and application data

The term *database* is used for many different kinds of resources. Examples are lexical and terminological databases, for instance, word nets, which represent semantic relations between lexical concepts. The following reference in the Modern Language Association's style is recommended by the publisher of WordNet, a lexical database for the English language, for reference to their online version:

Example 7:

Princeton University "About WordNet." WordNet. Princeton University. 2010.

This reference is somewhat underspecified, as it lacks information about the version, whereas several versions exist. Also, we recommend providing the *Locator* as a full URL, which in this example would be https://wordnet

.princeton.edu/, which does not point to the resource itself but to an information page with further instructions on how to access the resource. A more fully specified reference to a version of WordNet is given in example 8, in which the *Date* is the publication date of the specified *Version*.

Example 8:

Princeton University, 2006. Wordnet (version 3.0). Distributed by Princeton University, https://wordnet.princeton.edu/.

Application data are data sets or databases that are meant to be used in a particular application, for instance, in a system for machine translation, a finite state transducer, a parser. Example 9 points to a parallel corpus provided in part as a translation memory in Tile Map XML format for use in machine translation systems; the *Handle* resolves to a landing page with human-readable metadata.

Example 9:

Parra Escartín, Carla, 2012, Parallel Corpus of documents from the Technical Regulations Information System for German-Spanish (v0.3; TMX and TEI formats), Common Language Resources and Technology Infrastructure Norway (CLARINO) Bergen Repository, http://hdl .handle.net/11509/79.

7.3   Replication data sets or packages

In the common course of a research study, inputs from resources such as the ones mentioned herein are often further processed, refined, and analyzed. In recent years, it has become increasingly common—and required by funders and publishers—to make not only the raw data, but also processed data available to support the findings in a study. Processed data may consist of different resource types, such as spreadsheets, audio or video recordings and transcriptions, statistical code, software code, field notes, which are assembled into a data set that is made available to peers and the greater public.

Many replication data packages have been made for quantitative and qualitative data resulting from experiments, surveys, and similar methods. Such data are not language data in themselves, but measurements, judgments, attitudes, and so forth.

Example 10 shows a ready-made reference as generated and recommended by TROLLing:

Example 10a:

Ji, Yinglin, 2018, "Cognitive representation of spontaneous motion in a second language", https://doi.org/10.18710/N8KO4O, DataverseNO, V1.

We recognize several of the reference elements from our minimal template:

- *Author:* Ji, Yinglin; Date: 2018;
- *Title:* Cognitive representation of spontaneous motion in a second language;
- *Publisher:* DataverseNO (TROLLing is a special collection within the DataverseNO repository);
- *Locator:* https://doi.org/10.18710/N8KO4O (a DOI in the form of a fully expanded URL);
- *Version:* V1.

Furthermore, depending on the specified citation style, the tag "[dataset]" may be added to the reference to distinguish the referenced data from other types of materials.

Example 10b:

Ji, Yinglin, 2018, "Cognitive representation of spontaneous motion in a second language," https://doi.org/10.18710/N8KO4O, DataverseNO, V1. [dataset]

In example 10b, the reference points to a whole data set. TROLLing also assigns DOIs at file level, and thus you might want to refer to a particular file within a data set. Resuming our discussion of example 10a, based on the ready-made reference provided by TROLLing, the file "03_preference_data.txt" might be referred to as follows:

Example 11:

Ji, Yinglin, 2018, "03_preference_data.txt," *Cognitive representation of spontaneous motion in a second language*, https://doi.org/10.18710/N8KO4O /H9PDCL, DataverseNO, V1. [file]

If, in example 11, you choose to include a reference only at data set level, the in-text reference to the file has to be more fine-grained and should preferably include either the file name or the file DOI:

- (Yinglin 2018, 03_preference_data.txt)
- (Yinglin 2018, https://doi.org/10.18710/N8KO4O/H9 PDCL)

To round off this section, we would like to illustrate how the TROLLing data set would have been cited prior to publication. When submitting her article for submission, the author could have used the following (non-anonymized) reference:

Example 12:

> Ji, Yinglin, 2018, "Cognitive representation of spontaneous motion in a second language," https://doi.org/10.18710/N8KO4O, DataverseNO, DRAFT VERSION. [data set]

Once the journal article was accepted, the author would have published the data set, and replaced "DRAFT VERSION" with "V1" in the reference, before submitting the final version of the article to the journal publisher.

8 Reference management tools

Nowadays, several reference management tools are available that lessen the burden of keeping track of references and their formatting. Thus, it is paramount that reference managers have capabilities to handle at least the minimal items that we suggest. Unfortunately, widely used systems such as Zotero[9] and BibDesk[10] (based on BibTeX[11]) currently offer fragmentary support for describing research data, although changes are underway.

BibTeX does not have a dedicated type for research data among its standard reference types, but it has *url, webpage, electronic* (alias *online*), and *misc*. Our proposed elements *Author, Date, Publisher,* and *Title* can be mapped to BibTeX fields *Author, Date (or Year), Organization,* and *Title*, respectively. A role added for *Other Attribution* would be parsed as part of the name. For *Locator*, one can use *Url, Doi,* or *Howpublished* depending on the type. *Version* could go in *Howpublished*, as *Note*, or as part of the *Title*. *Date accessed* can be mapped to *URLdate* or *Lastchecked*.

The following is a BibTeX record that was automatically generated by the CLARINO Bergen Repository.[12] It has most of the important information, but it is unfortunate that the publisher is in the *Note* field and that *Copyright* is not a supported field for the *misc* type.

```
@misc{11509/73,
title={The Norwegian-Spanish Parallel Corpus},
author={Hareide, Lidun},
url={http://hdl.handle.net/11509/73},
note={Common Language Resources and Technology
Infrastructure Norway ({CLARINO}) Bergen Repository},
```

```
copyright={{CLARIN}\_{ACA}},
year={2013} }
```

BibLaTeX,[13] a newer alternative to BibTeX, has standard entry types for *software* and *dataset* since 2019. Whereas *software* is aliased to *misc*, the *dataset* entry type has its own definition, which includes several optional fields, including both *Publisher* and *Organization*. A possible modification and extension of the preceding example using some supported fields is the following:

```
@dataset{11509/73,
title={The Norwegian-Spanish Parallel Corpus},
author={Hareide, Lidun},
url={http://hdl.handle.net/11509/73},
location={Bergen, Norway},
publisher={Common Language Resources and Technology
Infrastructure Norway ({CLARINO}) Bergen Repository},
version={1},
note={[dataset]},
year={2013},
urldate={2020-01-17}}
```

The Research Information Systems (RIS) format, which can be imported in some bibliographic management systems, has ADVS (audiovisual material), DATA (data file), DBASE (online database), SOUND (sound recording), and so on, but no specific type for research data in general, so as to specify archives, replication packages, corpora, and such.

Zotero is a powerful bibliographic management system that also supports shared references in so-called group libraries. Currently, Zotero does not provide a dedicated citation item type for research data. However, this feature is planned to be included in the next major version upgrade.[14] As a transitional solution, Zotero recommends using the citation item type *Document* for data sets. Depending on how you create a reference in Zotero (e.g., manually vs. automatically using a web browser extension or a similar tool) you may have to edit the reference record in Zotero. In particular, you should pay attention to the following three fields, here illustrated with a data set from TROLLing. Note that the three pieces in the *Extra* field should be entered on separate lines. Do not include version if it is 1.

```
Item Type: Document
Publisher: DataverseNO
Extra: type: dataset
    version: 2
    DOI: 10.18710/BFFMPH
```

This solution works fairly well for some citation styles. Using the citation style for the seventh edition of the APA manual (American Psychological Association 2020), Zotero creates the following reference that includes the information from the *Extra* field:

> Holliday, J. J., Turnbull, R., & Eychenne, J. (2016). *K-SPAN (Korean Surface Phones and Neighborhoods)* (Version 2) [Data set]. DataverseNO. https://doi.org/10.18710/TWM79F

This reference contains all elements included in our recommended template for minimal bibliographic reference. However, fields are still lacking for other elements that might be recommended by resource providers, for example, an indicator of data fixity such as Universal Numerical Fingerprint, which is provided by the repository hosting the preceding data set.

If you want to refer to a *Subset* in your in-text citation using Zotero, you have to map this to *Part*, which is an alternative to *Page*. You may either refer to *Part* by file name or PID. For the preceding example, the in-text citation in APA style may look like this:

> (Holliday et al., 2016, pt. kspan_base.tab)

Currently, there is no convenient way to create fine-grained bibliographic references to research data using Zotero, but given the commitment and attention support services for research data management are receiving at present, this functionality is expected to come in a not-so-distant future.

9 Advice on metadata for repositories and other resource providers

Informative citation is dependent on metadata, that is, structured data describing the properties of the data. Metadata are normally entered when data are deposited in a repository. Obviously, such metadata should contain the elements necessary for citation. Metadata also serve other purposes, such as cataloging to support faceted search. For the purpose of citation, metadata should conform to the following.

- At minimum, the metadata should include the elements in the minimal templates recommended herein.
- Metadata should preferably be structured according to a standard format (e.g., component MetaData Infrastructure, RIS) so that information from it can be extracted by programs.

- Metadata should be available freely, without cost or restrictions, even if the data themselves have restrictions.
- The metadata should allow persistent reference to the data set, and to the metadata themselves, to avoid link rot. This implies that PIDs should be assigned to the data and to the metadata. Several identifiers have been proposed as standards. In the field of linguistics, the International Standard Language Resource Number[15] has been proposed (Mapelli et al. 2016). More inherently persistent identifiers are based on the Handle system,[16] which implements the identifier/resolution protocol (IRP) to enable persistence of the identifiers even if the data moves to different locations. The DOI system[17] is also based on IRP, but has additional specifications, such as those for minimal metadata.
- Data repositories and other resource providers should provide metadata in machine-readable as well as human-readable form and should preferably also generate ready-made citations, both in formats for export to reference managers and in textual format.

In a somewhat more distant future, it is expected that both data and metadata will be more inherently cloud-based, encapsulated as FAIR Digital Objects (De Smedt, Koureas, & Wittenburg 2019). This would introduce new ways for researchers and repositories to interact with data. Actionable digital objects will communicate with automated processes requesting access and data management and should be able to provide their own citations in a context-dependent way.

10 Advice for publishers

Apart from researchers and resource providers, the realization of the recommendations outlined in this chapter depends highly on the support from academic publishers. We thus strongly encourage publishers to adopt our recommendations in their work to make research more transparent and reusable. In particular, we recommend publishers to provide necessary guidance and resources for data citation to the different stakeholders in the ecosystem of scholarly communication. We are aware of the fact that several academic publishing houses and scholarly associations already have guidelines or are in the process of establishing those.

We recommend that publishers have a data policy that preferably requires authors to make data accessible at least for reviewers at the time of manuscript submission and to make data openly available at latest at the time of publication of the article or book. Publishers may also advise authors on where and how they should deposit their data, preferably based on information available in overviews such as the Registry of Research Data Repositories.[18] Author guidelines should include guidance on data availability statements and style sheets should have clear instructions for citation and bibliographies that cover different types of linguistic resources.

Links to cited data in published texts should be written in full. In electronic publications, these links should preferably be clickable.

We also recommend that publishers make the full metadata of published data openly and freely available to researchers, catalogs, and other resource providers. This is important, for example, for services that provide overviews about citations of data sets in article and book publications. Usually this can be done by providing metadata to Crossref or similar providers.[19]

In general, publishers should follow standards and best practice recommendations for electronic publishing of scholarly results, as promoted by, for example, Crossref and JATS4R.

Acknowledgments

The authors of this chapter wish to acknowledge all who through discussion or written comments have provided ideas for or feedback on the preparation of this chapter. In particular we wish to thank the Linguistic Data Interest Group of the Research Data Alliance for their work on the development of these citation guidelines, and the Linguistic Data Consortium for providing meeting space for one of our many face-to-face discussions.

Notes

1. https://makedatacount.org/.

2. https://www.rd-alliance.org/groups/linguistics-data-ig.

3. JATS4R (JATS for Reuse; https://jats4r.org/) is a working group devoted to optimizing the reusability of scholarly content by developing best-practice recommendations for tagging content in JATS (Journal Article Tag Suite) XML.

4. See https://www.hindawi.com/research.data/.

5. In reference management tools, the term "field" is often used instead of "element."

6. E.g., Cambridge University Press, https://www.cambridge.org/core/services/authors/open-data/data-citation.

7. On the Internet, a PID has the form of a PURL, which curates redirection by means of a resolver. This scheme attempts to solve the problem of transitory locators in location-based schemes such as HTTP. Example types of persistent identifiers are the Hangle the Digital Object Identifier (DOI), and the Archival Resource Key (ARK) There are also different types of globally unique identifiers that do not involve automatic curation by a resolver, such as the International Standard Language Resource Number (ISLRN).

8. http://hdl.handle.net/11495/D8B8-3970-851A-3@lfg234387, accessed February 2, 2020. Access to this data may require login.

9. See https://www.zotero.org/.

10. https://bibdesk.sourceforge.io/.

11. See http://www.bibtex.org/.

12. A repository based on CLARIN DSpace, http://clarino.uib.no/.

13. https://www.ctan.org/pkg/biblatex.

14. https://www.zotero.org/support/dev/translators/datasets.

15. http://www.islrn.org/.

16. https://www.dona.net/handle-system.

17. https://www.doi.org/.

18. https://doi.org/10.17616/R3D, accessed November, 19, 2020.

19. See https://www.crossref.org/.

References

Altman, Micah, and Gary King. 2007. A proposed standard for the scholarly citation of quantitative data. *D-Lib Magazine* 13 (3/4). https://doi.org/10.1045/march2007-altman.

American Psychological Association. 2020. *Publication Manual of the American Psychological Association*, 7th ed. Washington, DC: American Psychological Association. https://doi.org/10.1037/0000165-000.

Andreassen, Helene Nordgård, Andrea L. Berez-Kroeker, Lauren Collister, Philipp Conzett, Christopher Cox, Koenraad De Smedt, Bradley McDonnell, and the Research Data Alliance Linguistic Data Interest Group. 2019. Tromsø recommendations for citation of research data in linguistics, *Research Data Alliance*. https://doi.org/10.15497/RDA00040.

Ball, A., and M. Duke. 2015. How to cite datasets and link to publications. DCC how-to guides. Digital Curation Centre. http://www.dcc.ac.uk/resources/how-guides.

Berez-Kroeker, Andrea L., Helene N. Andreassen, Lauren Gawne, Gary Holton, Susan Smythe Kung, Peter Pulsifer, Lauren B. Collister, the Data Citation and Attribution in Linguistics Group, and the Linguistics Data Interest Group. 2018. *The Austin Principles of Data Citation in Linguistics*. https://site.uit.no/linguisticsdatacitation/austinprinciples/.

Berez-Kroeker, A. L., L. Gawne, S. S. Kung, B. F. Kelly, T. Heston, G. Holton, P. Pulsifer, et al. 2018. Reproducible research in linguistics: A position statement on data citation and attribution in our field. *Linguistics* 56 (1): 1–18. https://doi.org/10/gft4g7.

Borgman, C. L. 2016. Data, data citation, and bibliometrics. https://escholarship.org/uc/item/98r688tr.

Bos, Ton, Paul Donohoe, Melissa Harrison, Christina Von Raesfeld, and Kelly McDougall. 2018. Data availability statements, version 1.1. JATS4R (JATS for Reuse). https://jats4r.org/data-availability-statements.

Cousijn, Helena, Amye Kenall, Emma Ganley, Melissa Harrison, David Kernohan, Thomas Lemberger, Fiona Murphy, et al. 2018. A data citation roadmap for scientific publishers. *Scientific Data* 5 (November): 180259. https://doi.org/10.1038/sdata.2018.259.

DataCite DOI Display Guidelines. n.d. https://support.datacite.org/docs/datacite-doi-display-guidelines. Accessed December 15, 2019.

DataCite Metadata Working Group. 2019. DataCite metadata schema documentation for the publication and citation of research data, version 4.2. https://schema.datacite.org/meta/kernel-4.2/index.html.

De Smedt, Koenraad, Dimitris Koureas, and Peter Wittenburg. 2019. An analysis of scientific practice towards FAIR Digital Objects. EUDAT. http://doi.org/10.23728/b2share.e14269d07ce84027a7f79ee06b994ef9.

Hornik, Kurt, Duncan Murdoch, and Achim Zeileis. 2012. Who did what? The roles of R package authors and how to refer to them. *R Journal* 4 (1): 64–69. https://doi.org/10.32614/RJ-2012-009.

ISO 8601. 2019. *Wikipedia*. https://en.wikipedia.org/w/index.php?title=ISO_8601&oldid=895977129.

Johnson, Heidi. 2006. OLAC role vocabulary. http://www.language-archives.org/REC/role.html.

Mapelli, Valérie, Vladimir Popescu, Lin Liu, and Khalid Choukri. 2016. Language resource citation: The ISLRN dissemination and further developments. In *Proceedings of the Tenth International Conference on Language Resources and Evaluation* (LREC 2016), 1610–1613. Portorož, Slovenia: European Language Resources Association (ELRA). https://www.aclweb.org/anthology/L16-1254.

Martone, M., ed. 2014. *Data Citation Synthesis Group: Joint Declaration of Data Citation Principles*. San Diego: FORCE11. https://doi.org/10.25490/a97f-egyk.

Silvello, Gianmaria. 2018. Theory and practice of data citation. *Journal of the Association for Information Science and Technology* 69 (1): 6–20. https://doi.org/10/gcqfk2.

Wilkinson, Mark D., Michel Dumontier, IJsbrand Jan Aalbersberg, Gabrielle Appleton, Myles Axton, Arie Baak, Niklas Blomberg, et al. 2016. The FAIR guiding principles for scientific data management and stewardship. *Scientific Data* 3 (March): 160018. https://doi.org/10.1038/sdata.2016.18.

12 Metrics for Evaluating the Impact of Data Sets

Robin Champieux and Heather L. Coates

1 Introduction

Research is a social activity, involving a complex array of resources, actors, activities, attitudes, and traditions (Sugimoto & Larivière 2018). There are many norms, including the sharing of new work in the form of books and journal articles and the use of citations and acknowledgments to recognize the influence of earlier work, but what it means to produce impactful scholarship is difficult to define and measure. The goals, methods, metrics, and utility of evaluating the impact of data sets are situated within this broader context of scholarly communication and evaluation. An understanding of the dynamic history, current practices, concepts, and critiques of measuring impact for and beyond research data sets can help researchers navigate the scholarly dissemination landscape more strategically and gain agency in regard to how they and their work are evaluated and described.

What is research impact? As Roemer and Borchardt (2015) describe, the concept involves two important ideas: the change a work influences and the strength of this effect. These effects can include, but are not limited to, advances in understanding and decision making, policy creation and change, economic development, and societal benefits. For example, rich documentation of an endangered language might lead to and support community and governmental revitalization efforts. However, the linkages between a specific scholarly product and its effects are rarely direct, there are disciplinary differences between how research is communicated and endorsed, and some outcomes take a very long time to manifest (Greenhalgh et al. 2016). This makes the assessment of research impact very labor intensive, even at a small scale, so researchers and decision makers often rely on data and metrics that are regarded as indicative of certain kinds of impact.

Many communities, particularly those outlined herein, have been interested in and have contributed to data-based methods for assessing research impact. Libraries and librarians have a long relationship with research evaluation. In 1927, Gross and Gross published an article in *Science* describing a method for counting and analyzing the citations among chemistry journals to guide library support for graduate level training. The journal impact factor (JIF), which will be discussed in more detail in section 2, is rooted in this history, as it was originally developed to guide decision making for journal indexing and library collection development. Similarly, as institutionalized support for research has grown, largely since the mid-twentieth century, governments, universities, and other organizations have sought to track and benchmark the progress and outcomes of their investments (Sugimoto & Larivière 2018). Why and how metrics are used by such evaluators will be discussed in section 4, but recent examples of this intense interest in impact evaluation include the creation and application of assessment frameworks, such as the Australian Research Council's Research Impact Principles and Framework (Australian Research Council 2019), intended to capture the complex routes by which knowledge is created, shared, and applied (Greenhalgh et al. 2016), and the development of new metrics, such as the Relative Citation Ratio (Hutchins et al. 2016).

The development of *scientometrics*, the quantitative study of scholarly literature, as a field is connected to and has influenced this history. The creation of the Science Citation Index (Garfield 1963) made it possible to access and use data about the citation relationships between publications at a scale allowing for quantitative investigation and measurement of the growth and impact of science. Most of the metrics used today for evaluation purposes, such as the h-index, an author-level, citation-based metric, are an output of such scientometric research (Sugimoto & Larivière 2018).

Finally, it is worth highlighting the roles and influence of individual researchers within this landscape. They are often the focus of impact questions with high-stakes consequences and can be both the objects of evaluation and consumers of metrics. As such, researchers are some of the most prominent advocates for improving the ways in which their work is assessed. The Declaration on Research Assessment (DORA), for example, was initiated at the 2012 Annual Meeting of the Society for Cell Biology and argues against evaluating the quality and impact of research based upon where it is published; DORA has since been signed by "more than sixteen thousand" individuals and organizations, including the Linguistic Society of America (San Francisco Declaration on Research Assessment [DORA] n.d.)

DORA and the ideas, concerns, and practices described within it reflect a changing scholarly communication system. How scholarship is created and shared, when and where it is discussed, and how it is endorsed is evolving. Most scholarly work is now published online, and technology changes have made it possible to share research products more immediately. Scholarly communication is also taking place in informal spaces, such as Twitter and research blogs, which can be tracked. Additionally, ideas about what should be considered valuable and citable research products have expanded to include such things as data sets, protocols, and software, along with an increasing interest in making these products more accessible and reusable. As Cronin and Sugimoto (2014:9) observe, "today the scholarly communication system is less linear, less rigid, and less opaque than before; both the process and end products are being transformed."

These developments have influenced the ways in which research impact is understood and evaluated. Data about research, particularly citation-based data, are increasingly used to administer science and scholarship, from hiring and promotion decisions to grant funding and university rankings (Aksnes, Langfeldt, & Wouters 2019). However, while the strength and validity of citation-based metrics are regularly examined and debated within the scientometric community, evaluation-based users of metrics are often unaware of an indicator's limitations, which can lead to misuse (Hicks et al. 2015). Several initiatives and resources have emerged to draw attention to and address this issue, such as the Leiden Manifesto (Hicks et al. 2015),

which describes best practices for guiding metrics-based research evaluation, and the Metrics Toolkit (https://www.metrics-toolkit.org/), which uses a standardized schema to provide evidence-based information about metrics, including appropriate and inappropriate use cases. The availability of data that trace online and informal attention to and engagement with research products, and discussions about the types of impact these data reflect, are also increasingly a part of the modern impact landscape. Many data sources for online engagement have emerged and been integrated within traditional publishing and indexing platforms. Finally, the call to treat research data and other kinds of scholarly products as first-class research products has grown alongside the availability of new data sources for tracking and quantifying their impact.

Research impact is a complicated concept that exists within a highly dynamic scientific and scholarly communication ecosystem, and although this volume specifically deals with data and data management, metrics for data are best understood as components of research impact writ large. Understanding and participating in what can seem like a constant cycle of impact evaluation can be overwhelming; this chapter is designed to introduce foundational concepts for the understanding of impact and metrics, then specify how to apply these concepts to data. In section 2, we address fundamental metrics concepts, including the use of metrics for personal career advancement and by evaluators. Following that, we describe the practices that apply and are unique to research data and describe how to make use of them during data collection, analysis, and sharing. Our aims are (1) to help individual researchers develop metrics and evaluation literacy to make strategic decisions about how to share and disseminate research data and other scholarly products and (2) to equip them to be proactive participants in the research evaluation process who can effectively advocate for the value of their work.

2   Foundational metrics concepts

Here, we provide brief descriptions for the terms used throughout the rest of this chapter.

Activities: The ways in which users (scholars or machines) can interact with a scholarly product.

Altmetrics: The metrics and qualitative data that are calculated or derived from ways in which people interact online with scholarly content. These are often considered complementary or supplementary to traditional, citation-based metrics.

Awareness: The degree to which scholars within a particular group know about a product. This is strongly connected to the visibility and discovery of specific products.

Citation-based metrics: The metrics derived from citations. They are influenced by the content selected for indexing.

Dissemination: The process of distributing a scholarly product to relevant audiences.

Impact: The way(s) in which a scholarly product (or body of work) has affected the world. Often, this happens on a longer time scale than evaluation processes.

Indicators: An indicator is a quantified way of measuring a concept (e.g., impact, quality). The usefulness of an indicator depends on its explicit linkage to a concept and sufficient evidence that it is a valid measure for the concept (Gringas 2016). Gringas also suggests that indicators of different concepts should not be combined into a single composite indicator.

Normalization: A process for modifying data that are measured on different scales to produce values that share a common scale. This is necessary for valid comparisons of scholarly products.

Outcomes: The consequences or changes in a target that directly result from a research intervention, program, or discovery.

Quality: This is a broad concept that is operationalized differently across fields of research and which includes different elements such as novelty, creativity, and integrity depending on the field of research and methods employed. Data quality is often assessed based on its utility for a specified purpose. Similarly, the utility of a metric is influenced by the data on which it is calculated. No publication metric is a direct measure for quality because the standards for determining quality vary by individual, organization, discipline, setting, and many other factors. Despite its flaws, bibliometrics scholars (e.g., Gringas 2016; Waltman 2018) agree that there is no substitute for expert judgment via peer review in evaluating the quality and integrity of individual scholarly products or an author's body of work.

Scholarly product: The object the metric describes or applies to (e.g., journal, article, author).

Usage: The ways in which scholars use scholarly products. This encompasses viewing abstracts, skimming articles to filter for relevant information, reading online to scan for new ideas, downloading to save for later reference or citation, finding related articles and resources, storing and organizing into citation management databases for long-term use, text and data mining, and more.

Prior to the widespread adoption of network technologies for disseminating scholarly publications, metrics centered on analyzing the connections contained within citation data that exist between documents, authors, and journals. Many of the metrics not based on citations are simple counts of the ways in which users engage with products in an online environment. These are commonly referred to as altmetrics (short for "alternative metrics"). For example, in our current networked scholarly environment, a user can find, access, download, and export data about an item to their citation management tool. Each of these activities leaves a digital trace. Thus, we can see how many people on Twitter or how many media sources have mentioned the findings reported in a particular article. Altmetrics providers such as Altmetric and PlumX harvest and gather these digital traces for users to access and use. Other metrics are derived from more complex formulas; these include the JIF, the Eigenfactor Article Influence Score, and Field Normalized Citation Impact metrics. No single metric can reflect the full impact of an article, data set, or other product. In general, metrics are indirect indicators of impact, rather than direct measures.

A variety of terms are used to describe metrics about research. The term *publication metrics* is typically used to describe metrics for journal articles, books, and book chapters. As the processes for conducting research and disseminating the resulting knowledge have shifted online, it has become possible to capture interactions with a broader range of scholarly products. The field of *bibliometrics* uses statistical and network analysis techniques to analyze data related to scholarly products. This body of research often describes activities related to or relationships between three core objects—the scholarly product, authors, and the venue for dissemination, such as a journal or press. Many publication metrics are constructed from a few key attributes—citation, authorship, and institutional affiliation—and the relationships between them. *Altmetrics* is a more recent term coined in 2011 to describe a broader range of metrics derived from engagement with scholarly resources online and via social media (Priem et al. 2010). Altmetrics are often counts of specific activities that take place online, including views, downloads, endorsements (e.g., shares or likes, which vary by platform), and the use/reuse that takes place outside of the publication ecosystem described by journal indexes and citation databases. They are commonly seen as a supplement to citation metrics (i.e., metrics derived from citation data). The altmetrics manifesto (Priem et al. 2010) reflects frustration with the limitations of citation-based metrics and how they are used, particularly the JIF. Altmetrics are often siloed by social media platform; there is no metric, citation-based or altmetric, that is a reliable indicator of usage or engagement across all platforms. *Article-level metrics* are distinct from altmetrics; this term is used to describe both citation metrics and altmetrics about a particular article, as opposed to metrics about journals, such as the JIF. Finally, scientometrics is the "study of science, technology, and innovation from a quantitative perspective" (Leydesdorff & Milojević 2012), whereas *research impact metrics* is an umbrella term used to describe a range of metrics that speak to the impact of research. The rest of this chapter focuses on metrics about scholarly outputs or products, rather than metrics related to the inputs and outcomes of research.

Metrics are indicators, that is, indirect measures, rather than direct measures of impact. The many metrics just described exist because the data are available, not because they were designed to measure a particular concept for evaluation purposes (e.g., quality, impact, reputation). The strength of the relationship between a bibliometric indicator and the corresponding concept is crucial to the validity of the indicator (Sugimoto & Larivière 2018). Put simply, for an indicator to be valid, it must measure the concept that people expect it to and do it reasonably well. In the case of bibliometrics and altmetrics, the validity of the metric is often unclear to users, partly due to disciplinary differences in scholarship, publication, and the ways in which quality and impact are understood and valued. There is often a mismatch between the criteria that evaluators use (e.g., quality) and the metrics (e.g., citations). For instance, some administrators equate high impact research with publishing in a journal that has a comparatively high JIF. The JIF is "a measure reflecting the annual average (mean) number of citations to recent

articles published in that journal" (Metrics Toolkit Editorial Board 2019). The JIF is problematic for a number of reasons. First, it is a measure about a journal as a whole, rather than individual articles. Second, it is not a valid predictor for individual articles because the distribution of citations is highly skewed. Thus, the mean of a highly skewed range of citation counts is not representative of most of the individual citation counts. Most of the articles published in a journal will not receive the number of citations suggested by the JIF. In some cases, like that of the journal *Nature*, 75% of articles receive fewer citations than the average citations reflected in the JIF (Larivière et al. 2016).

Citation count is a common example of a metric that appears to be simple and consistent on the surface, but which has a tremendous amount of hidden variance. There is variance in meaning; scholars cite for many reasons—to acknowledge awareness of existing literature, to contradict or argue with previous findings, to support their own methodological decisions, and more (Bornmann & Daniel 2008). Neither the fact that article A cited article B nor the count of citations for article B inherently conveys meaning about the quality of article B, nor the quality of the research that led to its creation. Cultural norms and practices for when to cite also differ by discipline or research field. There is also substantial variance in the data available for different disciplines, publication languages, and regions of the world (Sugimoto & Larivière 2018). However, citations and derived metrics can be construed as an indicator for impact on a scholarly audience, given the appropriate context (Bornmann & Daniel 2008). Context is a tremendously important factor to consider when interpreting and using metrics (Paul-Hus et al. 2017). Over the last 50 years, we have learned much about the value of publication metrics as well as the dangers in using them to evaluate individual scholars. It is important to keep those lessons in mind as we construct and implement metrics about data sets so that we do not recreate the same biases, limitations, and challenges.

3 Understanding metrics for career advancement

Scholars are the subject of constant evaluation for hiring, publishing, funding proposal reviews, annual reviews, promotion and tenure, and recognition through awards. As candidates for promotion and tenure, scholars are expected to tell a compelling story about how their scholarship has affected the world, in addition to meeting disciplinary and institutional standards for quality, productivity, and often funding. The ways in which institutions and the schools and departments contained within them operationalize concepts such as quality, prestige, and impact vary widely. Early career scholars are expected to navigate these systems and construct their research programs to meet these expectations. In some cases, the expectations of institutions diverge from those of peer institutions; thus, scholars face the additional challenge of building a research program that is successful within their current institution and still viewed favorably by those at other institutions. Evaluation of scholars for hiring, promotion and tenure, and awards is often centered on notions of prestige, reputation, excellence, and impact. Often, these concepts are not sufficiently operationalized for the evaluation task, leaving evaluators to interpret and apply them within the limits of their own knowledge, expertise, and available time. At best, this results in inconsistent evaluation; at worst, it significantly disadvantages scholars whose work does not fit the expectations of the evaluators.

A scholar's ability to build reputation and gain access to resources is crucial to their career success. Successful scholars are effective at crafting a compelling narrative about the value of their work in grant proposals, reports, publications, and their dossier. Though these narratives may incorporate concepts such as "high-impact" and "prestige" that are used and valued by their institutions and disciplines, they frequently do so in very vague terms and without evidence to support the claims. There is a significant disconnect between the rhetoric used by both scholars and evaluators in describing scholarship and the evidence available to support those claims.

Uncertainty and the challenges of evaluating scholars as just described have contributed to an overreliance on easily available publication metrics, such as the JIF. Though not intentional, metrics have increasingly been used as proxies for values such as productivity, impact, and quality. This is problematic for two reasons. First, many metrics can be gamed; over time, people change their behavior to improve their performance according to the metric. The behaviors that result in metric improvement may compete with and win out over behaviors leading to better quality research and more reproducible results. Second, many metrics are not fit to be used in

evaluating scholars. A prime example is the JIF, which was initially designed to improve information retrieval and support collection development activities by librarians before the availability of electronic databases and the Internet. The JIF was not designed to be used in the evaluation of individual scholars, yet it frequently is.

3.1 Best practices for increasing the visibility of your scholarship

As the publishing ecosystem has changed, strategies for disseminating and discovering scholarship have also changed. These practices can enhance or constrain the metrics available for particular scholarly products. In the last decade, the following recommended practices have emerged to maximize dissemination of scholarly products and enable availability of publication metrics that support career advancement.

3.1.1 Own your scholarly profile First, scholars must create an online profile, or digital identity, that is independent from their institution. Institutional websites frequently change, and faculty may not be able to easily update or customize those sites. The core platforms recommended are ORCID (Open Researcher and Contributor ID; https://orcid.org/) and Google Scholar (https://scholar.google.com/). A structured profile, such as ORCID, can be exported to streamline and export bibliographic data for biosketches and other proposal and reporting requirements. Scholars who need a more robust digital identity or who engage with public and community audiences may want to consider creating a hosted site that helps their audiences understand and find their work. Core elements for these digital profiles are educational background, scholarly products, awards, and digital projects. It is crucial to provide clear and accessible information about scholarship that is geared toward a public audience. A digital profile can also increase the visibility of community-based service-learning projects or community-based participatory research. Links to scholarly profiles should be included in e-mail signatures, social media accounts, and other professional and institutional web pages to maximize discovery and visibility.

3.1.2 Share freely Once scholars have a digital profile that reflects their scholarly identity, the next step is to make the scholarly products as openly available as possible. Such products include journal articles as well as presentations, posters, book chapters, books, digital projects, data sets, and code or models, among other scholarly products. Because readers prefer one-click access, publications that are available openly are discovered and retrieved first. Greater access often leads to more citations (Piwowar et al. 2018; Colavizza et al. 2019; SPARC Europe, n.d.). Sharing freely does not necessarily require scholars to change their publishing practices; instead, they can utilize the expertise of librarians to identify which products can be shared openly and to deposit them into an appropriate repository or platform. The benefits offered by many institutional repositories include rich metadata and digital object identifier (DOI) registration to increase discovery, as well as a commitment to maintaining long-term access through archiving or preservation strategies. These services are typically available to affiliated scholars at no cost, as they are often subsidized by the library or research offices within the institution. The benefits of increased visibility and access take time to accrue, so creating a scholarly profile and sharing scholarly products freely are best completed as early as possible in a scholar's career trajectory.

3.1.3 Gather evidence

When preparing a dossier for promotion and/or tenure, a funding proposal, or an award package, scholars need evidence of the impact and influence of their work (Alperin et al., chapter 13, this volume). For some scholars, these points of need may be the first time they think about research impact metrics. However, the availability of rich evidence in support of their case may depend on proactive planning and strategies for disseminating their scholarship. While a substantial proportion of the Western, English-language literature in the physical and biomedical sciences is represented in citation indexes, this is less true for the social science, humanities, and interdisciplinary literature. Scholars should aim to gather a range of publication metrics (e.g., citation counts, normalized citation metrics, JIF) as well as altmetrics (e.g., Tweets, blog mentions, policy mentions) as potential evidence. With altmetrics, it is often the case that the stories behind the numbers are more compelling than the numbers themselves. When possible, normalized metrics are recommended. Field normalized metrics are a "ratio between the actual citations received by a publication and the average number of citations received by all other similar publications" (Metrics Toolkit Editorial Board 2018). Field normalized metrics in particular enable easy comparison by evaluators because they are standardized according to

the time of publication and research field. By intentionally disseminating their work, scholars can maximize its visibility, access, and use to generate evidence of attention, use, and impact.

3.1.4 Tell your story

Metrics should not drive the story. Scholars should develop their story first and use relevant metrics to support their case. Using a mix of qualitative and quantitative evidence to support the case is more effective than relying on a single type or source of evidence. Few candidates are well served by limiting the metrics used to those available in platforms such as Dimensions, Journal Citation Reports, Scopus, and Web of Science. In the case of tenure and promotion, the short pretenure time frame combined with the time it takes for citations to accrue means that it is rare for quantitative publication metrics alone to make the case. Selected metrics should describe the scholar's work (e.g., article level metrics, altmetrics), rather than the merits of the publisher or journal. Ultimately, the scholar's case and the evaluation of it are about more than the metrics. It is up to the scholar to tell a compelling story and demonstrate that they have met the requirements. Likewise, evaluation consists of more than comparing numbers. The expertise of evaluators is a crucial component of research evaluation. Neither the quality of scholarship nor its impact can be summed up in a metric.

4 How metrics are used by evaluators

Within academic and research institutions, the use of research impact metrics has increased for both hiring and promotion decisions. Their use in promotion and tenure decisions tends to be more formalized and documented than in other processes such as hiring, perhaps because the policies and processes for promotion and tenure are more formalized. However, these metrics do not hold absolute meaning. Rather, their meaning is socially constructed within the context of institutional practices (Leydesdorff, Wouters, & Bornmann 2016). Faculty reviewers serving on promotion and tenure committees are tasked with evaluating their peers according to the standards and processes of their institution. They bring to this work implicit assumptions and expectations about the meaning of prestige, high-quality scholarship, and impact. These assumptions often place higher value on products such as journal articles, which are vetted through the trusted (but imperfect) process of peer review, with correspondingly less value placed on presentations, posters, data, software, and such. (Alperin et al., chapter 13, this volume). There are also disciplinary or professional beliefs about the relative value of specific journals, conferences, and presses. These beliefs often favor historically significant or long-lived organizations but are not necessarily informed by evidence or a clear understanding of the scholarly ecosystem in which they are created, disseminated, assessed, valued, and consumed. Such implicit expectations and beliefs become problematic when they conflict with the disciplinary culture of the scholar under review.

Reviewers use research metrics for a variety of reasons. Anecdotally, reliance on metrics appears to be heaviest when time constraints are a factor and reviewers are unfamiliar with the field or discipline of the scholar under review. At large research institutions where committees review a hundred or more promotion cases per year, it is not possible for reviewers to read a sample of the publications produced by a candidate during the review period; neither are they experts in each candidate's field. Scholarly norms such as authorship conventions and the specific products that are valued can vary widely, even within disciplines. Additionally, reviewers are generally not aware of the limitations of and biases in the data used to generate citation metrics and altmetrics (Leydesdorff, Wouters, & Bornmann 2016). Despite insufficient training and support for this work, reviewers must do the best they can with limited information and resources. Changing the metrics used and how they are understood requires confronting complex and implicit beliefs held by each scholar. Beliefs about the value of scholarly products, ways of disseminating those products, and the metrics that serve as indicators of their visibility, use, and impact on the world influence evaluation decisions. Change will also require stakeholders to acknowledge the value systems enforced by their institutional policies and procedures for hiring and promotion. Finally, reviewers must recognize their own knowledge gaps and be willing to seek out expertise and support.

5   How data are shared and used

Having covered the foundational concepts and uses of metrics, we turn now to metrics for data. Importantly, data metrics highly depend on how they are shared. Dissemination of data occurs along a spectrum, ranging from the informal, such as posting data on a lab website, to the formal, such as peer-reviewed data papers. Callaghan et al. (2012) describe two models of data sharing: *publication* and *Publication*. The former refers to when data are shared without a formal commitment to discovery, reuse, or long-term availability. An example in linguistics is the Corpus of Regional African American Language (CORAAL) project website. In contrast, *Published* data are stored, described, and organized in a way that enables potential users to find, access, understand, use, and cite them. Mature examples of this model include subject repositories such as the Inter-university Consortium for Political and Social Research or The Tromsø Repository of Language and Linguistics (TROLLing) archive. An emerging model is that of data journals such as *Scientific Data* and *GigaScience*, in which data are described with rich metadata, associated with a persistent ID, usually a DOI, and supported by an organizational commitment to maintain access for some period of time into the future. Some journals in linguistics have sections devoted to data sharing, such as *Phonological Data and Analysis* and *Language Documentation and Conservation,* though these may not necessarily publish data sets on their own.

Many options for sharing data produce high value for both data producers and consumers (see Callaghan's model in Van den Eynden 2011), including depositing data to specialized data centers or open-access repositories. Sharing data on a research group website is a low-barrier option for the research group, but generally does not support effective discovery and reuse. Other researchers are not likely to find the data, unless they know that the group has this practice of sharing. Thus, neither the producer nor the consumer gains much value from data shared in this way. Similarly, decisions about sharing have substantial impact on the availability of metrics for the data set. The available metrics often depend on a number of factors related to the platform selected for sharing. Does the platform use server logs or web analytics tools to capture usage? Does the platform provide rich descriptive information that can be harvested by search engines such as Google Dataset Search or scholarly indexes such as DataCite (e.g., structured metadata)? Is a persistent identifier provided to ensure access, even as platforms and web links change? Is there a commitment to data retention? Is there a commitment to data preservation? Can a user access the usage statistics for their data sets?

Though many platforms are beginning to address some of these issues, most are focused on easily implemented solutions that provide immediate value without addressing long-term access and preservation. One such example is the proliferation of DOIs for data sets. While they are crucial in our current ecosystem for discovery and citation, they do not ensure that the data they point to will be available in ten years, even if the DOI and its associated metadata are maintained. For a more in-depth discussion of archiving linguistic data, see chapter 7 (Andreassen, this volume).

6 Metrics about data sets

6.1 Data citation

Citation has a pivotal role in the scholarly ecosystem, from both sociocultural and technical perspectives. In large part, citation has value because scholars believe that it has value. It represents our notion of credit and attribution within the research community (Kurtz & Bollen 2010). Like the citation of publications, citation of data serves a variety of needs. Data citation is a keystone practice for data sharing, discovery, access, and rewarding data creators for their work (Altman et al. 2015). The recent position paper by Berez-Kroeker et al. (2018) emphasizes the importance of data citation in supporting reproducible research in the field of linguistics. Developing and implementing standards for data citation is one way to address the lack of rewards for the important, but largely invisible, preprocessing work of preparing data for use. Citations are a familiar incentive for data creators to share their data because they are already embedded in hiring practices, career advancement, and awards and funding processes. A wide range of scholarly infrastructure and cultural norms influence data citation practices due to the many functions they have. Conzett and De Smedt (chapter 11, this volume) describe more fully the practices and principles of data citation. Here, we will focus on the role of data citation in attribution, discovery, and access as it shapes the availability of metrics.

Systematic data citation is a key element of the social and scholarly infrastructure that fosters trust in research (Funk et al. 2019). The linkages created between publications and data sets, particularly by machine actionable citation metadata and DOIs, are critical for enabling verification and validation of research conclusions (CODATA-ICSTI Task Group on Data Citation Standards and Practices

2013). Effective reuse depends on the data sets being usable digital objects (Borgman 2012). However, this additional value comes at a relatively high cost to the original research team and their institution; for data to be reused, the data must be managed, described, disseminated, and preserved. Researchers must choose how to invest their limited time in activities that are rewarded, such as data collection, analysis, and writing for publication, or in activities that are not rewarded, such as preparation of shareable data. For those who do not consider this work a core component of their research workflows, providing credit and recognition in the form of citations to data sets may be a motivating reward. Such rewards are crucial for changing the overall culture of research to one that values quality over quantity, reproducibility over novelty.

6.1.1 Discovery Though discovery is enhanced through data sharing and citation, the act of sharing data or making it available does not necessarily make it visible and discoverable to potential users. Borgman (2012) describes the discoverability of data as the ability to "determine the existence of a set of data objects with specified attributes." Such attributes commonly include data creator, date of creation, method of creation, description of contents, and its representation. One challenge is that those attributes deemed relevant and the terminology used to describe them differs across research disciplines and communities. Maximizing the visibility and discovery of data requires that they be well described in a way that both machines and humans can understand; data must also be identified uniquely and must be persistent and available in usable open formats (CODATA-ICSTI Task Group on Data Citation Standards and Practices 2013). By taking into account some of the important aspects of data citation outlined here and in Conzett and De Smedt (chapter 11, this volume), discovery may be enhanced and the relevant metrics that can show impact will be easier to collect and more meaningful.

The following examples illustrate how discovery can be affected by decisions related to description, registration, and citation.

Example 1: CORAAL

Citation: Kendall, Tyler, and Charlie Farrington. 2018. *The Corpus of Regional African American Language*. Version 2018.10.06. Eugene, OR: The Online Resources for African American Language Project. http://oraal.uoregon.edu/coraal.

Though this data set does not have a persistent identifier, the name is relatively unique. Thus, we can conduct a quick test of discovery. We performed phrase searching of "Corpus of Regional African American Language" in Dimensions, Google Scholar, Scopus, and Web of Science, as well as the subject database ProQuest Linguistics and Language Behavior Abstracts (LLBA). Our search results are in table 12.1.

The relevance of the results varies. In the subject database (LLBA), the phrase was found in nine items. Because the LLBA database does not include reference metadata, it is not possible to determine whether any of the items cite the CORAAL data set. In Dimensions, the results include several items that contain the phrase within the article title or in the references, many of which are not the data set itself. Google Scholar retrieved thirty-three items, of which twenty-four include the phrase in the title or full text. Both citation databases (Scopus and Web of Science) retrieved fewer results but with higher precision than Google Scholar. Without examining the articles, it is difficult to determine for all searches whether the retrieved items contain analyses based on the data set or simply discuss it. In this case, the creation of a DOI would uniquely identify the data set separately from articles citing or mentioning it. While the searches are not a perfect way to identify citation counts for a data source, it does lead us to those publications that might. Unfortunately, at least one article in the journal *American Speech* does analyze data from the CORAAL data set but does not cite it in the references. This may be an important use of the data set that is missed with some citation counting practices.

Example 2: TROLLing data set "Replication Data for: Seeing from without, seeing from within: Aspectual differences between Spanish and Russian"

Table 12.1

Results of phrase searches for "Corpus of Regional African American Language"

Source	Items retrieved
Dimensions	14
Google Scholar	33
ProQuest Linguistics and Language Behavior Abstracts (LLBA)	9
Scopus	11
phrase search References	7
phrase search TITLE-ABS-KEY-AUTH	
Web of Science	5

Citation: Janda, Laura A., and Antonio Fábregas. 2018. Replication Data for: Seeing from without, seeing from within: aspectual differences between Spanish and Russian. https://doi.org/10.18710/WR4Y0Q. DataverseNO, V1, UNF:6:v5Lkz2Vq1VjqBSIUTbLvrA== [fileUNF].

In example 2, we see that the repository TROLLing from DataverseNO network (Norway) has implemented a number of best practices that enable the creation of usage and citation metrics. The record contains rich metadata about the source, contact information, version information, and temporal coverage of the data, including terminology specific to the linguistic research community. A suggested citation is visible at the top of the record, which also includes a Universal Numerical Fingerprint (UNF) identifier. The UNF, similar to a checksum, allows users to confirm that the data set downloaded is the data set that was deposited. Users can also see the number of downloads for all files in this record.

The availability of features such as those described in the previous paragraph depends on the repository system selected and the decisions of those who manage it. There are many repository systems with different emphases on functionality (e.g., preservation, sharing), content (e.g., preprints, publications, research data), and users. Each system has limitations and strengths that can affect how discoverable data are by search engines and scholarly indexes. Generally, scholars need to be aware of the key features for discovery and ask questions of the repository managers about these features; these discovery features may help a scholar decide how to best increase the impact of their data and how to measure that impact. For more detail, see section 7.

6.1.2 Citation metrics Data citation as a practice is not new. The social sciences have had some tradition of data citation, at least since Dodd (1979) wrote about citing data from the General Social Survey. Developments in infrastructure and changing expectations for the dissemination of research products have created an environment in which data citation is possible and the benefits are clearer than ever before, as digital infrastructure makes counting citations and presenting metrics easier. So far, most data citation efforts are focused on prospective data citation, rather than looking backward to improve the record of data citations for prior publications (Mayernik et al. 2017). As such, sufficiently comprehensive studies of data citations are not yet possible, which limits the ability to put data metrics into context and develop normalized scores, for now. However, as data citation practices improve, so will the study of metrics examining data citation as a method of demonstrating impact.

Citation metrics for data are currently limited to raw citation counts; field normalized citation metrics are not yet possible for data sets. As with citations to publications, the context of the citation can be compelling, but it is not fully represented by metrics. The current scholarly communication infrastructure can capture the reuse of data in the form of citations when the references are contained in indexed publications such as journal articles, books, and book chapters, or in items shared via institutional or domain repositories. A central challenge for the visibility of data citations is the lack of a universal way to exchange information about links between publications and data. The availability of metadata about the linkages between publications and data varies widely; there is little exchange of usage data between systems at this point. The Scholix initiative seeks to improve the exchange of data citations between global aggregators such as DataCite, Crossref, and OpenAIRE to ensure that that metrics are accurate. Thus far, the initiative has developed an information model and a metadata schema for links. Scholix is developing exchange protocols and working to reach consensus across the community of publishers, data centers, and service providers to improve the exchange of links between data and literature. However, many other forms of knowledge sharing are not captured, including course syllabi, blogs, community and cultural heritage efforts, and projects that do not have a web presence. An ecosystem that excludes many of the ways in which data are reused limits our perspective on impact and tends to reward and reinforce the uses that we can easily measure, rather than what we value most.

> Example 3: TROLLing data set "Replication Data for: Automatic parsing as an efficient pre-annotation tool for historical texts"

> Citation: Eckhoff, Hanne, and Aleksandrs Berdicevskis. 2016. Replication Data for: Automatic parsing as an efficient pre-annotation tool for historical texts. https://doi.org/10.18710/FERT42 . DataverseNO, V1.

In example 3, we can see that the data set is related to a paper presented at the Workshop on Language Technology Resources and Tools for Digital Humanities. However, because the authors did not cite their own data in the references section of the paper and the proceedings are not indexed in any citation databases, the citation linkage is only visible on the TROLLing item record. Additionally, searching Google Scholar for the title retrieves the paper, rather than the data set. This potential confusion is one reason that some advocate for creating distinct titles for data sets and the publications based on them; this distinction would allow potential readers and data users to more easily find the item they are looking for, and for authors to more clearly understand who is citing their work and how.

From a scientometric perspective, citations between articles are an incomplete representation of the relationships between researchers (e.g., coauthorship) and research programs. Despite the importance of authorship in the discourse, no widely adopted metrics capture coauthorship contributions in a quantitative way; in part, this is due to the tremendous variety of authorship norms across disciplines and even journals. Some large research institutions deal with this issue by requiring authors to specify their contribution in percentages and getting confirmation of that effort from coauthors. There is a body of literature in scientometrics that describes coauthorship patterns and trends, but not for the purposes of evaluating individuals.

6.2 Altmetrics for data

The acceptance and use of altmetrics for data are highly localized to a few communities. A survey by Kratz and Strasser (2015) found that respondents valued citation and download counts over altmetrics and search rank. Indeed, the available metrics for data are thin and inconsistent, though expanding rapidly. Sharing data, whether via open or controlled mechanisms, is a prerequisite for data metrics to accrue (Costas et al. 2013). The altmetrics data are not yet reliable and consistent enough for scholars to trust that altmetrics for data sets can provide a reasonably accurate representation of their impact. Despite the widespread implementation of Altmetric and PlumX products by publishers, altmetrics are highly decentralized and generally dependent on the assignment of persistent identifiers such as DOIs to products.

The usage data, which the Kratz and Strasser (2015) survey indicates are of more interest to their respondents, are not typically captured by altmetrics vendors. These data, typically consisting of views, downloads, and user characteristics such as location, are siloed by the platforms on which they are created, requiring users to go to great lengths to gather and make sense of them. Even when such data are aggregated, it is currently impossible to compare or normalize them. In spite of these issues, usage metrics for data hold great potential for demonstrating engagement and use outside the scholarly environment. This potential depends on the development and adoption of common standards, data exchange or aggregation, and trust in the providers.

Key challenges for the adoption of altmetrics for data include (1) a lack of shared definitions and standards for gathering and reporting the data and (2) the decentralized storage of the data. In 2013–2016, the National Information Standards Organization led an initiative that explored a range of metrics beyond citations, including usage-based metrics, social media activities, and network behavioral analysis. The work resulted in a report, "Outputs of the NISO Alternative Assessment Metrics Project" (National Information Standards Organization 2016). The report identifies three themes or functions of metrics—showcase achievements, research evaluation, and discovery—and describes eight use cases that inform the recommendations. The report offers a helpful and relatively accessible overview and key recommendations related to data metrics.

7   A call to action

This chapter has described the complicated cultural and technical ecosystem in which data sharing and the evaluation of data sets as a scholarly product take place. This ecosystem includes many stakeholders whose knowledge and actions influence not only the success of individual researchers, but also the value of their scholarship. Thus, in conclusion, we have outlined practices that scholars, evaluators, academic institutions, publishers, and data repository managers can implement to facilitate good data sharing and its rewards.

Best practices for scholars:

- Develop a proactive strategy for disseminating your work to the most important audiences and systematically gather both qualitative and anecdotal evidence of use and impact.

- Use a combination of quantitative and qualitative evidence to support claims made in your case/story; do not let bibliometric data drive your case.

- Be aware of the limitations of the metrics used in evaluating you and your work, including your data (see the Metrics Toolkit; http://metrics-toolkit.org/).

- Use normalized metrics, statistically adjusted for publication date and field, when they are available. Examples include the Field Normalized Citation Impact (Field Weighted Citation Impact from Elsevier Scopus, Field Citation Ratio from Dimensions, or the Relative Citation Ratio for National Institutes of Health–funded work).

- Include the source for all metrics used (e.g., Scopus, Web of Science, Dimensions).

- Ask the editors of journals in which you publish to adopt standards and practices that support data citation, including contributing "Cited-by" metadata to Crossref.

  - Talk to the publishing arm of your professional society, if one exists, to ask the same and ask that they contribute to the Initiative for Open Citations (https://i4oc.org/).

- Get involved with groups such as the Research Data Alliance (RDA) Working Groups. RDA Working Groups typically have smaller committees that deal with data citation and measurement issues. For example, under the umbrella of the Joint RDA/World Data System Publishing Data Interest Group (https://rd-alliance.org /groups/rdawds-publishing-data-ig.html), several working groups have produced recommendations and guidance for issues related to the links between publications and data as well as metrics for publications and data. Two current working groups—Data Usage Metrics WG and the Data Citation WG—are especially relevant to this conversation. The Data Usage Metrics WG works closely with the Make Data Count project. Within RDA are several discipline-specific interest groups, including one for linguistics (https://rd-alliance.org/rda -disciplines/rda-and-linguistics), which works to apply data citation recommendations specifically to the field.

Best practices for evaluators:

- Be transparent and explicit regarding the assumptions about how indicators are valued and used within your institution and field—write them down, share them, and discuss them so that they are remembered during evaluation processes.

- Consider the value of scholarly products beyond journal articles, books or book chapters, and conference presentations. Refer to disciplinary guidance on the evaluation of these products, such as the Linguistic Society of America's Statement on Evaluation of Language Documentation for Hiring, Tenure, and Promotion (https://www.linguisticsociety.org/resource/statement -evaluation-language-documentation-hiring-tenure -and-promotion).

- Use evidence such as metrics to inform expert decision making, rather than using metrics to rank or compare individual scholars across disciplines or institutions.

- Consider evidence within the context of the candidate's case for advancement and disciplinary norms for scholarship.

- If expected to evaluate dissemination venues, choose the relevant data, put metrics into context, and use normalized metrics when possible.

- Balance consideration of dissemination venues with item- or article-level metrics.

- Ask your institution to provide training on research metrics for evaluation.

- In your evaluation toolkit/resource package, include information or point to resources that describe the appropriate uses, limitations, and biases of commonly used metrics (see the Metrics Toolkit).

Best practices for academic institutions:

- Provide relevant training to evaluators and sufficient support for hiring and review processes.

- Foster discussions about how institutional values should show up in evaluation processes; use data gathered from those discussions to inform guidance.

- Recognize that the university has shared responsibility for the long-term storage of scholarly records so that they remain available and accessible (Smith 2012).

- Commit sufficient resources to upholding the responsibility for ensuring the infrastructure that affiliated scholars need to do their work is maintained and well-functioning (Smith 2012).

- Make specific and explicit statements about the value of scholarly work such as data collection and data

management in evaluation, hiring, and promotion guidance.

Best practices for journal editors and publishers:

- Assign unique identifiers, such as a DOI, to your articles.

- Adopt clear policies and standards regarding data availability for research published in your journal. If possible, require authors to share their data, either openly or via controlled mechanisms.

- Adopt policies and standards that promote data citation in alignment with the Austin Principles of Data Citation in Linguistics (https://site.uit.no/linguisticsdataci tation/austinprinciples/).

- Contribute Cited-by metadata to Crossref (https:// www.crossref.org/services/cited-by/).

Best practices for managers of data repositories/archives/centers:

- Make it easier for users to judge relevance, accessibility, and reusability from the search summary. Some ways to do this include highlighting search terms, making the data availability and license clear, enabling a preview of the data, and displaying usage statistics (Wu et al. 2019).

- Make individual metadata records both readable and analyzable (Wu et al. 2019).

- Enable sharing and downloading of bibliographic references to data sets (Wu et al. 2019).

- Identify and/or aggregate duplicate metadata records for the same object (Wu et al. 2019).

- Make metadata indexed and searchable in ways compatible with Schema.org (Wu et al. 2019).

References

Aksnes, Dag W., Liv Langfeldt, and Paul Wouters. 2019. Citations, citation indicators, and research quality: An overview of basic concepts and theories. *SAGE Open* 9 (1): 2158244019829575. https://doi.org/10.1177/2158244019829575.

Altman, Micah, Christine Borgman, Mercè Crosas, and Maryann Martone. 2015. An introduction to the joint principles for data citation. *Bulletin of the Association for Information Science and Technology* 41 (3): 43–45. https://scholar.harvard.edu /mercecrosas/publications/introduction-joint-principles-data -citation.

Australian Research Council. 2019. Research impact principles and framework. *Australian Research Council.* March 27, 2019.

https://www.arc.gov.au/policies-strategies/strategy/research-impact-principles-framework.

Berez-Kroeker, Andrea L., Lauren Gawne, Susan Smythe Kung, Barbara F. Kelly, Tyler Heston, Gary Holton, Peter Pulsifer, et al. 2018. Reproducible research in linguistics: A position statement on data citation and attribution in our field. *Linguistics* 56 (1): 1–18. https://doi.org/10.1515/ling-2017-0032.

Borgman, Christine L. 2012. Why are the attribution and citation of scientific data important? In *Report from Developing Data Attribution and Citation Practices and Standards: An International Symposium and Workshop. National Academy of Sciences' Board on Research Data and Information*, ed. P. F. Uhlir, 1–8. Washington, DC: The National Academies Press. https://escholarship.org/uc/item/65b51130.

Bornmann, Lutz, and Hans-Dieter Daniel. 2008. What do citation counts measure? A review of studies on citing behavior. *Journal of Documentation* 64 (1): 45–80. https://doi.org/10.1108/00220410810844150.

Callaghan, Sarah. 2012. Data citation in the earth and physical sciences. In *For Attribution—Developing Data Attribution and Citation Practices and Standards: Summary of an International Workshop*, 49–54. Washington, DC: The National Academies Press. https://doi.org/10.17226/13564.

CODATA-ICSTI Task Group on Data Citation Standards and Practices. 2013. Out of cite, out of mind: The current state of practice, policy, and technology for the citation of data. *Data Science Journal* 12:CIDCR1–75. https://doi.org/10.2481/dsj.OSOM13-043.

Colavizza, Giovanni, Iain Hrynaszkiewicz, Isla Staden, Kirstie Whitaker, and Barbara McGillivray. 2019. The citation advantage of linking publications to research data, version 1. *ArXiv: 1907.02565 [cs.DL]*, July. http://arxiv.org/abs/1907.02565.

Costas, R., I. Meijer, Z. Zahedi, and P. F. Wouters. 2013. The value of research data: Metrics for data sets from a cultural and technical point of view. A Knowledge Exchange report. http://hdl.handle.net/1887/23586.

Cronin, Blaise, and Cassidy R Sugimoto. 2014. *Beyond Bibliometrics: Harnessing Multidimensional Indicators of Scholarly Impact*. Cambridge: MIT Press.

Dodd, Sue A. 1979. Bibliographic references for numeric social science data files: Suggested guidelines. *Journal of the American Society for Information Science* 30 (2): 77–82. https://doi.org/10.1002/asi.4630300203.

Funk, Cary, Meg Hefferon, Brian Kennedy, and Courtney Johnson. 2019. Trust and mistrust in Americans' views of scientific experts. *Pew Research Center*. August 2, 2019. https://www.pewresearch.org/science/2019/08/02/trust-and-mistrust-in-americans-views-of-scientific-experts/.

Garfield, Eugene. 1963. Science Citation Index. http://garfield.library.upenn.edu/papers/80.pdf.

Greenhalgh, Trisha, James Raftery, Steve Hanney, and Matthew Glover. 2016. Research impact: A narrative review. *BMC Medicine* 14 (1): 1–16. https://doi.org/10.1186/s12916-016-0620-8.

Gringas, Yves. 2016. *Bibliometrics and Research Evaluation: Uses and Abuses*. History and Foundations of Information Science. Cambridge: MIT Press. https://mitpress.mit.edu/books/bibliometrics-and-research-evaluation.

Gross, P. L. K., and E. M. Gross. 1927. College libraries and chemical education. *Science* 66 (1713): 385–389. https://doi.org/10.1126/science.66.1713.385.

Hicks, Diana, Paul Wouters, Ludo Waltman, Sarah de Rijcke, and Ismael Rafols. 2015. Bibliometrics: The Leiden manifesto for research metrics. *Nature News* 520 (7548): 429. https://doi.org/10.1038/520429a.

Hutchins, B. Ian, Xin Yuan, James M. Anderson, and George M. Santangelo. 2016. Relative citation ratio (RCR): A new metric that uses citation rates to measure influence at the article level. *PLOS Biology* 14 (9): e1002541. https://doi.org/10.1371/journal.pbio.1002541.

Kratz, John Ernest, and Carly Strasser. 2015. Researcher perspectives on publication and peer review of data. *PLOS One* 10 (2): e0117619. https://doi.org/10.1371/journal.pone.0117619.

Kurtz, Michael J., and Johan Bollen. 2010. Usage bibliometrics. *Annual Review of Information Science and Technology* 44 (1): 1–64. https://doi.org/10.1002/aris.2010.1440440108.

Larivière, Vincent, Véronique Kiermer, Catriona J. MacCallum, Marcia McNutt, Mark Patterson, Bernd Pulverer, Sowmya Swaminathan, Stuart Taylor, and Stephen Curry. 2016. A simple proposal for the publication of journal citation distributions. *BioRxiv* (September). https://doi.org/10.1101/062109.

Leydesdorff, Loet, and Staša Milojević. 2012. Scientometrics, version 1. *ArXiv:1208.4566 [cs.DL]*, August. http://arxiv.org/abs/1208.4566.

Leydesdorff, Loet, Paul Wouters, and Lutz Bornmann. 2016. Professional and citizen bibliometrics: Complementarities and ambivalences in the development and use of indicators—a state-of-the-art report. *Scientometrics* 109 (3): 2129–2150. https://doi.org/10.1007/s11192-016-2150-8.

Mayernik, Matthew S., David L. Hart, Keith E. Maull, and Nicholas M. Weber. 2017. Assessing and tracing the outcomes and impact of research infrastructures. *Journal of the Association for Information Science and Technology* 68 (6): 1341–1359. https://doi.org/10.1002/asi.23721.

Metrics Toolkit Editorial Board. 2018. Field Normalized Citation Impact. *Metrics Toolkit*. https://www.metrics-toolkit.org/field-normalized-citation-impact/.

Metrics Toolkit Editorial Board. 2019. Journal Impact Factor. *Metrics Toolkit*. https://www.metrics-toolkit.org/journal-impact-factor/.

National Information Standards Organization. 2016. Outputs of the NISO Alternative Assessment Metrics Project. *National Information Standards Organization.* https://www.niso.org/publications/rp-25-2016-altmetrics.

Paul-Hus, Adèle, Nadine Desrochers, Sarah de Rijcke, and Alexander D. Rushforth. 2017. The reward system of science. *Aslib Journal of Information Management* 69 (5): 478–485. https://doi.org/10.1108/AJIM-07-2017-0168.

Piwowar, Heather, Jason Priem, Vincent Larivière, Juan Pablo Alperin, Lisa Matthias, Bree Norlander, Ashley Farley, Jevin West, and Stefanie Haustein. 2018. The state of OA: A large-scale analysis of the prevalence and impact of open access articles. *PeerJ* 6 (February): e4375. https://doi.org/10.7717/peerj.4375.

Priem, Jason, D. Taborelli, P. Groth, and Cameron Neylon. 2010. Altmetrics: A manifesto. October 26, 2010. *Altmetrics.* http://altmetrics.org/manifesto/.

Roemer, Robin Chin, and Rachel Borchardt. 2015. *Meaningful Metrics: A 21st Century Librarian's Guide to Bibliometrics, Altmetrics, and Research Impact.* Chicago: The Association of College and Research Libraries, a division of the American Library Association.

San Francisco Declaration on Research Assessment (DORA). n.d. *DORA.* https://sfdora.org/. Accessed August 12, 2019.

SCHOLIX. n.d. SCHOLIX: A Framework for Scholarly Link eXchange. http://www.scholix.org/. Accessed December 3, 2019.

Smith, Mackenzie. 2012. Institutional perspective on credit systems for research data. In *For Attribution—Developing Data Attribution and Citation Practices and Standards: Summary of an International Workshop*, ed. National Research Council. Washington, DC: National Academies Press. http://www.nap.edu/catalog/13564.

SPARC Europe. n.d. Open Access Citation Advantage (OACA) list. https://sparceurope.org/what-we-do/open-access/sparc-europe-open-access-resources/open-access-citation-advantage-service-oaca/oaca-list/. Accessed August 3, 2019.

Sugimoto, Cassidy R., and Vincent Larivière. 2018. *Measuring Research: What Everyone Needs to Know.* New York: Oxford University Press.

Van den Eynden, Veerle. 2011. *Managing and Sharing Data: Best Practice for Researchers.* Colchester: UK Data Archive.

Waltman, Ludo. 2018. Responsible metrics: One size doesn't fit all. Slides presented at the 23rd International Conference on Science and Technology, Leiden, the Netherlands. https://www.slideshare.net/LudoWaltman/responsible-metrics-one-size-doesnt-fit-all.

Wu, Mingfang, Fotis Psomopoulos, Siri Jodha Khalsa, and Anita de Waard. 2019. Data discovery paradigms: User requirements and recommendations for data repositories. *Data Science Journal* 18 (1): 3. https://doi.org/10.5334/dsj-2019-003.

13 The Value of Data and Other Non-traditional Scholarly Outputs in Academic Review, Promotion, and Tenure in Canada and the United States

Juan Pablo Alperin, Lesley A. Schimanski, Michelle La, Meredith T. Niles, and Erin C. McKiernan

1 Introduction

Conducting a research program is becoming an increasingly complex enterprise for many academic faculty. In many fields, large volumes of research data are collected, and solutions must be found not only for interpretation and analysis, but also for aspects of data management such as organization, storage, sharing, transfer, and security, as well as management of software, hardware, and/or cloud services (Marx 2013). This can be the case not only in fields in which it might be expected (particle physics, genomics) (Marx 2013) but also in medicine (e.g., Margolis et al. 2014) and in fields that may incorporate both qualitative and quantitative approaches, such as the social sciences and humanities (e.g., Kaplan 2015).

As of 2010, the Linguistics Society of America has also recognized the diverse complexity in forms of scholarly work in the field, acknowledging the use and production of "not only grammars, dictionaries, and text collections, but also archives of primary data, electronic databases, corpora, critical editions of legacy materials, pedagogical works designed for the use of speech communities, software, websites, or other digital media" in its "Resolution Recognizing the Scholarly Merit of Language Documentation."[1] In this document, the Linguistics Society of America further recommends that these forms of work be recognized when hiring new faculty, as well as in tenure and promotion decisions, and acknowledges this will require developing methods to review these alternative forms of scholarship compared with more traditional works such as monographs, books, and journal articles.

In addition to navigating the complexities of academic research and scholarly activities, there are also expectations of faculty to contribute teaching and service at their institutions. In fact, for career advancement, expectations overall have increased over the last several decades. Whereas it was once sufficient for faculty to excel in either teaching or research, it is now typical to expect excellence in all three of the academic trifecta: research, teaching, and service (Gardner & Veliz 2014; Schimanski & Alperin 2018; Youn & Price 2009). That being said, there is also considerable evidence that the research component, supported mainly by scholarly outputs such as publications, is widely considered to be the most strongly weighted of the three (e.g., Acker & Webber 2016; Harley et al. 2010; Macfarlane 2007; and see Schimanski & Alperin 2018 for review). Nonetheless, significant contributions to academic service and teaching are required, and these rising demands of the academic faculty lead to time pressure to fulfill all obligations. Considering their limited time, faculty are in a position of needing to prioritize their activities to balance their own career objectives with those required by their institutions and departments for career advancement via the review, promotion, and tenure (RPT) process.

Those faculty serving on RPT committees also need to prioritize their time; when assessing the research outputs of other faculty, it is easier for committee members to rely on factors such as the prestige and reputation of the venues in which scholarly works are published including their impact factors (e.g., Adler, Ewing, & Taylor 2009; Harley et al. 2010; Malsch & Tessier 2015; McKiernan et al. 2019; Niles et al. 2020; Walker et al. 2010). Just as there is evidence that the prestige of the publisher matters for RPT—some institutions provide ranked lists of journals and publishing with university presses is most desirable for books (King et al. 2006; Thatcher 2007)—there is also evidence that various academic fields value some types of academic outputs more than others. Most commonly, the highly valued outputs include peer-reviewed journal articles and monographs, and to a lesser degree, books and submissions to academic conferences (Coonin & Younce 2009; Harley et al. 2010; Liner & Sewell 2009). However, faculty tend to produce a greater range of scholarly outputs, including but not limited to software, data sets, reports, preprints, creative performances, educational materials, articles in newspapers and magazines, blogs and social media, and various forms of public outreach. That faculty devote their time to such scholarly contributions indicates that they find value in these activities, despite the perception that they contribute less toward career advancement. This leaves us to ask: *What role do activities and outputs beyond those that appear in traditional publication channels such as journals, books, and academic conferences play in review, promotion, and tenure processes?* To investigate this topic, we focus on three related sub-questions:

1. What activities and outputs are mentioned in documents related to RPT?

2. How do the activities and outputs mentioned in documents related to RPT vary across institution types and disciplines?

Finally, and more specifically, given the topic of this handbook, we examine the following third sub-question:

3. To what extent and in which ways are data-related outputs mentioned in RPT documents?

In asking these questions, we must acknowledge that the framing of our research unintentionally pits "traditional" forms of scholarship against "other," "alternative," and "non-traditional" forms. We adopt this language from the existing literature, but acknowledge that doing so risks bias in favor of the status quo (Eidelman & Crandall 2012). With that warning in mind, we begin answering the research questions with a brief overview of previous research on the role that scholarly outputs play in the RPT process and, in the following two sections, we describe our methodological approach and our findings, including a summary statistics and specific examples of how outputs are discussed. We conclude the chapter with a discussion of how our findings fit into the wider literature on scholarly outputs and research evaluation.

2 The role of scholarly outputs in the RPT process

The types of scholarly outputs that are recognized in the assessment of research and publication may vary across institutions and the disciplines, but there are some overall trends discussed in previous research. In many disciplines (e.g., physical and life sciences, engineering, psychology, business), the peer-reviewed journal article is the gold standard and typical means for demonstrating productivity, as well as the quality and reach of one's research outcomes (Coonin & Younce 2009; Harley et al. 2010). In other disciplines (e.g., history, English, anthropology), monographs and edited volumes are the preferred medium (Estabrook & Warner 2003). RPT guidelines generally give credit for these traditional mediums in the communication of scholarly work.

For journal articles, it is generally understood that those published in peer-reviewed journals, in international journals, and in those with high journal impact factor are most highly valued in the RPT process (Dennis et al. 2006; Foos, Holmes, & O'Connell 2004; King et al. 2006; Seipel 2003; Walker et al. 2010). Although most would agree that having gone through the peer-review process should correspond to higher quality publications, it is less clear whether publishing in a journal perceived as prestigious, with good name recognition, and/or with a high journal impact factor really indicates high-quality scholarly work (Brembs 2018). Similarly, for monographs and books, publishing by presses with editorial boards and/or peer reviewers, and by university presses, may be taken to suggest higher quality (Thatcher 2007). The use of the venue of publication has been widely critiqued, most prominently in the Declaration on Research Assessment (DORA, n.d.) and in the Leiden Manifesto (Hicks et al. 2015), because they substitute in-depth assessment, using both qualitative and quantitative measures, of the scholarly work in question.

RPT committees may consider additional forms of scholarly outputs, but these tend to carry less weight toward the decision, if they are mentioned at all in the policies and guidelines for the process (e.g., Harley et al. 2010). These may include conference proceedings, textbooks, reports, websites, creative performances and compositions, exhibitions, development of software and instrumentation, patents, commercialization, databases, grant funding, social media, and more (Cabrera et al. 2017; Harley et al. 2010; Sanberg et al. 2014; Stevens, Johnson, & Sanberg 2011). In their survey of US faculty, Blankstein and Wolff-Eisenberg (2019), found a general belief that non-traditional scholarly works should receive less recognition, but also that about a third of faculty think that preprints, which are traditional publications that have not yet undergone peer review, should be valued equally to published traditional research publications. This number may continue to increase with efforts such as those of ASAPbio (https://asapbio.org), a non-profit organization promoting transparency in research communication, and changing editorial policies that promote the use of preprints (*Nature* 2019).

With regard to data management and sharing, there is a dearth of evidence in the published literature regarding their consideration in the RPT process. This lack of evidence may reflect a perceived risk of making research data available to others and losing one's first rights to uncover important findings in those data, as well as having others expose errors in one's work (e.g., Gorgolewski, Margulies, & Milham 2013; Kim & Adler 2015; Tenopir et al. 2015) despite evidence that sharing data tends to increase citations and funding opportunities (reviewed by (McKiernan et al. 2016; further discussion of data citations, also see Champieux & Coates, chapter 12, this volume). It may also reflect that data-sharing practices are relatively new, and that there is more room for embracing open data, especially in the social sciences, as discussed by Gawne and Styles (chapter 2, this volume). As such, their consideration in the RPT process may become more common as attitudes toward data continue to evolve, as they did during the period studied by Tenopir et al. (2015). Their surveys suggest that faculty (especially younger age groups) became more accepting of data sharing during 2009–2014. More recently, another survey found that over half of US-based researchers believe that data sharing is important to enable others to attempt to reproduce findings (Blankstein & Wolff-Eisenberg 2019). This shift in attitude is supported by policies encouraging or requiring data sharing from some journal publishers and from funders who have an interest in maximizing the benefits emerging from grant funding (Kim & Stanton 2016; McKiernan et al. 2016), and from projects like Make Data Count (https://makedatacount.org), which seeks to generate metrics to capture data usage (further discussion of the practice of data archiving and sharing can be found in Andreassen, chapter 7, this volume). Also, to bridge the gap between traditional outputs and the sharing of data sets, the notion of "data papers" has been suggested as a mechanism for sharing and explaining data sets (Gorgolewski, Margulies, & Milham 2013). The notion of data papers and efforts for data metrics

are both indicative of a perceived need of having data valued as part of the RPT process.

The collective evidence seems to suggest that RPT policy tends to focus on traditional academic outputs such as publication of journal articles and monographs/books, depending on discipline. However, if we directly evaluate documentation related to the RPT process, such as policies and guidelines, can we find evidence for non-traditional outputs and data-related works being valued in academic career evaluations?

3 Methods

This chapter presents selected findings from a larger study on RPT practices in the United States and Canada for which we collected and analyzed documents pertaining to the RPT process. A full description of the methods for selecting institutions, identifying documents, and analyzing them can be found in Alperin et al. (2019) and in the research note in the accompanying data set (Alperin et al. 2018).

Briefly, we used the 2015 edition of the *Carnegie Classification of Institutions* (Carnegie Foundation for the Advancement of Teaching 2015) and the 2016 edition of the Maclean's "University Rankings" (Rogers Digital Media 2016) to identify universities in both countries and proceeded to select a stratified random sample across three institutions types: those that focus on doctoral programs (i.e., research-intensive institutions; labeled R-type), those that predominantly grant master's degrees (labeled M-type), and those focused on undergraduate programs (i.e., baccalaureate degrees; labeled B-type). We then used a combination of web searches, crowdsourcing (i.e., calls on social media), and targeted e-mails to collect documents that pertain to the RPT process. We obtained a wide range of documents, including collective agreements, faculty handbooks, guideline documents, forms, and presentations. Some of the documents pertained to the university as a whole, whereas others were produced by a specific academic unit (i.e., a school, department, or faculty). We classified the latter group into three main disciplinary areas according to the National Academies' taxonomy (National Academy of Sciences 2006): life sciences (LS); physical sciences and mathematics (PSM); and social sciences and humanities (SSH). Units that could not be classified into a single discipline were deemed to be multidisciplinary and were coded as such.

In the end, we obtained 864 documents from 129 universities, with an intentional oversampling of R-type institutions given the prominent role that research and research outputs play at these institutions. This led to obtaining university-level documents from 57 R-type institutions, 39 M-type institutions, and 33 B-type institutions. We were also able to obtain at least one document from academic units at a subset of 60 universities, reaching a total of 381 distinct academic units. Due to the different sample sizes across institution types and a particular interest in the processes at research-intensive institutions, we limited our disciplinary analysis to academic units from the 57 R-type institutions. This analysis included 33 (28%) LS units, 21 (18%) PSM units, 39 (34%) SSH units, and 23 (20%) multidisciplinary units, spanning 43 (75%) of the 57 R-type institutions in the sample.

Documents were loaded into QSR International's NVivo 12 and grouped into two sets (i.e., NVivo nodes) corresponding to the institution-level guidelines and those for individual academic units following the procedure described in Alperin et al. (2019). We performed a series of text queries combined with manual revision and uncoding of irrelevant sections for an extensive set of terms that refer to research outputs. We took a maximalist approach to identifying the relevant terms, first by reading through the research or scholarship sections of a subset of documents chosen from each institution type and noting the outputs listed there. We then proceeded to perform a text query for each output and related variants, including plurals and alternate spellings, to identify all instances of those terms across the entire corpus regardless of where it appeared in the document. In manually reviewing every instance, we uncoded any instances where the term was used to refer to something other than a research output and identified additional terms to be included in the search. In this way, we expanded the original list of terms whenever a new type of output was mentioned in proximity to one already identified. A detailed description of all of the terms used, as well as the text query used to search for all variants of each term, can be found in the research note that accompanies the public data set (Alperin et al. 2018).

To our knowledge, there is no agreed-upon list of outputs or categories of outputs on which to base our work, and so we set out to construct our own list of terms and bespoke categories. Informed by the research team's experience on issues related to scholarly communications

and research assessment, we began with a deductive approach to identify the traditional outputs, including those discussed in the RPT literature. We complemented this approach by doing a close read of the RPT documents to identify the types of outputs that are recognized toward faculty evaluation. Following an open-coding and constant comparison approach (Strauss & Corbin 1990), we labeled each new term separately and compared it to the already existing terms and categories. If they referred to an output considered to be synonymous with one seen previously, they were grouped together. If the new term was judged to refer to something previously not seen, a new label was assigned to the term and, if necessary, a new category was created. In all cases we were careful to be inclusive of variations of spelling, terminology, and synonyms whenever querying for a new output. Several iterations of this process led to categories of variable size (described in detail in table 13.1). The data related to each individual term (prior to categorization) are publicly available along with the scripts used to perform aggregations by institution type and discipline to facilitate replication and further exploration (Alperin et al. 2019).

When counting the number of mentions per institution type, we considered there to be a mention when at least one document belonging to that institution or any of its academic units made mention of the output. Similarly, when counting the number of mentions per discipline, we considered there to be a mention when at least one of the documents belonging to that discipline at the institution in question made a mention of the output. For example, we have two university-level documents from the University of Utah and an additional eleven documents from ten different academic units. Of these, only one document, pertaining to the Department of Psychology, mentions a variant of the term "dataset." It does so in the following way: "Research/scholarship is sustained and ongoing, with evidence of work at all stages of the research process (e.g., publications, submitted manuscripts, draft manuscripts and conference presentations, collected *data sets*, plans for future work, intra- and/or extra-mural funding, and so on)" (emphasis added; University of Utah 2011). We would therefore consider this to be an example of an R-type mention (the University of Utah's Carnegie classification) as well as a SSH mention (the Department of Psychology's classification). In much the same way, we considered one of our defined category of outputs to be mentioned if at least one of the terms within that category was mentioned, as per the preceding description, in a given institution or discipline. Using the preceding example, we could consider the *data* category to have been mentioned at an R-type institution and in an SSH discipline.

4 Results

4.1 Types of outputs

We identified 127 different kinds of outputs in our corpus, which we grouped into twelve categories. In what follows we present a brief overview of the categories we arrived at, along with several examples of the terms included within each (table 13.1). A full description and a list of every term is available in the methodology note of the accompanying data set (Alperin et al. 2018).

The categories we created are varied in their composition. While some are made up of very few types of output (e.g., *preprints* and *data*), others represent a variety of output types (e.g., *arts*, *education*, and *events*). Four of the categories (i.e., *traditional*, *conventional*, *funding*, and *unspecified*) could be considered by some to fall under a broader definition of "traditional." We have chosen to analyze them separately, even though many of the outputs, especially those in the *unspecified* category, are likely to be referring to traditional and conventional outputs as well (see Schimanski & Alperin, 2018, for discussion of the values of different output types in RPT). To reflect the conceptual similarity in these four categories, they are grouped together in tables 13.1–13.3.

Table 13.1

Categories of outputs and examples of the outputs found in each

Category	Description	Examples
Traditional	Relating to the longest standing and most formal mediums of scholarly communication, verbal and written.	Books, journal articles, presentations
Conventional	Relating to other verbal and written work that caters to an academic audience.	Book reviews, editorials, posters
Funding	Relating to the acquisition of research funding.	Grants, funding
Unspecified	Relating to written dissemination of knowledge to an academic audience, format not specified.	Publications, outputs, papers, manuscripts
Arts	Relating to work that is in the realm of visuals, music, language, or performance.	Performances, creator works, exhibitions
Data	Relating to the creation or management of data.	Databases, databanks, data sets
Education	Relating to the creation of pedagogical materials or methods.	Textbooks, syllabi, lectures
Events	Relating to participation in a formally organized social occasion based around a topic with a specialized or academic audience.	Conferences, workshops, seminars
Information and Communication Technologies	Relating to the medium of work that is digital, audible, or visually recorded.	Audiovisual resources, aids, and materials; videos
Intellectual Property	Relating to work that results in intellectual property.	Patents, inventions, technology transfer
Preprints	Relating to documents typically intended for peer-review process, but published ahead of that process.	Preprint, working paper
Public Media	Relating to the dissemination of knowledge to a non-academic audience.	Newspaper articles, films, newsletters
Software	Relating to computer code in the form of software or programs.	Software, computer programs
Third-Party Collaborations	Relating to consulting or contract work where an individual is hired by a non-academic entity for their expertise.	Consulting works, policy analysis and reports, contract research and reports
Works in Progress	Relating to academic work that is in progress, has not been published, or is forthcoming.	Ongoing research, unpublished work, research in progress

4.2 Mentions of outputs across institutions and disciplines

As previously reported (Alperin et al. 2019), we found that terms referring to the most *traditional* outputs were ubiquitous, appearing in around 95% of all institutions across the three institution types (table 13.2). Although we consider the acquisition of grant funding a traditional output (Alperin et al. 2019), in this analysis, we separated terms related to *Funding* separately and found they were present in 82%–87% of institutions. We have also added terms for what we refer to as *conventional* outputs, which might be considered "traditional" and which were found in 82% of R-type, 62% of M-type, and 67% of B-type institutions. In this same vein, *unspecified* terms that are likely stand-ins for traditional outputs can be found in over 90% of institutions of each type—significantly more than almost every remaining category. The only other two categories that come close in prevalence are the *education* and *events* categories, both of which are found in 85%–91% of institutions of each type (table 13.2).

Overall, we found that R-type institutions were more likely to mention the whole range of outputs. With the exception of the *arts* and *third-party* categories, R-type institutions have proportionally more or equal mentions of every output category when compared to M-type and B-type institutions. This is especially true of the *intellectual property, information and communication technologies,* and *software* categories, all of which are mentioned in 65%–68% of the R-type institution documents, but only in 33%–38% of the M- and B-type institutions (table 13.2). The difference was also noticeable in the *data* and *preprints* categories, which were the least mentioned overall (more on the difference in data-related outputs in section 4.3).

In looking within the fifty-seven R-type institutions, we see a similar pattern across the academic units of the various disciplines. *Traditional* outputs are universally valued, with 94%–95% of academic units across the three disciplines, and 77% of the multidisciplinary units, mentioning their use (table 13.3). *Funding*-related output mentions can be found in 84%–94% in the units of each discipline, with the LS and PSM units having more mentions than those of SSH. *Unspecified* outputs are also universally mentioned, with 94%–97% of units in the three disciplines mentioning such terms along with 82% of the multidisciplinary units. Of the four categories that could be considered "traditional," the *conventional* outputs are the least mentioned in the academic unit documents. Outputs in this category can be found in 64% of multidisciplinary units, 68% of those of SSH, 70% of PSM, and 76% of LS.

Similarly, we found cross-disciplinary interest in *education*-related outputs, with 92%–95% of the each

Table 13.2

Presence of outputs in documents by institution type

Category of output	R-type (*n*=57)		M-type (*n*=39)		B-type (*n*=33)	
Traditional	53	93%	37	95%	31	94%
Conventional	47	82%	24	62%	22	67%
Funding	49	86%	34	87%	27	82%
Unspecified	55	96%	36	92%	30	91%
Arts	47	82%	33	85%	29	88%
Data	9	16%	4	10%	2	6%
Education	52	91%	33	85%	30	91%
Events	52	91%	35	90%	29	88%
Information and Communication Technologies	38	67%	15	38%	12	36%
Intellectual Property	39	68%	15	38%	11	33%
Preprints	13	23%	2	5%	4	12%
Public Media	39	68%	19	49%	11	33%
Software	37	65%	15	38%	12	36%
Third-Party Collaborations	25	44%	18	46%	12	36%
Works in Progress	34	60%	17	44%	16	48%

Table 13.3

Presence of outputs in documents of R-type institutions by discipline

Category of output	SSH (n=39)		PSM (n=21)		LS (n=33)		Multidisciplinary (n=23)	
Traditional	36	95%	19	95%	31	94%	17	77%
Conventional	26	68%	14	70%	25	76%	14	64%
Funding	32	84%	18	90%	31	94%	19	86%
Unspecified	37	97%	19	95%	31	94%	18	82%
Arts	29	76%	5	25%	13	39%	11	50%
Data	3	8%	0	0%	5	15%	1	5%
Education	35	92%	19	95%	31	94%	17	77%
Events	34	89%	19	95%	32	97%	19	86%
Information and Communication Technologies	24	63%	7	35%	21	64%	7	32%
Intellectual Property	10	26%	14	70%	22	67%	8	36%
Preprints	4	11%	4	20%	4	12%	2	9%
Public Media	22	58%	7	35%	19	58%	8	36%
Software	19	50%	7	35%	21	64%	8	36%
Third-Party Collaborations	14	37%	7	35%	15	45%	5	23%
Works in Progress	18	47%	7	35%	12	36%	6	27%

of the three disciplines mentioning this category along with 77% of the multidisciplinary units. The *events* category, which was mentioned in 91% of the R-type documents overall, showed a little more variation across disciplines, with 89% of the SSH and 86% of the multidisciplinary units mentioning outputs in this category, as compared to 95% and 97% of the PSM and LS units, respectively. Despite these variances, it is clear that *traditional* outputs, along with *education*- and *events*-related outputs are universally valued.

We note several other important differences across the disciplines in the categories that are much less frequently mentioned. In particular, the SSH units show the least acknowledgment of *intellectual property*–related outputs and of *preprints*, along with multidisciplinary units. This is not to say that SSH units had fewer mentions across all categories. Perhaps unsurprising, given that the SSH discipline includes arts and humanities fields, the *Arts*-related outputs were most widely found in SSH. We also observed that the PSM units had a lower proportion of mentions in the *information and communication technologies, software,* and *public media* categories. Lastly, we found that the LS units differ in their mention of *data* outputs, which we describe in the following section.

4.3 Data-related outputs

The mention of data-related outputs in RPT documents is relatively rare. They can be found in 16% of R-type

institutions, 10% of M-type institutions, and only 6% of the B-type institutions in our sample (table 13.2). Within the R-types, we found an uneven presence of data-related mentions across different disciplines in academic unit–level documents, with 15% of the LS units mentioning the term at least once, as compared to 8% of the SSH units, and none of the PSM units, although it should be noted that the number of mentions is small (five and three, respectively). PSM units did not mention *data* outputs at all.

To better understand how discussions around the importance of data are making their way into the documents that govern the RPT process, we did a closer reading of the three subterms included in this category: "data banks," "data bases," and "data sets" (all in their singular and plural, with spaces and without, as well as hyphenated versions, as described in the methodology note found in the accompanying data set for this chapter). Other data-related terms, such as "data management," were not present in our collection of RPT documents. Of the data-related terms we did find, the term "data-bases" and its variants were the most frequent (found in the documents of ten institutions and seven academic units), followed by "datasets" and its variants (found in the documents of three institutions and two academic units). A vast majority of these mentions were found as part of a longer list of outputs where the data-related item was closer to the end of the list than the beginning and in several cases was grouped into a "new" or "alternative" category of scholarship.

For example, we found this to be the case for the institution-level documents of the University of North Carolina at Chapel Hill, which state that "academic units should recognize that evaluation of new forms of scholarship often will come after publication" (University of North Carolina at Chapel Hill 2009). The document goes on to list examples, starting with "databases" and followed by "blogs, web sites, and other forms that do not resemble traditional journal articles or monographs."

When mentions were not found in a "new" or "alternative" section of the documents, these lists often place databases following a list of more traditional outputs, which might imply a lower importance relative to these other forms. For example, at the University of Calgary, this relative importance is made explicit, with databases and software being the two least valuable of the outputs mentioned:

> Promotion—scholarship will be judged, on a Department-specific basis, according to the quality of the research program, reflected *in roughly descending order* by the following kinds of publications: refereed books, book chapters, and articles, including major refereed research monographs; textbooks, edited books, other monographs and articles in non-refereed journals, book chapters, book reviews; other forms of scholarship, e.g., conference papers, research grants, editorship of journals, conference organization, development of computer-assisted learning, *data bases*, software. (University of Calgary 2005; emphasis added)

However, this is not universally the case. Another unit in what is now the same faculty (Faculty of Arts) contradicts this statement by stating that: "All research, scholarship and other creative activities shall be assessed on the merits of the work, regardless of the form in which they appear. Electronic publications—whether books, articles, journals, or databases—shall be considered equivalent to more traditional forms of publications if they are subjected to the same rigor of informed peer review or appropriate refereeing" (University of Calgary 2011).

5   Discussion and conclusions

When looking across institutions in the United States and Canada, there is a great deal of diversity in the kinds of research outputs that are presented to faculty in the documents that govern the RPT processes. Our analysis reveals that this diversity extends across institution types and disciplines. Most notably, the documents from R-type institutions offer a longer list of outputs to be considered, and within those institutions we see substantial differences in which outputs are mentioned in the documents of each discipline. This variability may be a sign that RPT processes are beginning to recognize research activities more broadly. If this is indeed the case, it is evident that this broader conception has not been adopted everywhere. On the other hand, greater specificity could be seen as a way to further constrain the outputs which are valued. Either way, traditional research outputs are universally presented to faculty as highly valued in RPT.

These two findings—the ubiquity of traditional outputs and the variability in the presence of other forms of scholarship—paint a complicated picture for those looking to understand what is valued for their academic career. Evidence suggests that in the face of ambiguous or incomplete information in the guidelines, committees revert to their own judgment and notions of disciplinary norms and expectations (Harley et al. 2010; May 2005; Schimanski & Alperin 2018). Such reliance on individual judgments of what is necessary for career advancement may be especially acute for pretenure faculty who will be evaluated by individuals from outside their institution who are less familiar with the institutional context and the corresponding guidelines. Even if internal and external evaluators rely on the documents that pertain to the candidates' RPT process, our analysis of the mentions of data-related outputs in these documents strongly suggests that new or alternative forms of scholarship (anything beyond the traditional peer-reviewed journal articles, books, and book chapters) are of lesser importance. This framing of non-traditional outputs, when they are mentioned at all, perpetuates the notion that faculty should focus on traditional research activities. In a context where faculty are asked to excel in every aspect of their work, including research, teaching, and service (Diamond & Adam 1998; Schimanski & Alperin 2018; Youn & Price 2009), and already do not spend as much time as they would like on research (Brownell 2018; Mamiseishvili, Miller, & Lee 2016), this message that some activities are less valued is likely to dissuade faculty from activities that result in non-traditional outputs. When it comes to data-related outputs and other forms of scholarship not mentioned in many RPT guidelines, it seems that while institutions are not dissuading faculty from undertaking such work, it is not actively encouraged or is devalued compared to traditional outputs.

This analysis supports various claims that current incentive structures are partly to blame for a lack of evolution in the state of research communications and in the push toward open science practices (G7 Science 2017; Harley et al. 2010; Wheeler et al. 2012). The need for change is evident, for example, in the growing reproducibility crisis, where researchers cite pressure to publish and incentive structures as important contributing factors (Baker 2016; Gawne & Styles, chapter 2, this volume). In linguistics, change may also be necessary to improve the participation of historically marginalized groups, such as Indigenous communities, so that research communications can serve to revitalize Indigenous languages (Ramos & Empinotti 2017; Young 2019). While there is no commonly accepted approach to research communication and activities, our findings suggest that current RPT guidelines found in the United States and Canada have not shifted to be more inclusive of non-traditional outputs. This is especially true for new forms of scholarship such as the production of data sets or the publication of preprints, both of which are mentioned in the documents of only a small percentage of all institutions.

The research presented here provides a benchmark against which future work can be measured, but we cannot observe from this single snapshot whether these practices are changing. For instance, it is possible that RPT committees do value data-related outputs in their decision-making process despite their absence or low valuation in the RPT documents. It has been observed that RPT documents typically espouse some degree of vagueness or flexibility in their requirements so as to allow committees to consider other information deemed appropriate for each unique faculty member's field of study (Macfarlane 2007; Schimanski & Alperin 2018; Smesny et al. 2007). This approach might allow for M-type and B-type institutions, which mentioned fewer output types in their RPT documents, to still be inclusive in assigning value to non-traditional forms of research output. However, the lack of explicit mentions of newer output forms, such as data sets and preprints, indicates that broad acceptance of these forms is not yet observable in RPT documents.

Despite the lack of mentions of data-related items in the RPT documents we examined, scholars are actively working on enhancing the profile of data-related endeavors in scholarship. For instance, the Make Data Count project has been working to make data a "first-class" research product by developing a framework to standardize and collect data usage metrics. Evidence of the acceptance and valuation of data work is also visible in other ways. In the field of computational linguistics, Wieling, Rawee, and van Noord (2018) found that by 2016, most researchers were willing to share data sets with other researchers, although sharing code occurred less frequently. Researchers appear to be driven by a desire to promote the reproducibility of research findings (Berez-Kroeker et al. 2018; Wieling, Rawee, & van Noord 2018) and to make data available in standard formats that facilitate their assessment by other parties (e.g., the "Cross-Linguistic Data Formats" initiative; Forkel et al. 2018). It will take future studies to determine whether calls for a greater valuation of data-related work are having an effect, and the valuation of data and other new forms eventually become encoded in RPT documents.

That said, our findings do indicate a wide range of outputs mentioned overall. This, and the high percentage of institutions that mention certain output categories (especially among the R-types), are signs that the academic community understands and values a broad notion of faculty work, even if it falls short of acknowledging the full range of outputs explicitly. As such, and in the spirit of fostering the positive cultural change to value and reward data sharing mentioned by Gawne and Styles (chapter 2, this volume), we believe that researchers can take steps to increase the likelihood that they receive recognition for data they create, curate, or publish. Perhaps most importantly, researchers should cite these data in any materials they present for review (e.g., curriculum vitae or tenure packages). Committees are likely to place these in the larger context of scholarly work, even if not yet recognizing them to the same degree as other scholarship. Moreover, as it becomes normal for data to appear in lists of outputs, it could, in time, lead to their inclusion among the explicitly recognized outputs. To be able to do so, we recommend that everyone follow good research data management practices. Good research data management reduces the work required to curate and publish data, making it easier to continue to fulfill existing expectations from RPT committees. These suggestions, we think, are equally valid for established researchers as they are for graduate students, whom we would already advise to follow good research data management practices and who are in a position to signal to more established colleagues that the next generation value working with data. Finally, for those who have the privilege to serve on RPT committees, we suggest that you familiarize yourself with efforts such as DORA and the Leiden Manifesto so that you can lead a conversation with your colleagues on how to recognize the diverse range of activities that make up faculty work because, as it stands today, our findings show that faculty are left navigating an uneven landscape that simultaneously values and undervalues different aspects of what they do.

Acknowledgments

We would like to acknowledge the critically important work of Carol Muñoz Nieves, who spent hours poring over the documents to identify and classify the outputs found here. We would also like to thank Kendal Crawford and Lisa Matthias for their relentless efforts to collect RPT documents necessary to enable this work in the first place, as well as the editors, two anonymous reviewers, and Daniella Lowenberg for their thoughtful feedback on earlier versions of this manuscript. Finally, we need to thank and acknowledge the OpenCon community who brought us together, and whose work inspires and invigorates us year after year.

Note

1. While the Linguistics Society of America refers to "speech communities," the diversity also includes communities for languages which are not spoken. Available at: https://www.linguisticsociety.org/resource/resolution-recognizing-scholarly-merit-language-documentation.

References

Acker, Sandra, and Michelle Webber. 2016. Discipline and publish: The tenure review process in Ontario universities. In *Assembling and Governing the Higher Education Institution*, ed. Lynette Schultz and Melody Viczko, 233–255. Palgrave Studies in Global Citizenship Education and Democracy. London: Palgrave Macmillan. https://doi.org/10.1057/978-1-137-52261-0_13.

Adler, Robert, John Ewing, and Peter Taylor. 2009. Citation statistics. *Statistical Science* 24 (1): 1–14. https://doi.org/10.1214/09-STS285.

Alperin, Juan Pablo, Carol Muñoz Nieves, Lesley A. Schimanski, Gustavo E. Fischman, Meredith T. Niles, and Erin C. McKiernan. 2019. How significant are the public dimensions of faculty work in review, promotion and tenure documents? *ELife* 8 (February). https://doi.org/10.7554/eLife.42254.

Alperin, Juan Pablo, Carol Muñoz Nieves, Lesley Schimanski, Erin C. McKiernan, and Meredith T. Niles. 2018. Terms and concepts found in tenure and promotion guidelines from the US and Canada. https://doi.org/10.7910/DVN/VY4TJE.

Baker, Monya. 2016. 1,500 scientists lift the lid on reproducibility. *Nature News* 533 (7604): 452. https://doi.org/10.1038/533452a.

Berez-Kroeker, Andrea L., Lauren Gawne, Susan Smythe Kung, Barbara F. Kelly, Tyler Heston, Gary Holton, Peter Pulsifer, et al. 2018. Reproducible research in linguistics: A position statement on data citation and attribution in our field. *Linguistics* 56 (1): 1–18. https://doi.org/10.1515/ling-2017-0032.

Blankstein, Melissa, and Christine Wolff-Eisenberg. 2019. Ithaka S+R US faculty survey 2018. https://doi.org/10.18665/sr.311199.

Brembs, Björn. 2018. Prestigious science journals struggle to reach even average reliability. *Frontiers in Human Neuroscience* 12:37. https://doi.org/10.3389/fnhum.2018.00037.

Brownell, Claire. 2018. Canadian university professors spend roughly half of their time on teaching. *Maclean's*, May 17, 2018. https://www.macleans.ca/education/canadian-university-professors-spend-equal-amounts-of-time-on-teaching-and-non-teaching-work/.

Cabrera, Daniel, Bryan S. Vartabedian, Robert J. Spinner, Barbara L. Jordan, Lee A. Aase, and Farris K. Timimi. 2017. More than likes and tweets: Creating social media portfolios for academic promotion and tenure. *Journal of Graduate Medical Education* 9 (4): 421–425. https://doi.org/10.4300/JGME-D-17-00171.1.

Carnegie Foundation for the Advancement of Teaching. 2015. *The Carnegie Classification of Institutions of Higher Education* (website). http://carnegieclassifications.iu.edu/. Accessed September 17, 2018.

Coonin, Bryna, and Leigh Younce. 2009. Publishing in open access journals in the social sciences and humanities: Who's doing it and why. In *ACRL Fourteenth National Conference*, 85–94. http://www.ala.org/acrl/sites/ala.org.acrl/files/content/conferences/confsandpreconfs/national/seattle/papers/85.pdf.

Dennis, Alan R., Joseph S. Valacich, Mark A. Fuller, and Christoph Schneider. 2006. Research standards for promotion and tenure in information systems. *MIS Quarterly* 30 (1): 1–12. https://doi.org/10.2307/25148714.

Diamond, Robert M., and Bronwyn E. Adam. 1998. *Changing Priorities at Research Universities: 1991–1996*. Syracuse, NY: Syracuse University.

DORA. n.d. Signers—DORA. San Francisco declaration on research assessment. https://sfdora.org/signers/. Accessed February 24, 2018.

Eidelman, Scott, and Christian S. Crandall. 2012. Bias in favor of the status quo. *Social and Personality Psychology Compass* 6 (3): 270–281. https://doi.org/10.1111/j.1751-9004.2012.00427.x.

Estabrook, Leigh, and Bijan Warner. 2003. *The Book as the Gold Standard for Tenure and Promotion in the Humanistic Disciplines.* Committee on Institutional Cooperation. http://citeseerx.ist.psu.edu/viewdoc/summary?doi=10.1.1.180.546.

Foos, Annabelle, Mary Anne Holmes, and Suzanne O'Connell. 2004. What does it take to get tenure? *Papers in the Geosciences,* paper 88. https://digitalcommons.unl.edu/cgi/viewcontent.cgi?article=1087&context=geosciencefacpub. Accessed December 7, 2020.

Forkel, Robert, Johann-Mattis List, Simon J. Greenhill, Christoph Rzymski, Sebastian Bank, Michael Cysouw, Harald Hammarström, Martin Haspelmath, Gereon A. Kaiping, and Russell D. Gray. 2018. Cross-Linguistic Data Formats, advancing data sharing and re-use in comparative linguistics. *Scientific Data* 5 (October): 180205. https://doi.org/10.1038/sdata.2018.205.

G7 Science. 2017. G7 science ministers meeting declaration. http://www.g7italy.it/sites/default/files/documents/G7%20Science%20Communiqu%c3%a9_1/index.pdf.

Gardner, Susan K., and Daniela Veliz. 2014. Evincing the ratchet: A thematic analysis of the promotion and tenure guidelines at a striving university. *Review of Higher Education* 38 (1): 105–132. https://doi.org/10.1353/rhe.2014.0045.

Gorgolewski, Krzysztof, Daniel S. Margulies, and Michael P. Milham. 2013. Making data sharing count: A publication-based solution. *Frontiers in Neuroscience* 7:9. https://doi.org/10.3389/fnins.2013.00009.

Harley, Diane, Sophia Krzys Acord, Sarah Earl-Novell, Shannon Lawrence, and C. Judson King. 2010. Assessing the future landscape of scholarly communication: An exploration of faculty values and needs in seven disciplines. *Center for Studies in Higher Education*, January. http://escholarship.org/uc/item/15x7385g.

Hicks, Diana, Paul Wouters, Ludo Waltman, Sarah de Rijcke, and Ismael Rafols. 2015. Bibliometrics: The Leiden Manifesto for research metrics. *Nature News* 520 (7548): 429. https://doi.org/10.1038/520429a.

Kaplan, Frédéric. 2015. A map for big data research in digital humanities. *Frontiers in Digital Humanities* 2:1. https://doi.org/10.3389/fdigh.2015.00001.

Kim, Youngseek, and Melissa Adler. 2015. Social scientists' data sharing behaviors: Investigating the roles of individual motivations, institutional pressures, and data repositories. *International Journal of Information Management* 35 (4): 408–418. https://doi.org/10.1016/j.ijinfomgt.2015.04.007.

Kim, Youngseek, and Jeffrey M. Stanton. 2016. Institutional and individual factors affecting scientists' data-sharing behaviors: A multilevel analysis. *Journal of the Association for Information Science and Technology* 67 (4): 776–799. https://doi.org/10.1002/asi.23424.

King, C. Judson, Diane Harley, Sarah Earl-Novell, Jennifer Arter, Shannon Lawrence, and Irene Perciali. 2006. Scholarly communication: Academic values and sustainable models. *Center for Studies in Higher Education*, July. http://escholarship.org/uc/item/4j89c3f7.

Liner, Gaines H., and Ellen Sewell. 2009. Research requirements for promotion and tenure at PhD granting departments of economics. *Applied Economics Letters* 16 (8): 765–768. https://doi.org/10.1080/13504850701221998.

Macfarlane, Bruce. 2007. Defining and rewarding academic citizenship: The implications for university promotions policy. *Journal of Higher Education Policy and Management* 29 (3): 261–273. https://doi.org/10.1080/13600800701457863.

Malsch, Bertrand, and Sophie Tessier. 2015. Journal ranking effects on junior academics: identity fragmentation and politicization. *Critical Perspectives on Accounting* 26 (February): 84–98. https://doi.org/10.1016/j.cpa.2014.02.006.

Mamiseishvili, Ketevan, Michael T. Miller, and Donghun Lee. 2016. Beyond teaching and research: Faculty perceptions of service roles at research universities. *Innovative Higher Education* 41 (4): 273–285. https://doi.org/10.1007/s10755-015-9354-3.

Margolis, Ronald, Leslie Derr, Michelle Dunn, Michael Huerta, Jennie Larkin, Jerry Sheehan, Mark Guyer, and Eric D. Green. 2014. The National Institutes of Health's Big Data to Knowledge (BD2K) initiative: Capitalizing on biomedical big data. *Journal of the American Medical Informatics Association* 21 (6): 957–958. https://doi.org/10.1136/amiajnl-2014-002974.

Marx, Vivien. 2013. The big challenges of big data. *Nature* 498: 255–260. https://www.nature.com/articles/498255a.

May, Daniel C. 2005. The nature of school of education faculty work and materials for promotion and tenure at a major research university. EdD dissertation, University of Pittsburgh. http://d-scholarship.pitt.edu/7274/1/DansETD2.pdf.

McKiernan, Erin C., Philip E. Bourne, C. Titus Brown, Stuart Buck, Amye Kenall, Jennifer Lin, Damon McDougall, et al. 2016. Point of view: How open science helps researchers succeed. *ELife* 5:e16800. https://doi.org/10.7554/eLife.16800.

McKiernan, Erin C., Lesley A. Schimanski, Carol Muñoz Nieves, Lisa Matthias, Meredith T. Niles, and Juan Pablo Alperin. 2019. Use of the Journal Impact Factor in academic review, promotion, and tenure evaluations. *ELife* 8:e47338 *https://doi.org/10.7554/eLife.47338*.

National Academy of Sciences. 2006. Taxonomy of fields and their subfields. *National Academies of Sciences, Engineering, and Medicine.* http://sites.nationalacademies.org/PGA/Resdoc/PGA_044522. Accessed November 18, 2019.

Nature. 2019. Springer Nature journals unify their policy to encourage preprint sharing. *Nature* 569:307. https://www.nature.com/articles/d41586-019-01493-z.

Niles, Meredith T., Lesley A. Schimanski, Erin C. McKiernan, and Juan Pablo Alperin. 2020. Why we publish where we do: Faculty publishing values and their relationship to review, promotion and tenure expectations. *PLOS ONE 15(3): e0228914.* https://doi.org/10.1371/journal.pone.0228914.

Ramos, Andre, and Marina Empinotti. 2017. Indigenous languages must feature more in science communication. *The Conversation.* December 19, 2017. http://theconversation.com/indigenous-languages-must-feature-more-in-science-communication-88596.

Rogers Digital Media. 2016. Maclean's university rankings. *Maclean's.* https://www.macleans.ca/education/unirankings/. Accessed November 1, 2019.

Sanberg, Paul R., Morteza Gharib, Patrick T. Harker, Eric W. Kaler, Richard B. Marchase, Timothy D. Sands, Nasser Arshadi, and Sudeep Sarkar. 2014. Changing the academic culture: valuing patents and commercialization toward tenure and career advancement. *Proceedings of the National Academy of Sciences* 111 (18): 6542–6547. https://doi.org/10.1073/pnas.1404094111.

Schimanski, Lesley, and Juan Pablo Alperin. 2018. The evaluation of scholarship in the academic promotion and tenure process: Past, present, and future. *F1000Research* 7:1605. https://doi.org/10.12688/f1000research.16493.1.

Seipel, Michael M. O. 2003. Assessing publication for tenure. *Journal of Social Work Education* 39 (1): 79–88.

Smesny, Andrea L., Jennifer S. Williams, Gayle A. Brazeau, Robert J. Weber, Hewitt W. Matthews, and Sudip K. Das. 2007. Barriers to scholarship in dentistry, medicine, nursing, and pharmacy practice faculty. *American Journal of Pharmaceutical Education* 71 (5): 91. http://www.ncbi.nlm.nih.gov/pmc/articles/PMC2064889/.

Stevens, Ashley J., Ginger A. Johnson, and Paul R. Sanberg. 2011. The role of patents and commercialization in the tenure and promotion process. *Technology and Innovation* 13 (3): 241–248. https://doi.org/info:doi/10.3727/194982411X13189742259479.

Strauss, Anselm, and Juliet Corbin. 1990. *Basics of Qualitative Research: Grounded Theory Procedures and Techniques.* Newbury Park, CA: Sage Publications.

Tenopir, Carol, Elizabeth D. Dalton, Suzie Allard, Mike Frame, Ivanka Pjesivac, Ben Birch, Danielle Pollock, and Kristina

Dorsett. 2015. Changes in data sharing and data reuse practices and perceptions among scientists worldwide. *PLOS ONE* 10 (8): e0134826. https://doi.org/10.1371/journal.pone.0134826.

Thatcher, Sanford G. 2007. The challenge of open access for university presses. *Learned Publishing* 20 (3): 165–172. https://doi.org/10.1087/095315107X205084.

University of Calgary. 2005. Faculty of social sciences: Policy guidelines relative to appointment, increment, promotion and tenure.

University of Calgary. 2009. Faculty of communication and culture guidelines for appointment, reappointment, promotion, tenure and merit assessment.

University of North Carolina at Chapel Hill. 2009. Report of the UNC task force on future promotion and tenure policies and practices.

University of Utah. 2011. Retention, promotion, and tenure criteria for the department of psychology.

Walker, Robin L., Lindsay Sykes, Brenda R. Hemmelgarn, and Hude Quan. 2010. Authors' opinions on publication in relation to annual performance assessment. *BMC Medical Education* 10:21. https://doi.org/10.1186/1472-6920-10-21.

Wheeler, Richard, Lauren Robel, P. Barry Butler, Philip J. Hanlon, Kim A. Wilcox, Karen Hanson, Ellen Weissinger, et al. 2012. Values and scholarship: Eleven research university provosts explain why they back open access—in Congressional legislation and on their campuses. *Inside Higher Ed.* February 23, 2012. https://www.insidehighered.com/views/2012/02/23/essay-open-access-scholarship.

Wieling, Martijn, Josine Rawee, and Gertjan van Noord. 2018. Reproducibility in computational linguistics: Are we willing to share? *Computational Linguistics* 44 (4): 641–649. https://doi.org/10.1162/coli_a_00330.

Youn, Ted I. K., and Tanya M. Price. 2009. Learning from the experience of others: The evolution of faculty tenure and promotion rules in comprehensive institutions. *Journal of Higher Education* 80 (2): 204–237. https://doi.org/10.1353/jhe.0.0041.

Young, David. 2019. Open-source software can revitalize Indigenous languages. *UNESCO Bangkok.* March 28, 2019. https://bangkok.unesco.org/content/open-source-software-can-revitalize-indigenous-languages.

14 Managing Sociolinguistic Data with the Corpus of Regional African American Language (CORAAL)

Tyler Kendall and Charlie Farrington

1 Introduction

This data management use case describes our work building and managing the Corpus of Regional African American Language (CORAAL; Kendall & Farrington 2020a), the first corpus devoted to making publicly available spoken language data sets for research on and education about African American Language.[1] While CORAAL is specifically focused on African American Language, it also represents a rare case where sociolinguistic interview recordings have been collected and published as an open access, public corpus. As such, we hope our work can act as a model for the publication and management of other sociolinguistic data. Publicly oriented sociolinguistic data sets are rare and published treatments of their design criteria and decision processes are even more rare. Thus, we hope this chapter can add to the limited literature on public sociolinguistic corpora and can aid in the development of best practices for linguistic data management and for sociolinguistic corpus building in particular (for other discussions see, e.g., Beal, Corrigan, & Moisl 2007a, 2007b; Kendall 2007, 2008, 2011; Poplack 1989; Yaeger-Dror & Cieri 2014). Readers are also encouraged to read the CORAAL *User Guide* (Kendall & Farrington 2020b), which is available from the CORAAL website (https://oraal.uoregon.edu/coraal).

Before proceeding, we should ask: Why African American Language? And, why public corpora? African American Language (AAL) is an intentionally broad term meant to encompass all varieties of language use in African American communities reflecting "differences in age/generation, sex, gender, sexuality, social and socioeconomic class, region, education, religion, and other affiliations and identities that intersect with one's ethnicity/race and nationality" (Lanehart 2015:3). Within sociolinguistics,

AAL has been one of the most studied varieties of English (or likely of any language). For over fifty years, researchers have turned to spoken language data from African American individuals and communities to investigate core, basic questions in sociolinguistics and in the history of American English. Researchers, since Labov et al. (1968) and Wolfram (1969), have also studied AAL to combat public myths and prejudice about language (see, e.g., Rickford 1999; Baugh 2000, 2005; or Wolfram 2008 for fuller discussions and Lanehart 2015 for a comprehensive treatment of AAL). Nonetheless, despite such an intense research tradition, almost no primary data are available for researchers or educators. As Kendall, Bresnan, and Van Herk (2011) discussed, research attempting to compare across AAL-speaking communities has been limited. As social science disciplines, and linguistics in particular, take more seriously issues of replicability, big data, and open access (see Berez-Kroeker et al. 2018; Gawne & Styles, chapter 2, this volume), it is, frankly, imperative, that publicly available data sets be developed and shared.[2]

2 CORAAL

CORAAL focuses on providing public access to recorded speech from regional varieties of AAL. CORAAL is a long-term corpus-building project conceived of in terms of several individual components. Each component includes audio recordings along with time-aligned orthographic transcription. The core components of CORAAL focus on AAL in Washington, DC, the nation's capital, a city with a long-standing African American majority, and the site of much early research on AAL (Farrington & Schilling 2019). CORAAL:DC, first released in January 2018, is composed of over one hundred sociolinguistic interviews with AAL speakers in DC born between 1890 and

2005. It consists of two sub-components, CORAAL:DCA, recorded around 1968 (Kendall, Fasold, et al. 2018), and CORAAL:DCB, recorded around 2016 (Kendall, Quartey, et al. 2018). In addition to CORAAL:DC, CORAAL is scheduled to increasingly include several smaller components to provide regional breadth. The three supplemental components available at the time of this writing are CORAAL:PRV (Rowe 2005; Rowe et al. 2018), which includes fifteen sociolinguistic interviews from a rural African American community in central North Carolina, CORAAL:ROC (King 2018; King et al. 2020), which includes thirteen sociolinguistic interviews from Rochester, a city in Western Upstate New York, and CORAAL:ATL (Farrington et al. 2020), which includes thirteen conversational interviews from Atlanta, Georgia. Additional supplemental components will be released in periodic updates as they become available. Updates typically include minor transcription revisions and new annotation versions, as well as new interviews and, when available, entire new supplemental components.

All CORAAL recordings are anonymized and orthographically transcribed with time alignment at the utterance level. Audio is available in high-quality uncompressed (.wav) format, and transcripts are available in three formats: Praat TextGrid (.TextGrid) files (Boersma & Weenink 2018), ELAN (.eaf) files (Wittenburg et al. 2006), and as plain text (.txt) files with tab-delimited fields. The corpus is intended to be downloaded by users for direct use, but CORAAL is also accessible through a website, CORAAL Explorer (see section 3.4), which provides browsing (audio and transcripts) and search capabilities directly in a web browser. A syntactically parsed version of much of the data is also scheduled for upcoming release.

3 Building CORAAL

Building CORAAL involved, and continues to involve, a combination of advanced planning and the development of a consistent workflow for data collection, processing, and sharing. In this section, we discuss each of these aspects of the project.

3.1 Collection

CORAAL's data come from two broad sources, legacy materials and new recordings collected specifically for the public corpus. By *legacy materials*, we mean sociolinguistic

recordings that were collected not intentionally for inclusion in CORAAL. This includes a subset of recordings from Ralph Fasold's foundational fieldwork in Washington, DC (Fasold 1972), which form the basis for CORAAL:DCA and were in many ways a motivating factor behind the entire CORAAL project. However, these legacy materials also include recordings from fieldwork projects contemporary with the development of CORAAL, for instance work by Sharese King for her dissertation (King 2018) on AAL in Rochester, New York (CORAAL:ROC).

For these legacy collections, the CORAAL development team makes arrangements with the collections' primary investigators to obtain the data. In the case of CORAAL:DCA, the reel-to-reel recordings were first digitized at the North Carolina State University Sociolinguistics Lab, and then uploaded to the Sociolinguistic Archive and Analysis Project (SLAAP; Kendall 2007; https://slaap.chass.ncsu.edu/) for storage. The development team then organized the recordings according to a 4×3 demographic table (see table 14.1), covering four age groups and three social classes. The social class groups, listed simply as classes 1, 2, and 3, are meant to capture broad social class differences and are not meant to represent theoretically motivated socioeconomic classes. Qualitative labels are included in the CORAAL *User Guide*, ranging from lower working class to upper middle class, with differences depending on the specific component (see tables 14.2 and 14.3). Our goal was to have two male and two female speakers for each demographic cell (48 speakers), but this was not always possible and when more data have been available, we have opted to include more than this many speakers per cell.

One of the goals of Fasold's (1972) study was a focus on teenagers, which resulted in a sample that was not balanced according to our designs for CORAAL. Furthermore, some of Fasold's recordings with the youngest speakers were quite short. Because of these factors, we

Table 14.1

Demographic matrix targeted for CORAAL:DC components

Age group	Social class 1		Social class 2		Social class 3	
	Male	Female	Male	Female	Male	Female
12–19	2	2	2	2	2	2
20–29	2	2	2	2	2	2
30–50	2	2	2	2	2	2
51+	2	2	2	2	2	2

Table 14.2

Demographic matrix for CORAAL:DCA component

Age group	Social class 1 (≈LWC)		Social class 2 (≈UWC)		Social class 3 (≈MC)	
	Male	Female	Male	Female	Male	Female
12–19	8	5	6	7	6	6
20–29	1	1	3	0	3	5
30–50	1	2	3	0	4	1
51+	2	0	1	1	2	0

LWC=lower working class; UWC=upper working class; MC= middle class (see *User Guide*).

Table 14.3

Demographic matrix for CORAAL:DCB component

Age group	Social class 1 (≈WC)		Social class 2 (≈LMC)		Social class 3 (≈UMC)	
	Male	Female	Male	Female	Male	Female
12–19	3	3	1	1	1	1
20–29	3	3	1	2	0	1
30–50	3	3	3	2	2	2
51+	2	1	1	5	2	2

WC=working class; LMC=lower middle class; UMC=upper middle class (see *User Guide*).

included at least twelve speakers in each of the social class groups for the youngest age group, for a total of sixty-eight speakers for CORAAL:DCA (see table 14.2 for the full demographic matrix of CORAAL:DCA).

For CORAAL:DCB (table 14.3), some demographic groups have been harder to recruit than others and so there too our actual sample of speakers diverges somewhat from our initial target. More information about speaker selection for CORAAL:DCA and CORAAL:DCB can be found in the "CORAAL:DCA (Washington, DC 1968)" and "CORAAL:DCB (Washington, DC 2016)" sections in the *User Guide*.

The non-core components within CORAAL target a smaller number of speakers, with a goal of two to three speakers per demographic cell (table 14.4) within a single social class. In the case of legacy collections, such as recordings from Princeville, North Carolina (Rowe 2005), recordings were selected from the larger collection (N=37) to fit this smaller demographic matrix.

Many additional resources, including the ones in SLAAP, are not fully publicly available and so will not become a part of CORAAL proper, but can be made available to bona fide researchers. In addition to CORAAL components,

Table 14.4

Demographic matrix targeted for other CORAAL components

Age group	Male	Female
18–29	2	2
30–50	2	2
51+	2	2

CORAAL also includes "Supplements", which are prepared and curated by the CORAAL team to highlight recordings and selections from larger datasets important to the field of sociolinguistics (https://oraal.uoregon.edu/coraal /supplements). CORAAL Supplements acts as a vehicle to help preserve and share other unique materials that do not fit the matrix criteria for CORAAL components, with the aim to promote greater public availability of diverse AAL data. We hope that CORAAL can help to promote the wider use of these resources and believe they can make valuable contributions to the overall coverage available in CORAAL.

For collections designed specifically for CORAAL, including the major fieldwork project led by Minnie Quartey in Washington, DC, for CORAAL:DCB but also data collected for a supplemental component for an urban Southern friend network in Atlanta (CORAAL:ATL), the corpus development team worked with fieldworkers to define demographic categories of targeted interest and interview protocols. For CORAAL:DCB, Quartey based her fieldwork recruiting on the matrix in table 14.1 and the available data for CORAAL:DCA. With several connections to the local community, interviews were done through friend of a friend networks. The interview schedule for CORAAL:DCB was designed to touch on several of the same general themes and topics as the CORAAL:DCA interviews did, while placing greater emphasis on engaging the participants in topics of interest to them that might promote conversational interactions. The six general categories of the interview schedule include general demographic information, neighborhood, family information, school days, friendship group, and work/occupation. A final category focused on DC-specific questions developed in consultation with our fieldworker and her primary interests.

Fieldworkers completed interview report forms for each sociolinguistic interview and administered informed consent documents for each participant. (All fieldwork and consent documents were designed in consultation with and approved by the overseeing university's—the University of Oregon's—human subjects research office.) Because the goal was intentionally to collect data that would be shared as widely as possible, consent forms explicitly asked the participants if they would allow us to use the recording for a public corpus on language diversity in the United States. Consent forms have four levels of permission from whether we can use the recording as researchers to the explicit recognition of the participant by name in the corpus. Once recordings were collected, the fieldworkers transmitted the files to the development team, at the Language Variation and Computation Laboratory (LVC Lab) in the Department of Linguistics at the University of Oregon.

3.2 Processing

Once the data were on hand in the LVC Lab, files were stored on a networked drive in the LVC Lab hosted by a Macintosh Pro desktop computer and backups were kept locally on an external hard drive in the LVC Lab. Each audio file was resaved with a unique code, following the naming conventions for SLAAP. Audio files and basic metadata were then uploaded to SLAAP, so the files could be accessed remotely by project members and to act as an off-site archival version for the original recordings.

3.2.1 Transcription   Each audio file was initially transcribed in Praat using Praat's TextGrid annotation features by an undergraduate research assistant. Our transcription process was designed to recognize that transcription is a process and one that does not yield a single, "correct" outcome (Bucholtz 2007; Du Bois et al. 1993; Edwards 2001; Kendall 2008, 2011; Mishler 1991; Ochs 1979). To quote Edwards (2001:321), "transcripts are not unbiased representations of the data. Far from being exhaustive and objective, they are inherently selective and interpretive. The researcher chooses what types of information to preserve, which descriptive categories to use, and how to display the information in the written and spatial medium of a transcript." The challenge for public corpora, especially for public "unconventional corpora" (see Kendall 2011), is to make choices about the transcription process that support diverse use cases and are not overly focused around a single research framework or perspective. At some level, this is an impossible task. For instance, our convention of delimiting the speech in transcripts into utterance-based units

(with pauses of a certain length as the boundaries; based on Kendall 2007) supports a number of different conceptions of spoken language data, but leads to different chunking than a conception based on syntactic units (e.g., clauses) or intonational groups (see, for instance, Chafe 1993) and therefore could hinder certain analytic uses. No single transcription convention can support every possible use. To this end, transcript conventions for CORAAL are laid out explicitly in the *User Guide*, giving users access to basically the same information used by the transcribers so that users have the ability to see our explicit decisions. We also chose not to implement certain conventions whatsoever in the transcripts. For example, we did not include quotation marks in the current versions of transcripts. While some cases of direct quotation are easy and uncontroversial to identify, other cases are highly subjective or come down to an analyst's conception of quotative marking (see Romaine & Lange 1991; Buchstaller 2006). Rather than risk arbitrary quotation marking we opted to forego all use of quotation marks to mark quotations.

After this initial round of transcription, subsequently each file went through at least two rounds of checking and editing. The first round involved editing primarily by the second author and was focused largely on the accuracy of the text and boundaries, and the second round of editing was to check for spelling convention consistency.

Transcription did not cover the entirety of each recording but focused on providing a forty-five to sixty minute sample of the conversational portion of the interview when possible. Audio for each file was trimmed to include only the transcribed portions. In a few cases, we have excised portions of interviews. This is occasionally by the request of the participant, and it is occasionally done as a decision of the project team based on the content of the interview. There are a few cases where we have excised content even though the participant gave us permission to include it. For example, in DCB_se1_ag4_f_01, a passage from 537.8 to 671.8 is excised because of a graphic personal story. Other excised content includes reading passages and word lists. In CORAAL:DCA, a majority of the recordings have other tasks (e.g., language games, described in Fasold 1972), while CORAAL:DCB includes reading passage data (including the "Please Call Stella" passage; Weinberger 2015). The CORAAL:DCB "Please Call Stella" passages are scheduled to be published in an upcoming release.

3.2.2 File naming

For the corpus publication, files were renamed from their SLAAP names for greater transparency to end users (for a discussion of data management practices, including file naming, see Mattern, chapter 5, this volume). Speaker and file names are labeled systematically based on speaker demographics. For example, *DCA_se2_ag1_m_05_1.wav* is an audio (WAV) file for DCA, the Washington, DC 1968 component of CORAAL. The file's primary speaker is in socioeconomic group 2 (se2), age group 1 (ag1; this is the youngest age group, see section 3.1), male (m) number 5 (i.e., the fifth speaker in the cell of the demographic matrix). The final 1 indicates the audio file number. For supplements that do not stratify the sample by socioeconomics (including CORAAL:PRV and CORAAL:ROC), se0 is used to notate that a speaker is uncategorized for socioeconomic group (not that the speaker is in group 0). For gender, three codes are used: f, for female; m, for male; and n, for non-binary.

3.2.3 Redaction

A guiding principle in the development of CORAAL is to protect the anonymity of its participants. Participants who were interviewed specifically for the corpus project (e.g., for CORAAL:DCB) were given the choice in the consent process of whether they wished to be recognized by name, with the default being that they will not be named. The majority of participants did ask to be recognized by name and we acknowledge them by name in the *User Guide*. For participants not interviewed by the project team (e.g., DCA, PRV, ROC, and some upcoming supplements), we do not disclose any names, unless there is an explicit (i.e., documented) permission given by the participant.

Our redaction process involved several steps. During the first round of transcription, transcribers marked different categories of sensitive information, such as names, street addresses, places of work, and other kinds of personally identifiable information. Additionally, transcribers noted the numbers of syllables of the item(s) to be redacted. The third round of transcription involved the creation of a redaction tier in Praat, where boundaries were placed directly around the portion of the interview to be redacted. The amount of material redacted varies widely by interview. Some interviews have only one or two redacted utterances while others have a

great many. Once completed, redaction "bleeps," which were generated to match the mean pitch and amplitude of the speech being redacted, replaced the sensitive information.

After the completion of all processing (transcription, file naming, redaction), the Praat TextGrids were automatically processed (by script) into tab-delimited text files and (by ELAN) into ELAN format files. All three formats are available for download.

3.3 Metadata files

Each component of CORAAL has its own metadata file that contains a range of information about the recordings and their speakers. These files are tab-delimited text files that can be readily opened in a spreadsheet program, such Microsoft Excel, or in R. The metadata files are downloadable with the rest of each corpus component's files. For example, metadata for CORAAL:DCA are in the file labeled DCA_metadata_2018.10.06.txt (for version 2018.10.06). This file can be accessed from http://lingtools.uoregon.edu/coraal/dca/2018.10.06/DCA_metadata_2018.10.06.txt.

All of the pretrimmed files are stored (in WAV format) on SLAAP. SLAAP often contains more files from a sociolinguistic fieldwork project than just those included in CORAAL. The SLAAP codes for the files are provided in a column the metadata file when appropriate and described in the CORAAL *User Guide*. For example, CORAAL:DCA SLAAP codes are reflective of the original codes used in Fasold (1972). In CORAAL:DCB and CORAAL:ROC, SLAAP codes were given to recordings by the date of completion. For CORAAL:PRV, SLAAP codes are reflective of the codes used when the audio tapes were digitized and uploaded to SLAAP in 2007 and 2008. While SLAAP access to the files is limited, this can facilitate the possibility of tracing a CORAAL file back to its original recording.

Several categories in the metadata spreadsheets apply to all CORAAL components, while others apply only to specific components. Metadata explanations and notes are available in the CORAAL *User Guide*. Metadata can vary across the components, but in many cases extremely rich information is available about each speaker. Most speaker files obtained from Ralph Fasold (DCA) came with an informant data sheet, where much of the CORAAL metadata information comes from. The informant data sheet collected basic demographic data, such as sex, age, address, birthplace, parents' birthplace, as well as a detailed socio-economic status determination. For CORAAL:DCB, interviewers were asked to complete a similar interview report form for each speaker, which collected similar kinds of demographic information as Fasold's informant data sheet. In addition to general demographic information, the interview report form contains additional interview notes (e.g., explanations about interruptions and background noise) as well as topics covered over the course of the interview. For CORAAL:PRV, some speaker information was gathered from the metadata on SLAAP, while other information was obtained from the content of the interviews themselves.

3.4 Sharing

The main CORAAL web page (https://oraal.uoregon.edu/coraal/) is housed on the Online Resources for African American Language (https://oraal.uoregon.edu) website, which is devoted to providing information and resources about language in the African American community, targeting educators, researchers, and the wider public. (ORAAL is a Drupal site, hosted as a part of the University of Oregon's Drupal services.) CORAAL data are hosted on and provided to the public via a virtual server (http://lingtools.uoregon.edu) managed by the University of Oregon's College of Arts and Sciences information technology services group. Originally (i.e., when CORAAL was first publicly released in January 2018), the data were provided in downloadable form only. That is, users could access the data by downloading a series of compressed file bundles (tar.gz format). Making the data available by download, but not including a web-based interface initially, was a design decision, based on our belief that truly public data means that the data themselves are public, and not simply that there are open interfaces to the data. Our first priority was ensuring that potential users had access to the entirety of the data. Following this initial release, we developed a set of webpages, the CORAAL Explorer site (http://lingtools.uoregon.edu/coraal/explorer/), which provide access to the individual interviews and to a search interface for the entire collection. We anticipate further developing the online tools over time, although we intend for the data to *always* be the main emphasis of the CORAAL project. Through the CORAAL Explorer site, users can also download and use CORAAL transcripts directly in the R programming environment.

3.5 Citation and attribution for CORAAL

CORAAL seeks to follow and support the *Austin Principles of Data Citation in Linguistics* (http://site.uit.no/linguisticsdatacitation/; see also Conzett & De Smedt, chapter 11, this volume). As such, the CORAAL *User Guide* provides suggested citations and version numbering for each individual component of CORAAL, as well for the main CORAAL project (Kendall & Farrington 2020a) and the umbrella ORAAL project (Kendall, McLarty, & Farrington 2020), which houses the corpus. Furthermore, individual files and speakers are given persistent and relatively transparent labels that can be used for uniquely referring to individual files (and further with resolution down to individual transcript line numbers or time stamps). This can aid in using the corpus to provide specific passages or examples from the discourse or of AAL features. For instance, (1) provides an example from CORAAL of negative inversion, a morphosyntactic feature of AAL.

(1) Negative Inversion in AAL: "Cause didn't nobody hardly stay home then."
DCA_se1_ag1_m_03_1 (2084.34–2086.31)

We can further provide a direct link to the transcript line and audio in the CORAAL Explorer website for the corpus: http://lingtools.uoregon.edu/coraal/explorer/browse.php?what=DCA_se1_ag1_m_03_1.txt&line=2006&settime=2084.34. One issue with this current approach is that the URLs are not persistent identifiers (that is, future updates could impact the integrity of the links; see Conzett & De Smedt, chapter 11, this volume).

To protect the privacy of the speakers in the corpus, individual speakers and files are only labeled with their CORAAL identifier, and no reference is made back to the speakers' actual names (see redaction discussion in section 3.2.3). However, we also wanted to acknowledge the contributions of the individual participants and many participants did not wish to remain anonymous. Thus, the *User Guide* explicitly acknowledges by name all of the participants who indicated in their informed consent process that they wished to *not* remain anonymous.

4   CORAAL now and in the future

As mentioned earlier, the first components of CORAAL were released publicly in January 2018. Now that there are several published components included in CORAAL, the development team's efforts center on adding to current components and revising what has already been published when errors or inconsistencies are discovered. Despite our close attention in the transcription creation and editing process, we regularly discover cases where our transcription practices have not been implemented as consistently as they could have been. (For instance, in v.2018.10.06, all instances of 'outta' and 'kinda' were changed to "out of" and "kind of" for internal consistency across each of the components.) The fact that we continue to find ways to improve CORAAL's transcripts does not surprise us, and, we hope, it will not disappoint CORAAL's users. We are also happy to receive from users corrections to mistranscribed elements. Sometimes users identify errors although at other times transcribers/listeners will just disagree about what they hear (Bucholtz 2000). Altogether, we anticipate periodically releasing corrections and we publish these in errata sections of the *User Guide*.

The decision to publish changes to transcriptions with periodic updates to the corpus means that different versions are in circulation. With the CORAAL Explorer website, updates to the corpus are also updated immediately on the Explorer website. In the metadata for each component, information about when each file was first added to CORAAL is included as well as the date of the most recent update for each file. We hope that whenever there is an update to the corpus, users will download the new update, although we cannot ensure that users do this. How to best manage versioning in a living, public corpus remains a question that we suspect we will be tackling for some time. We hope to improve our practices in future versions, for instance, by implementing a more formalized versioning system for the corpus, such as through Zenodo, GitHub, and/or other platforms.

5 Conclusion

CORAAL seeks to fill a major gap in linguistic research infrastructure by providing freely available sociolinguistic data sets for regionally situated AAL samples. The corpus is the first of its kind. Sociolinguistically oriented spoken language data raise a number of issues for corpus building, including sampling, metadata, and annotation (Beal, Corrigan, & Moisl 2007a, 2007b; Kendall 2007, 2008, 2011; Poplack 1989; Yaeger-Dror & Cieri 2014). The CORAAL development team has attempted to build as widely useful a resource as possible and hope to have

in place a distribution and data archiving plan that will prove robust over both the long and short terms. We hope the resources, as well as the lessons we have learned, are useful to the wider linguistics research and outreach community.

Notes

1. CORAAL, pronounced [ˈkoɹəl], is part of the Online Resources for African American Language (ORAAL) project at the University of Oregon. CORAAL and the larger ORAAL Project have been made possible by support from the U.S. National Science Foundation (grant no. BCS-1358724), by the University of Oregon, and by the contributions of many people. In addition to the authors, the main CORAAL development team has included Jason McLarty, Shelby Arnson, and Brooke Josler. Lucas Jensen, Emma Mullen, Chloe Tacata, Jaidan McLean, Deepika Viswanath, Savanah Ray, and Matthew Bauer have also contributed to the corpus transcription, annotation, and redaction. Fieldwork would not have been possible without the major contributions of Minnie Quartey, Carlos Huff, Patrick Slay Brooks, Sharese King, and Ryan Rowe. We also thank Ralph Fasold, Natalie Schilling, Charlotte Vaughn, Walt Wolfram, and Danica Cullinan for their many contributions to the project. In the CORAAL *User Guide* (Kendall & Farrington 2020b), we express our deep gratitude to the main individuals who contributed their speech to the corpus, as well as many additional colleagues who have supported the project in various ways. Please see that document for complete acknowledgments.

2. Note that the authors are not arguing that all data sets need to be shared or that data should never be kept private. There are many reasons for sociolinguistic data sets not to be shared (see Warner 2014; Holton, Leonard, & Pulsifer, chapter 4, this volume), and a half century of productive work has demonstrated that vast discoveries can be made from relatively small, private data collections. Nonetheless, our point is that new advances and better science can be done if there are *more* public and larger data sets.

References

Baugh, John. 2000. *Black Street Speech: Its History, Structure, and Survival*. Austin: University of Texas Press.

Baugh, John. 2005. Linguistic profiling. In *Black Linguistics: Language, Society, and Politics in Africa and the Americas*, ed. Arnetha Ball, Geneva Smitherman, and Arthur K. Spears, 155–168. London: Routledge.

Beal, Joan, Karen Corrigan, and Hermann Moisl, eds. 2007a. *Creating and Digitizing Language Corpora*. Vol. 1: *Synchronic Databases*. New York: Palgrave-Macmillan. http://doi.org/10.1057/9780230223936.

Beal, Joan, Karen Corrigan, and Hermann Moisl. 2007b. Taming digital voices and texts: Models and methods for handling unconventional synchronic corpora. In *Creating and Digitizing Language Corpora*. Vol. 1: *Synchronic Databases*, ed. Joan Beal, Karen Corrigan, and Hermann Moisl, 1–16. New York: Palgrave-Macmillan. https://doi.org/10.1057/9780230223936_1.

Berez-Kroeker, Andrea, Lauren Gawne, Susan Smythe Kung, Barbara Kelly, Tyler Heston, Gary Holton, Peter Pulsifer, et al. 2018. Reproducible research in linguistics: A position statement on data citation and attribution in our field. *Linguistics* 56 (1): 1–18. https://doi.org/10.1515/ling-2017-0032.

Boersma, Paul, and David Weenink. 2018. *Praat: Doing Phonetics by Computer* (computer program). Version 6.0.43. http://www.praat.org.

Bucholtz, Mary. 2000. The politics of transcription. *Journal of Pragmatics* 32: 1439–1465. https://doi.org/10.1016/S0378-2166(99)00094-6.

Bucholtz, Mary. 2007. Variation in transcription. *Discourse Studies* 9 (6): 784–808. https://doi.org/10.1177/1461445607082580.

Buchstaller, Isabelle. 2006. Diagnostics of age-graded linguistic behaviour: The case of the quotative system. *Journal of Sociolinguistics* 10:3–30. https://doi.org/10.1111/j.1360-6441.2006.00315.x.

Chafe, Wallace. 1993. Prosodic and functional units of language. In *Talking Data: Transcription and Coding in Discourse Research*, ed. Jane Edwards and Martin Lampert, 33–43. Hillsdale, NJ: Lawrence Erlbaum.

Du Bois, John W., Stephan Schuetze-Coburn, Susanna Cumming, and Danae Paolino. 1993. Outline of discourse transcription. In *Talking Data: Transcription and Coding in Discourse Research*, ed. Jane Edwards and Martin Lampert, 45–89. Hillsdale, NJ: Lawrence Erlbaum.

Edwards, Jane. 2001. The transcription of discourse. In *Handbook of Discourse Analysis*, ed. Deborah Tannen, Deborah Schiffrin, and Heidi Hamilton, 321–348. Malden, MA: Blackwell. https://doi.org/10.1002/9780470753460.ch18.

Farrington, Charlie, Tyler Kendall, Patrick Slay Brooks, Lucas Jenson, Chloe Tacata, and Jaidan McLean. 2020. *The Corpus of Regional African American Language: ATL (Atlanta, GA 2017)*. Version 2020.05. Eugene, OR: Online Resources for African American Language Project.

Farrington, Charlie, and Natalie Schilling. 2019. Contextualizing the Corpus of Regional African American Language, D.C.: AAL in the nation's capital. *American Speech* 94 (1): 21–35. https://doi.org/10.1215/00031283-7308060.

Fasold, Ralph W. 1972. *Tense Marking in Black English*. Arlington, VA: Center for Applied Linguistics.

Kendall, Tyler. 2007. Enhancing sociolinguistic data collections: The North Carolina Sociolinguistic Archive and Analysis Project. *Penn Working Papers in Linguistics* 13 (2): 15–26.

Kendall, Tyler. 2008. On the history and future of sociolinguistic data. *Linguistic and Language Compass* 2:332–351. https://doi.org/10.1111/j.1749-818X.2008.00051.x.

Kendall, Tyler. 2011. Corpora from a sociolinguistic perspective (Corpora sob uma perspectiva sociolinguística). In *Corpus Studies: Future Directions*, ed. Stefan Th. Gries, special issue of *Revista Brasileira de Linguística Aplicada* 11 (2): 361–389. http://dx.doi.org/10.1590/S1984-63982011000200005.

Kendall, Tyler, Joan Bresnan, and Gerard Van Herk. 2011. The dative alternation in African American English: Researching syntactic variation and change across sociolinguistic data sets. *Corpus Linguistics and Linguistic Theory*, 7 (2): 229–244. https://doi.org/10.1515/cllt.2011.011.

Kendall, Tyler, and Charlie Farrington. 2020a. *The Corpus of Regional African American Language*. Version 2020.05. Eugene, OR: The Online Resources for African American Language Project. http://oraal.uoregon.edu/coraal.

Kendall, Tyler, and Charlie Farrington. 2020b. *The Corpus of Regional African American Language User Guide*. Version 2020.05. Eugene, OR: The Online Resources for African American Language Project. http://lingtools.uoregon.edu/coraal/userguide.

Kendall, Tyler, Ralph Fasold, Charlie Farrington, Jason McLarty, Shelby Arnson, and Brooke Josler. 2018. *The Corpus of Regional African American Language: DCA (Washington DC 1968)*. Version 2018.10.06. Eugene, OR: The Online Resources for African American Language Project.

Kendall, Tyler, Jason McLarty, and Charlie Farrington. 2020. *ORAAL: Online Resources for African American Language*. Eugene, OR: Online Resources for African American Language Project. https://oraal.uoregon.edu/.

Kendall, Tyler, Minnie Quartey, Charlie Farrington, Jason McLarty, Shelby Arnson, and Brooke Josler. 2018. *The Corpus of Regional African American Language: DCB (Washington DC 2016)*. Version 2018.10.06. Eugene, OR: The Online Resources for African American Language Project.

King, Sharese. 2018. Exploring social and linguistic diversity across African Americans from Rochester, New York. PhD dissertation, Stanford University.

King, Sharese, Charlie Farrington, Tyler Kendall, Emma Mullen, Shelby Arnson, and Lucas Jenson. 2020. *The Corpus of Regional African American Language: ROC (Rochester, NY 2016)*. Version 2020.05. Eugene, OR: The Online Resources for African American Language Project.

Labov, William, Paul Cohen, Clarence Robins, and John Lewis. 1968. *A Study of the Non-Standard English of Negro and Puerto Rican Speakers in New York City*. Final Report, Research Project 3288. Washington, DC: United States Office of Education.

Lanehart, Sonja. 2015. Language use in African American communities: An introduction. In *The Oxford Handbook of*

African American Language, ed. Sonja Lanehart, 1–19. Oxford: Oxford University Press. https://dx.doi.org/10.1093/oxfordhb /9780199795390.001.0001.

Mishler, Elliot. 1991. Representing discourse: The rhetoric of transcription. *Journal of Narrative and Life History* 1 (4): 255– 280. https://doi.org/10.1075/jnlh.1.4.01rep.

Ochs, Elinor. 1979. Transcription as theory. In *Developmental Pragmatics*, ed. Elinor Ochs and Bambi Schieffelin, 43–72. New York: Academic Press.

Poplack, Shana. 1989. The care and handling of a megacorpus: The Ottawa-Hull French Project. In *Language Change and Variation*, ed. Ralph W. Fasold and Deborah Schiffrin, 411–444. Amsterdam: John Benjamins.

Rickford, John R. 1999. *African American English: Features, Evolution, and Educational Implications*. Malden, MA: Blackwell.

Romaine, Suzanne, and Deborah Lange. 1991. The use of *like* as a marker of reported speech and thought: A case of grammaticalization in progress. *American Speech* 66 (3): 227–279.

Rowe, Ryan. 2005. The development of African American English in the oldest Black town in America: Plural -*s* absence in Princeville, North Carolina. MA thesis, North Carolina State University.

Rowe, Ryan, Walt Wolfram, Tyler Kendall, Charlie Farrington, and Brooke Josler. 2018. *The Corpus of Regional African American Language: PRV (Princeville, NC 2004)*. Version 2018.10.06. Eugene, OR: The Online Resources for African American Language.

Warner, Natasha. 2014. Sharing of data as it relates to human subjects issues and data management plans. *Language and Linguistics Compass* 8 (11): 512–518. https://doi.org/10.1111/lnc3 .12107.

Weinberger, Steven. 2015. *The Speech Accent Archive* (website). George Mason University. http://accent.gmu.edu/.

Wittenburg, Peter, Hennie Brugman, Albert Russel, Alex Klassmann, and Han Sloetjes. 2006. ELAN: A professional framework for multimodality research. In *Proceedings of the 5th International Conference on Language Resources and Evaluation (LREC 2006)*, 1556–1559. http://hdl.handle.net/11858/00 -001M-0000-0013-1E7E-4.

Wolfram, Walter A. 1969. *A Sociolinguistic Description of Detroit Negro Speech*. Washington, DC: Center for Applied Linguistics.

Wolfram, Walt. 2008. Language diversity and the public interest. In *Sustaining Linguistic Diversity: Endangered and Minority Languages and Language Varieties*, ed. Kendall A. King, Natalie Schilling-Estes, Lyn Fogle, Jia Jackie Lou, and Barbara Soukup, 187–204. Washington, DC: Georgetown University Press.

Yaeger-Dror, Malcah, and Chris Cieri, eds. 2014. *Special Issue on Archiving Sociolinguistic Data*. *Language and Linguistics Compass* 8 (3).

15 Managing Data for Integrated Speech Corpus Analysis in *SPeech Across Dialects of English* (SPADE)

Morgan Sonderegger, Jane Stuart-Smith, Michael McAuliffe, Rachel Macdonald, and Tyler Kendall

1 Introduction: Large-scale speech corpus analysis

This data management use case discusses the SPeech Across Dialects of English (SPADE) project (for details, see https://spade.glasgow.ac.uk/.) SPADE was devised to carry out large-scale integrated speech corpus analysis across a subset of Englishes. In so doing, the project aims to facilitate large-scale integrated speech corpus analysis for the speech and linguistics research communities in two ways. First, the project will generate large, publicly available, derived data sets of acoustic measures for English speech sounds. Second, it will create freely accessible software for future use by other researchers for analyzing their own data sets: the Integrated Speech Corpus Analysis (ISCAN) system. The intended audience for this chapter thus includes (1) readers wishing to use the derived data sets of acoustic measures in their own work and seeking background on the SPADE project and how the ISCAN software works and (2) readers who would like to carry out their own large-scale integrated corpus analysis projects (as part of a research team) and would like to know about a previous effort.

The vision behind SPADE is to enable less and more experienced users to carry out large-scale automatic search and extraction of the same information about speech from numerous spoken corpora. The user should be able to carry out this analysis whether the corpus is public or private and independent of the corpus format, structure, complexity, and the dialect(s) it represents. As of October 2019, the project is two years in and has laid the groundwork by developing ISCAN (section 3). We are refining and testing this software for subsets of a single language, English, as represented by some forty existing public and private spoken data sets from the Old World (British Isles) and New World (North America) across an effective time span of over a hundred years. SPADE's research remit is to use ISCAN to investigate how segmental features of English, in particular vowels, sibilants, stops, and liquids, have changed over time and space.

SPADE was motivated by the desire to marry the availability of spoken language corpora with increasingly advanced speech processing tools and to make feasible the sharing of existing speech data sets through robust automated speech analysis. There are now vast resources of digital collections of transcribed speech, from many different languages, gathered for many different purposes: from oral histories to sociolinguistic interviews, large data sets for training speech recognition systems, legal interactions, and political debates. The benefits of being able to share diverse speech corpora for the high-quality automated acoustic analysis of *spoken* as well as written language have implications within and beyond speech and linguistic research, including technological, forensic, and clinical approaches (cf. Liberman 2019). This is especially so if such analyses are standardized, replicable, and *ethically non-invasive*, in other words, can produce anonymized acoustic measures or linguistic information (e.g., vowel formant measures or word frequencies), without the need for manual inspection or listening to speech from ethically restricted spoken corpora. However, notwithstanding cost and privacy, there are numerous barriers to sharing speech corpora, including the nature of the speech data sets themselves in terms of size, complexity, and diversity of storage formats.

The availability of digital speech data sets is matched by the availability of increasingly complex speech processing tools. Automatic speech recognition–based tools for *forced alignment* automatically segment and label speech recordings that have written transcriptions, resulting in word- and sound-level boundaries. These tools have become increasingly widely used over the past decade (e.g., FAVE [Forced Alignment and Vowel Extraction], Montreal Forced Aligner, LaBB-CAT, MAUS [Munich Automatic Segmentation System]; Rosenfelder et al. 2015; McAuliffe, Socolof, et al. 2017; Fromont & Hay 2012; Kisler, Schiel, & Sloetjes 2012), resulting in greatly reduced search time for "force-aligned" data sets. Machine learning–based software packages now allow for *automatic measurement* of some measures widely used in phonetic research (e.g., FAVE for vowel formants, Auto-VOT for voice onset time; Rosenfelder et al. 2015; Keshet, Sonderegger, & Knowles 2014). However, again, barriers prevent these tools from being widely used. Tools are generally specialized to particular data set formats and often require significant technical skill. For example, forced aligners require integration with electronic dictionaries that specify possible pronunciations of words, while measurement tools require command-line usage and some scripting in several programming languages (Python, R, Praat). Widely available speech analysis software such as Praat (Boersma & Weenik 2016) and EMU Speech Database Management System (EMU-SDMS; Winkelmann, Harrington, & Jänsch 2017) also allow users to write their own programs (scripts) for the semi- and fully automatic measurement of some simple acoustic measures reflecting pitch, loudness, and noise components of speech (e.g., F0, amplitude, spectra), based on preimplemented signal processing algorithms. But equivalent scripts are often written over and over again by different researchers, which has the methodological implication—reaching into theoretical inferences—that different acoustic analyses of the "same" aspect of speech sounds are not actually the same.

The ISCAN system developed within SPADE forms part of a general movement toward development of different speech database management systems (e.g., EMU-SDMS, LaBB-CAT, Phon [http://www.phon.ca/], Sociolinguistic Archive and Analysis Project [SLAAP; https://slaap.chass

.ncsu.edu/]; Rose et al. 2006; Kendall 2007). These differ in their goals and functionality, depending on intended use cases. The ISCAN system for SPADE is specialized for linking and analyzing multiple speech corpora, with flexibility for different use cases that do not assume users can necessarily access raw data.

ISCAN assumes that data annotation has been completed and performs data processing that can be carried out automatically and that does not necessarily require manual/visual access to raw speech/text data; though an additional "inspection interface" does permit access to raw audio, provided the user has the appropriate permissions. ISCAN requires minimally a collection of sound files, with accompanying word and segment-/phone-level time-stamped labeling (e.g., from forced alignment). Our approach to automated speech analysis assumes an abstraction away from the original speech data set format, whereby raw audio + text data sets are imported and enriched with a large range of acoustic measures, resulting in anonymized databases of acoustic measures with additional linguistic information. These data sets can then be queried, and the results exported, resulting in "derived data sets" (in comma-separated value [CSV]/spreadsheet format), for subsequent analysis (see figure 15.1). Depending on requisite user permissions, additional functionality is also available for token by token inspection of raw audio. Our workflow provides standardized, customizable linguistic and acoustic measures across speech data sets, which in turn will make reproducing and replicating investigation of speech much easier (Gawne & Styles, chapter 2, this volume).

The structure of our chapter is as follows. In section 2, we discuss SPADE's approach to *data sharing*, in terms of data collection and working with our data guardians; the *citation and acknowledgment* of data sets—both primary audio corpora, and secondary, derived data sets of speech measures produced by ISCAN; and *data*

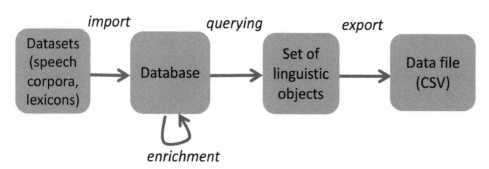

Figure 15.1
Data processing workflow for SPADE. Details are given in section 3.

archiving. In section 3 we discuss the technical workflow for ISCAN. This covers the core aspects of *data processing* and *storage* for SPADE, which result in standardized databases for each speech corpus, and *access* and *search* of these databases, from which users generate the derived data sets. To keep the discussion concrete, we exemplify using a SPADE project study, Stuart-Smith et al. (2019a), on English /s/-retraction, whereby /s/ in /str/ clusters (e.g., *street*) sounds more like /sh/. The research question is: to what extent is /s/ acoustically "retracted" relative to /ʃ/, as a function of onset structure (e.g., /sp st sk spr skr str/)? The data considered were from speakers of nine English dialects, from six spontaneous speech corpora (section 2).

2   Data sharing in SPADE

2.1   Sampling

Data set sampling for SPADE was constrained by theoretical factors of dialect coverage by *space* and *time*, and in particular, the aim of capturing the relationship between British English dialects from the Old World with those continued in the New World, in North American dialects of Canada and the United States. Spatial dialect coverage was determined by design and availability (figure 15.2). For the British Isles, we have standard and vernacular recordings from Ireland, Wales, Scotland, and England, and within England, Northern and Southern Englishes, as well as urban (e.g., London, Liverpool, Newcastle) and rural varieties (e.g., Devon, North-East Scotland),

ethnic varieties (e.g., Glasgow Asian, Bradford Panjabi English), and varieties with known historical links with North American English, such as West Country and East Anglian English. For North America, we aimed to cover the main recognized dialect regions following, for example, Thomas (2001). In terms of time, the speech data sets mainly date from the 1960s to the present. Many data sets contain either an apparent- or a real-time dimension: in other words, time depth is represented through recordings made at different times, or through containing speakers recorded at the same time point, but of different ages.

The speech data sets also vary by *speech style*. Most are largely of spontaneous speech, though some contain read speech (e.g., the International Corpus of English-Canada [ICE-Canada]; Newman & Columbus 2010) or are entirely read speech (e.g., the Intonational Variation in English corpus; Grabe, Post, & Nolan 2001). The spontaneous speech recordings range from interviews of different kinds (oral history, sociolinguistic, broadcast, police-suspect role-play), with differing numbers of speakers, to casual conversations with no interviewer present.

2.2   Data collection

The SPADE speech data sets fall into two main types, *public* and *private*. The public data sets include the Audio British National Corpus (AudioBNC; Coleman et al. 2012), the Buckeye Corpus (Pitt et al. 2007), the Dynamic Variability in Speech (DyViS) forensic corpus (Nolan et al. 2009), the Santa Barbara Corpus (Du Bois et al. 2000–2005), and the Scottish Corpus of Texts and Speech

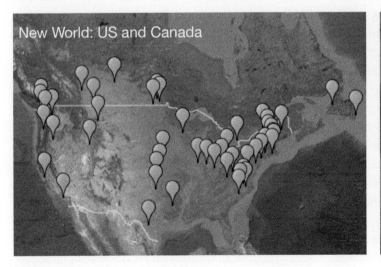

Figure 15.2

Approximate locations of the intended SPADE dialect coverage.

(SCOTS; Anderson, Beavan, & Kay 2007). These corpora are either freely accessible or are available for sharing via a fee. Some of the large public corpora include recordings from many different dialects (e.g., AudioBNC, Santa Barbara, SCOTS), while others were collected from a single dialect area (e.g., Buckeye, DyViS). Hence speech corpus does not necessarily equate to English dialect.

The private data sets are largely those that have been collected for a specific purpose, often sociolinguistic or phonetic, and from one or a few dialects. They can also be internally complex. For example, the Sounds of the City corpus (SoTC; Stuart-Smith et al. 2017), is a real-time corpus of Glaswegian English recorded from the 1970s to the 2000s, which itself consists of three sociolinguistic corpora, several sets of oral history interviews, broadcast recordings, and some other recordings. The Raleigh Corpus (Dodsworth & Kohn 2012) on the other hand, is an apparent-time corpus of Raleigh (North Carolina) English comprising only sociolinguistic interviews.

All SPADE data sets, public or private, are taken to have a *Data Guardian* (DG), that is, an entity, often an individual, with particular responsibility for one or more speech data set(s), which they have either collected personally for a specific purpose, overseen the collection of, or now curate (e.g., student projects, inherited collections of speech recordings).

A crucial aspect of the SPADE project has been working closely with our DGs to ensure *best ethical practice* for data sharing (see Holton, Leonard, & Pulsifer, chapter 4, this volume). Here, data sharing refers to two kinds of data: (1) primary data, the raw audio+text files, given by the DGs to SPADE for processing (mainly using ISCAN, but sometimes also for forced alignment, to extend dialect coverage); and (2) secondary data, anonymized derived data sets of acoustic measures and linguistic data produced by ISCAN for each speech data set, which SPADE then shares back with each DG, and—depending on DG permissions—SPADE uses for project research and publications, and/or for deposit for future speech and language research. The secondary data sets are not subject to the same level of scrutiny, because processing with ISCAN renders the primary data anonymous, but ethical practice but must still be considered.

Key *ethical* issues for SPADE relate to (1) the sharing of the primary data sets, because these were usually non-anonymous speech data sets, and hence included personal data, and sometimes also sensitive personal data

(i.e., in content, and/or specific metadata for, e.g., ethnicity, social practices), and (2) the purpose of the data sharing, specified by each DG. Other important issues arise from SPADE working in compliance with the General Data Protection Regulation (GDPR; legally applicable in the United Kingdom/European Union from May 2018): (3) SPADE must work with shared primary data according to the specific requirements of each DG (and not with a blanket set of requirements proposed by SPADE). In addition, (4) both "data holders" (in this case, the SPADE team members) and "data collectors" (the DGs) have to accept responsibility for the received (shared) data and the data that they share with the project, respectively. This means that SPADE has to ascertain, as far as is possible, that the DGs are sharing their data sets according to the wishes of the original participants and that they pass on any specific participants' requirements. So, for example, one speech data set can be acoustically analyzed, but the sound files may only be listened to by SPADE team members who were also members of the original research project team for that data set. In return, DGs have to respect best ethical practice in their sharing of the secondary derived data set provided to them by SPADE (see section 2.3).

We managed this aspect of data sharing through a primary/secondary data sharing agreement, which we call the *data transfer agreement* (DTA; cf. Collister, chapter 9, this volume). The DTA was drawn up in conjunction with the contracts team at the university of the lead project institution (Glasgow). The DTA not only confirms the responsibilities of data holders/data collectors, but it also allows DGs to specify what SPADE may (not) do with their data. Data processing for developing the ISCAN software was the minimum, but we also sought additional permission to use acoustic measures in SPADE research and outreach in different ways (e.g., publication of results, using anonymized sound extracts in presentations) and to deposit the derived data sets in a public repository. Through the DTA, DGs have agreed to all, some, or none of the additional data sharing purposes, for all or some of their data sets. For example, one DG allowed the use of anonymized sound extracts from all but nine speakers, as these individuals had not given permission for future use of their audio in this way. At the same time, that same data set allowed the use of acoustic measures from all speakers for ISCAN development.

Using the DTA, DGs have also indicated specific requirements, such as the exclusion of person and place names from analysis. For example, including the name of a tiny village in Scotland in a derived data set might lead to identification. We meet this requirement by minimally "whitelisting" derived data sets: anonymizing all words that are (1) <u>not</u> listed in large electronic English lexicons (Subtlex-US, -UK; Brysbaert & New 2009; Van Heuven et al. 2014); and (2) not marked as possible person/place names in the lexicons. Other DG specifications include citation of a representative publication for their data set, quotation of grant numbers, right of veto by the DGs for the use of their data set(s) for particular features, and so on. The main point here is that the DTA gives our DGs free rein to express their wishes, and then our procedures allow for these to be legally checked. All DGs in the British Isles and Canada were offered the opportunity to complete and sign the DTA, with the recommendation that DGs have the agreement signed by their institution on their behalf.

That the DTA could be drawn up for an international project like SPADE, consisting of institutions based in the United Kingdom and Canada that share EU data protection laws, and the United States, which does not, rested on two underlying agreements. The first was a research collaboration agreement between all participating institutions in all three countries, providing the basis for data sharing within the SPADE project team, especially for the secondary data sets. The second was a data sharing agreement drawn up between the UK and Canadian institutions to specify the basis for primary data set sharing; the US institutions were not able to participate in this second agreement. This means that the UK and Canadian teams cannot share primary data with the US teams, even that collected from the United States itself, because by law, primary data that enters the United Kingdom/European Union becomes subject to UK/EU GDPR (so the United Kingdom cannot return US primary data to the United States). As a result, SPADE observes the following workflow for collecting and sharing primary data:

- The main project site for software development is in Canada. This is also where the master data set repository is based.
- The UK (Glasgow) team collect primary data from British and Canadian DGs, and then share these with the Canadian team for data analysis using ISCAN. The UK team may also store and carry out data analysis of British and Canadian primary data sets.

- Only secondary, anonymized data sets, from British and Canadian DGs, can be shared with US teams.
- US teams collect primary data from US DGs and pass them directly to Canada for data processing (and/or process them themselves).

To ensure software development could begin, data collection took place in two phases. Most investigators for SPADE are also DGs, so phase 1 involved the collection of private data sets held by team members, specifically the Raleigh and SoTC corpora, and four key public corpora (Buckeye, Santa Barbara, ICE-Canada, and SCOTS). The sibilants study (Stuart-Smith et al. 2019a) is based on the dialects from these six corpora.[1] Phase 2 of data collection could only begin after the key data sharing agreements had been drawn up; no GDPR-compliant agreements already existed for us to adapt. The process was fairly lengthy given that the agreements were written while GDPR was coming into effect in the United Kingdom. However, our experience with the DTA has been positive, and we are happy to share the documentation and experience with others embarking on large-scale speech data sharing projects such as SPADE. While the details may differ for different jurisdictions, many similar issues may apply. For example, our DTA formed the basis for the agreement used for the US data collection. In terms of procedure, no primary data set transfer took place before the DTA was agreed, assuming the DG wanted to take up the DTA. Not all DGs wanted to, nor were obliged to, particularly for public data sets or those consisting only of read passages. Once data sets were received, they were checked and cleaned, before passing to the Canadian master repository.

2.3 Data citation and acknowledgment

Collecting a sociolinguistic corpus can be a substantial process that involves designing the sample, recruiting participants, interviewing/recording participants, and collating and transcribing the audio files. Not only do the wishes and rights of the original participants need to be respected by any future user (see section 2.2), we felt that it was essential that the researcher(s) who collected the corpora be given appropriate credit for their hidden labor, which can easily be overlooked. We also wanted to help set a precedent for future data sharing projects of this kind.

Our solution has been to adapt the following convention. The "SPADE Consortium" appears as the last author for all outputs that use private project-external data sets collected beyond phase 1. This coauthorship recognizes that the SPADE project, and especially the development of the ISCAN software, would not have been possible without the DGs who generously agreed to share their corpora with us. Their input has been so crucial that we consider the DGs collectively as coauthors of all SPADE-related outputs that make use of private, project-external, primary data sets. Listing all DGs as authors is impractical, and we therefore group them into the SPADE Consortium. In so doing, we have followed many of the conventions adopted by the Atlas of Pidgin and Creole Language Structures (Michaelis et al. 2013). This convention is adopted for all outputs, irrespective of which corpora are used as the basis of a particular analysis for presentation/publication. The detailed list of the members constituting the SPADE Consortium is given on the project website.

This means that citation of SPADE primary data sets is as follows. Preliminary outputs based on phase 1 acknowledged the private DGs (SoTC/Raleigh corpora) by coauthorship. All subsequent outputs that use primary or secondary data from SPADE must include the SPADE Consortium as last coauthor and give formal references for the specific corpora used for that output within the text/bibliography of that output. This citation requirement applies to project members, and to all who use the subsequently deposited secondary derived data sets. In this way, SPADE DGs can themselves track the future use of secondary data that their data sharing made possible. It especially enables reporting to funders for impact of their research, which is increasingly required in the United Kingdom.

2.4 Data archiving

The final core aspect of data sharing for SPADE is the responsible archiving of the primary and secondary data sets, and the databases (in Polyglot format; see section 3). This entails both adhering to the use of standard file formats and actual primary and secondary data set storage (Mattern, chapter 5, this volume; Andreassen, chapter 7, this volume).

The SPADE primary audio data are in standard file formats (e.g., waveform audio file format, .wav), usable on any computer. The speech data set text files are in various human-readable formats as per their deposit. The databases are in a hybrid database format, Polyglot, used by ISCAN (section 3.2.1). The secondary derived data sets of linguistic data and acoustic phonetic measures are comma-delimited files (.csv), which can be opened in R, Excel, and similar programs.

Project data storage is currently on servers at the Canadian and UK institutions (McGill, Glasgow University). Some US data are also stored at the US sites (North Carolina State University, University of Oregon), respecting ethical issues discussed in section 2.2. Storage is ensured for at least ten years and likely for many years afterward.

Secondary data sets containing the derived linguistic and acoustic measures from all public data sets, and all primary private data sets for which permission has been given, have been deposited in an Open Science Foundation public project, with a DOI (Sonderegger et al. 2020). The project contains secondary data sets (CSVs), along with documentation describing their contents and how they were generated using ISCAN (e.g., algorithm parameter values). This repository provides sustainable storage of the secondary data in perpetuity, at no cost to users, and will ensure backup and migration to new formats over time.

3 Data processing in SPADE: ISCAN software

Figure 15.3 shows the overall data processing pipeline in SPADE. In section 2, we discussed the initial and final stages of data management for the project: collection of the primary raw speech data sets and sharing of the secondary derived data sets. The steps in between are carried out using software developed for the core purpose of SPADE, scaling up phonetic investigations by carrying out the "same study" across many speech corpora. The ISCAN software can be configured for different types of cross-corpus analysis. This section describes the goals and design of ISCAN for this specific use case, to show how data processing, storage, access, and search are intended to work for cross-corpus phonetic analyses. Major development of ISCAN is complete. Its implementation is described in detail in the documentation for ISCAN (iscan.readthedocs.io) and PolyglotDB (polyglotdb.readthedocs.io) (see also McAuliffe et al. 2019).

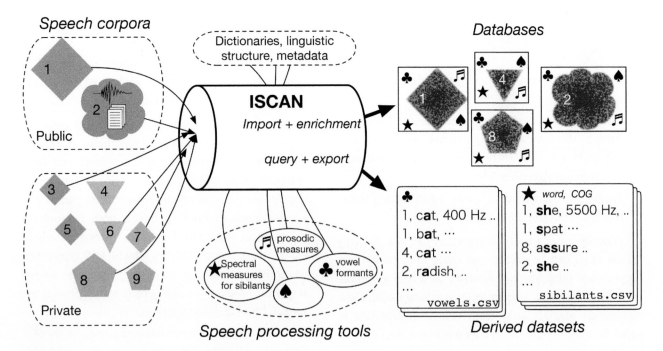

Figure 15.3
Schematic of the ISCAN system used for data management and processing in SPADE.

3.1 Design goals

The SPADE use case motivates a number of design goals that hold for any "big data" project using multiple speech corpora to study linguistic structure:

1. *Scalability*: Speech corpora can be large (one to fifty gigabytes each); even basic speech processing algorithms (e.g., pitch extraction) can be slow when run on hours of audio. The system must run in reasonable time as the amount of data grows (the SPADE target corpora contain over two thousand hours of speech).

2. *Abstraction away from corpus format*: Speech corpora are heterogeneous, with numerous formats used over the past twenty-five years to store annotations and metadata. Extensive scripting is required to perform similar operations on different corpora, despite substantial structural similarities across speech corpora. Users should be able to interact with corpora without understanding particularities of format.

3. *Minimization of technical skill and effort*: Ideally users should need minimal technical skill to manipulate and measure acoustic data, and even technical users should be able to minimize scripting by using a standard tool kit.

Each goal also applies for use cases addressed by existing speech data management systems—especially

EMU-SDMS, SLAAP, LaBB-CAT, and Phon, whose experiences have helped inform ISCAN development. Further design goals are motivated by SPADE itself, which hold for some but not all cross-corpus phonetic studies:

4. *Enabling multiple users, both local and remote*, to interact with the same data set—to account for use cases of a single user analyzing their own data (e.g., a DG), and of multiple users at remote locations analyzing the same data set. Both are needed for SPADE, where team members are in three countries.

5. *Working with restricted data sets*: Many speech data sets cannot be shared or even listened to by groups beyond the original research team (because speech inherently identifies speaker identity). However, neither is in principle necessary for many common phonetic analyses. It should be possible to carry out phonetic analysis on a data set without access to the raw data and also for different users to have different levels of access.

6. *Limited functionality to examine and modify individual tokens*: The original vision for SPADE was fully automated analysis without user inspection (section 1). However, during development we decided to include a limited postanalysis inspection capability (section 3.3.3) that is crucially restricted by user permissions.

A schematic of the system is shown in figure 15.3. A user goes from raw primary data to derived secondary data set by:

- Importing raw data into a common database format ("import")

- Adding linguistic structures and standardized measures to the database, using external speech processing tools, resources such as pronunciation lexicons, and internal algorithms ("enrich")

- Finding relevant tokens ("query") and writing information about them to a CSV file ("export")

(The optional step of "inspection" is not shown.) These steps can be carried out using either a Python application programming interface or a web graphical user interface (GUI; written in Django/AngularJS). Here we mostly abstract away from whichever interface is used, but assume that the reader would use the GUI.

3.2 Data processing and storage

The first step in processing a raw speech corpus is to import into a standardized database format, meeting the goal of abstracting away from corpus format. ISCAN assumes that minimally phone- and word-level time alignments exist (e.g., Praat "word" and "phone" tiers), such as the output of a forced aligner. ISCAN can currently import from various TextGrid-based forced aligners (Montreal Force Aligner, FAVE, LaBB-CAT) as well as BAS Partitur (used for MAUS: Schiel et al. 1998) and various idiosyncratic corpus-specific formats (TIMIT, Buckeye: Garofolo et al. 1993).

For example, for the /s/-retraction study, six heterogeneous speech corpora were imported: one with an idiosyncratic format (Buckeye) in annotation text files, one in LaBB-CAT format, and several in TextGrids from different forced aligners.

3.2.1 Database structure and "import" Use of a database presupposes a data model. There are two parts to ISCAN's data model, corresponding to the structure of transcribed speech and common measures:

1. *Annotation graphs* (Bird & Liberman 2001; also used in the EMU-SDMS, LaBB-CAT systems): A formalism based on graphs (in the sense of nodes and edges) that captures the logical structure underlying transcribed speech. Nodes and edges in the graph represent points in time, and intervals of time over which an annotation occurs (e.g., /k/ in the word *cat*).

2. *Time series*: Acoustic measures defined at fixed intervals over time, such as an F0 track.

Our corresponding custom database format, called *Polyglot*, uses two subdatabases, each matched to the structure of one aspect of the data:

1. Neo4j (https://neo4j.com/), a NoSQL *graph database*, is used to represent transcribed speech via annotation graphs, which capture linguistic objects and their temporal relationships. For example, in the initial import, word and phone information are parsed into a meaningful structure, reflecting both hierarchical information (e.g., which phones belong to which word; which phone follows which) and type-token relationships (such as what properties are shared across all productions and which words/phones are spoken by a particular speaker).

2. InfluxDB (https://www.influxdata.com/), a NoSQL *time-series database*, stores time series associated with a particular token of a linguistic object (e.g., the F0 track across a word).

The "polyglot persistence" design of our system, where different subdatabases are used for different data types, should maximize scalability, one of our key goals, because each subdatabase is already optimized for the structure of a particular data type. Our choice of a graph database in particular over a relational database (used in, e.g., EMU, LaBB-CAT, and SLAAP) was motivated by scalability. A disadvantage of this choice is the high storage footprint associated with graph databases. Empirically, for SPADE we have found that after enough enrichment is performed to do a typical phonetic study, the resulting Polyglot database is about as large as the original speech corpus.

3.2.2 Processing and storage loop: "Enrichment" The database resulting from importing a corpus is of limited use for phonetic studies—only word or phone durations can be examined. For a typical use case, the database is first built up through "enrichment": a loop of data processing and storage, to add different linguistic objects and phonetic measures of several types:

New linguistic units can be created, to enhance the structured hierarchy representing the corpus in the database. For example, words can be grouped together into larger chunks ("utterances") or phones into syllables.

Non-acoustic properties can be added to linguistic objects, including properties of words/phones/speakers, from external resources such as pronunciation lexicons (e.g., syllable stress, word frequency) or corpus metadata files (e.g., speaker gender, age), and measures based on hierarchical relationships—such as speech rate (e.g., "syllables per second") or number of phones in a word.

Acoustic measures can be stored, by processing the raw sound files using internal algorithms or integration with external tools (such as AutoVOT or REAPER [Robust Epoch and Pitch Estimator]: Talkin 2015). Currently available measures include F0, vowel formants (algorithm described in Mielke et al. 2019), and voice onset time, as well as anything computable by a user-specified Praat script in a certain format. Continuous-time measurements (such as F0) can be stored as single points (e.g., one F0 per vowel) or tracks (e.g., one F0 track per vowel).

For example, for the /s/-retraction study, enrichment included:

- Phone position in word, syllables, stress (from an external lexicon)
- Speaker dialect and gender (from corpus metadata)
- Acoustic measures for each sibilant token, such as center of gravity and spectral slope, calculated by a user-specified Praat script

Enrichment is a loop because all new information computed is stored, and subsequent enrichment steps usually depend on previously stored information. Anything encoded in enrichment is stored in the database and can be used again in the future. This design choice follows from the intended workflow of ISCAN: data processing and storage are only done once, can be slow, and require access to the original speech data. However, once the database is created, it exists independently of the original speech data, and can be used efficiently in different studies: querying the database and writing the results to a data file are designed to be fast.

3.3 Interacting with a Polyglot database: Access, search, inspection

Importing a speech corpus and carrying out enrichment results in one *Polyglot database* per corpus (top right of figure 15.3). Each database contains all information needed to carry out common phonetic analyses without access to the raw corpus itself. We now describe how users interact with these databases, in terms of *access*, *searching*, and *inspection*.

3.3.1 Access: System configuration and user access For our use case of cross-corpus analysis, we presume many existing Polyglot databases corresponding to different data sets; these need to be accessed by multiple users, possibly at different sites (goal 4), with access restrictions that respect ethical restrictions on some data sets (goal 5). Access to and interaction with the databases is managed via a Django web framework. The overall ISCAN system, which consists of several pieces managed by Docker (https://www.docker.com/), is called the *ISCAN server*.

An ISCAN server is installed on a static machine (e.g., a desktop), from where it can be used to interact with the databases locally by its installer. If the machine is a web server, the databases can also be accessed by remote users—which is the case we assume for the rest of this section, and the typical use case for SPADE. A fully fledged permissions system allows a user's access and functionality to be restricted for particular databases.[2] This is most relevant for "inspection" (section 3.3.3) to disable users' ability to listen to audio or see identifying information (e.g., parts of the transcript) for a data set. However, the permissions system could in principle be used more generally—such as to enable only searching for tokens but not exporting a data file, if a researcher wanted to let others explore the data they used for a study but is not able to provide a readable CSV, as for example, during a class.

To give a concrete example: an ISCAN server for the SPADE project has been set up on a web server at McGill, where users can log in by going to a web address. A user who has been given a tutorial account would only see the "iscan-tutorial" database (a subset of the ICE-Canada corpus) and would not see some functionality that has been disabled for purposes of the tutorial. A SPADE team member who logs in would see all available databases and all functionality.

3.3.2 Searching: "Query" and "export" However the ISCAN server is accessed (either locally or on a remote web server), a user primarily interacts with a Polyglot database by executing *queries*, to find a subset of linguistic objects (e.g., phones, words) of interest for a phonetic study. Queries are constructed either in a graphical interface (in the GUI; figure 15.4) or in a custom Python

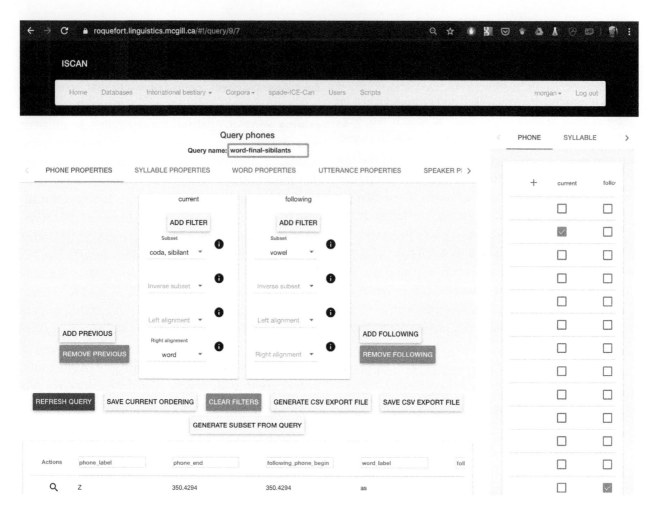

Figure 15.4
Screenshot of query interface for ISCAN.

query language (in the Python application programming interface)—no knowledge of underlying query languages of the subdatabases is assumed. Using a custom query language (as also in EMU-SDMS) minimizes the technical knowledge required from the user. Queries can reference properties of an annotation (e.g., "all phones which are labeled /s/ or /ʃ/"), user-defined subsets (e.g., "sibilants"), information from associated linguistic objects (e.g., following phone, syllable stress), and so on. For example, for the /s/-retraction study, the query found all word-initial sibilants in stressed syllables. Once the subset of objects has been found, information about them can be exported to a data file (a CSV), with one row per token and one column per variable. Any information referenced herein (in query, enrichment, import) can be exported as a column, including acoustic measures. For example, in the /s/-retraction study, the exported data

file included information about any following phones in the syllable onset, speaker demographics (dialect, gender), and acoustic measures associated with each sibilant (e.g., spectral center of gravity, peak).

3.3.3 Inspection The original vision of SPADE envisaged fully automatic analysis of speech, without user access to raw corpora. As ISCAN was developed and used team-internally, it became clear that *fully* automatic analysis is not yet realistic in many practical settings, such as when developing a new analysis pipeline to be applied across many corpora. For any phonetic study, even large-scale automated ones, some inspection of individual tokens may be important to get a handle on the data and to examine unusual cases. The ISCAN GUI thus contains functionality for inspection. Subject to user permissions, tokens returned by a query can be visually and auditorily inspected using a waveform, spectrogram, and a

TextGrid-like display showing the linguistic context (phones, words) (figure 15.5).

Importantly, this functionality is controlled by the permissions system: access to each aspect is defined on a per-corpus and per-user basis. For example, users' ability to actually play audio for individual tokens can be disabled—which addresses the primary privacy concern associated with sharing speech data. In this way, examination of individual tokens should be possible even for (some) private data sets.

ISCAN contains limited functionality to allow the user to change the database through inspection, in two ways which are important for augmenting "automatic" analysis. Tokens can be *excluded* from further analysis (e.g., due to a bad F0 track or incorrect forced alignment), and annotations can be *corrected*, though currently the latter

is restricted to fixing F0 tracks. While more extensive inspection capability is important for enabling large-scale studies, this direction is beyond the remit of the SPADE project. Inspection functionality is better developed in other speech database management systems (e.g., LaBB-CAT, Phon, EMU-SDMS) whose intended use cases centrally involve corpus annotation.

4 Future directions for ISCAN and SPADE

The SPADE project is a concrete instantiation, and first step, of developing our philosophy of speech data management for analyses of multiple speech corpora, where corpora are translated into standardized databases from which consistent high-quality acoustic measures can easily be extracted for analysis. The SPADE use case

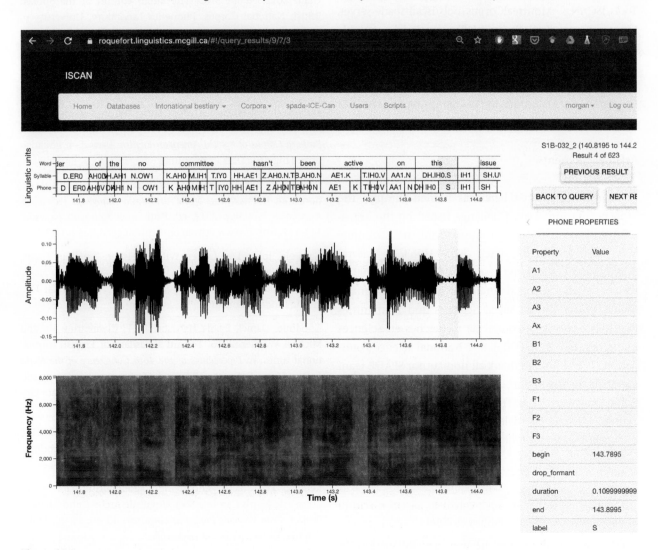

Figure 15.5

Screenshot of inspection interface for ISCAN.

necessarily focuses on subsets of speech segments in a subset of English dialects. Obvious extensions are to extend our sample to include overseas, native, and non-native Englishes, and to extend to other languages for crosslinguistic research (Sonderegger, McAuliffe, & Bang 2017). We also need to adapt ISCAN for large-scale study of suprasegmental speech phenomena, building on the parallel development of the system for smaller-scale cross-corpus analyses in the Intonational Bestiary project (Goodhue et al. 2016), as described in McAuliffe et al. (2019).

To this end, we also regard ISCAN as a step in a continually developing software system for integrated speech corpus analysis (ISCAN after all, continues Speech Corpus Tools; McAuliffe, Stengel-Eskin, et al. 2017). To address longevity of the system, all code is freely available and open source (on GitHub repositories: MontrealCorpusTools/ISCAN, MontrealCorpusTools/iscan-spade-server, MontrealCorpusTools/PolyglotDB), including stable releases. We hope and expect that the code will be taken up, extended, and cannibalized in the future, if not by ourselves, then by others who are also working toward the general scientific direction of scaling up phonetic data analysis.

Acknowledgments

The research reported here was funded through the 4th Digging into Data Challenge issued by the Trans-Atlantic Platform, through grants from the Economic and Social Research Council (ES/R003963/1), Natural Sciences and Engineering Research Council/Le conseil de recherches en sciences naturelles et en génie du Canada (RGPDD/501771–16), Social Sciences and Humanities Research Council/Le conseil de recherches en sciences humaines (869-2016-0006), and National Science Foundation (1730479). We thank all non-author SPADE team members for their contributions—especially Jeff Mielke, Robin Dodsworth, Erik Thomas, Vanna Willerton, James Tanner, Michael Goodale, and Arlie Coles—as well as Michaela Socolof for editorial assistance.

Notes

1. Materials for this study are archived in an Open Science Foundation project (Stuart-Smith et al. 2019b).

2. Such permissions systems are important for some other speech database management systems, such as SLAAP, which hosts mostly restricted data sets.

References

Anderson, Jean, David Beavan, and Christian Kay. 2007. SCOTS: Scottish Corpus of Texts and Speech. In *Creating and Digitizing Language Corpora*, ed. Joan Beal, Karen Corrigan, and Hermann Moisl, 17–34. London: Palgrave Macmillan.

Bird, Steven, and Mark Liberman. 2001. A formal framework for linguistic annotation. *Speech Communication* 33 (1): 23–60.

Boersma, Paul, and David Weenink. 2016. *Praat: Doing Phonetics by Computer*. Version 6.0.19. http://www.praat.org/.

Brysbaert, Marc, and Boris New. 2009. Moving beyond Kučera and Francis: A critical evaluation of current word frequency norms and the introduction of a new and improved word frequency measure for American English. *Behavior Research Methods* 41 (4): 977–990.

Coleman, John, Ladan Baghai-Ravary, John Pybus, and Sergio Grau. 2012. Audio BNC: The audio edition of the Spoken British National Corpus. Phonetics Laboratory, University of Oxford. http://www.phon.ox.ac.uk/AudioBNC.

Dodsworth, Robin, and Mary Kohn. 2012. Urban rejection of the vernacular: The SVS undone. *Language Variation and Change* 24 (2): 221–245.

Du Bois, John, Wallace Chafe, Charles Meyer, Sandra Thompson, Robert Englebretson, and Nii Martey. 2000–2005. *Santa Barbara Corpus of Spoken American English*. Parts 1–4. Philadelphia: Linguistic Data Consortium.

Fromont, Robert, and Jennifer Hay. 2012. LaBB-CAT: An annotation store. In *Proceedings of the Australasian Language Technology Association Workshop 2012*, ed. Paul Cook and Scott Nowson, 113–117. https://www.aclweb.org/anthology/volumes/U12-1/.

Garofolo, John, Lori Lamel, William Fisher, Jonathan Fiscus, David Pallett, Nancy Dahlgren, and Victor Zue. 1993. *TIMIT Acoustic-Phonetic Continuous Speech Corpus*. Philadelphia: Linguistic Data Consortium.

Goodhue, Daniel, Lyana Harrison, Y. T. Clementine Su, and Michael Wagner. 2016. Toward a bestiary of English intonational tunes. In *Proceedings of the 46th Conference of the North Eastern Linguistic Society (NELS)*, ed. Christopher Hammerly and Brandon Prickett, 311–320. Amherst, MA: GLSA (Graduate Linguistics Student Association).

Grabe, Esther, Brechtje Post, and Francis Nolan. 2001. *The IViE Corpus*. Department of Linguistics, University of Cambridge. http://www.phon.ox.ac.uk/IViE.

Kendall, Tyler. 2007. Enhancing sociolinguistic data collections: The North Carolina Sociolinguistic Archive and Analysis Project. *Penn Working Papers in Linguistics* 13 (2): 15–26. Philadelphia: University of Pennsylvania.

Keshet, Joseph, Morgan Sonderegger, and Thea Knowles. 2014. *AutoVOT: A Tool for Automatic Measurement of Voice Onset Time*

Using Discriminative Structured Prediction. Version 0.91. https://github.com/mlml/autovot/.

Kisler, Thomas, Florian Schiel, and Han Sloetjes. 2012. Signal processing via web services: The use case WebMAUS. In *Proceedings of the Digital Humanities Conference 2012*, ed. Clare Mills, Michael Pidd, and Esther Ward, 30–38. Sheffield, UK: HRI Online Publications.

Liberman, Mark. 2019. Corpus phonetics. *Annual Review of Linguistics* 5:91–107.

McAuliffe, Michael, Arlie Coles, Michael Goodale, Sarah Mihuc, Michael Wagner, Jane Stuart-Smith, and Morgan Sonderegger. 2019. ISCAN: A system for integrated phonetic analyses across speech corpora. In *Proceedings of the 19th International Congress of Phonetic Sciences*, 1322–1326. https://www.internationalpho neticassociation.org/icphs/icphs2019.

McAuliffe, Michael, Michaela Socolof, Sarah Mihuc, Michael Wagner, and Morgan Sonderegger. 2017. Montreal forced aligner: Trainable text-speech alignment using Kaldi. *Proceedings of Interspeech* (2017): 498–502.

McAuliffe, Michael, Elias Stengel-Eskin, Michaela Socolof, and Morgan Sonderegger. 2017. Polyglot and speech corpus tools: A system for representing, integrating, and querying speech corpora. *Proceedings of Interspeech* (2017): 3887–3891.

Michaelis, Susanne Maria, Philippe Maurer, Martin Haspelmath, and Magnus Huber, eds. 2013. *Atlas of Pidgin and Creole Language Structures Online*. Leipzig, Germany: Max Planck Institute for Evolutionary Anthropology. http://apics-online.info.

Mielke, Jeff, Erik Thomas, Josef Fruehwald, Michael McAuliffe, Morgan Sonderegger, Jane Stuart-Smith, and Robin Dodsworth. 2019. Age vectors vs. axes of intraspeaker variation in vowel formants measured automatically from several English speech corpora. In *Proceedings of the 19th International Congress of Phonetic Sciences*, 1258–1262. https://www.internationalphoneticas sociation.org/icphs/icphs2019.

Newman, John, and Georgia Columbus. 2010. *The ICE-Canada Corpus.* Version 1. University of Alberta. https://dataverse.library .ualberta.ca/dataverse/VOICE.

Nolan, Francis, Kirsty McDougall, Gea de Jong, and Toby Hudson. 2009. The DyViS database: Style-controlled recordings of 100 homogeneous speakers for forensic phonetic research. *International Journal of Speech, Language and the Law* 16 (1): 31–57.

Pitt, Mark, Laura Dilley, Keith Johnson, Scott Kiesling, William Raymond, Elizabeth Hume, and Eric Fosler-Lussier. 2007. *Buckeye Corpus of Conversational Speech.* 2nd release. Columbus: Department of Psychology, Ohio State University.

Rose, Yvan, Brian MacWhinney, Rodrigue Byrne, Gregory Hedlund, Keith Maddocks, Philip O'Brien, and Todd Wareham. 2006. Introducing Phon: A software solution for the study of phonological acquisition. In *Proceedings of the 30th Annual Boston University Conference on Language Development*, 489–500. http://www.cascadilla.com/bucld30toc.html.

Rosenfelder, Ingrid, Josef Fruehwald, Keelan Evanini, Scott Seyfarth, Kyle Gorman, Hilary Prichard, and Jiahong Yuan. 2015. *FAVE (Forced Alignment and Vowel Extraction) Program Suite.* Version 1.2.2. https://github.com/JoFrhwld/FAVE.

Schiel, Florian, Susanne Burger, Anja Geumann, and Karl Weilhammer. 1998. The Partitur format at BAS. In *Proceedings of the First International Conference on Language Resources and Evaluation*, 1295–1301.

Sonderegger, Morgan, Jane Stuart-Smith, James Tanner, Vanna Willerton, Rachel Macdonald, and Jeff Mielke. SPADE—Speech Across Dialects of English. OSF. osf.io/4jfrm. doi:10.17605/OSF. IO/4JFRM.

Sonderegger, Morgan, Michael McAuliffe, and Hye-Young Bang. 2017. Segmental influences on F0: Cross-linguistic and interspeaker variability of phonetic precursors. Paper presented at the 4th Workshop on Sound Change, Edinburgh, April 20–22.

Stuart-Smith, Jane, Brian José, Tamara Rathcke, Rachel Macdonald, and Erik Lawson. 2017. Changing sounds in a changing city: An acoustic phonetic investigation of real-time change over a century of Glaswegian. In *Language and a Sense of Place: Studies in Language and Region*, ed. Chris Montgomery and Emma Moore, 38–65. Cambridge: Cambridge University Press.

Stuart-Smith, Jane, Morgan Sonderegger, Rachel Macdonald, Jeff Mielke, Michael McAuliffe, and Erik Thomas. 2019a. Large-scale acoustic analysis of dialectal and social factors in English /s/-retraction. In *Proceedings of the 19th International Congress of Phonetic Sciences*, 1273–1277. https://www.internationalphonet icassociation.org/icphs/icphs2019.

Stuart-Smith, Jane, Morgan Sonderegger, Rachel Macdonald, Jeff Mielke, Michael McAuliffe, and Erik Thomas. 2019b. Large-Scale Analyses of English /s/-Retraction across Dialects. OSF. osf .io/bknrg. doi:10.17605/OSF.IO/BKNRG.

Talkin, David. 2015. REAPER: Robust Epoch and Pitch EstimatoR. https://github.com/google/REAPER.

Thomas, Erik. 2001. *An Acoustic Analysis of Vowel Variation in New World English.* Publication of the American Dialect Society 85. Durham, NC: Duke University Press.

Van Heuven, Walter J. B., Pawel Mandera, Emmanuel Keuleers, and Marc Brysbaert. 2014. Subtlex-UK: A new and improved word frequency database for British English. *Quarterly Journal of Experimental Psychology* 67 (6): 1176–1190.

Winkelmann, Raphael, Jonathan Harrington, and Klaus Jänsch. 2017. EMU-SDMS: Advanced speech database management and analysis in R. *Computer Speech and Language* 45:392–410.

16 Data Management at the uOttawa Sociolinguistics Laboratory

Shana Poplack

1 Introduction

This chapter details the data management principles and practices used in my Sociolinguistics Lab (http://www.sociolinguistics.uottawa.ca/thelab.html), home to hundreds of hours and millions of words of recorded spontaneous speech. The lab is the repository of nineteen major spoken language corpora in a variety of languages and eight corpora of language mixing in typologically similar and distinct language pairs, all constructed by our team. These include large-scale computerized data sets on spoken Canadian French spanning an apparent time period of a century and a half, Quebec English spoken before and after the passage of the Charter of the French Language (1977) that made it a minority language, and diaspora varieties of African American English, among others, as well as the Sociolinguistic Archives, collected by students in Urban Dialectology field methods courses between 1982 and 2018. It also houses two major written corpora of speech surrogates (*Ottawa Repository of Early African American Correspondence*, Van Herk & Poplack 2003; *Recueil historique des grammaires du français*, Poplack et al. 2015).

Much of this work was initiated in the early 1980s, well before data management became a popular topic in circles outside of variationist sociolinguistics, so some of the methods described here will appear (and in fact are) utterly antiquated by today's standards. Nonetheless, forty years down the road, there seems to be no danger of these materials "expiring" or getting "used up" any time soon, despite thousands of uses in the form of articles, books, talks, workshops, theses, dissertations, class papers, and other tangible products, generated by me, my students, lab assistants and associates, as well as colleagues far and wide. This is because all of these corpora have been properly preserved, if only by the seat of their pants, and remain discoverable, accessible (Bird & Simons 2003), and to the extent permitted by ethical considerations, shareable. Ensuing sections describe how we approached the ever-present tensions between the ideal and the feasible to achieve this.

2 Corpus creation

Recognizing that the linguistic materials at one's disposal exert the strongest constraint on what can ultimately be investigated, our data management practices begin with data acquisition. This inevitably raises the question of what to collect and from whom. The corpora housed in the Sociolinguistics Lab are conceived first and foremost as archives of potential answers to specific research questions. In keeping with the sociolinguist's mandate to study language issues of particular import to society, these typically emerge from public stakeholder discourse, but with a special focus on those of theoretical linguistic interest.

A notable example is the *Ottawa-Hull French Corpus* (Poplack 1989), the cornerstone of a still ongoing project that seeks to elucidate the extent to which minority status affects a language's permeability to influence from a majority language. The nature, extent, and even existence of contact-induced change have been the subject of much controversy in linguistics. It is also a long-standing concern of Canadian francophones, who fear that intense contact with and influence from English is destroying the structural integrity of French. Such concerns, which until recently, enjoyed relatively little empirical validation, dictate our methodology for corpus construction. The National Capital Region of Canada, situated on both sides of the geographic, provincial, and linguistic border between Quebec (French majority language) and Ontario (French minority language) was selected as the study site. Twenty-four native francophones, stratified according to age and gender were randomly sampled from each of five "French" neighbor-hoods, each differing according to intensity of contact with English at the local level. Another corpus (*Le français en contexte: Milieux scolaire et social*; Poplack 2015; Poplack & Bourdages 2005), originally built to test the popular belief that francophone youth are not acquiring "standard" French because their teachers do not master it themselves, is made up of 166 francophone high school students and their French language-arts teachers. Because these data were collected on the Quebec side of the National Capital Region twenty-five years later, this corpus contributes a real-time dimension. Together with a third corpus constructed from recordings made by folklorists in the 1940s and 1950s of rural Quebeckers born between 1846 and 1895 (*Récits du français québécois d'autrefois*; Poplack & St-Amand 2007), it extends the apparent time frame for the study of linguistic change to a century and a half, a span virtually unprecedented in the study of *speech*. The *Récits* also function as a precontact benchmark, crucial for any study of contact-induced change (Poplack & Levey 2010).

This comparative approach is also at the root of the *Early Black English* corpora (Poplack & Sankoff 1987; Poplack & Tagliamonte 1991). Inspired by the long-standing debate over the origins of African American Vernacular English (AAVE) as a prior creole or a dialect of English, these data address concerns of native speakers over the "quality" of their language, while responding to the caveat that any question of origins requires reference to an earlier stage of the language. The *Early Black English* corpora capitalize on speech recorded synchronically in three African American diaspora isolates settled between 1783 and 1824, with the goal of triangulating analysis of diagnostic linguistic features among them and relevant benchmarks to reconstruct the ancestor of contemporary AAVE (Poplack 2000; Poplack & Tagliamonte 2001).

For a full list of the lab's holdings, refer to Research Holdings (http://www.sociolinguistics.uottawa.ca/holdings.html) and the references therein. For the present purposes, suffice it to say that these are "unconventional" corpora (Beal, Corrigan, & Moisl 2007; Poplack 2007), insofar as they were specifically built to instantiate the conditions required to address a specific research question, rather than simply to represent some geographically or linguistically defined community, as is more often the case in (socio) linguistics. Thanks to the collection methods detailed herein, all of these data sets lend themselves readily to the study, both synchronic and diachronic, of just about

any linguistic feature that occurs freely in speech and can be apprehended from an audio recording. In addition, by virtue of the criteria motivating their constitution, they offer the less common advantage that the behavior of each feature can also be interpreted in terms of a more general research question, an inestimable added benefit of corpora built on such principles.

3   Data collection

As sociolinguists, our primary interest lies in the study of spontaneous language use, and in particular, the linguistic variability that is its hallmark. This variability typically involves alternation between ratified forms and their non-standard, often overtly stigmatized, counterparts. The latter are emblematic of the *vernacular*, valued as the most regular and systematic form of language (Labov [1966] 2006). Eliciting the vernacular spontaneously in the course of the formal data collection process is no simple matter. It requires, first and foremost, creating a situation in which its use is deemed appropriate by the speaker. While this may be straightforward enough in small-scale social network studies, which often involve long-term participant observation of and attendant familiarity with members, it turns out to be quite a challenge when the researcher is also seeking to constitute a representative and numerically adequate speaker sample. The major corpora housed in the Sociolinguistics Lab, for example, are made up of 120–183 individuals, who are in most cases unrelated. What such large-scale surveys offer in breadth and range they often lose in depth. The typical result is speech data that rarely transcend the more formal poles of the stylistic continuum, where the linguistic features of interest are either rare or altogether absent. This constitutes a real liability for the study of the vernacular.

Our response to this problem has been to adopt the ethnographically inspired methods developed by Labov and his associates (ourselves included) to resolve the *observer's paradox* (Labov 1972) by encouraging conversation that is a better approximation to the vernacular than that typically afforded by face-to-face interviews. The major tool here is the methodological instrument known as the *sociolinguistic interview* (Labov 1984). The antithesis of a standard interview schedule, this is rather a guide to eliciting casual speech through introduction of a wide range of conversational topics of a largely informal nature. These are adapted to the interests and concerns of the local populations by trained interviewers who, to the extent possible, are both linguists and community members themselves. To minimize the effect of the interview situation, including the power differential between interviewer and interviewee, the latter is encouraged to take the lead in the interaction, initiating transitions from topic to topic, as well as inclusion or exclusion of specific topics, all with limited intervention from the interviewer. The only exceptions involve the collection of metadata for each participant (section 4), which is introduced near the end of each recording session.

The results of these efforts, described in detail elsewhere (e.g., Poplack 1989; Poplack, Walker, & Malcolmson 2006), are a wealth of spontaneous speech, ranging in length from one to five hours per participant and featuring many narratives of personal experience, small-group discussions, and other highly informal discourse modes. These include the crucial vernacular variants targeted for study, in addition to (more easily accessible) careful speech styles. To the extent possible, we rely on linguists who are also community members to act as fieldworkers. They receive dedicated training, both in the lab and in the context of formal coursework, on how to administer the sociolinguistic interview, which is greatly enriched by their own insider knowledge of community mores. Perhaps our most successful endeavor of this kind is evidenced in the *African Nova Scotian English* corpus (Poplack & Tagliamonte 1991), a substantial compilation of largely informal speech collected by in-group members of tight-knit communities diglossic in Standard Canadian English and AAVE. Were it not for the local status—and skill!—of these fieldworkers, most of the vernacular grammatical features whose behavior we have since studied in detail would simply never have appeared during the recording sessions at all. This is because, where linguistic insecurity and at least some degree of diglossia coexist, "offending" forms are typically avoided with non-community members. This highlights the imperative to create appropriate conditions for data collection. Other notable examples of such prized but elusive linguistic features include multiword code-switching, or the French-Canadian informal register disparagingly referred to as *joual*. As observed in section 10, success at obtaining exemplars of the vernacular has often resulted in content too personal to disseminate publically, raising serious ethical concerns with respect to data sharing.

4 Metadata

Nowhere is the dictate that data cannot be divorced from their source(s) (Good, chapter 3, this volume; see also Holton, Leonard, & Pulsifer, chapter 4, this volume) more relevant than in sociolinguistic research. Recognizing that the speaker is a key source of the variability that characterizes language as well as the key agent of linguistic change, relevant speaker characteristics are explicitly incorporated into many of our analyses of linguistic structure. This section describes the metadata developed at the Sociolinguistics Lab to facilitate this endeavor. First, after each recording session, the fieldworker completes an *interview report* containing detailed demographic, sociological, and some language-related information about the participant(s) and their immediate families. At this time they also anonymize the interaction, providing each participant with a temporary pseudonym and speaker number, taking care to co-index these with every recording, interview report form, and any other documentation pertinent to the individual in question.[1] These are then transferred onto corpus-specific master metadata lists, which are continually updated as data acquisition continues, and even into preliminary analysis. Once data collection, transcription, and corpus construction have concluded, each participant is assigned a permanent unique number and pseudonym, consistently linking them to all their associated data. The result is a detailed inventory of potentially relevant characteristics. What is relevant can be expected to differ from variable to variable and community to community: one variable may be primarily socially conditioned, another may serve as a stylistic marker, and a third may display a distinct sociolinguistic profile depending on the speech community. Standard sociodemographic traits such as age, gender, neighborhood of residence, level of education, or approximate socioeconomic status are always taken into account, but we also capitalize on our knowledge of the community to incorporate local concerns into the analysis wherever feasible. Thus, speaker attitudes toward a majority language may prove explanatory in the analysis of variability in minority-language contexts (Poplack, Walker, & Malcolmson 2006); reported proficiency in a second language, or propensity to code-switch or to engage in lexical borrowing may be significant predictors in bilingual communities (Poplack 1989, 2018). These and other community-specific and more general factors are operationalized as factors via codes that can be readily incorporated into multivariate analyses to assess their relative contribution to the linguistic choices speakers make.

The resulting master catalogs are also useful in the creation of sub-corpora for specific studies. To name but one example, the question of whether copious code-switching leads to structural convergence could be addressed by comparing the behavior of a linguistic candidate for contact-induced change in a corpus made up of copious and sparse code-switchers identified from such metadata (Poplack, Zentz, & Dion 2012). Metadata also facilitate the construction of representative sub-samples, which are particularly useful for pilot or partial studies. The smallest such subsamples are made up of equal numbers of participants with maximally contrasting social characteristics (e.g., oldest vs. youngest, high-contact vs. low-contact neighborhood of residence) and are gradually expanded to include intermediate categories if exploratory studies warrant it. From participants with the targeted profiles, those whose recordings are most "successful" (in terms of length, stylistic range, vernacular features, and such) are then culled. The resulting subsamples obviate the need for a major investment in time and resources at the initial stage, while at the same time correcting for any (naturally occurring) imbalances in the larger sample. For example, while younger speakers tend to be more bilingual than their older counterparts in the wider *Quebec English Corpus* (Poplack, Walker, & Malcolmson 2006), the sub-sample maintains a perfect balance between those with low and high levels of bilingualism for each age cohort. Analysis of different variables in these pre-established sub-corpora enhances the generalizability of results.

A final type of metadata is afforded by a "corpus article" detailing the rationale behind the overall project, along with relevant methodological details regarding community type, data collection procedures, sample selection criteria, participant characteristics, transcription protocol, type of data, and such (e.g. Poplack 1989; Poplack, Walker, & Malcolmson 2006; Poplack & St-Amand 2007). Because data and findings can only be fully apprehended in the context of the norms of the community within which they were collected, prospective users are expected to familiarize themselves with these publications prior to receiving access to the corpora.

5 Annotation

Before describing the transcription protocols applied to the lab's corpora, recall that much of the data were collected decades before the advent of the wide variety of annotation schemes available today (e.g., Han, chapter 6, this volume; Beal, Corrigan, & Moisl 2007). Viewed in comparison with them, the solution we have adopted—manual transcription using standard orthography!—is not only technologically archaic, but to all appearances ridiculously vanilla. Yet even as increasingly sophisticated methods have gained more traction over the years, we have largely stuck with our original protocols for subsequent corpora, experience having shown us that they served our needs well. Our understanding of annotation as a *gateway* to analysis, as opposed to an end in and of itself, has dictated these choices.

For starters, once we experienced firsthand the formidable investment of time and money required to build a principled spoken-language corpus from scratch, we resolved to partition our own limited resources such that data *analysis* (i.e., actual linguistic research) would take precedence over data management, yet without unduly sacrificing the latter. Like many other corpus builders, we were torn between the lure of representing every linguistically interesting token and the desire to begin analysis of the large quantities of data that were flooding in. We were also sensitive to the hard lessons learned by colleagues whose ultra-detailed multilevel annotation systems eventually resulted in only a handful of fully transcribed recordings, having thus robbed precious time from analysis to support data handling for corpora that never materialized beyond a few speakers. This motivated our decision to maximize data entry (by getting initial transcriptions as quickly as possible) and multiply correction phases (totaling between three and six, both manual and automated, depending on the corpus). This meant giving up on many bells and whistles, despite hundreds of hours of labor from teams of seasoned transcribers.

An annotation scheme is only as good as the purposes it serves. We noted earlier that the corpora we construct lend themselves to the study of a wide variety of linguistic phenomena. Some may be known to us at the outset, but most emerge as the various projects evolve. Having no way of predicting what these might be, we (reluctantly) conceded that it would be unreasonable, if not impossible, to attempt to account for all of them during the transcription phase. As an example, because the research we carry out is largely based on detailed analyses of morphosyntactic variation, we resolved to ignore the myriad phonetic variants with which the data are rife, reasoning that any phonetician who wanted to exploit the lab's corpora from this perspective would prefer to analyze the raw recordings personally. The transcription protocol we adopted was largely determined by the goal of the automatic data manipulation phase of the project: construction of a computerized concordance in which the entire database is maximally accessible. To achieve this, the data must be rendered as faithfully and as consistently as possible. This is a particularly daunting challenge for spontaneous speech, which may include numerous and varied non-standard forms—sometimes, as in our case, in more than one language. Our objective was to preserve all the pertinent variation without needlessly multiplying entries, which has the effect of reducing retrieval.

The intended uses of the data, coupled with the determination to facilitate its automated treatment, led us to adopt an orthographic solution rather than a fine phonetic or prosodic transcription. This is described in detail in Poplack (1989), but in addressing the problem of how to treat each of the variant forms that a single word may have, the overall strategy has been to represent variation resulting from the operation of phonetic or phonological processes in standard orthography, regardless of the actual realization of the form. Thus, the main verb in (1), which was phonetically realized as [gɛrŋ], was transcribed <getting>, while variant forms affecting an entire morpheme, as in (2) (where the final [s] of 'trunks' represents the plural marker), were represented exactly as produced.

(1) And I said, "If things don't change around here, I'm <u>getting</u> out of here." (QEC.037.630)[2]

(2) That man had two <u>trunks</u>. Two <u>trunk</u> full of gold and silver and everything. Two <u>trunk</u>, big <u>trunks</u>. Full of gold and silver. (ANSE. NP.030.1323)

Our transcription protocol is generally consistent with accepted orthographic conventions in the language(s) in question, except where these violate our accessibility criteria. Thus, instead of using standard orthography for the recurrent Quebec French adverbial locution *à cette heure* 'now', containing the highly frequent (but in this context non-productive) function words *à* 'to' ($n=32,521$) and *cette* 'this' ($n=926$), we adopted the widespread dialect orthography *astheure* ($n=1,222$) so as to enhance retrievability. In a small number of cases, we created idiosyncratic orthographies, mainly to distinguish certain high-frequency forms from already high-frequency homographs. Thus, English quotative and discourse *like* ($n=37,449$), as in (3), was transcribed <lyke> to distinguish it from verbal and comparative homographs, rendered <like> ($n=9,723$).

(3) And all of a sudden, I'm lyke, "Why am I feeling grouchy?" (QEC.308.2210)

Another important departure involved inserting spaces after apostrophes replacing elided vowels in French articles to detach them from the lexical item they were qualifying (e.g., <j' ai>, <l' amie>), or to separate productive English contracted forms (e.g., <n't> from <do n't>, <did n't>), as illustrated in (4) with excerpts from the *Quebec English Corpus*. This facilitates their location in the alphabetical concordance (see sentence display 4).

(4)	301	45	that way? [301] He did	n't	want to and the school
	301	60	I was lyke, okay I do	n't	care. (laughter) Do n't
	304	570	I think back then it was	n't	at all. [2] Do you have a
	307	776	I think they just should	n't	be listening to music that
	314	501	It's the second last, is	n't	it? [Oh it is, driving, you
	315	1375	for, because he would	n't	stand there, 'cause it was
	316	231	ahold of that and it does	n't	cost us anything, so we
	318	445	remember that, I have	n't	thought of that for years. I
	319	162	[1] Oh yeah? [319] I ca	n't	tell you the stories about.
	319	671	never allowed to use "ai	n't	", so I mean, now
	320	608	close. Now they were	n't	people that uhm, were on

As a rule, however, no other effort was made to modify the form of the material in any way. Syntax, lexical choice, deletions, insertions, and neologisms of all sorts, as well as code-switching and borrowing, were all scrupulously reproduced.

An as-yet-unresolved problem concerns the many forms that are regularly deleted in speech, affecting a wide variety of linguistic categories. Over the years spent transcribing and correcting the various lab corpora, successive teams have grappled repeatedly with the issue of how to render these deleted items so as to facilitate their eventual retrieval. But the daunting number of disparate forms that would have to be coded as null, coupled with the difficulty of finding a unique representation for each (one capable of distinguishing a null subject from a null complementizer or a null inflection, for instance), eventually led to a point of diminishing returns, leading us to revert to manual retrieval of such items. Another notable challenge involved language tagging. Because several of our corpora are bilingual, constructed with the express purpose of facilitating the linguistic analysis of language mixing phenomena such as code-switching and lexical borrowing, we wanted to flag other-language incorporations. This turned out to be relatively straightforward for multiword stretches, as in (5), where each change of language is introduced by a code (here, <A> for *anglais* 'English' and <F> for *français* 'French').

(5) Tu sais, <u><A></u> I helped them <u><F></u> à comprendre le français pis à le parler. (OH.014.569)
     'You know, I helped them to understand French and to speak it.'

(6) On a faite nettoyer les <u>sewers</u> ici dans le projet parce c'était toute bloqué. (OH.027.2265)
     'We got the sewers here in the projects cleaned because it was all clogged up.'

But, unsurprisingly in retrospect, our francophone transcribers were no more able to reliably identify many established English-origin *loanwords* in French, such as *sewers* in (6) (initially represented as *sours*, reproducing community norms for its realization, but contravening our orthographic conventions) than most anglophones would be to flag words such as *terrace* or *lawyer* as having originated in French. Accordingly, to enhance consistency in the quantitative analysis of lexical borrowing and integration (e.g. Poplack & Dion 2012; Poplack 2018), we again resort to manual retrieval for lone other-language items.

Transcription, perhaps more than any other aspect of data management, requires ongoing decision making, especially when the protocols adopted blend annotation and some degree of analysis, as in our case. This process was greatly facilitated by the fact that our transcription teams were made up of trained linguists who, as noted, were generally also members of the community under study. All decisions, arrived at jointly, were incorporated into a continually evolving transcription guide to ensure their consistent application, not only to future occurrences of the same phenomena, but also retroactively to previous ones. Transcribers consulted (and, when necessary, updated) this document regularly during transcription and again at each correction phase.

6   Data correction

The goal of transcription is to yield a faithful reflection of what was actually said. As anyone who has worked with spontaneous speech data will attest, achieving it is perhaps the most arduous and time-consuming aspect of corpus construction. Our strategy of maximizing data entry, coupled with our requirements for retrievability, made efficient but effective correction even more of a priority, and one in which we invested considerable effort and experimentation. Teams of correctors, armed with the transcription protocol, alternated manual correction passes of the full transcript (at least one involving re-listening to the original audio recordings) with read-throughs of word lists and concordances. Automated "cleanup" programs targeting hundreds of recurrent transcription errors and spelling fluctuations (e.g., *favour* vs. *favor*) located additional inconsistencies. Interchanging documents among correctors at various correction stages further enhanced reliability. Progress was tracked on spreadsheets occupying large portions of the walls surrounding the workstations, where a dedicated column represented each correction phase for each recording. This enabled the team to ascertain at a glance where in the process each file was located, facilitating alternation of correctors and ensuring the full complement of correction passes, while minimizing the risk of (unplanned) duplication of effort. The result (described in detail in Poplack 1989) is a series of rather pristine corpora that can confidently be used to study morphosyntactic and lexical phenomena without recourse to original audio recordings.[3] And the simplicity of the single-level transcription protocol lends itself well to adaptation to other tools (e.g., concordance [section 7] or forced alignment [Mielke 2013]).

7 Data retrieval

The generalizations variationists make about language tend to be derived from large-scale quantitative analyses of actual linguistic behavior. Depending on the size of the data set and the corpus frequency of the linguistic phenomenon in question, our studies may be based on data ranging from only a few hundred tokens (e.g., English relative clauses; Poplack et al. 2006; Lealess & Smith 2011) to tens of thousands (e.g., the expression of negation in French [$n=85,447$]; Poplack 2015). Automated data handling is therefore essential. As explained in section 5, our corpora are not tagged for part of speech, nor indeed, in any other way beyond language and speaker. Instead we rely heavily on word concordance software. Many of these are readily available in the public domain, but few meet all of our specific needs. These include the imperative to associate each word with the specific speaker who produced it, while excluding those uttered by non-sample members (i.e., interviewers or other individuals present at the time of recording). We also want to ensure that extraneous elements present in the transcripts (metadata such as name of the interviewer or date, time, and location of the interview, and extralinguistic indications such as "(laughter)") do not figure in word counts or other calculations. Our current tool of choice is Concorder X (Edwards 2006), an in-house program based on existing open-source software (Concorder Pro; Fahrenbacher 2003) that was substantially modified to meet our conditions. Key among these is our requirement that all legal speech material (i.e., that produced by bona fide sample members) be properly associated with the speaker who produced it. Thanks to the basic format of the corpora going in, the data could be retrofitted to the requirements of the software with little to no conversion.

Concorder X is a versatile instrument that efficiently creates word lists and concordances in different configurations and orders (e.g., alphabetical, frequency). These can be efficiently generated for a single speaker, a corpus in its entirety, or a specified subsample thereof. The ability to consult a single word list or concordance (in contrast to as many such documents as there are speakers

in the sample) dramatically reduces the amount of time required to locate and extract relevant data. This is particularly valuable for quick-and-dirty feasibility assessments of the frequency (or even existence) in a corpus of targeted linguistic features and to facilitate identification of the speakers who make use of them. As illustrated in (4), the concordance displays each lexical item as a keyword in its immediately preceding and following linguistic context, along with speaker identifier and address in the transcript. Clicking on the keyword takes the user to its original location in the corpus, enabling access to the entire wider context.

Variationist analyses often take the form of determining why one competing variant is chosen over another in a previously specified *variable context*.[4] The variants in question may include such disparate forms as subjunctive versus indicative mood under subjunctive-selecting matrices, modal versus periphrastic versus simple present expressions of future temporal reference, or imperfect versus conditional tenses in protases of hypothetical *if*-complexes, among myriad others. The context view for each token displayed by the concordance is often sufficient to enable the analyst to code it according to factors hypothesized to affect variant choice (e.g., proximity in the future, polarity of the utterance, presence of intervening material between main and complement clauses, and so on). An important caveat, however, is that to locate a token, a lexical signpost must be queried, and the output of the search may be overspecified or fall outside the variable context. Thus, searching *que* 'that' will turn up a lot of complement clauses, but not only subjunctive-selecting ones, searching *si* 'if' will return *if*-clauses, but not only hypothetical ones. Outliers, which will differ according to the parameters of the variable context under investigation, must be detected and disposed of manually. As noted in section 5, location of relevant tokens is further complicated by the fact that many function words such as *que* or *that* are often deleted altogether, as are subjects, copulas, and prepositions, among many others. Some of these may be variants of the variable under study, and therefore must be considered alongside their overt counterparts. Retrieval is therefore based on a combination of automated searches (for forms with overt lexical representations) and manual extraction (for null elements and syntactic variants such as relativization or word-order alternation). Admittedly, manual retrieval is incredibly onerous, especially with large-scale corpora, but the silver lining is that it enables researchers to uncover the full set of variants of a given variable, a sine qua non for variationist analysis. Crucially, these may include variants that were not recognized or identified at the outset (e.g., selection of the conditional under French subjunctive-selecting matrices or absorption of prepositions in French relative clauses). Manual retrieval also forces researchers to continually (re)familiarize themselves with the data they are analyzing, which become exponentially more abstract as a function of the amount of annotation applied to them. In so doing, we respect another core tenet of the variationist paradigm, which is that linguistic elements must be studied in the *contexts* in which they occur.

However they are located, the extracted tokens are then *coded* according to a series of factors (themselves instantiations of hypotheses about what motivates variant choice) in preparation for statistical analysis. Data coding begins by transferring relevant tokens directly into Excel spreadsheets. Thousands of such tokens can be copied at a time, each automatically accompanied by speaker and line number, already split across columns with the keyword identified in bold red font. This not only ensures correct attribution of each token, but also enhances its visibility, which is particularly useful for correction purposes. We have marshalled many built-in features of Excel (e.g., filters, sorting and tabulating functions, the "hide columns" and subtotaling features) to facilitate coding and improve reliability. Here again, the simplicity of the original transcription protocol lends itself well to these efforts. The resulting strings encoding the targeted linguistic and social aspects of each token can then be fed into multivariate or other statistical analyses to assess the significance, relative magnitude, and direction of their effects. These results constitute the backbone of our analyses.

8   Data preservation

The data housed in the Sociolinguistics Lab were collected at different points in time and in a few cases (e.g., the *Récits du français québécois d'autrefois*, the *Ex-Slave Recordings*) by unaffiliated researchers. The material was therefore recorded using vastly different technologies resulting in different formats (ranging from reel-to-reel and cassettes to digital recordings). All recordings have been preserved in their original medium and subsequently digitized.[5] Digitized audio files were saved in the format most common at the time of digitization and are

updated as required. All of the data, from transcripts to token files, exist in multiple copies (digital and physical) stored in multiple secure locations, both within the lab's premises and without (i.e., on the university server).

9   Data life cycle

The large-scale research carried out at the Sociolinguistics Lab may span months, years, or even decades. Analyses and associated token files are frequently revisited, whether to alter them by recoding or eliminating factors that have not proved revealing, to update them by incorporating additional factors to test new hypotheses, to extend the original coding protocol to novel data sets, or any combination of these. Such tasks may sound straightforward, but as any researcher who has attempted them knows, this is far from the case—especially after a considerable amount of time has elapsed. To complicate matters, several researchers may be involved in different aspects of a single project simultaneously, and because turnover among them is not uncommon (students are enrolled for a set amount of time, the tenure of a postdoc or visiting scholar is by definition limited, and so on), rigorous record keeping and documentation at every stage are imperative for the survival and continuing utility of the data. Accordingly, we have invested a good deal of time and effort in establishing protocols to ensure this outcome. These range from labeling conventions identifying file types (e.g., *trans* for transcriptions, *ci* for coding instructions), designated abbreviations for variables (e.g., *NEG* for negation), or standardized cross-study coding for social characteristics, lexical items, and more. Dedicated file management procedures ensure that the relevant versions of project documents (including coding instructions, token files, or outputs of statistical analyses) can be readily accessed. All such documents are relabeled and dated each time they are worked on, taking care to retain older versions in case of data corruption, handling accidents, or simply for reference. They are stored in folders where they can be sorted chronologically or alphabetically. These and other practices have contributed enormously to our goals of replicating and/or reproducing earlier research.

10   Ethical considerations

All of the data housed in the Sociolinguistics Lab have been collected, handled, and stored in compliance with the ethical considerations outlined by both the relevant granting agencies (http://www.pre.ethics.gc.ca/eng/policy-politique_tcps2-eptc2_2018.html) and the University Research Ethics Board. Indeed, approval must be obtained before the project is even initiated. Our only departure from their requirements involves the principle that fully informed consent should precede data collection. Predictably enough, we have found that initiating interaction with a prospective participant by presenting the linguistic details of the project (which, according to some research ethics board members, should include describing the researcher's interest in use of the subjunctive or constraints on bilingual code-switching, for example), and the attendant reading, discussing, and signing of release forms, is antithetical to creating an atmosphere conducive to obtaining exemplars of unreflecting speech data, let alone any appreciable use of the vernacular. Instead, we explain the purpose of the interview in more general terms, but always including our interest in language use, and address the requirement of fully informed consent by debriefing participants immediately following the recording session (as stipulated by the research ethics board). Although participants are assured at the outset that consent may be withdrawn at any time with no penalty, this has never once occurred in the hundreds of interviews we have conducted. This is testimony to the skill and professionalism of the fieldworkers, all the more so considering that participation is wholly motivated by interest, no monetary incentive having ever been offered.

As noted, privacy and confidentiality of the data are ensured in several ways. The identity of participants is anonymized by means of pseudonyms and speaker numbers, and the material they provided, be it recorded or transcribed, is stored in a secure location under the supervision of the lab's research coordinator. Because of the personal nature of much of the material and the different ethical requirements to which the corpora are subject,[6] they have not been posted on the internet or otherwise distributed publicly. Instead, with the express consent of the participants, on-site access to the material is granted to applicants whose formal request to use the corpora has been approved by the lab's director. Approval is contingent upon the applicant's commitment to respect certain ethical conditions, including the following:

a. No information enabling identification of participants may be included in any paper or presentation based on the corpus.

b. Materials contained in the corpus will not serve as the basis for personal judgments about the opinions, personality, or language of the participant.

c. Materials contained in the corpus will only be cited verbatim in the interest of illustrating a linguistic point, and the content of any such citation must comply with conditions (a) and (b).

Such precautions are particularly important when the linguistic variety in question is non-standard or socially stigmatized, as is the case for much of the data housed at the Sociolinguistics Lab.

11   Data citation

As noted by Conzett and De Smedt (chapter 11, this volume), citation of data is not yet general practice. At the Sociolinguistics Lab, access to corpora is additionally contingent on the commitment to proper attribution, not only to the corpus from which the data were drawn (usually via citation of the published "corpus paper"), but also to the specific speaker who produced it. Any utterance that is reproduced must be attributed to its source via codes identifying the corpus name, speaker number, and utterance address, as exemplified in (1)–(3). The first citation of such an example must be accompanied by a footnote explaining the attribution codes (illustrated here in note 2) and referencing the appropriate corpus name and bibliographic reference, along with the clarification that examples are reproduced verbatim from speaker utterances. Such requirements make the data and associated claims readily verifiable, enhancing the reproducibility and accountability of any study based on them (Berez-Kroeker et al. 2018).

12   Applications

In keeping with our understanding that the utility of a corpus lies to a large extent in the versatility of uses to which it can be put, Sociolinguistics Lab corpora have lent themselves to the study of a wide variety of research questions. These include constraints on different manifestations of language contact (lexical borrowing, code-switching, grammatical convergence), issues involving language change (across the life span, contact-induced, resistance to by linguistic isolates, the role of the media in), grammaticalization (in English, French, and pan-Romance), heritage language maintenance, prescription versus praxis, and the origins of AAVE, among others. Linguistic variables marshalled to illustrate these issues include, but are not limited to, such disparate phenomena as copula deletion, dative alternation, question formation, word order variation, preposition stranding, relativization strategies, auxiliary alternation, the variable expression of present, past, and future temporal reference, mood alternation, gender assignment, and plural marking. For references to these and other publications based on lab corpora, see the lab's Publications page (http://www.sociolinguistics.uottawa.ca/publications.html).

13 Epilogue

In the current academic climate, the data-driven research that corpora enable is often denigrated as theoretically uninteresting linguistics—or even *not* linguistics—when not outright penalized. Outside of the narrow domain of (variationist) sociolinguistics, researchers are rarely (if ever) credited for the extreme efforts we undertake to collect, transcribe, organize, and share the vast quantities of precious spontaneous speech data that constitute many corpora. On the contrary, we are often chastised for the wonky distributions, empty cells, and sometimes less-than-optimal quantities of rare variants that characterize natural speech. It is not uncommon for leading linguistics journals, viewed as mouthpieces of the field, to reject or request major revisions of quantitative work reporting sparse or disproportionate data distributions, even when entire massive data sets have been systematically combed to yield those tokens. This while encouraging papers pushing complex and wide-ranging theories based on no production data at all beyond native speaker intuitions, often with little prospect of replicability or reproducibility. Linguists accustomed to painstaking analysis of language *as it is spoken* recognize that uneven distributions are the rule rather than the exception. But widespread unfamiliarity with the facts of actual spontaneous speech data, and the growing penchant for substituting it with more easily accessible surrogates (e.g., internet language), whose specific provenance we may know little or nothing about, have conspired to obscure these core characteristics. It is to be hoped that the practices outlined in this chapter, most of which have been staples of the methodology of variationist sociolinguistics since its inception over half a century ago, will contribute, along with the remainder of this volume, to rectifying this imbalance.

Acknowledgments

The work reported here was generously supported by the Social Sciences and Humanities Research Council of Canada through its Canada Research Chairs program and numerous research grants, as well as by the Killam Foundation, the Pierre Elliott Trudeau Foundation, the Ontario Ministry of Research and Innovation, the Canada Foundation for Innovation, and the Ontario Innovation Trust. I was first introduced to the concept of data management by the teachings and the example of William Labov. Respect for data and the speakers who provided it was at the core of his famous LIN 560 class at the University of Pennsylvania. Much of what I learned there formed the basis for my own data collection and handling practices at the Sociolinguistics Lab at the University of Ottawa, which I founded and have directed since the early 1980s, as well as for the Urban Dialectology courses we have been running here since then. My efforts have been immeasurably aided, and in fact surpassed, by generations of smart, committed, enthusiastic (and above all, incredibly organized!) students and associates, who have continued to translate those teachings into ever more productive and efficient ways of dealing with data. If I have been able to boast that we can reproduce or replicate an analysis ten years after the fact, it is thanks to them. I am also grateful to two anonymous reviewers for comments that enriched this chapter.

Notes

1. Real names are stored in a secure and confidential location during corpus construction and are disposed of when anonymization has been completed.

2. Codes in parentheses refer to corpus name, speaker number, and utterance address in the *Quebec English Corpus* (Poplack, Walker, & Malcolmson 2006) in (1) and (3), the *African Nova Scotian English Corpus* (Poplack & Tagliamonte 1991) in (2), and the *Ottawa-Hull French Corpus* (Poplack 1989) in (5) and (6). Examples are reproduced verbatim from speaker utterances.

3. One analysis of a 3.5-million-word corpus showed an average of one error per 520 words (including errors of all magnitudes, ranging from a missing space to a misspelled word), an excellent record by the standards of speech corpora.

4. The *variable context* is defined as the context in which variants alternate with no change in referential meaning.

5. With the exception of the older Sociolinguistic Archives recordings collected by students.

6. These have changed appreciably over the duration, with the result that different corpora are bound by different ethical conditions.

References

Beal, Joan, Karen Corrigan, and Hermann Moisl. 2007. *Creating and Digitizing Language Corpora*. Volume 1: *Synchronic Databases*. Houndmills: Palgrave-Macmillan UK.

Berez-Kroeker, Andrea L., Lauren Gawne, Susan Smythe Kung, Barbara F. Kelly, Tyler Heston, Gary Holton, Peter Pulsifer, et al. 2018. Reproducible research in linguistics: A position statement on data citation and attribution in our field. *Linguistics* 56 (1): 1–18.

Bird, Steven, and Gary Simons. 2003. Seven dimensions of portability for language documentation and description. *Language* 79 (3): 557–582.

Edwards, James. 2006. *Concorder X: Program and Documentation*. Ottawa: University of Ottawa Sociolinguistics Laboratory.

Fahrenbacher, Matt. 2003. *Concorder Pro 1.0: A Text-Analysis Tool for Mac OS X*. N.p.: Humongous Elephants and Tigers.

Labov, William. (1966) 2006. *The Social Stratification of English in New York City*. 2nd ed. Cambridge: Cambridge University Press.

Labov, William. 1972. *Sociolinguistic Patterns*. Philadelphia: University of Pennsylvania Press,

Labov, William. 1984. Field methods of the project on linguistic change and variation. In *Language in Use: Readings in Sociolinguistics*, ed. John Baugh and Joel Sherzer, 28–54. Englewood Cliffs, NJ: Prentice Hall.

Lealess, Allison V., and Chelsea Smith. 2011. Assessing contact-induced language change: The use of subject relative markers in Quebec English. *Ottawa Papers in Linguistics* 36: 20–38.

Mielke, Jeff. 2013. Ultrasound and corpus study of a change from below: Vowel rhoticity in Canadian French. *University of Pennsylvania Working Papers in Linguistics* 19 (2): article 16.

Poplack, Shana. 1989. The care and handling of a mega-corpus. In *Language Change and Variation*, ed. Ralph Fasold and Deborah Schiffrin, 411–451. Amsterdam: Benjamins.

Poplack, Shana, ed. 2000. *The English History of African American English*. Oxford: Blackwell Publishers.

Poplack, Shana. 2007. Foreword. In *Creating and Digitizing Language Corpora*, ed. Joan Beal, Karen Corrigan, and Hermann Moisl, ix–xiii. Houndmills: Palgrave-Macmillan UK.

Poplack, Shana. 2015. Norme prescriptive, norme communautaire et variation diaphasique. Variations diasystématiques et leurs interdépendances. In *Travaux de linguistique romane*, ed. Kristen Kragh and Jan Lindschouw, 293–319. Strasbourg: Société de linguistique romane.

Poplack, Shana. 2018. *Borrowing: Loanwords in the Speech Community and in the Grammar*. Oxford: Oxford University Press.

Poplack, Shana, and Johanne Bourdages. 2005. *Le français en contexte: Milieux scolaire et social*. Ottawa: University of Ottawa. (Social Sciences and Humanities Research Council of Canada research grant #410-2005-2108.)

Poplack, Shana, and Nathalie Dion. 2012. Myths and facts about loanword development. *Language Variation and Change* 24 (3): 279–315.

Poplack, Shana, Lidia-Gabriela Jarmasz, Nathalie Dion, and Nicole Rosen. 2015. Searching for "Standard French": The construction and mining of the *Recueil historique des grammaires du français*. *Journal of Historical Sociolinguistics* 1 (1): 13–56.

Poplack, Shana, Adrienne Jones, Allison V. Lealess, Martine Leroux, Chelsea T. Smith, Yukiko Yoshizumi, Lauren Zentz, and Nathalie Dion. 2006. Assessing convergence in contact languages. Paper presented at New Ways of Analyzing Variation 35. Ohio State University, Columbus, November 9–12.

Poplack, Shana, and Stephen Levey. 2010. Contact-induced grammatical change. In *Language and Space—An International Handbook of Linguistic Variation*. Volume 1: *Theories and Methods*, ed. Peter Auer and Jürgen E. Schmidt, 391–419. Berlin: Mouton de Gruyter.

Poplack, Shana, and David Sankoff. 1987. The Philadelphia Story in the Spanish Caribbean. *American Speech* 62 (4): 291–314.

Poplack, Shana, and Anne St-Amand. 2007. A real-time window on 19th century vernacular French: *The Récits du français québécois d'autrefois*. *Language in Society* 36 (5): 707–734.

Poplack, Shana, and Sali Tagliamonte. 1991. African American English in the diaspora: Evidence from old-line Nova Scotians. *Language Variation and Change* 3 (3): 301–39.

Poplack, Shana, and Sali Tagliamonte. 2001. *African American English in the Diaspora*. Oxford: Basil Blackwell.

Poplack, Shana, James A. Walker, and Rebecca Malcolmson. 2006. An English "Like no other"?: Language contact and change in Quebec. *Canadian Journal of Linguistics* 51 (2/3): 185–213.

Poplack, Shana, Lauren Zentz, and Nathalie Dion. 2012. What counts as (contact-induced) change. *Bilingualism: Language and Cognition* 15 (2): 247–254.

Van Herk, Gerard, and Poplack, Shana. 2003. Rewriting the past: Bare verbs in the Ottawa Repository of Early African American Correspondence. *Journal of Pidgin and Creole Languages* 18 (2): 231–266.

17   Managing Legacy Data in a Sociophonetic Study of Vowel Variation and Change

James Grama

1   Introduction: The focus of this data management use case

This data management use case provides a description of the workflow of a sociophonetic study of language variation and change using legacy data (Grama 2015). This study investigated change in the vowel system of Pidgin (known to linguists as Hawai'i Creole), an English-lexified creole spoken in Hawai'i. In that study, two existing corpora were used to conduct a trend study that compared Pidgin speakers at two time points: the 1970s and the 2000s. Analysis was conducted on acoustic vowel measurements taken from speech elicited using sociolinguistic-style interviews (cf. Labov 1972). This use case serves as a meta-analysis of the methods applied in the Grama study and is intended for researchers interested in using naturalistic legacy data to identify longitudinal change. Throughout the chapter, methodological considerations are made that concern sociophonetic studies, the management of legacy data (especially when that data was not originally designed to address sociophonetic research questions), and further issues that are relevant to variationist research.

The chapter is organized as follows: first, the language setting for the current study is described, along with a discussion of my positionality to Pidgin (section 2). Then, I discuss the way archived interviews were selected for analysis, as well as characteristics of the archived corpora used in Grama (2015) (section 3). This is followed by a description of the way vowel data was transcribed (section 4.1), force aligned (section 4.2), manually checked (section 4.3), extracted (section 4.4), cleaned (section

4.5), and normalized (section 4.6). Issues concerning data transparency (cf. Gawne & Styles, chapter 2, this volume), figure interpretability (section 5.1), and storing and sharing of data (section 5.2) are then briefly discussed. Throughout, the Grama study is evaluated in the context of best practices in sociophonetics, and deviations from optimal procedure are noted, where relevant.

I now turn to a brief discussion of the social setting of this study, as the social landscape of any variety is paramount to interpreting the results and understanding why the study took the shape it did.

2   A brief history of Hawai'i and the development of Pidgin

Hawai'i's complex history of contact began from its discovery. The islands were originally settled by Polynesian seafarers between 1190 and 1293 CE (Wilmshurst et al. 2011:1816; Walworth 2014:258), and the following two centuries saw intercultural movement among neighboring Polynesian cultures (Collerson & Weisler 2007). It is generally accepted that sustained contact between Hawai'i and other eastern Polynesians declined sharply in the fifteenth century (Drager 2012b:62). In 1778, Hawai'i was irrevocably altered by James Cook's arrival. European contact opened the floodgates for foreign influx at an unprecedented scale; the islands were quickly exploited for their sandalwood and used both as a strategic launching point during the whaling trade and a stopover point in the fur trade of the early 1800s (Reinecke 1969:24). Foreign presence was debilitating for Hawaiians and their language ('ōlelo Hawai'i).

The research discussed in this paper was made possible by funding from the Russell J. and Dorothy S. Bilinski Dissertation Fellowship Award and the University of Hawai'i at Mānoa. Many thanks are due to the editors of this handbook, Andrea L. Berez-Kroeker, Bradley McDonnell, Eve Koller, and Lauren B. Collister, to two anonymous reviewers, and to Melody Ann Ross for providing helpful feedback on earlier drafts. All remaining errors are my own. Greatest thanks go to the participants who graciously lent their voices to these collections.

Throughout the 1800s, the number of native Hawaiians dropped precipitously due largely to foreign disease (Stannard 1990:330). An increase in Christian missionaries in 1820 further contributed to the decline of ʻōlelo Hawaiʻi, as English was elevated as the language of the church, economic advancement, and social capital (Drager 2012b:63). The overt prestige of English was further entrenched by the steady growth of US influence in schools. A wealthy, English-speaking minority affected policies that gradually forced ʻōlelo Hawaiʻi schools to switch to English as the primary language of instruction. All of this was designed to prepare the youth of Hawaiʻi for "participation in an American-type community" (Stueber 1964:144). In July 1887, a group of wealthy US businessmen coerced King Kalākaua under threat of force to sign a new constitution that stripped the Hawaiian monarchy of its authority and disenfranchised native Hawaiians. A mere five years later, the Kingdom of Hawaiʻi was overthrown by a wealthy, white minority, and Hawaiʻi was illegally annexed by the US in 1898.

The rapidly changing social climate of Hawaiʻi in the nineteenth century was spurred on by the establishment of sugarcane plantations in 1835. The plantations lured laborers worldwide, initially, Cantonese and Portuguese, then Japanese, laborers from the Philippines, and later, from Germany, Korea, Puerto Rico, Spain, and islands throughout the Pacific. While the plantation foremen originally spoke ʻōlelo Hawaiʻi, English soon took its place, reflecting a changing social climate that was increasingly dominated by an English-speaking minority. Because many languages were used on the plantations with no shared first language among the workers, an English-based pidgin arose to facilitate communication. Children raised in this context commonly spoke both the language(s) of their parents and a creolized version of English—Hawaiʻi Creole, known locally as Pidgin (Kawamoto 1993). As English speakers solidified a position of overt economic power, Pidgin increasingly took on the role of lingua franca among Hawaiʻi Locals, and within three generations (by the 1930s), Pidgin was a distinct language from English (Roberts 2004).

Pidgin has become closely linked with a Local identity, due in part to its development alongside Hawaiʻi's changing demography. This identity encompasses many cultural backgrounds and ethnicities, the extent of which is beyond the scope of this use case (for detailed accounts, see Fujikane 1997; Rohrer 1997; Ohnuma

2002), but a crucial opposition places *Local* at conceptual odds with *Haole*. For many, the category "Local" comprises a non-white person, born in Hawaiʻi, with a familial connection to the plantations and Pidgin, while the category "Haole" comprises a white person whose presence on the islands is the result of historical exploitation via colonialism. "Haole" is a construct characterized by external forces (e.g., whiteness, the military, tourism, English dominance), while "Local" evinces solidarity against that force (Ohnuma 2002). Attitudes toward Pidgin and English reflect this opposition. Pidgin is marginalized by many as "broken English," while English is upheld as "proper" (Drager & Grama 2014). Moreover, English is often cited as a language of economic mobility, and despite Pidgin's use in publicly visible domains (e.g., politics, the news), it is nevertheless viewed by many as a language whose use should be restricted to the home and close personal relationships (see Marlow & Giles 2008, 2010).

2.1 A note on researcher positionality

The history of colonialism in Hawaiʻi cannot be ignored when discussing the present study. In keeping with the observation that data cannot be divorced from its source (Holton, Leonard, & Pulsifer, chapter 4, this volume), the researcher's positionality to the variety under study is key. In the context of Hawaiʻi, it matters greatly that I am a white, non-native Pidgin speaker from California. My very presence as a researcher in Hawaiʻi was the result of settler privilege. Because of this, the likelihood that I could elicit representative Pidgin speech data is low, given the long history of language hegemony (see Marlow & Giles 2008, 2010). Therefore, it was both prudent and methodologically necessary to make as much use of existing data as possible in lieu of collecting new data.[1]

Having established context, I now move on to describe the goals of the original study, as well as how legacy data were used to address those goals.

3   Using legacy data to achieve research goals

Building on phonological work on Pidgin (e.g., Bickerton 1976; Sakoda & Siegel 2008), the focus of Grama (2015) was to acoustically characterize changes in the vowel system of Pidgin over time, with considerations to both internal and external factors.[2] While phonological descriptions of Pidgin highlight that inter- and intra-speaker variation is clearly present in the language, relatively few studies have applied variationist methods to acoustic data to describe this variation (for exceptions in other creoles, see Kraus 2017; Lesho 2014; Rosenfelder 2009; Sabino 1996, 2012; Veatch 1991; Wassink 1999, 2001, 2006).

To characterize changes over time in Pidgin, Grama (2015) employed both real- and apparent-time data taken from archival recordings from two existing corpora on Kaipuleohone, the University of Hawai'i at Mānoa's digital ethnographic archive (Albarillo & Thieberger 2009; Berez 2013); one collection was recorded in the 1970s (with speakers born 1896–1946), and one was recorded in the 2000s (with speakers born 1947–1988). These data were appropriate for answering questions of language change over time because they represented two independent samplings of the Hawai'i speech community approximately thirty years apart, with speakers born over a ninety-year time frame. This allowed for real-time comparisons to be made across corpora and apparent-time comparisons to be made within each corpus. That the data were already extant was particularly beneficial, given that many of the recordings were conducted between native Pidgin speakers, and that my position as a migrant, white, non-native Pidgin speaker in Hawai'i limited my ability to reliably collect new data. These corpora—the Bickerton Collection and the Influences and Variation in Hawai'i Creole English—are discussed in the next section.

3.1 The corpora

3.1.1 The 1970s corpus (the Bickerton Collection) The Bickerton Collection includes materials elicited from Pidgin speakers and from speakers of a range of other languages. Recordings were made between 1970 and 1980 and include people born between the mid-1890s to the late 1940s. Speakers were represented across these birthdates, but they tended to be either in their mid-to-late sixties, or in their early thirties to mid-forties; this created a natural break in the corpus, where about half the speakers were older than fifty years of age and half were younger. The collection was amassed to describe the linguistic structure of Pidgin, with special attention paid to morpho-syntactic and phonological alternations (for studies based on this corpus, see Bickerton 1976;

Odo 1975, 1977). Interviews were conducted by both Pidgin and non-Pidgin speakers; the apparent dominant language of the interviewer became an important criterion for interview exclusion from Grama (2015) (see section 3.1.3). In all, the collection includes 168 recordings, which vary widely in duration. While many of the recordings are in the style of traditional sociolinguistic interviews, a number of them are recordings of radio and television programs or advertisements. Throughout the remainder of the chapter, this collection will be referred to as the 1970s corpus.

3.1.2 The 2000s corpus (Influences and Variation in Hawai'i Creole English) The Influences and Variation in Hawai'i Creole English collection comprises sociolinguistic-style interviews with Pidgin speakers. Recordings were made in the early-to-mid-2000s and include people born between the mid-1940s to the mid-1980s. Speakers were represented across these birthdates, but they tended to be either in their late forties, or in their early twenties, again creating a natural break in the corpus; here, approximately half the speakers were older than thirty years of age and half were younger. The corpus was amassed by Jeff Siegel and a number of research assistants to examine variation in Pidgin and the role played by external influences on language change (for studies based on this corpus, see Sakoda & Siegel 2003, 2008; Siegel 2007). Interviews were conducted by Pidgin speakers, with Pidgin speakers, and interviewees were typically friends, family members, colleagues, or otherwise previously known to the interviewer. In all, the collection includes 117 recordings, ranging from around six minutes to one hour and forty minutes. Throughout the remainder of the chapter, this collection will be referred to as the 2000s corpus.

3.1.3 Interview selection Selecting recordings from these corpora that were appropriate for a sociophonetic study of language change over time proved labor-intensive, largely because the original intent of each corpus was not to facilitate sociophonetic research. Recordings were prioritized that met five constraints. First, sufficient information had to be included in the metadata or in the recording itself to indicate that interviewees were born and raised in Hawai'i and not people who emigrated to Hawai'i later in life.[3] This constraint was implemented to be as certain as possible that speakers included in the study were native Pidgin speakers, and

not second-language learners, as later acquisition can impact phonological realizations (see, e.g., Flege, Shirru, & MacKay 2003). Second, interviews were prioritized where the interviewer was also a Pidgin speaker. Given the history of linguistic hegemony in Hawai'i, people are less likely to use Pidgin if their interlocutor does not also speak Pidgin. This is especially true in more formal domains (e.g., in a recorded conversation). Third, recordings with one interviewee were desirable because recordings with multiple interlocutors yield overlapping speech and uneven turn-taking, which makes preparing data for forced alignment more labor-intensive. Fourth, recordings needed to be of high-enough quality to undergo acoustic analysis. Quality issues rendered many recordings unusable; wind, excessive background noise, static, feedback, clipping, and quiet interviewees yielded recordings that were unlikely to produce reliable formant measurements. Fifth, recordings had to feature enough speech to map a speaker's vowel space.[4] Through conducting the original study, it became clear that interviews lasting around twenty minutes, or two thousand words, reliably produced enough vowel tokens across vowel category to accurately map the vowel space. Interviews that met each of these five constraints were candidates for inclusion in Grama (2015).

There was also a desire for a balanced number of speakers to ensure equal representation across demographic category. These categories consisted of *corpus* (1970s vs. 2000s), wherein real-time, longitudinal change could be tested; *relative age* within the corpus (relatively older vs. relatively younger speakers), so that change in apparent time could be tested, where relatively older speakers represent the language as it was in the past, and relatively younger speakers represent the language as it is spoken at the time of recording (Bailey 2004); and binary *sex* (female, male), to assess how females and males differed (if at all) in their participation in the identified changes. Pruning the two corpora based on these constraints resulted in a total of thirty-two total recordings. The distribution of speakers across the tested demographic categories included in Grama (2015) is reported in table 17.1.

Despite these restrictions, inherent differences exist between the two collections, particularly with respect to interview styles. In the 2000s corpus, interviewers and interviewees tended to be close friends or family members. The familiarity between speakers resulted in very

Table 17.1

Speaker numbers with age information across corpus, relative age, and sex

Corpus	Relative age	Sex	Mean age at time of recording	Mean birthdate	N
1970s	Old	Female	61	1913	4
		Male	65	1911	4
	Young	Female	40	1935	4
		Male	33	1940	4
2000s	Old	Female	49	1958	4
		Male	48	1959	4
	Young	Female	22	1985	4
		Male	22	1985	4
				Total	32

conversational interactions. By contrast, 1970s interviewers were less likely to be previously known to interviewees and tended to feature more monologic speech styles. Additionally, differences arose that reflected Hawai'i's changing social climate over a thirty-year period. Young 2000s speakers as a group, for example, completed more formal schooling than 1970s speakers, who typically did not achieve more than a high school education. By contrast, 1970s speakers were more likely to have worked in positions that required manual labor than 2000s speakers did. Appendix A provides a more detailed breakdown of demographic information for each speaker.

4 Data processing

The following section describes how data were processed in Grama (2015), including how interviews were transcribed and force aligned; how the resulting alignments were manually checked; and how vowel formants were extracted, cleaned, and normalized.

4.1 Transcription

After selection, interviews were orthographically transcribed at the utterance level. Research concerned with the acoustic properties of vowels ultimately relies on transcription of some kind. While there have been significant strides in automated speech recognition, fully automated transcription is far from accurate enough to replace human transcribers. Thus, manual transcription remains a necessary bottleneck to acquiring large amounts of high-quality vowel data (cf. Seifert et al.

2018:335). Currently, the industry standard for transcription is ELAN (Lausberg & Sloetjes 2009), which is under continual development. For this study, however, interviews were transcribed and time aligned in Transcriber (Barras et al. 2001). While Transcriber's interface has a gentler learning curve than ELAN's, this choice was made largely because Transcriber, not ELAN, interfaced with LaBB-CAT (Language, Brain and Behaviour – Corpus Analysis Tool) (Fromont & Hay 2012), the forced aligner used in Grama (2015) (see discussion in section 4.2). However as of writing, Transcriber suffers from a lack of upkeep. Prior to an update in March 2017, Transcriber had not been updated since 2005. Given that ELAN now interfaces with LaBB-CAT, it would be my choice of transcription software were I to undertake the study today.

A mean of twenty-two minutes, or two thousand words, was transcribed for each speaker for the original study. Transcription was of temporally contiguous sections, increasing the likelihood that an interviewee used roughly the same speech style. Overt discussions about Pidgin were avoided when possible, as this motivated some speakers to shift toward English; issues of recording quality also made it necessary to skip (usually short) sections of the interview until conditions improved. Table 17.2 summarizes the transcription statistics from each interview, noting word count as is typical in corpus descriptions.

4.2 Forced alignment

After interviews were transcribed, they were force aligned. Forced alignment refers to the process of automatically creating segmentations at the level of the phoneme using the acoustic signal (usually a .wav file) and an orthographic transcription (in this case, a .trs file). The rise of computational methods in the past decade has revolutionized research methods in phonetics, drastically increasing the speed of getting analyzable data (cf. Schiel, Draxler, & Harrington 2011). Choosing a forced aligner is therefore crucial, as they are now standard practice of workflows in many production-based sociophonetic studies.[5]

In Grama (2015), corpus storage and forced alignment were performed using a server build of LaBB-CAT housed at the Sociolinguistics Server (SOLIS) at the University of Hawai'i at Mānoa (Drager 2012a).[6] This choice was made both because of LaBB-CAT's ability to

Table 17.2

Transcription metadata

Age	Sex	Speaker pseudonym	Time transcribed (hr:min:sec)	Word count
Old 1970s	Male	Joseph	00:21:16	2,744
		Kawika	00:19:42	2,358
		Kimo	00:30:30	1,508
		Manny	00:32:06	2,831
	Female	Kaimana	00:18:45	2,324
		Keiko	00:15:13	1,689
		Kaimana	00:18:45	2,324
		Malia	00:27:56	2,766
Young 1970s	Male	Danny	00:19:36	1,735
		Eddie	00:19:23	2,245
		Glen	00:19:15	1,777
		Victor	00:14:42	2,045
	Female	Delia Jane	00:18:17	2,099
		Eddie	00:19:23	2,245
		Mona Lisa	00:18:40	1,858
		Teresa	00:26:58	1,930
Old 2000s	Male	Grant	00:17:06	1,976
		Keoni	00:14:11	1,952
		Kevin	00:18:36	1,910
		Palani	00:30:05	2,063
	Female	Carla	00:13:32	1,927
		Kahea	00:15:09	2,201
		Lani	00:14:05	1,727
		Pua	00:28:50	1,707
Young 2000s	Male	Alika	00:11:55	2,142
		Eric	00:27:37	2,018
		Kaleo	00:17:23	2,230
		Myko	00:21:48	2,038
	Female	Lena	00:27:30	1,941
		Mina	00:33:42	1,840
		Sarah	00:20:24	1,984
		Starla	00:24:09	1,966
		Total	11:16:29	66,100

automatically generate corpus annotations and because I had prior experience using the system. Transcriber files were uploaded along with their accompanying .wav files to SOLIS, and files were tagged with available metadata. Each uploaded transcript was automatically checked for words that were not in the English CELEX dictionary (Baayen, Piepenbroock, & Gulikers 1995), with which LaBB-CAT is designed to interface. Unfamiliar items in the dictionary were added using the grapheme-to-phoneme (G2P) mapping system that CELEX employs for British English.[7] Errors in the transcript (e.g., misspellings, unrecognized characters) were corrected in SOLIS with LaBB-CAT's transcription editing protocols. Forced alignment was produced using the Hidden Markov Model Toolkit, HTK (Young et al. 2009), via the default train/align procedure (see Fromont & Watson 2016), which produced automated boundaries around phonemes according to lexical data from CELEX.

Force-aligned data in LaBB-CAT can be accessed in two main ways. First, the user can access the *transcripts* tab to interface directly with the transcript and toggle available annotation layers on and off. These layers are programmed by the user and generated automatically. Information can then be extracted as a time-aligned file in several formats, for example, as a Praat TextGrid (Boersma & Weenink 2019). While the entire interview file can be exported as one Praat TextGrid (which is preferable if one-to-one correspondence between file and speaker is desired), Praat often has issues with larger files, making them difficult to work with if processing power is at a premium. The second way to extract the force-aligned data is via LaBB-CAT's *search* function. By

executing a search across the segments layer, LaBB-CAT returns all instances that fit the specified criteria. Individual segments can then be extracted, a process which yields TextGrids and .wav files for all aligned intervals that correspond to interval breaks in Transcriber or annotations in ELAN. For example, the user could specify one or more speakers in LaBB-CAT and query a specific vowel. Figure 17.1 shows an example of such a search executed for Myko, a young 2000s male.

This process was performed independently for each vowel category and individual speaker. The pairs of .wav files and TextGrids (between 25 and 350 files per vowel per speaker) were then extracted from SOLIS and stored on my personal computer in a folder organized by speaker by vowel. In accordance with best practices for data management, these files will be archived in the future in one of three locations: SOLIS, Kaipuleohone, or the Pacific and Regional Archive for Digital Sources in Endangered Cultures (PARADISEC).

Figure 17.1

LaBB-CAT's output for queried /o/ (represented by 5); first twenty tokens displayed.

4.3   Checking data

After forced alignment and extraction, vowel alignments were manually checked for accuracy and coded following the protocol described here. There is some debate in sociophonetics as to whether, and under what circumstances, manual checking of force-aligned vowel data is strictly necessary. For many, this comes down to what the research question is, trust in the force-aligned output, or more practical considerations (e.g., time). There are reasonable arguments for and against manually checking vowel alignments for accuracy. While some work demonstrates that force-aligned output produces inconsistent boundaries between vowels and sonorants (Strelluf 2016; Gonzalez, Grama, & Travis 2020), other work suggests that, given enough data, correcting force-aligned output only marginally improves formant measurements (Labov, Rosenfelder, & Fruehwald 2013:37–38; Gonzalez & Docherty 2018). However, much of the work that evaluates taking formant measurements from uncorrected data assesses the observed improvement in static vowel measures (e.g., single F1/F2 measurements for each vowel). Complications can arise if more measurements are taken from single vowels, as forced aligners are not as good at segmentation as humans are, despite doing the work much faster (Fromont & Watson 2016). In Grama (2015), there was the added complication of legacy data, where recordings were not performed in ideal scenarios, or where audio degradation impacted the quality of recordings prior to digitization. With such data, there is a higher risk that completely automated methods could yield spurious measurements. A middle ground is to check a random sample of vowel tokens, particularly those that occur in phonological contexts that disproportionately impact alignment (see Gonzalez, Grama, and Travis 2020). In my view, claims about the behavior of vowel trajectories necessitate more accurate alignments, given these concerns.

Given that the original study utilized legacy data and investigated vowels both statically and dynamically, it was prudent to take a more conservative approach and manually check all the force-aligned output. Each vowel was checked by hand and boundaries were corrected if necessary; then, the vowel was tagged with its appropriate lexical set (cf. Wells 1982). As is typical of sociophonetic studies, only vowels in stressed content words were prepared for analysis. Boundary correction

was done using a strict set of criteria, detailed in sections 4.3.1–4.3.3, and boundaries were placed at, or as close to a zero crossing in the waveform as possible. If the cues discussed in the following sections were not available, the token was excluded.

4.3.1 Obstruents   For vowels preceded by stops, the burst and aspiration were included in the consonant segment, not the vowel segment. Vowel onsets were marked where the waveform indicated periodicity and the spectrogram showed clear formant structure (e.g., rising F1). A perceptible decrease in amplitude served as an additional cue for vowels adjacent to voiced stops. Boundaries for vowels adjacent to voiceless fricatives were placed where formant structure was clear, and where the cessation of aperiodic energy coincided with a change in amplitude.

4.3.2 Sonorants   For vowels bordering nasals and laterals, boundaries were placed where decreased amplitude coincided with formant dampening or a lowered F1. Boundaries between vowels and pre-vocalic /r/ were marked at maximum F3, or F2, if F3 was unavailable. Where post-vocalic /r/ was present, boundaries were placed where a dip in F3 indicated oral closure consistent with /r/ articulation (see, e.g., Johnson 2012:140). Along with amplitude, boundaries for /w/ were placed where F1 and F2 began to diverge, and boundaries for /j/ were evaluated based on where F2 and F3 began to diverge.

4.3.3 Word-initial and word-final vowels   Vowel-initial words at the beginning of an utterance were often bordered by silence or glottal closure. The starting point of the vowel was therefore marked as the first relatively high-amplitude vocal pulse evident in the waveform. Vowel-final words at the end of an utterance were marked at the last high-amplitude vocal pulse evident in the waveform. In both cases, Praat's ability to track the formant structure factored into boundary placement.

4.4   Extracting formant values

Vowel checking and formant extraction was done for each speaker and vowel independently. Before extraction, a 15% subsample of each speaker's vowel category was checked to ensure that settings in Praat accurately captured formant behavior. While it is commonplace to use a standard set of values for vowel extraction (e.g., five formants under 5,500 hertz for females), this was not possible in every case given the aforementioned issues regarding recording quality. Therefore, manual assignment of formant settings during formant extraction was necessary. The specific extraction values supplied to the Praat script can be found in Grama (2015:296–307).

The Praat script used for this study was based on a script written by Mietta Lennes, which had been modified by Abby Walker and Katie Drager.[8] This script extracted vowel identity, the word in which the vowel appeared, the preceding and following phonological segments, the duration of the vowel, the fundamental frequency, and readings of the first three formants—F1, F2 and F3—from seven equidistant points, starting from 20% of the duration through the vowel and terminating at 80%. Speech rate was assessed using de Jong and Wempe's (2009) Praat script, which calculates speech rate as a function of the number of amplitude peaks over the duration of an interval. This process yielded two different types of data for each vowel: midpoint data, which were useful for assessing the overall picture of the vowel space and the target position of monophthongs, and transition data, which were useful for quantifying formant contours over the vowel's duration.

over fourteen vowel categories across thirty-two speakers. Formant measurements were checked in R over the duration of the vowel to ensure that accurate readings were taken by the Praat script. Radical deviations from expected patterns (e.g., an F2 in /u/ of 1,200 hertz at 30% of the vowel, followed by an F2 of 500 hertz at 40%) were treated as spurious measurements, and resulted in the exclusion of the vowel token. Each speaker's vowel space was plotted and checked for outliers. Tokens with formant measurements that fell outside the range of plausible adult physiological limits (e.g., an F1 of 2,000 hertz or an F2 of 300 hertz) were removed. Tokens that were phonologically unlikely (e.g., /i/ in the low back area of the vowel space) were evaluated in Praat and removed if they were judged to be measurement errors. Finally, a script was written to remove tokens whose formant measurements fell more than three standard deviations outside of a speaker's vowel distribution, calculated within speaker, within vowel (cf. Hughes 2014, discussed in Foulkes et al. 2018). Figure 17.2 presents an example of a speaker's /i/ and /æ/ before and after filtering.

A total of 353 vowel tokens were removed following these processes, yielding 11,198 tokens for analysis. A breakdown of the number of vowels per vowel class can be seen in table 17.3.

4.5 Cleaning the data

Speaker demographic information, along with formant and speech rate measurements were compiled into a single .csv file using R (R Core Team 2018) in wide format (i.e., where each row in the data frame corresponds to a single token). This yielded 11,551 vowel tokens

4.6 Normalizing vowel formants

Even when thoroughly cleaned, raw data are not usually the focus of direct analysis at the group level (cf. Han, chapter 6, this volume). Normalization is often a necessary step to interpreting patterns in vowel data. Vowel normalization seeks to neutralize differences between

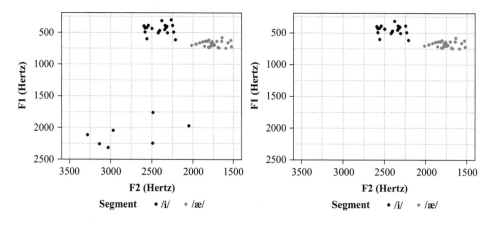

Figure 17.2
Raw formant measurements of /i/ (dark) from Eddie, a young 1970s man, before (left panel) and after (right panel) outlier filtering; /æ/ (light) included for reference.

Table 17.3

Distribution of vowel tokens in Grama (2015)

Vowel	n	Vowel	N
/i/	1,053	/u/	731
/ɪ/	1,093	/ʊ/	380
/e/	1,037	/o/	978
/ɛ/	1,158	/ʌ/	798
/æ/	1,154	/ɔ/	552
/aɪ/	899	/ɑ/	854
/aʊ/	412	/ɔɪ/	99

speakers that result from differences in physiology. For sociophoneticians, this typically means accounting for variation that stems from vocal tract length, a vital determiner of formant values; performing vowel normalization in this fashion means that any observed variation can be confidently ascribed to other factors.[9]

When and how to implement normalization is something of an ongoing discussion. If comparisons are made across groups (e.g., females to males, children to adults), normalizing vowels is uncontroversial (but consider methodological challenges pertaining to the automated vowel analysis of non-binary speakers discussed in Miles-Hercules & Zimman 2019), but normalization is typically unnecessary when investigating individual vowel spaces. Some argue against the need for normalization if comparisons are kept within group (e.g., males are compared to other males), pointing out that normalization warps the vowel space in such a way as to remove real patterns that emerge from the data (see Watson & Harrington 1999). Proponents of normalization argue that analyzing raw values is anti-conservative, and that assuming the comparability of raw formant frequencies even across speakers who share similar physiologies leads to uninterpretable data (cf. Watt, Fabricius, & Kendall 2010). Given that comparisons across speakers is precisely the goal of many sociophonetic studies, this is an especially vital point to consider. Practically speaking, my view is that normalizing is a relatively low-cost step to ensure the veracity of observed patterns, and it is often the case that well-normalized data bear considerable resemblance to unnormalized data.

The question of what normalization method is most appropriate is also a somewhat thorny issue in sociophonetics, and there are dozens of algorithms to choose from. Work that directly compares the efficacy of normalization techniques (e.g., Adank, Smits, & Van Hout 2004; Flynn & Foulkes 2011) tends to find that methods that are vowel-extrinsic, formant-intrinsic, and speaker-intrinsic are best at reducing variation that arises as a result of physiology, while preserving sociolinguistic variation. Vowel-intrinsic methods perform comparably worse by these same metrics. However, any vowel normalization technique shows improvement over raw hertz comparisons (Flynn & Foulkes 2011:686). A popular normalization choice is the Lobanov method (Lobanov 1971; but see Barreda & Nearey 2018), as it is vowel-extrinsic and produces interpretable plots.

The vowel data in this study were normalized using the Lobanov method, which requires that relatively equal samples of all (monophthongal) vowel categories be included to avoid artificial skewing. Lobanov converts raw hertz values to normalized z-scores by subtracting a speaker's mean formant frequency (μ_i) from a raw measurement (F_i), and then diving this by the standard deviation for that speaker's formant (σ_i), as in equation (17.1).

$$F_i^N = \frac{F_i - \mu_i}{\sigma_i} \qquad (17.1)$$

Because Lobanov produces values that are centered on (0, 0), it is not uncommon to scale these values back to hertz (see, e.g., Labov, Rosenfelder, & Fruehwald 2013:36), though this should only be performed after all values have been normalized. While easily performed manually or via script, normalization can also be performed using the *vowels* package (Kendall & Thomas 2018) in R, as can the Bark difference (Traunmüller 1997), ANAE (Labov, Ash, & Boberg 2006), Nearey (1977), and Watt and Fabricius (2002) methods.

5   Reporting, storing, and sharing the data

5.1   Reporting data

Transparent, clear reporting of data is an important aspect of any sociophonetic study. To this end, I include the raw formant values measured along the vowel's duration for all vowels across speakers (Grama 2015:308–337), as well as the normalized formant values across vowel, age, and sex (338–345). Moreover, clear figures and statistical analyses are key to achieving interpretable and reproducible findings. R is a powerful option for graphics creation

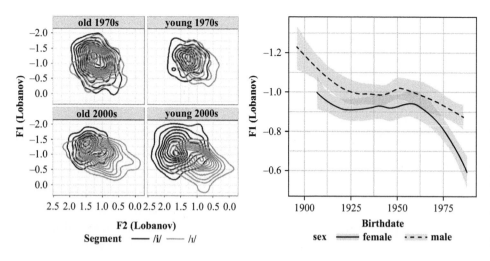

Figure 17.3

(Left) Two-dimensional kernel density plot of /i/ (dark) and /ɪ/ (light) over time across corpora and relative age. (Right) Local polynomial regression of /ɪ/ over birthdate for males (dashed line) and females (solid line).

and fitting statistical models. For graphing, ggplot2 (Wickham et al. 2019) is a popular and highly customizable option; for fitting statistical models, lme4 (Bates et al. 2019) allows the user to fit mixed models, and both lmerTest (Kuznetsova, Brockhoff, & Bojesen 2019) and pbkrtest (Halekoh & Højsgaard 2017) allow the user to derive *p*-values and interpretable model outputs from lme4.[10]

The original study strove to achieve clarity and statistical accountability. For example, the two-dimensional kernel density plots in the left panel of figure 17.3 show the distribution and overall shape of the data, giving the reader an understanding of the distribution of the overall vowel categories; this aids the interpretability of the plot. However, not every plot was equally well conceived. The right panel in figure 17.3 shows a localized polynomial regression with standard errors for the F1 of /ɪ/ over time. The regression indicates a sex difference; however, the figure lacks the data points on which the regression is based. Therefore, it is unclear how closely the regression fits the data and whether the data points vary consistently across the observed effect. A solution to this would be to include the individual data points in the plot in the right panel.

5.2 Storing and sharing the data

SOLIS served as the repository for transcribed interviews and the boundaries produced by forced alignment. Using this server allowed me to store raw data used in the original study in a password-protected online repository as I progressed through the collections. While this minimized the risk of data loss, the rest of my data (e.g., individual

formant measurements, R scripts, and statistical models) is on personal repositories. And while formant values are reported in Grama (2015), no officially archived data sheet exists. This is a key area where the original study was not in line with best practices (see Andreassen, chapter 7, this volume). One way to solve this issue would be to make further use of SOLIS. Because SOLIS uses LaBB-CAT architecture, it allows for detailed annotation stores. Formant values and other information could be uploaded to the server to allow the precise study to be replicated by anyone with access. In addition, manually checked Praat TextGrids could be uploaded to SOLIS to enrich the files currently housed on SOLIS. This would also constitute a step toward sharing the data, as access is, as of writing, restricted to SOLIS users or achieved through personal requests to me.

6 Conclusion

This use case serves as a guide for those wishing to undertake similar longitudinal studies of language variation and change, especially where legacy data are required. As a short-hand reference, a schematized version of the methodological steps detailed in this chapter is available in appendix B. As a final caveat, this methodology was employed between 2014 and 2015, meaning that there are aspects of it that may not stand the test of time. Nevertheless, the steps for processing the data discussed here, many of which are maximally conservative, should remain relevant in the future.

Appendix A: Detailed speaker demographic information in Grama (2015)

Table 17.4

Speaker demographic and social information in Grama (2015), including the collection file name, the corpus, and the speaker's relative age, assigned pseudonym, binary sex, age, date of birth, island of residence, listed ethnicity, highest education achieved, and occupation information

Collection file name	Corpus and relative age	Speaker pseudonym	Sex	Age	Date of birth	Island	Ethnicity	Highest education	Occupation
DB1–072	Old 1970s	Kawika	M	79	1896	Kauaʻi	Hawaiian	na	Retired motel owner
DB1–122	Old 1970s	Joseph	M	69	1906	Hawaiʻi	Portuguese	No high school	Retired plantation worker
CS1-JA-03	Old 1970s	Manny	M	58	1922	Hawaiʻi	Filipino	High school	Farmer, real estate
DB1–164	Old 1970s	Kimo	M	54	1921	Oʻahu	Part Hawaiian	High school	Retired roofer, plantation
DB1–073	Old 1970s	Miki	F	68	1907	Kauaʻi	Japanese	High school	Retired barber
DB1–066	Old 1970s	Malia	F	64	1911	Kauaʻi	Hawaiian	High school	Housewife
DB1–162	Old 1970s	Kaimana	F	57	1918	Oʻahu	Hawaiian, Haole	High school	Retired
DB1–056	Old 1970s	Keiko	F	55	1918	Kauaʻi	Japanese	High school	Home management
DB1–165	Young 1970s	Eddie	M	39	1936	Oʻahu	Part Hawaiian	High school	Construction worker
DB1–059	Young 1970s	Victor	M	37	1938	Kauaʻi	Portuguese	High school	NA
CS1-EA-03	Young 1970s	Danny	M	30	1942	Oʻahu	Filipino	High school	Floorer
CS1-GN-02	Young 1970s	Glen	M	25	1944	Hawaiʻi	Japanese	High school	Contract laborer
DB1–074	Young 1970s	Mona Lisa	F	48	1927	Kauaʻi	Filipino	High school	NA
DB1–075	Young 1970s	Leilani	F	42	1933	Kauaʻi	Hawaiian	High school	Housewife, retired
DB1–120	Young 1970s	Delia Jane	F	35	1940	Hawaiʻi	Filipino	High school	Adult education instructor
DB1–065	Young 1970s	Teresa	F	35	1940	Kauaʻi	Filipino	College	Air national guard
CS2–053	Old 2010s	Grant	M	56	1951	Oʻahu	Japanese	College	Government worker
CS2–029	Old 2010s	Kevin	M	52	1955	Hawaiʻi	Hawaiian	NA	Unemployed, ex-military/farmer
CS2–017	Old 2010s	Palani	M	44	1963	Hawaiʻi	Part Hawaiian	NA	Shop owner
CS2–030	Old 2010s	Keoni	M	40	1967	Hawaiʻi	Part Hawaiian	High school	NA
CS2–037	Old 2010s	Pua	F	58	1949	Oʻahu	Part Hawaiian	High school	NA
CS2–040	Old 2010s	Lani	F	49	1958	Oʻahu	Part Hawaiian	High school	Housewife
CS2–027	Old 2010s	Carla	F	46	1961	Hawaiʻi	Portuguese	High school	Unemployed
CS2–011	Old 2010s	Kahea	F	42	1965	Kauaʻi	Part Hawaiian	High school	Ranch worker
CS2–052	Young 2010s	Kaleo	M	22	1985	Maui	Hawaiian, Korean, Haole	College	Student
CS2–056	Young 2010s	Myko	M	22	1985	Kauaʻi	Portuguese	College	Student
CS2–046	Young 2010s	Eric	M	21	1986	Hawaiʻi	Chinese, Filipino	College	Student
CS2–051	Young 2010s	Alika	M	21	1986	Hawaiʻi	Japanese	College	Student
CS2–048	Young 2010s	Sarah	F	24	1983	Oʻahu	Chinese	College	MA Student
CS2–019	Young 2010s	Starla	F	23	1984	Hawaiʻi	Hawaiian, Chinese, Japanese	High school	NA
CS2–055	Young 2010s	Mina	F	21	1986	Kauaʻi	Japanese, Haole, Chinese, Hawaiian	College	Student
RK01	Young 2010s	Lena	F	19	1988	Kauaʻi	Filipino, Japanese	College	Student

F = female; M = male; NA = not available.

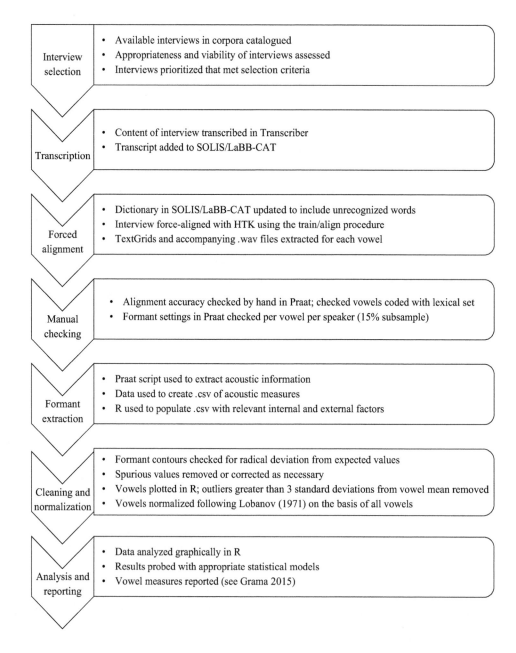

Appendix B: Data workflow for Grama (2015)

The chart schematizes the workflow for Grama (2015) from interview selection to analysis. It is meant as a short-hand reference for those wishing to replicate the methodology of this study. The transcription software and forced aligner listed could easily be altered to accommodate researcher preference.

Notes

1. This was especially true because time and financial considerations made hiring research assistants impractical during the completion of the original study.

2. One aim of Grama (2015) was to quantify vowel variation along the creole continuum (cf. DeCamp 1971; Sato 1993), a focus that falls outside the scope of the present chapter.

3. Metadata were missing or inconsistent across recordings; it is a researcher's duty to report these gaps, while being as vigilant as possible in our own studies to record metadata as thoroughly and representatively as possible (cf. Mattern, chapter 5, this volume). In some cases, accompanying corpus notes were mined for missing information to account for gaps in the metadata. When information crucial to the test variables was absent, the interview was excluded.

4. Recordings were excluded if they were shorter than ten minutes on these grounds.

5. Space does not allow for a fuller description of the range of factors that might govern the selection of a forced aligner; however, aligner choice should be based on the researcher's needs, as well as aligner performance and suitability. For a more thorough discussion of these factors, I direct the reader to Fromont and Watson (2016), McAuliffe et al. (2017), MacKenzie and Turton (2020), and Gonzalez, Grama, and Travis (2020).

6. The steps described here would be identical to those were the reader to use a local build of LaBB-CAT.

7. At the time, CELEX seemed preferable to the CMU Pronouncing Dictionary (the latter of which is optimized for US varieties), given the variable absence of post-vocalic /r/ in Pidgin. However, recent work demonstrates that automated alignment is not strongly affected by variety if the variety under study is not markedly different from the training variety (MacKenzie & Turton 2020), or if vowel coercion is performed (Gonzalez, Grama, & Travis 2020).

8. The original script is collect_formant_data_from_files.praat, available at https://github.com/lennes.

9. Some phoneticians (e.g., Rosner & Pickering 1994) argue that normalization is done to model cognitive processes that underpin vowel perception, though there is some debate in the phonetics literature as to whether listeners normalize vowels at all (see, e.g., Pisoni 1997). This chapter does not weigh in on this debate.

10. Because deriving p-values from linear and logistic mixed-effect models is not straightforward, I recommend consulting Luke (2017) for best practices.

References

Adank, Patti, Roel Smits, and Roeland van Hout. 2004. A comparison of vowel normalization procedures for language variation research. *Journal of the Acoustical Society of America* 116:3099–3107. https://doi.org/10.1121/1.1795335.

Albarillo, Emily E., and Nick Thieberger. 2009. Kaipuleohone, University of Hawai'i's digital ethnographic archive. *Language Documentation and Conservation* 3 (1): 1–14. http://hdl.handle.net/10125/4422.

Baayen, R. H., R. Piepenbroock, and L. Gulikers. 1995. *The CELEX Lexical Database* (CD-ROM). Philadelphia: Linguistic Data Consortium, University of Pennsylvania.

Bailey, Guy. 2004. Real and apparent time. In *The Handbook of Language Variation and Change*, ed. J. K. Chambers, Peter Trudgill, and Natalie Schilling-Estes, 312–332. Malden, MA: Blackwell. https://doi.org/10.1002/9780470756591.ch12.

Barras, Claude, Edouard Geoffrois, Zhibiao Wu, and Mark Liberman. 2001. Transcriber: Development and use of a tool for assisting speech corpora production. *Speech Communication* 33 (1–2): 5–22. https://doi.org/10.1016/S0167-6393(00)00067-4.

Barreda, Santiago, and Terrance M. Nearey. 2018. A regression approach to vowel normalization for missing and unbalanced data. *Journal of the Acoustical Society of America* 144 (1): 500–520. https://doi.org/10.1121/1.5047742.

Bates, Douglas, Martin Maechler, Ben Bolker, Steven Walker, Rune Haubo Bojesen Christensen, Henrik Singmann, Bin Dai, Fabian Scheipl, and Gabor Grothendieck. 2019. lme4: Linear mixed-effects models using "Eigen" and S4. R package version 1.1–21. https://github.com/lme4/lme4/.

Berez, Andrea L. 2013. The digital archiving of endangered language oral traditions: Kaipuleohone at the University of Hawai'i at C'ek'aedi Hwnaz in Alaska. *Oral Tradition* 28 (2): 261–270. doi:10.1353/ort.2013.0010.

Bickerton, Derek. 1976. *Change and Variation in Hawaiian English: Final Report on National Science Foundation Grant no. GS-39748.* Honolulu: Social Sciences and Linguistics Institute, University of Hawaii.

Boersma, Paul, and David Weenink. 2019. Praat: Doing phonetics by computer (computer program). Version 6.1. http://www.praat.org/.

Collerson, Kenneth D., and Marshall I. Weisler. 2007. Stone adze compositions and the extent of ancient Polynesian voyaging and trade. *Science* 317 (5846): 1907–1911. doi:10.1126/science.1147013.

DeCamp, David. 1971. Towards a generative analysis of post-creole speech continuum. In *Pidginization and Creolization of Languages*, ed. Dell Hymes, 349–370. Cambridge: Cambridge University Press.

de Jong, Nivja H., and Ton Wempe. 2009. Praat script to detect syllable nuclei and measure speech rate automatically. *Behavior Research Methods* 41 (2): 385–390. doi:10.3758/BRM.41.2.385.

Drager, Katie. 2012a. New directions in sociolinguistic methods. Paper presented at the *Linguistic Data Consortium 20th Anniversary Workshop*, Philadelphia, September 6–7.

Drager, Katie. 2012b. Pidgin and Hawai'i English: An overview. *Journal of Language, Translation and Intercultural Communication* 1 (1): 61–73. http://dx.doi.org/10.12681/ijltic.10.

Drager, Katie, and James Grama. 2014. "De tawk dakain ova dea": Mapping language ideologies on O'ahu. *Dialectologia* 12 (12): 23–51.

Flege, James E., Carlo Shirru, and Ian R. A. MacKay. 2003. Interaction between the native and second language phonetic subsystems. *Speech Communication* 40:467–491.

Flynn, Nicholas, and Paul Foulkes. 2011. Comparing vowel formant normalization methods. In *Proceedings of the 17th ICPhS*, ed. W. S. Lee and E. Zee, 683–686. Hong Kong: City University of Hong Kong. https://www.internationalphoneticassociation.org/icphs-proceedings/ICPhS2011/OnlineProceedings/RegularSession/Flynn/Flynn.pdf.

Foulkes, Paul, Gerry Docherty, Stefanie Shattuck Hufnagel, and Vincent Hughes. 2018. Three steps forward for predictability: Consideration of methodological robustness, indexical and prosodic factors, and replication in the laboratory. *Linguistics Vanguard* 42 (2): 1–11. https://doi.org/10.1515/lingvan-2017-0032.

Fromont, Robert, and Jennifer Hay. 2012. LaBB-CAT: An annotation store. In *Proceedings of the Australasian Language Technology Workshop*, 113–117. Otago University, December 4–6. https://www.aclweb.org/anthology/U12-1015.pdf.

Fromont, Robert, and Kevin Watson. 2016. Factors influencing automatic segmental alignment of sociophonetic corpora. *Corpora* 11 (3): 401–431. https://doi.org/10.3366/cor.2016.0101.

Fujikane, Candace. 1997. Reimagining development and the Local in Lois-Ann Yamanaka's "Saturday Night at the Pahala Theater." *Social Process in Hawai'i* 38:40–61.

Gonzalez, Simon, and Gerry Docherty. 2018. Measuring a stabilization point of uncorrected forced-aligned data. Paper presented at *SocioPhonAus2*, Brisbane, Australia, July 16–17.

Gonzalez, Simon, James Grama, and Catherine Travis. 2020. Comparing the performance of major forced aligners used in sociophonetic research. *Linguistics Vanguard* 6 (1). https://doi.org/10.1515/lingvan-2019-0058.

Grama, James. 2015. Variation and change in Hawai'i Creole vowels. PhD dissertation, University of Hawai'i at Mānoa.

Halekoh, Ulrich, and Søren Højsgaard. 2017. pbkrtest: Parametric bootstrap and Kenward-Roger based methods for mixed model comparison. R package version 0.4–7. https://myaseen208.github.io/pbkrtest/.

Hughes, Vincent. 2014. The definition of the relevant population and the collection of data for likelihood ratio-based forensic voice comparison. PhD dissertation, University of York.

Johnson, Keith. 2012. *Acoustic and Auditory Phonetics*, 3rd ed. Malden, MA: Wiley-Blackwell.

Kawamoto, Kevin Y. 1993. Hegemony and language politics in Hawai'i. *World Englishes* 12 (2): 193–207. https://doi.org/10.1111/j.1467-971X.1993.tb00021.x.

Kendall, Tyler, and Erik R. Thomas. 2018. Vowels: Vowel manipulation, normalization, and plotting. R package, version 1.2–2. https://cran.r-project.org/web/packages/vowels/.

Kraus, Janina. 2017. A sociophonetic study of the urban Bahamian Creole vowel system. PhD, dissertation, Ludwig-Maximilians-Universität München.

Kuznetsova, Alexandra, Per Bruun Brockhoff, and Rune Haubo Bojesen. 2019. lmerTest: Tests in linear mixed effects models. R package version 3.1–0. https://cran.r-project.org/web/packages/lmerTest/index.html.

Labov, William. 1972. *Sociolinguistic Patterns*. Philadelphia: University of Pennsylvania Press. https://doi.org/10.1017/S0047404500004528.

Labov, William, Sharon Ash, and Charles Boberg. 2006. *The Atlas of North American English*. New York: Mouton de Gruyter.

Labov, William, Ingrid Rosenfelder, and Josef Fruehwald. 2013. One hundred years of sound change in Philadelphia: Linear incrementation, reversal, and reanalysis. *Language* 89 (1): 30–65. https://doi.org/10.1353/lan.2013.0015.

Lausberg, Hedda, and Han Sloetjes. 2009. Coding gestural behavior with the NEUROGES-ELAN system. *Behavior Research Methods, Instruments, and Computers* 41 (3): 841–849. doi:10.3758/BRM.41.3.841.

Lesho, Marivic. 2014. The sociophonetics and phonology of the Cavite Chabacano vowel system. PhD dissertation, Ohio State University.

Lobanov, B. M. 1971. Classification of Russian vowels spoken by different speakers. *Journal of the Acoustical Society of America* 49 (2): 606–608. https://doi.org/10.1121/1.1912396.

Luke, Steven G. 2017. Evaluating significance in linear mixed-effects models in R. *Behaviour Research Methods* 46 (4): 1494–1502. https://doi.org/10.3758/s13428-016-0809-y.

MacKenzie, Laurel, and Daniel Turton. 2020. Assessing the accuracy of existing forced alignment software on varieties of British English. *Linguistics Vanguard* 6 (1). https://doi.org/10.1515/lingvan-2018-0061.

Marlow, Mikaela L., and Howard Giles. 2008. Who you tink you, talkin propah? Hawaiian Pidgin demarginalized. *Journal of Multicultural Discourses* 3 (1): 53–68. https://doi.org/10.1080/17447140802153535.

Marlow, Mikaela L., and Howard Giles. 2010. "We won't get ahead speaking like that!" Expressing and managing language criticism in Hawai'i. *Journal of Multilingual and Multicultural Development* 31 (3): 237–251. https://doi.org/10.1080/01434630903582714.

McAuliffe, Michaela, Michael Socolof, Sarah Mihuc, Michael Wagner, and Morgan Sondregger. 2017. Montreal Forced Aligner: Trainable text-speech alignment using Kaldi. *Proceedings of the 18th Conference of the International Speech Communication Association*, 498–502. doi:10.21437/Interspeech.2017-1386.

Miles-Hercules, DeAndre, and Lal Zimman. 2019. Normativity in normalization: Methodological challenges in the (automated) analysis of vowels among non-binary speakers. Paper presented at New Ways of Analyzing Variation 48 (NWAV48), Eugene, OR, October 10–12.

Nearey, Terrance M. 1977. Phonetic features system for vowels. PhD dissertation, University of Alberta. (Reprinted 1978 by the Indiana University Linguistics Club.)

Odo, Carol. 1975. Phonological processes in the English dialect of Hawai'i. PhD, dissertation, University of Hawai'i at Mānoa.

Odo, Carol. 1977. Phonological representations in Hawaiian English. *University of Hawai'i Working Papers in Linguistics* 9 (3): 77–85.

Ohnuma, Keiko. 2002. Local Haole—a contradiction of terms? The dilemma of being white, born and raised in Hawai'i. *Cultural Values* 6 (3): 273–285. https://doi.org/10.1080/13625170220 00007211.

Pisoni, David B. 1997. Some thoughts on "normalization" in speech perception. In *Talker Variability in Speech Processing*, ed. Keith Johnson and John W. Mullennix, 9–32. San Diego: Academic Press.

R Core Team. 2018. *R: A Language and Environment for Statistical Computing*. Vienna: R Foundation for Statistical Computing. http://www.R-project.org.

Reinecke, John R. 1969. *Language and Dialect in Hawaii*. Honolulu: University of Hawai'i Press.

Roberts, Sarah J. 2004. The emergence of Hawai'i Creole English in the early 20th century: The sociohistorical context of creole genesis. PhD dissertation, Stanford University.

Rohrer, Judy. 1997. Haole girl: Identity and white privilege in Hawai'i. *Social Process in Hawai'i* 38:138–161.

Rosenfelder, Ingrid. 2009. Sociophonetic variation in educated Jamaican English: An analysis of the spoken corpora of ICE-Jamaica. PhD dissertation, University of Freiburg, Germany.

Rosenfelder, Ingrid, Josef Fruehwald, Keelan Evanini, Scott Seyfarth, Kyle Gorman, Hilary Prichard, and Jiahong Yuan. 2014. FAVE (Forced Alignment and Vowel Extraction) Program Suite. Version 1.2.2. https://zenodo.org/record/9846#.X9hzldhKiUk.

Rosner, B. S., and J. B. Pickering. 1994. *Vowel Perception and Production*. Oxford: Oxford University Press.

Sabino, Robin. 1996. A peak at death: Assessing continuity and change in an underdocumented language. *Language Variation and Change* 8 (1): 41–61. https://doi.org/10.1017 /S095439450000106X.

Sabino, Robin. 2012. *Language Contact in the Danish West Indies: Giving Jack His Jacket*. Leiden: Brill Publishers. https://doi .org/10.1163/9789004230705.

Sakoda, Kent, and Jeff Siegel. 2003. *Pidgin Grammar: An Introduction to the Creole English of Hawai'i*. Honolulu: Bess Press, Inc.

Sakoda, Kent, and Jeff Siegel. 2008. Hawai'i Creole: Phonology. In *A Handbook of Varieties of English*. Volume I: *Phonology*, ed. Berndt Kortmann and Edgar W. Schneider, 729–749. Berlin: Mouton de Gruyter.

Sato, Charlene J. 1993. Language change in a creole continuum: Decreolization? In *Progression and Regression in Language: Sociocultural, Neuropsychological and Linguistic Perspectives*, ed. Kenneth Hyltenstam and Åke Viberg, 122–143. Cambridge: Cambridge University Press.

Schiel, Florian, Christian Draxler, and Jonathan Harrington. 2011. Phonemic segmentation and labelling using the MAUS technique. Paper presented at New Tools and Methods for

Very-Large-Scale Phonetics Research Workshop, University of Pennsylvania, January 28–31.

Seifert, Frank, Nicholas Evans, Harald Hammarström, and Steven C. Levinson. 2018. Language documentation twenty-five years on. *Language* 94 (4): e324–e345. doi:10.1353/lan.20 18.0070.

Siegel, Jeff. 2007. Recent evidence against the Language Bioprogram Hypothesis: The pivotal case of Hawai'i Creole. *Studies in Language* 31 (1): 51–88. https://doi.org/10.1075/sl.31.1.03sie.

Stannard, David E. 1990. Disease and infertility: A new look at the demographic collapse of Native populations in the wake of Western contact. *Journal of American Studies* 24 (3): 325–350.

Strelluf, Christopher. 2016. Overlap among back vowels before /l/ in Kansas City. *Language Variation and Change* 28 (3): 379–407. https://doi.org/10.1017/S0954394516000144.

Stueber, Ralph K. 1964. Hawaii: A case study in development education 1778–1960. PhD dissertation, University of Wisconsin.

Traunmüller, Hartmut. 1997. Auditory scales of frequency representation. http://www.ling.su.se/staff/hartmut/bark.htm.

Veatch, Thomas C. 1991. English vowels: Their surface phonology and phonetic implementation in vernacular dialects. PhD dissertation, University of Pennsylvania.

Walworth, Mary. 2014. Eastern Polynesian: The linguistic evidence revisited. *Oceanic Linguistics* 53 (2): 256–272. https://doi .org/10.1353/ol.2014.0021.

Wassink, Alicia B. 1999. A sociophonetic analysis of Jamaican vowels. PhD dissertation, University of Michigan.

Wassink, Alicia B. 2001. Theme and variation in Jamaican vowels. *Language Variation and Change* 13 (2): 135–159.

Wassink, Alicia B. 2006. A geometric representation of spectral and temporal vowel features: Quantification of vowel overlap in three linguistic varieties. *Journal of the Acoustical Society of America* 119 (4): 2334–2350. https://doi.org/10.1121 /1.2168414.

Watson, Catherine I., and Jonathan Harrington. 1999. Acoustic evidence for dynamic formant trajectories in Australian English vowels. *Journal of the Acoustical Society of America* 106 (1): 458–468.

Watt, Dominic J., and Anne H. Fabricius. 2002. Evaluation of a technique for improving the mapping of multiple speakers' vowel spaces in the F1~F2 plane. *Leeds Working Papers in Linguistics and Phonetics* 9 (9): 159–173.

Watt, Dominic J., Anne H. Fabricius, and Tyler Kendall. 2010. More on vowels: plotting and normalization. In *Sociophonetics: A Student's Guide*, ed. Marianna Di Paolo and Malcah Yaeger-Dror, 107–118. London: Routledge.

Wells, John C. 1982. *Accents of English*. Cambridge: Cambridge University Press.

Wickham, Hadley, Winston Chang, Lionel Henry, Thomas Lin Pedersen, Kohske Takahashi, Claus Wilke, Kara Woo, and Hiroaki Yutani. 2019. ggplot2: Create elegant data visualisations using the grammar of graphics. R package version 3.2.0. https://cran.r-project.org/web/packages/ggplot2/index.html.

Wilmshurst, Janet M., Terry L Hunt, Carl P. Lipo, and Atholl J Anderson. 2011. High precision radiocarbon dating shows recent and rapid initial human colonization of East Polynesia. *Proceedings of the National Academy of Sciences* 108 (5): 1815–1820. https://doi.org/10.1073/pnas.1015876108.

Young, Steve, Gunnar Evermann, Mark Gales, Thomas Hain, Dan Kershaw, Xunying Liu, Gareth Moore, et al. 2009. *The HTK book (for version 3.4)*. Cambridge: Cambridge University Engineering Department.

18 Managing Sociophonetic Data in a Study of Regional Variation

Valerie Fridland and Tyler Kendall

1 Introduction

The data that are the focus of this data management use case stem from our Vowels in America (VIA) project, a multiyear, multipronged project funded by the National Science Foundation, the University of Nevada, Reno, and the University of Oregon.[1] The larger aim of the project was to examine the role of regionally based social and linguistic experience in shaping speakers' production and perception of vowel quality. For the project, we collected speech production data and administered a series of speech perception tests in a number of research sites in the Northern, Southern and Western United States. While the research design, in large part, was fully conceived before beginning the project in 2005, several aspects of the research, and a number of field sites, were modified or added in subsequent stages. In the following sections, we overview the project from its initial stages to its current form, highlighting, in particular, our data collection, data processing, data storage, and data sharing procedures. While the discussions here are based on our specific experiences running this particular project, we hope that our discussions of our data management practices are relevant to a wider range of projects in regional language variation, dialectology, and sociophonetics.

2 Data in regional variation and dialectological studies

Historically, the study of regional variation has been the focus of the field of dialectology. Dialectological projects have centered on the use of elicitation and questionnaire-based techniques that are designed to elicit information about regional forms (see Chambers & Trudgill 1998). Early dialectology, in an effort to chart dialect boundaries, often presented data in the form of a linguistic atlas or dictionary (e.g., Cassidy & Hall 1985–2013; Kurath 1949; McDavid & O'Cain 1980; Pederson, McDaniel, & Adams 1986–1993). However, more recent interests have moved toward gaining a better understanding of the social processes by which regional variation is achieved, often focusing on diffusion within social space as well as across geographic space. This change in research goals has been accompanied by a parallel shift in looking more deeply at gradient phonetic/phonological variables and in using sophisticated data collection, measurement, and mapping tools.

For example, recent work in dialectology has moved to applying and developing geospatial statistical methods (in what is often called dialectometry; Wieling & Nerbonne 2015) and has also moved increasingly into online data collection and data presentation (e.g., Vaux & Golder 2003; Grieve, Asnaghi, & Ruette 2013; Huang et al. 2016). Recent work in sociophonetics has also taken a large interest in regional variation and examined dialectological questions based on speech recordings and close analyses of regionally variable pronunciation features (see Kendall & Fridland 2021). Based on a sample of over seven hundred speakers from urban areas across the United States, the *Atlas of North American English* (Labov, Ash, & Boberg 2006) has led this movement toward new, large-scale regional studies based on speech recordings. Our work on the VIA project is, at its core, about documenting linguistic differences across regional varieties, but we also share an interest in capturing the social dynamicity of regional shifts and view our work as a sociophonetically driven dialectological undertaking. As such, for its methods and management tools, the VIA project combines the need for large-scale data collection techniques informed by dialectology and the computationally driven instrumental data measurement and presentation techniques informed by sociophonetics.

3   Overview of our project

Using work by Labov, Ash, and Boberg (2006), Eckert (2008), and Clarke, Elms, and Youssef (1995) as a jumping off point, the VIA project was designed to look in more detail at inter- and intraregional distinctions in US dialects, in terms of comparing production-based participation in regional shift processes across a large sample of speakers in and across each regional field site and in terms of examining correlations between the vowel shifts and understudied phonetic aspects such as duration and vowel inherent spectral change. In addition, though the underlying assumption in most sociophonetic work on regional dialects is that productive choices are made as a result of variation in receptive input, there has been limited work measuring regionally diverse vowel perception. Thus, we simultaneously administered vowel perception tasks in each regional study site, with the goal to examine how regional dialect experience mediates both production and perception, building on work by Clopper and Pisoni (2004), Evans and Iverson (2004, 2007), Hay, Warren, and Drager (2006), Niedzielski (1999), and Sumner and Samuel (2009) that suggests regional background influences speech processing. In summary, our research project had several aims:

1. To examine the extent to which there is variable participation in regional vowel shifts within and across regionally situated locales (e.g., Kendall & Fridland 2012; Fridland & Kendall 2012)

2. To determine whether degree of individuals' vowel shift participation influences vowel perception, and whether this varies by region (Kendall & Fridland 2012, 2016, 2017; Fridland & Kendall 2012, 2015, 2017)

3. To investigate how other aspects of production such as duration and vowel inherent spectral change tie into vowel shift participation (Fridland, Kendall, & Farrington 2014; Kendall & Fridland 2017; Farrington, Kendall, & Fridland 2018)

4. To examine whether the addition of talker-specific social information alters listeners' performance during perception tasks (Fridland & Kendall 2018)

We shift now to describe in greater detail our data collection, storage, and processing procedures.

4   Data collection procedures

Our first step was to determine where and how to collect data. Initially, we started with at least one university-based field site in each of three regions (per the dialect regions identified by Labov, Ash, & Boberg 2006), where we were on faculty or had strong ties with local faculty (Memphis, Tennessee; Oswego, New York; and Reno, Nevada). The goal was to collect production data from fifteen to twenty speakers in each field site, as well as have participants complete a vowel categorization task (detailed in section 4.2). To do this in remote locations, local fieldworkers were recruited within each region through our faculty associates, and they received a stipend for their work. These fieldworkers, all of whom were local students with some basic linguistics experience, were trained on the recording equipment and on study and recruitment procedures by one of the primary investigators (PIs) and then were also provided with a summary information packet prepared for the project by the PIs that reviewed the instructions so that speech sample collection would be performed uniformly across field sites. These instructions and packet reviewed the participant requirements (e.g., native English speakers, living in the field site from minimally age four, with at least one parent from that region) and the recording procedures (instructions for using and ordering speech prompt materials and a review on how to use the recording equipment), and contained written-out scripts for fieldworkers to use to read to participants to make sure all subjects were presented with identical instructions across field sites and to control the study information/background given to participants. They also provided consent materials to participants, who signed a consent form (in person or online, depending on which aspect of the study they were involved in). Fieldworkers were tasked with recruiting subjects via the friend of a friend technique (Milroy 1980) or were students recruited by local faculty members. In Reno, Nevada, and Oswego, New York (and later also in Eugene, Oregon), the study was run through a university subject pool, and students received credit for participation. Due to the long-distance nature of the data collection, we occasionally had difficulty getting people willing to complete both the production and perception tasks, which prompted us to apply for a small grant from University of Nevada, Reno, to help cover a small stipend ($40) for participants upon completion of both production and perception tasks, for those not receiving academic credits.

As our research proceeded over the next few years, we were able to expand the research to include participants in several other locations within each region. Over the course of the project, we ended up with speech production and perception data from eight field sites in the United States: three within the Southern region (Memphis, Tennessee; Blacksburg, Virginia; and Raleigh, North Carolina), two within the Northern region (Oswego, New York, and Chicago, Illinois), and two within the West (Reno, Nevada, and Eugene, Oregon). We also obtained various California participants through our work in Oregon and Nevada and this enabled us to treat California as the third Western site (these participants were short-term residents of Oregon and Nevada, and we interpret these as best representative of their long-term hometown location). For the main vowel identification study, we were able to collect data from over 650 participants from across the three larger US regional dialect areas. A subset of over 90 of these participants also contributed production data (a reading passage and word list; see section 4.1), allowing us to compare a subset of our participants' production to their perception of target vowel pairs ($n=80$). Finally, for a follow-up study examining how social information affects vowel identification (Fridland & Kendall 2018), we also recruited participants for the perception part of the study from additional field sites in Alabama and Tennessee.

4.1 Production data

The research involved the collection of acoustic data elicited via a reading passage and word list, both of which were composed by the first author (Fridland 1998, 1999, 2001) to produce vowel variants in a variety of consonantal contexts, with a particular interest in Southern vowel features (one of the main regional dialects of focus initially). The reading passage and word list are provided in the appendix. As the project evolved, other contexts of interest emerged (e.g., lax front vowels preceding velar consonants, low back vowel merger), and a secondary word list, also included in the appendix, was created to provide additional tokens for those contexts. We chose to add a second word list rather than modify the first so that all participants would be presented the materials in the identical order, which helps to limit possible coarticulatory or prosodic differences across speakers. The reading passage and word list were printed on paper, double-spaced, with the word list printed down two columns per page.

The recordings were collected with a Tascam digital recorder and a Shure WH30XLR head-mounted microphone or with a Marantz digital recorder and a Shure SM93 lavalier microphone by a local fieldworker in a quiet

setting or, where possible, in a speech lab. All speakers read the same reading passage and word list(s) with the same instructions (to read the passage over before recitation and to pause briefly between each word list recitation).

4.2 Perception data

As the project was designed to investigate the link between use of regional vowel variants and the perception of these variants, our collection of speech production data was paired with a vowel identification task. The web-based vowel identification task was designed by first author Fridland and constructed by a computer science PhD student, Sohei Okamoto, who had taken linguistics coursework with Fridland at University of Nevada, Reno. The online task was designed to first present the online consent form, give a sound-level check (e.g., clicking a button to be sure the participant's volume setting was ideal), provide written instructions and request demographic information, and, finally, provide a practice vowel identification task (using a vowel not tested in the actual task). After this preliminary material was presented, participants were reminded one last time of the instructions (in written format), then presented with the actual perception experiment. This involved presenting for each stimulus token (randomized between and within blocks) the labels for the two continuum end points, such as *bait* and *bet* (each selectable to record a participant's response), and a PLAY button, which provided the aural stimuli when pressed. Once designed, it was run on a customized University of Nevada web server managed collaboratively by Okamoto and the university's information technology team. The use of a local, customized server was partly to provide full control of functionality but also avoided any confidential data being managed on a third-party server. It also allowed for better delivery of aural stimuli than commercial software allowed for at the time of development. The authors recognize that many projects are unable to develop a customized server for speech perception experiments, but note that the number of publicly available platforms, both commercially (such as Qualtrics) and via open source (such as PsyToolkit), are growing rapidly. The custom work that was done to develop our perception experiment platform is likely not needed today.

Those interested in being part of the study were provided the study URL, a log-in, and password and were able to take the study from any Internet-accessible computer. Participants, who were asked to use earphones, first answered a series of demographic questions about age, hearing ability, gender, and occupational and residence history. Participants were also prompted to fill in a text box with their first name, state abbreviation (which provided us quick field site information), and numerical street address (e.g., ValerieTN2760) as a means of providing each participant with a unique code so that their identifying information could be separately stored. The same code was used for their recorded production data, so they could be easily matched. As mentioned previously, in several field sites (Oswego, New York; Reno, Nevada; and Eugene, Oregon), we were able to collect a large amount of data on speech perception by recruiting through university subject pools. While this made geographically diverse large-scale data collection much easier, it did limit the age range of participants to the eighteen to thirty bracket for the most part.

The vowel identification stimuli were based on the synthesis of natural speech data provided by an adult male speaker from the Western United States with unmarked dialectal vocalic features per Clopper and Pisoni (2004). The speaker was recorded reading monosyllabic word pairs selected for vowel class and matched for consonantal environment (e.g., *date/debt, beat/bit*). The vowel identification test was designed by synthesizing consonant-vowel-consonant pairs for each vowel pair drawing from the labial, alveolar, and velar points of articulation, using the speaker's natural category means as a guide. Word pairs (minimal pairs) were selected for vowel categories with high dialectal variability across US dialects (/i/~/ɪ/, /e/~/ɛ/, /æ/~/ɑ/, /u/~/ɪ/, and /o/~/ʌ/). A pilot vowel categorization test using three consonantal environments suggested that bilabial and alveolar environments showed the greatest contrast in perception, and those two were selected for use in the final vowel identification test design. For each vowel pair studied, the continuum range was determined based on the sample speaker's production values for each of the two selected vowel categories. Based on these end points, the intermediate stimuli were created by Bartek Plichta through Akustyk, a vowel synthesis program he created. Using the web-based design just described, the experiment was set up so that one stimulus was presented per trial, and then participants were prompted to make a decision about what word they heard from two options (e.g., *bait* or *bet*). Each step in each vowel continuum was heard four times randomized over the course of the study. Generally, participants were given no background

on the speaker, other than what they could interpret from the signal source alone (e.g., male adult). For those participants contributing both speech production and speech perception data, they were instructed to do the online task at least one day prior to being recorded for the speech production study to minimize the possibility that participants' speech productions would be influenced by the perception task.

The software used to create the stimuli was available publicly as a part of Plichta's Akustyk plug-in for Praat until 2014 (Plichta 2004–2014), but the website and software are no longer maintained. While the stimulus synthesis software was made open source by the designer, we were not involved in the life of the software after our stimuli were created and, like other users of Akustyk, no longer have access to it. The downside to partnerships such as this is that the researcher is, in such an arrangement, limited in the ability to control what happens to software for the long term. Yet, the benefits and time savings of not duplicating software or scripts that already exist and utilizing resources created by researchers who are more experienced in design aspects of those tools often outweighs the risk of this loss of control of the software.

5 Data storage

Data storage efforts for this project have changed over the years. In short, as the project has evolved in its various ways, our data management practices have changed as well. For the purposes of this data management use case, we especially want to acknowledge that these changes have not always been improvements but rather reflect the practicalities of a large-scale project conducted across many field sites and universities, something we address in this section.

5.1 Production data

By *speech production data*, we mean the actual audio files of recordings (in waveform audio file format). We will return to discussing derived data sets, such as acoustic measurements. Speech production recordings were initially uploaded from the digital recorders to the PIs' computers for analysis and storage, as was the typical practice at the time we began the project, and followed the guidelines for participant confidentiality set forth in the consent documents. Subsequently, speech recordings were moved to the web server at University of Nevada that hosted the perception data, which acted as a centralized data repository for the project. These recordings were accessible to project staff through a simple, password-protected download interface. However, in 2011, we modified our human subjects protocol to allow us to store the data in a more formalized data archive environment instead, in line with field-based best practice to increase accessibility and data longevity. For more detailed discussion of data archiving and its benefits, we refer readers to Andreassen (chapter 7, this volume).

Based on earlier work developing the Sociolinguistic Archive and Analysis Project (SLAAP; Kendall 2007), the second author had developed a web-based archive for laboratory-based speech recordings at Northwestern University, the Online Speech/Corpora Archive and Analysis Resource (OSCAAR; Kendall 2010). Unlike SLAAP, whose architecture was designed around sociolinguistic interview recordings (relatively long recordings of multiparty conversational interactions), OSCAAR was designed around laboratory-based production recording collections, where recording files typically are quite short utterances (such a single sentence or word production) by a single speaker, with very many files per speaker, and where speech recordings relate to specific elicitation materials, such as word lists and reading passages. In short, OSCAAR, which housed other laboratory recordings, such as the Wildcat Corpus (Van Engen et al. 2010), was well suited to house our speech recordings. So, the recordings were stored centrally in OSCAAR for a few years. In 2013, however, OSCAAR began to be redesigned and the VIA and OSCAAR teams decided it no longer made sense for these data to reside at Northwestern University. (OSCAAR has since been further redesigned and renamed SpeechBox; it is available at https://speechbox.linguistics.northwestern.edu .) It was also the case that we had continued collecting perception and production data in the intervening years and the formal, archived collection in OSCAAR no longer represented our entire data set. The files were moved to a networked desktop server in the Language Variation and Computation Laboratory, directed by Kendall, at the University of Oregon. This computer was backed up regularly and also used to store and manage files for the Corpus of Regional African American Language (see Kendall & Farrington, chapter 14, this volume) and other projects. However, the computer's system was

never designed to be a full-fledged archive, and we admit the entire data collection remained somewhat underorganized for several years.

In the summer of 2017, the team undertook the project of organizing and reformatting all of the data for the project. The data now reside in SLAAP, which provides a centralized, password-protected interface to the production recordings and metadata. While SLAAP remains designed primarily around the storage and analysis of sociolinguistic interview recordings, and so is less well suited to these data than OSCAAR, its password protected web-based interface and storage capabilities provide a more robust long-term home for the VIA data. Per the consent arrangement with subjects, the actual recordings are not publicly available, but only accessible to the PIs and those working directly on the project.

5.2 Perception data

By *speech perception data*, we mean the responses obtained from the individual participants in the perception experiments. These basically represent fixed-choice responses summarized for each stimuli step (i.e., the percentage heard as one of the two choices for the four trials for each step), along with a range of metadata (including demographic information) collected from each participant. The web server software automatically generates and stores these data for each participant. It also calculates crossover points (where a participant goes from hearing mostly one variant to mostly the other variant) for each continuum.

These speech perception data have continued to reside on the web server developed by Okamoto at University of Nevada. The server has a password-protected customized interface to the perception data that lets us query perception data for individual participants or groups of participants and even generates simple plots and summary statistics of the perception data. It also allows for the exportation of query results. In addition to the server, the authors maintain local copies of the perception data. Local copies of the perception data have also been augmented over time based on our research interests. So, for example, around 580 participants were geocoded (with latitude and longitude of their self-reported hometown) for our dialectometric analysis of spatial patterns in perception (Kendall & Fridland 2016). Copies of the perception data are also stored on SLAAP along with the production data, although the primary storage for the perception data remains the original site through which they were collected.

6   Data processing

For analysis, the data are processed in various ways.

6.1   Production data

The speech recordings have been processed several times using different techniques. For our main set of studies (Fridland & Kendall 2012, 2015; Fridland et al. 2014; Kendall & Fridland 2012, 2017), vowel measurements were taken by hand using a customized set of Praat scripts (e.g., http://lingtools.uoregon.edu/scripts/vowel_capture_aug09.praat). These were done over a period of years, and actual measurements were done by a few different analysts, working under the guidance of the authors. Craig Fickle, an undergraduate student at the University of Oregon and the main Research Experience for Undergraduates

research assistant under our National Science Foundation grants, conducted the majority of hand-measurements, with second author Kendall checking and correcting his data. These measurements focused on a subset of the words in our word lists and reading passages, with an average of 133 tokens measured per speaker and an average of 10 tokens measured for each major vowel category per speaker. Most of our hand-measurements focused on taking two measurement points per vowel, one at one-third of the vowel's duration and one at two-thirds. Figure 18.1 displays a vowel plot for one speaker, exemplifying the set of vowel measurements taken for each speaker and demonstrating a common analytic and display technique for vowel data like these (see Thomas 2011). For some recent work (Farrington, Kendall, & Fridland 2018; Gunter, Vaughn, & Kendall 2020), measurements were taken using a new Praat script to support an interest in examining dynamic properties of vowels in greater detail. While the original hand-measurements delimited vowels

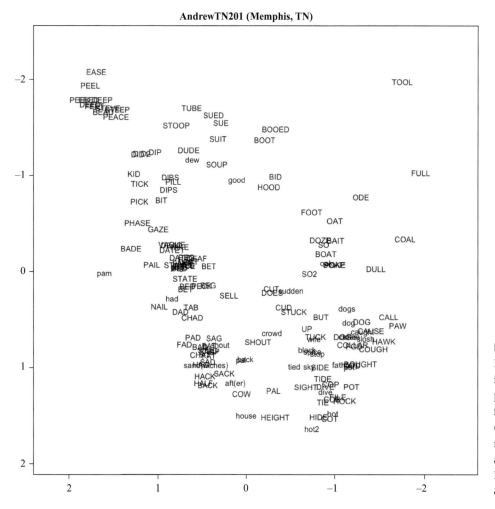

Figure 18.1

Example vowel plot showing one-third measurement point for 155 vowel tokens for participant AndrewTN201 (male from Memphis, Tennessee, between thirty-one and forty years old). Data are Lobanov normalized (Kendall & Thomas 2010).

manually, the data have been forced aligned using the Montreal Forced Aligner (McAuliffe et al. 2018) for these more recent interests. Recent approaches to vowel measurement, especially for US English, have increasingly relied on automated techniques, such as the use of the University of Pennsylvania FAVE (Forced Alignment and Vowel Extraction) Program (Rosenfelder et al. 2014). Future work with the VIA production data may follow this recent practice and use a tool such as FAVE to analyze the entirety of our collected data.

Kendall (2013) used the data stored in OSCAAR and tools built in to OSCAAR to examine speech rate variation in the reading passages. Kendall and Vaughn (2015, 2020) have used some of the speech recordings and hand-measured vowel data to explore a bootstrap measurement simulation process.

6.2   Perception data

Once retrieved from the server, perception data are processed in several ways. Many of our analyses (e.g. Kendall & Fridland 2012, 2017) examine the data through logistic (mixed-effect) regressions of the individual trials. For these analyses, the percentages stored on the server (i.e., an aggregate measure over the four instances each listener was presented for each stimulus step) were converted back to individual trial-level data points, with one categorical judgment per data row. For example, if a participant heard one step of the /ɑ/-/æ/ stimuli as 75% /æ/, this would be converted to three rows of "participant heard /æ/" and one row of "participant heard /ɑ/." We then typically presented this derived data using a vowel identification function, which shows a participant's averaged vowel identification along each step between the end points of the continuum. An example

showing vowel identification functions for three participants for the *bait~bet* continuum is shown in figure 18.2. This allows us to easily visualize individual or aggregate groups of speakers in comparison to one another. Though we have not found it to be a particularly useful metric for most of our subsequent analyses, we have also compared speakers on the basis of crossover points, or the point along the continuum at which vowel perception shifts from hearing one category to the next over 50% of the time (e.g., Kendall & Fridland 2016).

6.3   Analyzing perception and production

A large part of our initial interest was to examine the relationships between perception and production at both individual and community levels. This has required combining and processing our data in various ways. And more than any other aspect of our analyses, this has been the place we have spent the most effort on exploring our data. At its most basic, combining our perception and production data involves generating new independent variables for our perception data, where information from the production data is summarized in some way and then related to the perception data. This can involve, for instance, including a participant's Euclidean distance between /e/ and /ɛ/ (a summary measure generated for each speaker—we use this as an example as we have found it to be quite useful; see Fridland & Kendall 2012; Gunter, Vaughn, & Kendall 2020; Kendall & Fridland 2012) as a new potential predictor for each perception data point. However, the number of potential production measures that can be tested in relation to perception measures is boundless, and relationships between perception and production need not be linear (see Fridland & Kendall 2012). For the most part, our approach

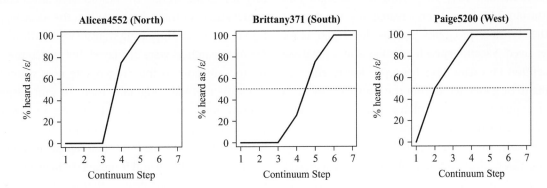

Figure 18.2

Identification functions for three participants for *bait~bet*.

to delimiting how to quantify production variables (as Euclidean distance, along a scale of F1 or F2 measures, in quartiles) has varied depending on the vowel in question and the type of vowel shift involved (backing, merger, relative movement). Much of this work is a process of trial and error, although trials are typically based in hypotheses about potential relationships between production and perception (such as that the distance between a participant's own /e/ and /ɛ/ vowel categories, in production, might relate to how that participant perceives the boundary between /e/ and /ɛ/).

7 Data sharing

Because we did not ask participants' permission to store their data in an open access format or to share it publicly, we did not set up the data archive to be publicly accessible. Thus, the audio recordings stored in SLAAP remain password-protected and not available publicly. However, we are able to share data in an anonymous format with other researchers on a permission-only basis. Likewise, about midway through the project we also changed the consent form on the online perception study to provide consent to share data more widely. Within the limitations imposed by the initial human subjects protocol, the PIs are hoping to make some of the anonymized metadata available more broadly and are currently in discussion about how best to approach this aim. Though we were not able to share our primary data publicly, our project has made available a number of products beyond publications. First, specialized software for vowel synthesis (as part of Akustyk) and phonetic data analysis and presentation scripts/code (e.g., three-dimensional plotting software; Fridland & Kendall 2009; http://lingtools.uoregon.edu /tools/durplot3d/) have been created for the project and other types of programs may be developed as we discover need. Second, speech samples and a database of perception task data have been previously and will continue to be generated during the course of the project, and, as just discussed, we plan to make some aspects of this data accessible more widely in an anonymized format. Finally, we also host public-facing information about the VIA project on Fridland's university webpage (https://packpages.unr.edu/fridland/), which seeks to make our research and findings available more widely to a non-specialist audience.

8 Lessons learned

The VIA project discussed here has been a fairly large-scale and long-term collaborative project. Our primary funding support ended in 2016, but nonetheless we continue to work with these data and the overall project continues to expand and grow. Our perception data continue to provide fuel for new insights into regional patterns of speech perception and linkages between perception and production, and our production data, in particular, form the basis for ongoing work on regional vowel patterns (Farrington, Kendall, & Fridland 2018; Fridland & Kendall 2019), as stimuli for new perception experiments (Gunter, Vaughn, & Kendall 2020), and as the basis for work on vowel analysis methods (Kendall & Vaughn 2015, 2020). We think it is fair to say that neither of the authors realized we were beginning such an expansive collaboration when we started to work together about a decade ago. As a part of this breadth and expansiveness, a number of issues have come up, several of which have been mentioned, and we believe this all provides some lessons for future data management and use for linguistic researchers. Before closing, we survey some specific points along these lines.

First, our project has relied on having a lot of "cooks in the kitchen." The breadth of our regional data collection, over 650 perception participants from across the United States, was only possible by partnering with fieldworkers local to our research field sites. And technical aspects of the project were facilitated by other collaborators. This was crucial for our project but also led to some problems. For instance, while the project's initial stimuli construction supported the development of a synthesis tool shared with the larger research community, it also meant that the PIs did have direct control or ownership over the software. When the Akustyk plug-in for Praat and its supporting website went offline, a number of researchers were dismayed, but it also meant that we too are now unable to generate new stimuli using the same methods originally used. To some degree this is not a huge issue because more tools and techniques are available now for vowel synthesis than were when we started this project, but it still represents an issue for possible replicability and it means we have been limited to expansions of our project that do not require small adjustments to our stimuli. Similarly, we have been extremely lucky and grateful to have the support of Sohei

Okamoto. Okamoto continued to help us by supporting the web server long after he completed his PhD dissertation and by providing his expertise on an ongoing basis. In part, this has been made possible because he continued at University of Nevada, Reno, in a post-doctorate position, and, also, because of his genuine interest in the project and good relationship with Fridland. However, without him we would be somewhat hindered in our ability to modify the database architecture that he set up to support the perception study and its database.

Second, while having a lot of research assistants has aided our data collection and analysis greatly, it has also created a sometimes chaotic situation for keeping up with how and where the data were stored and in what format. Each fieldworker was responsible for uploading the data to a shared server, but, depending on project and fieldworker, these were often in different folders and organized in different ways. In particular, our file-naming conventions have been irregular and not well organized. (For best practice in file naming and version control, see Mattern, chapter 5, this volume). Each fieldworker had different file-naming conventions and even differed in whether they recorded all recordings as one file or as multiple files. As well, it was often difficult to track the level of processing each sound file had been through (e.g., just raw data, Praat TextGrids, FAVE output), as we had difficulty ensuring all recordings were documented on the same master spreadsheet (several of which had been created over the course of the project, adding to the confusion). In some cases, this led to the need, at the data analysis phase of each project, to recreate the wheel. Recently, we have tried to make the data organization more transparent and clearer by having one research assistant go through and document the data and relabel everything with a more uniform practice. Our hope is that housing the data in the SLAAP archive will mean it remains more organized and centralized moving forward. However, when the data were put in OSCAAR originally, we did not expect to have to move them again. Overall, much wasted time and effort could have been saved had we been more calculated and meticulous in our data management practices from the outset.

9   Conclusion

As our ongoing project has evolved over the last ten years, our data collection, storage, and processing methods have needed to evolve as well. Partly this reflected the changing scope of our project and changing opportunities, but it also reflected a changing set of standards for how we might best manage data in linguistics. Best practices and standards have changed rapidly over the last ten years, and we have attempted to modify our procedures and data management as much as we could given the constraints of our original study design and human subjects protections. In retrospect, the main changes we would have made, based on our experience, would have been to have been more principled in our data labeling and archiving at the outset and to have set up our initial institutional review board protocol to allow for more public use of the data. However, we have created a number of public use and open-source materials during this work and also adapted our methods and data management as much as possible to allow our data to be processed and shared more effectively. We believe we've learned important lessons that inform our future research through this project and we hope this data management use case helps other researchers plan and manage their own data collections.

Appendix

Elicitation materials for production data.

Reading passage

Some mornings in the summertime, when the sky is fair and the lawn covered in dew, the good Duke Post and his wife Peg walk down to the brook by their house. There, beside the trees, is their favorite place to sit, talk and sip coffee. Her father, Don, and his dog, Bookie, often stop by to chat while their children, Betty and Kate, toss off their shoes and leap headfirst into the deep brook. It makes Peg feel like a kid again to watch them dive, shout and slosh around in the water and swing off the old black tire tied to the oak tree.

One hot, hazy, dull afternoon, she gave a call to their friends Pam and Ben Powder, inviting them over for supper. On the way, their truck got stuck in the mud and they showed up an hour late, for which they caught a good deal of teasing. But soon the crowd was having fun and the good hosts put out tunafish sandwiches, hot dogs, a big pot of bean soup and beer bread. When they were done eating, it was a sin that no one had saved room for Peg's tasty spice cake that was yet to come.

Word list 1

Dutch, Took, Cop, Dude, Shout, Bet, Collar, Cough, Town, Dock, Tide, Foot, Up, Bit, Tuck, Pail, Soap, Peel, Ghost, Dish, Deaf, Cause, Nail, Bade, Dip, Soup, Dive, Full, Seat, Beg, Bait, Poke, Same, Hock, Cow, Date, Pill, Kid, Call, Tool, Pot, Gate, Tick, Sue, Debt, Bid, Hood, Type, Gave, Boot, Tie, Cot, Dad, Bought, Paw, File, Dog, Did, Coal, Deep, Hawk, Bed, Sell, Sad, Does, Half, Deed, Peek, Dull, Pal, Bead, Date, Boat, Pod, Take, Booed, Pad, Doze, Did, But, So

Word list 2

Stayed, Fad, Vogue, Hug, Bad, Hack, Side, Dose, Stack, Tug, State, Ebb, So, Stuck, Tube, Feed, Bat, Hag, Sued, Sack, Suit, Height, Cut, Dead, Cod, Diss, Cud, Fatigue, Bet, Pick, Peace, Stoop, Bite, Pig, Hook, Bag, Sag, Dip, East, Back, Tab, Boutique, Bead, Sight, Feet, Phase, Tap, Ode, Steep, Dog, Dibs, Cob, Dips, Stag, Ease, Fake, Tease, Oat, Gaze, Step, Face, Chat, Seed, Fat, Peg, Peck, Steve, Hide, Chad, Vague, Pet, Regular, Pleasure, Bagel, Heck, Botany, Leg, Pagan, Measure, Lag, Egg, Shoot, Keg, Leggings, Treasure

Note

1. We are grateful to the National Science Foundation (grants BCS-0518264, BCS-1123460, and BCS-1122950), as well as the University of Nevada, Reno, and the University of Oregon for supporting the work described in this chapter. We especially thank Sohei Okamoto, Craig Fickle, Charlie Farrington, and Kaylynn Gunter for support with various aspects of the project. In addition, we want to acknowledge Bartek Plichta for his work helping to develop the stimuli, and the numerous faculty and students who helped recruit participants and collect data at field sites across the United States.

References

Cassidy, Frederic, and Joan Hall. 1985–2013. *The Dictionary of American Regional English*. Cambridge: Harvard University Press

Chambers, J. K., and Peter Trudgill. 1998. *Dialectology*. 2nd ed. Cambridge: Cambridge University Press.

Clarke, Sandra, Ford Elms, and Amani Youssef. 1995. The third dialect of English: Some Canadian evidence. *Language Variation and Change* 7:209–228.

Clopper, Cynthia, and David Pisoni. 2004. Some acoustic cues for the perceptual categorization of American English regional dialects. *Journal of Phonetics* 32 (1): 111–140.

Eckert, Penelope. 2008. Where do ethnolects stop? *International Journal of Bilingualism* 12 (1–2): 25–42.

Evans, Bronwen G., and Paul Iverson. 2004. Vowel normalization for accent: An investigation of best exemplar locations in northern and southern British English sentences. *Journal of the Acoustical Society of America* 115 (1): 352–361.

Evans, Bronwen G., and Paul Iverson. 2007. Plasticity in vowel perception and production: A study of accent change in young adults. *Journal of the Acoustical Society of America* 121 (6): 3814–3826.

Farrington, Charlie, Tyler Kendall, and Valerie Fridland. 2018. Vowel dynamics in the Southern Vowel Shift. *American Speech* 93 (2): 186–222.

Fridland, Valerie. 1998. The Southern Vowel Shift: Linguistic and social factors. PhD dissertation, Michigan State University.

Fridland, Valerie. 1999. The Southern Vowel Shift in Memphis, TN. *Language Variation and Change* 11 (3): 267–285.

Fridland, Valerie. 2001. Social factors in the Southern Shift: Gender, age and class. *Journal of Sociolinguistics* 5 (2): 233–253.

Fridland, Valerie, and Tyler Kendall. 2009. Mapping production and perception in regional vowel shifts: The effects of vowel duration and formant trajectories. Presentation given at the New Ways of Analyzing Variation Conference 38, University of Ottawa, Ottawa, Canada, October 22–25.

Fridland, Valerie, and Tyler Kendall. 2012. Exploring the relationship between production and perception in the mid front vowels of U.S. English. *Lingua* 122 (7): 779–793.

Fridland, Valerie, and Tyler Kendall. 2015. Within-region diversity in the Southern Vowel Shift: Production and perception. In *Proceedings of the International Congress on Phonetics (ICPhS) 2015*. Glasgow: University of Glasgow.

Fridland, Valerie, and Tyler Kendall. 2017. Speech in the Silver State. In *Speech in the Western States*. Volume 2: *The Mountain West*, ed. Valerie Fridland, Betsy Evans, Alicia Wassink, and Tyler Kendall, 139–164. Durham, NC: Duke University Press.

Fridland, Valerie, and Tyler Kendall. 2018. Regional identity and listener perception. In *Language Regard: Methods, Variation, and Change*, ed. Betsy Evans, Erica Benson, and James Stanford, 132–152. Cambridge: Cambridge University Press.

Fridland, Valerie, and Tyler Kendall. 2019. On the uniformity of the Low-Back-Merger Shift in the U.S. West and beyond. In *The Low-Back-Merger Shift: Uniting the Canadian Vowel Shift, the California Vowel Shift, and short front vowel shifts across North America*, ed. Kara Becker, 100–119. Durham, NC: Duke University Press.

Fridland, Valerie, Tyler Kendall, and Charlie Farrington. 2014. Durational and spectral differences in American English vowels: Dialect variation within and across regions. *Journal of the Acoustical Society of America* 136 (1): 341–349.

Grieve, Jack, Costanza Asnaghi, and Tom Ruette. 2013. Site-restricted web searches for data collection in regional dialectology. *American Speech* 88:413–440.

Gunter, Kaylynn, Charlotte Vaughn, and Tyler Kendall. 2020. Perceiving Southernness: Vowel categories and acoustic cues in Southernness ratings. *Journal of the Acoustical Society of America* 147 (1): 643–656.

Hay, Jennifer, Paul Warren, and Katie Drager. 2006. Factors influencing speech perception in the context of a merger-in-progress. *Journal of Phonetics* 34:458–484.

Huang, Yuan, Diansheng Guo, Alice Kasakoff, and Jack Grieve. 2016. Understanding U.S. regional linguistic variation with Twitter data analysis. *Computers, Environment and Urban Systems* 59:244–255.

Kendall, Tyler. 2007. The North Carolina sociolinguistic archive and analysis project: Empowering the sociolinguistic archive. *Penn Working Papers in Linguistics* 13 (2): 15–26.

Kendall, Tyler. 2010. Developing web interfaces to spoken language data collections. In *Proceedings of the Chicago Colloquium on Digital Humanities and Computer Science* 1.2. Chicago: University of Chicago. doi:10.6082/M1BK19HM.

Kendall, Tyler. 2013. *Speech Rate, Pause, and Sociolinguistic Variation: Studies in Corpus Sociophonetics*. Basingstoke, UK: Palgrave Macmillan.

Kendall, Tyler, and Valerie Fridland. 2012. Variation in perception and production of mid front vowels in the U.S. Southern Vowel Shift. *Journal of Phonetics* 40 (2): 289–306.

Kendall, Tyler, and Valerie Fridland. 2016. Mapping the perception of linguistic form: Dialectometry with perception data. In *The Future of Dialects*, ed. Marie-Hélène Côté, Remco Knooihuizen, and John Nerbonne, 173–194. Berlin: Language Science Press.

Kendall, Tyler, and Valerie Fridland. 2017. Regional relationships among the low vowels of U.S. English: Evidence from production and perception. *Language Variation and Change* 29 (2): 245–271.

Kendall, Tyler, and Valerie Fridland. 2021. *Sociophonetics*. Cambridge: Cambridge University Press.

Kendall, Tyler, and Erik R. Thomas. 2010. *Vowels: Vowel Manipulation, Normalization, and Plotting in R*. R package, version 1.1. Software Resource. http://lingtools.uoregon.edu/norm/.

Kendall, Tyler, and Charlotte Vaughn. 2015. Measurement variability in vowel formant estimation: A simulation experiment. In *Proceedings of the International Congress on Phonetics (ICPhS) 2015*. Glasgow: University of Glasgow.

Kendall, Tyler, and Charlotte Vaughn. 2020. Exploring vowel formant estimation through simulation-based techniques. *Linguistic Vanguard* 6 (s1): 1–13.

Kurath, Hans. 1949. *A Word Geography of the Eastern United States*. Ann Arbor: University of Michigan Press.

Labov, William, Sharon Ash, and Charles Boberg. 2006. *The Atlas of North American English: Phonetics, Phonology, and Sound Change*. New York: Mouton de Gruyter.

McAuliffe, Michael, Michaela Socolof, Sarah Mihuc, Michael Wagner, and Morgan Sonderegger. 2018. *Montreal Forced Aligner*. Version 1.0. http://montrealcorpustools.github.io/Montreal-Forced-Aligner/.

McDavid, Raven I., Jr., and Raymond O'Cain. 1980. *Linguistic Atlas of the Middle and South Atlantic States*. Chicago: University of Chicago Press.

Milroy, Leslie. 1980. *Language and Social Networks*. Baltimore, MD: University Park Press.

Niedzielski, Nancy. 1999. The effect of social information on the perception of sociolinguistic variables. *Journal of Language and Social Psychology* 18:62–85.

Pederson, Lee, Susan L. McDaniel, and Carol M. Adams, eds. 1986–1993. *Linguistic Atlas of the Gulf States*. 7 vols. Athens: University of Georgia Press.

Plichta, Bartłomiej. 2004–2014. *Akustyk*. Plug-in for Praat software.

Rosenfelder, Ingrid, Josef Fruehwald, Keelan Evanini, Scott Seyfarth, Kyle Gorman, Hilary Prichard, and Jiahong Yuan. 2014. *FAVE (Forced Alignment and Vowel Extraction)*. Program suite version 1.2.2. https://github.com/JoFrhwld/FAVE.

Sumner, Meghan, and Arthur Samuel. 2009. The effect of experience on the perception and representation of dialect variants. *Journal of Memory and Language* 60:487–501.

Thomas, Erik R. 2011. *Sociophonetics: An Introduction*. Basingstoke, UK: Palgrave Macmillan.

Van Engen, Kristin, Melissa Baese-Berk, Rachel Baker, Arim Choi, Midam Kim, and Ann R. Bradlow. 2010. The Wildcat Corpus of native-and foreign-accented English: Communicative efficiency across conversational dyads with varying language alignment profiles. *Language and Speech* 53 (4), 510–540.

Vaux, Bert, and Scott Golder. 2003. *The Harvard Dialect Survey*. Cambridge: Harvard University Linguistics Department.

Wieling, Martin, and John Nerbonne. 2015. Advances in dialectometry. *Annual Review of Linguistics* 1:243–264.

19   Data Management Practices in an Ethnographic Study of Language and Migration

Lynnette Arnold

1   Introduction

In this chapter, I discuss the data collection and management processes utilized in an ethnographic study of language and migration. While much linguistic research is ultimately concerned with understanding language itself, this research took a sociocultural linguistic approach, asking "how the empirical study of language illuminates social and cultural processes" (Bucholtz & Hall 2008:405). In this case, I used ethnographic methods to explore everyday communication among Salvadoran migrants living in the United States and their families back home to gain new insights into experiences of migration and transnational life (Arnold 2012, 2015b, 2019). In this project, the ethical aspects of data practices (Holton, Leonard, & Pulsifer, chapter 4, this volume) were clear from the outset, given the substantial power imbalances between myself, as an English-speaking, middle-class US citizen who can travel the world with ease and the monolingual Spanish-speaking research participants, residents of an impoverished Salvadoran village, who can only access transnational mobility at great risk. Given the population that I worked with and the types of data I gathered, this study presented ethical and practical challenges at each stage of the data life cycle (Mattern, chapter 5, this volume), including data collection, processing, and management. In what follows, I describe how I worked to resolve these concerns while also laying out how ethnographic research such as this complicates the open data model. To contextualize this discussion, I begin with a brief discussion of my research project and methods.

2   Project and methods

This research involved an ethnography of communication (Hymes 1964, 1972) conducted from 2009 to 2014 with families impacted by migration, specifically undocumented Salvadoran migrants in the United States and their relatives back home in El Salvador. Despite being unable to travel to visit one another, these families remained in regular contact through a range of digital communication technologies that are becoming increasingly available around the world. Everyday cross-border conversations within these families provide an important window into the impacts of migration, as language becomes the primary means for sustaining familial relationships and navigating the everyday concerns of family life when migrants and their loved ones must live stretched across borders for years at a time (Arnold 2016).

To capture the complete circuit of transnational family life, I conducted a multisited ethnography (for a more complete discussion of this method in linguistic research, see Dick & Arnold 2017). My research sites included research in a rural Salvadoran village and three different urban locations in the United States where migrants from this village had settled. This phase of the project involved video and audio recording twenty-four interviews with members of twelve transnational families—both migrants and non-migrants—as well as participant observation. I joined in many aspects of the families' daily lives, using field notes to track what I was learning about the role of communication in cross-border kinship. I saw individuals receive phone calls and other forms of communication from distant relatives and observed how families living together in either country would talk about these transnational conversations, discussing what needed to be communicated and who would be responsible to communicate it. Through attending carefully to such conversations, I began to understand the crucial but complex role that such phone calls in particular played in these families' lives. I therefore conducted a final five-month stage of intensive data collection with two multigenerational families.

In this phase of the study, I gathered recordings of everyday conversations, both on the phone and face-to-face, within the families. This intimate domain of study was made possible by ongoing relationships with the participants that were first forged during the four years that I spent living in El Salvador (2001–2005), when I worked with gender development and youth engagement programs primarily in the rural village that later became the hub of my research. Throughout the course of this study, I sought to honor the families' trust in me through careful consideration of data management practices at each stage of the data life cycle. In the following sections, I discuss data collection, data processing and storage, and data sharing and citation, describing key considerations and strategies for each in turn.

3 Data collection

Because of the multisited nature of the research, my data collection methods needed to work both in urban settings in the United States and in rural El Salvador, where access to electricity was unpredictable and there was no regular Internet connection. In addition, I needed methods that would allow for the recording of both face-to-face and remote, technologically mediated conversations. At the same time, it was crucial to me that family members be able to record data on their own as much as possible. On the one hand, this was a practical consideration, both to minimize the observer's paradox that is an inevitable part of sociolinguistic research (Labov 1972) and also to facilitate simultaneous data collection across multiple sites. At the same time, my interest in conducting "research with" (Cameron et al. 1993:87) also sprang from my ongoing ethical concern to gather data with as much sensitivity as possible to the intimate nature of the conversations themselves.

For the final intensive stage of data collection, I hired and trained a family research assistant in each family to assist with making recordings; I asked young adults to fill these roles, because they tended to have the best literacy skills and were also more accustomed to using digital technologies.[1] Although these young adults had full-time jobs, they generally had less extensive family responsibilities than the older adults did, leaving them more free time for such work. This collaborative model of working had its challenges: some data were inevitably lost during the process of learning to operate the

recording equipment. At the same time, working closely with these young people was crucial to the success of the project. Once the recordings were made, these research assistants provided vital background knowledge that helped to contextualize the conversations, providing feedback during regular face-to-face meetings or through digital correspondence. Family research assistants received a stipend of $100 per month and I also worked to provide mentoring. For instance, at their request, I took them to visit local colleges and libraries and helped them master the use of local public transportation systems (often with English-only signage), which gave them greater freedom of movement.

The family research assistants helped with the recording of both face-to-face and phone conversations. In-person conversations at each site were recorded using basic video cameras, tripods, and a sixteen-gigabyte microSDHC (secure digital high capacity) data card to store files. I passed all this equipment on to the families for their own use at the end of the study. Together, we gathered eighty-seven video recordings of spontaneous face-to-face interaction, totaling about fifty hours of video data. The recordings include everyday activities such as sharing meals, cooking, doing homework, and playing games, as well as special activities such as holiday and birthday celebrations. Phone conversations were recorded using a maximally flexible recording technology that would work regardless of the type of cell phone being used. The Olympus TP-8 consists of an earpiece with a microphone mounted on the back. Participants would wear this earpiece in their ear and connect it to an MP3 recorder (the Olympus VN-8100PC);[2] the phone was then held up to the ear with the earpiece so that phone calls could easily be recorded. These MP3 recorders were placed in carrying cases with carabiner clips, thus allowing the user to be as mobile as usual while making recordings of cell phone conversations. Although each recorder had two gigabytes of internal memory, I installed an eight-gigabyte microSDHC data card to be sure the recorders would not run out of space.

Using this methodology, sixty-seven transnational phone calls were recorded over the course of four months, ranging in length from two minutes to two hours, most averaging about twenty to thirty minutes, for a total of twenty-five hours of recordings. For both video and audio recorders, I showed the family research assistants how to delete recorded data, so that any conversations that had been recorded could be removed after the fact if anyone in the family had any concerns. I also reviewed all recordings before beginning analysis to identify any sensitive segments—particularly those concerning legal matters involving undocumented migrants—which I deleted permanently. The types, formats, and amounts of data gathered over the course of the project are shown in table 19.1.

4 Data processing and storage

The quantity of recordings and the diversity of types of data gathered created challenges at the next stages of the data life cycle—data processing and storage—which I will consider jointly here because they were very much interwoven in this project. In addition to managing large file sizes, particularly with the video recordings, I also worked to maintain the confidentiality of the data in both its processing and storage. These considerations led me to avoid using cloud-based storage options and instead to rely on external drives. All data files, whether audio or video, were copied from the cards on which they had been originally recorded onto a one-terabyte external drive, after which they were deleted from the recording device or cards. To minimize the possibility of data loss, I copied the entire contents of this drive onto a second backup drive using rsync (https://rsync.samba .org/), an open source utility that efficiently synchronizes files across hard drives by comparing file modification times and file sizes.[3] While this process allowed me to easily create a backup of my data by plugging both the original drive and the backup into my laptop and running the program, it did require me to manually update the backup drive as I continued to process the data,

revealing the challenges of an active storage process (see Mattern, chapter 5, this volume).

Data processing proceeded in the same way for all of my recordings, regardless of type, with the goal of tracing discourse patterns across the corpus. As a fluent second-language speaker of Salvadoran Spanish, I conducted all of my analysis with the original Spanish and only translated transcription excerpts for presentation and publication. Each audio or video file was first indexed using Excel, creating a time-stamped summary for each recording that included aspects of the content of the conversation as well as salient linguistic forms (see figure 19.1). The indexes averaged a new line of notation for every thirty seconds of conversation.[4] Based on an inductive coding of the indexes, I decided which parts of the recordings to transcribe. Time-aligned transcripts were made using ELAN, segmenting the data into intonation units. To obtain the waveforms necessary to help with this segmentation, I had to transform some of the data (see Han, chapter 6, this volume), converting all MP3 files to WAV format.[5]

Each audio or video recording thus had several derivative data files associated with it (an Excel spreadsheet index and three ELAN transcription files), while some audio files had both an MP3 and a WAV format. To keep all of the related files associated with one another, I followed a strict file-naming convention linked to a metadata spreadsheet that I used to process the data (see Mattern, chapter 5, this volume for more discussion of file naming).[6] I entered each separate recording on its own line of the spreadsheet, filling out each of the fields in order (see figure 19.2). Using the *concatenate* function in Excel, I then set up the spreadsheet to automatically compile the file name that I then copied and used for recordings, indexes, and ELAN files, simply changing the file format to the appropriate type.

I designed this file-naming system to explore the questions that had emerged from my ethnographic research, with each piece of the file name being tied to some crucial aspect of the data. The first indicator for each file was family name, which was crucial as I was concerned with how communication functioned within the family; similarly, the location where the data had been recorded was crucial for attending to the transnational dimensions of this communication. Tracking dates next allowed me to trace particular topics or themes of conversation over time. Finally, the event portion of the file name encoded

Table 19.1
Data gathered in this study

Type	Format	Quantity
Field notes	Word documents, non–optical character recognition PDF scans of handwritten notes	200 pages
Interviews	.mov and .wav files for each	24 interviews (45 hours of recordings)
Face-to-face interaction	.mov files	87 recordings (50 hours)
Phone conversations	.mp3 files	67 calls (25 hours)

Time	Index
0:00:00	brief greeting
0:00:10	OP issues complaint about her eye
0:00:25	OP asks F what he's doing - soccer game - minimal responses from F.
0:00:48	OP returns to eye issue
0:01:00	matching story by F - basura in his eye at work - OP matches with her pain
0:01:15	F continues story - OP asks about eye drops - tells her story
0:01:45	OP reports going to doctor - F asks about operation - technical terms - 'la carnosidad'
0:02:33	F asks about his grandfather - OP reports - lots of QS: he can't get up etc.
0:03:00	OP - reports on grandfather's health problems - QS: 'no voy a durar mucho'
0:03:35	OP & F talk about whether grandfather will be OK
0:03:50	OP reports what grandfather eats in great detail - more QS
0:04:35	F makes complaint about not having beans cooked for him to eat
0:04:45	OP continues with elaboration of grandfather's diet
0:05:05	OP: grandfather is like a child - more report about his diet
0:05:45	F continues/elaborates complaint about tortillas frias
0:06:00	OP reports on her diet - not allowed to eat tortillas but sends corn to molino
0:06:20	F asks who OP means (a woman who has something to do with molino) - he can't figure it out (OP reports who her parents are, where she lives)
0:06:40	F reports his day's activities: going to work and dentist
0:06:46	OP asks about more details of F's dental problems - sympathetic response
0:07:20	OP & F talk about dental details - pain and procedure
0:07:42	matching story by OP about her eye operation - 'todo duele'
0:08:14	OP tells F to be careful - reminds him of previous time he got sick with something she thinks is similar - although not clear with what
0:08:25	F denies similarity to previous case - 'los otros nervios no usted'
0:08:47	OP - well-wishing re: F's health

Figure 19.1

Sample index of phone conversation.

Family	Country	Year	Month	Day	Event	Format	Filename
Portillo	US	2013	11	09	Breakfast	mov	Portillo_US_2013-11-09_Breakfast.mov
Portillo	US	2013	11	10	Call-F-O	mp3	Portillo_US_2013-11-10_Call-F-O.mp3
Portillo	US	2013	11	10	Tamales1	mov	Portillo_US_2013-11-10_Tamales1.mov
Portillo	US	2013	11	10	Tamales2	mov	Portillo_US_2013-11-10_Tamales2.mov

Figure 19.2

Filename portion of metadata spreadsheet.

a shorthand description of the type of recording, for instance "Breakfast," "Tamales1," or "EveningGames"; phone calls were described as "call" and then appended with the pseudonym initial of all the participants in the order they spoke.[7] Multiple files with the same name were disambiguated numerically in sequential order (e.g., "Tamales1," and "Tamales2"). In addition to highlighting important aspects of each communicative event, utilizing consistent file-naming conventions across the complete data set was essential for keeping this large corpus organized and therefore as easy to work with as possible.

I did not complete the data processing alone, but rather with a group of undergraduate research assistants who helped primarily with the transcription in exchange for course credit and mentoring. Each semester, I found one or two students with the necessary linguistic background and trained them in the basics of discourse transcription using ELAN.[8] I maintained confidentiality of the data by consistently using participant pseudonyms with all of the research assistants throughout the data processing. Working with these students certainly accelerated the transcription, and as members themselves of extended transnational families, they shared keen insights into the nature of the data that have been fundamental to my ongoing research. Working with these students also created space for ongoing mentoring relationships, one of the ethical interventions whereby I sought to support the community that had helped me in my research. At the same time, this collaboration—like the one with the family research assistants during data collection—produced challenges in processing the data. Working with different assistants over a short period of time, each of whom was transcribing on their own, sometimes resulted in multiple ELAN files for a single recording, each with different parts of the recording transcribed. For instance, file 1 could have minutes 0–5 and 15–20 transcribed, while file 2 would have minutes 8–12 and 24–30 transcribed. This overlapping meant that syncing these separate files is not a straightforward, automatable undertaking. Moreover, I needed to check students' transcriptions before adding them to my main database of transcription. I created an ad hoc Excel sheet to track student transcriber assignments and files, but the lack of planning in data processing at this stage created a bottleneck in the workflow that future collaborative research would do well to avoid.

5   Sharing data

In the final stage of the data life cycle, data sharing, my ethnographic research diverges significantly from the open data model advanced in this volume, because I ultimately decided not to deposit my data with an archive nor to share it with other researchers. Nevertheless, considering research like mine that opts to maintain closed data can illuminate our thinking about the open data model, in particular revealing its limitations and challenges. For that reason, in this section I lay out the ethical and practical reasons that motivated my decision not to share data, while also outlining a non-academic form of public diffusion I engaged in at the request of my participants.

Maintaining closed data has long been, and still remains, a largely unquestioned norm within ethnographic research. This is reflected, for instance, in the fact that data citation practices in ethnographic journals almost never allow for particular segments to be traced back to their position in the larger corpus. In fact, I am often asked to remove reference to specific files and time stamps from examples in manuscripts submitted for publication and have thus opted to track this information for myself as part of my metadata spreadsheet. The pervasiveness of closed data is clearly tied to ethnographic epistemologies, in which knowledge emerges through the interaction between researcher and participants (Clifford & Marcus 1986; James, Hockey, & Dawson 1997). As such, ethnographic data do not easily lend themselves to interpretation and analysis by those not involved in the research process. In my research, for instance, the data I gathered were deeply embedded in the everyday lives of families, such that making sense of them at times required more background knowledge even than I had gathered in fifteen years of working with the participants. Such practical considerations were certainly part of my decision not to share my data.

It is possible that ethnographic data may be of interest to researchers pursuing other questions; for instance, my data could allow for a study of the lexical and morphosyntactic properties of Salvadoran Spanish. Questions of reproducibility alone are thus not sufficient to justify closed data. Beyond practicality, however, the question of whether to share data is fundamentally an ethical one, particularly when research involves working with minority language communities who have long been subject to extraction and misappropriation of their knowledge (Holton, Leonard, & Pulsifer, chapter 4, this volume). Although my research involved speakers of a majority language (Spanish), the political, economic, and social marginalization of undocumented immigrants in the United States meant that sharing data could potentially put some of my participants in danger of deportation. Other considerations, such as the intimate nature of the data gathered and the fact that children were often involved in the recordings, also factored into my decision-making process. For these reasons, it was clear that sharing any data in their raw form would be an ethical violation of the trust the participants had placed in me in allowing me to conduct my research. While the ethical implications of shared data were perhaps more stark in my project than in most linguistic scholarship, ultimately all our research involves people in one way or another. It is thus crucial for the field to take seriously the ethical implications of data sharing for all of the varied types of linguistic research.

Although the ethical imperative to maintain closed data was clear to me, at the same time, many of my participants emphasized that part of their motivation for participating in my research was that they wanted me to share their stories. They felt that US citizens did not sufficiently understand the realities of migrants' lives and their ties to family across borders. Because many of them had known me first as a community worker before I became a researcher, they saw me as an ally in the struggle for justice for immigrant communities, a positioning that I affirmed as well. They thus wanted me to share their stories with the broader public as a means of raising awareness about the full impact of US immigration policy on individuals living around the world. I thus felt the imperative to share particular aspects of my data with the broader public, beyond the narrow scope of academic publications and conference presentations, and have done so as best I can (Arnold 2015a, 2018, 2020; Hallett & Arnold 2016, 2018).

To facilitate the kind of public sharing that my participants were requesting, in my consent forms I incorporated questions about data sharing in three contexts: in presentations, in academic publications, and in broader public forums.[9] For each context, participants could select what level of sharing they were comfortable with, ranging from no sharing, sharing of anonymized recordings, to sharing of original recordings. Unsurprisingly, out of thirty participants who agreed to have their data shared publicly, only four were comfortable sharing materials that were not anonymized. Because most of my recordings involve several participants, this has effectively meant that any data I shared publicly must first be anonymized. This introduces a challenge, because full anonymization, particularly of video data, is quite labor intensive. Moreover, given the ethnographic nature of the data, it must be contextualized for the impact and breadth of the stories to be adequately conveyed to a broader audience.

I therefore experimented with using a blogging platform to publicly share segments of my data as part of larger stories about Salvadoran migration to the United States (for an example, see https://alasmigratorias.wordpress.com/2013/10/28/poverty/). To produce this shareable data, I combined anonymized audio with open access artwork to create short videos that tell individual migration stories. These videos are then embedded within a written narrative that recounts the history and current realities of unauthorized migration from El Salvador to the United States. This format works well, but it requires a great deal of time and effort that generally go unrecognized as valid academic labor for purposes of the job market or tenure and promotion. Nevertheless, in an era of virulent anti-immigrant sentiment, which is increasingly directed toward Central Americans, this form of data sharing is an ethical necessity.[10]

6   Conclusions

In this chapter, I have traced the data life cycle throughout an ethnographic study of language and migration, describing my data collection, processing, and sharing practices. Ultimately, although I chose not to archive or share my corpus as a whole, writing about data management nevertheless remains a key component of the openness that is a central principle of the social science data movement (see Gawne & Styles, chapter 2, this volume). Although ethnographic research ultimately does not strive toward replicability of particular studies as a means of asserting validity, I have shared my data practices here as a means of supporting future ethnographers of language and communication to think through their data management practices at each stage of the research. Such discussions are a crucial component of recent calls to incorporate ethnography as a more central methodological approach within linguistics (Snell, Shaw, & Copland 2015). More broadly, my project illustrates the benefits of collaboration with community members and students at multiple stages of the research process. In particular, I have pointed to unforeseen challenges that arose in the course of these collaborations, considerations that will be of use to those planning future collaborative research. Finally, it is my hope that consideration of research such as mine can be of help to proponents of more open data within linguistics. By highlighting the ethical complications and limitations of such an approach, I seek to contribute to an open data movement that does not let lofty goals override the absolute necessity of carefully implementing this approach in ways that are as variable as our research.

Acknowledgments

The research reported on in this chapter was made possible through the Jacob K. Javits Fellowship Program, the Chicano Studies Institute of the University of California at Santa Barbara, and the University of California

Institute for Mexico and the United States. I wish to thank two anonymous reviewers and Patrick Hall for their comments on this chapter, which have made it much stronger. Any remaining errors are my own.

Notes

1. Older adults in the families had often had little to no formal schooling, and my participants also included preliterate and school-aged children.

2. Given the degraded audio quality of phone calls, and in order to purchase several versions of the complete recording setup, I decided to opt out of the more expensive WAV recorders usually utilized for linguistic research.

3. I owe a debt of gratitude to Patrick Hall for introducing me to rsync and helping me set it up.

4. Many thanks to Mary Bucholtz for teaching me this method of processing sociocultural linguistic data.

5. Phone conversations were recorded in compressed format due to their degraded audio quality that made higher-quality WAV recorders useless.

6. Thanks to Laura Robinson and her graduate seminar on research methods for introducing me early on to the importance of file-naming conventions.

7. The calls generally involved a series of dyadic conversations that often involved several different individuals on both ends of the line, resulting in the sometimes long string of initials of pseudonyms.

8. I was fortunate to be able to find six students of Salvadoran descent who were able to understand my data.

9. There is a long-standing critique of informed consent and its mismatch with ethnography (Bell 2014) that I certainly experienced in my research. But my institutional affiliations and funding nevertheless made it necessary to follow these procedures.

10. Using social media and other online platforms also raises questions about reach, and I certainly don't think my blog posts were able to reach a very wide audience. A possible resolution to this consideration comes in the form of curated online venues (e.g., Medium https://medium.com/ and The Conversation https://theconversation.com/us) that help scholars present their research to a broader public. (See for instance, Arnold 2020, which has reached almost 6,000 unique readers from the time of publication to November 2020).

References

Arnold, Lynnette. 2012. "Como que era Mexicano": Cross-dialectal passing in transnational migration. *Texas Linguistics Forum* 55:1–9.

Arnold, Lynnette. 2015a. Deleting the I-word in Santa Barbara. *Center for California Languages and Cultures* (blog). January 28, 2015. http://www.ccalc.ucsb.edu/deleting-i-word-santa-barbara -guest-post-lynnette-arnold.

Arnold, Lynnette. 2015b. The reconceptualization of agency through ambiguity and contradiction: Salvadoran women narrating unauthorized migration. *Women's Studies International Forum* 52 (September): 10–19. https://doi.org/10.1016/j.wsif .2015.07.004.

Arnold, Lynnette. 2016. Communicative care across borders: Language, materiality, and affect in transnational family life. PhD dissertation, University of California, Santa Barbara.

Arnold, Lynnette. 2018. Imprisoning families is not the solution. *Youth Circulations* (blog). June 20, 2018. http://www .youthcirculations.com/blog/2018/6/20/imprisoning-families -is-not-the-solution.

Arnold, Lynnette. 2019. Language socialization across borders: Producing scalar subjectivities through material-affective semiosis. *Pragmatics* 29 (3): 332–356. https://doi.org/10.1075 /prag.18013.arn.

Arnold, Lynnette. 2020. Four tips for staying connected during coronavirus, from migrants who live far from family. *The Conversation*. March 30. https://theconversation.com/4-tips-for-staying -connected-during-coronavirus-from-migrants-who-live-far-from -family-134362.

Bell, Kirsten. 2014. Resisting commensurability: Against informed consent as an anthropological virtue. *American Anthropologist* 116 (3): 511–522. https://doi.org/10.1111/aman.12122.

Bucholtz, Mary, and Kira Hall. 2008. All of the above: New coalitions in sociocultural linguistics. *Journal of Sociolinguistics* 12 (4): 401–431.

Cameron, Deborah, Elizabeth Frazer, Penelope Harvey, Ben Rampton, and Kay Richardson. 1993. Ethics, advocacy, and empowerment: Issues of method in researching language. *Language and Communication* 13 (2): 81–94.

Clifford, James, and George E. Marcus, eds. 1986. *Writing Culture: The Poetics and Politics of Ethnography*. Berkeley: University of California Press.

Dick, Hilary Parsons, and Lynnette Arnold. 2017. Multisited ethnography and language in the study of migration. In *The Routledge Handbook of Migration and Language*, ed. Suresh Canagarajah, 397–412. London: Routledge, Taylor and Francis.

Hallett, Miranda Cady, and Lynnette Arnold. 2016. Detention, disappearance, and the power of language. *Anthropology News* 57 (11): e250–253. https://doi.org/10.1111/AN.241.

Hallett, Miranda Cady, and Lynnette Arnold. 2018. Compounding the crisis. *North American Congress on Latin America (NACLA)* (blog). July 24, 2018. https://nacla.org/news/2018/07 /24/compounding-crisis.

Hymes, Dell. 1964. Introduction: Toward ethnographies of communication. *American Anthropologist* 66 (6): 1–34. https://doi.org/10.1525/aa.1964.66.suppl_3.02a00010.

Hymes, Dell. 1972. Models of the interaction of language and social life. In *Directions in Sociolinguistics: The Ethnography of Communication*, ed. John Gumperz and Dell Hymes, 35–71. New York: Blackwell.

James, Allison, Jenny Hockey, and Andrew Dawson, eds. 1997. *After Writing Culture: Epistemology and Praxis in Contemporary Anthropology*. New York: Routledge.

Labov, William. 1972. *Sociolinguistic Patterns*. Philadelphia: University of Pennsylvania Press.

Snell, Julia, Sara Shaw, and Fiona Copland, eds. 2015. *Linguistic Ethnography*. London: Palgrave Macmillan UK. https://doi.org/10.1057/9781137035035.

Elliott M. Hoey and Chase Wesley Raymond

1 Introduction

This chapter describes how data are conventionally used in conversation analysis (CA; for overviews, see Sidnell & Stivers 2013; Clift 2016). We describe where it comes from, how it is collected and organized for analysis, and how it is distributed. Over the course of this description, we make some recommendations regarding best practices and potential improvements.

2 Data sources

CA research projects seek to uncover the orderliness of everyday social interactions often by locating *perspicuous settings*. These are everyday activities whose endogenous organizations naturally provide answers to the questions a researcher may have. For example, a researcher interested in how good/bad news is delivered may look to interactions involving cancer screenings, as these reveal the phenomenon of interest repeatedly and in perspicuous detail. Whatever the interest or setting, CA research relies on recordings of social interactions.

2.1 Recorded social interaction

The empirical basis of CA research is recorded audio/video of naturally occurring social interactions (see Sacks 1984; Mondada 2013). The use of such materials emerges from a commitment to examining the actual details of actual events, and an avoidance of data that are stipulated (imagined, recalled, intuited, and such), stimulated (staged, elicited, experimentally induced, and so forth), or otherwise produced via researcher involvement (cf. Speer 2002). The goal is to retain as much of an emic perspective as possible on activities as they are naturally organized by the participants. For this reason, recordings are preferred over field notes, interviews, and experiments, which fail to preserve the precise, embodied,

temporally unfolding ways that participants concertedly organize their situated activities as ordinary, practical achievements.

Recordings offer "good enough" documentation of what transpired in an interaction. They capture not only who said what, but also things that ordinarily elude noticing and memory, such as who stops laughing first (Jefferson 1985), or the words a speaker abandons before finding a suitable replacement (Schegloff, Jefferson, & Sacks 1977). Recordings can be played repeatedly and in slow motion, which, in the case of video data, permits detailed analyses of gaze, manual action, bodily comportment, engagement with objects, and so forth, all of which are routinely consequential for interaction (Mondada 2016a).

2.2 Existing data

CA research commonly relies on existing recordings of social interaction. These primarily differ in their provenance (collected by a researcher or by another entity) and purpose (for research or for another purpose). Many data sources are online. Some research corpora are freely available, notably TalkBank[1] (MacWhinney 2007), which holds well-known materials transcribed by Gail Jefferson (e.g., Newport Beach, Watergate), the Santa Barbara Corpus of Spoken American English, and the Corpus de Langue Parlée en Interaction, among others. Other research corpora are conditionally accessible, for instance after registration, ethics training, specification of research purpose, and sometimes payment. Such corpora include SamtaleBank,[2] the Language and Social Interaction Archive,[3] the One in a Million Archive of Primary Care Consultations,[4] and the Forschungs- und Lehrkorpus Gesprochenes Deutsch (FOLK).[5] Other online resources, while not made for research purposes, may be coopted for CA inquiry (Jones & Raymond 2012). These include YouTube videos and other "found" materials such as broadcasts of interviews and debates (Heritage & Clayman 2010).

Other avenues for accessing data involve more direct exchange between the researcher and those with rights to grant access (see Broth, Laurier, & Mondada 2014). Researcher-to-researcher sharing is probably the most common method. This operates informally over professional networks, with the sharing of "classic" data being especially commonplace. Researchers may also request access to data that was collected for non-research purposes. For Raymond (2014), the author petitioned numerous police departments for their automatically recorded emergency calls until one granted access. Less frequently, an organization may contact the researcher in the hopes of getting some data analyzed. For Hoey and Stokoe (2018), a university gave the researchers a set of telephone calls related to university admissions along with some specifications of what they wanted to discover.

2.3 "Classic" data

One distinctive research practice in CA is its long-standing reliance on a body of "classic" recordings made in the 1960s and 1970s. These were largely transcribed by Gail Jefferson, one of the founders of the discipline, and formed the basis for many seminal studies. There are a few reasons for this practice. First, the data are convenient. Using classic data precludes the need for the researcher to undertake the laborious work of recording and transcribing new interactions, because transcriptions of classic recordings already exist and are of reliably high quality. Additionally, because these recordings predate review boards, ethics approval is not needed to use them. Second, classic data are familiar within the CA research community. Many if not most CA practitioners know these materials, either from working with them directly or by encountering them repeatedly in papers, talks, and data sessions. They embody a kind of material culture for the discipline; not only are they well known, but particular snippets have become shorthand for particular phenomena. This familiarity contributes to CA's empirical rigor. Because classic recordings enjoy widespread recognition, analyses based on them may be more readily comprehended and consequently verified/contested. It is not uncommon for reviewers to cite these data as evidence for/against the claims in a given manuscript. And third, the data remain productive. Contemporary CA research continues to be informed by these materials some half a century later. As "living documents," these transcripts are routinely a source of

novel findings on their own (e.g., Holt 2017; Raymond, submitted) and also serve to corroborate analyses that are based on newer data (e.g., Clift 2014).

The practice of relying on classic data is not unproblematic, however. From a less flattering perspective, use of these data can inhibit scientific development and exclude particular groups. An immediately recognizable problem is that they capture social interactions between English-speakers in the 1960s and 1970s. Ethnographic and emic understandings of these settings may be less evident to younger generations of scholars. Relatedly, the practice contributes to an English-language bias in CA. While this is a natural consequence of CA's historical emergence (anglophones analyzing English data), it may unduly inform what questions we ask and where we look for answers and inspiration (see Raymond, submitted). Perhaps most perniciously, such anglocentrism can have an exclusionary effect. Papers using English data will be read/cited more than ones focusing on other languages. Another way that the practice may exclude is related to the communal familiarity of classic data. The extensive use of those sources and their cultural importance for the discipline produces the appearance of communal ownership—that everyone has these recordings and transcripts. This, however, is belied by the fact that access to the classic data is not equal, but tends to be confined to those with connections to CA's historical centers of gravity such as the University of California's Santa Barbara and Los Angeles campuses.

In short, classic recordings and transcripts are not merely the materials out of which we fashion our findings. Perhaps that is what they were at the time of recording, but today they also stand as objects that mediate professional relationships and shape disciplinary culture.

2.4 New data

Researchers also commonly make their own recordings, especially for PhD projects and grant-funded research. A major advantage to this is that the researcher gains greater ethnographic understanding of the examined activities. By contrast, relying on existing recordings necessarily means that some contextual details will remain unknown, for example, relevant off-camera occurrences, aspects of participants' relationships and histories, or participants' idiosyncratic conduct. The next section addresses the process of collecting new data.

3 Data collection

3.1 Preparation

Regarding what to record, any social situation is theoretically of interest since it is assumed that every social activity exhibits "order at all points" (Sacks 1984). The selection of a particular activity will be guided by some combination of access conditions, legal and ethical considerations, institutional requirements, and researcher interests, resources, and abilities.

A prerequisite to recording is gaining access to a setting of interest and developing some ethnographic understanding of its constitutive activities. This understanding of your research site—whether mundane or institutional—will inform the data collection process later on in terms of best recording conditions, placement of recording devices, and so forth. For institutional settings (Heritage & Clayman 2010), it is essential to understand the distinct participatory roles and the division of labor that give coherence to institutional activities. For crosslinguistic and cross-cultural projects, it is helpful to identify comparable contexts before recording. Enfield et al. (2007:97) refer to "maximally informal speech events" with minimal "structural constraints" (see Drew & Heritage 1992), offering as an example "the kind of verbal activity characterizing same-sex teenagers of the same hamlet in an idle moment."

In getting acquainted with your site of interest, you should talk with the participants whose activities you want to document. The aim of this is more than just securing formal consent; you want to ensure that participants understand what you will do and how you will use the recordings. Heath, Hindmarsh, and Luff (2010:17) suggest that participants are often willing to cooperate if you address the following: (i) the analytic necessity of recording; (ii) invasiveness of the recording equipment; (iii) commitment that the data will only be used for research and/or teaching; (iv) restricting data access; and (v) assurance that the data will not appear online, be broadcast, or used for commercial gain.

Ethical, legal, and organizational considerations are manifold, and different administrative locales, review boards, and funding agencies may have different requirements, so it is important that these inform the design of your research from the start (see Kung, chapter 8, this volume). Here are some basic considerations (n.b., these often also apply when using existing data):

- How will you brief participants when obtaining informed consent (see Holton, Leonard, & Pulsifer, chapter 4, this volume; Miller et al. 2012)? This is relevant when working with those who may not be able to give full informed consent, such as children or people with severe disabilities, or when obtaining individual consent is impractical, such as recording in busy public spaces.

- What is your plan if participants do something that may redound negatively on them? In the extreme case, you may be required to report illegal acts. In less severe cases, participants may gossip or talk in ways that are considered discriminatory or hateful. Even if "obviously" uttered in jest or irony, ethics boards will be concerned with your plan for such situations.

- How will you protect participants' confidentiality? Specify the range of sensitive objects (names, faces, logos), methods of protection (blurring, illustration, deletion), and circumstances for their use (talk/lecture, poster/slides, publication/blog).

- How will the data be kept and maintained (see Kung, chapter 8, this volume)? Consider the interrelated issues of storage medium (spinning disk hard drive, solid state flash drive), storage location (personal hard drive, institutional repository, commercial cloud service), file format (proprietary, open standard), security (encryption, password, physical lock and key), backup (number of copies, method, and frequency), and duration of retention. Ethics boards may suggest destroying recordings after a specified time. We recommend resisting such terms if possible and finding alternative means to satisfy ethics requirements without losing the data altogether.

- How will you handle access and ownership? Develop procedures for granting/declining requests from organizations, researchers, and the participants themselves; for apprising those with access of original agreements made with the participants; and for tracking who has what once you begin granting access.

3.2 Recording

In recording, the aim is to preserve the temporality, sequentiality, and ecology of the participants' activities.[6] For face-to-face interaction, video data are preferred over audio-only data. For non–face-to-face interaction (e.g., telephone, radio) audio-only data are acceptable.

Different options exist for automatically recording incoming/outgoing calls and creating audio files from radio broadcasts (see Raymond 2020).

For video, first consider what perspective(s) to capture. This should be informed by your analysis of what will best preserve the details of participants' conduct in their activity. When setting up, delimit the field so that all participants are in view. Resist privileging "active" participants over seemingly idle ones (e.g., teachers over students). Additionally, avoid directorial moves (zooming in/out, panning, following, and such) in general; using multiple recording devices usually mitigates the need for such movements. The camera(s) should also capture the participants' sites of focus (manual action, one another, a screen, and so on). For some studies, you may need to closely document material objects—such as institutional forms or records (e.g., Maynard, Freese, & Schaeffer 2010) or particular tools or technological interfaces (e.g., Heath & Luff 2000)—as these can impact participants' conduct and thus may become analytically relevant.

Regarding recording equipment and accessories, consider the affordances of the setting and activity. Stationary activities in spacious, quiet, well-lit spaces generally afford multiple cameras, tripods with large footprints, and table-top microphones. By contrast, circumstances involving mobile activities, restricted spaces, and limited visibility/audibility may require equipment adapted to such settings, such as cameras with vibration compensation, flexible "GorillaPod" tripods, lapel microphones, body cameras, wind dampeners, and so forth. These choices also intersect with analytic interests. Analyses of, for instance, phonetic detail, precise sites of gaze fixation, and computer-intensive interactions favor the use of high-quality microphones (Local & Walker 2005), eye-tracking glasses (Holler & Kendrick 2015), and screen capture software (Brown, McGregor, & Laurier 2013), respectively.

For your recording devices, you must also select technical settings. In general, we recommend recording in lossless formats (e.g., .wav) over lossy/compressed (e.g., .mp3), even though this requires more storage space and more frequently swapping out storage media. We also recommend open standard file types over proprietary ones, as these maximize future usability. During data processing, you can always convert to other formats for practical purposes. That said, it is fairly standard in CA to use QuickTime 7 Pro, which uses .wav and .mov formats and offers various listening and editing features (e.g., selecting, cropping) that subsequent versions lack. While Apple unfortunately no longer supports QuickTime 7, it remains downloadable.[7]

3.3 Data processing

If collecting data over several sessions, combine data collection with data processing (see Mattern, chapter 5, this volume). Establish a routine procedure after every session. This minimally involves transferring data from your recording devices to digital storage, checking for problems (e.g., was sound properly recorded), noting any needed modifications for the next session, and immediately creating backups. Keep the original files unconverted/uncompressed so they may be recovered in the event of data loss. It is helpful to label the folder something like "originals_DO_NOT_TOUCH." You will probably be renaming the files at this time, too. Devise a straightforward, consistent system for naming and file organization and describe that system in a text file. Create an index/spreadsheet of the data you have collected, identifying the date, time, place, activity, participants, pseudonyms, and other relevant metadata. Do not assume that you will be able to recall this information later or recover it from watching/listening to the data; you will be surprised at how much and how quickly you forget.

Postproduction is often required to get your data into a workable format (see Han, chapter 6, this volume). The originals are usually bulky, unplayable, and/or distributed across different files. Postproduction may involve some combination of file compression, conversion, and synchronization. Software such as Adobe Premiere,[8] Final Cut Pro,[9] and HandBrake[10] are commonly used for these purposes, and differ in terms of price and capability.

Once you have some workable audio/video files, the next step is usually transcription. Because this is more of an analytic activity than preanalytic, we describe it in the following section.

4 Analysis

4.1 Transcription

Transcription is one of the most flexible stages in CA research (see Mondada 2007), because different forms of transcripts are used at different points (data processing, data exploration, targeted analysis, coding, and publication/presentation). The main variable is the level of detail put into a transcript. This is inescapably an analytic activity. Because additional details can always be added, the inclusion/exclusion of any one is theoretically motivated (see Ochs 1979). The analytic issue is empirically determining the forms of conduct that participants treat as (potentially) *relevant* for the interaction (see Mondada 2018).

CA transcripts follow Gail Jefferson's conventions for verbal/vocal behavior (Jefferson 2004; Hepburn & Bolden 2017), which seek to capture not only phonetic/prosodic features of conversational speech, but also vocalizations that are typically viewed as marginal (e.g., disfluencies, sniffs, mouth-parting clicks) as well as the duration and precise location of silences. For visible/bodily behavior, Lorenza Mondada's conventions (2016b, 2018) are now widely used. Most analysts transcribe through repeated listening, sometimes aided by transcription software (e.g., Transana,[11] Computerized Language ANalysis [CLAN],[12] ELAN[13]). Transcription services are rarely used because they tend to be costly, insufficiently granular, and orthographically prescriptive. Additionally, the act/practice of transcribing is valuable because it incorporates analyses of turn-taking and other phenomena, which often aids in the germination of ideas (see Bolden 2015).

A word-for-word transcript, while permitting, for example, text searches and a basic grasp of what's happening, would be insufficient for CA research. Minimally, CA transcripts include timed silences and the precise placement of overlaps (see Roberts & Robinson 2004). More fully developed transcripts would show, among other things, prosodic details (intonation, rhythm, voice quality, intensity), pronunciational particularities, all manner of non-lexical sounds, morpheme-by-morpheme glosses, idiomatic translations, and relevant visible behavior, perhaps including images. New transcription conventions can be invented as necessary to capture certain phenomena as well—such as for crying (Hepburn 2004) or sighing (Hoey 2014).

Detailed transcripts would be used, for instance, in data sessions (see section 4.2), where such details are commonly part of developing ideas and arguments about the data. Somewhere between a more minimally and a more maximally detailed transcript are those made for presentation/publication. These transcripts often retain a fair amount of detail, but dispense with those that are not crucial for the argument being made or for comprehension of the data, decisions which may also be influenced by a publication's disciplinary interests or editorial

style. Transcripts made by another conversation analyst, while usually reliable enough, should be retranscribed as a precaution, especially for analysis and presentation/publication. Retranscription is also necessary to convert transcripts made with different conventions (e.g., CallFriend on TalkBank) into Jeffersonian-style transcripts.

4.2 Analysis

Analysis in CA characteristically begins with an observation about some concrete occurrence in a piece of data, followed by the collection and curation of various cases related to that observation.[14] The initial step of noticing often originates from what is known as *unmotivated looking*, wherein "the investigator as much as possible puts aside or brackets assumptions about how a domain of human action does or could operate," endeavoring instead to focus on whatever "phenomena that interaction itself presents" (Maynard 2013:18)—in other words, an altogether inductive approach. While this approach aligns closely with CA's distinctive analytic mentality, and may be especially fruitful in initial explorations, researchers can also be informed by prior work and guided by specific analytic interests (Clayman & Gill 2004:596–597).

Initial observations frequently originate in *data sessions*, where expert and novice CA practitioners gather to examine fragment(s) of data together. The data session is as much a method of developing analytic skills as it is a pedagogical exercise (Stevanovic & Weiste 2017), a form of live, informal peer review (Albert & de Ruiter 2018), and an arena for data exploration. Data sessions can also be seen as hypothesis-generating exercises. One or two observations in a data session can be used to form hypotheses that researchers can then assess by collecting additional cases afterward.

The main analytic objects in CA research are *cases* and *collections*. A case is an observation and analysis of a particular part of a transcript/recording. Cases are gathered across various recordings in the process of building a *collection* of cases. An intermediate step that targets all *candidate* cases may be relevant in assembling a collection. In investigating the syntactic and prosodic realization of "modular pivots,"[15] for instance, Clayman and Raymond (2015) first identified possible *candidate* cases based on syntactic criteria (clearly visible in transcripts), and then each candidate instance was subjected to auditory/acoustic analysis to determine whether its phonetic/prosodic packaging qualified it for inclusion in the core collection of "true" modular pivots. This serves as a reminder that transcripts, while clearly essential in analyses of data, should always be used in conjunction with—and not as a substitute for—the actual recordings themselves.

The assembly and organization of cases into various collections is the primary analytic activity of CA research (see Clift & Raymond 2018; Hoey & Kendrick 2018). Most researchers use some combination of text documents, folders, and spreadsheets in organizing various transcripts, (clips of) recordings, (sub)collections, lists, outlines, analytic observations, and manuscript drafts (White 2018). Spreadsheets are especially useful when dealing with numerous cases: They provide for a synoptic view of the collection(s), sorting/filtering/ordering cases along various features of interest, and coding and basic quantification (see Stivers 2015). This process is often supplemented or aided through various software programs for analytic activities such as mind-mapping (NVivo[16]), phonetic analysis and manipulation (Audacity,[17] Praat[18]), annotation (ELAN), and statistical analysis (RStudio[19]).

Sometimes collection building is done with students and/or research assistants. This is feasible for phenomena that are fairly frequent and easy to spot. For example, lexical items such as turn-initial particles (e.g., English *oh, well*; Finnish *siis, eli(kkä)*; Heritage & Sorjonen 2018) or reference forms (e.g., Enfield 2007; Fox 1987; Raymond 2016), morphosyntactic practices such as clausal markers (Ford & Mori 1994) or *do*-constructions (Raymond 2017), and embodied behaviors such as taking a drink (Hoey 2018), can be found in casual scanning of transcripts and recordings. Other phenomena, however, such as "fourth-position repair"[20] (Schegloff 1992), are relatively rare, which increases the time needed for collection, and/or are structurally more complicated, which means they may evade the notice of inexperienced analysts.

5   Distribution

5.1   Presentation

The data that are presented at scientific meetings, in academic publications, and other research outlets typically take the form of transcripts, sometimes accompanied by still images and audio/video clips. Regarding anonymization of these data, participants' consent forms and general ethical guidelines should be followed. For transcripts, identifying information such as the names of people, places, and employers is almost always pseudonymized.

For audio, software such as Audacity may be used to obscure (pitch shift, reverse, or otherwise garble) individual words/phrases. For images, it is common to blur or pixelate faces or logos (using, e.g., Adobe Photoshop[21]). A higher level of protection can be gained by graphically reproducing an image as a sketch or line drawing, either manually or automatically through programs such as AKVIS Sketch.[22] Anonymizing video recordings is more complicated because every frame must be edited, but it is possible (see Heath, Hindmarsh, & Luff 2010). When especially sensitive data are shown (e.g., police interviewing children suspected of abuse; Fogarty, Augoustinos, & Kettler 2013), presenters should take greater care to protect the participants by, for example, requesting that transcripts be returned after the talk, and/or that no pictures be taken or posted on social media.

Practices surrounding the citation of data sources (see Conzett & De Smedt, chapter 11, this volume) are not quite standardized in CA, but some conventions have emerged. This is clearest when the data do not belong to the researcher. In this case, an acknowledgment may appear in a footnote/endnote, such as, "I am grateful to Candy and Chuck Goodwin for allowing the use of the tapes and the accompanying transcripts I have used for this article" (Fox 1999:58). The body of the paper often has a basic description of the data specifying the activity recorded, setting, corpus/collection size, and how the data were collected. For example, "The database consists of 30 videotaped conversations with aphasic Finnish speakers collected by Minna Laakso in speech therapy sessions and at home" (Helasvuo 2004:5). If no specific entity is named as the data collector, it is usually assumed that the data are drawn from a body of semicommunal classic data (see section 2.3) or some other corpus of everyday/mundane conversation. For instance, "[the data come from] transcribed telephone conversations recorded in both Britain and America" (Holt & Drew 2005:39).

Apart from prosaic descriptions of data sources, transcript titles may also disclose identifying information. Some titles specify a great deal about the recording, such as "Holt:X(C)85:1:1:1:6" (Holt & Drew 2005:36), which, while opaque to the outsider, refers to the corpus collected by Elizabeth Holt, recordings from Christmastime of 1985, tape 1 of those recordings, side 1 of that tape, call 1 from that side, and transcript page number or page range. This level of detail tends to be the exception, however. More commonly, transcript titles are informative only to the researcher who collected the data, such as "RCE25, 21:48" (Hoey 2015:445), which references a file that the researcher has access to and a time stamp within that recording. Even less informative are titles such as "extract 3," which only make sense within the context of that article. When a data extract is taken from an already published paper, a regular in-text citation is given, for example, "Example (29) from Sacks et al. (1974:733)" (Lindström 2006:83).

5.2 Sharing and accessibility

CA is a research tradition whose approach to data is grounded in empiricism and transparency. We have already mentioned some forms of data sharing and accessibility in CA. There is the widespread practice of researcher-to-researcher data sharing, especially classic data. Researchers already make use of published transcripts as if they were public, usable, and freely reproducible, and many corpora and transcripts are available for download in online databases. Intertwined with these practices is the presentation of data extracts in the form of transcripts, images, and clips of recordings in papers and presentations. Though not substitutes for full access to the data, these make the data sufficiently available so that others may check—and, in principle, replicate—an analysis. Indeed, the use of detailed transcription conventions is in part directed toward closing the gap between those with access to the data and those without.

Technological advancements in the digitization of recordings and international telecommunications infrastructure have opened up new possibilities for CA research. Transcripts may be supplemented by the recordings themselves. Notably, Emanuel Schegloff, one of the most important figures in CA, has endeavored to make available on his web site all the clips he has analyzed in his publications. More recently, a new journal *Social Interaction: Video-based Studies of Human Sociality* was created in part to allow video data to accompany its papers.

CA's historical record offers a strong foundation for further progress to be made in the archiving, accessing, and sharing data. Specifically, we believe that the CA community would be open to creating an institutionalized repository for recorded materials and transcripts and a protocol for archiving data in that repository. We support efforts by professional bodies such as the International Society for Conversation Analysis for undertaking such an endeavor, as they have the representation, visibility, and membership fees to support it.

The promotion of open science in this way would serve several needs. First, while there is the sense that "everyone" has access to certain classic recordings, their actual distribution is unequal, with potentially exclusionary effects. Archiving these classic recordings in the repository and making them available would do much to resolve this tension. Second, while some organizations provide their researchers with the resources to responsibly archive, maintain, and share their materials, not all do. The repository and protocol would address this lack. Those who wish to put up the recordings for their papers may do so—both for those papers already published and those that are forthcoming. Complete data sets could also be added for research and teaching purposes. Particularly for languages that are underrepresented in CA research, a communal database would offer enhanced opportunities for research and collaboration, which would both address the field's current English-language bias, as well as facilitate crosslinguistic, cross-cultural studies. Finally, researchers would be able to rely on an institutionally legitimated archive and its procedures in specifying and justifying plans for data collection/management, which would aid in the production of things such as grant applications, research proposals, and ethics permissions.

Acknowledgments

We are grateful to Liz Holt and Lorenza Mondada for their input on prior versions of this chapter.

Notes

1. https://ca.talkbank.org/.

2. https://samtalebank.talkbank.org/.

3. http://www.sfsu.edu/~lsi/.

4. https://data.bris.ac.uk/data/dataset/l3sq4s0w66ln1x20sye7s47wv.

5. http://agd.ids-mannheim.de/folk.shtml.

6. For further reading on technical and practical aspects of video recording (equipment, technical specifications, framing, placement, and such), see, e.g., Derry et al. (2010); Heath, Hindmarsh, and Luff (2010); Luff and Heath (2012); and Mondada (2013).

7. https://support.apple.com/kb/DL923.

8. https://www.adobe.com/products/premiere.html.

9. https://www.apple.com/final-cut-pro/.

10. https://handbrake.fr/.

11. https://www.transana.com/.

12. https://talkbank.org/software/.

13. https://tla.mpi.nl/tools/tla-tools/elan/.

14. For in-depth discussions and practical guides to the analytic process in CA, see Heritage (2011), Sidnell (2013), Clift and Raymond (2018), and Hoey and Kendrick (2018).

15. Something like the address term *Jen* in the following sentence acts as a "modular pivot" between the potential ending of one turn and the contingent beginning of the next: *You don't look it Jen I must be honest* (Clayman & Raymond 2015:391).

16. https://www.qsrinternational.com/nvivo/home.

17. https://sourceforge.net/projects/audacity/.

18. http://www.fon.hum.uva.nl/praat/.

19. https://www.rstudio.com/.

20. Schegloff (1992:1321) provides the following instance of fourth position repair (line 4):

01	Marty:	Loes, do you have a calendar,
02	Loes:	Yeah ((reaches for her desk calendar))
03	Marty:	Do you have one that hangs on the wall?
04	Loes:	Oh, you <u>want</u> one.
05	Marty:	Yeah

21. https://www.adobe.com/products/photoshop.html.

22. http://akvis.com/en/sketch/index.php.

References

Albert, Saul, and Jan Peter de Ruiter. 2018. Improving human interaction research through ecological grounding. *Collabra: Psychology* 4 (1): 24.

Bolden, Galina. 2015. Transcribing as research: "Manual" transcription and conversation analysis. *Research on Language and Social Interaction* 48 (3): 276–280.

Broth, Mathias, Eric Laurier, and Lorenza Mondada, eds. 2014. *Studies of Video Practices: Video at Work*. London: Routledge.

Brown, Barry, Moira McGregor, and Eric Laurier. 2013. iPhone in vivo: Video analysis of mobile device use. In *Proceedings of the SIGCHI Conference on Human Factors in Computing Systems*, 1031–1040. Philadelphia: Association for Computing Machinery.

Clayman, Steven, and Virginia Gill. 2004. Conversation analysis. In *Handbook of Data Analysis*, ed. Alan Byman and Melissa Hardy, 589–606. Beverly Hills: Sage.

Clayman, Steven, and Chase Wesley Raymond. 2015. Modular pivots: A resource for extending turns at talk. *Research on Language and Social Interaction* 48 (4): 388–405.

Clift, Rebecca. 2014. Visible deflation: Embodiment and emotion in interaction. *Research on Language and Social Interaction* 47 (4): 380–403.

Clift, Rebecca. 2016. *Conversation Analysis*. Cambridge: Cambridge University Press.

Clift, Rebecca, and Chase Wesley Raymond. 2018. Actions in practice: On details in collections. *Discourse Studies* 20 (1): 90–119.

Derry, Sharon J., Roy D. Pea, Brigid Barron, Randi A. Engle, Frederick Erickson, Ricki Goldman, Rogers Hall, et al. 2010. Conducting video research in the learning sciences: Guidance on selection, analysis, technology, and ethics. *Journal of the Learning Sciences* 19 (1): 3–53.

Drew, Paul, and John Heritage, eds. 1992. *Talk at Work: Language Use in Institutional and Work-Place Settings*. Cambridge: Cambridge University Press.

Enfield, Nick J. 2007. Meanings of the unmarked: How "default" person reference does more than just refer. In *Person Reference in Interaction: Linguistic, Cultural and Social Perspectives*, ed. Nick J. Enfield and Tanya Stivers, 97–120. Cambridge: Cambridge University Press.

Enfield, Nick J., Stephen C. Levinson, Jan Peter de Ruiter, and Tanya Stivers. 2007. Building a corpus of multimodal interaction in your field site. In *Field Manual Volume 10*, ed. Asifa Majid, 96–99. Nijmegen, the Netherlands: Max Planck Institute for Psycholinguistics.

Fogarty, Kathryn, Martha Augoustinos, and Lisa Kettler. 2013. Re-thinking rapport through the lens of progressivity in investigative interviews into child sexual abuse. *Discourse Studies* 15 (4): 395–420.

Ford, Cecilia, and Junko Mori. 1994. Causal markers in Japanese and English conversations: A cross-linguistic study of interactional grammar. *Pragmatics* 4 (1): 31–61.

Fox, Barbara. 1987. *Discourse Structure and Anaphora: Written and Conversational English*. Cambridge: Cambridge University Press.

Fox, Barbara. 1999. Directions in research: Language and the body. *Research on Language and Social Interaction* 32 (1–2): 51–59.

Heath, Christian, Jon Hindmarsh, and Paul Luff. 2010. *Video in Qualitative Research*. London: Sage Publications.

Heath, Christian, and Paul Luff. 2000. *Technology in Action*. Cambridge: Cambridge University Press.

Helasvuo, Marja-Liisa. 2004. Searching for words: Syntactic and sequential construction of word search in conversations of Finnish speakers with aphasia. *Research on Language and Social Interaction* 37 (1): 1–37.

Hepburn, Alexa. 2004. Crying: Notes on description, transcription and interaction. *Research on Language and Social Interaction* 37:251–290.

Hepburn, Alexa, and Galina Bolden. 2017. *Transcribing for Social Research*. Thousand Oaks, CA: Sage.

Heritage, John. 2011. Conversation analysis: Practices and methods. In *Qualitative Research*, ed. David Silverman, 208–230. London: Sage.

Heritage, John, and Steven Clayman. 2010. *Talk in Action: Interactions, Identities, and Institutions*. Oxford: Blackwell-Wiley.

Heritage, John, and Marja-Leena Sorjonen. 2018. *Between Turn and Sequence: Turn-Initial Particles across Languages*. Amsterdam: John Benjamins.

Hoey, Elliott M. 2014. Sighing in interaction: Somatic, semiotic, and social. *Research on Language and Social Interaction* 47 (2): 175–200.

Hoey, Elliott M. 2015. Lapses: How people arrive at, and deal with, discontinuities in talk. *Research on Language and Social Interaction* 48 (4): 430–453.

Hoey, Elliott M. 2018. Drinking for speaking: The multimodal organization of drinking in conversation. *Social Interaction: Video-Based Studies of Human Sociality* 1 (1). https://doi.org/10.7146/si .v1i1.105498.

Hoey, Elliott M., and Kobin H. Kendrick. 2018. Conversation analysis. In *Research Methods in Psycholinguistics and the Neurobiology of Language: A Practical Guide*, ed. Annette M. B. de Groot and Peter Hagoort, 151–173. Hoboken, NJ: Wiley and Sons.

Hoey, Elliott M., and Elizabeth Stokoe. 2018. Eligibility and bad news delivery: How call-takers reject applicants to university. *Linguistics and Education* 46:91–101.

Holler, Judith, and Kobin H. Kendrick. 2015. Unaddressed participants' gaze in multi-person interaction: Optimizing recipiency. *Frontiers in Psychology* 6:article 98.

Holt, Elizabeth. 2017. Indirect reported speech in storytelling: Its position, design, and uses. *Research on Language and Social Interaction* 50 (2): 171–187.

Holt, Elizabeth, and Paul Drew. 2005. Figurative pivots: The use of figurative expressions in pivotal topic transitions. *Research on Language and Social Interaction* 38 (1): 35–61.

Jefferson, Gail. 1985. An exercise in the transcription and analysis of laughter. In *Handbook of Discourse Analysis*, vol. 3, ed. Teun A. Van Dijk, 25–34. New York: Academic Press.

Jefferson, Gail. 2004. Glossary of transcript symbols with an introduction. In *Conversation Analysis: Studies from the First Generation*, ed. Gene H. Lerner, 13–31. Amsterdam: John Benjamins.

Jones, Nikki, and Geoffrey Raymond. 2012. "The camera rolls": Using third-party video in field research. *Annals of the American Academy of Political and Social Science* 642 (1): 109–123.

Lindström, Jan. 2006. Grammar in the service of interaction: Exploring turn organization in Swedish. *Research on Language and Social Interaction* 39 (1): 81–117.

Local, John, and Gareth Walker. 2005. Methodological imperatives for investigating the phonetic organization and phonological structures of spontaneous speech. *Phonetica* 62 (2–4): 120–130.

Luff, Paul, and Christian Heath. 2012. Some "technical challenges" of video analysis: Social actions, objects, material realities and the problems of perspective. *Qualitative Research* 12 (3): 255–279.

MacWhinney, Brian. 2007. The Talkbank Project. In *Creating and Digitizing Language Corpora*, ed. Joan C. Beal, Karen P. Corrigan, and Hermann L. Moisl, 163–180. London: Palgrave Macmillan.

Maynard, Douglas W. 2013. Everyone and no one to turn to: Intellectual roots and contexts for Conversation Analysis. In *Handbook of Conversation Analysis*, ed. Jack Sidnell and Tanya Stivers, 12–31. Malden, MA: Wiley-Blackwell.

Maynard, Douglas W., Jeremy Freese, and Nora C. Schaeffer. 2010. Calling for participation: Requests, blocking moves, and rational (inter)action in survey introductions. *American Sociological Review* 75 (5): 791–814.

Miller, Tina, Melanie Birch, Maxine Mauthner, and Julie Jessop, eds. 2012. *Ethics in Qualitative Research*. London: Sage.

Mondada, Lorenza. 2007. Commentary: Transcript variations and the indexicality of transcribing practices. *Discourse Studies* 9 (6): 809–821.

Mondada, Lorenza. 2013. The conversation analytic approach to data collection. In *Handbook of Conversation Analysis*, ed. Jack Sidnell and Tanya Stivers, 32–56. Malden, MA: Wiley-Blackwell.

Mondada, Lorenza. 2016a. Challenges of multimodality: Language and the body in social interaction. *Journal of Sociolinguistics* 20 (3): 336–366.

Mondada, Lorenza. 2016b. Conventions for multimodal transcription. https://franzoesistik.philhist.unibas.ch/fileadmin /user_upload/franzoesistik/mondada_multimodal_conventions .pdf. Accessed December 24, 2018.

Mondada, Lorenza. 2018. Multiple temporalities of language and body in interaction: Challenges for transcribing multimodality. *Research on Language and Social Interaction* 51 (1): 85–106.

Ochs, Elinor. 1979. Transcription as theory. In *Developmental Pragmatics*, ed. Elinor Ochs and Bambi Schieffelin, 43–72. New York: Academic Press.

Raymond, Chase Wesley. 2014. Entitlement to language: Calling 911 without English. *Language in Society* 43 (1): 33–59.

Raymond, Chase Wesley. 2016. Linguistic reference in the negotiation of identity and action: Revisiting the T/V distinction. *Language* 92 (3): 636–670.

Raymond, Chase Wesley. 2017. Indexing a contrast: The *do-*construction in English conversation. *Journal of Pragmatics* 118:22–37.

Raymond, Chase Wesley. 2020. Negotiating language on the radio in Los Angeles. In *Spanish in the Global City*, ed. A. Lynch, 406–229. New York: Routledge.

Raymond, Chase Wesley. 2021. Tense and aspect in sequences of action. Unpublished manuscript.

Roberts, Felicia, and Jeffrey D. Robinson. 2004. Inter-observer agreement on "first-stage" conversation analytic transcription. *Human Communication Research* 30:376–410.

Sacks, Harvey. 1984. Notes on methodology. In *Structures of Social Action: Studies in Conversation Analysis*, ed. J. Maxwell. Atkinson & John Heritage, 21–27. Cambridge: Cambridge University Press.

Sacks, Harvey, Emanuel A. Schegloff, and Gail Jefferson. 1974. A simplest systematics for the organization of turn-taking for conversation. *Language* 50:696–735.

Schegloff, Emanuel A. 1992. Repair after next turn: The last structurally provided defense of intersubjectivity in conversation. *American Journal of Sociology* 97 (5): 1295–1345.

Schegloff, Emanuel A., Gail Jefferson, and Harvey Sacks. 1977. The preference for self-correction in the organization of repair in conversation. *Language* 53 (2): 361–382.

Sidnell, Jack. 2013. Basic conversation analytic methods. In *Handbook of Conversation Analysis*, ed. Jack Sidnell and Tanya Stivers, 75–99. Malden, MA: Wiley-Blackwell.

Sidnell, Jack, and Tanya Stivers, eds. 2013. *The Handbook of Conversation Analysis*. Malden, MA: Wiley-Blackwell.

Speer, Susan A. 2002. "Natural" and "contrived" data: A sustainable distinction? *Discourse Studies* 4 (4): 511–525.

Stevanovic, Melisa, and Elina Weiste. 2017. Conversation-analytic data session as a pedagogical institution. *Learning, Culture and Social Interaction* 15:1–17.

Stivers, Tanya. 2015. Coding social interaction: A heretical approach in conversation analysis? *Research on Language and Social Interaction* 48 (1): 1–19.

White, Sarah J. 2018. Guest blog: A survey of CA craft skills. *Research on Language and Social Interaction—Blog*. June 18, 2018. https://rolsi.net/2018/06/18/guest-blog-a-survey-of-ca-craft -skills/#more-4906.

21 Managing Sign Language Data from Fieldwork

Nick Palfreyman

1 Introduction: Fieldwork on sign languages in the global South

Language documentation has become increasingly important as a paradigm in linguistic research (Austin 2016), and this is as true for signed languages as for spoken ones. For sign language documentation, however, some of the issues that fall under the heading of data management are rarely discussed and almost never written about (Schembri 2019). Accounts of sign language data invariably jump from collection methods to transcription, annotation, and analysis without stopping for long, if at all, to explain how data are processed, stored, or shared (see, e.g., contributions to Pfau, Steinbach, & Woll 2012; Orfanidou, Woll, & Morgan 2015). The lack of attention to these issues has become ever more conspicuous with the steady growth of literature on sign language documentation and ethics (Fischer 2009; Dikyuva et al. 2012; Kusters 2012, 2015; Nyst 2015; Hou 2017; Hochgesang & Palfreyman forthcoming).

Among a few notable exceptions is the special issue of *Sign Language and Linguistics* (Bergman et al. 2001), which deals with database storage of sign information as well as sign transcription, but naturally some of the details therein have become obsolete over the intervening years. Indeed, most of those documenting sign languages in the field in 2001 were still rewinding and fast-forwarding their way through video cassette tapes or recording signs using notation systems.[1] For the large part, researchers had nothing resembling the multimedia tools or dedicated multitier coding and annotation software that is now in common use. My own earliest experiences of data collection (2010–2011) entailed capturing conversational data onto video cassette tapes—a fact requiring some explanation to the latest generation of researchers familiar only with digital technology.

This case study outlines issues related to processing, storing, sharing, and citing data reported in the literature on sign language documentation. I also draw on my own experience documenting Indonesian Sign Language (BISINDO) from 2010 onward and share a few of the mistakes that I have made along the way. There is some overlap with Crasborn (chapter 39, this volume), but the discussion of data management here reflects some of the particular challenges of being based in the United Kingdom while conducting fieldwork in what is termed the "global South."

2 Sign language documentation and corpora

2.1 Local and distant language documentation

When considering the management of sign language data, it is helpful to make a distinction between two types of documentation that have emerged in sign language research. The first type, which I refer to as *local documentation*, is conducted by researchers based in or near to the community where the sign language is used (Nyst 2015:108), and most of the sign language corpora to have emerged so far fall into this type. Examples include the Auslan (Australian Sign Language) corpus (Johnston 2008), the British Sign Language (BSL) corpus (Schembri et al. 2011), the Corpus NGT (Sign Language of the Netherlands) (Crasborn, Zwitserlood, & Ros 2008), the Corpus Project of Finland's sign languages (Salonen et al. 2016) and the PJM (Polish Sign Language) corpus (Rutkowski et al. 2013).[2]

These corpora usually contain data collected in several regions, but often in relatively controlled environments such as universities and deaf organizations that generate comprehensive records, with good lighting, multiple cameras filming at different angles, and so on (Perniss 2015). Most if not all of these corpora have research teams that include or are even led by deaf members. The process of liaising with the community is possible because networks are strong, while the community's leaders and at least some of its members are aware of what research is taking place and how it might be important.

The second type, which I refer to as *distant documentation*, is conducted by researchers in countries other than their own and resembles more traditional notions of fieldwork. Linguists of this type have typically been from the global North, documenting sign languages used in non-WEIRD[3] countries of the global South—including Adamorobe Sign Language (Nyst 2012), BISINDO (Palfreyman 2013, 2016, 2019), Inuit Sign Language (Schuit 2013), Kata Kolok (de Vos 2012, 2016), Kenyan Sign Language (Morgan 2017), Malinese Sign Language (Nyst, Magassouba, & Sylla 2011) and San Juan Quiahije Chatino Sign Language (Hou 2016). They usually work with consultants and research assistants, who may need training on linguistics, data collection techniques, ethics, and literacy skills (Nyst 2015).

While the local-distant distinction is not clear-cut, the target language communities for each type are generally rather different. Members of deaf communities in the global South often have fewer resources and less access to education or communication technology for example (Nyst 2015), which might explain why these projects are often led, at least initially, by researchers from the global North. This has important consequences for data management because, as a result of these issues, many researchers have reservations about making data available to other researchers at all (see section 3).

2.2 Types of sign language corpora

A second useful distinction can be discerned in the literature from different emphases that are placed on the attributes of language corpora by researchers from different academic traditions: the first approach is associated with corpus linguists, while the second approach to the corpus is linked with those who identify as documentary linguists. The concerns of corpus linguistics are outlined by McEnery and Wilson (2001:14), who foreground the corpus as representative, finite, machine-readable, and a standard reference. The language documentation approach to the corpus is described by Woodbury (2011:181) using the terms *diverse, ongoing, distributed,* and *opportunistic,* following in the tradition of Franz Boas (Epps, Webster, & Woodbury 2017). Of course, the two approaches are not mutually exclusive, but the distinction is crucial, not least because those creating corpora do not always specify how their corpus relates to these approaches.

Much of the burgeoning work on sign language corpora arguably includes elements from both approaches. On the one hand, considerable effort has been expended on creating machine-readable corpora, with crosslinguistic glossing and annotation conventions emerging to support this (see section 6 for further details). On the other hand, almost all of the sign language corpora developed to date have drawn largely on data produced for the corpus, defying what has been described as a common practice in corpus linguistics of using existing examples of language rather than creating data for the purpose of linguistic analysis (Stubbs 2001:221; Cox 2011:250). One of the few studies that does use existing examples, available online, is described by Hou, Lepic, and Wilkinson (chapter 40, this volume), but paradoxically their corpus is opportunistic and not machine-readable.

2.3 The BISINDO corpus

BISINDO has been used since at least the 1950s (Palfreyman 2019:76), though the language was named in 2006 (from an acronym based on *Bahasa Isyarat Indonesia,* "Indonesian Sign Language") by Gerkatin, the Indonesian Association for the Welfare of the Deaf (Palfreyman 2019:288). The BISINDO corpus comprises nine hours of spontaneous conversational data from 131 participants in six different islands across Indonesia.

Retrospectively, data collection has occurred in two stages.[4] For the first stage (2010–2015), three hours of data were collected from Solo (Central Java) and Makassar (South Sulawesi) using funding obtained from an international non-governmental organization.[5] These data were collected primarily for a comparative study looking at the grammatical domains of completion and negation (Palfreyman 2015), but they were glossed and annotated with the intention of creating a corpus that could be used to answer other research questions.

The second stage (2016–2019) was conducted with funding obtained in 2016 from the Leverhulme Trust.[6] Six hours of data were collected from four locations: Padang (West Sumatra), Pontianak (West Borneo), Singaraja (Bali), and Ambon (Maluku). This was seen as highly desirable to increase geographical representativeness, and the corpus now has a much wider geographic scope.

The choice of field site was also motivated by a desire to reflect better the religious makeup of Indonesia—Pontianak has a high level of ethnic diversity, while the community in Singaraja is mostly Hindu. Singaraja is also the town nearest to the village where Kata Kolok, an unrelated sign language, is used (see section 8), enabling potentially valuable comparisons between a village sign language and the dominant sign language used in the surrounding province. Other considerations include a desire to collect data from places with a relatively long attested history of sign language use (deaf people from Padang were among the earliest from outside of Java to attend the first deaf school, set up in the Dutch East Indies), and the existence of a local community able to work with the researchers.

The BISINDO corpus is best described as an example of distant documentation (see section 2.1), albeit with the intention of moving corpus creation closer to local documentation in future (see section 5). As I mentioned, many sign language corpora encompass elements of both language documentation and corpus linguistics, and the BISINDO corpus is similar in this respect: the corpus is ongoing and opportunistic, with the aim of creating a diverse corpus that is also machine-readable.

3   Informed consent

Informed consent is not always obtained in written format, and researchers such as Austin (2010) have relied on oral consent from hearing people in many endangered indigenous communities. Likewise, for the BISINDO corpus, the conventional method for obtaining informed consent—an information sheet and a consent form—was not used, for three reasons. First, it was difficult to explain to the informants what they were consenting to before they had actually taken part in data collection, because they had no prior experience or understanding of the notion of "research." Second, handing out an information sheet saturated with text is oppressive and inappropriate for a community that has a low literacy rate. Third, an explanation of the research prior to the collection of data would have made it harder to obtain natural data, because this would have prompted unwarranted expectations on the part of informants regarding what was required of them (see Schembri 2008).

With these points in mind, informants who wished to take part were filmed first, and informed consent was obtained afterward, with explanation in sign language as to how the data would be used. This meant that participants now had a clearer understanding as to what they were consenting to. It was hard to explain about the right to withdraw data at a later stage because the informant had only just given consent for their data to be included, so the idea of withdrawal caused some confusion. I therefore informed local deaf community leaders that those who took part in the research could withdraw at any time if they later changed their mind, and that these leaders should let me know if anyone expressed any concerns about their involvement at any stage (Palfreyman 2019:114–115).

Having taken these steps, it is still not possible to say that optimally informed consent has been obtained from all of the participants. In our target communities, some deaf people have not been to school, while those who have been to school had little to no access to the language of instruction. Only a very small number of deaf Indonesians to date have been able to enter further and higher education institutions. While hearing people who have not been to university may be able to draw on general knowledge gleaned from information (over) heard on the radio, the television, or in conversation to understand what might be meant by "research," many deaf Indonesians do not have access to such knowledge.

Although a corpus may be compiled with the aim of linguistic analysis in mind, its participants are sharing their thoughts, stories, experiences, and feelings. Nathan (2011) notes that spontaneous, naturalistic speech "can easily include content that might cause embarrassment, or worse, for the speakers" (112) and cites examples of corpus conversations that reveal illegal activities or damaging statements about other community members. In the BISINDO corpus, there are moments where participants talk about distressing situations, sometimes appearing emotional as they recount what happened, and these can make for uncomfortable viewing. As researchers collecting a large amount of data, we did not observe conversations taking place—to reduce the effects of the observer's paradox—and we did not always have the opportunity to view the data ourselves for several weeks. As a result, we were sometimes not aware of the content of the data before leaving the field.

A longer amount of time in the field may have made it possible to take a different approach: for example, each participant could have been able to review their data and decide whether they should be permitted. This entails several assumptions, however; for example that each person has the time and inclination to review the data (which is not always the case). It also assumes that participants are able to make decisions based on the range of potential people who might see the data, how they might use them, and how they feel about such people using and viewing them, which is a big ask. As Crasborn (2010) implies, even seasoned researchers cannot know exactly how digital data will be used, especially given ongoing advances in data capacity.

Such caution is not restricted to signed languages (see Gawne & Styles, chapter 2, this volume); spoken language researchers also collect data from informants who may not have a full understanding of what is involved (Thieberger & Musgrave 2007:30–32). The notion of archiving texts that can be accessed via the Internet is not easily understood by people in remote locations with no access to computers. Nathan (2011) notes how those researching endangered languages may regard themselves as having "an ongoing custodial role" (118), controlling access on behalf of their informants.

Sign languages do not have a written tradition (see Crasborn, chapter 39, this volume), and it has been widely noted that video recording is essential when documenting visual-gestural languages (Wilcox 2003; Fischer 2009; Crasborn 2010). The use of space plays a critical role in sign language grammars (Perniss 2012), while facial expressions have important functions at different levels of linguistic organization—including grammar and prosody (Pfau & Quer 2010; Sandler 2012). Full anonymity may therefore seem an impossibility: if documentation efforts are not to lose their value, researchers must retain the faces of their signers, thus increasing the risks associated with making data more widely available (Hochgesang & Palfreyman forthcoming).

4   Responding to the challenge of anonymity

One of the affordances of language documentation is that other researchers can view the primary material on which linguistic analyses are based (Thieberger et al. 2015). There is tension between "formulating, implementing and maintaining access restrictions, and, on the other hand, making materials accessible to the right people for the right purposes" (Nathan 2011:113). In other words, it is important to protect against risks to participants while acknowledging the requirement to build and safeguard academic knowledge.

In response to this challenge, the model that Nathan (2011) proposes, which is based on the Endangered Languages Archive, would be suitable for sign languages. The protocol section allows for several options in terms of who can access corpus content:

- Anyone
- Certain people or groups
  - Research community members
  - Language community members
  - Certain named people or bodies
- Depositor is asked permission for each request
- Only the depositor has access
  (117)

These provide a means of "developing further ways for depositors and users to communicate; allowing users to contribute moderated content; and providing detailed reports to depositors detailing accesses of their materials." The aim of such an approach is to encourage a shift in how archives are perceived—as a "dynamic resource at the center of sharing and discussion" (9) rather than simply a set of files. Building up such a community is also a way to ensure that the records can be accessed by users of the language and their descendants (Thieberger et al. 2015).

Johnston (2016) explains how corpus data can be enriched according to the availability of time and resources, by input from successive researchers, who may make annotation passes with similar or different research questions in mind. This approach is used on the BSL corpus website (Schembri et al. 2014) that encourages applications from volunteers and researchers alike.

Another possible solution to the anonymity problem lies in sign language avatar technology, which is becoming ever more sophisticated as research brings together expertise on sign language linguistics, computational linguistics, computer animation, mathematics, and other fields. To date, most of this research focuses on translation between spoken or written texts and a signed language, which is challenging for many reasons (Kipp, Heloir, & Nguyen 2011). Relatively, it is much easier to use this technology simply to replicate text from a human signer on a signing avatar. The ability of avatars to replicate the nuance of sign language production has increased enormously over the past few years, and this creates considerable potential for revisiting the anonymity problem of sign language data.

If software can be programmed to identify manual and non-manual parameters and reconstruct data from signers in avatar form, in a way that captures hand configurations, spatial distinctions, and subtle facial movements such as blinks and eye gaze as well, it may then be possible to treat video data in a way that removes features that identify signers without damaging the precision of representation. Signers and speakers can also be identified by what they say, and content may require additional anonymization. But, as Crasborn (chapter 39, this volume) notes, it is highly likely that automated processing of videos will lead to the identification of phonetic features, and those collecting data should encourage those working on avatars to investigate the application of their work to these ends.

5 Collecting data with the community

There is a considerable literature on conducting research in ways that bring benefits to language communities (Wolfram 1993; Cameron 1998; Benedicto, Modesta, & McLean 2002; Grinevald 2003; Czaykowska-Higgins 2009), and it may be appropriate for researchers to correct erroneous ideas and misconceptions in the community (Labov 1982). Yet, as Nathan (2011:112–113) notes, "by most criteria, the increasing amount of documentation has in itself provided few positive outcomes for communities that want to maintain their languages, or for the evolution of a linguistics discipline that could help them to do so."

Austin (2010:36) draws attention to reciprocity: the researcher should contribute to the community in some way in exchange for the contributions that community members make to the research project. For the documentation of languages used by marginalized or vulnerable communities, researchers might wish to consider how they can use their influence to challenge stigmatized languages (Hochgesang & Palfreyman forthcoming). Certainly, in the case of deaf communities, language documentation and description has been described as "the core activity for sign language vitalization and community empowerment" (Hoyer 2013:43).[7]

Several models have emerged for how linguists can work with deaf communities (see Hochgesang & Palfreyman forthcoming), and Dikyuva et al. (2012) share their experiences as deaf researchers from the global South, offering helpful perspectives on the complex business of negotiating the form that such reciprocity should take.

It is all too easy to take an idealistic view of how the relationship with the community should work, perhaps moving from coworking to co-owning, but in practice it is likely that what is possible will be shaped by many constraints. With this in mind, Dikyuva et al. (2012) refer to virtue ethics, which places emphasis on the researcher's moral character, including their ability and willingness "to discern situations with potential ethical ramifications as they arise in the research practice" (Kubanyiova 2008:507). At the very least, one might apply this to data management by paraphrasing Austin (2010:36): "do not manage your data in a way that will make people regret working with you."

Those conducting research in other communities often exchange stories about how they came to enter into the community, and this can be an important consideration from an ethical point of view (Hochgesang & Palfreyman forthcoming). I entered the Indonesian sign community as a volunteer, rather than a researcher, and after working with deaf organizations on capacity building (2007–2009), I switched roles to researcher, documenting BISINDO in a way informed by typology and sociolinguistics (Palfreyman 2019). While I feel fortunate to have worked with the Indonesian sign community for over twelve years, this was not a planned course of action, at least from the start. In my case, the research journey has been shaped by factors as varied as who I volunteered with, funding applications (some accepted, others rejected), and chance encounters, both with certain academics and with informants who wanted to become more involved in research.

Having gained experience of documentation in the first stage of data collection (see section 2.3), data for the second stage were collected in partnership with Pusat Penelitian Tuli (PUPET), a social research foundation set up in 2014 with Muhammad Isnaini, a deaf Indonesian man. Isnaini had assisted with transcription in the first stage and went on to work with me on data collection and transcription for the second stage. This brought knowledge and experience of documentation in-country, placing Isnaini in a position to pass this on to other interested persons, especially deaf members of the sign community wishing to document their own language (further details about this approach appear in Hochgesang & Palfreyman forthcoming).

6   Choice of metalanguage and other data processing decisions

The glossing and enrichment of sign language data entails many decisions, not least concerning the use of annotations to specify different types of signs—such as lexical signs, fingerspelling productions, pointing signs, gestures, depicting signs, and so on (chapters in Pfau, Steinbach, & Woll 2012 give a helpful overview to these and other types of signs). It makes good sense to follow common conventions, developing, challenging, and adapting as necessary, and the most comprehensive annotation guidelines for sign language data to date were created for the machine-readable Auslan corpus (Johnston 2016). A recent project, Digging into Signs, builds on this by identifying annotation standards that are emerging crosslinguistically (Crasborn, Bank & Cormier 2015), while the Global Signbank (signbank .science.ru.nl) offers a standardized template that those documenting a sign language can use to create a database of lexical entries.[8]

These guidelines are specifically crafted for the purpose of creating a machine-readable corpus and lexical database, and this kind of work continues to be both labor-intensive and time-consuming. The BISINDO corpus team currently has three members (including the author) working on it part time, which is far from optimal. That said, technological fixes continue to appear that aim to automatize processes such as creating video clips and organizing signs according to sublexical parameters, which promises to accelerate the business of organizing and annotating sign language corpora in due course.

Another issue requiring more attention is the lack of guidelines for documentary corpora of sign languages (section 2.2). For situations where researchers lack the resources to make a corpus machine-readable, or are not aiming to compile a machine-readable corpus, guidelines would be valuable, and to continue without such guidelines as the field of sign language documentation expands will most likely result in ever more fragmented sign language data management practices.

A further issue concerns the selection of a metalanguage for glossing. Instead of allocating a random alphanumeric code for each sign, it is common to use glosses or labels: these are invariably words from a metalanguage that make it possible to analyze sign language corpora (Johnston et al. 2011:12). For sign language documentation, the metalanguage is almost always a written language with which the sign language has contact (Lucas 2013).

For the BISINDO corpus, the metalanguage for glosses and free translation is Indonesian, which "enhances the accessibility for the research consultants and for future researchers in Indonesia—most of whom will not have a good command of English, but will have a working knowledge of Indonesian" (Palfreyman 2019:99). With find-and-replace functions and annotation programs such as ELAN (Sloetjes 2014) now offering multiple language options, it will then be possible to translate the metalanguage into English with relative ease, which enables greater access for the international academic community.

Indeed, the Global Signbank manual (Crasborn et al. 2018) specifies that a parallel gloss must be created in English, to enable cross-corpora analysis. Once again, however, a balance must be struck between ensuring that the corpus can be accessed by the international academic community and by the community that uses the target language, which is challenging for several reasons. Academics often face more pressure, from funders for example, to prepare data for other academics than for the sign or speech communities concerned. Further to this, when working with sign communities with low literacy levels, there are issues around the accessibility of the metalanguage. One of the ways to make the metalanguage more accessible is to set up links between glosses and a lexical database (such as the Lexicon service linking ELAN with the Signbank) so that written glosses can be viewed as signs, but this does not solve the accessibility of annotations and the like.

7   Learning about sign language data management

Many of those documenting sign languages at postgraduate level and beyond will have learned more about linguistics and comparatively much less about data management, although research culture is changing swiftly in this area. Bad practices that take root in one's early research tend to persist if unchallenged, and for many good reasons, it makes sense to remain attuned to developments in data management. While a few research teams are dedicated to sign language documentation, it is still common for sign language researchers to find themselves in university departments that focus on spoken language research, and the ensuing isolation is compounded in the case of deaf researchers who do not always enjoy access to information.

Summer schools can be an excellent way to learn, although there is usually a heavy bias toward spoken languages, with course leaders who do not always remember that some languages are signed rather than spoken. Very occasionally, sessions deal specifically with sign languages: for example, on several recent occasions at the Leiden Summer School in Linguistics.

Online forums are an excellent place to seek advice from those with experience of sign language documentation, and it is worth posting queries to groups such as Deaf Linguists, who are usually very happy to share their own practices. Conferences also offer an opportunity to ask for advice: presentations dealing with technical aspects of data management are still lamentably rare, but it can only be a good thing for researchers to open up and share their approaches to managing data. In my experience, issues around sign language documentation have arisen informally during conversation at international gatherings such as the SIGN conference series and the Sign CAFÉ workshops.

Optimal or recommended technical specifications for compatibility with annotation software such as ELAN should be available in the user manuals, including file type (.mp4, .wmv, and so on), frame height, and frame rate, and these can be useful to ensure that recordings are compatible with the software. It is sensible to look for advice on preferred recording formats and settings elsewhere in the documentary linguistic literature, and/or in training institutes and online forums, so that recordings are in line with current best practice recommendations for long-term media preservation and reuse. The technical requirements of language archives must also be met. In sum, planning ahead is always beneficial: data recorded in the wrong format will have to be converted, and converting large numbers of files unnecessarily is best avoided where possible, especially when working in the field.

The consequences of files with incompatible specifications may not always be immediately apparent, but I have had experiences where the same video files have worked with annotation software on one computer, while producing indecipherable output on another computer. Unfortunately, on at least one such occasion the latter output was in Indonesia and I was in the United Kingdom, which held up data analysis considerably.

Despite a plethora of data-sharing options, it remains difficult to share very large files internationally, and sound planning—making sure that the right files are left securely with the right team member in the right country—really does pay dividends.

8 Data management for sign language documentation: Future directions

Perhaps the most inevitable future direction for language documentation entails collecting and managing data from the Internet, now that more signers are posting videos on Facebook, Instagram, and other social media platforms in different sign languages (including BISINDO). As the Internet creates communicative spaces and transforms real-life practices, it generates immense opportunities as well as dilemmas that researchers need to engage with, linked for example to ethics and the collection of metadata (see Hou, Lepic, & Wilkinson, chapter 40, this volume).

The use of data from sign communities that are in contact with "deaf tourism," and other language contact situations, is another promising area for sign language documentation. This is especially pertinent for Indonesia because Bali receives a regular stream of deaf tourists from around the world, and several deaf-led enterprises have emerged to cater for them (Moriarty Harrelson 2019). Two major projects examining contact situations, Sign Multilingualism (Zeshan & Webster 2019) and Deaf Communication without a Shared Language[9] answer theoretical questions using data mostly collected in laboratory settings, but thus far few data have been collected in situations where languages are naturally in contact.

As described in section 2.1, filming in the laboratory has obvious and important benefits—including control over lighting and the use of numerous cameras—but also limitations, especially for those wishing to elucidate the use of language in situ. The Kata Kolok corpus (de Vos 2016) is arguably richer in this respect than most others, as all data were collected in and around the village where the language is used. While the BISINDO corpus also comprises data filmed in situ, Kata Kolok signers were also recorded in a range of cultural contexts, such as informal gatherings and religious ceremonies (de Vos 2016:211). I conclude by suggesting that we need more of this kind of in situ language documentation: these data offer multiple insights to linguists, sociolinguists, and anthropologists and offer an important counterbalance to data collected in the controlled settings of the laboratory.

Notes

1. As with many spoken languages, sign languages have no widespread written form and nothing resembling the International Phonetic Alphabet (Nyst 2015). Rudimentary systems such as Stokoe Notation and SignWriting have been developed to encode the sublexical components of signs, but they are not in common use in most countries, and the availability of video recording has replaced the use of such notation.

2. A publicly available corpus for American Sign Language (ASL) has not yet been created; several documentation projects are underway—including the ASL Signbank (Hochgesang, Crasborn, & Lillo-Martin 2019), which provides a collection of ASL signs linked with identification glosses—but these are not sign language corpora.

3. WEIRD stands for Western, educated, industrialized, rich, democratic.

4. Due to the funding required to collect data from sites across such a vast country, the expansion of the corpus was highly desirable but far from certain during the first stage. The general dearth of long-term funding highlighted by this case is, unfortunately, quite common, and made it harder to plan the corpus in advance.

5. CBM (Christian Blind Mission), an organization for disability-inclusive development.

6. Leverhulme Trust Early Career Research Fellowship, ECF-2016-795.

7. Many of the world's deaf people continue to face discrimination; lack of access to sign language, education, and information, in particular, create disparities and make deaf people more vulnerable than their hearing counterparts (for more information see Hochgesang & Palfreyman forthcoming).

8. One of the main aims of the Signbank is to facilitate cross-linguistic comparison.

9. This project is run by Prof. Onno Crasborn at Radboud University 2017–2022.

References

Austin, Peter K. 2010. Communities, ethics and rights in language documentation. In *Language Documentation and Description* 7, ed. Peter K. Austin, 34–54. London: SOAS.

Austin, Peter K. 2016. Language documentation 20 years on. In *Endangered Languages and Languages in Danger: Issues of Documentation, Policy, and Language Rights*, ed. Luna Filipović and Martin Pütz, 147–170. IMPACT: Studies in Language and Society 42 Amsterdam: John Benjamins. https://doi.org/10.1075/impact.42.02gri.

Benedicto, Elena, Dolores Modesta, and Melba McLean. 2002. Fieldwork as a participatory research activity: The Mayangna linguistic teams. In *Proceedings of the Twenty-Eighth Annual Meeting of the Berkeley Linguistic Society* 28 (1): 375–386.

https://journals.linguisticsociety.org/proceedings/index.php/BLS/article/view/3852.

Bergman, Brita, Penny Boyes-Braem, Thomas Hanke, and Elena Pizzuto, eds. 2001. Sign

transcription and database storage of sign information. Special issue, *Sign Language and Linguistics* 4 (1/2).

Cameron, Deborah. 1998. Problems of empowerment in linguistic research. *Cahiers de l'ILSL* 10:23–38.

Cox, Christopher. 2011. Corpus linguistics and language documentation: Challenges for collaboration. *Language and Computers* 73:239–264.

Crasborn, Onno. 2010. What does "informed consent" mean in the internet age? Publishing sign language corpora as open content. *Sign Language Studies* 10 (2): 276–290.

Crasborn, Onno, Inge Zwitserlood, and Johan Ros. 2008. *The Corpus NGT: A Digital Open Access Corpus of Movies and Annotations of Sign Language of the Netherlands*. Nijmegen, the Netherlands: Centre for Language Studies, Radboud Universiteit Nijmegen.

Supplementary material: http://hdl.handle.net/hdl:1839/00-0000-0000-0004-DF8E-6. ISLRN: 175-346-174-413-3.

Crasborn, Onno, Inge Zwitserlood, Els van der Kooij, and Anique Schüller. 2018. *Global Signbank Manual*. Version 1. Nijmegen, the Netherlands: Radboud University, Centre for Language Studies.

Crasborn, Onno, Richard Bank, and Kearsy Cormier. 2015. Digging into Signs: Towards a gloss annotation standard for sign language corpora. Technical report. http://doi.org/10.13140/RG.2.1.2468.5840.

Czaykowska-Higgins, Ewa. 2009. Research models, community engagement, and linguistic fieldwork: Reflections on working within Canadian indigenous communities. *Language Documentation and Conservation* 3 (1): 15–50.

de Vos, Connie. 2012. Sign-spatiality in Kata Kolok: How a village sign language of Bali inscribes its signing space. PhD dissertation, Max Planck Institute of Psycholinguistics, Nijmegen.

de Vos, Connie. 2016. Sampling shared sign languages. *Sign Language Studies* 16 (2): 204–226.

Dikyuva, Hasan, Cesar Ernesto Escobedo Delgado, Sibaji Panda, and Ulrike Zeshan. 2012. Working with village sign language communities: Deaf fieldwork researchers in professional dialogue. In *Sign Languages in Village Communities*, ed. Ulrike Zeshan and Connie de Vos, 313–344. Berlin: de Gruyter & Ishara Press. https://doi.org/10.1515/9781614511496.313.

Epps, Patience L., Anthony K. Webster, and Anthony C. Woodbury. 2017. A holistic humanities of speaking: Franz Boas and the continuing centrality of texts. *International Journal of American Linguistics* 83 (1): 41–78.

Fischer, Susan. 2009. Sign language field methods: Approaches, techniques, and concerns. In *Taiwan Sign Language and Beyond*, ed. James H.-Y. Tai and Jane Tsay, 1–19. Chia-Yi, China: Taiwan Institute for the Humanities, National Chung Cheng University.

Grinevald, Colette. 2003. Speakers and documentation of endangered languages. In *Language Documentation and Description*, vol. 1, ed. Peter K. Austin, 52–72. London: SOAS.

Hochgesang, Julie A., and Nick Palfreyman. Forthcoming. Sign language corpora and the ethics of working with the community. In *Sign Language Corpora*, ed. Jordan Fenlon and Julie A. Hochgesang. Washington, DC: Gallaudet University Press.

Hochgesang, Julie A., Onno Crasborn, and Diane Lillo-Martin. 2019. *ASL Signbank*. New Haven, CT: Haskins Lab, Yale University. https://aslsignbank.haskins.yale.edu/.

Hou, Lynn Y-S. 2016. "Making hands": Family sign languages in the San Juan Quiahije community. PhD dissertation, University of Texas at Austin.

Hou, Lynn, Y-S. 2017. Negotiating language practices and language ideologies in fieldwork: A reflexive meta-documentation. In *Innovations in Deaf Studies: The Role of Deaf Scholars*, ed. Annelies Kusters, Maartje De Meulder, and Dai O'Brien, 339–359. Oxford: Oxford University Press.

Hoyer, Karin. 2013. *Language Vitalization through Language Documentation and Description in the Kosovar Sign Language Community*. Nijmegen, the Netherlands: Ishara Press. www.oapen.org/download?type=document&docid=442947.

Johnston, Trevor. 2008. *Auslan Corpus*. London: SOAS, Endangered Languages Archive. https://elar.soas.ac.uk/Collection/MPI55247. Accessed April 12, 2019.

Johnston, Trevor. 2016. *Auslan Corpus Annotation Guidelines*.

https://media.auslan.org.au/attachments/Johnston_Auslan-CorpusAnnotationGuidelines_February2016.pdf.

Johnston, Trevor, Adam Schembri, Kearsy Cormier, Jordan Fenlon, and Ramas Rentelis. 2011.

Type/token matching in annotated SL corpora: Examples from Auslan and BSL corpus projects. Presentation at the workshop Building Sign Language Corpora in North America, Gallaudet University, Washington, DC, May 21–22.

Kipp, Michael, Alexis Heloir, and Quan Nguyen. 2011. Sign language avatars: Animation and comprehensibility. In *Intelligent Virtual Agents. IVA 2011*, ed. Hannes H. Vilhjálmsson, Stephan Kopp, Stacy Marsella, and K. R. Thórisson, 113–126. Lecture Notes in Computer Science 6895. Berlin: Springer. https://doi.org/10.1007/978-3-642-23974-8_13.

Kubanyiova, Maggie. 2008. Rethinking research ethics in contemporary applied linguistics: The tension between macro- and microethical perspectives in situated research. *Modern Language Journal* 92 (4): 503–518. https://doi.org/10.1111/j.1540-4781.2008.00784.x.

Kusters, Annelies. 2012. Being a deaf white anthropologist in Adamorobe: Some ethical and methodological issues. In *Sign Languages in Village Communities: Anthropological and Linguistic Insights*, ed. Ulrike Zeshan & Connie de Vos, 27–52. Berlin: de Gruyter.

Kusters, Annelies. 2015. *Deaf Space in Adamorobe: An Ethnographic Study in a Village in Ghana*. Washington, DC: Gallaudet University Press.

Labov, William. 1982. Building on empirical foundations. In *Perspectives on Historical Linguistics*, ed. Winfred P. Lehmann and Yakov Malkiel, 17–92. Amsterdam: John Benjamins.

Lucas, Ceil. 2013. Methodological issues in studying sign language variation. In *Sign Language Research, Uses and Practices: Crossing Views on Theoretical and Applied Sign Language Linguistics*, ed. Laurence Meurant, Aurélie Sinte, Mieke Van Herreweghe and Myriam Vermeerbergen, 258–308. Berlin: de Gruyter & Ishara Press. https://doi.org/10.1515/9781614511472.285.

McEnery, Tony, and Andrew Wilson. 2001. *Corpus Linguistics*. Edinburgh: Edinburgh University Press.

Morgan, Hope. 2017. The phonology of Kenyan Sign Language (Southwestern Dialect). PhD dissertation, University of California, San Diego. https://escholarship.org/uc/item/9bp3h8t4.

Moriarty Harrelson, Erin. 2019. An ethnography of deaf tourist mobilities. Presented at ASL Lecture Series, University of Pennsylvania School of Arts and Sciences, November 20.

Nathan, David. 2011. Archives 2.0 for endangered languages: From disk space to MySpace. *International Journal of Humanities and Arts Computing* 4 (1-2): 111–124. https://doi.org/10.3366/ijhac.2011.0011.

Nyst, Victoria. 2012. *A Reference Corpus of Adamorobe Sign Language: A Digital, Annotated Video Corpus of the Sign Language used in the Village of Adamorobe, Ghana*. Leiden, the Netherlands: Leiden University Centre for Linguistics.

Nyst, Victoria. 2015. Sign language fieldwork. In *Research Methods in Sign Language Studies: A Practical Guide*, ed. Eleni Orfanidou, Bencie Woll, and Gary Morgan, 107–122. Malden, MA: Wiley Blackwell.

Nyst, Victoria, Moustapha Magassouba, and Kara Sylla. 2011. *A Digital Annotated Video Corpus of the Local Sign Language used in Bamako and Mopti, Mali*. Leiden, the Netherlands: Leiden University Centre for Linguistics.

Orfanidou, Eleni, Bencie Woll, and Gary Morgan, eds. 2015. *Research Methods in Sign Language Studies: A Practical Guide*. Oxford: Wiley Blackwell.

Palfreyman, Nick. 2013. Form, function and the grammaticalization of completive markers in the sign language varieties of Solo and Makassar. In *Tense, Aspect, Modality and Evidentiality in Languages of Indonesia*, ed. John Bowden, 153–172. NUSA 55. http://hdl.handle.net/10108/74331.

Palfreyman, Nick. 2015. Sign language varieties of Indonesia: A linguistic and sociolinguistic perspective. PhD dissertation, University of Central Lancashire.

Palfreyman, Nick. 2016. Colour terms in two Indonesian sign language varieties: A preliminary analysis. In *Semantic Fields in Sign Languages*, ed. Ulrike Zeshan and Keiko Sagara, 269–300. Berlin: de Gruyter and Ishara Press. https://doi.org/10.1515/9781501503429-008.

Palfreyman, Nick. 2019. *Variation in Indonesian Sign Language: A Typological and Sociolinguistic Analysis*. Berlin: de Gruyter Mouton. http://doi.org/10.1515/9781501504822.

Perniss, Pamela. 2012. Use of sign space. In *Sign Language: An International Handbook*, ed. Roland Pfau, Marcus Steinbach, and Bencie Woll, 412–431. Berlin: de Gruyter.

Perniss, Pamela. 2015. Collecting and analysing sign language data: Video requirements and use of annotation software. In *Research Methods in Sign Language Studies: A Practical Guide*, ed. Eleni Orfanidou, Bencie Woll, and Gary Morgan, 55–73. Oxford: Wiley-Blackwell.

Pfau, Roland, and Josep Quer. 2010. Non-manuals: Their grammatical and prosodic roles. In *Sign Languages*, ed. Diane Brentari, 381–402. Cambridge: Cambridge University Press. https://doi.org/10.1017/CBO9780511712203.018.

Pfau, Roland, Markus Steinbach, and Bencie Woll, eds. 2012. *Sign Language: An International Handbook*. Berlin: de Gruyter. https://doi.org/10.1515/9783110261325.

Rutkowski, Pawel, Joanna Lacheta, Piotr Mostowski, Joanna Filipczak, and Sylwia Lozinska. 2013. The corpus of Polish Sign Language (PJM): Methodology, procedures and impact. Presentation at Research, Records and Responsibility: Ten Years of the Pacific and Regional Archive for Digital Sources in Endangered Cultures, December 2–4. https://ses.library.usyd.edu.au/handle/2123/13310. Accessed December 19, 2019.

Salonen, Juhana, Ritva Takkinen, Anna Puupponen, Henri Nieminen, and Outi Pippuri. 2016. Creating corpora of Finland's sign languages. In *Workshop Proceedings of the Seventh Workshop on the Representation and Processing of Sign Languages: Corpus Mining / Proceedings of the Tenth International Conference on Language Resources and Evaluation (LREC 2016)*, ed. Eleni Efthimiou, Stavroula-Evita Fotinea, Thomas Hanke, Julie Hochgesang, Jette Kristoffersen, and Johanna Mesch, 179–184. Paris: European Language Resources Association (ELRA).

Sandler Wendy. 2012. Visual prosody. In *Sign Language: An International Handbook*, ed. Roland Pfau, Marcus Steinbach, and

Bencie Woll, 55–76. Berlin: de Gruyter. https://doi.org/10.1515/9783110261325.55.

Schembri, Adam. 2008. The British Sign Language Corpus Project: Open access archives and the observer's paradox. Presentation at Workshop on Construction and Exploitation of Sign Language Corpora, LREC, Marrakech, Morocco, May 26–June 1.

Schembri, Adam. 2019. Making visual languages visible: Data and methods transparency in sign language linguistics. Presentation at TISLR13, Hamburg, September 27.

Schembri, Adam, Jordan Fenlon, Ramas Rentelis, and Kearsy Cormier. 2011. *British Sign Language Corpus Project: A Corpus of Digital Video Data of British Sign Language 2008–2011*. 1st ed. London: University College London. http://www.bslcorpusproject.org.

Schembri, Adam, Jordan Fenlon, Ramas Rentelis, and Kearsy Cormier. 2014. *British Sign Language Corpus Project: A Corpus of Digital Video Data and Annotations of British Sign Language 2008–2014*. 2nd ed. London: University College London.

Schuit, Joke. 2013. Signs of the Artic: Typological aspects of Inuit Sign Language. PhD dissertation, University of Amsterdam.

Sloetjes, Han. 2014. ELAN: Multimedia annotation application. In *The Oxford Handbook of Corpus Phonology*, ed. Jacques Durand, Ulrike Gut, and Gjert Kristoffersen, 305–320. Oxford: Oxford University Press.

Stubbs, Michael. 2001. *Words and Phrases: Corpus Studies of Lexical Semantics*. Oxford: Blackwell.

Thieberger, Nick, and Simon Musgrave. 2007. Documentary linguistics and ethical issues. In *Language Documentation and Description*, vol. 4, ed. Peter K. Austin, 26–37. London: SOAS.

Thieberger, Nick, Anna Margetts, Stephen Morey, and Simon Musgrave. 2015. Assessing annotated corpora as research output. *Australian Journal of Linguistics* 36 (1): 1–21. https://doi.org/10.1080/07268602.2016.1109428.

Wilcox, Sherman. 2003. The multimedia dictionary of American Sign Language: Learning lessons about language, technology and business. *Sign Language Studies* 3 (4): 379–392.

Wolfram, Walt. 1993. Identifying and interpreting variables. In *American Dialect Research*, ed. Dennis Preston, 193–221. Amsterdam: Benjamins.

Woodbury, Anthony C. 2011. Language documentation. In *The Cambridge Handbook of Endangered Languages*, ed. Peter K. Austin and Julia Sallabank, 159–186. Cambridge: Cambridge University Press.

Zeshan, Ulrike, and Jenny Webster, eds. 2019. *Sign Multilingualism*. Lancaster, UK: Ishara Press and de Gruyter.

22 Managing Data in a Language Documentation Corpus

Christopher Cox

1 Introduction

This chapter presents a case study in data management in the context of documentary linguistics, a subfield of the language sciences that is concerned with issues in the development and application of records of linguistic practices and knowledge (Himmelmann 1998; Woodbury 2003, 2011; McDonnell, Berez-Kroeker, & Holton 2018). In contrast to some other areas of linguistics, attention to data management practices and procedures has been a central theme in the emergence of documentary linguistics over the past twenty years, following in part from the emphasis that definitional work in this area placed on defining linguistic data types and their relationship to one another (e.g., Himmelmann 2012) and the preservation and reuse of language records in research (e.g., as supported by language archives; cf. Henke & Berez-Kroeker 2016). Even with this attention to data management issues, what individual documentarians and language documentation teams actually *do* to develop documentation—the actual nuts and bolts of running a documentation project from start to finish—has, somewhat surprisingly, been described in the literature less often than more abstract "best practice" or "good practice" recommendations. This imbalance has begun to be addressed by published descriptions of individual documentary collections and the projects that have developed them (e.g., Schembri et al. 2013; Salffner 2015; Gawne 2018), which often include some discussion of data management issues. This chapter has a similar aim to these publications, albeit with a somewhat narrower focus on data management concerns specifically, rather than the full range of ethical and other issues that come with work in language documentation (cf. Rice 2006; Czaykowska-Higgins 2009, 2018; Holton, Leonard, & Pulsifer, chapter 4, this volume).

As important as this attention to language records and their management has been to documentary linguistics as a subfield within the language sciences, data management practices in actual language documentation projects are diverse, and what is described in this use case should not be assumed to be representative of all contexts in which documentation is being undertaken today. The sections that follow present one illustration of how common data management practices in language documentation have been applied in one particular documentation project and do not attempt to offer either exhaustive coverage of practices across the entire field or a general-purpose guide to data management in documentary linguistics, in general. Fortunately, further guidance on data management practices in language documentation can be found in sources such as Bowern (2015) and Meakins, Green, & Turpin (2018), who approach these issues from a field linguistics perspective, but whose advice applies here no less well. The discussion found in Thieberger & Berez (2012) also offers valuable insights into a wider range of data management issues in documentary linguistics. This chapter attempts to complement the treatment of data management practices found in sources such as these by illustrating the principles and practices that they describe, paying particular attention to the kinds of data that emerge in the course of a language documentation project and how they are stored, organized, and drawn on.

The overall workflow described in this chapter also shares some similarities with those described in a number of other data management use cases in this volume. Although this chapter focuses on the documentation of a spoken language that still has an appreciable number of first-language users, many of these same data management practices are also shared with work with historical documentation for language reclamation (Lukaniec, chapter 25, this volume) and with sign languages (Crasborn, chapter 39, this volume; Palfreyman, chapter 21, this volume). As well, while the focus of the project described here is on the creation of multipurpose primary data representing language in use, rather than on particular structural or grammatical features of that language, many language documentation corpora contain records of both kinds. In these cases, there is likely to be some overlap with data management practices in descriptive linguistic fieldwork (Daniels & Daniels, chapter 26, this volume), as well, as is evident from the connection between fieldwork and documentation often made in the wider literature (e.g., Bowern 2015, among others).

2 Background, planning, and community considerations

The data management practices in language documentation that this chapter discusses are centered on Plautdietsch (ISO 639-3: pdt; Glottocode: plau1238), a diasporic West Germanic language spoken by minority communities throughout the Americas (primarily Belize, Bolivia, Brazil, Canada, Mexico, Paraguay, and the United States), Europe (Germany), and Asia (primarily Kazakhstan and the Russian Federation). Plautdietsch is spoken today primarily by Dutch-Russian Mennonites and their descendants, a pacifist Christian denomination with roots in the radical Protestant Reformation (Dyck 1993). The documentation project at the heart of this chapter was conducted from 2010 to 2015 and concentrated on Plautdietsch as spoken in central Saskatchewan, Canada, one of the larger Mennonite settlement regions in western Canada and a historically important waypoint for international Mennonite migrations during the twentieth century (Guenter et al. 1995). No prior linguistic research had been conducted in these communities before this project began, and ongoing language shift toward English had left Plautdietsch endangered in the region, with most first-language users from the region in their sixties or older.[1] Documentation activities came about as part of a larger, local response to this pattern of language shift, paralleled by a growing interest in second-language education programs for members of the local community (e.g., classes for adult learners). Outside of bilingual dictionaries developed in other Mennonite communities in Canada, there were relatively few resources available for language learners and

teachers at the time that this project started. Many community members also noted considerable linguistic variation between individuals and communities in the region that needed to be taken into consideration when developing language programs and materials, but on which little linguistic or sociodemographic information was available. This was one area where (socio)linguistic research based on newly developed documentation seemed particularly promising, being well aligned with both the immediate need for serviceable information on how Plautdietsch was being spoken in the region, as well as broader questions about how linguistic variation is distributed in diasporic, religious minority communities such as these.

Preparing for documentation projects that aim to contribute both to the immediate issues identified as priorities by members of this language community and to the resources available for *language work* (which here includes efforts focused on education, revitalization, and supporting resource material development, as well as research focused on linguistic and sociolinguistic aspects of the language community's practices reflected in the final documentation) in the longer term often involves both initial and ongoing consultation with members of the language community (Czaykowska-Higgins 2009). Contacting, consulting with, and staying in touch with members of the language community present their own small data management tasks in terms of organizing contact information (e.g., contributors' phone numbers, mailing addresses, and physical addresses) and scheduling meetings related to the project. In this project, contributors' contact information was kept in a spreadsheet where each row represented a single contributor (maintained in Microsoft Excel, although in retrospect, Unicode-encoded CSV/TSV would have provided a more platform-neutral alternative), and meeting schedules were maintained in a separate word processing document (kept in Microsoft Word, although again, a simple text file or a digital calendar would have likely handled this just as well, if not better). Both of these documents were intentionally kept separate from other data in this project: because some of this information, such as phone numbers and home addresses, might be considered sensitive, an effort was made to keep these data separate from other sources of information assembled in this study.

Through the initial discussions that took place with members of the language community over the initial planning phase of this project, it quickly became clear that we would need to be mindful of the diversity of contributors' backgrounds, varieties, and patterns of language use. While almost all of the contributors grew up in families in which Plautdietsch was the primary language of the home, most noted that their use of the language had significantly decreased over their lifetimes, with relatively few using the language on a day-to-day basis outside of interactions with their age-mates and other individuals who they knew were able to speak the language. Contributors also observed possible linguistic differences between different Mennonite settlement areas in central Saskatchewan and frequently commented on social divisions between Mennonite denominations that had historically contributed to limited interaction between groups within the Mennonite population. To help ensure that these kinds of geographical and sociolinguistic factors weren't overlooked in documentation, a basic questionnaire was developed that gave attention to individuals' places and dates of birth, levels of formal education, knowledge of languages present in the community (e.g., besides Plautdietsch, also English and Mennonite High German), and more.

These questionnaires were delivered to contributors on paper, and the completed forms were scanned (as PDF documents, although in retrospect, uncompressed TIFF at a minimum of 300 DPI would probably have been preferable from an archiving perspective) and stored alongside the meeting and contact information documents, keeping them separate from other documents in this project. The responses from these scanned forms were then entered into a contributor metadata spreadsheet (maintained as Unicode-encoded CSV), with each column representing one question and each row representing one completed questionnaire. Each contributor was assigned a unique, anonymous identifier in this spreadsheet (e.g., M01, F23), which served an important function later

in this study, allowing the demographic and sociolinguistic information in this spreadsheet to be linked to transcripts of contributors' speech in project recordings (through the participant metadata in the corresponding ELAN transcripts; see section 4). Figure 22.1 shows a sample of this spreadsheet. Although the "master" copy of this document contained personally identifying details about contributors (e.g., names of contributors' parents), and was thus not immediately suitable for being shared more widely, an anonymized subset of these columns was later exported for use in analysis, allowing a large part of this information to be used in the study and shared more widely without compromising contributors' anonymity.

Another outcome of the discussions that took place at the outset of this project was general agreement about the need for more written resource materials in Plautdietsch, both to support second-language learners and adult language programs and first-language speakers who wanted to see their language in writing (both as an aid to literacy development and as a means to promoting respect for the language locally). This eventually led to the development of an illustrated *Fibel* [ˈfiːbəl], or "primer," which followed the model of books of the same name that were historically a key element of the traditional Mennonite educational system (cf. Cox 2015:56). As seen in figure 22.2, each page in this book presented a target sound, an English word whose Plautdietsch equivalent contained this sound in a consistent phonological environment, and an English sentence that presented the target word in context. By incorporating linguistically variable features reported for other Mennonite Plautdietsch speech communities in the previous literature into these example sentences, the final *Fibel* was able to serve not only as the basis for a new

	A	B	C	D	E	F	G	H
1	AnonID	Gender	POB	DOB	Age	ChurchDenomination	ChurchLocation	ParentsPOB
2	F00	F	RABBIT LAKE	1935	78	Mennonite Church Canada	SASKATOON	UkraineUkraine
3	F01	F	CARMEL	1922	91	Roman Catholic	CARMEL	UkraineUkraine
4	F02	F	Aberdeen	1938	75	Bergthaler	Warman	CanadaCanada
5	F03	F	Langham	1926	87	Mennonite Church Canada	SASKATOON	USAUSA
6	F04	F	CARMEL	1925	88	Roman Catholic	CARMEL	CanadaUkraine
7	F05	F	Kronsthal	1933	80	Old Colony	Neuhorst	CanadaCanada
8	F06	F	Hepburn	1928	85	Mennonite Church Canada	Osler	UkraineUkraine
9	F07	F	Osler	1933	80	Mennonite Church Canada	SASKATOON	UkraineUkraine
10	F08	F	Osler	1934	79	Mennonite Church Canada	SASKATOON	UkraineUkraine
11	F09	F	Osler	1939	74	Mennonite Church Canada	Osler	CanadaUkraine
12	F10	F	Hague	1940	73	Mennonite Church Canada	SASKATOON	CanadaCanada

Figure 22.1

An excerpt of the contributor metadata spreadsheet.

Figure 22.2

An example page from the *Fibel*.

Source: Adapted from the original photograph "Bears" by Flickr user davipt, released under a Creative Commons Attribution-NonCommercial-ShareAlike license (CC BY-NC-SA; https://creativecommons.org/licenses/by-nc-sa/2.0/).

resource for language learners, but also as a translation task that provided a baseline of information of linguistic variation among speakers of Plautdietsch in central Saskatchewan, complementing the spontaneous conversations and discussions that were also often recorded with contributors (cf. Lüpke 2009 on the use of linguistic tasks such as these in language documentation).

This document was initially developed as a rough set of text and images in Microsoft PowerPoint, which allowed for quick incorporation of contributors' feedback into the draft layouts and text of early revisions of this document. Images were drawn from public domain or Creative Commons–licensed sources, with the appropriate acknowledgments and license information kept in a separate spreadsheet (maintained as a Unicode-encoded CSV file). These slides were later exported from PowerPoint as a PDF document and as individual PNG images, which were stored alongside the other project-internal files. A copy of the *Fibel* was also printed in color, laminated, and spiral bound for easy use in the consultation sessions with contributors that followed.

3 Recording

With a printed copy of the *Fibel* in hand, consultation sessions were arranged with speakers of Plautdietsch from throughout central Saskatchewan to review and translate

the *Fibel* and converse in Plautdietsch. As is common in language documentation projects, we wanted to make sure that these recordings were of the highest possible quality and that the formats and standards that we chose to follow at this stage in the project would allow for many possible future uses of the recordings that each speaker contributed (cf. Nathan 2010). This led us to use a dedicated, solid-state audio recorder (initially an Edirol R-09HR, accompanied by a stereo Sound Devices MixPre preamplifier; later, a Sound Devices 702), together with omnidirectional ear set microphones (Countryman E6i; cf. Lee 2013), for producing audio recordings of these sessions in the contributors' homes.[2] Recordings were made in uncompressed WAV format (48 kHz/24-bit samples), with each microphone recorded on a separate channel. Figure 22.3 shows one such session with Mrs. Nettie Boehr, one of the contributing speakers, as we reviewed the *Fibel* together.[3]

Immediately after each day's language meetings were finished, the audio recordings were copied from the recording devices' memory card onto a laptop, renamed and organized into directories by session, and copies then made onto multiple external hard drives for backup.[4] A standard session would result in a single folder containing files that looked something like this:

```
2011-07-23-pdt-NB-CDC-Warman/2011-07-23-pdt-NB-
CDC-Warman-Edirol-01.wav
2011-07-23-pdt-NB-CDC-Warman/2011-07-23-pdt-NB-
CDC-Warman-Edirol-01.wav.md5
2011-07-23-pdt-NB-CDC-Warman/2011-07-23-pdt-NB-
CDC-Warman-Edirol-01.wav.sha1
```

Figure 22.3

Reviewing the *Fibel* with Nettie Boehr.

While having consistent file naming and organization practices made later processing and annotation steps much more straightforward, our file naming conventions at the time were, in retrospect, unnecessarily baroque, including not only the recording date (July 23, 2011) and ISO 639-3 language code (pdt), but also the initials of the contributors (NB), of the recorder (CDC), the recording location (Warman, Saskatchewan, Canada), the recording device (Edirol R-09HR), and a track number (01). Much of this information could have safely been kept in separate, session-level metadata, whether in another text-based spreadsheet or in an XML-based format such as the Open Language Archives Community (OLAC; Bird & Simons 2003), ISLE Metadata Initiative (IMDI; Broeder et al. 2001), or Component Metadata Initiative (CMDI; Broeder et al. 2012) metadata schemas. It probably would have been better to keep these file and session names much simpler than this; in more recent documentation projects, I generally include only the language code (pdt), a unique project identifier (OS, *Onse Spröak* "Our Language"), the recording date, and the number of the session that day (01 for the first session that day, 02 for another session later that same day, etc.), with individual files being identified by track numbers (01 for the first recording made in the session, 02 for the second, etc.):

```
pdt-OS-20110723-01/pdt-OS-20110723-01-01.wav
pdt-OS-20110723-01/pdt-OS-20110723-01-01.wav.md5
pdt-OS-20110723-01/pdt-OS-20110723-01-01.wav.sha1
```

As mentioned above, once all of the day's recordings had been renamed and properly organized into sessions, we concatenated all of the tracks in each session into a single, long WAV in CD format (44.1 kHz, 16-bit stereo) and burned copies of this onto audio CDs for each of the contributors. This was done using Audacity,[5] an open source audio editing application, although this could have also easily been automated using a utility such as FFmpeg.[6] Once all of this had been done, copies of all of these files were made on several external hard drives, as well as in a private account with a cloud-based storage provider. Having multiple copies stored in multiple physical (and virtual) locations helped lessen the potential for catastrophic data loss, which is in keeping with the principle of LOCKSS (Lots of Copies Keeps Stuff Safe; cf. Austin 2006:89). Because these audio recordings were essentially static—we weren't planning on editing them

directly in later work—keeping copies in multiple places was relatively easy, as we didn't need to worry about multiple versions of the same file circulating in the same project. Each of these storage options presents its own ethical and practical issues (e.g., in the case of cloud-based storage providers, the possibility of files being stored in jurisdictions where access may be granted to government agencies and other third parties without users' approval), and it is worth considering which of these options may be best suited to the particular context in which documentation is being undertaken.

4 Processing and annotating

With the recordings now properly organized and backed up safely in multiple locations, we set about annotating each recording's contents. We used ELAN, an open source software tool for annotating audiovisual materials that is the de facto standard for this kind of task in language documentation (Sloetjes 2014). Using ELAN allowed us to directly associate text (transcriptions of the original audio, as well as accompanying translations, working notes, and coding) with time-aligned segments of each recording, thereby creating a fully text-searchable speech database of all of the contributors' recordings.[7] Each recording was annotated by an ELAN transcript sharing the same file name (ending in .eaf, with a corresponding display preferences file ending in .pfsx automatically created by ELAN), for example:

```
pdt-OS-20110723-01/pdt-OS-20110723-01-01.wav
pdt-OS-20110723-01/pdt-OS-20110723-01-01.eaf
pdt-OS-20110723-01/pdt-OS-20110723-01-01.pfsx
```

Similar to the procedure that Nagy and Meyerhoff (2015) describe for sociolinguistic research, each ELAN transcript served not only as the place in which speech in the original recordings was transcribed, but also where contributors' translations of individual words and sentences in the *Fibel* were identified and linguistic variables that were represented in contributors' translations of *Fibel* prompts were coded. Thus, a translation of the *Fibel* prompt sentence 'You should leave the big, brown bear alone' would be annotated in ELAN as seen in example (1) (reproduced from Cox 2015:135, example (9), with data types added in boldface), with the third line containing JSON–like strings that identified individual linguistic variables (e.g., the form of the singular masculine definite article in the accusative case) and their values in this utterance (e.g., here, *dän*) (see sentence display 1):

From a logistical perspective, including this kind of coding directly in the ELAN transcripts made sense: this kind of variation often required some review of the corresponding portions of the source recording to analyze, so having these codes time-aligned with the original audio made for much quicker work. This also opened the door to a much wider range of later uses of these transcripts (because we could instantly retrieve the audio associated with any text that was of interest), increasing the overall value of the investment that was made to produce time-aligned transcripts in the first place.[8]

5   Applying and sharing

Having the results of the sociolinguistic questionnaire, the original recordings, and our time-aligned annotations all organized consistently in non-proprietary, well-supported formats provided a number of benefits when it came time to apply these data to the tasks identified as priorities in this project. Managing our data in this way made it possible to develop scripts in Python and R that automatically extracted all of the tagged instances of variation directly from the corpus and fed these tokens directly into various forms of visualization and analysis (e.g., into dialectometric tools such as Gabmap [Nerbonne et al. 2011], which went a long way toward determining the extent to which differences between speakers represented in the corpus might be conditioned by features of local demographics and geography). Where these semi-automated processes drew attention to errors in the original annotations (e.g., a typo in a particular annotation), it was trivial to open the corresponding ELAN transcript, review and correct the relevant annotations, and re-run the entire analysis on the freshly corrected corpus. This kind of reproducible workflow not only made it feasible

to analyze the quantity of data assembled here (contributions from nearly fifty speakers across twenty-seven hours of audio recordings), but also freed up time to delve into questions that we likely wouldn't have been able to get to otherwise if we had needed to do this kind of data wrangling by hand (including digging into apparent instances of personally patterned variation in these communities, a relatively rare finding from the perspective of sociolinguistic typology; cf. Dorian 2010; Cox 2015:244–247). Scripts that took care of data processing and analysis tasks were stored in their own "analysis" folder, separate from the primary recordings, ELAN annotations, and contributor metadata, which stayed in a consistent location that these scripts could refer to.[9]

Along with making it more straightforward to apply computational and quantitative methods in analysis, developing this collection of language materials in line with current good practice recommendations in documentary linguistics also allowed for easier citation of individual data points in later publications. In particular, using ELAN to create time-aligned transcripts of the contents of these recordings made a noticeable difference for citing excerpts from the corpus in ways that allow for quick reference back to the primary data. In one study based on these materials (Cox 2015), whenever data from the corpus were being cited, a reference was made to the corresponding session and track number, the unique identifier(s) of the contributing speaker(s), and the start and end times of this segment in the audio—all information that could be gleaned immediately from the ELAN transcripts. This is the case in example (2), where contributors M00 and F20 share their perceptions of two of the words for "girls" that are in use in the local community (reproduced from Cox 2015:178, example (13)):

(2)   **M00:** *Mejalles,* [.] *Mäakjes.*
        CDC: Is there a difference there, or, uh . . . ?

(1)   **text:**   Du   su'st   dän   grooten,   bruunen
        gloss: you.SG   should:2SG   the.ACC   big.ACC   brown.ACC
                       Boa   tochloten.
                       bear   leave.alone:INF
        coding: S07: { lxShould2S: "su'st", lxMascAccThe: "dän", lxMascAccDefBig: "grooten", lxMascAccDefBrown: "bruunen" }
        free-translation: 'You should leave the big, brown bear alone.'
        (*Fibel* sentence S07; F28, 2011-10-27, 4m45s890–4m48s490)

F20: *Na*, [.] *"Mejalles"* is a little more slang.

M00: Yeah, a little more crude.

F20: *"Määkjes"* is a little more proper.

(2011-08-09 (02), 00m29s906–00m40s570)

Managing the data from this project in this way also contributed to addressing a number of the questions that motivated this work in the language community, as well. The results of the analysis of variation described herein pointed to a relatively small number of subgroups of speakers within the larger Plautdietsch-speaking community in central Saskatchewan who shared similar constellations of linguistic features. In some cases, this mirrored the intuitions of members of the language community: at least two groups of Plautdietsch varieties were widely reported within the community, although the exact nature of the linguistic differences between them wasn't always clear. Having serviceable information about a wider range of the varieties present in these communities, as well as the linguistic and sociodemographic features that typically characterized them, left us in a better position to make informed decisions about how language resource materials and language programs might be developed (e.g., in which varieties, and with which possible contributors). It also made it much simpler to see how individual *Fibel* responses, annotated in ELAN, could be transformed back into printable and/or online learning resources, merging the text and audio for individuals' responses in the ELAN transcripts with the templates that were developed for the *Fibel* to create copies that presented each contributor's translations.

It is common in many language documentation projects for teams to make sure that the assembled materials are and remain accessible to members of the contributing language community, both in the short and long terms. As mentioned above, while copies of all of the recorded sessions were returned to the contributing speakers, this in itself did not guarantee that the larger collection of language resources would be available to the larger language community in the area. Instead, arrangements were made for a complete copy of all of the materials from this project to be deposited with the archives of a local Mennonite historical society, which has a mandate to preserve and facilitate access to records such as these for community use into the future. Having this kind of support for long-term, local access was important to a documentation project like this that aimed to support

both linguistic research and community language initiatives. It would also be helpful to have copies of these materials archived with an institution whose mandate also included facilitating discovery of and access to these resources for a wider, potentially non-local audience as one way of encouraging further research on Plautdietsch, although this would require further discussion with members of the language community to determine how this could best be accomplished (especially as there are presently no publicly accessible language archives in Canada, meaning that these materials would either need to be entrusted to a suitable organization outside of the country, which may be of concern to some contributors, or to one inside of Canada that does not participate in the wider community of language archives).

In this project, investing the effort required to develop language resources in ways that reflected our understanding of current recommended practices in documentary linguistics—creating our recordings using non-proprietary, uncompressed formats on equipment that would produce relatively high-quality results; favoring open standards and open source software tools wherever possible for managing our recordings, metadata, and annotations; and trying to keep materials organized consistently when it came to directory structures and file names—made many of the later uses described above not only possible, but actually practicable. While we would recommend that documentation teams consider the possible benefits that implementing similar data management practices may have in their own contexts, it is also important to recognize that not every team may necessarily find itself in a position to bring all of these recommendations to bear immediately on their own work. Although the situation is rapidly improving with step-by-step guides, learning resources, and training opportunities becoming available to documentation teams around the world, training and resources that support these kinds of data management practices are still unevenly distributed. We would likely do well to heed the observation made by Carpenter et al. (2016:4) that "unworkable standards and a dogmatic insistence on 'best practices' in digital technologies and language documentation, set by scholars and funding agencies, can have a disempowering effect on individuals and communities" and consequently take care to ensure that data management practices such as these are shared and implemented in ways that support and amplify the efforts of documentation teams that choose to adopt them.

Notes

1. The median age of contributors to this project was 79 (with a standard deviation of 8.7 years), which gives a sense of the demographic skew that had resulted from language shift in the region.

2. As one reviewer noted, it may be preferable to choose directional (e.g., cardioid or hypercardioid) microphones for capturing spoken language under circumstances such as these, both to reduce the amount of ambient noise that is recorded and to improve the degree of separation between individual speakers' voices. We agree, although it may be important to weigh these benefits against other possible trade-offs. Directional microphones sometimes exhibit proximity effects that amplify low-frequency sounds, which may affect the usability of recordings made with this kind of equipment in later acoustic analyses of phonetic features such as nasality and voice quality (cf. Plichta 2010).

3. This documentation project did not involve any video recording. While this may not have been critical to the parts of these consultation sessions that involved reviewing and translating the *Fibel*, it would almost certainly have been worthwhile for the conversations that were frequently recorded before and after this work, where being able to see each of the contributors as they spoke would no doubt expand the range of possible future uses of these materials (and likely make them more engaging on a personal level for future users, as well). If we had the chance to do this project again, I would hope that it would be possible to incorporate video to the degree that contributors thought it was appropriate.

4. Since none of these devices offered any safeguards against bit rot or other forms of data corruption over time, we also produced both MD5 and SHA-1 checksums of each of the audio files immediately after they were renamed and organized, storing them in the same folder as the corresponding recordings (the files ending in .md5 and .sha1). Although not a perfect solution, these "digital fingerprints" provided at least one way for us to confirm the integrity of the audio recordings over time by checking that each checksum algorithm returned the same value for each audio recording as it did when it was first applied shortly after the recordings were made. A copy of all of the project materials was later made on a network-attached storage system that performed automatic integrity checking and error correction and that maintained an additional off-site mirror of these files onto a remote computing cluster that offered nightly backups.

5. https://www.audacityteam.org/.

6. https://ffmpeg.org/.

7. Although this sounds attractive in theory, in practice, creating time-aligned annotations for the dozens of hours of audio recorded in this project was no small task. This "transcription bottleneck" is well known in the documentary linguistic literature (see Reiman 2010; Boerger 2011; Seifart et al. 2018:e335–e336; Himmelmann 2018; among others) and posed a serious logistical challenge to the overall success of this project. While recent work drawing on techniques from natural language processing and computational linguistics aims to lessen this burden (e.g., Cox, Boulianne, & Alam 2019), in this project, we were fortunate to have the help of two dedicated annotators, Adrienne Findlay and Chelsea Cox, who assisted in creating empty annotations around segments of speech for each of the contributors in each recording, which ultimately made the transcription and coding described here feasible.

8. At the outset of this work, we coded instances of variation by hand, relying on ELAN's multitranscript regular expression search facilities to retrieve particular variants in the transcribed text of all of our transcripts. This turned out to be quite time-consuming, because ELAN offered limited facilities for users to batch edit the results returned from these kinds of queries. In the end, we developed two small scripts that helped with this work: one that performed the same kinds of regular expression searches as ELAN did, saving the results into a Unicode-encoded CSV spreadsheet together with cross-linked audio clips that could be reviewed and edited quickly and another that reintegrated the contents of these edited spreadsheets back into the ELAN transcripts from which they had been drawn (see Cox 2015:136 for details). The final result of using these two scripts was the same as if we had done all of this annotation inside of ELAN—a fully time-aligned spoken corpus with all identified instances of variation tagged as such—but took a fraction of the time it otherwise would have to accomplish.

9. It would have been possible at the time when this project was underway (and even easier now) to integrate this analysis directly into the academic writing that presented it using tools such as Sweave (Leisch 2002) and knitr (Xie 2015), which allow snippets of "live" code to be embedded into documents. Tools like these can be used to help ensure that the output of analyses stay in sync with the contents of a documentary corpus when the latter is still being actively corrected and expanded (which is often the case in documentation projects, where annotations are continually being refined as the corpus is used and understandings of the language develop), making reproducible research practices easier to implement in this context (cf. Berez-Kroeker et al. 2018; Berez-Kroeker et al., chapter 1, this volume, for further discussion of reproducible research in linguistics).

References

Austin, Peter K. 2006. Data and language documentation. In *Essentials of Language Documentation*, ed. Jost Gippert, Nikolaus P. Himmelmann, and Ulrike Mosel, 87–112. Berlin: Mouton de Gruyter.

Berez-Kroeker, Andrea L., Lauren Gawne, Susan Smythe Kung, Barbara F. Kelly, Tyler Heston, Gary Holton, Peter Pulsifer, et al. 2018. Reproducible research in linguistics: A position statement on data citation and attribution in our field. *Linguistics* 56 (1): 1–18. doi:10.1515/ling-2017–0032.

Bird, Steven, and Gary Simons. 2003. Extending Dublin Core metadata to support the description and discovery of language resources. *Computers and the Humanities* 37 (4): 375–388. doi:10.1023/A:1025720518994.

Boerger, Brenda H. 2011. To BOLDly go where no one has gone before. *Language Documentation and Conservation* 5:208–233. http://hdl.handle.net/10125/4499.

Bowern, Claire. 2015. *Linguistic Fieldwork: A Practical Guide.* 2nd ed. New York: Palgrave Macmillan.

Broeder, Daan, Freddy Offenga, Don Willems, and Peter Wittenburg. 2001. The IMDI metadata set, its tools and accessible linguistic databases. In *Proceedings of the IRCS Workshop on Linguistic Databases*, ed. Steven Bird, Peter Buneman, and Mark Liberman, 48–55. Philadelphia: Linguistic Data Consortium.

Broeder, Daan, Menzo Windhouwer, Dieter van Uytvanck, Thorsten Trippel, and Twan Goosen. 2012. CMDI: A component metadata infrastructure. In *Proceedings of the Workshop on Describing Language Resources with Metadata: Towards Flexibility and Interoperability in the Documentation of Language Resources*, ed. Victoria Arranz, Daan Broeder, Bertrand Gaiffe, Maria Gavrilidou, Monica Monachini, and Thorsten Trippel, 1–4. Istanbul: European Language Resources Association. http://www.lrec-conf .org/proceedings/lrec2012/workshops/11.LREC2012%20Meta data%20Proceedings.pdf.

Carpenter, Jennifer, Annie Guerin, Michelle Kaczmarek, Gerry Lawson, Kim Lawson, Lisa P. Nathan, and Mark Turin. 2016. Digital access for language and culture in First Nations communities. Knowledge Synthesis Report. Vancouver: Social Sciences and Humanities Research Council of Canada. http://www.ideas -idees.ca/sites/default/files/sites/default/uploads/general/2016 /2016-sshrc-ksg-turin_et_al.pdf.

Cox, Christopher. 2015. Quantitative perspectives on variation in Mennonite Plautdietsch. PhD dissertation, University of Alberta. http://hdl.handle.net/10402/era.40446.

Cox, Christopher, Gilles Boulianne, and Jahangir Alam. 2019. Taking aim at the transcription bottleneck: Integrating speech technology into language documentation and conservation. Paper presented at the 6th International Conference on Language Documentation and Conservation (ICLDC), University of Hawai'i at Mānoa, Honolulu, HI, February 28–March 3. http://hdl.handle.net/10125/44841.

Czaykowska-Higgins, Ewa. 2009. Research models, community engagement, and linguistic fieldwork: Reflections on working within Canadian Indigenous communities. *Language Documentation and Conservation* 3 (1): 15–50. http://hdl.handle.net/10125 /4423.

Czaykowska-Higgins, Ewa. 2018. Reflections on ethics: Rehumanizing linguistics, building relationships across difference. In *Reflections on Language Documentation 20 Years after Himmelmann 1998*, ed. Bradley McDonnell, Andrea L.

Berez-Kroeker, and Gary Holton, 110–121. Language Documentation and Conservation Special Publication 15. Honolulu: University of Hawai'i Press. http://hdl.handle.net/10125/24813 .

Dorian, Nancy C. 2010. *Investigating Variation: The Effects of Social Organization and Social Setting.* Oxford: Oxford University Press.

Dyck, Cornelius J. 1993. *An Introduction to Mennonite History.* 3rd ed. Scottdale, PA: Herald Press.

Gawne, Lauren. 2018. A guide to the Syuba (Kagate) Language Documentation Corpus. *Language Documentation and Conservation* 12:204–234. http://hdl.handle.net/10125/24768.

Guenter, Jacob G., Leonard Doell, Dick Braun, Jacob L. Guenther, Henry A. Friesen, Jacob W. Loeppky, John P. Doell, et al., eds. 1995. *Hague-Osler Mennonite Reserve: 1895–1995.* Saskatoon, Canada: Hague-Osler Reserve Book Committee.

Henke, Ryan, and Andrea L. Berez-Kroeker. 2016. A brief history of archiving in language documentation, with an annotated bibliography. *Language Documentation and Conservation* 10:411–457. http://hdl.handle.net/10125/24714.

Himmelmann, Nikolaus P. 1998. Documentary and descriptive linguistics. *Linguistics* 36 (1): 161–195. doi:10.1515/ling.1998.36 .1.161.

Himmelmann, Nikolaus P. 2012. Linguistic data types and the interface between language documentation and description. *Language Documentation and Conservation* 6:187–207. http://hdl .handle.net/10125/4503.

Himmelmann, Nikolaus P. 2018. Meeting the transcription challenge. In *Reflections on Language Documentation 20 Years after Himmelmann 1998*, ed. Bradley McDonnell, Andrea L. Berez-Kroeker, and Gary Holton, 33–40. Language Documentation and Conservation Special Publication 15. Honolulu: University of Hawai'i Press. http://hdl.handle.net/10125/24806.

Lee, Nala Huiying. 2013. Review of Shure WH30XLR cardioid headset microphone and Countryman E6 omnidirectional earset microphone. *Language Documentation and Conservation* 7:177–184. http://hdl.handle.net/10125/4595.

Leisch, Friedrich. 2002. Sweave: Dynamic generation of statistical reports using literate data analysis. In *Compstat 2002: Proceedings in Computational Statistics*, ed. Wolfgang Härdle and Bernd Rönz, 575–580. Heidelberg: Physica Verlag. https://doi .org/10.1007/978-3-642-57489-4_89.

Lüpke, Friederike. 2009. Data collection methods for field-based language documentation. *Language Documentation and Description*, vol. 6, ed. Peter K. Austin, 53–100. London: School of Oriental and African Studies. http://www.elpublishing.org/PID /071.

McDonnell, Bradley, Andrea L. Berez-Kroeker, and Gary Holton, eds. 2018. *Reflections on Language Documentation 20 Years after Himmelmann 1998.* Language Documentation and Conservation

Special Publication 15. Honolulu: University of Hawai'i Press. http://hdl.handle.net/10125/24800.

Meakins, Felicity, Jennifer Green, and Myfany Turpin. 2018. *Understanding Linguistic Fieldwork*. New York: Routledge.

Nagy, Naomi, and Miriam Meyerhoff. 2015. Extending ELAN into variationist sociolinguistics. *Linguistics Vanguard* 1 (1): 271–281. doi:10.1515/lingvan-2015–0012.

Nathan, David. 2010. Sound and unsound practices in documentary linguistics: Towards an epistemology for audio. In *Language Documentation and Description*, vol. 7, ed. Peter K. Austin, 262–284. London: School of Oriental and African Studies. http://www.elpublishing.org/PID/088.

Nerbonne, John, Rinke Colen, Charlotte Gooskens, Peter Kleiweg, and Therese Leinonen. 2011. Gabmap—a web application for dialectology. *Dialectologia: Revista electrònica*. Special Issue 2, 65–89.

Plichta, Bartłomiej. 2010. Microphones used in recording speech. *AKUSTYK* (website, via Wayback Machine Internet Archive). https://web.archive.org/web/20130406095648/http://bartus.org/akustyk/microphones.php. Accessed July 21, 2013.

Reiman, D. Will. 2010. Basic oral language documentation. *Language Documentation and Conservation* 4:254–268. http://hdl.handle.net/10125/4479.

Rice, Keren. 2006. Ethical issues in linguistic fieldwork: An overview. *Journal of Academic Ethics* 4:123–155. doi:10.1007/s10805-006-9016-2.

Salffner, Sophie. 2015. A guide to the Ikaan language and culture documentation. *Language Documentation and Conservation* 9:237–267. http://hdl.handle.net/10125/24639.

Schembri, Adam, Jordan Fenlon, Ramas Rentelis, Sally Reynolds, and Kearsy Cormier. 2013. Building the British Sign Language Corpus. *Language Documentation and Conservation* 7:136–154. http://hdl.handle.net/10125/4592.

Seifart, Frank, Nicholas Evans, Harald Hammarström, and Stephen C. Levinson. 2018. Language documentation twenty-five years on. *Language* 94 (4): e324–e345. doi:10.1353/lan.2018.0070.

Sloetjes, Han. 2014. ELAN: Multimedia annotation application. In *The Oxford Handbook of Corpus Phonology*, ed. Jacques Durand, Ulrike Gut, and Gjert Kristoffersen, 305–320. Oxford: Oxford University Press.

Thieberger, Nicholas, and Andrea L. Berez. 2012. Linguistic data management. In *The Oxford Handbook of Linguistic Fieldwork*, ed. Nicholas Thieberger, 90–118. Oxford: Oxford University Press.

Woodbury, Anthony C. 2003. Defining documentary linguistics. In *Language Documentation and Description*, vol. 1, ed. Peter K. Austin, 35–51. London: School of Oriental and African Studies. http://www.elpublishing.org/PID/006.

Woodbury, Anthony C. 2011. Language documentation. In *The Cambridge Handbook of Endangered Languages*, ed. Peter K. Austin and Julia Sallabank, 159–186. Cambridge: Cambridge University Press.

Xie, Yihui. 2015. Dynamic documents with R and knitr. 2nd ed. Boca Raton, FL: Chapman and Hall/CRC. https://yihui.name/knitr/.

23   Managing Data for Writing a Reference Grammar

Nala H. Lee

1   Introduction to the project

A fundamental challenge for any reference grammar project is the actual management of the massive amount of data that would usually be collected. Both data and metadata are important in informing the findings of the grammar, and findings in a respectable reference grammar must be substantiated by a good number of examples. The efficient use of data and metadata for grammar-writing calls for some amount of preplanning, but overall allows for data to be much more easily retrieved, especially if the actual writing of the grammar takes place sometime after data collection. The system of careful data management described in this chapter facilitated the writing of a dissertation with over five hundred pages and eight hundred examples (fully citable and referenced to individual locations within an archive) in the short span of six months.

The grammar of Baba Malay was developed as a PhD dissertation project at the University of Hawai'i at Mānoa. It was part of a larger language documentation project that was undertaken between the years of 2012 and 2014 (Lee 2014). Data from the project has been archived at Kaipuleohone (https://scholarspace.manoa.hawaii.edu/handle/10125/4250), the digital language archive hosted by the University of Hawai'i at Mānoa. The data management system utilized for this project was informed by a language documentation methods course conducted by Andrea Berez-Kroeker in 2012 and held at the university. The software that was utilized included SayMore (https://software.sil.org/saymore/), FLEx (FieldWorks Language Explorer; https://software.sil.org/fieldworks/), and ELAN (https://tla.mpi.nl/tools/tla-tools/elan/), in addition to Audacity, Word, and Excel, which was required for the archive's metadata management. SayMore is a tool that enables the organization of files and metadata, transcription, and conversion of common file types for archiving.

FLEx supports various tasks such as transcription, glossing, and dictionary development, while ELAN allows for transcription, translations, and glosses to be interlinearized with audio or video streams. While effort was made to maintain a data management system throughout the duration of the project, I make suggestions at the end of this chapter for a possible improved system and am open to further recommendations. Also, this chapter focuses mostly on methodology for data management. For perspectives on grammar-writing, the reader may wish to consult Ameka, Dench, and Evans (2006), Nakayama and Rice (2014), or Camp et al. (2018).

Baba Malay is a contact language spoken in Singapore and Malaysia. Formed by early intermarriages between Hokkien-speaking Chinese traders and Indigenous women speaking a variety of Malay as early as the fifteenth century, the language is spoken by their descendants, the Peranakans (Lee 2014). The language is considered to be critically endangered at both locations, due to a number of factors (Lee 2019). Many Peranakans shifted to English as a home language following English-medium education during the period of British colonization. Due to the small community size, marriages between Peranakans these days are rarer, and therefore the language is also not popularly used in the home domains. The grammar that this chapter describes focuses on the language of the Peranakans in Singapore for the most part, with a chapter detailing some differences found between both the Singapore variety and the Malacca variety as they are spoken at both locations. The urban context in which documentation takes place enables the type of digital data management steps taken—all digital hardware and software requisite for the project could be fully utilized.

The grammar that ensued was 532 pages in length, had over eight hundred examples that were fully citable and referenced to individual locations within the archive, following methods that allow for persistent identification (see Kung, chapter 8, this volume), such as the one advocated by Thieberger (2009) and used by Berez (2011). The grammar also included a Baba Malay–English, English–Baba Malay glossary with approximately 1,100 headwords, and three fully time-aligned and interlinearized transcripts archived as ELAN .eaf files, in addition to transcripts of Baba Malay poems written by a language consultant, and a number of other word lists. This reference grammar is by no means the largest or most exhaustive in terms of its coverage of grammatical topics, or the numbers of examples that were utilized, but the actual writing and formatting of such a grammar was completed in a reasonable time frame of six months. This time frame would not have had been possible had the data management aspect of the project not been preplanned.

2   Overall data management steps

The overall flow of the project was a seemingly standard one (see for example, Crowley 2007)—I would plan the data collection sessions with the language consultants in advance, deciding on what it was that I wanted to record or elicit (including narratives, procedures, and conversation, as well as traditional data elicitation in which I asked for how a word or a sentence was said in the language). I would carry out the interview session, make audio recordings of the session, take meticulous notes in my field notebook, transfer the data onto my computer where I could add the necessary metadata, and then systematically process the data through SayMore, FLEx, and ELAN, depending on what the end goal was for each individual session. Details of how these programs were used will be covered later in this chapter. With the limited time available for the project, bearing in mind that the data collected here would form the basis of a PhD dissertation, it would have been unrealistic to expect that every session with a language consultant would be fully transcribed, translated, and interlinearized. As an indication of how much data one-and-a-half years' worth of fieldwork can amount to (with about three interview sessions a week), this project resulted then in ninety-two hours of Baba Malay data. While the goal of language documentation is to create records that are representative, long-lasting, and multipurpose (Himmelmann 2006), it becomes clear that a language may never

be satisfactorily documented in this way to its fullest extent (see Himmelmann 2018). Immediate goals are also clearly important, and the immediate goal of this project was to produce a grammar of Baba Malay that would ideally have all its examples citable and traceable back to their time codes within the individual recording and to a particular file within the digital archive. In addition, the grammar I had in mind would have at least three fully interlinearized transcripts representing different genres. These goals ultimately informed my data management workflow.

2.1   The unstated role of a digital language archive and metadata in fieldwork data organization

From the onset of the project, an archive was identified for the storage of material that was to be collected from the field (see Kung, chapter 8, this volume). Kaipuleohone was chosen for the purpose of this project, as it has a strong focus on languages in the Asia-Pacific region. Kaipuleohone also conforms to international archiving standards for digital archives and is a member of the Open Language Archives Community (http://www.language -archives.org/), which potentially increases the searchability and visibility of the data deposited. With the archive in mind, it was much easier to figure out what types of metadata information I required or that the data would require to be complete. I could label my session in my field notebook with the same titles I was using for the relevant files in the archive and collect the relevant and necessary information from my language consultants during the elicitation sessions. See figure 23.1 for an example of a page within my field notebook. The title on this page, "NL1–056: Adverbials Part 3," corresponds mostly with the information of the archived file within Kaipuleohone. The file-naming convention here follows that which Kaipuleohone uses: my name was used for the name of the collection, and therefore my initials NL are used here, 1 indicates that this is the first collection, and 56 indicates the item number within the collection. Note that the archive only requires this information but not the extra information—"Adverbials Part 3 with Victor." This information was written down for my own use, and had to be deleted from the title before depositing the file in the archive, but was added to notes about the file within the archive's metadata spreadsheet.

My sessions were preplanned and organized by the types of information that I perceived would be relevant

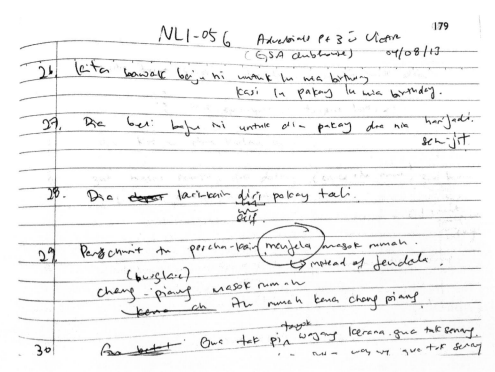

Figure 23.1
Field notebook page with session information.

to the grammar that I was writing. I had sessions dedicated to verbs or adjectives, for example, although they were not always thematically sorted linguistically, and could be a conversation, a narrative, or centered on a map task to get at different ways of asking for directions. The content of the session would be reflected mostly in the title of the recording, which would be listed in the metadata spreadsheet that I had to fill in for Kaipuleohone, as well as in my field notebook. For example, in figure 23.1, the metadata information includes the name of the speaker (Victor), date (April 8, 2013), the location of recording (a clubhouse), the content of the session (adverbials), and the title of the audio file generated from the session (NL1–056). Likewise, if I wanted to look for words for body parts, I knew that the relevant data might be found within the file "NL1–70: Body Part 3 with Victor Wee," based on the information on my Kaipuleohone metadata spreadsheet (see figure 23.2 for a sample portion of it).

Such methods ensured that I could find relevant examples quickly when writing a particular section, for example, a section on relative clauses. There are clearly different opinions on whether elicitation provides the most natural data (see Camp et al. 2018), but I found that it was necessary to balance more naturally occurring data with elicited data to ensure that paradigms were fully fleshed out. It is also always possible to check the naturalness or well-formedness of elicited data with a number of speakers other than the speaker from whom the data was elicited (bearing in mind speaker confidentiality or anonymity if the speaker so wishes). Other types of information recorded for the metadata spreadsheet of the archive also helped in the process of writing the grammar (see figure 23.2). For example, it was necessary at various points to check that a particular construction was not idiosyncratic for a speaker, and sorting through the metadata spreadsheet, it was easier to pick up possible sessions of instances where a different speaker might have been interviewed on the same topic. Ideally, it would have been preferable to have every single session fully transcribed on software that allows constructions to be easily searchable, for example in FLEx or even within Word itself. However, this was not possible within the limitations of a dissertation time line, and transcribed data sometimes had to be used in conjunction with data that could only be found within a recording. Therefore, having well-organized metadata helped in the process of writing the grammar itself, allowing the grammar to be much more quickly and efficiently written than if there had been no organized metadata. That there was a digital archive identified from the outset of the project meant that metadata had to be kept, and it was definitely easier to immediately file away metadata at the end of each recording than to do it later on (Thieberger and Berez 2012).

*NOTES (Prose description of the contents of the item)	ORTHOGRAPHY (any notes about orthography that are required to understand the metadata)	LENGTH OF REEL-TO-REEL Tape in Meters	RUNNING TIME OF REEL-TO-REEL tapes	RECORDING SPEED OF REEL-TO-REEL Tapes	RELATION (if this item is related to other items in the collection, select ONE of the following types, followed by the item number of the related item, e.g. HasTranscript ALB01-005.txt. IsCopyOf, IsCopiedBy, Requires, IsRequiredBy, HasPart, IsPartOf, HasVersion, IsVersionOf, Replaces, isReplacedBy, HasTranscript, Transcribes)	RIGHTS (Access conditions specific to this item if different from most of collection, as you specified on your Deposit of Materials agreement)	*ROLE AND PERSON (select from the Annotator, artist, author, copier, consu...	
NL1-070: Body part 3 with Victor							Interviewer Nala Lee	Speaker Victor
NL1-071: Notes on previous recordings NL1-032, NL1-043, difference between toksa and jangan, and some quantifiers, with Victor							Interviewer Nala Lee	Speaker Victor
NL1-072: Transcript of NL1-022: Pear Story with Peter Wee					Transcribes NL1-022		Transcriber Nala Lee	Speaker Peter Wee
NL1-073: Transcript of NL1-028: Pear story version 2 with Victor					Transcribes NL1-028		Transcriber Nala Lee	Speaker Victor
NL1-074: Transcript of NL1-034: Story of the enormous turnip with Victor							Transcriber Nala Lee	Speaker Victor
NL1-075: Transcript of NL1-035. Story of the three little pigs with Victor					Transcribes NL1-034		Transcriber Nala Lee	Speaker Victor
NL1-076: Conversation about Tan clan. Mostly in English, some Peranakan.					Transcribes NL1-035			Speaker Peter Wee (60s, Sing... Speaker Alfred (70s, M...
NL1-077: Differences between Malay and Peranakan terms for some household items								Speaker Peter Wee Ban Keng Speaker Alfred (70s, M...
NL1-078: Notes on previous recordings NL1-044 and NL1-045, clarifying lexical meanings with Victor							Interviewer Nala Lee	Speaker Victor
NL1-079: Conversation between Lilian, Peter Wee, Kim Choo and Nala at the Katong Antique House.							Speaker Peter Wee	Speaker Lilian (50s)
NL1-080: Peter Wee on the telephone talking about purchasing leaves for dumplings							Recorder Nala Lee	Speaker Peter Wee
NL1-081: Verbs part 3 with Victor							Interviewer Nala Lee	Speaker Victor
							Speaker Irene /79. Stop	Speaker Victor

Figure 23.2

A portion of the Kaipuleohone depositor's metadata spreadsheet.

2.2 Matching time codes in field notes to audio stream

In addition to the notes I made about each recording, I also took down notes of what was being said as best as I could. Another method that did actually help the process of writing was taking note occasionally of the time codes on the digital audio recorder that was being used for the purpose, particularly when something interesting was said. There were instances during the writing of the grammar that I wanted to find particular examples from files that were not already fully transcribed. In a session that was an hour long, I would have at least five time codes written, and this helped to demarcate the file to an extent. I knew where these examples were in a rough sense because that information was in my metadata file, but it would have been difficult to look for these examples in real time within the actual audio file itself had there not been various time codes written at various points in my field notebook (see figure 23.3).

So, even if I did not have a time code written for every individual example, I would still be able to find the ones I needed quite easily, if they were found between two time codes or close to a time code. While this can feel like a tedious process to have to manage in tandem with the rest of the recording session, it was a way of matching up my digital audio files with my physical handwritten notes, and it was a process that I found particularly helpful while writing the grammar.

Following the interview sessions, the audio files were immediately transferred off the SD (secure digital) cards (straight from the recorder) and onto three separate types of storage—my personal computer, a primary portable external hard drive, and a second backup portable external hard drive—given the importance of proper data storage (see Thieberger and Berez 2012). All the necessary metadata required are also written down at this point on the Excel sheet provided by the archive. These are activities that are preferably done on the day the interview is carried out. The other editing that I did at this point was to include spoken metadata in the audio recording, if for some reason, this information was not included in the recording. Any postrecording addition of metadata was carried out in Audacity, a free-to-use audio editor. At the beginning of each recording, I usually included basic spoken metadata, such as "This is the second of July 2013, and I am recording with Auntie Jane Quek and today we are talking about directions."

This is important because it is useful for an audio file to be self-identifiable in the event that any written metadata are not accessible or become inaccessible. The other process that was carried out in Audacity was the deletion of names in conversations that would otherwise identify individuals in ways that were not appropriate, for example, in conversations where gossip inevitably took place. If the content of the conversation was entirely unsuitable or ethically problematic, regardless of the fact that permission had been given by the language consultants to record the conversation, the recording would be purged completely from the collection. Besides the time codes themselves, I found it useful to enter an "*" and a time code in my field notebook every time something that was potentially contentious was said, so that again, information in my field notebook could be easily matched to information within my digital audio files. The parts of the recordings that I would prefer to delete would be easily found with the relevant time code information that I had. Otherwise, I would have had to listen to entire audio files in real time to find this information or take ethical risks by not paying attention to the potentially problematic portions of the recordings (which I clearly could not do).

2.3 Transcription, translation, glossing, and time alignment with audio stream

The postinterview processing that took place after batches of sessions was to decide whether this was a session that should be fully transcribed, time-aligned, and interlinearized (so that there would be at least a main transcription tier, a word or morpheme tier, a word or morpheme gloss tier, and a free translation tier) or whether the session needed only transcription and free translation. These would include in particular the recordings that would form the basis of the transcripts in the appendix of the grammar. Otherwise, the data that would inform the grammatical description and form the basis of the examples just had to be at the very least searchable, so that they could be produced and provided in a citable form within the grammar.

Full transcripts of the interview sessions that were included in the grammar were one conversation and two narratives, where the language consultants provided the bulk of the content. For these, the goals were to transcribe and free translate quickly, provide word glosses (and create a Baba Malay–English dictionary and reversal index at the same time), and then merge various information in a time-aligned form together with the

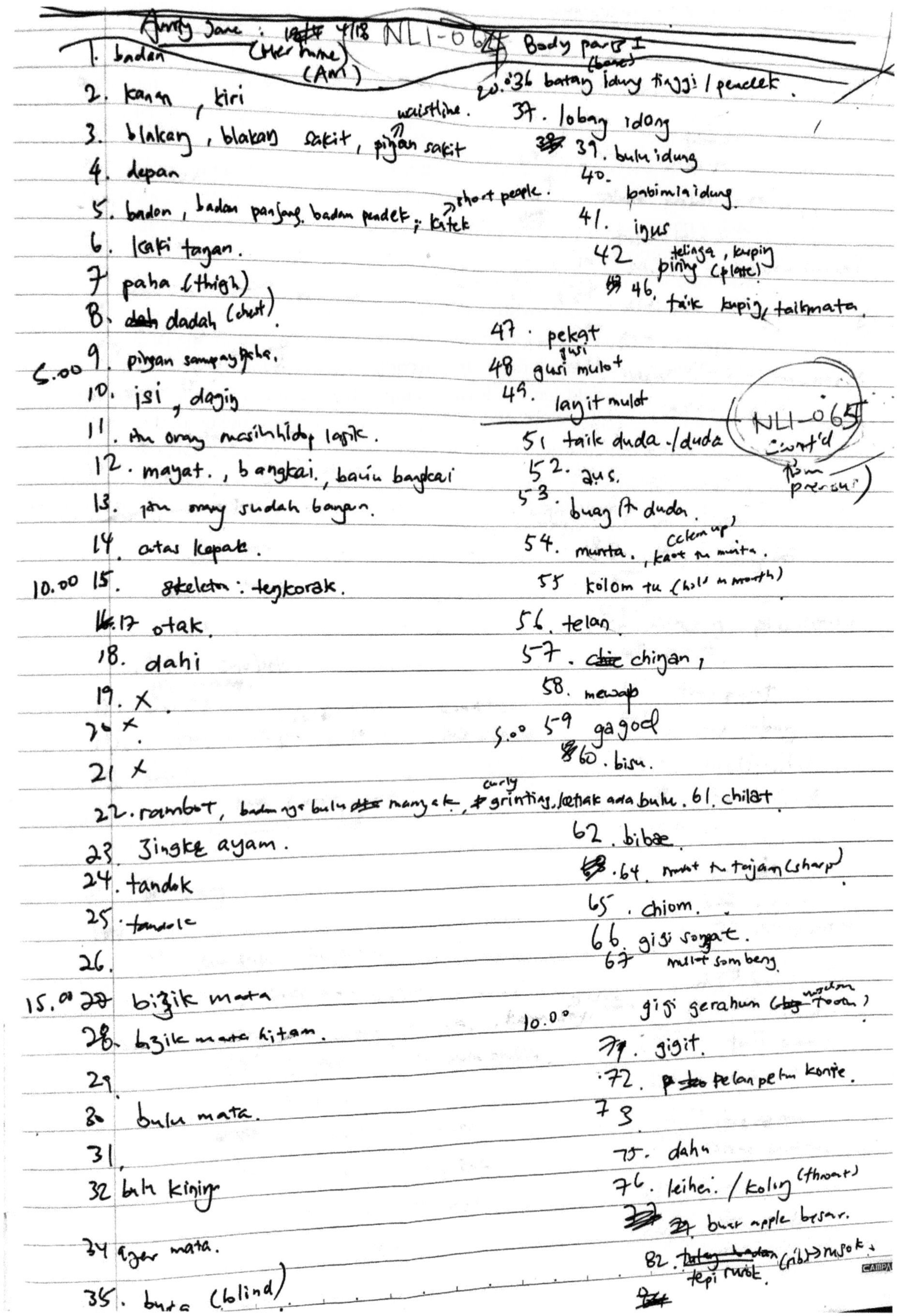

Anny Jane : 9/18 NLI-06 Body part I
(her name)   (bars)
(AM)

1. badan
2. kanan , kiri
3. blakan , blakan sakit , pigan sakit   waistline
4. depan
5. badan , badan panjang. badan pendek ; kitek   → short people
6. kaki tagan.
7. paha (thigh)
8. dadah (chest).
5.00 9. pigan sampay pehe.
10. isi , daging
11. Au orang masih hidop lagik.
12. mayat. , bangkai , baun bangkai
13. jau orang sudah bangan.
14. atas kepak.
10.00 15.   skeleton : tengkorak.
16.17 otak.
18. dahi
19. X
20. X
21. X
22. rambot , badan yg bulu manyek , → grinting , letak ada bulu . 61. chilat
                                    curly
23. Jingke ayam.
24. tandok
25. tandok
26.
15.00 27. bizik mata
28. bizik mata hitam.
29.
30. bulu mata.
31.
32. bulu kining
34. ajer mata.
35. buta (blind)

20.036 batang idung tingji / pendek.
37. lobang idong
39. bulu idung
40. babi mia idung
41. igus
42. telinga , kuping
     piring (plate)
46. taik kupi , taik mata.
47. pekat
48. gusi mulot
49. layit mulot
51 taik duda / duda
52. aus.
53. buang A duda.
54. munta , kaot m munta.   (clean up)
55 kolom tu (hole m mouth)
56. telan
57. chigan ,
58. mewap
5.00 59 gagod
60. bisu.
62. bibe
64. maut n tajam (sharp)
65 . chiom.
66. gigi songat.
67 mulot somberg
     gigi gerahun (toorn)
10.00 71. gigit.
72. pelan pelan konje.
73
75. dahu
76. leihei / koling (throat)
77 buer apple besar.
82 badan (ribs) musok
     tepi musok.

NLI-065
cont'd
Bm pre sau)

Figure 23.3
Field notebook page with noted time intervals.

audio content (so that the final product was a fully time-aligned and interlinearized transcript with four tiers: intonation unit, word, word gloss, and free translation). The software I used for these purposes were SayMore, FLEx, and ELAN. SayMore was used for the first initial transcription and free translation pass (see figure 23.4 for a screenshot of how SayMore was used).

FLEx was used to quickly fill in the glosses for individual words as well as to create a Baba Malay–English dictionary as well as an English–Baba Malay reversal index. Figure 23.5 shows how FLEx was used to fill in word glosses, and figure 23.6 demonstrates the lexicon function in FLEx.

The information was then all merged in ELAN, so that the transcript would be time-aligned. Figure 23.7 is a screenshot of ELAN being used to time align transcription, words in the language, glosses, and free translation.

The final transcripts that were used in the grammar were edited and ordered Word versions exported from ELAN.

2.3.1 Transcription and free translation in SayMore The SayMore process is a rather straightforward one. Within a single project, multiple sessions can be created, each representing a different recording. The relevant recording is uploaded for each session. Before transcribing and

translating, the audio file is first segmented into intonation units. As a way of making the segmentation process more efficient, the autosegmentation tool in SayMore is utilized as a first pass—the autosegmentation tool here is essentially a silence recognizer. The segments are then checked manually and extended or reduced accordingly. This was a much quicker process than manually segmenting the data entirely. The software then allows for transcription and free translation to be carried out rather quickly. I would recommend choosing and sticking to a single method of transcription from the start, so that the transcription stays consistent and time does not have to be wasted thinking about how best to transcribe in the middle of the project. The method of transcription I utilized was a modified and simplified version of Du Bois et al.'s (1992) discourse transcription method, which chunks utterances into intonation units. Note that SayMore does not allow for more than a single speaker tier, nor does it handle overlap well. To indicate different speakers in a conversation, the initials of the speaker followed by ";" would be entered in the transcription column.

2.3.2 Glossing and dictionary development in FLEx Once the transcription and free translation had been carried out, the SayMore session would be exported as a FLEx

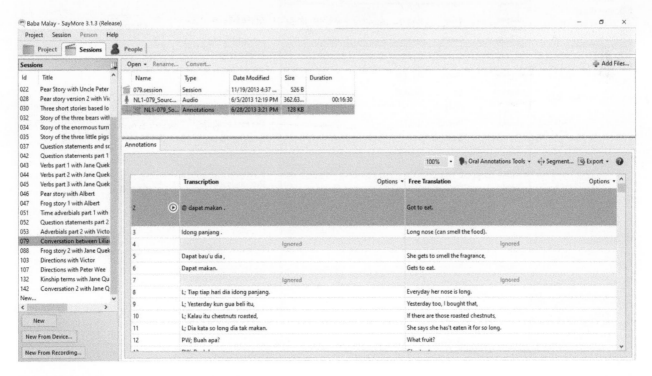

Figure 23.4
Transcription and free translation in SayMore.

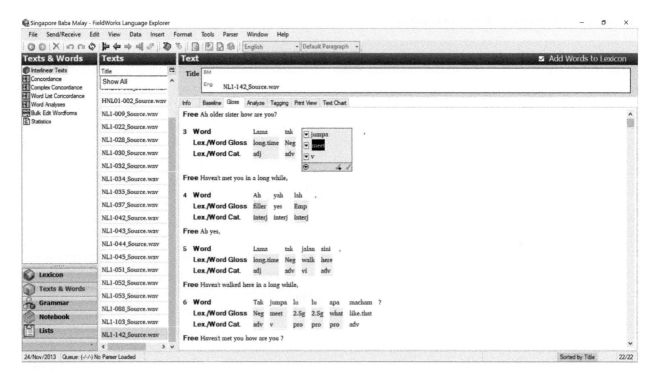

Figure 23.5
Glossing in FLEx.

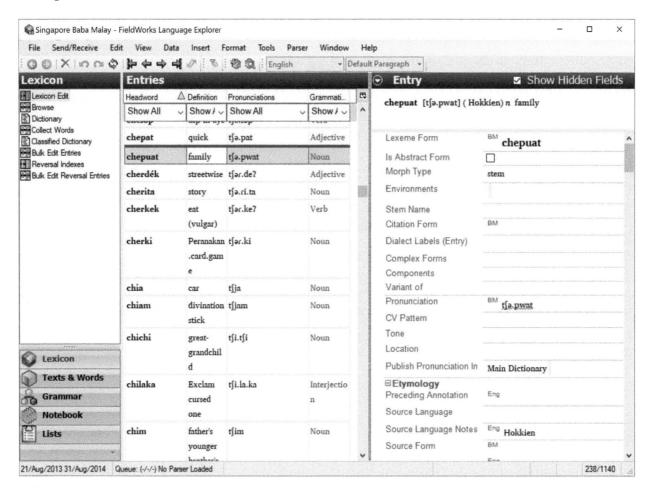

Figure 23.6
The lexicon function in FLEx.

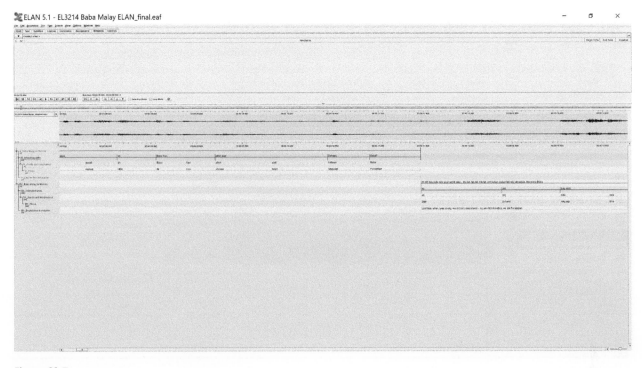

Figure 23.7
Time alignment in ELAN.

interlinear text (flextext extension, a format designed for use with ELAN). It was much easier keeping track of the files generated by the different software by naming them with the same conventions, save for the file extensions that would allow them to be properly recognized by the relevant software. Within FLEx's Text & Words function, the transcription and free translation tiers could then be imported. After import, the relevant metadata are added (including title of the text), and glossing can then take place with the Gloss function. The Gloss function automatically remembers the gloss and part of speech associated with the word if the relevant setting is chosen (ensure that the tick plus button is clicked after a new gloss is entered to automatically populate the gloss and part of speech boxes every time the same word occurs). The autoglossing should still be checked, especially in instances where a word has multiple meanings. Importantly, I wanted to create a two-way lexicon/dictionary in FLEx. The headword would be the word that appears, while the definition in some sense for this lexicon would be provided by the gloss. For the two-way lexicon to be automatically compiled, the Add Words to Lexicon box has to be checked before any glossing takes place at all. Note that after all the

relevant texts had been glossed in the SayMore environment, it is useful to check that information in the Lexicon function. Using Lexicon Edit, other types of information, such as the pronunciation of the word in the International Phonetic Alphabet and the etymology of the word, can be added. After all the data entry had taken place in FLEx, I was able to export the Baba Malay–English lexicon and the reversal index using the Pathway add-on. The lexicon and reversal index formed a crucial part of the grammar's appendix. Another function that I found to be particularly useful in FLEx was the Concordance function, where I was able to search for relevant examples while writing the grammar and look at what was happening in the environment of the word. Note that time alignment with the audio stream does not take place in FLEx. For transcripts that did not require time alignment, such as the bulk of the data that would inform the grammar and be used for various examples throughout the grammar, the transcription process could technically stop here because the data are searchable and usable in FLEx. If the time code of the utterance is required, the information can be easily found in the ELAN file that can be quickly generated in SayMore (see figure 23.8).

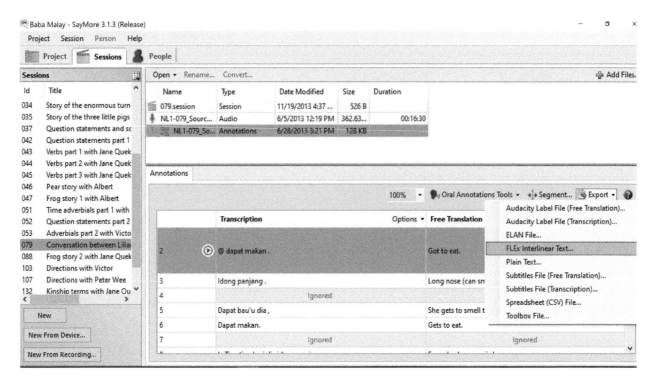

Figure 23.8
Generating an ELAN file in SayMore.

2.3.3 Time alignment in ELAN For transcripts that required further time alignment, and to consolidate all the information earlier produced from SayMore (transcription and free translation) and FLEx (words and gloss), the FLEx output was exported from FLEx and imported back into SayMore. These imports and exports all take place in the FLExtext format. SayMore itself does not reflect the word and word gloss tiers, but that information is retained with the data, and these data are viewable and accessible when exported into ELAN. The final product in ELAN includes a numbering tier, a transcription tier (intonation units in this case), a words or morphemes tier, a words or morphemes gloss tier, and a free translation tier. The durations of each major chunk—in this case the intonation unit—can be time-aligned to the audio stream. The final product can then be exported for Microsoft Word in an XML format and modified in whatever ways necessary for use in the grammar or for other purposes.

2.3.4 Understanding data formats The data import and export processes among SayMore, FLEx, and ELAN may appear tenuous, particularly when the desired products can be produced in FLEx (dictionary) and ELAN (interlinearized time-aligned transcript) separately or using just the two programs. For example, ELAN can be

used for creating the initial transcription (for example at the intonation unit level) and free translation, and the product from ELAN can be exported to FLEx in FLExtext format for segmenting the intonation units or sentences into words or morphemes, glossing at the word or morpheme level, and for almost automatically creating the two-way index or dictionary. The data together with the gloss in FLEx can be then exported back into ELAN, so that there would now be tiers for the main intonation units or sentences, a word or morpheme tier, a word or morpheme gloss tier, and a free translation tier. However, the version that I was working on while preparing these transcripts did not allow for such an import-export process, and even now, while the software allows for it, I find it much faster to carry out my initial transcription and free translation in SayMore. Do note, however, that the SayMore-FLEx-ELAN process does not allow for the representation of speech from two speakers in two separate lines—the solution to this at least for the transcripts used in the grammar was to modify them in Word so that the speakers are represented on separate lines in a transcript of a conversation, for example. Otherwise, it would be possible now with the current versions of FLEx and ELAN to directly import and export data between both programs (bearing in mind that the tiers have to be set up appropriately at the start for this to take place).

Essentially, it is important to be aware of what data formats each individual software supports and what data formats can be used for imports and exports between programs (see Bird and Simons 2003). It is also a good idea to keep track of how the various file types map onto each other. I labeled the files with the same name if they were from the same project and had a separate form in Excel with information regarding what stages the transcription were at and which files those stages of transcription resulted in. Otherwise a file labeled NL1–030 interlinear. flextext would not by itself be very informative. The name of the file itself does not indicate what stage of the transcription has taken place—or in this case, that the word for word glossing has entirely taken place, unless the file is opened and checked in FLEx itself.

2.3.5 Archiving and backup
After transcribing, data that were archived in Kaipuleohone included the audio files, the .xml generated files from ELAN and FLEx depending on where the process was halted for each session, as well as the human-readable Word files (for the grammar itself, but not the archive). The metadata spreadsheet details what each file comprises. It is possible for the transcriber to pick up the transcription where it was left off for files that have not been fully transcribed, but it is good to back up all possible file versions where possible. Where backup is concerned, the various versions of files that are generated from each step of transcription are also doubly backed up in two external portable hard drives. It is not the best idea to have a single backup, especially just on one's personal computer. It was also especially important to create multiple backups, where this project was concerned, because data could not be submitted online for Kaipuleohone, and I had to submit them in bulk on a disk or by being physically there in person with one of my portable external hard drives in Hawai'i. It is much more secure with the data being multiply stored before any backup can take place to the digital archive. Since the time I was writing the grammar, the digital archive's interface has been updated, and it is now possible to submit data and metadata online if the collection has already been set up, but users are still encouraged to submit data offline.

At the end of the day, what helped was having clear goals, both for the project and for the data generated from each individual recording session. These, together with the software tools, allowed my grammar to take the shape that it did. Following Thieberger (2009) and Berez (2011), an example in my grammar (Lee 2014) could appear as in the following, indicating that the example, which was uttered by the speaker Peter Wee, can be found on the Kaipuleohone web site in the file labeled NL1–042 and, more specifically, that the utterance can be heard between 00:02:44.4 and 00:02:46.0.

(1) *Dia   chakap   sama   dia.*
    3SG   speak   with   3SG
    'He speaks with him.'

    (Peter Wee, oai:scholarspace.manoa.hawaii.edu:
    NL1–042, 00:02:44.4–00:02:46.0)

The importance of producing reproducible and citable data is discussed at length by Berez-Kroeker et al. (2018). What this case study hopes to show is that it is possible to do so with some foreplanning.

3 What might have been done differently

Reflecting on how the data in this grammar project was managed, there are clearly things that could have been done differently and better.

In the process of fieldwork, the time codes that I had written down in my field notebook were helpful in bringing together information in my physical notes and my digital audio files, but I could have done this more consistently, and perhaps notes of the topic of conversation could be taken at a more regular interval of every five minutes (in addition to noting down time codes where interesting data were shared). This would accelerate that process of matching field notes and audio data, particularly when I am searching for the bit of audio that matches up to interesting data when reviewing my field notes. At the time of this grammar project, there were limitations on what could be done in terms of producing a digital field notebook, but current possibilities include entering field notes directly onto a digital tablet and converting handwriting to digital text on the same device. This would make referencing one's field notes a lot easier, and these would be a lot easier to upload into a digital archive too. My notebooks from that project require scanning before I can upload them anywhere.

Other ways in which the data could have been better managed include keeping a separate personal metadata spreadsheet with other types of information that the archive metadata spreadsheet does not request—including content-related information, such as the ages of the speakers (which I have in my field notebook but is separate from the data otherwise), and file-related information, such as the type of software used to generate a particular data format, and its version number. Keeping track of version numbers of various software would have been immensely useful too. For example, while the earlier versions of FLEx and ELAN did not allow for an easier way of transferring data between the two programs, I do not have on hand the information regarding which versions of the software these were. There are also particular combinations of operating systems and software versions that do not work very well together. This is important information when beginning a new project or when teaching software, as I do in my language documentation classes.

Another issue concerns the name of the collection in the digital archive—I continue to collect data from Baba Malay that I intend to upload, but this time as a joint effort with my research assistants. The collection was created with my name instead of using a more generic name such as that of the language. This feels somewhat awkward, at least for myself, and I plan on changing the name of the collection.

Finally, cloud computing has come some way, and it is not as expensive as it was in the past to back up data directly onto the cloud. This makes the data more easily accessible than on a physical external portable hard drive, although I would advocate at least having two backups, in addition to backing up to a digital archive. My current data backups include using a particular cloud service, in addition to using portable external hard drives, although it is important to check that the cloud computing system allows for a layer of encryption, especially for sensitive data. It also needs to be said that the cloud storage should only be used as a redundant backup, not as a permanent solution for archiving, and it is necessary to check that the cloud service chosen does not own the data in ways that are going to be problematic down the line.

All that being said, there are evidently multiple ways of managing data for a grammar, and this is just one of them. The main message in actuality is that the process of grammar-writing can take place much more smoothly if data are properly managed and organized. While the foreplanning is somewhat tedious, once data management plans are set in place, the system can be quickly learned and adopted, which beats listening in real time to a hundred or more audio files at half an hour to an hour each, for eight hundred–odd examples to include in one's grammar and allows for the data to be used for other purposes in the future.

References

Ameka, Felix K., Alan C. Dench, and Nicholas Evans, eds. 2006. *Catching Language: The Standing Challenge of Grammar Writing*. Trends in Linguistics: Studies and Monographs 167. Berlin: Mouton de Gruyter.

Berez, Andrea. 2011. Directional reference, discourse and landscape in Ahtna. PhD dissertation, University of California, Santa Barbara.

Berez-Kroeker, Andrea L., Lauren Gawne, Susan Smythe Kung, Barbara F. Kelly, Tyler Heston, Gary Holton, Peter Pulsifer, et al. 2018. Reproducible research in linguistics: A position statement on data citation and attribution in our field. *Linguistics* 56 (1): 1–18. https://doi.org/10.1515/ling-2017-0032.

Bird, Steven, and Gary Simons. 2003. Seven dimensions of portability for language documentation and description. *Language* 79 (3): 557–82. https://doi.org/10.1353/lan.2003.0149.

Camp, Amber, Lyle Campbell, Victoria Chen, Nala H. Lee, Matt Magnuson, and Samantha Rarrick. 2018. Writing grammars of endangered languages. In *Oxford Handbook of Endangered Languages*, ed. Kenneth L. Rehg and Lyle Campbell, 271–304. Oxford: Oxford University Press.

Crowley, Terry. 2007. *Field Linguistics: A Beginner's Guide*. Oxford: Oxford University Press.

Du Bois, John, Susanna Cumming, Stephan Schuetze-Coburn, and Danae Paolino, eds. 1992. *Discourse Transcription*. Santa Barbara: University of California, Santa Barbara.

Himmelmann, Nikolaus P. 2006. Language documentation: What is it and what is it good for? In *Essentials of Language Documentation*, ed. Jost Gippert, Nikolaus P. Himmelmann, and Ulrike Mosel, 1–30. Berlin: Mouton de Gruyter.

Himmelmann, Nikolaus P. 2018. Meeting the transcription challenge. In *Reflections on Language Documentation 20 Years after Himmelmann 1998*, ed. Bradley McDonnell, Andrea L. Berez-Kroeker, and Gary Holton. Special issue, *Language Documentation and Conservation* 15:33–40.

Lee, Nala H. 2014. A grammar of Baba Malay with sociophonetic considerations. PhD dissertation, University of Hawai'i at Mānoa.

Lee, Nala H. 2019. Peranakans in Singapore: Responses to language endangerment and documentation. In *Documentation and Conservation of Contact Languages in Southeast Asia and East Asia: Current Issues and Ongoing Initiatives*, ed. Mário Pinharanda-Nunes, and Hugo C. Cardoso. Special issue, *Language Documentation and Conservation*.

Nakayama, Toshihide, and Keren Rice, eds. 2014. *The Art and Practice of Grammar Writing*. Language Documentation and Conservation Special Publication 8. Honolulu: University of Hawai'i Press.

Thieberger, Nicholas. 2009. Steps toward a grammar embedded in data. In *New Challenges in Typology: Transcending the Borders and Refining the Distinctions*, ed. Patricia Epps and Alexandre Arkhipov, 389–408. Berlin: Mouton de Gruyter.

Thieberger, Nicholas, and Andrea L. Berez. 2012. Linguistic data management. In *The Oxford Handbook of Linguistic Fieldwork*, ed. Nicholas Thieberger, 90–118. Oxford: Oxford University Press.

24 Managing Lexicography Data: A Practical, Principled Approach Using FLEx (FieldWorks Language Explorer)

Christine Beier and Lev Michael

Wherever I turned my view,
there was perplexity to be disentangled,
and confusion to be regulated;
choice was to be made out of boundless variety . . .
—Samuel Johnson, 1755, preface to *A Dictionary of the English Language*

1 Introduction

In this chapter, we describe a methodology and workflow for developing lexical resources for underdocumented languages in the context of language documentation projects dedicated to one or both of the following goals: (1) to create and distribute a *dictionary* to a user community; and (2) to create a multipurpose *extensible lexical resource* that forms an integral part of a language documentation and is interdependent with other components of the project, including a text corpus and grammatical analyses. In particular, we describe a workflow that makes use of FieldWorks Language Explorer (FLEx),[1] a lexical and text corpus database application, together with an XML[2]-to-(Xe)LaTeX[3] Python[4] script, from which one can produce professional-quality typeset PDF files for paper or digital publications. All the software and applications we discuss are open source and/or free to obtain and use and have been stably supported for decades. In addition, we describe the methodology we have developed over more than twenty years of language documentation and description in Peruvian Amazonia that addresses concerns about both data *sharing* and data *validity* in the context of the lexicographical practicalities of documentation projects focused on underdocumented languages.

2 Lexicography and language documentation

Lexical resources occupy a prominent place in modern language documentation. A dictionary, for example, is often one of the outcomes of linguistic research that is most valued by the members of heritage communities of languages that are shifting. Being responsive to community priorities thus often means emphasizing the early development of a variety of lexical resources. Lexicographic work is also indispensable to the documentation and description of underdocumented languages, forming part of the classic Boasian trilogy, together with a grammar and a translated text corpus (Woodbury 2011). The methodology and workflow we describe in this chapter reflect our commitment to both long-standing motivations for lexicographic work and the influence of the principles and best practices of digital data management and preservation that have emerged in recent decades (see, e.g., Bird & Simons 2003; Bowern 2008).

As Nichols and Sprouse (2003:99) observe, "producing easily usable, professional-looking descriptive dictionaries on a shoestring budget in a short time span is a priority for documentation, but hard to achieve." The magnitude of the challenge can be appreciated by considering the technical and ethical desiderata that many language documentation projects face in carrying out lexicographic work. In the *short term*, a methodology and workflow are needed that will generate outputs that are useful and appropriate to host community collaborators on the one hand, and to linguistic scholarship on the other, in as short a time frame as possible, at as low a cost as possible. This methodology and workflow design, must, in the *medium term*, anticipate expansion, refinement, and adaptation of the project's structures and products as the project evolves over time. And finally, in the *long term*, the methodology and workflow need to be successful in producing data, analyses, infrastructures, and concrete products that are durable, secure, sharable, reusable, and archivable; while community-directed materials should be easy to access and easy to reproduce, both digitally and on paper, without the need for continual expert maintenance.

The methodology and workflow desiderata we've out-lined must also be responsive to the practical realities that face many linguists' host community collaborators—especially their political and economic marginalization, often compounded by their geographical distance from urban political centers; lack of access to educational opportunities and corresponding low levels of literacy; lack of access to the Internet and other digital resources; and their desire for straightforward, easy-to-use language-learning materials. Here, these considerations are as important to project design and output as are the desiderata responsive to academic and scholarly practices.

These high-level desiderata also entail requirements for the digital tools we employ for lexicography in language documentation projects. First, the lexical database must have flexibility in organizing, categorizing, annotating, coding, sorting, and searching data. Second, our digital tools must have the autonomy, stability, and portability necessary for being able to work in situ and offline. Third, the system must be as simple and flexible as possible for the production of different types of print and digital outputs that themselves are portable and inexpensive. And finally, the digital tools must be as low cost or freely available as possible, so that neither access nor longevity constitute obstacles to sharing or preservation. The reader with a targeted interest in the technical aspects of our discussion may wish to skip ahead to sections 4.2 and 7.

3   Background

The lexicographic methodology we describe here, and the priorities that motivate it, have emerged dynamically since 1999 when we first began doing lexicographic work with various Amazonian communities, most of whom have experienced dramatic language shift toward Spanish over the last few generations.[5] In this context, our lexicographic objectives have been:

1. To gather as much *target language* lexical data as possible,

   1a. with glosses and definitions in the *local* (i.e., con-tact) *language* (typically Spanish, but also Quichua in two cases),

   1b. and with equivalent plus additional descriptive and analytical material in English;

2. then to organize and interpret that data in order to produce:

2a. free, accessible, photocopiable print resources, generated from archivable, web-accessible PDFs, that we deliver rapidly to our local collaborators and other interested members of the heritage community;

2b. and archivable results for scholars and unknown future users.

In practical terms, how we have operationalized these objectives has been shaped, in each project, by a core set of factors that we address briefly: project time frame (section 3.1) and scale (section 3.2); scope of dictionary content (section 3.3); and teamwork (section 3.4) and data sharing (section 3.5) as organizing principles.

3.1   Project time frames

In some cases, our projects have had specifically delimited time frames for fieldwork and production of the lexical resources, as in the case of our "rapid" projects with the Andoa, Muniche, and Záparo communities, where we were limited to a single in situ fieldwork visit (typically about two months) and an additional calendar year (sometimes less) for the creation of lexical (and other) resources. In other cases, the projects have been more open-ended, as in the case of our work with the Iquito[6] and Máíhùnà[7] communities, which remain ongoing. Even in these more open-ended projects, however, we have prioritized producing versions of lexical resources promptly and on a regular basis for community members and other project participants.

3.2   Project scale

The scale of each project that we have carried out has had a significant impact on the kinds of lexical resources we have sought to develop, as has the user community that we have sought to serve. Because most of our lexicographic work has been with "target" languages that no longer have active speech/user communities, but whose inheritors expected our fieldwork with them to result in materials that give them access to knowledge of and about the language and its history, we have chosen to make bilingual or trilingual dictionaries, with head-words in the target language and descriptive/definitional content in the contact language(s) that have replaced the target language in its heritage community. In some circumstances, we have opted for an alphabetically ordered dictionary only (e.g., the Iquito and Máíhǐ̀kì dictionaries), while in other cases, we have included thematically organized content as well (e.g., the Muniche and Záparo dictionaries; see also Mosel 2011). In some cases, we have also produced pamphlets focused on particular semantic domains for pedagogical purposes, to complement the alphabetically ordered dictionary. As we discuss in detail in sections 7.2 and 8, the tools that are built into FLEx for organizing, categorizing, labeling, and sorting lexicographic data, as well as their extensibility, are indispensable to creating these varied types of language-specific outputs.

3.3 Scope of dictionary content

For the larger dictionaries we have developed, an important decision that we have made is to include as much "encyclopedic" information as we can—cultural, historical, and ecological—precisely because there is no other obvious place in which to systematically document, organize, circulate, and preserve this type of knowledge, which is of great interest to the communities with whom we work and, we hope, to future scholars. For the same reason, we have attempted to maintain high standards when it comes to defining ethnobiological terminology, aiming to provide descriptions and scientific names to the best of our abilities. We have thus avoided relatively uninformative definitions such as "bird species" or "type of tree" (unless that is literally all the local knowledge that remains of the lexeme). This encyclopedic goal, and the resulting data management requirements for such an internally complex data set, is a key reason that the preparation of certain of our dictionaries has been so time-consuming, but we have felt that a commitment to this scope is demanded by the circumstances of linguistic and cultural endangerment in which we tend to work. A more nuanced discussion of sources for lexical data is offered in section 5; relevant methodological strategies are offered in sections 8 and 10.

In sum, our typical output is a bilingual, bidirectional, quasi-encyclopedic PDF-based print dictionary that is designed to (1) describe the lexicon of the language as comprehensively as possible and (2) serve as an organized repository of diverse cultural knowledge associated with the language.

3.4 Teamwork as an organizing principle

Turning to methodological specificities, because all of our field projects have involved teamwork—minimally, the two of us, but in some projects, a team of six to nine collaborating researchers—we have been driven by necessity to develop methods and workflows that permit shared use and shared management of a lexical database and related resources. In this respect, we have found that the two most important elements of successful collaborative methodologies are, first, developing and documenting explicit detailed procedures, workflows, and standards that all team members use and, second, systematizing the means for adding metadata to the lexical database to ensure that there is a chronological record of the developments and changes made by identified participants.[8] For this approach to work, accommodating multiple collaborators and multiple project periods (e.g., fieldwork seasons), we have found that users of the lexical database must be committed to creating metadata and documenting work history at every step along the way; we explore this matter in greater detail in section 11.

3.5 Open linguistic data and sharing as an organizing principle

In every project, an important organizing principle has been to return usable outputs of our fieldwork to our collaborators and host community at the end of every field season. In our experience, doing this is a demonstration of respect and commitment that has a long-lasting positive impact on everyone involved. In practice, what this has meant is creating lexicographic materials that are designed for being harvested and shared in this time frame. For longer-term projects, this has meant producing "draft" dictionaries, clearly labeled as such, that can be exported, printed, circulated, and corrected by local collaborators and community members and which serve as good-faith down payments on the eventual production of a non-draft version.

A parallel commitment to sharing data and outputs with other scholars has led us to make durable digital materials available, including drafts of dictionaries, as soon as possible, through our own web sites and/or through digital archives, including, at different points, the Endangered Languages Archive,[9] the Archive of the Indigenous Languages of Latin America,[10] and the California Language Archive[11] (see also Buszard-Welcher, chapter 10, this volume).

4   Starting out on a lexicography project

4.1 General considerations for lexicography work

Having sketched out the frame around our own work, we now broaden our view to some general considerations. In beginning any lexicography project, we are embarking on a tremendously intricate and time-consuming undertaking (see Frawley, Hill, & Munro 2002a for an excellent summary), and we must calibrate our objectives to the temporal, material, financial, and human resources available.

We start by addressing fundamental questions asked by all lexicographers, including: Who is our audience? What is our time frame? What is the intended scope of our project? What are the intended outputs? What are the ethical entailments of the project? What will we do to ensure the long-term storage, protection, and dissemination of data and outputs? What will be the internal composition of, and division of labor among, the lexicography team? We think carefully about orthography design and the challenges of standardization. We consult with local collaborators about orthography, as well as ethics and permissions (see also Holton, Leonard, & Pulsifer, chapter 4, this volume; Collister, chapter 9, this volume). We consider whether, and how, to handle multiple media within, or associated with, the lexical database and whether the project will have an online component. Finally, we contemplate how to determine when the lexical database is "good enough" to publish in dictionary form and when and how to archive (all or part of) the data set (see also Andreassen, chapter 7, this volume; Buzsard-Welcher, chapter 10, this volume). To explore these and related issues further, we refer readers to resources on basic lexicography theory and practice (e.g., Atkins & Rundell 2008; Landau 2001; Zgusta 1971, among many others, as well as the *International Journal of Lexicography*) and to resources that specifically address lexicographic work in the context of language documentation and preservation (e.g., Frawley, Hill, & Munro 2002b; Mosel 2011; Haviland 2006; Ogilvie 2011; Rice 2018).

4.2   Overview of our lexicographic methodology and workflow

Returning our focus now to the specific lexicographic methodology presented in this chapter, the key sequential (and in some cases iterative) steps that guide our

workflow are laid out in table 24.1; subsequent sections explicate the content summarized in the table.

5   Sources of lexical data

Clearly, fundamental to any good dictionary are broad, diverse, and nuanced lexical data. In our projects, we use a complementary set of methods for data collection, five of which we briefly discuss here.

5.1   Lexical data from parsed texts

Audio- or video-recorded texts that are transcribed,[12] translated, and subsequently parsed using FLEx (see section 7.2) are an obvious and excellent foundation for a FLEx lexical database. Not only do parsed texts yield glossed roots and stems that serve as the kernel of entries in the short term, but also, in the long term, this corpus provides numerous examples of the use of more common roots and stems, helping you to refine the definition and senses of the lexemes in question. And just as texts are invaluable for the investigation of grammatical phenomena because they manifest phenomena that are either difficult to elicit or that may not occur to the investigator to elicit, texts are also a rich source of lexical data that are either difficult to elicit or are not obvious candidates for lexicalization. Despite the great value of texts, however, it is important to emphasize that they are far from a panacea for lexicographic work. First, many lexemes of a language simply do not appear in corpora of the size typically developed in language documentation projects focused on underdocumented languages. This reflects the fact that low-frequency lexemes surface only sporadically in such corpora. For example, fewer than 25% of the large number of Iquito ethnobiological terms in our database actually surface in our quite extensive Iquito corpus. Similarly, we have found that less common senses of even high-frequency lexemes are often not represented in texts. To address these weaknesses, thoughtful and careful elicitation is indispensable.

5.2   Lexical data from stimulus word lists

Without a doubt, stimulus word lists that provide contact-language lexical items to be translated into the target language can be useful tools for quickly acquiring a large number of lexemes. Great care must be taken with this approach, however. Word lists of this sort suffer from

Table 24.1
Guide to workflow for our lexicographic methodology

Sequential step (i = iterative)	Type of work • Done by whom	Core tasks	Main discussion section(s)
1. Create a new project in FLEx	FLEx work • Linguist	• Set up orthography • Select built-in fields to structure your database • Create custom fields as needed per project	8
2(i). Document lexicon	Fieldwork • Linguist(s) with language users	• Gather lexical data	3.3, 5
3(i). Create FLEx Entries	FLEx work • Linguist(s)	• Start Entry History • Write definitions and other text using existing fields	7, 9
4(i). Develop FLEx Entries	FLEx work • Linguist(s) and consultants	• Expand, refine • Check, correct • Exemplify	10
5(i). Categorize FLEx Entries	FLEx work • Linguist(s)	• Populate existing fields • Add custom fields based on your analytical needs and output types	8
6. Export XML version of database	FLEx work • Linguist	• Export LIFT* file of lexicon	7.2
7. Create/obtain script, adapt it to project and output	Python work • Linguist and programmer	• Script structure will depend on desired content and form of output(s).	7.3
8. Run script	Python work • Programmer	• Process LIFT file to generate TeX file	7.3
9. Prepare TEX file	LaTeX work • Linguist and programmer	• Create/obtain preamble • Create/obtain mappings from XML-based tags to LaTeX commands	7.4
10(i). Create and share PDF	LaTeX work • Linguist	• Typeset TeX file • Disseminate PDFs of successive versions and types of dictionary	2, 3.5

* LIFT (Lexicon Interchange FormaT) is an XML format for storing lexical information.

two major types of weakness. First, they are typically based on whichever concepts are lexicalized in the contact language, and these may exhibit quite different patterns of lexicalization than those of the target language. This mismatch can be frustrating for both linguist and consultant in elicitation contexts. Second, the cultural and physical contexts presupposed by the word list may be quite different from those relevant to contemporary users of the target language, and/or relevant historically for the society in which the target language was used vitally, in the case of highly endangered languages. In such cases, the word list may be replete with concepts not lexicalized in the target language, while simultaneously lacking numerous important concepts that *are* lexicalized in the target language. In some regions of the world, scholars have developed areal or regional lexical elicitation lists that mitigate these problems to some degree.

For these reasons, we generally do not recommend starting lexical data collection through elicitation using word list stimuli. However, such lists can be very useful when employed strategically to identify gaps in lexical data collection, once the researchers who are compiling the lexical data have developed a familiarity with the patterns of lexicalization in the language and with the cultural and physical environments.

5.3   Lexical data from stimulus activities

Activity-based elicitation sessions (audio-/video-recorded or not) are another excellent source of lexical data. Concretely, for example, the lexicographer can accompany someone when they carry out an activity, such as going fishing, doing laundry, cooking, harvesting from a garden, going shopping, fixing a motor, or caring for a child, and ask a range questions about all the objects and actions that emerge: "What is that?" "What are you (is he/she) doing?" "Why are you (is he/she) doing that?" Alternatively, it may be the case that it is wisest to simply record words for future focused consultant work, rather than interrupting the activity.

5.4   Systematic exploration of semantic domains

In semantically cohesive and well-defined domains such as kinship terms, color terms, body parts, ethnobiology (mammals, birds, plants, and so on), and actions of particular types, such as cutting and breaking, it is fruitful to build up lexical data by exploring the semantic domain in a systematic way. This type of systematic exploration benefits substantially from specific methodologies and stimuli (such as using diagrams, color chips, ethnobiological publications, and the like), but some early progress can be made with *free listing*, that is, asking consultants to recall as many terms in a given semantic domain as possible.

5.5   Participant observation of language in use

Developing your conversational abilities in the target language and then participating in regular conversations, either as an interlocutor or as an accepted overhearer, is another excellent way of identifying lexemes that have not yet been documented via other methods, as well as for developing insights into the definitions of, or new senses of, lexemes that you have already recorded. For example, a few days before departing the Iquito community last month, in the flow of a conversation with us about a loud party near her house, one of our consultants used a word for "loud," *ihɨrana*, that we had never previously encountered. This word had never appeared in a text, and when we had explored the concept "loud" in prior elicitation sessions, we had only ever obtained the word *amátanana*, which has a broader range of meanings that include "strong" and "fast." But sure enough, when we asked another consultant about

ihɨrana, he instantly recognized it and confirmed it as meaning "loud," while confirming that *amátanana* is used more commonly.

6   Structuring the dictionary as a whole

A common basic structure for a dictionary consists of either three or four main parts. The first part, the *front matter*, contextualizes the dictionary; describes the project that produced it; and identifies and thanks all participants, supporters, and funders. It also describes how to use the dictionary and provides essential grammatical information.[13] The second part, the *main body*, presents the lexical content of the dictionary, ordered alphabetically by target language headwords. The optional third part, the *thematic content*, presents the same lexical content as the main body but organized by semantic fields or themes. The final part provides the *reversals* from contact language(s) to the target language. In our workflow, each of these second, third, and fourth parts is the output of a different subset of our lexical database content, which is ordered, formatted, and typeset using specifications that are made possible by using LaTeX (see sections 7 and 8). Regardless of the structure you choose, note that it is essential to provide, before the main body, a detailed description of *how to read an entry*, along with a description of how to interpret the set of categories, labels, and abbreviations that you have used in your different types of entry.

7   Choosing digital tools for a lexicography project

In this era, we would not undertake lexicographic work without making use of flexible digital tools for data management and the production of outputs such as dictionaries. Here we describe the digital tools that we currently employ in our workflow.

7.1   A bird's-eye view

We use FLEx to house and organize our lexical data and the combination of Python and LaTeX to produce attractive, well-formatted outputs. Our use of Python and LaTeX is a response to the limited output options for FLEx. After trying out several variants, we settled on a digital pipeline that takes the native XML output from FLEx and converts it to (Xe)LaTeX markup using a Python script. The first version of this pipeline was created in 2012 by Máíhɨ̃̀kì Project team members Greg Finley and Stephanie Farmer, and it served to produce the 2012, 2013, and 2014 drafts of the *Diccionario Bilingüe Máíj̀ɨ̠kì—Castellano y Castellano—Máíj̀ɨ̠kì* (Michael et al. 2013). The results were so satisfying that we have used updated and customized versions of this pipeline for all our FLEx-based dictionary outputs since then, including the *Diccionario Trilingüe Záparo* (Beier et al. 2014) and the dictionaries published by the Iquito Language Documentation Project (Beier et al. 2019; Michael et al. 2019). For the Iquito Language Documentation Project dictionaries, the Python script has been significantly reworked by Ronald Sprouse to handle the more complex database and dictionary organization required.[14]

7.2 FLEx

FLEx is a free, open source application, developed and made available by SIL International. FLEx is designed to create linked text corpus and lexical databases, where the lexical database can serve to parse texts in the corpus, and parsed texts can serve as one of the sources of data for the lexical database. The pros and cons of FLEx are laid out in table 24.2.

7.3 Python

Python is a high-level programming language widely used in academia for scientific programming. The pros and cons of Python are laid out in table 24.3.

7.4 LaTeX and XeLaTeX

LaTeX is a free and widely used document preparation and typesetting system that produces PDF documents of high typographical quality; XeLaTeX is an extension to LaTeX that accommodates Unicode in its native TeX files, thereby accommodating a vast range of characters. The pros and cons of LaTeX are laid out in table 24.4.

8 Structuring FLEx lexical database records

Regardless of which lexical database tools you use, the most consequential data management task you will face is the structuring of the *Entry*, by which we mean the unique database record that corresponds to a single headword. Since there are good resources available that discuss the essentials and logic of dictionary entry creation in general (e.g., Atkins & Rundell 2008; Landau 2001), we will note here only the most important elements of structure that

Table 24.2
FLEx: Pros and cons

Pro	Con
Easy to obtain and install; project backup is also quick and easy.	Relatively poor documentation makes it difficult to learn, use, fully exploit, or troubleshoot.
Backed by significant institutional infrastructure and commitment from SIL International, therefore likely to remain a viable tool for the foreseeable future.[15]	Native to PC and Linux, but not to Mac OSX (we have had mixed success using PC and Linux emulators on Mac OSX devices) and requires substantial RAM to run smoothly.
Accommodates Unicode characters—a crucial feature for orthographies that incorporate non-ASCII characters and diacritics.	The user has relatively limited control over the types and design of outputs.
Widely used among linguists, therefore it is relatively easy to share projects with colleagues, as well as to obtain guidance and advice from other linguists who use FLEx for similar purposes.	Has a relatively small online user community for purposes of sharing knowledge and experiences, or for troubleshooting.
Different versions of the database can be synchronized online via the built-in Language Depot tool, or by synchronizing copies on storage devices such as USB drives, which facilitates collaboration across multiple computers.	SIL International is a Christian missionary organization and the ethical considerations of having one's professional activities crucially dependent on such an organization are significant (Dobrin 2009; Epps & Ladley 2009 concerning Amazonia in particular).
The database can be exported in a variety of formats, including XHTML and XML, which allows repurposing and manipulation of the data using other tools.	
Has the capacity to add custom fields, as well as to bulk edit and merge fields, allowing for flexibility as the database evolves with use.	

Table 24.3

Python: Pros and cons

Pro	Con
Free, flexible, expandable, adaptable, powerful, and well-supported.	Requires a relatively high level of programming expertise to develop the script and employ it for the FLEx-to-LaTeX pipeline described here.
It is relatively easy to find people with Python programming experience.	The script employed for the FLEx-to-LaTeX pipeline must be tailored to the specific FLEx fields one wishes to typeset in LaTeX.
Python scripts developed for handing FLEx exports (e.g., XML) can be adapted from one project to another.	

Table 24.4

LaTeX: Pros and cons

Pro	Con
Free and easily accessible.	Requires learning its markup language, which involves a learning curve.
Very stable—in two different senses. First, whereas the files of applications such as Word can become quite unstable when they are both large and incorporate complicated formatting, LaTeX files never do. Second, whereas commercially popular applications change their features and encoding with some regularity, resulting in the permanent loss of formatting in older files, LaTeX files made decades ago are as readable now as they were when they were made.	Many publishers don't accept LaTeX files (although many academic publishers do); in such cases, only the PDFs it produces could be submitted.
Very powerful, well-designed, and seemingly limitless tool for producing publishable documents on one's own time frame, using in-house labor. Basic functions, plus a vast set of extensions (packages) satisfy a plentitude of linguists' specific needs, such as interlinearization, flexible example numbering, and tree diagrams.	
LaTeX and its variants have a huge and active user community that helps tremendously in learning and troubleshooting.	

we have come to rely on in the type of work we do using FLEx.

8.1 Basic components of an Entry

The default FLEx lexicon record, called an Entry, includes a very large number of built-in fields, of two types: fields that pertain to an Entry as a whole, and fields that pertain to Senses within an Entry. To a large degree, the earliest stages of developing the structure of FLEx database records involves selecting which fields to employ and which ones to suppress. Many of these choices will be obvious, based on a general familiarity with dictionaries (e.g., creating citation forms, parts of speech, and definitions), but others are perhaps less so. We will discuss some important fields of the latter type, and considerations involved in their use—but first, we offer two overarching observations.

First, it has been our experience that as our knowledge of the grammar of a language has deepened, we have discovered new aspects of lexical or grammatical irregularity, or relationships between lexemes, that merit documentation. In the Iquito case, for example, we discovered a large number of irregular plurals, morphologically conditioned root allomorphy, and active/middle verb pairs related by ablaut and consonant mutation, for all of which we eventually created dedicated custom fields in FLEx. In short, it is not possible to know at the outset all the fields that you will want or need, and it is helpful to accept from the outset that you'll continue to develop the structure of your Entries as your lexical documentation advances.

Second, in this context, a powerful advantage of the FLEx-Python-LaTeX pipeline described here is that the fields that make up a FLEx Entry can, to a large degree, be reordered at will via the Python script, in so far as the final output document is concerned. We have even taken advantage of this capability to display, in different parts of the dictionary entries, subtypes of a single FLEx field (e.g., the Variants field, discussed in section 8.2), in effect splitting a single FLEx field into distinct dictionary entry fields. In short, there is much about the structure of your output dictionary entry that can be reworked via the pipeline described here.

The single aspect of FLEx record structure that cannot be so easily finessed in this way is the distinction between fields linked to the Entry as a whole (e.g., Citation Form), and fields linked to particular Senses (e.g.,

Gloss and Definition). This is arguably most significant for the various types of note fields (see section 7.3), some of which are Entry-level fields and others of which are Sense-level fields. In this light, it is important to contemplate whether the note field you want to use supplies information that is relevant at the level of the Entry as a whole or at the level of an individual Sense associated with the lexeme.

Now let us turn our attention to several specific field types that are extremely useful in developing the structure of a FLEx Entry.

8.2 Variant forms

In FLEx, it possible to establish a Variant relationship between distinct Entries, such that one Entry is treated as the Main Entry, and the other as a Minor Entry that points back to the Main Entry. These Variant relationships are extremely useful for addressing both sociolinguistic variation and dialectal diversity. Significantly, it is simple to create customized Variant types by which to categorize your Variants. For example, a particular variant can be identified as pertaining to a specific dialect or as a "playful variant" or an "archaic form" of the Main Entry. For our Iquito dictionary, we also use the Variant relationship for a number of irregular form types, such as irregular third-person possessives, irregular imperfective roots, and irregular plurals. Importantly, because each Variant type is directly associated with the FLEx Entry in the XML that we export from FLEx, it is possible to customize both where and how these Variants appear in the associated dictionary entry, resulting in considerable power and flexibility in organizing the structure of the dictionary entry in the final output.

8.3 Built-in Note fields

The types of note fields built into FLEx—including Grammar Note, Semantic Note, and Anthropology Note, among many others—are excellent tools for organizing and categorizing different types of descriptive information and data (see section 5) related to an Entry. Using these various note fields means that, at the point of generating a dictionary, you are able to choose which of them will appear in the output. Similarly, if it turns out that you have overdifferentiated, it is possible to merge the contents of different note fields together using FLEx's Bulk Edit function.

8.4 Semantic domains

If one of your objectives is to create a dictionary resource that is organized thematically, the Semantic Domain tool in FLEx is indispensable. A highly elaborate tree of Semantic Domains is built into FLEx, but we have preferred to set up our own custom Semantic Domain categories, based on the type and quantity of data we have for a given project. (For example, for Iquito, it serves us well to have as distinct domains the following: Plants, Plants: medicinal, Plants: parts, Body parts, and Body parts: human.)

8.5 Custom fields

In the lexical databases that we have designed to serve as a source for multiple types of output, we have come to rely on the tremendous usefulness of creating custom fields. Custom fields allow us to annotate, categorize, and label multiple facets, and organizing principles, of content that is unique to a particular project (see sections 3 and 5). Thus, we have created custom fields not only to house information that is destined to be output for a dictionary entry, but also for categorizing FLEx Entries as candidates for certain outputs, as well as for managing workflow. For example, in the Iquito database, we have a field for tagging the subset of Entries that will appear in the teaching dictionary and another to label every Entry whose Spanish content has been proofread by a native Spanish user.

The most important by far of our custom fields, however, is the Entry History field, which we use to communicate with one another, and our future selves, regarding the creation, development, and editing of the Entry. We discuss this field at greater length in section 11.

9 What counts as a headword in your dictionary?

A decision that will have significant ramifications for your lexicographic project is settling on a principle that divides words that you select as headwords from those that you do not. From the perspective, common among linguists, that considers the lexicon to be the locus of unpredictable form-meaning pairings that constitute the input into grammatical processes and structures, this is, in principle, an easy decision: headwords should be restricted to morphologically simplex words and morphologically complex words with non-compositional semantics; while morphologically complex words with compositional semantics should be excluded as headwords.

While this is an excellent guiding principle, there are multiple ways in which matters can be more complicated. First, it has been our experience that as our knowledge and understanding of a language's lexicon deepens, we have discovered areas of the lexicon that exhibit gradience between compositionality and non-compositionality. Second, while a phenomenon may be compositional, its permissible realizations may not be predictable. We illustrate this with the example of Iquito pluractional suffixes and classifiers. The semantics of verbs and adjectives, respectively, when they bear these morphemes *is* entirely predictable on the basis of the verbal and adjectival stems involved. However, what *is not* entirely predictable is which verbal or adjectival stems can bear these morphemes. Our solution was to create a Related Forms field that allowed us to record these forms in the relevant verb or adjective Entry, but not to promote them to headwords.

Finally, a different issue is raised by the fact that the contact language will typically lexicalize concepts that are not lexicalized in the target language, in which these concepts may be expressed via entirely productive processes such as verb serialization or derivation. Especially in contexts of significant language shift, however, users may search for words on the basis of concepts lexicalized in the contact language. Take the example of Spanish *ladrón* "thief," whose translational equivalent in Iquito is a wholly productive nominalization of a verb glossable as *robar* "steal." This kind of situation presents the following dilemma: if one does not include the nominalized form as a headword, then someone looking for the translational equivalent of *ladrón* will fail to find it, which may be frustrating to them (and incidentally, give them a dim view of the dictionary). On the other hand, if we organize the dictionary around concepts lexicalized in the contact language, the documentation of the target language can be significantly distorted. The solution we adopted was to include the form for *ladrón* in the Related Forms field in the Entry for the Iquito verb meaning "steal." This way, the word for *ladrón* is included and findable (especially via search functions on PDF versions of the dictionary), but it does not impose Spanish lexicalization onto the principles for what counts as a headword for Iquito.

10   Checking, verifying, and expanding dictionary content

Lexicography is partly a *science* (in the spirit discussed by Berez-Kroeker et al. 2018:6–7; see also Berez-Kroeker et al., chapter 1, this volume; Gawne & Styles, chapter 2, this volume) but it is also an *art* in a significant sense, and in the case of endangered language lexicography, it is a research endeavor so heavily dependent on the knowledge of a small number of specific individuals that the totality of the qualitative results cannot be considered reproducible. Nonetheless, the methodology presented here is principled, rigorous, reproducible, and valid. And to the degree that dictionary work is linked to and exemplified by textual materials, a reasonable degree of intersubjectivity and verifiability can be obtained, for which we discuss some methods and strategies next.

10.1   Establishing the validity of lexical data

The glosses, definition(s), and exemplification that a consultant provides on any single occasion for a particular lexeme have a complex relationship to the meaning(s) and function(s) of that lexeme that emerge after prolonged study. Though consultants often do provide highly insightful and nuanced definitions that cannot be significantly improved, this is not always the case. In particular, the information a consultant provides on a given occasion may suggest either a narrower, or a broader, meaning or function than the precise picture you'll be able to present after more extensive investigation. Often, this is because the specific situation or discourse context that is evoked on a single occasion strongly affects how the consultant construes the word. Simultaneously, there may be crucial mismatches between forms available in the contact language used to gloss or translate words in the target language, on the one hand, and the meaning of the words in the target language itself, on the other.

The principle strategy that we now rely on for both verifying our data and clarifying our definitions is to consider the development of a definition as a multistep process through which we build up a coherent view of the meaning of a headword from multiple vantage points. This multiperspectival view can be developed by examining multiple uses of the lexeme in texts; by asking multiple consultants to reflect on the meanings of the form; and by asking the same consultants to do this on different occasions, such as during different field seasons. It also includes asking consultants to reflect on translations provided by others, and, in some cases, to explicitly evaluate the hypotheses we develop about the meaning of the form. This outcome of this process is a stable, intersubjectively valid entry for the form, with its steps and participants annotated as appropriate in the Entry History (see section 11).

10.2   The role of exemplification

Example sentences that illustrate the meaning and/or grammatical properties of the definition (or senses) of a headword serve multiple ends. Most importantly, they provide evidence for the generalizations presented in the entry, while the process itself of obtaining examples is a valuable method for checking, evaluating, testing, and further developing an entry.

An obvious and excellent source for example sentences are texts that have been recorded and transcribed (and ideally parsed in FLEx as well; see section 5.1) as part of the broader documentation project, and such texts should, in many cases, be prioritized as a source of example sentences. That said, our experience suggests that the corpus available for a language that is the focus of language documentation will typically not be sufficient as the sole source of example sentences. Not only may the relevant lexemes simply be missing from the corpus (see section 9.1), but also the sentences found in the corpus may not clearly exemplify important aspects of meaning or function, or they may be overly long or otherwise unwieldy. Elicitation of examples in one form or another thus becomes inescapable.

We have found the following three methods for example elicitation especially fruitful. First, ask consultants to make up sentences including the lexeme in question. If a consultant is experiencing difficulties with doing this from scratch, we find it useful to ask about common contexts in which the lexeme would be used; then, after fleshing out the context, we ask the consultant to produce an utterance (or utterances) appropriate in that context.

Second, in collaboration with a consultant, adapt a sentence already in the corpus so that it exemplifies the meaning or function of a lexeme more clearly or succinctly. And finally, in collaboration with a consultant, develop a target-language translation of a contact-language sentence, which is sometimes the most practical and efficient means of focusing on a very specific aspect of meaning or function. As with all the strategies discussed in this section, sentences obtained in this way should evaluated with the multiperspectival approach sketched in section 10.1.

10.3   Verification and validation through principled comparisons

A third important method for checking and expanding generalizations regarding meaning(s) and function(s) is by drawing out and identifying the differences between two or more similar lexemes. We approach this elicitation-based strategy in two primary ways: first, by comparing lexemes within a given semantic domain, and second, by comparing lexemes that bear similar or identical glosses or reversal-list meanings. For example, Iquito exhibits two verbs that consultants readily gloss as "break," further qualifying that they apply to slender, rigid objects such as sticks and bones: *tihaka* and *nasikata*. But only when asked to compare and contrast these two forms were our consultants able to articulate the difference: the former entails that the two parts are completely separated, while the latter entails that the two parts remain connected in a flexible manner (e.g., a broken stick whose two parts remain connected by a piece of green bark). In addition, this comparison-based strategy has also proved very successful in helping consultants to identify variants of various types, including dialectal variants, archaisms, and synonyms with particular affective flavors.

11   Tracking and managing the development of an entry

As the preceding discussion makes clear, the development of any single lexical Entry is typically a prolonged process; it typically involves contributions from multiple consultants, and it may also involve the contributions of multiple linguists, as has been the case for several of the dictionaries that we have developed. Both of these factors—a prolonged development period and multiple contributors—make it likely that, without efforts to address the issue, relevant information will be forgotten and complementary viewpoints—or discrepant ones—overlooked.

The solution we have developed for addressing this specific issue is to create an Entry History field in our FLEx databases, which serves as a running log of changes made to the Entry. This field is absolutely indispensable for knowing what has been done when, by whom, and with whom, as well as for annotating what remains to be done, by whom, and with whom. It is a place to note complementary or discrepant information from different sources, to spell out apparent problems in the

Table 24.5

Entry History examples from the Iquito Language Documentation Project FLEx lexical database

FLEx Entry	FLEx Entry History
headword • Part of speech glosses	• Participants are identified by three initials. • At first use, abbreviations are spelled out between square brackets. • CHECK or TODO means not yet checked or done, while CHCK or TD means already checked or done.

mɨɨsaji
 • Noun
  1. woman
  2. female
	LDM 23.09.2006 added lx [new lexeme Entry];
	 LDM 23.10.2006 JPI now says 'tiene pausa' so recheck hw [headword];
	 LDM 24.10.2006 mod [modified] hw mɨsáji > mɨɨsáji, expanded def [definition] with JPI, now 2 senses;
	 BGG Praat [segment lengths annotated];
	 CMB 12sep2015 RNLT [removed non-lexical tone mark];
	 2015CHCK confirm tone is non-lexical;
	 2015TD WED [write English definitions];
	 LDM 25sep2015 conf [confirmed] non-lex tone, WED [wrote English definitions];

iitimɨra • Noun irregular plural of: *mɨɨsaji*	LDM 23.09.2006 added lx; LDM 28.09.2006 mod hw itímɨra > itimɨra; LDM 23.10.2006 conf lx with JPI; 2015CHCK all; LDM 13oct2015 hw itimɨra > iitimɨra, RNLT, WED; 2015TD conf for humans only? yes: pɨsɨkɨ mɨɨsajika; LDM 15jul2017 ELY has n/poss [possessed vs. non-possessed] alt, nu-iItim+ra; LDM 10jun2018 confirmed, added to IrregPoss [field]; 2019CHECKJPI GrammNote: confirm and add what to use in non-human cases
awasi • Noun digit, finger, or toe	LDM 05.09.2006 added lx; LDM 08.11.2006 lx def; LDM 06jun2016 JPI conf lx, irreg.pl.; LDM 18jun2016 JPI conf def, WED; LDM 28jul2016 ELY has toneless awAsi for nposs [non-possessed] form; 2016TD add this variant; 2016CHCKJPI to see if he has same? he does not; 2017CHCKELY again on her variants; 23jun2017 ELY confirms nposs form is toneless, poss form is Awasi; 2017TD discuss w/CMB what to do in such cases where JPI does not show a variation; LDM 24jun2017 hw áwasi > awasi, created hw for poss form áwasi; 2017CHCKELY plurals for poss, nposs forms; LDM 06jul2017 ELY has awasi no lextone for nposs, but nAwasi, nawAsika for poss; 2017TD deal with how to annotate JPI variants? added to GramNote [field]; LDM 15jul2017 ELY confirmed n/poss alt, added to IrregPoss [field]; CMB 13nov2019 added 3.poss.Var [populated Variant field to generate a Minor Entry]

entry, and to summarize how problems were resolved. In our work, the Entry History has allowed us to identify, among other things, subtle errors in representation (e.g., by noting discrepancies between different contributing linguists' representations of lexemes), and dialectal or sociolinguistic variation (e.g., by noting differences among consultants).

In practice, every annotation in the running Entry History begins with the initials of the annotating linguist and the date of the annotation, followed by terse but specific prose, and also including a consultant's initials when relevant. In addition, we have employed the Entry History field to tag or spell out tasks that remain to be

carried out, such as exactly what to check with consultants on various aspects of the entry. Three illustrative examples, edited for readability, are given in table 24.5.

12 Conclusion

It is our hope that this chapter has presented one approach to managing lexicography data with sufficient motivation and methodological detail that interested readers will be able build on this methodology for their own lexicography projects. The work of lexicography is neither simple nor swift, but it can be an immensely rewarding contribution to a language and its users.

Notes

1. https://software.sil.org/fieldworks/.

2. https://www.w3.org/TR/REC-xml/.

3. https://www.latex-project.org/.

4. https://www.python.org/psf-landing/.

5. This has included work with users/rememberers of: Nanti (ISO 639-3: cox; 1995–2010), Iquito (iqu; 2001–present), Omagua (omg; 2003–present), Aʔiwa (ash; 2008, 2010), Andoa (anb; 2009), Muniche (myr; 2009–2010), Máíhɨ̃kì (ore; 2009–present), Caquinte (cot; 2010), Matsigenka (mcb; 2010–present), and Záparo (zro; 2010–2011). Each of these projects has resulted in tangible, usable outputs for community members or for scholars or both.

6. A growing collection of materials of the Iquito Language Documentation Project is available at the California Language Archive at http://dx.doi.org/doi:10.7297/X2PC30JV.

7. A growing collection of materials of the Berkeley Máíhɨ̃kì Project is available at the California Language Archive at http://dx.doi.org/doi:10.7297/X2DR2SGD.

8. For managing work on Iquito, we have, in addition, used a separate Wiki to coordinate some multiparty procedures and workflow.

9. https://www.soas.ac.uk/elar/.

10. https://www.ailla.utexas.org/.

11. http://cla.berkeley.edu/.

12. Our digital tool for text transcription and translation work is ELAN Linguistic Annotator, available at https://tla.mpi.nl/tools/tla-tools/elan/.

13. Time permitting, including a *grammatical sketch* in the front matter is extremely useful to users, particularly to help them connect the roots and citation forms in your dictionary with the more complex forms that they encounter in interactions and texts.

14. If you are interested in acquiring a version of our script to adapt for a project of your own, please contact Lev Michael at levmichael@berkeley.edu.

15. Over the years, we have witnessed a number of efforts to develop alternatives or competitors to FLEx or its antecedents. Unfortunately, not one has yet been backed by the long-term institutional infrastructure necessary, in our view, for such tools to be a responsible and defensible choice for a researcher to make.

References

Atkins, B. T. S., and Michael Rundell. 2008. *The Oxford Guide to Practical Lexicography*. New York: Oxford University Press.

Beier, Christine, Brenda Bowser, Lev Michael, and Vivian Wauters. 2014. *Diccionario Záparo Trilingüe*. Quito, Ecuador: Ediciones Abya-Yala.

Beier, Christine, Lev Michael, Jaime Pacaya Inuma, Ema Llona Yareja, Hermenegildo Díaz Cuyasa, and Ligia Inuma Inuma. 2019. *Diccionario Escolar Ikíitu Kuwasíini—Tawɨ Kuwasíini (Iquito—Castellano)*. Iquitos, Peru: Cabeceras Aid Project. https://escholarship.org/uc/item/03m736sz.

Berez-Kroeker, Andrea, Lauren Gawne, Susan Smythe Kung, Barbara F. Kelly, Tyler Heston, Gary Holton, Peter Pulsifer, et al. 2018. Reproducible research in linguistics: A position statement on data citation and attribution in our field. *Linguistics* 56 (1): 1–18. https://doi.org/10.1515/ling-2017-0032.

Bird, Steven, and Gary Simons. 2003. Seven dimensions of portability for language documentation and description. *Language* 79:557–582.

Bowern, Claire. 2008. *Linguistic Fieldwork: A Practical Guide*. New York: Palgrave MacMillan.

Dobrin, Lise. 2009. SIL International and the disciplinary culture of linguistics: Introduction. *Language* 85:618–619.

Epps, Patience, and Herb Ladley. 2009. Syntax, souls, or speakers? On SIL and community language development. *Language* 85:640–658.

Frawley, William, Kenneth C. Hill, and Pamela Munro. 2002a. Making a dictionary: Ten issues. In *Making Dictionaries: Preserving Indigenous Languages of the Americas*, ed. William Frawley, Kenneth C. Hill, and Pamela Munro, 1–22. Berkeley: University of California Press.

Frawley, William, Kenneth C. Hill, and Pamela Munro, eds. 2002b. *Making Dictionaries: Preserving Indigenous Languages of the Americas*. Berkeley: University of California Press.

Haviland, John. 2006. Documenting lexical knowledge. In *Essentials of Language Documentation*, ed. Jost Gippert, Nikolaus P. Himmelmann, and Ulrike Mosel, 129–161. Berlin: Mouton de Gruyter.

Landau, Sidney. 2001. *Dictionaries: The Art and Craft of Lexicography*. 2nd ed. Cambridge: Cambridge University Press.

Michael, Lev, Christine Beier, and Stephanie Farmer, compilers. 2013. *Diccionario Bilingüe Máíjɨ̃kì–Castellano y Castellano–Máíjɨ̃kì. Borrador Agosto 2013*. Iquitos, Peru: Cabeceras Aid Project. http://www.cabeceras.org/mai_ore_diccionario2013.pdf.

Michael, Lev, Christine Beier, Jaime Pacaya Inuma, Ema Llona Yareja, Hermenegildo Díaz Cuyasa, and Ligia Inuma Inuma. 2019. *Iquito—English Dictionary*. Quito, Ecuador: Ediciones Abya-Yala.

Mosel, Ulrike. 2011. Lexicography in endangered language communities. In *The Cambridge Handbook of Endangered Languages*, ed. Peter K. Austin and Julia Sallabank, 337–353. Cambridge: Cambridge University Press.

Nichols, Johanna, and Ronald L. Sprouse. 2003. Documenting lexicons: Chechen and Ingush. In *Language Documentation and Description*, vol. 1, ed. Peter K. Austin, 99–121. London: SOAS.

Ogilvie, Sarah. 2011. Linguistics, lexicography, and the revitalization of endangered languages. *International Journal of Lexicography* 24 (4): 389–404. http://dx.doi.org/doi:10.1093/ijl/ecr019.

Rice, Keren. 2018. Reflections on documenting the lexicon. In *Reflections on Language Documentation 20 Years after Himmelmann 1998*, ed. Bradley McDonnell, Andrea L. Berez-Kroeker, and Gary Holton. Special issue, *Language Documentation and Conservation* 15: 180–190. http://hdl.handle.net/10125/24819.

Woodbury, Anthony C. 2011. Language documentation. In *The Cambridge Handbook of Endangered Languages*, ed. Peter K. Austin and Julia Sallabank, 159–186. Cambridge: Cambridge University Press.

Zgusta, Ladislav. 1971. *Manual of Lexicography*. The Hague: Mouton.

25 Managing Data from Archival Documentation for Language Reclamation

Megan Lukaniec

1 Introduction

Archival documentation can provide us with an invaluable (albeit partial) record of the language, society, and culture of a community at an earlier point in time. While invaluable, working with archival documentation poses unique challenges, as it can be a disorderly, cryptic, and frustratingly non-interactive collection of materials. This chapter discusses the management of archival documentation with the specific goal of advancing language reclamation efforts. Here, *archival documentation* refers to all materials that were previously created and contain linguistic data, whether that be written materials, audio recordings, video recordings, or some combination of these media. The intended audience, breadth, depth, age, physical location, ease of accessibility, among other factors varies dramatically among different instances of archival, or historical, documentation. For example, within the context of Indigenous North America, which will be the wider context for the following discussion, the age of these materials can vary greatly, dating from the early sixteenth century onward. As one would expect, much of this earlier documentation was a product of colonization, which carries its own host of problems.

Interestingly enough, sometimes the purpose(s) of creating this documentation often runs counter to the purpose(s) of engaging with this documentation in the present day. For members of Indigenous language communities, linguists, language reclamation practitioners, and those whose role overlaps these categories, a common goal is to use the data found in this archival documentation for reclaiming the language. *Language reclamation*, in the context of this discussion, refers to both revitalizing the language and decolonizing the role of the language within the wider community (Leonard 2011). In other words, in addition to striving toward the creation of new speakers, strengthening or reinstating intergenerational transmission, and expanding the use of the language into more domains of everyday life, the aim is to also recover positive attitudes toward the language and restore the value of the language for community members.

For some Indigenous language communities with living language users, archival documentation is used simply to supplement already existing resources for the language. This documentation can provide a snapshot of an earlier state in the language, supplying lexical items that may have fallen out of use, information on different registers that may have been eroded, more robust information about dialect differences that have been merged, or simply an idea of how the language has changed over time. For other communities, perhaps those with language users that are only able to support reclamation efforts in limited ways (e.g., because they are at an advanced age or unwell), documentation then becomes more important as a source of information about the language. Yet, for still other language communities, archival documentation represents the sole means by which a community can reawaken their language. These communities have experienced a complete shift from the heritage language to another language, typically a language of the colonizer (such as English, French, or Spanish). The language then falls into disuse and becomes dormant. The term extinct that was once widely used to describe these languages is inaccurate and inappropriate (see Leonard 2011), because the language can be reawakened by using existing documentation.

Focusing on language reclamation as a goal, this chapter discusses how to manage not necessarily the archival documentation itself, but the *data* found within it. Although this chapter is within a wider handbook of linguistic data management, I feel conflicted about the word *data* when it is applied to the Indigenous languages of North America. On the one hand, it is a useful term that concisely and precisely refers to the information found within this documentation. On the other hand, its use could be perceived as further disconnecting the language from its heritage community and objectifying it as small, discrete pieces for the all-consuming science of linguistics. In this vein, Indigenous scholar Rodriguez-Lonebear (2016) comments that although the singular form *datum* means 'something given' in Latin, "indigenous experiences under colonial control suggest that [it] more often means 'something taken'" (255). It is not hard to see how this manifests itself in linguistics, where "data from American languages" are characterized as "grist for the mill" that is linguistic theory and have been considered as such "since the days of Boas and Sapir" (Beck & Gerdts 2017:10). Nevertheless, in the absence of a better term, and following Indigenous scholars Kovach (2009) and Wilson (2008) discussing Indigenous research methods, the term *data* will be used in this chapter (see also Holton, Leonard, & Pulsifer, chapter 4, this volume, for a discussion of Indigenous data sovereignty).

Finally, this chapter is situated within the context of my work as a linguist and language reclamation practitioner from the Huron-Wendat community of Wendake, Quebec. Our language, Wendat (also known as Huron), was dormant for over 150 years, and therefore our current reclamation efforts are based on archival documentation created by missionaries during the seventeenth and eighteenth centuries. Along with other members of the language reclamation team, I have been trying to "manage" the data found in this documentation for many years. The following discussion is based on these experiences, discussing steps that I have taken to handle these data, steps that I am currently putting into action, and, in retrospect, steps that I should have taken to better handle these data.

Before delving into specific steps to manage the data found in archival documentation, I begin with a discussion of the ways in which archival materials vary (section 2) followed by some examples of why and how to engage with these materials thoughtfully and carefully (section 3). Section 4 discusses how data are commonly organized and presented in written archival documentation, and the following section (section 5) presents some suggested steps toward transforming the data. Analyzing the data is the subject of section 6 and finally,

repurposing this information for language reclamation is discussed in section 7.

2 Types of archival documentation

As previously mentioned, *archival documentation* refers to any and all previously collected materials, whether or not they are located in a physical archive or held in a private collection (see also Buszard-Welcher, chapter 10, this volume). Some of the more relevant types of archival documentation for language include textual materials, audio recordings, video recordings, drawings or other art (which could record gestures for sign languages), and cartographic materials (see also Good, chapter 3, this volume, about the scope of linguistic data). Textual materials include handwritten or typed pages of language content, whether that be in the form of word lists, field notes, dictionaries, grammars, texts, or other content types. Audio recordings may have been made over a century ago on wax cylinders or they may be more recent, "born digital" recordings, and they can contain elicitation sessions, conversation, texts, music, or other content. Video recordings have the added capacity of containing information about gesture, and this type of information was earlier captured through drawings or other pictorial representations. Finally, cartographic materials can contain toponyms and other land-based knowledge.

While there is a variety of archival documentation, it stands to reason that written documentation in the form of textual materials, without any accompanying audiovisual materials, leaves us with the most unanswered questions. Audio recordings of spoken language and video recordings of either spoken or signed language contain data that are, in my opinion, easier to manage. This is for the simple reason that regardless of how much time has passed from the date of the original recording, you are able to hear or see the language being spoken or signed. The analysis and resources created for reclamation do not have to depend solely on someone else's interpretations and transcriptions of the language. Furthermore, there is software available for phonetic analysis (e.g., Praat[1]) and time-aligned transcribing (e.g., ELAN[2]). There are, of course, complicating factors that can arise from these types of data. For example, wax cylinder recordings are particularly difficult to use as data, because there is great deal of background noise that renders any fine-grained phonetic analysis near to impossible. However, for the most part, audiovisual recordings and the data found within them tend to be easier to manage, due to the fact that documentary linguistics has grown as a field with this technology.

Aside from the physical media and the general content of the documentation, there are many other factors that differentiate these materials, and this is with regard to the purpose of creating this documentation, the intended scope of the materials, and their intended audience.[3] In other words, there are questions to ask of the documentation, and the answers to these questions will help to shape how you (are able to) work with the data. Many of these same questions were presented in a course titled "Working with Archival Materials" that was taught by Susan Gehr and myself at the 2016 iteration of CoLang (the Institute on Collaborative Language Research) at the University of Alaska, Fairbanks.

One of the first questions to ask is why did the individual or individuals collect these data. A common reason for someone to document the language is a concern for preservation. Within Indigenous North America, this could be due to seeing evidence of language shift, believing in the myth of the "vanishing Indian," a combination of the two, or yet another motivation (see Rosenblum & Berez-Kroeker 2018 for a critical description of historical and contemporary documentation practices in North America). Another reason may have been to create a lasting record of the culture, which like language, was (and still is) considered to be disappearing at an alarming rate (e.g., Boas 1911:56; Nettle & Romaine 2000:26). Franz Boas, one of the major figures in earlier documentation of North American Indigenous languages, considered "much of the content of culture, e.g. rituals, oratory, narrative, verbal art and onomastics, [to be] linguistic in nature" (Woodbury 2011:163), and therefore, preserving culture meant creating a record of the language.

Others may have decided to document the language for religious reasons, without a regard for preserving language or culture. This is the case for most documentation created by missionaries, who collected information about the language in order to convert an Indigenous group to Christianity. Still others may have documented some of the language for practical reasons, such as those who saw the need to be able to communicate in the local Indigenous language, due to the fact that they became settlers in the area, hoped to exploit the natural resources in the area, or both.

A related question to ask of the documentation is the reason or reasons for language users, or members of the Indigenous language community, to collaborate in producing the documentation. Why would language users contribute to the documentation? What are their motivations in doing so? In some cases, the language users are the individuals who created the documentation. In others, even if they are not the ones who are writing, drawing, or recording this information, they sometimes share the same reasons for doing so. In other words, language users may choose to contribute to the documentation due to concerns about preserving language and culture for future generations. Some language users may have already converted to Christianity and decided to aid the missionaries in their efforts to convert the rest of their community. In other cases, because of the overarching "power imbalance in the documentary encounter" (Dobrin & Berson 2011:189), language users may have felt pressured to participate in the documentation process because of economic, political, educational, or other factors.

The reasons for individuals to participate in the documentation have direct impacts on the resulting materials. In other words, because the documentation process is a "historically contingent social activity" (Dobrin & Berson 2011:188), the relationships between these individuals and their motivations for engaging in this work can and do shape the archival record we have today. There is no easy way to uncover this information, especially for much older documentation. In some families, communities, and even the archival record itself, there are stories of the ways in which language users have intentionally misinformed individuals creating the documentation in an effort to subvert and resist the documentation process. For example, in the 1633 *Relation* of his time among the Innu, the Jesuit missionary Paul Le Jeune complained that his primary Innu consultant Pierre Pastedechouan would often intentionally provide the wrong word in Innu-aimun when Le Jeune asked him for a translation (True 2015:56). These interactions have an effect on the archival documentation we work with today. The best we can try to do is understand the human dynamics behind these archival records: the purpose of creating the documentation, the motivations for doing so, both on the part of the documenter and the members of the Indigenous language community (although they may be one and the same), and the relationships between the different participants.

3 Engaging with archival documentation

As alluded to in the previous section, for Indigenous languages in the North American context, archival documentation is often a product of colonization. In general, the older the documentation is, the more likely that it was not created for the benefit of the heritage language community. In fact, these materials might have been explicitly created to erase or suppress specific aspects of the culture, worldview, and peoplehood of the heritage language community. For example, the Jesuit documentation of Wendat was created in order to learn the language and better convert the Wendat people to Christianity. It was not intended to be a lasting record of the language to be used by future generations of the language community, although ironically, it is now being used in that very respect.

Therefore, using this documentation, for any purpose, needs to be done thoughtfully and carefully. If the documentation was indeed created to advance the colonial project, it is as much a record of language as it is a record of that particular colonial encounter. At the very least, we need to be aware of the potentially harmful (i.e., retraumatizing) aspects of engaging with this documentation, as it can be "emotionally heavy" work (Rosenblum & Berez-Kroeker 2018:349). For example, the Jesuit documentation of Wendat contains many utterances relating to particular types of historical trauma, including smallpox epidemics, the disruption of Wendat lifeways, and the forced conversion to Christianity. That being said, working with this documentation may not pose a problem for some, but it certainly will have effects on others, especially those from the Indigenous language community themselves.

From another perspective, engaging with this documentation can also be incredibly positive. Archival documentation presents a way in which present community members can reconnect with the past, whether the materials be from years, decades, or centuries ago. For documentation with metadata about the particular community members who participated in its creation, it is possible for individuals to see (and sometimes hear) the contributions from their relatives. Rematriating (instead of repatriating) documentation and repurposing it for language reclamation remains a positive act for the heritage language community and provides a way to move toward healing from the effects of language shift. To put it simply,

overall there needs to be some thought put into the potential implications of engaging with such documentation.

4 Organization and presentation of data in archival documentation

This section discusses the organization and presentation of data within archival documentation and, in particular, on spoken language data in textual materials without any accompanying audiovisual materials. As mentioned in section 2, textual materials stand to be the most frustrating to work with of all the types of materials, because we have to rely solely on the transcriptions of the documenter(s). Because of this, and because of my familiarity with working with written documentation, we will be examining the organization and presentation of data from these types of archival materials. However, these strategies may also be helpful for other types of documentation.

To understand how to work with these materials, it is important to try and understand the scope and intended audience of the documentation, as well as the organization and presentation of the data (again, see also Good, chapter 3, this volume). The scope of written documentation can vary from lengthy manuscript dictionaries and grammars to shorter word lists or individual words and glosses scattered throughout field notes. These materials could also be composed of texts, whether that be transcriptions of traditional stories, historical accounts, ceremonial speeches, conversation, catechisms, song lyrics, or some other genre. The documentation will always be incomplete, because it can never possibly record the entirety of a language, but in some cases, pages will also be missing or illegible, which further limits the materials we have to work with, but is still part of the intended scope of these materials.

The intended audience has a clear bearing on the metadata, if any, found in the documentation (see also Austin 2013). If the creator assumed that there is a possibility that others would like to consult these materials in the future, there might be some metadata that can at the very least situate the materials in time and space, providing information about when and where they were created. These metadata can provide us with an idea of how much time has passed since its creation, which then could be useful in considering the role, if any, of diachronic change in the analysis process, and where it was created, which could then be useful for understanding dialect features as well as characteristics of the social, cultural, and political landscape.

However, if the creators of the documentation only intended it to be used by themselves, there may have been little need to record any information about when or where it was created, whom they were speaking to, and even, who the documenters were. For example, the Jesuit manuscript dictionaries of Wendat were intended only to be used by these missionaries as field manuals. Therefore, most of these dictionaries do not contain the missionary's name or the year it was transcribed, and none of them identify the name of the particular Wendat village in which they were living or the names of any individuals who contributed to this work. This obscures the reconstruction of dialect differences among the numerous villages of the Wendat confederacy. Furthermore, because most of these manuscripts are not dated, it is difficult to determine whether differences among them are due to diachronic change, dialect differences, synchronic variation, transcription errors, or some combination of these possibilities.

The organization of the data within these materials may or may not be straightforward. On the one hand, the organization may simply reflect the way in which the data were gathered. For example, field notes will (or perhaps, most likely will) follow the chronological order in which interactions between the documenter(s) and consultant(s) occurred. However, for some collections of materials, there may have also been a subsequent (re)organization of the data. For example, the ethnologist Marius Barbeau, who did fieldwork with the Wendat and Wyandot[4] in Quebec, Ontario, and Oklahoma, cut up some of his field notebooks into small slips of paper in order to rearrange his notes by semantic category, which is how much of these materials are found today in the Fonds Marius Barbeau.[5]

Another example of reorganization pertains to the Wendat-French dictionaries created by the Jesuits. The Jesuits organized these dictionaries by conjugation class (i.e., classes are defined by the initial segment or segments of the verb base, which then determines the shape of the pronominal prefixes) and then arranged these verb bases alphabetically within conjugation classes. Creating an index of the materials can be a way in which to alleviate these issues of organization and also prepare for the process of transforming the data.

Finally, before delving into working with the archival documentation, it is worth the time to develop a data management plan that specifies how you plan on transforming, analyzing, and repurposing the information found in the archival documentation (see Kung, chapter 8, this volume). As stated earlier, given that much of this archival documentation will not have been created for community reclamation needs, it is especially important to think through how to best repurpose this information. For example, keeping in mind the goal of supporting language learning and teaching, in what form or forms should these data be? How should they be presented? How should they be organized? These questions are important to ask before starting to transform the data from the archival documentation.

5   Transforming data from archival documentation

To analyze and repurpose data from archival documentation for language reclamation efforts, we need to transform the data (see also Han, chapter 6, this volume). At the end of this transformation process, ideally, the corpus will be "cleaned up," searchable, sortable, and editable. In my experiences of working with written archival documentation, this means that the data need to be transcribed and tagged, or encoded, in some sort of structure. For textual materials that were not born digital, the first step toward a workable corpus is transcribing the data. The transcription process may seem simple, but it can be quite complex depending on certain characteristics of the documentation. First, some portions of the archival documentation may be illegible, which hinders the transcription process. For example, as shown in figure 25.1, the legibility of the handwriting in the seventeenth-century French-Wendat dictionary attributed to the Jesuit Pierre Joseph Marie Chaumonot varies substantially, even on a single page, which is an obstacle for transcription purposes.

Second, there may be symbols used in the documentation that do not belong to a recognized transcription system such as the International Phonetic Alphabet or the North American Phonetic Alphabet. For example, the Jesuits occasionally transcribed a dieresis over the letter *n* (often, this was to signal that the *n* was the second half of a nasal vowel digraph and not the onset of the following syllable), which is not a common use of this diacritic. Identifying representative samples of each part of the documentation to transcribe will help to identify most, if not all, of the symbols used in the documentation. (We are not yet concerned with understanding

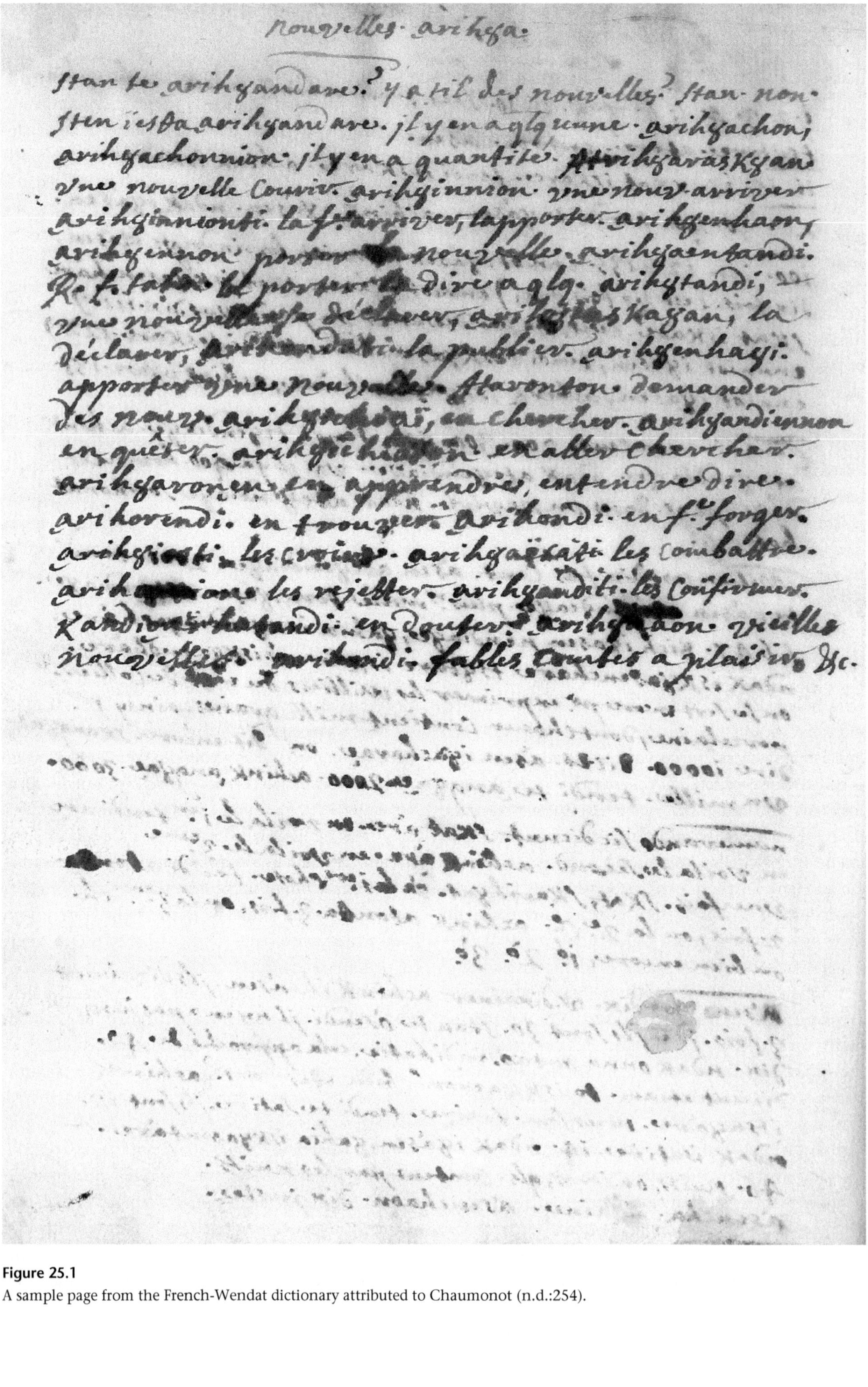

Nouvelles· arihça·

Stan te arihçandare? y a t'il des nouvelles? Stan· non·
Sten iesta arihçandare. il y en a qlqu'une. arihçachon;
arihçachonnion· il y en a quantité.
une nouvelle Courir. arihçinnion· une nouv. arriver
arihçinnionti· la f. arriver, l'apporter. arihçenhaon,

Figure 25.1
A sample page from the French-Wendat dictionary attributed to Chaumonot (n.d.:254).

the sound(s) that are represented by each symbol. That is part of the analysis process, although transforming and analyzing the data tend to overlap one another.) By inventorying these symbols, it is then possible to create a custom keyboard, or even just keyboard shortcuts, to facilitate the transcription process.

Transcription is a lengthy process, and depending on the quantity of documentation, it may be helpful to have more than one transcriber. With a team of at least two individuals, each person can proof the other's transcription, checking for errors or inconsistencies. Instead of relying on human transcribers, some may choose to work with optical character recognition (OCR) software, which attempts to convert static images of text into editable text. Although this software is promising for transcription projects in the future, it is unclear whether pursuing an OCR option at this time is worthwhile, given the current state of the technology (e.g., see Christy et al. 2017), because a large amount of this documentation is handwritten, bi- or multilingual, and contains orthographic symbols that are unattested in many of the languages that OCR is trained to handle.

While transcribing the documentation, we also need to preserve the data structure. The minimal structure of these data would be the distinction between data in the target language and the gloss. The target language data could be separated in different ways. For example, the data (and corresponding gloss) could be on the level of the word, intonation unit, sentence, utterance, or some other unit, and this could vary throughout the documentation. For example, in polysynthetic languages such as Wendat, an individual, conjugated verb will sometimes be the entirety of a data point, whereas in other circumstances, the data point consists of a multiword utterance. A more complicated data structure would involve more than these two types of information. In Wendat-French dictionaries, the Jesuits typically also included grammatical information in the entry. Not only does this information need to be transcribed, but it also needs to be tagged as belonging to a specific category of data (e.g., aspect-mood suffixes, pronominal prefix paradigms). The transcription process will itself lead to a categorization of the data structure, and therefore the tagging and the transcription process work in tandem.[6]

Finally, in addition to tagging the structure of the data, or finding a way to preserve the relationships between the different pieces of information in the archival materials, it is also helpful to decide on a system for flagging items of interest. Working with the same manuscripts over the years, I often stumble on certain dictionary entries or utterances that are of interest for cultural or linguistic reasons. To mark an interesting entry or example for later consultation, initially, I simply bookmarked the page that contained the interesting item (either digitally on the PDF files or physically on the printed copies of the digitized manuscripts). Yet, due to this practice, I was unable to easily retrieve any of them because they were not searchable. I have since switched to a digital system (making notes in .txt files) to flag interesting aspects of the archival materials and can now search through this list. Ideally, however, these flags would be incorporated directly into the body of transcribed data.

The data transformation process as discussed here implies the use of some type of software, platform, or technology to implement these practices. At the time of writing, there is no single technology that was specifically designed to manage linguistic data from archival documentation for the goals of both linguistic analysis and language reclamation (i.e., designing materials for language teaching and learning and for facilitating language learning). Unfortunately, general linguistic analysis software is typically not built to handle archival documentation. Taking FieldWorks Language Explorer[7] (FLEx) as an example, the lexicon module of the software is not designed to encode multiple sources for a single entry. With multiple instances of the same lexical item across different manuscripts or sections of the documentation, it would make sense to be able to merge these tokens into a single type entry, preserving the transcription and source information for each token. However, FLEx has a single field for source information. Therefore, to represent multiple tokens of the same entry, these additional tokens must be recorded in some other way, such as variants in a single entry (whether or not the transcriptions actually vary from one another and whether or not the variation is representative of actual speech variation or transcription errors).

Furthermore, there is no way to view the image of the archival materials as part of the entry, which is important for proofing transcriptions, among other things (however, it is possible to link to these images, which then open in a different software program). Finally, there are no fields dedicated to performing historical-comparative reconstruction, which, as will be discussed, is an important step for certain types of archival documentation. To support reconstruction, the software would have to minimally include fields for cognate information, sources for the cognate information, and the reconstructed forms. FLEx does allow for custom fields to be integrated into the database, yet having tested this option myself, the "workaround" becomes quite a significant undertaking. Ultimately, I abandoned this software due to these issues.

One piece of technology that addresses many of the needs for transforming data found in archival materials is the Indigenous Language Digital Archive (Baldwin et al. 2019). This software had its start as the Miami-Illinois Digital Archive, a project specific to the goals and needs of one language community (Baldwin, Costa, & Troy 2016; Baldwin, Hinton, & Pérez-Báez 2018). This online repository contains digitized images of manuscript pages and searchable transcriptions of these data that allow users to more easily conduct research with the archival documents. While it is a promising tool for archival research, there are some of the same drawbacks as FLEx, because it is a token, not type, database (yet, this may fit the needs of some language communities using archival documentation). Finally, as of the time of writing, the software is not open source and it exports the data only in .csv files (Baldwin et al. 2019).

As it stands, there is no ideal out-of-the-box technology that can manage data for archival-based language reclamation projects. However, one flexible option is to use the Text Encoding Initiative[8] (TEI) guidelines to encode the text found in archival documentation in TEI P5 XML. This option is increasingly explored for encoding legacy materials (e.g., Czaykowska-Higgins, Holmes, & Kell 2014; Lillehaugen et al. 2016; Thieberger 2016). Because the transcriptions are human-readable, and the technology is a "mature, reliable, flexible standard" (Czaykowska-Higgins, Holmes, & Kell 2014:1), this could be a (more) sustainable way to transform the data and analyze it for the purposes of language reclamation,[9] which is the topic of the next section.

6   Analyzing data from archival documentation

Although the data transformation process is presented separately from the linguistic analysis, these two components of managing the data often go hand in hand. Here, I focus only on the tools of linguistic analysis that are particular to the needs of analyzing archival data

for language reclamation (see also Amery 1995, 2000; Spence 2018). The analysis of this specific type of language data depends on deciphering and reinterpreting the transcriptions of the documenter(s) (see also Austin & Crowley 1995). This is no easy task, and it can take years of careful analysis to fully understand the workflow and transcription system of the individual or individuals who created the documentation.

Because language reclamation is the goal of this work, there is a concern for recovering language from this documentation that is as faithful as possible to how it was spoken at the time of recording. One of the analytical tools of linguistics that can help achieve this is historical-comparative reconstruction using the comparative method. However, because the primary goal of the reconstruction is not to reconstruct the proto-language, but to repair errors in the archival transcription, I use the term *reclamation-driven reconstruction* to describe this process. This type of reconstruction is an essential step in the process of reclaiming Wendat, due to the fact that the Jesuit transcribers were unable to consistently hear glottal stops and aspiration. By identifying cognates in other Northern Iroquoian languages, I am able to restore missing laryngeals, clarify other ambiguities in transcription, and ensure, to the extent possible, that the reconstructed forms are close to how Wendat was spoken at the time of transcription.

In addition to reclamation-driven reconstruction, the other analytical tool of linguistics that can be useful for archival data is reconstitution. This process aims to fill gaps in the data, either by borrowing lexical items from a related language and adapting them to the target language's phonology and grammar or by innovating new forms. An example from Wendat of reconstitution by borrowing pertains to a traditional winter game called snowsnake. Although Wendat people played this game historically, no lexical items related to this game have been found in the archival documentation. Therefore, using the process of reconstitution, we borrowed the word *gahwę́hdaʔ* 'snowsnake' (Woodbury 2003:1355) from Onondaga, a closely related Northern Iroquoian language. This noun, which refers to both the game itself and the stick used to play it, was then adapted to the phonology and standardized orthography of Wendat to yield *yahwenhta'*. Reconstitution by borrowing or by lexical innovation is typically indispensable, especially for dormant language communities, as the communicative needs of language learners and teachers do not always match the content found in archival documentation.

Finally, because much of the documentation created in Indigenous North America stems from colonial encounters, another analytical goal is to work toward "undoing" the colonial gaze that permeates some of these materials. As an example, the Jesuit missionaries routinely characterized Wendat spiritual practices as "superstition." This is a very explicit example of how the information captured in this documentation reflects the biases and beliefs of the documenter, rather than the members of the language community, yet there are more covert ways in which colonial ideologies infiltrate the archival record. For example, the Wendat manuscript dictionaries contain far fewer entries relating to women's activities in comparison to those relating to men's activities. In this case, it is not the colonial gaze that needs to be removed, but rather it is grappling with the silence of the colonial record with respect to these matters. Notwithstanding that all documentation reflects the biases of its creator(s), the impact of colonial forces is particularly distorting to the archival record. There is no one way to counteract these effects, but it is good to have some foundation or grounding in cultural, social, and political practices and histories when analyzing these types of data.

7 Repurposing archival data for language reclamation

While transforming and analyzing the data, the most pressing question becomes 'how do you repurpose or curate the data found in this documentation for language reclamation?'. While the specific goals of language reclamation can differ widely across communities, in many cases, we are working toward revalorizing the language, widening the domains of use for the language, restoring or repairing intergenerational transmission, creating speakers of the language, and other goals. To achieve these goals, we need to support and facilitate language learning and teaching by drawing on the linguistic (and cultural) information found in the archival documentation. The resources made from this information could be reference materials, such as dictionaries and grammar aids (charts of inflectional affixes, descriptions of different aspects of grammar, and such). It could also consist of purely pedagogical materials, such as curricula, classroom teaching aids, exercises, games, stories, and songs adapted for language learning.

To create these materials for language learning and teaching, it is helpful to start with a corpus of data that is cleaned up (this can be reconstructed, transliterated in a community orthography, or both), searchable (from the transcription of the data), sortable (from the tagging of the data structure), and editable. Unsurprisingly, the way in which the language data need to be organized for language teaching and learning tends to look remarkably different from how they were organized in the original archival documentation or how they are organized for purposes of linguistic analysis. For example, some Indigenous language communities design their curricula around cultural norms and activities, such as the traditional calendar or seasonal cycles. Furthermore, in building these curricula, it could be helpful to organize and sort language content by skill (speaking, listening, reading, writing) and level (beginner, intermediate, advanced). Being able to tag the data in terms of culturally and pedagogically relevant parameters would facilitate the process. Therefore, the way in which we handle linguistic data from archival documentation, including the technology or technologies used to transform and analyze the data, then needs to be flexible enough to accommodate the ever-evolving needs of language reclamation practitioners, linguists, language learners, and language teachers.

8 Conclusion

Using archival documentation requires working toward understanding the nature of that particular documentation and how it was created and then using that information to shape the overlapping processes of transforming, analyzing, and repurposing the data found within it. By engaging with this documentation, we are creating a new layer of information over the archival record, and that also should be archived at regular intervals (see Andreassen, chapter 7, this volume, on archiving).

Finally, as mentioned earlier, much of the archival documentation produced in Indigenous North America were products of colonization. However, the management of the information within archival documentation, especially when it is undertaken by members of the Indigenous language community, can be a potential space for decolonization. Decolonization can be defined as "the intelligent, calculated, and active resistance to the forces of colonialism that perpetuate the subjugation and/or exploitation of our minds, bodies, and lands"

(Wilson & Yellow Bird 2005:2). The very act of reclaiming a language is decolonial. Engaging with this documentation, which may have itself had a role in perpetuating colonization, is a positive step toward reclaiming language and culture and reaffirming self-determination.

Notes

1. http://www.praat.org.

2. https://tla.mpi.nl/tools/tla-tools/elan/.

3. The scope and intended audience of the materials will be discussed in section 4.

4. Wendat and Wyandot (also spelled Wyandotte, Wandat, and Wa^{n}dat) are dialects of the same language.

5. The Fonds Marius Barbeau is a collection of materials that were either gathered or created by Barbeau. Within this collection are the "Huron-Wyandot" materials that date from between 1911 and 1964. The collection is held in the Canadian Museum of History in Gatineau, Quebec, Canada.

6. I discuss different technologies that can be used for this work later in this section.

7. https://software.sil.org/fieldworks/.

8. https://tei-c.org/guidelines/P5/.

9. I am currently using TEI for encoding the Wendat archival documentation, in collaboration with Martin Holmes from the Humanities and Computing Media Centre of the University of Victoria.

References

Amery, Rob. 1995. Learning and reviving a language from historical sources. In *Paper and Talk: A Manual for Reconstituting Materials in Australian Indigenous Languages from Historical Sources*, ed. Nicholas Thieberger, 147–164. Canberra, Australia: Aboriginal Studies Press.

Amery, Rob. 2000. *Warrabarna Kaurna! Reclaiming an Australian Language*. Lisse, the Netherlands: Swets and Zeitlinger.

Austin, Peter, and Terry Crowley. 1995. Interpreting old spelling. In *Paper and Talk: A Manual for Reconstituting Materials in Australian Indigenous Languages from Historical Sources*, ed. Nicholas Thieberger, 53–102. Canberra, Australia: Aboriginal Studies Press.

Austin, Peter K. 2013. Language documentation and meta-documentation. In *Keeping Languages Alive: Documentation, Pedagogy, and Revitalization*, ed. Mari C. Jones and Sarah Ogilvie, 3–15. Cambridge: Cambridge University Press.

Baldwin, Daryl, David J. Costa, and Douglas Troy. 2016. Myaamiaataweenki eekincikoonihkiinki eeyoonki aapisaataweenki: A Miami language digital tool for language reclamation. *Language Documentation and Conservation* 10:394–410.

Baldwin, Daryl, Jaecie Hall, Gabriela Pérez-Báez, Carson Viles, and Jerome Viles. 2019. The Indigenous Languages Digital Archive (ILDA) for depth, breadth and rigor in archive-based research for revitalization. Paper presented at the 6th International Conference on Language Documentation and Conservation, Honolulu, Hawai'i, February 28–March 3.

Baldwin, Daryl, Leanne Hinton, and Gabriela Pérez-Báez. 2018. The Breath of Life workshops and institutes. In *The Routledge Handbook of Language Revitalization*, ed. Leanne Hinton, Leena Huss, and Gerald Roche, 188–196. New York: Taylor and Francis.

Barbeau, Marius. 1911–1964. Fonds Marius Barbeau: Huron-Wyandot. Canadian Museum of History, Gatineau, Quebec.

Beck, David, and Donna B. Gerdts. 2017. The contribution of research on the languages of the Americas to the field of linguistics. *International Journal of American Linguistics* 83 (1): 7–39.

Boas, Franz. 1911. Introduction. In *Handbook of American Indian Languages*, part 1, ed. Franz Boas, 1–83. Smithsonian Institution Bureau of American Ethnology Bulletin 40. Washington, DC: Government Printing Office.

[Chaumonot, Pierre Joseph Marie?]. n.d. [*French-Huron Dictionary and Vocabulary*]. Indigenous Collection. John Carter Brown Library, Brown University, Providence, RI. https://archive.org/details/frenchhurondicti00chau.

Christy, Matthew, Anshul Gupta, Elizabeth Grumbach, Laura Mandell, Richard Furuta, and Ricardo Gutierrez-Osuna. 2017. Mass digitization of early modern texts with optical character recognition. *ACM Journal on Computing and Cultural Heritage* 11 (1): article 6.

Czaykowska-Higgins, Ewa, Martin D. Holmes, and Sarah M. Kell. 2014. Using TEI for an endangered language lexical resource: The Nxaʔamxcín Database-Dictionary Project. *Language Documentation & Conservation* 8:1–37.

Dobrin, Lise M., and Josh Berson. 2011. Speakers and language documentation. In *The Cambridge Handbook of Endangered Languages*, ed. Peter K. Austin, and Julia Sallabank, 187–211. Cambridge: Cambridge University Press.

Gehr, Susan, and Megan Lukaniec. 2016. Working with archival materials. Course taught at the 2016 Institute on Collaborative Language Research (CoLang), University of Alaska, Fairbanks, June 20–July 1, July 5–23. http://bit.ly/CoLang2016docs.

Kovach, Margaret. 2009. *Indigenous Methodologies: Characteristics, Conversations, and Contexts*. Toronto: University of Toronto Press.

Leonard, Wesley Y. 2011. Challenging "extinction" through modern Miami language practices. *American Indian Culture and Research Journal* 35 (2): 135–160.

Lillehaugen, Brook Danielle, George Aaron Broadwell, Michel R. Oudijk, Laurie Allen, May Plumb, and Mike Zarafonetis. 2016. Ticha: A digital text explorer for Colonial Zapotec, 1st ed. http://ticha.haverford.edu/.

Nettle, Daniel, and Suzanne Romaine. 2000. *Vanishing Voices: The Extinction of the World's Languages*. Oxford: Oxford University Press.

Rodriguez-Lonebear, Desi. 2016. Building a data revolution in Indian country. In *Indigenous Data Sovereignty: Toward an Agenda*, ed. Tahu Kukutai and John Taylor, 253–272. Canberra, Australia: Australian National University Press.

Rosenblum, Daisy, and Andrea L. Berez-Kroeker. 2018. Reflections on language documentation in North America. In *Reflections on Language Documentation 20 Years after Himmelmann 1998*, ed. Bradley McDonnell, Andrea L. Berez-Kroeker, and Gary Holton. Special issue, *Language Documentation and Conservation* 15:340–353.

Spence, Justin. 2018. Learning languages through archives. In *The Routledge Handbook of Language Revitalization*, ed. Leanne Hinton, Leena Huss, and Gerald Roche, 179–187. New York: Taylor and Francis.

Thieberger, Nick. 2016. Daisy Bates in the digital world. In *Language, Land and Song: Studies in Honour of Luise Hercus*, ed. Peter K. Austin, Harold Koch & Jane Simpson, 102–114. London: EL Publishing.

True, Micah. 2015. *Masters and Students: Jesuit Mission Ethnography in Seventeenth-Century New France*. Montreal: McGill-Queen's University Press.

Wilson, Shawn. 2008. *Research Is Ceremony: Indigenous Research Methods*. Halifax, Canada: Fernwood Publishing.

Wilson, Waziyatawin Angela, and Michael Yellow Bird. 2005. Beginning decolonization. In *For Indigenous Eyes Only: A Decolonization Handbook*, ed. Waziyatawin Angela Wilson and Michael Yellow Bird, 1–8. Santa Fe: School of American Research Press.

Woodbury, Anthony C. 2011. Language documentation. In *The Cambridge Handbook of Endangered Languages*, ed. Peter K. Austin and Julia Sallabank, 159–186. Cambridge: Cambridge University Press.

Woodbury, Hanni. 2003. *Onondaga-English/English-Onondaga Dictionary*. Toronto: University of Toronto Press.

Don Daniels and Kelsey Daniels

1   Introduction

In this chapter we describe the data management work-flow we have used in our fieldwork in Madang Province, Papua New Guinea. The bulk of the chapter is devoted to the data management practices we used during the first author's time as a postdoctoral researcher at the Centre of Excellence for the Dynamics of Language at the Australian National University. During this period, the authors conducted a pair of two-month field trips together in 2016, and the first author also conducted a solo trip in 2018. These were all to the Astrolabe Bay area of Madang. In D. Daniels's doctoral research, he conducted solo trips to a different part of the province, the Middle Ramu. We briefly describe the data management workflow used for this project later in the chapter.

In both cases, the goals of this research were primarily descriptive: We were documenting and describing a few essentially undescribed Papuan languages of the Rai Coast and Sogeram branches of the Madang branch of Trans New Guinea (Pawley & Hammarström 2018; Daniels 2015). But one of D. Daniels's primary research interests is historical-comparative linguistics (e.g., Daniels 2014, 2017, 2019), and this interest informed the research agenda in important ways. Most notably, it meant that we conducted shorter stints of research in multiple communities, rather than a longer spell in one community. For the Rai Coast project our research goal was to be able to write a decent grammatical sketch for each of three languages (Bongu, Soq, and Jilim) with the data we collected on these trips. In practical terms, this meant that, for each language, we hoped to collect word lists, conduct basic grammatical elicitation, and record and transcribe a sizeable corpus of naturalistic speech (we hoped for an hour per language per trip). We discuss how the historical orientation of the first author's research agenda influenced the research program toward the end of the chapter.

It will be helpful to describe the logistical situation in Astrolabe Bay before discussing the actual workflow. The villages that we worked in—Bongu, Kaliku, and Jilim—are all rural. The first two are usually serviced by a road during the dry season, but not the wet; during the wet season, the villages are accessible via small motorboats that travel along the coast. Jilim has no road access but is reached by a three-hour walk from the coastal road. None of the villages have electricity, but in each village, there are a few generators around—often in various states of disrepair—that individuals have acquired for one reason or another. A primary difficulty of fieldwork in this context is keeping your electronic equipment, especially laptops, functioning.

The bulk of this chapter is devoted to describing our data management process, which we do in the next section. Section 3 describes some of the differences between this process and the data management practices the first author used in previous research. Section 4 discusses the ways a focus on historical research informed our choices on the field, and we offer some concluding thoughts in section 5.

2   Fieldwork with portable solar panels

The process of managing data consists of three phases. The most involved workflow takes place in the villages where we conduct the fieldwork; this is where primary data collection and processing take place (section 2.1). Then when we return from the villages to the provincial capital of Madang we process some of the collected materials (section 2.2), and we complete the data processing once we return home (section 2.3).

2.1   Data management in the village

There is a lot to do in the village. We have broken our process down into three broad steps: making recordings (section 2.1.1), transcribing recordings (section 2.1.2), and what we call "end-of-day processing," a daily routine of backing up files and processing metadata (section 2.1.3). An added task is equipment management, which is ongoing (section 2.1.4). A key point about this phase of data collection is that routine is paramount (Mattern, chapter 5, this volume). There are so many tasks to perform, and so much to keep track of, that without a solid routine to guide the researcher, the number of decisions to be made quickly becomes overwhelming.

2.1.1 Making recordings

Three types of recordings are made on each trip: elicitation (both lexical and grammatical), natural-language recordings, and informed consent. Before arriving in the village, a field notebook is prepared with a word list based on Z'graggen (1980) and basic grammatical elicitation paradigms. After arriving in the village, the word list is usually the first recording made, if possible, with two language users. Elicitation of basic grammatical paradigms follows soon after. This includes verbal subject-agreement paradigms for several categories, including present, future, multiple pasts, habitual, imperative, and switch reference, and pronominal paradigms for transitive subject, object, and possessor. This initial skeletal session is later supplemented with additional elicitation. In each case, the session is recorded in audio but not video, and transcriptions are recorded in the prepared notebook.

Natural-language sessions are recorded in both audio and video format. We generally try to record a diverse corpus, with representation of men and women, multiple clans (Stanford 2009), and a variety of genres.

Informed consent is usually obtained after each recording so language users are fully aware of what stories or personal information they might be disclosing to others. A description of the purpose and use of the recordings is provided to each language user both in speech and in writing, but, due to low levels of literacy in the area, consent is recorded orally (see Collister, chapter 9, this volume, and Holton, Leonard, & Pulsifer, chapter 4, this volume, for more discussion around consent and rights to data).

Metadata about each recording and each language user is recorded in field notebooks. The first two pages of each notebook contain a table of contents for that notebook; recording metadata are listed next, usually on pages 3–6, and language user metadata around pages 7–10. Recording metadata include the original file names created by the recording devices, name(s) of the language user, and the title of the recording (often in two or three languages). If multiple audio and video recorders, or multiple secure digital (SD) cards, are being used, we also note which device and which memory card a recording was created on.[1] Language user metadata include name, date of birth, level of education, clan membership, childhood residence, languages used, marital status, and number of children. An example is given in figure 26.1.

2.1.2 Transcription

Before natural-language recordings are transcribed, audio files are entered into a program called SayMore (Moeller 2014), where we segment the recording into intonation units. SayMore was chosen for a few reasons. It creates an ELAN file (.eaf) for each recording that makes the data easy to import into other programs. It has simple interfaces for audio segmentation and transcription; this helps engage consultants in the work of transcription, and the interfaces are easier to teach to advanced consultants than are the corresponding interfaces in a more powerful program, such as ELAN. Finally, SayMore automatically generates a file directory for each language project, which helps with keeping files organized.

After the audio file has been segmented, SayMore's transcription interface presents an ELAN tier for the target language transcription and another for the analysis language translation, each consisting of the same time-aligned audio segments. Clicking inside any segment automatically plays the corresponding audio on loop to facilitate the transcription or translation of that text.

We spend most of our days in each village transcribing texts. Transcription typically involves one of the authors sitting at a laptop with one language user, each of us with a pair of earbuds in our ears. (Our field laptops typically do not have good built-in speakers.) We play a chunk of the recording, which the consultant repeats slowly so we can transcribe it. Then the consultant translates the chunk into Tok Pisin, and we transcribe that as well.

As we proceed, we also take notes about the recording. SayMore works well for time-aligned line-by-line transcription and translation, but there is no place to record transcription notes or word-by-word translations. For this reason, we write word-by-word translations and other notes in our notebooks. To save time, we typically write only the first letter of each target language word with the word-by-word translation and notes below that. We also often conduct spontaneous elicitation inspired by the text we are transcribing, and this is also

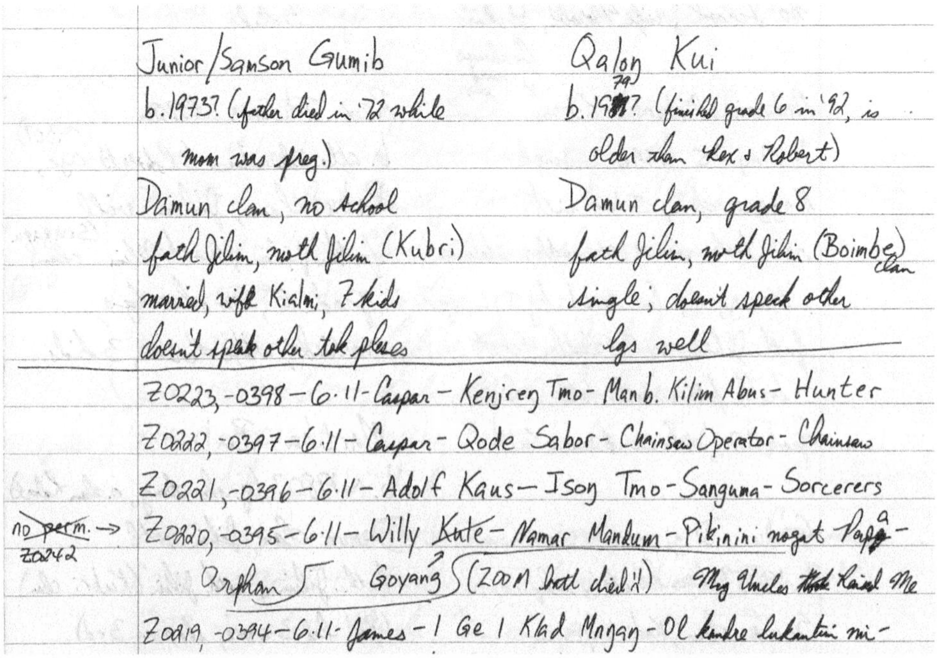

Junior/Samson Gumib
b.1973? (father died in '72 while mom was preg.)
Damun clan, no school
fath Jilim, moth Jilim (Kubri)
married, wife Kialmi, 7 kids
doesn't speak other tok ples

Qalon Kui
b.1979? (finished grade 6 in '92, is older than Rex & Robert)
Damun clan, grade 8
fath Jilim, moth Jilim (Boimbe clan)
single; doesn't speak other lgs well

Z0223, -0398 - 6.11 - Caspar - Kenjiren Tmo - Man b. Kilim Abus - Hunter
Z0222, -0397 - 6.11 - Caspar - Qode Sabor - Chainsaw Operator - Chainsaw
Z0221, -0396 - 6.11 - Adolf Kaus - Isoŋ Tmo - Sanguma - Sorcerers

Figure 26.1
An excerpt from a field notebook, showing speaker metadata and recording metadata.

recorded in the notebooks. A sample is given in figure 26.2. These notebooks are then scanned when we arrive back in town.

2.1.3 End-of-day processing At the end of each day, all files are saved to an external hard drive, and all metadata from the field notebooks are entered in a master spreadsheet. Once all the recording devices have been collected, the contents of each SD card (photos, audio files, video files, and such) are copied to the external hard drive. Copies of all new audio files are also copied to the SayMore directory.

While these files are copying, metadata from all new recordings are copied from the field notebook to the master spreadsheet.[2] The master spreadsheet includes all the recording metadata contained in the field notebooks; it also includes information about corresponding SayMore names for each natural-language recording, the notebook locations of transcription notes, and the transcription status for each natural-language recording (i.e., whether it is untranscribed, only segmented, partially transcribed, or fully transcribed).

One of the most important steps at the end of each day is to standardize the files across the hard drive and both laptops. Copying an updated SayMore transcription file to another laptop requires overwriting the previous SayMore file on that laptop; therefore, it is extremely important for us to save a copy of the updated SayMore transcription file to the hard drive before overwriting any laptop files. This process of transferring and updating files on all the various devices easily gets confusing, so we created a column in the master spreadsheet as a "transfer log" to systematically document which files are most up-to-date and which files have been copied to which devices. The master spreadsheet is copied to the hard drive each day. At the end of this process, both laptops and the external hard drive have a copy of the most recent SayMore transcripts. All photos, videos, and audio recordings are stored both on the original SD cards and on the external hard drive. Depending on how much work is accomplished throughout the day, this process can take up to an hour every afternoon.

It is important to note that the challenges of version control mentioned have long been addressed by software engineers—for example, one reviewer suggested the use of an application such as Git, which can permanently store previous file versions to avoid the hazards of accidentally overwriting or deleting transcriptions. We did not use Git in the field, however, primarily because (1) we did not know about it, and (2) we did not have Internet access to sync laptop versions. Such version control applications seem promising for fieldwork situations like ours, but they require more a bit more investigation before implementation.

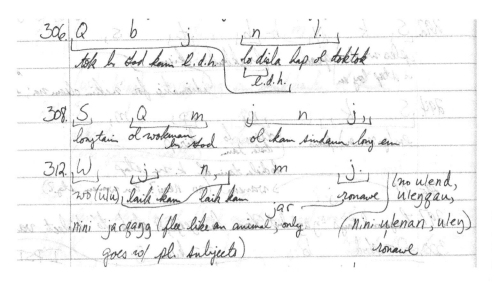

Figure 26.2
An excerpt from a field notebook, showing transcription notes.

2.1.4 Equipment management

Working in rural villages with no electricity requires advanced planning and consistent routines to keep all the devices and batteries charged. To ease this burden somewhat, we have chosen, whenever possible, to use recording devices and transmitters that require AA batteries. And before leaving the United States, we buy the batteries we need, as the life spans of those bought in Papua New Guinea tend to be quite short.

The camera that we use requires a lithium ion rechargeable battery that we recharge using a small portable universal charger—bought in Papua New Guinea—that transfers power from AA batteries to the camera battery. We always bring a few spare lithium ion batteries, allowing us to charge one while we are using another.

Likewise, the two 24,000 mAh PowerGorilla power banks that charge the laptops must regularly be reconnected to solar panels. When we first arrive in the village, D. Daniels finds a trustworthy homeowner whose roof gets decent access to direct sunlight and asks them if we can install the canvas solar panels on their roof. After installing them, each morning D. Daniels goes to their house to check that the panels are functioning properly and to unplug the charged power bank and plug in the recently used power bank. Throughout the day, we alternate which laptop is connected to the power bank. Additionally, the laptops are always set to power-saving mode, to the lowest screen-brightness setting, and to airplane mode. These power banks and solar panels can usually power the laptops for approximately five to six hours a day for a bit more than one week. Data processing is particularly power-intensive, as the external hard drive we use draws power from the laptops, further draining their batteries.

When both laptops and the power banks are depleted, everything needs to be recharged using a generator. In each village we worked in in 2016, at least one person owned a generator. We purchased fuel for them, and they allowed us to recharge all our devices using their generator over the course of an evening. One danger in using locally owned generators is power surges. Depending on the quality of the generator, surges of power can abruptly run through the power cords setting fire to the laptop chargers and the power banks. On one occasion when this happened, we were fortunately able to buy a replacement charger from a computer supply store on our next trip to town. Because of this risk, it is important for someone to be near the generator at all times while it is running, to unplug electronics in case of a surge. Once all the laptops and the power banks are recharged, we can usually operate our devices using only the solar panels and power banks for another week. Another risk with using local generators is that the generator simply will not work; this happened in 2018 and meant that for the last few days in the village, the first author had to rely on solar power. Due to this, he is now planning on buying a high-quality generator for the village.

Another aspect of equipment management is preparing field notebooks. We use two-hundred-page composition notebooks and archival-quality pens, which ensure that ink does not run if it gets wet. Before arriving at the field site, we enter a notebook title and a table of contents on the first page, leave six or seven pages for recording metadata[3] after that, and then prepare any elicitation tasks we plan to complete (word lists, grammatical elicitation, and so on). We also number every page in the notebook, which aids tremendously in tracking data after it has been entered into FieldWorks Language Explorer (FLEx) and other analysis programs.

We must also consider the safety of the equipment. Equipment is most vulnerable during travel, so we take special care when packing our bags to minimize the risk. All electronics are placed in dry-bags to prevent water damage. If we are transporting data (that is, if we are leaving the village), we try to ensure that duplicates are spread across different bags. For example, if SD cards with original recordings are in one bag, the hard drive with backups is put in another bag. In this way, most data will be safe even in the event of a lost or stolen bag.

2.2 Data management in town

When we return from the village, our data are primarily located in two places: field notebooks and an external hard drive. The field notebooks contain consultant metadata, basic metadata about recordings, transcripts of elicitation sessions, and notes from transcription sessions. The hard drive contains all our recordings and photos, the metadata spreadsheet, and transcripts of the naturalistic recordings. Redundant copies of these files are also located on SD cards and our field laptops.

Upon arriving in town, we have two primary tasks. The first is to scan the field notebooks. We use the offices of some friends to do this and copy the scans to our hard drive. The second task is then to copy everything from our first hard drive (the "village" hard drive) to our "town" hard drive. Then, if we return to the villages for more fieldwork, the town hard drive stays with friends in town. If it is time to leave the country, we once again distribute all data between our bags before boarding our flight home.

2.3 After returning from the field

Once we have arrived home, hopefully with all our hard drives intact, there is still a considerable amount of work to be done. In section 2.3.1, we describe the work involved in archiving the materials we collected, and in section 2.3.2, we describe preparing those materials for our own research.

2.3.1 Archiving One of the primary goals of this research is to produce an enduring and open record of the languages and communities under investigation (Gawne & Styles, chapter 2, this volume). As such, we archive the materials we collect in D. Daniels's (2018) Pacific and Regional Archive for Digital Sources in Endangered Cultures (PARADISEC) collection.[4] Preparing them for

archiving involves preparing more detailed metadata, renaming the files, and delivering them to the archive.

D. Daniels maintains a personal metadata spreadsheet (Daniels 2010a), which contains significantly more detail than our field metadata spreadsheet, and filling this in is the first item of business after returning home. The field spreadsheet is organized by recording files. Each separate audio or video file is given its own line. This information is copied into the personal spreadsheet, but the personal spreadsheet also organizes recordings into events. This way, for example, an audio and a video recording of the same story are grouped together. The personal spreadsheet also includes a description of the content of each recording event, which is produced from memory at this stage in the workflow. Metadata about transcripts—both those in the field notebooks and ELAN transcripts produced with SayMore—is also entered into this spreadsheet. For the audio, video, and transcription files, the spreadsheet includes personal file names (which are meaningful) and the PARADISEC file names (which are not). It also includes detailed information about language users, which is copied from the field notebooks.

Once the personal metadata spreadsheet is filled out, copies of the files produced during fieldwork are created. They are renamed in accordance with PARADISEC's file-naming conventions and given to PARADISEC. This involves copying a subset of the metadata from the personal metadata spreadsheet onto PARADISEC's intake spreadsheet and transferring that, along with the renamed files, to PARADISEC. Personal copies of the files are retained with the first author's personal file-naming conventions.

In our experience, it is important to attend to data processing as soon as possible after returning from the field (see also Mattern, chapter 5, this volume). In our own process, responsibility for this stage of work has fallen to the first author, and he has found that there are invariably hiccups in the process that are much easier to get through when the whole experience is fresh in your memory. The longer data processing is delayed, the longer it takes, and the higher the likelihood that some information will be lost or corrupted (Han, chapter 6, this volume). D. Daniels generally expects the whole process to take two full weeks of eight-hour days.

2.3.2 Preparing materials for research Once everything is archived, it is time for D. Daniels to begin moving materials through the research workflow. This can be conceived of as using primary data to create different kinds of more abstract data (Good, chapter 3, this volume; Han, chapter 6, this volume). At this stage he is primarily working with transcripts in FLEx. The first author also has experience using Toolbox, and he has found FLEx to be more powerful, more reliable, and far more useful. The ability to edit morphological analyses as one goes, in particular, is essential for an analyst working with an unfamiliar language. The search functionality is significantly better, as is the technical support from the developer. FLEx also interfaces much better with other programs, most importantly SayMore and ELAN. This allows the analyst to take advantage of ELAN's very powerful "Structured Search Multiple eaf" function.

How data are entered into FLEx depends on the type of data being entered. Transcripts created in SayMore can be automatically imported (Pennington 2014). First they are exported from SayMore by highlighting the relevant transcript and selecting "Export>FLEx interlinear text," which creates an XML file with a ".flextext" extension. This file is then imported into FLEx as an interlinear text, which imports each vernacular line with its Tok Pisin free translation and preserves the time stamps for future exporting. As each text is imported into FLEx, basic metadata about the text are copied to the "Info" tab.

D. Daniels also creates additional "texts" to store other kinds of multimorphemic data, such as morphological paradigms and syntactic elicitation. This is necessary so this data can be morphologically parsed. D. Daniels generally makes four of these dummy texts: one for verb paradigms, one for noun paradigms, one for all other multimorphemic utterances he has recorded, and one for all utterances he has recorded as being ungrammatical. Creating a special place for storing ungrammatical utterances ensures that (1) he will have access to that information when he is conducting research on a particular feature in FLEx, and (2) he will see immediately whether something is ungrammatical based on the text it is in.

Lexical data from our field notebooks needs to be copied manually into FLEx. Word lists can be entered in the Lexicon view or using the "Collect words" interface (this is more useful when dealing with a single semantic domain, such as words for trees, because all entries can be automatically tagged as belonging to the same semantic field). The notebook page where a word is recorded is entered into that lexeme's "Source" field, to facilitate double-checking the source material when necessary.

The final step is parsing. In each text in FLEx, whether it is a genuine transcript of a recording or a dummy text storing morphological paradigms, the user can parse words morphologically. In this process, the user splits the word into its constituent morphemes and tells the program which specific lexical entry each morpheme corresponds to. This turns the texts into a searchable database and allows the analyst to bring up all tokens of a particular morpheme at will. The first author enters lexical glosses in English in FLEx. This means that word-by-word and morpheme-by-morpheme translations are English, but line-by-line translations, which are imported directly from field transcripts, are in Tok Pisin. These choices are largely driven by convenience. The use of Tok Pisin in the field is dictated by the language abilities of our consultants. The use of English at the morphological level means that example sentences can be exported directly into papers and presentations; if Tok Pisin were used here, exporting would mean translating every morpheme afresh, each time.

D. Daniels prefers to proceed with morphological parsing by moving through field notebooks. He begins by parsing in FLEx whatever is recorded on the first pages of field notebook 1 and completes notebook 1 before continuing on to notebook 2. As he parses, he has SayMore open so that he can play back any line in the text that he is working on. He also has a skeleton outline of a grammar sketch open in Word. As he encounters interesting examples, or constructions that he does not understand, he copies them into the appropriate section of the sketch (for instance, an example involving a nominalized verb would go into a section on verb nominalization). He also keeps a list of follow-up questions to ask on his next field trip.

3 Fieldwork without portable solar panels

In the preceding sections we have primarily described the data management practices we used during two trips we went on together in 2016, and during a trip the first author conducted alone in 2018. But for the first author's PhD fieldwork, which he conducted between 2010 and 2014, he worked without field laptops or solar panels, and consequently had to develop different data management practices. We would not recommend this approach over the more technology-heavy approach described in section 2—we have found that the added hassle of solar panels and laptops is more than compensated for by the added capabilities they provide. Nevertheless, we recognize that it may not always be possible to acquire all the gear needed for this kind of fieldwork in remote locations, so in this section we briefly describe the differences between the 2016–2018 fieldwork and the 2010–2014 fieldwork.

The main difference, as mentioned, was that for the 2010–2014 fieldwork D. Daniels did not bring a laptop to the village, which meant he did not need a solar panel. All the power he needed was provided by AA batteries, which could power his camera, his audio recorder, and his video recorder. This difference in equipment primarily affected the work in two ways. It changed the transcription process, and it limited the amount of metadata recording that was possible in the field.

Without a laptop, all transcription had to be done in field notebooks. Transcription is always a time-intensive task, but this limitation made the process even slower. Additionally, audio files couldn't be cut into intonation units before meeting with a speaker but had to be rewound manually and played back. For this reason, audio recorders were selected based, in part, on their built-in playback capabilities. D. Daniels opted for the Olympus LS-10 and LS-14, which enabled him to manually fast-forward and rewind through a recorded file and play back portions of it as needed. After returning from the village, the fact that all transcripts were handwritten in field notebooks also meant that they then needed to be typed into FLEx; the ease of exporting typed transcripts from SayMore to FLEx is a major improvement in this regard.

All metadata also had to be recorded in the notebooks and could not be converted to electronic form until leaving the village. This made the task of entering metadata more time-consuming because it had to be delayed until weeks after many recordings had been made.

4 Historical research

Readers will have noted that relatively little of the fieldwork methodology we have chosen seems to have anything to do with historical linguistics, even though the first author's work is primarily historical (e.g., Daniels, Barth, & Barth 2019; Daniels 2010b, 2020a,b) and this chapter is ostensibly about managing data for historical research. This impression is mostly correct: the research agenda in the field is primarily designed to produce data for synchronic description. We see historical linguistics as

something that is done *after* synchronic analysis has been carried out and consequently aim to collect material with which to write grammatical descriptions.

Nevertheless, there are some ways that D. Daniels's historical research goals did inform our choices in the field. One is the collection of a standard word list. We collected a list of meanings based on Z'graggen's (1980) work for every language, which increased the odds of finding cognates for lexical reconstruction. Another is that we prioritized elicitation of formal linguistic features over less easily visible ones. By this we mean linguistic features that have a formal, phonological realization, as opposed to features that are simply stored in speakers' memory but have no overt realization. For example, a verb's morphologically irregular inflectional form is realized with overt phonological material, while that verb's subcategorization frame is not. We spent significantly more time collecting information of the former kind than the latter because it would be more likely to be useful for historical reconstruction.

D. Daniels's historical-linguistic goals also informed his choices during data processing and analysis. As he analyzed and described the data we had collected, he maintained a document with notes about constructions that might be cognate. This was particularly useful because he was not just interested in lexical cognates, but also syntactic ones, and prose notes could more easily express relations of cognacy between, for example, a particular stem shape in one language and a serial verb construction in another.

For keeping track of more traditional lexical and morphological cognates, the first author simply used spreadsheets. Separate worksheets were devoted to various morphological categories (one for verb suffixes, one for pronouns, one for lexemes, and so on), but each worksheet was organized similarly. Each language was given a column, and each row consisted of semantically similar forms. In cases of semantic innovation, where a form in one row was cognate with a form in another, D. Daniels used color coding to keep track of cognacy relations.

5 Conclusions

We hope these reflections will be useful to fieldworkers in the future and will help researchers design metadata workflows that are effective for their particular situations. We recognize that every project, every researcher, and every language community is different, and we encourage readers to adapt from our workflow those things that they find useful and to ignore those things that seem ill-suited to their situation. Our primary recommendation is to set up a solid routine: create a set of daily expectations and stick to them. Like any chore, staying on top of data is manageable if it is done regularly, but it quickly becomes unmanageable if delayed for a few days. This is especially true if, as will hopefully be the case, fieldwork is going well, and you are recording lots of data.

Another recommendation we have is to pay attention to your relationships in the field. We hope this goes without saying, but fieldwork is much more than an exercise in collecting data. Although for this chapter we focused on the nuts and bolts of how to record and manage data, successful fieldwork will also involve making friends, building collaborative relationships, and learning how to navigate what will often be a very foreign cultural landscape. These aspects of fieldwork probably deserve even more attention than data, but that is a topic for another time.

Notes

We are grateful to the editors and two anonymous reviewers for comments on earlier versions. We are also immensely grateful to people in the various communities where we have conducted fieldwork for their tireless help and steady companionship. All remaining errors are our own. The authors' joint fieldwork was supported by the ARC Centre of Excellence for the Dynamics of Language.

1. We have found it helpful to distinguish SD cards by affixing a unique sticker to each one.

2. Although SayMore has specified fields for recording metadata, we have chosen to record this information in spreadsheets because the first author used spreadsheets when he first started his career in linguistics and because spreadsheets are easier for searching for and copying information.

3. As mentioned, SayMore can easily store metadata about texts and speakers; however, we choose to write this information in our field notebooks as they are more readily accessible when we are recording stories with speakers.

4. PARADISEC is an archive focused on preserving language materials, with a historical connection to the Pacific region.

References

Daniels, Don. 2010a. Metadata spreadsheet. doi:10.4225/72/56 F00F2CCA5E9. http://catalog.paradisec.org.au/collections/DD1 /items/068. Accessed December 12, 2018.

Daniels, Don. 2010b. A preliminary phonological history of the Sogeram languages of Papua New Guinea. *Oceanic Linguistics* 49 (1): 163–193.

Daniels, Don. 2014. Complex coordination in diachrony: Two Sogeram case studies. *Diachronica* 31 (3): 379–406.

Daniels, Don. 2015. A reconstruction of Proto-Sogeram: Phonology, lexicon, and morphosyntax. PhD dissertation, University of California, Santa Barbara.

Daniels, Don. 2017. A method for mitigating the problem of borrowing in syntactic reconstruction. *Studies in Language* 41 (3): 577–614.

Daniels, Don. 2018. Papuan Languages Collection. Pacific and Regional Archive for Digital Sources in Endangered Cultures (PARADISEC). http://catalog.paradisec.org.au/collections/DD1. (Archival collection, 960 items).

Daniels, Don. 2019. Using phonotactics to reconstruct degrammaticalization: The origin of the Sirva pronoun *be*. *Diachronica* 36 (1): 1–36.

Daniels, Don. 2020a. *Grammatical reconstruction: The Sogeram languages of New Guinea*. Berlin: Mouton.

Daniels, Don. 2020b. The history of tense and aspect in the Sogeram family. *Journal of Historical Linguistics* 10 (2): 167–208. doi:10.1075/jhl.18012.dan.

Daniels, Don, Danielle Barth, and Wolfgang Barth. 2019. Subgrouping the Sogeram languages: A critical appraisal of historical glottometry. *Journal of Historical Linguistics* 9 (1): 92–127. doi:10.1075/jhl.17011.dan.

Moeller, Sarah Ruth. 2014. SayMore, a tool for language documentation productivity: From SIL International. *Language Documentation and Conservation* 8:66–74.

Pawley, Andrew, and Harald Hammarström. 2018. The Trans New Guinea family. In *The Languages and Linguistics of the New Guinea Area: A Comprehensive Guide*, ed. Bill Palmer, 21–195. Berlin: De Gruyter Mouton.

Pennington, Ryan. 2014. Producing time-aligned interlinear texts: Towards a SayMore–FLEx–ELAN workflow. Unpublished manuscript, SIL International.

Stanford, James N. 2009. Clan as a sociolinguistic variable: Three approaches to Sui clans. In *Variation in Indigenous Minority Languages*, ed. James N. Stanford and Dennis R. Preston, 463–484. Amsterdam: John Benjamins.

Z'graggen, John A. 1980. *A Comparative Word List of the Rai Coast Languages, Madang Province, Papua New Guinea*. Pacific Linguistics D 30. Canberra, Australia: Pacific Linguistics.

27 Managing Historical Data in the Chirila Database

Claire Bowern

1 Introduction

For as long as linguists have been researching language variation, typology, and change, they have been organizing their data. Historical linguistics is both one of the oldest areas of linguistics and one of the most cutting-edge. It is the focus of interdisciplinary work together with genetics, anthropology, and archaeology, a crucial source of information about the human past. Contemporary historical linguistics includes reconstruction and philology, but it also includes work involving computational approaches to historical linguistics, such as phylogenetics (see Bowern 2018; List, Greenhill, & Gray 2017; Greenhill, Blust, & Gray 2008).

This use case is based on the Chirila database, a database of the contemporary and historical lexical data for Australian languages. The project was begun in 2007 and is described in some detail in Bowern (2016).[1] This use case concentrates on the use of data in historical linguistic and language reclamation research. I briefly describe the database, before providing some discussion of the structure of the database in terms of data types in historical linguistics. Because the data structures for Chirila were already described in detail in Bowern (2016), I concentrate here on the consequences of decisions made early in the Chirila project. Many of these decisions have consequences for how the database can be used later on. This database is both repository and research tool and serves a varied audience. Here I use the metaphor of a "choose your own adventure" novel to describe the process of decision making for a complex research database; with twelve years of work on Chirila, we can now look back at where the "choices" went right and where they could (or should) have been different. In the next section, I discuss some of the issues that arise in historical linguistics research based on the points made in the contributions to part I of this volume.

2 General considerations

Historical databases can either contain single languages at different points in time, or be comparative, with multiple languages, possibly also from different periods. Chirila is a comparative database, containing both multiple languages and records that span two centuries.

2.1 Overview of the database

First, following Good (chapter 3, this volume) I describe the "scope" of a database. Chirila is a set of relational databases, currently stored in FileMaker Pro, along with limited web viewing. The rationale for using FileMaker Pro was discussed in Bowern (2016). However, so much of the data pipeline is now done outside of FileMaker, I am investigating the feasibility of moving the database entirely to a plain text file + Python and R. See also sections 2.4 and 4 for further discussion. A summary of the database structure is given in figure 27.1.

The database covers primarily lexical data; however, there is also a collection of grammatical features and a secondary database of geocoded languages that includes information about other linguistic ontologies (Glottolog, ISO-639, and the AIATSIS[2] language codes), georeferencing, and classification. Its uses include comparative, typological, and historical research involving both traditional comparative and phylogenetic methods.

A lexical database was chosen because so many of the languages are recorded and exhibited only in the form of word lists. If the aim is continent-wide consistent comparison, it needs to be word lists, because that is the only data available for much of the country. Contexts of use were never recorded for these languages. However, that does not prevent us from using ancillary data to check different hypotheses. For example, we can generate ideas about phonological structure from studying the sound systems of a few languages.

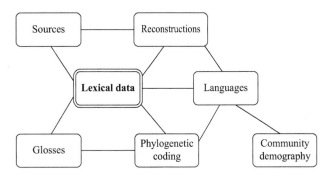

Figure 27.1
Core data structures for the Australian lexical database (from Bowern 2016).

Chirila includes both public and restricted data. The restrictions arise mostly from archives. Several archives place restrictions on reuse of data; one Aboriginal community preferred their language material be not shared, and several linguists placed limits on data use pending community consultation and permission. These restrictions have been respected.

A few sample entries from the linking databases are given in table 27.1. It shows the kinds of data that are collected from original sources, the processing of the original data, and the linking to other material within the databases.[3] The fields are further explained in Bowern (2016).

Chirila also contains grammatical data. Ninety languages were coded for 250 structural features in morphology, semantics, and syntax. These features were based on a combination of the Constenla Umaña (1991) typological survey, WALS features, and the Sahul project "pioneers of Island Melanesia."

Holdings of Chirila (as of September 2019), include 1,140 sources, 474 standard languages with more than 50 items, and 2,988 "variety" names (not necessarily distinct varieties, but records of language/variety names across sources). There are 874,165 items in the lexical database.

The database has been used over the last ten years for research involving structural reconstructions of phonology, morphology, and semantics on the one hand, and language change and population spreads using lexical data on the other.[4] Its metadata have been used to make public language maps. It has also been used as an informal research tool for sourcing early word attestations.

Crosscutting the interlocking structures illustrated in figure 27.1 and table 27.1 are the research strata in the database. These strata do not concern the type of data

directly (in the sense of lexical data or morphology data types). Rather, they concern the relationship between the data items and their place in the research process, more akin to the distinction between primary and secondary data or the documentation materials versus analytical materials described by Himmelmann (1998) and subsequent work. These strata are described next.

First, there is the part of the database that is concerned with the keeping of the actual *primary* data as represented in the original source materials. This part of the database aims to reproduce the original language items as faithfully as possible, including the glosses and orthographic representations from the original source. For example, if a word for the bird of the genus *Dacelo* is glossed as "laughing jackass"—rather than the much more common and contemporary word "kookaburra"—the original gloss would be recorded. This is illustrated in table 27.1 by material in the columns labeled "original." This component of the database is primarily archival.

Another set of fields comprise the *regularization* of the primary data. This allows systematic comparison of disparate sources through the regularization of forms. Producing standardized forms from language-specific orthographies is automatic in some cases, but not for the majority of nineteenth- and early twentieth–century sources.[5] Even quasi-automatic regularization and conversion requires specialist knowledge of the language and documentation conventions of different regions (see, for example, Thieberger 1995). At the very least, it involves conversion of orthographies. Glosses are also problematic (see Bowern 2016 and Everson et al., in prep., for examples specific to Australia). In my previous example, "laughing jackass" is standardized to "kookaburra," because the latter is the term that is more widely used and much more likely to be searched for. An example of orthography standardization is given in the Ngiyambaa example in table 27.1.

Han (chapter 6, this volume) discusses data transformation, which as can be seen is a crucial aspect of making data in Chirila comparable. Note also that evaluating the accuracy of data import and transformation often also requires specialist knowledge; automatic computational validation of entries alone will not catch errors. Automated validation lets us see whether a field is empty when it should be filled, IDs are not unique, or a variety is assigned to multiple standard languages. But it won't tell us if a form has been standardized incorrectly.

Table 27.1

Schematic sample entries for different tables in the Chirila database

Data

Variety	[a]Std language	Original gloss	[b]Std gloss	Original form	Std form	Part of speech	[c]Abbrev source
Bardi	Bardi	boat	boat	yandilybar(a)	yantilypara	N	akl99
Ngarluma	Ngarluma	boat, ship	boat	yandilybara	yantilypara	N	ASEDA0037
Biri	Biri	boat	boat	gumbara	kumparra	N	Terrell
The Lower Macleay River	Ngiyambaa	boat	boat	olpino	wulpinu [unc]	N	Curr185
DDY	Gumatj	boat, ship	boat	mitjiyaŋ	mityiyaŋ	N	Zorc
DDY	Gumatj	large boat, steamship	ship	gapala(')	kapala(?)	N	Zorc

[a]Language

Standard language name	ISO639	Glottolog	AIATSIS code	Family	Latitude	Longitude	Number of entries (all varieties)
Bardi	bcj	bard1255	K15	Nyulnyulan	-16.5	122.93	9801
Ngiyambaa	wyb	ngiy1239	D22, D18	Pama-Nyungan	-31.28	146.05	2589
Gumatj	guf	guma1253	N141	Pama-Nyungan	-12.25	136.8	4949

[b]Gloss

Standard gloss	Entry count	Part of speech	Wordnet form	Concepticon name	Semantic field(s)	Sutton/ Walsh (1980) category	Cognate code
boat	201	N	boat.n.01	BOAT	water, material culture	D	—
ship	94	N	ship.n.01	SHIP	water, material culture	D	—

[c]Source

Abbreviated source name	Author/ Compiler	Title	Access	Published	Reliability	Year	Number of items
akl99	Aklif, Gedda	Ardiyooloon Bardi Ngaanka: One Arm Point Bardi Dictionary	open	yes	1	1999	1547
Curr185	Spencer, Charles		open	yes	3	1886	215

Superscript letters show links between database tables.

Third, historical data, just like other data, require metadata. Metadata are the data about the data, the data about the languages in the sample, the source materials, the linguists who collected them, and the like (Good 2003). Metadata are part of the archival component of the database but may require additional research of themselves and may also be the subject of research.[6] Bowern (2014, 2015) describes some of the Chirila outputs based on the metadata research. Metadata for a historical database should also include documentation of the regularization conventions that were required for each data set. This was not done explicitly in the Chirila database, but there is a three-point scale for reliability of the transcription at the level of the source. A score of 1 is given to sources that are phonemically represented and likely to be accurate representations of the lexical items; 2 is given to sources that are regular, but which are idiosyncratic in some way (e.g., under-differentiated phonemes); and 3 is given to materials that are not consistently represented and whose phonological representation cannot be automatically inferred.

Finally, there is the comparison part of the database: this is the identification of cognate forms, the identification of loans, and the tracking of the aspects of language history that are crucial to doing research involving diachrony. This also requires expert knowledge of the data. Only at that point, once we have primary data, metadata, and cognate links, do we have the database forms that are the output for the historical research itself: that is, inferring trees, loan patterns, and other research. We might call this the iceberg principle of databases: that underneath the visible outputs of research questions are all the invisible decisions and codings that nonetheless impact how data can be obtained and used.

Ideally, the curatorial aspects of a database are kept distinct from research questions involving historical analysis of the data. I did not separate these parts of the database in earlier work, and they are now intertwined, making some aspects of data use unwieldy. For example, in 2013 I experimented with mapping the outputs of cognate sets by writing a script that produced kml-formatted entries for display in Google Earth. This required several columns that I put in the main lexical database, along with match field queries in the database structure. Although this mapping is now superseded (by scripts, in R), the match queries are now used in other database functions, and the mapping columns, though not actually used, cannot easily be removed.

2.2 Reproducibility and recoverability of hidden decisions

The contents of the Chirila data are primary data in that it is an original research contribution and feeds into the secondary analysis of language change. Such work does not clearly fit into a description versus documentation dichotomy (cf. Himmelmann 1998), as it is itself a combination of reporting and analysis, of compilation and synthesis in a loop that becomes more accurate as more knowledge is obtained. The intertwined nature of the data and analysis for historical databases has, in my opinion, been underappreciated in work on synchronic language documentation based on field methods, where authors have focused greater attention on the field to write-up "pipeline." One may also compare the Chirila database with the TerraLing/SSWL database (Koopman & Guardiano, chapter 55, this volume), which includes statements about grammatical features in languages but does not explicitly track how those decisions are made.

A further way in which the primary/secondary data distinction fails here is that diachronic databases contain material which is all, to a greater or lesser extent, *secondary*, in that the database records are abstracted representations of speech signals, presented in isolation.[7] These discussions have practical relevance when considering the analytical paper trail: how much manipulation of data is done, to what end, and how is that tracked and recovered if necessary (see also Han, chapter 6, this volume).

While data processing may be a pipeline, the decisions about *how* to process the data perhaps resemble a "choose your own adventure" novel. More technically, it resembles a process where prior choices shape the possibilities for subsequent work. Regularizing data, for example, allows comparisons to be made more easily and systematically. But irrecoverably regularizing means that it is then impossible to examine the ways in which words are variably represented in earlier sources. Another example of consequence is how to treat synonyms and multiple glosses or senses of a lexical item. Should the entry be split, so that each entry contains a single gloss or sense, or should all senses be in a single entry? The former makes it easier to tag disparate senses, to make it clear which words are recorded in some sentences but not others, and to track semantic change. However, this comes at the expense of proliferation of entries, which becomes unwieldy in cognate coding. The alternative is to add another layer of structure (a "lexeme" layer) where cognates are marked, and which has senses and variant spellings as daughters.

Furthermore, it is vital to have some way of documenting decisions about such choices in analysis and considering what implications of those choices might be. For example, in Chirila, doculects are assigned to *reference languages* (similar to a standard language, allowing for typological comparison across varieties of roughly equivalent genetic distance).[8] In many cases, assigning a doculect to a reference language is straightforward; in others, it requires extensive additional research and may rely on implicit assumptions about the accuracy of underlying sources. If later work reveals that the doculect was mis-assigned, it can affect later analyses. This is particularly problematic where all the sources are sparse. For example, there are three vocabularies that are all tentatively assigned to the standard language Bigambal. Because they do not contain a lot of overlapping vocabulary, the cognate list for Bigambal includes words attested from only one of each of the three word lists. Where the word lists do overlap, they do not always have the same word. If later research shows that more than one language is represented in these vocabulary lists, this affects not just the mapping between varieties and languages, but cognate coding as well.

Gawne and Styles (chapter 2, this volume) and earlier Berez-Kroeker et al. (2018) describe a framework by which linguistic research, even if not fully replicable, should be reproducible at key points. That is, even if we cannot do all the steps to redo an analysis from scratch, it should be possible to trace all the steps and understand where all the data came from. This is also key for Chirila, where original sources are fully sourced, and major points in analysis are documented. Data sets like these are easier to use to replicate analyses; for example, as in the case of the discussion in PNAS between Haynie and Bowern (2016) and Nash (2017), and the reply at Bowern and Haynie (2017).

2.3 Summary: The "data science" of historical linguistics

This description of the database is somewhat similar to taking a data science view of the work of the database;

that is, seeing the data as part of a research pipeline from the original research questions, to data questions and identification, to the actual analysis and its write-up. While I have treated the historical database as a single entity, in practice identical data sets may be used in very different ways depending on the particular research question. For example, Swadesh word lists have been used for Australian language historical research in studying the distribution of sound correspondences and sound change (Babinski & Bowern 2018); studying the phylogenetic signal in phonological inventories and phonotactics (Macklin-Cordes & Round 2015; Macklin-Cordes, Bowern, & Round, 2021; building a tree of languages (Bouckaert, Bowern, & Atkinson 2018; Bowern & Atkinson 2012); studying sound symbolism (Haynie, Bowern, & LaPalombara 2014); examining the distribution of loans and retentions across a large number of languages (Haynie et al. 2014); and public outreach.

3 Use case problems

The most challenging issues for this database have been the software components, an adequate pipeline for the many different types of data, and the separation of the research and simple data processing aspects of the database. Each of these issues is discussed in turn.

3.1 Software

Interfacing with pipelines for analysis requires other software. For example, the advantage of structured data of this type is that they can eventually feed in, possibly automatically, to tools for language analysis such as LingPy (List, Greenhill, & Forkel 2017; List, Greenhill, & Gray 2017). Statistical packages such as those in the R platform (R Core Team 2017) can use data from text formats and manipulate strings, but they are not very graphically user-friendly. FileMaker Pro, on the other hand, is user friendly for some types of operations. Complex searching, for example, is straightforward; building, changing, and manipulating joins in relational databases to construct complex queries is far easier in FileMaker than in SQL. Its spreadsheet visualization functions make it straightforward to use for manual data comparison, loan investigation, and lexical reconstruction using the principles of the comparative method (Weiss 2015). But these same advantages also bring disadvantages. For example, it is difficult to undo operations in a FileMaker database. It is possible, with three mouse clicks, to irrecoverably delete all the data in a table (unless a backup has been made). It does not easily fit into a data pipeline, such as can be constructed in R or Python, where the original underlying data set is untouched and subsequently manipulated.

A reviewer of this chapter brought up the point of advocating for proprietary software and the dangers of using such software, which may cease to be maintained or may render data inaccessible when the software is upgraded. This is a serious concern. However, on these dimensions, free open source is not necessarily better. Having used open source software for many years, I see two issues that cause particular problems for language projects: the lack of stable development and problems with backward compatibility. For example, R packages that have become integral to a pipeline cease to be maintained and become incompatible with platform updates. While such issues do not affect the underlying data, they can render a project unusable or results undisplayable.

My choices for databases at the time were to use FileMaker (with its imperfections), learn SQL and web interfaces and create an architecture from scratch, or pay someone to create a database. A major advantage of File-Maker was that I could experiment with database structures while still doing language research; I did not have to wait for the database to be ready and be beholden to someone else's schedule for development (something I have subsequently found to be a problem for databases such as this). At the time, Chirila was unique—the models of other comparative databases either weren't exactly equivalent (such as the Austronesian Basic Vocabulary Database; cf. Greenhill & Gray 2008) or were not available to be viewed. I wanted to create something that would be an archive, a research tool, and a data and analysis collation tool together. Using FileMaker allowed both historical-linguistic and database structure research to take place organically. Given the options available, FileMaker was the right choice.

If I were starting again from scratch now, however, I would probably use plain text files, stored in .json format or an equivalent, with field manipulation through R or Python, and data viewing in something like a Jekyll site (that serves content from static pages). Alternatively, I would keep the master files as text or .json files and use FileMaker for the research coding. That is, I would use FileMaker as a data visualization end point, not as the main repository. However, I still believe that for most of what I do interactively with the database, there is no better solution than FileMaker.

In summary, whatever software is used for storage, analysis, and display, the principles of data sustainability apply. Data should be backed up, code should be backed up, and both in ways that retain accessibility as much as possible. Chirila holdings are frequently exported as Unicode plain text tables, and waypoints in the File-Maker databases are also saved before any major changes (and periodically at other times; see section 3.4).

3.2 Pipelines, bottlenecks, and "life cycles" of data

Three metaphors are in common usage in talking about data and its processing: *data pipelines* refer to the process of working with original data, processing and cleaning it and analyzing it for a specific purpose. *Bottlenecks* are points in that pipeline where the processing takes more time, leading to less data being available. For example, in the Chirila database, one bottleneck is the assignment of standardized English glosses to dictionary entries, which has to be done manually. Another is the digitization of handwritten notes. The *data life cycle* is a third metaphor and will be discussed further in section 3.4.

Data pipelines are structured by protocols. These are procedures for processing data in a particular way, in a predefined order, to make sure that all necessary steps are followed correctly. Protocols ensure that crucial steps are followed in the appropriate order and that data are treated consistently. However, it is difficult to get student researchers to keep to detailed protocols when many temporary student workers are involved. The training may end up taking more time than they spend on the data itself. This has meant for Chirila that some languages are better represented than others, simply because the original data were more accessible to student researchers, and that some protocols were not followed, meaning subsequent emendations were required. For example, one student did not follow instructions about not representing underlined characters with Excel underline markup; when the data were imported into the main database, all underlines (and the distinction between retroflex and apical consonants) were lost.

3.3 Research and data

For long-term and intensive database work, it is crucial to prepare for an *evolving* research project; that is difficult when the nature of the research means that future possibilities cannot be known. For example, when Chirila was first constructed, none of the software tools that I now most commonly use in my research were available. Both historical linguistics and linguistics more generally were considerably less quantitative. Being transparent and flexible in the data structures is crucial.

3.4 Ethics

Ethical considerations (Holton, Leonard, & Pulsifer, chapter 4, this volume) are everywhere. The ethical issues are complex, because individuals have different views of what should happen to their language data. Three particular issues that arise with Chirila are (1) consultation about data use, (2) negotiation with archives, and (3) sharing.

Language work in Aboriginal Australia typically proceeds with the assumption that many members of a language community will be consulted before work begins. This was simply not feasible with Chirila, given the number of languages involved and the number of languages without clear community presence. When compiling Chirila, I consulted with representative bodies, such as local language centers, and individuals at the 2007 inaugural Aboriginal Languages Conference in Adelaide. My aim was to do things ethically, but also with the concern that when negotiating access and publication where different people have different opinions, it's impossible to please everyone, and both restricting and releasing data have positive and negative ethical consequences. Too often, I think, we focus on the positives of restricting and the negatives of releasing, without considering the positives of releasing data.[9] Indeed, one of the primary community user groups of Chirila has been members of the Stolen Generations using the resource to find out more about their languages. Some have done this in part by looking up words (e.g., words for grandparents) that they remember from early childhood. By definition they would not have been able to do this if the availability of resources had been dependent on giving permission in advance.

In discussions about language data, Aboriginal people have stressed that consultation is important. The communities and individuals I have consulted with have been almost unanimously in favor of some type of data release. Linguists have usually also been in favor of data release. The exceptions have been mostly where linguists have not wished to give an answer on behalf of the community or communities they worked with and have needed time to consult them.

Data backup and curation are ethical issues, not just logistic ones. This database is a record of thousands of hours of work between Aboriginal communities and linguists and represents a major repository of cultural patrimony. Taking care of that material should not be taken lightly. Chirila is itself an archive of a sort. The solution for Chirila has been a version of LOCKSS (Lots of Copies Keeps Stuff Safe; Bird & Simons 2003). In addition to multiple copies of the FileMaker databases (backed up in Dropbox and Yale's institutional backup service and the FileMaker server), the material is privately backed up with Zenodo (zenodo.org), the data archive run by CERN.

Zenodo allows the publication and citation of data sets with DOIs, both increasing version control and making citations more visible and trackable (cf. Conzett & De Smedt, chapter 11, this volume). Chirila's citation issues are complicated, because someone working with Chirila data needs to be able to cite both the original source(s) and the Chirila database itself.

Finally, some work has recently discussed the data life cycle (e.g., Mattern, chapter 5, this volume). I'm not in favor of the metaphor of the life cycle for linguistic data of this type, given what it implies about end of cycle and how the very existence of this database shows that the metaphor is misplaced.[10] I also do not think that ending up in an inaccessible archive is good "end of life" care for data, particularly given the social backdrop against which so many Australian languages have been documented.

3.5 Recommendations

In summary, here are the recommendations of decisions taken for Chirila that turned out to be good ones, even if the choice was not obvious at the time. I also include some decisions that in retrospect were not good ones. This summary builds on the discussion of key points in this chapter.

Including both standardized and original data was a good decision. Some other databases have only presented standardized materials (or only original materials). Having both data types allows for new projects, such as studying the ways in which nineteenth-century researchers represented the sounds they were hearing. It also made it possible to catch errors that would otherwise have gone undetected.

Where possible, separate the basic data from particular views or additions to the database that are used for particular projects. For example, I created some mapping fields which proved useful for a particular representation of some lexical data for a subset of languages, but these are in columns in the main lexical database. A better decision would be to pull the underlying database material into a new frame, using virtual links.

Geocoding both standard languages and varieties, where possible (Bowern 2017), was also very helpful in unforeseen ways. This has made it possible to do much more geospatial analysis of cognacy than was dreamed of when the database was first constructed. It has also made it possible to construct outreach materials (e.g., maps based on words for items in particular languages).

A problem that is still ongoing is how to represent recursive subgrouping in a hierarchical database. When I started compiling Chirila, we had family data, major subgroup data (within Pama-Nyungan), but no fully articulated tree (that came with Bowern & Atkinson 2012 and Bouckaert, Bowern, & Atkinson 2018). Hierarchical subgroups with different layers are not easy to represent in a table-based database such as this. Currently, I include family, subgroup, and major grouping as per Bowern and Atkinson (2012).

FileMaker does not make it straightforward to incorporate changelogs, but we do have some basic data tracking (such as the date and time last edited, and the username of the person who last modified the entry). This has proven invaluable on more than one occasion. Issue tracking is highly recommended. Document decisions and back up before and after major data changes. I once accidentally replaced all the cognate codes with language codes, destroying hundreds of hours of work. However, I was able to restore a prior copy of the database (from ten minutes before).

Consider the consequences of decisions not just for immediate projects but for all conceivable future projects. It is helpful to ask variations of the question "If I organize it this way, will I be able to do X, Y, Z?" For example, if I do this, how will I get data back out? How will I be able to analyze the forms with another software program? If I split all glosses, will I be able to recover the words that were glossed together in the original sources?

Considering carefully what properties are properly attributes of which pieces of data is crucial. For example, words can be geocoded so they can be represented on a map, but words are part of doculects, so the geocoded entity is technically the doculect, and words inherit their geocoding by which doculect they represent.

Most of the biggest problems have stemmed from areas of data processing where we lack good data management practices. One issue is that just as Chirila is a work in progress, so too are some of the data sources that underlie it. Language centers such as Wangka Maya and the Goldfields continue to work on languages and release updates, corrections, and new works. Some of those works are based in part on earlier editions. We do not want to include errors from previous sources, nor can we simply replace one source with its update.

Another area where problems have arisen is in language names. It has been difficult to standardize language names across all projects, leading to confusion and time lost in having to match languages to codes. For example, the first geocoding of polygons for language names (Bowern 2017) was done in Google Earth before some language names were standardized. Thus, the FileMaker database and the Google Earth files ended up with alternative spellings for some languages. Matching these needs to be done manually. Furthermore, there are three major standard codes for Australian languages (the AIATSIS codes, Glottolog, and the ISO-639 three-letter codes). These are not directly comparable, as they have slightly different coverage and classification.

4 Conclusions

Computational and statistical approaches that combine with historical linguistics require complex data management. The Chirila database has evolved over its twelve years of development as the field has changed; this has created both a test of flexibility in data structures and an illustration of the need to be careful about data curation decisions.

Notes

1. Although the database is still under active use and data are still being added and processed, the underlying structure of the database has been stable since 2013. Development of the database has been supported by NSF BCS-0844550 and BCS-1423711.

2. See https://collection.aiatsis.gov.au/austlang/search/.

3. While all links in the Chirila database are done with unique and persistent ID numbers, here only the labels are given. Fields are omitted for clarity; only the most common fields are given.

4. References include (Bowern 2011; Bowern 2012; Haynie & Bowern 2016; Bowern et al. 2014; Epps et al. 2012; Bouckaert, Bowern, & Atkinson 2018), among others.

5. There were 379 sources published before 1920, comprising 84,635 words.

6. For example, the information about how many standard languages are represented in the database is the main data for a chapter in the forthcoming *Oxford Handbook of Australian Languages* on how many languages were used in Australia at European settlement.

7. For my purposes, I distinguish original field documentation, published analyses (which might be based on preprocessed original documentation, such as Wafer, Lissarrague, & Harkins 2008; Ash, Giacon, & Lissarrague 2003; and others), and work that I have subsequently done that regularizes materials for the purpose of comparison. That is, we could distinguish "interpretation" from "regularization"; the latter is a substitution algorithm, whereas the former requires special linguistic knowledge of the particular language. Others may make different distinctions.

8. The term *doculect* is due to Good and Cysouw (2013).

9. To take one example, I have an informal data-sharing arrangement with the Resource Network for Linguistic Diversity (rnld.org), who run workshops on language reclamation for individuals who are members of the Stolen Generations and their descendants. Keeping language data highly restricted would further deprive those communities of their cultural rights. Is it truly ethical to say that members of the Stolen Generation cannot further discover details of their cultural heritage (which colonial institutions deprived them of) because of rules restricting access that are created by archives (another type of colonial institution)? Compare further projects such as http://www.decolonisingthearchive.com.

10. For further discussion of metaphors of death in documentary linguistics, see Perley (2012), Davis (2017), and Hill (2002).

References

Ash, Anna, John Giacon, and Amanda Lissarrague. 2003. *Gamilaraay, Yuwaalaraay and Yuwaalayaay Dictionary*. Alice Springs, Australia: IAD Press.

Babinski, Sarah, and Claire Bowern. 2018. Mergers in Bardi: Contextual probability and predictors of sound change. *Linguistics Vanguard* 4 (s2): 20170024. https://doi.org/10.1515/lingvan-2017-0024.

Berez-Kroeker, Andrea L., Lauren Gawne, Susan Smythe Kung, Barbara F. Kelly, Tyler Heston, Gary Holton, Peter Pulsifer, David I. Beaver, Shobhana Chelliah, and Stanley Dubinsky. 2018. Reproducible research in linguistics: A position statement on data citation and attribution in our field. *Linguistics* 56 (1): 1–18.

Bird, Steven, and Gary Simons. 2003. Seven dimensions of portability for language documentation and description. *Language* 79 (3): 557–582.

Bouckaert, Remco R., Claire Bowern, and Quentin D. Atkinson. 2018. The origin and expansion of Pama–Nyungan languages across Australia. *Nature Ecology and Evolution* 2:741–749.

Bowern, Claire. 2011. Loans in the basic vocabulary of Pama-Nyungan languages. LSA Conference Presentation presented at the 85th Annual Meeting of the Linguistic Society of America, Pittsburgh, Pennsylvania, January 6–9.

Bowern, Claire. 2012. The riddle of Tasmanian languages. *Proceedings of the Royal Society B: Biological Sciences 279 (1747): 4590–4595*. https://doi.org/10.1098/rspb.2012.1842.

Bowern, Claire. 2014. Data "big" and "small"—Examples from the Australian lexical database. *Linguistics Vanguard* 1 (1): 295–303. https://doi.org/10.1515/lingvan-2014-1009.

Bowern, Claire. 2015. Pama-Nyungan phylogenetics and beyond. Presented as the Plenary Address to Leiden Lorentz Center Workshop on Phylogenetic Methods in Linguistics, Leiden, The Netherlands, October 26–30. https://zenodo.org/record/3032846.

Bowern, Claire. 2016. Chirila: Contemporary and historical resources for the Indigenous languages of Australia. *Language Documentation and Conservation* 10:1–44. http://scholarspace.manoa.hawaii.edu/handle/10125/24685.

Bowern, Claire. 2017. Files for Australian language locations. Zenodo. doi:10.5281/zenodo.848646. https://zenodo.org/record/848646. Accessed May 19, 2019.

Bowern, Claire. 2018. Computational phylogenetics. *Annual Review of Linguistics* 4 (1): 281–296. http://www.annualreviews.org/doi/full/10.1146/annurev-linguistics-011516-034142.

Bowern, Claire, and Quentin Atkinson. 2012. Computational phylogenetics and the internal structure of Pama-Nyungan. *Language* 88 (4): 817–845.

Bowern, Claire, and Hannah J. Haynie. 2017. Reply to Nash: Color terms are lost, despite missing data. *Proceedings of the National Academy of Sciences* 114 (39): E8132–E8133. doi:10.1073/pnas.1714258114.

Bowern, Claire, Hannah Haynie, Catherine Sheard, Barry Alpher, Patience Epps, Jane Hill, and Patrick McConvell. 2014. Loan and inheritance patterns in hunter-gatherer ethnobiological systems. *Journal of Ethnobiology* 34 (2): 195–227. doi:10.2993/0278-0771-34.2.195.

Constenla Umaña, Adolfo. 1991. *Las lenguas del área intermedia: Introducción a su estudio areal.* San José: Editorial de la Universidad de Costa Rica.

Davis, Jenny L. 2017. Resisting rhetorics of language endangerment: Reclamation through Indigenous language survivance. In *Language Documentation and Description*, vol. 14, ed. Wesley Y. Leonard and Haley De Korne, 37–58. London: EL Publishing.

Epps, Patience, Claire Bowern, Cynthia Hansen, Jane Hill, and Jason Zentz. 2012. On numeral complexity in hunter-gatherer languages. *Linguistic Typology*16 (1): 41–109.

Everson, Rebecca, R Tom McCoy, and Claire Bowern. In preparation. Standardizing glossing from dictionary sources: A case study from Australia. Unpublished manuscript, Yale University.

Good, Jeff. 2003. *A Gentle Introduction to Metadata.* UBIR. http://ubir.buffalo.edu/xmlui/handle/10477/38681. Accessed September 30, 2019.

Good, Jeff, and Michael Cysouw. 2013. Languoid, doculect, and glossonym: Formalizing the notion "language." *Language Documentation and Conservation* 7:331–359. http://scholarspace.manoa.hawaii.edu/handle/10125/4606.

Greenhill, S. J., R. Blust, and R. D. Gray. 2008. The Austronesian basic vocabulary database: From bioinformatics to lexomics. *Evolutionary Bioinformatics Online* 4:271–283.

Haynie, Hannah J., and Claire Bowern. 2016. Phylogenetic approach to the evolution of color term systems. *Proceedings of the National Academy of Sciences* 113 (48): 13666–13671.

Haynie, Hannah, Claire Bowern, Patience Epps, Jane Hill, and Patrick McConvell. 2014. Wanderwörter in languages of the Americas and Australia. *Ampersand* 1:1–18.

Haynie, Hannah, Claire Bowern, and Hannah LaPalombara. 2014. Sound symbolism in the languages of Australia. *PLoS One* 9 (4): e92852.

Hill, Jane H. 2002. "Expert rhetorics" in advocacy for endangered languages: Who is listening, and what do they hear? *Journal of Linguistic Anthropology* 12 (2): 119–133.

Himmelmann, Niklaus. 1998. Documentary and descriptive linguistics. *Linguistics* 36 (1): 161–196. doi:10.1515/ling.1998.36.1.161.

List, Johann-Mattis, Simon Greenhill, and Robert Forkel. 2017. *LingPy: A Python Library for Quantitative Tasks in Historical Linguistics.* Jena, Germany: Max Planck Institute for the Science of Human History.

List, Johann-Mattis, Simon J. Greenhill, and Russell D. Gray. 2017. The potential of automatic word comparison for historical linguistics. *PLoS One* 12 (1): e0170046. doi:10.1371/journal.pone.0170046.

Macklin-Cordes, Jayden L., and Erich R. Round. 2015. *High-definition Phonotactics Reflect Linguistic Pasts.* Tübingen, Germany: Universitätsbibliothek Tübingen.

Macklin-Cordes, Jayden L., Claire Bowern, and Erich R. Round. 2021. Phylogenetic signal in phonotactics. *Diachronica* 38. https://doi.org/10.1075/dia.20004.mac.

Nash, David. 2017. Loss of color terms not demonstrated. *Proceedings of the National Academy of Sciences* 114 (39): E8131. doi:10.1073/pnas.1714007114.

Perley, Bernard C. 2012. Zombie linguistics: Experts, endangered languages and the curse of undead voices. *Anthropological Forum* 22 (2): 133–149. doi:10.1080/00664677.2012.694170.

R Core Team. 2017. *R: A Language and Environment for Statistical Computing.* Vienna: R Foundation for Statistical Computing. http://www.R-project.org.

Thieberger, N., ed. 1995. *Paper and Chalk: Manual or Reconstituting Materials in Australian Indigenous Languages from Historical Sources.* Canberra, Australia: Aboriginal Studies Press.

Wafer, Jim, Amanda Lissarrague, and Jean Harkins. 2008. *A Handbook of Aboriginal Languages of New South Wales and the Australian Capital Territory.* Nambucca Heads, Australia: Muurrbay Aboriginal Language and Culture Co-operative.

Weiss, Michael. 2015. The comparative method. In *The Routledge Handbook of Historical Linguistics*, ed. Claire Bowern and Bethwyn Evans. Routledge Handbooks Online. Abingdon, UK: Routledge. June 27, 2014. doi:10.4324/9781315794013-16. Accessed November 19, 2018.

28 Managing Historical Linguistic Data for Computational Phylogenetics and Computer-Assisted Language Comparison

Tiago Tresoldi, Christoph Rzymski, Robert Forkel, Simon J. Greenhill, Johann-Mattis List, and Russell D. Gray

1 Introduction

Computational phylogenetics is a relatively recent branch of historical linguistics that uses quantitative techniques to investigate the history of related languages. As the classical comparative method is less explicit on the techniques for constructing phylogenies of language families (see discussion in Jacques & List 2019), such a new approach can complement traditional techniques for sub-grouping based on shared innovations (Ross & Durie 1996).

The popularization of computer-based methods has led to a greater awareness of issues resulting from limited data sustainability and proper data management (see, in particular, Mattern, chapter 5, this volume, for general discussion and Daniels & Daniels, chapter 26, this volume, for discussion of historical linguistic data). As linguistic data compiled for purposes other than phylogenetic reconstruction might be difficult to adapt to the needs of such analyses, we find an increasing number of attempts to prepare the original data in ways amenable to qualitative inspection and quantitative investigations. However, because the practice of data preparation has not been standardized so far, scholars employ a variety of custom formats as the backbone of their phylogenetic analyses. Such formats range from inadequate coding in which connections to the original sources have been lost, to very detailed and complex formats that can only be processed by specific programs, which may at times not be publicly available. As a result, it is difficult for newcomers to find good instructions on data handling and conversion. Additionally, data reuse is hampered because crucial information on the sources, the languages under investigation, or questionnaires used as basis for word comparisons are usually not supplied in a standardized form.

Ideally, all linguistic data should be "FAIR" in the sense of Wilkinson et al. (2016): Findable, Accessible, Interoperable, and Reusable. FAIR not only implies that studies should be maximally reproducible, starting from the initial design of a project (cf. Berez-Kroeker et al. 2018), but also that specific attention to "fairness" during all intermediate stages of preparing, curating, and transforming the data is needed. Instead of enumerating the many possibilities of coding and using linguistic data to conduct phylogenetic analysis, we illustrate our suggestions for phylogenetic data management in a workflow based on a concrete study. We illustrate these suggestions with the help of a published data set, exploring the information, file formats, processes, and software involved, and explaining/demonstrating how to collect and store crosslinguistic information, how to guarantee that data sets are crosslinguistically comparable, how to store intermediate and final results of the analyses, and how to share data in a reusable form. While phylogenetic methods are not restricted to lexical data, the use of *cognate sets* (i.e., sets of related words identified by the comparative method or computer-assisted approaches) has become a quasi-standard in the discipline and will be the only method explored here (for alternative proposals using various types of structural features, see Macklin-Cordes & Round 2015; Greenhill et al. 2017; Ringe, Warnow, & Taylor 2002; Longobardi et al. 2015).

Our analysis uses the data set of Lieberherr and Bodt (2017), which the authors made publicly available, consisting of lexical entries for a hundred concepts, derived from the concept lists of Haspelmath and Tadmor (2009) and Swadesh (1971), and translated into twenty-two "highly divergent, endangered, and poorly described" languages of the Kho-Bwa sub-group of the Sino-Tibetan language family. We then selected twenty varieties, which were all based on the authors' field notes and reflect a unified source. The study is accompanied by a tutorial that conveniently mirrors the sections and tasks presented, allowing readers to experiment with the data set—or their own data—by following our instructions step-by-step.

2   Phylogenetic data life cycle

The initial stage of a computational phylogenetic study requires acquiring and converting digital sources to machine-readable format, which is in most cases a tabular word list (see stage 1 in section 2.1). The second stage involves adding cognate judgments to the word list, which can be done *manually*, relying on experts or on information from the literature, *automatically*, by relying on software for automated cognate detection, or *semiautomatically*, by checking automatically inferred cognates (List 2016, see stage 2 in section 2.3). Once these data are available, we carry out the actual phylogenetic analysis. The investigation starts with exploratory data analysis (Morrison 2014, see stage 3 in section 2.4) to visualize the signal in the data by, for example, producing a Neighbor-Net or splits graph (a network convenient for inspecting the major patterns in the data; Bryant & Moulton 2003; Huson 1998), or calculating various summary statistics that quantify the signal and noise in the data set, such as consistency and retention indexes (Farris 1989), δ-scores, and Q-residuals (Holland et al. 2002; Gray et al. 2010). This also ensures that there are enough common data points among the languages (List, Walworth, et al. 2018). Following this step, a detailed phylogenetic analysis using a range of different methods can be performed. Currently, the best-performing methods are based on Bayesian models that can provide a dated and rooted phylogeny (see stage 4 in section 2.5). Independent of the stage of the analysis, we recommend that scholars publish their data in a FAIR form, allowing colleagues to review and reuse them (see stage 5 in section 2.6).

2.1   Data collection (stage 1)

Before we can make phylogenetic analyses, the data have to be assembled, which can be done in multiple ways, including original fieldwork; corpus analyses of texts (both modern and ancient); or consulting dictionaries, word lists, or glossaries. Once we have identified the sources that can deliver the data, we need to extract them and store them in a format convenient to access with software. In the following section, we will introduce the very general abstract data model we recommend to authors and give concrete recommendations on data storing and curation.

2.1.1 General remarks on data management   The data model that many linguists still use was popularized by Morris Swadesh, the pioneer in the large-scale collection of word lists in form of tabular data for quantitative analyses (Swadesh 1952). The crucial aspect of this data model is the semantic alignment of information, starting from a list of non-cultural concepts, at times expanded and modified, which was successively translated into the target languages of various studies. Linguists often think of the multilingual word lists produced by this procedure as a simple table, in which the rows refer to the concept labels (or elicitation glosses) and the columns capture the lexical entries in the sampled languages. This format has many plain advantages for non-computational usage. It is simple, easy to inspect, and easy to produce, and tables can be edited with common text processing or spreadsheet software. In fact, Lieberherr and Bodt (2017) originally provided their data in this form. Table 28.1 provides a small sample of these data in multilingual word list forms.

The simplicity of multilingual word list data provided in this form, however, is apparent and restricted to lexicographic entries, creating multiple complications once scholars include other information besides the translations for elicitation glosses across languages. What should one do, for example, if unable to decide for one of several alternatives to translate a concept? Should one list the synonyms separated by a comma, a slash, a dash, or even a vertical pipe (|), as in many existing data sets? Or should one get rid of synonyms, either following Swadesh's practice of selecting the most common form (mostly decided in terms of perceived frequency of usage; see Swadesh 1955:125–126) or Gudschinsky's (1956:179) advice of "flipping a coin"? Likewise, there is no consensus on how to annotate specific entries to

Table 28.1

Sample word list from the Kho-Bwa data set, showing words glossed as "big," "bird," and "blood" for different language varieties, in the traditional word list form

Concept	Dikhyang	Wangho	Rawa
"Big"	əpõː	eboᵘ	arai
"Bird"	fuə	fua	pədoː
"Blood"	əfuɛ	efua	fui

include information such as cognacy. The most common solution is to add an extra column storing information on cognacy to the right of the one devoted to each language variety, as in the STARLING software package (Starostin 2000) and as in the data provided by the authors of our data set, which is illustrated in table 28.2.

A better strategy is to follow the insights of relational databases (Codd 1970), while adopting long-table formats (Forkel et al. 2018; List, Walworth, et al. 2018). In this data structure, we give each cell containing a word form in table 28.1 its own row. Table 28.3 provides an example corresponding to the data from table 28.2. The first column of the long table is an identifier (usually a numerical identifier), and the consecutive columns define the different aspects of the word in question, for example, language, pronunciation, concept, and also cognate identifier. Although it may look redundant at first sight, this format has many advantages. We can display synonyms without separating the content in a cell (by adding an alternative entry for a given concept as an extra row of our table). We can also easily annotate cognates and even append arbitrary information by simply adding a new column.

Table 28.2
Sample word list from the Kho-Bwa data set, derived from table 28.1, with cognate judgments added in extra columns labeled "Cog"

Concept	Dikhyang	Cog	Wangho	Cog	Rawa	Cog
"Big"	əpõː	1	eboᵘ	1	arai	2
"Bird"	fuə	3	fua	4	pədoː	4
"Blood"	əfuɛ	5	efua	5	fui	5

Table 28.3
Sample word list from the Kho-Bwa data set, as listed in table 28.2, in long form

ID	Language	Concept	Entry	Cogset
1	Dikhyang	BIG	əpõː	BIG-1
2	Wangho	BIG	eboᵘ	BIG-1
3	Rawa	BIG	arai	BIG-2
4	Dikhyang	BIRD	fuə	BIRD-1
5	Wangho	BIRD	fua	BIRD-1
6	Rawa	BIRD	pədoː	BIRD-2
7	Dikhyang	BLOOD	əfuɛ	BLOOD-1
8	Wangho	BLOOD	efua	BLOOD-1
9	Rawa	BLOOD	fui	BLOOD-1

2.1.2 The Cross-Linguistic Data Formats initiative

Because long tables are computationally speaking nothing more than tables, we can store them in the same format in which we would store "traditional" word list tables. To increase data comparability and FAIRness, however, it is worth using additional tables for adding other information about the entities in our data, especially in terms of reference catalogs that facilitate data set aggregation. For language identification, for example, it is useful to link each variety to its corresponding code in Glottolog (https://glottolog.org; Hammarström et al. 2021). For comparative concepts, the Concepticon initiative (https://concepticon.clld.org; List, Rzymski, et al. 2021) offers identifiers for standardized concept sets. Linking our data to these two catalogs offers useful additional information (e.g., geographic locations from Glottolog, semantic categories or frequencies of word use from Concepticon). For the handling of the form part of the linguistic sign, the Cross-Linguistic Transcription Systems initiative increases the accessibility and interoperability of phonetic transcriptions by explicitly specifying which speech sounds are represented by which symbol combinations in the data. In this way, the specification greatly facilitates automated sequence comparison or enhanced interfaces for cognate annotation (see stage 2).

To standardize the representation of data for computational phylogenetics and historical language comparison, the Cross-Linguistic Data Formats initiative (CLDF, https://cldf.clld.org; Forkel et al. 2018) offers standard formats for different data types in historical linguistics and linguistic typology, including word lists, structural data, dictionaries, and parallel texts. To render one's data in CLDF word list format, normal spreadsheet editors can be used, but the initiative also offers software solutions that facilitate conversion from other structured formats. CLDF encourages data set maintainers to use the above-mentioned reference catalogs and also offers tools to validate the content of a CLDF data set. The formats are supported by some important software tools for computational phylogenetics, such as BEASTling (Maurits et al. 2017) and LingPy (List & Forkel 2021) and libraries for reading and writing CLDF data are available for the Python (pycldf; Forkel, Bank, Greenhill, et al. 2021) and R (rcldf, https://github.com/SimonGreenhill/rcldf) programming languages. Additionally, with CLDFBench (Forkel and List 2020), a Python package is available that helps to automatize and customize the creation of data sets in CLDF format. Given the increasing importance of CLDF as a standard for data storing and sharing, as well as the growing amount of early adopters who have used the framework for data sharing (Hill & List 2017; Kaiping & Klamer 2018; Sagart et al. 2019; Wu et al. 2020) or for data aggregation (Rzymski et al. 2020), we recommend all those who are interested in computational phylogenetics applications to code their data in the formats of the CLDF initiative. Our supporting tutorial instructs how this can be done, explaining how a CLDF data set can be created (tutorial 2.1.1; for all tutorials, see Supplementary Material) and loaded with LingPy (tutorial 2.1.2), and how existing data sets can be retrieved from online repositories (tutorial 2.1.3). Lieberherr and Bodt (2019) is the CLDF version of the original data set that we use in the subsequent analyses.

2.2 Cognate identification (stage 2)

Information on the etymological relations between words in different languages is occasionally already available in the form of classical sources, such as etymological dictionaries or lexicostatistic data sets (see, e.g., McElhanon 1967). However, the annotation of cognate words for phylogenetic investigations can still be tedious, in particular when working with tabular data that follows the "classical" model shown in table 28.1. If sufficient information on the history of the languages under investigation is not available, scholars will have to apply the classical workflow of the comparative method to infer regular sound correspondences crucial for identifying cognate words. Automated methods for cognate identification (List 2014; Rama et al. 2018) and sound correspondence patterns (List 2019) may come in handy, specifically in a computer-assisted framework where the data are preprocessed by the software and then thoroughly reviewed and corrected by experts. To annotate, correct, and modify cognate sets, we recommend the use of interfaces designed for these purposes (see, e.g., the EDICTOR tool by List 2017; https://digling.org/edictor), as this may help to avoid errors when working with large data sets.

Our accompanying tutorial illustrates how software for automated sequence comparison may be used to align the data automatically (tutorial 2.2.1), how cognates can be automatically inferred with different methods and evaluated against a gold standard (tutorial 2.2.2), and how the data can be curated with the help of lightweight web-based interfaces (tutorial 2.2.3).

2.3 Exploratory data analysis (stage 3)

Data prepared in CLDF are easily amenable to a range of phylogenetic analyses. First, it is easy to extract distances between languages by assuming that the more similar languages are, the more related they are. This is the fundamental assumption of the classical, and problematic, approach of lexicostatistics (Swadesh 1950, 1952). Using the same languages from the examples in tables 28.1–28.3 and the entire data set, with a hundred concepts, we get the matrix of similarities.

Similarity matrices, as in table 28.4, can be converted without effort to a tree using algorithms such as Unweighted Pair Group Method with Arithmetic Mean (UPGMA) or Neighbor-Joining (Saitou & Nei 1987), which mimic lexicostatistics (figure 28.1). These algorithms are implemented, among others, in the LingPy library (List & Forkel 2021), a library used in the tutorial and in R's APE (analyses of phylogenetics and evolution) library (Paradis, Claude, & Strimmer 2004). We can also load distances into other statistical inference procedures such as cluster analysis, as done in Lieberherr and Bodt (2017).

One common distance-based approach to data exploration in computational historical linguistics is building a neighbor-net network (Bryant & Moulton 2003; Huson 1998). This visualization (see figure 28.2) constructs branches proportional to the amount of change between languages where conflicting signals are represented by box-like structures. These networks provide a useful way of visualizing overlapping and conflicting signals, such as that caused by borrowing or dialect-chain processes (Heggarty, Maguire, & McMahon 2010; Gray et al. 2010). These networks are constructed in the SplitsTree package (Huson 1998), and we can easily convert the CLDF data set into a format suitable for SplitsTree. Other exploratory approaches that can be used to quantify the signal and noise in a data set are analyses through

Table 28.4

Similarity matrix of a subset of Kho-Bwa languages

	Dikhyang	Wangho	Rawa
Dikhyang	0.00	0.07	0.54
Wangho	0.07	0.00	0.52
Rawa	0.54	0.52	0.00

Language pairs with scores closer to 0.0 are more similar; scores closer to 1.0 are more dissimilar.

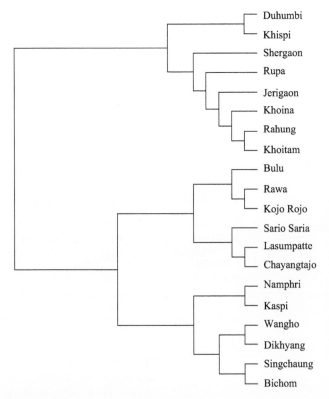

Figure 28.1

Phylogenetic visualization of the Kho-Bwa data set, with an UPGMA tree mimicking lexicostatistics.

consistency and retention indexes (Farris 1989), δ-scores, and Q-residuals (Holland et al. 2002; Gray et al. 2010). Our accompanying tutorial illustrates how to perform these tasks (tutorial 2.3).

2.4 Phylogenetic analysis (stage 4)

After the simpler distance-based approaches for data exploration, it is common to perform more advanced analyses. Currently, the most powerful phylogenetic approach is a set of tools known collectively as Bayesian phylogenetic methods (Huelsenbeck et al. 2001). These methods build trees in a way that mimics that of the traditional linguistic comparative method, identifying where cognate sets are innovated and retained. Furthermore, these tools model uncertainty and error in our estimated phylogenies such that we can measure support for different sub-grouping hypotheses. Greenhill and Gray (2009) provide a more detailed overview of how Bayesian approaches work. Bayesian phylogenetic packages such as BEAST (Bayesian Evolutionary Analysis Sampling Trees; Bouckaert et al. 2014) tend to require data in a specific format called NEXUS (Maddison, Swofford, & Maddison

1997) that can be generated from word list or CLDF data sets with tools such as LingPy.

Here we analyze the Kho-Bwa data set using a Bayesian phylogenetic approach implemented in BEAST2 (Bouckaert et al. 2014, version 2.5.1). We use a binary covarion model (Penny et al. 2001) that allows cognate sets to be gained and lost at different rates over time. We implemented a relaxed-clock model (Drummond et al. 2006) that allows each branch to change at a different rate and this distribution of rates to be estimated from the data. The results are shown in figures 28.3 and 28.4. The study indicates that all three methods show strong similarities in their overall sub-grouping and are consistent with the results presented in Lieberherr and Bodt (2017) based on hierarchical clustering. All methods split the family into three major branches: (1) the Western Kho-Bwa (Duhumbi, Khispi, Shergaon, Rupa, Jerigaon, Khoina, Rahung, Khoitam), (2) Bugun (Bichom, Singchung, Dikhyang, Wangho, Kaspi, Namphri), and (3) Puroik (Bulu, Rawa, Kojo Rojo, Sario Saria, Lasumpatte, Chayangtajo). Within these branches, the patterning is similar to that presented in Lieberherr and Bodt (2017), despite some notable differences that in most analyses are reported to the experts for investigation. Among the benefits of Bayesian approaches is the fact that we could further model variation in rate change for testing hypotheses on the evolution, which can also be reported to the experts. The discussion on Bayesian analyses goes beyond the purposes of data management of this user case, but our tutorial shows how to prepare data for BEAST2 (tutorial 2.4).

The availability of a data set collected and published in a long-form table, and converted to CLDF with ease, allowed us to apply different methods of investigation to support or disprove hypotheses of the original work. The analysis tried to emphasize how rewarding an adequate management of phylogenetic data can be in scientific terms. Researchers benefit from it not only by saving the time usually spent in data collection and preparation, but also because of the facilitated collaboration and the suggestions of future work offered by the results. More specifically, we not only have quantitative bases on which questions should be investigated next, such as the placement of the Bugun and Puruik clades in the tree, but also anyone is able to apply other quantitative methods or combine these data with different data sets for new research questions (for example, Sino-Tibetan collections offering additional data points in CLDF, as presented, e.g.,

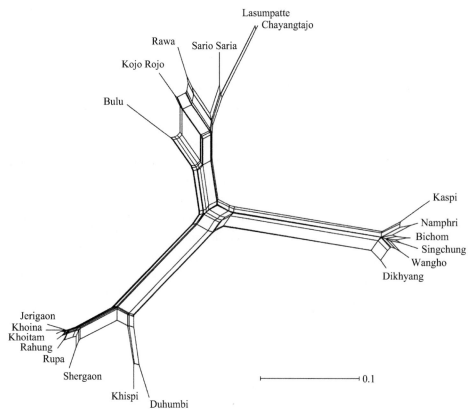

Figure 28.2

Phylogenetic visualization of the Kho-Bwa data set, with a Neighbor-Net network visualization.

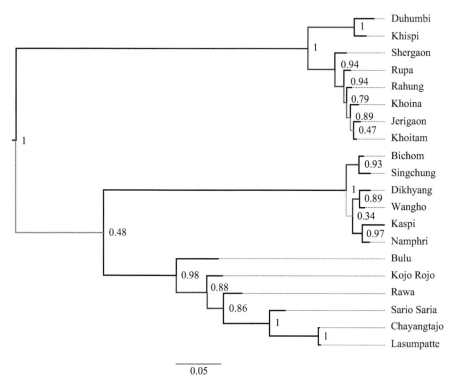

Figure 28.3

Phylogenetic visualization of the Kho-Bwa data set, with a maximum clade credibility tree of the posterior probability distribution from a Bayesian phylogenetic analysis.

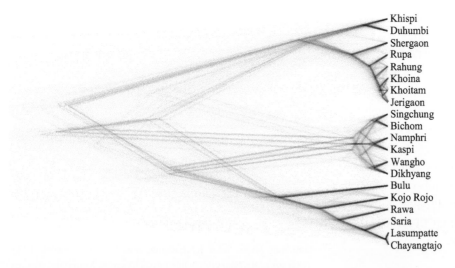

Khispi
Duhumbi
Shergaon
Rupa
Rahung
Khoina
Khoitam
Jerigaon
Singchung
Bichom
Namphri
Kaspi
Wangho
Dikhyang
Bulu
Kojo Rojo
Rawa
Saria
Lasumpatte
Chayangtajo

Figure 28.4

Phylogenetic visualization of the Kho-Bwa data set by means of a DensiTree (Bouckaert 2010) showing only consensus trees from the Bayesian analysis, highlighting the uncertainties in some splits and the confidence in terms of the three main groups.

in Sagart et al. 2019). In all cases, this results in desirable prospects for language groups that are still poorly understood from a historical linguistic perspective.

2.5 Data sharing and deployment (stage 5)

We encourage and practice data sharing, creating, and maintaining reusable data in linguistics (Berez-Kroeker et al. 2018). The modular architecture of CLDF allows researchers to combine and mix, more or less freely, what might best fit their individual pipelines and requirements. The main idea of this pipeline is not to enforce any theoretical constraints, but to ensure that once a research project is finished, data and results will be findable and accessible. For this reason, besides providing easily analyzable data, CLDF data sets were designed for convenience in sharing and deployment. While plain data sets can be shared with little effort on platforms such as GitHub and Zenodo, the related Cross-Linguistic Linked Data project (Forkel, Bank, & Rzymski 2019) allows users to deploy data into browsable web applications, as showcased in a study on colexification patterns (Database of Cross-Linguistic Colexifications 3; Rzymski et al. 2020), the typological survey of the World Atlas of Language Structures (https://wals.info; Dryer & Haspelmath 2013), a study on horizontal lexical transfer in the World Loanword Database (https://wold.clld.org; Haspelmath & Tadmor 2009), the retro-standardized version of the Tableaux phonétiques des patois suisses romands (Geisler, Forkel, & List 2020), and a collection of French and Franco-Provençal dialects (Gauchat, Jeanjacquet, & Tappolet 1925), among others. Our tutorial discusses how CLDF data sets can be shared and deployed (tutorial 2.5).

3 Conclusion

Our plan with this use case was to present principles of data management as applied to computational phylogenetics and computer-assisted language comparison, showcasing the solutions we recommend. We are confident that, no matter how it will evolve, historical linguistics will benefit from good practices in the representation and management of its data. Methods, questions, and solutions come and go; interdisciplinarity will evolve from its current shape; concept lists will routinely be expanded and reduced; cognate sets as basic characters of analysis might be supplemented or replaced by other data; and Bayesian phylogenetic inference might lose its momentum and be replaced by new quantitative or symbolic models, and so on, but the general principles of linguistic data management, and of phylogenetic data and CLDF in particular, acknowledge that such evolution is inevitable and instruct us to prepare data for all future manipulations that might be required.

Supplementary material

The supplementary material can be downloaded from https://doi.org/10.5281/zenodo.4311308 (Tresoldi et al. 2020). It contains the accompanying tutorial along with the data and the code needed to reproduce the analyses discussed in this study.

Acknowledgments

We thank Timotheus Bodt and Ismael Lieberherr for providing help with the parsing of their data and the interpretation of their results and Gereon Kaiping for providing help with the development of interfaces between the LingPy software package and CLDF. This research would not have been possible without the generous support by many institutes and funding agencies. J.-M. List and T. Tresoldi were funded by the European Research Council Starting Grant 715618 Computer-Assisted Language Comparison (https://digling.org/calc/). S. J. Greenhill was supported by the Australian Research Council's Discovery Projects funding scheme (project number DE 120101954) and the Australian Research Council Center of Excellence for the Dynamics of Language grant (CE140100041).

References

Anderson, Cormac, Tiago Tresoldi, Thiago C. Chacon, Anne-Maria Fehn, Mary Walworth, Robert Forkel, and Johann-Mattis List. 2018. A cross-linguistic database of phonetic transcription systems. *Yearbook of the Poznań Linguistic Meeting* 4 (1): 21–53.

Berez-Kroeker, Andrea L., Lauren Gawne, Susan S. Kung, Barbara F. Kelly, Tyler Heston, Gary Holton, Peter Pulsifer, et al. 2018. Reproducible research in linguistics: A position statement on data citation and attribution in our field. *Linguistics* 56 (1): 1–18.

Bouckaert, Remco R. 2010. DensiTree: Making sense of sets of phylogenetic trees. *Bioinformatics* 26 (10): 1372–1373.

Bouckaert, Remco, Joseph Heled, Denise Kühnert, Tim Vaughan, Chieh-Hsi Wu, Dong Xie, Suchard Marc A., Andrew Rambaut, and Alexei J. Drummond. 2014. BEAST 2: A software platform for Bayesian evolutionary analysis. *PLoS Computational Biology* 10 (4): 1–6.

Bryant, David, and Vincent Moulton. 2003. Neighbor-Net: An agglomerative method for the construction of phylogenetic networks. *Molecular Biology and Evolution* 21 (2): 255–265.

Codd, Edgar F. 1970. A relational model of data for large shared data banks. *Communications of the ACM* 13 (6): 377–87.

Drummond, Alexei J., Simon Y. W. Ho, Matthew J. Phillips, and Andrew Rambaut. 2006. Relaxed phylogenetics and dating with confidence. *PLOS Biology* 4 (5): e88.

Dryer, Matthew S., and Martin Haspelmath, eds. 2013. *WALS Online.* Leipzig, Germany: Max Planck Institute for Evolutionary Anthropology.

Farris, J. S. 1989. The retention index and the rescaled consistency index. *Cladistics* 5:417–419.

Forkel, Robert, Sebastian, Bank, Simon J. Greenhill, and Gereon Kaiping. 2021. cldf/pycldf: pycldf, Version 1.22.0. Leipzig, Germany: Max Planck Institute for Evolutionary Anthropology. https://pypi.org/project/pycldf/1.22.0/.

Forkel, Robert, Sebastian Bank, and Christoph Rzymski. 2021. clld/clld: clld - A toolkit for cross-linguistic databases, Version 7.4.2. Leipzig, Germany: https://pypi.org/project/clld/7.4.2.

Forkel, Robert, and Johann-Mattis List. 2020. CLDFBench: Give your Cross-Linguistic data a lift. In *Proceedings of the Twelfth International Conference on Language Resources and Evaluation,* 6997–7004. Marseille, France: European Language Resources Association.

Forkel, Robert, Johann-Mattis List, Simon J. Greenhill, Christoph Rzymski, Sebastian Bank, Michael Cysouw, Harald Hammarström, Martin Haspelmath, Gereon A. Kaiping, and Russell D. Gray. 2018. Cross-Linguistic Data Formats, advancing data sharing and re-use in comparative linguistics. *Scientific Data* 5:180205.

Gauchat, Louis, Jules Jeanjacquet, and Ernest Tappolet. 1925. *Tableaux phonétiques des patois suisses romands.* Neuchâtel, France: Attiger.

Geisler, Hans, Robert Forkel, and Johann-Mattis List. 2020. *The Tableaux phonétiques des patois suisses romands online.* Jena, Germany: Max Planck Institute for the Science of Human History.

Gray, Russell D., David Bryant, and Simon J. Greenhill. 2010. On the shape and fabric of human history. *Philosophical Transactions of the Royal Society of London. Series B, Biological Sciences* 365 (1559): 3923–3933.

Greenhill, Simon J., and Russell D. Gray. 2009. Austronesian language phylogenies: Myths and misconceptions about Bayesian computational methods. In *Austronesian Historical Linguistics and Culture History: A Festschrift for Robert Blust,* ed. K. A. Adelaar and A. Pawley, 375–397. Canberra, Australia: Pacific Linguistics.

Greenhill, Simon J., Chieh-Hsi Wu, Xia Hua, Michael Dunn, Stephen C. Levinson, and Russell D. Gray. 2017. Evolutionary dynamics of language systems. *Proceedings of the National Academy of Sciences* 114 (42): E8822–E8829.

Gudschinsky, Sarah C. 1956. The ABC's of lexicostatistics (glottochronology). *Word* 12 (2): 175–210.

Hammarström, Harald, Robert Forkel, Martin Haspelmath, and Sebastian Bank. 2021. Glottolog 4.4. Leipzig, Germany: Max Planck Institute for Evolutionary Anthropology. https://glottolog.org.

Haspelmath, Martin, and Uri Tadmor, eds. 2009. *WOLD.* Leipzig, Germany: Max Planck Institute for Evolutionary Anthropology.

Heggarty, Paul, Warren Maguire, and April McMahon. 2010. Splits or waves? Trees or webs? How divergence measures and network analysis can unravel language histories. *Philosophical Transactions of the Royal Society of London. Series B, Biological Sciences.* 365:3829–3843.

Hill, Nathan W., and Johann-Mattis List. 2017. Challenges of annotation and analysis in computer-assisted language comparison: A case study on Burmish languages. *Yearbook of the Poznań Linguistic Meeting* 3 (1): 47–76.

Holland, Barbara R., Katharina T. Huber, Andreas Dress, and Vincent Moulton. 2002. δ-plots: A tool for analyzing phylogenetic distance data. *Molecular Biology and Evolution* 19 (12): 2051–2059.

Huelsenbeck, John P., Fredrik Ronquist, Rasmus Nielsen, and Jonathan P. Bollback. 2001. Bayesian inference of phylogeny and its impact on evolutionary biology. *Science* 294:2310–2314.

Huson, Daniel H. 1998. SplitsTree: Analyzing and visualizing evolutionary data. *Bioinformatics* 14 (1): 68–73.

Jacques, Guillaume, and Johann-Mattis List. 2019. Save the trees: Why we need tree models in linguistic reconstruction (and when we should apply them). *Journal of Historical Linguistics* 9 (1): 128–166.

Kaiping, Gereon A., and Marian Klamer. 2018. LexiRumah: An online lexical database of the Lesser Sunda Islands. *PLOS ONE* 13 (10): 1–29.

Lieberherr, Ismael, and Timotheus A. Bodt. 2017. Sub-grouping Kho-Bwa on shared core vocabulary. *Himalayan Linguistics* 16 (2): 26–63.

Lieberherr, Ismael, and Timotheus A. Bodt. 2019. CLDF data set derived from Lieberherr and Bodt's "Comparative Wordlists of Kho-Bwa" from 2017, Version 0.9. Zenodo. December 8. https://doi.org/10.5281/zenodo.4925670.

List, Johann-Mattis. 2014. *Sequence Comparison in Historical Linguistics*. Düsseldorf: Düsseldorf University Press.

List, Johann-Mattis. 2016. *Computer-assisted Language Comparison: Reconciling Computational and Classical Approaches in Historical Linguistics*. Jena, Germany: Max Planck Institute for the Science of Human History.

List, Johann-Mattis. 2017. A web-based interactive tool for creating, inspecting, editing, and publishing etymological data sets. In *Proceedings of the 15th Conference of the European Chapter of the Association for Computational Linguistics. System Demonstrations*, 9–12. Valencia, Spain: Association for Computational Linguistics.

List, Johann-Mattis. 2019. Automatic inference of sound correspondence patterns across multiple languages. *Computational Linguistics* 45 (1): 1–24.

List, Johann-Mattis, Cormac Anderson, Tiago Tresoldi, and Robert Forkel. 2021. *Cross-Linguistic Transcription Systems*, Version v2.1.0. Leipzig: Germany: Max Planck Institute for Evolutionary Anthropology. http://clts.clld.org.

List, Johann-Mattis, and Robert Forkel. 2021. *LingPy: A Python Library for Quantitative Tasks in Historical Linguistics*, Version 2.6.7. Leipzig, Germany: Max Planck Institute for Evolutionary Anthropology. https://lingpy.org.

List, Johann-Mattis, Christoph Rzymski, Simon Greenhill, Nathanael Schweikhard, Kristina Pianykh, Annika Tjuka, Carolin Hundt, and Robert Forkel. 2021. *Concepticon: A Resource for the Linking of Concept Lists*, Version 2.5.0. Leipzig, Germany: Max Planck Institute for Evolutionary Anthropology. https://concepticon.clld.org.

List, Johann-Mattis, Mary Walworth, Simon J. Greenhill, Tiago Tresoldi, and Robert Forkel. 2018. Sequence comparison in computational historical linguistics. *Journal of Language Evolution* 3 (2): 130–144.

Longobardi, Giuseppe, Silvia Ghirotto, Cristina Guardiano, Francesca Tassi, Andrea Benazzo, Andrea Ceolin, and Guido Barbujan. 2015. Across language families: Genome diversity mirrors linguistic variation within Europe. *American Journal of Physical Anthropology* 157 (4): 630–640.

Macklin-Cordes, Jayden L., and Erich R. Round. 2015. High-definition phonotactics reflect linguistic pasts. In *Proceedings of the 6th Conference on Quantitative Investigations in Theoretical Linguistics*, ed. Johannes Wahle, Marisa Köllner, Harald Baayen, Gerhard Jäger, and Tineke Baayen-Oudshoorn. Tübingen, Germany: University of Tübingen.

Maddison, David R., David L. Swofford, and Wayne P. Maddison. 1997. Nexus: An extensible file format for systematic information. *Systematic Biology* 46 (4): 590–621.

Maurits, Luke, Robert Forkel, Gereon A. Kaiping, and Quentin D. Atkinson. 2017. BEASTling: A software tool for linguistic phylogenetics using BEAST 2. *PLoS ONE* 12 (8): e0180908.

McElhanon, Kenneth A. 1967. Preliminary observations on Huon Peninsula languages. *Oceanic Linguistics* 6:1–45.

Morrison, David A. 2014. Is the Tree of Life the best metaphor, model, or heuristic for phylogenetics? *Systematic Biology* 63 (4): 628–638.

Paradis, Emmanuel, Julien Claude, and Korbinian Strimmer. 2004. APE: Analyses of phylogenetics and evolution in R language. *Bioinformatics* 20:289–290.

Penny, David, Bennet J. McComish, Michael A. Charleston, and Michael D. Hendy. 2001. Mathematical elegance with biochemical realism: The Covarion model of molecular evolution. *Journal of Molecular Evolution* 53 (6): 711–723.

Rama, Taraka, Johann-Mattis List, Johannes Wahle, and Gerhard Jäger. 2018. Are automatic methods for cognate detection good enough for phylogenetic reconstruction in historical linguistics? In *Proceedings of the North American Chapter of the Association of Computational Linguistics*, 393–400. Stroudsburg, PA: Association for Computational Linguistics.

Ringe, Donald, Tandy Warnow, and Ann Taylor. 2002. Indo-European and computational cladistics. *Transactions of the Philological Society* 100 (1): 59–129.

Ross, Malcom, and Mark Durie. 1996. Introduction. In *The Comparative Method Reviewed: Regularity and Irregularity in Sound Change*, ed. Mark Durie, 3–37. New York: Oxford University Press.

Rzymski, Christoph, Tiago Tresoldi, Simon J. Greenhill, Mei-Shin Wu, Nathanael E. Schweikhard, Maria Koptjevskaja-Tamm, Volker Gast, et al. 2020. The Database of Cross-Linguistic Colexifications, reproducible analysis of cross-linguistic polysemies. *Scientific Data* 7:13.

Sagart, Laurent, Guillaume Jacques, Yunfan Lai, Robin Ryder, Valentin Thouzeau, Simon J. Greenhill, and Johann-Mattis List. 2019. Dated language phylogenies shed light on the ancestry of Sino-Tibetan. *Proceedings of the National Academy of Science of the United States of America* 166:10317–10322.

Saitou, Naruya, and Masatoshi Nei. 1987. The neighbor-joining method: A new method for reconstructing phylogenetic trees. *Molecular Biology and Evolution* 4 (4): 406–425.

Starostin, Sergej A. 2000. *The Starling Database Program*. Moscow: RGGU.

Swadesh, Morris. 1950. Salish internal relationships. *International Journal of American Linguistics* 16 (4): 157–67.

Swadesh, Morris. 1952. Lexico-statistic dating of prehistoric ethnic contacts. *Proceedings of the American Philosophical Society* 96 (4): 452–463.

Swadesh, Morris. 1955. Towards greater accuracy in lexicostatistic dating. *International Journal of American Linguistics* 21 (2): 121–137.

Swadesh, Morris. 1971. *The Origin and Diversification of Language*, ed. Joel Sherzer. Chicago: Aldine.

Tresoldi, Tiago, Christoph Rzymski, Robert Forkel, Simon J. Greenhill, Johann-Mattis List, and Russell D. Gray. 2020. Supplementary code tutorial and data for "Managing Historical Linguistic Data for Computational Phylogenetics and Computer-Assisted Language Comparison," Version 0.9. Zenodo. December 8. https://doi.org/10.5281/zenodo.4311308.

Wilkinson, Mark D., Michel Dumontier, IJsbrand J. Aalbersberg, Gabrielle Appleton, Myles Axton, Arie Baak, Niklas Blomberg, et al. 2016. The fair guiding principles for scientific data management and stewardship. *Scientific Data* 3 (1): 160018.

Wu, Mei-Shin, Nathanael E. Schweikhard, Timotheus Bodt, Nathan Hill, and Johann-Mattis List. 2020. Computer-assisted language comparison: State of the art. *Journal of Open Humanities Data* 6 (2): 1–14.

29   Managing Computational Data for Models of Language Acquisition and Change

Matthew Lou-Magnuson and Luca Onnis

1   Introduction: Outline of work presented

The goal of this data management use case is two-fold: first, to illuminate how computational modeling works to augment traditional scientific methods and, second, to suggest ways in which computational models exist as a kind of data in and of themselves, and as such need to be properly archived.

The chapter begins with some background information on two specific models that form the object of the discussion. Next a brief overview of the process of computational modeling is presented and followed by some theoretical perspective on how models present unique challenges as data for archiving. In the longest portion of the chapter, these points are examined stage-by-stage in a case study, highlighting the decision process and ideals for data management involved. Finally, a unifying ideal for archiving computational models that generalizes the details of the case study is given.

1.1   Case studies presented

In this chapter, two computational models of language evolution are discussed. The term language evolution is used generally to refer to the biological evolution of the faculties necessary for human language, as well as traditional work on language change taken at a broader, systemic level; the models presented here are of the latter category. In particular, the models we discuss attempt to capture the interaction between the development of morphological complexity[1] and the structure of human social networks, but differ in the level of granularity at which they formalize the problem. Lou-Magnuson and Onnis (2018) developed a so-called *high-level model* of the fundamental conditions for morphological complexity to emerge; it seeks to answer the question: does a particular social network structure support the capacity

for sustained development of morphological complexity? The second, *low-level model*, presented in Lou-Magnuson (2018), builds on the results of the prior high-level model, but at a more fine-grained level of computational detail. It seeks to answer the question of observable language change: given the capacity for morphological complexity, as predicted by the low-level model, does more complex morphology actually emerge? It is beyond the scope of this chapter to explain in detail both models and the phenomena they capture; however, some further explanation in broad strokes is provided.

Both computational models share an identical framework for studying language evolution: computational agents are created and embedded in a social network that constrains who is allowed to communicate with whom. Each agent is able to produce expressions that carry some phonological and semantic form, as well as learn how to produce these expressions from usage examples. The agents are allowed to communicate with each other for a set period of time, after which each is replaced by a new agent that learns de novo how to produce expressions solely from the examples heard by the agent it replaces. This process of intergenerational transfer is allowed to repeat over and over again, and changes in the structure of expressions produced by the agents are analyzed.

The distinctions between the high-level and low-level models are in the level of detail in the expressions produced by the agents and the learning mechanisms involved. In the high-level model, the expressions are holistic collections of values (one representing a meaning, and few others the phonological content) that the agents pass between each other. Learning amounts to choosing a set of expressions (one for each meaning) to use in the next generation, potentially with some minor alterations to the values. The details are presented in Lou-Magnuson and Onnis (2018), but, conceptually, language for the agents in the high-level model is like a deck of playing cards. To communicate, they exchange these cards among themselves, and each generation selects a playing card for each meaning, occasionally making a small change, such as turning a nine of clubs into a ten of clubs.

In contrast, each linguistic expression in the low-level model is a pair of two compositionally complex representations: a tree structure encoding the meaning, and a string of phonological symbols encoding the utterance that represents this meaning. In this model, the agents use an information theoretic method to learn a context-free rewrite system (such as a context-free grammar, but defined over these meaning and phonological structures) that they use to produce their own expressions and parse the expressions of other agents. Similarly, language in the low-level model is conceptually a modern natural language processing system on a smaller scale (see details in Lou-Magnuson 2018:chapter 3).

To investigate whether social structure potentially affects language change, the two models discussed above were run over thousands of generations on different social network topologies. Each topology captured a different social dynamic, for example, a society of intimates or a society with deep hierarchical leveling, that has been suggested in the literature to affect the morphological evolution of the language used in such communities over time. The high-level model provided insight into how these different structures affected the potential for morphological change in a given network; however, as the expressions produced and received by the agents were indivisible with respect to traditional linguistic units of analysis (i.e., sememes and morphemes), the model was only suggestive of the relationship between social structure and morphological structure. In the low-level model, though, the expressions exchanged by agents were at a level of detail such that actual grammars could be learned by the agents and the typology of the language quantitatively assessed.

The models represent computer simulations at two contrasting scales and scopes of development, each highlighting different challenges for data management. The high-level model is relatively lightweight in computational assumptions, implementation in code, and size of data outputs. In contrast, by attempting a more granular examination, the low-level model requires many more assumptions to be made, traditional software engineering practices to manage the code base, and data outputs that are difficult to store and analyze on a single, conventional workstation. These differences of scale allow for a comparison of data management principles that may not generally arise in lab-based human studies or the collection of language data in the field.

2 Modeling social science

When compared to work done with human participants, computational modeling not only shares a number of data management concerns, but also presents several additional challenges stemming from the implementation of the model in code. These more modeling-specific challenges will be the primary focus. For example, the general principles of the data life cycle as discussed in Mattern (chapter 5, this volume) will not be presented again, but rather we will discuss how those concerns translate to the management of a code base as opposed to collections of language use. Again, the data being managed here is not the output of the models, but the models and code in which the models are written.

Of particular importance for data management in the context of computational modeling is understanding how computational work relates to the traditional scientific method as practiced in the social sciences (see figure 29.1[2]). Before we examine this process with respect to the high- and low-level models, we first provide a brief summary of each stage. After this process is presented, we also touch on how it creates new data management concerns in terms of preserving the model code, as well as documenting the stages and rationale of model creation.

2.1 Model

In this stage the task is to translate the complexity of the real world, into a set of simplifying assumptions. For example, the model of Newtonian kinematics takes the complexity of physical objects and motion and abstracts the world into Euclidean space—just three dimensions and time. This is not a statement that properties such as shape or volume are not important aspects of physical reality, but that for determining where objects are and where they are going, these details are less relevant, and add more difficulty than clarity. The goal of modeling is to replace a system that is too complex to readily understand with a simpler one that is able to be analyzed and yield insights. The goal of modeling is not to replicate

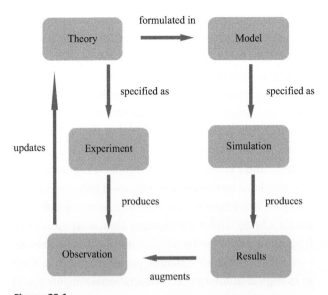

Figure 29.1

Parallels between computational modeling and the scientific method. A simplified version of the traditional empirical research cycle (theory, experiment, observation) is presented on the loop to the left, while its complementary stages of computational modeling (model, simulation, results) are presented on the outer loop to the right.

reality closely, for if such a feat is even possible, then one complex system has just replaced another.

In the realm of the social sciences, including linguistics, the models built must not only consider how to model the environment, but also abstract human beings into artificial agents. This often takes the form of reducing human behavior down to the cognitive processes relevant for the tasks of study. For example, Lou-Magnuson (2018) modeled language acquisition in agents as the ability to perform pattern abstraction and categorization. In addition to the interactions between environment and agent, models of language evolution must also consider a third artifact, language itself. There is no one best answer to this or any of the modeling questions, save perhaps simply the heuristic of how the modeling choices trim reality down to the core elements relevant for study.

2.2 Simulation

Having formulated a mathematical model, in other words, the equations and algorithms, the next step is to translate it into an explicit computable form, a piece of software written in one or more computer programming languages. At this stage, two competing aspects are in play: engineering and design. Typically, the process of

formulating a model allows for the design of experiments that would not be possible in reality. For example, having replaced living human beings with computational agents, one can simulate hundreds or thousands of generations, recording exactly the languages and learning processes of each. However, even if such a scenario is definable using the model, there are limits on what can be actually run on modern computer hardware. Thus, there is a trade-off between the limits of the engineering ingenuity in designing the software and the limits of what can be realistically explored in the possible space of the model. A practical aspect to consider is whether the desktop or laptop computer available to the researcher is sufficiently powerful, or whether a dedicated machine needs to be purchased or high-performance computing services rented on the cloud.

2.3 Results

The data recorded from simulations are generally analogous to those recorded in conventional experimental settings, and likewise, modern statistical techniques are used to analyze digital experiments. However, with simulations involving agents, and especially language, it is usually not clear how the effects of the model map the effects in real life. For example, is the amount of language change seen in a generation of digital agents comparable to the linguistic change seen in a generation of human beings, or is the space of meanings expressible by the language model in the simulation of the same scope as that of a natural human language?

These questions are, more likely than not, empirically unanswerable. Yet, in much the same way that the goal of defining a model was not to reproduce the complexities and nuances of reality, the goal of social science simulation is not to reproduce the same metrics as reality. The ideal result of traditional experiment analysis is to discover whether a given manipulation produced a statistically significant difference with meaningful effect size. The ideal result in the analysis of a simulation is to discover whether a statistically significant relationship exists between variables in the model, and perhaps even more important, new patterns of emergent behavior. These two things provide insight into the general mechanisms that drive the observations of reality and past experiments and suggest future areas of exploration that otherwise may have been unclear or inconceivable.

3 Implications for data management

In discussing lab-based psycholinguistics research versus computational modeling work, Dijkstra and De Smedt (1996) summarize the differences in terms of information specification. They invoke the notion of information processing at three levels of detail, as defined by Marr (1982) in organizing his pioneering work on the human visual system: *computation, algorithm,* and *implementation.* Briefly, the computational level is the specification of the inputs and outputs of a system to be studied—it defines the representations and transformations. The algorithmic level defines the procedures involved in making those transformations, and finally, the implementation level defines the physical system in which these algorithms are performed.

To better understand these levels, let us imagine a hypothetical understanding of human object detection. At the computational level, we might define the inputs as being visual information originating in the eye and the outputs being mental representations of the object. The transformation process is one of refinement from a set of physical stimuli to one or more internal, cognitively useful representations.

At the algorithmic level of understanding, let us posit two possibilities. First, that visual information is passed through sequential layers of feature detectors (as happens in actual human vision) eventually leading to the production of object-level representations. Second, we could imagine a vast store of previous visual experiences and associated objects, and that a distance is computed between new inputs and past experiences, and the closest memory pair is chosen. That is, we posit either that visual inputs are progressively refined until the final mental representation has been built from these refinements, or alternatively, that visual information is compared directly against past experiences and the closest mental representation is retrieved from memory in a one-off match.

At the implementation level, either algorithm could be posed as a task to a feed-forward neural network architecture (mimicking human biology). The first, progressive algorithm could be implemented as a so-called *deep neural network,* where layers of computation are stacked one after the other until the final level produces the desired representation. The second, one-shot algorithm could be a *shallow network,* wherein a direct mapping from visual input to mental representation is learned. Alternatively, the first algorithm could be more efficiently computed in less biologically plausible, convolutional neural network architecture, as is commonly done in computer vision and natural language processing work (Bengio et al. 2003; Krizhevsky, Sutskever, & Hinton 2012). Likewise, the second could be computed by storing the images and labels pairs, use Euclidean distance to find the five closest pairs in memory, and let the majority label be the chosen output—a procedure called k-nearest neighbors in the machine learning literature (Bishop 2006). There are multiple alternatives for specifying the mechanism by which these algorithms are executed that appeal to different practical concerns, such as biological mimicry and computational efficiency, and the designer of the model may have specific assumptions to prefer one or the other: the goals of a biologist doing theoretical research versus those of an applied computer vision engineer.

Dijkstra and De Smedt (1996) argue that, in general, traditional social scientists design human experiments working almost exclusively at the highest, computational level. They observe and reason about stimuli and responses and suggest mappings that exist between them. Furthermore, Dijkstra and De Smedt argue that this has been such a successful endeavor because the lower levels of analysis are essentially fixed: the algorithmic and implementation details are supplied naturally by the human brain and its neural architecture. In so far as the brains of participants are comparable to one another, these details need not be understood fully by social scientists before devising and testing hypotheses defined at the computational level alone.

It is here that we see that stark contrast and need for additional data management by those doing computational modeling. To produce a runnable simulation, one cannot neglect any of Marr's levels of understanding. A computational modeler must explicitly set forth the process that will transform the inputs into the outputs and physically implement it in some concrete system. As the example illustrated, there may be more than one viable process at the algorithmic level and usually many more options at the implementation level. The motivations behind these choices are far from arbitrary and usually are borne out from the researcher's assumptions and goals.

In terms of the model as an object of data management, computational modeling poses at least two novel requirements on the researcher beyond the need to redundantly and safely store the simulation outputs. First, they must track the software that was engineered to implement the model and run the simulations. That is, a computational model requires preserving the technical means by which to rerun and verify the software itself. Second, they must record the decisions made to define the algorithmic and implementation levels of the model. The level of detail, both conceptual and technological is non-trivial and can even affect the simulation outcomes in unforeseeable ways. Revisiting the object-detection example, while the shallow neural network and *k*-means implementations can ostensibly execute the same algorithm, they interject different biases: the neural network is heavily dependent on the data used to train it, whereas the *k*-means results can be drastically altered by initial random conditions (Bishop 2006).

The necessity to account for these two additional factors largely stems from the increasing need for reproducibility in the social sciences, as discussed by Gawne and Styles (chapter 2, this volume) in regard to experimental work and more generally in linguistics by Berez-Kroeker et al. (chapter 1, this volume). For simulations to provide valuable insights, it is not enough that the output results are properly archived so that the findings can be verified. As discussed in section 2, the metrics are generally not directly comparable to human measures, and with the ability to arbitrarily increase sample sizes with more simulation runs, eventually some significant findings will emerge. What is important are the patterns of behavior that emerge in simulations and their impact on interpreting traditional lab-based work. In the absence of the human brain providing a common ground, the decisions involved in specifying Marr's levels of the model and in engineering the software itself become crucial elements that must be documented and preserved.

4 Case studies stage by stage

In this section the stages of computational modeling identified in the previous sections will be revisited. At each step an example of the decision *process* for the high-level and low-level models will be presented, followed by a discussion of the *data management* issues and how they were (or should have been) addressed. Although conceptually the scientific method and computational modeling follow a sequence of stages, the conceptualization

and actual work done typically jumps around. For example, one may try to implement a particular algorithm only to discover that it cannot efficiently be done and be forced to reconceptualize the scope of a simulation. It is an increasingly desirable practice that the researcher explicitly documents this iterative decision-making process itself, as it increases reproducibility (Freedman et al. 2018).

For the case study in this chapter, both the high- and low-level model codes and supporting documentation can be found in the *main repository* (https://github.com /skagit/ntu_thesis.git). Any and all materials referenced in the following section can be found at this location. The main repository was initially used for Lou-Magnuson (2018), but an additional folder has been added—*data_ management*—for this chapter. It is expected that the reader consults these materials actively while reading the following sections.

4.1 Model: Process

At this stage, the task is to abstract the core elements of theory into a mathematical form, omitting as many extraneous details as possible. The phenomenon to be modeled was the development of grammatical complexity and, further, the relationship to the social network of language users. The research goal was ultimately to construct a model with a sufficient level of detail to measure synthesis (the morpheme-to-word ratio) directly. However, such computational operations on hierarchical data structures are expensive in terms of computation time, and many simulations would need to be run to explore the effects of varied social network parameters.

Thus, before work on the simulation coding began, we decided to create two related models: the high-level one that would be relatively light computationally but provide indirect support for our primary hypothesis, and the low-level model that would be computationally expensive but provide direct support for the hypothesis. In effect, the high-level model would be used to explore the space of model parameters and social network configurations, while the low-level model would be invoked to dive deeply into specific scenarios of interest.

Besides the decision to split the model for computational considerations, at this stage the relevance for the results to human studies was also decided. Within the field of language change, there exists a relatively recent, lab-based paradigm known as iterated learning used to simulate intergenerational transfer of knowledge (Kirby,

Cornish, & Smith 2008). At the time of our work, a number of small studies had been conducted looking at the emergence of compositionality in human communication (see Smith & Kirby 2012, chapter on compositionality, for comprehensive overview). However, the existing methods were unable to incorporate social network structures and were unable to operate at scales. To make sure the behavior of our models could be comparable with this growing body of work, the scope of what the model language could express was designed to match as closely as possible the stimuli used in the human experiments. Similarly, the procedure used for communication was designed to match that used in the human studies.

Beyond the desire to make the simulation results applicable to a set of existing studies, there is a strong hypothesis in the greater field of cognitive science that much of what the human mind does is learn using a simplicity bias (Chater & Vitányi 2003). There exists a well-defined mathematical principle that models this kind of simplicity-based learning and even specific algorithms that use the principle to learn context-free grammars from unstructured data, and model processes of language acquisition and evolution (Onnis, Roberts, & Chater 2002; Roberts, Onnis, & Chater 2005). To place the simulation results in this emerging, unifying context of simplicity-based learning, the decision was made to adapt the existing grammar learning algorithm into the model structure and use this principle as the basis for the agent's actions.

4.1.1 Model: Data management

This is the stage most often underrepresented in the archiving of simulation data. While the design decisions are explained in part in the research products for the two models, there is no direct indication in our collection of source files and simulation data that makes clear that certain assumptions of the model relate to specific studies already conducted or to broader scientific principles. As suggested in Dijkstra and De Smedt (1996), the decisions at this stage correlate with Marr's (1982) levels that squarely distinguish computational studies from human-based ones.

In future projects, we suggest that a document be added to the archive with sections corresponding to Marr's levels of analysis: computation, algorithm, and implementation. Inside the data management folder of the main repository, we have added a brief example of such a document for the high-level model—*model_exposition*. To keep the example reasonably short, we have omitted the details of the social network simulation,

which were also omitted in the preceding presentation of the case studies.

This document has a section for each of Marr's levels. In the computation section the overall objective of the model is given, as well as the inputs, outputs, and transformation process. The algorithmic section provides a broad overview of how the inputs are transformed to the outputs and, importantly, provides the rationale for the various steps involved. The mathematical details have not been included, nor would we recommend they be. The purpose is not to provide a document that enables reproducibility, but one that explains the design decisions involved. For example, it mentions the kinds of computations, such as probabilistic process, that are used, but rather than specify probabilities or parameters, it mentions why the process was designed the way it was. Crucially, it links the rationale of the algorithm design to the computation goals.

4.2 Simulation: Process

The simulation stage is largely the engineering of the software that runs the model. One of the first issues to be settled is the programming language used to code the model and specific scenarios to be run. For these projects, we considered different programming languages. Throughout the social sciences, Python has become the lingua franca for computational work for three reasons, it has a large ecosystem of available tools for almost every common task, performant libraries for linear algebra and matrix-bases computations (a staple representation used in the hard sciences), and a shallow learning curve with code that reads very similar to natural language. However, in contrast to the physical sciences, much of linguistic theory is based on symbolic manipulations (cf. phonological substitution rules) that are not easy to express as matrix operations. With these kinds of computations, Python is one of the least performant languages and a poor choice for constructing flexible, scalable models. In contrast, Julia is every bit as easy to learn and as clear as Python, but with execution speeds that are among the fastest available. Thus, our decision was set on the emerging language Julia.

4.2.1 Simulation: Data management

Perhaps more than any other stage, data management is most pervasive in the preparation of the source code files used in the simulation. While one does not need to be a professional software engineer to program simulations, a number of best practices are crucial for maintaining the relevance of the code throughout its life cycle.

The main point to keep in mind is that unlike with professional software projects, one is not producing a final software product to be consumed by users. Instead, the researcher produces a computational model, and the effort should be placed on making that model as transparent as possible for other researchers to read, understand, and potentially reuse. Thus, organizational and code decisions should be guided first and foremost by clarity of the model.

Organization of the code should be kept as modular as possible, and minimally, the code that deals with the main steps defined at the algorithmic level should be kept apart from one another. For a large software project, such as the low-level model code in the main repository, we can see that there are a number of source code files defining natural concepts of the algorithm: the model deals with agents and networks, grammars and rules, and each of these is compartmentalized in a single place. In contrast, for small software projects such as that of the high-level model, there is but a single source file. For the high-level model, despite having the same fundamental components, the entirety of its source code is smaller than most individual pieces of the low-level model. Rather than spread the code over dozens of files, each just a few lines in length, it was kept together in one place. Additionally, it was written more linearly, whereby the smallest pieces of the model are presented first, followed by the code that uses them. This makes the source more like a narrative, introducing new concepts in a bottom-up fashion, from least to most complex.

Another aid to clarity is to write your code to be read and not just run. While it is easier to simply write code using abbreviated names and without comments, it will be extremely difficult to decipher yourself several weeks or months later, let alone for readers who are trying to understand it for the first time. Take for example the code that defines a linguistic construction and a language, located at the top of the main source file for the high-level model, and partially reproduced in figure 29.2. Even if you have never seen a single line of code in the programming language Julia before, there are plain English sentences explaining what each section does and the intent behind them. Additionally, items in the code are given long and so-called self-documenting names:

```
### DATA TYPES
mutable struct Construction
# a Construction has a meaning, some original source signal pattern,
# and a level of reanalysis
meaning::Int64
origin::Int64
level::Int64
end
mutable struct Language
# a Language is a collection of meanings and constructions
# its primary importance is not to model human language, but to keep global variables such as id numbers coordinated over the agents, but local to the simulation in multiprocessing
meanings::Int64
origins::Int64
construction_i::Int64
constructions::Array{Construction,1}
end
```

Figure 29.2
Write to read.

again, not knowing anything about Julia, you could certainly direct your attention to the part dealing with a *construction* versus the part dealing with a *language*, and the comments clue you in on the details.

A common pitfall, especially when eager to get running code for some initial results, is to leave such comments out and use abbreviations to save yourself typing out long names. If I was being lazy I could have just named the first object *con* and given its components names with their first letters, *m*, *o*, and *l*, respectively. While writing the code, I would surely remember that *con* was short for construction and that *m* was short for meaning. However, how could an external reader of the code be expected to know what those symbols meant?

A further blow to clarity (as well as engineering) is not dividing one's code into small units of logical work. For example, on lines 325–329 (reproduced in figure 29.3) of the high-level model code there is a small function called *select_events*. First, note that thanks to the naming, it is clear that this piece of code is responsible for selecting some events, and thanks to the comments, we know that those events are the conversations that happen among the agents. The meat of the code is a single line (327) that

```
#select the conversations to happen this round of
communication
function select_events()
return shuffle(network.connections)
end
```

Figure 29.3
Small logical units.

simply implements the command "randomize a list of values" (which again, thanks to good naming, you know are the connections in a network). This single line would be trivial to write out on its own in the few places it occurs in the code. However, it captures a fundamental idea, how the agents' exchanges are chosen.

We could easily imagine a future in which, rather than at random, the agents chose their partners in some other manner. If we had not broken this piece of code out into a single reusable function, it would be much more error-prone to change: we would have to hunt down every location this happens and copy and paste the new selection code in its place. The more that code was used, the more likely it is that we will miss a piece or make a mistake in replacing it. In terms of clarity, the reader might not know what this code does each place we find it. We could add a comment explaining it, but we again run the risk of forgetting to comment it every place it occurs, or worse, forgetting to update a comment when changing it again. By keeping it in a single place, we make sure that it is easy to change (just this one place) and signal to the reader of the code that (however trivial and small) this code is important.

There are many more software engineering tips that could be given here, but these were selected primarily on the grounds of making the code a readable object for those wishing to engage the model in detail. To reiterate, beyond the engineering principles involved, strive to make the model clear to the reader of the code, including yourself.

4.3   Results: Process and data management

At this stage, the main concerns are relating the data to existing work and organizing the archive for easy consumption. The process of relating data to existing work is typically handled in the research output, such as a journal article or white paper, where one cites relevant studies and explains how they relate; for computational modeling this is no different than for traditional academic work. For that reason, we will focus on aspects of preparing the model source code for consumption.

In section 4.1.1 we introduced an exposition file and emphasized the importance it plays in linking the rational between the computational and algorithmic levels. Similarly, it provides a chance to link the source itself to those algorithmic steps. In the implementation section of that file, we make direct references to key parts of the algorithmic steps and how those steps can be found in greater detail in pseudo-code files.

Pseudo-code, as the name suggests, is a computational description of your model's code that one could implement in any given programming language but is itself not code in some particular language. It has all the details required to be translated fully into an implementation of your algorithms, but is written as closely as possible to plain English (or any other natural language), so that the reader can understand what your model code does without having to understand the programming language you chose to code in. The virtue of pseudo-code is that it exposes the lowest-level details of the model, that is, how your algorithmic steps were turned into and executable implementation, but without placing technical burden on your reader.

In the algorithmic section of the exposition file, two main steps of the model are clarified: an exchange stage where the agents communicate, and a transfer stage where new agents learn the language and replace the old. In the final, implementation section of the exposition file, these stages are each linked to individual pseudo-code files, contained in a pseudo-code directory alongside the model code. For example, looking at the *diffuse* file (a portion of which is reproduced in figure 29.4) you can see the details of the computations that happen during the exchange stage. Importantly, the exchange and transfer stages correspond to the two main theoretically driven concepts in language change, and keeping these stages separate and identifiable within the computer code helps any researcher to relate the algorithmic level with the computational level. In other words, organizing and labeling the code in ways that mirror the conceptual assumptions and theoretical choices of the researcher can promote reproducibility, as well as further expansions, and modifications of the model in follow-up studies.

For instance, in the exposition file we mentioned that agents attempt to decode expressions (called signals

```
Exchange (speaker, hearer)
pick a random meaning
pick a random signal from speaker's actives for the
meaning
IF hearer Can Understand OR speaker Can Repair
add speaker id and signal to hearer history
add signal to passive if not already present
IF signal already in passive AND chance <= 0.25
add signal to hearer active
END
ELSE
create new zero level signal
add signal to each agent's active and passive
add each agent's id and signal to each other's history
END
END

Can Understand (speaker signal, hearer)
FOR EACH passive signal hearer has for meaning
IF meanings and origins match
IF reanalysis levels within 1 OR speaker signal level
is zero
RETURN true
    END
  END
  RETURN false
END
```

Figure 29.4
Exchange and *Can Understand*: pseudo-code.

```
function canunderstand(target, hearer)
knowns=hearer.passive[target.meaning]

if target.level==0 #paraphrastic phrases are always
understood
return true
end

for known in [network.language.constructions[index]
for index in knowns]
#phonetics share same origin, and changes not great,
then understood
if known.origin==target.origin && abs(known.level-
target.level) <= 1
return true
end
end

return false
end
```

Figure 29.5
Can Understand: Julia code.

in the code) of others, and do so if a given signal they encounter is close enough to a signal they already know. Here we can see exactly how "close enough" is defined in terms of the integer values used in the simulation. It may seem unnecessary to specify such a simple computation like this in pseudo-code but compare it to the actual Julia implementation in lines 252–264 of the high-level model source code (reproduced in figure 29.5).

The intent of this code, despite the comments, is obfuscated by the mechanics of accessing the required variables and syntax unique to Julia: in the pseudo-code the plain English *reanalysis levels are within one* corresponds to the Julia *abs(known.level − target.level) <= 1* where the reader must know the naming conventions and data layout of the *known* and *target* signals, that the *abs* call is to a Julia library function that computes the absolute value, and must finally reason that testing that

absolute value of a difference of two integers is less than or equal to another integer captures mathematically the idea of being within a range. The important concept for the model is what was stated in the pseudo-code, and everything else is just circumstantial to Julia and the software engineering decisions made by the coder. Another advantage of detailing pseudo-code next to the code is for debugging. Anyone knowledgeable of the specific programming language inspecting the code can verify whether the actual code does implement what the pseudo-code intends to code, or whether a bug or a typo may need correcting (for instance, something as trivial as the use of a +sign instead of −in the *abs* example above).

Finally, something that may strike a reader familiar with archives of other social science studies is that the raw data themselves are missing. Simulations, often more so than human experiments, generate a tremendous volume of data. For example, in our low-level model, a single run of a single condition easily produces five gigabytes of data, which is already large for many consumer laptops to hold in memory. Even more problematic, there were dozens of conditions to be run, where each condition was replicated fifty to one hundred times. Thus, the raw data for any one condition would require keeping hundreds of gigabytes of data in memory and storing many terabytes of data in the archive in all. This is not practical.

However, where differences between people generate differences in behavior in human studies, computational simulations make use of pseudo-random number generators to generate randomness. While there are many algorithms in use, a crucial commonality is that they require some initial input (usually an integer) to start the process, called the seed. Such generators are not truly random, as even though the sequences they generate are statistically random, they are totally determined by the seed—the same seed value will produce the same sequence every time. To make a computational model truly reproducible, the seed values used to generate the data must be clearly documented. When done so, only the code is required to be stored, as any portion of a massive data collection can be reproduced on demand.

5 Conclusion and suggestions for best practices

To meet greater demands of open science in the social sciences and linguistics, there is a much greater burden on the computational modeler to bridge the gap between how theories are typically presented in plain language, and their expression as mathematical objects that are amenable to implementation as a computer program. Indeed, this decision-making process is non-arbitrary and explicitly aligns the model with particular existing experiments and theoretical camps within the discipline. As such these decisions need to be a focus of documenting and archiving models in a manner that makes them reproducible and multipurpose.

Ideally, a model archive should contain an exposition document that outlines the assumptions made while developing it. As suggested in Dijkstra and De Smedt (1996), the three conceptual levels outlined in Marr (1982)—computation, algorithm, and implementation—provide a principled organizational base. There should also be pseudo-code available for the algorithmic steps, and the exposition document should make clear which pseudo-code corresponds with which step. In this way, not only are the assumptions documented, but interested readers can understand the computations without having to know the particular programming languages used to code the model. Especially as programming languages come and go, the model itself does not become irrelevant as the computations are preserved in a form that is universal.

For computational modeling to advance as a relevant and complementary method in linguistics, both models themselves must evolve beyond incidental artifacts of research. That is, it is no longer sufficient to just publish the source code, or even worse, just a binary executable file in an archive. Instead, any model (code and process) must become reproducible and informative in its own right. While there is no gold standard for how this should be done, this chapter has outlined the abstract differences between computational models and traditional experimental studies and, moreover, provided a framework for data management and preservation of computation models as data.

Notes

1. There does not exist any singular measure of the complexity of a language, nor any singular measure of the complexity of a language's morphology. In the two works presented in this chapter, morphological complexity was defined as the measure of synthesis (Greenberg 1960), which is average number of morphemes per word over a corpus of language use. Again, this is not the only measure of morphological complexity, and it is not without problems; for a discussion of alternatives and rationale for usage, the reader is directed to Lou-Magnuson (2018). Henceforth, the term *complexity*, unless otherwise specified refers to morphological complexity quantified as synthesis.

2. This figure is inspired by figure 1.1 in Dijkstra and De Smedt (1996), in which they discuss computational modeling in the context of psycholinguistics. In the original, the traditional scientific method is not shown in full.

References

Bengio, Y., R. Ducharme, P. Vincent, and C. Jauvin. 2003. A neural probabilistic language model. *Journal of Machine Learning Research* 3:137–1155.

Bishop, C. M. 2006. *Pattern Recognition and Machine Learning*. New York: Springer.

Chater, N., and P. Vitányi. 2003. Simplicity: A unifying principle in cognitive science? *Trends in Cognitive Sciences* 7 (1): 19–22.

Dijkstra, T., and K. De Smedt, eds. 1996. *Computational Psycholinguistics: AI and Connectionist Models of Human Language Processing*. London: Taylor and Francis.

Freedman, G., M. Seidman, M. Flanagan, M. C. Green, and G. Kaufman. 2018. Updating a classic: A new generation of vignette experiments involving iterative decision making. *Advances in Methods and Practices in Psychological Science* 1 (1): 43–59.

Greenberg, J. H. 1960. A quantitative approach to the morphological typology of language. *International Journal of American Linguistics* 26 (3): 178–194.

Kirby, S., H. Cornish, and K. Smith. 2008. Cumulative cultural evolution in the laboratory: An experimental approach to the origins of structure in human language. *Proceedings of the National Academy of Sciences* 105 (31): 10681–10686.

Krizhevsky, A., I. Sutskever, and G. E. Hinton. 2012. Imagenet classification with deep convolutional neural networks. *Advances in Neural Information Processing Systems* 25 (2): 1097–1105.

Lou-Magnuson, M. E. 2018. Intimate connections: An agent-based model of the relationship between social network structure and language typology. PhD dissertation, Nanyang Technological University, Singapore.

Lou-Magnuson, M., and L. Onnis. 2018. Social network limits language complexity. *Cognitive Science* 42 (8): 2790–2817.

Marr, D. 1982. *Vision: A Computational Investigation into the Human Representation and Processing of Visual Information*. Cambridge: MIT Press.

Onnis, L., M. Roberts, and N. Chater. 2002. Simplicity: A cure for overregularizations in language acquisition? In *Proceedings of the 24th Conference of the Cognitive Science Society*, 720–725. Mahwah, NJ: Lawrence Erlbaum.

Roberts, M., L. Onnis, and N. Chater. 2005. Acquisition and evolution of quasi-regular languages: Two puzzles for the price of one. In *Language Origins: Perspectives on Evolution*, ed. Maggie Tallerman, 334–356. Oxford: Oxford University Press.

Smith, K., and S. Kirby. 2012. Compositionality and linguistic evolution. In *The Oxford Handbook of Compositionality*, ed. Wolfram Hinzen, Edouard Machery, and Markus Werning, chapter 24. Oxford: Oxford University Press. doi:10.1093/oxfordhb/9780199541072.013.0024.

30 Managing Sign Language Acquisition Video Data: A Personal Journey in the Organization and Representation of Signed Data

Julie A. Hochgesang

1 Introduction

In this chapter, I describe my own personal and evolving experiences over the years with regard to better understanding and doing video data management for sign language acquisition, specifically for American Sign Language (ASL). There are no standing practices for managing sign language acquisition data, and in this data management use case, I describe the workflows that I've developed in a reflective manner, making this somewhat a personal piece. From this personal recollection, however, are some more general lessons that can be relevant to the reader—a few lessons are more meta in terms of thinking about how data are represented in text (a point I focus on first before diving into a description of my sign language acquisition management work) and some lessons are more practical and can be adopted by others managing sign language data (acquisition or not). Bear with me as I first briefly focus on how signs are typically represented in the field of signed language research, then I'll turn to the management I've done with child sign language acquisition data.

In this chapter I focus on the management of sign language acquisition data, drawing on my experiences from the last fifteen years. Much of my work—the decisions I make, the behavioral habits I have, the products I create—revolve around my own experiences as a Deaf[1] person and ASL user. These experiences are deeply affected by how I can access information in the world around me (see also Holton, Leonard, & Pulsifer, chapter 4, this volume). I do not have access in the same way that most people who have "normal hearing" do, and this awareness carries over into my work. Everyone who is reading this (assuming you often think about language research) knows that how information is represented is an essential, though often overlooked or even downplayed,

aspect of language research. The representational system itself encodes aspects about what you are sharing.

Signed languages do not have any widespread conventionalized written systems of their own. But for signed languages to be useful to researchers who like to count, sort, and organize instances in the data, signed forms need to be represented in machine-readable text. To that end, a signed language is usually represented through the written system of an ambient spoken language (glossing), during which signs or parts of signs are shoehorned into the nearest equivalents in the written language. The chosen written gloss then brings all of the associations from the original word to what is actually being represented. For example, in ASL to refer to people or things, we can point ☞. Because ☞[2] can refer to so many things, it's especially tricky to textually label. When we use English, we then think about how ☞ would be represented in English. We start using words such as *I, me, you, he, she, it,* and *they,* which then backfires because with those English words, we understand that other grammatical senses are represented—person (first person in *I* or *me* and second person *you*), number (singular in *I* and plural in *we*), grammatical case (the nominative *I* vs. the accusative *me*). All of these senses in the English words can then bleed back into our understanding of the form (☞ in ASL), which doesn't have any of those senses other than number. Rather, this ASL sign ☞ points and ASL signers use their understanding of the language, the discourse events, and the physical surroundings to figure out the intended references. But the side effect of glossing, especially as the main choice of textual representation, is that it obscures the original form. This is just one example of many.

The problems with representing signed language data using written glosses are widely acknowledged (e.g., Johnston 2001; Pizzuto & Pietrandrea 2001; Frishberg,

Hoiting, & Slobin 2012), yet glossing remains the predominant representational system (most noticeably in publications),[3] a problem that Slobin (2008) refers to as "the tyranny of glossing." It is a problem that I constantly think about.[4]

To further discuss how ASL (or any signed language) is usually represented, consider how the English word in all uppercase letters, LAPTOP, is used to represent the ASL sign for "laptop." The orthographic representation of the English word bears no resemblance to the phonological form of the ASL sign as shown in figure 30.1. The ASL sign is two-handed with one hand held stationary in front of the signer's torso. The other hand, palm down, is on top of the base hand and rotates up so that the ulnar side of the hand is the only part in contact with the base hand. The only reason why LAPTOP is used to represent this ASL sign is because it is the closest approximate meaning in English.

Yet many publications focusing on signed language phonology—which makes the production of signs its primary focus—use written glosses with no immediate reference (by way of notation, photo, or movie) to the actual signed form. Publications in other topics in signed language linguistics may be even more reliant on these written glosses without any direct visual reference to the original signed language forms they are studying. For instance, there are articles that discuss syntax in ASL relying solely on written glosses leading people like me who use ASL in their everyday lives to wonder exactly what signs these are. What the forms of signs look like may not be as relevant to the topics discussed in those articles where discussions of meaning or syntactic function prevail—but the choice of representation matters to

the Deaf signing communities. It matters when I'm reading a paper that discusses an analysis of my language and I'm unable to reproduce what is being shared about ASL in written English (and the same can be said for any signed language represented in their usual ambient written language). All of this means I'm hyperaware about representation of data at all stages—during data collection, organization, processing, and dissemination—and am constantly striving to maintain links between signed forms and their textual representations.

In the following sections, after first describing the sign language acquisition projects that I have been or am currently involved in (sections 2.1–2.5) and ethics of working with signed language communities (section 2.6), I touch on some data management considerations or current practices related to our projects in different stages: data collection (section 3), organization (section 4), annotation (section 5), and sharing (section 6). I conclude with brief thoughts about open data (section 7). As already stated, this chapter will draw from my personal experiences related to the management of sign language acquisition data (colored by my preoccupation with representation). The entry will also touch on (1) issues common to any sign language project that collects data—usually in video format given the visual nature of signed languages—that then leads to a variety of secondary consequences (e.g., large file sizes, varying compression rates, rapidly changing technology); (2) the fact that we are working with a signed language community, one that is historically marginalized and often studied by outsiders who do not sign well (or at all) and are perhaps not aware of the specific needs and preferences of the signing communities; and (3) the unfortunate reality that signed languages do not yet have conventionalized written systems that can be used for representation.

2   Research projects

I have been involved in four research projects related to child acquisition studies. I helped film, record lab notes, digitize the videos, digitally organize the videos and lab notes, annotate the primary data, develop and maintain data organization and annotation protocols, prepare the annotations for sharing, create and maintain a lexical database (the ASL Signbank; Hochgesang, Crasborn, & Lillo-Martin 2020), and supervise others doing the same.

Figure 30.1
ASL sign for "laptop."
Source: Image from ASL Signbank, 2020.

I also used the acquisition data I helped collect and manage for my own dissertation (Hochgesang 2013) in which I examined different notation systems and the ability to represent handshapes in a way that illuminated questions related to acquisition.

2.1 Project 1

From 2006 to 2009, I was a research assistant for Deborah Chen Pichler's Effects of Bilingualism on Word Order and Information Packaging in ASL, a Gallaudet Research Institute Priority Grant, which eventually became a part of BiBiBi (see section 2.2). During this three-year project, we followed the language development of the same few hearing children of deaf adults (Codas) or, as the project itself used, kids of deaf adults (Kodas) on a weekly basis. The children started with the project when they were about one year old and were actively acquiring two languages in two modalities (aka bimodal bilingual acquisition), specifically English and ASL. During the weekly one-hour-long sessions, research assistants such as myself would film one child playing with another assistant or caretaker in a naturalistic environment (reading books, playing with blocks, imaginary play, and so on). The language we targeted alternated weekly—one week we surrounded the child with ASL-using adults and vice versa for English. This project was built on Chen Pichler's research involvement with Diane Lillo-Martin's work in sign language acquisition, especially during the Cross-Language Early Syntax Study (CLESS) (Lillo-Martin & Chen Pichler 2008).

2.2 Project 2

From 2009 to 2015, Lillo-Martin and Ronice de Quadros were primary collaborators with Chen Pichler for the Development of Bimodal Bilingualism project[5] (Lillo-Martin, Quadros, & Chen Pichler 2016) (https://slla.lab.uconn.edu/bibibi/), for which I worked as a lab manager for three years. I even contributed a hearing child of my own to the project. This was a joint longitudinal acquisition project between the University of Connecticut, Gallaudet University, and Universidade Federal de Santa Catarina (Florianópolis, Brazil) that studied how children acquired both a sign language and a spoken language (e.g., Quadros et al. 2015). The participants included Kodas and deaf children of deaf parents using cochlear implants for spoken language. The research assistants who worked with the children were usually either Deaf or Codas, although a few were hearing second-language (L2) signers.

2.3 Project 3

From 2009 to 2011, just as I became a new faculty member for Gallaudet in the Department of ASL and Deaf Studies, I worked as a consultant for the ID Gloss Project[6] (https://slla.lab.uconn.edu/past-projects/; Fanghella et al. 2012). "An ID-gloss is the (English) word that is consistently used to label a sign within the corpus, regardless of the meaning of that sign in a particular context or whether it has been systematically modified in some way" (Johnston 2010:119; see section 5.2 for more). The ID Gloss Project focused on developing consistent or comparable transcription conventions for ASL across different research labs (Boston University, Gallaudet University, University of Connecticut, and University of Texas, Austin) by building a database containing clips of frequent ASL signs along with the annotation (ID gloss) labels and additional information about the signs for machine-readability. This project, which personally appealed to me in the way it addressed our field's problem of relying on glosses as the main representation, eventually evolved into the ASL Signbank (see sections 2.4 and 5.3).

2.4 Project 4

More recently, I have been a consultant for Sign Language Acquisition, Annotation, Archiving and Sharing (SLAAASh) (2014–2019) (https://slla.lab.uconn.edu/slaaash/). The SLAAASh team is working to create and share a digitized video corpus of Deaf children's use of ASL, collected as spontaneous production data from four Deaf children of Deaf parents, ages 1;04–4;01 (the CLESS data; Lillo-Martin & Chen Pichler 2008). The primary video data are being annotated systematically using SLAAASh ID glosses and annotation conventions (Hochgesang 2016; 2020). ID glosses are maintained in a "signbank," a lexical database that stores and organizes ID glosses (see Crasborn, chapter 39, this volume), specifically the ASL Signbank (Hochgesang, Crasborn, & Lillo-Martin 2020). Reconsenting protocols (Chen Pichler, Hochgesang, Simons, et al. 2016) have been developed to obtain permission from the participant children, now all adults, as well as others in the primary data to share their data. All together these activities serve as a basis for an annotation, archiving, and sharing infrastructure that can be used by other research projects also studying ASL.

2.5 When I first started

I got into sign language data management during my second year of graduate school in the Department of Linguistics at Gallaudet University. Because it was 2006 and it was around this time that the first corpus for Auslan (Johnston 2001) was initiated and earlier large collections such as Sociolinguistic Variation in American Sign Language (Lucas, Bayley, & Valli 2001) were not yet digital,[7] most of my professors unsurprisingly did not have much experience in managing large-scale digital data sets. Chen Pichler, a professor in the department, had just hired me as her research assistant along with some other students. Together we made use of the resources available to us and just kept asking around, hobbling around online, and reading about other research projects trying to get a sense of what we should do for our own. Most of what we read was for spoken language acquisition and, especially for our representation of spoken language in our data sets, we drew heavily from Child Language Data Exchange System (CHILDES) and its Codes for the Human Analysis of Transcripts (better known as CHAT transcription) (MacWhinney 2000; see https://childes.talkbank.org). CHILDES, with over 130 consistently prepared corpora, provides access to language acquisition data.

For the signed language component, however, there was little available to us for data protocols of sign language acquisition research (with the exception of Baker, Bogaerde, & Woll 2005, in which general research practices are described) and what was available focused mainly on analyses and results and data interpretation with little mention of their own methodology. And often the data that were available were shared through written glosses alone. We stumbled our way through using ELAN annotation software (http://tla.mpi.nl/tools/tla-tools/elan/; Crasborn & Sloetjes 2008) to link videos to the annotations and figuring out how to best represent the data for our needs and machine-readability (Chen Pichler et al. 2010; Chen Pichler, Hochgesang, & Lillo-Martin 2015). Through trial and error and ongoing dialogue with our research participant families as well as fellow researchers, we created data collection and organization methods for management of both signed language and spoken language (Quadros, Lillo-Martin, & Chen Pichler 2014; Chen Pichler, Hochgesang, Lillo-Martin, et al. 2016).

2.6 Ethics of working with signed language communities

"It's an exchange. We as research participants give up our privacy in allowing ourselves to be filmed, but in return, the researchers must respect our preferences and wishes." This sentiment was shared by one of the deaf women participating in a focus group meeting in which we solicited feedback from the community regarding reconsenting protocols (Chen Pichler, Hochgesang, Simons, et al. 2016). Our language acquisition work collects snapshots of real lives, and we are grateful for such contributions. We try to honor these contributions by good research practices, including ethical considerations (See Holton, Leonard, & Pulsifer, chapter 4, this volume). We strive to practice activities that the signing communities value, especially language-wise. For instance, our lab meetings at Gallaudet are conducted in ASL. Because we knew that whoever was in the room would affect communication dynamics, we scheduled the Deaf or Coda ASL-using research assistants to film and/or play with the child participants during ASL-targeted sessions and vice versa. When we present at conferences, we present in ASL. We give access to our work online through websites or social media. In all aspects of our data management, we continually reflect on our research practices in light of the signing communities we are working with (e.g., Harris, Holmes, & Mertens 2009; Hochgesang et al. 2010; Hochgesang 2018).

3 Data collection

3.1 Filming signed language data with just one camera and little equipment

Given that signed languages are of the visual-gestural modality, the best recording medium is filming; thus, our primary data are videos of signing. During our projects, we used one camera on a tripod usually about five feet away from the participants (actual distance varied depending on the filming environment and preferences of the participants). Contemporary signed language corpora (with all adult participants) usually use multiple cameras to capture a more comprehensive view (e.g., Fenlon, Schembri, et al. 2015) because pointing a camera directly at a signer will always obscure some aspect of the sign or, when having more than one participant, the communicative event. Having multiple cameras also provides a backup in case one of the cameras should fail. Despite these advantages, we opted for one camera for convenience and comfort. We did not want to over-whelm our participants with too many cameras in the room. And given the young ages of our main participants (ranging from the age of one year to five years for the longitudinal data collection), it was also better to have fewer shiny objects in the room or run the risk of exploring little hands resulting in shaking angles—not ideal when having to watch video playback to annotate signed language.

Given budget limitations and the fact that we were working with young children, we did not use additional filming equipment other than microphones connected to the camera and child participants (via harness or toy backpack). For lighting, we tried to use well-lit areas. If we were filming at a family's house, we tried to find a brightly and consistently lighted area with the light source behind the camera. We also tried to reduce as much as we could in the background such as finding a blank solid-colored wall. Well-lit footage with little detail in the background allows for clearer viewing of signing. Such clear viewing is even more important for signed languages when considering that non-manual behavior such as eye gaze direction, head movement, eyebrow movement, and so on are essential yet highly detailed and tiny components of signing that are challenging to capture on camera. Even though we forewent additional filming equipment that would have ensured the high-quality footage ideal for the sign language researcher, we still managed to capture suitably clear footage using the strategies I've outlined here as well as in section 3.2.

3.2   Our filming setup

We collected "naturalistic spontaneous" production data (that is, no structured elicitation tasks).[8] Usually one person was in charge of the camera, and one person was playing with the child participant.[9] Ideally one research assistant would be monitoring the camera and adjusting it to follow the child participants who usually did not feel the need to remain seated in one place for the entire duration of the filming session (which usually lasted about an hour depending on the child's willingness). The person monitoring the camera also had a designated notebook (one per main child participant) in which specific notes from the session were logged about interesting language productions ("Wow, this is the first time we've seen her sign this!"), non-target forms ("Still signing MOTHER using the index finger rather than all extended fingers"), behavioral notes ("Cranky

today because recovering from cold, not much production"; "great string of language productions from 00:10 to 03:15"). The other adult—either another research assistant or a caretaker of the child—sat with the child encouraging language production. While there was a microphone placed on the child (in a bear backpack or harness) to capture sound for English productions, the adult playing with the child was responsible for ensuring the child remained in the view of the camera. If the child turned their back to the camera and started signing ASL, that would be undecipherable later. Some strategies included bringing whatever toy piqued the child's interest to the table, positioning themselves so that the child would have to turn, or even picking the child up and putting them back in the chair by the table.

3.3   Staying on camera

The participants must also be careful about signing off-camera. Unlike spoken language where sound carries and can be perceived even when off-camera, signed language production needs to be on-screen to be perceived. If any participant communicates with someone off-camera, then comprehension can be limited later to any-one who views the video. Ways of minimizing this were simply not communicating off-camera, the person off-camera moving into view if necessary, or the participant on-camera could summarize what happens off-camera ("They [pointing off-camera] just asked me if we needed to leave early today").

In addition to ensuring all language productions were accessible by way of amplification by microphone or remaining in frontal view of the camera, we wanted all of our data to be as accessible as possible. If there was any content that was not easily viewed by the camera—storybooks for example—the adult playing with the child might hold up the pages of the storybook to the camera or the filming research assistant got the book at the end of the session and scanned the pages. This is especially important when the participants point or depict because complete information about the communicative event includes referents (i.e., who they were pointing at or depicting).

3.4   Working with children

One of the first concerns is usually becoming familiar to the child and to make sure the environment is a comfortable and safe one. This basically means taking time to know the child and their family and being sensitive to their needs and preferences. Once, when one of the children we worked with was new to the project, she did not want to come in the room and talk with any of us. The lone camera on tripod in the room and the unfamiliar room was intimidating to her. While the child stood on the side with her mother, I took a toy bear and sat down with it at the table. I didn't look at the child at all but addressed all of my comments to the bear in ASL, and when the bear responded, I had the arms move as if it were signing ASL back to me. The child watched this for a while and when she started smiling, I turned the bear itself to her and used it to ask her in ASL if she wanted to play. She walked in with her mother still nearby and sat next to the bear. They played together with my guidance (i.e., I made the bear's arms move in ASL accompanied by my face directly above the bear's head for facial expressions) for a bit then after a few minutes, she looked at me and offered me a toy. Then we were able to play directly without too much guidance from the bear itself.

3.5   Toys occupy hands that could be signing

The last concern I will mention here for data collection from children who sign is that toys occupy hands. When making a naturalistic environment for children, it makes sense to use a playroom and toys to put them at ease. But when it comes to signing, toys that occupy hands are not ideal for eliciting signed language production. These toys also take up eye gaze—meaning the children are busy looking at their toys and not the adults who are trying to address them. Sometimes we would pick up children from their day care/school and walk them to the filming location—we found that the children were often more talkative during this walk and then when they entered the playroom, they were quiet and committed to their playing.[10] We tried to find ways around this by suggesting hands-free activities such as reading books (which are placed flat on the table) or doing imaginary play. Or playing with toys ourselves and asking them to describe what we were doing, which is wonderful for depiction.

3.6   Encouraging sign language production in children

To continue the last point, while we strived for a naturalistic play environment, we also tried encouraging language production. Many hearing adults draw on their own memories and experiences of how to engage with a child—songs, rhymes, a certain cadence to their speech to grab the attention of the child and engage in spoken conversation. Because of educational experiences where signed language is often actively ignored or suppressed, there is not much collective knowledge to draw on while playing with the child and encouraging language. To this end, I created a video called "Working with Children on Camera"[11] to share with other adults who played with our child participants in order to draw out more ASL. This video showed clips from one Deaf mother who was skilled in language strategies that encouraged ASL production (figure 30.2).

Each clip focused on different strategies. In the first clip, the Deaf mother gives ASL vocabulary when the child points at things in the room. It actually turned into a game where the child gleefully and in increasing speed pointed at things all over the room. Another clip shows a strategy where the older child keeps pointing but is capable of producing ASL signs for those referents; therefore the mother tries eliciting ASL signs ("What's that?" "I don't know what that is."). The third clip focuses on demonstrating depiction when the child plays with toys and the mother depicts his actions in ASL. In figure 30.2b, the mother has two hands with extended index fingers up facing one another representing the two toy figures that her son is playing with. You can see he is looking at her and entertained by her language production. In the "collaborative storytelling" clip, the mother and the child worked together to create a story. Sometimes child participants are tired or hungry and the last two clips "motivation" and "different involvement strategies" show how the adult participant can involve the child ("Boy, I'm so tired. I just don't want to read a book. Oh, you want to read a book. Hmm, I'm not so sure . . ." then the child starts asking for the mother to read the book).

4   Data organization

As detailed in section 3, our data collection is largely complete, and we are currently in the research phase, thus our data organization is motivated by what we need for research. We have not yet progressed to long-term archiving but are working toward such in order to share the work with other researchers and the signing communities. Our primary means of organizing and storing

Figure 30.2
Screenshots of different clips from video "Working with Children on Camera." (a) The mother signs "door" in ASL when the child points to the door. (b) The mother demonstrates depiction as the child plays with his toys. (c) The child is pointing off-camera while the mother looks at him with a questioning face about to prompt him to go beyond pointing. (d) The mother is engaging her child who isn't all that keen to be filming that day. (e) In a bit of collaborative storytelling, the mother is signing "dress" in ASL while the son is signing "red." (f) The mother is attempting an involvement strategy (particularly playful discourse) when the child is upset.

our data has been local lab computers and encrypted and password-protected external hard drives as well as cloud-based platforms—university-provided secure servers, Dropbox, or G Suite for Education (including Google Drive). Like most digital documentation projects, we organize our content by thematic bundles, use consistent file names and versions, and back up our data in multiple locations. Many folders have "read me" documents that provide detail about folder content.

4.1 Our primary data

All primary data (videos and filming logs) were usually digitized shortly after the recording event. While perhaps it is ideal to store raw video footage for better preservation and any data recovery, we were unable to do that with some video data after switching to digital cameras because of the huge storage capacity they would require[12] (which is an ongoing problem in language documentation—how to best archive space-hogging video data in the long term). Instead, especially for the BiBiBi data collection when cloud-based platforms were not readily available, videos were compressed using the highest playback quality (usually 1080p whenever possible) using software such as iMovie or QuickTime player. For more recent collection of videos especially for the ASL Signbank, we have been able to store the raw unedited video using Google Drive (as well as backed up on external hard drives) along with the edited videos for sharing on ASL Signbank (also backed up on Dropbox).

Each session was named using a three-digit number after the main child participant's code name, for example, BEN_001 for the first session with BEN. Those became the file names of each video. The written session notes were also typed up and saved with appropriate file names. Both videos and notes are saved on local lab computers as well as stored on a secure password-protected server or cloud-based platforms (Google Drive or Dropbox) and external hard drives (including off-site backup).

4.2 Metadata

We also collect metadata in our digital logs on shared folders in Google Drive (and backed up on our lab computers and external hard drives). Each spreadsheet log for each child contains sheets organizing metadata about sessions (participant code names, target language, date of filming, age of child, filming duration, and miscellaneous comments) and transcription progress. Our metadata

organization also includes other kinds of information: participant metadata (family background, educational experience, and such), project materials (e.g., guides to filming and data organization, project proposal, institutional review board materials), annotation files, coding materials, and supplemental materials (e.g., a maintained file of pseudonyms or initials for all participants, research assistants, principal investigators for history of project along with pictures).

5 Data annotation

To make our primary video data machine-readable, we annotate using ID glosses (Johnston 2010) and free translations at the sentence/utterance level to provide access to all of the spoken and signed words and communicative actions on camera. We use ELAN annotation software (Crasborn & Sloetjes 2008) in which video is linked or time-aligned with the annotations. This constant indexical link between the primary data and the transcript (textual annotations—ID glosses and free translations) allows us to minimize the "tyranny of glossing" (Slobin 2008) because the link allows for the viewing of the primary data (the signs) along with the textual annotations. Our lab has observed best practices in annotation of signed language data (e.g., Johnston 2010; Cormier, Crasborn, & Bank 2016) and documented our transcription practices (e.g., Chen Pichler et al. 2010; Chen Pichler, Hochgesang, & Lillo-Martin 2015; Hochgesang 2016; 2020). Most recently, we are using the SLAAASh data annotation protocols, which are primarily concerned with the use of ID glosses that are organized in a signbank (Cassidy et al. 2018) along with our latest set of annotation conventions. I describe this recent set of protocols herein.

5.1 Spoken language annotation

For the annotation of spoken language in our data, we follow conventions outlined in the CHAT manual for the CHILDES project (MacWhinney 2000). Some exceptions to the CHAT guidelines due to our bilingual bimodal discourse environments have been outlined in Chen Pichler et al. (2010).

5.2 Signed language annotation: ID glosses

For the annotation of signed language in our data, we rely on a more machine-readable version of glossing along with a set of conventions (Hochgesang 2018). As briefly described earlier in section 2.3, an ID gloss is a consistent textual label using a word in uppercase from a written language that is used to link to a sign. We use written English to label ASL signs. Figure 30.3 provides some examples.

Once a written English word is used to label an ASL sign, it cannot be used for another ASL sign. When I first started annotating, we did not have a reference list of ID glosses. So, as I built one, I just went by the principle of using different English words to label different ASL signs. If more than one ASL sign needed to share the same English representation (consider the English word "light" which can be associated with multiple ASL signs [one means "lightweight" and the other signify different kinds of "electric lights"], I used lowercase tags appended to the uppercase glosses to distinguish them—LIGHTweight, LIGHTchin, LIGHTneutral, and so on).

In the earlier stages (prior to the ID Gloss Project described in section 2.4), we used local resources to organize our shared ID glosses—a single folder on my computer organized by file names and tags, a shared Google Drive account also organized by file names and tags, then a shared Dropbox account so we could sync across lab computers. Quickly we discovered that these attempts were inefficient (information wasn't always synced across files and devices) and that we needed to use a database such as a signbank.

5.3 ASL Signbank

The ASL Signbank (https://aslsignbank.haskins.yale.edu; Hochgesang, Crasborn, & Lillo-Martin 2020) is a lexical database modeled on already existing signbanks starting with Auslan (Johnston 2001) and developed specifically for ASL with the help of a team at Radboud University, including Onno Crasborn, Wessel Stoop, Micha Hulsbosch, and Susan Even (see Crasborn, chapter 39, this volume), who based the ASL Signbank software on Nederlandse Gebarentaal (NGT) (Sign Language of the Netherlands) Signbank. The software is available for developers under a public license at http://github.com/Signbank/Global-Signbank/. Although the ASL Signbank is built on the idea of a lexical database that could model how words are related to one another, it is primarily meant to store our annotation labels (ID glosses) so we can more easily retrieve them during annotation,

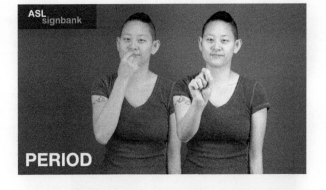

Figure 30.3
Four ASL signs with their English ID glosses.
Source: Images from ASL Signbank, 2020.

by direct linking to ELAN (Crasborn et al. 2016) as part of version 5.0 (released October 2017). The entries in the ASL Signbank are produced and coded by a team headquartered at Gallaudet University, and the ASL Signbank is hosted by Haskins Laboratories and Yale University.

When we began using the ASL Signbank, we shifted to using lemmatization principles that changed our ID glossing decisions (Hochgesang, Crasborn, & Lillo-Martin 2018). We generally follow lemmatization principles similar to those used by the British Sign Language (BSL) Signbank (Fenlon, Cormier, & Schembri 2015) although we still use lower case tags to distinguish between two phonological variants of the same lemma. We are also collaborating with the team building ASL-LEX (Caselli et al. 2017), a publicly available database that includes subjective frequency and iconicity judgments as well as phonological information on one thousand ASL signs (and more to come). Our collaboration involves sharing ID glosses (via comma-separated value exports of their database and ours and merging them into a shared spreadsheet on Google Drive and sharing sign videos via Dropbox), so that signs that are common across the databases can be easily accessed, as well as phonological information, so that the signs have consistent and comparable coding.

Figure 30.4 shows a screenshot of one of the entries in the ASL Signbank. Each entry gets a video, picture, Lemma ID Gloss, Annotation ID Gloss, and other sections that provide additional information about the sign to enhance searchability and analysis (phonology, morphology, morphosyntax, relations to other signs, frequency, publication status, notes, and other media).

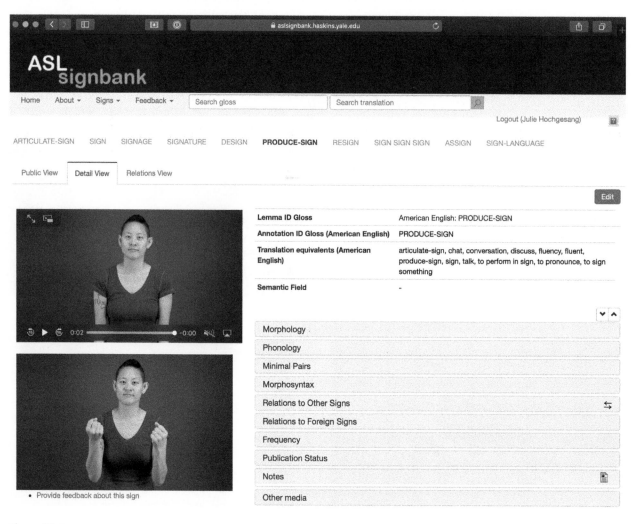

Figure 30.4

Screenshot of one of the ASL Signbank entries, PRODUCE-SIGN.

Source: Image from ASL Signbank, 2020.

The ASL Signbank is open through its public view—in which complete entries along with professionally produced videos and pictures are made public (through Publication Status seen in figure 30.4). Limited information is provided per sign as can be seen in figure 30.5.

The annotation ID gloss, translation equivalents, and sign distribution (where it's used in North America) are available under the public view. Any visitor to the site can access the Home, About, and Terms of Use pages that are full of hyperlinks to additional resources (e.g., a PDF of our annotation manual; GitHub link to the source code for the signbank software; YouTube videos explaining different aspects of the ASL Signbank including ID glosses in both ASL and English). Registration is required for an account to access complete details for all entries as well as a comma-separated value export. Access to the images and videos in the ASL Signbank is provided under a Creative Commons license.[13] The ASL Signbank is not a solution to long-term preservation of video data but is a tool for making primary video data

accessible (i.e., searchable) and thus important in making video data accessible in the long term.

5.4 Maintenance of ID glosses

New signs and their ID glosses (or even suggestions about existing ID glosses) are possible through a feedback form on the site, directly signing in as an editor and using our protocols for suggesting, or contacting me directly. ID glosses are usually proposed by annotators who regularly use the SLAAASh annotation conventions (which I discuss briefly herein) and the ASL Signbank. One person (currently myself) is responsible for approving ID glosses and making the appropriate changes to the ASL Signbank as well as communicating ongoing changes through an ID gloss Digest (figure 30.6).

The screenshot in figure 30.6 shows how the digest serves as versioning of the ID glosses because, as of 2019, there are no revision histories currently stored on the ASL Signbank website. Glosses that have been added, changed, deleted, rejected, or tagged as "need to discuss"

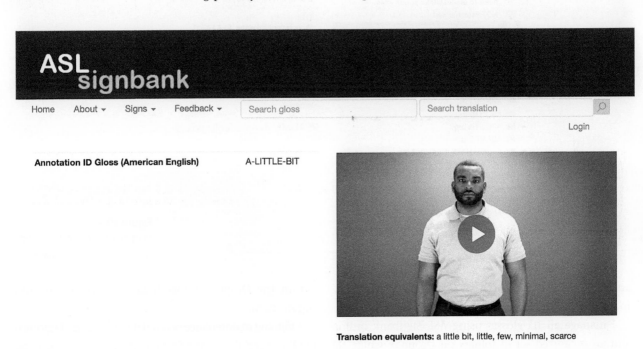

Figure 30.5

Screenshot of one of the ASL Signbank entries, A-LITTLE-BIT (public view).

Source: Image from ASL Signbank, 2020.

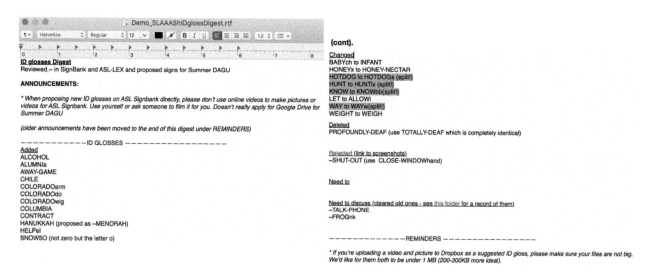

Figure 30.6

Screenshot of ID gloss Digest.

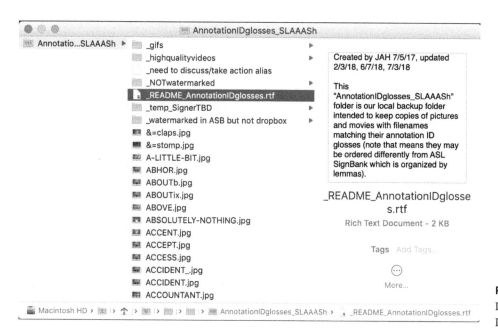

Figure 30.7

Dropbox folders of ASL Signbank ID gloss videos and images.

are identified in this digest, along with reminders of how to use the ASL Signbank or ID glosses.

I manage all ID glosses using ASL Signbank online and an organized set of folders on Dropbox where ID gloss pictures and videos are also backed up (figure 30.7) and synced across lab computers for SLAAASh using the Dropbox Desktop app.

Maintenance of ID glosses involves different activities such as reviewing proposed glosses, considering glosses from ASL-LEX, and incorporating feedback from annotators or community. There are different questions or concerns that arise during the process and need to be processed by a member of the research team. Using subfolders

within the Dropbox folder helps organize these tasks (figure 30.8).

Ongoing maintenance of our data (including ID glosses) requires careful and ongoing coordination, especially by the principal investigators and lab managers. Explicit documentation, clear protocols, and ongoing communication helps in making smoother workflows.[14]

5.5 Annotation files

We use ELAN to annotate our primary data. An ELAN template file with a specified set of tiers and an External Controlled Vocabulary (ECV) link to the ASL Signbank helps maintain consistency across annotation files. Our

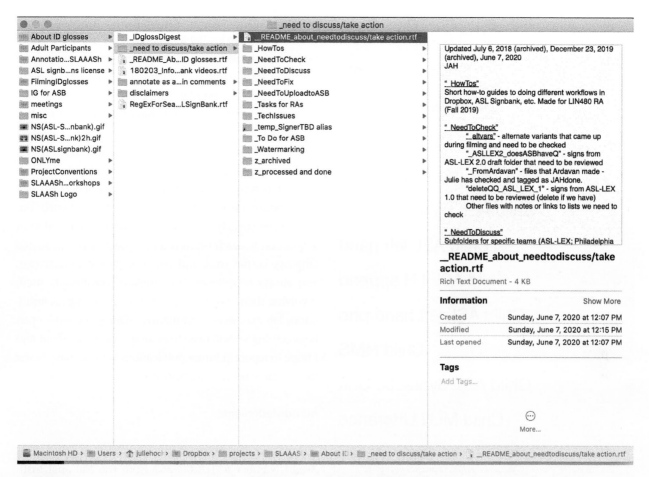

Figure 30.8
Screenshot of finder window showing folder organization for ID gloss maintenance.

tiers (figure 30.9) serve to provide machine-readable access to bilingual bimodal production as well as initial analysis.

The same set of tiers is listed for each participant on camera in a single ELAN Annotation File (EAF). Annotation is not a single-step process but rather a multistep one in which annotation,[15] proofing, and coding activities are coordinated through lab management and tracking. Along with transcription progress noted in a Google spreadsheet, the file name also contains information about its status SessionName_Language_YYMMDD (Name of the session, which language has been annotated—ASL and English using capitalization to indicate its status [0=not yet started, lowercase=in progress, uppercase=done]; and date of last annotation).

6 Data sharing

Currently our primary data and accompanying metadata and annotation files are in protected locations and are only available to researchers who have obtained the appropriate permissions. We are also working with others to develop a web-based platform for sign language data sharing. While the primary data are currently protected, our data management protocols for annotation and archiving are available online through our project website[16] and the ASL Signbank as previously described. On the website for the ASL Signbank, we previously linked to Dropbox Showcases, which were digital collections of various files hosted on Dropbox. As of January 2021, Dropbox discontinued this service, and we have since used Figshare collections,[17] a better, open-access alternative.

As was described earlier, the ASL Signbank is open, especially through the public view. We also share information through social media accounts, Instagram[18] and Twitter,[19] to engage with the community. We use YouTube to share videos in ASL and written English via captions. These are meant to make our work accessible to the community by making the content easily available (rather than having to go through the library to access a paywalled article that is written in dense academic

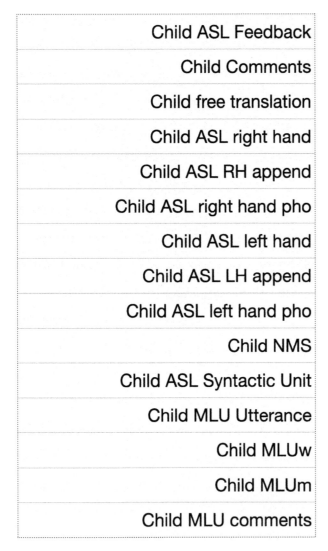

Child ASL Feedback

Child Comments

Child free translation

Child ASL right hand

Child ASL RH append

Child ASL right hand pho

Child ASL left hand

Child ASL LH append

Child ASL left hand pho

Child NMS

Child ASL Syntactic Unit

Child MLU Utterance

Child MLUw

Child MLUm

Child MLU comments

Figure 30.9
Screenshot of tiers in ELAN for one participant.

speak) and directly accessible by making the content more bilingual or bimodal than it ever could be in a written article. These multimedia platforms also allow for much freer use of photos and videos, which means ASL is much more visible and used.

7 Thoughts about open data

The data management use case authors in this volume were instructed to describe our data management practices "with regard to open linguistic data." Most of the work I have done with sign language acquisition and described here has actually resulted in digital records that are confidential and protected, especially for the BiBiBi project. This is both because we are working with child data (remember the primary data are filmed and

it is difficult to ensure confidentiality when access to faces are directly available) and because we really didn't know how to make our data open. But the purpose of the SLAAASh project is to be able to share the data with other researchers and planning is underway.

In general, our work to date has primarily been focused on making our primary video data accessible for searches on the computer and ready for analysis by our research teams. To that end, we have been more concerned with developing protocols that allow us to better represent data without a conventionalized writing system. As demonstrated, our ongoing practices have been influenced by best practices in acquisition research (spoken and signed) as well as signed language corpus work and our own personal preferences and always considering the language community itself, involving them whenever possible (focus group, as annotators, lab managers, consultants). Making our work open is something we will need to be more conscious about and I hope to report in future publications how we have better incorporated open data principles wherever possible.

Acknowledgments

The project described in this chapter is supported by Award Number R01DC009263 from the National Institute on Deafness and Other Communication Disorders (United States). The content is solely the responsibility of the authors and does not necessarily represent the official views of the National Institute on Deafness and Other Communication Disorders or the National Institutes of Health (United States). Additional support was provided by a Gallaudet priority grant, and by Conselho Nacional de Desenvolvimento Científico e Tecnológico (Brasilia) grants 200031/2009–0 and 470111/2007–0.

The research reported here was supported in part by the National Institute on Deafness and Other Communication Disorders of the National Institutes of Health under award number R01DC013578 and award number R01DC000183. The content is solely the responsibility of the authors and does not necessarily represent the official views of the National Institutes of Health.

Along with Diane Lillo-Martin as principal investigator and Julie A. Hochgesang and Deborah Chen Pichler as consultants, the SLAAASh research team includes research assistants Amelia Becker, Donovan Catt, Anna Lim Franck, Ardavan Guity, Carmelina Kennedy, Laura Mahan, Matthew Nardozza, Lettie Nazloo, Deborah Peterson, Lee Prunier, Doreen Simons, Phoebe Tay, and

Jacob Veeder, and all of the ASL Signbank actors (slla.lab.uconn.edu).

The ASL Signbank was developed at Radboud University by Onno Crasborn, Wessel Stoop, Micha Hulsbosch, and Susan Even.

I appreciate the feedback given by Andrea Berez-Kroeker, Oswald V. Cameron, Onno Crasborn, Deborah Chen Pichler, Jennifer Hochgesang, and Diane Lillo-Martin on earlier drafts of this chapter.

And I am truly grateful to Deborah Chen Pichler, Diane Lillo-Martin, and Ronice de Quadros for inviting me to work with them.

Notes

1. The use of d/D in "deaf" is controversial (e.g., Kusters, De Meulder, and O'Brien 2017; Pudans-Smith et al. 2019). While I'm still undecided on this issue, here I follow the practice of not capitalizing "deaf" unless the status has already been identified in previous literature.

2. Please note that ☞ is used here as an icon for an actual real-world sign. That is, I am using the emoji ☞ as a representation for the ASL sign that looks the same and is, among other functions, pronominally used to point to referents (real-world or those established in discourse) and could be interpreted into English as "he," "she," "it," and so on.

3. In a review of an earlier draft of this chapter, Onno Crasborn notes that "ID-glosses in the sense of Johnston (2010) are not intended to be representational but indexical, they point to an entry in a lexical database." I agree, however, the sense I'm discussing here in this chapter is a more general reference to the practice of glossing especially in dissemination (presentations and publications). Later in section 5, I discuss ID glosses and note that they help minimize the glossing problem but as noted by Crasborn as well, people will still see the textual labels first and may not even check the sign form itself in the ID glossing databases.

4. That this is a problem I often think about was highlighted by the Twitter hashtag #GlossGesang, created by colleague Carl Börstell after a presentation I gave at the Doing Reproducible and Rigorous Science with Deaf Children, Deaf Communities, and Sign Languages: Challenges and Opportunities, Deaf X Lab Pre-TISLR13 Workshop at Humboldt University, Germany (Hochgesang 2019a). "#GlossGesang: 'Always present sign language data in a visual format (videos/images) without relying solely on glossing'" (https://twitter.com/c_borstell/status/1177498599992610823).

5. The two projects from 2006 to 2015 are sometimes informally referred to as BiBiBi which stands for "Binational Bilingual Bimodal" and incidentally when fingerspelling these letters in ASL also looks like the fingerspelled form for "baby," a fitting resemblance given the focus of the research.

6. This project has no website or other online presence, but the work started for this project was continued in project 4 discussed in section 2.4.

7. Many are still not digital or if they are, they remain inaccessible from a machine-readable point of view. Current efforts are underway by colleagues and myself at Gallaudet to make them accessible (see "Gallaudet University Documentation of ASL," https://doi.org/10.6084/m9.figshare.c.5223824).

8. This is true for the projects I was involved with. The principal investigators of these projects conducted additional projects that had experimental components or even within the same project (BiBiBi) added experimental tasks (see Quadros et al. 2014).

9. Sometimes, given scheduling conflicts or lack of staffing, there was only one adult in the room doing all activities, which is not recommended.

10. We even tried bringing a camera during these pick-up walks. But sans camera stabilizers and microphones, the content of those videos was great but the quality not so much.

11. Hochgesang (2019b), https://doi.org/10.6084/m9.figshare.9943586.v1.

12. When I started with Chen Pichler as a research assistant, we were using cameras that recorded to mini-DV tapes. Those tapes were labeled and placed in organizing bins in locked file cabinets. Because those have a limited life span, they are considered backups.

13. Creative Commons Attribution-NonCommercial-ShareAlike 4.0 International (CC BY-NC-SA 4.0); https://aslsignbank.haskins.yale.edu//about/copyright/.

14. A project management or task manager tool would probably be useful, but we've always relied on a mixture of e-mail and shared documents on a cloud-based resource such as Dropbox or Google Drive.

15. Annotation of the signed language production is done by native or early users of ASL (either deaf or Coda).

16. https://slla.lab.uconn.edu/slaaash/#.

17. https://doi.org/10.6084/m9.figshare.c.5233700.v2 and https://doi.org/10.6084/m9.figshare.c.5236682.v1.

18. Our Instagram account (@ASLSignbank; https://www.instagram.com/aslsignbank/) has gotten a lot of attention. Over eighteen thousand followers in less than a year after the account opened. While it has gotten a lot of interest from people who want to learn ASL, there are many comments from fluent ASL users who have provided information that turned out to be useful to our the ASL Signbank (a kind of crowdsourcing of sorts)—usage information (regional or other kind of demographic information on where a sign is used), describing variants of existing signs, and even engaging in general discussions about how signs are actually used (or they think should be used) in the community.

19. Our Twitter account: @ASLSLAASH; https://twitter.com/AslSlaash.

References

Baker, Anna, Beppie van den Bogaerde, and Bencie Woll. 2005. Methods and procedures in sign language acquisition studies. *Sign Language and Linguistics* 8 (1–2): 7–59. https://doi.org/10.1075/sll.8.1.03bak.

Caselli, Naomi, Zed Sevcikova, Ariel Cohen-Goldberg, and Karen Emmorey. 2017. ASL-LEX: A lexical database for ASL. *Behavior Research Methods* 49 (2): 784–801. https://doi.org/10.3758/s13428-016-0742-0.

Cassidy, Steve, Onno Crasborn, Henri Nieminen, Wessel Stoop, Micha Hulsbosch, Susan Even, Erwin Komen, and Trevor Johnston. 2018. Signbank: Software to support web based dictionaries of sign language. In *Proceedings of the Eleventh International Conference on Language Resources and Evaluation (LREC 2018)*, ed. Nicoletta Calzolari, Khalid Choukri, Christopher Cieri, Thierry Declerck, Sara Goggi, Koiti Hasida, Hitoshi Isahara, et al., 2359–2364. Paris: ELRA. http://www.lrec-conf.org/proceedings/lrec2018/summaries/499.html.

Chen Pichler, Deborah, Julie A. Hochgesang, and Diane Lillo-Martin. 2015. BiBiBi Project ASL annotation conventions. Poster presented at Digging into Signs Workshop: Developing Annotation Standards for Signed Language Corpora, University College London, London, March 30–31. https://bslcorpusproject.org/events/digging-workshop/, https://doi.org/10.6084/m9.figshare.9741728.v1.

Chen Pichler, Deborah, Julie A. Hochgesang, Diane Lillo-Martin, and Ronice de Quadros. 2010. Conventions for sign and speech transcription in child bimodal bilingual corpora. *Languages, Interaction and Acquisition* 1 (1): 11–40. https://doi.org/10.1075/lia.1.1.03che.

Chen Pichler, Deborah, Julie A. Hochgesang, Diane Lillo-Martin, Ronice de Quadros, and Wanette Reynolds. 2016. Best practices for building a bimodal bilingual child language corpus. *Sign Language Studies* 16 (3): 361–388. https://doi.org/10.1353/sls.2016.0007.

Chen Pichler, Deborah, Julie A. Hochgesang, Doreen Simons, and Diane Lillo-Martin. 2016. Community input on reconsenting for data sharing. In *Proceedings of the LREC 2016 7th Workshop on the Representation and Processing of Sign Languages: Corpus Mining, 10th International Conference on Language Resources and Evaluation (LREC 2016)*, ed. Eleni Efthimiou, Stavroula-Evita Fotinea, Thomas Hanke, Julie Hochgesang, Jette Kristoffersen, and Johanna Mesch, 29–34. Paris: ELRA. https://www.sign-lang.uni-hamburg.de/lrec/lrec/pubs/16028.pdf..

Cormier, Kearsy, Onno Crasborn, and Richard Bank. 2016. Digging into signs: Emerging annotation standards for sign language corpora. In *Proceedings of the LREC 2016 7th Workshop on the Representation and Processing of Sign Languages: Corpus Mining, 10th International Conference on Language Resources and Evaluation (LREC 2016)*, ed. Eleni Efthimiou, Stavroula-Evita Fotinea, Thomas Hanke, Julie Hochgesang, Jette Kristoffersen, and Johanna Mesch, 35–40. Paris: ELRA. https://www.sign-lang.uni-hamburg.de/lrec/lrec/pubs/16015.pdf.

Crasborn, Onno, Richard Bank, Inge Zwitserlood, Els van der Kooij, Anique Schüller, Ellen Ormel, Ellen Nauta, Merel van Zuilen, Frouke van Winsum, and Johan Ros. 2016. Linking lexical and corpus data for sign languages: NGT Signbank and the Corpus NGT. In *Proceedings of the LREC 2016 7th Workshop on the Representation and Processing of Sign Languages: Corpus Mining, 10th International Conference on Language Resources and Evaluation (LREC 2016)*, ed. Eleni Efthimiou, Stavroula-Evita Fotinea, Thomas Hanke, Julie Hochgesang, Jette Kristoffersen, and Johanna Mesch, 41–46. Paris: ELRA. https://www.sign-lang.uni-hamburg.de/lrec/lrec/pubs/16023.pdf.

Crasborn, Onno, and Han Sloetjes. 2008. Enhanced ELAN functionality for sign language corpora. In *Proceedings of the LREC 2008 3rd Workshop on the Representation and Processing of Sign Languages: Construction and Exploitation of Sign Language Corpora, 6th International Conference on Language Resources and Evaluation (LREC 2008)*, ed. Onno Crasborn, Thomas Hanke, Eleni Efthimiou, Inge Zwitserlood, and Ernst Thoutenhoofd, 39–43. Paris: ELRA. https://www.sign-lang.uni-hamburg.de/lrec/lrec/pubs/08022.pdf.

Fanghella, Julia, Leah Geer, Jon Henner, Julie Hochgesang, Diane Lillo-Martin, Gaurav Mathur, Gene Mirus, and Pedro Pascual-Villanueva. 2012. Linking an ID-gloss database of ASL with child language corpora. In *Proceedings of the LREC 2012 5th Workshop on the Representation and Processing of Sign Languages: Interactions between Corpus and Lexicon, 8th International Conference on Language Resources and Evaluation (LREC 2012)*, ed. Onno Crasborn, Eleni Efthimiou, Evita Fotinea, Thomas Hanke, Jette Kristoffersen, and Johanna Mesch, 57–62. Paris: ELRA. https://www.sign-lang.uni-hamburg.de/lrec/lrec/pubs/12026.pdf.

Fenlon, Jordan, Kearsy Cormier, and Adam Schembri. 2015. Building BSL Signbank: The lemma dilemma revisited. *International Journal of Lexicography* 28 (2): 169–206. https://doi.org/10.1093/ijl/ecv008.

Fenlon, Jordan, Adam Schembri, Trevor Johnston, and Kearsy Cormier. 2015. Documentary and corpus approaches to sign language research. In *Research Methods in Sign Language Studies: A Practical Guide*, ed. Eleni Orfanidou, Bencie Woll, and Gary Morgan, 156–172. Malden, MA: Wiley-Blackwell.

Frishberg, Nancy, Nini Hoiting, and Dan I. Slobin. 2012. Transcription. In *Sign Language: An International Handbook*, ed. Roland Pfau, Markus Steinbach, and Bencie Woll, 1045–1075. Berlin: De Gruyter Mouton.

Harris, Raychelle, Heidi M. Holmes, and Donna M. Mertens. 2009. Research ethics in sign language communities. *Sign Language Studies* 9 (2): 104–131. https://doi.org/10.1353/sls.0.0011.

Hochgesang, Julie A. 2013. Is that a Y or. . . . ? Representation of hand configuration data in different notation systems for child acquisition of ASL. PhD dissertation, Gallaudet University.

Hochgesang, Julie A. 2016. SLAAASh ID glossing principles and annotation conventions. Unpublished manuscript, University of Connecticut and Gallaudet University. https://doi.org/10 .6084/m9.figshare.9741656.v1.

Hochgesang, Julie A. 2018. SLAAASh and the ASL Deaf communities (or "so many gifs!"). In *Proceedings of the LREC 2018 Workshop 8th Workshop on the Representation and Processing of Sign Languages: Involving the Language Community, 11th International Conference on Language Resources and Evaluation (LREC 2018)*, ed. Eleni Efthimiou, Evita Fotinea, Thomas Hanke, Julie Hochgesang, Jette Kristoffersen, and Johanna Mesch, 63–68. Paris: ELRA. https://www .sign-lang.uni-hamburg.de/lrec/lrec/pubs/18049.pdf.

Hochgesang, Julie A. 2019a. Tyranny of glossing revisited: Reconsidering representational practices of signed languages via best practices of data citation. Invited presentation at Doing Reproducible and Rigorous Science with Deaf Children, Deaf Communities, and Sign Languages: Challenges and Opportunities: Deaf X Lab Pre-TISLR13 Workshop, Humboldt University of Berlin, September 23. https://doi.org/10.6084/m9.figshare.9941807.v1.

Hochgesang, Julie A. 2019b. *Working with Children on Camera for Signed Language Data* (online video). Figshare, Oct. 6, 2019. https://doi.org/10.6084/m9.figshare.9943586.v1.

Hochgesang, Julie A. 2020. SLAAASh ID Glossing Principles, ASL Signbank and Annotation Conventions, Version 3.0. figshare. https://doi.org/10.6084/m9.figshare.12003732.v3.

Hochgesang, Julie A., Onno Crasborn, and Diane Lillo-Martin. 2018. Building the ASL Signbank: Lemmatization principles for ASL. In *Proceedings of the LREC 2018 8th Workshop on the Representation and Processing of Sign Languages: Involving the Language Community, 11th International Conference on Language Resources and Evaluation (LREC 2018)*, ed. Eleni Efthimiou, Evita Fotinea, Thomas Hanke, Julie Hochgesang, Jette Kristoffersen, and Johanna Mesch, 69–74. Paris: ELRA. https://www.sign-lang .uni-hamburg.de/lrec/lrec/pubs/18048.pdf.

Hochgesang, Julie A., Onno Crasborn, and Diane Lillo-Martin. 2020. *ASL Signbank* (website). New Haven, CT: Haskins Lab, Yale University. https://aslsignbank.haskins.yale.edu/.

Hochgesang, Julie A., Pedro Pascual Villanueva, Gaurav Mathur, and Diane Lillo-Martin. 2010. Building a database while considering research ethics in sign language communities. In *Proceedings of the LREC 2010 4th Workshop on the Representation and Processing of Sign Languages: Corpora and Sign Language Technologies, 7th International Conference on Language Resources and Evaluation (LREC 2010)*, 112–116. Paris: ELRA. https://www.sign-lang .uni-hamburg.de/lrec/lrec/pubs/10055.pdf.

Johnston, Trevor. 2001. The lexical database of Auslan (Australian Sign Language). *Sign Language and Linguistics* 4 (1/2): 145–169. https://doi.org/10.1075/sll.4.12.11joh.

Johnston, Trevor. 2010. From archive to corpus: Transcription and annotation in the creation of signed language corpora. *International Journal of Corpus Linguistics* 15 (1): 104–129. https:// doi.org/10.1075/ijcl.15.1.05joh.

Kusters, Annelies, Maartje De Meulder, and Dai O'Brien, eds. 2017. Innovations in Deaf Studies: Critically mapping the field. In *Innovations in Deaf Studies: The Role of Deaf Scholars*, 1–54. New York: Oxford University Press.

Lillo-Martin, Diane, and Deborah Chen Pichler. 2008. Development of sign language acquisition corpora. In *Proceedings of the LREC 2008 3rd Workshop on the Representation and Processing of Sign Languages: Construction and Exploitation of Sign Language Corpora, 6th International Conference on Language Resources and Evaluation (LREC 2008)*, ed. Onno Crasborn, Thomas Hanke, Eleni Efthimiou, Inge Zwitserlood and Ernst Thoutenhoofd, 129–133. Paris: ELRA. https://www.sign-lang.uni-hamburg.de /lrec/lrec/pubs/08035.pdf.

Lillo-Martin, Diane, Ronice Müller de Quadros, and Deborah Chen Pichler. 2016. The development of bimodal bilingualism: Implications for linguistic theory. *Linguistic Approaches to Bilingualism* 6 (6): 719–755. (Invited keynote paper for epistemological issue.)

Lucas, Ceil, Robert Bayley, and Clayton Valli. 2001. *Sociolinguistic Variation in American Sign Language*. Washington, DC: Gallaudet University Press.

MacWhinney, Brian. 2000. *The CHILDES Project: Tools for Analyzing Talk*. 3rd ed. Mahwah, NJ: Lawrence Erlbaum Associates. https://doi.org/10.21415/3mhn-0z89.

Pizzuto, Elena, and Paola Pietrandrea. 2001. The notation of signed texts: Open questions and indications for further research. *Sign Language and Linguistics* 4 (1–2): 29–45. https:// doi.org/10.1075/sll.4.12.05piz.

Pudans-Smith, Kimberly K., Katrina R. Cue, Ju-Lee A. Wolsey, and M. Diane Clark. 2019. To deaf or not to deaf: That is the question. *Psychology* 10 (15): 2091–2114. https://doi.org/10 .4236/psych.2019.1015135.

Quadros, Ronice Muller de, Diane Lillo-Martin, and Deborah Chen Pichler. 2014. The development and use of sign language acquisition corpora. In *Spoken Corpora and Linguistic Studies*, ed. Tommaso Raso and Heliana Mello, 84–102. Amsterdam: John Benjamins. https://doi.org/10.1075/scl.61.03qua.

Quadros, Ronice Müller de, Deborah Chen Pichler, Diane Lillo-Martin, Carina Rebello Cruz, Laura Kozak, Jeffrey Levi Palmer, Aline Lemos Pizzio, and Wanette Reynolds. 2015. Methods in bimodal bilingualism research: Experimental studies. In *The Blackwell Guide to Research Methods in Sign Language Studies*, ed. Eleni Orfanidou, Bencie Woll and Gary Morgan, 250–280. Malden, MA: Wiley-Blackwell. https://doi.org/10.1002/9781118346013.ch14.

Slobin, Dan I. 2008. Breaking the molds: Signed languages and the nature of human language. *Sign Language Studies* 8 (2): 114–130. https://doi.org/10.1353/sls.2008.0004.

31 Managing Acquisition Data for Developing Large Sesotho, English, and French Corpora for CHILDES

Katherine Demuth

1 Introduction

Research into the acquisition of language began with diary data in the 1800s (Darwin 1877), constituting the early beginnings of corpus construction, which has become central to language acquisition research. Although experimental methods have also had a major impact on the field of developmental psycholinguistics, these often involve cross-sectional studies at different ages, where data from many participants are collated to provide a picture of what the "typical" child of a certain age might perceive or produce. Language acquisition corpora, which often involve the longitudinal study of only a few children, provide a complementary picture of development over time. As such they also provide a rich amount of detail regarding the different steps along the way to becoming a competent user of a language, how this is resolved simultaneously at multiple levels of linguistic structure, and how this developmental trajectory is similar to and/or varies from one individual to the next.

If the child corpora contain spoken input from parents, other caregivers, and/or siblings, these can also be extremely useful for addressing issues about the nature of child-directed speech, as well as the discourse use of the language. This is a critical aspect of the design of a corpus, essential for understanding what types of linguistic information the learner is exposed to, and how this may change as the child becomes a more competent user of the language.

Different types of language acquisition corpora are typically collected for different reasons, focusing on specific research questions. Brown's (1973) longitudinal corpus of Adam, Eve, and Sara's interactions with their parents was specifically designed to address the order of acquisition of grammatical morphemes, forming one of the first comprehensive studies of the acquisition of

English grammar. The Manchester Corpus (Theakston et al. 2001), on the other hand, was designed to provide a "dense" corpus of frequent recordings of several children's speech to facilitate research questions of lexical use and how this develops over time. The Demuth Sesotho Corpus (Demuth 1992), described herein, was collected to address issues of children's acquisition of Sesotho morphosyntax, but has also yielded new insights about the structure of the language (e.g., Demuth, Machobane, & Moloi 2009; Demuth et al. 2005; Machobane, Moloi, & Demuth 2007). In contrast, the Providence and Lyon corpora were collected to examine the emergence of grammatical morphemes (Demuth, Culbertson, & Alter 2006; Demuth & Tremblay 2008).

The specific goal of each corpus thus determines the number and ages of the children in the corpus, the frequency and type of recording, and the nature of the interlocutors. Nonetheless, a corpus may be useful for addressing many research questions not originally envisioned during the initial corpus design. In many cases, corpus data can also provide pilot data for designing future experiments and/or future corpora designed to address issues not possible given current resources. This has been the case with all the corpora discussed in this chapter.

Given the different types of corpora collected for different purposes, different results may be found depending on the nature of the corpus and the research question. For example, spoken and written corpora typically yield very different distributions in terms of lexical frequencies. For example, the language used in newspaper text differs from that of poetry or novels in many obvious respects. The same is true of more formal versus less formal speech styles, including narratives, news broadcasts, and everyday speech interactions. None of these different types of language data is capable of capturing all of what humans know about language. Thus, given a particular research question, new corpora may need to be collected. It is thus advisable to report the type of corpus used in any study, even if it was not specifically designed for the research question at hand. This can then address the important issue of replicability. But perhaps more important, before constructing a corpus, is to collect consent from those in the study to have their data made publicly available. This is especially critical for any data containing video.

The first corpus discussed here is the Demuth Sesotho Corpus (Demuth 1992). This was designed as an exploratory study, investigating the acquisition of morphosyntax in Sesotho, a southern Bantu language. It was collected as part of Demuth's dissertation research. Later funding and computational assistance from Mark Johnson enabled the entire corpus to be computerized, tagged, the audio files linked, and contributed to the Child Language Data Exchange System (CHILDES) database. It is still one of the only corpora on the acquisition of an African language.

The second two corpora (the Providence Corpus [American English] and the Lyon Corpus [French]) were collected at the same time as part of the same project, and they used similar workflow and data management procedures (Demuth, Culbertson, & Alter 2006; Demuth & Tremblay 2008). These "parallel" corpora were collected for the purpose of exploring the emergence of grammatical morphemes in children's early speech in two prosodically different languages (stress-timed English, with trochaic feet vs. syllable-timed French with phrase-final prominence). Many of the data collection methods employed and transcription procedures used were thus designed to be as similar as possible. As it was always envisioned that these data would be contributed to the public domain, parental consent to do so was obtained during enrollment in the study. Further details of these three different corpora are outlined in sections 2–4.

2   The acquisition of morphosyntax: The Demuth Sesotho Corpus

The Demuth Sesotho Corpus (Demuth 1992) was collected in the southern African country of Lesotho from 1980 to 1982. Like other Bantu languages, Sesotho is highly agglutinative, with pervasive agreement on nominal modifiers and the verb: the verb can thus constitute a full sentence on its own, with resulting free word order (cf. Demuth 1992; Doke & Mofokeng 1985 for a description of Sesotho). This raises many interesting questions regarding how the language is acquired. The data for this corpus were collected in a small mountain village of 550 people in the district of Mokhotlong, where it was possible to establish close rapport with both the children and their families. The corpus contains a longitudinal study of four target children's language development as they interacted with members of their extended family including mothers and/or grandmothers, older siblings, cousins, and peers. Three of the target children were aged two to three years, with an older child aged three to four years. This older girl and one of the younger ones were cousins living in the same household and were, therefore, recorded together. Monthly, three- to four-hour recordings of spontaneous speech took place over one year per child, resulting in a corpus of ninety-eight hours of speech containing approximately 13,250 utterances with lexical verbs (approximately 500,000 morphemes).

The original goal of the study was to examine the acquisition of the tense/aspect system. However, it quickly became apparent that these systems are very complex, and that the semantic theories of the day were not up to addressing such issues. Nonetheless, it has been possible to address many issues of morphosyntactic acquisition, leading to early studies of passives (Demuth 1989, 1990) and relative clauses (Demuth 1995), as well as an overall assessment of morphosyntactic abilities in general (Demuth 1992). Because about 40% of the corpus contains utterances from the four target children, and about 40% are adult utterances, with the remaining 20% from peers or older siblings, it has also been possible to have an excellent understanding of the characteristics of the child-directed speech these children hear, providing much-needed new insight into the nature of the target grammar (Demuth et al. 2005; Demuth, Machobane, & Moloi 2009; Machobane, Moloi, & Demuth 2007). Thus, although part of the data management challenge for a lesser studied language is to know what learners may be hearing in the environment around them, investigating this issue is often only made possible by exploring discourse interactions with children.

This corpus was collected and transcribed in the early 1980s, before the advent of portable computers and/or solar batteries for powering electronic devices. Thus, orthographic and broad phonemic transcription was carried out by hand (by Demuth, in consultation with the mothers/grandmothers of the children), and then verified by a Sesotho native speaker at the University of Lesotho who listened to the tape recordings.

Sesotho is also a tonal language, like all other Bantu languages (except Kiswahili), and like (most) other Niger-Kordofanian languages. A series of follow-up grants were therefore written to explore the acquisition of Sesotho tone, and other syntactic constructions, complementing the use of the Demuth Sesotho Corpus with new experiments. These grants then also provided funding to computerize and morphologically tag the Demuth Sesotho Corpus using the Codes for the Human Analysis of Transcripts and accompanying formatting tools, to prepare it for donation to the CHILDES database (see MacWhinney 2000; https://childes.talkbank.org). It was also then possible to digitize and link the audio files, providing the mechanism for listening to the audio and conducting analysis of the children's acquisition of tone (Demuth 1993). Mark Johnson was instrumental in constructing the Sesotho Morphological Parser to morphologically tag the corpus, 'learning' from an initial hand-tagged set of data to provide options for a human to select the appropriate parse from a list of alternatives. Morphemes that constitute 'words' are connected with a hyphen in the gloss: ke-a-e-rek-a sm1s-t^p-om9-v^buy-m^in 'I'm buying it.' Fusion of two morphemes was indicated with a slash / in the morphological tags: ke-u-rek-ets-e sm1s-om2s-v^buy-ap/t^pf-m^in 'I bought (it) for you.' A full list of tags was then provided in the manual and resulting publications.

A summer of research by Demuth, Johnson, and research assistants was needed to render the Sesotho Corpus computerized and morphologically tagged. This, plus the contribution to the CHILDES database, has put these data in the public domain, where others can now freely use them for exploring issues of broad theoretical interest, including research on child language acquisition, the typology of linguistic systems/learnability, Bantu linguistic structures, and computational issues involving morphological parsing and/or machine translation.

Initial analyses using the Demuth Sesotho Corpus, such as the early work on the acquisition of passives (Demuth 1989, 1990), was carried out by hand. Once the Demuth Sesotho Corpus was tagged and computerized, it was possible to return to these initial analyses and check

them for reliability. The correlation was very strong (cf. Demuth & Kline 2006; Kline & Demuth 2010), providing a reliability check for these early analyses. These findings have since been confirmed with a series of perception, production, and generalization experiments using novel verbs (cf. Demuth, Moloi, & Machobane 2010). Thus, although paper transcripts have been extremely useful throughout the ages, the computerization (and morphological tagging) of such corpora not only preserve them for future generations, but also make it possible for both the original researchers, as well as those to come, to explore the data much more systematically and reliably than would otherwise be possible.

3   The emergence of grammatical morphemes in American English: The Providence Corpus

Since at least Brown's (1973) corpus of Adam, Eve, and Sarah, researchers had realized that children acquire grammatical morphemes gradually during the preschool years, and that there are periods in development when children may produce a given morpheme only variably—perhaps 50% of the time, or less. The mechanisms for this gradual acquisition process had been attributed to a lack of either semantic (Brown 1973) or syntactic (Wexler 1994) knowledge. However, the type of longitudinal corpus data needed to evaluate these claims, and explore the potential phonological contributions to this process, did not exist as these previously collected corpora began too late (after the age of two years) and/or had neither the phonetic transcriptions of children's imperfect attempts at grammatical morphemes nor the linked acoustic files needed to conduct a phonetic analysis of what was said. To be able to address the possibility that the emergence of grammatical morphemes might be influenced by phonological or prosodic factors (à la Gerken 1996), it was therefore necessary to collect a new corpus of English, starting earlier (from the age of one year), with audio and video files linked. But this would also be a large undertaking and not possible without several years of funding.

With the help of a large grant and the assistance of talented undergraduates, the Providence Corpus was compiled over a period of six years (Demuth, Culbertson, & Alter 2006). The corpus contains longitudinal audio/video recordings of six monolingual English-speaking children's language development from one to three years during spontaneous interactions with their parents (usually the mother) at home. The aim of the study was to provide a corpus of phonetically transcribed data, with linked acoustic files, for the purpose of studying early phonological and morphological development. The participants included three girls and three boys, each recorded for approximately one hour a week between the ages of one and three years, beginning at the onset of first words. The full corpus consists of 364 hours of audio/video data, linked to PhonBank (Rose & MacWhinney 2014).

Both adult and child utterances were orthographically transcribed using CHILDES transcription conventions, with the audio/video files linked. Trained transcribers then carried out broad phonemic transcription using the Speech Assessment Methods Phonetic Alphabet, a computer-readable phonetic script transcription of the child utterances. These were then later transferred to Unicode/International Phonetic Alphabet. Stress was only transcribed if it occurred in an unpredictable location (as in the case of child Lily "stressing" articles at age 1;10 [cf. Demuth & McCullough 2009b]). A second trained coder then retranscribed 10% of each file. Reliability scores ranged from 80% to 98% (discounting voicing errors).

These data were then contributed to the CHILDES database. These have been useful for addressing a wide range of issues from phonological/prosodic effects on the acquisition of both inflectional morphemes (e.g., third-person singular) (Song, Sundara, & Demuth 2009) and articles (Demuth & McCullough 2009b). Other studies have explored some of the acoustics of the children's and mothers' speech, with a special focus on the acquisition of coda consonants (Song et al. 2013, Song, Shattuck-Hufnagel, & Demuth 2015). The Providence Corpus has also been useful for teaching language acquisition classes, where students can log on to the CHILDES database and conduct either cross-sectional and/or longitudinal group and/or individual research projects. Some of these have resulted in honors theses/publications (e.g., Evans & Demuth 2012 on pronoun reversal). Many others have used the Providence Corpus for a wide range of studies of child speech, child-mother interactions, and computational modeling of word segmentation (Börschinger, Johnson, & Demuth 2013; Johnson et al. 2014). The Providence Corpus was also one of the first to be included in the new Databrary database (https://www .databrary.org), which is available to researchers of child development. Thus, contribution to the public domain

has again made these data widely available to a broad range of researchers for the investigation of issues not originally envisioned.

4 The emergence of grammatical morphemes in French: The Lyon Corpus

Addressing theoretical issues regarding the nature of the acquisition process in one language raises many questions about the generalizability of these processes to other languages. Thus, as it became clear that phonological and prosodic factors might influence how and when grammatical morphemes were acquired, it became necessary to explore these issues crosslinguistically. Because English and French are prosodically very different (English has [trochaic] lexical stress, and French has phrase-final prominence), the collection of a comparable corpus of French acquisition became paramount.

The methods for collecting and annotating the Lyon Corpus were thus as similar as possible to those used for the Providence Corpus. It contains longitudinal audio/video recordings of five monolingual French-speaking children's language development from ages one to three years during spontaneous interactions with their mothers at home. (Two additional children were also recorded; transcription is still in progress). All files are audio/video linked and available in PhonBank (Rose & MacWhinney 2014).

Once again, the aim of the study was to provide a corpus of phonetically transcribed data, with linked acoustic files, for the purpose of studying early phonological and morphological development. The participants included two boys and three girls, each recorded for one hour every two weeks beginning at the onset of first words (around one year) and continuing until the age of three. The corpus currently consists of 185 hours of speech.

Both adult and child utterances were orthographically transcribed using CHILDES transcription conventions, with the audio/video files linked. Trained transcribers then carried out a broad phonemic (Speech Assessment Methods Phonetic Alphabet > Unicode) transcription of the child utterances. Ten percent of each recording was then retranscribed by a second trained coder, with segmental reliability scores ranging from 90% to 98%.

Issues of reliability can now be addressed across different French corpora as well, where article/determiner acquisition has been well documented by several different groups of researchers (e.g., Veneziano & Sinclair

2000; Bassano, Maillochon, & Mottet 2008; Demuth & Tremblay 2008). The corpus has also provided the means for exploring other issues of phonological interest, such as the acquisition of consonant clusters, both in French and crosslinguistically (Demuth & Kehoe 2006; Demuth & McCullough 2009a; Kehoe et al. 2008).

5   Conclusions

In sum, the collection, annotation, and preparation of language acquisition corpora, though extremely labor-intensive, have made, and continue to make, an enormous contribution to science. Access to underlying data sets allows not only for reliability and verification of original results, but also provides a wealth of additional information that can continue to be tapped in years to come to address a wide range of research questions. These data resources are enhanced by the inclusion now not only of the transcriptions, but also audio files so that researchers can hear what was actually said. This, plus the inclusion of video files, allows for a better understanding of the discourse context as well—that is, who was talking to whom, looking where, and so on. (See Holton, Leonard, & Pulsifer, chapter 4, this volume, for further discussion of ethical issues of video sharing.)

As an example, intonation (and information structure more generally) play a critical role in understanding the meaning of what was said, both in English, and in other languages. Without access to the acoustic signal, all this information is missing. As Ochs (1979) once noted, the very act of transcription involves a reduction of information. Thus, the inclusion of audio files, as well as video of those interacting, provides a much more complete picture of the discourse interactions, including potentially helpful or even essential information regarding the nature of language use, including its development. Technology is now available for ensuring that future corpus construction can include both audio and video information, preserving a more complete record of the discourse situation. Both types of information also facilitate accurate transcription, which is still one of the bottlenecks for corpus development.

Acknowledgments

Collection of the Demuth Sesotho Corpus was supported in part by Fulbright-Hays Doctoral Dissertation Grant and Social Science Research Council International Doctoral Grant for Research in Africa dissertation funding. Computerization and tagging of the corpus was supported in part by National Science Foundation grants BNS-08709938 and SBR-9727897. Collection and annotation of the Providence Corpus and the Lyon Corpus were funded by National Institutes of Health grant R01MH60922 (Demuth & Johnson, Jisa). Additional funding for the Lyon Corpus was provided by two grants from Action Concertée Incitative (Terrains, techniques et théories et Internationalisation des sciences humaines et sociales), as well as support from the Délégation générale à la langue française and the Ministère de l'Enseignement supérieur et de la Recherche. None of these corpora would exist without the ongoing participation of the children and their families who have allowed us into their homes for several years: they have provided abundant insight into their language, their culture, and their children's language development. We thank them, as well as the many students and research assistants in Lesotho, the United States, and France, who contributed hours to the transcription and preparation of these corpora to ready them for donation to the CHILDES database.

References

Bassano, Dominique, Isabelle Maillochon, and Sylvain Mottet. 2008. Noun grammaticalization and determiner use in French children's speech: A gradual development with prosodic and lexical influences. *Journal of Child Language* 35 (2): 403–438.

Börschinger, Benjamin, Mark Johnson, and Katherine Demuth. 2013. A joint model of word segmentation and phonological variation for English word-final/t/-deletion. *Proceedings of the 51st Annual Meeting of the Association for Computational Linguistics* 1:1508–1516.

Brown, Roger. 1973. *A First Language: The Early Stages*. Cambridge: Harvard University Press.

Darwin, Charles. 1877. A biographical sketch of an infant. *Mind* 2 (7): 285–294.

Demuth, Katherine. 1989. Maturation and the acquisition of the Sesotho passive. *Language* 65 (1): 56–80.

Demuth, Katherine. 1990. Subject, topic and Sesotho passive. *Journal of Child Language* 17 (1): 67–84.

Demuth, Katherine. 1992. Acquisition of Sesotho. In *The Cross-Linguistic Study of Language Acquisition*, ed. Dan Slobin, 557–638. Hillsdale, NJ: Lawrence Erlbaum Associates.

Demuth, Katherine. 1993. Issues in the acquisition of the Sesotho tonal system. *Journal of Child Language* 20 (2): 275–301.

Demuth, Katherine. 1995. Questions, relatives, and minimal projection. *Language Acquisition* 4 (1–2): 49–71.

Demuth, Katherine, Jennifer Culbertson, and Jennifer Alter. 2006. Word-minimality, epenthesis and coda licensing in the early acquisition of English. *Language* 49 (2): 137–173.

Demuth, Katherine, and Margaret Kehoe. 2006. The acquisition of word-final clusters in French. *Catalan Journal of Linguistics* 5 (1): 59–81.

Demuth, Katherine, and Melissa Kline. 2006. The distribution of passives in spoken Sesotho. *Southern African Linguistics Applied Language Studies* 24 (3): 377–388.

Demuth, Katherine, Malillo Machobane, and Francina Moloi. 2009. Learning how to license null noun-class prefixes in Sesotho. *Language* 85 (4): 864–883.

Demuth, Katherine, Malillo Machobane, Francina Moloi, and Christopher Odato. 2005. Learning animacy hierarchy effects in Sesotho double object applicatives. *Language* 81 (2): 421–447.

Demuth, Katherine, and Elizabeth McCullough. 2009a. The acquisition of clusters in French. *Journal of Child Language* 36 (2): 425–448.

Demuth, Katherine, and Elizabeth McCullough. 2009b. The prosodic (re)organization of children's early English articles. *Journal of Child Language* 36 (1): 173–200.

Demuth, Katherine, Francina Moloi, and Malillo Machobane. 2010. 3-Year-olds' comprehension, production, and generalization of Sesotho passives. *Cognition* 115 (2): 238–251.

Demuth, Katherine, and Annie Tremblay. 2008. Prosodically-conditioned variability in children's production of French determiners. *Journal of Child Language* 35 (1): 99–127.

Doke, Clement Martyn, and S. Machabe Mofokeng. 1985. *Textbook of Southern Sotho Grammar*. 2nd ed. Cape Town: Longman.

Evans, Karen E., and Katherine Demuth. 2012. Individual differences in pronoun reversal: Evidence from two longitudinal case studies. *Journal of Child Language* 39 (1): 162–191.

Gerken, LouAnn. 1996. Prosodic structure in young children's language production. *Language* 72 (4): 683–712.

Johnson, Mark, Anne Christophe, Emmanuel Dupoux, and Katherine Demuth. 2014. Modelling function words improves unsupervised word segmentation. *Proceedings of the 52nd Annual Meeting of the Association for Computational Linguistics.* Vol. 1, *Long Papers,* 282–292.

Kehoe, Margaret, Geraldine Hilaire-Debove, Katherine Demuth, and Conxita Lleó. 2008. The structure of branching onsets and rising diphthongs: Evidence from the acquisition of French and Spanish. *Language Acquisition* 15 (1): 5–57.

Kline, Melissa, and Katherine Demuth. 2010. Factors facilitating implicit learning: The case of the Sesotho passive. *Language Acquisition* 17 (4): 220–234.

Machobane, Malillo, Francina Moloi, and Katherine Demuth. 2007. Some restrictions on Sesotho null noun class prefixes. *South African Journal of African Languages* 27 (4): 166–180.

MacWhinney, Brian. 2000. *The CHILDES Project: Tools for Analyzing Talk.* 3rd ed. Mahwah, NJ: Lawrence Erlbaum Associates.

Ochs, Elinor. 1979. Transcription as theory. *Developmental Pragmatics* 10 (1): 43–72.

Rose, Yvan, and Brian MacWhinney. 2014. The PhonBank Project: Data and software-assisted methods for the study of phonology and phonological development. In *The Oxford Handbook of Corpus Phonology,* ed. Jacques Durand, Ulrike Gut, and Gjert Kristoffersen, 380–401. Oxford: Oxford University Press.

Song, Jae Yung, Katherine Demuth, Karen Evans, and Stefanie Shattuck-Hufnagel. 2013. Durational cues to fricative codas in 2-year-olds' American English: Voicing and morphemic factors. *Journal of the Acoustical Society of America* 133 (5): 2931–2946.

Song, Jae Yung, Stefanie Shattuck-Hufnagel, and Katherine Demuth. 2015. Development of phonetic variants (allophones) in 2-year-olds learning American English: A study of alveolar stop/t, d/codas. *Journal of Phonetics* 52:152–169.

Song, Jae Yung, Megha Sundara, and Katherine Demuth. 2009. Phonological constraints on children's production of English third person singular -s. *Journal of Speech, Language, Hearing Research* 52 (3): 623–642.

Theakston, Anna L., Elena V. M. Lieven, Julian M. Pine, and Caroline F. Rowland. 2001. The role of performance limitations in the acquisition of verb-argument structure: An alternative account. *Journal of Child Language* 28 (1): 127–152.

Veneziano, Edy, and Hermine Sinclair. 2000. The changing status of "filler syllables" on the way to grammatical morphemes. *Journal of Child Language* 27 (3): 461–500.

Wexler, Ken. 1994. Optional infinitives, head movement and the economy of derivations in child grammar. In *Verb Movement,* ed. David Lightfoot and Norbert Hornstein, 305–350. Cambridge: Cambridge University Press.

32 Managing Phonological Development Data within PhonBank: The Chisasibi Child Language Acquisition Study

Yvan Rose and Julie Brittain

1 Introduction

Since 2006, the PhonBank database project (https://phonbank.talkbank.org) has provided computer-assisted methods for the management and analysis of child language phonological data. These methods are assembled within Phon (https://www.phon.ca), an open-source software program that supports all of the data annotation standards required for the building and analysis of PhonBank corpora.[1] PhonBank is a component of the larger TalkBank database system (https://talkbank.org), alongside CHILDES (the long-standing Child Language Data Exchange System; MacWhinney & Snow 1985) and other specialized databases such as FluencyBank and AphasiaBank. Each of these projects, as well as their continuous funding, has historically relied on public granting agencies as well as on significant levels of commitment within the research community. Just as scholars must use computer programs such as Phon to build and analyze their corpus data, the very existence of these programs and databases such as those of TalkBank is fully dependent on data sharing, which effectively transforms each corpus-building endeavor into a long-term investment for research and associated activities (e.g., educational, clinical), as we will exemplify.

Within the TalkBank family, PhonBank is unique in its organization around the Phon software program; all of the other databases center on the CLAN program https:// (dali.talkbank.org/clan). While Phon and CLAN offer similar basic functionality (e.g., time alignment; standardized annotation system; query functions), Phon differs from CLAN in that it offers specialized functions for the study of phonetics and phonology (Rose & MacWhinney 2014). While these functions were originally designed and implemented to study phonological development, they can also be used to study virtually all topics related to

phonology and acoustic phonetics (e.g., speech disorders, dialectal variation, sociophonetics, or field studies, among many others). In a nutshell, Phon is a database software program that integrates several tools for textual, phonological, and acoustic analysis. Phon also incorporates dedicated functions for the study of language acquisition and language disorders. For analyses based on textual forms, Phon can be used to encode text and incorporate lexical or morphosyntactic annotations, each of which is stored in dedicated data fields. These annotations can then be used as search criteria within powerful yet easy-to-use query functions to extract precise information relevant to the analysis at hand. Concerning phonetics and phonology, Phon automatically builds the phonological data structure from phonetically transcribed words. The transcriptions are internally analyzed by the program's specialized algorithms to identify all phones, phonological features, and positions (within the syllable, word, relative to word stress, and so on). Phon also fully integrates with Praat software for acoustic analysis. Already existing Praat (TextGrid) data can be imported into Phon, and new TextGrids can be generated directly from within Phon. Given these combined functions, and the reduced need to manually enter phonological annotations into the corpus, we can perform an unlimited number of phonological and phonetic (acoustic) analyses, the results of which can be interpreted in light of all other information contained within the Phon database (e.g., speaker information, phonological context).

In this chapter, we describe the general methods of corpus building and analysis available within Phon, contextualizing our account by taking the Chisasibi Child Language Acquisition Study (henceforth, CCLAS) as a primary example. CCLAS is particularly relevant to the present Handbook in that it combines descriptions of the phonetic, phonological, and morphosyntactic units of Cree, a polysynthetic (Algonquian) language, as well as children's recorded behaviors during their acquisition of these linguistic units.[2]

2   The Chisasibi Child Language Acquisition Study

The primary aim of CCLAS, a community-initiated project that began in 2004, is to document the acquisition of Cree as a first language.[3] The project began following some years of discussion between linguists at Memorial University and members of the Cree community in Chisasibi, with whom our department had a long-standing research relationship. The Cree School Board was particularly invested in the dialogue, having a nuanced understanding of the potential applications of the research, and they made the formal invitation to initiate CCLAS; they have been our community partner for the past fifteen years. Detailing the project's practical applications is beyond the scope of this chapter; suffice to say, offering support to the community's speech-language pathologists is a priority. Within the community there was a concern that more children than the expected average were being diagnosed with speech-language problems, an overdiagnosis, some felt, resulting from screening in a second language (English or French) due to the lack of Cree language tools; clearly, adequate first-language (Cree) screening tools were required to begin to address the issue. We say more about this herein.

CCLAS falls within the general tradition of naturalistic, longitudinal studies of language acquisition, which consists of samples of child language productions obtained at regular intervals through the recording of linguistic interactions within the child's regular environment. The long-term objectives of CCLAS are to contribute to current debates in contemporary linguistic theory, especially within the subdiscipline of first language acquisition; to contribute to the descriptive literature for Cree, an underdescribed and potentially endangered language (Wurm 1998; Brittain & MacKenzie 2016); and to assist in maintaining the vitality of the Cree language by sharing research findings with educators and speech-language clinicians who work in the Cree-speaking environment. Research published to date has been primarily based on our data sets from two children, code-named "Ani" (child A1) and "Billy" (child B3). Further information can be obtained from the project's website (https://www.mun.ca/cclas).

CCLAS is unique in that it is, to our knowledge, the first and only research project on the acquisition of an Algonquian language. CCLAS is also the only project on the acquisition of any Indigenous language to contribute data to a publicly accessible database. A subset of Ani's data was simultaneously contributed to the CHILDES and PhonBank databases in 2013. We are currently working toward expanding this data set with the publication of the other children's data.

Cree is typically spoken in multilingual contexts; in Chisasibi, for example, most people are fluent in English and in French to a lesser extent, and both languages are used in domains such as education. We have thus utilized a set of annotations to identify code switches, which help to contextualize aspects of both phonological and morphosyntactic development, for example, concerning the development of phones and phone combinations that are unique to either the Cree or the English phonological systems (Bryant 2013). Finally, and perhaps more relevant to the purpose of the current chapter, the CCLAS database combines phonetic, phonological, and morphosyntactic annotations structured within Phon in ways that facilitate the parallel study of different aspects of the Cree language. As a result, phonological analyses can be informed by morphosyntactic observations, or vice versa, using a unified set of data transcriptions and annotations.

In the following sections, we describe how we proceeded with the most central aspects of this research and discuss how we responded to the many challenges it raised along the way. It is worth noting that CCLAS and the larger context within which it exists, namely Phon and PhonBank, have all emerged in virtual synchrony and have been tightly intertwined from the outset because all three projects constitute the ongoing work of researchers and computer scientists at Memorial University. In this regard, CCLAS has served as both a source of inspiration and testing ground for many of the annotation and query methods currently available within Phon.

3   Managing phonological data in a first language acquisition study: The CCLAS experience

As we alluded to, our building of the CCLAS database came with a unique set of challenges, which we tried to tackle in a pragmatic way, following the "agile" approach to corpus building highlighted in Voormann and Gut

(2008). Under this approach, corpus building consists of a series of sweeping data processing steps that apply over the full corpus in a way that ensures that methodological adjustments, unavoidable in virtually all corpus-building endeavors, are applied to the entire data set in a uniform fashion to ensure corpus and analytic consistency. We describe the most essential steps we took toward the building of our Cree data set, which together have enabled us to obtain interrelated observations (phonetic, phonological, morphosyntactic) about the children's language performance throughout extensive developmental periods, observations that are supplemented with additional information (e.g., situational), helping us interpret these data within their proper context. We then describe some of the ways in which we have been disseminating our research outcomes within the Cree community and for scholarly research.

3.1 General context

Since its inception, CCLAS has been operating in two main locales, Chisasibi, Québec, the community in which our research is situated, and Memorial University in St. John's, Newfoundland, where most of the work on data transcription and analysis has taken place. Fieldwork sessions with the project-affiliated Cree language consultants take place at both of these research sites. Another defining characteristic of this project, and principal driver of the methods we have developed at different stages in our research, is the fact that while Algonquianists specializing in Cree and related languages have been involved in the project since its inception, none of the team members based in St. John's is a native speaker of Cree. In the following sections, we describe how we have adapted to these challenges in building the CCLAS database and in analyzing it. As we will see, conducting first language acquisition work on an underdocumented language imposes the double task of performing fieldwork to describe the grammatical and phonetic aspects of the Cree (adult) system being acquired by the children and then analyzing the children's patterns of language development in light of the descriptions obtained from fieldwork. This is the only way to ensure that we interpret the children's patterns of language development in their proper contexts.

3.2 Data collection

The CCLAS database comprises ninety-seven audio-video digital recordings made over a thirty-month period (November 2004 to April 2007), which cover the language-learning journey of six Cree-speaking children. These child participants fall into two age cohorts: the children from cohort A (children A1, A2, A3) were approximately 1;8 when recording began, while the children of cohort B (children B1, B2, B3) were approximately 3;6. Three of the six participants yielded corpora of a substantial nature, that of child A1 Ani (thirty-seven recordings), B1 "Daisy" (thirty-two recordings), and B3 Billy (nineteen recordings), amounting to approximately fifty-six hours of recording.[4] The children were filmed by a Cree-speaking resident of Chisasibi who also served as CCLAS's on-site project manager. During the recording sessions she was also the children's caregiver, engaging with them in activities that elicit language—playing with toys, talking about recent activities, and so on; she is identified as "the adult" interlocutor in all the recordings. While recordings took place primarily in Cree, a minority of interactions also occurred in English, in contexts when the children preferred to use English words or phrases.

3.3 Data processing

The processing of these original recordings then followed a series of steps that took place at either of our sites, as will be described, and involved a combination of linguists and Cree language consultants. We summarize these steps herein.

Data segmentation consists of the identification of the time intervals on these recordings and their associated utterances. Each session recording received from Chisasibi is first identified with the date of the recording as well as the names of the participants. Using the segmentation function in Phon, every utterance recorded is then time-stamped and associated with its corresponding speaker (e.g., the child participant or the adult interlocutor), a task that can only be performed by someone who understands what the speakers are saying, necessarily, that is, a Cree speaker. To achieve this step in the processing sequence, the Phon data files are transferred to the Cree language consultant in Chisasibi, who works within Phon to do the segmentation.

After the segmentation step is completed, the Cree consultant provides an *orthographic transcription* (using roman script) and an English *translation* for each utterance (record). Translation is a key requirement bearing in mind the fact that none of the researchers are fluent in the language. The updated files are then sent back to the researchers at Memorial University.

We then engage in the *phonetic transcription* of each child utterance. This step is rather difficult, primarily due to the fact that we do not have access to native Cree speakers trained for the task. To further alleviate some of the shortcomings related to the transcription of a language one does not speak (e.g., potential misperception of phonetic categories), we provide dedicated training on Cree transcription to undergraduate and graduate research assistants in linguistics who are native speakers of English. In addition, we rely on the double-blind transcription protocol, followed by consensus-based validation of the transcripts, as follows: Two independent transcribers first perform their phonetic transcriptions within dedicated interfaces, each without access to the other's work. After they have completed their individual transcriptions, the same transcribers then work together to compare each of their respective transcriptions, select the one deemed the most valid, and, whenever needed, improve the selected transcription with additional details noted during the comparison. In cases where the transcribers cannot reach a consensus, even with the help of a third person or through other methods such as spectrographic inspection of the signal, the records are excluded from further research.

This brings us to the stage of *data processing*. Either in Chisasibi or in St. John's, the team members work together to better understand the child language captured in the videos and to audio-record the "target" (adult) forms corresponding to each child utterance. This target form provides a baseline to assess the child's productive abilities. The different kinds of information gathered in these work sessions, which generally run for about a week, are entered into the appropriate tiers in Phon. With regard to better understanding the language, the principal goals here are to clarify linguistically relevant context, to identify "incorrect" child productions, and to discuss grammatical constructions unfamiliar to the linguists. We now consider each of these in a little more detail.

For the non-native–Cree-speaking members of the team, understanding the context of the language, particularly the child utterances, is challenging because Cree has very liberal argument omission patterns so that knowing who is doing what to whom, so to speak, is dependent on being able to track complex functional forms, bound and free, across what can be relatively large spans of discourse. Viewing the recordings as a team, contextual information is clarified and observations are recorded in Phon. The Cree consultant also identifies cases where the form a child produces is not "on target," differing from the adult form in some manner (phonology, morphology, syntax, lexical choice, and so on). Target forms are audio-recorded for all the child utterances and these are transcribed phonetically using the International Phonetic Alphabet (IPA) and entered into Phon by research assistants. For each child utterance (which corresponds to a data record within Phon), we have an IPA representation of the target and actual forms, allowing us to identify cases where the child falls short in her production. While this comparison can be done within Phon without the help of a Cree speaker, reviewing each utterance with the consultant provides invaluable information regarding, in particular, types of grammatical error or potential factors that might yield the errors observed; in some more extreme cases, an "error" may only be apparent but not actual in that it simply reflects the types of phonetic patterns that occur in familiar or frequently used expressions, aspects of which fly in the face of prescriptive language descriptions (e.g., the pronunciation of *potato* as [pteɾo] instead of [pəteɾo] in English). Finally, because Cree in general, and Northern East Cree in particular, is underdescribed, as we discuss both child and adult language, we frequently identify areas of the grammar where further fieldwork is required. The more theoretically oriented work undertaken on the project is dependent on the descriptive; for example, the adult stress system Northern East Cree was detailed within the context of the project (Dyck, Brittain, & MacKenzie 2006), work that facilitated a case study of the acquisition of this area of the grammar (Swain 2009). To disseminate this descriptive work more widely, our findings are also published on https://www.eastcree.org, a website oriented toward a Cree-speaking audience.[5]

The orthographic transcriptions provide the basis for our *morphological breakdown* of the utterances, which is performed by members of our research team with the relevant expertise. We input the morphological and related semantic information into dedicated fields within the Phon database, with the aid of a parser built specifically for this work and integrated into Phon. The screen shot in figure 32.1 illustrates the outcome of this work

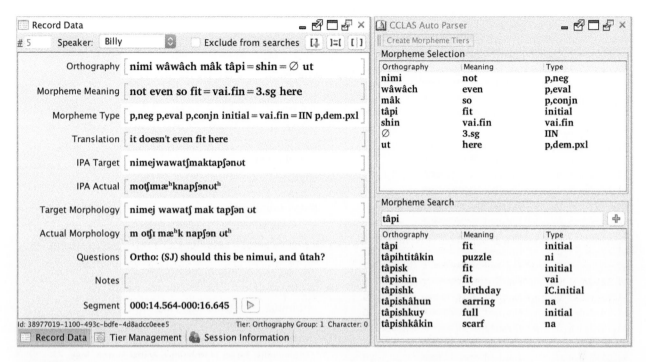

Figure 32.1
Data record, alongside morphological parser for Cree data.

through one data record from Billy's corpus, displayed alongside the CCLAS parser interface.

3.4 Data analysis

As discussed extensively in Rose and Inkelas (2011), beyond the work involved in the building of a longitudinal corpus of child language development, data interpretation arguably represents one of the most difficult challenges for any acquisition study. This is especially true in the context of CCLAS, given the frequent need to engage in fieldwork in order to set a basis to interpret the child data. Following the needs of the research at hand (e.g., on Cree speech phonetics, phonological or morphological development), we work in concert with graduate students and Cree language consultants to obtain the required data descriptions, which we maximally incorporate within our database, where they become not only useful in the current context but also available for future research. Also maintaining a pragmatic approach to database building, we typically expand our annotations on a need base and restrict annotation work only to the set of data records relevant to the study at hand. While this approach gets in the way of exhaustiveness for certain types of annotations, it also makes possible analyses that would otherwise be too time-consuming;

this approach also optimizes research output relative to database-building time.

After all the necessary annotations are entered into our database, we proceed with data analysis. Phon supports different methods for database mining. To make powerful queries readily available to linguists, which would otherwise call for expertise in programming or scripting, we designed a series of query forms such as the one in figure 32.2, which provide intuitive guidance but leave much of the technical (programmatic) details out of the interface.

For example, one can look for particular morpheme types (e.g., the preverb, represented by the "pvb" text expression in figure 32.2) and display all the corresponding morphological or phonetic data within and across session transcripts, either for all participants or for a subset of the participants.

Similarly, we can look for a given phone class (e.g., obstruent stops) and study its development over time, within and across positions within the syllable or word; each time developmental or otherwise variable patterns are detected in the data, further queries can be formulated to identify the origins of these patterns. The current version of Phon also incorporates general measures such as the PMLU (Ingram 2002) or the percentage

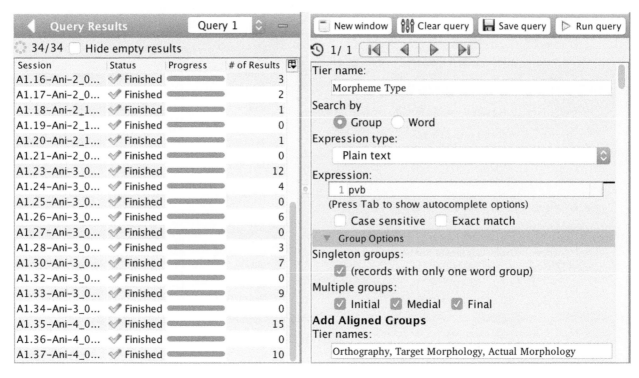

Figure 32.2
Example of a query form.

of consonants correct (Shriberg et al. 1997) as well as "detector" algorithms for phonological patterns such as fricative stopping or consonant harmony. These measures, which are commonly used in research on phonological development and speech disorders, can also be applied in the context of research on second-/foreign-language acquisition or dialectal variation or, in the case of the PMLU, to obtain broad measures of phonological complexity and related productivity.

Finally, to engage in acoustic analysis (beyond spectrographic visualization, readily available in Phon), we must perform a few additional preparatory steps. The first of these consists of obtaining TextGrids, which can be generated from within Phon to immediately incorporate tier data such as orthographic and phonetic transcriptions of the forms produced by the speaker. These transcriptions, in turn, serve as the basis for TextGrid alignment, where word, syllable, phones, or other measurable phenomena such as pauses serve as useful labels for the time intervals of the audio recordings that they represent. Although we are planning on integrating technology to automate the TextGrid alignment process, the current version of Phon only supports manual alignment of the TextGrid data.[6] After TextGrid alignment is

complete, we then identify the phones or phonological contexts to be measured through regular (orthographic or phonetic) data queries. After completion of a query, we can run one or more acoustic measurements on the data returned by the query. For example, one can look for broad measures such as pitch measurements on word forms; one can also employ narrow acoustic measures targeting specific phones such as high vowels produced in stressed versus unstressed syllables, and compare vocalic production across these two prosodic contexts based on a combination of formant, duration, intensity, or pitch data. (Other analyses include voice onset time and spectral moments, which are useful to study the production of obstruent stops and fricatives, respectively.) The interface to select the desired analyses is illustrated in figure 32.3. For each acoustic analysis, we can set specific parameters, following all the methods readily available in Praat, which we incorporated within Phon in close collaboration with the developers of Praat.[7]

Because of the integration between Phon database and Praat acoustic measurement functions, acoustic data can be easily combined with other annotations within the database. For example, still keeping the general mixed-language context of the Cree community in

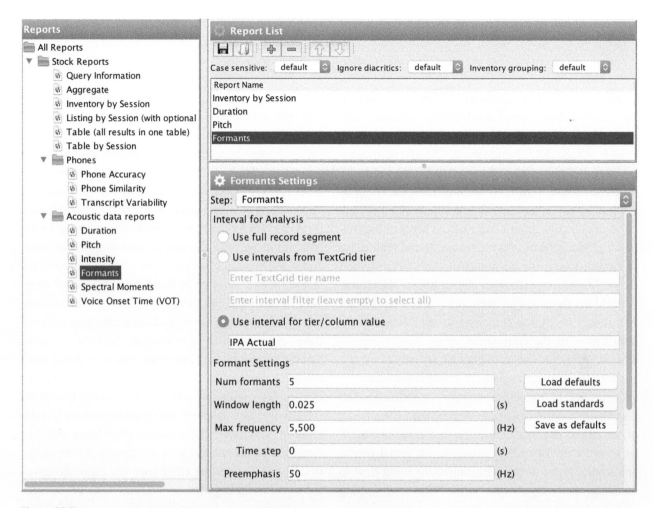

Figure 32.3
Report selection, combining textual and acoustic measurement data.

Chisasibi, we can compare phonetic units of production found in native Cree words with those observed in the English loanwords documented within our database.

Every report from textual, phonological, or acoustic analysis generated by Phon is displayed within a dedicated Phon window. From this window, the reports can be saved in a number of formats, again depending on the current need. Print-ready reports can be saved in HTML format. More typically in the context of scholarly research, Phon reports can be saved for postprocessing as Excel spreadsheets and workbooks, or exported as CSV files, for use in Open/LibreOffice or within most statistical software packages (e.g., SPSS, R).

3.5 Results dissemination and anonymized data sharing

As important as the dissemination of scholarly findings is our commitment to share our research outcomes with the Cree community; to this end, team members make regular presentations to educators and speech-language pathologists working within the community (e.g., Brittain et al. 2005; Brittain & MacKenzie 2010a, b) and to the community at large (e.g., Brittain, Johansson, & Rose 2011; Johansson 2012b), including being guests on the Cree-medium community radio. We are also committed to finding practical applications that support the language, and, to date, these contributions have been in two principal areas: supporting the work of speech-language clinicians (Brittain 2014) and contributing to the documentation and description of the language. As we have said, the active CCLAS database consists of three corpora, for which reason our output takes the form of case studies of various areas of the grammar. Although the database lacks the statistical power required to create screening tools for speech-language pathologists, which typically rely on normative data obtained from larger-scale sampling, we have proceeded on the assumption that the in-depth analyses we obtain from longitudinal case studies can provide useful information toward the building of these tools.

We maintain documentation of these outcomes on the CCLAS website, which also includes academic works on the acquisition of morphosyntactic (Terry 2010; Rose & Brittain 2011; Johansson 2012a) and phonological categories (Swain 2009; Rose et al. 2010; Bryant 2013), phonetic studies of the Cree language independent of its acquisition (Dyck, Brittain, & MacKenzie 2006; O'Neill 2014) as well as systematic comparisons between the children's productions of native Cree words and their usage of English loanwords (Bryant 2013; Pile 2018). Beyond their contributions to theories of linguistics and language acquisition, these studies offer many resources toward educational or clinical initiatives as well as additional information to the community about multilingualism or more practical considerations such as that of raising a child within a mixed-language linguistic community.

Returning to the larger context of CHILDES and PhonBank, we also began our work toward the sharing of our corpus data with our research community. Similar to our corpus-building initiative, our initial corpus publication posed a number of questions about how to maximize data output while at the same time keeping within ethical boundaries in the areas of data anonymity and cultural propriety. Key to this was the removal of any contextual identifier so that members of the Cree community unaware of what particular children participated in our study would have no way to trace the data back to any individual child or related family. As video can never offer full anonymity, an early decision was to limit media publication to the audio tracks of the videos we recorded with the children. Beyond this obvious decision, a trickier challenge was that names of people and places are often mentioned as part of verbal interactions with the children, in particular these individual children's names and that of their relatives. This is one of the drawbacks of the naturalistic approach; avoiding this type of issue is much easier through guided data elicitation (e.g., picture- or word-naming tasks). To remove this information, we first perused through our data transcripts to identify all of the names and dates present in data records. Using the time stamps of these records as a starting point, we then identified the exact time intervals containing these identifiers and replaced the sound

information with "pink" noise, which can be described as a non-aggressive, low-intensity version of white noise, making the listening of these intervals, which are often found within larger utterances, more comfortable to the listener than the white noise itself. After each media file was fully deidentified using this method, we then proceeded with the replacement of the names within the corresponding transcript by meaningless strings such as "nnn," to which we can still attach morphological or other types of labels as a unit of morphological analysis, also making sure to remove the IPA Target and Actual forms corresponding to the original name. Using a similar method, we were also able to remove names of places and dates, including the participants' birth dates and the recording dates present in the original transcript metadata. We only left child's age (at recording time), a timeless measure in the absence of corresponding calendar dates, as a means to map developmental data over time. Finally, in the face of potential concerns about one's ability to identify speakers based on the characteristics of their own voice, we add the observation that given the changes that toddlers' voices undergo during childhood, it is unlikely that someone other than, possibly, direct family members (who are already aware of the study), can identify the child speakers, especially given the relatively long period between the time of the original recording and the time when the (anonymized) data are uploaded to the online database (over a decade for the first subset of our corpus).

Resulting from this work is a data set that remains fully analyzable from both linguistic and developmental perspectives, but which is otherwise impossible to trace back to the original child speaker. This level of deidentification, and the relatively easy method employed to obtain it, makes the documents conform to the letter of our informed consent; it is also perfectly sufficient to meet the requirements of the EU General Data Protection Regulation (https://gdpr.eu), arguably the most restrictive international policy statement to date in the area of confidentiality for electronic documentation worldwide.

We then submitted our corpus to CHILDES and PhonBank through the TalkBank contribution system (https://talkbank.org/share/contrib.html), where it was curated and then published in both Phon and CHAT (Codes for the Human Analysis of Transcripts) formats, the latter being the format used by CLAN. The curation steps were minimal in this case, as the original corpus was already within the Phon format, which is fully compliant with the general standards of TalkBank. In addition to the media and transcript files, corpus submission only requires a summary description of the corpus as well as a short list of references. According to the general sharing rules of TalkBank, any individual who benefits from the published data has an obligation to cite one or more of these references to the original authors' works as part of any new study that builds on shared data. This view of data sharing and referencing is essentially an honor system that has supplied researchers and students with invaluable resources and methods since its inception in the early 1980s (MacWhinney 2000; MacWhinney et al. 2012; Rose & MacWhinney 2014). It also provides corpus contributors with an additional window to publicize works based on their original data set.

4 Conclusion

We have provided an overview of the building, analysis, and dissemination of corpus data on the first language acquisition of an Indigenous language. This work, still ongoing, has raised a number of difficulties, primarily due to its setting across multiple sites and the absence of a native speaker of Cree among our team in St. John's. We have streamlined a methodology whereby data processing is undertaken in these different locales, by the non-Cree speakers in St. John's, by the Cree speakers in Chisasibi, and, crucially, by these two groups meeting on a regular basis and working together to pool their expertise. We have also offered an overview of the types of analyses we can run within Phon, as well as some of the most important steps toward anonymous corpus data publication on PhonBank (or other similar databases within TalkBank).

In conclusion, we would like to highlight that very little of the work we described would have been possible without all the types of sharing we benefited from at every step along the way. As several people have shared their time, knowledge and expertise since the beginning of CCLAS, the whole TalkBank architecture for data sharing also rests on the premises that sharing effectively turns the large amounts of resources spent on corpus development and analysis into long-term investments into research and society more generally. In this context, it is our hope that our publication of Cree acquisition data will encourage similar initiatives with additional Indigenous languages, ideally within the context of TalkBank. This would yield many opportunities for cross-language, cross-corpus comparisons, thereby opening additional windows of understanding into each language involved and their acquisition.

Notes

1. The early development of Phon was funded by grants from the Social Sciences and Humanities Research Council of Canada, the Canada Fund for Innovation, as well as by a Petro-Canada Award for Young Innovators. Since 2006, the development of Phon and PhonBank has been funded primarily through grants from the US National Institutes of Health (R01 HD051698, R01 HD051698–06A1, and R01 HD051698–11).

2. The CCLAS database is Northern East Cree (ISO 639-3: crl).

3. CCLAS has been funded primarily by the Social Sciences and Humanities Research Council of Canada (Standard Research Grants 410-2004-1836 and 410-2008-0378 and Insight Grant 435-2013-1297), internal funding from Memorial University, and through financial and in-kind support from institutions within the Cree community, namely the Cree Nation of Chisasibi, the Cree School Board of Québec, and the Anjabowa Childcare Centre in Chisasibi.

4. In 2006, child A3 was diagnosed with atypical language development; for the present time, we exclude this child's nine recordings. Children A2 and B2 were withdrawn from the study after only four recordings were made for each.

5. https://www.eastcree.org/cree/en/grammar/sounds-east-cree.

6. Users with the relevant level of expertise can also align the Phon-generated TextGrids using forced-alignment systems such as those built within LaBB-CAT, the Montreal Forced Aligner, or MAUS. More information about these and other forced aligner technologies can be found at https://github.com/pettarin/forced-alignment-tools.

7. We owe special thanks to Dr. Paul Boersma for his collaboration on this aspect of Phon development.

References

Brittain, Julie. 2014. Resonance screening tool for speakers of Northern East Cree. *Cree Board of Health and Social Services of James Bay.* http://www.creehealth.org/library/resonance-screening-tool-northern-east-cree.

Brittain, Julie, Sara Johansson, and Yvan Rose. 2011. How children learn language and what we know about Cree. Public presentation, James Bay Eeyou School Library, May 22.

Brittain, Julie, and Marguerite MacKenzie. 2010a. The Chisasibi Child Language Acquisition Study: Bridging the gap—How to make our data serve a practical use. Presentation to clinicians, Montreal Children's Hospital, May 27.

Brittain, Julie, and Marguerite MacKenzie. 2010b. The future of Cree. Presentation to Council of Commissioners for the Cree School Board, Montréal, February 1.

Brittain, Julie, and Marguerite MacKenzie. 2016. Language endangerment and revitalization strategies. In *The Routledge Handbook of Linguistic Anthropology*, ed. Nancy Bonillain, 433–446. New York: Routledge.

Brittain, Julie, Marguerite MacKenzie, Carrie Dyck, and Yvan Rose. 2005. First language acquisition and the Chisasibi Child Language Acquisition Study (CCLAS). Presentation to the Board of Directors of Anjabowa Childcare/Headstart Centre, Chisasibi, April 25.

Bryant, Kayla. 2013. The development of segmental phonology in a mixed language environment: A case study from Northern East Cree. MA thesis, Memorial University of Newfoundland.

Dyck, Carrie, Julie Brittain, and Marguerite MacKenzie. 2006. Northern East Cree accent. In *Proceedings of the 2006 Annual Conference of the Canadian Linguistics Association*. http://cla-acl .ca/actes-2006-proceedings/.

Ingram, David. 2002. The measurement of whole-word productions. *Journal of Child Language* 29 (4): 713–733.

Johansson, Sara. 2012a. Learning words before learning grammar: A case study of passives and unaccusativity in Northern East Cree first language acquisition. MA thesis, Memorial University of Newfoundland.

Johansson, Sara. 2012b. Learning words before learning grammar: (Part of) the story of a child learning Cree as a first language. Public presentation, James Bay Eeyou School Library, June 7.

MacWhinney, Brian. 2000. *The CHILDES Project: Tools for Analyzing Talk*. 3rd ed. Mahwah, NJ: Lawrence Erlbaum Associates.

MacWhinney, Brian, and Catherine E. Snow. 1985. The child language data exchange system. *Journal of Child Language* 12:271–295.

MacWhinney, Brian, Leonid Spektor, Franklin Chen, and Yvan Rose. 2012. Best Practices in the TalkBank Framework. In *Proceedings of Best Practices for Speech Corpora in Linguistic Research, 8th International Conference on Language Resources and Evaluation (LREC)*, ed. Michael Haugh, Sukryie Ruhi, Thomas Schmidt, and Kai Wörner, 57–60. http://lrec.elra.info/proceedings/lrec2012 /workshops/03.Speech%20Corpora%20Proceedings.pdf.

O'Neill, Katharine. 2014. A phonetic study of word-final phenomena in Northern East Cree. MA thesis, Memorial University of Newfoundland.

Pile, Stephanie. 2018. Monolingual language acquisition in a mixed language community: A case study of Northern East Cree. MA thesis, Memorial University of Newfoundland.

Rose, Yvan, and Julie Brittain. 2011. Grammar matters: Evidence from phonological and morphological development in Northern East Cree. In *Selected Proceedings of the 4th Conference on Generative Approaches to Language Acquisition North America (GALANA 2010)*, ed. Mihaela Pirvulescu, María Cristina Cuervo, Ana T. Pérez-Leroux, Jeffrey Steele, and Nelleke Strik, 193–208. Somerville, MA: Cascadilla Press.

Rose, Yvan, Julie Brittain, Kevin Terry, and Erin Swain. 2010. Grammatical analysis in early morphological development: Evidence from (Northern East) Cree. Paper presented at the Canadian Linguistics Association 2010 meeting (Congress of the Social Sciences and Humanities), Concordia University, May 29.

Rose, Yvan, and Sharon Inkelas. 2011. The interpretation of phonological patterns in first language acquisition. In *The Blackwell Companion to Phonology*, ed. Colin J. Ewen, Elizabeth Hume, Marc van Oostendorp, and Keren Rice, 2414–2438. Malden, MA: Wiley-Blackwell.

Rose, Yvan, and Brian MacWhinney. 2014. The PhonBank Project: Data and software-assisted methods for the study of phonology and phonological development. In *The Oxford Handbook of Corpus Phonology*, ed. Jacques Durand, Ulrike Gut, and Gjert Kristoffersen, 380–401. Oxford: Oxford University Press.

Shriberg, Lawrence D., Diane Austin, Barbara A. Lewis, Jane L. McSweeny, and David L. Wilson. 1997. The percentage of consonants correct (PCC) metric: Extensions and reliability data. *Journal of Speech, Language, and Hearing Research* 40 (4): 708–722.

Swain, Erin. 2009. The acquisition of stress in Northern East Cree: A case study. MA thesis, Memorial University of Newfoundland.

Terry, Kevin. 2010. The emergence of intransitive inflection in Northern East Cree: A case study. MA thesis, Memorial University of Newfoundland.

Voormann, Holger, and Ulrike Gut. 2008. Agile corpus creation. *Corpus Linguistics and Linguistic Theory* 4 (2): 235–251.

Wurm, Stephen A. 1998. Methods of language maintenance and revival, with selected cases of language endangerment in the world. In *Studies in Endangered Languages*, ed. Kazuto Matsumura, 191–211. Tokyo: Hituzi Syobo.

33 Managing Oral and Written Data from an ESL Corpus from Canadian Secondary School Students in a Compulsory, School-Based ESL Program

Philippa Bell, Laura Collins, and Emma Marsden

1 Introduction

Compulsory schooling throughout the world frequently includes the studying of a/some language(s) other than the language of instruction. In some contexts, students may be learning academic content through the new language, in conditions that provide a substantial number of hours of exposure to the language (e.g., French immersion in English-speaking Canada; English Content Language and Integrated Learning in mainland Europe). More common, however, is for the study of second language (L2)/foreign language in school settings to occur in a gradual fashion—students receive a relatively small number of hours of instruction per week over many years (Collins & Muñoz 2016). Due to the small number of hours available for learning, and thus limited input, structuring lessons to optimize learning is essential. This remains a challenging objective, though, in the absence of a clear sense of what students are able to learn and how this learning develops throughout the years of limited exposure to the target language through compulsory schooling. The data detailed here come from a corpus created to address this research objective.

In this chapter, we provide a detailed account of the creation of oral (approximately 44,000 words) and written (approximately 31,000 words) corpora and associated metadata from 230 first-language (L1) French students with no other languages aged twelve to seventeen years studying in the Quebec regular English as a Second Language (ESL) compulsory program. Although Canada is officially a bilingual French-English country, French is the only official language of Quebec. For many students, especially outside the Montreal area, the only opportunity to interact in the language, and thus learn it, comes from their school program. Any additional exposure afforded by multimedia and social interaction is done of their own individual initiative, and thus, this is similar to many foreign-language contexts throughout the world. The following account is divided into five sections documenting the necessary first steps prior to data collection (section 2), data collection (section 3), data processing and metadata tagging to create the corpora (section 4), data storage (section 5), and data sharing (section 6).

2 Organizing data collection

The organization of data collection is a key step as it is at this juncture that decisions are taken that impact all subsequent steps. For example, decisions on types and the number of tests to include affect data collection and processing in terms of their duration, personnel requirements, and cost. In addition to methodological decisions, certain practical considerations also need to be considered, which also affect subsequent steps. It is for this reason that what follows details our organizational process comprehensively. We begin by briefly summarizing our piloting, which we then refer back to frequently, given that it affected all steps in our organizational process. The remaining topics in this section describe further aspects of our procedure—obtaining ethics approval, accessing participants, securing informed consent, identifying equipment needs, and training research assistants. It ends with a description of the eight measures we prepared for data collection.

2.1 Piloting

With the exception of obtaining ethics approval, all decisions were finalized following extensive piloting, which is an essential part of data planning in the data life cycle (Mattern, chapter 5, this volume). It takes time and grant money, but its importance cannot be overstated for creating valid data sets. Our piloting, which is detailed in Bell, Collins, and Marsden (2020), was conducted in five classrooms with 145 students. Data were collected from primary school students aged ten and eleven in grades five and six (the final two years of primary) and secondary school students aged fourteen and fifteen in the final three years of secondary. Piloting informed a range of procedural and analysis decisions detailed in the coming sections. It also allowed us to make the final selection of the elicitation tasks in terms of (1) the suitability of the topics for students of different ages, (2) the effectiveness for eliciting students' full linguistic repertoire regardless of proficiency level, and (3) the wording and language (French L1 or English L2) needed for clear instructions. It further guided our decisions on the most appropriate grade levels to target: the limited output elicited from the grade five and six primary students due to their very low proficiency in English demonstrated to us that our corpora should focus on secondary school students only.

2.2 Ethics approval

This section refers to the necessary administrative steps for ethics approval rather than questions relating to ethical use of participants' data (see Holton, Leonard, & Pulsifer, chapter 4, this volume for information on ethical use of data). To conduct research with humans in Canada, it is necessary to obtain ethics approval, which is accorded by the university at which the principal investigator (main grant holder) works. Obtaining approval requires the completion of an extensive form that ensures the research does not contravene any laws and that the participants will not be negatively affected by the research. Completion of the form requires a thorough understanding of how data collection will be conducted, even though pilot testing may change some of the original plans. It is standard practice to provide drafts or samples of all documents that will be used with the participants including consent forms, which are closely evaluated. In Quebec, students over sixteen are allowed to sign alongside a parent so we had one consent form for students aged fifteen and younger, and one for students sixteen and older. It is important to bear in mind that obtaining approval can take some time (approximately two months during term time in our context, longer if the process is undertaken during the summer break).

2.3 Access to participants (collection sites)

Accessing participants to contribute data can be time-consuming and extremely challenging within school settings. Schools in Quebec are governed by school boards that may have their own ethics approval process that must be completed before gaining access to schools and classes. Administrative steps to gaining access vary by school, school board, age of participants, to name a few, and as such, the protocol to be followed varies considerably. We gained access through approaching ESL pedagogical advisors who work with ESL teachers at different school boards. Initially, we wrote an information letter detailing the goals of the research and specific information on what students and their teachers would need to do. The advisors sent this document either to teachers they believed would be interested or to all teachers with whom they worked. The teachers then contacted the researchers directly.

The time interval from sending out the letters to pedagogical advisors to starting data collection in a school varied from two weeks to two months, with shorter delays usually being associated with more experienced teachers as they knew whom to ask for permission, if needed, and were organized in terms of distributing and collecting consent forms. This process also included a lot of communication with several teachers who ultimately could not participate for different reasons. We needed to control for L1 background, for example, and some classes had too many non-native speakers of French for our purposes. Some teachers realized they could not accommodate our needs. This last point is important to bear in mind for this type of data collection as our time needs (approximately one hour with all students and one to two hours in a setting where a small number of students could be seen individually for approximately ten minutes) were difficult to meet in contexts where teachers only worked with a class for as little as sixty minutes per week.

2.4 Informed consent

As soon as data collection was organized with a teacher, consent forms were sent to the school. In some situations, it may be necessary for the research team to present the forms to the students in person. When working with children under seventeen years of age in Quebec, consent needs to be provided by their parents/guardians, although those sixteen years and older can also provide contingent consent. As such, for these participants, we provided two versions of the consent form—one which only asked for the parents'/guardians' signature and one which included a space for the students to sign. Obtaining consent could take over a week if teachers only saw their students once a week. To increase the likelihood of parents providing consent, we offered to send them information on the results of the research project two years after its completion, which approximately two-thirds requested. We also divided consent into two sections—participation in the current project and consent for data to be used for future research projects. This was done to ensure we had explicit consent to use the data for other projects, as well as to provide parents with an option if they were uncomfortable not knowing how the data would be used in the future. In this study, no participant/parent opted out of data being used in the future. In total, consent was not provided by 81 students/parents of 354 that received the forms.

2.5 Data collection equipment

Successful oral and written data collection requires appropriate recording equipment, and piloting was an excellent means of understanding true equipment needs. When collecting oral data, audio recorders are the main piece of equipment. Piloting allowed us to ascertain that our audio devices were suitable, and that lapel microphones were undesirable as they led to lost data when students played with them. Nor did they notably improve the facility with which we could transcribe the oral data. Our audio devices were purchased on Amazon.ca at a cost of either C$26.99 or C$29.99. The two models were both EVISTR mini voice recorders (L157 and L169) with 8 GB of storage equivalent to 560 hours of taped audio. Two models were purchased due to an insufficient quantity of one model being available. The audio files were saved in .wav format.

For collecting written data, no specialized equipment was needed. Some researchers may wish to collect typed texts to reduce transcription time (Gilquin 2015), but this was not feasible in our context. As we needed to collect written data from all students in a class simultaneously due to the limited number of ESL class hours, this would have meant the provision of up to thirty-four computers at one time as schools cannot guarantee

access to computers/laboratories. This was beyond our budget and would not have been a useful long-term purchase. In addition, as children are still more accustomed to handwriting than typing in class, we did not want children's typing skills to become a confound in our data, as the nature of their productions (such as deviations from the norm) could either be attributable to typing skills or a true reflection of their written language.

One of the proficiency measures, the elicited imitation (Ortega 2003), required sentences to be read aloud, which were then repeated and recorded by each student. To this end, we needed a laptop and speakers. Piloting allowed us to ascertain correct volume levels and optimal speaker placement within a classroom. Despite our efforts to ensure that our intended procedure would be appropriate, the majority of these data were ultimately unanalyzable due to noise issues—our piloting classroom for this test only was an extremely quiet grade five primary classroom, which in the end did not adequately reflect the noise challenges in secondary school classrooms.

Piloting also demonstrated the importance of having clear information on when and where each data collection would occur to ensure that all equipment (audio recorders, speakers, laptop, paper copies of tests, and so on) was in the right place at the right time. As different research assistants collected data on different days, this information, which we presented in an Excel sheet, needed to be shared with all assistants and updated regularly. We achieved this by using Dropbox. In this document, we included explicit instructions on where equipment would be taken after one data collection and how this equipment would be transferred to another research team for the next data collection.

2.6 Training research assistants

To ensure all tasks were completed in the allotted time and to ensure all students received the same instructions and had the same interactions with the different assistants, extensive training was required. Without such training, there is a risk of data collection lacking consistent standards (poor reliability) across collection sites and times. Training also minimizes the likelihood of tasks not being completed or being administered incorrectly.

The need to adjust and expand training became evident during pilot testing. For the oral data collection, students worked individually with an assistant. Piloting demonstrated that the interactions between students and different assistants (seven in total) varied greatly. Some assistants provided much more help than others, which meant, for example, certain language forms may have been primed (McDonough & Trofimovich 2008) by the assistants for some students, but not for others.

Following pilot testing, we created a checklist and a script for both oral and written data collection. The checklist allowed assistants to verify they had all the materials and equipment needed for data collection. We also used the oral checklist for assistants to write down the number of each audio file alongside each student's name. This had the added benefit of reminding assistants to stop and start the file after each oral measure and between students. Use of these protocol documents ensured that instructions and order of tests were identical across all participants, which helped to ensure that any influence that undertaking one test had on undertaking another was experienced equally across all participants.

2.7   Final data collection materials

Four tasks were used to collect data for the corpus. Four other measures were used to provide further information on the participants (metadata). The process we undertook before finalizing our data collection materials, including task selection, has been fully documented in a previous publication (Bell, Collins, & Marsden 2020) whose goals included methodological transparency to reduce research biases and to improve overall data collection (Gawne & Styles, chapter 2, this volume; Marsden 2019). Here, we present an overview of the different measures.

2.7.1 Written argumentative task   Students were given twenty minutes to respond to one of two questions, which were both yes/no questions. Students chose the question to which they responded and they were asked to provide three reasons to justify their response.

1. Should students be allowed to use their cell phones in school?

2. Do aliens exist?

2.7.2 Written narrative task   Students were given a time limit of twenty minutes to write a story based on an image of two police officers at the house of a young boy and his mother. The instructions asked them to look at the image, to imagine what has happened, what is

happening now, and what will happen. This measure was adapted from a measure used in published research with Quebec ESL students aged ten to twelve (Collins et al. 1999; Collins & White 2011).

2.7.3 Oral argumentative task   Students were given a handout containing images and the following sentences, each of which appeared next to the relevant image.

> Alex is studying for his math exam tomorrow. Emma cannot study because her parents are out having dinner. She is babysitting her baby brother. Emma copies her friend Alex's answers. Alex sees her.

Students were asked to provide oral responses to each of the following questions:

If you were Emma, would you have cheated? Why?

If you were Alex, what would you do? Why?

No time limit was provided.

2.7.4 Oral narrative task   Students were given eleven images from the book *Frog, Where Are You?* (Meyer 1969), which has been used as an instrument in other studies (for examples and some elicited data, see https://www.iris-database.org/iris/app/home/search?query=frog). Students were asked to recount the story. No time limit was provided.

2.7.5 Student questionnaire   To help interpret the data, we obtained biographical information from each participant in a questionnaire containing seventeen questions that could be completed in under ten minutes. In our context and in line with our research objectives, it was important to collect data from francophone students who did not have any additional languages other than L2 English learned in the Quebec compulsory education program. The questionnaire included questions on home languages, schools where they had previously studied, study outside Canada, and exposure to all languages. It is also here that one can ask students to evaluate their proficiency in all their languages. As has been argued elsewhere, proficiency in the language of the corpus should be measured as objectively as possible (Bell & Payant 2020; Thewissen 2013), but self-evaluation for other languages is probably sufficiently fit-for-purpose and can be collected quickly and may help explain counterintuitive results about use of the target L2 (Sinclair 2005).

The questionnaire responses identified twenty-one students who had too much experience with English to be included in the study—English-speaking parents or close family or previous study at an English-medium school or in a special program in which exposure to English is far more frequent than in the regular, compulsory program. For those students who identified a parent or family member as speaking English, but who also wrote they only spoke French, we assessed their written and oral texts to see whether the student appeared to be more proficient in English than would be expected.

Eighteen students identified a language other than English or French as being the main language used at home. These students also identified their proficiency in this language as being the same or better than their French proficiency. Their data were thus excluded.

We chose to write our questionnaire in French to ensure that students, regardless of English proficiency, could understand. Nevertheless, it is still important to pilot the questionnaire to ensure the questions are written clearly and that they generate the intended information for the research project. In our prepilot questionnaire, we referred to different Quebec ESL programs (e.g., Intensive English, core, enriched), but many students were not familiar with these terms alone. We thus provided more detailed information to ensure we gathered the required information.

2.7.6 Proficiency measures Two measures of proficiency (an elicited imitation and a yes/no vocabulary measure) were used to ensure that the oral and written texts constituting the corpora could be classified based on objective measures of proficiency. We chose to include two measures, as our preferred measure (the elicited imitation) requires students to use audio recorders, which increases the likelihood of lost data. Furthermore, as the proficiency measures had to be collected from all students simultaneously, we were concerned that the elicited imitation would be difficult to analyze due to background noise. We thus included the yes/no test, which is quick and easy to administer, and has been widely used as a general proficiency measure (Harsch & Hartig 2016).

2.7.6.1 Proficiency measure 1: Elicited imitation An elicited imitation test was selected as a general proficiency measure. This test asks participants to repeat aural sentences aloud after a time delay to encourage reconstruction of meaning, not direct imitation. The test was adapted from an extant measure that can be found on

IRIS, a digital repository for second language researchers (https://www.iris-database.org/iris/app/home/detail?id=york%3a852670&ref=search; Ortega et al. 2002) and has been normed across eight languages.

2.7.6.2 Proficiency measure 2: Yes/no test The yes/no test (Meara & Buxton 1987; see Collins & White 2011, https://www.iris-database.org/iris/app/home/detail?id=york%3a934278&ref=search for a version of this test) was chosen to provide an independent means of assessing each student's proficiency (Hasko 2013). In this vocabulary test, students have to say whether they know or do not know a word. The test includes real words (two-thirds) and pseudo-words (one-third). The target words came from Meara's X-Lex test (2005), which were drawn from the 5,000 most frequent words of English in five bands reflecting 1,000 words each. Thirty words (20 real; 10 pseudo) from each of the five 1,000-word levels were included for a total of 150 words for students to judge (Harsch & Hartig 2016). The test can be marked in a number of ways. We followed Cobb's example (personal e-mail correspondence, August 11, 2017) used on Compleat Lexical Tutor (https://www.lextutor.ca). For each real word that is identified as known, the participant receives one point. For each pseudo-word identified as known, the participant loses two points.

2.7.7 Teacher questionnaire The teacher questionnaire, containing eleven open-ended questions written in English, was included to understand the teachers' teaching philosophy in terms of types of activities used in the classroom, use of French, school board teaching requirements, and beliefs on the teaching of grammar and vocabulary. It took approximately fifteen minutes to complete and was sent via e-mail to the teachers and returned at their convenience. This questionnaire was deemed important to help interpret, if applicable, any differences found between classes.

3 Data collection

The extensive pilot testing and intensive planning allowed for the data collection to be completed with only one major problem—the elicited imitation data were largely unanalyzable. In the following paragraph, we provide detailed information about minor problems that were encountered. Two key elements to facilitate data collection of the type we were conducting are (1) having sufficient numbers of research assistants to manage the flow of tasks and students (particularly during the individual oral testing sessions), which should include an assistant whose role is to ensure student movement between classrooms and assigning students to assistants waiting for another student, and (2) budgeting sufficient amount of time to set up the equipment and materials and organize the configuration of the oral testing rooms. Given the restrictions of the students' timetables, as little as a five-minute delay in testing could mean one measure would not be given to a set of students, which in turn either leads to rescheduling (often impossible) or lost data.

Other minor problems encountered in data collection in classroom contexts merit highlighting. Public address systems are common in Quebec schools, so interruptions during in-class testing had to be managed. This was of importance during the administration of the elicited imitation as all students were closely listening to audio and then repeating. The research assistants were told to be next to the laptop so that if the address system was used, the audio recording could be stopped immediately. On occasion, the regular teacher was replaced by a substitute who was not aware of our research so it was important that all research assistants felt comfortable providing a brief summary of the research and its goals. Some teachers did not realize that they would have to teach during the oral data collection class, which demonstrated the need to better prepare teachers for the procedures in any future data collections. As we were speaking individually with students, teachers needed to teach their normal class while letting four or five students out at a time to meet with the research assistants. Finally, it is useful to let other teachers and administrative staff be aware of the testing to reduce the likelihood of interruptions, which happened during oral testing when curious teachers poked their heads round the door of the classroom in which we were working to see what was happening.

4   Data processing

After data collection, the data must be processed to create the corpus (for more information on transforming data, see Han, chapter 6, this volume). Concretely, this process includes transcription, verification, and annotation, although it is also at this time that format standards and file naming (key practices for responsible and consistent data management; see Mattern, chapter 5, this

volume) will occur (discussed in section 5 on data storage). Transcription requires the written and oral texts be rendered into a chosen format based on a set of norms. We chose to transcribe using the Codes for the Human Analysis of Transcripts (CHAT; (MacWhinney 2000), which is the transcription system of the TalkBank system (MacWhinney 2007). CHAT requires the integration of texts and tags (both in-line tags and independent tagging lines) rather than the separation of the original text and any annotation (XML format). These two differing approaches affect transcription with corpus linguists recommending separation (Sinclair 2005), while researchers using TalkBank must use the integrated approach. Our choice to use CHAT was based on recommendations in the field of second-language acquisition (Myles 2005; MacWhinney 2017a), the first author's knowledge of this transcription system, and the possibilities for automatic analyses using natural language processing steps within TalkBank.

Data processing is enormously time- and labor-intensive, which is one important argument for the field to develop a collaborative ethic and, for example, share instruments through IRIS (Marsden, Mackey, & Plonsky 2016) and share their corpora (despite valid concerns in areas such as ethical data use; see Holton, Leonard, & Pulsifer, chapter 4, this volume) and corpora representativeness for future users (Sinclair 2005). Processing oral data is particularly arduous with many transcription decisions needing to be made (Cottier, Wlodarski, & Bell 2019). However, even with written data, issues related to the interpretation of handwriting exist. It has been mentioned that written corpora are now often already word processed (Gilquin 2015), but this is likely more realistic when collecting data from adults. In our context, the only means of collecting word processed documents would have been through our providing individual laptops for all students, and it would have introduced a confound in the data.

Our transcription conventions were taken from the CHAT manual (MacWhinney 2000), which allowed us to copy the students' texts as written. However, as CHAT requires words to be spelled correctly for them to be recognized and analyzed by the Computerized Language Analysis program (MacWhinney 2017b), it was necessary to change incorrect spellings, which then required in-line annotation to ensure later analysis could be conducted transparently (i.e., it was possible to know whether a participant's word had been spelled incorrectly in their original production). It is perhaps worth noting that CHAT was originally created for oral language transcription and for L1 participants, thus orthographic representation of (non-native) sounds was less of an issue during the development phase of CHAT.

After transcription, all texts were verified by another person to ensure the reliability of transcription. Even though this step takes longer for oral data, it is also vital for written data as it is at this juncture that mistakes can be found.

5 Data storage

As discussed by Mattern (chapter 5, this volume), responsible and consistent data management practices are vital if corpora are to be considered reliable. First, we present the file-naming system employed. Then, how all the files are stored will be discussed.

We used an Excel sheet as the master list, although other open use programs or accessible formats (e.g., .csv) could be used. In accordance with the ethics protocol we followed, this sheet is the only document in which participants are fully identified. It is only accessible to the main researcher and the head research assistant whose access will end once the sheet is finalized and any data cleaning or analysis requiring names is complete.

The file-naming system was created prior to data processing to ensure consistency across files from the data set. Data from piloting were also included in this system, which explains the inclusion of files from two years of primary school students. This allows us to include the pilot data for certain analyses, although these data cannot be made available to the wider research community as ethics approval for the piloting was restricted to use by the research team only. First, a four-digit number was employed to identify the grade level: 1000: primary grade five; 2000: primary grade six; 3000: secondary grade one; 4000: secondary grade two; 5000: secondary grade three; 6000: secondary grade four; 7000: secondary grade five.

Participants within each grade level were then identified using a number, which was integrated into the four-digit grade level number. For example, the student identified as number 1 in secondary grade one was given the code 3001, student 2 was 3002. The data within each grade level are not identified based on class (students at each grade level came from multiple classes) as the corpora focuses on individuals in terms of grade level rather than in terms of which class they were in (this would be useful/necessary, for example, if the corpora were designed to address instructional practices). The head researcher has access to this information, but there was no reason to provide this a priori to respond to the main research objectives. As little information was collected in terms of potential class differences (apart from teachers' brief self-report about their teaching philosophy in the survey), it is unlikely the corpora will be analyzed based on class in the future.

Each measure was given a code: oral argumentative (OA), oral narrative (ON), written argumentative (WA), written narrative (WN), elicited imitation (EI), student questionnaire (Q), and teacher questionnaire (TQ).

Separate files (CHAT format) for each student were created for the four tasks that formed the corpus (OA, ON, WA, WN). Each file integrated the grade level, the student identification number, and the task. For example, 3061.OA referred to the oral argumentative text from a secondary grade one student whose identification number was 61.

As CHAT files had to be verified, we added .v to verified files. Thus, the final version for analysis would be 3061.OA.v. In hindsight, it may have been more sensible to label unverified files with a longer file name, which could then be deleted after verification (e.g., 3061.OA.u where the u stands for unverified).

After the verified files had been automatically analyzed for parts of speech, the file name had .M added to it to indicate that it had been analyzed using the MOR program in the CHILDES suite of programs.

Storage includes paper and electronic data, and many of the decisions involve following established ethics protocols. Paper copies of all the measures have been scanned to create electronic copies. The hard copies, including consent forms, are in a locked filing cabinet in the head researcher's office, as they have the participants' names on them. Electronic files are anonymous aside from one Excel sheet that acts as a master copy, which also includes the student questionnaire data and scores on the two proficiency measures. This file is only available to the head researcher and the head research assistant. Electronic files are in a variety of formats—the four transcribed oral and written texts are in .cha, the electronic copies of hard copies are in PDF, the audio files are in .wav. All electronic files are stored on two external hard drives and in the Dropbox of the head researcher. Assistants working on transcription/verification also have access through Dropbox to the files they need.

6 Data sharing

Gawne and Styles (chapter 2, this volume) discuss the centrality of openness in terms of methodological transparency and the importance of making data accessible to other researchers aside from those initially involved. Indeed, second language researchers now have a digital repository, IRIS (https://www.iris-database.org), in which instruments, materials, and data are shared and made highly searchable due to its fine-grained, domain-specific metadata (Marsden, Mackey, & Plonsky 2016). This collaborative effort has been an important step in advancing research practice and methodology.

In terms of data sharing, specifically, it is important to also share the detailed methodological steps undertaken in creating the corpus. In other words, data sharing should only occur if sufficient information is provided for researchers to understand the data in-depth (Sinclair 2005). Researchers can often contact the original researchers with queries, but this requires the secondary researchers to pose specific questions and the original researchers to be available. In reality, many methodological decisions that could affect the data will not be considered in any single study. For example, a secondary researcher may not consider whether participants contributing to the corpora were allowed to use outside resources such as dictionaries/spell-check. However, the inclusion/exclusion of external resources during the production of texts that make up the corpora should be taken into account during data analysis and interpretation to meet certain research objectives.

The data from the corpora are not finalized so are not yet ready for sharing. As previously discussed, the corpus files are in CHAT format and thus, the TalkBank regulations regarding sharing will be used. This does mean the audio files will need to be manually cut to delete the initial interactions that identify the school and the participant by name and to add a participant identification number. Even though the addition of this number to the audio file itself could be seen as superfluous (as the name of the audio file links to the relevant transcript), it is deemed necessary in case file labels are changed inadvertently,

resulting in the loss of the participant's identification number. This process will be conducted by a research assistant using an open-source program such as Audacity.

7 Conclusion

The goal of this chapter was to present pertinent information on the creation and storage of a corpus of oral and written texts from learners of ESL in compulsory schooling in Quebec, Canada. The different steps undertaken by the research team have been described to help promote understanding of corpus building and maintenance in general and with respect to contextual factors. Noteworthy for our project were the decisions and procedures that were dictated by working with intact classes in schools and child participants. Certain issues become more or less important depending on the context, and we believe our discussion highlights a number of decisions that must be taken to ensure the validity, reliability, sustainability, and usefulness of these types of data sets.

References

Bell, P., L. Collins, and E. Marsden. 2020. Building an oral and written learner corpus of a school programme: Methodological issues. In *Learner Corpus Research and Second Language Acquisition*, ed. B LeBruyn and M. Paquot, 214–242. Cambridge: Cambridge University Press.

Bell, P., and C. Payant. 2020. Designing Learner Corpora: Collection, Transcription, and Annotation. In *The Routledge Handbook of Second Language Acquisition and Corpora*, ed. N. Tracy-Ventura and M. Paquot. New York: Routledge.

Cobb, Thomas. n.d. Compleat Lexical Tutor v.8.3. https://lextutor.ca. Accessed January 29, 2019.

Collins, L., R. H. Halter, P. M. Lightbown, and N. Spada. 1999. Time and the distribution of time in L2 instruction. *TESOL Quarterly* 33 (4): 655–680. https://doi.org/10.2307/3587881.

Collins, L., and C. Muñoz. 2016. The foreign language classroom: Current perspectives and future considerations. *The Modern Language Journal* 100 (1): 133–147. https://doi.org/10.1111/modl.12305.

Collins, L., and J. White. 2011. An intensive look at intensity and language learning. *TESOL Quarterly* 45 (1): 106–133.

Cottier, D., N. Wlodarski, and P. Bell. 2019. The impact of methodological decisions in transcribing written data on research findings. Paper presented at the American Association of Applied Linguistics Conference, Atlanta, March 9–12.

Gilquin, G. 2015. From design to collection of learner corpora. In *The Cambridge Handbook of Learner Corpus Research*, ed. S. Granger, G. Gilquin, and F. Meunier, 9–34. Cambridge: Cambridge University Press. https://doi.org/10.1017/CBO9781139649414.002.

Harsch, C., and J. Hartig. 2016. Comparing C-tests and yes/no vocabulary size tests as predictors of receptive language skills. *Language Testing* 33 (4): 555–575.

Hasko, V. 2013. Capturing the dynamics of second language development via learner corpus research: A very long engagement. *The Modern Language Journal* 97 (S1): 1–10. https://doi.org/10.1111/j.1540-4781.2012.01425.x.

MacWhinney, B. 2000. *The CHILDES Project: Tools for Analyzing Talk.* 3rd ed. Mahwah, NJ: Lawrence Erlbaum Associates.

MacWhinney, B. 2007. The TalkBank Project. In *Creating and Digitizing Language Corpora: Synchronic Databases,* vol. 1, ed. J. C. Beal, K. P. Corrigan, and H. L. Moisl, 163–180. Houndmills: Palgrave-Macmillan.

MacWhinney, B. 2017a. A shared platform for studying second language acquisition. *Language Learning* 67 (S1): 254–275.

MacWhinney, B. 2017b. Tools for analyzing talk, part 2: The CLAN Program. https://childes.talkbank.org/. PDF document downloaded May 2, 2017.

Marsden, E. 2019. Methodological transparency and its consequences for the scope and quality of research. In *Routledge Handbook of Research Methods in Applied Linguistics*, ed. J. McKinley and H. Rose, 15–28. New York: Routledge.

Marsden, E., A. Mackey, and L. Plonsky. 2016. The IRIS Repository: Advancing research practice and methodology. In *Advancing Methodology and Practice: The IRIS Repository of Instruments for Research into Second Languages,* ed. A. Mackey and E. Marsden, 1–21. New York: Routledge.

McDonough, K., and P. Trofimovich. 2008. *Using Priming Methods in Second Language Research.* New York: Routledge.

Meara, P. M. 2005. *X_Lex: The Swansea Vocabulary Levels Test.* Version 2.05. Swansea, UK: Lognostics.

Meara, P., and B. Buxton. 1987. An alternative to multiple choice vocabulary tests. *Language Testing* 4 (2): 142–154.

Meyer, M. 1969. *Frog, Where Are You?* New York: Dial Press.

Myles, F. 2005. Review article: Interlanguage corpora and second language acquisition research. *Second Language Research* 21 (4): 373–391.

Ortega, L. 2003. Syntactic complexity measures and their relationship to L2 proficiency: A research synthesis of college-level L2 writing. *Applied Linguistics* 24 (4): 492–518.

Ortega, L., N. Iwashita, J. M. Norris, and S. Rabie. 2002. An investigation of elicited imitation tasks in crosslinguistic SLA research. Paper presented at the Second Language Research Forum, Toronto, October 3–6.

Sinclair, J. 2005. Corpus and text: Basic principles. In *Developing Linguistic Corpora: A Guide to Good Practice*, ed. M. Wynne, 1–16. Oxford: Oxbow.

Thewissen, J. 2013. Capturing L2 accuracy developmental patterns: Insights from an error-tagged EFL learner corpus. *The Modern Language Journal* 97 (S1): 77–101.

34 Managing Second Language Acquisition Data with Natural Language Processing Tools

Scott A. Crossley and Kristopher Kyle

1 Introduction

Second language (L2) data in the form of learner corpora are linguistically untidy when compared to the majority of language data corpora because L2 corpora are rife with grammatical errors, neologisms and borrowed terms, unique phrasal items, misspellings, punctuation problems, and ill-formed syntactic constructions. Nonetheless, much of second language acquisition (SLA) research investigates patterns of learning within large learner corpora that may be composed of either naturalistic or elicited language production. Working with L2 learner corpora introduces unique sets of qualifiers and limitations that may not exist in more standardized data sets (such as first-language production samples). Thus, the management of L2 data requires specific insight to avoid potential pitfalls that may make data analyses less robust, leading to erroneous conclusions. This becomes even more important when researchers rely on natural language processing (NLP) tools to automatically assess the content of L2 learner corpora because these NLP tools process language literally without knowledge of text content, learner background, or the data collection context.

The purpose of this chapter is to introduce proper data management techniques specific to L2 data analyses that rely on NLP tools and learner corpora. Specifically, we introduce and discuss the limitations of both NLP tools and learner corpora. We then provide details about proper data management workflow unique to L2 corpora and NLP tools (section 2). We next present a hands-on case study to guide the reader through the process of an NLP analysis of a learner corpus (section 3). We follow this with a discussion of the analysis and a guide to interpreting NLP results (section 4). We conclude with a general statement about the strengths and limitations of both NLP analyses and learner corpora (section 5).

1.1 Natural language processing

NLP encompasses all computerized approaches to analyzing language in order to measure linguistic features to better understand various features of language use (e.g., developmental trajectories, register variation). All NLP tools are computer programs that rely on a sequence of instructions that tell the program how to complete a task. NLP also requires, at some level, knowledge of language that can either be derived explicitly or implicitly. Explicit language knowledge can be provided to computer programs as databases of lexical items or rules for part-of-speech tagging. Implicit language knowledge can be derived by through neural network models that then inform NLP approaches. The strength of NLP programs is their efficiency in analyzing massive amounts of data by repeating analyses objectively and literally, something that is time consuming and difficult for humans to accomplish.

The two main purposes of NLP analyses are to better understand language and cognition (i.e., gather information on how we understand language and use language; a cognitive science approach) or to respond appropriately to humans using natural language (i.e., an artificial intelligence approach). For example, researchers may want to study the quality and the content of L2 writers' essays longitudinally to better understand L2 writing development. Alternatively, researchers may want to develop NLP algorithms to provide feedback to (L2) writers about the quality of their texts to help guide the writers through the revision process. NLP tools are generally not used in isolation and are instead mixed with statistical methods that are based on inferential techniques or machine learning algorithms based on probabilistic models to increase the reliability and validity of their output. In addition, NLP tools can be used to complement qualitative analyses by providing objective support for more nuanced examinations of language.

NLP tools can also be used to assess a number of domains within language studies, including language acquisition, reading ability, speaking proficiency, and writing development (Crossley et al. 2011; Kyle, Crossley, & Berger 2018; Crossley & McNamara 2013). NLP tools can also be used to assess the mental states of students in terms of engagement, boredom, confidence, and openness as well as individual differences related to prior knowledge, reading skills, persistence, language ability, native language used, and working memory (Allen & McNamara 2015; Allen, McNamara, & McCrudden 2015; Allen, Mills, et al. 2016; Allen, Perret, & McNamara 2016; Crossley & McNamara 2012; Crossley, Salsbury, & McNamara 2012). Beyond assessing student and learning development and characteristics, NLP has many other educational applications, including but not limited to, assessing text readability, predicting math proficiency, categorizing text disciplines and registers, and predicting task types (Biber 1988; Biber & Conrad 2009; Crossley et al. 2018; Crossley, Skalicky, et al. 2017; Crossley, Russell, et al. 2017; Guo, Crossley, & McNamara 2013; Kyle & Crossley 2016).

There are a number of freely available NLP tools that have been developed recently to help non-specialists conduct NLP analyses (Crossley, Kyle, & Dascalu 2018; Kyle & Crossley 2017; Kyle, Crossley, & Berger 2018). Most of these are in English, but some tools are multilingual (MacWhinney 2014; Dascalu et al. 2015). Linguistically, the tools can provide information about text cohesion, lexical attributes of a text, syntactic complexity metrics, and emotion and affective features. In turn, these features can be used to better understand L2 production in learner corpora.

1.2 Learner corpora

Learner corpora are electronic collections of spoken, signed, and/or written language produced by individuals who are learning a particular second (third or fourth, and so on) language. Learner corpora vary widely in their characteristics and in the metadata available. Learner corpora are often characterized by the nature of the data collection (e.g., natural conversations, semistructured interviews, timed production tasks), the particular L2(s)

that are represented, the first-language (L1) group(s) that are included, and the types of metadata included (production quality scores, standardized proficiency scores, age, gender, educational settings, time spent learning the L2). Furthermore, learner corpora are distinguished with regard to whether the data are cross-sectional or longitudinal in nature. Given the difficulty in collecting longitudinal data (e.g., attrition), most learner corpora are cross-sectional in nature, though a number of longitudinal corpora have been recently made available (e.g., LANGSNAP [Languages and Social Networks Abroad Project]; Tracy-Ventura et al. 2016). Cross-sectional and quasi-longitudinal corpora allow researchers to examine trends across (usually a large number of) learners of different proficiency levels. These corpora help researchers create and refine assessment criteria, set learning benchmarks, and discover potential developmental trends. Longitudinal corpora, which are usually much smaller due to participant recruitment and attrition issues, allow researchers to examine the actual developmental trajectories of language learners. These trajectories can be non-linear (Verspoor et al. 2017), which cannot be captured in cross-sectional and quasi-longitudinal corpora, demonstrating their limits.

2 SLA data management workflow

2.1 Corpus collection

Most SLA NLP analyses depend on the use of learner corpora. These corpora form the foundation for NLP analyses and need to be developed and/or selected carefully and conscientiously. Mistakes in collecting wide enough corpus parameters, specifically metadata, can prove extremely problematic to interpretations of results. Some elements that need to be controlled for when collecting and/or analyzing learner corpora are L1 influence, age-related variables, gender, proficiency level, task, prompts and topics, and parallelisms between corpora that are combined in analyses.

Some analyses will require research to control for L1 influence. This will be the case when a corpus includes data from speakers of multiple L1s. Researchers can use a corpus that is composed of L2 users from the same L1. However, such an approach will not allow for findings to be generalized beyond the L1 represented in the corpus, which will limit any interpretations of the data. If multiple L1s are represented in a corpus, researchers have a few options. First, a corpus or a subcorpus of a larger corpus can be analyzed wherein the participants speak similar languages within a larger language family. This would allow for some generalizability of the findings beyond a single language group. However, the best approach is to use a corpus that affords representation from a variety of L1s and not a subsection of that corpus or corpus that represents only a single L1 background. Using a corpus that includes multiple L1s allows for greater generalizability of findings and can be robust if principled statistical analyses are used to factor in crosslinguistic influence of the L1s. For instance, the L1 of a participant can be included as a categorical fixed effect in mixed-model analyses, or a continuous variable such as linguistic distance can be used (Chiswick & Miller 2005).

Age is another important factor to consider when using NLP tools on learner corpora. Much research has demonstrated differences in L2 performance based on the age at which individuals began learning a particular L2 (referred to as age of onset; Abrahamsson & Hyltenstam 2009; Hyltenstam & Abrahamsson 2003). While it is feasible to analyze a corpus that contains participants of the same age of onset and even potentially the same learning experience background, it is unlikely. A robust learner corpus will contain this metadata for all participants such that researchers can control for age-related effects in mixed-effects models.

The most important variable to control for in a corpus (and one that likely supersedes data on L1 or age-related variables) is L2 language proficiency. A large body of research has indicated that the language produced by L2 users varies greatly by proficiency (Kyle & Crossley 2015, 2017; Lu 2011; Laufer & Nation 1995). In the absence of proficiency level information, it is difficult to interpret findings from NLP tools.

Beyond controlling for individual differences such as L1, age-related variables, and proficiency, NLP analyses need to carefully control for context. The two most obvious contextual factors are the task and the topic, both of which can exert influence on language production (Biber & Gray 2013; Kyle & Crossley 2016; Kyle, Crossley, & McNamara 2016). In terms of task, a good example is the difference in linguistic output that occurs between independent tasks that require participants to rely on existing knowledge or integrated tasks that require participants to incorporate information from outside sources. Multiple studies have shown that these two tasks produce different linguistic output from participants (Guo, Crossley, & McNamara 2013; Kyle & Crossley 2016). If task is not controlled for, interpretation of results may be problematic. Similarly, topic can exert a strong influence on linguistic production with many studies indicating that the formality of the topic or the difficulty of the topic matter can lead to different types of linguistic production (Biber & Gray 2013; Hinkel 2009). In some cases, researchers will focus on a single task with a single topic, but this limits the generalizability of findings. It is best to control for task and topic in statistical analyses.

Another key consideration is parallelism in corpora. Often, researchers will combine corpora to develop as large a sample as possible to better reflect L2 learning. While this is not problematic on its own, and, in fact, can be good practice, researchers need to ensure that combined corpora are comparable (Sinclair 2005). In addition, often researchers will have to select which reference corpus in a specific NLP tool they want to use to best match the corpora at hand. That is to say, there are many instantiations for NLP indices based on different corpora and researchers need to select the appropriate corpus for their analysis. For instance, if a researcher is interested in examining lexical growth in classroom writing in terms of word frequency, the reference corpus used to develop the frequency measure is an important consideration. If the class is an English for Academic Purposes class, it would be best to use frequency counts from an academic corpus. However, an academic corpus may not be appropriate for a class that focuses on journal writing or narrative writing.

2.2 Corpus preprocessing

Once a corpus has been rigorously developed and/or selected, a number of preprocessing decisions need to be made. Chief among these are decisions about text formatting, text cleaning, and spelling correction. In terms of text formatting, most NLP analyses need to be conducted on texts that are in plain text formats (e.g., .txt). Plain text formats contain no special formatting (e.g., images, objects, and other elements such as headings, footnotes, or special font characteristics) and, as such, preserve the basic linguistic information in the text in a format that is machine-readable.

Researchers also need to make decisions about cleaning texts of unneeded and unwanted information. For instance, many times during transcription, text conversion, or when text files are switched between operating systems, a number of opportunities for non-Unicode characters to permeate texts occur. These characters will cause difficulties for many NLP tools because they will not recognize the characters, possibly causing the tools to shut down. Researchers need to carefully examine a percentage of texts to make sure they only include Unicode characters. In addition to non-Unicode characters, researchers need to make principled decisions about the inclusion or exclusion of disfluencies (i.e., false starts, attention signals, word repetition, and filler words). Such disfluencies are common in speech and NLP tools will process them regardless of structural concerns. However, the inclusion of disfluencies could strongly influence outcomes, especially lexical outcomes. If L2 learners use "yea" or "okay" to signal that they are paying attention, an NLP tool will assume the learner is using very frequent words more often, even though these words may not represent actual production. The same may be true if false starts are included or filler terms such as "you know," "I mean," or "like" are included.

Lastly, researchers need to make a principled decision about spell-correcting L2 data (specifically written data). L2 written data is rife with spelling errors and these errors may not represent wider language knowledge, but only knowledge of spelling conventions. However, they do represent actual production and researchers may want to maintain the independence of the data. Problems also arise with spelling correction at the conceptual and practical levels. Conceptually, it may be difficult to accurately fix all misspellings because of context. Additionally, many L2 learners may use words from their L1 (either cognates or non-cognates) and it will not be clear to researchers which words represent actual production and which ones are guesses, estimates, or non-words. Practically, when dealing with large data sets, it is difficult to spell-correct texts without the aid of computer code. While spelling correction engines exist or can be programmed for specific purposes, they will likely be less accurate than human judgments.

2.3 Text processing

Once the corpora have been selected or developed and preprocessed, the easy part of using NLP tools comes into play: the actual text processing. Many NLP tools are extremely user-friendly, while some require a certain amount of familiarity with computer science or fluency in a computer science language. For the purposes of this chapter, we introduce the readers to the Suite of Automatic Linguistic Analysis Tools (SALAT) developed by the authors of this chapter.

SALAT contains freely available desktop tools that work on Windows, Mac OSX, and (in many cases) Linux operating systems. They allow users to process large numbers of texts in a (relatively) short period of time. All texts must be formatted in ASCII or eight-bit Unicode transformation format and saved as plain text (.txt) files to preserve Unicode formatting. The tools provide different processing options, but generally allow users to select specific indices (e.g., content word frequency) or index categories (e.g., clausal complexity). After index selection has been completed, the user indicates where the desired files to process are located, selects a name and location for the output file(s) (i.e., where the results of the analyses will be written), and presses the Process Texts button. The internal processes of each tool differ somewhat, but generally speaking each text is lemmatized, tagged for part of speech, and possibly parsed using Stanford CoreNLP (Manning et al. 2014). The processed texts are then analyzed using Python scripts that either look up each item of interest (e.g., word, *n*-gram, or syntactic structure) in a database (e.g., of word naming response times) or conduct a formal analysis (e.g., number of words per clause) and provide average scores for each text. After the program has processed each text, values are written to a machine (and human) readable output file in .csv format. Users can then analyze their data in other programs such as R.

2.4 Text length

Once the tools are processed through the NLP tools, it is likely that the length of each text will become available. The length of a text needed for robust NLP analyses is difficult to pin down because the number of words needed to provide an accurate profile of a learner's language skills is an open question. A common rule of thumb is that texts should be long enough to provide enough linguistic coverage to accurately portray the linguistic knowledge of the person that produced that text. However, the exact number of words needed is unknown and may fluctuate among learners and contexts. Little work in this vein has been conducted in L2 learner research. Work in educational sciences and other fields indicates that language analyses benefit from longer text samples

(Allen, Snow, & McNamara 2015; Crossley 2018; Varner et al. 2013; Vyas & Uma 2018; Young et al. 2018; Zhang, Huang, & Zhao 2018) because longer texts provide stronger and more reliable NLP results that better represent language profiles. Of the studies conducted using NLP tools with L2 learner data, an agreed upon threshold seems to be around one hundred words in order to support reliable results (Crossley et al. 2011; Crossley & McNamara 2013).

2.5 Data organization

One problem with many NLP tools is that their output can be overwhelming. For instance, Tool for the Automatic Analysis of Lexical Sophistication (TAALES) will produce a spreadsheet that may have over five hundred columns for every text for which it calculates features. Many of the features calculated may not be of interest to the user and many may be redundant. Thus, it is generally a good idea to preselect indices of interest that will help address the research questions in a study. Preselecting indices will help control the number of features in a spreadsheet and will also help control for type 1 errors in one's statistical analysis (Larson-Hall 2015).

It is generally recommended to put data in the format that best answers a particular research question. For instance, a long (or narrow) format comprises a column that contains the context of the values found in another column containing the values of interest. Long formats may contain multiple variable types in a single column. Most L2 NLP data are best fit into wide formats wherein each column represents an NLP feature of interest and each row represents a text from which those data were collected.

Data can also be represented in various file types, the most common being comma separated values (.csv) and Excel files. In practice, it is easier to use .csv files to store data because they are more easily accessible to statistical and machine learning programs. For instance, R (R Core Team 2014) will read .csv files quite easily while Excel files need more manipulation. As well, machine learning packages such as WEKA (Frank, Hall, & Witten 2016) will also read .csv files (but not Excel files).

2.6 Statistical analysis

Once the data from the NLP tools is suitably organized, analyses of the data can begin. Because researchers will likely be looking at thousands of data points and each

point is represented by an incidence or ratio score, statistical or machine learning approaches are required. In addition, with such large samples, there are a number of statistical concerns that must be addressed including normality of data, multicollinearity of the data (i.e., when various features measure the same construct), overfitting, and suppression effects (for more information, see Field 2013).

While normality of the data is not an assumption in all analyses, it is important to examine the incidences of zero features found in a text. While not common, it is possible that some features measured by an NLP tool will not be found in texts and these texts will report a zero for that feature. As an example, consider the argument overlap features reported in Tool for the Automatic Analysis of Cohesion. A researcher interested in overlap between paragraphs (i.e., global cohesion) in L2 writing may find that many students don't produce writing samples that contain more than one paragraph. In these cases, the tool will report zeroes for paragraph argument overlap. While this may not affect statistical analyses, it will make generalizations to new data or new tasks problematic. A similar concern can be found with the academic word sublists found in TAALES. In some instances, the words in these lists may not occur in L2 data either because of the rarity of the words or the shortness of the L2 texts. If data are non-normally distributed, certain statistical and machine learning approaches cannot be used and alternatives will have to be used. Researchers may also decide to remove these features because they do not accurately represent learners' language profiles.

With hundreds of variables reported by NLP tools and many variables being conceptually redundant (e.g., multiple frequency features), researchers have to be careful not to include similar variables. The easiest solution to this problem is to control for multicollinearity among variables, which can be done with simple correlational analyses. Generally, multicollinearity is set at $r \geq .700$ or researchers use variance inflation values below 5 (Field 2013). These thresholds ensure that variables are not strongly correlated, but allows similar variables to be included (i.e., lexical variables such as concreteness and frequency, which measure different lexical constructs, will be included).

Overfitting may also be a problem in certain contexts. Briefly, overfitting occurs when a statistical model (e.g., a linear regression) attempts to use all variables to predict an outcome regardless of whether the derived model predicts future observations. Simply put, the regression model will force unwarranted variables to fit the data and explain a greater amount of variation regardless of whether the variation explained represents the model or represents statistical noise. Because NLP tools calculate hundreds of variables, researchers may try to incorporate all of them into a model for a relatively small corpus, producing a model that contains more variables/parameters than are justified. A general rule of thumb is that researchers should include one variable for every fifteen items (see, e.g., Tabachnick & Fidell 2013). Thus, if your learner corpus contains samples from three hundred learners and the outcome variable is learner level, the researcher should limit the number of NLP features to twenty (i.e., one variable for every fifteen items in the analysis).

Researchers need to also be careful with including variables that show flipped signs (i.e., suppression effects) in statistical models. A statistical model may include a variable that raises the amount of variance explained because it accounts for residual variance left over after other variables have been added. It is possible that the residual variance explained by this variable is not due to its association with the dependent variable (in this case writing quality score), which can often be seen because of flipped signs between the correlation of the variable on its own and within a model. For example, when examining links between L2 writing quality and lexical variables, it is likely that frequency will negatively correlate with quality such that more frequent words are found in lower quality writing samples. However, if frequency is added into the model late, perhaps after other lexical variables have been added such as concreteness, the reported co-efficient may be positive instead of the expected negative seen in the initial correlation. This is a strong indicator that there is a suppression effect in which case the frequency variable should be removed. To control for suppression effects, researchers should check initial statistical patterns (e.g., correlations, t-tests, or ANOVAs) between the independent variables and the dependent variables in isolation to the patterns reported in statistical models.

3 Case study

3.1 Data

As a case study, we present an examination of L2 lexical development over the course of a semester of study. The data in this case study has been previously used in two other studies examining lexical development in terms of word concreteness, familiarity, meaningfulness, age of acquisition (Crossley & Skalicky 2019) and word frequency (Crossley et al. 2019). In this case study, we examine lexical development in terms of word-naming times for words produced by L2 learners during naturalistic oral output with both English L1 and L2 users. The users included 50 non-matriculated L2 English learners enrolled in an intensive English program. These 50 intensive English program students conversed with 50 matriculated L1 and L2 speaking students (25 L1 and 25 L2) enrolled in undergraduate- and graduate-level TESOL courses over the course of a semester. The L2 students were recorded at minimum twice during the semester and at maximum four times. More information about these data can be found in Crossley and Skalicky (2019) and Crossley et al. (2019).

We specifically use these data because they afford control for a number of demographic, task, and individual differences in the learners as we have discussed. These include distance from the users' L1s to English using a language distance measure (Chiswick & Miller 2005) to control for potential crosslinguistic influence as well as age, gender, L2 proficiency level (as measured by standardized language assessment tests), order of data collection session, and whether the interlocutor was an L1 or L2 user.

3.2 Word-naming index

The word-naming norms used in this study were derived from a standard psychological task for measuring word recognition. In word-naming tasks, participants are presented with an orthographic word that they then must name aloud. The time it takes for the participant to begin pronouncing the word is measured as the response time. The word-naming response times used in this case study were derived from the English Lexicon Project, a large publicly available behavioral and descriptive data set (Balota et al. 2007). This data set includes word-naming response norms from 816 participants, with 2,500 per participant for the word-naming tasks. In total, response times were calculated for 40,481 words. All participants were native English users. Previous research has demonstrated that L2 learners produce words that are named more quickly over time and that learners rated as more lexically proficient by human raters produced words that are named more slowly (Berger, Crossley, & Kyle 2019).

However, this previous research did not control for demographics, individual differences, or task features.

3.3 Statistical analysis

We used linear mixed-effects models in R (R Core Team 2014) using the lme4 package (Bates et al. 2015) to examine any potential for changes in word-naming response times over time. The model tested whether any independent variables significantly predicted changes in word-naming response times (i.e., the dependent variable). In the model, we entered age, gender (female or male), language distance, English proficiency (advanced, high intermediate, low intermediate, or high beginning), session order (1–4), and pair language match (i.e., L1/L2 or L2/L2) as predictor variables (i.e., fixed effects).

The baselines comparison for our proficiency variable was advanced. Baseline for gender was female and baseline for pair language match was L2/L2. We also included subjects as random effects as well as a random slope of session order fit to participants. Lastly, within the model, we fitted an interaction between session order and English proficiency to measure whether English proficiency influenced word frequency production over time. We used lmerTest (Kuznetsova, Brockhoff, & Christensen 2017) to derive p values from the models, multcomp (Hothorn, Bretz, & Westfall 2008) to obtain full pairwise comparisons between the four proficiency levels (advanced, high intermediate, low intermediate, and high beginner), the effects package to retrieve model information for our figures, and the MuMIn package (Nakagawa & Schielzeth 2013) to obtain two measures

of variance explained: marginal R^2, which measures the variance explained by the fixed effects only, and conditional R^2, which measures the variance explained by both the fixed and random effects.

4 Results

The linear mixed-effects model reported a significant main effect for age, and a significant interaction between English proficiency (high intermediate learners compared to advanced learners) and session order. In the case of the interaction, the high intermediate participants' word-naming response times for the words they produced was significantly lower during earlier sessions when compared to advanced participants, but then increased significantly as session order increased. This interaction is visualized in figure 34.1. This model reported a marginal R^2 of .281 and a conditional R^2 of .393. Table 34.1 displays the estimates, standard errors, t values, and p values for the fixed effects entered into this model.

5 Discussion and conclusion

We present an overview of how data derived from NLP tools are best managed and provide a sample analysis to highlight the overview. The sample analysis follows the suggestions in the overview by examining a longitudinal learner corpus in terms of lexical development while controlling for a number of variables known to interact with linguistic features including age, gender, language proficiency, and L1 considerations. The findings from

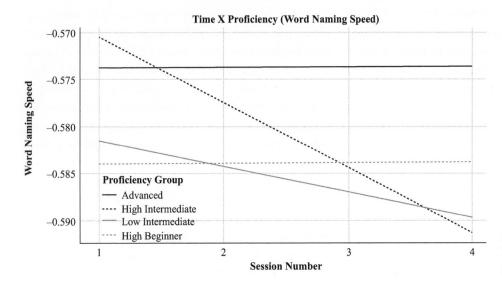

Figure 34.1

Interaction between proficiency and session order.

Table 34.1

Linear mixed-effects model predicting word-naming response times

Fixed effects	Estimate	Standard error	t	p
(Intercept)	−0.602	0.009	−65.181	<.001
Sex: male	0.002	0.004	0.599	.552
Match: L1-L2	−0.005	0.004	−1.124	.267
Age	0.001	0.000	5.649	<.001
Proficiency				
High intermediate	0.010	0.010	1.057	.294
Low intermediate	−0.005	0.009	−0.582	.563
High beginning	−0.010	0.011	−0.932	.354
Session order	0.000	0.002	0.015	.988
Language distance	−0.003	0.004	−0.914	.365
Proficiency × session order interaction				
High intermediate	−0.007	0.003	−2.143	<.050
Low intermediate	−0.003	0.003	−0.949	.345
High beginning	0.000	0.004	0.006	.995

Baselines for categorical variables are as follows: sex = female; match = L2-L2; proficiency = advanced.

the sample analysis indicate that L2 learners show a significant interaction with time and proficiency such that high intermediate learners show significant decreases in word-naming speed across time while learners from other proficiency levels do not. Age was also a significant predictor, indicating that older participants produced words with higher word-naming times. In total, the analysis indicates that older participants produce more sophisticated words and that high intermediate learners show a trend toward producing less sophisticated words over time when compared to other proficiency level learners.

This simple case study demonstrates some of the strengths of using NLP tools to examine SLA data. First and foremost, the measures reported by the NLP tool are objective and are calculated similarly across learners. This provides credibility to the study in terms of reproducibility (i.e., the ability to reproduce this analysis) and replication (i.e., the ability to reproduce this study using new data following similar research methods). Concerns about subjective rating scales, differences in material designs, and human coding are mitigated by NLP tools' intrinsic designs. In addition, the measures reported by NLP tools are generally transparent. The word-naming scores used in this study can be traced back to the original data set released by Balota et al. (2007), which provides extensive information about the collection techniques (although this is not always the case). In addition, a tool such as TAALES provides additional information to ensure greater transparency including output that shows word-naming scores for each individual word and percentage of words in each text that have word-naming scores. Lastly, the website that supports the tool (linguisticanalysistools.org) provides supplementary information related to how the indices are calculated.

There are limitations to using NLP tools for SLA analyses. Among these are depth of features reported by NLP tools; the production of words, phrases, or structures not recognized by an NLP tool; and the breadth of indices available. From a depth perspective, it should be noted that NLP tools often only measure surface level features of text (though there are many exceptions) and the tools do not have the capability to measure the context in which words are used and whether the language structures produced are appropriate for the discourse at hand. Thus, while NLP tools can measure many linguistic features, they cannot assess features related to style, strength of argumentation, effect on interlocutor, or other contextual variables. NLP tools often rely on databases that provide the linguistic knowledge needed to analyze a text. If the database does not contain the words or structures produced by the participant, it may not be possible to present a fully accurate linguistic profile. In the case of L2 learners, this is especially true because L2 student data may contain neologisms, unique phrasal combinations, or uncommon syntactic and grammatical constructions.

These data may not be captured by NLP tools. Another problem with NLP tools is the sheer breadth of features they produce, which may overwhelm researchers. For instance, TAALES reports over 150 frequency features each with their own specific calculations, domains, and dictionaries. Without experience, researchers may select incorrect frequency features that do not match their research questions. In many cases, the NLP tools in SALAT contain component scores developed using statistical analysis that convert related indices into linearly uncorrelated, aggregated variables. For instance, Kim, Crossley, and Kyle (2018) combined hundreds of lexical indices into twelve core lexical components that are available in the newest version of TAALES. These and similar component scores can help researchers narrow down the number of features they analyze.

References

Abrahamsson, N., and K. Hyltenstam. 2009. Age of onset and nativelikeness in a second language: Listener perception versus linguistic scrutiny. *Language Learning* 59:249–306.

Allen, L. K., and D. S. McNamara. 2015. Promoting self-regulated learning in an intelligent tutoring system for writing. In *AIED 2015: Artificial Intelligence in Education*, ed. C. Conati, N. Heffernan, A. Mitrovic, and M. Verdejo. Lecture Notes in Computer Science, vol. 9112. Cham: Springer. https://doi.org/10.1007/978-3-319-19773-9_125.

Allen, L. K., D. S. McNamara, and M. T. McCrudden. 2015. Change your mind: Investigating the effects of self-explanation in the resolution of misconceptions. In *Proceedings of the 37th Annual Meeting of the Cognitive Science Society*, ed. D. C. Noelle, R. Dale, A. S. Warlaumont, J. Yoshimi, T. Matlock, C. D. Jennings, and P. Maglio. Austin, TX: Cognitive Science Society.

Allen, L. K., C. Mills, M. E. Jacovina, S. A. Crossley, S. K. D'Mello, and D. S. McNamara. 2016. Investigating boredom and engagement during writing using multiple sources of information: The essay, the writer, and keystrokes. In *Proceedings of the 6th International Learning Analytics and Knowledge (LAK) Conference*, 114–123. https://doi.org/10.1145/2883851.2883939.

Allen, L. K., C. Perret, and D. S. McNamara. 2016. Linguistic signatures of cognitive processes during writing. In *Proceedings of the 38th Annual Meeting of the Cognitive Science Society*, ed. J. Trueswell, A. Papafragou, D. Grodner, and D. Mirman, 2483–2488. Philadelphia: Cognitive Science Society.

Allen, L. K., E. L. Snow, and D. S. McNamara. 2015. Are you reading my mind? Modeling students' reading comprehension skills with natural language processing techniques. In *Proceedings of the 5th International Conference on Learning Analytics and Knowledge*, ed. P. Blikstein, A. Merceron, and G. Siemens, 246–254. New York: Association for Computing Machinery.

Balota, D. A., M. J. Yap, M. J. Cortese, K. A. Hutchison, B. Kessler, B. Loftis, J. H. Neely, et al. 2007. The English Lexicon Project. *Behavior Research Methods* 39 (3): 445–459.

Bates, D., M. Maechler, B. Bolker, and S. Walker. 2015. Fitting linear mixed-effects models using lme4. *Journal of Statistical Software* 67 (1): 1–48.

Berger, C. M., S. Crossley, and K. Kyle. 2019. Using native-speaker psycholinguistic norms to predict lexical proficiency and development in second-language production. *Applied Linguistics* 40 (1): 22–42.

Biber, D. 1988. *Variation across Speech and Writing*. Cambridge: Cambridge University Press.

Biber, D., and S. Conrad. 2009. *Register, Genre, and Style*. Cambridge: Cambridge University Press.

Biber, D., and B. Gray. 2013. *Discourse Characteristics of Writing and Speaking Task Types on the TOEFL iBT Test: A Lexico-grammatical Analysis*. TOEFL iBT Research Report 19. Princeton, NJ: Educational Testing Service.

Chiswick, B. R., and P. W. Miller. 2005. Linguistic distance: A quantitative measure of the distance between English and other languages. *Journal of Multilingual and Multicultural Development* 26 (1): 1–11.

Crossley, S. A. 2018. How many words needed? Using natural language processing tools in educational data mining. In *Proceedings of the 10th International Conference on Educational Data Mining*, 630–633.

Crossley, S. A., K. Kyle, and M. Dascalu. 2018. The Tool for the Automatic Analysis of Cohesion 2.0: Integrating semantic similarity and text overlap. *Behavior Research Methods* 51:1–14.

Crossley, S. A., and D. S. McNamara. 2012. Detecting the first language of second language writers using automated indices of cohesion, lexical sophistication, syntactic complexity, and conceptual knowledge. In *Approaching Language Transfer through Text Classification: Explorations in the Detection-Based Approach*, ed. S. Jarvis and S. A. Crossley, 106–126. Bristol, UK: Multilingual Matters.

Crossley, S. A., and D. S. McNamara. 2013. Applications of text analysis tools for spoken response grading. *Language Learning and Technology* 17 (2): 171–192.

Crossley, S. A., J. Ocumpaugh, M. Labrum, F. Bradfield, M. Dascalu, and R. Baker. 2018. Modeling math identity and math success through sentiment analysis and linguistic features. In *Proceedings of the 11th International Conference on Educational Data Mining*, ed. K. E. Boyer and M. Yudelson, 11–20. International Educational Data Mining Society.

Crossley, S. A., D. Russell, K. Kyle, and U. Römer. 2017. Applying natural language processing tools to a student academic writing corpus: How large are disciplinary differences across science and engineering fields? *Journal of Writing Analytics* 1:48–81.

Crossley, S. A., T. Salsbury, and D. S. McNamara. 2012. Predicting the proficiency level of language learners using lexical indices. *Language Testing* 29 (2): 243–263.

Crossley, S. A., T. Salsbury, D. S. McNamara, and S. Jarvis. 2011. What is lexical proficiency? Some answers from computational models of speech data. *TESOL Quarterly* 45 (1): 182–193.

Crossley, S. A., and S. Skalicky. 2019. Examining lexical development in second language learners: An approximate replication of Salsbury, Crossley, and McNamara (2011). *Language Teaching* 52 (3): 385–405.

Crossley, S. A., S. Skalicky, M. Dascalu, D. McNamara, and K. Kyle. 2017. Predicting text comprehension, processing, and familiarity in adult readers: New approaches to readability formulas. *Discourse Processes* 54 (5–6): 340–359.

Crossley, S. A., S. Skalicky, K. Kyle, and K. Monteiro. 2019. Absolute frequency effects in second language lexical acquisition. *Studies in Second Language Acquisition* 41 (4): 721–744.

Dascalu, M., S. Trausan-Matu, D. S. McNamara, and P. Dessus. 2015. ReaderBench—Automated evaluation of collaboration based on cohesion and dialogism. *International Journal of Computer-Supported Collaborative Learning* 10 (4): 395–423.

Field, A. 2013. *Discovering Statistics Using IBM SPSS Statistics*. Thousand Oaks, CA: Sage.

Frank, E., M. A. Hall, and I. H. Witten. 2016. The WEKA workbench. Online appendix for *Data Mining: Practical Machine Learning Tools and Techniques*. 4th ed. Burlington, MA: Morgan Kaufmann.

Guo, L., S. A. Crossley, and D. S. McNamara. 2013. Predicting human judgments of essay quality in both integrated and independent second language writing samples: A comparison study. *Assessing Writing* 18 (3): 218–238.

Hinkel, E. 2009. The effects of essay topics on modal verb uses in L1 and L2 academic writing. *Journal of Pragmatics* 41 (4): 667–683.

Hothorn, T., F. Bretz, and P. Westfall. 2008. Simultaneous inference in general parametric models. *Biometrical Journal* 50 (3): 346–363.

Hyltenstam, K., and N. Abrahamsson. 2003. Maturational constraints in SLA. In *The Handbook of Second Language Acquisition*, ed. C. Doughty and M. Long, 539–588. Malden, MA: Blackwell.

Kim, M., S. A. Crossley, and K. Kyle. 2018. Lexical sophistication as a multidimensional phenomenon: Relations to second language lexical proficiency, development, and writing quality. *Modern Language Journal* 102 (1): 120–141.

Kuznetsova, A., P. B. Brockhoff, and R. H. B. Christensen. 2017. lmerTest package: Tests in linear mixed effects models. *Journal of Statistical Software* 82 (13). doi:10.18637/jss.v082.i13.

Kyle, K., and S. A. Crossley. 2015. Automatically assessing lexical sophistication: Indices, tools, findings, and application. *TESOL Quarterly* 49 (4): 757–786.

Kyle, K., and S. A. Crossley. 2016. The relationship between lexical sophistication and independent and source-based writing. *Journal of Second Language Writing* 34:12–24.

Kyle, K., and S. A. Crossley. 2017. Assessing syntactic sophistication in L2 writing: A usage-based approach. *Language Testing* 34 (4): 513–535.

Kyle, K., S. Crossley, and C. Berger. 2018. The tool for the automatic analysis of lexical sophistication (TAALES): Version 2.0. *Behavior Research Methods* 50 (3): 1030–1046.

Kyle, K., S. A. Crossley, and D. S. McNamara. 2016. Construct validity in TOEFL iBT speaking tasks: Insights from natural language processing. *Language Testing* 33 (3): 319–340.

Larson-Hall, J. 2015. *A Guide to Doing Statistics in Second Language Research Using SPSS and R*. London: Routledge.

Laufer, B., and P. Nation. 1995. Vocabulary size and use: Lexical richness in L2 written production. *Applied Linguistics* 16:307–322.

Lu, X. 2011. A corpus-based evaluation of syntactic complexity measures as indices of college-level ESL writers' language development. *TESOL Quarterly* 45:36–62.

MacWhinney, B. 2014. *The CHILDES Project: Tools for Analyzing Talk*. Volume 2: *The Database*. New York: Psychology Press.

Manning, C. D., M. Surdeanu, J. Bauer, F. Finkel, S. J. Bethard, and D. McClosky. 2014. The Stanford CoreNLP natural language processing toolkit. In *Proceedings of the 52nd Annual Meeting of the Association for Computational Linguistics: System Demonstrations*, 55–60.

Nakagawa, S., and H. Schielzeth. 2013. A general and simple method for obtaining R^2 from generalized linear mixed-effects models. *Methods in Ecology and Evolution* 4:133–142.

R Core Team. 2014. *R: A Language and Environment for Statistical Computing*. R Foundation for Statistical Computing, Vienna, Austria. http://www.R-project.org/.

Salsbury, T., S. A. Crossley, and D. S. McNamara. 2011. Psycholinguistic word information in second language oral discourse. *Second Language Research* 27 (3): 343–360. doi: 10.1177/0267658310395851.

Sinclair, John. 2005. Corpus and text: Basic principles. In *Developing Linguistic Corpora: A Guide to Good Practice*, ed. M. Wynne, 1–16. Oxford: Oxbow Books.

Tabachnick, B. G., and L. S. Fidell. 2013. *Using Multivariate Statistics*. Boston: Pearson.

Tracy-Ventura, N., R. Mitchell, and K. McManus. 2016. The LANGSNAP longitudinal learner corpus: Design and use. In *Spanish Learner Corpus Research: State of the Art*, ed. M. Alonso Ramos, 117–142. Philadelphia: John Benjamins.

Varner, L. K., G. T. Jackson, E. L. Snow, and D. S. McNamara. 2013. Does size matter? Investigating user input at a larger bandwidth. In *Proceedings of the 26th International Florida Artificial Intelligence Research Society (FLAIRS) Conference*, ed. C. Boonthum Denecke and G. M. Youngblood, 546–549. Menlo Park, CA: AAAI Press.

Verspoor, M., W. Lowie, H. P. Chan, and L. Vahtrick. 2017. Linguistic complexity in second language development: Variability and variation at advanced stages. *Recherches en didactique des langues et des cultures. Les cahiers de l'Acedle* 14 (1): 1–27.

Vyas, V., and V. Uma. 2018. An extensive study of sentiment analysis tools and binary classification of tweets using rapid miner. *Procedia Computer Science* 125:329–335.

Young, T., D. Hazarika, S. Poria, and E. Cambria. 2018. Recent trends in deep learning based natural language processing. *IEEE Computational Intelligence Magazine* 13 (3): 55–75.

Zhang, T., M. Huang, and L. Zhao. 2018. Learning structured representation for text classification via reinforcement learning. In *Proceedings of the 32nd Association for the Advancement of Artificial Intelligence Conference*, 6053–6060.

35 Managing Data Workflows for Untrained Forced Alignment: Examples from Costa Rica, Mexico, the Cook Islands, and Vanuatu

Rolando Coto-Solano, Sally Akevai Nicholas, Brittany Hoback, and Gregorio Tiburcio Cano

1   Introduction: Why did we use untrained forced alignment?

Forced alignment is a technique to align the audio signal of a spoken utterance with its transcription, so that the boundaries between words, and even between phones,[1] can be determined automatically (Wightman & Talkin 1997). Figure 35.1 shows an example of this in Spanish, where the spectrogram of an utterance is accompanied by lines indicating the approximate temporal limits of words and individual phones within the recording. The main advantage of this technique is that it accelerates phonetic research: the algorithm can tag these boundaries approximately thirty times faster than expert humans can (Labov, Rosenfelder, & Fruehwald 2013).

Forced alignment depends on a language model that describes the spectral features that characterize each of the phones in the sample provided to the algorithm, as well as the probabilities for the occurrence of different phones and words within the language sample. These probabilities are derived from a supervised training set: annotated examples are provided to the algorithm, so that it can learn to connect spectral features to phones. Training these requires large amounts of data (e.g., twenty-five hours for the American English model in the Forced Alignment and Vowel Extraction [FAVE]-align aligner [Rosenfelder et al. 2011]). Because such large data sets are not available for most Indigenous and minority languages, a technique called *untrained* forced alignment has been devised (DiCanio et al. 2013; Strunk, Schiel, & Seifart 2014). In untrained forced alignment, the model for one language (e.g., English) is used to process the phones of a different language (e.g., Cook Islands Māori). This is possible because, even though the words for both languages are completely different, many of the phones are acoustically similar, so that bootstrapping is possible. For example, the

'm' phones in both English and Cook Islands Māori have similar spectral cues, so the English model's idea of an 'm' can also find 'm's in the Cook Islands Māori data. Many of the phones are not similar. For example, the glottal stop of Cook Islands Māori /ʔ/ has no direct equivalent in American English, French, Spanish, or other European languages with available models. However, the phones that are not available in English can be approximated. For example, the /ʔ/ stops the air flow like /t/ and /k/ do, and these similarities have been exploited to detect /ʔ/ in languages such as Triqui (DiCanio et al. 2013). These transformations allow for the use of an existing model with audio from another language, and because the model has not been explicitly trained on data from the Indigenous language, we say that this method is untrained forced alignment.

This untrained method has been fruitfully applied to languages such as Triqui from Mexico (DiCanio et al. 2013), Nikyob from Nigeria (Kempton 2017), Nambo and Matukar Panau from Papua New Guinea (Kashima et al. 2016; González et al. 2018), Australian Kriol (Jones et al. 2017, 2019), and Tongan (Johnson, Di Paolo, & Bell 2018). Research teams have also created pan-language models to take advantage of the similarities across an entire language family and pooled together the resources from these various underresourced languages to increase the size of the training set, such as the Australian language aligners in WebMAUS (Strunk, Schiel, & Seifart 2014).

On first encountering this technique, we tested and confirmed its potential to accelerate phonetic research in underresourced languages, as well as to contribute to the larger program of natural language processing (NLP). We investigated the potential of using forced alignment to create new data sets for the training of other NLP techniques, including speech recognition, automatic part-of-speech tagging, and parsing. Finally, the data

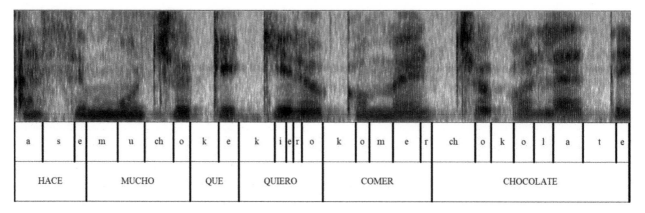

Figure 35.1
Praat (Boersma 2001) spectrogram and TextGrid with the Spanish phrase 'I've been wanting to eat chocolate for a long time,' with words and phones aligned.

sets we generated can themselves be corpora that can be used by linguists and community members for their research. As we did this, we found numerous challenges in data management given the many intermediate steps between transcriptions and completed TextGrids, and the many intermediate files generated along the way. We also faced issues with sharing the data in accordance with community principles of access and sharing.

The following sections report on these challenges. Section 2 focuses on our initial attempts and shows a 'typical' attempt to combine NLP and linguistics: disorderly and with little replicability. Think of it as a guide to how not to perform forced alignment. Section 3 reports our attempts to improve the data management flow, from collection to sharing, as well as the incorporation of consultation for the purpose of public archiving and reuse of data for language revitalization and to train other NLP applications. Section 4 focuses on software maintenance and replicability of the algorithms themselves across different platforms and users. Sections 5 and 6 present our ideas about a functional workflow for data management in forced alignment, and our recommendations for those who wish to replicate this technique.

While doing this, each section will also present six use cases of adaptation of forced alignment to six underresourced languages: Bribri, Cabécar and Malecu (Chibchan, Costa Rica), Me'phaa Váthàá (Otomanguean, Mexico), Cook Islands Māori (Austronesian, Cook Islands), and Denggan (Austronesian, Vanuatu).

Before we begin, it is useful to clarify that this is just one way of performing forced alignment, and there are in fact numerous other aligners and ways of doing

alignment. In addition to the P2FA (University of Pennsylvania Phonetics Lab Forced Aligner) algorithm (Yuan & Liberman 2008), which is used in FAVE-align (Rosenfelder et al. 2011), there are other algorithms for forced alignment, such as the Montreal Forced Aligner (McAuliffe et al. 2017), which is used in the Dartmouth Linguistic Automation, or DARLA, website (Reddy & Stanford 2015). There are also EasyAlign (Goldman 2011), Prosodylab-Aligner (Gorman, Howell, & Wagner 2011), LaBB-CAT (Fromont & Hay 2012), and the Munich Automatic Segmentation System, or MAUS (Strunk, Schiel, & Seifart 2014). Despite this wealth of options, we believe the workflow presented here represents a valid case for data management in forced alignment studies.

2 Good alignment, bad data management: Forced alignment and languages in the Americas

Our first attempt to run these algorithms on linguistic data was with languages of the Americas. We tested the feasibility of the technique by using previously existing recordings from three Chibchan languages from Costa Rica: Bribri, Cabécar, and Malecu (ISO 639-3: bzd, cjp, gut) (Coto-Solano & Flores Solórzano 2016, 2017). After that, we ran the algorithms using fieldwork-collected data from the Otomanguean language Me'phaa Váthàá (no specific ISO 639-9 code, Glottocode: zila1239) in order to study its tonal phonetics (Coto-Solano 2017).

The phonological systems of these languages have numerous elements that are different from those in European languages that could potentially pose challenges for English language models or other models based on well-resourced languages. For example, three of the languages are tonal (Bribri, Cabécar, and Me'phaa Vátháá), while Malecu has phonemic vowel length. The Chibchan languages all have liquids that don't appear in English, French, or Spanish, such as /l, r, ɾ/ for Bribri and Cabécar and /l, r, ɾ/ for Malecu. Bribri, Cabécar, and Me'phaa Vátháá have contrastive vowel nasality, and Me'phaa Vátháá has aspirated and prenasalized stops: /p, pʰ, m, ᵐb/, /t, tʰ, d, ⁿd/. Given all of these differences, we tested the performance of English and French language models to align Chibchan data (Coto-Solano & Flores Solórzano 2016), and after determining that the English model had better performance, we used it to align Me'phaa data (Coto-Solano 2017). We used a web-based interface for the aligner (Rosenfelder et al. 2011), and the performance of the algorithm was satisfactory: 8% error when aligning the center of words (i.e., the center of the word was off by 8% of the duration of the word), and 23% error when aligning the center of vowels compared to alignment made by a human expert.[2] However, after our initial publications, we found that we had a mess of files and experiments strewn all over our personal computers, with little hope of being able to replicate it without starting from scratch.

Figure 35.2 shows the workflow for generating and processing information from forced alignment algorithms.

In particular, it shows fourteen steps where files are generated, modified, or susceptible to updates and changes. These files include the source files for the recording and its transcription (steps 1 and 2), Python code to generate intermediate transformations of the data (steps 5, 8, and 9), and text files that contain those intermediate transformations (steps 3, 4, and 6). Using all of these, we generate Praat TextGrids (Boersma 2001) with the alignment of the audio and transcription (steps 7 and 11), as well as comma-separated values data sets (steps 10 and 13) that are then processed using statistical software such as R (step 14) (R Core Team 2017).

The main challenge is to transform the data into a form that can be processed by an English aligner (the *data preparation* section of figure 35.2), and then to undo those transformations so that the data are not 'deformed' by having fit it into an English language mold. Critical to this is the *glyph management*. This entails three processes: First, we have to study the way in which the alignment system expresses the phonology of English. For example, FAVE-align uses the Arpabet transcription system (Zue & Seneff 1996). *Arpabet* is an English-based phonetic alphabet that expresses a word such as 'read' using the following glyph sequence: R IY1 D. The glyphs R and D represent the phones 'r' and 'd', while the glyph IY1 represents the vowel. The number 1 represents the fact that the vowel

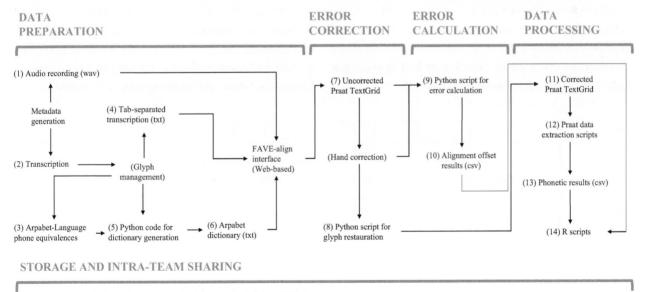

Figure 35.2
Workflow for untrained forced alignment with FAVE-align. The numbers indicate steps where data files are generated during the alignment process.

is in the stressed syllable of the word. (Arpabet also uses 0 for unstressed syllables and 2 for syllables with secondary stress). Second, in the glyph management process, we have to decide which phones of the original language correspond to which glyphs in English Arpabet, so we can express the Chibchan words in the recording using the Arpabet transcription system. For example, the Bribri phones /a/ /aɟ/, /à/ /aˈ/, and /á/ /aˈ/ only have one equivalence in English Arpabet: AE1. This means that both the words *alà* /aɟ.ˈɟaˈ/ 'child' and *alá* /aɟ.ˈɟaˈ/ 'thunder' will have the English Arpabet AE1 L AE1. (The tonal contrast between these two words is lost at this point, but it will be recovered on step 8 of figure 35.1, *glyph restoration*.) The third issue in glyph management has to do with encoding compatibility. Depending on its configuration, the aligner might be unable to process Unicode characters that appear in ELAN transcriptions (Wittenburg et al. 2006). This means that a mark such as that for nasalization, which is written with a line under the vowel (e.g., ṵ /ũɟ/ 'pot'),[3] had to be expressed in some other way in the tab-separated transcription that will become the input for the aligner. For example, the glyph {h}, which is not used in the Bribri orthography, was chosen to represent nasality, so that nasal /u/ with a high tone (ṵ́) becomes ùh in the tab-separated transcription. Python scripts deal with both problems of glyph management, creating a dictionary (steps 5 and 6) and then transforming the uncorrected TextGrids from Arpabet (AE L AE1) back to the original representation of the language (*alà*) (step 7). If the reader is interested in the specifics of how these dictionaries are structured, section 2.1 of Coto-Solano and Flores Solórzano (2017) provides a detailed explanation.

These dictionaries are used not only to instruct the aligner on the phones of our languages, but they are also used to reconstruct phonemic contrasts that were lost during the alignment process. Figure 35.3 shows TextGrid tiers for the Bribri phrase *ì kuéki wìm òr darèrè* 'why does the monkey shout so loud' (Jara Murillo & Segura 2009). Figure 35.3a shows the output of the aligner, with the glyphs still in Arpabet. Some of the phonemic distinctions of Bribri are not represented. For example, the word *ì* 'what' has a high tone oral vowel /iˈ/, whereas the final phoneme of the word *kuéki* /kwéˈkiɟ/ 'because' has a low tone nasal vowel /ĩɟ/. Despite these two being different, they are both represented by the Arpabet IY1. Figure 35.3b shows the TextGrid where the Arpabet has been replaced with the original labels for each glyph (i.e., {ì} and {ih}). These changes are effected by Python code (available in the GitHub repository https://github .com/rolandocoto/cim-aligned). This code goes through the dictionary and looks for the phones that were originally in the word. This restores any lost phonemic distinctions and leaves the TextGrid in a form that is usable for phonetic research.

A second issue in data management came with the correction of the raw results from the forced alignment (the uncorrected TextGrid in step 7 of figure 35.2). After performing the forced alignment, the resulting Praat TextGrids need to be checked and hand-corrected so that the boundaries detected by the system correspond to the actual boundaries of the phones.

This is an exacting process and is best achieved by a multiperson team with specialized knowledge in phonetics, where the team is jointly deciding on the

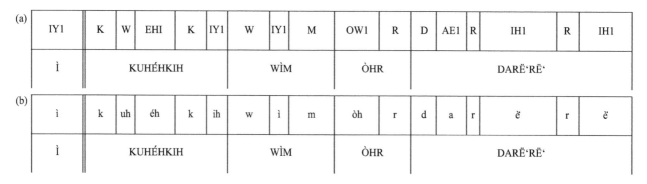

Figure 35.3
Praat TextGrid tiers with phones and words from Bribri: *ì kuéki wìm òr darèrè* 'why does the monkey shout so loud?' (a) The phone tier has Arpabet glyphs. (b) The phone tier now has the phones in a form closer to the standard spelling of Bribri, and phonemic distinctions such as tones have been reinserted into the TextGrid.

numerous issues that will arise during boundary marking. For example, phones can be phonetically combined or reduced to the point where it's difficult to neatly separate them from others (Ernestus & Warner 2011), and the correction team will need to make decisions about how to manage these reductions. This marking will have an impact on the type of data that can be extracted for research down the line.[4]

A third issue in data management was the sharing of transcriptions, recordings, and TextGrids, so that they could be accessed by all team members and backups could be kept. At this stage we used consumer-level password-controlled cloud storage (e.g., Google Docs). We used relatively simple versioning,[5] with file names indicating the latest edition of each file, and regular backups limited only to the main inputs of the alignment algorithm (source recordings and transcription: steps 1 and 2), the main outputs (the TextGrids: steps 7 and 11) and some of the code (the R scripts: step 14).

The management of the other files did not take sharing or future use into account. Much of the code that generates the intermediate data transformations was only accessible to one member of the team (the person who ran the NLP algorithm), and it was not accessible at all by other scholars. As for the dictionary, no effort was made to generate one 'large' dictionary that contained all the words from all the transcriptions. Instead of creating one large file that could serve as a main dictionary and progressively populating it with the words from each recording (so that in the future we have a dictionary like the English Carnegie Mellon University Pronouncing Dictionary), we used a minidictionary that we had to generate for each recording. Finally, the code for the aligner itself was being used from a third-party interface (Rosenfelder et al. 2011), which meant that we didn't have to access the code itself to run the program. Having a prebuilt interface made it easy to use the aligner at the time, but as we discuss in section 4, it proved to be a vulnerability once that server was taken offline.

In summary, at this point of our work, the data management of the project was haphazard. This is probably typical of other linguists using NLP tools: files stored only in the researchers' devices, code that isn't shared, and complex software that the researchers use but ultimately don't control.

3 Sharing our results: Alignment in Cook Islands Māori

The real overhaul came with the work on Southern Cook Islands Māori (CIM; ISO 639-3: rar). Here, we attempted to involve the community members in our decisions for data management and dissemination, and we also improved the versioning of the files in the project.

CIM is an East Polynesian language originating from the Southern Cook Islands and spoken by approximately 1,500 people in the Cook Islands and in diaspora populations in New Zealand and Australia. Within the language community, the majority of whom reside in a diaspora, there are very low rates of intergenerational transmission and, as such, there is a very advanced shift toward English as the main language of communication (Nicholas 2018:46). There have been recent efforts to increase the documentation for the language (Nicholas 2017) that have resulted in a corpus of spoken CIM of approximately eighty hours. The manual orthographic transcription of this collection is in progress; at the time of writing, about 30% of it has been transcribed using ELAN. The existence of these transcriptions has allowed the possibility of using untrained forced alignment to study the phonetics of the language. For example, we used this method to describe the distribution of glottal stop realizations throughout the Southern Cook Islands. These realizations range from a full glottal stop (e.g., *ta'i* ['ta.ʔi] 'one') on some islands, to a realization without glottal closure but with creaky voice on the vowels on other islands (e.g., *ta'i* ['ta.ḭ] 'one') (Nicholas & Coto-Solano 2019).

The input for the CIM alignment came from a documentation project that had been ongoing for multiple years, with many speakers and sources for the recordings, as well as different file formats. This meant that the data required more metadata and curation to manage them. For example, the recordings were captured with both audio and video, significantly increasing both the number and size of the files to be managed. In addition to this, many of the recordings involve naturalistic conversation, which is linguistically rich, but difficult to prepare for NLP processing. The audiovisual material of the corpus (Nicholas 2012) is stored and made publicly available at the Pacific and Regional Archive for Digital Sources in Endangered Cultures (PARADISEC; http://www.paradisec.org.au), but when we first began the forced alignment for CIM, the file transcriptions were stored in the main researcher's personal computer, which was different from the computer where the data were being aligned. To add to these issues of file management, early on we found a divergence in transcription styles: sometimes the needs for 'linguistically oriented' documentation were not the same as those of the alignment algorithm. The following are three examples of these differences: First, linguistically oriented transcriptions need to retain punctuation and case sensitivity, whereas transcriptions for forced alignment usually need to be as simple as possible, eliminating punctuation and reducing the number of glyphs in the text to those that correspond to sounds in the recording. Second, linguistically oriented transcriptions also have multiple tiers, including tiers for translations, annotations of linguistic features (e.g., morphemic glossing, discourse level tags), while forced alignment transcriptions need to be separated by speakers and almost completely free of data that are not directly related to the signal. Third, linguistically oriented transcriptions need to include instances of code-switching (e.g., between Spanish and Bribri or between Bislama and Denggan) to present a complete picture of the linguistic patterns of the speakers. Processing multilingual data, however, would further complicate the use of untrained forced alignment, as well as the generation of training sets for further NLP tools.

One final difference between linguistically oriented and alignment-oriented transcription styles is that transcriptions for forced alignment need to have a more precise temporal delimitation of each separate utterance. In linguistically oriented transcriptions, the temporal limits for each utterance can include noise or even phrases in other languages without degrading its usability. Noise, on the other hand, can engage the alignment at the wrong points of the recording. 'Noise,' by the way, includes roosters, children, pigs, dogs, wind, and cicadas, elements that are common to all the fieldwork settings presented in this chapter. Because those are constant, their influence has to be managed and minimized. In the future, we hope to bring noise-robust speech recognition techniques from large languages to help with this in fieldwork settings (Liao & Gales 2008; Seltzer, Yu, & Wang 2013). The interruptions of other people and other background conversations can also result in errors in alignment. When eliciting word lists, for example, false starts of words or half-utterances can fool the alignment

program into thinking that they're the beginning of the word, and then an indiscriminate vowel sound or hesitation might extend a real target's ending. All of these details of the transformation from transcription to the 'tab-separated transcription' intended as input to the aligner demanded attention and time when generating the input for the forced alignment algorithm.

As described in section 2, TextGrids generated from forced alignment need to be corrected to make sure that the boundaries are aligned with the phones correctly, a time-consuming process that benefits from a multiperson workforce. These corrections distributed across a larger team, combined with the many intermediate files generated during the alignment process, quickly caused an organizational chaos that forced us to rethink our file management process. We started pushing critical files (e.g., uncorrected, partially corrected, and completely corrected TextGrids) onto a GitHub repository (in this case https://github.com/rolandocoto/cim-aligned). This has been shown to provide effective versioning for code and for linguistic data (Partanen 2016), so we could have files at different versions of progress and work on them asynchronously. Very quickly it was obvious that other files, such as ELAN files, the Arpabet dictionaries, and the R and Python code would also benefit from stable backups and versioning.

This process brought to the fore questions about the public availability of our data. Complete access to data is not always desirable in the context of Indigenous language work because the data might contain data that are private to a family, private for religious or cultural reasons, or that constitutes an intangible cultural or intellectual property of the community, and are therefore susceptible to appropriation or theft (cf. Dwyer 2006; Kukutai & Taylor 2016; Keegan 2019). Great care must be taken to make sure the needs of the language community are being met in this regard. In the Cook Islands context, there is widespread support for open access to most types of linguistic materials due to the perception that this approach provides the best chance for successful language revitalization. During the documentation process, the contributors are always given the option to exclude their recording, or part of it, from the open access corpus or to ask for it to be excluded at a later date. However, we must always remain responsive to the wishes of the contributors, and we must continue to make sure contributors understand what might happen to and result from their recordings and keep them informed as these possibilities change with technological advances.

In addition to public access for the data sets, the goals of the documentation project included contributing to the revitalization efforts of CIM. Therefore, alongside our data management needs for supporting the scholarly use of the results of forced alignment, we also needed to overhaul the mechanisms to report our findings to make sure that they would produce materials accessible to the language community that would benefit their revitalization efforts. As it stands, the community has several ways to access the raw data. The audiovisual recordings themselves, as well as the aligned and corrected TextGrids can be accessed through PARADISEC (Nicholas 2012). There is also a text-based corpus in the Annotation of Information Structure search and visualization platform (Centre of Excellence for the Dynamics of Language & Nicholas 2019). Finally, the code, TextGrids, and ELAN files needed to replicate the alignment are available on a GitHub repository. However, these formats are not layperson friendly, so we've had to think of a number of ways for community members to use our materials so that they can use them when teaching the language to themselves or others. These community-oriented resources need to occupy less bandwidth, be topically focused, and be easily accessible through a wide range of devices. The most well-populated of these resource channels are the YouTube channel *Araara Māori Kuki Airani* (Nicholas 2019a) and the GERLINGO collection of CIM narrations (Nicholas 2019b). We are also currently engaged in an ongoing educational relationship with the language community. Specifically, we work with primary and secondary school language teachers, coordinating classes on how to use all these community-facing resources as well as how to contribute to creating more of them.

Finally, we have taken the wealth of well-annotated data that the forced alignment workflow has generated and started using it to train NLP algorithms, in the hopes of accelerating the documentation process. We have begun training automatic speech recognition algorithms so that the transcription can be automated and turned into a process of mere correction and verification. As we produce more transcribed data, these could be fed into the algorithm again, increasing the accuracy of the automated transcription (Foley et al. 2018; Foley, Van Esch, & San, chapter 36, this volume). We have also used the data to train part-of-speech tagging (Coto-Solano,

Nicholas, & Wray 2018), which is currently working with 92% accuracy (currently at http://cimpos.appspot.com). We hope to create a 'virtuous circle' where more documentation can be used to train more NLP tools. This will not only help with the documentation process but also help us bring the language closer to the computer devices that permeate people's lives, thereby creating a 'symbolic impact' in favor of language reclamation (Aguilar Gil 2014; Jones & Ogilvie 2013; Terrill 2002) and expanding the domains of usage of CIM.

Figure 35.4 shows a summary of the workflow for the untrained forced alignment of CIM data, including the data transformations, and the process for storage, archiving, and sharing research outputs with the community and with academia.

As we learned more about managing our files, new challenges emerged. One of them led us in a new direction: How can we make sure that other researchers can replicate the workflow, and that they can run the code and use untrained forced alignment to work on their languages?

4 Maintaining reproducibility: Vanuatu and the future

After early successes in using untrained forced alignment to generate research on Meʼphaa Vátháá and CIM phonetics, we decided to expand this technique to a new language. Denggan, formerly known as Banam Bay Language or Burmbar (ISO 639-3: vrt), is a language spoken in the Pacific archipelago of Vanuatu. Denggan is an Austronesian language spoken by an estimated nine hundred language users and has recorded word lists of 300–1,500 words (Tryon 1976; Charpentier 1982), but it is otherwise undocumented. While it still maintains high vitality and intergenerational transmission, it is considered endangered based on the small speaker population and the prominence of the national language, Bislama, in official domains such as church and government and in communication with people from different language backgrounds throughout Vanuatu. Our immediate goal was to use fieldwork recordings of both casual and elicited speech (i.e., Swadesh word lists) to plot F1 and F2 formants, so that we could start the documentation of the vowels. This is part of a larger project by Hoback to document the grammar of the language and aid in creating language maintenance resources.

The lessons learned from the archiving of CIM data and community sharing were useful for the Vanuatu

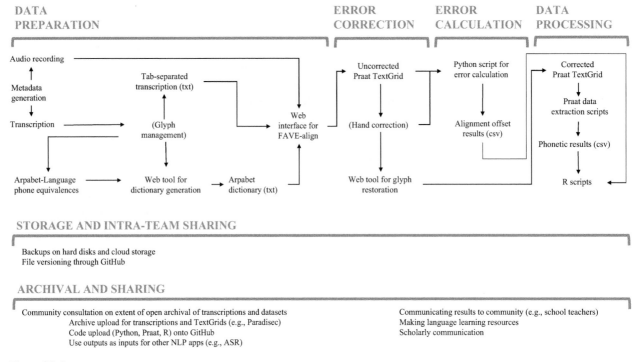

Figure 35.4
Workflow for CIM data. ASR = automatic speech recognition.

case, given that this had a formal requirement for its related files to be archived in the Endangered Languages Archive (ELAR; https://www.soas.ac.uk/elar/), and that it belongs to a much larger language documentation project. Like with the CIM archival materials, the resources for Denggan were archived both as sound files, ELAN transcriptions, and corresponding TextGrid files (Hoback 2019; ELAR deposit identifier: 0549). These were bundled together through CMDI Maker (Zimmer 2014) and can be accessed separately for use of the community (of which audio files or transcriptions would be the most useful). It can also be accessed as a full bundle, including aligned TextGrids, which can be accessed to provide accountability and replicability of the phonetic analysis. The majority of these resources are open access to registered users of ELAR. For the community, this means that there is one registered account for the whole community that individuals can use to access the resources in ELAR. As found in the CIM project, accessing the files of interest can be difficult for speakers through this interface. It also requires downloading the files (e.g., video files of several gigabytes), which is not the most economical way of accessing materials through mobile data, which is the main Internet access for the majority of community members. We are therefore trying to use other means to

distribute language resource files, particularly through social media sites such as YouTube or Facebook, whose interfaces are familiar to Denggan speakers.

Denggan presented some challenges that were now familiar: When transforming the data, we found numerous phones that did not correspond to any English Arpabet glyphs. For example, Denggan has the prenasalized consonant /ᵐb/, as well as a uvular fricative [χ]~[ʁ] that also affects the acoustic characteristics of the surrounding vowels. More importantly, the recordings from Denggan were more multilingual than the ones we had processed before were. The Chibchan and Me'phaa recordings were almost exclusively monolingual. The CIM recordings had code-switching among English, CIM, and occasional words in Te Reo Māori from Aotearoa/New Zealand. However, the recordings from Vanuatu constantly used at least three languages: English, Bislama, and Denggan. English and Bislama were used as contact languages and as a way to elicit Denggan data. Because the transcriptions were segmented into continuous conversation chunks, the aligner would pick up the prompt in the contact language if there was a sound that also corresponded to an expected English phone. This caused the alignment to begin at the prompt and extend, usually, to the end of the actual target word. In addition to this, the phonotactics

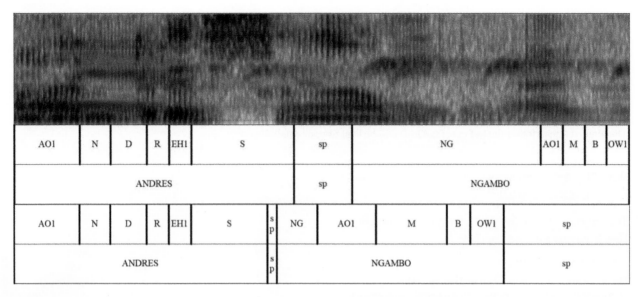

AO1	N	D	R	EH1	S	sp	NG	AO1	M	B	OW1
	ANDRES					sp		NGAMBO			

AO1	N	D	R	EH1	S	sp	NG	AO1	M	B	OW1	sp
	ANDRES					sp		NGAMBO				sp

Figure 35.5
Alignment of word-initial /ŋ/ in Denggan data. The first TextGrid tier shows an automatic alignment for /ŋ/ that extends beyond the end of its word. The third tier shows the hand-corrected alignment.

of Denggan would sometimes affect the alignment. For example, the velar nasal /ŋ/ can occur word-initially (as shown in figure 35.5). Because English phonotactics do not allow for this, the English-trained algorithm had problems identifying them in the Denggan recordings and would often misalign word boundaries. This resulted in more manual hand-correction and a workflow similar to that for CIM.

One new challenge, however, had a major impact on the project: While working on CIM, and right before we started working with Denggan, we lost access to the web interface for the aligner software. This website was taken offline, and this left the community of FAVE-align users scrambling to find solutions. The most common fix was to download the FAVE-align code to our own computers and run it via Python. Here, the problems of encoding and code maintenance came back with a vengeance. We were working on multiple operating systems (Windows, Ubuntu, and Mac OSX), and while we installed the software, trained ourselves in running it manually, and made sure our transcriptions were compatible across all platforms, the temporary files piled up in multiple computers with little thought given to versioning or backups.

Our first attempt to deal with this issue was to create a short manual with command line instructions, so that we could run it on our personal computers. This worked for a while, but it was highly dependent on the experience that each user had with command line work

(which in this case was the *bash* command language). Our second attempt was to run our code using a remote virtual machine, instantiated using an Amazon Web Service AWS-EC2 CentOS (https://aws.amazon.com/es/ec2/) and accessible through a secure shell protocol.[6] We ran a workshop using this method, and while it was intimidating to new users, they could use this remote text-based interface to align novel data after about four to five hours of training.[7] These solutions worked, but they still presented formidable obstacles to first-time users. Ultimately, a solution where all the team needs programming experience is completely unsustainable.

After this workshop, we decided that a web-based graphical interface was necessary. This new interface would both allow us to customize the code and give the users an easy way to run the scripts and automate the data transformations without resorting to text-based instructions to a Python script. The resulting interface can be used at http://icldc-align.appspot.com. This new interface operated using the AWS storage and virtual machines as the back end for the processing, and a Java-based interface for the front end. Figure 35.6 shows a screenshot of the instructions to align a recording.

We were able to test this new interface at a workshop in the International Conference on Language Documentation and Conservation conference at the University of Hawai'i, in two sessions attended by over a hundred people (Coto-Solano et al. 2019). Each of the

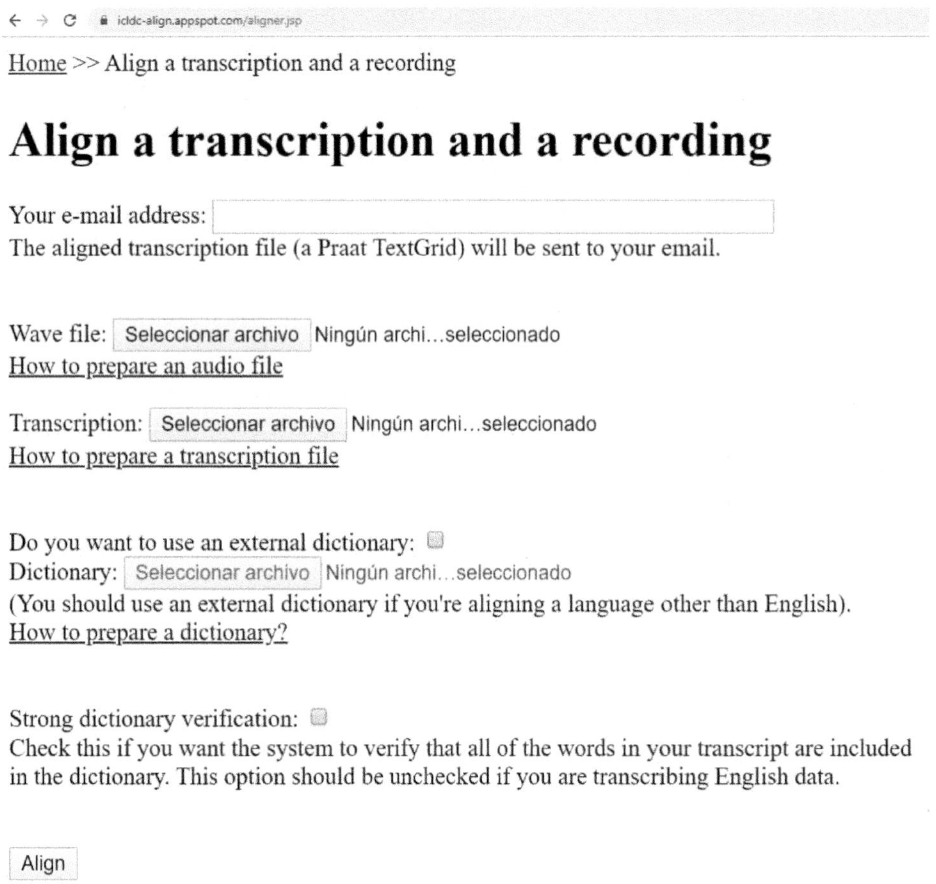

← → C 🔒 icldc-align.appspot.com/aligner.jsp

Home >> Align a transcription and a recording

Align a transcription and a recording

Your e-mail address: [   ]
The aligned transcription file (a Praat TextGrid) will be sent to your email.

Wave file: [Seleccionar archivo] Ningún archi...seleccionado
How to prepare an audio file

Transcription: [Seleccionar archivo] Ningún archi...seleccionado
How to prepare a transcription file

Do you want to use an external dictionary: ☐
Dictionary: [Seleccionar archivo] Ningún archi...seleccionado
(You should use an external dictionary if you're aligning a language other than English).
How to prepare a dictionary?

Strong dictionary verification: ☐
Check this if you want the system to verify that all of the words in your transcript are included
in the dictionary. This option should be unchecked if you are transcribing English data.

[Align]

Figure 35.6
Interface to align audio and transcription using FAVE-align.

sessions lasted about ninety minutes, and users were able to generate alignment for previously untrained languages during that time. This new interface also has an important element: we added tutorials for how to download the code and run all the steps of the alignment from a user's personal computer. We also pointed users to the GitHub repository and to the documentation there. By taking these steps we are adding a layer of protection so that users can run the code on their own in case our own website goes offline. We hope that this will increase the reproducibility of this method of linguistic research.

5   Key elements of data management and future work

As we developed the methods of untrained forced alignment, we quickly found that linguistic data management is linked to the ethics of fieldwork and documentation, to Indigenous data sovereignty, and to the intersection of these with ideas from the open access and open science movements. As figure 35.4 shows, the life cycle of

the data includes not just the input and the output for the NLP algorithm, but also considerations of (1) how the data and the outputs will benefit the community that speaks the language, (2) how much of it can be shared with researchers are do not belong to the community, and (3) how the publicly shared outputs can serve multiple stakeholders, including other academics, language learners and teachers, and activists involved in language reclamation projects. These ethical considerations are a key part of the data management process, as they will determine which data are archived where, who has access to backups and intermediate files, and how the data will continue to inform research on the language.

The untrained forced alignment workflow also made us examine the reproducibility of computer code environments and the creation of asynchronous workflows for large teams. This made us recapitulate the principles of open source code and thinking of our in-house code as objects that could potentially be useful to other researchers. Also, the concept of data sovereignty directly affected us. We needed to understand the code and create an environment where we could ensure its future execution so we could continue to use this technique.

One key element is that many of the issues we found were recurrent across these six very disparate languages. The issues in CIM glyph and data management were mirrored in Denggan, for example, and therefore such issues can be addressed and resolved similarly. We are increasingly confident that this technique is replicable and that it can be used by other teams for phonetic research. Exploring these questions has also made us reconsider what has happened to the data from previous projects. For example, could the data from the Chibchan experiments be reused by other researchers? The public archiving of the Me'pha͟a Vátháá data has also begun as a result of improvements in the management of CIM and Denggan data.

The workflow presented in figure 35.4 is just one example of how the untrained forced alignment technique can be applied, and there are numerous improvements that we would like to implement. For example, we would like to write scripts that automatically push partially corrected Praat TextGrids into GitHub repositories. We would also like to improve the support of non-Roman systems from any operating system, so that a wider range of languages can be analyzed using this technique. As we explore improvements, we find ourselves coming back to the same questions: How do we keep this complex task coordinated among the team participants, and how do we make sure that our research has an impact in both academia and in language reclamation efforts? These are elements that remain constant even as the NLP algorithms and their environments change.

6 Conclusions

We have presented an example of a workflow for managing the data involved in untrained forced alignment. During this process we faced the task of organizing and keeping coordinated numerous data transformations across teams of linguists and data annotators, and we found that online platforms that provide explicit versioning helped us with this task. We also had to figure out ways to appropriate the computer code for the algorithm so we could ensure the replicability of our results. In doing these, we explored the ethics of community-based language documentation and research (Czaykowska-Higgins

2009), as well as the issues of research replicability and data reusability in linguistics. In light of the need for work on Indigenous languages, we need to bring in tools that can help get more work done, and we hope that these results will provide ideas for how to use existing NLP tools and knowledge to help the speakers of these languages in their goals of language documentation and reclamation.

Acknowledgments

We want to thank Dr. Christian DiCanio (whose work first introduced us to this technique), Dr. Tyler Peterson, Dr. Miriam Meyerhoff, Dr. Samantha Wray, Dr. Bradley McDonnell, Dr. Sofía Flores, and Alí García Segura; software testers at Victoria University of Wellington, Jawaharlal Nehru University in New Delhi, and the International Conference on Language Documentation and Conservation in Honolulu; as well as audiences at University of Costa Rica, Accenture Costa Rica, Dartmouth College, University of the South Pacific in Suva and Rarotonga, University of Auckland, and the National Library of New Zealand. We also thank the anonymous reviewers of this chapter for their revisions and useful suggestions for tool improvement. In addition to them, we also thank the Fulbright Foreign Student Program, the Tinker Foundation, the Center for Latin American Studies of the University of Arizona, and the Graduate and Professional Student Council at the University of Arizona (grant RSRCH-201FY16) for funding the work on Me'pha͟a alignment, as well as the Me'pha͟a Vátháá teachers of School Sector 76 in Guerrero, Mexico, for their support with the Me'pha͟a project.

We would also like to acknowledge the many CIM speakers who have contributed to this project and particular thanks must go to the 2018 cohort of the Diploma in Pacific Vernacular Languages (Cook Islands Māori) at the University of the South Pacific Rarotonga. In that respect we would like to acknowledge the recent passing of Mama Kairangi Daniel and Uriaau George, *moe mai ra e te ngā taeake*. We would also like to thank the staff and students of Ma'uke School, our most prolific collaborator Jean Tekura Mason, *ē tō Ake kōpū tangata kātoatoa*. Together we will make our language thrive again.

Finally, we would like to acknowledge the communities of S. E. Malekula and speakers of Denggan for the active interest and participation in the language project and for their patience providing recordings. Also to

Brittany's partner, Jim, who has been a constant help transcribing and explaining phonological features hand-in-hand with our visual analyses of his language. We would like to acknowledge Victoria University of Wellington and the Endangered Languages Documentation Programme SOAS University of London for funding for the Banam Bay Language Documentation Project (grant IGS0329) and one more time Dr. Miriam Meyerhoff for her insight and supervision during this and subsequent phases of the research. *Sipa ran emdro ran naut Banam Bay nge mun matbafi nenggis san enge san sor Denggan. Sipa ran fafu raru, boti fana sangk, boti nating raru, Isaac boti Jeffry.*

Notes

1. We will use the word *phone* for any unit of sound in a word that can be transcribed using a symbol in the International Phonetic Alphabet, regardless of its status as a phoneme or allophone in a language.

2. This amount of error is comparable to that of aligning nonstandard English dialects. When performing untrained forced alignment on British dialects such as Sunderland or Westray English (MacKenzie & Turton 2019), approximately 80% of the phones have errors of less than twenty microseconds when marking their onset. When marking the onset of Bribri phones, 80% of the vowels have an error of less than thirty-one microseconds, and 80% of the consonants have an error of less than twenty-nine microseconds (Coto-Solano & Flores Solórzano 2017).

3. Bribri has several spelling conventions. Nasalization can be written either as a line underneath the vowel (*ṳ* /ū̃/ 'pot') or as a tilde above the vowel (*ũ* 'pot') (Jara Murillo & Segura 2009).

4. For example, when a glottal stop loses its closure but you still have vocalic laryngealization, do you keep a 'glottal stop' interval in the Praat script? Our solution in Nicholas and Coto-Solano (2019) was to mark the smallest possible interval to indicate that a glottal stop was expected there, but so small that we could easily filter it out. Other solutions are possible. For example, adding additional tiers with full transcriptions or explanations is also a possibility for retaining phonological information, as is done in the Corpus of Spontaneous Japanese (NINJAL 2006).

5. *Versioning* or 'version control' refers to the practice of keeping track of the small differences between iterative versions of a complex documents as they are developed and edited, commonly computer code, but in our case ELAN files or Praat TextGrids.

6. We also considered deploying a container-like environment on a platform such as Docker (Merkel 2014). However, this presented the same challenge in terms of user interface and usability.

7. This workshop saw some of the biggest challenges in terms of file encoding. The current FAVE-align algorithm (implemented on Python 2) has issues using Indic and other complex writing systems.

References

Aguilar Gil, Yásnaya Elena. 2014. *¿Para qué publicar libros en lenguas indígenas si nadie los lee?* E'px, September 10. https://archivo.estepais.com/site/2014/para-que-publicar-libros-en-lenguas-indigenas-si-nadie-los-lee/.

Boersma, Paul. 2001. Praat: A system for doing phonetics by computer. *Glot International* 5 (9–10): 341–345.

Centre of Excellence for the Dynamics of Language and S. A. Nicholas. 2019. *Cook Islands Māori.* ANNIS. http://www.corpus.dynamicsoflanguage.edu.au/. Accessed September 29, 2019.

Charpentier, J. M. 1982. *Atlas linguistique du Sud-Malakula (Vanuatu).* Vol. 1. Paris: Société d'Études Linguistiques et Anthropologiques de France, Peeters Publishers.

Coto-Solano, R. 2017. Tonal reduction and literacy in Me'phaa Vátháá. PhD dissertation, University of Arizona.

Coto-Solano, R., and S. Flores Solórzano. 2016. Alineación forzada sin entrenamiento para la anotación automática de corpus orales de las lenguas indígenas de Costa Rica. *Káñina* 40 (4): 175–199. https://doi.org/10.15517/rk.v40i4.30234.

Coto-Solano, R., and S. Flores Solórzano. 2017. Comparison of two forced alignment systems for aligning Bribri speech. *CLEI Electronic Journal* 20 (1): 21. https://doi.org/10.19153/cleiej.20.1.2.

Coto-Solano, R., S. A. Nicholas, and S. Wray. 2018. Development of natural language processing tools for Cook Islands Māori. In *Proceedings of the Australasian Language Technology Association Workshop 2018*, ed. S. Mac Kim and X. J. Zhang, 26–33. Dunedin, New Zealand: Australasian Language Technology Association. https://www.aclweb.org/anthology/U18-1003/.

Coto-Solano, R., S. A. Nicholas, S. Wray, and T. Petersen. 2019. Accelerating the analysis of your audio recordings with untrained forced speech alignment. Paper presented at the 6th International Conference on Language Documentation and Conservation (ICLDC), University of Hawai'i at Mānoa, March 3. http://hdl.handle.net/10125/44886.

Czaykowska-Higgins, E. 2009. Research models, community engagement, and linguistic fieldwork: Reflections on working within Canadian indigenous communities. *Language Documentation and Conservation* 3 (1): 182–215.

DiCanio, C., H. Nam, D. H. Whalen, H. Timothy Bunnell, J. D. Amith, and R. C. García. 2013. Using automatic alignment to analyze endangered language data: Testing the viability of untrained alignment. *Journal of the Acoustical Society of America* 134 (3): 2235–2246. https://doi.org/10.1121/1.4816491.

Dwyer, A. M. 2006. Ethics and practicalities of cooperative fieldwork and analysis. In *Essentials of Language Documentation,* ed. J. Gippert, N. Himmelmann, and U. Mosel, 31–66. Trends in Linguistics: Studies and Monographs 178. Berlin: Mouton de Gruyter. https://doi.org/10.1515/9783110197730.31.

Ernestus, M., and N. Warner, eds. 2011. An introduction to reduced pronunciation variants. In *Speech Reduction*. Special issue, *Journal of Phonetics* 39 (3): 253–260. https://doi.org/10.1016/s0095-4470(11)00055-6.

Foley, B., J. T. Arnold, R. Coto-Solano, G. Durantin, T. M. Ellison, D. van Esch, D.,S. Heath, et al. 2018. Building speech recognition systems for language documentation: The CoEDL Endangered Language Pipeline and Inference System (ELPIS). In *Proceedings of SLTU*, 205–209. https://doi.org/10.21437/sltu.2018-42.

Fromont, R., and J. Hay. 2012. LaBB-CAT: An annotation store. In *Proceedings of the Australasian Language Technology Association Workshop*, ed. P. Cook and S. Nowson, 113–117. Dunedin, New Zealand: Australasian Language Technology Association. https://www.aclweb.org/anthology/U12-1015/.

Goldman, J. P. 2011. *EasyAlign: An Automatic Phonetic Alignment Tool under Praat.* http://latlcui.unige.ch/phonetique/easyalign.php.

González, S., C. E. Travis, J. Grama, D. Barth, and S. Ananthanarayan. 2018. Recursive forced alignment: A test on a minority language. In *Proceedings of the Seventeenth Australasian International Conference on Speech Science and Technology*, ed. J. Epps, J. Wolfe, J. Smith, and C. Jones, 145–148. Sydney, Australia: Australasian Speech Science and Technology Association. https://assta.org/proceedings/sst/SST-2018/SST_2018_Proceedings_Rev_A_IDX.pdf.

Gorman, K., J. Howell, and M. Wagner. 2011. Prosodylab-aligner: A tool for forced alignment of laboratory speech. *Canadian Acoustics* 39 (3): 192–193.

Hoback, B. 2019. *Banam Bay Language: Documentation and Endangered Language Maintenance*. London: SOAS, Endangered Languages Archive. (Deposit ID: 0549). https://elar.soas.ac.uk/Collection/MPI1202117.

Jara Murillo, C., and A. G. Segura. 2009. *Se' e'yawö bribri wa. Aprendemos la lengua bribri*. San José: Editorial de la Universidad de Costa Rica.

Johnson, L. M., M. Di Paolo, and A. Bell. 2018. Forced alignment for understudied language varieties: Testing Prosodylab-Aligner with Tongan data. *Language Documentation and Conservation* 12:80–123.

Jones, C., K. Demuth, W. Li, and A. Almeida. 2017. Vowels in the Barunga variety of North Australian Kriol. In *Proceedings of Interspeech*, 219–223. https://doi.org/10.21437/interspeech.2017-1552.

Jones, C., W. Li, A. Almeida, and A. German. 2019. Evaluating cross-linguistic forced alignment of conversational data in north Australian Kriol, an under-resourced language. *Language Documentation and Conservation* 13:281–299.

Jones, M. C., and S. Ogilvie, eds. 2013. *Keeping Languages Alive: Documentation, Pedagogy and Revitalization*. Cambridge: Cambridge University Press. https://doi.org/10.1017/cbo9781139245890.

Kashima, E., D. Williams, T. Mark Ellison, D. Schokkin, and P. Escudero. 2016. Uncovering the acoustic vowel space of a previously undescribed language: The vowels of Nambo. *Journal of the Acoustical Society of America* 139 (6): EL252–EL256. https://doi.org/10.1121/1.4954395.

Keegan, T. 2019. Language normalisation through technology: Te Reo Māori example. In *6th International Conference on Language Documentation and Conservation (ICLDC)*. http://hdl.handle.net/10125/44883.

Kempton, T. 2017. Cross-language forced alignment to assist community-based linguistics for low resource languages. In *Proceedings of the 2nd Workshop on the Use of Computational Methods in the Study of Endangered Languages*, 165–169. https://doi.org/10.18653/v1/w17-0122.

Kukutai, T., and J. Taylor. 2016. *Indigenous Data Sovereignty: Toward an Agenda*. Vol. 38. Canberra, Australia: ANU Press.

Labov, W., I. Rosenfelder, and J. Fruehwald. 2013. One hundred years of sound change in Philadelphia: Linear incrementation, reversal, and reanalysis. *Language* 89 (1): 30–65. https://doi.org/10.1353/lan.2013.0015.

Liao, H., and M. J. F. Gales. 2008. Issues with uncertainty decoding for noise robust automatic speech recognition. *Speech Communication* 50 (4): 265–277. https://doi.org/10.1016/j.specom.2007.10.004.

MacKenzie, L., and D. Turton. 2019. Assessing the accuracy of existing forced alignment software on varieties of British English. *Linguistics Vanguard* 6 (s1): 1–14.

McAuliffe, M., M. Socolof, S. Mihuc, M. Wagner, and M. Sonderegger. 2017. Montreal Forced Aligner: Trainable text-speech alignment using Kaldi. In *Proceedings of Interspeech*, 498–502. https://doi.org/10.21437/interspeech.2017-1386.

Merkel, D. 2014. Docker: Lightweight Linux containers for consistent development and deployment. *Linux Journal* 2014 (239): 2.

Nicholas, S. A. 2012. *Te Vairanga Tuatua o te Te Reo Māori o te Pae Tonga: Cook Islands Māori* (Southern dialects) (sn1). Digital collection managed by PARADISEC. [Open Access]. doi:10.4225/72/56E9793466307. http://catalog.paradisec.org.au/collections/SN1.

Nicholas, S. A. 2017. *Ko te Karāma o te Reo Māori o te Pae Tonga o Te Kuki Airani*: A grammar of Southern Cook Islands Māori. Unpublished PhD thesis, University of Auckland. http://hdl.handle.net/2292/32929.

Nicholas, S. A. 2018. Language contexts: *Te Reo Māori o te Pae Tonga o te Kuki Airani* also known as Southern Cook Islands Māori. *Language Documentation and Description* 15:36–64.

Nicholas, S. A. 2019a. *Araara Māaori Kuki Airani* (YouTube channel). https://www.youtube.com/channel/UCXow-aTZOg3hEk BYAz7F8Cw. Accessed October 1, 2019.

Nicholas, S. A. 2019b. *Cook Islands Māori*. https://www.gerlingo .com/language_detail.php?langID=26. Accessed September 29, 2019.

Nicholas, S. A., and R. Coto-Solano. 2019. Glottal variation, teacher training and language revitalisation in the Cook Islands. In *Proceedings of the 19th International Congress of Phonetic Sciences, Melbourne, Australia*, ed. S. Calhoun, P. Escudero, M. Tabain, and P. Warren, 3602–3606. Canberra, Australia: Australasian Speech Science and Technology Association.

NINJAL (National Institute for Japanese Language and Linguistics). 2006. Construction of the Corpus of Spontaneous Japanese. https://pj.ninjal.ac.jp/corpus_center/csj/en. Accessed December 8, 2019

Partanen, Niko. 2016. Using a Git repository for language documentation corpora (web log message). https://langdoc.github .io/2016-05-20-langdoc_with_Git.html.

R Core Team. 2017. *R: A Language and Environment for Statistical Computing*. Vienna: R Foundation for Statistical Computing. https://www.R-project.org/.

Reddy, S., and J. N. Stanford. 2015. Toward completely automated vowel extraction: Introducing DARLA. *Linguistics Vanguard* 1 (1): 15–28. https://doi.org/10.1515/lingvan-2015-0002.

Rosenfelder, I., J. Fruehwald, K. Evanini, K. Seyfarth, S. Gorman, K. Prichard, and J. Yuan. 2011. *FAVE (Forced Alignment and Vowel Extraction) Program Suite*. https://doi.org/10.5281/zenodo.9846. Accessed December 2020.

Seltzer, M. L., D. Yu, and Y. Wang. 2013. An investigation of deep neural networks for noise robust speech recognition. In *2013 IEEE International Conference on Acoustics, Speech and Signal Processing*, 7398–7402. IEEE. https://doi.org/10.1109/icassp.2013 .6639100.

Strunk, J., F. Schiel, and F. Seifart. 2014. Untrained forced alignment of transcriptions and audio for language documentation corpora using WebMAUS. In *Proceedings of the Ninth International Conference on Language Resources and Evaluation (LREC '14)*, ed. N. Calzolari, K. Choukri, T. Declerck, H. Loftsson, B. Maegaard, J. Mariani, A. Moreno, et al., 3940–3947. Reykjavik, Iceland: European Language Resources Association. https:// www.aclweb.org/anthology/L14-1123/.

Terrill, Angela. 2002. Why make books for people who don't read? A perspective on documentation of an Endangered Language from Solomon Islands. *International Journal of Society and Language* 2002 (155–156): 205–219. https://doi.org/10.1515/ijsl.2002.029.

Tryon, D. T. 1976. *New Hebrides languages: An internal classification*. Canberra: Department of Linguistics, Research School of Pacific Studies, the Australian National University.

Wightman, C. W., and D. T. Talkin. 1997. The Aligner: Text-to-speech alignment using Markov models. In *Progress in Speech Synthesis*, ed. J. P. H. Santen, J. P. Olive, R. W. Sproat, and J. Hirschberg, 313–323. New York: Springer. https://doi.org/10 .1007/978-1-4612-1894-4_25.

Wittenburg, P., H. Brugman, A. Russel, A. Klassmann, and H. Sloetjes. 2006. ELAN: A professional framework for multimodality research. In *Proceedings of the Fifth International Conference on Language Resources and Evaluation (LREC '06)*, ed. N. Calzolari, K. Choukri, A. Gangemi, B. Maegaard, J. Mariani, J. Odijk, and D. Tapias, 1556–1559. Genoa, Italy: European Language Resources Association. https://www.aclweb.org/anthology/L06 -1082/.

Yuan, J., and M. Liberman. 2008. Speaker identification on the SCOTUS corpus. *Journal of the Acoustical Society of America* 123 (5): 3878. https://doi.org/10.1121/1.2935783.

Zimmer, S. 2014. *CMDI Maker 2.20*. https://beta.cmdi-maker .uni-koeln.de/. Accessed December 8, 2019.

Zue, V. W., and S. Seneff. 1996. Transcription and alignment of the TIMIT database. In *Recent Research towards Advanced Man-Machine Interface through Spoken Language*, ed. H. Fujisaki, 515–525. Amsterdam: Elsevier Science BV. https://doi.org/10.1016 /b978-044481607-8/50088-8.

Ben Foley, Daan van Esch, and Nay San

1 Introduction

This chapter provides a mid-level introduction to speech recognition technologies, with particular reference to Elpis (Foley et al. 2018), a tool designed for people with minimal computational experience to accelerate their language documentation transcription workflows by taking advantage of modern speech recognition technologies (e.g., Kaldi [Povey et al. 2011] and ESPnet [Watanabe et al. 2018]). By a *mid-level introduction*, we mean that the chapter focuses on the *whats* and *whys*, rather than low-level *hows* (e.g., click button X, then . . .); such how-to descriptions are provided via the latest stable version of the Elpis project's documentation (Foley, Lambourne, & San 2020). On the other hand, for a more comprehensive, high-level introduction to speech recognition models, we recommend Jurafsky and Martin (forthcoming).

Elpis is intended to be used in situations where there might not be the large quantities of already transcribed recordings typically required for training commercially viable speech recognition systems (which are usually trained on hundreds to thousands of hours of transcribed recordings). Even in language documentation contexts where people may only have one or two hours of transcribed recordings, using speech recognition can be beneficial to the process of transcription. A speech recognition system can be built using small quantities of recordings and used to generate a rough "best guess" for untranscribed audio. This new transcription can be corrected and used to retrain the system, improving the quality of the rough transcription with each iteration.

Moreover, in becoming more familiar with the types of data and metadata necessary to train a speech recognition system (as well as best practices for their organization), language documentation teams may develop a better-informed data management plan that facilitates the adoption of semi-automated workflows.

In the first section, we describe the motivations for this work, provide an overview of various components of a speech recognition system, and describe their roles within the overall system. Subsequently, we discuss how to plan and prepare data for use with Elpis. The technologies discussed here are designed to learn from acoustic features of spoken language and are not effective for signed languages.

1.1 Motivations

The motivations for developing Elpis are two-fold. The first is to further amplify the many ongoing efforts of people transcribing recordings of spoken language, particularly endangered and under-resourced languages. The second is to bring the possibility of using speech recognition technologies, which are currently restricted to very few languages and inaccessible for people without specialist training, to many more of the world's languages.

A transcription is the textual representation of language, typically made by writing while listening to or watching a recording. Transcriptions can be created by typing into a text file, by using software such as ELAN (ELAN 2019), or even by writing by hand on paper. When done from scratch without assistance from automatic speech recognition software, transcription tends to be slow—a survey of linguists in 2017 reported an average of forty minutes taken to transcribe one minute of speech (Foley et al. 2019). While digital technologies make it easy to record large quantities and varieties of knowledge, this bottleneck of transcription limits the amount that may be turned into written text.

Indeed, this transcription bottleneck has long been recognized (Himmelmann 2018). With recent advances in the field of automatic speech recognition, there has been an increasing amount of interest in employing speech recognition tools in language documentation contexts, and various interdisciplinary collaborations are reporting promising results. For example, Michaud et al. (2018) describe the positive change in workflow experienced by using Persephone for phonemic transcription of Na language. Seneca transcribers report approximately 40% reductions in both the time taken and transcription word error rate when using the Kaldi speech recognition tool kit (Jimerson et al. 2019).

However, a widespread uptake of state-of-the-art tool kits such as Kaldi and ESPnet for use on many of the world's languages is hindered by two primary barriers. The first has traditionally been the general availability of adequate quantities of recordings and transcriptions to train speech recognition systems. With many language communities now proactively making their own language recordings and crowdsourcing the transcription work, this first barrier has been substantially lowered for many languages.

Still, the specialist expertise required to design, build, or even run an existing speech recognition system are beyond the reach of many. Elpis aims to lower the barrier of entry to help people work toward implementing speech recognition systems for their own language by providing an easy-to-use interface. In particular, Elpis was designed with language workers and linguists to provide a graphical user interface to assist the preparation of files for training and recognition using Kaldi for orthographic transcription. Elpis has since been extended to provide an accessible interface for phonemic transcription using ESPnet.

1.2 Overview

Automatic speech recognition (ASR) is a technology used to generate a written transcription of an audio signal. In general, the term is used to refer to a process that involves stages of preparation of existing recordings and transcriptions, using this existing data to train the system, and then using the trained system to infer an automatic transcription for untranscribed audio (this automatic transcription is called the *machine hypothesis*). ASR is used in applications such as speech interfaces on devices such as Google Assistant, Amazon Alexa, or Apple Siri, but beyond such consumer use cases, it can also be beneficial for assisting in workflows of transcribing speech recordings (Michaud et al. 2018).

For orthographic transcription, Elpis uses a statistical ASR system to determine the likelihoods that acoustic units occur in particular sequences, based on the acoustic and textual information provided in the training data. Currently, the default method used is based on a combination of hidden Markov models (HMMs) and Gaussian mixture models (GMMs). The decision to use the HMM+GMM–based technique is based on the attributes of the recordings that the users involved in the first stage of design of Elpis had access to: collections of recordings less than tens of hours in total duration. In general, for languages with large quantities of training material, neural network techniques perform better. However, for small quantities of recordings, HMM+GMM systems are computationally efficient and have comparable performance to neural networks. In future, neural networks for orthographic transcription will be added to Elpis to benefit users with larger quantities of training data.

For phonemic transcription, Elpis uses ESPnet (Watanabe et al. 2017), another speech processing tool kit that is compatible with Kaldi-style input data (and hence can be used with the data preparation procedures Elpis facilitates).

ESPnet provides an "end-to-end" approach, which generally requires more data though reduces the need to prepare "hand-crafted" intermediary data, such as a pronunciation lexicon (introduced below).

Specifically, ESPnet in Elpis uses a hybrid CTC-attention model (Watanabe et al. 2017) with a three-layer BiLSTM encoder and a single layer decoder.

Elpis can be installed on local computers or networked servers, suiting the needs of different users. By running entirely on local hardware, such as a laptop or a desktop, recordings do not have to be uploaded to the cloud, which would pose a privacy and data sovereignty concern for many language communities (Holton, Leonard, & Pulsifer, chapter 4, this volume).

Each ASR technology has data preparation needs that differ according to the requirements of the system. In the following sections, we describe how to prepare language recordings and transcriptions to use with Elpis.

2 Components: Acoustic model, language model, pronunciation lexicon

In this section, we describe the components of the Kaldi orthographic transcription system, which uses a statistical method. For details of the phonemic transcription system used in Elpis, see Adams et al. (2020).

Statistical ASR systems are typically composed of three main parts: an acoustic model, a pronunciation model, and a language model. These models are trained or built separately using some previously transcribed audio and text. The models are then combined and used to provide a hypothesis about the text representation of untranscribed audio.

The acoustic model aims to produce a phonemic transcription for a given input audio recording. It is trained by providing speech recordings along with an orthographic transcript of each utterance. This orthographic transcript is turned into phonemes at training time, and the model is trained by feeding in segments of the waveform along with the appropriate phoneme labels to output.

The pronunciation model prepared by Elpis is simply a pronunciation dictionary, a list of all the words in the lexicon and a representation of how each word is pronounced. These representations are typically phonemic transcriptions. Depending on the degree of orthographic transparency of the target language, these phonemic transcriptions can be straightforwardly derived from the orthography through letter-to-sound rules, or they may need to be curated manually on a word-by-word basis.

The language model is a statistical representation of the occurrence of word sequences in the language. It is trained on the transcription text but may also additionally be trained on any other text-only material that may be available. When combined at runtime, the acoustic model first provides a set of best guesses as to the series of phonemes contained within a previously unseen snippet of audio. The pronunciation model then turns these phonemic transcription candidates into a list of word candidates. The language model then helps further disambiguate these candidates according to what it knows are the most likely series of words that tend to follow each other (learned from the training data).

When a system is trained on small quantities of recordings, typically with few speakers, it will not generalize well to new speakers. In the language documentation context for which Elpis was designed, it is rare to have access to large quantities of recordings to build general conversation systems that can scale for many speakers. However, in the context of language documentation with few speakers, scaling can be less of an issue if most of the speakers are previously observed. It is also important to acknowledge that the resulting system is somewhat limited in its ability to transcribe audio with very different characteristics: for example, if there is little background noise in any of the original audio recordings, the system will struggle to transcribe new recordings with significant amounts of background noise. Another limitation is that the trained system can generally only emit words that have been observed in the original training data, either in the text-and-audio pairs, or in the text-only supplemental materials.

3 Using Elpis

The process of using Elpis for either orthographic or phonemic transcription begins with planning and organizing your recordings and transcriptions. Cleaning, normalizing, and standardizing the transcription text is critical, and effort spent here will make a positive impact on the performance of the system. For detailed steps, refer to tutorial information provided in Foley, Lambourne, and San (2020).

Elpis can be used either locally on high-end laptops or desktop computers or as software on a cloud server. When using Elpis locally, no network connection is needed, making it ideal for fieldwork use in areas with limited connectivity. Local use can also be helpful in enabling the use of automatic speech transcription in situations where privacy/security requirements or data ownership concerns make uploading recordings to cloud services for transcription infeasible. Using a cloud version of Elpis can provide access to large amounts of computing power, reducing the time it can take to train the system. It may also be possible to use local university-run computer clusters to run Elpis. Choosing which method of running Elpis will depend on the particular needs of your language.

3.1 Workflow

A typical workflow begins with making recordings and manually transcribing some of the recordings. For orthographic transcription, a file that maps letters in the orthography to symbols representing how they are pronounced is also prepared. This file is not required for phonemic transcription. The recordings, transcriptions, and letter-to-sound file would then be added to Elpis. For orthographic systems, the pronunciation dictionary is generated by Elpis, and the results are checked and edited. Then the models are trained. After training, untranscribed audio can be passed through the trained model to obtain a hypothesis transcription. The transcription can be viewed and downloaded as a text or ELAN file.

Currently, using Elpis is a linear workflow, requiring retraining when new training data is added to the corpus. For example, if we train a system with three hours of data, we could obtain a hypothesis for fifteen minutes of untranscribed audio and edit the hypothesis. The new transcription can then be added to the corpus. We would then create a new collection of files in Elpis. The pronunciation dictionary may need to be regenerated if there are new words in the new data, and the training would be rerun. This would be repeated for each new, edited hypothesis we wanted to include in the training corpus. Adding data into the training corpus after editing is not mandatory, but it allows the system to learn and potentially correct similar mistakes when transcribing more audio.

3.2   Planning and preparing data

The quality of results that we can obtain from an ASR system depends on the quality and quantity of the recordings and text used to train the system. To build an ASR system's acoustic model, audio is analyzed to learn various examples of each phoneme, or unit of speech. The clearer the recordings that are provided, the better clarity the system will have in "hearing" the difference between phonemes. High-quality audio is said to have a high signal-to-noise ratio, meaning that the voice signal is clear and there is little interfering background noise. Other significant factors include managing multiple people speaking during the activity and repetition of utterances.

Before adding the transcription files to Elpis, the transcriptions must be cleaned to correct typographic errors, normalize orthography, and remove non-lexical text and codes from the annotations. Cleaning transcriptions can take time, but the effort put into cleaning will improve the results of the system. When starting a new language documentation project using an ASR system, make sure to pay careful attention to the consistency of the transcriptions.

For an example of the data used to train Elpis refer to the Abui toy corpus,[1] a tiny selection of transcriptions from a larger corpus of a Papuan language of Alor Island,

Indonesia (Kratochvíl 2007), which has been cleaned and prepared according to the steps outlined herein.[2]

3.2.1 Planning for clean recording   Audio quality can be affected by many factors ranging from the location in which recording happens, the social activity surrounding the recording event, the types of equipment used to make the recording, and the formats used in storing the recordings. Thus, when planning a recording session, try to use a location in which ambient noise can be controlled, such as a room in which air-conditioners can be turned off, or locations that minimize surrounding animal or traffic noises. When recording outside, the impact of wind on a recording can be minimized by using wind shields on microphones, putting up barriers to block wind, or recording in portable structures such as Green's signadome (Green, Woods, & Foley 2011); structures such as the signadome also provide shade for participants, keep out wayward dogs and children, and focus participants' attention on the recording activity at hand. For a detailed guide to planning and recording a language documentation activity in a fieldwork context, see Meakins, Green, and Turpin (2018).

3.2.2 Managing multiple speakers   When planning a recording activity for ASR with multiple speakers, two key factors will affect the ability to use the recordings: separating speakers as audio sources, and overlapping speech.

Directional head-mount microphones with multi-track recording devices are ideal for isolating speakers to individual tracks. Where possible, provide each speaker with a microphone and record to separate tracks on the recording device. This will enable individual speakers to be more easily used in training a multiple-speaker system, by keeping each speaker's voice unmixed. Elpis currently cannot separate the acoustic signal of speakers when they talk over each other. Prior to recording, encourage speakers to be conscious of talking over the top of others and making back-channel interjections. Minimizing the occurrence of overlapping speech during the recording will lead to a cleaner acoustic signal for training.

3.2.3 Repetition   The more instances of each phoneme that can be provided, the more opportunities the ASR system will have to learn, and consequently the ASR system will be more robust. When recording an elicitation activity, try to have a few utterances that are repeated a few times, and aim for some variation in what is recorded, for example, slightly faster and slightly slower speech, some expressive prosody, and some flatter delivery. For multiple speaker systems, try to record repetitions by each speaker. Supply all of these recordings (along with their matching transcriptions) as training data to expose the system to variations in the sounds.

3.2.4 Audio format   When recording, use a lossless format such as WAV rather than a format such as MP3 that discards and compresses audio information (Mattern, chapter 5, this volume). Set the device to record at the highest setting it is capable of—contemporary recording equipment will typically record at 48 kHz or higher. Elpis expects mono (single-channel), 16-bit sample depth, 44.1 kHz sample rate, WAV format audio. If the supplied audio is different to these specifications, Elpis will convert the source to match. Note that it is good to record at higher sample rates and allow Elpis to downsample, as this will provide more flexibility for future reuse of the recordings.

3.2.5 File handling   It is good practice for language recordings to have unique file names, which will ensure that recordings can be uniquely identified. It is particularly important for Elpis that file names are unique across the corpus, so as to prevent erroneous associations of transcriptions to audio when the audio and transcription files are uploaded and added to the collection of training files.

Elpis requires that the base names (the file name part before the period and extension) of each file in a pair of audio and transcription match, with a differing extension, for example: audio1.wav, audio1.eaf, audio2.wav,

audio2.eaf. Prior to your recording activity, set your recording device to use a file-naming template, following good data management planning practices such as those mentioned in Kung (chapter 8, this volume). If the recording device doesn't have a naming template, rename the files after getting them off the device. Rather than doing this manually, use batch-renaming software to save time.

3.2.6 Annotation segmentation   Elpis requires the existing audio and transcriptions to be aligned at an utterance level, meaning that it is sufficient to transcribe in chunks or segments that are approximately ten seconds in duration or less (see figure 36.1). Word- or phoneme-level segmentation of the training data is not necessary.

3.2.7 Typographic errors   Check the transcriptions for typographic errors. For now, this is a manual process that is best done using the software that the transcriptions are written with; however, planned Elpis work includes the ability to edit the transcripts directly in the interface. Pay attention to spelling errors, and for consistency in spelling across the corpus, especially for transcriptions that may have developed over many years as the transcribers' knowledge of the language evolved.

3.2.8 Orthographic consistency   To maximize the frequency of occurrence of words, consistency in orthography within the training data is important. Spelling the same word in multiple ways will confuse the language model and dilute the frequency count for that word among the number of spellings used. The challenge for many languages is that there may not be a standard orthography, or the orthography may change over time

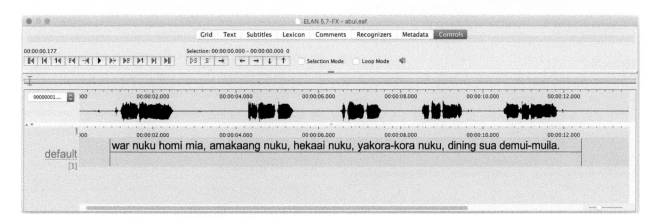

Figure 36.1

Annotation segment in ELAN approximately ten seconds in duration.

in response to changes in social-political and/or linguistic influences. Even in these contexts, developing a *working orthography* just used for training Elpis, and conforming your training transcriptions to this orthography will benefit the system (even if some speakers and/or language experts do not agree on adopting this orthography as a broader standard).

3.2.9 Faithful transcriptions Ensure that everything in the speech signal is transcribed faithfully and that only human speech is transcribed. For example, if the speaker says 'hello hello', then both *hellos* should be transcribed. Likewise, transcriptions should not include references to non-speech sounds. If dogs are barking, or someone is laughing in the audio, do not transcribe as "dogs barking" or "people laughing"; just leave the descriptions out or make an annotation describing the audio on a different tier if using ELAN.

3.2.10 Non-lexical forms Non-lexical numbers and shorthand forms of words should be replaced in the transcriptions with full lexical forms. For example, replace "9" with "nine"; if someone says 'for example', check that the transcript reflects what is said, and is not written as "e.g." Likewise, for abbreviations, check that the transcription reflects what was spoken. This cleaning stage is an important step in ensuring that what is written is as close as possible to the acoustic signal.

3.2.11 Speaker and language codes Other common transcription artifacts that are among the transcription text, such as speaker and language codes (see figure 36.2), should be removed (see figure 36.3) and kept as tier attributes, in separate transcription tiers (if using ELAN), or in metadata files.

DvE NLD Have you seen the turtles? They are usually in the lake.

Figure 36.2
Original transcription has speaker (DvE) and language codes (NLD).

Have you seen the turtles? They are usually in the lake.

Figure 36.3
Speaker and language codes removed from the transcription.

| DvE | Have you seen the turtles | | Yeah right |
| BF | | They are in the lake | |

Figure 36.5
Tiers for each speaker.

Although it is possible to train multilingual ASR systems, Elpis is currently configured to train single-language systems. If the recordings contain multiple languages, separate the languages to different tiers (if using ELAN) or delete the second-language transcriptions from the data. When removing languages from the transcriptions, work with a copy of the data, as this is a destructive process.[3]

Similarly, for multiple speakers, rather than including speaker codes in a single tier (see figure 36.4), annotate each speaker on a separate tier, labeled with the speaker's name, or add the speaker's name as a tier attribute (see figure 36.5) (see sentence figure 36.4).

3.2.12 Automatic cleaning After thoroughly cleaning and normalizing the audio and transcription files, they can be added to Elpis. When they are added, some further processing stages occur, including automatic removal of English words and other text that you can specify, stripping punctuation, and changing the corpus to lowercase. Elpis uses the Natural Language Toolkit (NLTK) English corpus to identify words in the transcriptions that match and removes them. For utterances that are greater than 10% English in total, the whole utterance is excluded from the data. Elpis will remove certain punctuation marks, including periods, commas, single and double quotation marks, and so forth. The set of punctuation marks to be removed can be customized by the user.

3.3 Pronunciation lexicon

For orthographic transcription, a plain text file that lists the characters used in the transcription, along with symbols that represent the pronunciation, is used to create a pronunciation lexicon. The text file is also referred to as grapheme-to-phoneme (G2P), letter-to-phoneme, or letter-to-sound mapping. The letter-to-sound mapping in Elpis is crude, intended to be a rough draft that can be improved iteratively.

DvE: Have you seen the turtles   BF: They are in the lake   DvE: Yeah right   **Figure 36.4**
Original single-tier structure.

```
m m
ng ŋ
n n
r r
y j
l l
q q
v w
# vowels
uu u:
u u
ii i:
```

Figure 36.6
A section of a letter-to-sound file.

The letter-to-sound text file is prepared by listing all the characters used in the orthography in one column. In a second column, separated by a space, a symbol is placed to represent the pronunciation, such as an International Phonetic Alphabet (IPA) or X-SAMPA symbol (Elpis accepts many consistent phonemic transcription systems). Comments can be written in the file with a # starting the comment line (see figure 36.6).

After uploading the letter-to-sound file, Elpis generates a pronunciation dictionary (see figure 36.7). It does this crudely by splitting each word in the lexicon into individual characters and replacing them with the pronunciation symbol. This works better for languages where the orthography closely matches the pronunciation. Regardless, this is a stage where the results will need to be reviewed and edited.

When reviewing the results, corrections can be made directly in the interface for individual words, or system-wide changes can be made by updating the letter-to-sound.txt file. Check words that have been transcribed with consecutive matching characters. Do they represent one sound or two? If there is only one, add a line to the letter-to-sound.txt file, mapping the consecutive characters to a single symbol and rebuild the lexicon.

For example, if a word 'singer' is erroneously mapped to "singer s i n g ə" in the lexicon, where for Australian English it should have a single velar nasal *ŋ* instead of an alveolar nasal *n* followed by a velar stop *g*, add "ng ŋ" to letter-to-sound.txt above the entry for "n n" (see figure 36.8), upload it again, and rebuild the lexicon. The results should be collapsed lexicon entry "singer s i ŋ ə".

```
di d I
ba b a
amakaang a m a k a: ŋ
botol b O t O l
yaari j a: r I
dining d I n I ŋ
hekaai h E k a: I
kamar k a m a r
mui m u I
dong d O ŋ
hepikaai h E p I k a: I
muila m u I l a
ayoku a j O k u
hada h a d a
mia m I a
ong O ŋ
kaai k a: I
homi h O m I
hayei h a j E I
deina d E I n a
del d E l
```

Figure 36.7
A pronunciation dictionary generated by the letter-to-sound map.

```
ng ŋ
n n
```

Figure 36.8
Specifying consecutive characters and prioritizing the order of entries.

Make sure to put these replacements earlier in the letter-to-sound file, above single characters.

When working iteratively to develop the pronunciation lexicon, incrementally name the letter-to-sound file when you make changes to it. Use the same name as the name for this step in Elpis. This way you can track which version you are using and which improvements you have made.

A dictionary can be manually created and used to train a model with other tools such as Phonetisaurus (Novak, Minematsu, & Hirose 2016), but this is not currently supported in Elpis.

3.4 Language model

The language model is a probabilistic approach to predicting the order of words occurring in the language, as observed in the training text. It is used to disambiguate the occurrence of words that have the same pronunciation, for example, identifying which is the correct option from *you're book* or *your book*. A probabilistic language model is also known as a grammar, but this is quite a different, somewhat simpler, sense of the word than a linguist's grammar.

3.4.1 N-grams

For orthographic transcription, the language model is learned from sequences of consecutive words in the training files: chiefly, the audio-and-text pairs, but optionally also any supplementary text-only materials such as word lists, bible translations, dictionaries. The number of words in a sequence is referred to as an *n-gram*, with individual words being a *unigram*, word pairs are *bigrams*, three words in a row are *trigrams*, four words are *4-gram*, and so on. For example, given the sentence "The quick brown fox jumped . . . ," the language model can be trained to learn single words (unigrams) or words with their neighbors (bigrams, trigrams, and so on), as follows:

Unigrams: the, quick, brown, fox, jumped

Bigrams: the quick, quick brown, brown fox, fox jumped

Trigrams: the quick brown, quick brown fox, brown fox jumped

The n-gram value is a setting that can be chosen in the Elpis interface prior to starting the training process. The optimal n-gram value for a language will be different depending on the training transcription text used. Although larger n-gram values (larger groups of words) generate more information, in language documentation it can be difficult to record enough instances of larger structures to give statistical value to the structures, especially for languages with small quantities of training recordings.

Consider a tiny corpus with three sentences: "I like to play tennis with Daan"; "I like to play tennis with Nay"; and "I like to play football with Nay." In this tiny corpus, a 7-gram structure would have the maximum amount of information. However, we would only see a single occurrence of each instance, so a probabilistic system would not be able to choose a likelihood between the options, each being equally likely. If we used a smaller n-gram, our model would see higher occurrences of the bigrams "play tennis" and "with Nay" because there are two occurrences of those bigrams in the training text. In this way, our model would learn a higher likelihood of certain word structures, with each of those structures

occurring twice compared with the lower probability of "play football" and "with Daan" only occurring once.

Unseen word sequences are determined using a technique called *back-off*, which looks for the probability of a word sequence at the previous n-gram level. For example, if we are using trigrams, and no trigram structure of a hypothesis occurs, the system can back-off and try bigram structures. If no bigrams are known, we could fall back to using unigrams. This is clearly not how the human mind works, but it is remarkably effective for machines.

3.5 Diagnostics

3.5.1 Word error rates

When Elpis trains a model on a new data set, it splits off part of the data set to use as a *held-out test set*. This test set is used to evaluate the speech recognition model during and after the training process by producing an accuracy metric known as *word error rate*, or WER. This metric is computed by comparing the machine transcription of the audio in the test set to the human-provided transcription of this audio, which is assumed to be correct. Because the test set is not included in the training data, this provides a fair assessment of the level of quality that could be expected on similar entirely new, untranscribed data that is fed into Elpis for transcription. By similar, we mean data with the same characteristics, such as in terms of topic, background noise levels, and so on. In general, the closer the data characteristics are to the training data, the better the model will perform.

Lower WERs correspond to better performance: put simply, WERs reflect the number of words transcribed incorrectly within the test set, and fewer errors are better. Specifically, WER is calculated by counting three types of errors:

1. Deletions, where a word is not transcribed but it should have been. For example, 'hello world' is mistranscribed as "hello" with the word *world* missed.

2. Insertions, where a word is transcribed where no word should be transcribed. For example, 'hello world' is mistranscribed as "hello world people" with the word *people* incorrectly inserted.

3. Substitutions, where a word is transcribed incorrectly, replacing another word. For example, mistranscribing 'hello world' as "hello moon" incorrectly substitutes the word *world* with the word *moon*.

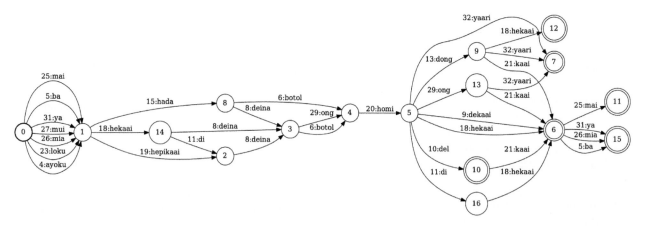

Figure 36.9
Lattice generated for an Abui utterance.

To produce the WER, the number of errors is then added up and divided by the number of words in the correct transcription. WERs will vary depending on the complexity of the language and the recordings, but in general, you should expect to see the WER drop over time as you include more training data for the models.

When performing phonemic transcription with ESPnet, Elpis reports a *phoneme error rate* (PER), an equivalent system for reporting phonemic errors rather than word errors.

3.5.2 Lattices When Elpis orthographically transcribes new audio, it runs the audio through the acoustic, pronunciation, and language models to produce a transcription. Under the hood, however, modern speech recognition systems do not generate just one transcription. Instead, they produce a *lattice* of options, which you can read as different ways the audio could be transcribed.

Reading from left to right in figure 36.9, there are multiple options for the first word, and then a number of different paths leading into different *states* of the lattice. These all represent potential transcriptions of the audio, and Elpis returns the most likely of the paths going through this lattice as the final transcription. In some cases, however, the model's second guess may actually turn out to be correct.

Up to the time of writing this chapter, the main focus of Elpis development has been on consultatively creating a user-friendly interface for data preparation for Kaldi and ESPnet. As this stage of the development stabilizes, we are experimenting with approaches to providing the diagnostic information (e.g., WER, lattices) in a user-friendly manner and in ways that can be easily integrated into typical language documentation transcription workflow patterns.

4 Conclusion

We have described the main components of statistical speech recognition systems and described what is required to prepare data to use Elpis, along with the reasons why data preparation is required. This chapter provided information in addition to what is covered in Elpis tutorials, to provide a greater contextualization of the steps involved in using Elpis.

By following the guidance given here in preparing, cleaning, and normalizing files, the value of the recordings and transcriptions will be maximized for training Elpis, other ASR systems, and other language technologies. It is often thought that only supplying greater quantities of data to a system will improve the system, but in fact, there is much to be gained (and learned) from improving the quality of existing material.

We hope that this chapter has provided an understanding of the data preparation requirements and the potential for automatic speech recognition to be used in language documentation workflows.

Notes

1. https://github.com/CoEDL/toy-corpora

2. We thank František Kratochvíl for graciously offering the Abui data for use during the first iteration of the Elpis workshop (June 28, 2017) and Elpis-related demonstrations beyond.

3. See Han (chapter 6, this volume) for considerations in planning and managing data transformation processes.

References

Adams, O., B. Galliot, G. Wisniewski, N. Lambourne, B. Foley, R. Sanders-Dwyer, J. Wiles, et al. 2020. User-friendly automatic transcription of low-resource languages: Plugging ESPnet into Elpis. *Proceedings of the 4th Workshop on the Use of Computational Methods in the Study of Endangered Languages (ComputEL)*. Vol. 1. Online.

ELAN, version 5.7 (Computer software). 2019. Nijmegen, the Netherlands: Max Planck Institute for Psycholinguistics. https://tla.mpi.nl/tools/tla-tools/elan/.

Foley, B., J. T. Arnold, R. Coto-Solano, G. Durantin, T. M. Ellison, D. van Esch, S. Heath, et al. 2018. Building speech recognition systems for language documentation: The CoEDL Endangered Language Pipeline and Inference System (Elpis). In *The 6th International Workshop on Spoken Language Technologies for Under-Resourced Languages (SLTU)*, ed. S. S. Agrawal, 200–204. https://www.isca-speech.org/archive/SLTU_2018/pdfs/Ben.pdf.

Foley, B., G. Durantin, A. Ajayan, and J. Wiles. 2019. Transcription Survey. Paper presented at the 52nd conference of the Australian Linguistic Society (ALS2019), Sydney, Australia, December 11–13.

Foley, B., N. Lambourne, and N. San. 2020. *Elpis documentation*. Zenodo. December 27. https://doi.org/10.5281/zenodo.4394816.

Green, J., G. Woods, and B. Foley. 2011. Looking at language: Appropriate design for sign language resources in remote Australian Indigenous communities. *Sustainable Data from Digital Research: Humanities Perspectives on Digital Scholarship*. http://ses.library.usyd.edu.au/handle/2123/7949.

Himmelmann, N. P. 2018. Meeting the transcription challenge. In *Reflections on Language Documentation 20 Years after Himmelmann*, ed. B. McDonnell, A. L. Berez-Kroeker, and G. Holton, 33–40. Honolulu: University of Hawaiʻi Press. https://scholarspace.manoa.hawaii.edu/handle/10125/24806.

Jimerson, R., R. Hatcher, R. Ptucha, and E. Prud'hommeaux. 2019. Speech technology for supporting community-based endangered language documentation. Poster presented at the 6th International Conference on Language Documentation and Conservation (ICLDC), Honolulu, Hawaiʻi, February 28–March 3.

Jurafsky, D., and J. H. Martin. Forthcoming. *Speech and Language Processing*, 3rd ed. https://web.stanford.edu/~jurafsky/slp3/.

Kratochvíl, F. 2007. *A Grammar of Abui*. Doctoral thesis, Leiden University. http://hdl.handle.net/1887/11998.

Meakins, F., J. Green, and M. Turpin. 2018. *Understanding Linguistic Fieldwork*. Abingdon, UK: Routledge.

Michaud, A., O. Adams, T. A. Cohn, G. Neubig, and S. Guillaume. 2018. Integrating automatic transcription into the language documentation workflow: Experiments with Na data and the Persephone toolkit. *Language Documentation and Conservation* 12:393–429. https://scholarspace.manoa.hawaii.edu/handle/10125/24793.

Novak, J. R., N. Minematsu, and K. Hirose. 2016. Phonetisaurus: Exploring grapheme-to-phoneme conversion with joint n-gram models in the WFST framework. *Natural Language Engineering* 22 (6): 907–938. https://doi.org/10.1017/S1351324915000315.

Povey, D., A. Ghoshal, G. Boulianne, L. Burget, O. Glembek, N. Goel, M. Hannemann, et al. 2011. The Kaldi Speech Recognition Toolkit. Paper presented at IEEE 2011 Workshop on Automatic Speech Recognition and Understanding. Hilton Waikoloa Village, Big Island, Hawaii.

Watanabe, S., T. Hori, S. Kim, J. R. Hershey, and T. Hayashi. 2017. Hybrid CTC/attention architecture for end-to-end speech recognition. *IEEE Journal of Selected Topics in Signal Processing* 11 (8): 1240–1253.

Watanabe, S., H. Takaaki, K. Shigeki, H. Tomoki, N. Jiro, U. Yuya, N. E. Y. Soplin, et al. 2018. *Espnet: End-to-end speech processing toolkit*. arXiv preprint. arXiv:1804.00015.

37 Managing Data and Statistical Code According to the FAIR Principles

Laura A. Janda

1 Introduction: The FAIR principles

In linguistic studies that draw on empirical data and statistical code, the linguistic community needs full access not just to the scholarly article or report of the findings but also to the data and statistical code that stand behind them. Ideally researchers should post a resource that includes all of the researcher's data as well as the necessary tools for interpretation and analysis in a format that is accessible, transparent, and explicit enough to allow a second researcher to carry out the same analysis on that data or on similar data. The idea is simple, but making it work in practice requires the author of a study to take several issues into consideration.

This chapter contains recommendations for linguists working with data sets that are analyzed with statistical code to conform to the FAIR principles for data management (cf. Wilkinson et al. 2016):[1]

- Findable: Attaching metadata to a post that is indexed in an archive makes it possible for other researchers to find the data and code.
- Accessible: Using an archive that is publicly available makes it possible for other researchers to access resources that contain the data and code.
- Interoperable: Using file formats that are persistent and open-source makes it more likely that other researchers will be able to open and use the files.
- Reusable: Providing adequate description of the files, their contents, the variables, and their values, as well as annotation for the statistical code, will make it possible for other researchers to understand and reuse the data and code.[2]

Adherence to the FAIR principles with regard to data and code for statistical analysis entails additional work, but there are benefits both for the scholar and for the

field as a whole. Linguistics is a relative late-comer to the scientific frontier of replicable research, and our performance thus far leaves a lot to be desired (see Gawne & Styles, chapter 2, this volume). Berez-Kroeker et al. (2017) and Gawne et al. (2017) surveyed linguistics articles, dissertations, and descriptive grammars published in 2003–2012 and found that for most journals, fewer than 50% of authors provided descriptions of methodology or citations of the sources of linguistic examples. Archiving of data was likewise found lacking among linguists: only twelve of fifty dissertations and ten of fifty grammars had archived data at the time of publication.

We can all contribute to the prestige of our field by setting ethical standards for best practices in data management and collaboration. Posting reusable data and code fosters horizontal learning across the community of researchers, facilitating the propagation of new methods. It is also a safeguard against research fraud. Under pressure to get published in prestigious journals, some researchers have fabricated or fudged data to impress reviewers, a problem that has been particularly acute in the field of medicine (cf. Fanelli 2009). Publication of data and code will not eliminate the possibility of fraud, but it will make fraud easier to detect, and, if practiced regularly, will improve the overall level of accountability and integrity in the field. Such posts can additionally help eliminate unnecessary duplication of efforts, because researchers can more easily discover whether a given study has been conducted. And there is also the possibility that a set of data and/or statistical code will have unforeseen uses, analogous to Velcro, which was developed for use by astronauts in space and is now common in clothing and widely used by earthlings.

The benefit of integrity builds the reputation of the individual researcher, because backing up arguments with the facts they are based on contributes to the legitimacy of one's claims. Furthermore, one never knows when one might need to go back to a data set, either to squeeze another analysis out of it or to use it as a recipe for a parallel analysis of new data. If the data and code are adequately annotated and archived, this will be easy to do, even if time has erased the meanings of all the abbreviations and code that were so obvious when working on the original project from the researcher's personal memory. After several mishaps with data that were lost, corrupted, or otherwise became uninterpretable, along with discontinuance of site licenses and backward-incompatible software upgrades that permanently separated me from my data and analyses, I have come to appreciate the value of things that are open-access, open-source, and generally portable across time and platforms (see Mattern, chapter 5, this volume, and Collister, chapter 9, this volume).

Here I present two examples from resources that I have created in the spirit of adhering to the FAIR principles. I think that I have been partly successful in these examples, but I have also made my share of mistakes. I present these two resources "warts and all" and point out some places where I could have done a better job. These resources (also referred to as posts) are available in the TROLLing archive: the Tromsø Repository of Language and Linguistics (https://dataverse.no/dataverse/trolling), which I use as an example in this chapter (see also Andreassen, chapter 7, this volume). As a discipline-specific archive, TROLLing offers added value to the post (Alter & Gonzalez 2018:149) and comes with three features that are particularly desirable for archiving linguistic data and statistical code: (1) public access, (2) professional management, and (3) harvestable metadata. In addition, TROLLing adheres to the FAIR principles and assists authors in achieving these goals.

2   A resource that adheres to FAIR principles, but is not user-friendly

The first resource that I use as an example is available at https://doi.org/10.18710/4XTXMH. It was created in connection with Janda and Antonsen (2016), a study of a language change in which a synthetic possessive construction with a possessive suffix is being replaced by an analytic construction with a reflexive pronoun in the North Saami language. We collected a data set with over two thousand examples across three generations of speakers and performed a statistical analysis to determine the influence of various factors on the ongoing change. We also made some graphs to visualize our data and results. Next I demonstrate how this resource adheres to FAIR principles.

Findable: Because the metadata can be searched, data and code become findable when posted in an archive with harvestable metadata. In the metadata section of this post I added Keywords: "North Saami, possessive suffix, Uralic, S-curve, vocative, possession, language change, complexity"; and selected Topic Classifications: "morphology, diachronic, affixes." Kind of Data is listed as "corpus." Other kinds of data could include "questionnaire" and "experiment," and in both cases one would need to make sure that no personal identifiers are present so that the data can be publicly archived. In the case of experimental data, it would be useful to include files representing the stimuli. This TROLLing post additionally lists the Geographic Coverage as: "Norway, Sweden, Finland, Sápmi, Northern Scandinavia."

Accessible: A unique identifier and URL make data and code accessible. The first thing that happens when a user initiates a TROLLing post is that the site generates a unique identifier and URL for the data set (previously this was achieved with a "handle," or hdl, as in this example, but now the system produces a digital object identifier, or DOI, for each post). The unique URL exists right from the start and persists no matter how many times the TROLLing post is updated, although it is not visible to others until it is submitted. The advantage to this is that the TROLLing post can be cited in an article, in addition to citing the article in the TROLLing post, so cross-referencing is achieved in both directions. However, it is not necessary to have a published article to create a post. Any data set can be posted, regardless of whether there is an accompanying article. This includes data representing so-called negative results, which can be challenging to publish, but can be very valuable to the greater scientific community nevertheless.

Interoperable: The use of appropriate formats makes data and code usable across platforms. A crucial issue for sharing data and code is that they be presented in formats that can be accessed by anyone and at any future time (see Mattern, chapter 5, this volume). For this reason, it is best to select persistent non-proprietary open formats such as .pdf and .txt, as required in the TROLLing repository (cf. TROLLing guidelines, https://site.uit

.no/dataverseno/deposit/prepare/#what-are-persistent -file-formats; Andreassen, chapter 7, this volume). This will hopefully safeguard data and code against a situation that would lack any device or software needed to access them. Using such formats can mean losing the direct connection to software that comes along with an item such as an R script. This can be handled by providing duplicate files in different formats.

Reusable: In addition to the information in the metadata, particularly the Description and the citation of the related article, the next most important item is a readme file. Ideally the readme file should explain what all the other files in the post are, providing details of the data files including all of the factors and what their values are. In TROLLing, it is also possible to attach a description to each file. Providing details about data and code can be a tedious process, but it is essential to make them reusable.

In the post about North Saami possessive constructions I did some things right and there were other things I could have done better. I did make a readme file in a persistent open format (Readme file for Diachronica-CART.txt), but that readme file is not the first file that a user sees—it is the seventh of ten because TROLLing lists the files in alphabetical order according to their titles. I have since learned that one should give the readme file a name like "01Readme.txt" so that it will be put at the beginning of the list. Another problem with my readme file is that it does not provide a guide to all the files in the post; instead I relied on the descriptions attached to each file. While most of these descriptions are reasonably straightforward, such as "This is the R code for the CART analysis," the fact that the files have been alphabetized means that the logical order of the files is a bit jumbled in addition to the fact that information has been scattered across the ten files. A strategy to improve this would be to give all the files names starting with "01," "02," and so on. But even so, it would be better to have all the file descriptions in one place connected in a coherent way, namely in a "01Readme" file.

My readme file describes the factors and values used in one file that has a lot of factors and values, namely the one called DiachronicaCART.csv. That description is quite thorough, as shown in this example:

Column A/PossCon: This column represents the possessive construction (PossCon), and the values are NPx (noun + possessive suffix) and Refl (analytic construction with reflexive genitive pronoun).

Given this information, most researchers should be able to decipher all of the abbreviations used to name both the factors and their values.

Worse, however, is the fact that the data in DiachronicaCART.csv are just the annotations for the sentences that we analyzed. The sentences themselves are presented in a file called AnnotatedSentences.txt, which has this attached description in the TROLLing post:

This file contains the sentences that constitute our database, along with their annotations. Most of the annotations are explained in the Readme file for Diachronica CART. This file additionally cites the works of the authors that the sentences are taken from and gives some additional details concerning the semantic classes of possessums.

It is possible to identify most of the annotations from the readme file, but only because the first eleven factors appear in the same order and use all the same abbreviations. However, after that we have some additional information, the name of the literary work and the page number where the example is found, inserted before the last two factors are listed. In other words, the information is there, but it is not very user-friendly.

Another problem with DiachronicaCART.csv is that it is in .csv (comma-separated values) format, which has some quirks. This format is not fully standardized, it runs into problems with data fields that contain commas, and it can include data that use other marks of separation such as semicolons. A better alternative is tab-separated values (.tab or .tsv), because this format is more widely supported. One possibility would be to save duplicate data sets in both formats to preserve some benefits of the original file and also protect the file against future incompatibilities.

Our article about North Saami possessive constructions (Janda & Antonsen 2016) contains three figures, and our TROLLing post presents both the data and the code needed to produce these figures. Figure 1 in our article shows the longitudinal development of the language change. The relevant data for figure 1 in our article is presented in Scurve.csv, and in the TROLLing post I give details about the columns and values in the description attached to this file, because in this case there are only five columns and those contain values that are easy to describe (names of authors, year of birth). ScurveCode.txt, as shown in sample file 37.1, contains the R code used to generate the plot (labeled figure 1 in our article) from Scurve.csv.

Code for S-curve

```
> Sdat=read.csv(file=file.choose(), header=T)
#Choose Scurve.csv
> print(Sdat)
name year NPx Refl PropRefl
1 A Larsen 1870 132 11 0.07692308
2 J Turi 1895 88 24 0.21428570
3 KN Turi 1895 38 3 0.07317073
4 HA Guttorm 1907 250 9 0.03474903
5 M Bongo 1923 14 1 0.06666667
6 AO Eira 1927 31 3 0.08823529
7 JA Vest 1948 498 365 0.42294320
8 K Paltto 1947 114 50 0.30487800
9 EM Vars 1957 152 153 0.50163930
10 JM Mienna 1972 17 68 0.80000000
11 MA Sara 1983 49 63 0.56250000
> plot(Sdat$year,Sdat$PropRefl, type= "n", xlab="Year
of Birth", ylab="Proportion of ReflN")
>
text(Sdat$year,Sdat$PropRefl,as.character(Sdat$name),
cex=0.7)
> lines(lowess(Sdat$year,Sdat$PropRefl))
```

Sample file 37.1
ScurveCode.txt.

While this is an accurate representation of the statistical code needed to plot figure 1 in our article, there is not much annotation here (the only annotation is #Choose Scurve.csv, telling the user which file to use as input data) and this file has not been set up in such a way that it can be fed directly into R (one would need to delete the > characters and add # before all the rows of the table of Sdat). It would have been desirable to add annotations explaining what the last three lines of code do, namely create the plot, add the text, and add the locally weighted scatterplot smoothing line. The file Scurve.pdf shows what the result should look like (our figure 1). And because all three of these files begin with "Scurve" they are conveniently listed together.

The representation of the R code for the classification and regression tree (CART) analysis is somewhat more successful in the sense that it can be directly fed into R and is given in both .R and .txt file formats (DiachronicaCode.R, DiachronicaRcode.txt). But again, there should have been more annotation, particularly to identify the parts of the code that produce the plots that are in figures 2 and 3 in our article. Furthermore,

the names of the files could have been more informative, something like "CARTanalysis.txt." "Diachronica" here refers to the journal that the article was published in, a piece of information that was useful to me on my personal computer, but is not so useful for another user.

3 A resource that is somewhat more successful

The second example is of the TROLLing post at https://doi.org/10.18710/VDWPZS for data and statistical code from Janda and Tyers (2018), an article about Russian paradigms. This post both conforms to the FAIR principles and does a better job in terms of user-friendliness. Sample file 37.2 shows an example of an R script in this TROLLing post for which I provided better annotation:

```
#This R script is supplementary to the article
#"Less is More: Why All Paradigms are Defective, and
Why that is a Good Thing"
#by Laura A. Janda and Francis M. Tyers
#This script shows how to create the plot in Figure 1:
#Correspondence Analysis for Masculine Animate Lexemes
#The same code can be used (just changing the names of
the files)
#to make similar plots for the other groups of nouns.
#This code also shows how to get the data for Tables
4a-b and 5.
#First load the languageR package.
#Note that if you do not have that package, you will
need to install it first.
library(languageR)
#Then load the data that we need:
mascanim<-read.csv(file.choose(), header=T)
#We name this data mascanim because it shows the
grammatical profiles
#of masculine animate nouns.
#Choose this file: procent-I-m.aa.csv
#Notice that this same code can be used to load any of
the other datasets,
#but of course each one should get a corresponding
name.
#Check to make sure that this file has loaded
correctly:
head(mascanim)
#There is one item that has accidentally been included
in this file,
#кто-то 'someone' is actually a pronoun and needs to
be removed.
```

```
#You can see it here:
mascanim[mascanim$lemma=="кто-то",]
#Notice that this same code can be used to look at the
grammatical profile
#of any noun in the dataset.
#This tells us that кто-то is on line 20, so that is
the line to remove.
#Remove it with this code:
mascanim<-mascanim[-20,]
#Now we need to subset the data to take only the
columns that we need
#for the correspondence analysis, namely the lemma
(column 2) and
#the grammatical profile (the percentages listed in
columns 5 through 16).
#Here is how we do that:
mascanimdata <- mascanim[, c(2, 5:16)]
#Now we need to make this into a dataframe:
mascanimdataframe <- data.frame(mascanimdata)
#Now we run the correspondence analysis:
mascanimdataframe.ca <-
corres.fnc(mascanimdataframe[2:13])
#And then we plot the result:
plot(mascanimdataframe.ca,
rlabels=mascanimdataframe$lemma, rcex=0.75)
#This is the plot found in Figure 1.
#Note that you can use the following code to get the
values for
#Factor 1 and Factor 2 from the correspondence
analysis:
mascanimCoor=attr(mascanimdataframe.ca,
"data")$origOut$rproj
#You can see what this looks like here:
head(mascanimCoor)
#And you can add these into the dataframe so that they
are aligned
#with the lemmas:
mascanimdataframe$Factor1 <- mascanimCoor[,1]
mascanimdataframe$Factor2 <- mascanimCoor[,2]
#Now they are in your dataframe, as you see here:
head(mascanimdataframe)
#It is also possible to order lemmas according to
their
#Factor 1 values, for example:
mascanimdataframe[order(mascanimdataframe$Factor1),]
```

Sample file 37.2

Paradigms.R (also presented as Paradigms.R.pdf).

This annotation is far more explicit, even giving directions that would enable the reader to engage further with the data and analysis. However, this post is not perfect either. The name of the file is not very helpful; "Paradigms" merely tells the user that this is a file related to paradigms, which is what the whole post is about. It would have been better to give this file a more descriptive name, like "RScriptForCorrespondenceAnalysisOfMasculineAnimateParadigms.pdf."

4 Closing recommendations

Solid data management principles are fairly new to most linguists, something that we are just beginning to wrap our heads around. In this situation, we are better off helping each other out and learning from each other. Gone are the days of the solo linguist like Mr. Higgins in his cozy library. For many scholarly works today, no single individual can command all of the relevant areas of expertise. Making linguistic data and code accessible according to FAIR principles is one way to promote collaboration and raise competence within the field. And there is evidence that this actually works: a couple of years ago while serving on a dissertation committee, I discovered that the candidate had downloaded one of my TROLLing posts and used it as a model for the analysis of his own data.

Because we all have limited time and energy, making data and code reusable can seem like one more burden. And even when one takes on this extra burden, like so many other things, every time one goes back to a post, it is possible to identify ways in which it could have been improved. Hopefully this set of guidelines will convince other researchers that it is worth trying and will help to streamline the process and avoid pitfalls.

To make these tasks more manageable, one could begin working on documentation early in the research process, with a data management plan (see Kung, chapter 8, this volume), and make sure that readme files and annotated R scripts are created early on and updated periodically, rather than tackling the whole job after a publication is accepted. Giving files informative names and ordering them in a logical fashion is helpful. All files should be presented in persistent open-source formats and should be archived in a public discipline-specific archive that collects harvestable metadata in conformity with scholarly standards.

Notes

1. Brief statements of the FAIR principles are also available at https://www.force11.org/group/fairgroup/fairprinciples and https://www.go-fair.org/fair-principles/.

2. I have opted to use *reusable* instead of "reproducible" or "replicable" as it is the term adopted in the FAIR principles statements.

References

Alter, G., and R. Gonzalez. 2018. Responsible practices for data sharing. *American Psychologist* 73 (2): 146–156. http://dx.doi.org/10.1037/amp0000258.

Berez-Kroeker, Andrea L., Lauren Gawne, Barbara F. Kelly, and Tyler Heston. 2017. *A Survey of Current Reproducibility Practices in Linguistics Journals, 2003–2012*. https://sites.google.com/a/hawaii.edu/data-citation/survey.

Fanelli, Daniele. 2009. How many scientists fabricate and falsify research? A systematic review and meta-analysis of survey data. *PLoS One* 4 (5): e5738. https://journals.plos.org/plosone/article?id=10.1371/journal.pone.0005738.

Gawne, Lauren, Barbara F. Kelly, Andrea L. Berez-Kroeker, and Tyler Heston. 2017. Putting practice into words: The state of data and methods transparency in grammatical descriptions. *Language Documentation and Conservation* 11:157–189. http://hdl.handle.net/10125/24731.

Janda, Laura A., and Lene Antonsen. 2016. The ongoing eclipse of possessive suffixes in North Saami: A case study in reduction of morphological complexity. *Diachronica* 33 (3): 330–366. http://dx.doi.org/10.1075/dia.33.3.02jan.

Janda, Laura A., and Francis M. Tyers. 2018. Less is more: Why all paradigms are defective, and why that is a good thing. *Corpus Linguistics and Linguistic Theory* 14 (2). doi.org/10.1515/cllt-2018-0031.

Wilkinson, Mark D., Michel Dumontier, IJsbrand Jan Aalbersberg, Gabrielle Appleton, Myles Axton, Arie Baak, Niklas Blomberg, et al. 2016. The FAIR Guiding Principles for scientific data management and stewardship. *Scientific Data* 3:160018. https://doi.org/10.1038/sdata.2016.18.

Stefan Th. Gries

1   Introduction

This chapter discusses data management and preparation issues that would arise in a fictitious corpus study using data from the British National Corpus World XML edition (BNC; BNC Consortium 2001); for overview and discussion of corpus linguistics as a field and its relation to notions such as *theory* and *method*, see the 2010 special issue of the *International Journal of Corpus Linguistics* (Pope 2010) and McEnery and Hardie (2011). This corpus consists of approximately 100 million words—4,049 files with 10 million words from spoken and 90 million words from written data—that were compiled to represent British English of the 1980s and is by now downloadable for free from the Oxford Text Archive (http://ota.ox.ac.uk /desc/2554). Specifically, for this chapter, I am discussing a hypothetical study of the so-called dative alternation between a ditransitive construction as in (1a) and the often-available prepositional dative with *to* in (1b); we will restrict our attention to sentences in the active voice.

(1) a. Captain Picard gave Commander Data a new phaser.
     b. Captain Picard gave a new phaser to Commander Data.

To study this kind of alternation, a corpus-linguistic analysis would typically begin from a concordance display that shows instances of each construction in context, as shown in a screenshot in the appendix. This is so that the user can read each example and annotate it for the large number of variables that seem to jointly affect the dative alternation. These include, but are not limited to, morphological, syntactic, semantic, information-structural, psycholinguistic, and other factors and have been identified in a large number of corpus-linguistic and quantitative studies of this alternation (see Gries 2003 for one of the earliest multifactorial studies and Bresnan et al. 2007

for the first one involving mixed-effects regression modeling). However, even if this alternation is fairly well understood by now, this example is still instructive for a variety of reasons:

- The BNC has been one of the most widely used corpora.
- Its XML annotation is fairly comprehensive and, on the morphosyntactic side of things, includes part-of-speech tags, some multi-word annotation, and lemma annotation.
- Its annotation does not include syntactic parse trees.

Given the BNC's annotation scheme and the absence of syntactic parses, retrieving syntactic constructions of the above-mentioned kind from the BNC is typically not possible in a fully automatic way and, therefore, involves the following, quite common corpus-linguistic search process, which will be discussed in what follows.

The user begins by running a query/search that is based on as much existing annotation as possible, here words/lemmas and parts of speech. For a study of the dative alternation, we will imagine that we want to find all instances of the dative alternation (with *to*) that involve one of the following ten verb lemmas that are frequently used in the dative alternation:

- Four verb lemmas that strongly prefer the ditransitive: *tell, give, show,* and *ask.*
- Three verb lemmas that strongly prefer the prepositional dative: *bring, sell,* and *pass.*
- Three verb lemmas that are relatively neutral with regard to the two constructions: *send, lend,* and *write.*

These preferences are based on Gries and Stefanowitsch (2004).

If the part-of-speech and lemma annotation is perfect (which would mean that instances of *show* or *shows* used as nouns would not be retrieved), a query/search for these verb lemmas will lead to perfect recall for these ten verb lemmas with a user-defined context such as, for now, the complete sentence in which they are used. All their uses will be found and thus all their uses in the dative alternation (in corpora other than the BNC such as learner corpora, the user might have to deal with misspellings and other things). However, this result, the concordance lines, will come with fairly bad precision: all the verbs' uses will be found, in other words, also all uses in intransitive or monotransitive constructions or in phrasal verbs, prepositional verbs, and so on. Thus, the second step is to go over the concordance lines and prepare them for two kinds of annotation.

The first kind of annotation serves to identify false positives in the search result: that is, to identify the hits that involve the verbs but not the constructions in question so that we know which search results not to annotate for linguistic/contextual variables. However, given the size of the BNC and the relatively high frequencies of these verbs, we will not want to read all hits returned by the search, but only a subset/sample of them, and I will discuss ways to arrive at such a subset/sample (sections 2 and 3). Once the true positives—uses of forms of the verb lemmas that instantiate one of the two constructions—have been identified, the second kind of annotation is to (also usually manually) annotate each constructional use for the linguistic/contextual variables whose effect on the dative alternation is to be studied and to do that in such a way that facilitates subsequent statistical analysis; this part of the process is often partially outsourced to research assistants, which has some implications for the data management (section 3).

The final step in the process leading up to the actual analysis is to do some final checking and preparatory steps for the following statistical analysis (section 4). However, to make the whole endeavor as precise, consistent, and replicable as possible, I will make a variety of suggestions for this along the way; admittedly, some of these are general best practices for the management of corpus data and do not only apply to studies based on the BNC.

2   Retrieval

The first step of data management is to extract a first version of the concordance lines from, here, the BNC. The relevant part of the annotation of the corpus is represented in example 38.1 (see Han, chapter 6, this volume for more discussion of annotation) in which <u> is

```
<u who="D8YPS006">
<s n="80"><w c5="CJC" hw="and" pos="CONJ">And
</w><w c5="UNC" hw="erm" pos="UNC">erm </w><pause/><w
c5="DT0" hw="that" pos="ADJ">that </w>
<w c5="VBD" hw="be" pos="VERB">was </w><w c5="VVN"
hw="consider" pos="VERB">considered</w><c
c5="PUN">.</c></s>
</u>
<u who="D8YPS002">
<s n="81"><w c5="ITJ" hw="yes" pos="INTERJ">Yes </w><w
c5="CJS" hw="if" pos="CONJ">if </w><w c5="PNP"
hw="you" pos="PRON">you </w>
<w c5="VVD-VVN" hw="look" pos="VERB">looked </w><w
c5="PRP" hw="after" pos="PREP">after </w><w c5="AT0"
hw="a" pos="ART">a </w>
<w c5="NN1" hw="child" pos="SUBST">child</w><c
c5="PUN">.</c></s>
</u>
```

Example 38.1
Two one-sentence utterances from the BNC World edition, file D8Y.xml.

an utterance tag with a who attribute–value pair marking the speaker; <s> is a sentence number tag; <c> is a punctuation mark tag; and <w> is a word tag with two part-of-speech tags (a fine-grained "c5" version and a coarse-grained "pos" version) and a lemma tag ("hw" for head word). The corpus files are in UTF-8 encoding.

The BNC can be accessed online and with a variety of (free and commercial) corpus-processing tools, but these options restrict the analyst's freedom too much, so the best way to process corpus data is operating on a downloaded version with a programming language; many people are using Python, but I personally find R (R Core Team 2019) to be the altogether better choice (and Gries 2016 provides a detailed book-length introduction to corpus/text processing with R).

Recall, the task is to create a concordance of the ten above-mentioned verb lemmas from all of the BNC. There are two main ways this text processing/retrieval task can be approached in R: one is applying regular expressions to the files on a line-by-line basis, and the other is using packages such as XML (Lang & the CRAN Team 2019) or xml2 (Wickham, Hester, & Ooms 2018) that utilize the complete XML markup tree structure. In many cases, however, we want to retrieve the data in a way that maximally facilitates subsequent data processing and statistical analysis, which means we want to end up with a file in the so-called case-by-variable, or long, format, which has the following characteristics:

- Every measurement of the dependent variable, every data point, to be studied—here, the constructional choice—gets its own row (in a spreadsheet-like representation).

- Every variable or every feature with regard to which each measurement/data point is annotated gets its own column (see Gries 2021: section 1.4 for more discussion of this format).

Given this secondary goal—getting as close as possible to the case-by-variable format—we will proceed with the regular expression option. This is because the output of the XPath queries in R offered by, say, the XML package do not return two output lines for two instances of the same verb (say, *give*) in the same sentence—at least not straightforwardly. For example, if there was a corpus sentence such as "Picard showed Data a phaser and then Data showed it to Riker," then the case-by-variable format requires that each use of *showed* is in its own row, as shown here in table 38.1, which is not what the XML package would immediately provide.

Without delving into actual R coding too much (again, see Gries 2016), the regular expression route means we could essentially proceed with two loops: one (outer) loop that loads every corpus file (using the right file encoding, which typically is UTF-8) so that its sentences can be searched for the verb lemmas in question, and an inner loop that retrieves every instance of each of the ten verb lemmas from the sentences with, here, the whole sentence as the context; note that often gathering more context can be essential, for example, to annotate discourse-functional/ information-structural variables such as givenness/accessibility. Note the arrangement of the loops: because the loop that loads the files from the hard drive is the outer one, our script requires 4,049 hard drive accesses—if we had made the loop that loads the files the inner one, the one

nested into the ten verb lemmas, we might need 40,490 file accesses, which would be considerably slower.

As we are writing the script to gather this output, we should make sure that the output we are generating is more comprehensive than what table 38.1 suggests. For instance, the following pieces of information are "cheap" to obtain as we are doing the concordancing but could be useful or even vital either for data processing (e.g., sampling, sorting, filtering) or for the statistical analysis later. Thus, in addition to collecting the mere concordance data, there are some other kinds of information that are routinely useful to collect:

- Every concordance line should have a separate case number so that each case (i.e., row in the spreadsheet) can be uniquely identified by that number.

- It is often useful to include information about the circumstances of production of a data point: this could include register information, but it should minimally include the mode, in other words, whether the file contains spoken or written data, which we can extract either from the teiHeader in the first line of each BNC file or from the file's text type tag in the second line.

- We should not just retain the exact verb form found (as in the Match column in table 38.1) but also the verb lemma in a separate column (so that all forms of irregular verbs, such as *be* in a study of subject complementation, can be sorted together).

- It is nearly always useful or even necessary to save not only the file name in which a match was found, but also the line/sentence number. Many linguistic phenomena are subject to priming effects. That means the processes of planning to produce a construction are affected by whether that construction was processed before and how long ago that happened. Retaining the line/sentence numbers shown in figure 38.1 allows us to control for priming effects by computing the distance between two uses of a construction (see Gries 2018 and references discussed therein). (Along the same lines, it can be useful, in the case of spoken/conversational data, to include the speaker from the utterance tag in yet another column, which we will skip here.)

- Finally, it can be useful to immediately clear the output of parts of the annotation that are not going to be required anymore or that would make reading (during the subsequent manual annotation process) harder. In this case, we might delete part-of-speech tags, sentence

Table 38.1

The case-by-variable format for two matches in one sentence

Preceding	Match	Subsequent
Picard	showed	Data a phaser and then Data showed it to Riker
Picard showed Data a phaser and then Data	showed	it to Riker

number tags (because we have the sentence number in a separate column anyway), and so on, but for some applications it might be useful to retain some tags such as overlap markers, unclear word tags (which might also indicate disfluencies), and others.

The final product is then ideally saved into a raw text file (a tab-delimited .csv file ideally still with UTF-8 encoding) that has column headers for all columns (which are separated by tab stops), and that has been cleaned up as well (e.g., no excess spaces anywhere); also, during any such steps, great care needs to be exercised to not compromise the identity and structure of the data. For instance, R, and also spreadsheet software, may need to be told explicitly how to handle single and double quotes, number/pound signs, and so on, which may occur in a corpus file, but must not disrupt R's/the spreadsheet software's parsing of the files column structure; this was also the reason why the columns in the output should be tab-delimited because tabs, unlike commas, are not part of the regular corpus file content and, thus, are no threat to recognizing the structure of the file (see ?read.table and ?write.table in R and check the settings of the Text Import Assistant in spreadsheet software).

Two related brief comments on preparing this output file: First, it is useful to do as much as of this as possible with code in an R script rather than manually or semi-manually (e.g., using database lookup functions) in a spreadsheet. This is because the output usually needs to be fine-tuned over multiple attempts and so it will save time and prevent errors if R does nearly everything with a script rather than when a human has to intervene over and over again manually with the point-and-click interface of a spreadsheet software.

Second, and more generally, it is always tempting to quickly hack together a script that somehow accomplishes the task, but I would encourage you to spend a bit time on thinking and planning this properly. One particularly relevant aspect is that it is often worth the extra five to ten minutes to think about whether (i) the code you're writing scales up to bigger research projects—if not, it is often worth the extra effort to change the code to make it run more efficiently, and (ii), relatedly, the code can be parallelized, that is, it can use the multiple cores or threads that contemporary computer processors now routinely offer.

As for the former, hacking together some code that just about works, but maybe inelegantly so (*elegance* not referring to aesthetics, but computational efficiency),

might seem like "it's good enough for now," but it often happens that slight changes or additions need to be made as the scope of a study changes, among other reasons, and then having an elegant script is nearly always a good return on the investment (of the time that went into improving and streamlining the code).

As for the latter, running a script that does all of this on the BNC using R's default of just using a single thread of the computer's processor might take twenty minutes or more (depending on the user's hardware, obviously), but the script that I used for all of this used ten threads on a laptop with a 6-core Intel i5 processor and hyper-threading (using the R packages foreach and doParallel) and finished all the data retrieval and preparation discussed in this chapter within less than three minutes, a speed that even only a few years ago would have been nearly impossible to attain.

Section 3 deals with preparing and performing the annotation processes after the first concordance has been generated and saved.

3 Annotation

The next steps involve (i) preparing to weed out false positives and (ii) adding annotation with regard to the variables that might affect the dative alternation to the true positives. This part of the process is often done by research assistants, so it is useful to be maximally consistent and minimize the risk of errors in data entry, among other things, but, in all honesty, I have applied the same kind of precautions even in cases where I knew I was going to annotate the data myself. In a manner of speaking, I was protecting myself against my own errors, laziness, and such.

With regard to (i), in my experience it is most useful to prepare for the annotation by adding (still in the R script) an additional column to the data that is to the right of the column with the match that is called, say, Construction. That column can contain a placeholder for now, but it will contain the labels *ditrans*, *prepdat*, *other* for the constructions instantiated by the verb uses. Plus, it needs to be able to also contain some other code(s) to be able to, for instance, indicate that the row has been looked at but needs further attention (e.g., to disambiguate).

Also, I always recommend adding a column called Problem, whose only purpose is to (i) be empty if there is no problem whatsoever in any other column of the same row/case, but to (ii) contain the letter of the column that *does* contain something problematic requiring further attention to disambiguate or that might lead to the case being discarded. For instance, if a match for one of the verb forms was found but something in the subsequent context column K makes you think that maybe this case should not be included, then the Problem column would contain the letter "K" to indicate that, because of column K, this line merits a second look. A lot of students, but also more senior practitioners, do something like this by changing the font color or the background of the problematic cell, but these are things that cannot easily be sorted by or find/filter in a spreadsheet that has, say two hundred thousand rows, but a code in a separate column is something that can be found/filtered/sorted by. Thus and more generally, if information needs to be added to the data, add it into a column, not with formatting, because only if information made it into a cell of a column can all the data processing power of R/spreadsheet software be applied to it efficiently.

Next, we need to select a sample of concordance lines to read to determine whether they actually instantiate one of the two constructions of the dative alternation. The biggest mistake to avoid here is to draw a random sample of, say five thousand concordance lines out of all concordance lines. While this practice is still widespread, it is a really bad idea for two reasons: First, many phenomena are susceptible to priming effects, which means that to analyze an example of a ditransitive in file EFS.xml, it is most likely necessary to see what construction was used last before that and how similar that use was to the current one. But if we sample randomly from all concordance lines, the current line will be separated from all others in the same file, which makes such annotation much harder than necessary. Second, many corpus studies of this type these days are analyzed with mixed-effects models or similar kinds of tools, one selling point of which is that they can control for speaker-, file-, or lexically specific variability in the data. However, if the one ditransitive in file EFS.xml that I am looking at right now is the only one that made it into my random sample (although there are actually many ditransitives and prepositional datives in there, which were just not sampled), then I am not giving my later statistical analysis the chance to determine whether there is something special to this speaker or file.

Thus, what we should do here is make the file the subsetting/sampling unit: choose files (pseudorandomly) to be part of our subset/sample and then look at all concordance lines from that file. Obviously, there are many straightforward ways in which such sampling might be implemented, so I will just mention two of them that provide an additional perspective on this part of the process. The first alternative could involve tabulating all files (in 4,049 rows) with all verb lemmas (in ten columns) to see which verb lemma is attested how often in each file. Then we could decide to only consider files for sampling that contain say, at least eight of the ten lemmas at least, say, twice. Of those files, we could begin with the file with the smallest number of verb lemma tokens and add all concordance lines from files—recall, the sampling unit are files, not lines—with successively more verb lemma tokens until we reach a desired number of concordance lines. The reason for this seemingly convoluted scheme is that (i) it would make sure that the files sampled contain a "decent variety" of relevant verb lemmas and that (ii) we sample a "decent" number of files (which makes sure that no one huge file and its idiosyncrasies could affect our analysis too much).

The second alternative could begin as we did for the first—identifying files with a decent number of matches to begin with—and then randomly sample complete files from those; in such a case, it is absolutely essential to set a random-number seed before any sampling is done (in R: set.seed) so that the sampling is random, but also replicable.

Finally, it is often helpful to sort the complete output in a useful way. This could be sorting by, for instance:

- Whether a file/concordance line is "in the sample" to be studied or not (so that all to-be-annotated items in the sample are together).

- The file name (so that all lines from the same file are together).

- The sentence number (so that all lines from the same file are in order of occurrence in the file).

- The length of the preceding context (so that multiple hits in the same sentence are sorted in order of occurrence in the line).

Ideally, everything so far in this process would be performed with a single fully automated script that, when run on the same data, would give you the same output and would require as little human intervention as possible (in the interest of speed and replicability). This would entail, for instance, that file locations (of the input and output files are hard-coded into the script). Also, the code/script should be extremely heavily commented, which is useful if ever you want to share the script with others and which is *necessary* to remind your future self what you did and why a year ago (when you submitted the paper to that special issue). A useful check as well as documentation of all your activities during this stage, but also during the later statistical analysis, would be to generate two things: (i) a variety of output files (interim results for fast debugging as well as final results) in useful file formats (such as .rds for everything to be used only within R and tab-delimited .csv for everything that might be loaded into other software), and (ii) an HTML report or an R Markdown document that contains all your code, all your commentary, and all the results that would have been in the console/on the screen in a single shareable HTML file, which ensures proper error checking (because otherwise the report won't compile in the first place) and transparency (to others and your future self).

Then, and only then, do we stop using R for a moment and we can begin to actually annotate (i) whether concordance lines are the right construction(s) and (ii) what their characteristics are that might have affected the speaker's choice. For this part of the process, I recommend using a spreadsheet software such as LibreOffice Calc (which has characteristics such as full-fledged regular expressions and better filtering functionality that, to my mind, make it more useful than competing spreadsheet software; see the

appendix for what we are aiming for). Crucially, I recommend using the Data: Validity functionality, which allows a user to limit the number of options that can be entered into a cell. Consider figure 38.1, which shows the first of three tabs of the menu option Data: Validity in LibreOffice Calc. In the Criteria tab, we can list the elements that the user is allowed to enter into the cells of column J, which are then shown in a drop-down selection list for entering with a mouse click; in the Input Help tab, we can enter a title and a help text that is shown when a user clicks on a cell to enter something; and in the Error Alert tab, we can enter what should happen and what feedback should come up when the user tries to enter something they are not supposed to enter.

This feature makes it much easier to avoid data entry errors because, for instance, we can define a list of admissible entries (as shown here), we can only permit numbers or dates, and such, and the pop-up help constantly reminds an annotator of all the possible options that are at their disposal—just make sure there also are options for the annotator to indicate they have a problem and cannot annotate a certain data point decisively yet.

Once all annotation of the relevant variables is complete, we turn to the last data management stage, the final steps before a subsequent statistical analysis.

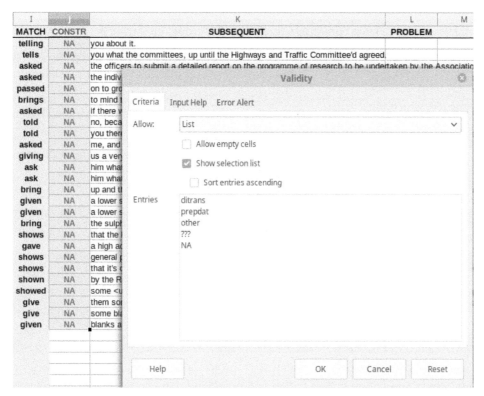

Figure 38.1

The use of the Data: Validity function to guide and constrain data entry.

4   Preparation and documentation

Once the relevant data points—the uses of the two constructions—have been identified and annotated for the factors targeted in the study (e.g., length, animacy, definiteness) there are several final things that need to be done to make sure the data are in good shape for subsequent (statistical) analysis.

The first of these is performing a general sanity check of the data as a whole but specifically the annotation that was entered. This can be done in two ways: in the spreadsheet software (or any more specialized annotation software) with which the annotation was performed and within the software used for statistical analysis (these days, typically, R). As for the former, I recommend using the spreadsheet's filtering function to determine whether a column contains only sensible entries, for example, only the animacy levels you intended to code or only reasonable ages of speakers. This is more important than you might think: I recently met with a student whose spreadsheet (with more than twenty thousand rows) contained a column named Age of Speaker (supposedly measured in years), which upon inspection was found to contain a variety of values exceeding 170. This arose from an unintentional use of dragging down a cell with a numeric value that was not repeated as intended, but

incremented instead; obviously, these kinds of things need to be addressed prior to any analysis. Figure 38.2 shows how the Data: Autofilter functionality can be used to check, here, that the Lemma column contains only the lemmas it is supposed to contain.

Similarly, if data entry was not restricted with the Data: Validity tool, annotators often unintentionally add spaces to labels—for example, using the labels "animate" and "animate·"—which will create problems for the later statistical analysis. Microsoft Excel does not even flag this in its filtering function, but in LibreOffice Calc, this would be obvious from the kind of filtering display shown in figure 38.2. Therefore, we want to check for all sorts of other problems including plain typos ("animat"), other implausible values (decimal values in a column that should only contain integers such as length of an NP in words or characters), and many similar problems.

As for the latter kind of sanity check (in R), I recommend loading the .csv file into a data frame in R and explore it, minimally, with the summary function (to get first frequency tables of all categorical variables and numerical summaries of all numeric variables: if you intended to restrict your speakers to younger people and the median age value in the summary output is forty-eight, then you might want to look at your code and your (interim) output files again.

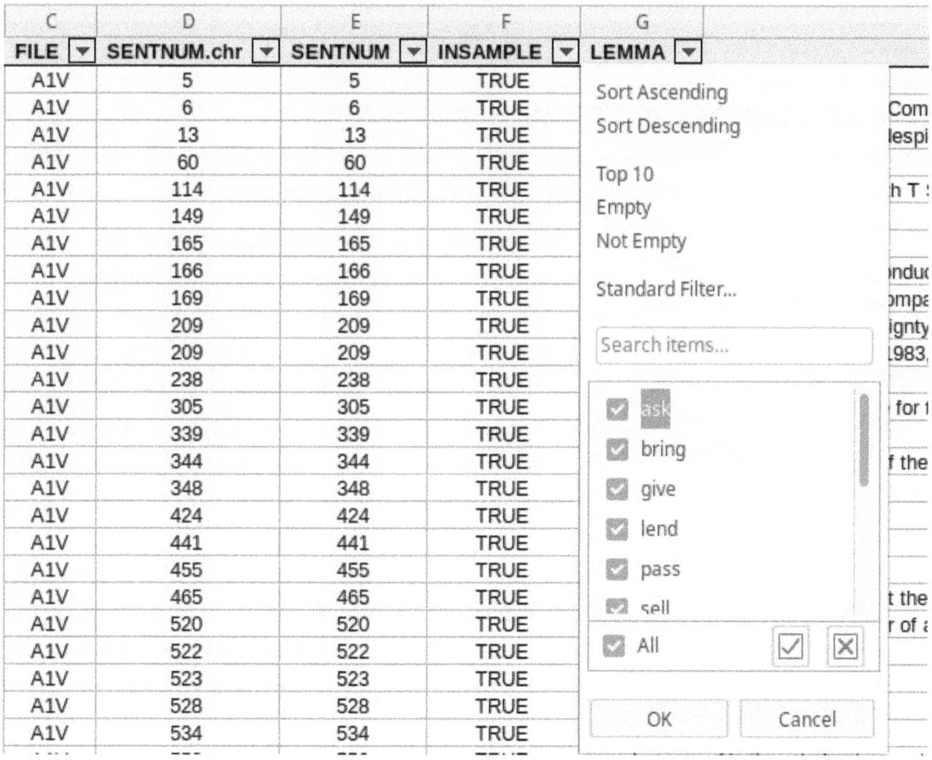

C	D	E	F	G
FILE ▼	SENTNUM.chr ▼	SENTNUM ▼	INSAMPLE ▼	LEMMA ▼
A1V	5	5	TRUE	
A1V	6	6	TRUE	Com
A1V	13	13	TRUE	lespi
A1V	60	60	TRUE	
A1V	114	114	TRUE	h T
A1V	149	149	TRUE	
A1V	165	165	TRUE	
A1V	166	166	TRUE	nduc
A1V	169	169	TRUE	mpa
A1V	209	209	TRUE	ignty
A1V	209	209	TRUE	1983,
A1V	238	238	TRUE	
A1V	305	305	TRUE	for
A1V	339	339	TRUE	
A1V	344	344	TRUE	f the
A1V	348	348	TRUE	
A1V	424	424	TRUE	
A1V	441	441	TRUE	
A1V	455	455	TRUE	
A1V	465	465	TRUE	t the
A1V	520	520	TRUE	r of a
A1V	522	522	TRUE	
A1V	523	523	TRUE	
A1V	528	528	TRUE	
A1V	534	534	TRUE	

Filter dropdown overlay on column G (LEMMA):
Sort Ascending / Sort Descending / Top 10 / Empty / Not Empty / Standard Filter… / Search items… / ☑ ask / ☑ bring / ☑ give / ☑ lend / ☑ pass / ☑ sell / ☑ All / ☑ / ☒ / OK / Cancel

Figure 38.2
The use of Data: Autofilter to check data entry.

Finally, and this is beginning to move away from the core processing of corpus data per se and toward initial statistical processing, there are a few exploratory steps that have implications on the data structure you're working with. For instance, it is straightforward, but very useful, in R to quickly check for each column of your data how many unique types it contains and what their frequency distribution is and looks like when visualized in a statistical plot. This kind of information is useful because it often offers suggestions with regard to (i) which column (especially of categorical variables) might contain more unique values than it should, (ii) which column (especially of categorical variables) might contain more super-rare values than is useful for a subsequent statistical analysis, and (iii) which column (especially of numerical variables) has distributional characteristics that are problematic for whatever subsequent analysis was planned and thus needs to be transformed. If such exploration leads to new columns—because levels of a categorical variable are conflated or because numerical variables are log-transformed—it is usually a good idea to leave the old columns in the data frame in case you unexpectedly need to go back and use the original values again. However, if you have been doing what I've recommended—diligently documenting all steps in a code file and creating many interim results files—revisiting an earlier variable state should be unproblematic anyway. Note that sometimes you might even have to combine multiple columns into one to disambiguate information for the later analysis: Imagine a case where speaker IDs are simply numbers from 1 to n in each corpus file. This would mean that concordance line one thousand might be from a speaker labeled as "1," as might be concordance line two thousand—but the two concordance lines might be from different files! Thus, you would need to create a new column that conflates the file name and the speaker name into one string so that the former becomes, say, "D8Y. xml_1" and the latter becomes "EFS.xml_1." The BNC speaker codes include the file name, which avoids this problem, but it is useful to be on guard for such or similar situations; for instance, this careful separation of speaker codes is also important for experimental data.

A final comment that is more general than the specific scope of this chapter—data management with the BNC—but still so important that I feel compelled to make this point anyway: I strongly recommend the adoption of a rigorous practice of naming files and documenting workflow across files. Too often, I see students as well as senior practitioners presenting me with files called somescript.r, newscript.r, betterversion.r, and ten different output files whose names make no sense even to the users themselves anymore once even only a moderate amount of time has passed (see https://xkcd.com/1459/). My recommendations for a corpus study of the type I've discussed, with the BNC or any other corpus, are the following:

- Create a new folder for each project.
- Name nearly all files in the folder so they are numbered in order of creation and indicate what they produce.
- Name all files having to do with the paper or slides you produce from the data 01a_paper.odt, for example, with major successive revisions being called 01b_paper.odt, 01c_paper.odt, and so on. This makes sure they are shown at the top of the folder.
- Number all files involved in the analysis as follows: The script that generates the first concordance from the corpus is called 02a_concordance.r, which might generate an output file called 02b_concordance.csv. That file is then also saved as an .ods file 02b_concordance.ods, which is used for annotating the data and which, when the annotation is complete, is saved as 03_annotated.ods and, for R, as a tab-delimited version called 03_annotated.csv, and so forth.
- Note that the R script that reads this file and contains the statistical analysis of 03_annotated.csv is called 04a_eval.r and might produce output files 04b_. . . . csv via 04e_. . . . rds to 04h_. . . . png and so on.
- Create the first file in the folder and name it 00_overview.txt. This file contains your notes that state for every file in the folder (i) its name, (ii) what it does (and what its input files are), and (iii) its output file.

As obsessive as this may seem, corpus studies of large corpora often lead to huge amounts of results, not to mention the possibility that multiple slightly different attempts to come to grips with the data may have been made, which quickly can lead to an explosion of files. (I have seen many times, during office hours, the inability of a student to even locate "the current analysis.") In the interest of proper data management and, hopefully, the increase in precision, transparency, and replicability of our corpus studies, these kinds of scenarios—see http://phdcomics.com/comics/archive.php?comicid=1323—need to be avoided. If you follow the guidelines in this chapter, they will be; of course, you can also use git or similar tools.

02c_concordance.ods - LibreOffice Calc

File   Edit   View   Insert   Format   Styles   Sheet   Data   Tools   Window   Help

A1 | fx Σ =   CASE

	CASE	MODE	FILE	SENTNUM	SENTNUM.chr	INSAMPLE	LEMMA	PRECEDING	MATCH	CONSTR	SUBSEQUENT	PROBLEM
2	8597	w	A30	8	8	TRUE	give	In 1988 the foster parents	gave	NA	notice of their application to adopt the child.	
3	8598	w	A30	15	15	TRUE	give	reasons and that a reasonable woman in her position would	give	NA	her consent.	
4	8613	w	A30	46	46	TRUE	ask	After retiring the jury returned with a notice	asking	NA	whether the co-defendant was charged with gross indecency	
5	8599	w	A30	50	50	TRUE	give		giving	NA	the judgment of the court, said the appellant did not sugge	
6	8576	w	A30	92	92	TRUE	tell	MR JUSTICE SAVILLE,	told	NA	the International Bar Association conference in Strasbourg.	
7	8634	w	A30	105	105	TRUE	write	ional Health Service, Stephen Gilchrist, a London solicitor,	writes	NA	Patricia Wynn Davies.	
8	8577	w	A30	106	106	TRUE	tell	the Association of British Travel Agents warned yesterday,	told	NA	the conference.	
9	8578	w	A30	112	112	TRUE	tell	exotic trips likely to incur larger increases, Sidney Perez	told	NA	about an invention which could curb kidnapping and the i	
10	8614	w	A30	123	123	TRUE	ask	The conference was also	asking	NA	' is to be treated in exactly the same way as Dr Wyatt'.	
11	8637	w	A30	143	143	TRUE	bring	'All I am	brought	NA	in by social workers or others with suspicion of abuse, or th	
12	8615	w	A30	146	146	TRUE	ask	Of the 82 'index' children — those	asking	NA	whether I am still confident about the children in which I r	
13	8616	w	A30	159	159	TRUE	ask	repared to diagnose, she says, and because Dr Wyatt started	asking	NA	whether sexual abuse might be the problem in cases which	
14	8617	w	A30	176	176	TRUE	ask	'We have to	ask	NA	why this is such a horrendous issue to raise.'	
15	8618	w	A30	178	178	TRUE	ask	She	asks	NA	how it can be made easier for abusers, who suffer a compuls	
16	8645	w	A30	212	212	TRUE	pass	where, unless you live in a marginal constituency elections	pass	NA	you by on the other side.	
17	8600	w	A30	239	239	TRUE	give	ms elect several candidates in multi-member constituencies,	giving	NA	due weight to minority votes.	
18	8601	w	A30	245	245	TRUE	give	The Single Transferable Vote	gives	NA	voters a free choice of candidates in multi-member constitu	
19	8579	w	A30	256	256	TRUE	tell	Robin Cook	told	NA	delegates that tax concessions for private medical insuranc	
20	8580	w	A30	260	260	TRUE	tell	s ambulanceman's uniform, won a standing ovation after he	told	NA	delegates: 'Mrs Thatcher and her ministers are extremely q	
21	8635	w	A30	273	273	TRUE	write	we summed up the general consensus: "We've been stuffed.",	writes	NA	John Pienaar.	
22	8581	w	A30	292	292	TRUE	tell	As he	told	NA	the story, he did not seem too worried.</div><div level="	
23	8609	w	A30	303	303	TRUE	show	ssued in Scotland, but even the 'official doctored figures'	showed	NA	that 700,000 people had not paid.	
24	8602	w	A30	308	308	TRUE	give	orkers' union USDAW, said non-payment campaigners were	giving	NA	false hope to the vulnerable.	
25	8646	w	A30	316	316	TRUE	pass	The Social Democrats	passed	NA	a motion at their conference in Brighton last month calling	
26	8619	w	A30	319	319	TRUE	ask	clear 84 per cent majority and then the Campaign was then	asked	NA	to submit a draft statement to the policy review.	
27	8603	w	A30	331	331	TRUE	give	many things by my political opponents, but I have just been	given	NA	'the kiss of death.'	
28	8647	w	A30	345	345	TRUE	pass	nored the call for complete immunity in tort which the TUC	passed	NA	to the conference.	
29	8648	w	A30	346	346	TRUE	pass	Under the resolution overwhelmingly	passed	NA	by Labour delegates, unions would be subject to fines and	

Figure 38.3
Concordance display.

References

BNC Consortium. 2001. *The British National Corpus, Version 2 (BNC World)*. Distributed by Oxford University Computing Services on behalf of the BNC Consortium. http://www.natcorp.ox.ac.uk/.

Bresnan, Joan, Anna Cueni, Tatiana Nikitina, and R. Harald Baayen. 2007. Predicting the dative alternation. In *Cognitive Foundations of Interpretation*, ed. Gerlof Bouma, Irene Kraemer, and Joost Zwarts, 9–94. Amsterdam: Royal Netherlands Academy of Science.

Gries, Stefan Th. 2003. Towards a corpus-based identification of prototypical instances of constructions. *Annual Review of Cognitive Linguistics* 1 (1): 1–27.

Gries, Stefan Th. 2021. *Statistics for Linguistics with R*. 3rd rev. and extended ed. Berlin: De Gruyter Mouton.

Gries, Stefan Th. 2016. *Quantitative Corpus Linguistics with R*. 2nd rev. and extended ed. London: Routledge, Taylor & Francis Group.

Gries, Stefan Th. 2018. Syntactic alternation research: Taking stock and some suggestions for the future. *Belgian Journal of Linguistics* 31 (1): 8–29.

Gries, Stefan Th., and Anatol Stefanowitsch. 2004. Extending collostructional analysis: A corpus-based perspective on "alternations." *International Journal of Corpus Linguistics* 9 (1): 97–129.

Lang, Duncan Temple, and the CRAN Team. 2019. XML: Tools for Parsing and Generating XML within R and S-Plus. R package version 3.98–1.20. https://CRAN.R-project.org/package=XML.

McEnery, Tony, and Andrew Hardie. 2011. *Corpus Linguistics: Method, Theory and Practice*. Cambridge: Cambridge University Press.

Pope, Caty Worlock, ed. 2010. The bootcamp discourse and beyond. Special issue, *International Journal of Corpus Linguistics* 15 (3).

R Core Team. 2019. *R: A Language and Environment for Statistical Computing*. Vienna: R Foundation for Statistical Computing. https://www.R-project.org/.

Wickham, Hadley, James Hester, and Jeroen Ooms. 2018. xml2: Parse XML. R package version 1.2.0. https://CRAN.R-project.org/package=xml2.

Onno Crasborn

1   Introduction

With the arrival of video on desktop computers at the start of this century, the use of data in the study of signed languages saw substantial changes. Where before, few larger data sets were created (primarily for observational data in first-language acquisition), from 2004 onward many research groups started constructing sign language corpora (Crasborn et al. 2007; Johnston 2009). These corpora were virtually all elicited, rather than harvested from external sources, as such sources simply did not exist in sufficient quantities. Even today, it is debatable whether YouTube and similar online platforms contain a large enough collection of the use of a particular sign language from which a balanced sample could be created (Crasborn & van Winsum 2014). In addition, the available metadata are often limited and legal and ethical issues also make it difficult to actually use such data for research purposes. An exception is the TV-recorded weather reports that were interpreted from spoken German to German Sign Language (Deutsche Gebärdensprache, or DGS), and collected in a corpus by Rheinisch-Westfälische Technische Hochschule Aachen for the purpose of developing sign language technologies (Bungeroth et al. 2006). Such a limited domain of language use has its advantages for developing automatic sign recognition and machine translation of sign to speech. Because the topic of language use is constrained, the "type-token ratio" of signs will be better (fewer signs occurring only once, for instance).

The corpora that are based on elicitation generally serve a wide variety of purposes in linguistic research and also for applied uses. They form the first large-scale documentation efforts for the sign languages involved, enable research in a variety of linguistic domains, allow for the development of corpus-based lexicography, and

are used by teachers and learners. Because of the lack of a written tradition for any sign language, film or video is crucial for each of these domains and consequently, sign language corpora are having major impact on research and are promising to have a long-term impact on the language communities as well (see Gawne & Styles, chapter 2, this volume).

This impact comes almost directly from the documentation of the language: for the first time, both laymen and experts have access to a record of the language in all its present-day diversity. Lacking a commonly used writing system and the concomitant lack of a written tradition, a sign language "library" in the past two decades consisted of printed dictionaries with photos and a set of CD-ROMs and DVDs, if at all. In the construction of sign language corpora, age is always a parameter (e.g., see Johnston & Schembri 2006; Crasborn & Zwitserlood 2008; Schembri et al. 2013; Bono et al. 2014): we know from observation and some research (e.g., Frishberg 1975 and Supalla & Clark 2014 on American Sign Language) that sign languages throughout the world have changed over the last century and continue to change in part due to educational and language policies. In that sense, present-day sign language corpora are "snapshots" of the language: they are recorded at one point in time, rather than harvested from sources that may span multiple decades. There is not at present a monitor corpus of any sign language that keeps recording new data as time progresses.

More indirectly, the availability of annotated corpora allows for the development of language technologies such as machine translation that are becoming ever more important. Currently, many deaf and hard of hearing users are using spoken language technologies such as automatic speech recognition to aid in specific situations. The development of sign language recognition and synthesis has certainly made progress (see, for example, the collection of presentations from the most recent Conference on Language Resources and Evaluation, or LREC, workshop on the representation and processing of sign languages; Efthimiou et al. 2020), but is far from being ready for a wide range of applications (Crasborn 2010a). The need for manual transcription and annotation is hampering the development of the very large data sets that are used by state-of-the-art machine learning techniques.

In terms of research data management, the relatively young history of multimodal annotation and archiving and the privacy-sensitive nature of video make sign language corpora different from text and audio corpora and similar to audiovisual data sets collected to study nonverbal behavior. This chapter aims to discuss some of the data management issues that the developers of sign language corpora are faced with. The different parts of the data life cycle, from data collection to sharing are discussed in turn, focusing on the use of ELAN for transcription and annotation (used for most sign language corpora).

2   Data collection

Video data are the primary data for all sign language corpora, sometimes supplemented by infrared (Kinect) or three-dimensional video recordings to obtain depth information (Jayaprakash & Hanke 2014). While for more experimental studies, motion tracking is also used (and can sometimes be displayed and analyzed by the same software as where the annotations are created), this has not been done for larger sign corpora yet.

This inevitable use of video as primary data calls for extra attention in the protection of privacy (see Kung, chapter 8, this volume). Anonymization of the video images themselves is impossible without destroying the value of the video recordings (Crasborn 2010b). Given the importance of facial expressions in signed interactions (Baker-Shenk 1983; Crasborn 2006; Herrmann & Steinbach 2011), it is important that people's faces are not only recognizable but also recorded at such an orientation and resolution that fine facial movements can even be detected when signers rotate their head in various directions. This implies a separate camera on each of the interlocutors and either a high-resolution camera (like the present-day high definition, 1920×1080 pixels)

or a dedicated camera zoomed in on the head. Either way, good lighting is imperative to record high-quality video. In terms of research data management, two approaches can be taken. Research participants can be asked to give informed consent for public distribution, acknowledging that this means eternal availability for anyone and permitting for uncertainty as to what future technologies will be able to do with the data (Crasborn 2010b). Although public, "copyleft" licenses are getting more and more common, it is debatable whether researchers will actually be able to enforce the conditions of the license (such as the Creative Commons conditions "no commercial use" and "share alike"); see also Collister (chapter 9, this volume) for further discussion. Alternatively, the video data are shielded off from public use and shared only with researchers who sign a restrictive end user license. This limits the potential impact on and use by any given sign language community, but makes it more likely that signers can agree to their recordings being archived and reused.

As with audio(visual) corpora of spoken languages, some of the metadata that make the data most interesting for research use concern person variables such as age, gender, and linguistic skills (Trippel 2004). For signers, given the heterogeneity of the deaf community in terms of language background, further information about family history can be crucial: Did their parents and grandparents use sign language? Were they deaf or hearing? For archives (including those such as the Language Archive [TLA] of the Max Planck Institute for Psycholinguistics that house sign language collections), it is important that metadata are all public so that data sets can be located. However, the combination of all the signer properties that researchers may wish to have access to are so specific that they will easily lead to unique individuals in the (often small) language communities, even without having the video. Following discussions in a workshop on the documentation of sign language heritage ("Metadata for Sign Language Corpora" workshop of the European Cultural Heritage Online [ECHO] project, Nijmegen, the Netherlands, May 8–9, 2003), an elaborate and a reduced set of metadata categories was considered, the latter being recommended as a standard (Crasborn & Hanke 2003). This proposed standard included information about the deafness of participants and their parents, for instance, as well as the age of acquisition of their sign language. Further details about their hearing status, such as the use of hearing aids or the precise hearing loss in decibels, were considered unnecessary and too privacy-sensitive, especially because metadata are often publicly accessible even if the data are not. More detailed information can still be included in an archive when protected under a (more restricted) end user license. If the metadata profile permits, corpus-level statistics can also be published independent of the individual videos, stating, for instance, that 85% of the signers in the data set acquired the primary sign language under the age of six years. What is considered sensitive information may differ between communities, and the involvement of deaf signers (whether as informants, assistants, or researchers) is of key importance for large as for small language communities (cf. Pollard 1992; Harris, Holmes, & Mertens 2009; Singleton, Martin, & Morgan 2015).

Many sign language corpora collected in the last fifteen years are remarkably similar, which importantly promotes reproducible research across corpora and languages (Gawne & Styles, chapter 2, this volume). They tend to focus on dialogues rather than monologues and multilogues, where narratives are also recorded in a dialogue setting. Narrative tasks such as recounting fable stories or the Tweety and Sylvester cartoon "Canary Row" complement more interactive tasks such as discussions of deaf-related themes and relatively free interaction. While this makes for comparable data sets across sign languages, it also restricts our view of language use in deaf communities (cf. Good, chapter 3, this volume). The narrative tasks are not necessarily the most ecologically valid samples of language use. Increasingly, we see collections of more spontaneous data resulting from fieldwork being archived in the same way as the sign language corpora of Australian Sign Language (Auslan), Sign Language of the Netherlands (Nederlandse Gebarentaal, NGT), British Sign Language, and other signed languages.

These interactions are typically recorded by multiple video cameras, combining frontal views of signers with a view of the whole scene and top shots or zoomed-in recordings of the face. Recordings tend to use dark plain backgrounds and have signers wearing fairly plain clothing without too many patterns, contrasting well with their skin color. One specific technical point of attention is use of manual focus, as automatic focusing in many cameras can be ineffective with moving hands at short range. The resulting video data form the primary data for a sign language corpus, and the quality of these recordings is therefore paramount. While for some annotation and analysis tasks low-resolution video may suffice, for others the full frame of standard definition or high definition will be important. For instance, if there is only one camera recording a frontal view of each signer, fine facial movements may not be visible in a reduced frame. Details of body positions and movements are better visible at higher temporal resolutions and with the use of good lighting and professional cameras: the in-camera compression used by cheaper cameras is especially detrimental in poor light conditions. The current rise of 4K video (quad high definition) at high frame rates (fifty or sixty frames/second) promises a great step forward for future sign corpora, with a concomitant impact on storage space. Although it may still be a challenge for annotation software to play back multiple synchronic video streams at such high resolutions, it is no longer necessary to create low-resolution working copies of primary data in addition to full-resolution archive copies (see also Mattern, chapter 5, this volume).

3   Data processing

Multimodal annotation of sign language data is not fundamentally different from that of other types of multimodal data; there is more convergence in the tools that are used within the sign language linguistics community. The large majority of researchers use the open-source stand-alone tool ELAN developed by TLA at the Max Planck Institute for Psycholinguistics (Wittenburg et al. 2006),[1] with a few exceptions of research groups that use the proprietary server-based software iLex, developed by the University of Hamburg to integrate the annotation of discourse with a lexical database (Hanke, Rodriguez, & Paz Suarez Araujo 2002).[2]

A general requirement of annotation workflows applies just as much to sign language data sets as to any other type of annotation: to use clear and systematic setups of annotation documents (using different tier types for different types of information), separating annotations for individuals on different tiers, using participant labels in ELAN, and so forth. Figure 39.1 illustrates how this has been approached in the Corpus NGT.

ELAN cannot enforce the application of a template across a corpus, so extra attention is needed and possibly some scripting to find inconsistencies and remove these.

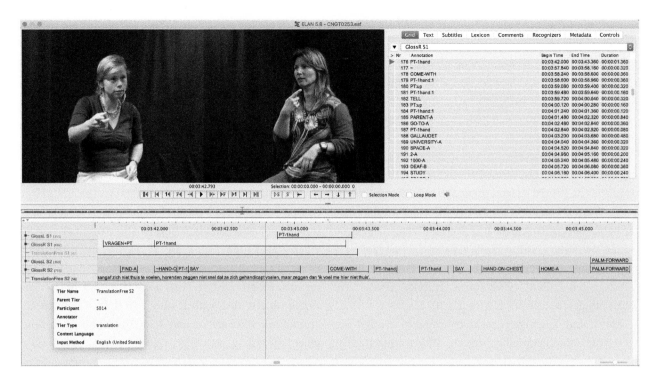

Figure 39.1

An annotation file for the Corpus NGT, illustrating how tier names use "S1" and "S2" to refer to the signer on the left and the right, respectively, in a dialogue. The pop-up menu shows further tier information, including a participant code that uniquely identifies each individual.

Explicit annotation guidelines and the use (or development) of a lexical database are vital especially for glossing, as there is no shared sign language orthography that is in common use by any deaf community nor linguistics community. The use of "ID glossing" has been extensively discussed in the literature surrounding sign language corpora (Johnston 2008), and the annotation guidelines of the Auslan corpus (Johnston 2016) have served as a model for all other sign language corpora.[3] A Digging into Data project in 2015 led to a summary of shared glossing practices between the British Sign Language and NGT corpora, which highlights the categories sign language researchers are likely to want to distinguish in the manual channel (Crasborn, Bank, & Cormier 2015). Figure 39.2 shows how different gloss tiers have been set up for the left and right hands in the Corpus NGT, enabling independent alignment of annotations for the activity of the left and right hands (see Crasborn & Sáfár 2016 for further discussion of this annotation scheme).

The transcription and annotation of non-manual channels is generally not done across the board, with the exception of mouth actions (Crasborn & Bank 2014). The intensive code mixing that can be observed in the use of mouthings (mouth actions stemming from spoken words) brings many lexical elements into interactions that will inform linguistic analyses at other levels. The transcription and annotation of features such as eye gaze, eye brow states, or nose wrinkles appear to have a much worse trade-off between effort and general benefit. These are then added to specific segments when a corpus is actually used for dedicated linguistic studies.

As ELAN saves its information in XML documents (ELAN Annotation Format; extension .eaf) and ELAN is still being actively developed and maintained, basic future compatibility is ensured. However, the version of the ELAN Annotation Format file format has been changing slowly over the years, and old annotation files sometimes need to be updated to work with (all features of) new versions of the software. At present (version 6.1), ELAN does not offer an automated way to update files for a whole corpus of dozens or even thousands of files. For this and other corpus-wide processing, the development of scripts that work on large batches of annotation documents can be useful. The integrated and server-based approach offered by iLex clearly has its advantages in this respect.

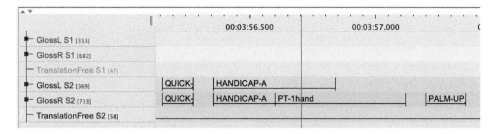

Figure 39.2

Independent alignment of glosses for each hand enable the transcription of so-called spreading behavior, where one hand of a two-handed sign (here, HANDICAP-A) is held while the other hand articulates the next sign.

A larger concern in using archived data lies in any lexicon links that have been used. The online lexicon will likely have evolved after archiving the annotation data, and inconsistencies of various types might arise. More generally, the use of external controlled vocabularies (containing list of values for a certain annotation layer) that are not part of the archive but keep changing if they are used for new data sets and adapted because of new insights can lead to such inconsistencies. Values may have disappeared from the vocabulary or acquired a new meaning. It is therefore recommended to also archive vocabularies along with the annotation files. For a Signbank lexicon or older LEXUS lexicons (the two types that ELAN 6.1 can link to), it is at present not clear how an archived version could be created. As a minimal option, a comma-separated values dump of the lexicon could be archived along with the annotation files. Although not a user-friendly option for researchers who want to use the archived data, archiving text versions of external controlled vocabularies (which are already in XML format) at least ensures interpretability of the data.

For the Corpus NGT, there are now four public releases of the annotation files, which complement the archiving of the video files in TLA in 2008.[4] These successive releases not only include a step-by-step growth of the number of annotated files, but also corrections to obvious errors, and changes to glosses that came about during relemmatization of the Global Signbank data set for NGT since 2008.

4 Storing

There are two primary archives that currently host sign language data sets: the Endangered Languages Archive presently includes the Auslan corpus and data from twelve other sign languages, and TLA hosts the Corpus NGT and data from some ten other sign languages. Some other sign language corpora are stored on local university servers. The two large archives share metadata standards: earlier ISLE Metadata Initiative (IMDI), and now Component Metadata Initiative (CMDI) files are required to archive data. The European Common Language Resources and Technology Infrastructure (CLARIN) project and similar language resource projects have contributed to this converging standard. The extension to the IMDI standard can be flexibly implemented in a CMDI profile, with room for variation.

Global Signbank, an outgrowth of the NGT Signbank that was based on the Auslan Signbank software (Cassidy et al. 2018), currently hosts data sets from eleven different sign languages, most of them in their initial stages of language documentation, corpus creation, or historical research across sign languages. It also hosts shadow copies of ASL Signbank (English; American Sign Language), VGT Signbank (Dutch; Vlaamse Gebarentaal), and an English/French LSFB (Langue des Signes de Belgique Francophone) lexical data set to facilitate research on "international sign," the highly dynamic language contact practices between users of different sign languages.

Although the software of the different Signbank systems all go back to the original one for Auslan, the details of the systems vary. In particular, the degree to which morphological information is encoded and the level of detail in the phonological description differs. This can make direct comparison of data sets rather difficult. In this sense, and in the lack in registration in larger databases of language resources, the Signbank data sets are still far from the FAIR (Findable, Accessible, Interoperable, and Reusable) principles.

5 Sharing

Although anonymity is difficult if not impossible to maintain in video-recorded interactions of signed languages, many researchers are opting for open access publication following the choice of the Corpus NGT to be open access in 2008. They feel that the difficult if not endangered position of signed languages in many countries calls for maximal visibility. The limited availability of video resources for language learning and the lack of written resources make for a potentially large impact of open access corpora. The Corpus NGT, for instance, is widely used in deaf education, for training sign language interpreters and sign language teachers, and for entry-level courses to NGT. The first sign language corpus created for Auslan was made with funding support of the Endangered Languages Documentation Programme following a successful case for the endangerment of Auslan (Johnston 2004). Sign language corpora can thus be seen as documenting languages under pressure, but they can also be seen as instruments for language (re)vitalization (McKee & Manning 2015). Ethical concerns around the publication of a person's data (see Holton, Leonard, & Pulsifer, chapter 4, this volume) are taken seriously but, with people's explicit consent, are mitigated by the need for data inside and outside the academic world.

6 Future perspectives

The biggest difference between corpora for signed as opposed to spoken language corpora lies in the need for manual annotation. There is currently no equivalent of automatic speech recognition that could aid in the basic transcription of sign language use. This is likely to change rapidly in the coming decade. Researchers recording and archiving new sign language corpora might therefore want to prioritize the collection of more primary data over the annotation of those data: once automated processing of videos will lead to, first, phonetic features and later, with advances in machine learning, tokenization of manual signs, data sets can be processed and made available for linguistic research that are much larger than the thirty to three hundred hours of video that we see nowadays. Interestingly, the increase of (semi)automated annotation may well alleviate our present concerns with privacy of signers in video recordings, as many studies will become possible based on transcriptions of signed interactions without the need for access to the original videos.

7 Conclusion

Sign language corpora have had an enormous impact on sign language linguistics. With the lack of a writing system and the late arrival of technology to record, store, and share recordings of signers, only now have linguists been enabled to do research on the basis of published data sets. At the same time, many aspects of the technologies involved are still under development. Although the ELAN annotation tool has become a de facto standard, it lacks many of the advanced corpus management features that the proprietary tool iLex has. The creation of lexical databases dedicated to sign language data is currently seeing rapid development, and here too, only since very recently have such lexical data sets become available for use by a wider research community. In the coming decade, further developments are expected that will impact research data management, including the improved integration between ELAN and the Signbanks, the FAIR publication of lexical data sets, and the addition of new data coming from automated analysis of videos using computer vision and pattern recognition.

Resources

For an overview of sign language corpora, see the survey of the DGS-Korpus team at Hamburg University: https://www.sign-lang.uni-hamburg.de/dgs-korpus/index.php/sl-corpora.html.

Notes

1. https://tla.mpi.nl/tools/tla-tools/elan/.

2. https://www.sign-lang.uni-hamburg.de/ilex/.

3. More information can be found at http://www.auslan.org.au/about/annotations/. The latest version of the annotation guidelines is published on https://mq.academia.edu/TrevorJohnston.

4. https://hdl.handle.net/1839/00-0000-0000-0004-DF8E-6.

References

Baker-Shenk, Charlotte L. 1983. A microanalysis of the nonmanual components of questions in American Sign Language. PhD dissertation, University of California, Berkeley.

Bono, Mayumi, Kouhei Kikuchi, Paul Cibulka, and Yotaka Osugi. 2014. A colloquial corpus of Japanese Sign Language: Linguistic resources for observing sign language conversations. In *Proceedings of the Ninth International Conference on Language Resources and Evaluation*, ed. Nicoletta Calzolari, Khalid Choukri, Thierry Declerck, H. Loftsson, Bente Maegaard, Joseph Mariani, Asuncion Moreno, Jan Odijk, and Stelios Piperidis, 1898–1904. Paris: ELRA.

Bungeroth, Jan, Daniel Stein, Philippe Dreuw, Morteza Zahedi, and Hermann Ney. 2006. A German Sign Language corpus of the domain weather report. In *Proceedings of the Fifth International Conference on Language Resources and Evaluation (LREC)*, ed. Nicoletta Calzolari, Khalid Choukri, Thierry Declerck, Hrafn Loftsson, Bente Maegaard, Joseph Mariani, Asuncion Moreno, Jan Odijk, and Stelios Piperidis, 2000–2003. Paris: ELRA.

Cassidy, Steve, Onno Crasborn, Henri Nieminen, Wessel Stoop, Micha Hulsbosch, Susan Even, Erwin Komen, and Trevor Johnston. 2018. Signbank: Software to Support Web Based Dictionaries of Sign Language. In *Proceedings of LREC 2018*, ed. Nicoletta Calzolari, Khalid Choukri, Christopher Cieri, Thierry Declerck, Sara Goggi, Koiti Hasida, Hitoshi Isahara, Bente Maegaard, Joseph Mariani, Hélène Mazo, Asuncion Moreno, Jan Odijk, Stelios Piperidis, Takenobu Tokunaga, 2359–2364. Paris: ELRA.

Crasborn, Onno. 2006. Nonmanual structures in sign languages. In *Encyclopedia of Language and Linguistics*, 2nd ed., ed. Keith Brown, vol. 8, 668–672. Oxford: Elsevier.

Crasborn, Onno. 2010a. The Sign Linguistics Corpora Network: Towards standards for signed language resources. In *Proceedings of the 8th Conference on Language Resources and Evaluation (LREC)*, ed. Nicoletta Calzolari, Khalid Choukri, Bente Maegaard, Joseph Mariani, Jan Odijk, Stelios Piperidis, Mike Rosner, and Daniel Tapias, 457–460. Paris: ELRA.

Crasborn, Onno. 2010b. What does "informed consent" mean in the Internet age? Publishing sign language corpora as open content. *Sign Language Studies* 10 (1): 276–290.

Crasborn, Onno, and Richard Bank. 2014. An annotation scheme for the linguistic study of mouth actions in sign languages. In *Beyond the Manual Channel: 6th Workshop on the Representation and Processing of Sign Languages*, ed. Onno Crasborn, Eleni Efthimiou, Stavroulou-Evita Fotinea, Thomas Hanke, Julie Hochgesang, Jette Kristoffersen, and Johanna Mesch, 23–28. Paris: ELRA.

Crasborn, Onno, Richard Bank, and Kearsy Cormier. 2015. Digging into Signs: Towards a gloss annotation standard for sign language corpora. Project deliverable, Nijmegen, the Netherlands, and London. https://www.ru.nl/sign-lang/projects/completed-projects/digging-signs/.

Crasborn, Onno, and Thomas Hanke. 2003. Additions to the IMDI metadata set for sign language corpora. Unpublished manuscript, Radboud University. http://sign-lang.ruhosting.nl/echo/docs/SignMetadata_Oct2003.pdf.

Crasborn, Onno, Johanna Mesch, Dafydd Waters, Annika Nonhebel, Els van der Kooij, Bencie Woll, and Brita Bergman. 2007. Sharing sign language data online: Experiences from the ECHO project. *International Journal of Corpus Linguistics* 12 (4): 535–562. doi:10.1075/ijcl.12.4.06cra.

Crasborn, Onno, and Anna Sáfár. 2016. An annotation scheme to investigate the form and function of hand dominance in the Corpus NGT. In *A Matter of Complexity: Subordination in Sign Languages*, ed. M. Steinbach, R. Pfau, and A. Herrmann, 231–251. Berlin: Mouton de Gruyter.

Crasborn, Onno, and Frouke van Winsum. 2014. NGT online: A first inventory. Poster presented at Exploring New Ways of Harvesting and Generating Sign Language Resources: Legal, Technical, and Crowd-Sourcing Issues, CLARIN workshop, Hamburg, December 13–14, 2014. https://www.ru.nl/sign-lang/events/past-events/clarin-workshop/.

Crasborn, Onno, and Inge Zwitserlood. 2008. The Corpus NGT: an online corpus for professionals and laymen. In *Construction and Exploitation of Sign Language Corpora: 3rd Workshop on the Representation and Processing of Sign Languages*, ed. Onno Crasborn, Eleni Efthimiou, Thomas Hanke, Ernst Thoutenhoofd, and Inge Zwitserlood, 44–49. Paris: ELRA.

Efthimiou, Eleni, Stavroulou-Evita Fotinea, Thomas Hanke, Julie Hochgesang, Jette Kristoffersen, and Johanna Mesch 2020. *Proceedings of the 9th Workshop on the Representation and Processing of Sign Languages: Sign Language Resources in the Service of the Language Community, Technological Challenges and Application Perspectives*. Paris: ELRA.

Frishberg, Nancy. 1975. Arbitrariness and iconicity: Historical change in American Sign Language. *Language* 51:696–719.

Hanke, Thomas, M. González Rodriguez, and C. Paz Suarez Araujo. 2002. iLex—A tool for sign language lexicography and corpus analysis. Presented at the LREC 2002 Conference, Las Palmas de Gran Canaria, Spain, May 27–June 2.

Harris, Raychelle, Heidi M. Holmes, and Donna M. Mertens. 2009. Research ethics in sign language communities. *Sign Language Studies* 9 (2): 104–131. doi:10.1353/sls.0.0011.

Herrmann, Annika, and Markus Steinbach. 2011. Nonmanuals in sign languages. *Sign Language and Linguistics* 14 (1): 3–8. doi:10.1075/sll.14.1.02her.

Jayaprakash, Rekha, and Thomas Hanke. 2014. How to use depth sensors in sign language corpus recordings. In *Beyond the Manual Channel: 6th Workshop on the Representation and Processing of Sign Languages*, ed. Onno Crasborn, Eleni Efthimiou, Stravroula-Evita Fotinea, Thomas Hanke, Julie Hochgesang, Jette H. Kristoffersen, and Johanna Mesch, 77–80. Paris: ELRA.

Johnston, Trevor. 2004. W(h)ither the deaf community? Population, genetics and the future of Auslan (Australian Sign Language). *American Annals of the Deaf* 148 (5): 358–375. doi:10.1353/aad.2004.0004.

Johnston, Trevor. 2008. Corpus linguistics and signed languages: No lemmata, no corpus. In *5th Workshop on the Representation and Processing of Signed Languages: Construction and Exploitation of Sign Language Corpora*, ed. O. Crasborn, E. Efthimiou, T. Hanke, E. Thoutenhoofd, and I. Zwitserlood, 82–87. Paris: ELRA.

Johnston, Trevor. 2009. Creating a corpus of Auslan within an Australian National Corpus. In *HCSNet Workshop on Designing the Australian National Corpus: Mustering Languages*, ed. Michael Haugh, Kate Burridge, Jean Mulder, and Pam Peters, 87–96. Somerville, MA: Cascadilla Proceedings Project.

Johnston, Trevor. 2016. *Auslan Corpus Annotation Guidelines*, February 2016 version. Macquarie University. http://www.auslan.org.au/about/annotations/.

Johnston, Trevor, and Adam Schembri. 2006. Issues in the creation of a digital archive of a signed language. In *Sustainable Data from Digital Fieldwork*, ed. L. Barwick and N. Thieberger, 7–16. Sydney: University of Sydney Press.

McKee, Rachel Locker, and Victoria Manning. 2015. Evaluating effects of language recognition on language rights and the vitality of New Zealand Sign Language. *Sign Language Studies* 15 (4): 473–497. doi:10.1353/sls.2015.0017.

Pollard, Robert Q., Jr. 1992. Cross-cultural ethics in the conduct of deafness research. *Rehabilitation Psychology* 37 (2): 87–101. doi:10.1037/h0079101.

Schembri, Adam, Jordan Fenlon, Ramas Rentelis, Sally Reynolds, and Kearsy Cormier. 2013. Building the British Sign Language Corpus. *Language Documentation and Conservation* 7:136–154.

Singleton, Jenny L., Amber J. Martin, and Gary Morgan. 2015. Ethics, deaf-friendly research, and good practice when studying sign languages. In *Research Methods in Sign Language Studies: A Practical Guide*, ed. Eleni Orfanidou, Bencie Woll, and Gary Morgan, 7–20. West Sussex, UK: John Wiley and Sons.

Supalla, Ted, and Patricia Clark. 2014. *Sign Language Archeology*. Washington, DC: Gallaudet University Press.

Trippel, Thorsten. 2004. Metadata for time aligned corpora. In *Proceedings of the LREC 2004 Workshop: A Registry of Linguistic Data Categories within an Integrated Language Repository Area*, ed. Thierry Declerck, Nancy Ide, Key-Sun Choi, and Laurent Romary, 49–55. Paris: ELRA.

Wittenburg, Peter, Hennie Brugman, Albert Russel, Alex Klassmann, and Han Sloetjes. 2006. ELAN: A professional framework for multimodality research. In *Proceedings of the LREC 2006 Conference*, ed. Nicoletta Calzolari, Khalid Choukri, Aldo Gangemi, Bente Maegaard, Joseph Mariani, Jan Odijk, and Daniel Tapias, 1556–1559. Paris: ELRA.

40 Managing Sign Language Video Data Collected from the Internet

Lynn Hou, Ryan Lepic, and Erin Wilkinson

1 Introduction

Research on spoken languages relies extensively on the use of written text. The speech signal is a continuous stream of acoustic information, and spoken language is usually accompanied by visible information such as facial expressions and co-speech gestures. However, linguists are comfortably accustomed to analyzing spoken language data using standardized text systems such as the International Phonetic Alphabet and the Leipzig Glossing Rules (but see, e.g., Pawley & Syder 1983 and Linell 2011 on the biases caused by over-reliance on written text conventions). Written language is also the primary object of study in the analysis of literary and digital texts. In contrast, while there have been a number of attempts to create orthographic systems for sign language users such as Sutton SignWriting, and transcription systems for sign language linguists such as the Hamburg Notation System, no system has yet been adopted as a suitable and generally accepted standard for textually representing sign language data (see Crasborn 2015). Sign languages are essentially unwritten, and this poses a considerable challenge for the representation, management, and accessibility of sign language data.[1]

Though sign language researchers have not reached general consensus on a standardized system for text-based representation of sign forms, research on sign languages has nevertheless progressed, through the common practice of representing signs with metalinguistic, meaning-based glosses. For American Sign Language (ASL), researchers typically use English glosses to represent manual signs and, when necessary, they superimpose these glosses with additional diacritics to represent facial expressions and body movements. Such meaning-based glossing is highly idiosyncratic and is fundamentally shaped by the researcher's analysis

of the phenomenon at hand. Thus, readers often can only guess which signs are referred to and must imagine how glossed examples would be signed. This means that when reading scholarly publications about a given sign language, even competent users of the language generally do not have adequate access to the primary data being discussed. Researchers have adopted different strategies to address this issue of data accessibility. For example, Edward Klima and Ursula Bellugi's (1979) essential volume, *The Signs of Language*, popularized representing some signs with line drawings of human bodies in motion, and many of the illustrations that artist Frank Paul created for the volume, and others from around that time, continue to be widely circulated and re-used to this day.

However, as video recording and digital storage have become increasingly accessible and affordable, so too have they been increasingly embraced by signers and linguists alike to capture sign language data for future viewing.[2] One outcome of this use of digital video recording has been an expansion of sign language videos on the internet, particularly for ASL. Among other things, such videos open up new opportunities for researchers to work with naturalistic data from members of the ASL-signing community and to mitigate some of the problems of accessibility caused by the lack of standardized text-based systems for representing sign language data.

Accordingly, in this Data Management Use Case, we illustrate some of the practical considerations for working with digital video recordings of sign language data for language description purposes. We describe our efforts to analyze ASL signing on the internet, from data collection to sharing and citing, in a way that (we hope) can serve as a working guide for readers who may want to work with video data on the internet for the purposes of (sign) language description and documentation.

2 Working with digital video recordings of elicited (sign) language data

Here, we briefly describe some practical considerations for managing digital recordings of elicited sign language data. In many ways, managing sign language data is quite similar to managing spoken language data (see, for example, Holton, Leonard, & Pulsifer, chapter 4, this volume; Mattern, chapter 5, this volume; Kung, chapter 8, this volume; Hoey & Raymond, chapter 20, this volume; and Daniels & Daniels, chapter 26, this volume). One primary difference between spoken language research and sign language research is that, as described in section 1, sign language linguistics lacks a standardized transcription system for representing visual sign language data textually (see Palfreyman, chapter 21, this volume; Crasborn, chapter 39, this volume; and Hochgesang, chapter 30, this volume). As a result, all textual data and meta-data must be managed using the written form of another language, such as English.

High-definition digital video recordings are currently the preferred, if not the standard, means for recording and archiving sign language data. At a minimum, researchers will need at least one video camera, a tripod, a high-capacity memory card, a computer, video editing software, and an external hard drive or cloud service for storing large video files. Tight shots of multiple signers participating in signed discourse are best captured with multiple video cameras, including (at least) one camera for each signer. However, when working with multiple cameras, it also becomes necessary to synchronize all video recordings in the coding process, to simultaneously view both participants on the computer screen. The choice of video editing software may depend on editing requirements and technical knowledge. Investing in a large, reliable storage and data plan will save you from the heartache of losing your data.

Laboratories, filming studios, and other controlled environmental settings are very common for maximizing the quality of sign language data collected, especially when researchers are building a sign language corpus and filming signers with at least two cameras (e.g., Fenlon et al. 2015). Such settings allow researchers to construct an optimal layout for multiple participants and cameras (Perniss 2015). There are two main types of sign language data commonly distinguished in the field of sign language research, *elicited* and *naturalistic*. For collecting elicited data, researchers utilize a variety of elicitation tasks that involve visual stimuli such as pictures and video clips and written stimuli such as children's stories, semi-structured interviews for obtaining lexical and grammatical constructions, and elicited narratives. For collecting naturalistic data, there are at least two approaches. In sociolinguistic variation studies, researchers videotape groups of signers for one- to two-hour periods in public and/or social spaces such as deaf club events, schools, and conferences (Lucas, Bayley, & Valli 2001; McCaskill et al. 2011). In corpus studies, researchers may assign a pair of acquaintances or friends, or a pair of interlocutors who share similar demographic backgrounds such as age and/or region, and prompt them to engage in spontaneous conversation for half an hour in a filming studio (Fenlon et al. 2015). The idea is to reduce the effects of the "observer's paradox" (Labov 1972) by making some methodological accommodations with the intrusive nature of videotaping to obtain more naturalistic signing from the participants.

Linguistic research that involves primary language data collection from consultants typically falls under the umbrella of human subjects research, meaning that all data collection procedures should be approved by an Institutional Review Board (IRB) or a similar ethical committee. Fortunately, many descriptive linguistic projects are considered socio-behavioral (as opposed to medical) research, and because humans naturally use language every day, there are few risks associated with descriptive linguistic research, outside of boredom and fatigue for language consultants. When working with video data, however, the researcher also needs to be aware, and communicate to the ethical review board as well as to language consultants, that video data poses an inherent risk of loss of confidentiality and privacy for consultants. Typically, it is sufficient to anonymize data by assigning consultants pseudonyms (unless they request their real names to be used) in all data management and reporting, and to include questions on the consent form that ask consultants to determine whether their videos (1) can be viewed by other researchers, (2) can be shown at academic conferences, (3) can be published in academic papers, and, ideally, (4) can be archived in data repository sites for future research.

3 Working with digital video recordings of (sign) language data from the internet

In section 2 we outlined basic considerations for recording, managing, and sharing digital recordings of sign language data for language description purposes. In this section we describe the additional advantages and issues that arise when analyzing sign language data from videos on the internet. Here we primarily consider ASL, the language that we have worked with in this capacity. As a globally dominant sign language, ASL is relatively well attested in signing videos on the internet. However, we expect that the suggestions we make here should be broadly applicable to any body of video data on the internet, for spoken and sign languages alike.

In essence, studying ASL signing on the internet involves searching for videos that have been produced by members of the ASL-signing community, creating a researcher copy of the videos, and analyzing them. In comparison to researcher-elicited video data, which we consider to include semi-naturalistic data obtained in controlled laboratory settings, what sets internet-based studies apart is that signers decide on their own to share their language in public internet spaces. Table 40.1 outlines the differences stemming from there, providing a general overview of the points made throughout this chapter.

3.1 Language sampling from internet data

Traditionally, research on ASL structure and use has targeted only a limited population of deaf signers who use one variety of ASL, and this pattern of recruitment follows from particular language ideologies and language attitudes that researchers hold about ASL and its users (Hill 2013). However, the ASL-signing community is heterogeneous, and the conservative approach that researchers take in recruiting language consultants has shaped how ASL varieties are represented to the wider research community. Acknowledging these facts leads to a bigger question: What does it mean to analyze ASL that is representative of the ASL-signing community?

Table 40.1

Comparison of ASL data types: Researcher-elicited data versus internet-based data

	Researcher-elicited	Internet-based
Interaction between participants and researchers		
Participant recruitment	Required	No recruitment needed
IRB (or ethical review board) protocol	Required	Depends on the institution and research question; if contacting individuals to collect information, then IRB is required
Profile of participant pool	Typically homogenous (e.g., educated, white, deaf of deaf, able-bodied) Individual recruitment	Potentially diverse; however, analyses (e.g., variationist studies) will depend on research goals and available data
Data authenticity		
Data elicitation	Planned elicitation tasks, including prompted naturalistic conversation	No elicitation involved
Observer's paradox	Although researchers may create naturalistic environments for consultants, knowing that video recordings will be shared publicly may affect language use	Contributors voluntarily post their videos in public forums (e.g., Facebook and Twitter), indicating that they acknowledge that others will view and even share their videos
Data sampling and sharing		
Genres	Typically limited variety	Typically wider variety
Language sampling	Given the nature of elicitation tasks, including naturalistic conversation in controlled settings, elicitation could generate adequate materials for very particular research questions	While internet-based ASL data may be more representative in terms of language usage, researchers may not easily find adequate materials to answer very particular research questions
Data distribution by researchers (for example to archives or repositories)	Not standard; researchers typically maintain closed databases	Any online videos that are available to one researcher are also available to *any* researcher, for as long as they remain public. However, it is still necessary for researchers to consider archiving videos

Historically, well-educated, white, deaf signers from signing deaf families have been considered representative users of a prestige variety of ASL. This prestige variety is what is represented in many scholarly publications on ASL. Some exceptions include research on sociolinguistic variation in ASL among Black and white deaf signers of varying socio-economic backgrounds (Lucas, Bayley, & Valli 2001; Lucas et al. 2001; Lucas & Bayley 2005) and the Black ASL Project, a study of a constellation of ASL varieties that emerged in segregated residential schools for Black deaf children and transmitted to subsequent generations of users in Black deaf families and communities (McCaskill et al. 2011). The Black deaf community is identified as "one of the underrepresented, underdocumented, and underreported populations in the literature on ASL and Deaf studies" (Hill & McCaskill 2016:62). Thus, it seems that the variety of ASL represented in most sign language research can be considered largely based on a specific demographic group, rather than as a representative sample of the ASL-signing population.

Fewer than 10% of the deaf signing population are born into signing families; these individuals are referred to as native signers or deaf (children) of deaf (parents). While there is no systematic and direct data available about ASL usage in the United States (Mitchell et al. 2006:307),[3] approximately 95% of American deaf children are born to hearing parents who do not know any sign language. Despite the heavy representation of native-signing ASL users in the literature, then, the majority of deaf, signing Americans do not acquire ASL from fluent signing caregivers as children (Mitchell & Karchmer 2004). Instead, many deaf children begin to learn ASL when they enroll in a school for the deaf or socialize with other deaf children in afterschool programs, camps, or other (in)formal gatherings; others may not learn ASL until well into adolescence or even adulthood (Erting & Kuntze 2008; Morford & Hänel-Faulhaber 2011).

In principle, looking at ASL data on the internet has the potential to spur research that represents the heterogeneous nature of the ASL-signing community more directly. Like other members of the public, researchers have access to any videos of ASL signing that are posted publicly. In practice, however, access to the internet and the drive to post videos to the internet are likely influenced by demographic and socio-economic considerations such as technological literacy and fluency in prestige varieties of ASL. In our estimation, many popular

videos are produced by the same group of white, well-educated deaf signers that have been favored by researchers in the past. At the same time, there are other videos showcasing a more diverse pool of deaf signers producing different varieties of ASL, offering researchers a larger sample that is potentially more representative of the ASL community. We expect that diverse representations of ASL signing on the internet, and indeed of sign languages other than ASL, will only increase over time, meaning that in the long term, internet data hold the potential to grant researchers and signing populations unprecedented access to underrepresented language varieties within the ASL-signing community.

A related consideration in analyzing ASL videos from the internet is selecting which videos to work with. It may not be possible to identify a "random" sample of internet data for linguistic analysis. Ultimately, data sampling will depend on the particular research question, weighed against the videos that are available. We propose to minimize "cherry-picking" internet data with the following suggestions, especially for researchers who are interested in issues of frequency, language change, and variation. First, do not consider only an individual signer, but rather a variety of signers, including those who are established vloggers and those who occasionally vlog.[4] Second, consider including all videos from an established vlogger or perhaps a number of videos from a single channel over a certain period of time. In the latter case, consider adopting the standard practice of random data sampling by selecting the videos produced at equal intervals across a time period of the channel, for example, one video from each week for one year. Researchers can also consider contacting the vloggers for demographic background information, to ensure more variety, though this will likely require ethical review approval from the researcher's institution. In the long run, it will also be possible to compare older video sources used in recent publications with newer video sources.

Because ASL videos necessarily reveal the face and body of the signer, researchers who are interested in language variation and change may guess at certain demographic variables of the signer such as age, gender, sex, race, ethnicity, location, and even language background of the signer.[5] However, we urge caution on this front: appearances can be deceiving, and researchers are not immune to language attitudes and ideologies (Hill 2013). It is especially crucial to realize that signers may "read" as belonging to a particular demographic group, but may identify as members of underrepresented and marginalized minorities including but not limited to African Americans, Native Americans, Latinx/Chicanx, and trans, non-binary, gay, lesbian, and queer persons. Making unfounded assumptions about the background and identity of a signer not only introduces the possibility of inaccurate data, but it also shows a lack of respect for the signer as well as their language and community. Researchers interested in sociolinguistic variation should therefore plan to collect such background information to make their data sampling as principled and ethical as possible.

We also want to comment on genre. Internet-based ASL videos include ASL news sources such as the Daily Moth; vlogs by individual signers touching on a wide range of topics such as politics, car repairs, and cooking; videos sponsored by organizations such as ASLized!; and commercial videos for ASL-signing consumers or for university students who are taking ASL classes. These videos represent a wide range of genres and registers: monologues with and without live audiences, face-to-face and videophone interviews, dyadic and group conversations, rehearsed narratives based on children's stories, and so on. Thanks to inexpensive, accessible video technology, signers are producing a massive number of ASL videos on the internet, resulting in a rich variety of online genres and topics in naturalistic environments. There may even be new genres and subgenres of discourse that have emerged from the interaction of video-recording technological affordances and the visual-manual modality of sign languages. Thus, we encourage researchers who are interested in studying ASL usage on the internet to be mindful of these many genre types.

Finally, researchers should also be aware that vlogs are often subject to some degree of audience design and that vloggers may (metaphorically or literally) edit their content to construct a digital persona. Above all, a primary advantage of internet data is that public ASL videos constitute authentic instances of ASL use, which also encompasses a wide variety of genres. ASL use from the videos should not be considered separate from the use of ASL in "real life"; the internet encompasses part of real life for signers who participate in signing communities online.

3.2 Ethical considerations with internet data

From a researcher's and institutional perspective, videos (and text) that have been posted publicly to the internet, such as vlogs, are generally categorized as "previously collected data" or "no risk studies" and are therefore exempt from institutional ethical review. However, this may vary across educational institutions (Lucas et al. 2013). Given the public nature of internet data, there is, by default, no participant recruitment by researchers. The lack of interaction between the researchers and the video contributors minimizes potential influence from the researcher, including the signers' reaction to the social characteristics of the researchers, on the language data to be studied.

However, researchers need to be aware of potential legal and ethical considerations having to do with video ownership, copyright, and privacy (e.g., Giglietto, Rossi, & Bennato 2012). Videos embedded in *public* posts on social media websites such as Facebook, Instagram, and Twitter do not require an account or log-in for viewing. We recommend that researchers consider only these public posts when working with internet data. However, vloggers may later choose to change their posts to *private*, meaning that they are no longer openly viewable, but rather are shared only with the user's curated list of "friends." Videos embedded in private posts require a user to be friends with the other user who publishes them on their social media page as well as to be part of the same social network to view these videos. Considering these types of private posts as data should involve a comprehensive discussion with the researcher's IRB, including procedures for contacting individuals for permission to analyze their videos.

Relatedly, another ethical concern involves video contributor meta-data. While some contributors disclose information regarding their personal background in their videos, others may only give limited information (e.g., geographical region). As mentioned, given the visual nature of videos, researchers may be tempted to speculate on contributors' age, gender, ethnicity, and other relevant background variables, if contributors do not disclose their identity. We again emphasize the need for caution and reflection on the part of the researcher. If it happens that researchers have insider knowledge on particular contributors, for instance if they are from similar social circles or have mutual connections, then to what extent should the researcher include identifiable information on those contributors? Where do we draw the line? If researchers want to collect demographic information about the signers, they should obtain ethical review approval from their institution. Although we are experiencing a social transformation of the internet with respect to linguistic and communicative practices in sign languages, there are continuing questions regarding ethical and legal issues of video contributions on different social media platforms, and we as a research community need to continually consider potential changes in ethical practices of collecting internet data.

3.3   Internet data as compared to open data

An additional consideration, related to the discussion of ethical research practices in section 3.2, has to do with copyright ownership as it relates to individual websites' terms of use. There will certainly be legal issues to consider before re-uploading any videos online, including storing videos collected from the internet in any digital data repository (see Collister, chapter 9, this volume). To err on the side of caution, we recommend that researchers contact video creators to request copies of videos and request explicit permission to store the video in an online data repository. This process in turn requires institutional ethics approval as described. We suggest that you consider taking this course of action and have an IRB-approved consent form as soon as possible, because videos may be moved to another website, made private, or taken down at any time, without warning. A permanent link to the videos in a digital data repository will contribute to and promote the practice of reproducible research and open access, making research more transparent and accessible for future scrutiny. This approach is not limited to sign language videos, but any study working with language videos from the internet.

The rise of the internet has also enabled the shift of practices and standards for sharing sign language data: some recently published works incorporate film stills of individual signs along with URLs to the video source from which the signs have been extracted (see Lepic 2019 for a recent example). Other papers are published with selected video clips that are available on a journal-sponsored website (such as *Sign Language and Linguistics*; Zeshan & Panda 2015, for example, provide a link to the video sources used in their article). Still others provide links to the video sources in an online corpus, which may require registration for access; additionally, annotations of the sign language videos may be provided on a digital data repository (see Oomen & Kimmelman 2019 for an example). In each of these cases, the primary

data remain accessible to readers for as long as the links remain active. However, there is no guarantee that the links will indeed remain active, and these practices are not yet the norm for most journal publications.

Thus, for the time being, we encourage researchers to provide links to internet-based ASL videos in their conference presentations and scholarly publications, so that other researchers can access and assess the data directly. We also encourage researchers to consider taking steps to deposit their research data, including videos, annotations, and translations, in an open access digital repository. It is not yet the norm in sign language linguistics to make research data, whether elicited in the lab or collected from the internet, available in an archive. However, we hope that this will soon change: the use and citation for internet-based sign language data may help researchers to recognize the benefits of having primary data available for evaluating analyses and for planning future studies. This appreciation may then scaffold data persistence and reproducibility of sign language data sources. This long-term strategy would minimize the ongoing practice of sign language data sets to be short-lived within the limits of a single study.

In the spirit of this push toward using accessible internet data as a bridge to truly open data, we next discuss the handful of small-scale internet-based studies of ASL. Our intention is to highlight the benefits of using internet data for advancing linguistic analyses.

4   Examples of small-scale internet-based studies of ASL

There are a handful of examples of small-scale internet-based studies of ASL. To our best knowledge, Wilkinson was the first investigator to analyze internet-based ASL data, in her corpus analyses on frequency effects on NOT collocations (2016) and the functions of SELF (2006, 2013a, 2013b). The study on NOT collocations included 9.1 hours of internet-based data as a part of the larger data set, which was retrieved during 2006–2007 from the website called DeafRead: Best of Deaf Blogs and Vlogs (http://www.deafread.com). The study investigated the distribution of token and type frequency of NOT collocations, and analysis revealed the three highest-frequency two-sign collocations were identified as [NOT HAVE-TO], [WHY NOT], and [NOT UNDERSTAND]. These phonologically reduced collocations have undergone changes in semantic-pragmatic function, compared to non-reduced two-sign constructions. This indicated that "signers are not processing sequential relations of two distinct forms, but instead are accessing the chunking unit directly as the collocation has become autonomous in form and meaning" (2016:98), indicating grammaticalization of NOT collocations is taking place in ASL.

The incorporation of internet data in a larger data set also led Wilkinson (2013a, 2013b) to discover genre effects on the usage of three related forms of the sign SELF among American and Canadian signers. The first analysis (2013a) found a robust pattern of SELF usage in vlogs, compared to in narratives and two-person conversations for Americans. The second, variationist study (2013b) compared the American data with Canadian data to explore whether there were differences in patterns of SELF usage among American and Canadian ASL signers. The study identified morphosyntactic variation in ASL in the distribution SELF usage in a variety of genres, revealing that, for example, American vloggers demonstrated a robust preference for employing SELF signs in their vlogs but not in live presentations, whereas Canadian signers showed a more balanced use of SELF forms in vlogs and live presentations.

Two other studies of phonological reduction and morphosyntactic variation in ASL signing on the internet are Lepic (2016) and Lepic (2019). Lepic (2016) documents compound formation processes in contemporary ASL and identifies 104 unique compounds from eighty-seven minutes of ASL signing from fifteen public You-Tube channels. These 104 compounds were classified as either *fingerspelled compounds*, which are likely calques of English compounds (e.g., [C-O-N-T-E-N-T QUESTION] "a content question"); *chain compounds*, which are instances of English-ASL bilingual repetition (e.g., [F-I-L-T-E-R FILTER] "filter"); or *sign-sign compounds*, which juxtapose two ASL signs to create a larger unit (e.g., [EXAMPLE SENTENCE] "an example sentence"). Lepic (2016:234) suggests that naturalistic signing on the internet is essential for collecting novel as well as more conventionalized instances of ASL use. This view is also taken up in Lepic (2019), which draws on examples of ASL signing on the internet to examine the gradual erosion of structure in multiword expressions, fingerspelled words, and morphologically complex signs as a function of their frequent use. Many of the ASL examples discussed are linked directly to the relevant video on YouTube, setting the stage for more

open and reliable access to (sign) language example sentences in the coming years.

A third internet-based study is Hou, Lepic, and Anible (2018), which investigates the distribution and grammatical functions of the family of LOOK-AT signs in ASL. The data include over eight hundred tokens, from a larger data set of almost fifteen hours' worth of internet-based videos, consisting of eighty-six vlogs from fifty-five unique signers. The data were divided into three broad genre types: conversations (one hour), monologues (four hours and twenty minutes), and broadcast journalism (over nine hours). The sign LOOK-AT corresponds to a prototypically one-handed sign and has been traditionally described as a directional verb that marks the object of visual perception and that codes number and aspect (Klima & Bellugi 1979; Liddell 2003). This sign also participates in other constructions that are literally or metaphorically related to vision; such constructions are often labeled with other English glosses such as ADMIRE, OBSERVE, PERSPECTIVE, and READ, in ASL dictionaries and lexical databases. The English glosses give the impression that these signs are distinct and separate lexical entries. However, looking at the functions within the family of LOOK-AT signs, the investigators find that signers use a variety of LOOK-AT signs in a network of related constructions relating to a wide array of visual and metaphorical perceptions, and these signs exhibit polysemy across all genres. Similar to the studies of Wilkinson and Lepic, the incorporation of internet-based ASL data allowed Hou, Lepic, and Anible to re-examine previous analyses of LOOK-AT signs and to capture the emergence of linguistic structure and meaning among these signs in spontaneous signing across different genre contexts.

What we can learn from the aforementioned studies is that internet-based ASL data have allowed researchers to investigate frequency, language change, and variation and to come up with new analyses that were not previously available using elicited data. Not only have these analyses contributed to the study of sign language linguistics, they have advanced our understanding of sign languages with respect to general linguistic phenomena that have been documented for spoken languages. Finally, these analyses are in principle reproducible, as the data remain open for as long as the links to the videos that were analyzed remain active. The same cannot necessarily be said for the majority of previous ASL studies, in which access to primary data remains quite closed. The use and re-use of internet data has potential for shifting current research standards and practices toward more reproducible research in sign language research, in light of Berez-Kroeker et al.'s (2018) call for reproducibility in linguistics. Some of the shifts would involve greater transparency about data sources and research methodologies, more direct access to primary data and analyses, and even citations of data sets.

5   Future directions for internet-based (A)SL research

The internet holds a trove of naturalistic data that can be used to chart out new directions in sign language research. An inherent benefit to using internet data is that these videos are authentic examples of ASL as produced by members of the ASL-signing community. While these videos are likely subject to some degree of audience design, there is virtually no risk of researchers compromising the integrity of the available data, as the data are not solicited by experimenters in any way. In addition, videos that have been posted in public spaces online remain visible beyond the time of their original creation and posting. Depending on various factors, many of these videos could remain visible for quite some time.

Internet-based ASL data offer researchers the opportunity to document lexical, grammatical, and sociolinguistic variation from deaf signers across diverse genres and text types, such as monologues and broadcast journalism. Furthermore, internet data also offer fertile opportunities for conducting synchronic and diachronic research. In the case of diachronic research of ASL, one can combine ASL data from the Historical Sign Language Database (Supalla & Clark 2015) and modern ASL signing on the internet to investigate grammaticalization in ASL. Internet data can also reduce and perhaps eliminate the need to conduct metalinguistic elicitation sessions, although this depends on the particular research question. But the potential of internet data is enormous, to the point where researchers can minimize the recruitment and "recycling" of the same language consultants for their studies, while maximizing the opportunity to study underrepresented minority signers within their signing communities.

Internet data also offer researchers the opportunity to document the impact of technology on signing practices, as a growing number of deaf signers are communicating through video chat applications (e.g., FaceTime and Facebook); filming themselves in naturalistic environments such as at their homes, in cars, and in public; and posting their vlogs online (Lucas et al. 2013). Given how the internet has connected signers from near and far in the United States (and their transborder connections also permit them to reach out to other (A)SL signers outside of the United States), the language ecology of the ASL community is changing; signers are broadening their social circles beyond their traditional practices of convening at deaf schools, social clubs, and deaf-oriented events in near proximity to their residences and workplaces. Moreover, as more deaf signers are increasingly encountering each other at international events such as festivals and conferences and through deaf tourism (Friedner & Kusters 2015), signers are also connecting through the internet, making more unprecedented transnational connections possible.

However, there remain a number of challenges related to collecting and managing internet-based ASL videos and in particular sharing and archiving these videos. There are not yet standardized mechanisms for identifying and tagging ASL videos on the internet. We as a field are also still determining the legal and ethical considerations that govern appropriate research practices with internet-based data. In particular, here we have identified the lack of standardized text-based representation systems and the issue of making internet data open and available, beyond the circumstances of individual content creators or website platforms, as tricky problems for which there is not yet a perfect solution.

In this chapter, we have attempted to situate these practical and ethical concerns that stem from studying sign language data on the internet, relative to more traditional methods for obtaining sign language data from language consultants. We are optimistic that as open research and data sharing become increasingly the norm in linguistics, so too will sign language linguists benefit from the push toward open methods.

Notes

1. Indeed, since the very beginning of sign language linguistics, a central concern has been how to best analyze and represent sign language data: William Stokoe's seminal analysis of ASL, for example, demonstrated that individual signs can be described as combinations of structural primes constituting the "tabula" (now typically referred to as *location*), "designator" (*handshape*), or "signation" (*movement*) of the sign, with each structural prime having its own written symbol (Stokoe 1960; Stokoe, Casterline, & Croneberg 1965). However, while

this general approach is still central to sign language analysis, Stokoe's particular symbols are not widely used today.

2. For example, Ted Supalla and others have studied patterns of historical change in ASL, which is made possible by the past efforts of the National Association of the Deaf to preserve videotaped examples of ASL use from 1910 to 1920, as well as the work of deaf filmmakers such as Charles Krauel to document everyday ASL use starting in the 1920s (Supalla 1991; Supalla & Clark 2015).

3. When we say *American Sign Language*, we are referring to signing varieties that emerged naturally among deaf Americans in signing families and residential schools for the deaf and have been transmitted to subsequent generations of deaf people. This is distinct from any artificial signing system such as Signed Exact English invented specifically to teach deaf people the grammar of English. At the same time, we acknowledge the high degree of language contact between ASL and English in the daily lives of deaf people, because signing communities are microcosms of speaking communities, and this presents sign language researchers the challenge of characterizing what constitutes ASL (Lucas & Valli 2010).

4. *Vlog* is short for "video log" or "video blog." A *vlogger* is an internet user who regularly posts vlogs online for others to view.

5. One exception is the Linguistic Video Collection at Gallaudet University, because the videos contain some demographic information about the signers.

References

Berez-Kroeker, Andrea L., Lauren Gawne, Susan Smythe Kung, Barbara F. Kelly, Tyler Heston, Gary Holton, Peter Pulsifer, et al. 2018. Reproducible research in linguistics: A position statement on data citation and attribution in our field. *Linguistics* 56 (1): 1–18. https://doi.org/10.1515/ling-2017-0032.

Crasborn, Onno A. 2015. Transcription and notation methods. In *Research Methods in Sign Language Studies: A Practical Guide*, ed. Eleni Ofanidou, Bencie Woll, and Gary Morgan, 74–88. West Sussex, UK: Wiley-Blackwell.

Erting, Carol J., and Marlon Kuntze. 2008. Language socialization in deaf communities. In *Encyclopedia of Language and Education*, vol. 8, ed. Patricia Duff and Nancy H. Hornberger, 287–300. New York: Springer Press.

Fenlon, Jordan, Adam Schembri, Trevor Johnston, and Kearsy Cormier. 2015. Documentary and corpus approaches to sign language research. In *The Blackwell Guide to Research Methods in Sign Language Studies*, ed. Eleni Orfanidou, Bencie Woll, and Gary Morgan, 156–172. Oxford: Blackwell.

Friedner, Michele, and Annelies Kusters. 2015. *It's a Small World: International Deaf Spaces and Encounters*. Washington, DC: Gallaudet University Press.

Giglietto, Fabio, Luca Rossi, and Davide Bennato. 2012. The Open Laboratory: Limits and possibilities of using Facebook, Twitter, and YouTube as a research data source. *Journal of Technology in Human Services* 30 (3–4): 145–159. https://doi.org/10.1080/15228835.2012.743797.

Hill, Joseph. 2013. Language ideologies, policies, and attitudes toward signed languages. In *The Oxford Handbook of Sociolinguistics*, ed. Robert Bayley, Richard Cameron, and Ceil Lucas, 680–697. Oxford Handbooks in Linguistics. Oxford: Oxford University Press.

Hill, Joseph, and Carolyn McCaskill. 2016. Reflections on the Black ASL Project. *Sign Language Studies* 17 (1): 59–63.

Hou, Lynn, Ryan Lepic, and Benjamin Anible. 2018. When looks count: The function and distribution of LOOK-AT in American Sign Language. Presented at the Sign CAFE 1, Birmingham, UK, July 30.

Klima, Edward, and Ursula Bellugi. 1979. *The Signs of Language*. Cambridge: Harvard University Press.

Labov, William. 1972. *Sociolinguistic Patterns*. Philadelphia: University of Pennsylvania Press.

Lepic, Ryan. 2016. The great ASL compound hoax. In *Proceedings of the High Desert Linguistics Society Conference*, vol. 11, ed. A. Healey, R. Napoleão de Souza, P. Pešková, and M. Allen, 227–250. Albuquerque: University of New Mexico.

Lepic, Ryan. 2019. A usage-based alternative to "lexicalization" in sign language linguistics. *Glossa: A Journal of General Linguistics* 4 (1): 23. https://doi.org/10.5334/gjgl.840.

Liddell, Scott K. 2003. *Grammar, Gesture, and Meaning in American Sign Language*. Cambridge: Cambridge University Press.

Linell, Per. 2011. *Written Language Bias in Linguistics: Its Nature, Origins and Transformations*. New York: Routledge.

Lucas, Ceil, and Robert Bayley. 2005. Variation in ASL: The role of grammatical function. *Sign Language Studies* 6 (1): 38–75.

Lucas, Ceil, Robert Bayley, Ruth Reed, and Alyssa Wulf. 2001. Lexical variation in African American and white American Sign Language. *American Speech* 76 (4): 61–111.

Lucas, Ceil, Robert Bayley, and Clayton Valli. 2001. *Sociolinguistic Variation in American Sign Language*. Washington, DC: Gallaudet University Press.

Lucas, Ceil, Gene Mirus, Jeffrey Levi Palmer, Nicholas James Roessler, and Adam Frost. 2013. The effect of new technologies on sign language research. *Sign Language Studies* 13 (4): 541–564.

Lucas, Ceil, and Clayton Valli. 2010. *Language Contact in the American Deaf Community*. San Diego: Academic Press.

McCaskill, Carolyn, Ceil Lucas, Robert Bayley, and Joseph Hill. 2011. *The Hidden Treasure of Black ASL: Its History and Structure*. Washington, DC: Gallaudet University Press.

Mitchell, Ross E., and Michael A. Karchmer. 2004. Chasing the mythical ten percent: Parental hearing status of deaf and hard of hearing students in the United States. *Sign Language Studies* 4 (2): 138–163.

Mitchell, Ross E., Travas A. Young, Bellamie Bachelda, and Michael A. Karchmer. 2006. How many people use ASL in the United States? Why estimates need updating. *Sign Language Studies* 6 (3): 306–335.

Morford, Jill P., and Barbara Hänel-Faulhaber. 2011. Homesigners as late learners: Connecting the dots from delayed acquisition in childhood to sign language processing in adulthood. *Language and Linguistics Compass* 5 (8): 525–537. https://doi.org/10.1111/j.1749-818X.2011.00296.x.

Oomen, Marloes, and Vadim Kimmelman. 2019. Body-anchored verbs and argument omission in two sign languages. *Glossa: A Journal of General Linguistics* 4 (1): 42. https://doi.org/10.5334/gjgl.741.

Pawley, Andrew, and Frances Hodgetts Syder. 1983. Natural selection in syntax: Notes on adaptive variation and change in vernacular and literary grammar. *Journal of Pragmatics* 7 (5): 551–579. https://doi.org/10.1016/0378-2166(83)90081-4.

Perniss, Pamela. 2015. Collecting and analyzing sign language data: Video requirements and use of annotation software. In *The Blackwell Guide to Research Methods in Sign Language Studies*, ed. Eleni Orfanidou, Bencie Woll, and Gary Morgan, 55–73. Oxford: Wiley-Blackwell.

Stokoe, William C. 1960. *Sign Language Structure: An Outline of the Visual Communication Systems of the American Deaf.* Buffalo, NY: University of Buffalo.

Stokoe, William C., Dorothy C. Casterline, and Carl G. Croneberg. 1965. *A Dictionary of American Sign Language on Linguistic Principles*. Silver Spring, MD: Linstok Press.

Supalla, Ted. 1991. Deaf folklife film collection project. *Sign Language Studies* 70:73–82. https://doi.org/10.1353/sls.1991.0027.

Supalla, Ted, and Patricia Clark. 2015. *Sign Language Archaeology: Understanding the Historical Roots of American Sign Language*. Washington, DC: Gallaudet University Press.

Wilkinson, Erin. 2006. Does it behave as a reflexive pronoun in American Sign Language? Talk presented at the High Desert Linguistics Society 7 (HDLS 7), Albuquerque, NM, November 9–11.

Wilkinson, Erin. 2013a. A functional description of SELF in American Sign Language. *Sign Language Studies* 13 (4): 462–490. https://doi.org/10.1353/sls.2013.0015.

Wilkinson, Erin. 2013b. Morphosyntactic variation in American Sign Language: A corpus-based investigation on SELF in Canada and the United States. In *Sign Language Research Uses and Practices: Crossing Views on Theoretical and Applied Sign Language Linguistics*, ed. Laurence Meurant, Aurélie Sinte, Mieke van Herreweghe, and Myriam Vermeerbergen, 259–284. Berlin: De Gruyter Mouton.

Wilkinson, Erin. 2016. Finding frequency effects in the usage of NOT collocations in American Sign Language. *Sign Language and Linguistics* 19 (1): 82–123. https://doi.org/10.1075/sll.19.1.03wil.

Zeshan, Ulrike, and Sibaji Panda. 2015. Two languages at hand: Code-switching in bilingual deaf signers. *Sign Language and Linguistics* 18 (1): 90–131.

41 Managing Data from Social Media: The Indigenous Tweets Project

Kevin P. Scannell

1 Introduction

Social media sites such as Facebook, Twitter, and Instagram provide a rich source of linguistic data for hundreds of languages in real time. They also play an important role in language revitalization efforts for many Indigenous and minority languages, serving to connect members of language communities that may be geographically scattered. This chapter is a case study in collecting and managing linguistic data from Twitter as part of the Indigenous Tweets project, which was founded in 2011 as a way of promoting the use of Indigenous and minority languages in social media. Our principal aim in this chapter is to describe our data management procedures in sufficient detail that linguists, sociolinguists, lexicographers, or community language activists with some programming skills can begin experimenting with Twitter data themselves.

The primary home of the Indigenous Tweets project is the website IndigenousTweets.com (see figure 41.1), where we track statistics on users tweeting in 185 languages, ranging from a few languages with more than ten thousand users and millions of tweets (e.g., Irish, Welsh, Basque) to others with only one or two users and just a handful of tweets. Each language has a home page that displays the top five hundred users in that language with each user's individual statistics (number and percentage of tweets in the language, number of followers, and such), along with up-to-date "Trending Topics" for the language (e.g., figure 41.2). In practical terms, the language pages serve as a kind of "menu" for accounts someone might choose to follow in their own language community, but they also play an important role in increasing the visibility of some very small language communities whose voices might otherwise be drowned out on a platform dominated by global languages such

as English, Spanish, French, and Arabic (Scannell 2011). In terms of language revitalization, there has been an unexpected competitive aspect to the project, in which some people have been encouraged to tweet more often in their native language in order to move up in the rankings on the site.

Behind the scenes, the site makes use of the Twitter Application Programming Interface (API)[1] and statistical language identification to collect tweets in each of the target languages; the details of this process and the structure of the resulting data sets are provided in sections 2 and 3, respectively. Unfortunately, Twitter's Terms of Service do not allow corpora of tweets to be redistributed, even for research purposes; we discuss this issue and its impact on reproducibility of research in section 4. Despite these limitations, the Indigenous Tweets data sets provide an up-to-the-minute snapshot of how these languages are used in an informal context and have proved useful in both linguistic research and in the development of natural language processing resources. We list a few of these applications in section 5.[2]

2 Data collection methodology

Twitter is a social networking service that allows users to post short messages (*tweets*) of up to 280 characters. It is one of the most widely used social networks in the world, with over three hundred million active monthly users. It is a social network in the sense that users are able to *follow* other users, which means they will see those users' tweets when logged into the service. Users can follow friends, family, or work colleagues, as well as politicians, celebrities, and other public figures.

Shortly after Twitter's launch in 2006, the company released the first version of the Twitter API, a set of software tools that allows third-party developers to access the

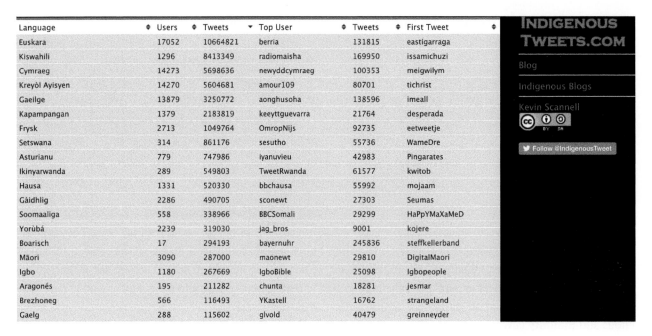

Language	Users	Tweets	Top User	Tweets	First Tweet
Euskara	17052	10664821	berria	131815	eastigarraga
Kiswahili	1296	8413349	radiomaisha	169950	issamichuzi
Cymraeg	14273	5698636	newyddcymraeg	100353	meigwilym
Kreyòl Ayisyen	14270	5604681	amour109	80701	tichrist
Gaeilge	13879	3250772	aonghusoha	138596	imeall
Kapampangan	1379	2183819	keeyttguevarra	21764	desperada
Frysk	2713	1049764	OmropNijs	92735	eetweetje
Setswana	314	861176	sesutho	55736	WameDre
Asturianu	779	747986	iyanuvieu	42983	Pingarates
Ikinyarwanda	289	549803	TweetRwanda	61577	kwitob
Hausa	1331	520330	bbchausa	55992	mojaam
Gàidhlig	2286	490705	sconewt	27303	Seumas
Soomaaliga	558	338966	BBCSomali	29299	HaPpYMaXaMeD
Yorùbá	2239	319030	jag_bros	9001	kojere
Boarisch	17	294193	bayernuhr	245836	steffkellerband
Māori	3090	287000	maonewt	29810	DigitalMaori
Igbo	1180	267669	IgboBible	25098	Igbopeople
Aragonés	195	211282	chunta	18281	jesmar
Brezhoneg	566	116493	YKastell	16762	strangeland
Gaelg	288	115602	glvold	40479	greinneyder

Figure 41.1
Home page of the Indigenous Tweets project.

	Cleachdaiche	Gàidhlig	Iomlan	% Gàidhlig	'Ga leantainn	A' leantainn	An drannd mu dheireadh
1	sconewt	27303	31209	87.5	19	0	2013-06-11 20:25:53
2	Gaidhlig_Tweets	13626	25109	54.3	554	309	2019-01-13 10:48:22
3	bbcnaidheachdan	12413	13407	92.6	3463	264	2019-09-13 20:15:51
4	Gaidhlig_	11756	29712	39.6	1074	270	2016-08-29 12:13:16
5	ForamnaGaidhlig	8426	13875	60.7	2375	2123	2019-09-14 15:07:02
6	NaidheachdanAAA	8422	10356	81.3	600	820	2019-09-14 14:49:42
7	BBCSpors	8120	10020	81.0	2149	969	2019-09-14 15:49:46
8	gaelic_tweets	7206	34151	21.1	1046	230	2019-05-20 05:39:25
9	GaelicTweets	7148	20179	35.4	2220	18	2013-05-14 09:08:40
10	bordnagaidhlig1	7030	11754	59.8	5033	1345	2019-09-11 21:41:44
11	isleofsouthuist	6179	64409	9.6	37843	15100	2019-09-14 23:10:23
12	am_broc	5375	8935	60.2	1227	520	2019-09-14 20:20:39
13	Bliadhnaichean	5358	744453	0.7	3145	591	2019-09-14 23:22:39
14	Maigheach	5159	81636	6.3	3995	1167	2019-09-14 08:08:20
15	ParlAlba	4826	6034	80.0	2774	959	2019-09-12 10:50:25
16	akerbeltzalba	4780	5467	87.4	1118	128	2019-09-13 16:23:54
17	LearnGaelicScot	4719	11466	41.2	13758	290	2019-09-14 14:30:09

Figure 41.2
Language page for Scottish Gaelic.

Twitter database from their own programs. When a developer uses the Twitter API, they are essentially performing a remote database query to retrieve some information about users or tweets directly from Twitter's servers. For example, to retrieve information about a particular user, a developer can make use of the query users/show, which returns metadata such as the user's account name, numerical user ID, location (if specified), number of followers, total number of tweets, and so on. There are dozens of

such queries available (usually referred to by developers as "API endpoints") that return rich information related to users, tweets, followers, lists, direct messages, trends, geolocations, and so on. API queries can be made using almost any programming language.

The Indigenous Tweets site gathers the data it needs from the Twitter API using the Perl module Net::Twitter written and maintained by Marc Mims.[3] For our purposes, we need only make use of a small number of (read-only)

API endpoints, namely `statuses/user_timeline`, `users/show`, `followers/ids`, `friends/ids`, `statuses/show`, and `search/tweets`. The parameters and return values of these API endpoints are well-documented on Twitter's Developer site.[4]

The Indigenous Tweets project relies heavily on code and data sets from the Crúbadán web crawler (Scannell 2007), a long-running project that involves crawling the web for texts in about 2,200 languages.[5] In particular, the Crúbadán project implements a statistical language identifier based on frequencies of words and character sequences, and we apply this language identifier to tweets collected using the Twitter API. Twitter text is sufficiently different from typical web texts (e.g., news articles, government reports, blog posts, Bible texts) that we have found it beneficial to fold samples of tweets from each language into the statistical models used by the language identifier. By doing this sufficiently often, the language identifier can benefit from common hashtags, proper names, and such in current use by a language community to help detect tweets in the language more accurately. However, even with these tweets included in the models, it is important to note that the language identifier is not perfect; it sometimes mislabels very short tweets or is confused by bilingual tweets or code-switching.

Data collection for the Indigenous Tweets site works as follows. For each of the 185 supported languages, we maintain a database of users known to have tweeted in the language at least once. Twice a week we make queries to `statuses/user_timeline` for each of these users to collect their most recent tweets and retweets, and then we apply the language identifier to discard any tweets not in the target language. At present, we are discarding tweets that are rejected by the language identifier to save space in the database, but we plan to change this behavior in the future because it could provide some insight into the linguistic behavior of multilingual tweeters. Each query to `statuses/user_timeline` returns up to two hundred tweets, so except for the most prolific users, a single query twice a week suffices to track each user's full output of tweets. We refer to one such pass through the database of users as a *crawl*. Because this endpoint is currently rate-limited by Twitter at a generous nine hundred queries per fifteen-minute window, it does not take long to process all of the users in our database.

This discussion assumes the existence of some users tweeting in a language. We have four main techniques

for finding new members of a language community on Twitter:

1. Searching characteristic words: As part of the Crúbadán project, we maintain lists of "statistically unique" words in each of the 2,200+ languages the crawler recognizes. These are words that have high frequency in the target language, but which do not appear in any other language, or if they do, with very low frequency. Examples are words such as *oedd* or *mewn* in Welsh, *bhfuil* in Irish, or *airson* in Scottish Gaelic. Using the Standard Search API provided by the endpoint `search/tweets`, we periodically search for users who have posted tweets containing these words, and then scan their full history for tweets in the target language if they are not already in our database. This is the most effective technique for finding users in languages we are not yet tracking because it only relies on existing word lists and language identification models provided by the Crúbadán project. Indeed, the great majority of the 185 languages on the site were added in this way, with the others coming from lists of users provided by members of the language community.

2. Retweets: When collecting tweets via `statuses/user_timeline` we make no distinction between original tweets and retweets or quoted tweets. Therefore, if an existing user A in our database retweets user B who is not in our database, we apply the language identifier to the text of the retweet as usual. If it is identified as being in the target language, we can safely add user B to the database and retroactively scan their history for additional tweets in the language.

3. Followers: If a user tweets in the target language frequently, we assume that anyone following that user has at least a passive knowledge of the language. So we periodically generate a list of all followers of users that tweet in the target language more than a given percentage of the time (the threshold varies from language to language), remove any users already in our database, and then scan each remaining user's history for tweets in the language.

4. Crowdsourced suggestions: Each language page on the Indigenous Tweets site has a text input box labeled "Anyone missing?" that users of the site can use to suggest a username not yet appearing in our lists. Because the site only displays the top five hundred tweeters in each language, we sometimes get suggestions of users

already in our database but not in the top five hundred, and these are simply discarded. A number of communities have been energetic in contributing in this way, submitting hundreds or thousands of suggested users, most notably the Kapampangan, Irish, Asturian, Aragonese, Frisian, Cornish, and Māori communities.

Two final technical constraints. First, Twitter puts a limit on how far back in a user's history one can go using `statuses/user_timeline` (currently capped at the most recent 3,200 tweets). For users who tweet frequently in the target language, this is not a serious problem because we generally pick up on those users quickly via one of the four approaches just described. Occasionally, however, we miss someone and therefore cannot examine their full tweet history if they already have more than 3,200 tweets when we first discover them. Second, for most languages we only access a given tweet a single time via the API, and so any variable metadata attached to that tweet (for example, the number of likes or the number of retweets) is never updated after the initial crawl. Although we are not currently using any such metadata on the Indigenous Tweets site itself, for the author's primary languages of interest (Irish, Scottish, and Manx Gaelic) we have some applications that make use of this information (see section 5). As a result, for these three languages we have additional processes in place to requery the metadata attached to a subset of tweets to ensure they remain up to date.

3   Data management process

For each language tracked by the Indigenous Tweets site, there are two main tables in the database, one for users and one for tweets. We distinguish *upstream metadata*, by which we mean metadata available directly from the Twitter API, from *derived metadata*, meaning information that we generate through some additional analysis of the upstream metadata. All upstream and derived metadata are fully updated for all users in the database with each semi-weekly crawl.

Upstream metadata are partially documented on Twitter's Developer site, but they are subject to change with each new version of the API. Upstream metadata for users currently includes attributes such as a unique user ID, number of followers, total number of tweets, a link to the user's profile picture, self-reported location from the user profile, the chosen user interface language

on the Twitter website, and many additional attributes that are not important for our purposes, such as the background color of the user's profile. The upstream metadata for tweets includes a time stamp, the text of the tweet itself, information about whether it is a reply, retweet, quoted tweet, and so forth, and additional data unlikely to be useful for our purposes. We do not retain all of the upstream metadata attached to users or tweets even though failing to do so has caused some minor difficulties in the past. For example, at one point we examined the relative usage of the Irish Twitter interface among native versus non-native speakers, but because we originally did not store the user's chosen interface language in the database, we were forced to go back and add that attribute through additional queries to the API.

Derived metadata for users includes the number and percentage of tweets in the target language according to the language identifier, the time stamp of the last time the user was crawled by our site, and the numerical identifier of their most recent tweet in our database (which can be passed to `statuses/user_timeline` to avoid reanalyzing tweets we have seen before). For many users we also derive an approximate latitude and longitude from their self-reported location in the user profile by running these through an online geolocation service; this enables some of the geographical visualizations discussed in section 5.

Tweets, when viewed as linguistic data, are more richly structured than simple plain text (Good, chapter 3, this volume). For example, tweets can be posted in reply to other tweets, revealing complex patterns of conversation among multiple users, or they can quote or retweet other tweets. Very often they are posted together with media objects of various types (e.g., images, videos, animated GIFs) and the Twitter API provides URLs for these objects. We currently make no attempt to download, store, or analyze the content of associated media objects, primarily because the project depends on software for *written* language identification. We would like to rectify this in the future because these media objects sometimes contain interesting linguistic information, for example, text embedded in an image, the spoken or signed language used in a video, or even the association between the plain text of a tweet and an image. This would also enable us to extend the project to sign languages and unwritten languages.

In addition to the two primary tables storing users and tweets, we maintain three auxiliary data sets that facilitate the data collection process described in section 2. First, for each language we maintain a list of "discarded" user IDs for which we have scanned the user's history without finding any tweets in the target language. This prevents a lot of repeated effort when using the social graph to search for new members of the language community. For example, the Irish language television station TG4 tweets from the account @TG4TV and more than 60% of their tweets are in Irish, but the majority of their 36,000+ followers have never tweeted in the language, so we do not bother rechecking those users over and over. This runs the risk of missing someone who might make a conscious decision to begin using the language at some later date, but we hope to detect such users through one of the other three methods discussed, which do not make use of the discarded list.

Second, for the three Gaelic languages, we maintain Twitter lists of the top users in each language (top five hundred for Irish, top one hundred for Scottish Gaelic, and the top ten for Manx).[6] These are updated automatically based on the number of tweets in the respective language over the previous six-month period, and membership requires that users maintain a certain minimum percentage of tweets in the language. These lists are used in some of the applications described in section 5.[7]

Finally, each language has a queue of candidate user IDs that arise from one of the four techniques for finding new users described in section 2. These are queued up and processed between crawls to avoid running into issues with API rate limits.

We make all of the derived metadata available under a Creative Commons Attribution-ShareAlike license. Data related to the number and percentage of tweets in the language are available on the Indigenous Tweets site, and we have additional derived data sets relating to geolocation available on GitHub.[8] We do not distribute corpora of tweets, for reasons we will discuss in section 4. Nevertheless, a number of researchers have made use of data from Indigenous Tweets in their sociolinguistic research, for example Keegan, Mato, and Ruru (2015), Ní Bhroin (2015), Lillehaugen (2016), and Mato (2018), and we believe there is much more that can be done with these data sets, in terms of both individual languages and cross-linguistic analysis.

4   Twitter's Terms of Service and reproducibility

This chapter is likely to be an outlier among the Use Cases presented in this book in that we are not permitted to distribute the most interesting and useful data coming out of the project, namely, the corpora of tweets in the 185 languages we are tracking. According to the Twitter Terms of Service, anyone making use of the public API is bound by the Twitter Developer Agreement and Developer Policy.[9] The Developer Policy (here we are referencing the version that went into effect on November 3, 2017) is explicit regarding redistribution of Twitter content. For example, section I.F.2 of the agreement specifies that "if you provide Twitter Content to third parties, including downloadable datasets of Twitter Content or an API that returns Twitter Content, you will only distribute or allow download of Tweet IDs, Direct Message IDs, and/or User IDs." There are also restrictions on the number of tweet IDs that can be distributed (1.5 million per thirty-day period), although there is an exception for non-commercial research in academic institutions (and almost all of our corpora are small enough that this limit is not an issue in practice).

Before 2011 there were at least two large Twitter corpora available online, one created at Stanford containing the text of more than 500 million tweets (Yang & Leskovec 2011) and another created at Edinburgh containing the text of about 97 million tweets (Petrović, Osborne, & Lavrenko 2010). Unfortunately, these are no longer available because they now violate the Terms of Service. It has since become standard practice to distribute Twitter corpora as lists of tweet IDs and/or user IDs, sometimes together with software tools for retrieving the actual tweets via the API (see, e.g., McCreadie et al. 2012; McMinn, Moshfeghi, & Jose 2013; Scheffler 2014). Note that there may also be concerns around copyright when distributing corpora of tweets, because Twitter's Terms of Service state that users retain rights to any content they submit, post, or display on the service (cf. Collister, chapter 9, this volume).

Although distributing tweet IDs complies with the Terms of Service, it presents major difficulties in terms of the reproducibility of research based on such corpora (Berez-Kroeker et al., chapter 1, this volume). Twitter users have the ability to delete tweets at any time after posting them; they can choose to make their account private (and public again later); or they can delete their account entirely. The tweets in question would then no longer be accessible via the Twitter API, meaning that only a subset of the original corpus would be available. Even for the tweets that are still available, certain tweet attributes may be inconsistent with the original corpus because some of the upstream metadata are subject to change. These issues were recognized, for example, by McCreadie et al. (2012) who tried to mitigate the problem by asking users of their Twitter corpus (participants in an information retrieval "shared competition") to regenerate the corpus of tweets within a short time frame to minimize differences. Nevertheless, it remains the case that linguistic research or evaluation of natural language processing resources based on Twitter corpora distributed as tweet IDs is not fully reproducible in the long term. For more detailed discussions of the impact of Twitter's Terms of Service on social media research, we recommend the papers by Wheeler (2018) and Bruns and Burgess (2016).

Setting these issues aside, there is also a practical problem with distributing tweet IDs in that it can be time-consuming to regenerate very large corpora using only the statuses/show API endpoint. One workaround is to provide both user IDs and tweet IDs and regenerate the corpora by retrieving batches of tweets for a given user ID via statuses/user_timeline and keeping only those tweet IDs in the given list. In addition to the problems with deleted tweets that we've noted, this approach may also run into the 3,200-tweet limit for user timelines that was noted earlier.

For those not engaged in academic research and for whom reproducibility is not a major concern, it may be easier to abandon the notion of redistributable corpora of tweets entirely and instead create custom corpora on demand using one of the many open-source tools for doing so (for example, Bazo, Burghardt, & Wolff 2013; Ljubešic, Fišer, & Erjavec 2014).

5 Applications

Our primary focus with the Indigenous Tweets project has been to provide resources that help users of Indigenous and minority languages communicate online. In this section, we mention four applications that have emerged from the project.

Twitter offers translations of tweets into many languages using Microsoft's Bing Translator, but almost none of the languages on the Indigenous Tweets site are supported. Over the last several years, the author has developed a machine translation engine that translates between the three Gaelic languages (Scannell 2014) and has deployed this engine on a third-party site to provide translations of tweets in Scottish and Manx Gaelic into Irish, facilitating online communication between members of these closely related language communities. All of the tweets coming from the Twitter lists mentioned in section 3 are translated, and the translations are presented as mouse-over "annotations," so that a user can attempt to read the tweet in the original language and get help for difficult words or possible false friends through these annotations.

Users very frequently include links to external content in their tweets, and links contained in tweets written in a particular language often point to material on the web in that same language. We therefore gather all such links and use them as seed URLs for the Crúbadán web crawler, greatly enhancing that resource with up-to-date content. In the case of Irish, we also incorporate external links into a news aggregator called *chuala .me* ("I heard" is the English for *Chuala mé*).[10] This site aggregates links embedded in Irish language tweets with others gathered from public Facebook posts, blog posts, and RSS feeds and displays the top one hundred stories, updated hourly and ranked by level of engagement in the form of likes, retweets, comments, replies, and such by the Irish-speaking community.

We have also used data from Indigenous Tweets to generate visualizations of language communities on Twitter. For example, a language community can be visualized as an abstract graph in which users are nodes, and a directed edge is drawn between two users when one follows the other (or when one mentions or retweets the other, and so on). We can then use standard network analyses such as eigenvalue centrality to find and plot the most influential users in each language community.[11]

Finally, the geography of Indigenous and minority language communities on social media is a largely unexplored area of research. A relatively small percentage of users on Twitter have geolocation activated so that when they tweet from a mobile device, their latitude and longitude is attached to the tweet and can later be retrieved via the API. A less precise method (and one that is less problematic from a privacy perspective) is to make use of a user's self-reported location in their profile to assign them a latitude and longitude at the granularity of a town or city. Once these data are in place, a number of different geographic visualizations are possible, for instance heat maps of Twitter activity in a given language,[12] maps illustrating conversations between users on Twitter,[13] or the distribution of word usage as in a traditional linguistic atlas.[14]

6 Conclusion

This chapter introduced the Indigenous Tweets project and provided details on how the project uses the Twitter API to gather and process linguistic data for 185 Indigenous and minority languages. We proceeded to address the constraints imposed by Twitter's Terms of Service, which prohibit the redistribution of full-text corpora of tweets, and the impact this has on reproducible research involving Twitter data. This was followed by a description of several applications of the Indigenous Tweets data sets, above and beyond the main IndigenousTweets.com website. The aim of all of this work is the same: to provide tools to users of Indigenous and minority languages that facilitate online communication and hopefully in turn serve to strengthen these languages.

Anyone with some programming experience can begin experimenting with Twitter data through the Twitter API. We mentioned the Perl library Net::Twitter, and there are similar libraries for more than a dozen programming languages (including Python, Ruby, PHP, and Java) listed on the Twitter Developer Site.[15] Most of these libraries come with basic sample programs that can be used out of the box for simple queries or that can be modified as needed for more ambitious experimentation.

Notes

1. The Twitter API is a resource that allows external software developers to make programmatic queries of the Twitter database. See section 2 for details.

2. I am grateful to the enthusiastic community of users of the Indigenous Tweets site for their many contributions over the years, especially Michael Bauer, Edmond Kachale, Keola Donaghy, Jean Came Poulard, and Luistxo Fernandez. While the majority of this work was completed at Saint Louis University, I spent six months as a Visiting Scientist at Twitter during a sabbatical leave in 2011–2012.

3. https://metacpan.org/pod/Net::Twitter.

4. https://developer.twitter.com/.

5. http://crubadan.org/.

6. https://twitter.com/IndigenousTweet/lists.

7. The focus on the Gaelic languages is only because these are the author's main languages of interest; there would be no technical obstacle to extending these lists to the other Indigenous Tweets languages.

8. https://github.com/kscanne/itweets-geodata.

9. https://developer.twitter.com/en/developer-terms/agreement; https://developer.twitter.com/en/developer-terms/policy.

10. http://chuala.me/.

11. E.g., https://twitter.com/kscanne/status/917767416242941953 showing the top 421 users in Irish in 2017.

12. E.g., https://twitter.com/kscanne/status/1031498648482406401 clearing showing Gaeltacht regions.

13. See http://indigenoustweets.blogspot.com/2013/12/mapping-celtic-twittersphere.html.

14. E.g., https://drive.google.com/open?id=1EBTQXo3xc2vKJ5-dHyxvVDIC0x4&usp=sharing showing the distribution of different words for *potato* in Irish.

15. https://developer.twitter.com/en/docs/developer-utilities/twitter-libraries.html.

References

Bazo, Alexander, Manuel Burghardt, and Christian Wolff. 2013. TWORPUS—An easy-to-use tool for the creation of tailored Twitter corpora. In *Language Processing and Knowledge in the Web*, ed. Iryna Gurevych, Chris Biemann, and Torsten Zesch, 23–34. Berlin: Springer. doi:10.1007/978-3-642-40722-2_3.

Bruns, Axel, and Jean Burgess. 2016. Methodological innovation in precarious spaces: The case of Twitter. In *Digital Methods for Social Science*, ed. Helene Snee, Christine Hine, Yvette Morey, Steven Roberts, and Hayley Watson, 17–33. London: Palgrave Macmillan. doi:10.1057/9781137453662_2.

Keegan, Te Taka, Paora Mato, and Stacey Ruru. 2015. Using Twitter in an Indigenous language: An analysis of Te Reo Māori tweets. *AlterNative: An International Journal of Indigenous Peoples* 11 (1): 59–75. doi:10.1177/117718011501100105.

Lillehaugen, Brook Danielle. 2016. Why write in a language that (almost) no one can read? Twitter and the development of written literature. *Language Documentation and Conservation* 10:356–393.

Ljubešic, Nikola, Darja Fišer, and Tomaz Erjavec. 2014. TweetCaT: A tool for building Twitter corpora of smaller languages. In *Proceedings of LREC*, ed. Nicoletta Calzolari, Khalid Choukri, Thierry Declerck, Hrafn Loftsson, Bente Maegaard, Joseph Mariani, Asuncion Moreno, Jan Odijk, and Stelios Piperidis, 2279–2283. European Language Resources Association.

Mato, P. J. 2018. Mā te hangarau te oranga o te reo Māori e tau-toko ai? Can technology support the long-term health of the Māori language? PhD dissertation, The University of Waikato, Hamilton, New Zealand.

McCreadie, Richard, Ian Soboroff, Jimmy Lin, Craig Macdonald, Iadh Ounis, and Dean McCullough. 2012. On building a reusable Twitter corpus. In *Proceedings of the 35th International ACM SIGIR Conference on Research and Development in Information Retrieval*, 1113–1114. ACM. doi:10.1145/2348283.2348495.

McMinn, Andrew J., Yashar Moshfeghi, and Joemon M. Jose. 2013. Building a large-scale corpus for evaluating event detection on Twitter. In *Proceedings of the 22nd ACM International Conference on Information and Knowledge Management*, 409–418. ACM. doi:10.1145/2505515.2505695.

Ní Bhroin, Niamh. 2015. Social media-innovation: The case of Indigenous Tweets. *Journal of Media Innovations* 2 (1): 89–106. doi:10.5617/jmi.v2i1.974.

Petrović, Saša, Miles Osborne, and Victor Lavrenko. 2010. The Edinburgh Twitter corpus. In *Proceedings of the NAACL HLT 2010 Workshop on Computational Linguistics in a World of Social Media*, ed. Ben Hachey and Miles Osborne, 25–26. Los Angeles: Association for Computational Linguistics.

Scannell, Kevin P. 2007. The Crúbadán Project: Corpus building for under-resourced languages. In *Building and Exploring Web Corpora: Proceedings of the 3rd Web as Corpus Workshop*, vol. 4, ed. Cédrick Fairon, Hubert Naets, Adam Kilgarriff, and Gilles-Maurice de Schryver, 5–15. Louvain-la-Neuve, Belgium: Presses universitaires de Louvain.

Scannell, Kevin P. 2011. Welcome/Fáilte! *Indigenous Tweets* (blog). March 17. http://indigenoustweets.blogspot.com/2011/03/welcomefailte.html.

Scannell, Kevin P. 2014. Statistical models for text normalization and machine translation. In *Proceedings of the 1st Celtic Language Technology Workshop*, ed. John Judge, Teresa Lynn, Monica Ward, and Brian Ó Raghallaigh, 33–40. Dublin: Dublin City University and Association for Computational Linguistics.

Scheffler, Tatjana. 2014. A German Twitter snapshot. In *Proceedings of LREC*, ed. Nicoletta Calzolari, Khalid Choukri, Thierry Declerck, Hrafn Loftsson, Bente Maegaard, Joseph Mariani, Asuncion Moreno, Jan Odijk, and Stelios Piperidis, 2284–2289. European Language Resources Association.

Wheeler, Jonathan. 2018. Mining the first 100 days: Human and data ethics in Twitter research. *Journal of Librarianship and Scholarly Communication* 6 (2): 1–23. doi:10.7710/2162–3309.2235.

Yang, Jaewon, and Jure Leskovec. 2011. Patterns of temporal variation in online media. In *Proceedings of the Fourth ACM International Conference on Web Search and Data Mining*, 177–186. ACM. doi:10.1145/1935826.1935863.

42 Managing Semantic Norms for Cognitive Linguistics, Corpus Linguistics, and Lexicon Studies

Bodo Winter

1 Introduction

Bloomfield (1933:140) famously noted that "the statement of meanings is the weak point in language study." One issue is that meaning is difficult to measure objectively. It is relatively straightforward to quantify linguistic phenomena that have surface manifestations, such as words or particular grammatical constructions. Meaning, however, is much more elusive because it ultimately resides within the language user's head.

This chapter will discuss data management in the domain of semantics. It will be argued that meaning can be fruitfully studied using *norms*. This term is used by psycholinguists when they collect ratings for linguistic items, generally words. As an example of a norm data set, consider the emotional valence norms collected by Warriner, Kuperman, and Brysbaert (2013), who asked hundreds of native English speakers to rate words for how good or bad they are. The word *vacation* received a rating of 8.53 on the nine-point rating scale for these emotional valence norms, which is 3.47 valence points above the mean emotional valence of 5.06. This indicates that the word *vacation* overall appeared to be very positive to the raters in this study. The same word received a rating of 3.14 on Brysbaert and colleagues' five-point concreteness scale (Brysbaert, Warriner, & Kuperman 2014), which is quite close to the average concreteness ($M = 3.03$), indicating that native speakers felt that the word *vacation* was neither particularly concrete nor particularly abstract.

The "norming" of stimuli is standard procedure within psycholinguistics. However, the resultant norms are also increasingly being investigated as an object of study in their own right, or they are used in conjunction with corpora as means of quantifying particular semantic dimensions. This chapter will present two linguistic examples where researchers commonly do *not* use norms to elucidate some of the problems that may arise for norm-less semantics with respect to the reproducibility of these studies (section 2); followed by an overview of some common norm data sets (section 3); and, finally, a discussion of methodological challenges of norm-based research and how norm-based linguistics fits within contemporary efforts to facilitate reproducible research (section 4).

2 Norm-less semantics: Two examples

2.1 Corpus linguistics: Semantic prosody

It is widely known that word meaning depends on context. Take, for example, the verb *to cause*, which, when seen in isolation appears to be a rather neutral term. However, when using a corpus to look at the contexts this term tends to occur in (e.g., via a concordancer), it becomes apparent that by and large, only bad things get caused (Stubbs 2001), which is exemplified by the concordance lines from the Corpus of Contemporary American English (COCA; Davies 2009) shown in table 42.1.

The idea that words consistently occur in certain types of attitudinal or emotional contexts has been dubbed *semantic prosody* in the British tradition of corpus linguistics (Hunston 2007; Louw 1993; Stewart 2010; Whitsitt 2005), and the fact that language users can so greatly mischaracterize the "connotation" of words when they introspect on them in isolation is a major argument for using corpus methods when looking at word meaning. In this field, other headwords that have been studied with respect to semantic prosody include *to set in* (Sinclair 1991) and *utterly* (Louw 1993), both of which tend to occur in negative contexts. As another example, consider the plural form *days*, for which Louw (1993) claims

Table 42.1

Ten concordances of *cause* (verb) + noun from the Corpus of Contemporary American English (Davies 2009)

. . . that the flapping of a butterfly's wings can	cause	tornadoes.
. . . because he lacked intent to	cause	injury or property damage.
. . . were not welcome were ones that were only meant to	cause	offense without furthering a dialogue or conversation.
Space is full of all sorts of garbage that can	cause	problems, including some of the stuff we send up . . .
. . . relief against a use of a mark that might	cause	dilution by blurring or dilution by tarnishment . . .
. . . that the manufacturer's use of the mark is likely to	cause	dilution by blurring or tarnishment.
. . . and especially intramedullary instrumentation	cause	bone marrow extravasation and release of fat emboli . . .
. . . for a free Samsung-sponsored concert—but also	cause	crowd concerns.
Interfascicular dissection may additionally	cause	a disruption in the segmental vascular supply . . .
. . . to educate themselves about the factors that	cause	dogs—all dogs—to bite.

that it tends to occur in contexts invoking a sense of nostalgia.

A major methodological issue in the study of semantic prosody is that concordances are usually hand-classified for their emotional connotation, such as whether they are overall positive or negative. As noted by Bednarek (2008:122), it is "difficult to establish objectively" whether something is negative or positive. Similarly, Stewart (2010:91) notes in a critique of semantic prosody research that "one analyst's meat is another analyst's poison."

If the analysis of a semantic prosody relies on subjective introspection without any clear criteria for what makes a positive or negative context, it is strictly speaking not *reproducible*. That is, if the same data set is given to a different researcher (who has not conducted the original study), they may draw different conclusions. Without inter-reliability checks (which are not often conducted in at least some areas of corpus linguistics and cognitive linguistics), linguistic intuitions are by definition not reproducible because they are contingent on one person's beliefs.

Moreover, the cumbersome method of hand-classifying concordances for whether they are positive or negative has also been a constraining factor with respect to the scope of research on semantic prosody, which has been criticized for focusing on the meaning of only a few isolated headwords (Stewart 2010; Whitsitt 2005). This focus on a small set of linguistic items is a natural outgrowth of the fact that classifying concordances by hand is a very time-consuming process.

Norms provide a solution to both of these issues; they allow reproducible research on semantic prosody that is furthermore *scalable*, which affords more generalizable claims that expand beyond isolated examples.

While it is a time-consuming and expensive process to collect a norm data set, once it has been established, it can be used for a whole range of applications by different researchers. For example, the above-mentioned emotional valence norms can be used in conjunction with corpora to see whether the words surrounding a given headword in a concordance line are overall positive or negative, which was an approach taken by some researchers (Dilts & Newman 2006; Snefjella & Kuperman 2016; Winter 2016). In these studies, the subjective judgment has been "outsourced" to a norming study. This means that given the same concordances and the same norming data set, different researchers will reach the same conclusions, thus ensuring reproducibility. The scalability of this type of research is demonstrated, for example, by Winter (2016), who showed that taste words have overall more positive semantic prosodies than smell words. Such claims—characterizing hundreds of words rather than a few isolated headwords—are practically impossible when hand-classifying concordances.

Thus, norms provide an opportunity to free the phenomenon of semantic prosody from the shackles of a time-consuming classification process that is difficult to reproduce and that is difficult to extend to larger chunks of the English lexicon.

2.2 Cognitive linguistics: Sensory language and perceptual metaphor

As another example of norm-less linguistics, consider perceptual language, including the study of perception verbs such as *to see* and *to hear* (Evans & Wilkins 2000; Matlock 1989; Sweetser 1990; Viberg 1983), or the study of perceptual adjectives as they occur in metaphorical expressions such as *smooth melody* (Ronga et al. 2012;

Strik Lievers 2015; Williams 1976; Winter 2019). As one particular finding in this field, consider the hypothesis that there is a "hierarchy of the senses," following the order touch > taste > smell > sight/sound (Ullmann 1959). This hypothesis was formed based on the observation that sensory adjectives are more likely to extend from "lower" senses to the "higher" senses, as evidenced by expressions such as *smooth melody* (touch to sound) and *rough smell* (touch to smell), as opposed to the ill-formed *squealing feeling* (sound to touch) or *barking taste* (sound to taste).

At the basis of any generalization of sensory language is a categorization of sensory words according to perceptual modality, such as classifying *smooth* as a touch word, or classifying *squealing* as a sound word. Such classifications are often assumed to be self-evident, which may in fact be the case for some isolated examples. However, there are also numerous examples that are hard to classify. For example, how is one to categorize dimension words such as *long* and *thick* according to sensory modality? And how does one deal with highly multisensory words, such as *harsh*, which can be used to describe a *harsh sound*, a *harsh feeling*, or even a *harsh smell* or *harsh taste*? The literature in this field is ripe with examples where different researchers have classified the same words differently. For example, Ronga et al. (2012) mention how the same dimension words are either classified as sight-related (Williams 1976) or touch-related (Popova 2005). These examples show that it is generally not straightforward to classify words according to senses, and criteria for doing so need to be made explicit in order for research on perceptual language to be reproducible.

Luckily, there are by now multiple data sets of sensory norms for English (Lynott & Connell 2009, 2013; Speed & Majid 2017; Winter 2016). These norms have been used to make research on perceptual words more reproducible. For example, Winter (2019) re-analyzed data on perceptual metaphor using norms, showing that the hierarchy of the senses needs to be reinterpreted when using more reproducible research methods. Strik Lievers and Winter (2018) used sensory norms to show that sound concepts are more lexically differentiated in the verbal as opposed to adjectival domain (there is a disproportionate number of sound verbs in English). Winter, Perlman, and Majid (2018) used sensory norms to argue that the English language is overall visually dominant.

3 Norm data sets and examples of norm-based linguistics

There is by now a wealth of linguistic norms available. Many of these norms have so far only been applied to psycholinguistic experiments, which leaves a lot of room for future corpus linguistic research or analyses of the lexicon using norms.

Collecting norms has a long history in the language sciences. The first large norming studies were conducted in the 1950s and 1960s, such as those discussed in *The Measurement of Meaning* (Osgood, Suci, & Tannenbaum 1957). One of the oldest norm data sets that was used for a long time in psycholinguistics was Paivio's, which included concreteness, imageability, and meaningfulness ratings for 925 English words (Paivio, Yuille, & Madigan 1968).

These days, norms are often collected via crowdsourcing platforms in large "megastudies" (Keuleers & Balota 2015), such as the above-mentioned concreteness norms, which have been collected for 40,000 English words using data from over 4,000 participants. Another fruitful semantic dimension for norming has been emotional valence, for which a large norming data set exists for about 14,000 English words (Warriner, Kuperman, & Brysbaert 2013). As mentioned, researchers have begun to apply these norms to the study of semantic prosody, but an even more wide-spread application is the domain of *opinion mining* or *sentiment analysis* in computer science and in industry, where rating data are used to classify texts such as online reviews with respect to whether they are overall positive or negative.

As a result of the collective efforts of hundreds of researchers, there is by now a wealth of freely available data sets available. Some perhaps unexpected dimensions of meanings that have been "normed" include roughness, hardness, and size of touch adjectives (Stadtlander & Murdoch 2000), the color and motion-relatedness of nominal concepts (Medler et al. 2005), or the graspability and pain-relatedness of object terms (Amsel, Urbach, & Kutas 2012). There are also norms for dimensions that are not strictly speaking exclusively semantic, such as the Bochum English Countability Lexicon that includes expert annotator's ratings for whether nouns are mass or count (Kiss et al. 2016).

A lot of norming data sets are traditionally published in the journal *Behavior Research Methods*, although a bewildering amount of norming data is hidden in published studies that are otherwise focused on answering substantive rather than methodological questions. These data sets may be difficult to find. An issue with the massive amount of data that is already available is that many particular data sets don't have a lot of visibility, which also means that researchers within certain subareas of linguistics may not know that norms are an available methodological option for answering their research questions. For example, corpus linguists studying semantic prosody may continue to hand-classify concordances simply because they are unaware that emotional valence norms exist.

Luckily, there are by now a few websites that allow easy access to norm data sets. One of them is the LAB, the Linguistic Annotated Bibliography (Buchanan, Valentine, & Maxwell 2018). Another one is the language goldmine (languagegoldmine.com). These websites facilitate searching for specific norm data sets, and they encourage exploration of the wealth of available data sets that exist.

Besides the above-mentioned norm-based studies on sensory linguistics and semantic prosody, it is worth pointing out a few more studies that have used norms to showcase the utility of this approach. Warriner and Kuperman (2015) used emotional valence norms to test the *Pollyanna hypothesis*, which is the hypothesis that overall, speakers have a prosocial need to talk about positive things more often than about negative things—this hypothesis was supported by looking at both the type and token frequencies of positive words. The English language has more positive words than negative words overall, and positive words are also used more frequently than negative words in various corpora. In another norm-based study, Lupyan and Winter (2018) used concreteness norms to argue that language is much more abstract than is commonly assumed by "embodied" approaches to cognition.

There are also a number of norming studies for figurative language, for example, Katz et al. (1988) normed more than four hundred literary and non-literary metaphors for various semantic dimensions, such as metaphor goodness, comprehensibility, or metaphoric imagery (for a replication, see Campbell & Raney 2016). Littlemore et al. (2018) normed metaphors for goodness and then correlated these norms with ratings from other norm data sets to show that metaphors judged to be "good" exhibit asymmetries in word frequency and emotional valence, but not concreteness.

A by-now quite extensive line of research has used *iconicity norms*. These norms quantify the degree to which participants feel that a word's form resembles its meaning. For example, the English words *hissing, click, humming, gurgle, beep,* and *screech* tend to receive high ratings in these norms, whereas for words such as *moss, beginning, faucet, onion,* and *atom,* participants do not feel that the word sounds like what it means (Perry, Perlman, & Lupyan 2015; Perry et al. 2017). Iconicity norms were first collected for signed languages (Caselli et al. 2017; Grote 2013; Vinson et al. 2008), and this idea was subsequently extended to spoken languages, including English and Spanish (Perry, Perlman, & Lupyan 2015). These norms have led to a number of interesting findings. For example, the norms were useful in showing that iconicity disproportionately resides in the perceptual part of the English vocabulary (Sidhu & Pexman 2018; Winter et al. 2017) or that words with more semantic neighbors are less likely to be iconic (Sidhu & Pexman 2018). Iconicity norms have also been used to show that children's language is relatively more iconic compared to adult's language (Perry, Perlman, & Lupyan 2015) and that adults increase the frequency of iconic words when talking to their children (Perry et al. 2017). The iconicity norms have also been used to compare signed and spoken languages (Perlman et al. 2018).

4 Methodological issues and reproducibility in the context of norms

Norms facilitate reproducibility because given the same norm data set, a different researcher can reproduce an analysis, not having to rely on another researcher's subjective evaluation of particular linguistic items. That said, norm data are still subjective, as they rely on native language user judgments. The word *banker*, for example, may be judged to be neutral by some but negative by others. The idea of using a norm data set rather than relying on the single linguist's intuition is that one can benefit from the "wisdom of the crowd" effect, where individual differences in subjective judgment are less influential due to averaging over many people's intuitive responses.

That said, the subjectivity of norms needs to be kept in mind when doing analyses with norm data sets. For example, in the case of iconicity norms, it is not always clear what native language users base their iconicity judgments on. For example, Perry, Perlman, and Lupyan (2015) collected norms on a scale from −5 to +5, with −5 indicating that a word sounds like "the opposite of what it means." Many of the words with negative iconicity scores are questionable, such as *dandelion* (iconicity: −2.8), *silent* (−2.17), and *would* (−2.1). It is not clear why participants felt that these words sounded like the opposite of their respective meanings. As a result of this, when Sidhu and Pexman (2018) used these norms, they made the analytical decision to exclude words at the lower end of the scale.

This example shows that it is important to consider *construct validity* for norming studies, which refers to the question of whether a study measures the construct that one intends it to measure. While it may be theoretically well defined that a word sounds like what it means (such as the onomatopoetic word *beep* mimicking the corresponding sound), it is not so clear what it means for a word to sound the opposite of what it means. As another example of construct validity, consider a norming study conducted by Engelthaler and Hills (2018), who collected ratings for whether words were humorous or not, with words such as *nitwit*, *tinkle*, and *egghead* receiving high ratings, compared to words such as *trauma*, *oxide*, and *cleaver*. Their rating study was word-based, but the literature on humor generally considers humor to be something that arises over sequences of words. Thus, it is not clear whether the humor ratings actually measure that what humor researchers call humor, and the correspondence between the norms and specific theories in humor research is not straightforward. As another example of potentially limited construct validity, consider the fact that sensory norms have also been collected for highly abstract words. What does it *mean* to ask a participant to rate words such as *freedom* or *vulnerability* as relating to sight, touch, sound, taste, or smell? And, can we trust the resulting ratings?

Another issue that stems from the fact that norms are subjective has to do with infrequent and little-known words. Winter (2019) lists several examples in the sensory norm data sets commonly used in psycholinguistics for which participants clearly misunderstood a word, presumably because they did not know its meaning very well. For example, the word *brackish* was classified by participants as predominantly touch-related (Lynott & Connell 2009) even though dictionary definitions list its meaning as "slightly salty." Similarly, the word

clamorous has an auditory meaning listed in dictionaries, but was rated to be higher in tactile than in auditory strength (Lynott & Connell 2009). Given that both of these words are rather infrequent, it seems likely that word knowledge (and its lack thereof) needs to be taken into account. Analyses should not be performed on words that are not sufficiently known by participants. After all, what did participants rate if they did not know the meaning of these words? To alleviate these concerns, the analyst may want to take data from large-scale word knowledge studies into account (Brysbaert et al. 2016; Keuleers et al. 2015).

Norming studies should also compute *inter-rater reliability statistics* (e.g., Engelthaler & Hills 2018), such as the intra-class coefficient for continuous data. *High inter-rater reliability* means that participants of a norming study agree with each other, and *low inter-rater reliability* means that participants differ in their judgments. Low inter-rater reliability could suggest that participants used different criteria for performing judgments or that the overarching construct is not well defined, with different participants interpreting the instructions differently. Here, it is important to keep in mind that the agreement of raters may not be uniform across all the words from a norm data set. Pollock (2018) brings up the important issue that the standard deviation of ratings is higher for words in the middle ranges of norming studies. For example, it may be clear that *murder* is negative and that *happiness* is positive, which means that different participants rate these words very consistently and the standard deviations across participants are low for these words. But a seemingly more neutral word such as *banker* may be rated positively by some participants and negatively by others. The word would end up with a neutral score, even though some participants may have felt very strongly about this word. Thus, researchers doing norm-based linguistics should keep the standard deviation of norms in mind, with Pollock (2018) recommending that researchers may want to exclude words with very high standard deviations.

The standard deviation of a particular word's ratings may also be higher when words are highly polysemous, which is another factor that needs to be taken into account. Given that norming studies generally present words in isolation, the context may not be enough to disambiguate certain meanings. This invites the possibility that different participants rate different meanings of the same word form. As an example of this, consider the fact that the noun *firm* was rated to be high in tactile strength in Lynott and Connell (2013). This was presumably the case because participants rated the (much more frequent) adjective *firm* (to the touch), even though the noun sense was clearly implied by the study's focus on nouns.

All of these constraints of norm data need to be recognized, but they should not cause researchers to shy away from using norms for their research, so as long as norms are used cautiously. Any method is characterized by advantages and disadvantages, and the advantages of norms are that they allow researchers to avoid hand-classification, which facilitates reproducibility (if using the same norm data set) and generalizability (via the opportunity to analyze many more words automatically). In general, given that judgments for any individual word may be off, norm-based linguistics is best done on large sets of words, so that the noise inherent in the judgment for particular words is less influential.

In part due to the methodological concerns outlined herein, it is desirable to replicate specific analyses with different norm data sets. In this context, it is important to distinguish replication from reproducibility (see Gawne & Styles, chapter 2, this volume). Whereas a replication refers to the process of conducting the same experiment or study again with new data, reproducible research is the more basic requirement that even for a given study, another researcher can come to the same conclusion, in other words, all analytical decisions are transparent (see Berez-Kroeker et al., chapter 1, this volume). As an example of how replication can be done within the remit of norm-based linguistics, consider Winter's (2016) analysis of taste and smell language. The claim that taste and smell words are more emotional than other types of sensory words was substantiated by using three different emotional valence data sets. This shows that this result is not contingent on the specific norm set chosen by the analyst, and it shows how one can perform the same analysis using multiple different norm data sets to ensure that a particular claim rests on a firm foundation.

Finally, it is worth pointing out that general standards of reproducible research are even more important in the domain of norms than they may be in other areas of the language sciences. Because norm-based research is easy to conduct if the analyst has the relevant analytical and computational skills, and because there are myriad decisions to make in observational and often exploratory research

with norms (e.g., whether to exclude words with high standard deviations or not), it is important to be maximally transparent about one's analytical decisions. At a bare minimum, this requires sharing one's data and code, which should preferably be done via a publicly accessible repository, such as via the Open Science Framework. This way, other researchers can follow all analytical steps, and if they disagree with specific analytical decisions, they have the option of performing a re-analysis.

In addition, it is worth stressing that norm-based research—even though it is entirely observational—can still be *preregistered*. That is, the researcher specifies their analysis plan in advance, so that other researchers can know whether a researcher has deviated from their analysis (for a discussion of preregistration in linguistics research, see Roettger 2019). Preregistration does not mean straitjacketing the analyst, as the registration report can be updated when unforeseen problems arise in a data analysis. However, preregistration allows clearly demarcating the boundary between confirmatory (hypothesis-testing) and exploratory (hypothesis-generating) research.

5   Conclusion and outlook

Traditionally, a large amount of linguistic theorizing has been based on the intuitions of linguists. The over-reliance on introspective judgments from single individuals has been criticized by a number of researchers across the language sciences. However, rather than throwing the baby out with the bath water, intuitions should still play an important role in linguistics. Dąbrowska (2016:55) mentions that introspective judgments still "provide the most direct source of information about some aspects of language, notably meaning." The recommendation defended here is that rather than relying on a single linguist, intuitions should be aggregated over hundreds of individuals. Although, as discussed, this approach is not without its caveats (see also Pollock 2018), it is still better than relying *exclusively* on the hand classification of meanings, which lacks reproducibility and scalability.

To make a norm-based linguistics feasible in the long run, more norm data sets need to be collected. The big picture idea for the future of norm-based linguistics is that any important dimension of meaning that is of interest to the analyst can be quantified via collecting suitable ratings. Future research also needs to branch out to other languages. There exist norming data sets of various lexical characteristics for such languages as German (Schmidtke et al. 2014; Vo et al. 2009), Polish (Riegel et al. 2015), Dutch (Speed & Majid 2017), and Chinese (Chen et al. 2019), all of which are from major world languages. Much more work needs to be done so that norm-based linguistics is not restricted to the analysis of English and major world languages.

Though norms may thus prove no panacea, they are an important component of the methodological tool kit of modern linguistics. As emphasized by Dąbrowska (2016:57), "when it comes to understanding something as complex as human language, it will be most productive to use every method that is available."

References

Amsel, B. D., T. P. Urbach, and M. Kutas. 2012. Perceptual and motor attribute ratings for 559 object concepts. *Behavior Research Methods* 44 (4): 1028–1041. https://doi.org/10.3758/s13428-012-0215-z.

Bednarek, M. 2008. Semantic preference and semantic prosody re-examined. *Corpus Linguistics and Linguistic Theory* 4 (2): 119–139.

Bloomfield, L. 1933. *Language.* Chicago: Chicago University Press.

Brysbaert, M., M. Stevens, P. Mandera, and E. Keuleers. 2016. How many words do we know? Practical estimates of vocabulary size dependent on word definition, the degree of language input and the participant's age. *Frontiers in Psychology* 7:1116.

Brysbaert, M., A. B. Warriner, and V. Kuperman. 2014. Concreteness ratings for 40 thousand generally known English word lemmas. *Behavior Research Methods* 46 (3): 904–911.

Buchanan, E. M., K. D. Valentine, and N. P. Maxwell. 2018. LAB: Linguistic Annotated Bibliography—A searchable portal for normed database information. *Behavior Research Methods* 51 (9): 1878–1888.

Campbell, S. J., and G. E. Raney. 2016. A 25-year replication of Katz et al.'s (1988) metaphor norms. *Behavior Research Methods* 48 (1): 330–340.

Caselli, N. K., Z. S. Sehyr, A. M. Cohen-Goldberg, and K. Emmorey. 2017. ASL-LEX: A lexical database of American Sign Language. *Behavior Research Methods* 49 (2): 784–801.

Chen, I.-H., Q. Zhao, Y. Long, Q. Lu, and C.-R. Huang. 2019. Mandarin Chinese modality exclusivity norms. *PloS One* 14 (2): e0211336. https://doi.org/10.1371/journal.pone.0211336.

Dąbrowska, E. 2016. Looking into introspection. In *Studies in Lexicogrammar: Theory and Applications*, vol. 54, ed. G. Drożdż, 55–74. Amsterdam: John Benjamins.

Davies, M. 2009. The 385+ million word Corpus of Contemporary American English (1990–2008+): Design, architecture, and linguistic insights. *International Journal of Corpus Linguistics* 14 (2): 159–190.

Dilts, P., and J., Newman. 2006. A note on quantifying "good" and "bad" prosodies. *Corpus Linguistics and Linguistic Theory* 2 (2): 233–242.

Engelthaler, T., and T. T. Hills. 2018. Humor norms for 4,997 English words. *Behavior Research Methods* 50 (3): 1116–1124.

Evans, N., and D. Wilkins. 2000. In the mind's ear: The semantic extensions of perception verbs in Australian languages. *Language* 76 (3): 546–592.

Grote, K. 2013. "Modality relativity": The influence of sign language and spoken language on conceptual categorization. PhD thesis, Hochschulbibliothek der Rheinisch-Westfälischen Technischen Hochschule Aachen.

Hunston, S. 2007. Semantic prosody revisited. *International Journal of Corpus Linguistics* 12 (2): 249–268. https://doi.org/10.1075/ijcl.12.2.09hun.

Katz, A. N., A. Paivio, M. Marschark, and J. M. Clark. 1988. Norms for 204 literary and 260 nonliterary metaphors on 10 psychological dimensions. *Metaphor and Symbol* 3 (4): 191–214.

Keuleers, E., and D. A. Balota. 2015. Megastudies, crowdsourcing, and large datasets in psycholinguistics: An overview of recent developments. *Quarterly Journal of Experimental Psychology* 68 (8): 1457–1468.

Keuleers, E., M. Stevens, P. Mandera, and M. Brysbaert. 2015. Word knowledge in the crowd: Measuring vocabulary size and word prevalence in a massive online experiment. *Quarterly Journal of Experimental Psychology* 68 (8): 1665–1692.

Kiss, T., F. J. Pelletier, H. Husic, R. N. Simunic, and J. M. Poppek. 2016. A sense-based lexicon of count and mass expressions: The Bochum English Countability Lexicon. Paper presented at the 10th Language Resources and Evaluation Conference, Portorož, Slovenia, May 23–28.

Littlemore, J., P. P. Sobrino, D. Houghton, J. Shi, and B. Winter. 2018. What makes a good metaphor? A cross-cultural study of computer-generated metaphor appreciation. *Metaphor and Symbol* 33 (2): 101–122.

Louw, B. 1993. Irony in the text or insincerity in the writer? The diagnostic potential of semantic prosodies. In *Text and Technology: In Honour of John Sinclair*, ed. M. Baker, G. Francis, and E. Tognini-Bonelli, 157–176. Amsterdam: John Benjamins.

Lupyan, G., and B. Winter. 2018. Language is more abstract than you think, or, why aren't languages more iconic? *Philosophical Transactions of the Royal Society B: Biological Sciences* 373 (1752): 20170137.

Lynott, D., and L. Connell. 2009. Modality exclusivity norms for 423 object properties. *Behavior Research Methods* 41 (2): 558–564.

Lynott, D., and L. Connell. 2013. Modality exclusivity norms for 400 nouns: The relationship between perceptual experience and surface word form. *Behavior Research Methods* 45 (2): 516–526.

Matlock, T. 1989. Metaphor and the grammaticalization of evidentials. *Annual Meeting of the Berkeley Linguistics Society* 15:215–225.

Medler, D. A., A. Arnoldussen, J. R. Binder, and M. S. Seidenberg. 2005. *The Wisconsin Perceptual Attribute Ratings Database.* http://www.neuro.mcw.edu/ratings/.

Osgood, C. E., G. J. Suci, and P. H. Tannenbaum. 1957. *The Measurement of Meaning.* Champaign: University of Illinois Press.

Paivio, A., J. C. Yuille, and S. A. Madigan. 1968. Concreteness, imagery, and meaningfulness values for 925 nouns. *Journal of Experimental Psychology* 76 (1): 1–25.

Perlman, M., H. Little, B. Thompson, and R. L. Thompson. 2018. Iconicity in signed and spoken vocabulary: A comparison between American Sign Language, British Sign Language, English, and Spanish. *Frontiers in Psychology* 9:1433. https://doi.org/10.3389/fpsyg.2018.01433.

Perry, L. K., M. Perlman, and G. Lupyan. 2015. Iconicity in English and Spanish and its relation to lexical category and age of acquisition. *PloS One* 10 (9): e0137147. https://doi.org/10.1371/journal.pone.0137147.

Perry, L. K., M. Perlman, B. Winter, D. W. Massaro, and G. Lupyan. 2017. Iconicity in the speech of children and adults. *Developmental Science* 21 (3): e12572. https://doi.org/10.1111/desc.12572.

Pollock, L. 2018. Statistical and methodological problems with concreteness and other semantic variables: A list memory experiment case study. *Behavior Research Methods* 50 (3): 1198–1216.

Popova, Y. 2005. Image schemas and verbal synaesthesia. In *From Perception to Meaning: Image Schemas in Cognitive Linguistics,* vol. 29, ed. B. Hampe, 395–419. Berlin: Mouton de Gruyter.

Riegel, M., M. Wierzba, M. Wypych, Ł. Żurawski, K. Jednoróg, A. Grabowska, and A. Marchewka. 2015. Nencki affective word list (NAWL): The cultural adaptation of the Berlin affective word list–reloaded (BAWL-R) for Polish. *Behavior Research Methods* 47 (4): 1222–1236.

Roettger, T. 2019. Researcher degrees of freedom in phonetic research. *Laboratory Phonology: Journal of the Association for Laboratory Phonology* 10 (1): article 1.

Ronga, I., C. Bazzanella, F. Rossi, and G. Iannetti. 2012. Linguistic synaesthesia, perceptual synaesthesia, and the interaction between multiple sensory modalities. *Pragmatics and Cognition* 20 (1): 135–167.

Schmidtke, D. S., T. Schröder, A. M. Jacobs, and M. Conrad. 2014. ANGST: Affective norms for German sentiment terms, derived from the affective norms for English words. *Behavior Research Methods* 46 (4): 1108–1118.

Sidhu, D. M., and P. M. Pexman. 2018. Lonely sensational icons: Semantic neighbourhood density, sensory experience and iconicity. *Language, Cognition and Neuroscience* 33 (1): 25–31.

Sinclair, J. M. 1991. *Corpus, Concordance, Collocation.* Oxford: Oxford University Press.

Snefjella, B., and V. Kuperman. 2016. It's all in the delivery: Effects of context valence, arousal, and concreteness on visual word processing. *Cognition* 156:135–146.

Speed, L. J., and A. Majid. 2017. Dutch modality exclusivity norms: Simulating perceptual modality in space. *Behavior Research Methods* 49 (6): 2204–2218.

Stadtlander, L. M., and L. D. Murdoch. 2000. Frequency of occurrence and rankings for touch-related adjectives. *Behavior Research Methods, Instruments, and Computers* 32 (4): 579–587.

Stewart, D. 2010. *Semantic Prosody: A Critical Evaluation.* Abingdon, UK: Routledge.

Strik Lievers, F. 2015. Synaesthesia: A corpus-based study of cross-modal directionality. *Functions of Language* 22 (1): 69–95.

Strik Lievers, F., and B. Winter. 2018. Sensory language across lexical categories. *Lingua* 204:45–61.

Stubbs, M. 2001. *Words and Phrases.* Oxford, UK: Blackwell.

Sweetser, E. 1990. *From Etymology to Pragmatics.* Cambridge: Cambridge University Press.

Ullmann, S. 1959. *The Principles of Semantics.* Glasgow: Jackson, Son & Co.

Viberg, Å. 1983. The verbs of perception: A typological study. *Linguistics* 21 (1): 123–162.

Vinson, D. P., K. Cormier, T. Denmark, A. Schembri, and G. Vigliocco. 2008. The British Sign Language (BSL) norms for age of acquisition, familiarity, and iconicity. *Behavior Research Methods* 40 (4): 1079–1087.

Vo, M. L., M. Conrad, L. Kuchinke, K. Urton, M. J. Hofmann, and A. M. Jacobs. 2009. The Berlin affective word list reloaded (BAWL-R). *Behavior Research Methods* 41 (2): 534–538.

Warriner, A. B., and V. Kuperman. 2015. Affective biases in English are bi-dimensional. *Cognition and Emotion* 29 (7): 1147–1167.

Warriner, A. B., V. Kuperman, and M. Brysbaert. 2013. Norms of valence, arousal, and dominance for 13,915 English lemmas. *Behavior Research Methods* 45 (4): 1191–1207.

Whitsitt, S. 2005. A critique of the concept of semantic prosody. *International Journal of Corpus Linguistics* 10 (3): 283–305.

Williams, J. M. 1976. Synaesthetic adjectives: A possible law of semantic change. *Language* 52 (2): 461–478.

Winter, B. 2016. Taste and smell words form an affectively loaded and emotionally flexible part of the English lexicon. *Language, Cognition and Neuroscience* 31 (8): 975–988.

Winter, B. 2019. *Sensory Linguistics: Language, Perception, and Metaphor.* Amsterdam: John Benjamins.

Winter, B., M. Perlman, and A. Majid. 2018. Vision dominates in perceptual language: English sensory vocabulary is optimized for usage. *Cognition* 179:213–220.

Winter, B., M. Perlman, L. K. Perry, and G. Lupyan. 2017. Which words are most iconic? Iconicity in English sensory words. *Interaction Studies* 18 (3): 433–454. https://doi.org/10.1075/is.18.3.07win.

43   Managing Treebank Data with the Infrastructure for the Exploration of Syntax and Semantics (INESS)

Victoria Rosén and Koenraad De Smedt

1   Introduction

Data from annotated corpora greatly facilitate empirical research on linguistic properties of authentic texts. However, traditional corpora that are annotated at word level (e.g., lemmas, morphology, and parts of speech) offer only a limited view of the structure of sentences. In contrast, corpora that are syntactically and sometimes semantically annotated, commonly called *treebanks*, support the investigation of a wider range of linguistic phenomena.

Treebanks allow the study of many aspects of grammar. They make it possible to find which words occur in certain grammatical constructions, and how often. One can also study how the occurrence of certain grammatical constructions varies among time periods, genres, or even individual authors. It is also possible to induce a computational grammar from all the structures in a treebank. Furthermore, the addition of semantic structures makes it possible to study, for instance, stereotypical meaning relations, such as the association of the verb *sew* with female agents and *butcher* with male agents, as recently was shown in a study on Norwegian.[1] There are many more possible ways of using a treebank in the study of a language or in building computational models of a language.

Treebank annotations often reflect syntactic constituency in traditional tree structures (hence the name). Figure 43.1 shows tree diagrams for sentence (1) from the German TIGER Treebank in two different visualization modes (see sentence display 1).

A well-known example of a *constituency treebank* is the Penn Treebank (Marcus, Santorini, & Marcinkiewicz 1993). Further developments of the Penn Treebank include the Proposition Bank (PropBank), in which sentences are semantically annotated with verbal propositions and their arguments (Kingsbury and Palmer 2002), and the Penn Discourse Treebank (Prasad et al. 2008).

Dependency treebanks represent relations between words. Dependency treebanks for a large number of languages have been constructed through a community effort using Universal Dependencies (UD) as a grammatical framework (Nivre et al. 2016). Lexical-Functional Grammar (LFG) treebanks have at least two levels of representation: a c-structure for constituency and an f-structure for grammatical relations and features (Bresnan 2001). Head-driven Phrase Structure Grammar (HPSG) analyses are composed of feature structures, but the unification of these can be represented as trees (Pollard & Sag 1994). Researchers intending to investigate grammatical structures should consider what type of representation is best suited to their methodologies.

In addition, treebanks may have annotations for relations between sentences. Some treebanks include relations across sentence boundaries, such as coreference, but this is rare. A *parallel treebank* consists of two or more treebanks, usually in a translational relation,[3] which are aligned, usually on the sentence level; each of the monolingual treebanks may not only have different provenance but also different types of annotation. In sum, treebanks tend to have complex, detailed annotation that requires sophisticated data management.

As treebanks are important resources both for basic research and for the development of language technology, it is important that they are easily accessible by

(1) IBM   und   Siemens   gelten   nicht   mer   als   Schimpfworte.
     IBM   and   Siemens   count   not   more   as   swear words
"IBM and Siemens are no longer considered swear words."

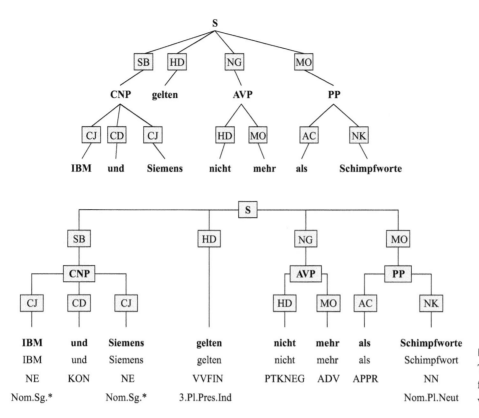

Figure 43.1

Two views of the tree structure for sentence (1) in different visualization modes.[2]

researchers. Their availability is also important for purposes of verification and replicability of research results. Good data management, including good documentation; clear conditions on their use; and good ways to find, explore, and cite the data greatly facilitate the use of treebanks by researchers.

The landscape of available tools that address these aspects is too extensive to present in this chapter. We will limit ourselves to discussing the most important issues in data management for treebanks that are intended for public research and development, and as a use case for how these issues can be addressed, we will present INESS, the Infrastructure for the Exploration of Syntax and Semantics.[4] INESS is both a tool for creating treebanks and for accessing and exploring treebanks online (Rosén, De Smedt, et al. 2012).

This chapter is primarily addressed to researchers intending to produce a treebank and planning for its data management but it will also be useful background information for researchers wishing to explore treebanks and wishing to know how to use and cite data obtained from them. More extensive introductions to building and using treebanks can be found in the literature (e.g., Abeillé 2003).

2 Data collection

The choice of texts to be included in a treebank depends on the intended use (Abeillé 2003:xiii–xxvi). Treebanks may be specialized with regard to genre, modality, and so on, or they may attempt to be a balanced sample of a language. Some treebanks cover a large time period, such as the Icelandic Parsed Historical Corpus (Rögnvaldsson et al. 2012), but most treebanks are contemporary.

As with other corpora, intellectual property rights and privacy must be respected. Issues related to rights clearance and personal data for the source texts should be addressed already at the data collection stage (Collister, chapter 9, this volume). Choosing documents in the public domain is simplest, but it restricts the text types. If the inclusion of copyrighted literature is desired, permission for minimally restricted user groups should be sought from the rights holders. In the case of large treebanks for which it is impractical to contact the rights holders of each text, alternative approaches can be taken, depending on the laws of the individual country. Because the scope of syntactic annotation is usually limited to the sentence level, one may consider selecting a percentage of sentences from each text and scrambling them to stay within the limits of legally accepted quotation. However, this has the disadvantage that some ambiguities cannot easily be resolved due to lack of context.

Care must be taken in the handling of personal data. In transcriptions of spontaneous speech, or collections of student essays, there are bound to be expressions identifying the author or other people. In such cases, permission must be obtained to use the texts, and it may be necessary to anonymize them (Holton, Leonard, & Pulsifer, chapter 4, this volume).

Furthermore, the rights to the annotations themselves, and the conditions for their use, should be determined already at the data collection stage. Standard end user license conditions, for example, those based on the Creative Commons license family,[5] can be an advantage when negotiating with rights holders, and they are also familiar to most users. In case the license is more restricted than Creative Commons "No rights reserved" (CC0), a data management system should authenticate users and ask them to agree to the licensing conditions before they are authorized to access the treebank.

3   Data processing

Treebanks are produced with a variety of annotation methods, ranging from manual annotation (with appropriate editing tools) to automated parsing. In the latter case, the treebank is often called a *parsebank*. Semi-automatic methods may involve parsing with manual adjustments.

Parsing with a computational grammar followed only by manual disambiguation, but not correction, does not aim for full coverage, but guarantees that the grammar and the structures are always compatible with each other. In contrast, parsing with manual correction may attempt to fully annotate all sentences, also those outside the scope of the grammar, which may result in ad hoc structures that are not theoretically motivated (Rosén & De Smedt 2007).

INESS offers online tools for parsing and efficient interactive disambiguation based on discriminants, which provide easy identification of relevant differences between a potentially large number of analyses (Rosén, Meurer, & De Smedt 2009; Rosén, Meurer, et al. 2012). INESS also supports online editing of dependency structures.

A parsebank may be reparsed after the grammar and lexicon are adjusted to improve coverage. This incremental method of building a treebank was first used by the Redwoods initiative (Oepen et al. 2004). It is also used for NorGramBank, a large-scale treebank for Norwegian created within the INESS project (Dyvik et al. 2016). Any method for incremental treebank construction requires versioning as well as tools for monitoring grammar coverage. An example of version monitoring in INESS is shown in figure 43.2.

If texts are obtained by optical character recognition, preprocessing may be required for cleaning them up and correcting them before annotation is undertaken. Furthermore, it can be necessary to identify words unknown to the grammar if a parser is to be applied. INESS has an interface for these preprocessing steps (Rosén, Meurer, et al. 2012).

A treebank may also be constructed stepwise by starting with a chunker and then deepening the structural analysis (Volk, Marek, & Samuelsson 2017), or a treebank can be derived from another treebank by mapping structural elements to corresponding elements in a different format (Forst 2003; Przepiórkowski & Patejuk 2019).

Many contemporary approaches involve automatically annotating a large treebank through training on a smaller corpus (a *gold standard*) that has been manually annotated, corrected, or disambiguated. This can be achieved, for instance, by a machine learning algorithm trained on manual annotations or on disambiguated parse results in a parsebank (Dyvik et al. 2016) or by inferring a robust statistical parser from the manual treebank.

Manual work in treebank annotation should preferably be carried out by at least two annotators, with an adjudicator resolving any differences. Good guidelines are crucial for achieving annotation that is consistent with the intentions and for promoting *interannotator agreement*. Annotation guidelines, or at least detailed descriptions of the annotation, should be made available to researchers using the treebank so that they will be able to correctly interpret the annotation.

The UD initiative for dependency treebanks has created common annotation guidelines that are partly universal and partly language-dependent (Nivre et al. 2016). Many UD treebanks have been converted from earlier annotation formats. Starting from another angle, the

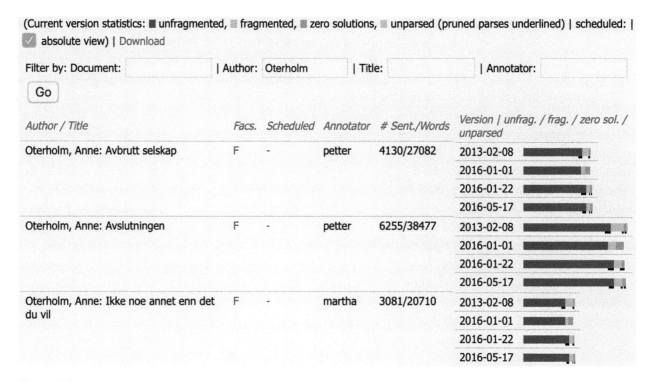

(Current version statistics: ■ unfragmented, ▨ fragmented, ▨ zero solutions, ▨ unparsed (pruned parses underlined) | scheduled: | ☑ absolute view) | Download

Filter by: Document: [   ] | Author: [Oterholm] | Title: [   ] | Annotator: [   ]

[Go]

Author / Title	Facs.	Scheduled	Annotator	# Sent./Words	Version	unfrag. / frag. / zero sol. / unparsed	
Oterholm, Anne: Avbrutt selskap	F	-	petter	4130/27082	2013-02-08	
					2016-01-01	
					2016-01-22	
					2016-05-17	
Oterholm, Anne: Avslutningen	F	-	petter	6255/38477	2013-02-08	
					2016-01-01	
					2016-01-22	
					2016-05-17	
Oterholm, Anne: Ikke noe annet enn det du vil	F	-	martha	3081/20710	2013-02-08	
					2016-01-01	
					2016-01-22	
					2016-05-17	

Figure 43.2
Screenshot from an INESS monitoring tool showing grammar coverage for versions of parse results for selected texts in NorGram-Bank. The leftmost section of the bar indicates complete (unfragmented) parses.

Parallel Grammar project (ParGram) has enabled cooperation on parallel grammar development for a number of languages, based on a common approach to computational grammar design and a common parsebanking platform (Butt et al. 2002). This approach has then been demonstrated through the construction of a small parallel parsebank with ten languages (Sulger et al. 2013).

Treebanks, especially those created in part by manual or heuristic methods (the latter, e.g., in the conversion of annotation tags) may contain errors or inconsistencies. Thus, tools that support the systematic search for inconsistencies or the correction of such errors may be helpful (Dickinson & Meurers 2003, 2005; Wisniewski 2018; De Smedt, Rosén, & Meurer 2015).

4   Data storing

In treebank data management, several formats for storing and distributing treebank data may be considered. INESS imports treebanks in most common formats and stores them on disk, with appropriate backup. Some common exchange formats for treebanks have been based on the shared tasks organized by the Conference on Computational Natural Language Learning (CoNLL) (Buchholz & Marsi 2006). Whatever storage and exchange format is chosen by a treebank depositor, the data should be well formed and valid and the format should be documented.

In INESS, imported treebanks are processed to an efficient internal format for the purpose of indexing in order to allow fast access through a relational database. In INESS Search (Meurer 2012), the indices are static and are stored in files on disk; those index files are mapped onto virtual memory addresses. This implementation implies *demand* paging that ensures that only those parts (pages) of the index files that are actually needed are loaded into main memory, thus obviating the need for loading the files entirely into main memory, as was done in the older TIGERSearch (Brants et al. 2004). Nevertheless, storing large treebanks with rich annotation, including their indices and the relational database to support searching, requires some non-trivial disk storage, while querying them greatly benefits from substantial central processing unit (CPU) power as well as a large internal memory.

5   Documentation and metadata requirements

The complexity and theory dependence of treebank data make good documentation necessary. Treebank depositors should provide documentation that not only covers the usual items for language data (such as provenance, data format, licensing, size, languages), but also more specialized information. The documentation of the annotation method should at least distinguish between manual annotation, automatic parsing with manual correction, automatic parsing with manual disambiguation, stochastic parse ranking, and deterministic parsing. Any editors or other tools that have been used should also be mentioned. Documentation of the annotation itself can be elaborate; in the case of any manual intervention, the codebook or stylebook that the annotators have used as guidelines may be very useful for end users of the finished treebank as well.[6] For a treebank produced by automatic parsing with a computational grammar, the documentation of that grammar itself is important.

Metadata should be structured in a machine-readable format that can be harvested by language resource catalogs, where they can be found by researchers. Like other participants in CLARIN, INESS uses component metadata based on the Component Metadata Infrastructure (CMDI) (Broeder et al. 2012).[7] These metadata are harvested by the Virtual Language Observatory (VLO),[8] an international inventory of language resources maintained by CLARIN, the European infrastructure for language resources and technology (Van Uytvanck et al. 2010). CMDI metadata can be edited using downloadable or online editors, such as the online Component Metadata Editor (COMEDI) (Lyse Samdal, Meurer, & De Smedt 2015). CMDI metadata have a hierarchical but flexible structure based on profiles consisting of components. For treebanks, corpusProfile can be used; in its Corpus info component, the attribute Corpus type should then have the value Treebank. Likewise, there are attributes for size, language, annotation type, and so forth. Figure 43.3 shows a small part of the metadata for NorGramBank children's fiction in Norwegian Nynorsk,[9] one of the treebanks in the NorGramBank collection.

In creating metadata for parallel treebanks, information should be provided for each of the monolingual treebanks; in addition, the alignment itself is an independent annotation layer that requires its own documentation and metadata, including a license (Losnegaard et al. 2013:51).

6   Data sharing

Sharing a treebank with researchers presupposes that treebanks can easily be found and that they can either be acquired or explored online by end users. Catalogs such as the aforementioned VLO may help in locating treebanks. Normally the data archive where a treebank is deposited will assign a persistent identifier (PID) to each resource to improve the persistence of references stored in such catalogs. Such a PID will normally lead the intended user to a landing page with at least a summary of the metadata, a license that perhaps must be accepted by the user, and a link to the treebank itself. This link can either be to a downloadable file or to an online environment for querying the treebank. INESS uses the Handle[10] system for its PIDs.

The rich information in treebanks makes effective access to the information in the treebank non-trivial. Traditionally treebanks have been difficult to access for the research community in general, often requiring that users download not only the treebank itself but also special tools for viewing the analyses. This was the case for the German TIGER treebank (Brants et al. 2004), which had to be downloaded together with the TIGERSearch tool in order to perform searches (Lezius 2002; Brants et al. 2004).

A newer approach is to offer online treebank searching through a web browser. In recent years, a range of online tools have become available for the online distribution, construction, and/or querying of treebanks. INESS currently provides access in this way to more than five hundred treebanks in seventy languages. Some other online treebanking systems include the following:

- Treebank search maintained by the University of Turku in Finland[11]
- Prague Markup Language (PML) Tree Query, maintained by the Charles University in Prague[12]
- Kontext, maintained by the Charles University in Prague[13]
- Grew-match, maintained by Inria (Institut national de recherche en informatique et en automatique) in Nancy, France[14]

Language info

Language id: nn

Language name: Norwegian Nynorsk

Modality info

Modality type: writtenLanguage

Size info

Size: 106434

Size unit: sentences

Size info

Size: 1043260

Size unit: words

Annotation info

Annotation type: syntacticAnnotation-treebanks

Annotation standoff: false

Segmentation level: sentence

Annotation format: XLE (Packed c- and f-structures in Prolog)

Tagset:
http://prosjekt.digital.uni.no/projects/inesspublic/wiki/NorGram_Lexical_Categories_(Preterminals);
http://prosjekt.digital.uni.no/projects/inesspublic/wiki/NorGram_Phrase_Structure_Categories;
http://prosjekt.digital.uni.no/projects/inesspublic/wiki/NorGram_F-structure_Features

Theoretic model: Lexical Functional Grammar (LFG)

Annotation mode: mixed

Annotation mode details: Automatic parsing, manual disambiguation using discriminants.

Annotation manual unstructured

Role: annotationManual

Document unstructured: http://clarino.uib.no/iness/page?page-id=_NorGram_annotator_guidelines_

Annotation tool

Target resource name URI: LFG Parsebanker

Figure 43.3

Part of the metadata for a treebank in the NorGramBank collection, showing detailed information on size and annotation. The full metadata are much more extensive.

Treebank Selection

Select a set of treebanks to work with. ?

Languages: All · Afrikaans (1) · Ancient Greek (to 1453) (13) · Arabic (7) · Basque (6) · Belarusian (1) · Bulgarian (7) · Buriat (1) · Catalan (4) · Chinese (7) · Church Slavic (8) · Classical Armenian (1) · Coptic (2) · Croatian (7) · Czech (16) · Danish (8) · Dutch (10) · English (24) · Estonian (7) · Faroese (1) · Finnish (15) · French (13) · Galician (7) · Georgian (7) · German (19) · Gothic (6) · Hebrew (6) · Hindi (6) · Hungarian (9) · Icelandic (3) · Indonesian (8) · Irish (6) · Italian (11) · Japanese (4) · Kazakh (4) · Korean (1) · Latin (19) · Latvian (5) · Lithuanian (1) · Marathi (1) · Modern Greek (1453-) (7) · (1) · Northern Kurdish (1) · Northern Sami (26) · Norwegian (5) · Norwegian Bokmål (40) · Norwegian Nynorsk (13) · Old English (ca. 450-1100) (5) · Old French (842-ca. 1400) (1) · Old Norse (4) · Old Russian (20) · Persian (6) · Polish (21) · Portuguese (15) · Romanian (6) · Russian (10) · Sanskrit (2) · Serbian (1) · Slovak (3) · Slovenian (10) · Spanish (10) · Swedish (13) · Swedish Sign Language (2) · Tamil (5) · Telugu (1) · Turkish (6) · Uighur (3) · Ukrainian (3) · Upper Sorbian (1) · Urdu (4) · Vietnamese (3) · Wolof (3) · Yue Chinese (1)

Treebank Collections: All · Acquis (7) · Alpino (1) · BulTreeBank (1) · CLARIN-PL (5) · DELPH-IN (2) · GEGO (4) · GeoGram (4) · HunGram (3) · ISWOC (9) · JOS (1) · Menotec (4) · Mercurius (1) · NDT (4) · NorGram (42) · NorGramBank (26) · POLFIE (15) · PROIEL (10) · PaHC (2) · ParGram (12) · ParTMA (14) · Sami-open (15) · Sami-restricted (7) · Sofie (9) · TOROT (22) · TiGer (3) · Universal Dependencies 1.1 (19) · Universal Dependencies 1.2 (36) · Universal Dependencies 1.3 (53) · Universal Dependencies 1.4 (63) · Universal Dependencies 2.0 (63) · Universal Dependencies 2.1 (103) · WolGram (3) · XPar (2)

Treebank Types: All · lfg (37) · constituency (19) · constituency-alpino (1) · dependency (45) · dependency-cg (373) · dependency-tuebadz (1) · hpsg (2)

Figure 43.4
Screenshot of the treebank selection page in INESS.

7   Interface

Online environments for managing treebanks must have good interfaces to guide users in their exploration efforts and present relevant parts of the data in understandable ways. The interface of INESS, with its main components, is described briefly in this section.

7.1   Selection

The user can choose one or more treebanks to search in. Treebank selection is made through first choosing a language, an annotation type, or a treebank collection. After the first choice is made, a list of all treebanks compatible with that choice is presented. The user may then make further choices in these three categories or choose one or more of the listed treebanks. The user can also restrict the selection to parallel treebanks. Many treebanks are available to any user, but authentication as a researcher provides access to a larger number of treebanks. A screenshot of the treebank selection page is shown in figure 43.4.

7.2   Metadata

When a treebank is selected, an easily readable overview of the basic metadata is shown, as illustrated in figure 43.5. The license must be accepted. If the treebank has a restricted license, the user must also be authenticated, that is, must be logged in.

7.3   Browse and search

The user can browse sentences/analyses, or search for sentences matching certain properties by writing a search expression specified in the query language INESS Search, which is a reimplementation and extension of TIGER-Search. INESS Search has support for LFG (whose structures are general directed graphs, not just trees), HPSG, dependency, and constituency treebanks. An example of a search result in the LFG treebank NorGramBank is displayed in figure 43.6.

The query in (2) specifies a c-structure node CPnom (#x) that projects to an f-structure node #y that is the value of the object (OBJ) attribute in the f-structure node #z. In other words, this search expression finds nominal clauses that function as objects. Such a search can

NorGram Newspaper text (30 documents from the years 2006 - 2009) in Norwegian Bokmål from the Norwegian Newspaper Corpus

Full metadata record:

hdl:11495/DB24-E23E-5F86-1

Persistent identifier for the resource:

hdl:11495/DB24-E30D-55EA-1

Links:

http://clarino.uib.no/iness/landing-page?resource=nob-newspaper&view=short (landing page @ INESS)

http://clarino.uib.no/iness/landing-page?resource=nob-newspaper (full metadata)

http://clarino.uib.no/iness/landing-page?resource=NorGramBank&view=short (The collection of which this treebank is part)

Contact Person: Rosén, Victoria

This resource is licensed under the following terms:

Creative Commons-BY (CC-BY)
BY

Please click on the link to read the license terms.

By accepting the terms of the license you will be granted access to the resource.

Accept

Attribution:

Please use the following text to cite this resource:
NorGram Newspaper text (30 documents from the years 2006 - 2009) in Norwegian Bokmål from the Norwegian Newspaper Corpus. Created by *Infrastructure for the Exploration of Syntax and Semantics.* Distributed by the INESS Portal: hdl:11495/DB24-E30D-55EA-1

Size: 246397 sentences , 3157558 words

Language(s): Norwegian (no), Norwegian Bokmål (nb)

Description:

The "NorGram Newspaper text (30 documents from the years 2006 - 2009) in Norwegian Bokmål from the Norwegian Newspaper Corpus" treebank is a syntactically annotated corpus based on 30 documents taken from the years 2006 - 2009 from the Norwegian Newspaper Corpus (NCC). This treebank is part of INESS NorGramBank collection (see URL in metadata).

Note that the available treebank contains only those newspaper articles from 2012 and 2013 that have been manually preprocessed; see details otherwheres in the metadata.

Figure 43.5

Screenshot of a metadata page, including license that must be accepted. Clicking on Full metadata record will reveal more detailed information.

be useful for researching the syntactic functions that nominal clauses can fill in a language. Figure 43.6 shows the c- and f-structures for the sentence in (3),[15] providing an illustration of a nominal clause as an object of a preposition.

The values of node variables and features included in the search expression may be displayed in tabular format, sortable by column. This may be useful, for instance, when searching different treebanks in different languages. The query in (4) searches for fixed expressions in the selected

(2) #x: CPnom >> #y & #z >OBJ #y

(3) Etter   at   hun   sluttet,   forsvant   plagene.
    after   that   she   quit   disappeared   the afflictions
    "After she quit, her afflictions disappeared."

C-structure

F-structure

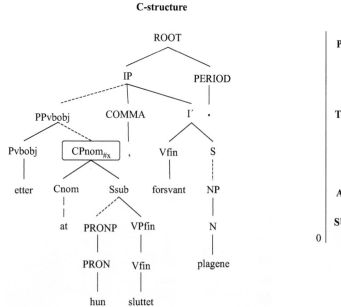

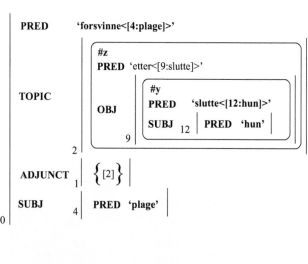

Figure 43.6
Structures for one of the search results returned by query (2).

treebanks. The result of this query, given in figure 43.7, is a table with the values of the metavariable *lang* displayed together with the number of matches.

(4) #x_ >fixed #y_ :: lang

7.4 Properties

All indexed attributes and their possible values are listed for each treebank (alphabetically or by frequency) so that the user knows what properties can be included in search expressions. As an example, figure 43.8 shows the list of parts of speech (*pos*) in one of the UD treebanks.

7.5 Visualization

A sentence selected by the user can be visualized in ways that are appropriate for the treebank type, as shown in several examples herein. For constituency treebanks, two different views are supported, as illustrated in figure 43.1. For dependency treebanks, both tree view and linear view are supported, as illustrated in figure 43.9. Highlighting of various properties of the representations aids the user in reading the graphs. Nodes targeted in a search expression are marked in red in the graphs produced in INESS. In addition, mousing over certain elements highlights information associated with them; what is highlighted is dependent on the annotation type. Visualizations in INESS are discussed in further detail by Meurer, Rosén, and De Smedt (2019).

8 Data citation

Repositories or platforms providing access to treebanks should provide not only documentation and metadata, but also citation information. Ideally, citation information is provided in textual format, ready to be used in a publication, as well as in various database formats (e.g., BibTeX or RIS). The essential enabler of proper treebank citation (as for any other data) is a PID. Citation should at least include a brief description and a PID. The following is an example for a treebank of Old English made accessible by INESS:

> ISWOC—Ælfric's Lives of Saints. Created by ISWOC—Information Structure and Word Order Change in Germanic and Romance Languages. Distributed by INESS: hdl:11495/DB24-D3F8-A861-1.

When different versions of a treebank are stored (for instance, when they are repeatedly parsed with newer versions of a grammar), INESS clearly distinguishes between them in their name and documentation and assigns them separate PIDs. In the case of parallel treebanks, each of the component monolingual treebanks has its own PID, and the alignment layer also has a PID. Sometimes, however, there is no PID for the individual treebanks that are part of a collection; this is the case, for instance, for the UD treebanks, which only have one PID for every version of the entire collection.

Count	globals: *lang*
55680	fra
10669	rus
9905	cat
8066	ron
7204	ces
5854	nld
3203	kor
3052	ara
2040	eng
1976	por
1678	fas
1585	heb
1386	ita
1128	fin
819	lat
800	ind
782	hin
738	bul
707	hrv
495	dan
418	jpn
290	eus
266	glg
236	gle

202	pol
202	hye
188	mlt
185	slk
156	deu
138	est
105	cop
104	kmr
100	bel
98	hsb
94	grc
91	ell
88	lit
88	myv
69	bua
58	lav
57	pcm
30	bam
25	fro
5	kom
4	bre
4	mar
3	amh
3	got
1	akk

Figure 43.7

Table showing the number of occurrences of fixed expressions in selected treebanks (here all treebanks in the collection Universal Dependencies 2.3),[16] sorted by language code.

Click on an attribute to see the values it assumes in the treebank.

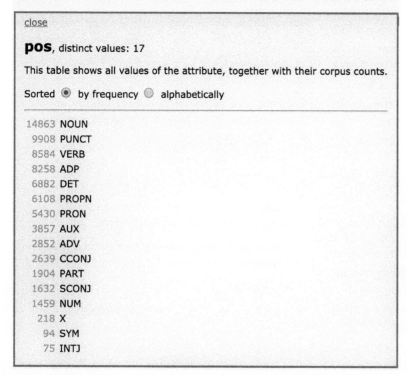

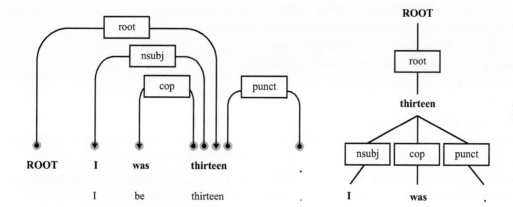

Figure 43.8
Screenshot showing the frequencies of the seventeen parts of speech in the Universal Dependencies version of syntax annotations from the GUM corpus, one of the English treebanks in the UD 2.3 collection.

Figure 43.9
Dependency structures in linear view (at left) and tree view (at right) for the sentence *I was thirteen*.[17] Mousing over any word in the linear view highlights all edges to and from that word. In the interface, incoming edges are marked in red and outgoing edges in blue, making it easier to read the structure.

Furthermore, research publications may want to cite individual samples from a treebank. Although readers can retrieve samples by entering queries to search for them, this process is cumbersome and error prone. An alternative solution is for treebanks to allow each sentence to be addressed by means of a unique identifier.[18] In INESS, such PIDs can be obtained by clicking on "Copy sentence URL" on a sentence page in INESS. This PID can then be shared so that using it in a browser will always get to the same sentence.

Additionally, it may be desirable to cite search results by making the search easily replicable. INESS has two ways of achieving this, either as the intension or the extension of the search. On the one hand, INESS allows search expressions to be stored and publicly shared, so that people can easily replicate treebank queries instead of going through the error-prone process of typing them in. On the other hand, a set of sentences obtained as the result of a query can be saved as a custom treebank and shared.

9   Conclusion

Treebanks are syntactically annotated corpora targeted at researchers wishing to undertake empirical studies of grammatical constructions. Due to their complexity, treebanks require good tools and often substantial manual intervention for their construction; furthermore, their exploration also requires powerful tools for search and visualization. These requirements make treebanks costly, so that good data management is important for their optimal dissemination and exploitation in research.

Our suggested guidelines for the data management of treebanks can be summarized as follows. First make a plan for all aspects of data management and obtain a budget for carrying it out. Already in this stage it is recommended to get in touch with a treebanking infrastructure or other distribution service that will provide curation and access to researchers. Choose corpus materials and secure the rights to their intended use, as formulated in an end user license. Choose an annotation type and method based on theoretical and practical considerations as well as a format for sharing the data. Obtain tools and recruit annotators depending on the chosen approach. Be prepared for a long annotation phase. Deposit your results, make sure they get appropriate PIDs, and provide users with all documentation necessary for the intended use and for citation.

Notes

1. Dyvik, Helge, *Far leser og mor syr* (blog), September 11, 2018. https://norgramtall.w.uib.no/2018/09/11/far-leser-og-mor-syr/.

2. Sentence PID: http://hdl.handle.net/11495/D8B8-3970-851A-3@dep100995.

3. A parallel treebank may also consist of different annotations of the same text: for example, a dependency treebank and a constituency treebank.

4. http://clarino.uib.no/iness/.

5. https://creativecommons.org/.

6. E.g., http://bultreebank.org/wp-content/uploads/2017/06/BTB-TR05.pdf—the stylebook for the BulTreeBank.

7. CMDI is standardized under number 24622 of the International Organization for Standardization.

8. http://vlo.clarin.eu.

9. PID for the resource: hdl:11495/D963–33EA–65BD-0.

10. https://www.handle.net/.

11. http://bionlp-www.utu.fi/dep_search/.

12. http://lindat.mff.cuni.cz/services/pmltq/#!/home.

13. https://lindat.mff.cuni.cz/services/kontext/corpora/corplist.

14. http://match.grew.fr/.

15. Sentence PID: http://hdl.handle.net/11495/D8B8-3970-851A-3@lfg3834598. May require login.

16. Treebank collection PID: hdl:11495/E026–161F-546A-6.

17. Sentence PID: http://hdl.handle.net/11495/D8B8-3970-851A-3@dep7308861. May require login.

18. E.g., http://hdl.handle.net/11495/D8B8-3970-851A-3@lfg234387. May require login.

References

Abeillé, Anne, ed. 2003. *Treebanks: Building and Using Parsed Corpora*. Text, Speech and Language Technology 20. Dordrecht, the Netherlands: Kluwer Academic Publishers.

Brants, Sabine, Stefanie Dipper, Peter Eisenberg, Silvia Hansen-Schirra, Esther König, Wolfgang Lezius, Christian Rohrer, George Smith, and Hans Uszkoreit. 2004. TIGER: Linguistic interpretation of a German corpus. *Research on Language and Computation* 2 (4): 597–620. https://doi.org/10/cv6j8w.

Bresnan, Joan. 2001. *Lexical-Functional Syntax*. Malden, MA: Blackwell.

Broeder, Daan, Menzo Windhouwer, Dieter Van Uytvanck, Twan Goosen, and Thorsten Trippel. 2012. CMDI:

A component metadata infrastructure. In *Proceedings of the Workshop on Describing LRs with Metadata: Towards Flexibility and Interoperability in the Documentation of LRs*, ed. Victoria Arranz, Daan Broeder, Bertrand Gaiffe, Maria Gavrilidou, Monica Monachini, and Thorsten Trippel, 1–4. Paris: ELRA. http://www.lrec-conf.org/proceedings/lrec2012/workshops/11 .LREC2012%20Metadata%20Proceedings.pdf #page=8.

Buchholz, Sabine, and Erwin Marsi. 2006. CoNLL-X shared task on multilingual dependency parsing. In *CoNLL-X '06: Proceedings of the Tenth Conference on Computational Natural Language Learning*, ed. Lluís Màrquez and Dan Klein, 149–164. Stroudsburg, PA: Association for Computational Linguistics. https:// www.aclweb.org/anthology/W06-2920.

Butt, Miriam, Helge Dyvik, Tracy Holloway King, Hiroshi Masuichi, and Christian Rohrer. 2002. The parallel grammar project. In *COLING-GEE '02 Proceedings of the 2002 Workshop on Grammar Engineering and Evaluation*, ed. John Carroll, Nelleke Oostdijk, and Richard Sutcliffe, 1–7. Stroudsburg, PA: Association for Computational Linguistics. https://www.aclweb.org /anthology/W02-1503.pdf.

De Smedt, Koenraad, Victoria Rosén, and Paul Meurer. 2015. Studying consistency in UD treebanks with INESS-Search. In *Proceedings of the Fourteenth Workshop on Treebanks and Linguistic Theories (TLT14)*, ed. Markus Dickinson, Erhard Hinrichs, Agnieszka Patejuk, and Adam Przepiórkowski, 258–267. http:// tlt14.ipipan.waw.pl/files/4614/5063/3858/TLT14_proceedings .pdf.

Dickinson, Markus, and W. Detmar Meurers. 2003. Detecting inconsistencies in treebanks. In *Proceedings of the Second Workshop on Treebanks and Linguistic Theories (TLT 2003)*, ed. Joakim Nivre and Erhard Hinrichs. Växjö, Sweden: Växjö University Press. http://www.sfs.uni-tuebingen.de/~dm/papers/dickinson-meurers -tlt03.pdf.

Dickinson, Markus, and W. Detmar Meurers. 2005. Prune diseased branches to get healthy trees! In *Proceedings of the Fourth Workshop on Treebanks and Linguistic Theories (TLT 2005)*, ed. Montserrat Civit, Sandra Kübler, and M. Antònia Martí. Universitat de Barcelona, Publicacions i Edicions. http://www.sfs .uni-tuebingen.de/~dm/papers/dickinson-meurers-tlt05.pdf.

Dyvik, Helge, Paul Meurer, Victoria Rosén, Koenraad De Smedt, Petter Haugereid, Gyri Smørdal Losnegaard, Gunn Inger Lyse, and Martha Thunes. 2016. NorGramBank: A "deep" treebank for Norwegian. In *Proceedings of the Tenth International Conference on Language Resources and Evaluation (LREC'16)*, ed. Nicoletta Calzolari, Khalid Choukri, Thierry Declerck, Marko Grobelnik, Bente Maegaard, Joseph Mariani, Asunción Moreno, Jan Odijk, and Stelios Piperidis, 3555–3562. Paris: ELRA. http://www.lrec-conf.org/proceedings/lrec2016/summaries /943.html.

Forst, Martin. 2003. Treebank conversion: Creating a German f-structure bank from the TIGER Corpus. In *Proceedings of*

the *LFG03 Conference*, ed. Miriam Butt and Tracy Holloway King, 1989–1993. Paris: ELRA. http://web.stanford.edu/group /cslipublications/cslipublications/LFG/8/pdfs/lfg03forst.pdf.

Kingsbury, Paul, and Martha Palmer. 2002. From TreeBank to PropBank. In *Proceedings of the Third International Conference on Language Resources and Evaluation (LREC'02)*, 252–256. http:// lrec-conf.org/proceedings/lrec2002/pdf/283.pdf.

Lezius, Wolfgang. 2002. TIGERSearch—Ein Suchwerkzeug Für Baumbanken. In *Proceedings Der 6. Konferenz Zur Verarbeitung Natürlicher Sprache (KONVENS 2002)*, ed. Stephan Busemann, 107– 114. https://konvens.org/proceedings/2002/pdf/03V-lezius.pdf.

Losnegaard, Gyri Smørdal, Gunn Inger Lyse, Anje Müller Gjesdal, Koenraad De Smedt, Paul Meurer, and Victoria Rosén. 2013. Linking Northern European infrastructures for improving the accessibility and documentation of complex resources. In *Proceedings of the Workshop on Nordic Language Research Infrastructure at NODALIDA 2013, May 22–24, 2013, Oslo, Norway*, ed. Koenraad De Smedt, Lars Borin, Krister Lindén, Bente Maegaard, Eiríkur Rögnvaldsson, and Kadri Vider, 44–59. NEALT Proceedings Series 20. Linköping Electronic Conference Proceedings. Linköping, Sweden: Linköping University Electronic Press. http://www.ep.liu.se/ecp/089/005/ecp1389005.pdf.

Lyse Samdal, Gunn Inger, Paul Meurer, and Koenraad De Smedt. 2015. COMEDI: A component metadata editor. In *Selected Papers from the CLARIN 2014 Conference, October 24– 25, 2014, Soesterberg, the Netherlands*, ed. Jan Odijk, 82–98. Linköping Electronic Conference Proceedings 116. Linköping, Sweden: Linköping University Electronic Press. http://www.ep .liu.se/ecp/article.asp?issue=116&volume=&article=8#.

Marcus, Mitchell P., Beatrice Santorini, and Mary Ann Marcinkiewicz. 1993. Building a large annotated corpus of English: The Penn Treebank. *Computational Linguistics* 19 (2): 313–330.

Meurer, Paul. 2012. INESS-Search: A search system for LFG (and other) treebanks. In *Proceedings of the LFG '12 Conference*, ed. Miriam Butt and Tracy Holloway King, 404–421. LFG Online Proceedings. Stanford, CA: CSLI Publications. http:// cslipublications.stanford.edu/LFG/17/papers/lfg12meurer.pdf.

Meurer, Paul, Victoria Rosén, and Koenraad De Smedt. 2019. Interactive visualizations in INESS. In *LingVis: Visual Analytics for Linguistics*, ed. Miriam Butt, Annette Hautli-Janisz, and Verena Lyding, 55–85. Stanford, CA: CSLI Publications.

Nivre, Joakim, Marie-Catherine de Marneffe, Filip Ginter, Yoav Goldberg, Jan Hajič, Christopher D. Manning, Ryan McDonald, et al. 2016. Universal Dependencies v1: A multilingual treebank collection. In *Proceedings of the Tenth International Conference on Language Resources and Evaluation (LREC'16)*, ed. Nicoletta Calzolari, Khalid Choukri, Thierry Declerck, Sara Goggi, Marko Grobelnik, Bente Maegaard, Joseph Mariani, et al., 1659–1666. Paris: ELRA. http://www.lrec-conf.org/proceedings/lrec2016/pdf /348_Paper.pdf.

Oepen, Stephan, Dan Flickinger, Kristina Toutanova, and Christopher D. Manning. 2004. LinGO Redwoods: A rich and dynamic treebank for HPSG. *Research on Language and Computation* 2 (4): 575–596.

Pollard, Carl, and Ivan A Sag. 1994. *Head-Driven Phrase Structure Grammar*. Chicago: University of Chicago Press.

Prasad, Rashmi, Nikhil Dinesh, Alan Lee, Eleni Miltsakaki, Livio Robaldo, Aravind Joshi, and Bonnie Webber. 2008. The Penn Discourse TreeBank 2.0. In *Proceedings of the Sixth International Conference on Language Resources and Evaluation (LREC'08)*, ed. Bente Maegaard Nicoletta Calzolari, Khalid Choukri Joseph Mariani, Jan Odijk, Stelios Piperidis, and Daniel Tapias, 2961–2968. Paris: ELRA. http://www.lrec-conf.org/proceedings/lrec2008/pdf /754_paper.pdf.

Przepiórkowski, Adam, and Agnieszka Patejuk. 2020. From lexical functional grammar to enhanced universal dependencies: The UD-LFG treebank of Polish. *Language Resources and Evaluation* 54:185–221. https://doi.org/10.1007/s10579-018-9433-z.

Rögnvaldsson, Eiríkur, Anton Karl Ingason, Einar Freyr Sigurðsson, and Joel Wallenberg. 2012. The Icelandic Parsed Historical Corpus (IcePaHC). In *Proceedings of the Eighth International Conference on Language Resources and Evaluation (LREC'12)*, ed. Nicoletta Calzolari, Khalid Choukri, Thierry Declerck, Mehmet Uğur Doğan, Bente Maegaard, Joseph Mariani, Asuncion Moreno, Jan Odijk, and Stelios Piperidis, 1977–1984. Paris: ELRA. http://www .lrec-conf.org/proceedings/lrec2012/pdf/440_Paper.pdf.

Rosén, Victoria, and Koenraad De Smedt. 2007. Theoretically motivated treebank coverage. In *Proceedings of the 16th Nordic Conference of Computational Linguistics (NoDaLiDa-2007)*, ed. Joakim Nivre, Heiki-Jaan Kaalep, Kadri Muischnek, and Mare Koit, 152–159. Tartu, Estonia: Tartu University Library.

Rosén, Victoria, Koenraad De Smedt, Paul Meurer, and Helge Dyvik. 2012. An open infrastructure for advanced treebanking. In *META-RESEARCH Workshop on Advanced Treebanking at LREC2012*, ed. Jan Hajič, Koenraad De Smedt, Marko Tadić, and António Branco, 22–29. http://www.lrec-conf.org/proceedings /lrec2012/workshops/12.LREC%202012%20Advanced%20 Treebanking%20Proceedings.pdf.

Rosén, Victoria, Paul Meurer, and Koenraad De Smedt. 2009. LFG Parsebanker: A toolkit for building and searching a treebank as a parsed corpus. In *Proceedings of the Seventh International Workshop on Treebanks and Linguistic Theories (TLT7)*, ed. Frank Van Eynde, Anette Frank, Gertjan van Noord, and Koenraad De Smedt, 127–133. Utrecht: Landelijke Onderzoekschool Taalwetenschap.

Rosén, Victoria, Paul Meurer, Gyri Smørdal Losnegaard, Gunn Inger Lyse, Koenraad De Smedt, Martha Thunes, and Helge Dyvik. 2012. An integrated web-based treebank annotation system. In *Proceedings of the Eleventh International Workshop on Treebanks and Linguistic Theories (TLT11)*, ed. Iris Hendrickx,

Sandra Kübler, and Kiril Simov, 157–167. Campo Grande, Portugal: Edições Colibri. http://tlt11.clul.ul.pt/ProceedingsTLT11.tgz.

Sulger, Sebastian, Miriam Butt, Tracy Holloway King, Paul Meurer, Tibor Laczkó, György Rákosi, Cheikh Bamba Dione, et al. 2013. ParGramBank: The ParGram parallel treebank. In *Proceedings of the 51st Annual Meeting of the Association for Computational Linguistics*, vol. 1, ed. Hinrich Schütze, Pascale Fung, and Massimo Poesio, 550–560. Stroudsburg, PA: Association for Computational Linguistics. http://www.aclweb.org/anthology /P13-1054.

Van Uytvanck, Dieter, Claus Zinn, Daan Broeder, Peter Wittenburg, and Mariano Gardellini. 2010. Virtual language observatory: The portal to the language resources and technology universe. In *Proceedings of the Seventh International Conference on Language Resources and Evaluation (LREC'10)*, ed. Nicoletta Calzolari, Khalid Choukri, Bente Maegaard, Joseph Mariani, Jan Odijk, Stelios Piperidis, Mike Rosner, and Daniel Tapias, 900–903. Paris: ELRA.

Volk, Martin, Torsten Marek, and Yvonne Samuelsson. 2017. Building and querying parallel treebanks. In *Annotation, Exploitation and Evaluation of Parallel Corpora*, ed. Silvia Hansen-Schirra, Stella Neumann, and Oliver Čulo, 9–35. Berlin: Language Science Press. https://doi.org/10.5281/zenodo.283438.

Wisniewski, Guillaume. 2018. Errator: A tool to help detect annotation errors in the Universal Dependencies project. In *Proceedings of the Eleventh International Conference on Language Resources and Evaluation (LREC'2018)*, ed. Nicoletta Calzolari, Khalid Choukri, Christopher Cieri, Thierry Declerck, Sara Goggi, Koiti Hasida, Hitoshi Isahara, et al., 4489–4493. Paris: ELRA. http://www.lrec-conf.org/proceedings/lrec2018/pdf/652.pdf.

44 Managing Data in a Formal Syntactic Study of an Under-Investigated Language (Uzbek)

Vera Gribanova

1 Introduction

In this data management use case, I describe the considerations and decision points that arose in the course of organizing and making accessible certain parts of the data I collected through fieldwork on the morphosyntax of Uzbek, an under-studied Turkic language of Central Asia. The discussion will focus on one such data set—on the syntax of cleft constructions—that draws on, and documents the results of, empirical studies that formed the basis of my work on the syntax and morphosyntax of Uzbek between 2009 and 2019. The kind of fieldwork involved in this study involves native speaker[1] judgments about the grammaticality of sentences or morpheme combinations in words and occasionally judgments about interpretation as well; this approach will be more or less familiar to most theoretical linguists and involves fieldwork practices that are already very well described in textbooks and articles on fieldwork methodology (e.g., Bowern 2008; Vaux, Cooper, & Tucker 2007, among many others). I therefore do not focus especially on this aspect of the data management process in this chapter, except where it touches on fieldwork choices I made that were specific to Uzbek or to my investigation of it. Rather, my focus is on what motivated the organizational choices I made when it comes to managing data sets involving numerous moving parts. Secondarily, I will also discuss the motivations behind my decision to make publicly accessible the results of these studies and the various logistical decisions I faced when doing so.

As will become clear in the second and third sections of this chapter, the process that eventually led to the existence of the online Uzbek language data archive described here was initiated in the context of a constellation of circumstances and language-specific factors that is not likely to hold across a particularly broad range of investigative situations. It is nevertheless the case that the lessons learned in this process may be useful to readers who are considering engaging in such a project, using data that they have collected via fieldwork, especially if—like me—they have little to no training in language documentation and tend to work with fieldwork-collected language data in service, primarily, of syntactic analysis.

2 Uzbek

Uzbek is an under-studied Turkic language spoken by about eighteen million people, primarily in Uzbekistan. Because of the history of Soviet occupation and the geography of Uzbekistan, very few native speakers of Uzbek are monolingual: Russian, Tajik, and languages of neighboring Turkic-speaking regions (Kazakh, Kyrgyz, Turkmen) are common second and third languages, with English as an ever more prominent contender, especially among younger generations. I collect basic information about the speakers I work with, including their region of origin and their range of languages used; to the extent possible, I try to work with consultants whose primary language is Uzbek, rather than Russian. All of this is especially relevant in light of the fact that in the course of my work on this language (since about 2009), one of my most rewarding and challenging discoveries has been that there is a great deal of not only phonological and lexical, but also morphological and syntactic variation among speakers. As far as I am able to tell, this variation is conditioned primarily by generation and region. The fact of variation across age groups is not surprising: with independence from the Soviet Union in 1991 came a great number of changes, among them a resurgence of national pride and pride in the Uzbek language, which was reflected in numerous educational policy decisions.

Young people's education stopped being centered on the acquisition of Russian as a professional language and as a lingua franca; in the majority of cases, Uzbek became the primary language of schooling. I suspect, but cannot know for sure, that this brought with it numerous other small shifts in the syntactic patterns of young people's language. The regional variation is perhaps even less surprising. Uzbekistan is bordered by five countries, three of them with Turkic national languages; Uzbek speakers along borders with these languages tend to adopt certain features of the neighboring language. This is quite directly observable phonologically, for example, from the fact that standard Uzbek has no vowel harmony, but regional variants close to the border with Kazakhstan, Kyrgyzstan, and Turkmenistan have vowel harmony. Regional variation in Uzbek, and its role in Uzbek dialect classification, is discussed primarily on the basis of observable differences in lexical choice and phonetic variation, as in, for example, the work of Turaeva (2015). Although morphosyntactic variation is not—to my knowledge—documented in the descriptive literature on Uzbek, it is nevertheless the case that investigation of the language led me to find a situation where judgments, upon first impression, did not always systematically align across native speaker consultants. Further investigation showed that this lack of alignment in judgments was not random: it was limited to certain syntactic and morphosyntactic domains and displayed certain patterns of covariation that called for a deeper explanation.

A second circumstance that required some thought about the organizational principles I would apply to structuring collected data is that Uzbek is an underinvestigated language. When I began work on the language in 2009, although there were some high-quality descriptive grammars (Bodrogligeti 2003; Kononov 1960; Sjoberg 1963), there was no sustained, theoretically driven work on the structural properties of Uzbek, as far as I was aware. While the existence of descriptive resources provided me with an invaluable point of departure for my work, they were in some cases outdated, they provided no negative evidence, and they also provided no insight into the morphosyntactic variation I ultimately encountered. Finally, it is unsurprising that my theoretical perspective often led me to look for information about the structure of Uzbek that was not encompassed in descriptive grammars. Taken together, all of this led me to think that the areas of contemporary Uzbek grammar that I

was interested in investigating required more systematic data collection—for example, in the form of wellformedness surveys of entire morphological paradigms, rather than just the forms of immediate interest to me—so that I could both get a holistic sense of the relevant patterns and get a handle on the variation, where I was finding it.[2] The resulting data sets involved patterns with a lot of moving parts, in terms of the grammatical features that were at play. It became apparent relatively quickly that I needed a way to sort and tag my data so that I could visualize how these factors were interacting. As I will discuss, besides the many obvious benefits this kind of organization brought with it, this approach led to significant analytical findings that most likely would not have emerged otherwise.

3   Data collection and organization: Uzbek clefts

The project I describe here is the first of an ongoing series; every project in this series involves examination of distinct components of Uzbek clause structure and morphosyntax, but they share some common themes, one of which is the observation that certain sub-components of the relevant patterns involve a significant degree of variation in judgment. In all cases, including the project discussed in detail here, the basic methodology for treating data collection is quite simple: in the typical case, I prepare examples I want to ask native speaker consultants about in a raw text file, editing that file as I go through the session with every individual speaker. I keep a separate file with information about speakers' area of origin, educational history, approximate age, and gender. Elicitation sessions inside each text file are labeled with keywords, the consultant's name, and the date.

I generally do not record elicitation sessions. Audio recording can be very helpful, and it is often the norm in the kind of data collection I am describing here. However, in certain socio-cultural contexts it is also inappropriate, and can hinder the process of building trusting relationships between the language investigator and the language consultant. In the case of Uzbek, most of the people I work with are old enough to have grown up in a Soviet context, or else their parents did. Audio recording in this context gives rise to an automatic distrust of the investigator, even if the materials being recorded are not sensitive. Secondarily, many of the Uzbek consultants I work with have known me for the course of almost a decade, and we have formed strong friendship ties. Unfettered by audio recordings, our elicitation sessions can toggle smoothly from discussions of our lives—academic and work pursuits; children's growing pains; discussions of Uzbek culture, abroad and at home—back to Uzbek example words and sentences. This would never be possible in a context where consultants knew that they were being recorded, and I believe that the freedom offered by not having to restrict the discussion narrowly to the Uzbek language at any given moment is an important one for building long-term relationships with consultants.

Recording language users' reactions to the materials I prepare for evaluation in a text file is usually sufficient when I am working with data and judgments Linzen and Oseki (2018:3) call "Class II"—these are "judgments that illustrate uncontroversial facts about the grammar of the language." Each of the cases I discuss required further investigation, in large part because they involved variation in judgments that illustrate more subtle contrasts that are crucial to theory-building (Linzen and Oseki label these "Class III").

3.1 Uzbek sluicing-like constructions and cleft strategies

The investigation I discuss here took place around 2009–2011, during which time I worked with Uzbek language consultants in Uzbekistan, Russia, and the United States. Much of the discussion that follows is drawn from Gribanova (2013), which contains far more detail than I can provide here. A portion of the data that was collected for this investigation is now archived, through the Stanford Digital Repository, at https://purl.stanford.edu/qs579kq8188—more detail about this aspect of the project is provided in section 4.

Like all Turkic languages, Uzbek uses the WH-*in-situ* strategy to form content questions (1). Uzbek also makes use of a construction (as in (2)) that looks on the surface like *sluicing*: ellipsis of some roughly clause-sized material, stranding a WH-phrase. For the sake of neutrality, I adopt the term *sluicing-like construction* (SLC) to describe the phenomenon in Uzbek.

(2) Siz   kim-ga-dir   pul   ber-a-siz,   lekin
    You   some-DAT-one   money   give-PRS-2SG   but
    kim(-ga)-lig-i-ni   bil-ma-y-man.
    who(-DAT)-COMP-3SG.POSS-ACC   know-NEG-PRS-1SG
    "You give money to someone, but I don't know who."

This combination of possibilities is surprising, from a typological perspective, for prominent theories of the nature of ellipsis. One of the best-defended ideas in this domain is that in constituent ellipsis, the elided constituent is unpronounced but nevertheless fully articulated and present as far as the syntax is concerned (Merchant 2001; Ross 1969). Ellipsis of the type in (1) is therefore typically taken to be the result of WH-movement—the operation that fronts WH-phrases to the left edge of clauses in languages like English—and an ellipsis operation that targets a clause-sized constituent. According to such an approach, languages without an overt WH-movement operation (among them, Uzbek) should not countenance genuine sluicing. The major thrust of Gribanova (2013) is that Uzbek SLCs such as (2) should be derived not from a clause featuring WH-movement—a

(1) a. Umida universitet-da O'zbek   til-ni   o'qi-y-di.
        Umida university-LOC Uzbek   language-ACC learn-PRS-3SG
        'Umida learns Uzbek at the university.'

    b. Kim universitet-da O'zbek til-ni o'qi-y-di?
        who
        'Who learns Uzbek at the university?'

    c. Umida   qayer-da   O'zbek til-ni o'qi-y-di?
                where-LOC
        'Where does Umida learn Uzbek?'

    d. Umida universitet-da qaysi til-ni   o'qi-y-di?
                               which language-ACC
        'Which language does Umida learn at the university?'

strategy that would be incompatible with the organizing syntactic principles of the language—but rather from a clause that is underlyingly either copular or a cleft.[3] The challenge for such a proposal is to show that the various properties of SLCs follow from the properties of copular and cleft constructions; such a strategy therefore requires an independent investigation of copular and cleft clauses in the language.

Investigation of the copular and cleft structures of Uzbek (illustrated schematically in (3)) turned out to be a challenge, in part because there are two cleft strategies that share some features and can look similar. The idea that cleft constructions may actually correspond to two different structural possibilities in a single language is very well established (Jespersen 1927, 1937; Pinkham & Hankamer 1975), but has been difficult to show for languages like English (Gundel 1977).

(3)

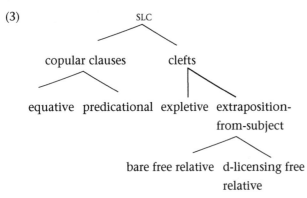

The two cleft strategies of interest to us in Uzbek are shown in (4) and (5); they differ in (i) whether the copula agrees, (ii) whether the pivot shows case connectivity, (iii) whether the pivot can be an adjunct, (iv) whether extraposition from subject position (of the cleft clause or free relative) is optional or obligatory, and (v) whether the clause extraposed from subject position is a free relative or a cleft clause.

(4) Extraposition from subject (EFS)
  a. Men   ko'r-gan,   siz   e-di-ngiz.
     I   see-PST.PTCP   you   COP-PST-2SG
     "Who I saw was you."
  b. U   siz   e-di-ngiz,   men   ko'r-gan.
     3SG   you   COP-PST-2SG   I   see-PST.PTCP
     "It was you, who I saw."

As noted in (5), the EXPL strategy is not available to all speakers whom I consulted, and within (5), there is variation especially as to whether an accusative nominal can serve as the pivot of the cleft—a pattern I will return to next.

3.2 Organizing the data and identifying patterns

On the surface, the cleft data I was eliciting was difficult for me to make sense of by just looking at individual examples of grammatical and ungrammatical possibilities. There were two sources for this difficulty: first, the fact that there are five properties of these clefts, listed in (i)–(v) in section 3.1, which ultimately point to two underlying structures; and second, the fact that a subpart of the overall patterns exhibits variation.

Tackling the first problem is what initially led me to take a more systematic approach to data organization and management than the basic methodology that I outlined at the beginning of section 3. While there are probably far more technologically sophisticated approaches I could have taken, for my purposes it sufficed to list all the cleft structures I had elicited in an Excel file. Each sentence was annotated with information about speaker judgment(s) and was tagged for a subset of the various pieces of information in (i)–(v).[4] I ended up doing this for an extensive set of sentences, and by using the "sort data" (by tags) function in Excel, I was able to understand how clusters of properties were patterning together. This revealed, for example, that the EFS strategy

(5) Expletive (EXPL)
  a. Siz-ga   e-di,   men   pul   ber-gan-im.   [*subject to variation*]
     you.DAT   COP-PST.3SG   I   money   give-PST.PTCP-1SG.POSS
     "It was to you that I gave money."
  b. Siz-ni   e-di,   men   ko'r-gan-im.   [*subject to variation*]
     you-ACC   COP-PST.3SG   I   saw-PST.PTCP-1SG.POSS
     "It was you that I saw."

always required a non-case-marked nominal in its pivot and that this same cleft strategy required agreement on the copula. This is distinct from the EXPL cleft, where no copular agreement is ever attested and a broader range of constituents is permitted in the pivot position. Table 44.1 summarizes the entire range of properties.

Configuring the data set in this way also revealed gaps in my exploration—it turned out that there were pairings of properties I had implicitly assumed would or would not co-occur, but had not actually tested in my initial elicitations. Once I had put all the data I had into a spreadsheet, I was able to see what kinds of clusterings or pairings of properties I did not yet have data for and to follow up on those pairings. After a few rounds of this, I was able to visualize the data and to conclude that I was looking at two patterns that were only superficially similar. The next step was to connect these clusters to structural analyses that could provide a principled explanation as to why the various properties in table 44.1 pattern the way they do.

Dealing with the second challenge required me to home in on the empirical domains where the variation was found. Once I had gone through the initial stages of organizing the data it became clear that not all speakers would accept EXPL clefts at all. I designed a further survey that contained primarily the types of strings where I knew there was some variation. This survey demonstrated that those speakers who did accept the EXPL cleft exhibited further variation as to whether they accepted accusative-marked nominal pivots—a pattern that is also found in Japanese (Kizu 1997) and Turkish (Merchant 1998) clefts. A direct benefit for my analysis of adding these data to my data set was that the variation in

acceptability of accusative-marked pivots turned out to be directly correlated to whether speakers would accept an accusative-marked WH-remnant in an SLC configuration. This co-variation between cleft and SLC behavior ended up being one of the strongest and most satisfying pieces of evidence in Gribanova (2013) for the analytical claim that SLCs were in fact derived from cleft and copular constructions in Uzbek. Figure 44.1 gives a partial snapshot of the survey data, although certain columns in the spreadsheet were collapsed for the purposes of fitting the spreadsheet on the page. The crucial result—all and only the speakers who accept accusative pivots in clefts also accept accusative remnants in the SLC—can be seen in columns A–J, where each column represents a judgment by a native Uzbek speaker.

4 Archiving and transparency

4.1 Motivations for archiving data from syntax field research on Uzbek

The process of putting the evidence I had collected together and annotating that data led me to consider the question of whether to make the data publicly accessible. Important considerations specific to archiving methodology, archiving ethics, and intellectual property are discussed extensively by Andreassen (chapter 7, this volume); Holton, Leonard, and Pulsifer (chapter 4, this volume); and Collister (chapter 9, this volume), respectively. My aim here is to try to articulate why I was driven to archive my own data and the considerations involved in doing so. These considerations are especially relevant, given that there are many reasons such a task may be difficult to undertake. Preparing data

Table 44.1
The distinctive properties of EXPL and EFS clefts

Extraposition	Expletive
The copula agrees with the most accessible nominal	The copula bears default agreement
No case connectivity on the pivot	Case connectivity on the pivot
The pivot is an argument	The pivot is an argument or an adjunct
Subject position contains a free relative or a third-person pronoun	No overt element fills the subject position; null expletives only
Extraposition of the free relative from subject position is optional	Extraposition of the cleft clause from object position is obligatory
The free relative is a genuine headless relative clause (one of two types)	The cleft clause is not a traditional relative clause

parse	gloss	A	B	C	D	E	F	G	H	I	J	clause type	[remnant/pivot] [case/category]
Men ol-ib kel-gan-im Farhod-dan e-di.	1SG take-CV come-PST.PTCP-1SG.POSS Farhod-ABL COP-PST					ok	ok	ok		ok		copular clause	ablative
Men ol-ib kel-gan-im Toshkent-dan e-di	1SG take-CV come-PST.PTCP-1SG.POSS Tashkent-ABL COP-PST						ok	ok		ok		copular clause	ablative
U kim-dan-dir pul ol-di, lekin kim-dan-lig-i-ni bil-ma-y-man.	3SG who-ABL-one money take-PST but who-ABL-NMLZ-3SG-ACC know-NEG-PRS-1SG	ok	ok	ok	ok	ok	ok	ok	ok	ok		SLC	ablative
U kim-dan-dir pul ol-di, lekin kim-dan ekan-lig-i-ni bil-ma-y-man.	3SG who-ABL-one money take-PST but who-ABL EVID-NMLZ-3SG-POSS-ACC.POSS-ACC know-NEG-PRS-1SG	ok	ok	ok	ok	ok	*		ok	ok		SLC	ablative
U kim-dan-dir pul ol-di, lekin u kim-dan ekan-lig-i-ni bil-ma-y-man.	3SG who-ABL-one money take-PST but 3SG who-ABL EVID-NMLZ-3SG-POSS-ACC.POSS-ACC know-NEG-PRS-1SG	*	*	*	ok	*		ok	*	*		SLC	ablative
Siz-ni e-di, men ko'r-gan-im.	2SG-ACC COP-PST 1SG see-PST.PTCP-1SG.POSS	ok	*	*	*	*	*	*	ok	ok	ok	cleft	accusative
U siz-ni edi, men ko'r-gan-im.	3SG 2SG-ACC COP-PST 1SG see-PST.PTCP-1SG.POSS		*	*	*	*	*	*	*			cleft	accusative
Men kim-ni-dir ko'r-d-im, lekin kim-ni-lig-i-ni bil-ma-y-man.	1SG who-ACC-one see-PST-1SG but who-ACC-NMLZ-3SG.POSS-ACC know-NEG-PRS-1SG	ok	*	*	*	*	*	*	ok	ok	ok	SLC	accusative
Men kim-ni-dir ko'r-d-im, lekin kim-ni ekan-lig-i-ni bil-ma-y-man.	1SG who-ACC-one see-PST-1SG but who-ACC EVID-NMLZ-3SG-POSS-ACC.POSS-ACC know-NEG-PRS-1SG	?						*				SLC	accusative
U chiroy-li e-di, men ko'r-gan-im.	3SG beauti-ful COP-PST 1SG see-PST.PTCP-1SG.POSS	*		*	*	ok	*	*	*	*		cleft	AP
Men ko'r-gan-im chiroy-li e-di.	1SG see-PST.PTCP-1SG.POSS beauti-ful COP-PST	*		ok	ok	*	ok	*	ok	ok		copular clause	AP
Men ko'r-gan qiz chiroy-li e-di.	1SG see-PST.PTCP girl beauti-ful COP-PST	ok		ok	ok	ok	ok	ok	ok	ok		copular clause	AP
U siz e-di-ngiz, men ko'r-gan-im.	3SG 2SG COP-PST-2SG 1SG see-PST.PTCP-1SG.POSS	ok	ok	ok	ok	*	ok	ok	*	ok		cleft	bare
Men ko'r-gan-im, siz e-di-ngiz.	1SG see-PST.PTCP-1SG.POSS 2SG COP-PST-2SG	ok	ok	ok	ok	ok	ok	ok	ok	ok		copular clause	bare
Men ko'r-gan-im siz e-di.	1SG see-PST.PTCP-1SG.POSS 2SG COP-PST	*		*	*	*	*	*	*	*		copular clause	bare
Men kim-ni-dir ko'r-d-im, lekin u kim ekan-lig-i-ni bil-ma-y-man.	1SG who-ACC-one see-PST-1SG but 3SG who EVID-NMLZ-3SG-POSS-ACC.POSS-ACC know-NEG-PRS-1SG	ok	ok	ok	ok	ok	ok	ok	ok	ok		SLC	bare
U kim-ga-dir pul ber-di, lekin u kim ekan-lig-i-ni bil-ma-y-man.	3SG who-DAT-one money give-PST but 3SG who EVID-NMLZ-3SG-POSS-ACC.POSS-ACC know-NEG-PRS-1SG	ok	ok	ok	ok	ok	ok	ok	ok	ok		SLC	bare
Men sovg'a qil-gan-im, siz-ga e-di.	1SG present do-PST.PTCP-1SG.POSS 2SG-DAT COP-PST						ok	*	ok		ok	copular clause	dative
U kim-ga-dir pul ber-di, lekin kim-ga-lig-i-ni bil-ma-y-man.	3SG who-DAT-one money give-PST but who-DAT-NMLZ-3SG-POSS-ACC know-NEG-PRS-1SG	ok	ok	ok	ok	ok	ok	ok	ok	ok		SLC	dative
U kim-ga-dir pul ber-di, lekin u kim-ga ekan-lig-i-ni bil-ma-y-man.	3SG who-DAT-one money give-PST but 3SG who-DAT EVID-NMLZ-3SG-POSS-ACC.POSS-ACC know-NEG-PRS-1SG	*	*	*	ok	*	*	*	ok	ok		SLC	dative
U kim-ga-dir pul ber-di, lekin kim-ga ekan-lig-i-ni bil-ma-y-man.	3SG who-DAT-one money give-PST but who-DAT EVID-NMLZ-3SG-POSS-ACC.POSS-ACC know-NEG-PRS-1SG	ok	ok	ok	ok	ok	ok	ok	ok	ok		SLC	dative
Men sovg'a qil-gan-im, siz uchun e-di.	1SG present do-PST.PTCP-1SG.POSS 2SG for COP-PST						ok	*	ok		ok	copular clause	PP

Figure 44.1

Variation in the acceptability of accusative pivots.

for archiving requires resources, in the form of time and money. And as Berez-Kroeker et al. (2019) and Alperin, Schimanski, La, Niles, and McKiernan (chapter 13, this volume) have pointed out, a major de-motivating factor is that our field on the whole does not have clear guidelines for attributing credit for data stewardship for the purposes of tenure and promotion.

Despite these difficulties, once I had organized the data I had collected for myself, I was quite motivated to make it accessible; there were clear benefits both to my own work and to the community of native Uzbek speakers with whom I worked. The central benefit to my own work and analytical process was knowing that I could be open and transparent about areas where judgments were subject to variation, and I was able to let go of the pressure to present an idealized snapshot of the language. Putting all of the elicited materials online has enabled me to embrace the actual linguistic situation as I have found it; this has fed back into my analytical claims in a tremendously beneficial way, as I discussed in section 3. On the logistical side of things, there is also a clear sense in which working on an under-investigated language requires papers to be on the longer side, and this can be a source of tension or difficulty in the publication process. It is almost always the case that not all the data collected in an investigation can be provided in any reasonable-length manuscript. It has been beneficial for me to be able to refer, in submitted papers, to the entire range of data archived online. This has enabled me to feel I am being responsible to the full range of facts I have collected, and to the language itself, without necessitating that the entirely of the collected data be in the materials I submit for publication.

It is important to acknowledge that open archiving of data collected via fieldwork is not always the appropriate choice for every community; for a useful discussion, see Holton, Leonard, and Pulsifer (chapter 4, this volume). Such decisions will hinge at least in part on the specific language, type of data, and the language politics associated with the community of speakers. In the case of the Uzbek-speaking community, both in Uzbekistan and in the diaspora, the speakers I worked with felt proud that their language was receiving a scholarly kind of attention.[5] After decades of linguistic oppression in the Soviet context, many Uzbek speakers are happy to see their language thriving in the context of Uzbek national language policy, and the fact that someone studies their language has generally been, in my experience, a source of excitement.

A final and important motivation for making public the results of fieldwork-based data collection in syntactic investigations is that this can help to address many of the perennial empirical challenges associated with judgment-based studies. Sprouse, Schütze, and Almeida (2013) demonstrated experimentally that English-based judgments collected using a relatively small sample can be quite reliable. While this was shown to be true for English, the situation for judgments collected about certain grammaticality contrasts in other majority languages—Hebrew and Japanese—have been shown to be far less reliable (Linzen & Oseki 2018). One reason this might be the case—as suggested by both Phillips (2009) and Linzen and Oseki—is that English-based judgments are exposed to scrutiny by speakers of English in the review process, providing more opportunities for questionable judgments to be flagged. This same situation does not always hold for other languages, and it *especially* does not hold for languages with few or no native speaker linguists that have the kind of generative training required to serve as reviewers for the relevant journals. What this means for a language like Uzbek is that the core evidence on which analyses are based is subject to less scrutiny; as a consequence, there is a greater risk that contrasts or data points may be incorrect or not reliable.

The first step in remedying this situation is to be aware of it; in my case, it has also helped to take the extra step of being as transparent as possible about the data that I collect, so that interested parties—language specialists, native speaker linguists of all traditions, language consultants, and others—can access the original judgments on which I am basing my analysis and challenge those judgments, or use them to make the case for an alternative understanding of the empirical space. In at least one recent case, graduate students working on Uzbek for a field methods course developed a project looking at some overlapping areas of interest with mine and were able to draw on the data I had collected on predicate formation,[6] in combination with further independent fieldwork, to formulate their own analysis (Donovan & Nematova 2019). I see this as an early, positive sign that making data publicly accessible in this way can lead to real scientific progress.

4.2 Logistics

There are several decisions I made with respect to how the data I collected should be represented and made accessible online. I will recount those decisions here in case the same considerations arise for other scholars considering a similar move, acknowledging simultaneously that many of these decisions are specific to my subfield, the language in question, and my institution. Kung (chapter 8, this volume) provides a detailed discussion of the kinds of considerations that may be at stake in making decisions about data management and organization, whether or not that data ends up being publicly accessible.

A major factor that made this process easier for me was the existence of the Stanford Digital Repository,[7] which is run by the Stanford Library system and which is designed for managing and depositing scholarly information resources of a variety of forms. The ready availability of a digital archive with solid data management practices and institutional support made a world of difference to me. The repository makes scholarly data available through the library catalog and provides a

permalink for each folder in the digital archive, so that I can link to data in publications without being worried that the link will change. Similar repositories already exist or are being developed across universities internationally; the Linguistic Society of America has a useful discussion of considerations in choosing an archive for language data and provides a list of a range of digital repositories.[8] After a bit of research and deliberation I decided that using the .csv file format would be the most accessible way to present and disseminate the data I had collected; the remaining decisions concerned what kind of information to put in each data set online.

To maximize accessibility,[9] I used the Latinate writing system for Uzbek (even though Cyrillic still continues to be used quite productively in Uzbekistan). For each token, I typically provided the linguistic utterance as an Uzbek speaker would write it, then provided a morpheme-by-morpheme parse, and a gloss. Apart from this, I provided information about judgments of any speakers that were asked about the string and any comments they might have made about it in a separate "notes" field. Separate from this, the only information provided in the body of each .csv file was the series of tags associated with each sentence; these tags, in combination with the ability to sort data by tag, were very useful to me in my own analytical work, so it made sense to leave this information in the posted files as well.

For each .csv file that contains judgments, there is an associated file, sometimes containing information about speakers, and noting any abbreviations used in the tagging or morpheme-by-morpheme glosses. Speakers were given a random letter to cross-reference their judgment in the main file with any data I reported about them in the metadata file. Information I reported, for certain studies, included gender, approximate age, and region of origin. This balance of information on the one hand, with some opacity about speakers' individual identities on the other, is what I found to be both fair and optimal from the perspective of protecting speakers' privacy, but each situation will be different.

Finally, as I mentioned in section 4.1, preparing data for online accessibility takes resources: I was using Excel files as a starting point for my own private use, and the gap between that and what was posted online is not insignificant: I needed to provide morpheme-by-morpheme glosses and definitions of abbreviations and tags, all of which is work-intensive. Early in my time on the tenure track at Stanford, I was fortunate to have a grant from Hellman Foundation to fund my work on Uzbek. I used some of this funding to train an undergraduate research assistant, Allison Dods, and later to train a native speaker linguist, Sharifa Djurabaeva, to assist me in preparing the files for public use. Without this help it is unlikely that I would have had the time I needed to undertake the endeavor on my own. This speaks volumes, I think, about how far even a relatively small amount of seed funding can go in helping archiving efforts along.

5 Conclusion

I learned many lessons from my attempts to make data I have collected via fieldwork publicly accessible, and with each project I become more careful about how the data are structured and how thoroughly and transparently things are organized. A lesson to be taken from these experiences is that especially when it comes to under-investigated languages, some effort can go quite a long way, even if that effort is coming from someone who lacks explicit training in language documentation and archiving.

Notes

1. As Uzbek is a spoken language, I will use the term *speaker* here in place of the more inclusive *user*.

2. This approach the investigation of a linguistic system, with due attention to the whole system rather than to isolated subparts of the system, reflects my commitment to what Sandy Chung has called "whole-language description."

3. Analogous strategies had already been applied successfully, by this point, for typologically similar languages such as Japanese (Kizu 1997) and Turkish (Merchant 1998). But the alternative view—in which some sort of exceptional WH-movement is forced in languages that are typically WH-in-situ in order to give rise to a genuine sluicing construction—is well attested as well (Ince 2006, 2012; Takahashi 1994), and so the Uzbek discussion was meant to weigh in on a matter of some debate.

4. This having been my first attempt at such an approach, I was less systematic in my tagging than I probably ought to have been. Later projects, including one on predicate formation strategies in the language—http://purl.stanford.edu/bq499mh5981—used a more thorough system for tagging each token for various properties that I thought would be important.

5. I obtain oral permission from speakers for these materials to be posted online. Individual speaker names/identities are never revealed in the archived materials. Relatedly, I ask speakers whether they want to be acknowledged by name in papers I ultimately publish.

6. http://purl.stanford.edu/bq499mh5981.

7. https://library.stanford.edu/research/stanford-digital-repository.

8. https://www.linguisticsociety.org/content/finding-archive-your-endangered-language-research-data.

9. Uzbekistan has implemented a Latinate alphabet gradually since it became an independent Republic in 1991, so it seemed to me that using the Latinate system would make the data accessible both to the majority of Uzbek speakers and to the scholarly community at large.

References

Berez-Kroeker, Andrea, Lauren Gawne, Susan Smythe Kung, Barbara Kelly, Tyler Heston, Gary Holton, Peter Pulsifer, et al. 2019. Reproducible research in linguistics: A position statement on data citation and attribution in our field. *Linguistics* 56 (1): 1–18.

Bodrogligeti, András J. E. 2003. *An Academic Reference Grammar of Modern Literary Uzbek*. LINCOM Studies in Asian Linguistics 50. Munich: LINCOM.

Bowern, Claire. 2008. *Linguistic Fieldwork: A Practical Guide*. London: Palgrave MacMillan.

Donovan, Michael, and Shakhlo Nematova. 2019. What counts as second-to-last? The case of the Uzbek question particle. Presented at the 93rd Annual Meeting of the LSA, New York, January 3–6.

Gribanova, Vera. 2013. Copular clauses, clefts, and putative sluicing in Uzbek. *Language* 89 (4): 830–882.

Gundel, Jeanette. 1977. Where do cleft sentences come from? *Language* 53 (3): 53–59.

Ince, Atakan. 2006. Pseudo-sluicing in Turkish. In *University of Maryland Working Papers in Linguistics 14*, ed. Nina Kazanina, Utako Minai, Philip J. Monahan, and Heather L. Taylor, 111–126. College Park: University of Maryland, Department of Linguistics.

Ince, Atakan. 2012. Sluicing in Turkish. In *Sluicing: Cross-linguistic Perspectives*, ed. Andrew Simpson and Jason Merchant, 248–269. Oxford: Oxford University Press.

Jespersen, Otto. 1927. *A Modern English Grammar*, vol. 3. London: Allen and Unwin.

Jespersen, Otto. 1937. *Analytic Syntax*. London: Allen and Unwin.

Kizu, Mika. 1997. Sluicing in *Wh-in-situ* languages. In *Proceedings of the Chicago Linguistic Society 33*, ed. Kora Singer, Randall Eggert, and Gregg Anderson, 231–244. Chicago: Chicago Linguistic Society.

Kononov, Andrei Nikolaevič. 1960. *Grammatika sovremennogo Uzbekskogo literaturnogo jazyka*. Moscow: Akademija Nauk SSSR, Institut Vostokovedenija.

Linzen, Tal, and Yohei Oseki. 2018. The reliability of acceptability judgments across languages. *Glossa* 3 (1): 1–25.

Merchant, Jason. 1998. "Pseudosluicing": Elliptical clefts in Japanese and English. In *ZAS Working Papers in Linguistics 10*, ed. Artemis Alexiadou, Nanna Fuhrhop, Paul Law, and Ursula Kleinhenz, 88–112. Berlin: Zentrum für Allgemeine Sprachwissenschaft.

Merchant, Jason. 2001. *The Syntax of Silence: Sluicing, Islands and the Theory of Ellipsis*. Oxford: Oxford University Press.

Phillips, Colin. 2009. Should we impeach armchair linguists? *Japanese/Korean Linguistics* 17:49–64.

Pinkham, Jessie, and Jorge Hankamer. 1975. Deep and shallow clefts. In *Papers from the Eleventh Regional Meeting of the Chicago Linguistic Society*, ed. R. E. Grossman, L. J. San, and T. J. Vance, 429–450. Chicago: Chicago Linguistic Society.

Ross, John Robert. 1969. Guess who? In *Papers from the 5th Regional Meeting of the Chicago Linguistic Society*, ed. Robert Binnick, Alice Davidson, Georgia M. Green, and Jerry L. Morgan, 252–286. Chicago: Chicago Linguistic Society.

Sjoberg, Andrée. 1963. *Uzbek Structural Grammar*. Uralic and Altaic Series 18. Bloomington: Indiana University Press.

Sprouse, Jon, Carson Schütze, and Diego Almeida. 2013. A comparison of informal and formal acceptability judgments using a random sample from *Linguistic Inquiry* 2001–2010. *Lingua* 134:219–248.

Takahashi, Daiko. 1994. Sluicing in Japanese. *Journal of East Asian Linguistics* 3:265–300.

Turaeva, Rano. 2015. Linguistic ambiguities of Uzbek and classification of Uzbek dialects. *Anthropos: International Review of Anthropology and Linguistics* 110:463–476.

Vaux, Bert, Justin Cooper, and Emily Tucker. 2007. *Linguistic Field Methods*. Eugene, OR: Wipf and Stock.

45 Managing Data for Theoretical Syntactic Study of Underdocumented Languages

Philip T. Duncan, Harold Torrence, Travis Major, and Jason Kandybowicz

1 Introduction: Project backdrop and methods of data collection

To shed light on helpful data management principles for theoretical syntax, this chapter draws from a recent and ongoing collaborative project to document two Indigenous Ghanaian languages, Ikpana (ISO 639-3: lgq) and Avatime (ISO 639-3: avn). Ikpana and Avatime are both underdocumented Ghana-Togo Mountain languages, spoken in the mountainous Volta region, in an area northwest of the regional capital Ho and east of Lake Volta. Data for this project were collected over a six-week period from July to August 2018, working with speakers in Logba Alakpeti, Amedzofe, Dzokpe, and Ho. Our eight-person research team divided into two groups, each dedicated to either Avatime (including authors Torrence and Major with Blake Lehmann and Kerri Devlin) or Ikpana (including authors Kandybowicz and Duncan with Bertille Baron Obi and Hironori Katsuda).[1] Given that extant work on Ikpana and Avatime remains limited, documenting general properties of the grammar of each language was a major focus of the project overall. To collect thematically unified data that would facilitate comparison between the two languages and give the project a more concrete direction, each group dedicated a majority of time to the documentation of interrogatives, which is what we highlight herein. Individuals also collected data for several interface topics (syntax-phonology, syntax-semantics, syntax-discourse, and so on), meaning that the data collection and management needed to be relevant and curated for robust linguistic inquiry across multiple subdomains.

Our methods of data collection included structured, direct elicitations, grammaticality judgments, and text collection across multiple genres (including short autobiographies, regional histories, and traditional *Ananse* [spider/trickster] stories, which are well-known in Ghana and other areas of West Africa, and still passed down among families there). For purposes of exemplification in this chapter, we primarily orient herein to principles underlying management of elicited material, though these do extend to our treatment of texts. The nature of our specific project—that is, non-Indigenous "outsider" (Ameka 2018) scholars working with Indigenous peoples and with Indigenous languages—informs aspects of data management that we feel are important to note but, given the purview of our chapter, are unable to elaborate on in detail. In particular, this includes taking appropriate steps to ensure that data use is transparent, aligned with language users' (and, when necessary, broader community) desires and expectations, and that data management and use are done in ways that promote Indigenous sovereignty, self-determination, and self-governance (see Holton, Leonard, & Pulsifer, chapter 4, this volume, and citations therein for discussion of data management issues specific to working with Indigenous peoples/nations/communities/families/individuals).

Our chapter is organized as follows. In section 2, we discuss aspects of our project pertaining to curating data, touching on themes such as data and file preparation practices that facilitate ease of interaction with the data along a typical syntax research pipeline, which involves cyclic integration of data collection, transcription, exploration, analysis, dissemination, and archiving. This highlights some of the more mechanical aspects of file preparation and management for the purposes of syntactic inquiry. Section 3 turns to conceptual and methodological issues. We reinforce what we see as a need for constant negotiation of descriptive and theoretical needs throughout data collection, which also has implications for data management (e.g., file curation, annotating transcriptions, and performing calls on data) in order to facilitate exploration of grammatical properties. Section 4 concludes.

Before proceeding, we would like to offer clarification on our use of *theoretical* in relation to syntax and field-work in this chapter. We recognize that *theoretical syntax* encompasses a plurality of diverse approaches, perspectives, and theoretical orientations. We intend the issues we discuss to be germane to theoretical syntax in the broad sense. This includes, but is by no means limited to, the generative framework in which we happen to operate (which itself is not singular). However, given that we exemplify various issues that arise in theoretical syntactic research with our own work, at times our discussion may be colored by peculiarities specific to one theoretical framework, that is, generativism (as among the many applications of theory that exist for syntax). By using the phrase *theoretical* in contrast to *non-theoretical*, then, we do not intend the misleading dichotomy of *generative* in contrast to *other approaches*.

2   Data management and project design

Underlying our data management was a file-oriented "database"[2] design informed by four interrelated principles: simplicity, ease of implementation, ease of deployment, and versatility. *Simplicity* here means that the interface, structure, and ability to interact with/access the data introduce as little complexity as possible and ensure that there is not-too-steep a learning curve. *Ease of implementation* for us means that the database could be constructed by leveraging existing technologies, architectures, and functionalities that are already present by default on personal computers. Relatedly, *ease of deployment* means that the database could be deployed seamlessly across multiple platforms (e.g., Windows, Mac, and Linux operating systems). Finally, *versatility* for our purposes was primarily directed toward output: we aimed to ensure that the initial formatting and data transformation would best prepare for dissemination (presentations and publications), as well as archiving (see Andreassen, chapter 7, this volume). Orienting to these principles is important in our project because it positions us to meet practical, ethical, and professional needs in ways that intersect with current best practices. We recognize from the outset that the approach we outline here is a bit ad-hoc and that ad-hoc solutions can provide challenges in linguistic data management. However, the reality of the current landscape is such that there is no single application or software that meets project needs universally.

Even with a project-specific database, though, we stress the importance of forward- and multipurpose-thinking in design, so as to facilitate the production of accessible, replicable, and durative materials.

All files in the database followed consistent naming conventions with persistent file formats (see Mattern, chapter 5, this volume, for issues related to data sustainability and file naming). This included, for example:

- Audio recordings from elicitation sessions and text production/performances as uncompressed and lossless WAV files
- Video recordings of text production/performances as MPEG-4 files
- Scans of handwritten transcriptions and notes, either as PDF/A (which is specialized for archiving) or compressed and lossless PNG files
- Typed transcriptions (completed following elicitation sessions based on original handwritten notes and review of audio) as plain text files with UTF-8 encoding

Our file-naming conventions were based on "semantic file naming" (Thieberger & Berez 2011:103), incorporating the following information:

- Target language's ISO 639-3 code
- Date, according to international format (YYYYMMDD)
- Ordered letter, if more than one file for a single day
- Initials of language consultants, listed alphabetically
- Genre of the data (e.g., elicitation, text)
- Initials of linguists participating in the session, with "ALL" appended for group sessions with all researchers present
- File extension

For example, the file LGQ_20180723b_KA_NH_RD_elic_ALL.wav is an audio file from a group elicitation session with three Ikpana speakers on July 23, 2018. The aforementioned elements are also embedded in the metadata added to transcription files, along with additional information such as location, provenance, and explanations/definitions of percent sign (%) tags used.

Though these types of details about file formatting and naming conventions are nowadays fairly typical for language documentation projects, we feel that they are important to note here because they begin to form the basis for the file-oriented database we implemented in our project. To preserve the relationships between files, all associated files from a single data collection event would be placed in a parent folder with the same semantic file name as the audio file (e.g., the folder LGQ_20180723b_KA_NH_RD_ elic_ALL would minimally contain the .wav audio file, one or more .txt transcription files, and .pdf files of linguists' handwritten transcriptions and notes). Folders pertaining to data collection events are in turn contained in parent folders for their associated language, and these two language folders are one level under the folder for the entire project. This provides a by-language chronological organization that is easily navigable when individual files need to be reviewed, and the directory structure allows for querying the data, which is a simple but indispensable feature.

With respect to data entry within transcription files, we used the three-tier glossing system, but without numbering or additional formatting (for reasons we discuss shortly).[3] In lieu of an added numbering system, project members used a text editor with built-in line numbering, such as Notepad++ for Windows (https://notepad-plus -plus.org/), BBEdit (https://www.barebones.com/products /bbedit/) for Mac OS, or Atom for either environment (https://atom.io/). Morphological glosses follow the Leipzig Glossing Rules (https://www.eva.mpg.de/lingua /resources/glossing-rules.php) to the extent possible. To annotate examples for grammatical information, we used % tags, which were entered in the line immediately following the English gloss. These tier tags are initially derived from descriptive grammatical properties, and they can be further added to in order to annotate examples based on theory-specific points or domains of grammar outside of syntax proper (e.g., a pragmatic feature or intonational pattern). Thus, a typical numbered example would be split across four lines as seen in figure 45.1, which shows, from Ikpana, four lines associated with each of two constructions: a transitive sentence in lines 30–33 and an object *wh*-question in lines 35–38.

The built-in numbering is helpful in cases where group members need to quickly identify and discuss or review a particular example within a .txt file. The primary reason that we avoided additional document-internal numbering relates to the distinction "between the *form* of the presentation of the data and its *content*" (emphasis in original). In addition to the need to accommodate multiple platforms for doing data entry, we also wanted to ensure that the content would "derive many presentation forms" (Thieberger & Berez 2011:94). Among members of our project, this included creating documents (papers/ articles, handouts) and presentations, with products in the Microsoft Suite, Google Suite, and LaTeX (the choice being either personal preference or a requirement, say, of a particular journal). Organizing the workflow in this way means that further formatting and editing is required, but this can be minimized through scripting. For example, we partnered with a colleague to create a simple Python script that could take plain text files as input and generate LaTeX-ready numbered examples (see Han, chapter 6, this volume, for detailed discussion of converting data into different forms). Running the script on an example like the first of the two seen in figure 45.1 can generate the following gb4e-style numbered example:

```
\beging{exe}
\ex
\gll Fafá o-kplò ìdzɔ́ afàn udânt∫ì(ɛ).\\
Fafa 3\textsc{sg}-cook yam home morning\\
'Fafa fried yams at home this morning.'
\end{exe}
```

This reduces time taken to format and typeset examples (gb4e uses single spacing to left-align elements in the gloss), and it also provides a different way to call and interact with data. For example, an entire text file can

```
29
30    Fafá o-kplò i-dzɔ́ afàn udânʃì(ɛ).
31    Fafa 3SG-cook CL-yam home morning
32    'Fafa fried yams at home this morning.'
33    %transitive %declarative %mass noun %temporal adverbial %bare prepositional phrase
34
35    Mé Fafá o-kplò afàn udântʃì(ɛ)?
36    what Fafa 3SG-cook home morning
37    'What did Fafa cook at home this morning?'
38    %transitive %temporal adverbial %bare prepositional phrase %content question %object wh-question
39
```

Figure 45.1
Entering linguistic examples in a plain text editor (Atom shown) using a three-tier format and % tags.

be generated. Alternatively, the script can search across files and subfolders within a directory based on features such as % tags. A LaTeX engine can then easily create a searchable PDF for team or community members to use, because PDF readers are readily available, and such files can be opened in browsers if a PDF reader is not available. At this point in our project, though, we do not have as easy of a way to prepare linguistic examples for numbering in proprietary formats such as Microsoft Word, which for us still require manual formatting/typesetting.

The system we adopted for data management also can be integrated into workflows that require use of more specialized linguistic software and tools, including ones that are quite standard among documentary linguistics, such as ELAN (https://tla.mpi.nl/tools/tla-tools/elan/).[4] For example, some members of our project were interested in exploring issues related to the syntax-phonology interface. While the % tags in our system can be used to indicate features relevant to any domain of grammar associated with a particular entry (e.g., "%F0 rise on right edge" to mark specific intonation on a prosodic unit), ELAN is more suited to exploring phonetic and prosodic properties of sentences and utterances because it can be used to synchronize annotation tiers with A/V. For linguists who want to use ELAN in addition to adopting our system for data management, constructing a template within ELAN that exports into the format that we utilized is rather straightforward. This allows one to separate the large ELAN files from the text files, which is desirable when, for example, one is trying to work with a database, but does not need to access the audio.

Although as Dimitriadis and Musgrave (2009) note, the type of file-oriented database we've described has weaknesses, such as being less suited to highly "data-intensive" projects, we find that it has many advantages, such as rapid implementation, a drastically reduced learning curve, and ease of shareability of work product. Because the database leverages existing structures, this reduces computing power needed, and it also means that users interact with data in a way that is already familiar, which is helpful for researchers, as well as for language users who may wish to access the data. The database is also not operating system–dependent, which means that it can be easily deployed. These two components also allow for a means of interacting with data that is crucial in theoretical syntax, in particular: searching for, reviewing, and compiling examples based on grammatical features. In addition to building search features into scripting, a more basic way to achieve this is through the use of regular expressions (regex). In our project and database design, we can use regex to return files based on properties of a file name. For example, the regex (.txt and "elic") will return all elicitation files in the directory. Regex can also be performed on elements within a text file, by searching for, for example: a string in the target language, a particular morpheme in the gloss tier, or a particular grammatical feature listed in the % tags. The learning curve for using regex is not steep, and it does not require additional software (e.g., these can be entered into the Spotlight tool or Finder window in Mac OS, or a Windows folder). We also use additional % tiers to tag examples to simplify future regex queries that return examples based on more theory-oriented properties. For instance, if one is investigating *wh*-questions in a particular language or set of languages, there are a variety of properties that should be tracked throughout the data-entry process. Some examples include *wh*-in-situ, partial movement, full movement, arguments versus adjuncts. Elicitation sessions are often organized to investigate these particular issues, but this organization is lost when the entire database is considered. Tagging example sentences is a way of maintaining the content of the examples at a global level across the database (for instance, %FM+Q=full movement with question particle, %PM-Q=partial movement without a question particle, %IS+Q=in situ with question particle, and so on).

3   Data collection

3.1   Planning for data collection: Preparing for what is known and what is unknown

The basic challenge confronting the researcher in data collection for theoretical syntax is a familiar one that is common to scientific and/or scholarly investigation more broadly (Logan 2009). To borrow an infamously lampooned but surprisingly insightful comment from former US Secretary of Defense Donald Rumsfeld, "There are known knowns. . . . There are known unknowns. . . . But there are also unknown unknowns." That is, there are things we know, things that we don't know but know more or less about their existence, and things that we don't know, which we don't really know exist. Theoretical syntactic research—especially when working with an underdocumented Indigenous language—is by necessity characterized by continuous navigation of these three components. This is partly because at the outset one often begins without necessarily knowing what will be theoretically interesting from the perspective of the language(s) investigated. This should not be taken to mean that one falls blindly into research. Instead, we advocate a cyclic, reflective approach, one that is based on using known knowns and known unknowns derived from theoretical and descriptive work to illuminate known unknowns and unknown unknowns. The idea is that over time the unknowns both become reduced and serve as the impetus for continued investigation. It is therefore simultaneously crucial to stay abreast of theoretical developments and their application to the language(s) of study and to understand the language(s) in theoretically neutral terms. The theory-neutral emphasis ensures that one's research is (1) accessible to non-linguists as well as linguists, (2) relevant to researchers of other frameworks, and (3) sound in description to be sound in theory (whatever theory).[5] In short, data collection for theoretical purposes begins with language description, just as data collection does for non-theoretical purposes.

The data collection process for this project began by consultation of prior work on Avatime and Ikpana. In this regard, the existence of excellent descriptive and analytical work (Ford 1971; Schuh 1995a, 1995b; Dorvlo 2008; van Putten 2014; Defina 2016), although they did not focus on *wh*-question formation, provided critical baseline data that allowed us to make much more progress than would have been possible otherwise.

We chose to look at *wh*-questions for reasons both theoretical and practical. On the theoretical side, some of us (Kandybowicz and Torrence) had already investigated *wh*-questions in the Akan group (Asante Twi, Bono, Wasa) and in Krachi, a North Guang language (Kandybowicz & Torrence 2013, 2015). These studies revealed some of the complexities of the construction in languages of the area. It seemed likely that Avatime and Ikpana would also share such complexity, which would be of theoretical interest. On the practical side, first, all languages have *wh*-questions, so we could be assured that we would find them in the languages. In addition, given the large theoretical and descriptive literature on *wh*-question formation, we could readily compare the Avatime and Ikpana data to what has been found in other languages. Finally, there was a limited time window in which the fieldwork could be carried out because

of scheduling conflicts among team members. Typically, we would not go into a fieldwork situation on a "new" language with a theoretical agenda. This is because of the simple fact that it cannot be predicted which areas of the grammar will be of the most theoretical interest and one cannot know in advance where the evidence for theoretical analysis will be found. Related to this point, we basically agree with Dixon (2007:13), who states that a poor reason for doing fieldwork is to test or prove a theoretical point. If one knows nothing about the language, then we concur. However, if one knows a great deal about a language then testing a theoretical point is an excellent reason for conducting fieldwork!

3.2 Types of data and their use in theoretical syntax

3.2.1 Elicited material One way in which fieldwork for theoretical linguistics differs from classical descriptive fieldwork is that elicitation can play a central role in data collection for theoretically minded analysts. As a whole, our impression is that fieldworkers are divided on the role of elicitation, both within and across theoretical orientations. However, we take it as a given that the methods employed depend on the questions that one is trying to answer. If a theory makes a prediction about what stress pattern should be found or what word order should be ungrammatical, elicitation provides a straightforward way of testing the theory (although there are other, less immediately practical means). As Rice (2001:244) says, "given a particular theoretical claim, one should expect to find certain things are grammatical and other things are ungrammatical." Similarly, Aissen succinctly summarizes the importance of direct, controlled elicitation in theoretically oriented (in this case, generative) fieldwork by saying, "While nothing in generative linguistics excludes text collection, direct elicitation is unavoidable. The view of a generative grammar as a hypothesis about the internalized knowledge of the native speaker . . . makes central the classification of tokens as well-formed or ill-formed since the predictions of these hypotheses concern well- and ill-formedness. While well-formedness can be supported (though not established) by the existence of attested examples, ill-formedness cannot be supported by their absence" (1992:9).

Regarding "grammatical elicitation," Dixon enjoins fieldworkers that "such elicitation should play no role whatsoever in linguistic fieldwork." However, he goes on to say that "What I do is make up Jarawara sentences (that are generated by the grammatical rules I am positing) and ask if these are bona fide utterances. . . . Or else I will quote some sentence that I know is alright (because I have heard it in a text or conversation) and ask about variants of it, perhaps changing the verb . . . or adding or subtracting an affix or a word. Consultants get the idea of what I am trying to do and either confirm that my made-up sentence is correct, or else offer an appropriate correction" (2007:23). Because this is almost exactly what we do in eliciting data for theoretical purposes, we take it that the differences in the role of elicitation among theoretical fieldwork approaches, and even in non-theoretical-oriented fieldwork, is one of degree, not quality. The only difference that we can readily discern in methodology is that, unlike Dixon, we see no problem in asking for translations from the contact language. If we imagine asking for the translation of a sentence from the contact language into the target language, Dixon correctly observes that the construction in the contact language may or may not literally correspond to a similar construction in the target language. However, this is a general property of translation, independent of fieldwork. The same issue arises, for example, if one were to ask for the Spanish translation of "I like puppets" and then assume that the subject "I" in English must be expressed as a subject in Spanish. With theoretically oriented fieldwork, analytical problems of this kind can probably be avoided entirely if one simply does not assume that *translations* must correspond to isomorphic structures across languages.

One advantage of working in a community of users of the target language is that the linguist may be able to work with users of different dialects, ages, and genders, for example. For theoretically oriented fieldwork, this is important because it may yield critical information about the range and sociolinguistic determinants of variation in the phenomenon under investigation. Expressing a similar view (specifically for syntax, but of more general applicability), den Dikken et al. (2007:339) note that "for the generative syntactician, the more informants [*sic*] you have, the more data from individual grammars you have, which gives you the potential to find micro-variants you might otherwise not have found (this is not unlike the general desire to study as many 'languages' as possible)." Certainly, in generative syntax, there is a long tradition of theoretical studies that makes crucial use of dialectal variation to argue for particular analyses (Bayer 1984; Henry 1995; Munaro 1997;

Zanuttini 1997; Aboh 2004; Barbiers 2009, among others). The main point here though, is that it is that, by being embedded in the community, we were able to work with language users from a variety of social backgrounds. Thus, while we consider data collection from a single language user to be entirely legitimate (and we do this ourselves), while working in the Ikpana and Avatime communities we took it as imperative that we should seek out speakers from a variety of backgrounds to the extent we could. For descriptive/documentary purposes, this would yield a snapshot (although imperfect) of language variation in the community. Additionally, for our theoretical orientation, we hoped that this would result in a clearer idea of the factors that correlate with differences between individual grammars ("I-language[s]," Chomsky 1965, 1986).

3.2.1 Texts For this project, we also collected various genres of text, but the focus was on traditional stories. We also attempted, to the extent that we could, to find any previously written material that we could in either language. Given our focus on theoretical analysis, the role of text in theoretically oriented fieldwork is not the same as in other kinds of fieldwork. Unlike classical Boasian fieldwork (with its focus on text collection and the construction of a grammar and dictionary), the collection of negative data is necessary in theoretically oriented fieldwork, and ungrammatical data (with exceptions such as speech errors and stops and starts, and such) are not found in texts. This follows from the basic fact that native language users do not speak ungrammatically. This is a limit on the usefulness of texts. However, this does not mean that texts cannot be enormously useful in theoretically oriented fieldwork.

Concerning texts, Aissen (1992:9) observes that "while generative linguists may collect texts, publishing them has no place in the generative literature." Indeed, texts have not played a prominent role as data sources in the development of generative theoretical linguistics. However, fieldwork for theoretical purposes should include text collection, both audio and video if possible. For theoretically oriented fieldwork, texts are important because they are extremely rich sources of linguistic information. A text may reveal constructions that the linguist would never have thought to elicit explicitly. It is not surprising that there are limits to the usefulness of elicitation, just as with any other data source. In addition to "new" constructions, texts may also provide discourse contexts that license particular word orders, for example. Based on the text, the theoretical linguist could then, based on the text, provide a felicitous discourse context to check sentence acceptability through direct elicitation, as suggested by Dixon. In our (i.e., authors Kandybowicz and Torrence) work on Krachi, we were able to obtain a copy of the New Testament book of Mark (GILLBT 2011). From this, we found a number of complex verbs that would have been practically impossible to find through direct elicitation. We then used these verbs in direct elicitation with the Krachi consultants. Probing the syntactic properties of these complex verbs proved critical in our analysis of predicate clefts in Krachi (Kandybowicz & Torrence 2015, 2016). For the present project, we were given a copy of the New Testament book of Mark. This text was useful because of the many examples it has involving question particles. These examples were then checked with the native speaker consultants, and we were able to get a clearer picture of the (very) complex distribution of these particles. The text also proved useful because the language is high register. The consultants would note that certain passages, while grammatical, sounded very formal and not at all like ordinary speech. This naturally led to elicitation about how one would express the Bible passage in "regular" speech, which revealed new constructions of theoretical interest. As part of the current project, we have collected audio and video texts of traditional folktales. It was intended that the great complexity of textual material could contribute to both the descriptive/documentary aspects of the project and the theoretical ambitions.

4 Conclusions

In this chapter, we discussed key principles of data management for doing theoretical syntax, including aspects related to database design, data collection and entry, and multipurpose data curation. We recommend that a database be simple, easy to implement, easy to deploy, and versatile. Attending to these interrelated principles enables high functionality and ensures that best practices can be followed—even with a highly project-specific implementation. In terms of practical and mechanical aspects, keeping in mind the distinction between data presentation form and content is essential. At the content level, tagging linguistic examples with grammatical features during data entry allows for performing calls on data and returning subsets bearing specific features. This, we

feel, is an indispensable functionality, as it gives theoreticians the ability to interact with, probe, and explore data with theoretical issues and questions in mind. Methodologically, for data collection we advocate using an array of techniques, especially when a project requires more open-ended exploration of linguistic properties as a precursor to theoretical analysis. Finally, a major theme that we highlighted herein is that data collection for theoretical purposes (regardless of theoretical orientation) begins with language description, just as data collection does for non-theoretical purposes. Adopting a descriptive stance while doing theoretically oriented work has implications across the cycle of data collection and management and provides a solid foundation for robust theoretical inquiry.

Notes

1. On behalf of all the members of our project, we would like to express heartfelt gratitude to the speakers we have had the privilege of working with: Mary Akum, Kwame Amedzro, Vivian Anka, Edward Antwi, Raymond Dzakpo, Nelson Howusu, Ogordor, Gifty Amu, Peace Awunyama, Akos Mawulorm, Vincent Azafokpe, Wisdom Ekissi, Kwame Jones, Philomena Kumatse, Paul Kwawu, and Agbenya Wisdom. We also thank two anonymous reviewers and the volume editors for many helpful insights. This research was supported by a grant from the National Science Foundation (BCS EAGER DEL—1748590), which we gratefully acknowledge.

2. We recognize that *database* is a general term that encompasses a wide spectrum of structured data collections. For the purposes of this chapter, we use *database* primarily to refer to a structured file system residing on a local computer or cloud-based web application.

3. Additionally, we used the IPA as the basis for our transcription, and not, for example, an Akan-based romanization that is regionally prevalent and typically used for rendering Ghanaian languages orthographically.

4. From the Max Planck Institute for Psycholinguistics, the Language Archive, Nijmegen, the Netherlands (see Brugman & Russel 2004, among others).

5. Ultimately, then, the goal is to be sound in description *and* sound in theory. Here, we intend to highlight the importance of a good descriptive foundation for theoretical inquiry and analyses.

References

Aboh, Enoch. 2004. *The Morphosyntax of Complement–Head Sequences: Clause Structure and Word Order Patterns in Kwa*. New York: Oxford University Press.

Aissen, Judith L. 1992. Fieldwork and linguistic theory. In *International Encyclopedia of Linguistics*, vol. 2, ed. William Bright, 9–11. New York: Oxford University Press.

Ameka, Felix K. 2018. From comparative descriptive linguistic fieldwork to documentary linguistic fieldwork in Ghana. In *Reflections on Language Documentation 20 Years after Himmelmann 1998*, ed. B. McDonnell, A. L. Berez-Kroeker, and G. Holton, 224–239. Honolulu: University of Hawai'i Press.

Barbiers, Sjef. 2009. Locus and limits of syntactic variation. *Lingua* 119 (11): 1607–1623.

Bayer, Josef. 1984. COMP in Bavarian syntax. *Linguistic Review* 3 (3): 209–274.

Brugman, Hennie, and Albert Russel. 2004. Annotating multimedia/multi-modal resources with ELAN. In *Proceedings of LREC 2004, Fourth International Conference on Language Resources and Evaluation*, ed. M. T. Lino, M. F. Xavier, F. Ferreira, R. Costa, and R. Silva, 2065–2068. Paris: European Language Resources Association. http://www.lrec-conf.org/proceedings/lrec2004/pdf/480.pdf.

Chomsky, Noam. 1965. *Aspects of the Theory of Syntax*. Cambridge: MIT Press.

Chomsky, Noam. 1986. *Knowledge of Language: Its Nature, Origin, and Use*. New York: Praeger.

Defina, Rebecca. 2016. Events in language and thought: The case of serial verb constructions in Avatime. PhD dissertation, Radboud University.

den Dikken, Marcel, Judy B. Bernstein, Christina Tortora, and Raffaella Zanuttini. 2007. Data and grammar: Means and individuals. *Theoretical Linguistics* 33 (3): 335–352.

Dimitriadis, Alexis, and Simon Musgrave. 2009. Designing linguistic databases: A primer for linguists. In *The Use of Databases in Cross-Linguistic Studies*, ed. M. Everaert, S. Musgrave, and A. Dimitriadis, 13–75. Berlin: Mouton de Gruyter.

Dixon, R. M. W. 2007. Field linguistics: A minor manual. *Sprachtypologie und Universalienforschung* 60 (1): 12–31.

Dorvlo, Kofi. 2008. A grammar of Logba (Ikpana). PhD dissertation, Leiden University, Landelijke Onderzoekschool Taalwetenschap Dissertation Series. Utrecht, the Netherlands.

Ford, Kevin. 1971. Aspects of Avatime syntax. PhD dissertation, University of Ghana.

Ghana Institute of Linguistics, Literacy, and Bible Translation (GILLBT). 2011. *Maakı ɛ Kyıkyeı*. Tamale, Ghana: GILLBT.

Henry, Alison. 1995. *Belfast English and Standard English: Dialect Variation and Parameter Setting*. New York: Oxford University Press.

Kandybowicz, Jason, and Harold Torrence. 2013. Comparative Tano interrogative syntax: The view from Krachi and Bono. In *Selected Proceedings of the 43rd Annual Conference on African Linguistics*, ed. Olanike Ola Orie and Karen W. Sanders, 222–234. Somerville, MA: Cascadilla Press.

Kandybowicz, Jason, and Harold Torrence. 2015. Wh-question formation in Krachi. *Journal of African Languages and Linguistics* 36 (2): 253–286.

Kandybowicz, Jason, and Harold Torrence. 2016. Predicate focus in Krachi: 2 probes, 1 goal, 3 PFs. In *Proceedings of the 33rd West Coast Conference on Formal Linguistics*, ed. Kyeong-min Kim, Pocholo Umbal, Trevor Block, Queenie Chan, Tanie Cheng, Kelli Finney, Mara Katz, Sophie Nickel-Thompson, and Lisa Shortern, 227–236. Somerville, MA: Cascadilla Press.

Logan, David C. 2009. Known knowns, known unknowns, unknown unknowns and the propagation of scientific enquiry. *Journal of Experimental Botany* 60 (3): 712–714.

Munaro, Nicola. 1997. *Proprietà strutturali e distribuzionali dei sintagmi interrogativi in alcuni dialetti italiani settentrionali*. PhD dissertation, University of Padua.

Rice, Keren. 2001. Learning as one goes. In *Linguistic Fieldwork*, ed. Paul Newman and Martha Ratliff, 230–249. New York: Cambridge University Press.

Schuh, Russel G. 1995a. Aspects of Avatime phonology. *Studies in African Linguistics* 24 (1): 31–67.

Schuh, Russel G. 1995b. Avatime noun classes and concord. *Studies in African Linguistics* 24 (2): 123–149.

Thieberger, Nicholas, and Andrea L. Berez. 2011. Linguistic data management. In *The Oxford Handbook of Linguistic Fieldwork*, ed. N. Thieberger, 90–118. Oxford: Oxford University Press.

van Putten, Saskia. 2014. Information structure in Avatime. PhD dissertation, Max Planck Institute for Psycholinguistics.

Zanuttini, Raffaella. 1997. *Negation and Clause Structure: A Comparative Study of Romance Languages*. New York: Oxford University Press.

Matthew Wagers

1 Introduction: Reproducibility and data management in experimental syntax

This use case considers some data management workflows that can help in studies of experimental syntax and sentence processing. For concreteness, I will use the example of data generated by an acceptability judgment experiment—a familiar sort of workhorse study in *experimental syntax* (Bard, Robertson, & Sorace 1996; Cowart 1997; Schütze 1996; Sprouse 2007). Acceptability judgments play an important role in many domains of linguistics, such as psycholinguistics and the study of sentence processing (Dillon et al. 2018), semantics, pragmatics, as well as any other linguistic domains where classes of stimuli can be discriminated by "goodness" in some sense. In an acceptability judgment experiment, participants are presented with a list of experimentally controlled sentences and respond to their acceptability, naturalness, felicity, or some related quality. The dependent variable is most commonly a binary choice (yes/no, acceptable/unacceptable) or a response along a labeled or numeric scale. Sometimes experimenters record decision-related variables such as judgment time/response time and confidence.

Acceptability judgment experiments may seem, at first blush, to have simple designs and to generate relatively uncomplicated experimental data. And yet they pose some challenging data management questions, ones that recur across a number of types of language experiments. Here I will discuss the choices that have routinely faced myself and my collaborators, and the decisions we've made—or sometimes, the ones we would aspire to make in a better world. I divide my discussion into three phases: *design, execution,* and *analysis.* I'd particularly like to highlight the idea that designing an experiment is itself a data-generating activity. Berez-Kroeker et al. (2018) have urged a culture of reproducible research in linguistics, whose

goal is "scientific accountability" and whose means is transparency. Transparency is achieved by access not only to *source data* (observations of some linguistic behavior or function) but also to the *methods of data collection.* In a language experiment, those methods are themselves the consequences of myriad decisions about such practical issues as what lexical items to use, what presentation parameters to select, how to word the instructions, and so forth. While research reports do routinely provide that information, under a "Materials and Methods" section, it is often only in a fragmentary or ambiguous way. Having more comprehensive access to the process by which the experiment was constructed can often be just as important to evaluating a claim as being able to inspect the source data yourself. Therefore, part of managing and sharing the data of an experimental study is managing and sharing the documents and scripts that precede the actual execution of the study.

To make this point, we must consider how an acceptability experiment is designed. Suppose a researcher is interested in whether sentences with longer syntactic dependencies are less acceptable than sentences with shorter ones (they are, usually) and whether a discourse-linked *wh*-phrase dependent can counteract that length effect (it can, sometimes).[1] The researcher would design an experiment using sentences that systematically explore a logical space of dependency lengths and *wh*-phrase types. In (1) I've provided a set of sentences that span four points in that space. Observe that each token in this set exemplifies a single type of sentence, or *condition,* in the experiment: (a) long distance + bare *wh*-phrase; (b) long + D-linked *wh*-phrase; (c) short distance + bare; and (d) short + D-linked.

(1) a. Who does Nora suspect the judge must appoint?

  b. Which guardian does Nora suspect the judge must appoint?

c. Who suspects the judge must appoint someone?

d. Which guardian suspects the judge must appoint someone?

In a typical acceptability judgment experiment, a participant would see just one sentence token from (1a–d). At the same time, they would also need to see sentence tokens from all the possible conditions.[2] Therefore, there must be other groups of related sentence tokens, called *item sets* or just *items*. In a typical experiment, the number of item sets a researcher uses is a multiple of the number of conditions. For example, if there are four conditions, the researcher may create sixteen to forty item sets, depending on the sensitivity of the experiment and the expected effect size. Example (2) is another item set with the same four conditions as are in (1).

(2) a. Who was Tom worried that the patient couldn't recognize?

b. Which relatives was Tom worried that the patient couldn't recognize?

c. Who was worried that the patient couldn't recognize anyone?

d. Which relatives were worried that the patient couldn't recognize anyone?

While the items (1) and (2) instantiate the same abstract template, they necessarily vary in lots of particulars. The range and structure of that variation is determined by the researchers, who have to make decisions about what differences are allowable. They are guided by considering how differences in individual words or sentences could interact with the contrasts that the conditions are set up to measure, and whether they could help, or hurt, in obscuring from the participant the design of the experiment. For example, just comparing (1) versus (2), we can ask: is it OK that the embedded predicate is negated in (2) but not in (1)? Or that the embedding predicate is verbal in (1) but adjectival in (2)? Should the grammatical number of the *wh*-phrase be allowed to differ, as it does in (1) and (2), or should it be the same across all items?

Documenting not only the answers, but also the rationale, to such questions of item design is thus part of the data generated by the experiment. In the next sections, we consider ways to organize and preserve this data for the many other questions that arise regarding presentation of materials, selection of participants, plans of analysis, and other situations. Table 46.1 lists some of the types of data that will routinely be generated in an experimental syntax study and that will be expanded later in this chapter. Along its rows are the phases of data generation. Along its columns, I've divided the data types into *process* versus *product* data. By *product* I mean the data we need to evaluate a researcher's claims. And by *process* I refer to the information we need to exactly reproduce a researcher's study. This distinction is only heuristic, but it helps, I think, to give a sense of the complexity of even a "simple" acceptability judgment experiment.

The strongest possible view is that both the process and the product data from all phases of a study should be archived, disseminated, and cited. This view is not, I believe, deeply at odds with community standards that have emerged in psycholinguistics and experimental syntax in recent years. For some time now it has been standard to make at least the item sets public (some journals require it). And it has become increasingly common for reviewers to also request a version of the data themselves and perhaps the analysis scripts. Barriers to a more total archiving practice in this realm of experimental syntax are less social[3] and more practical—it takes

Table 46.1

Data-generating phases, and data types, in an experimental syntax study

Phase	Processes	Products
Design	Generation rubric/guidelines Lexical sets Norms, corpus queries Counterbalancing dimensions	Item sets Text Audio/video files Images
Execution	Scripts or other program data Presentation parameter settings	Experimental observations Demographic surveys Debriefings
Analysis	"Pipeline" scripts (cleaning, formatting, and shaping data) Scripts to explore, summarize, and model data	Descriptive and inferential statistics, both summative and item/participant specific Data charts or visualizations

time and forethought to collate and annotate the data. What privacy issues that exist are slight and can be solved straightforwardly by anonymizing the data sets. (Incidentally, these reasons make a basic acceptability judgment experiment a great arena for a beginning investigator to explore, play around with, or polish their familiarity with the resources and tools of data management.)

2 Data related to the design of a study

2.1 Item sets

Item sets consist of particular lexicalizations of abstract syntactic templates, as illustrated in (1) and (2). The ultimate product of the design phase of an experiment consists of a list of all item sets to be used. Practically this often exists in two forms: a *human-readable file*, which the experimenters edit themselves, and a *machine-ready file* formatted for the experiment presentation software. Preserving the human-readable file is arguably the most helpful for future researchers, who may wish to use different software, as a matter of preference, or in case the original software has become deprecated or otherwise difficult to deploy. The human-readable data should be stored in a delimited text file format[4] so that it can be directly transformed into the format required by the presentation and acquisition software; our lab uses CSV files, with commented header fields. While some currently used types of presentation software use input files with minimal formatting, such Linger (Rohde 2003), others can attain greater flexibility with more extensible, and complex, formats. Ibex (Drummond 2013) uses JSON, an open standard and language-independent file format that is organized by attribute-value pairs and that supports array data. Figure 46.1 illustrates both formats for two sentence tokens. The JSON data structure can be more richly annotated, and here that richness serves to preserve structured information about how response options were presented.

While item sets themselves are product data, there is a broad array of process data that describe the history of the item set. Most common are *norms*—data about the particular lexical items and grammatical constructions used in the study, values such as frequency or familiarity. For the tokens illustrated in figure 46.1, my collaborators and I collected information about the transitivity of the verb *praise*: how often that verb appears with and without a direct object in various corpora. While such norms could mainly serve to filter items during the design process, they might also be useful to future investigators who wish to conduct further analysis on the data. They should be preserved, therefore, to increase the transparency of the study. The norm itself, as a value, can be added in the materials file as an extra field. But it is also necessary to include descriptions of how the norms were collected—such data as corpus queries or even survey data. Indeed, norms are routinely derived from small experiments that precede the main one (see, e.g., Gahl, Roland, & Jurafsky 2004).

```
Itm,Cnd,Sentence
4,a,Who do you assume that the controversial politician would praise?
4,c,Which author do you assume that the controversial politician would praise?


[["Aa",4], DS, {s: "Who do you assume that the controversial politician would
praise?"},Question,{q: "Please indicate your confidence",as: ["Very
confident","Somewhat confident","Not confident"],randomOrder:
false,presentHorizontally: false}],
[["Ac",4], DS, {s: "Which author do you assume that the controversial
politician would praise?"},Question,{q: "Please indicate your confidence",as:
["Very confident","Somewhat confident","Not confident"],randomOrder:
false,presentHorizontally: false}]
```

Figure 46.1
Two sentence tokens in human-readable and machine-ready formats. In the upper panel, two sentence tokens from item set 4 are given. In the lower panel, the same tokens are embedded in the JSON array used by Ibex.

Another kind of process data in an acceptability judgment experiment comes from counterbalancing. *Counterbalancing* is the process by which features of the materials that are incidental or orthogonal to the design of the experiment are "balanced" against one another in a particular distribution—usually a uniform distribution, but they can also be matched to some relevant theoretical or empirical distribution (e.g., natural occurrence rate in a corpus). For example, item sets (1) and (2) include sentences with a proper name in matrix subject position, but the item set in figure 46.1 uses the local pronoun *you*. That such variation is allowed is the result of an experimenter decision to use several different subject types in the experiment, each in an equal number of item sets. For the study I've been describing, there were at least seven dimensions of counterbalancing and those dimensions were grounded in particular justifications, judgments, or prejudices–which another experimenter might not have made or held. Ideally, therefore, those justifications would be included and preserved as part of the data archive. Such data are no longer the discrete single values or expressions easily coded in a spreadsheet. They are qualitative: arguments, citations, and persuasive prose. As such, the format for preservation will be more open-ended. I prefer plain text README files structured in Markdown.

2.2 Presentation parameters

Presentation parameters are critical to the reproducibility of an experimental syntax study. For example, were sentences presented for free inspection for an unlimited amount of time on a screen? Or, were they presented in auto-paced text blocks? If they were auto-paced, how long did each chunk remain on screen? Or, were the items printed as a list in a survey? How were they randomized? How were the response options framed, and how long could the participant deliberate in making their selection?

An obvious way to preserve these data would be to archive the scripts or program files themselves used in presenting the stimuli and acquiring the data. This is advisable, but it may not be sufficient if the programs become impractical or impossible to use in the future, or simply because they may not be interpretable by everyone who would like to access the information. This concern is genuine, especially if proprietary software is used. A researcher may additionally want to consider a writing a simple "parameters" file, or folding this information redundantly into the README file.

In this context I'd like to mention pre-registration as another tool that can help to tie together the preservation of both intangible design process factors (like why certain counterbalancing procedures were adopted) and other more straightforward ones (like a list of presentation parameters). *Pre-registrations* are standardized and immutable design-and-analysis-plan documents that are registered and deposited on a server before an experiment is run. The stated reason for having such documents is to provide a public basis for distinguishing between confirmatory and exploratory analyses of a data set; as such, they can be quite bare-bones—just brief answers to a few questionnaire prompts. However, they can also be granular documents that encode more of the researchers' intentions about how the experiment will be executed. In this guise, I've found them to be useful "drafts" of the process data in an experiment (as long as any departures from the pre-registration are recorded later). Some tools, such as AsPredicted (https://aspredicted.org), are purposely very simple and user-friendly; others are more powerful or customizable, such as the facilities offered by the Open Science Framework (OSF).

3 Data collected from individual participants

3.1 Target-dependent measures

An acceptability judgment experiment generates trial-by-trial observations about the judgments participants make and, often, how long they take to make them. These direct observations are paired with the information about exact item presentation order. These observations are usually saved by the data acquisition software into files corresponding to individual participants, or to whole studies. As with presentation parameters, it is advisable to archive this "raw" data, in tandem with a reshaped version of it.

How those data are shaped depends on the analysis goals of the experiment. In a language experiment, a "long" tabular format is often the most conducive to an analysis sensitive to subject and item random effects: in this format, each row of a spreadsheet consists of a single observation or the data produced by one trial. The columns correspond both to metadata that index the trial—for example, participant, item, condition, ordinal position in the experiment/block—and to the target-dependent measures—for example, binomial judgment, or rating, judgment time, confidence. Additionally, some software may compute derived measures automatically, such as correctness of the response.

The reshaped version should be preserved in an open standard format. In most experimental syntax and behavioral psycholinguistics experiments, a plain text CSV file is the most suitable.

3.2 Observational and survey data

Information about the participants themselves are typically collected via a survey and includes such details as the participant's age and language background. Other kinds of questions are possible, though less routinely relevant in experimental syntax—information such as gender, handedness, use of corrective lenses or hearing aids, and so on. There is generally no cause to retain information that is directly personally identifiable, such as a name or ID number. These may serve a temporary administrative function, such as to grant course credit, or to pay someone on a web platform, but the information necessary to serve that function should be kept separate from the target data and destroyed as soon as feasible. Special care should be taken that any (de-identified) biographical details relevant to the analysis—and thus in need of being preserved—be stored separately from personally identifiable information.

A final kind of observational data collected in an experimental syntax study comes from the debriefing. The debriefing is the portion of the experiment in which the researcher discusses the goals or topics of the experiment and potentially reveals any misdirection (which is, frankly, uncommon in experimental syntax). In a structured debriefing, participants can be encouraged to discuss their perception of the experiment, what they believed it to get at, or whether/how they developed a response strategy. The researcher may seek targeted feedback about particular experimental items (e.g., sentences, constructions). In my own experience, the debriefing is most routinely viewed as a pro forma requirement, one ensuring that experimenters discharge their ethical obligations to the participant. But I think it would behoove us all to embrace it as another data-gathering opportunity (see, e.g., Blanck et al. 1992). The details that participants volunteer about their response strategies may be especially germane when extra-syntactic extra-grammatical factors are already theoretically implicated.[5] As such, preserving them can provide valuable clues to other investigators, particularly if future attempts at replication do not

succeed. When my collaborators and I have been careful enough to collect detailed debriefing notes, we simply record them in a narrative-style text file. However, this is not a particularly consistent standard, so there are open questions, and opportunities, about how to better manage this data, and how to incorporate it with the more quantitative observations that are easily encoded in the tabular format.

4 Data related to the analysis of a study

The only reliable way to precisely and unambiguously replicate the analysis that underwrites particular research conclusions is to have access to the exact scripts that the original researcher used. Published research reports provide some of the products of this analysis, such as tables of descriptive statistics, data charts, or regression tables. However, behind those "surface" representations of the data are many decisions the experimenter made about transforming the raw data—questions of scaling, of participant exclusions, of outlier policies, among others. These decisions are sometimes reported in an article, but there is still often vagueness or ambiguity about what exactly occurred. This is much like the issues discussed earlier with materials design: for maximum transparency, and total replicability, the process data must be preserved as well.

In experimental syntax and psycholinguistics, the R language/environment is the de facto standard for statistical analysis (R Core Team 2019). It is free software distributed under the GNU General Public License. At a minimum, therefore, researchers should archive the analysis scripts, commented amply and clearly, that link specific chunks of code to parts of the published text (figures, tables, results paragraphs). My collaborators and I use R Markdown (Allaire et al. 2018; Xie, Allaire, & Grolemund 2018), a literate programming tool that allows documentation in a plain text markup language to be "woven" together with R code chunks. Archiving these R Markdown files with the target data themselves is a nearly complete solution for replicability.

5 Data format and dissemination

For experimental syntax, and many behavioral psycholinguistic studies, file formats can usually be kept relatively simple. In all cases, open formats are preferred (see Mattern, chapter 5, this volume, and Han, chapter 6, this volume). For the lightly reshaped cumulative data files, as well as for the item files or norms, CSV-formatted text is usually sufficient. And for supporting process materials, such as explanations of norming decisions or debriefing records, plain text is still preferable for its light footprint and searchability. Here my collaborators and I construct Markdown-formatted README files.

In more recent research, when we have been especially conscientious of reproducibility, my collaborators and I have begun using the version-control system Git (https://git-scm.com; see Chacon & Straub 2014) during the creation and revision of materials, writing or customization of experiment presentation scripts, and in the analysis phase. Version control is not strictly necessary for reproducibility, but it helps the researcher to track changes and alternative versions, in other words, to create a record of the process of design and analysis itself. (And the Ibex software package currently can integrate directly with Git repositories, an attractive feature for managing the transition from design to execution).

For dissemination I have taken advantage of two resources. The first is an institutional tool, the California Digital Library (https://www.cdlib.org), owned and therefore supported by the University of California. The second is the OSF (https://osf.io). OSF is a powerful platform because it brings together pre-registration, data storage, and pre-print/post-print hosting. Static snapshots of a project can be registered and associated with a digital object identifier (DOI) as well. The power of the DOI in "setting down a marker" for tracking and identifying a contribution before publication has served as a real impetus to making myself and my collaborators more open to publicly sharing data, even during review (an option that may vary as a function of journal requirements and whether authors are willing to unmask themselves during review). These snapshot versions of the project can be archived redundantly in another repository as well. In the references, I have pointed the reader to two sample OSF repositories (Dillon, Wagers, & Andrews 2018; Wagers & Chung 2018). See Andreassen (chapter 7, this volume) for greater discussion of these matters.

6   Taking stock

In this use case, I have moved through three phases of an acceptability judgment study: design, execution, and analysis. In each phase, a considerable amount of

data is generated that relates not only to the proximal inputs and outputs of the experiment—that is, the items or the observations—but also to records of the researchers' decision making. Greater transparency is achieved if access is preserved to both classes of data, which are potentially more informative when interpreted jointly. It is probably impossible to keep an exhaustive and strictly veridical record of the process. But if researchers are tuned to the data-generation events that occur across the life cycle of an experiment—and create a data management plan of even modest scope (see Kung, chapter 8, this volume)—it should be possible to produce data archives and documentation in experimental syntax that more closely approach reproducibility.

Notes

1. Specifically, this design tests the effect of *discourse-linking* or *D-linking;* see Goodall (2015) for background. For purposes of illustration, I have simplified and adapted the design of an unpublished actual experiment conducted with my collaborator Brian Dillon (University of Massachusetts, Amherst), whose permission I gratefully acknowledge in describing it here. The item sets may be accessed here: https://github.com/mattwagers/killmonger.

2. Most studies in experimental syntax are *within subjects* and *within items*. What this means is that each participant (subject) is exposed to all conditions, ranging across items, and that each item set is associated with data from all conditions, ranging across subjects. There are definite advantages to a *within subjects, within items* design. For example, it can moderate strategic responding, and it can lead to improved statistical power. But it may not be appropriate for all questions or adaptable to all linguistic expressions.

3. Undoubtedly reticence does exist when it comes to sharing all details of the analysis, and I trace some of that to insecurity or uncertainty about doing a good job. Standards of statistical analysis have changed rapidly in just the past decade; a comparison of Baayen's (2004) influential critique and recent "state of the art" reviews by Vasishth and Nicenboim (2016) and Nicenboim and Vasishth (2016) give a sense of that. Linguists, and the academic units they belong to, are all grappling with how best to obtain or implement the training necessary to achieve stronger standards.

4. Here we focus on experiments that use text. Audiovisual presentation may be better suited to the experimental question at hand or to the population participating in a study. Nonetheless, an items file, as a record of the structure of the experiment, will still be a plain text file with fields: those fields could directly contain the sentences being tested or file names for the digital versions of that material.

5. As an example—here from "experimental semantics"—Anand et al. (2011) investigated the influence of monotonicity on the exclusive interpretation of plural nominals. In one of their experiments, some trials paired images to be verified with quantificational sentences whose domains were null; for example, a sentence such as "Each castle surrounded by a moat is gray" paired with a picture in which no castle was surrounded by moat. They discovered, only via debriefing, that there were some participants who accommodated these null quantificational domains, while others consistently rejected them as presupposition violations. When the data were split based on the debriefing report, presupposition-violation responders were found to be much more likely to interpret plurals as exclusive.

References

Allaire, J. J., Yihui Xie, Jonathan McPherson, Javier Luraschi, Kevin Ushey, Aron Atkins, Hadley Wickham, Joe Cheng, and Winston Chang. 2018. *RMarkdown: Dynamic Documents for R*. R package version 1.9. https://CRAN.R-project.org/package=rmarkdown.

Anand, Pranav, Caroline Andrews, Donka Farkas, and Matthew Wagers. 2011. The exclusive interpretation of plural nominals in quantificational environments. In *Proceedings of the 21st Semantics and Linguistic Theory Conference*, ed. Neil Ashton, Anton Chereches, and David Lutz, 176–196. Linguistic Society of America. https://doi.org/10.3765/salt.v21i0.2617.

Baayen, R. Harald. 2004. Statistics in psycholinguistics: A critique of some current gold standards. *Mental Lexicon Working Papers* 1 (1): 1–47.

Bard, Ellen Gurman, Dan Robertson, and Antonella Sorace. 1996. Magnitude estimation of linguistic acceptability. *Language* 72 (1): 32–68.

Berez-Kroeker, Andrea L., Lauren Gawne, Susan Smythe Kung, Barbara F. Kelly, Tyler Heston, Gary Holton, Peter Pulsifer, et al. 2018. Reproducible research in linguistics: A position statement on data citation and attribution in our field. *Linguistics* 56 (1): 1–18.

Blanck, Peter David, Alan S. Bellack, Ralph L. Rosnow, Mary Jane Rotheram-Borus, and Nina R. Schooler. 1992. Scientific rewards and conflicts of ethical choices in human subjects research. *American Psychologist* 47 (7): 959–965.

Chacon, Scott, and Ben Straub. 2014. *Pro Git*. Berkeley, CA: Apress.

Cowart, Wayne. 1997. *Experimental Syntax: Applying Objective Methods to Sentence Judgments*. Thousand Oaks, CA: Sage.

Dillon, Brian, Caroline Andrews, Caren M. Rotello, and Matthew Wagers. 2018. A new argument for co-active parses during language comprehension. *Journal of Experimental Psychology: Learning, Memory, and Cognition* 45 (7): 1271–1286. doi:10.1037/xlm0000649.

Dillon, Brian, Matthew Wagers, and Caroline Andrews. 2018. *A New Argument for Co-Active Parses during Language Comprehension*. OSF. August 25. doi:10.17605/OSF.IO/SD3HU.

Drummond, Alex. 2013. *Ibex*. Version 0.3.6. https://code.google.com/archive/p/webspr/. Accessed April 1, 2019.

Gahl, Susanne, Douglas Roland, and Daniel Jurafsky. 2004. Verb subcategorization frequencies: American English corpus data, methodological studies, and cross-corpus comparisons. *Behavior Research Methods, Instruments and Computers* 36 (3): 432–443.

Goodall, Grant. 2015. The D-linking effect on extraction from islands and non-islands. *Frontiers in Psychology* 5:1493. doi:10.3389/fpsyg.2014.01493.

Nicenboim, Bruno, and Shravan Vasishth. 2016. Statistical methods for linguistic research: Foundational ideas—Part II. *Language and Linguistics Compass* 10 (11): 591–613.

R Core Team. 2019. *R: A Language and Environment for Statistical Computing*. Vienna: R Foundation for Statistical Computing. https://www.R-project.org/.

Rohde, Doug. 2003. *Linger*. Version 2.88. Available from https://web.archive.org/web/20191220181934/http://tedlab.mit.edu/~dr/Linger/.

Schütze, Carson T. 1996. *The Empirical Base of Linguistics*. Chicago: University of Chicago Press.

Sprouse, Jon. 2007. A program for experimental syntax. PhD dissertation, University of Maryland.

Vasishth, Shravan, and Bruno Nicenboim. 2016. Statistical methods for linguistic research: Foundational ideas–Part I. *Language and Linguistics Compass* 10 (8): 349–369.

Wagers, Matthew, and Sandra Chung. 2018. *Chamorro Relative Clause Processing*. OSF. May 31. doi:10.17605/OSF.IO/B8ZWQ.

Xie, Yihui, J. J. Allaire, and Garrett Grolemund. 2018. *R Markdown: The Definitive Guide*. Boca Raton, FL: CRC Press.

47 Managing Web Experiments for Psycholinguistics: An Example from Experimental Semantics/Pragmatics

Judith Degen and Judith Tonhauser

1 Introduction

This chapter reports on the organization of an experimental semantics/pragmatics project that investigated the extent to which variability in a content's projectivity is predicted by that content's at-issueness (Tonhauser, Beaver, & Degen 2018). The project included four web-based experiments in which participants adjusted sliding scales to provide projectivity and at-issueness ratings for close to three hundred items. The workflow and best practices we report here are generalizable to any sufficiently similar web-based study, as well as to in-lab studies and dependent measures that differ substantially from the reported ones, for example, online measures such as eye movements. The workflow further easily accommodates computational project components including cognitive models and corpus analyses, though the current chapter does not include these components. The chapter also describes best practices within the first author's interActive Language Processing Lab at Stanford (ALPS) at the time of writing. We close with some reflections on what we would do differently if we were we to start this project again from scratch.

2 Research hypothesis: The less at-issue a content is, the more it projects

The project whose organization is described in this chapter was published in Tonhauser, Beaver, and Degen (2018) and addressed the following two questions, which we explain further in this section:

1. Is there variability in the extent to which the content associated with an expression projects?
2. If there is variability, is degree of projection predicted by a content's at-issueness?

For instance, the verb *regret* is typically taken to be a factive predicate. This means that even when embedded under so-called entailment-canceling operators such as polar questions as in (1) or negation as in (2), the content of its complement—here *that Mike visited Alcatraz*—is taken to project, in other words, the speaker of (1) and (2) is taken to be committed to Mike having visited Alcatraz.

(1) Does Felipe regret that Mike visited Alcatraz?
(2) Felipe doesn't regret that Mike visited Alcatraz.

This is in contrast to (3) and (4), where the speaker is not taken to be committed to the content of the complement of the non-factive predicate *think*.

(3) Does Felipe think that Mike visited Alcatraz?
(4) Felipe doesn't think that Mike visited Alcatraz.

While intuitions appear to be clear regarding the projection of some contents, there is evidence that content varies in its projectivity (Karttunen 1971; Smith & Hall 2011; Xue & Onea 2011). Our goal was to investigate this potential projection variability systematically and test the hypothesis, based on previous work (Abrusán 2011; Beaver et al. 2017; Simons et al. 2010), that projection of content is predicted by the extent to which that content is not-at-issue, in other words, the extent to which the content is taken to be background information.

To address research questions 1 and 2, we conducted four web-based experiments: in experiments 1a and 1b, we collected projection ratings and at-issueness ratings for the projective contents of two sets of expressions. In experiments 2a and 2b, we collected at-issueness ratings for the same contents as in experiments 1a and 1b using a different at-issueness diagnostic. We found that there is variability in the projectivity of content associated with different expressions, both across and within expressions, and that this variability is systematically predicted by at-issueness: the less at-issue a particular content is, the more it projects.

While this project investigated issues at the core of formal semantics/pragmatics, the project management structure described herein is general enough to extend to experimental studies in any area of linguistics.

3 Data management: The organizational framework

In this section we present the workflow and organization of the project and offer comments on the general workflow of any experimental project we conduct. To orient the reader to the management spirit of this and all other projects conducted within ALPS Lab: we aim for all experiments and analyses reported in papers to be directly reproducible (see also Berez-Kroeker, McDonnell, Collister, & Koller, chapter 1, this volume; Gawne & Styles, chapter 2, this volume; Mattern, chapter 5, this volume). This means that we aim to freely share as much of a project as possible and avoid using proprietary software whenever possible. For the current project, all experimental files, data files, and analysis files are freely available online. Moreover, all of the software used to generate the experiments, manage the connection between the experiment and the experiment hosting platform, and analyze the data, are open source.

3.1 The organizational framework for collaboration

While every project starts with an idea, its organization starts with the creation of a dedicated project directory that serves to store experimental materials, data, analysis scripts, and documentation. The collaborative nature of many experimental (and computational) projects requires a framework to manage file sharing and communication between collaborators. To this end, we use GitHub,[1] Git,[2] and Slack,[3] described in the following.

As a matter of course, we immediately turn a new project directory into a GitHub repository so all materials—experimental files, data files, and analysis files—are openly shared online. GitHub is a file hosting platform that includes version control and allows people to work together on projects. We recommend the use of GitHub as a way of sharing project materials openly regardless of the number of project collaborators. The repository that accompanies this chapter can be found at https://github.com/judith-tonhauser/how-projective.

In this project (and in general for ALPS Lab projects), we used Git to keep track of the project's progress. Git is a version control system. Originally it was developed for tracking changes in software development, but it has the broader application of tracking changes in any file, which makes it useful for tracking changes in research projects generally. We use Git to locally keep track of changes we make to files, and via integration with GitHub, these changes are also visible to our collaborators and anybody with internet access at large. We additionally used Slack, a collaboration tool that is essentially a messaging system and allows for (groups of) users to create channels dedicated to specialized topics or research projects and to exchange messages about the project. We used Slack's GitHub integration feature to link the GitHub repository to our dedicated project channel, which allows Slack to follow any changes made to the GitHub repository and to automatically post as messages in Slack the commit messages created by the researcher when a change is made to the repository. This allows collaborators on the project to be notified when a change is made to the repository and to see what the nature of the change is (provided the researcher making the change has written an informative commit message). Together, Git/GitHub/Slack comprise the collaboration framework used in this project and in all of ALPS Lab's projects. Note that for the reader interested in following the structure of the project, Slack is not necessary, though we recommend it as a tool for collaborative research projects to manage communication. Similarly, for readers who have not integrated Git/GitHub into their workflow, using these tools is not necessary for viewing or emulating the project structure, though we strongly recommend integrating these tools into your own workflow as they increase ease of collaboration, increase project transparency and shareability, and assuage fears of losing data or not being able to revert to a previous version of a file.

In the following, you can (a) view the project in the browser at https://github.com/judith-tonhauser/how-projective; (b) download the project repository from that same URL and follow along locally on your machine; or (c) if you have installed Git, clone the repository from the command line and follow along locally:

```
git clone https://github.com/judith-tonhauser/how-projective.git
```

3.2 Project repository structure

The project repository, like ALPS Lab repositories in general, has the following content:

1. A *README* markdown file in the root directory of the repository, which contains information about the repository's contents.

2. An *experiments* directory, which stores all the files required to run the experiments. This directory is further divided into sub-directories: one for each experiment, named appropriately, and a *_shared* directory that contains JavaScript libraries required for any of the experiments to run.

3. A *results* (or *analysis*) directory, which stores all the files required to analyze the collected data. This directory is further divided into sub-directories that mirror the structure of the *experiments* directory, that is, each experiment in *experiments* has its corresponding directory in *results*. It also contains files with helper functions required by all analysis scripts (in this case, aptly named *helpers.R*) as well as a separate directory for any analyses spanning multiple experiments.

4. A *paper* (or *writing*) directory, which contains the files that generate the final submitted version of the paper. When this is a more general *writing* directory, it may contain multiple writing projects, organized as separate sub-directories.

A project repository routinely contains the following additional directories:

5. A *data* directory, if the project is complex and the researchers want to keep all relevant data files in one place.

6. A *models* directory, if the project encompasses a computational cognitive modeling (separate from the statistical analysis) component, as is frequently the case in ALPS Lab.

7. A *talks* directory, where slides from talks given about the project are stored.

Some projects may also encompass corpus searches. Depending on the status of these searches—whether they constitute the main studies of the project or whether they are used to extract information to be used in the analysis of the main studies—they may either merit their own top-level directory (e.g., *corpus_analysis*) or be included in the *experiments* or *analysis* directories. Finally, each repository also contains a *.gitignore* file, which specifies files that Git should ignore (i.e., not track changes in, and not push to the online GitHub repository). We say more on this in section 4.

We consider this to be an optimal project repository structure and have not yet encountered a project that doesn't benefit from this organizational structure.

Cleanly separating the files used to generate the experiments from the analysis of the data collected in said experiments is useful because it naturally separates two aspects of the replicability pipeline: (a) the reproducibility of the *experimental methodology* (including the exact task, materials, trial structure, and instructions) and (b) the reproducibility of the *data analysis* (and thereby hopefully the replicability of the results). An external party interested in reproducing the analysis but not in re-running the experiment may therefore directly operate only on the *results* directory without having to wade through the *experiments* directory. In contrast, an external party interested only in seeing exactly what participants' task was can easily navigate to and open the .html file corresponding to the experiment of interest without having to search very hard.

In sections 4 and 5 we describe the contents of the *experiments* and the *results* directories and the associated workflows, which we consider the main components of the project.

4 Data collection (experiments directory)

Each experiment in the project was run via Amazon's Mechanical Turk,[4] a crowdsourcing platform that allows individuals to post so-called Human Intelligence Tasks (HITs, e.g., experiments) for workers to complete. Running web-based experiments via Mechanical Turk and similar online platforms such as Clickworker[5] and Prolific Academic[6] has many advantages over in-lab studies, including a larger and more diverse participant population than is typically available on university campuses, as well as very rapid completion times (Buhrmester, Kwang, & Gosling 2011; Mason & Suri 2012).[7] Moreover, many classic results from the cognitive psychology literature have been replicated via Mechanical Turk, suggesting that data from online participants are generally reliable (Buhrmester, Kwang, & Gosling 2011; Crump, McDonnell, & Gureckis 2013). Measures that increase data reliability and reduce dropout include paying participants reasonable rates,[8] running studies in the morning on weekdays, including attention checks, and including a progress bar so that participants have an estimate of the remaining length of the experiment.

In the following, we describe one way the workflow for a Mechanical Turk experiment can be managed; this workflow was used for the current project and is the standard workflow for any web-based experiment in ALPS Lab. Its advantages include a large degree of flexibility in the choice of experimental design and task, automated infrastructure for posting experiments and retrieving data, and a high degree of reproducibility. The initial learning curve is, we believe, very much justified by the payoff.

Each experiment was programmed as an external website using HTML[9]/ JavaScript[10]/CSS[11] and posted to Mechanical Turk. While generating experiments directly using HTML/JavaScript/CSS initially involves a learning curve for the user uninitiated in web programming, we recommend it over using the Mechanical Turk templates or out-of-the box services such as Qualtrics. The reason is that programming one's own experiments allows for more flexibility and control regarding tasks and experimental design than out-of-the-box services do. While the current experiment involved a simple continuous slider rating task in a two-block design with randomization of trials within blocks, we have used the same general infrastructure to run truth-value judgment studies, response time studies, self-paced reading studies, perception studies, free and forced production studies, studies involving drag-and-drop functionality, and many others. Example templates for such studies within the same framework used for this study are provided at https://github.com /thegricean/LINGUIST245B. We encourage interested readers to use the files we have provided as the basis for their own experiments. The internet abounds with good web-programming tutorials to aid in the process of modifying the experiments.

To run the experiments, we uploaded each experiment to J.T.'s university web space to be accessed through an external URL.[12] To link the experiment website to Mechanical Turk as a HIT we used the Submiterator tool (now superseded by Supersubmiterator[13]), which provides an intuitive wrapper around the Mechanical Turk command line tools.[14] The experiment ran until all the data were collected (no longer than a few hours for any of the experiments). Again using Submiterator, the data file was downloaded from Mechanical Turk, participant worker IDs[15] anonymized, and the data reformatted in such a way that the resulting .csv file contained one data point per row with all the relevant information for statistical analysis. This data file was then copied into the corresponding data sub-directory in the results directory, which concluded the data collection process.

4.1 Experiment files

We find it useful to label the directories corresponding to the individual experiments that were run in ascending order (e.g., by prefacing the directory names with 1_, 2_). This serves as a reminder of the chronological order in which the experiments were run. In this case, there is only a small number of experiments so this may seem less relevant, but for projects that require a lot of piloting, this ascending labeling is extremely useful. Alternatively, we have found it useful in other projects to include *pilots* and *main* sub-directories that contain the pilot experiments and main experiments to be reported, respectively.

Each of the sub-directories in the experiments has the same structure and consists of the following:

1. An *experiment.html* file that specifies the elements of the experiment and can be opened in a browser to view the experiment.[16]

2. A *js* directory that contains an *experiment.js* JavaScript file that determines the logical flow of the experiment.

3. A *css* directory that contains .css style files that determine stylistic elements of the experiment.

4.2 Interfacing with Mechanical Turk

Once the experiments were ready to be deployed, we used Submiterator, a python program originally written by Dan Lassiter and extended by Erin Bennett, to post the experiment to Mechanical Turk, subsequently retrieve the data, and anonymize participants' worker IDs. As noted, this tool has since been superseded by Supersubmiterator, written by Sebastian Schuster, which has the following convenient features; features 2 and 3 were not yet available with Submiterator:

1. One simple command each for (a) posting the experiment, (b) retrieving the results, and (c) reformatting the Mechanical Turk results file (which comes back as one participant's data per row) into a .csv file with one data point per row for easy analysis in R with already anonymized worker IDs.

2. No interaction with the no longer supported Mechanical Turk Command Line Tools is necessary. Simply specify a .config file with all relevant information about the HIT (see the Supersubmiterator documentation for more details, and see figure 47.1 for an example .config file for Experiment 1a).

3. Built-in batch support that makes sure that the total number of assignments (participants) is spread over

```
1   {
2   "liveHIT":"yes",
3   "title":"Language study",
4   "description":"You will rate short dialogs.",
5   "experimentURL":"https://web.stanford.edu/~jdegen/exp1a/",
6   "keywords":"language research fun cognitive science linguistics university",
7   "USonly?":"yes",
8   "minPercentPreviousHITsApproved":"95",
9   "frameheight":"650",
10  "reward":"1.00",
11  "numberofassignments":"250",
12  "assignmentduration":"1800",
13  "hitlifetime":"2592000",
14  "autoapprovaldelay":"60000"
15  }
```

Figure 47.1

Example .config file for posting experiments to Mechanical Turk with Supersubmiterator.

batches of no more than nine each. This is relevant because, at the time of writing, Amazon charges a 40% fee for HITs with more than nine assignments, but only 20% for HITs with up to nine assignments. The reformatting command automatically generates one merged data file for analysis.

Running Supersubmiterator requires only installing the tool, whereas Submiterator additionally required installing the no longer supported Mechanical Turk Command Line Tools (highly discouraged, given the lack of future support). Additionally, any requirements associated with Mechanical Turk studies generally— including having an Amazon Payments account and a Mechanical Turk requester account—are necessary.

Because using Supersubmiterator means that multiple HITs with nine participants are generated, the issue of how to prevent participants from taking the experiment multiple times is relevant: the Unique Turker[17] service provides that functionality. Setup notes are provided on the first author's LINGUIST 245B "Methods in Psycholinguistics" GitHub repository[18] along with setup notes for the rest of the web-based experiment pipeline used in ALPS Lab and useful Mechanical Turk–related tips.

For the current project, the steps involved in running each experiment were:[19]

1. Program experiment as external website and copy it to web space.

2. Create *mturk* directory inside the *experiments* directory where all Mechanical Turk–related files are stored and from where the Submiterator command will be called.

3. Create *experiment.config* file (see example in figure 47.1) in *mturk*.

4. Run from command line to post experiment to Mechanical Turk:

   `submiterator posthit experiment`

5. Run from command line to retrieve data from Mechanical Turk:

   `submiterator getresults experiment`

6. Run from command line to reformat data for worker ID anonymization and easy analysis in R:

   `submiterator reformat experiment`

7. Copy generated data file *experiment.csv* to its corresponding *data* directory in *results* directory.

Step 7 is necessary because the project repository's *.gitignore* file specifies that all files inside of directories called *mturk* are to be ignored. This is a safety measure to ensure that deanonymized participant data does not end up visible to the public on the internet. It does introduce one step of potential human error if the wrong file is copied or is copied to the wrong place. We consider this preferable to the potential for exposing deanonymized data. A record of participant worker IDs is thus only kept on the local machine of the researcher who ran the experiment.

5 Data analysis (results directory)

For this project, and in ALPS Lab generally, we used the open-source statistical software package R (R Core Team 2017) in conjunction with the integrated development environment RStudio (RStudio Team 2016) to analyze the data. Reasons why RStudio is highly recommended include the ease of managing multiple active analysis scripts and plots, workspace visualization, syntax highlighting and prediction, and seamless integration with R Markdown[20] and knitr.[21]

Useful packages we used in this project (1–4 we use routinely) include:

1. *lme4* (Bates, Maechler, & Dai 2009) for conducting mixed-effects analyses.

2. *brms* (Bürkner 2017) for conducting Bayesian mixed-effects analyses.

3. *tidyverse* (Wickham 2017) for tidy data wrangling in R.

4. *ggplot2* (Wickham 2016) for data visualization.

5. *lsmeans* (superseded by *emmeans*; Lenth 2016) for computing pairwise comparisons.

The directory structure of *results* roughly mirrors that of *experiments*, in that each experiment receives its own directory in *results*. Each experiment directory further contains sub-directories *data*, *graphs*, and *rscripts*, which cleanly separates data files (e.g., the *experiment.csv* file generated by Submiterator reformat), R analysis files,[22] and graphs generated in the analysis process.

The *rscripts* directory contains separate R scripts for pre-processing the raw data from Mechanical Turk (mostly for the purpose of performing data exclusions, *preprocessing.R*), creating useful visualizations that are saved to the *graphs* sub-directory (*graphs.R*), and analyzing the data using mixed-effects models (*analysis.R*). All scripts should contain enough comments to allow the reader to reproduce the analyses reported in the paper and to follow what was done at each step. This particular way of separating the scripts is not necessary, though it can be helpful to separate preprocessing, visualization, and analysis.

6   Concluding remarks

We believe the reported organizational framework for web-based studies is a useful one: it cleanly separates relevant components of the reproducibility pipeline and openly stores all components for others to reproduce and build off of, with the exception of Mechanical Turk–related files that contain confidential participant information.

6.1   Generalization to other types of studies

The organizational framework we reported in this chapter generalizes to any project using web-based experiments. Experience suggests that it also easily generalizes to projects that use computational cognitive modeling or corpus searches in addition to (or instead of) behavioral experiments.[23] It also generalizes to lab-based experiments and experiments conducted in the field—storing experimental scripts is a general property of the framework and is not specific to web-based or even more specifically Mechanical Turk experiments. An issue arises when proprietary software, such as E-Prime, is used. In this case, less material

can be shared. We consider this a reason to use open-source software whenever possible.

A different problem arises for studies that require storing very large data sets, as is often the case with eye-tracking or ERP studies. GitHub has limits on how much data can be stored within one repository: at the time of writing, no one file can be larger than one hundred megabytes; repositories have a hard limit of one hundred gigabytes; and it is recommended that repositories be kept under one gigabyte in size. While large file storage solutions are constantly being developed, an option for those wanting to remain within the GitHub universe is to use Git Large File Storage (Git-LFS).[24] Another option is to upload downsampled or otherwise compressed data files and keep the raw data files backed up locally.

6.2   What would we change?

In general, we consider this an instance of a well-organized and easily shareable project that we recommend as a model to others. However, given the rapid pace at which discussions regarding best practices in open and transparent science are progressing, we have already identified one key issue that we would handle differently, were we to start from scratch: preregistration. The Open Science Framework (OSF) makes it easy to preregister hypotheses, experimental design, and analyses (Foster & Deardorff 2017). The literature suggests that preregistration reduces the potential for many pitfalls in scientific practice, including avoiding problematic researcher degrees of freedom in fiddling with exclusion criteria, determining stopping criteria for running participants, and running exploratory analyses that are framed as planned analyses in the resulting papers (Roettger 2019; Simmons, Nelson, & Simonsohn 2011). Indeed, in current follow-ups to this project we have preregistered our hypotheses (see OSF preregistration at https://osf.io/hn8px/), and the policy we have implemented in ALPS Lab is that any hypothesis-driven experiment must be preregistered. This excludes experiments that only serve norming purposes or are acknowledged to be exploratory experiments that serve a subsequent hypothesis-generation purpose, though we have begun to preregister even those simply to note in an official place what the point of the experiment is. This is not to say that we see preregistration as the solution to all replicability problems, nor that there is anything wrong with conducting exploratory analyses—indeed, we are fans of fully

Table 47.1

Overview of tools used

Use	Tool	More information
Communication	Slack	https://slack.com
Version control	Git	https://git-scm.com
	GitHub	https://github.com
Experiment development	HTML/JavaScript/CSS	https://www.w3schools.com/html/default.asp
Mechanical Turk interface	Supersubmiterator	https://github.com/sebschu/Submiterator
Data analysis	R	https://www.r-project.org
	RStudio	https://rstudio.com
Preregistration	Open Science Framework	https://osf.io

exploring and becoming intimate with one's data sets. Preregistering hypotheses simply allows for a clear separation between confirmatory and exploratory analyses (for discussion, see Nicenboim et al. 2018; Roettger 2019).

A second thing we might do differently is to use R Markdown files instead of simple R files for running and documenting analyses. R Markdown allows for weaving together text written in the Markdown language with R source code to generate a coherent document that contains both the output of R code that is run (e.g., visualizations or tables of model coefficients) as well as prose descriptions of the analysis. The resulting document can be compiled into multiple output formats, including HTML and PDF. It can thus function as an internal lab notebook or even as a full paper.

6.3 Adopting the organizational framework

We are aware of the steep learning curve involved in adopting the workflow outlined in this chapter for those who have never used any of the described tools, but we believe it is worth it in the long run for all the reasons discussed in this chapter. The reader need not adopt all components of the framework at once. Table 47.1 provides an overview of the tools we discussed. You can add these tools to your own workflow incrementally, which is what we did over the years. Each addition yielded an improvement in transparency and organization of our projects, and we hope the same will be true for you.

Notes

1. https://github.com.

2. https://git-scm.com.

3. https://slack.com.

4. https://www.mturk.com.

5. https://www.clickworker.com.

6. https://www.prolific.co.

7. We routinely complete studies that require three hundred participants within a few hours of posting.

8. ALPS Lab typically aims to pay participants at a rate of $12–$14 per hour. At the time of writing, US federal minimum wage is $7.25 and California minimum wage is $12. Workers typically get paid about $3 per hour on Mechanical Turk, which has been documented as a serious and systematic case of labor exploitation (Pittman & Sheehan 2016).

9. https://www.w3schools.com/html/.

10. https://www.w3schools.com/js/.

11. https://www.w3schools.com/css/.

12. The experiments have since been taken off of J.T.'s Ohio State university web space. We provide a lasting example of Experiment 1a at https://web.stanford.edu/~jdegen/exp1a/experiment .html—this is the same experiment that is viewable by the reader by opening the file experiments/exp1a/experiment.html in a browser on your local machine if you have cloned the repository as described in section 3.

13. https://github.com/sebschu/Submiterator.

14. Other tools or entire frameworks that provide interfaces with Mechanical Turk and other crowdsourcing platforms and include some functionality for experiment development directly include psiTurk (http://psiturk.org/) and _magpie (https://magpie -ea.github.io/magpie-site/), among many others.

15. A Mechanical Turk worker ID is a unique identifier associated with a participant, linked to their e-mail address, and thus provides personal identifying information. These IDs must therefore never be posted online.

16. To view the HTML and JavaScript code, open any of the files in your favorite editor. We like Sublime Text (https://www

.sublimetext.com) and recommend avoiding built-in editors such as Notepad.

17. https://uniqueturker.myleott.com.

18. https://github.com/thegricean/LINGUIST245B.

19. The experiments for this project were run before the existence of Supersubmiterator, so these commands assume the use of Submiterator.

20. https://rmarkdown.rstudio.com.

21. https://yihui.name/knitr/.

22. Researchers may use different statistical software packages for data analysis. For example, for someone who uses python wanting to replicate our workflow, the only difference should be in the *rscripts* directory. We have no recommendations for researchers using SPSS or other drop-down menu software packages except to switch to R or python, for the simple reason that they offer more control, better shareability, automation and consequently increased reproducibility of analysis steps, comparatively easy identification of analysis errors, better online documentation, and, thanks to its large developer base, many more methods than are implemented in SPSS.

23. Examples of recent lab repositories with computational components: https://github.com/thegricean/RE_production.

24. https://git-lfs.github.com/.

References

Abrusán, M. 2011. Predicting the presuppositions of soft triggers. *Linguistics and Philosophy* 34 (6): 491–535. https://doi.org/10.1007/s10988-012-9108-y.

Bates, D., M. Maechler, and B. Dai. 2009. lme4: Linear mixed-effects models using S4 classes. R package version 0.999375–31.

Beaver, D. I., C. Roberts, M. Simons, and J. Tonhauser. 2017. Questions under discussion: Where information structure meets projective content. *Annual Review of Linguistics* 3: 265–284. https://doi.org/10.1146/annurev-linguistics-011516-033952.

Buhrmester, M., T. Kwang, and S. D. Gosling. 2011. Amazon's Mechanical Turk: A new source of inexpensive, yet high-quality, data? *Perspectives on Psychological Science* 6 (1): 3–5. https://doi.org/10.1177/1745691610393980.

Bürkner, P.-C. 2017. brms: An R package for Bayesian multilevel models using Stan. *Journal of Statistical Software* 80 (1): 1–28. https://doi.org/10.18637/jss.v080.i01.

Crump, M. J. C., J. V. McDonnell, and T. M. Gureckis. 2013. Evaluating Amazon's Mechanical Turk as a tool for experimental behavioral research. *PloS One* 8 (3): e57410. https://doi.org/10.1371/journal.pone.0057410.

Foster, E. D., and A. Deardorff. 2017. Open Science Framework (OSF). *Journal of the Medical Library Association* 105 (2): 203–206. https://doi.org/10.5195/JMLA.2017.88.

Karttunen, L. 1971. Implicative verbs. *Language* 47 (2): 340–358.

Lenth, R. V. 2016. Least-squares means: The R package lsmeans. *Journal of Statistical Software* 69 (1): 1–33. https://doi.org/10.18637/jss.v069.i01.

Mason, W., and S. Suri. 2012. Conducting behavioral research on Amazon's Mechanical Turk. *Behavior Research Methods* 44 (1): 1–23. https://doi.org/10.3758/s13428-011-0124-6.

Nicenboim, B., S. Vasishth, F. Engelmann, and K. Suckow. 2018. Exploratory and confirmatory analyses in sentence processing: A case study of number interference in German. *Cognitive Science* 42:1075–1100. https://doi.org/10.1111/cogs.12589.

Pittman, M., and K. Sheehan. 2016. Amazon's Mechanical Turk a digital sweatshop? Transparency and accountability in crowdsourced online research. *Journal of Media Ethics: Exploring Questions of Media Morality* 31 (4): 260–262. https://doi.org/10.1080/23736992.2016.1228811.

R Core Team. 2017. *R: A Language and Environment for Statistical Computing.* https://www.r-project.org.

Roettger, T. B. 2019. Researcher degrees of freedom in phonetic research. *Laboratory Phonology: Journal of the Association for Laboratory Phonology* 10 (1): 1. https://doi.org/10.5334/labphon.147.

RStudio Team. 2016. *RStudio: Integrated Development ENvironment for R.* https://rstudio.com.

Simmons, J. P., L. D. Nelson, and U. Simonsohn. 2011. False-positive psychology: Undisclosed flexibility in data collection and analysis allows presenting anything as significant. *Psychological Science* 22 (11) 1359–1366. https://doi.org/10.1177/0956797611417632.

Simons, M., J. Tonhauser, D. Beaver, and C. Roberts. 2010. What projects and why. *Semantics and Linguistic Theory* 20:309–327. https://journals.linguisticsociety.org/proceedings/index.php/SALT/article/viewFile/2584/2332.

Smith, E. A., and K. C. Hall. 2011. Projection diversity: Experimental evidence. In *Proceedings of the ESSLLI 2011 Workshop on Projective Meaning*, 156–170. https://citeseerx.ist.psu.edu/viewdoc/download?doi=10.1.1.646.290&rep=rep1&type=pdf.

Tonhauser, J., D. I. Beaver, and J. Degen. 2018. How projective is projective content? Gradience in projectivity and at-issueness. *Journal of Semantics* 35 (3): 495–542. https://doi.org/10.1093/jos/ffy007.

Wickham, H. 2016. *ggplot2: Elegant Graphics for Data Analysis.* New York: Springer-Verlag. https://ggplot2.tidyverse.org.

Wickham, H. 2017. *tidyverse: Easily Install and Load the "Tidyverse."* https://CRAN.R-project.org/package=tidyverse.

Xue, J., and E. Onea. 2011. Correlation between presupposition projection and at-issueness: An empirical study. In *Proceedings of the ESSLLI 2011 Workshop on Projective Meaning*, 171–184. https://citeseerx.ist.psu.edu/viewdoc/download?doi=10.1.1.646.290&rep=rep1&type=pdf.

48 Managing, Sharing, and Reusing fMRI Data in Computational Neurolinguistics

Hiroyuki Akama

1 Introduction

The word *corpus* derives from Latin, in which it has several meanings, including *body*, *element*, or *principal component*. For this reason, it is used to refer to various anatomical components, such as the fiber bundle connecting the hemispheres of the brain: the corpus callosum. However, the broader meaning of the term can be applied to language science; thus, the term corpus linguistics now encompasses a vast range of topics, including a new discipline that could be called *corpus neurolinguistics* or *computational neurolinguistics* (Hudson 1979; Murphy et al. 2010). This interdisciplinary field of language study integrates functional anatomy with document analysis. Specifically, several informatics techniques can be used to bridge the gap between neural and lexical data, namely correlation analysis, statistical hypothesis testing, multivariate pattern analysis in machine learning, Bayesian inference, and so on.

2 Neurolinguistics and functional magnetic resonance imaging

Neurolinguistics data are usually obtained through noninvasive measurement of brain response to language stimuli or tasks using electroencephalography, magnetoencephalography, transcranial magnetic stimulation, or MRI. In some neurocognitive linguistic experiments, volunteers are subjected to these techniques while performing covert or overt tasks involving sets of words or sentences. Data are normally averaged across participants to allow group-level analysis (hypothesis testing) and draw conclusions that can be generally accepted and established as fact.

However, many researchers also release information about the functional images of individual subjects. In this regard, because anatomical images are anonymized,

single-subject data could be reused. Moreover, such data may be more useful in computational neurolinguistics models because cross-subject analysis is less accurate when predicting the neural responses of individuals based on the features of other brains (Akama et al. 2014). They shape their neurolinguistics data sets parted into each subject's information although the anatomical structure of the brain is standardized with a same shared template instead of using a native space (original data leaving room for personal identification). For example, in functional MRI (fMRI), neural activation is recorded in terms of volume at the level of the pixel (*voxels*) corresponding to a particular language stimulus or task condition. To this end, three-dimensional (3D) images of each brain at various time points are used to compile 4D data. The original data from each subject are then subjected to motion correction and realignment of the 3D volumes; the anatomical and functional scans are then co-registered and adapted into standard brain templates (Montreal Neurological Institute [MNI] space or Talairach space). In some cases, they are smoothed to increase the signal-to-noise ratio (Friston et al. 1995). Therefore, the neurolinguistics data of each fMRI participant can be opened to the public to allow users to reconstruct their functional brain maps, provided that the following are available: (1) the general information of the experiment, including the timing and condition order of the stimuli, (2) the time series of signal intensity for all voxels, saved as a 4D array, (3) metadata related to the scan protocols, and (4) information about volume slicing or spatial resolution in the standardized brain.

3 Computational neurolinguistics as a new approach

In this regard, the fMRI data set derived from the computational neurolinguistic research led by Tom Mitchell is particularly noteworthy (Mitchell et al. 2008). This data set is packaged for each subject as a MATLAB file, with subject number *x* (MATLAB is a programming language developed by MathWorks). A typical file name takes the form "data-science-Px.mat." In these files, the variables are categorized according to the following three rubrics: (1) *info* (information about each presentation trial), (2) *data* (image intensity data values), and (3) *meta* (general information about the data set).[1] In Mitchell's study, nine subjects were placed in an fMRI scanner and asked to think about the properties of sixty concrete nouns. Using a text corpus in Web 1T 5-gram (Google Inc.), the subjects' neural activation patterns were regressed to determine the probability of co-occurrence between the nouns and various semantic features (twenty-five basic verbs). Using the open-source data set (http://www.cs.cmu.edu/afs/cs/project/theo-73/www/science2008/data.html), the paper's readers could replicate this predictive modeling, or at least depict, on a standard brain, the average fMRI responses of each subject to the stimulus nouns. In this respect, functional anatomy is instantiated through the mapping of structural and functional semantic processing information at the single-subject level. The cortical and sub-cortical space of individual brains can then be treated as a 3D "dictionary," whereby each word is allocated to a set of particular brain areas or even voxels that are sensitive to its meaning and implication. Such neurolinguistic data are useful for drawing regions or clusters of semantic memory on a brain atlas—at least in the case of concrete nouns. The activation patterns then take on properties of distributed representation, whereby the neural correlates of category-relevant knowledge are scattered and condensed across the brain.

Interestingly, the neural underpinnings of lexical representation can also be predicted for words that are not yet represented by fMRI data. The time for which any one subject can stay in an fMRI scanner is limited, as is the number of words that can be used as fMRI stimuli. Regions selectively involved in the semantic processing of words for which no neurolinguistic data are available will only be revealed by machine learning models if the arrangement of words in a semantic space is extracted as "external knowledge" from language corpora using the techniques of natural language processing. Presumably, the semantic similitude between words would be correlated with that of their corresponding neural response patterns. To prove this, intermediate meaningful words are selected as *semantic features* from language resources or even from word-association norms. They are then used to build a basis function, which is a distance matrix used to position new words in a semantic space. Using this function, the virtual activation signatures of the individual brain can be computed. This method can then be evaluated using leave-out cross-validation, and a *walking or a talking* dictionary can be constructed, whereby each single word is assigned to a particular voxel in the cortex. This method was used by Huth et al. (2016) to construct their semantic atlas. They were inspired by the computational neurolinguistics method of Mitchell et al. (2008). However, their technique was criticized by the cognitive linguist Laurence Barsalou, who used the denigrating term *semantic tiling* (Barsalou 2017). Specifically, in the fMRI experiment of Huth et al. (2016), the seven subjects in the scanner listened to a *Moth Radio Hour* program. Based on the co-occurrence between each word in the stories, as well as on 985 common words from a large corpus, a 3D functional brain map was drawn to locate the neurosemantic space representing each word and semantic category (series of words sharing a paradigm). For instance, at the voxel with the coordinate values [10, 69, 77] of their semantic map, the words *situation, suspected, victim, suspect, arrest,* and *evidence* were tagged together (the semantic maps of the Gallant Lab can be retrieved from this URL: http://gallantlab.org/huth2016). According to Barsalou, however, many things remain to be uncovered in terms of the algorithmic-level mechanisms of lexiconeural mapping. In particular, to gain a deeper understanding of how the brain understands the meaning of words, researchers must bridge the gap between the representation and processing mechanisms well established by Huth et al. (2016). In connectionist models that provide instances of lexiconeural mapping, an algorithmic "black box" remains between the computational level assigned to semantic and conceptual functions and the implementation level wherein we ought to argue the biological neural configuration. Such defects tend to be amplified in state-of-the-art engineering artifacts, in other words, convolutional neural networks in deep learning, which are, although inspired by biology, neither representative of neural architecture nor computations that occur within the brain.

4 Semantic and neural networks from language and fMRI databases

The neural correlates of the semantic memory of each word sometimes include many outland zones of the brain—this has previously been called *distributed representation* and likely occurs because words, as well as their contextual implications and extended meanings, are semantically processed via the *motor-perceptual* modality.[2] These neural components may also have implicit functional links that reflect conceptual free association and property generation of words as manifestations of external knowledge. This hodological structure can be represented as a spreading activation network of semantic memory, as illustrated in the famous Collins and Loftus (1975) model. It is for this reason that semantic networks sampled from associative concept dictionaries are useful for providing lexicosemantic distance matrices that can be used to train neurolinguistic predictive machine learning models. For example, the free association norms of Nelson et al. (1998) constitute one typical English-language associative concept dictionary, as do Roget's thesaurus (http://www.gutenberg.org/ebooks/10681) and the Edinburgh Associative Thesaurus of English (EAT) (https://github.com/dariusk/ea-thesaurus). These corpora list word-pair data from psychological experiments in which volunteers provided semantically related response words to given stimulus words. By chaining these pairs, in which the same word is allocated to a single node (vertex), semantic networks can be built in the form of lexical adjacency graphs, with the edges representing semantic relatedness. In fact, this technique can be applied to WordNet data, which has also been transformed into a type of semantic network. If you are inadept at writing programs using scripting languages such as MATLAB, Python, R, or Mathematica, you may resort to using the graphical user interface (GUI) service of WordNet::Similarity interface (http://wn-similarity.sourceforge.net),[3] where you can fill in the text fields of word 1 and word 2 and select various measures to derive a similarity value. Although this system is supported by huge lexicons, the word association norms are arranged in a compact and convenient fashion as a semantic network, allowing users to measure lexical-relatedness in terms of similarity in neural activation patterns. The starting point of this computation is an adjacency matrix, which is a mathematical expression of an adjacency graph; it is square in all cases, symmetrical in the direction of association, and binary when making the linkage weights uniform. It takes the value of 1 at the cell position (i, j) if there is a tie between the nodes i and j, otherwise its value is 0.

Various distance definitions for these graphs are widely known, such as the Jaccard and Simpson indices. However, Akama et al. (2015) successfully proposed an original index to replicate Mitchell et al.'s (2008) fMRI modeling using another external knowledge source (EAT) combined with a new technique for measuring relevance in a semantic space (the Markov inverse-F measure [MiF]), which takes advantage of geodesic information (random walk on the graph) and co-occurrence adjustment (degree balance and distribution). To compute the MiF between vertices x and y, the number of paths connecting them with I steps must be counted and normalized using the weighted harmonic mean of all i-step paths leaving them. Using this technique, Akama et al. (2015) measured the effectiveness of the MiF for predicting neural activity recorded during conceptual processing in the human brain. When applied to the fMRI data sets of Mitchell et al. (2008), the MiF of linguistic graph EAT word association information allows researchers to obtain, with utmost predictive accuracy, a scalar parameter that specifies the degree to which each voxel in the brain is activated by each word.

The other merit of such a graph-based approach is that researchers can overlay the semantic network onto the functional connectivity of the brain rather than atomizing the location of words in a semantic map with univalent correspondence. For example, by calculating the Pearson's correlation between (1) the activation values of the selected feature voxels for fMRI nouns and (2) the principal component scores computed from any distance matrix, with rows for fMRI nouns and columns for semantic features (intermediate important words), a bipartite graph can be computed between corpus and neural information. The product of the adjacency and transposed matrices of this graph forms a *neural context*, which can shed light on the functional relatedness of the featured voxels (cf. "Supporting Information" of Akama et al. (2015): https://journals.plos.org/plosone/article?id=10.1371/journal.pone.0125725#sec010). Importantly, other than the bipartite graph approach, several other techniques have been designed to mediate external linguistic knowledge and internal neural resources, such as Canonical Correlation Analysis (CCorA; see section 6).

The approaches we have introduced here do not embrace other attempts at neurosemantic modeling. Specifically, the choice of semantic features is not limited to language corpora and word association norms, which, although flexible and apt to reflect graph-form semantic memory structure, may not be immune to noise such as redundancy, misstatement, conceptual error, or idiosyncratic reaction of informants. We can also resort to any basic conceptual system, stable and universal, commonly shared by linguistic researchers such as ontological mapping or concept lists (List, Cysouw, & Forkel 2016). Starting from what Swadesh called basic vocabulary, there is a long research tradition of systematizing the exhaustive range of concepts in the lexicon, and leveraging tools based on this idea could be fruitful for predictive modeling in computational neurolinguistics. Further to that, it would be quite useful to categorize neurocognitive topics as top-level categories for hierarchically constructing external knowledge in the form of a dendrogram, arranging "neurally plausible semantic features" (Wang, Cherkassky, & Just 2017) within a middle layer, and determining external stimuli such as fMRI task words at the bottom. In that case, neurological researchers could let a small number of experts judge, in a binary fashion, the relevance of each semantic feature to each stimulus word (Wang, Cherkassky, & Just 2017), or adopt a large cohort of people who intuitively rate the degree of relevance, such as anonymous workers for the Amazon Mechanical Turk (Binder et al. 2016; Anderson et al. 2016). The matrices thus created could be served in a linear regression for predictive analysis as sets of topic vectors instead of using those representing co-occurrence probability or relaxed semantic similarity. The classification accuracy of machine learning based upon these neurologically determined ontological catalogs were significant even for sentence comprehension and at the level of cross-subject modeling.

5 Databases of neuroimaging meta-analysis

In this section, we introduce another type of neurolinguistics database as a corpus, because it plots clusters of voxels that are closely related to human-centered topic words. Some fMRI researchers have advanced an original methodology whereby more global and more abstract semantic maps of the brain can be made. In this regard, there is a vast literature that could be shaped by recycling many fMRI results, especially coordinates of peak activation pertaining to particular subject matters, as presented in the papers mentioned. This technique in fMRI meta-analysis consists of hypothesis testing across a large-scale set of shared data to extract significant areas relevant to given topics, key terms, and such.

Among the databases of maximal information of brain imaging, we highlight Neurosynth (http://neurosynth .org/), a platform for large-scale, automated synthesis of fMRI data that comprises 347,911 activations reported in 9,721 prior studies, providing interactive and downloadable statistical maps of 3,099 selected features of functional anatomy (Yarkoni et al. 2011; Poldrack & Gorgolewski 2014). For instance, if a user is interested in brain areas pertaining to semantics, they need only enter that term into the text field to display it in the browser and download it as files of the Neuroimaging Informatics Technology Initiative (NIfTI) format (https://nifti.nimh .nih.gov/). The maps elicit, after setting the threshold of the z-scores, the voxel-wise significant likelihood that the given term has been used in a study based on the presence of reported activation (association map) and the likelihood that a region has been reported as activated when a study uses that term (uniformity map). The original maps (NIfTI images), prior to the threshold setting by false discovery rate (FDR) as a method of statistical correction (multiple comparison), can be downloaded from GitHub (https://github.com/neurosynth/), wherein all the voxel-wise probability values are needed for computation. The relevant positional information of the voxel indicated by the cursor is displayed on the GUI of Neurosynth when the user presses the *What's here?* button to display the coordinates of that voxel. Studies reporting activation within six millimeters of the coordinates designated by the cursor are listed under first tab, with links to relevant journal papers; the second tab links to meta-analysis maps, providing a catalogue of terms that share similar paradigms at the same coordinates.[4]

However, to carry out fully-fledged meta-analyses, it is better to run the command line (No-GUI) programs of Neurosynth after installing a Python package with the same name and directly manipulate the voxel-wise values. If you are a user of MATLAB, these values can be extracted as a 3D array with its accompanying metadata using the built-in functions of *niftiread(filename)* and *niftiinfo(filename)*. For the topic word of *color*, for example, they can be executed using commands such as *data=niftiread('color_z.nii.gz'); info=niftiinfo('color_z.nii.gz').*[5] The alternative and more versatile way of treating NIfTI images has been used on the Statistical Parametric Mapping (SPM) software package (https://www.fil.ion.ucl.ac .uk/spm/), which is a free toolbox on MATLAB for analyzing brain imaging data (run *info=spm_vol('color_z.nii.gz'));* *data=spm_read_vols(info)* after launching SPM by running *spm fmri* in the command window of MATLAB). Information regarding voxels per brain region can be obtained from the data image of a regional *mask*, whereby a binary value of 1 is assigned to the voxels inside. Each mask is calculated from a brain atlas, whereby the voxels in the same region share the same numbering label. One of the most conventional brain atlases is the Automated Anatomical Labeling (AAL) template (aal.nii.gz), which is available in SPM through both the AAL toolbox (http://www.gin.cnrs .fr/en/tools/aal-aal2/; Tzourio-Mazoyer et al. 2002) and MRIcron (http://people.cas.sc.edu/rorden/mricron)—a GUI-based free software package for analyzing and visualizing MRI data. When applied to a functional image, brain masks enable users to extract quantitative information from a particular circumscribed region.

6 Connecting language and neuroscience databases

It is interesting to explore the multifaceted macroscopic relationship between fMRI meta-analysis of the brain and results from language corpora, which were originally impertinent to neuroscience. CCorA can be used to elucidate the relatedness of two multivariate sets of random variables that are related to both the corpus (in this case, keywords of neuroscience) and fMRI measured from the same subject. This technique is also used for a more complicated purpose in the context of fMRI, as in the case of the Poldrack et al. (2012), which aimed to identify the relationship between mental disorders using Neurosynth. Nonetheless, CCorA, which can be carried out using the MATLAB function of *canoncorr*, would allow us to extract copious information through cross-covariance of matrices built from two information sources, such as linguistic and neural ones, which are independently assigned to the same topic words of interest. However, before running the CCorA for both domains, users must prepare a matrix of keywords by brain region as an index for degree of relativity (abbreviated here as M1). To this end, they must compute the product of the image body (whole brain) and each

region-of-interest (ROI) mask based on AAL. The mean z-scores in each region can then be calculated. On the other hand, to measure the co-occurrence probability in a large-scale corpus, a distance or similarity matrix (abbreviated here as M2) should be produced between the same keywords and semantic features as a set of basic words or of intermediate words found along the shortest path connecting any two words within a semantic network built on a dictionary. Next, the M1 and M2 are used to find the vectors of principal component loading (abbreviated here as PCL_M1 and PCL_M2, respectively) with the rows of topic words, as well as the vectors of principal component scores (abbreviated here as PCS_ M1 and PCS_M2, respectively) with the rows of semantic features and brain regions. CCorA can be executed between the PCL vectors of M1 and M2, which outputs two *factor structure* matrices—FS_M1 and FS_M2— which isolate the PCL rows each by themselves, as well as the columns of shared variates called *canonical variables* (CVs). The CVs can thus be considered as dimensions representing the association between the two sets. This structure allows users to interpret the relationship between the two information sources based on the original variables that are highly correlated with the CVs. As a result, researchers should be able to understand, using CVs, how a group of topic words belonging to the same semantic category is mapped onto regions in close proximity and should therefore be considered as recruited to the functions implied by these words (figures 48.1a and 48.1b).[1]

7 Conclusion

In this chapter, we have simplified information for linguistics researchers wishing to address a major challenge in human brain mapping that pertains to semantics. Indeed, many thorny debates surround the deep mechanism at the algorithmic level (according to Barsalou), which may explain why a particular semantic unit is processed in particular voxels or brain regions. The embodiment cognition theory combines meaning-, understanding-, and modality-specific neural correlates of motion and perception. In addition, we can assume that a supramodal region may act as a memory space for implementing a genuine pattern difference in signs.

---

1. Color versions of Figures 48.1a, 48.1b, 48.2a, and 48.2b can be viewed at http://hdl.handle.net/10125/73279.

Several open questions remain to be answered, and these issues should be addressed head-on using computational neurolinguistics applied to both open text corpus databases and shared fMRI data sets, including the results of meta-analysis. It may be that humans carry a 3D dictionary in their brains. This could lend insight into the development of artificial intelligence that can perfectly simulate our language response behavior.

Notes

1. Note that the StarPlus fMRI data published by Marcel Just et al. at Carnegie Mellon University follows a similar format: http://www.cs.cmu.edu/afs/cs.cmu.edu/project/theo-81/www/.

2. It is worth noting here the importance of embodiment cognition theory, which posits a mechanism of semantic processing in the general context of body and mind, action and perception, movement and imagery (Pulvermüller 2005; Willems & Casasanto 2011).

3. This data set was used to measure lexical distances in the study of Fairhall and Caramazza (2013) and to delimit the neural spheres of supramodal semantic processing.

4. Another type of fMRI coordinate-based meta-analysis is founded on activation likelihood estimation (ALE), which consists of treating the coordinates of peak activation reported in previous studies as foci of a 3D Gaussian distribution, taking into account the range of data fluctuation (Turkeltaub et al. 2002; Laird et al. 2005). The free ALE software (GingerALE) is published through the BrainMap project (http://brainmap.org /ale/). The ALE map for the journal of *Brain and Language* is quite similar to the Neurosynth coordinate-based meta-analysis applied to the topic terms of *syntactic* and *semantic*. We will treat the latter in note 5.

5. To extract voxels that appear as significant in the results of an association test between *syntactic* and *semantic*, the following script should be run in the command window of MATLAB of a version later than R2017b after downloading from the Neurosynth website: 'syntactic_association-test_z_FDR_0.01.nii .gz' and 'semantic_association-test_z_FDR_0.01.nii.gz'.

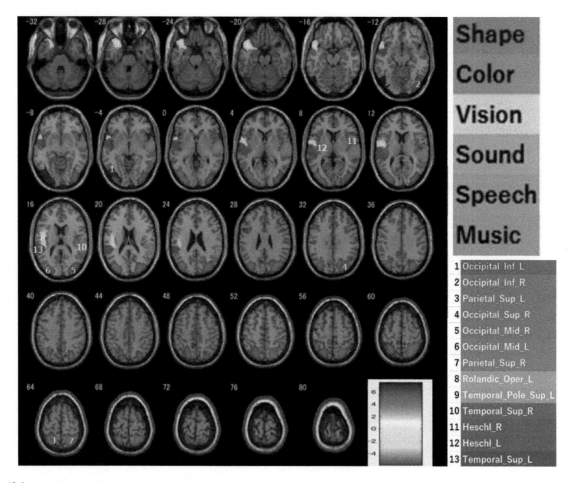

Figure 48.1

(a) Example of the CCorA with the keywords: *shape, color, vision, sound, speech,* and *vision.* This figure was built on the Neurosynth data set by retrieving the corresponding meta-analytical maps of these keywords as topics and measuring the contribution weights of the ROIs segmented in the AAL atlas.

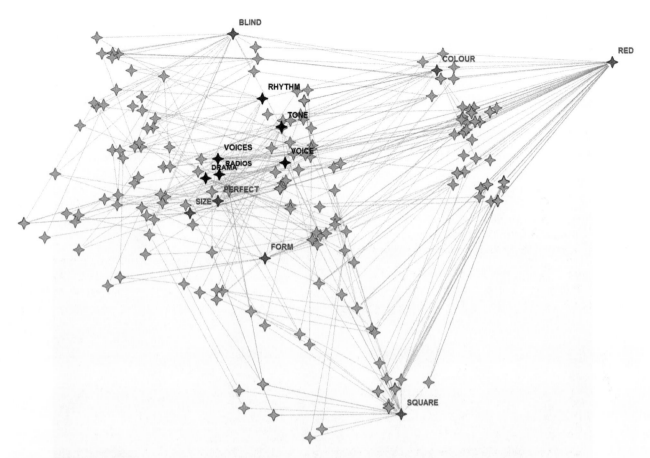

Figure 48.1 (continued)

(b) This graph was computed by applying MiF to the semantic network of the EAT involving these keywords as end nodes and all the mid words found between them. The relationships between the FS_M1 and FS_M2 were visualized with the rainbow color scale (except for the node colors of the right graph) by leaving and emphasizing the ROIs and the mid words of the highest (or the lowest) PCS_M1 and PCS_M2. This figure gives a glimpse of the interlocking cluster structure in the modality-specific (i.e., auditory and visual related) brain regions and linguistic paradigms.

```
data1=niftiread('syntactic_association-
test_z_FDR_0.01.nii.gz');
data2=niftiread('semantic_association-
test_z_FDR_0.01.nii.gz');
V=data1.*data2;
info=niftiinfo('syntactic_association-
test_z_FDR_0.01.nii.gz');
niftiwrite(V,
'shared_syntactic_semantic.nii',info);
```

If you happen to be a Python user, you can run this script in a notebook such as IPython (https://ipython.org/) after installing the Nipy package—a Python project for analysis of structural and functional neuroimaging data (http://nipy.org/packages/nipy/index.html).

```
import numpy as np
from nipy import load_image, save_image
from nipy.core.api import Image
import os
datalist=['syntactic', 'semantic']
```

```
fname='shared_syntactic_semantic.nii.gz'
loaded_images=[()]*len(datalist)
image_data=[()]*len(datalist)
all_image_data=[()]*len(datalist)
for i in range(len(datalist)):
loaded_images[i]= load_image(datalist[i]+
'_association-test_z_FDR_0.01.nii.gz')
image_data[i]=loaded_images[i].get_data()
if i==0:
all_image_data[i]=image_data[i]
else:
all_image_data[i]=all_image_data[i-1] *
image_data[i]
all_images=Image(all_image_data[i],loaded_image
s[i].coordmap)
save_image(all_images, fname)
os.system('gzip -cd '+ fname+'>'+''
+fname[:-3])
```

You will then be able to display the resulting image—"shared_syntactic_semantic.nii" or "shared_syntactic_semantic

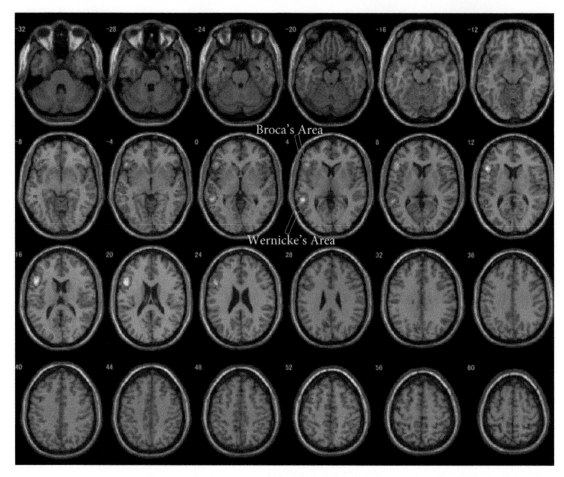

Figure 48.2
(a) Visualizing results of the computation explained in note 5 for extracting the shared clusters between the topics of *syntactic* and *semantic*.

.nii.gz"—using MRIcron by overlaying it onto the AAL template (aal.nii.gz) to derive information about the location of the voxels that are significantly in common. The two input images were originally similar, but we now understand more clearly that the shared voxels between the topics of *syntactic* and *semantic* extensively cover two classical brain regions: Broca's (left inferior frontal gyrus) and Wernicke's areas (posterior part of left superior temporal gyrus) (Libben 2017) (figure 48.2).

References

Akama, H., B. Murphy, M. M. Lei, and M. Poesio. 2014. Cross-participant modelling based on joint or disjoint feature selection: An fMRI conceptual decoding study. *Applied Informatics* 1:article 1. doi:10.1186/2196-0089-1-1.

Akama, H., M. Miyake, J. Jung, and B. Murphy. 2015. Using graph components derived from an associative concept dictionary to predict fMRI neural activation patterns that represent the meaning of nouns. *PLoS One* 10 (4): e0125725. doi:10.1371/journal.pone.0125725.

Anderson, A. J., J. R. Binder, L. Fernandino, C. J. Humphries, L. L. Conant, M. Aguilar, X. Wang, D. Doko, and R. D. S. Raizada. 2016. Predicting neural activity patterns associated with sentences using a neurobiologically motivated model of semantic representation. *Cerebral Cortex* 27 (9): 4379–4395. https://doi.org/10.1093/cercor/bhw240.

Barsalou, L W. 2017. What does semantic tiling of the cortex tell us about semantics? *Neuropsychologia* 105:18–38. doi:10.1016/j.neuropsychologia.2017.04.011.

Binder, J. R., L. L. Conant, C. J. Humphries, L. Fernandino, S. B. Simons, M. Aguilar, and R. H. Desai. 2016. Toward a brain-based componential semantic representation. *Cognitive Neuropsychology* 33 (3–4): 130–174. doi:10.1080/02643294.2016.1147426.

Collins, A. M., and E. F. Loftus. 1975. A spreading activation theory of semantic processing. *Psychological Review* 82 (6): 407–428.

Fairhall, S. L., and A. Caramazza. 2013. Brain regions that represent amodal conceptual knowledge. *Journal of Neuroscience* 33 (25): 10552–10558.

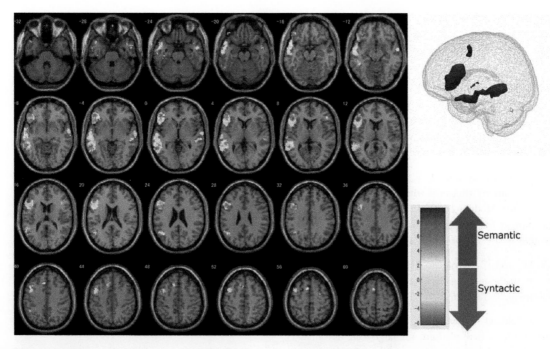

Figure 48.2 (continued)

(b) Voxel-wise fine-grained representation of the functional bias in semantic against syntactic factors within the language-related brain areas. We used the meta-analytical maps without z-score thresholding, which can be downloaded from the Neurosynth GitHub site. Because all the voxels contain non-zero z-scores, the voxel-wise division followed by a logarithmic transformation was overall possible between the arrays that constitute the statistical image bodies for these topic terms. Note that the top 5% voxels were selected as belonging to the intersection (seen as "linguistic") areas according to the magnitude of the Hadamard power of these arrays. The intriguing property of this bias map is that within the left inferior frontal gyrus there are small but distinct sub clusters pertaining to semantic and syntactic factors, respectively.

Friston, K. J., A. P. Holmes, K. J. Worsely, J.-P. Poline, C. D. Frith, and R. S. J. Frackowiak. 1995. Statistical parametric maps in functional imaging: A linear approach. *Human Brain Mapping* 2 (4): 189–210.

Hudson, P. 1979. What is computational neurolinguistics anyway? *Behavioral and Brain Sciences* 2 (3): 468–469. doi:10.1017/S0140525X00063809.

Huth, A. G., W. A. de Heer, T. L. Griffiths, F. E. Theunissen, and J. L. Gallant. 2016. Natural speech reveals the semantic maps that tile human cerebral cortex. *Nature* 532 (7600): 453–458.

Laird, A. R., P. M. Fox, C. J. Price, D. C. Glahn, A. M. Uecker, J. L. Lancaster, P. E. Turkeltaub, P. Kochunov, and P. T. Fox. 2005. ALE meta-analysis: Controlling the false discovery rate and performing statistical contrasts. *Human Brain Mapping* 25 (1): 155–164.

Libben, G. 2017. Brain and language. In *Contemporary Linguistics: An Introduction*, ed. W. O'Grady, J. Archibald, M. Aronoff, and J. Rees-Miller, 463–484. Boston: Bedford/St. Martin's.

List, J. M., M. Cysouw, and R. Forkel. 2016. Concepticon: A resource for the linking of concept lists. In *Proceedings of LREC 2016*, 2393–2940. http://www.lrec-conf.org/proceedings /lrec2016/summaries/127.html.

Mitchell, T. M., S. V. Shinkareva, A. Carlson, K. M. Chang, V. L. Malave, R. A. Mason, and M. A. Just. 2008. Predicting human brain activity associated with the meanings of nouns. *Science* 320 (5880): 1191–1195.

Murphy, B., K. K. Chang, and A. Korhonen. 2010. Proceedings of the NAACL HLT 2010 First Workshop on Computational Neurolinguistics. *Proceedings of the NAACL HLT 2010 First Workshop on Computational Neurolinguistics*, 70–78. https://www .aclweb.org/anthology/W10-0600/.

Nelson, D. L., C. L. McEvoy, and T. A. Schreiber. 1998. The University of South Florida word association, rhyme, and word fragment norms. http://w3.usf.edu/FreeAssociation/.

Poldrack, R. A., and K. J. Gorgolewski. 2014. Making big data open: Data sharing in neuroimaging. *Nature Neuroscience* 17 (11): 1510–1517.

Poldrack, R. A., J. A. Mumford, T. Schonberg, D. Kalar, B. Barman, and T. Yarkoni. 2012. Discovering relations between mind, brain, and mental disorders using topic mapping. *PLoS Computauional Biology* 8 (10): e1002707. doi:10.1371/journal.pcbi.1002707.

Pulvermüller, F. 2005. Brain mechanisms linking language and action. *Nature Reviews Neuroscience* 6:576–582. doi:10.1038/nrn 1706.

Turkeltaub, P. E., G. F. Eden, K. M. Jones, and T. A. Zeffiro. 2002. Meta-analysis of the functional neuroanatomy of single-word reading: Method and validation. *Neuroimage* 16 (3 Pt 1): 765–780.

Tzourio-Mazoyer, N., B. Landeau, D. Papathanassiou, F. Crivello, O. Etard, N. Delcroix, and M. Joliot. 2002. Automated anatomical labeling of activations in SPM using a macroscopic anatomical parcellation of the MNI MRI single-subject brain. *Neuroimage* 15 (1): 273–289.

Wang, J., V. L. Cherkassky, and M. A. Just. 2017. Predicting the brain activation pattern associated with the propositional content of a sentence: Modeling neural representations of events and states, human brain mapping. *Human Brain Mapping* 38 (10): 4865–4881.

Willems, R. M., and D. Casasanto. 2011. Flexibility in embodied language understanding. *Frontiers in Psychology* 2:116. doi:10.3389/fpsyg.2011.00116

Yarkoni, T., R. Poldrack, T. Nichols, D. Van Essen, and T. Wager. 2011. NeuroSynth: A new platform for large-scale automated synthesis of human functional neuroimaging data. *Frontiers in Neuroinformatics Conference Abstract: 4th INCF Congress of Neuroinformatics.* doi:10.3389/conf.fninf.2011.08.00058.

49 Managing Phonological Data in a Perception Experiment

Rory Turnbull

1 Introduction

In this chapter, I'll be walking through the data management workflow used in the study reported by Turnbull and Peperkamp (2017). This study investigated phonological priming in French. Simplifying somewhat, the experiments involved participants hearing a prime word followed by a target word; the task was to decide whether the target was a lexical word or a non-word (a *lexical decision* task). The experimental manipulation was the degree and type of phonological overlap between the prime and target. For example, the target word *bac* /bak/ "tray" could have as a prime any of *bac* /bak/ "tray," *sac* /sak/ "bag," *banque* /bɑ̃k/ "bank," *baffe* /baf/ "slap," or *mangue* /mɑ̃g/ "mango." If you're interested in the theoretical background and the implications of our results, I refer you to the original paper. For the rest of this chapter, I'll refer to the Turnbull and Peperkamp (2017) experiments as "TP17."

I've chosen the TP17 experiments for this data management use case as, methodologically speaking, they're rather mundane. They use standard methods for perception experiments in phonology, phonetics, and psycholinguistics, and it should be fairly straightforward to find correspondences between the data components of these experiments and many others.

I assume that you, the reader, have a basic familiarity with experimental methods in linguistics. Nevertheless, I've tried to avoid jargon and be clear and explicit in this chapter. If I've been successful, then this chapter should be easy to follow even if you're unfamiliar with these methods. (And if so, hello, welcome to the world of experimental linguistics!)

1.1 What is a phonological perception experiment?

For the purposes of this chapter, *phonological perception experiment* is intended as a big-tent term for an experiment with auditory linguistic stimuli and non-auditory responses, where the focus of investigation relates to the form of the stimuli, rather than their meaning. Crucially, the research question in these studies relates to the mechanisms of perception and related processes. This includes artificial language learning experiments (e.g., Finley 2011, 2012; Katz & Fricke 2018); speech intelligibility studies (e.g., Warren et al. 1995; Youngdahl et al. 2018); word comprehension eye-tracking tasks (e.g., Brouwer, Mitterer, & Huettig 2012; Ito & Speer 2008); phoneme monitoring tasks (e.g., Damian & Bowers 2010; Hay, Drager, & Gibson 2018); phoneme identification tasks (e.g., McGurk & MacDonald 1976; Mitterer 2006); prosody perception tasks (e.g., Cole, Mo, and Hasegawa-Johnson 2010; Turnbull et al. 2017); and many others. Many of the best practices associated with these kinds of experiments can be extended to similar but different tasks, such as (non-linguistic) psychophysical perception studies (e.g., Ladd et al. 2013), or perception studies with a production component (e.g., Wiener & Turnbull 2016).

Still, even this broad definition excludes perception research on signed languages, which use a visual rather than auditory modality. I suspect that many of the issues discussed in this chapter will map reasonably well to experiments on signed languages, such as Dye and Shih (2006), substituting "auditory" for "visual" as appropriate. Nevertheless, the rest of the discussion in this chapter will refer exclusively to studies of spoken language.[1] For data management of sign language data in various contexts, see Hou, Lepic, and Wilkinson (chapter 40, this volume), Hochgesang (chapter 30, this volume), Crasborn (chapter 39, this volume), and Palfreyman (chapter 21, this volume).

1.2 Chapter overview

In experimental linguistics, the term *data* is often used synonymously with the recorded responses from the experiment. "Let's look at the data" is usually an invitation to examine the experiment's results. However, the entire research process, from experiment conceptualization through to sharing the results involves a great deal of data and data generation. Each of these kinds of data have different management needs.

In this chapter, I discuss in turn the following topics: organizational principles; stimuli; participant information; experimental script(s); experiment responses; statistical analysis script(s); and storing, sharing, and citing. For each of these, I first describe the management we employed (or, in some cases, ought to have employed!) for TP17, followed by more general considerations for other projects.

A common thread running through these topics is that of documentation. "Always include a readme file" is a common (but often ignored!) edict in software engineering, and the same is true of each step of the experimental research process. Work as though another person is going to have to see and understand everything you've done. This other person might be a collaborator, a supervisor, or—the most likely case—your future self. Make your future life easier and document as much as you can.

Your documentation needs to be *interpretable*; the main points should be easily gleaned from the opening. Even if you have no plan to share any of these details, the documentation you write now will surely help your future self when you return to the project in a month's time, a year's time, or even a decade's time. The whole point of the documentation is to make life for your future self (and other future readers) easier.

Your documentation also needs to be *accessible*. Have you ever tried to open a WordPerfect file from 1995 on a modern computer? While not impossible, it's a lot more difficult than it has any right to be. Have you ever opened a file and all the formatting is messed up? The phonetic symbols and non-roman characters have been transformed into gibberish like *æ–‡å—åŒ–ā*? Your documentation ought to be as future-proof as possible. For that reason, I recommend using plain text files (.txt), with a Unicode standard encoding such as UTF-8 (eight-bit Unicode Transformation Format).

Writing this kind of documentation is a curious exercise, especially when your target audience is yourself. Surely you understand what this code is doing, how these stimuli are organized, why you chose this particular sampling frequency? My personal experience suggests that I greatly overestimate the intelligence of my future self.[2]

There's an adage coined by Douglas Hofstadter (1979) called *Hofstadter's Law*: "It always takes longer than you expect, even when you take into account Hofstadter's Law." I hope I do not do too much damage to this law by suggesting a related law: your documentation always needs more detail than you expect, even when you've taken this law into account.

With that framing in mind, let's begin.

2   Organizational principles

You're beginning a new project. You create a new folder on your computer and then add a few files to that folder. Maybe you have a couple of documents with notes, some saved e-mails with ideas from collaborators, and a couple of interesting papers that are relevant to the project. As the project develops, you add more and more files, until eventually it's a sprawling mess of files, with no organization, no clear hierarchy, and not even a way to know which files are the most up-to-date. Does this sound familiar? If so, you're not alone, and treatment is available.

Let's consider how we can improve on this method. First, clarity through structure. Each distinct form of data should have its own folder within the main project folder. Second, clarity through documentation. Each folder should have a readme file that explains the contents of the directory. The main project folder should have its own readme file for the entire project. Each of the kinds of data discussed in this chapter—stimuli, experimental script, experimental responses, statistical analysis—should have its own folder, and each folder its own readme. Depending on how you organize your files, you may also want a folder of relevant papers, a folder for conference presentations based on this data, a folder for the manuscript you're writing, and others.

Using this method is no guarantee that the project will be perfectly organized. Changes in ideas and plans often necessitates a change in structure. Keeping readme files up to date requires attention. But using this method will make it less likely that your project folder will descend into chaos. With these organizational principles outlined, let's turn to our discussion of different data types.

3   Stimuli

The *stimuli* are an important part of any experiment, and often something that are relatively easily shared with others. I distinguish three main kinds of stimulus data: the (master) stimulus list, the stimulus media, and the presentation lists. Finally, I end with a cautionary note about character encodings.

3.1 Stimulus list

Also called a "master" list or "grand" list, this is a list of all the stimuli used in the experiment. For TP17, developing this list took many hours of work, as we wanted French words of consonant-vowel-consonant, or CVC, shape with several phonological competitors to serve as primes. Ultimately this work involved carefully combing through the French lexical database Lexique (New et al. 2001) to find appropriate words. Lexique includes frequency counts and other psycholinguistically relevant information, which we incorporated into our list. We also had to create nonwords with plausible real word competitors and obey various constraints of counterbalancing.

Recall the design of this experiment—participants heard a prime word, followed by a target item that may or may not be a word and that has some particular phonological relationship to the prime. In designing the stimuli, we had multiple possible primes for each target. As can be seen in figure 49.1, the first target is *bac*, which could be preceded by any of *bac*, *sac*, *banque*, *baffe*, or *mangue* as primes. Note that some combinations were impossible and that there are empty cells: there are no onset competitors or vowel competitors for *bègue*.

While the organization in figure 49.1 is pleasant to look at and relatively easy to understand, it is not so helpful for generating lists of stimuli for presentation to participants. It also does not show the word metadata, such as frequency, morphological information, number of neighbors, and so on. Indeed, to get this metadata, we'd need at least an additional five columns per kind of metadata.

For this reason, our final stimulus list was a spreadsheet file with one row per stimulus word. An excerpt is shown in figure 49.2. This organization loosely follows the principles of "tidy data" (Wickham 2014).[3] Each set of target and prime words is given a unique identifier

(ID) number, enabling the data to be transformed into the structure shown in figure 49.1 without fuss. Because each word has its own row, there is only a need for a single column for each of our kinds of metadata. (The metadata here was lifted straight from Lexique.)

The conditions in the Condition column are prefixed with the letters *A* through *F*; rather than writing "Target," we've written "ATarget"; instead of "Homophone," we have "BHomophone"; and so on. This was solely so that when we sorted the spreadsheet by the Condition column, we'd see the conditions in the order we wanted them. This is helpful to us, the spreadsheet makers, but not helpful to spreadsheet readers without explanation. Indeed, more confusingly, the terms used in this spreadsheet are different from those we ended up using in figure 49.1 and in the final paper (where we used, e.g., "_VC" rather than "OnsetMP"). Consequently, the readme file in the stimulus folder explains the correspondences between the published paper and the spreadsheet.

Other details in the readme file include how to interpret the details from Lexique, such as the phonological transcriptions and the morphological parse.

3.2 Stimulus media

This category includes audio recordings and any other media used, such as video recordings or images. For TP17, the prime words and target words were recorded by separate talkers. We used a custom-made MATLAB[4] script to facilitate our recordings. This script presented the talkers with the stimulus words to be recorded and made a single Waveform Audio File (WAV) file of the microphone input during that particular word. The WAV file was automatically trimmed to remove silence around the edges. The recordings were then amplitude-normalized via a Praat[5] script (Boersma & Weenink 2020).

We didn't report most of this detail in our paper, as the particulars of *how* we segmented the recordings aren't really germane to the methods section and don't impede replicability. But for internal purposes, we documented each stage of this, including what scripts were

Target	CVCPrime	_VCPrime	C_Cprime	CV_Prime	UnrelatedPrime
la bague	une bague	une vague	un bogue	plus basse	qu'il mange
un bac	la bac	le sac	une banque	une baffe	la mangue
un bègue	le bègue			elle baigne	la soeur
plus belle	très belle	le gel	une balle	une benne	les pognes
je me baisse	il baisse	une caisse	un bus	la base	elles fouillent

Figure 49.1
Example sets of prime/target pairs from TP17.

WordTrial	Condition	ID	Phrase	Orth	Phon	Class	Gender	Number	Frequency	Morphology	Neighbours
Word	ATarget	1	un	bac	bak	NOM	m	s	9.03		32
Word	BHomophone	1	un	bac	bak	NOM	m	s	9.03		32
Word	COnsetMP	1	le	sac	sak	NOM	m	s	105.96		27
Word	DVowelMP	1	une	banque	b@k	NOM	f	s	70.79		10
Word	ECodaMP	1	une	baffe	baf	NOM	f	s	1.41		27
Word	FUnrelated	1	la	mangue	m@g	NOM	f	s	0.73		13
Word	ATarget	2	je	file	fil	VER			36.47	imp:pre:2s	27
Word	BHomophone	2	je	file	fil	VER			36.47	imp:pre:2s	27
Word	COnsetMP	2	de	Gilles	Zil	NOM	m	p	2.43		22
Word	DVowelMP	2	la	foule	ful	NOM	f	s	25.95		19
Word	ECodaMP	2									
Word	FUnrelated	2	pas	russe	Rys	ADJ		s	24.85		21
Nonword	ATarget	152	les	duche	dyS						
Nonword	ECodaMP	152	la	dune	dyn	NOM	f	s	1.55		13
Nonword	ATarget	153	un	veauf	vof						
Nonword	COnsetMP	153	tu	chauffes	Sof	VER			0.42	ind:pre:2s;	10
Nonword	ATarget	154	la	guèffe	gEf						
Nonword	COnsetMP	154	des	chefs	SEf	NOM		p	15.46		11

Figure 49.2
Extract from the grand stimulus list from TP17.

used, and we retained a copy of the raw recordings in a separate subfolder. The relevant scripts themselves were kept in their own subfolder, as they are a key part of the project and should not be separated from it.

TP17 was fairly ordinary terms of stimulus media, but for speech perception research involving artificially generated or manipulated stimuli, there are a lot of steps here to document. Your documentation here should essentially be a how-to guide so that someone with only limited technical expertise can reproduce your steps to arrive at functionally equivalent stimulus media.

3.3 Presentation lists

This category includes the actual lists involved in the experiment, if necessary. That is, these are the lists of stimuli, in order, that are presented to each participant. For within-subjects designs, these lists are essentially reordered (pseudorandomized) versions of the grand stimulus list. For between-subjects designs like those used in TP17, generation of these lists can involve a lot of careful counterbalancing. We ended up with four distinct lists, each a proper subset of the master list.

3.4 A note about character encodings

It would be remiss of me at this point to fail to mention character encodings (see also Han, chapter 6, this volume). Character encodings are the techniques used to represent symbolic data—for example, in Morse code, the letter *A* is encoded as "dot dash," while in ASCII,[6]

A is represented as the number "65." The Lexique database downloadables are encoded in ISO 8859-1, a character encoding designed for western Europe. If the files are read as if they're UTF-8 (a common modern Unicode standard and the default encoding for many operating systems), several accented characters will display incorrectly. Therefore, at an early stage in constructing the stimulus lists, we converted the Lexique database to UTF-8 to avoid other problems. However, care should be taken to ensure that the experimental presentation software is capable of correctly displaying the encoding you're using. Indeed, some older software does not work well with Unicode. Encoding problems are frustrating, so plan ahead to save a headache, especially if you're working with non-Latin orthographies.

4 Participant information

Experiments have participants, and we need to collect information on those participants. This information comes in two kinds: legally required information and documentation, and research-relevant information and documentation. The first kind satisfies the legal (and ideally ethical) obligations we have to our participants, while the second kind of information is driven by some research-related motivations.

I'm deliberately excluding from this category any *behavioral responses*, that is, the results of the main task of the experiment; instead, this category is usually information *about* the participants and could perhaps be termed "participant metadata."

4.1 Legal paperwork

The details here will differ depending on your jurisdiction, but this will likely involve, at a minimum, documentation of informed consent. Other aspects may include debriefing forms, compensation receipts, evidence of prior ethical approval from a board (e.g., an institutional review board in the United States), and so on. These documents are, in some sense, the most important pieces of data for your entire project, as there can be stiff administrative and legal consequences if things are out of order. For TP17, we collected paper consent forms with signatures, along with documentation of receipt of compensation.

4.2 Research paperwork

These are data relating to participants that is not legally required, nor is it part of the experiment proper, but still constitutes useful information. I've called this "paperwork" as it's often collected in the form of a paper questionnaire, but many researchers choose to collect this via computer.

For TP17, the research paperwork consisted of a questionnaire about the participant's language background. The responses to these questionnaires were then collated into a digital spreadsheet. Note that individual participants were identified in the research paperwork solely by a unique ID number. No names were used here, thus helping with anonymity requirements. This ID was also used to link participant metadata to participant responses in the statistical analysis.

Other elements of research paperwork include a list of all participants (facilitating the application of exclusion criteria), scheduling information, and all logistical details related to participants actually participating.

5 Experimental script

By *script* I mean the computer file(s) that will present the experimental stimuli and record responses. In TP17, the we used the PsychoPy experimental presentation software (Peirce et al. 2019), and our script is therefore constituted of the PsychoPy code file, the presentation list comma-separated values, or CSV, files it reads, and the folders of WAV files it accesses to present the stimuli.

There are many options in the world of experimental presentation software, each with distinct implications

for data management. One advantage of PsychoPy is that it's open source, so anyone can use it and see the details of the script without needing to install expensive software. Had we used a closed-source, proprietary system (such as, e.g., E-Prime[7] or SuperLab[8]), it would be harder for researchers in subsequent decades to examine exactly what the script did, especially if those companies do not exist any longer. While this might sound far-fetched, this scenario can and has happened. SensoMotoric Instruments (SMI), a prominent maker of eye-tracking hardware, was acquired by Apple in 2017. Apparently, the corporate leadership at Apple wanted a new direction, and as of this writing (early 2019), SMI no longer makes new trackers or repairs old ones. For existing users of SMI products, their customer support is still active, but it's not clear whether it always will be. If, ten years from now, you are trying to examine a script written with SMI's software, how are you going to figure it out?

This problem is not unique to proprietary systems (although I contend it's more likely to happen with proprietary than with open systems), and consequently the best way to future-proof your experiment is to write extensive documentation in plain text. This documentation should explain exactly what the script presents to the participants, in as much detail as possible. While writing this sounds like a chore, you're going to write (a version of) this *anyway* in the methods section of your paper.

A crucial nuance to consider when writing documentation is that the script is a set of instructions for the computer in what to do, often at a relatively low level. The documentation, on the other hand, primarily describes the participant experience. The script may direct the computer to load a sound file into the memory buffer in preparation for the next trial, so that the auditory stimulus onset is synchronous with a visual stimulus onset; the documentation would state that the stimulus onsets were simultaneous. That's not to say that the documentation *shouldn't* contain technical details—it definitely should, when appropriate!—but that the primary goal of the documentation is to allow another human researcher to understand and reproduce the experiment.

In other words, the documentation is not simply a recapitulation of the script in human-readable format. It is a high-level description of what is presented to the participant and how the responses are recorded. This high-level description can also help with cross-platform issues when trying to (re)implement the experiment on a different computer with a different operating system. For example, the TP17 PsychoPy script was developed and tested on a machine running Debian configured to British English language settings, but the experiment was conducted on machines running Windows 7 with French language settings and a slightly different set of input hardware. Thanks to the explicit documentation, there were no issues in getting the script to work on the different machines.

6   Responses from the experiment

Finally, we get to the "real" data. Depending on your experimental presentation software, this will vary in format—for example, SuperLab and PsychoPy output text files by default, while E-Prime uses its own proprietary E-DataAid format (which can be converted to text files via E-Prime software tools).

Data files are nearly always unintelligible without documentation. The data files from TP17 have thirty-seven columns of data each, many of them with some variation of "resp" in the name. These include the following: key_resp_leftorright.keys, key_resp_leftorright.rt, key_resp_begin.keys, key_resp_begin.rt, key_resp_lexdec.keys, key_resp_lexdec.rt, key_resp_end_of_training.keys, key_resp_end_of_training.rt, key_resp_memory_test.keys, key_resp_memory_test.corr, key_resp_memory_test.rt, key_resp_memory_end.keys, and key_resp_memory_end.rt. Which one is the response to the experimental task? The first part of each column name, namely "key_resp," tells us that these columns record information about some kind of key response. The middle part of the name, for example, "lexdec" or "end_of_training," refers to the kind of trial this response was for. The column names ending in ".rt" list reaction times (i.e., the time elapsed between the presentation of the trial and the participant pressing a button), and the ones ending ".keys" show which key was pressed in response. The responses to the lexical decision task are therefore contained in key_resp_lexdec.keys, and the reaction times for these responses are in key_resp_lexdec.rt. Some other columns are less important, for example, the column key_resp_leftorright.rt tells us how quickly the participant answered the question about whether they were right-handed or left-handed.

From the perspective of the person who coded the experiment, the meaning of these column titles is relatively clear, but this system is rather opaque for anyone else. Here, again, having plain text documentation to accompany the data is key. This documentation should explain what each column represents—or at the very least, which columns can be ignored—and how to read the contents of each column.

7   Statistical analysis scripts

The first step in data analysis is data preparation. For TP17, we had a data preparation R[9] script that read each of the data files into a data frame, removed unnecessary columns (such as frame rate information) and rows (such as practice trials), calculated response accuracy, merged in the stimuli metadata (such as word frequency) and participant metadata, resulting in a data frame that was ready to be used as input to a statistical model.

The beginning of the R script contains a description of what the script does. This information carries a degree of redundancy with the script's description in this folder's readme file, although the R script description is more detailed and uses more technical language. It also states that the script is not intended to be run on its own, but instead it is called directly by the main analysis script. As before, documentation is key here.

For your own project, you need documentation. Even if you don't write a data preparation script—even if you just copy and paste each individual data file into one big Excel file (please don't do this)—write a plain text document describing what you did in more detail than you think necessary.

The other script we had for TP17 was our main analysis script. This is the one that the user actually runs to implement our analysis. The code is (somewhat) commented, explaining what the script does at both a high level (e.g., "compare the unrelated primes to the related primes") and a low level (e.g., "this function automatically re-codes factor contrasts into Helmert coding after using droplevels()").

Finally, there is a plain text readme file in this directory. This document describes each of the files in the directory, and what files to run in what order to carry out the analyses reported in the paper.

8   Storing, sharing, and citing

For TP17, due to data privacy restrictions, we are not able to share the raw data (i.e., the log files output by the PsychoPy script) publicly. Nevertheless, here are a few considerations relating to the storage, sharing, and citation of data.

Storing data during a project is an issue everyone has to deal with. It's not uncommon for projects to have multiple collaborators, each of whom requires access to some portion of the data. A good way to achieve this while minimizing conflicting copies of data is for each collaborator to have a local copy of the data that is synchronized to a "master" copy somewhere. There are several commercial solutions such as Dropbox,[10] Google Drive,[11] Bitbucket,[12] and GitHub[13] that allow for easy cloud-based synchronization and, depending on the service, some degree of version control.[14] The cloud is just someone else's computer and is therefore sensitive to data security vulnerabilities. It's also possible to avoid using "the cloud" (thereby sidestepping possible data security vulnerabilities) via the combined use of distributed (non-cloud-based) syncing tools such as Resilio Sync and version control software such as Git or Apache Subversion, or SVN.[15]

Once the data are ready to share with the public, the question of hosting arises. Two prominent nonprofit repositories for hosting experimental data include the Tromsø Repository of Language and Linguistics (TROLLing)[16] and the Open Science Foundation (OSF).[17] Both TROLLing and OSF are able to assign a DOI (digital object identifier) to any repository, making the citation of these repositories straightforward. For more detailed discussion of these issues, see Andreassen (chapter 7, this volume) and Buszard-Welcher (chapter 10, this volume).

9 Conclusion

From this overview, an overall structure for data management emerges. Each distinct form of data should have its own directory, and each directory has an accompanying readme file explaining the contents of the directory. The readme file should also make clear the data processing workflow required—for example, describing the use of the relevant Praat script, data preparation code, or experimental procedures. Without these aids, the value of the data is significantly diminished. While in common parlance, *data* simply refers to the results of the experiment (the output of the experimental script), best practices in data management for a phonological perception

experiment require the recognition that every step in the research process involves data.

Notes

1. This choice is a pragmatic one, not an ideological one. Like many linguists, my education in the linguistics of signed languages was extremely sparse, and I don't have the expertise to give the issues the discussion they deserve. I'm working to remedy this gap in my knowledge so that the next generation of linguists will have a better understanding of the world's languages in all modalities.

2. Perhaps that of my present self too, if we're being quite honest.

3. Wickham's definition of *tidy data* is essentially equivalent to third normal form in relational database management.

4. MATLAB: https://www.mathworks.com/products/matlab.html.

5. Praat: http://www.fon.hum.uva.nl/praat/.\.

6. *ASCII,* the American Standard Code for Information Exchange, is an influential (and relatively limited) character encoding developed in the 1960s. It is still widely used today and forms the basis for many Unicode encodings.

7. E-Prime: https://pstnet.com/products/e-prime/.

8. SuperLab: https://www.cedrus.com/superlab/.

9. R: https://www.r-project.org/.

10. Dropbox: https://dropbox.com.

11. Google Drive: https://www.google.com/drive.

12. Bitbucket: https://bitbucket.org.

13. GitHub: https://github.com.

14. Services that are primarily marketed for software engineering projects (such as GitHub and Bitbucket) usually have version control as a fundamental part of the system, while services such as Google Drive or Dropbox may have only rudimentary built-in version control. Note, however, that one can easily make a local Git repository and synchronize it with a Dropbox folder, thus combining the version control capabilities of Git with the ease of use of Dropbox.

15. Nothing is immune from security vulnerabilities, including distributed synchronization systems. However, it could be argued that a large system such as Google Drive is a more likely target for an organized hack attempt than a distributed synchronized system of a group of academics. Perrin (2007) termed this feature "accidental security through obscurity."

16. TROLLing: https://dataverse.no/dataverse/trolling.

17. OSF: https://osf.io.

References

Boersma, Paul, and David Weenink. 2020. Praat: Doing phonetics by computer [computer program]. Version 6.1.36. http://www.praat.org/.

Brouwer, Susanne, Holger Mitterer, and Falk Huettig. 2012. Can hearing *puter* activate *pupil*? Phonological competition and the processing of reduced spoken words in spontaneous conversations. *Quarterly Journal of Experimental Psychology* 65 (11): 2193–2220.

Cole, Jennifer, Yoonsook Mo, and Mark Hasegawa-Johnson. 2010. Signal-based and expectation-based factors in the perception of prosodic prominence. *Laboratory Phonology* 1 (2): 425–452.

Damian, Markus F., and Jeff S. Bowers. 2010. Orthographic effects in rhyme monitoring tasks: Are they automatic? *European Journal of Cognitive Psychology* 22 (1): 106–116.

Dye, Matthew W. G., and Shui-I Shih. 2006. Phonological priming in British Sign Language. In *Laboratory Phonology*, vol. 8, edited by Aditi Lahiri, 241–261. Berlin: de Gruyter Moutin.

Finley, Sara. 2011. The privileged status of locality in consonant harmony. *Journal of Memory and Language* 65:74–83.

Finley, Sara. 2012. Testing the limits of long-distance learning: Learning beyond a three-segment window. *Cognitive Science* 36:740–756.

Hay, Jennifer B., Katie Drager, and Andy Gibson. 2018. Hearing r-sandhi: The role of past experience. *Language* 94 (2): 360–404.

Hofstadter, Douglas. 1979. *Gödel, Escher, Bach: An Eternal Golden Braid.* New York: Basic Books.

Ito, Kiwako, and Shari R. Speer. 2008. Anticipatory effects of intonation: Eye movements during instructed visual search. *Journal of Memory and Language* 58:541–573. http://doi.org/:10.1016/j.jml.2007.06.013.

Katz, Jonah, and Melinda Fricke. 2018. Auditory disruption improves word segmentation: A functional basis for lenition phenomena. *Glossa* 3 (1): 38.

Ladd, D. Robert, Rory Turnbull, Charlotte Browne, Catherine Caldwell-Harris, Lesya Ganushchak, Kate Swoboda, Verity Woodfield, and Dan Dediu. 2013. Patterns of individual differences in the perception of missing-fundamental tones. *Journal of Experimental Psychology: Human Perception and Performance* 39 (5): 1386–1397.

McGurk, Harry, and John MacDonald. 1976. Hearing lips and seeing voices. *Nature* 264 (5588): 746–748.

Mitterer, Holger. 2006. On the causes of compensation for coarticulation: Evidence for phonological mediation. *Perception and Psychophysics* 68:1227–1240.

New, Boris, Christophe Pallier, Ludovic Ferrand, and Rafael Matos. 2001. Une base de données lexical du français contemporain sur internet: LEXIQUE. *L'Année Psychologique* 101:447–462.

Peirce, Jonathan, Jeremy R. Gray, Sol Simpson, Michael MacAskill, Richard Höchenberger, Hiroyuki Sogo, Erik Kastman, and Jonas Kristoffer Lindeløv. 2019. PsychoPy2: Experiments in behavior made easy. *Behavior Research Methods* 51:195–203.

Perrin, Chad. 2007. The value of accidental security through obscurity. *TechRepublic* (blog). December 13. https://www.techrepublic.com/blog/it-security/the-value-of-accidental-security-through-obscurity/.

Turnbull, Rory, and Sharon Peperkamp. 2017. The asymmetric contribution of consonants and vowels to phonological similarity: Evidence from lexical priming. *Mental Lexicon* 12 (3): 404–430.

Turnbull, Rory, Adam J. Royer, Kiwako Ito, and Shari R. Speer. 2017. Prominence perception is dependent on phonology, semantics, and awareness of discourse. *Language, Cognition and Neuroscience* 32 (8): 1017–1033.

Warren, Richard M., Keri R. Riener, James A. Bashford, and Bradley S. Brubaker. 1995. Spectral redundancy: Intelligibility of sentences heard through narrow spectral slits. *Perception and Psychophysics* 57 (2): 175–182.

Wickham, Hadley. 2014. Tidy data. *Journal of Statistical Software* 59 (10): 1–23.

Wiener, Seth, and Rory Turnbull. 2016. Constraints of tones, vowels and consonants on lexical selection in Mandarin Chinese. *Language and Speech* 59 (1): 59–82.

Youngdahl, Carla L., Eric W. Healy, Sarah E. Yoho, Frédéric Apoux, and Rachael Frush Holt. 2018. The effect of remote masking on the reception of speech by young school-age children. *Journal of Speech, Language, and Hearing Research* 61 (2): 420–427.

Anne Cutler, Mirjam Ernestus, Natasha Warner, and Andrea Weber

1   Speech perception data sets

Sizeable sets of speech perception data can be highly valuable to researchers; consider that the early reports on the identification of American English vowels (Peterson & Barney 1952) and consonants (Miller & Nicely 1955) have racked up citation counts, respectively, of 4329 and 2455 (in June 2021; after more than half a century, the citations are still coming in). Understandably, most experiments on the perception of speech are focused on specific questions (testing models of spoken-language comprehension, comparing processing across structurally different languages, assessing perceptual outcomes for differing listener populations) and accordingly use the minimum data set size necessary for their target statistical power (although see Sedlmeier & Gigerenzer 1989). But other reasons to collect speech perception data can make for large data sets with wide relevance or usefulness.

One reason might be to build the basis for a computational system such as an automatic speech recognizer. A database of human recognition achievement to support such a computational system will need to have broad scope; for example, it should include all phonemes or syllables of the language in question, ideally in every potential phonemic context. This then makes for a data set on which comparative perceptual questions of many other kinds can be tested. Another reason might be to set norms for useful stimulus selection control measures, such as the relative effects of word occurrence frequency in listening, or the effects of vocabulary structure such as word class. Again, once the norms are established, the data sets remain useful for answering a range of further questions. As long as the data sets are easily accessible, they can be put to many uses, similar to the method of "virtual experiments" suggested by Kuperman (2015). Thus, these large data sets on speech perception can be viewed both as "big data" and as "open data" (Borgman 2015).

The following section covers four data sets. The first two indeed came into being in service of a computational model: SHORTLIST-B (Norris & McQueen 2008), a Bayesian model of human spoken-word recognition that draws its probability estimates from human recognition scores for all possible two-phoneme speech sound sequences in all their legal contexts in the language (which in this case is actually the two languages Dutch and English, enabling two language-specific SHORTLIST-B instantiations). These two studies were nicknamed DADDY (the Dutch Auditory Diphone Database) and EDDY (the English Diphone Database), respectively, but given their identical design and guiding principles they are described together in section 2.1. The third study was analogously nicknamed NINNY (Noise-masked Identifications by Native and Non-native listeners) and as described in section 2.2 was aimed mainly at providing a larger-scope data set able to clear up contradictory claims based on smaller-scale studies, many of these incorporating also confounding properties such as variations in lexical familiarity. The fourth study (section 2.3) was motivated by the proven usefulness of an existing data set of responses in a lexical decision study using visually presented stimuli; it was the first set of such lexical decision data using auditory presentation and was accordingly named BALDEY, because it was then the Biggest Auditory Lexical Decision Experiment (Yet). In the following sections, we approach each data set from the questions of "Why?" (what was the goal of the project), "How?" (how was the study done), "What?" (main results), "For whom?" (who the users of the data set are), and "Where?" (data management and storage).

Accessibility of such data is here defined as open access (OA) to the speech stimuli presented and the resulting listener responses. These four data sets all include both stimuli and responses (the latter being response times, or identification choices, or both). Participant-identifying features are anonymized; the issues here for language data are discussed by Warner (2014). Each of the data sets in section 2 has been made available in more than one OA way, and together they cover several options. The choices we have made about how to make these data sets available, and about what information to store in them, relate to the issues of data management and planning discussed by Mattern (chapter 5, this volume). Even when the plan from the beginning is to create a large data set and make it publicly available, the issues Mattern discusses still lead to challenges. All of these data sets are freely licensed for use by others. Authors using these data sets should cite the relevant publication reporting each data set in order to give credit appropriately. Because the purpose of all of these data sets is basic science, we considered this sufficient without requiring other researchers to ask our permission for further use. See Collister (chapter 9, this volume) for discussion of copyright issues for such data sets.

Further questions arise with respect to the use of large OA data sets on speech perception such as these. An obvious initial question is: how do other researchers find such data sets? One method of making data sets known is based in traditional scientific publication: for each of the projects discussed herein, the research team published one or more papers on specific analyses of the data set before making the data publicly available, with each such publication, from the first one on, at least mentioning the availability of the data set for other researchers. The research teams also gave talks at major conferences that served both to present specific results from the data sets and to publicize their availability for further studies to other researchers. Internet searches are a likely method of turning up such data sets when one is seeking them. However, it would be desirable to find additional ways to publicize the existence of such data sets that would continue to reach audiences after conference talks on the projects have concluded.

A separate issue concerns how other researchers who succeed in finding and downloading these data sets then make use of and maintain them. Individual researchers are encouraged to download a copy of the data files for local use. A given researcher is likely to edit the data file to add additional columns during the process of analyzing the data to answer their own questions. At this point, other researchers using these data files need to take responsibility for keeping track of any restructuring they have done and for citing the source of the original data correctly.

2 DADDY, EDDY, NINNY, and BALDEY

2.1 Diphones: Identification of sounds in two-sound sequences over time

2.1.1 The goal (Why?)   The goal of the Diphones project (DADDY: Smits et al., 2003; EDDY: Warner, McQueen, & Cutler, 2014) was to provide information about how listeners extract acoustic cues to segments from *all* possible sequences of two sounds of a language over time. Data were collected for two languages: Dutch and English. Many detailed findings were already available on how native listeners perceive specific sequences of sounds, such as /ba, da, ga/, /f/ versus /θ/ before vowels, and so on. However, those studies did not all use the same methods so that the results are not comparable.

The principal stimulus for the project was to provide input data for a probabilistic model of spoken-word recognition, the SHORTLIST-B model of Dutch spoken-word recognition (Norris & McQueen 2008), and a corresponding English model. The Diphones data provide an account of what sounds listeners think they are hearing as the speech signal unfolds. This information can then be fed into the model of what words are consequently considered as candidates for word recognition. For example, if the input is actually "book," the Diphones data show at what probability listeners believe that they are hearing /bʊ/ and then /ʊk/ as the signal progresses. The data also provide information about the probability at any given time with which the listeners may think they have heard something else, such as /bu/, /bʌ/, or /pʊ/. This information probabilistically influences the model's estimation of how likely the listener is to think they are hearing the word *book* as opposed to the words *boot, but,* or *put.* For this purpose, the data must include information for all diphones that could occur in the language, even across word boundaries, to allow modeling of recognition of any string of words.

Thus for example the English Diphones stimulus set includes vowel-vowel (VV) diphones such as /oᵘaᵘ/ (as in "row out") and consonant-consonant (CC) /pʃ/ (as in "upshot") as well as the more commonly studied CV (/ba/ but also the less common /ðoⁱ/) and VC (/ab/ but also /ʊv/). All diphones that cannot be ruled out as impossible in the language are included, even if they could only occur across a word or morpheme boundary, as for example /ðv/, which does not occur within any word of English, but could occur in the sequence "loathe vegetables." Thus, phonotactically impossible diphones such as /ɛh/ are the only ones excluded (in English, no syllable can end in a lax vowel like /ɛ/ and /h/ cannot appear in a syllable coda, so this diphone cannot occur even across a word boundary).

2.1.2 The study (How?) The stimuli for each study comprised a list of all the possible two-sound sequences of the language, whether CV, VC, CC, or VV (e.g., /ba, iz, fp, ioᵒ/). For diphones containing a vowel, a version with the vowel stressed and a separate version with the vowel unstressed were used, thus there was a stressed and an unstressed /ba/ diphone, and four /ioᵒ/ diphones (stressed-stressed, stressed-unstressed, unstressed-stressed, and unstressed-unstressed). Each of these languages has almost 2,300 possible diphones, when stress is counted in this way.

Each diphone (two-sound sequence) was gated at six time points at thirds of the duration of each segment, so that on Gate 1, listeners heard only the first third of the first segment, while on Gate 5 they heard from the beginning of the diphone through two-thirds of the duration of the second sound. Gate end points were placed at thirds of the duration of each segment for most segment types. Thus, for example, Gate 1 of /sa/ would allow listeners to hear from the beginning of the /s/ up until one-third through the /s/; Gate 3 would allow them to hear from the beginning up to the end of the /s/; and Gate 5 would allow them to hear from the beginning of the /s/ up to two-thirds through the /a/. (Only for stops and affricates, the end points of Gate 2 or Gate 5 were set just before the onset of the burst rather than at two-thirds through the duration, so that the burst and aspiration/frication noise always occurred within the same gate.) At the gate end point, the amplitude of the speech was ramped down over the course of five milliseconds while the amplitude of a square wave was simultaneously ramped up and added to the speech wave. The square wave (resembling a computer beep) then continued for a few hundred milliseconds. The amplitude ramp from speech to square wave and presence of the square wave prevents the creation of artifactual cues to some sound. The beep also helps encourage

listeners to believe that more sound would follow if they were allowed to hear the entire string. Regardless of gate, the listeners' task was always to identify what two sounds they heard or might have heard the start of, even though at Gate 1 they might be extremely unsure. Full details of methods and stimulus creation appear in Smits et al. (2003) and Warner, McQueen, and Cutler (2014). There were over 12,000 stimuli for each language.

Eighteen Dutch and twenty American English native listeners participated in the experiments (each for only their own language). Each listener heard all the stimuli for their language once, visiting the lab for a series of up to thirty sessions, which were each an hour long. All stimuli were randomized. On hearing each stimulus, listeners had to identify both the first and second sound. For a Gate 6 stimulus, the listener might hear both sounds of a stimulus /az/ clearly and be able to identify both sounds correctly. However, at Gate 1 of the same stimulus, the listener might be only somewhat sure what the first segment was and have no idea what the second segment was at all, as Gate 1 ends at one-third through the duration of the first segment, and very little information about the upcoming /z/ spreads into the first third of the preceding /a/. In this case, the listener would have to respond to the second segment by guessing. For each stimulus, listeners saw a computer screen showing buttons for every phoneme of the language on the left half of the screen for the first segment response and the right half of the screen for the second segment response. They used the computer mouse to select what two sounds they heard or might have heard from among the full phoneme set of the language. See Smits et al. (2003) and Warner, McQueen, and Cutler (2014) for additional details. Because each listener gave two judgments (first and second segment) for each of the more than 12,000 stimuli, the total data set across both languages comprises approximately a million judgments.

2.1.3 Main results (What?) The Diphones studies of Dutch and English have elucidated or confirmed many patterns about the timing of speech perception. For example, the results (for Dutch also in Warner et al. 2005) make the difference very clear between segments that strongly change quality over the course of the segment (diphthongs and affricates) and those that remain relatively stable. Listeners seem to perceive whatever sound they hear during the stimulus as a phoneme and do not allow for the possibility that additional acoustic cues to the sound they are currently hearing could still follow. Therefore, if the stimulus ends during the closure of an affricate (e.g., Gate 5 of /a͡tʃ/, which ends just before the burst), listeners typically respond with a stop rather than the affricate. The data for affricates therefore shows very poor perception up until the frication noise, and then a very steep and sudden improvement in perception accuracy when the stimulus includes frication noise of the release. A similar effect for diphthongs at the stimulus that first includes the second quality of the vowel means that patterns of recognition for diphthongs are delayed relative to the patterns for recognition of monophthongs. Diphthong perception accuracy generally lags behind accuracy for monophthongs by one gate (one-third of duration of the segment).

The Diphones studies also allow comparison of speech perception in English and Dutch. One major comparative finding is that unstressed vowels are recognized far more poorly than stressed ones in English, while this effect is small and limited to a few vowels in Dutch. In Warner and Cutler (2017), we argue that this difference comes not from acoustic differences in the unstressed vowel space, but rather from listeners' differing need to distinguish among unstressed vowel qualities. Dutch has more unstressed vowels with full vowel quality (not schwa-like quality), while unstressed English vowels are usually schwa. Hence there is more potential for the quality of an unstressed vowel to aid the listener in determining what word they are hearing in Dutch. Dutch listeners therefore pay more attention to vowel quality even in unstressed vowels than English listeners do.

2.1.4 The users (For whom?) The Diphones data set is primarily of interest for two groups of researchers: those interested in questions about speech perception, and those interested in modeling spoken-word recognition. The data can most straightforwardly be used to answer questions about what information listeners can extract from the acoustic signal at what time point. In addition to our own work, graduate students at other institutions have contacted us about uses they are making of the data for speech perception topics. For modeling of spoken-word recognition, the Diphones data provide input data for SHORTLIST-B, but could also be used for other models. Indeed the Diphone studies are cited by these primary interest groups. However, the papers have also been regularly cited on issues of language

acquisition (Altvater-Mackenson, van der Feest, & Fikkert 2014; Law & Edwards 2015; Wagensveld et al. 2013) and more recently also with respect to clinical research (Hajiaghbaba, Marateb, & Kermani 2018) and historical linguistics (Minkova 2016).

2.1.5 The data management (Where?) The Dutch diphones data were initially made available through the Max Planck Institute for Psycholinguistics (Nijmegen) website, and a reference to this site was included in the 2003 publication. None of the authors still work there, however, and the website has been radically upgraded several times, making it difficult to maintain the accessibility. That data set was also deposited in the Alveo Human Communication Science Virtual Lab, a secure Australian repository accessible from Research Data Australia (http://researchdata.ands.org.au/human -communication-science-virtual-laboratory-hcs-vlab). At the time of writing, the Dutch materials remain available at MPI (https://www.mpi.nl/world/dcsp/diphones /index.html). Both the Dutch and English diphones data sets are available through Warner's website and her lab's website (https://nwarner.faculty.arizona.edu/content/7). We plan to deposit the data at an online location that is intended as a long-term archive, such as the University of Arizona library system's archive.

For both Diphones projects, all stimuli and all responses are available. Researchers can thus calculate any response percentages or confusion matrices they seek, or they can work directly with the raw individual responses. A large zipped file containing all the stimulus sound files (including the appended square wave beep) can be downloaded for each project, enabling acoustic analyses of the stimuli for comparison to responses. Both languages' data sets also have a README file documenting transcription systems, file organization, and such. The Dutch files on the MPI site contain some additional materials, such as premade confusion matrices and the label files used to create the stimuli from the recordings (which contain information about where boundaries were placed).

2.2 NINNY: Noise-masked Identifications by Native and Non-native listeners

2.2.1 The goal (Why?) Adverse listening conditions, for example noisy backgrounds, disrupt listening to non-native speech more strongly than they disrupt listening to native speech (see Garcia Lecumberri, Cooke, & Cutler 2010 for a review). The main goal of the study

NINNY (Cutler, Weber, Smits, & Cooper, 2004) was to identify the source of this asymmetry. One obvious possibility was that this disadvantage for non-native listeners was due to greater difficulty in phoneme identification. Where the phoneme categories of a non-native language fail to match those of the native language, phonetic decisions can be influenced by the native repertoire (e.g., Strange 1995), and this influence may become stronger when stimuli are harder to perceive, for example, because they are embedded in noise. In order to render higher-level factors such as lexical frequency or contextual plausibility irrelevant, Cutler et al. tested phoneme identification in VC or CV syllables in noise. Identification responses by American English (native) and Dutch (non-native) listeners to all American English vowels and consonants were collected under three levels of noise masking.

Phonetic identification data of any kind are highly valuable for speech comprehension research. They are valuable because sounds differ in how easily they can be recognized (even in native listening), and the data sets provide identification accuracy and confusion patterns sound by sound. It is also possible to estimate the contribution of phoneme perceptibility to recognition of any spoken word with such data sets. Such large data collections are scarce, however, because collecting the data is time-consuming and laborious. Data for non-native listening are even harder to find, because data for any given language pair might not provide a full set of answers relevant to another language pair.

2.2.2 The study (How?)

For the NINNY data set, native speakers of American English and Dutch non-native speakers of English listened to English syllables and identified either the consonant or the vowel. All 645 possible standard CV and VC sequences of American English, excluding those with schwa, were recorded by a female native speaker and centrally embedded in one second of multi-speaker babble noise. The multi-speaker babble was combined with the test syllables at three levels of signal-to-noise ratios (SNRs): zero, eight, and sixteen decibels. These SNRs were chosen on the basis of a pretest to yield difficult, intermediate, and easy English phoneme perception for Dutch non-native listeners. Sixteen native listeners of American English and sixteen non-native Dutch listeners who were highly proficient in English were presented with the syllables in noise, and identified each phoneme of each syllable at each noise

level separately (3,870 trials per listener). Testing was spread across eight sessions, each lasting approximately thirty to forty minutes. To guide listeners' responses, illustrative words for all phonemes were shown on a display (e.g., the word *very* for the consonant response /v/), and listeners signaled responses by clicking on the word matching the phoneme they decided was presented. Collected responses comprised correct responses (e.g., a click on *very* when identifying the consonant in the syllable /vi/) as well as errors (e.g., a click on *very* when identifying the consonant in the syllable /bi/). The full identification response set contains 123,840 data points in total: 32 participants, each taking part in eight sessions and contributing 3,870 identification responses.

2.2.3 Main results (What?)

With these isolated syllables, all listeners were adversely affected by an increase in noise, and the phoneme identification performance of non-native listeners was overall less accurate than that of native listeners. Crucially, however, the disadvantage for non-native listeners was not proportionally greater at higher noise levels. It was concluded that the frequently reported asymmetry of non-native versus native listening under difficult listening conditions is not due to greater masking and hence greater difficulty of phoneme identification, but rather to non-native listeners' lesser, and less efficient use of, higher-level information (e.g., lexical and statistical information) for recovery from the effect of noise masking.

The combination of native and non-native phonetic identification data is important because it allows us to distinguish the roles of general auditory and language-independent processes from those involving prior knowledge of a given language. Thus a principal theory-driven finding of the NINNY study was that non-native listeners do not need better low-level evidence than native listeners do (i.e., a less noisy environment) to overcome listening difficulties; instead, they could best match native performance by having a larger vocabulary and increased listening experience.

2.2.4 The users (For whom?)

The NINNY data set is of interest for researchers who work on either native listening or non-native listening (in comparison to native listening). By November 2019, the 2004 NINNY study had received 280 citations (Google Scholar). The data have been analyzed to compare phoneme confusion patterns to predictions of speech perception models (e.g., Silbert & de Jong 2007) and to guide the selection of sound contrasts for word recognition studies (e.g., Darcy, Daidone, & Kojima 2013; Escudero, Hayes-Harb, & Mitterer 2008; Weber & Cutler 2004). Although most citations are in publications on the central issue of native versus non-native speech perception, the study has also been cited on non-nativeness effects at higher levels of linguistic processing (e.g., Hopp 2010; Van Engen & Bradlow 2007), on the effect of multi-speaker babble as a type of masking noise (e.g., Garcia Lecumberri & Cooke 2006), and for comparisons with clinical data due to age-related hearing deficits (Kumar Kalaiah et al. 2016) or cochlear implant use (Lee & Mendel 2016).

2.2.5 The data management (Where?)   The 2004 study again listed the MPI website as a location for accessing the data. All stimuli in WAV format and all individual identification responses were made available there (https://www .mpi.nl/people/cutler-anne/research), and at the time of writing, they are still available. The data set was again also deposited in the Alveo Human Communication Science Virtual Lab. In 2018, both the primary research data (identification responses and audio files) and metadata according to ISO 24622-1 (CMDI) were further archived in the Tübingen CLARIN-D Repository (https://talar.sfb833 .uni-tuebingen.de/about/). CLARIN-D (https://www .clarin-d.net/en/) is a research-oriented infrastructure for the Humanities and Social Sciences and covers a wide range of expertise ranging from annotated corpora to psycholinguistic experiments and from speech databases to web-based services for language and speech processing. Archiving in CLARIN-D is sustainable, data are stored in non-proprietary formats, and data sets can easily be found by different search engines (as attested by the awarded Data Seal of Approval; https://www.datasealofapproval .org/en/). With the Virtual Language Observatory (https:// vlo.clarin.eu/?4), CLARIN-D also offers a search engine that specializes in finding available metadata for language resources worldwide, including of course resources from the Tübingen CLARIN-D Repository.

2.3   BALDEY: Biggest Auditory Lexical Decision Experiment Yet

2.3.1 The goal (Why?)   One of the word recognition researcher's favorite workhorses is the lexical decision task. The literature reports thousands of lexical decision experiments. The studies have taught us about multiple different aspects of written and spoken language

processing, for instance about where semantic processing takes place in the brain (e.g., Beeman et al. 1994) or which lexical characteristics affect ease of word recognition (e.g., Connine et al. 1990; Schreuder & Baayen 1995), providing information for language and speech processing models. For every new research question, a new experiment is typically designed, with a small number of target words fulfilling all kinds of constraints related to the research question.

The English Lexicon Project (ELP; Balota et al. 2007), in contrast, contains a huge visual lexical decision experiment, with 40,481 real words and 40,481 pseudowords. Because the data are freely available on the internet, researchers can test hypotheses about visual word processing without conducting new experiments. The frequent citation of the ELP data set in all kinds of analyses proves that this indeed occurs and suggested that it would also be worth conducting a large auditory lexical decision experiment to similarly further the research needs of spoken-word recognition, in particular by including word types for which almost no auditory data were previously available. BALDEY (Ernestus & Cutler, 2015) was designed for this purpose.

2.3.2 The study (How?)   The 5,541 BALDEY experimental stimuli consist of 2,780 spoken Dutch real content words and 2,761 pseudowords, the latter differing from real words in just one or two segments. The words represent a large number of categories differing in word class (adjective, noun, or verb), morphological structure (simple or complex, with a restricted set of derivational and inflectional affixes), the position of stress (initial vs. non-initial), and the number of syllables in the stem (one or two). Most of these features have not been systematically varied in prior studies. The stimuli were recorded by a single female speaker and presented to twenty native listeners of standard Dutch (ten male, ten female). Each participant heard all words, distributed over ten experimental sessions, which were an hour long and were held one week apart. The final data set thus contains both accuracy and reaction times of 110,820 responses.

2.3.3 Main results (What?)   Two initial analyses were presented at a conference (Ernestus & Cutler 2014) and were included in the publication (Ernestus & Cutler 2015) to illustrate how the data set might be exploited. The first analysis concerned the point at which a word has no further neighbors and effectively reaches the criterion for recognition. Listeners' response times were more strongly predicted by the duration of the spoken item than by any property of the word's competitor population, indicating that listeners adopt a rational approach to the task of auditory lexical decision (including the possibility that the input may be a pseudoword), and their responses are driven by these task-based considerations. The second analysis was concerned with how well four different measures of frequency of occurrence (from written corpora, spoken corpora, subtitles, and frequency ratings by listeners) predicted the study outcomes. The results were better predicted by form frequencies in a very large database compiled from film subtitles than by subjective ratings, or by frequencies of forms in written text, or by frequencies in spoken corpora, either of spontaneous or rehearsed speech. The size of the subtitles corpus and its constant objective of naturalness in dialogue were suggested to be the primary underlying drivers of its greater predictive power.

2.3.4 The users (For whom?) The data set is of interest to all researchers working on human or automatic spoken-word recognition. Examples of studies based on BALDEY include Ernestus and Cutler (2014) on spoken-word identification points and which frequency measure best reflects a listener's experience, Brysbaert et al. (2016) on the impact of a word's prevalence on its recognition, and ten Bosch, Boves, and Ernestus (2013), who tested their computational model of spoken-word recognition (Diana) on BALDEY. Although most citations to date have occurred in the context of discussion of large-scale studies, including recently a similar collection of auditory lexical decision data for English (Tucker et al. 2018), the study has also been cited on issues of morphological processing (Goodwin Davies 2018) and of cross-modality consistency (Hasenäcker, Verra, & Schroeder 2018).

2.3.5 The data management (Where?) BALDEY is available as supplemental information for the published article (https://journals.sagepub.com/doi/suppl/10.1080/17470218.2014.984730). In addition, all data are freely available at two other sites: (a) at the first author's site http://www.mirjamernestus.nl/Ernestus/Baldey/index.php and (b) via the Language Archive of the Max Planck Institute for Psycholinguistics (https://archive.mpi.nl).

The OA package contains a list of all stimuli, specifying the phonological and morphological properties of each stimulus, including number of phonemes, number of syllables in the stem, stress location, word class, morphological stem, affixes, and such. The frequency information lists each stimulus' frequencies of occurrences in several databases. The identification point information lists for several definitions of these points their locations in the stimuli. The database also contains the acoustic signals with text grids aligned at phone level. Furthermore, the database lists participant information (e.g., age, gender, handedness, language background), and their accuracy and reaction times for every stimulus. All information is arranged in files that can easily be imported in the statistical package R.

3 Summary

As these four case studies show, there are multiple reasons why large speech perception data sets should be collected, leading in consequence to multiple prompts for them to become OA and multiple ways in which that goal can be realized. We have not exhausted the possibilities. For instance, some journals insist on accepted publications providing OA data sets and contribute to maintaining secure and lasting storage sites for such data. If a speech perception study is accepted by such a journal, then that is another way for speech perception data sets to be sharable via OA, though they may not qualify at all as Big Data.

One way for megastudies in speech perception to become known is similar, in that it involves participation in a special issue or the like devoted to Big Data (as for our BALDEY case). This does not necessarily involve a guarantee of permanent storage, however. The majority of large speech perception data sets are collected for research reasons devised by the collectors, and at the time when we carried out these studies, accessibility was initially dependent on university or personal sites. We are in favor of the establishment and use of more permanent sites, which may best be managed by long-term agreements between multiple universities and professional associations, and, if funding organizations require OA from grant recipients, they should ideally contribute to the permanent maintenance of such sites. Services such as GitHub are a welcome addition to the means of data sharing, for maintaining long-term access to data; the future will probably bring a range of accessible sites, from minimally supervised depositories to professionally curated archives.

It is now twenty years since the earliest of these studies (DADDY) was first designed, and in that time not only has researchers' knowledge of best practices in collection and sharing of large behavioral data sets developed considerably, but available technology has multiplied. The chapters in the rest of this volume attest to the explosion of knowledge in this area, plus the associated maintenance and communication options. It is tempting to consider what we might have chosen to do had alternative options been available two decades back. Nonetheless, these four large data sets on speech perception are available and in use, so they apparently meet a need. We therefore look forward to the speech perception community providing many more shared troves of useful data!

Acknowledgments

The order of authorship is alphabetical. The research described in this contribution was financially supported by the Max Planck Society and all authors were previously associated with the Comprehension Group at the Max Planck Institute for Psycholinguistics in Nijmegen, The Netherlands. Additional funding for part of the work was provided by a Spinoza award to the first author from the Dutch Scientific Research Council (NWO), and by NICHD Grant No. 00323 to Winifred Strange.

References

Altvater-Mackenson, N., S. van der Feest, and P. Fikkert. 2014. Asymmetries in early word recognition: The case of stops and fricatives. *Language Learning and Development* 10 (2): 140–178. http://dx.doi.org/10.1080/15475441.2013.808954.

Balota, D. A., M. J. Yap, K. A. Hutchison, M. J. Cortese, B. Kessler, B. Loftis, J. H. Neely, D. L. Nelson, G. B. Simpson, and R. Treiman. 2007. The English Lexicon Project. *Behavior Research Methods* 39 (3): 445–459. http://dx.doi.org/10.3758/BF03193014.

Beeman, M., R. B. Friedman, J. Grafman, E. Perez, S. Diamond, and M. B. Lindsay. 1994. Summation priming and coarse semantic coding in the right hemisphere. *Journal of Cognitive Neuroscience* 6 (1): 26–45. http://dx.doi.org/10.1162/jocn.1994.6.1.26.

Borgman, C. L. 2015. *Big Data, Little Data, No Data: Scholarship in the Networked World*. Cambridge: MIT Press. https://doi.org/10.7551/mitpress/9963.001.0001.

Brysbaert, M., M. Stevens, P. Mandera, and E. Keuleers. 2016. The impact of word prevalence on lexical decision times: Evidence from the Dutch Lexicon Project 2. *Journal of Experimental Psychology: Human Perception and Performance* 42 (3): 441. http://dx.doi.org/10.1037/xhp0000159.

Connine, C. M., J. Mullennix, E. Shernoff, and J. Yelen. 1990. Word familiarity and frequency in visual and auditory word recognition. *Journal of Experimental Psychology: Learning, Memory, and Cognition* 16 (6): 1084–1096. http://dx.doi.org/10.1037/0278-7393.16.6.1084.

Cutler, A., A. Weber, R. Smits, and N. Cooper. 2004. Patterns of English phoneme confusions by native and non-native listeners. *Journal of the Acoustical Society of America* 116 (6): 3668–3678. http://dx.doi.org/10.1121/1.1810292.

Darcy, I., D. Daidone, and C. Kojima. 2013. Asymmetric lexical access and fuzzy lexical representations in second language learners. *Mental Lexicon* 8 (3): 372–420. https://doi.org/10.1075/ml.8.3.06dar.

Ernestus, M., and A. Cutler. 2014. BALDEY: The Biggest Auditory Lexical Decision Experiment Yet. Paper presented at the 9th International Conference on the Mental Lexicon, Niagara, Ontario, September 30–October 2.

Ernestus, M., and A. Cutler. 2015. BALDEY: A database of auditory lexical decisions. *Quarterly Journal of Experimental Psychology* 68 (8): 1469–1488. https://doi.org/10.1080/17470218.2014.984730.

Escudero, P., R. Hayes-Harb, and H. Mitterer. 2008. Novel second-language words and asymmetric lexical access. *Journal of Phonetics* 36 (2): 345–360. http://dx.doi.org/10.1016/j.wocn.2007.11.002.

Garcia Lecumberri, M. L., and M. Cooke. 2006. Effect of masker type on native and non-native consonant perception in noise. *Journal of the Acoustical Society of America* 119:2445–2454. http://dx.doi.org/10.1121/1.2180210.

Garcia Lecumberri, M. L., M. Cooke, and A. Cutler. 2010. Non-native speech perception in adverse conditions: A review. *Speech Communication* 52:864–886. http://dx.doi.org/10.1016/j.specom.2010.08.014.

Goodwin Davies, A. J. 2018. Morphological representations in lexical processing. PhD dissertation, University of Pennsylvania.

Hajiaghbaba, F., H. R. Marateb, and S. Kermani. 2018. The design and validation of a hybrid digital-signal-processing plug-in for traditional cochlear implant speech processors. *Computer Methods and Programs in Biomedicine* 159:103–109. http://dx.doi.org/10.1016/j.cmpb.2018.03.003.

Hasenäcker, J., L. Verra, and S. Schroeder. 2018. Comparing length and frequency effects in children across modalities. *Quarterly Journal of Experimental Psychology* 72 (7): 1682–1691. http://dx.doi.org/10.1177/1747021818805063.

Hopp, H. 2010. Ultimate attainment in L2 inflection: Performance similarities between non-native and native speakers. *Lingua* 120:901–931. http://dx.doi.org/10.1016/j.lingua.2009.06.004.

Kumar Kalaiah, M., D. Thomas, J. S. Bhat, and R. Ranjan. 2016. Perception of consonants in speech-shaped noise among young and middle-aged adults. *Journal of International Advanced*

Otology 12 (2): 184–188. http://dx.doi.org/10.5152/iao.2016 .2467.

Kuperman, V. 2015. Virtual experiments in megastudies: A case study of language and emotion. *Quarterly Journal of Experimental Psychology* 68 (8): 1693–1710. https://doi.org/10.1080 /17470218.2014.989865.

Law, F., and J. R. Edwards. 2015. Effects of vocabulary size on online lexical processing by preschoolers. *Language Learning and Development* 11 (4): 331–355. http://dx.doi.org/10.1080 /15475441.2014.961066.

Lee, S., and L. L. Mendel. 2016. Effect of the number of maxima and stimulation rate on phoneme perception patterns using cochlear implant simulation. *Clinical Archives of Communication Disorders* 1 (1): 87–100. http://dx.doi.org/10.21849/cacd .2016.00066.

Miller, G. A., and P. E. Nicely. 1955. An analysis of perceptual confusions among some English consonants. *Journal of the Acoustical Society of America* 27:338–352. http://dx.doi.org/10 .1121/1.1907526.

Minkova, D. 2016. From stop-fricative clusters to contour segments in Old English. In *Studies in the History of the English Language VII: Generalizing vs. Particularizing Methodologies in Historical Linguistic Analysis*, ed. D. Chapman, C. Moore, and M. Wilcox, 29–59. Berlin: de Gruyter. http://dx.doi.org/10 .1515/9783110494235-003.

Norris, D., and J. M. McQueen. 2008. Shortlist B: A Bayesian model of continuous speech recognition. *Psychological Review* 115 (2): 357–395. http://dx.doi.org/10.1037/0033-295X.115.2.357.

Peterson, G. E., and H. L. Barney. 1952. Control methods used in a study of the vowels. *Journal of the Acoustical Society of America* 24 (2): 175–184. http://dx.doi.org/10.1121/1.1906875.

Schreuder, R., and R. H. Baayen. 1995. Modeling morphological processing. In *Morphological Aspects of Language Processing*, ed. L. B. Feldman, 131–157. Hillsdale, NJ: Erlbaum.

Sedlmeier, P., and G. Gigerenzer. 1989. Do studies of statistical power have an effect on the power of studies? *Psychological Bulletin* 105 (2): 309–316. http://dx.doi.org/10.1037/0033-2909.105 .2.309.

Silbert, N. H., and K. J. de Jong. 2007. Laryngeal feature structure in 1st and 2nd language speech perception. *Proceedings of the Sixteenth International Congress of Phonetic Sciences* 16:1901–1904.

Smits, R., N. Warner, J. M. McQueen, and A. Cutler. 2003. Unfolding of phonetic information over time: A database of Dutch diphone perception. *Journal of the Acoustical Society of America* 113 (1): 563–574. http://dx.doi.org/10.1121/1.1525287.

Strange, W. 1995. *Speech Perception and Linguistic Experience: Issues in Cross-language Speech Research*. Baltimore, MD: York Press.

ten Bosch, L., L. Boves, and M. Ernestus. 2013. Towards an end-to-end computational model of speech comprehension: Simulating a lexical decision task. In *Proceedings of Interspeech 2013*, 2822–2826.

Tucker, B., D. Brenner, D. K. Danielson, M. C. Kelley, F. Nenadic, and M. Sims. 2018. The Massive Auditory Lexical Decision (MALD) database. *Behavior Research Methods* 51 (3): 1187–1204. http://dx.doi.org/10.3758/s13428-018-1056-1.

Van Engen, K. J., and A. R. Bradlow. 2007. Sentence recognition in native- and foreign-language multi-talker background noise. *Journal of the Acoustical Society of America* 121 (1): 519–526. http://dx.doi.org/10.1121/1.2400666.

Wagensveld, B., E. Segers, P. van Alphen, and L. Verhoeven. 2013. The role of lexical representations and phonological overlap in rhyme judgments of beginning, intermediate, and advanced readers. *Learning and Individual Differences* 23 (1): 64–71. http://dx.doi.org/10.1016/j.lindif.2012.09.007.

Warner, N. 2014. Sharing of data as it relates to human subject issues and data management plans. *Language and Linguistics Compass* 8 (11): 512–518. http://dx.doi.org/10.1111/lnc3.12107.

Warner, N., and A. Cutler. 2017. Stress effects in vowel perception as a function of language-specific vocabulary patterns. *Phonetica* 74 (2): 81–106. http://dx.doi.org/10.1159/000447428.

Warner, N., J. M. McQueen, and A. Cutler. 2014. Tracking perception of the sounds of English. *Journal of the Acoustical Society of America* 135:2995–3006. http://dx.doi.org/10.1121/1.4870486.

Warner, N., R. Smits, J. M. McQueen, and A. Cutler. 2005. Phonological and frequency effects on timing of speech perception: A database of Dutch diphone perception. *Speech Communication* 46 (1): 53–72. http://dx.doi.org/10.1016/j.specom .2005.01.003.

Weber, A., and A. Cutler. 2004. Lexical competition in non-native spoken-word recognition. *Journal of Memory and Language* 50 (1): 1–25. http://dx.doi.org/10.1016/S0749-596X(03)00105-0.

51 Managing and Analyzing Data with Phonological CorpusTools

Kathleen Currie Hall, J. Scott Mackie, and Roger Yu-Hsiang Lo

1 Introduction

Phonological CorpusTools (PCT; Hall et al. 2018) is a free, open-source, cross-platform software tool that is designed to facilitate the phonological analysis of transcribed corpora.[1] It is written in the Python programming language and features both a graphical user interface and a (more limited) command-line interface (see also Hall, Mackie, & Lo 2019, for more details). In this chapter, we first explain the overall rationale for and structure of the software and then discuss how it can be used in conjunction with two different kinds of data: pre-existing corpora and original or fieldwork data.

2 Background

Over the past few decades, there has been an increasing interest in using corpus data to understand phonological phenomena (see, e.g., Durand, Gut, & Kristoffersen 2014 and chapters therein). As Hall (forthcoming) points out, there is a sense in which using *any* collection of empirical data to address a phonological question is *corpus phonology*. At the same time, corpus linguistics is generally thought to be a relatively new field (i.e., developed in the twentieth century), and this comes from the particular use of empirical data in a *post hoc manner*. That is, a corpus of data is collected independently of the specific research question being posed, rather than being collected for the purpose of answering that question.

In the realm of phonology, corpus methods have been usefully applied to a number of areas, including phonological variation and change (e.g., Cedergren & Sankoff 1974; Fosler-Lussier & Morgan 1999; Bybee 2001; Phillips 2006; Piantadosi, Tily, & Gibson 2011; Gahl, Yao, & Johnson 2012; Wedel, Jackson, & Kaplan 2013; Wedel, Kaplan, & Jackson 2013; Durand 2014; Pinnow & Connine 2014),

phonological acquisition (e.g., Jakobson [1941] 1968; Peperkamp et al. 2006; Rose 2014), and "core" phonological phenomena such as phonotactics, vowel harmony, syllable weight, and phonological relationships (e.g., Frisch 2012; Ryan 2014; Goldsmith & Riggle 2012; Hall & Hall 2016). Indeed, any phonological question that can be addressed by examining a collection of phonologically transcribed data can be informed by corpus work.

For a new approach such as corpus phonology to move forward, the methodologies involved must be understandable and replicable by others; indeed, this is good scientific practice more generally (see also Berez-Kroeker et al., chapter 1, this volume; Mattern, chapter 5, this volume). One recurrent problem with data-heavy analysis techniques such as corpus-based linguistics is that the level of detail needed to understand and replicate any given study is often far greater than is typically included in a traditional journal publication. While researchers are increasingly aware of this problem and may share computer code as part of the "supplementary materials" that accompany a project, such programs are often still unique to a particular type of data set and/or written in a programming language that another researcher may not be familiar with. Thus, one of the primary rationales behind the development of PCT as a resource was to streamline parallel analyses of similar data sets by a wide range of researchers. That is, PCT provides relatively accessible, parameterized versions of a number of the recently developed algorithms for doing phonological corpus analysis, so that an analysis performed within PCT can be straightforwardly replicated by another researcher and/or on another language, with the guarantee that the computation of the measures is identical across studies. Furthermore, PCT itself is extensively documented with detailed and accessible descriptions of how each function is calculated (https://corpustools

.readthedocs.io/en/latest/), and the code for the software itself is also openly available (https://github.com /PhonologicalCorpusTools/CorpusTools). These measures are intended to maximize the transparency and replicability of phonological corpus research.

The basic workflow of PCT is as follows. First, a user loads a corpus into the software. For the purpose of PCT, a *corpus* is simply a structured list of words, consisting of their spellings, transcriptions, and frequencies; PCT is designed for analysis of individual words rather than of the running context in which those words may have originally appeared. (Sections 3 and 4 provide much more detail in terms of how a corpus might be obtained.) Once a corpus has been provided, the user must also tell PCT how to interpret the transcriptions in terms of phonological features (see section 3.1 for more detail). Finally, the user is in a position to do phonological searches and analyses on the corpus itself (see sections 3.2 and 3.3).

It should be noted that PCT is specifically intended to be software for this last step, in other words, doing analysis of phonologically transcribed corpora, rather than designed to help with the collection, management, and storage of the corpus data themselves. There are other tools out there to facilitate such practices, including, for example, Phon (Rose & Brittain, chapter 32, this volume; Rose & MacWhinney 2014; and https://www.phon.ca /phon-manual/misc/Welcome.html); the Online Linguistic Database (OLD; https://www.onlinelinguisticdatabase .org/); ELAN (see discussion in Sloetjes 2014); EMU (see John & Bombien 2014); and Alveo (https://alveo.edu.au/). Naturally, because of the nature of trying to provide standalone software, some of these tools *also* include some tools for phonological analysis, and in turn, PCT includes some functionality for creating or modifying corpora (see more in section 4; see also discussion in Han, chapter 6, this volume). Users should remember, however, that each tool has its own particular uses and should be accessed with those purposes in mind.

Having a proliferation of tools can make learning any one of them somewhat difficult, as certain amounts of time and effort are needed to properly understand how any given tool functions. We think that having accessible, pre-existing data sets or example exercises are a valuable way of helping new users train themselves on new software, and we are encouraged by the increasing support for communication about such tools (such as satellite/training workshops often held at conferences

such as Laboratory Phonology and the Annual Meeting on Phonology, and the existence of handbooks such as the current one).

3   Example 1: Working with pre-existing corpora

As mentioned, it can be daunting to try to use a new analysis tool on one's own data without any prior familiarity. While it means a slight delay in terms of getting to the actual analysis of data, we think it is more efficient in the long run to get to know a new tool on data that have been formatted ahead of time, such that the user can see how the data need to be structured for the software to process them in the way(s) the user is interested in.[2]

In terms of getting started with PCT, one of the best resources is the Irvine Phonotactic Online Dictionary of English (IPhOD; Vaden, Halpin, & Hickok 2009). IPhOD is a dictionary of American English (transcribed using ARPAbet notation using the Carnegie-Mellon Pronouncing Dictionary; Weide 1994) that also includes the token frequencies of each word as found in the SUBTLEX$_{US}$ database (Brysbaert & New 2009, which is based on frequencies of occurrence in subtitles of TV shows and movies). IPhOD is itself freely available from www.iphod .com, but its developers have also given permission for a version of the database to be distributed with PCT directly. Thus, upon downloading PCT, one can choose to download and open the IPhOD corpus. Although the full IPhOD database includes extensive pre-calculated information about characteristics such as phoneme, biphone, and triphone probabilities, the version loaded with PCT contains only the essential information that is required to be considered a corpus in PCT, that is, orthographic representations, transcriptions, and token frequencies of each word (see figure 51.1; frequencies are occurrences per million words).

3.1   Transcription systems and feature files

To actually use a corpus in PCT, it needs to be associated with a feature file. This feature file is crucial for the success of PCT's analysis algorithms and is also the source of PCT's flexibility when it comes to phonological representations (see also section 4). The feature file is a delimited text file (e.g., a .csv file) that lists the transcription symbols used in the corpus in the first column and then all of the phonological feature values for each symbol in the subsequent columns (see figure 51.2).

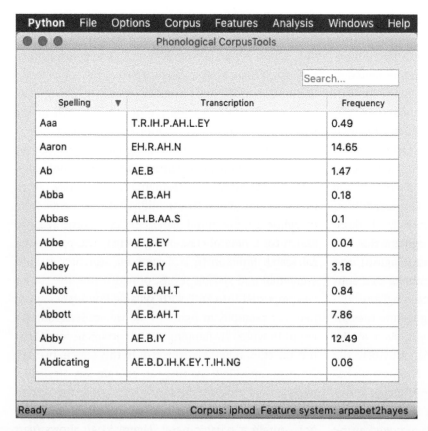

Figure 51.1
The IPhOD corpus (Vaden, Halpin, & Hickok 2009) loaded into PCT.

Edit feature system

symbol ▼	anterior	approximant	back	consonantal	constricted glottis	continuant	coronal	delayed_release	diphthong	distributed	dorsal	front
AA	0	+	+	-	-	+	-	0	-	0	+	-
AE	0	+	-	-	-	+	-	0	-	0	+	+
AH	0	+	+	-	-	+	-	0	-	0	+	-
AH L	+	+	0	+	-	+	+	0	0	-	-	0
AH N	+	-	0	+	-	-	+	0	0	-	-	0
AO	0	+	+	-	-	+	-	0	-	0	+	-
AW	0	+	-	-	-	+	-	0	+	0	+	-
AY	0	+	-	-	-	+	-	0	+	0	+	-
B	0	-	0	+	-	-	-	-	0	0	-	0

Change feature systems
Transcription and feature file

arpabet2hayes

Modify the feature system

Add segment

Edit segment

Add feature

Corpus inventory coverage

Hide all segments not used by the corpus

Show all segments

Check corpus inventory coverage

Display options

Display mode: Matrix

Save changes to this feature system   Cancel   Help

Figure 51.2
The ARPAbet-to-Hayes feature file for the IPhOD corpus.

Because the feature file is customizable by the user, *any* transcription system (including one of the user's own invention) can be interpreted by PCT. (Note that most common encoding systems are accepted, e.g., UTF-8, ASCII.) When using the IPhOD corpus, the feature file also comes pre-loaded; the transcriptions are in ARPA-bet notation. The featural interpretation that is loaded by default is based on the phonological features used in Hayes (2009), a widely used introductory phonology text-book with a fairly standard and transparent set of features.

It is important to note that these features are intended to be primarily descriptive rather than analytical; they are used to allow phonological search and analysis functions to work, not to provide a theoretical interpretation of the segment inventory of a language. Thus, redundant features are of no particular consequence, and every segment in the inventory must be fully specified for each feature. Features can, however, be specified with any type of value; for example, [+], [–], and [0] are all common feature specifications. To be maximally descriptive, the Hayes feature set has also been enhanced by the addition of a few descriptive features used to distinguish diphthongs: [+diphthong] is used for any segment that is a diphthong (e.g., [aɪ], [aʊ], [ɔɪ] in American English), and [+front-diphthong] is used for any diphthong that ends in a front vowel (e.g., [aɪ], [ɔɪ] in American English).

PCT comes with several pre-existing feature files for use with common transcription systems, such as the International Phonetic Alphabet (IPA), ARPAbet, the Extended Speech Assessment Methods Phonetic Alphabet (X-SAMPA), the Computer Phonetic Alphabet (CPA), and the Distinct Single Character set (DISC). Each of these transcription systems can be interpreted using either the Hayes (2009) features or with features that are based on Chomsky and Halle (1968), referred to as SPE. As will be discussed in section 4, these pre-existing feature files can be adapted for more customized use.

3.2 Basic descriptions and searches

With a corpus and feature file in place, basic statistics can be calculated. A good place to start with a corpus is examining its segmental inventory. PCT will try to automatically organize a corpus based on the specified phonological features. These features will be necessary for any analysis function to work (or at least, for the function to produce meaningful output), so it is best to check here first and ensure that the inventory is organized as expected. If it is not, the inventory can be managed using a separate menu option in which one can, for example, specify which features distinguish vowels from consonants, or the feature file can be edited to have PCT automatically re-organize the inventory along new featural dimensions. Figure 51.3 shows the consonantal inventory of the IPhOD corpus, automatically sorted into an IPA-style table by PCT. Clicking on any given segment will show both its type and token frequency in the corpus, both in raw counts and in percentages.

One of the most basic but flexible aspects of PCT is the ability to do *phonological searches* within a corpus. This allows researchers both to calculate general statistics on particular phonological sequences or patterns and to find individual examples of such sequences. Figure 51.4 illustrates a basic phonological search in the CELEX corpus (Baayen, Piepenbrock, & Gulikers 1995).[3] An individual environment or environments can be specified using the typical format for writing phonological contexts, using non-segmental symbols (e.g., word or morpheme boundaries), individual segments (e.g., to define a non-natural class), and/or features (e.g., to search for a natural class of segments). The phonological search function in PCT supports searches on both segmental and syllabic levels, provided that the corpus was imported into PCT with syllable boundaries specified. For example, in figure 51.4a, we are searching for words in which /t/-flapping, which occurs in some English varieties, might be expected. In this search, two syllables are specified; the first can contain any [+syllabic] nucleus that receives primary stress, while the second must contain [t] in onset position, be unstressed, and not contain a syllabic nasal. Figure 51.4b shows (part of) the overall summary results for this search, listing the type and token frequencies for each of the resulting environments. Finally, figure 51.4c shows (part of) the individual word results for this search, listing out individual words from the corpus that match specific environments that were included in the search.

In terms of data management per se, it is useful to note that particular search parameters (and not just the results of searches) can be saved to be used across sessions or across corpora. The five most recent searches are automatically saved in PCT and are retrievable across sessions with different corpora. In addition, any particular search that is performed can be saved and then applied to another session and/or another corpus. This option is especially useful for doing cross-linguistic comparisons and ensuring that the parameters of the search are both replicated exactly and precisely reportable in any subsequent descriptions of the process (see also Han, chapter 6, this volume).

3.3 Analysis algorithms

Finally, the true *goal* of PCT is to facilitate the analysis of phonological patterns within a corpus. The algorithms included in PCT are ones that help researchers

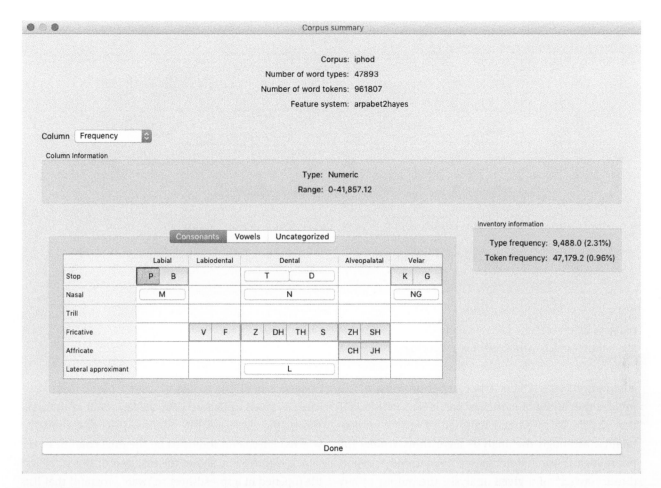

Figure 51.3
Segmental inventory of the IPhOD corpus, with type and token frequency information for the segment [p].

find, describe, and quantify phonological patterns within a corpus. It is important to note that while these can then be used to theorize about more abstract phonological structure, they are only directly able to inform about surface-level patterns (unless the corpus itself is transcribed at a deeper level).

There are several algorithms that can be used, including:[4]

- Measures that examine how similar strings are to each other (*string similarity*; see, e.g., Frisch, Pierrehumbert, & Broe 2004; Khorsi 2012), how many phonologically similar "neighbors" any given word has (*neighborhood density*; see, e.g., Greenberg & Jenkins 1964; Luce & Pisoni 1998; Yao 2011), and how likely any particular string is (*phonotactic probability*; see e.g., Vitevitch & Luce 2004).

- Measures of phonological relationships, both in terms of how much work a phonological contrast does in the language (*functional load*; see, e.g., Hockett 1966;

Surendran & Niyogi 2003; Wedel, Jackson, & Kaplan 2013; Wedel, Kaplan, & Jackson 2013) and in terms of how close to or distant from complementary distribution a pair of sounds might be (*predictability of distribution*; see, e.g., Hall 2009, 2012; and *Kullback-Leibler divergence*; see, e.g., Kullback & Leibler 1951; Peperkamp et al. 2006).

- Measures of how likely some sound is based on other components of its environment_transitional probability_; see, e.g., Saffran et al. 1996; (*informativity*; see, e.g., Cohen Priva 2008, 2015; and *mutual information*; see, e.g., Brent 1999; Goldsmith & Riggle 2012).

As we've mentioned, one of the particular advantages to using a program such as PCT to analyze data, rather than writing original analysis scripts for different research projects, is that multiple researchers can be sure that they are using the same algorithms when approaching their data, enabling more direct

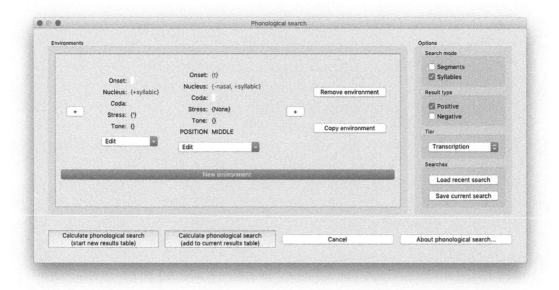

Figure 51.4a

Phonological search specification for /t/-flapping.

comparison.[5] At the same time, any given analysis will involve the setting of particular parameters within PCT that should be saved and reported to ensure comparability. Although the analysis algorithms, unlike the phonological search function, do not currently support direct "saving" of a given analysis, the output of any analysis includes a record of all parameters in addition to the relevant calculated result. These outputs can themselves be saved as .csv files and referred to in future work, and it is good practice to do so, rather than simply recording the parameters that seem relevant in the moment.

As an example, consider how one could calculate the functional load of the [i]/[u] contrast in the IPhoD corpus, shown in figure 51.5. Figure 51.5a shows PCT's interface for an analysis of functional load. Notice that multiple parameters can be selected by the user. In this case, PCT is told to calculate functional load by counting the number of minimal pairs that occur in the corpus (rather than the change in entropy of the corpus upon merger); to output the results in terms of the raw counts (rather than e.g., normalizing them to the corpus size); to distinguish homophones from each other (so that e.g., "seen"/"soon" and "scene"/"soon" count as two separate minimal pairs); to also save a list of the actual minimal pairs in the corpus to a .txt file for future reference; and to only include words that have a minimum token

frequency of 2. The results window, with all parameters listed, is given in figure 51.5b; the key result of the analysis is that there are 145 minimal pairs that meet the selected criteria (as indicated by the final column in the table). Figure 51.5c shows the first part of the saved .txt file (opened in a spreadsheet software program) that lists out these 145 pairs, in both orthographic and phonetic representations.

Note that in the results window shown in figure 51.5b, the user is given the option to save these summary results to a .csv file for later reference. We recommend saving these kinds of results to an archive (see Andreassen, chapter 7, this volume), at least once a final analysis has been arrived at, as these files contain all the information necessary for reproducing the analysis in addition to the actual results.

The results window also offers the option to return to the analysis function window, where all of the user-selected options are still displayed. As long as a current results window remains open, a user can continue to run the same algorithm multiple times with different parameters, with the new results appended to the existing ones, and then export the full set of results together. For example, in the settings shown in figure 51.5a, switching off the parameter of distinguishing homophones results in there being only seventy-eight minimal pairs in the corpus, and this information (including the changed

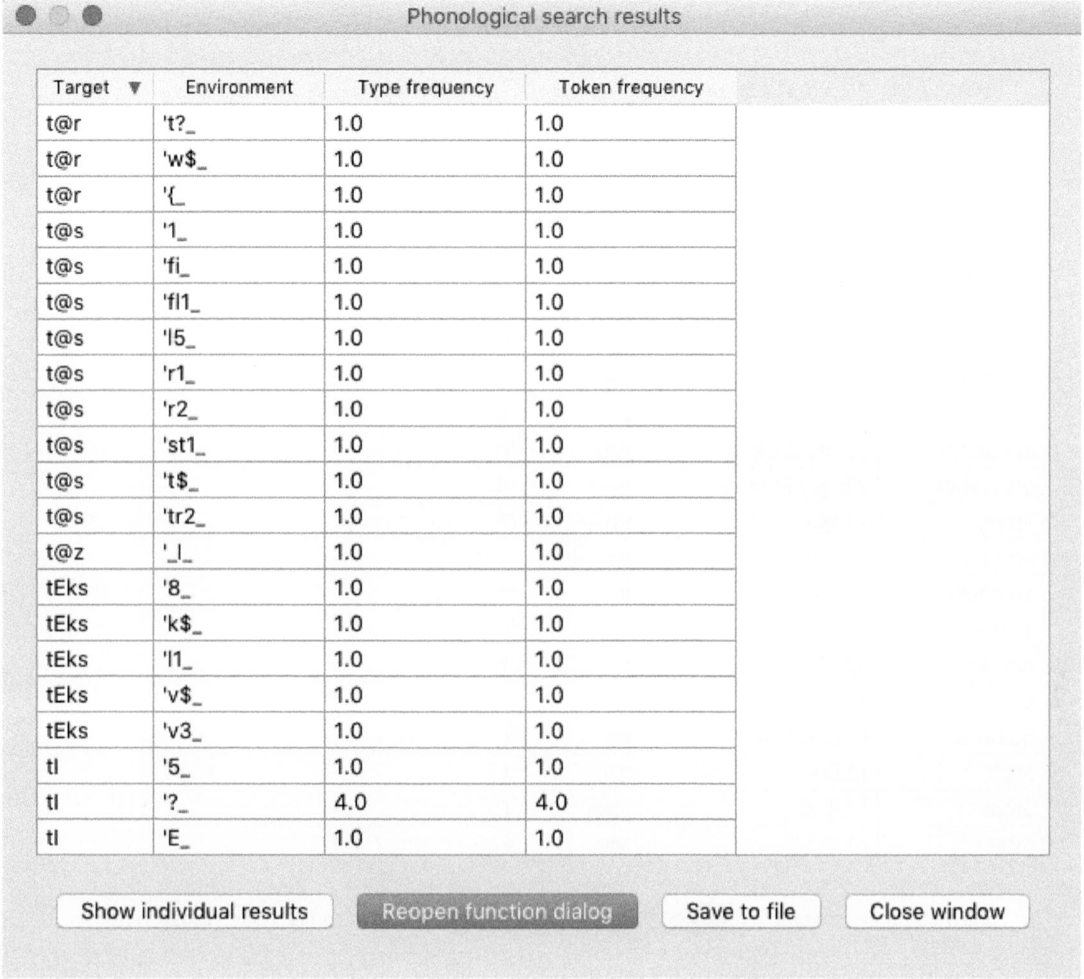

Target	Environment	Type frequency	Token frequency
t@r	't?_	1.0	1.0
t@r	'w$_	1.0	1.0
t@r	'{_	1.0	1.0
t@s	'1_	1.0	1.0
t@s	'fi_	1.0	1.0
t@s	'fl1_	1.0	1.0
t@s	'l5_	1.0	1.0
t@s	'r1_	1.0	1.0
t@s	'r2_	1.0	1.0
t@s	'st1_	1.0	1.0
t@s	't$_	1.0	1.0
t@s	'tr2_	1.0	1.0
t@z	'_I_	1.0	1.0
tEks	'8_	1.0	1.0
tEks	'k$_	1.0	1.0
tEks	'l1_	1.0	1.0
tEks	'v$_	1.0	1.0
tEks	'v3_	1.0	1.0
tl	'5_	1.0	1.0
tl	'?_	4.0	4.0
tl	'E_	1.0	1.0

Figure 51.4b
Summary results from the search.

parameters that gave rise to the different result) could be added to the results window and exported.

3.4 Other pre-existing corpora

In addition to the IPhOD corpus, which is directly distributed with PCT, it is possible to import other pre-existing corpora into the software. In these cases, the user must independently have access to a copy of the corpus, and sometimes, this involves purchasing access rights (e.g., the Linguistic Data Consortium (https://www.ldc.upenn.edu/) stores and distributes hundreds of corpora and databases to its paying members).[6] In other cases, a corpus may be freely available, but the user must personally register with the owner of the corpus to get access (e.g., the Buckeye Corpus of Conversational Speech [Pitt et al. 2007] requires acceptance of the license agreement and individual registration, but the corpus is available free of charge).

Any corpus that is in PCT's standard format of a .csv file with columns for orthography, transcription, and frequency can be imported into PCT. As mentioned in section 3.1, a transcription/feature file will also need to be loaded into PCT to make use of its search and analysis functions. That said, PCT does facilitate the use of some common corpora through the existence of additional resources. In particular, the Buckeye corpus (Pitt et al. 2007) has a file structure that is more complex than a single .csv file, but can be automatically converted into such a structure and directly loaded into PCT from a local copy. PCT also comes with transcription/feature files that interpret the transcription systems of this corpus as well as the CELEX (Baayen, Piepenbrock, &

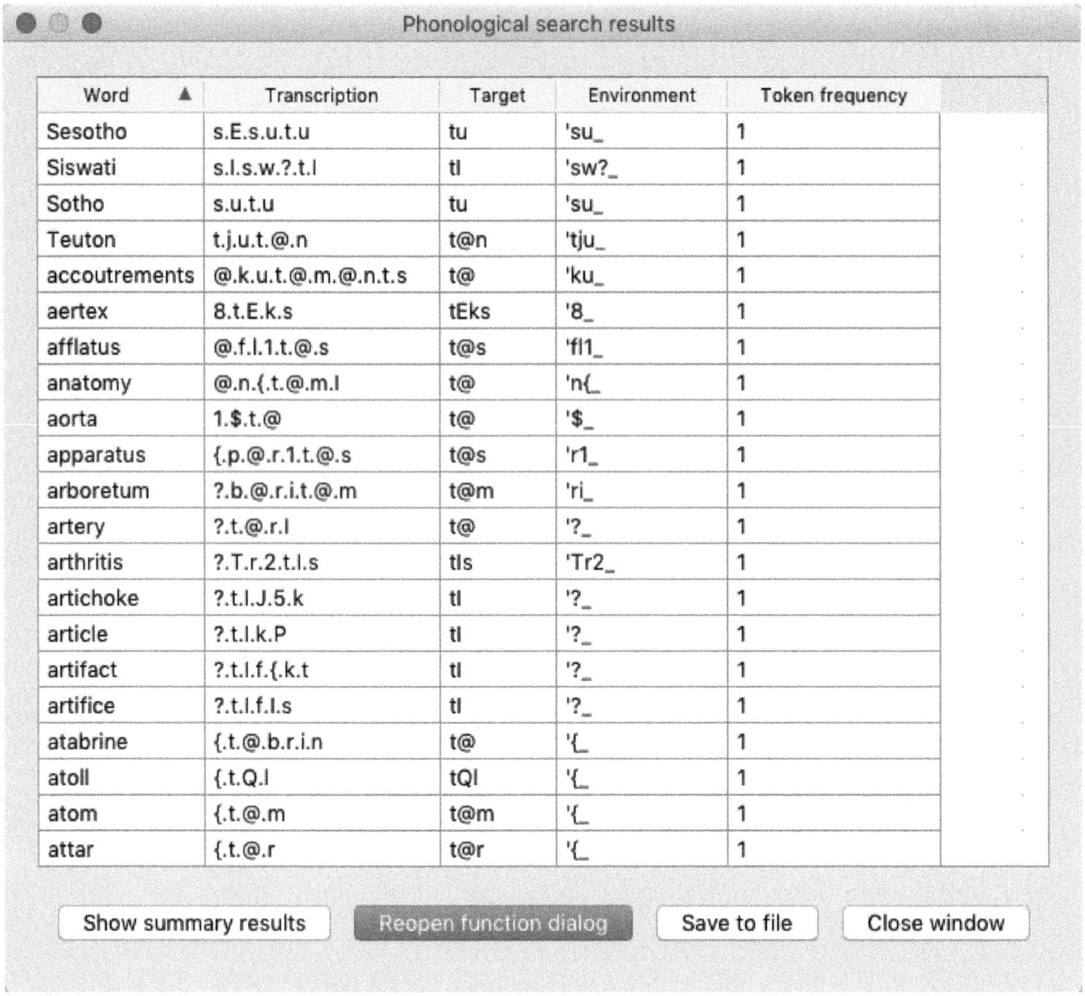

Word	Transcription	Target	Environment	Token frequency
Sesotho	s.E.s.u.t.u	tu	'su_	1
Siswati	s.I.s.w.?.t.I	tI	'sw?_	1
Sotho	s.u.t.u	tu	'su_	1
Teuton	t.j.u.t.@.n	t@n	'tju_	1
accoutrements	@.k.u.t.@.m.@.n.t.s	t@	'ku_	1
aertex	8.t.E.k.s	tEks	'8_	1
afflatus	@.f.l.1.t.@.s	t@s	'fl1_	1
anatomy	@.n.{.t.@.m.I	t@	'n{_	1
aorta	1.$.t.@	t@	'$_	1
apparatus	{.p.@.r.1.t.@.s	t@s	'r1_	1
arboretum	?.b.@.r.i.t.@.m	t@m	'ri_	1
artery	?.t.@.r.I	t@	'?_	1
arthritis	?.T.r.2.t.I.s	tIs	'Tr2_	1
artichoke	?.t.I.J.5.k	tI	'?_	1
article	?.t.I.k.P	tI	'?_	1
artifact	?.t.I.f.{.k.t	tI	'?_	1
artifice	?.t.I.f.I.s	tI	'?_	1
atabrine	{.t.@.b.r.i.n	t@	'{_	1
atoll	{.t.Q.l	tQl	'{_	1
atom	{.t.@.m	t@m	'{_	1
attar	{.t.@.r	t@r	'{_	1

Figure 51.4c
First part of the individual word results from the search.

Gulikers 1995) and TIMIT (Garofolo et al. 1993) corpora into both the SPE and Hayes-style feature systems as we've described. Thus, depending on the research questions of interest, PCT can be used for analysis with relatively little pre-manipulation of the data if a pre-existing corpus is available.

4 Example 2: Working with original/fieldwork data

PCT is also intended, however, to be used with *original data*, that is, with corpora that have been developed by individual researchers (see also Hall, Pine, & Schwan 2018). To maximize the utility of the software across linguistic methodologies, there are three different formats from which such corpora can be created.

First, if a researcher has a .csv file that contains words, their transcriptions, and their frequencies, then this can be easily uploaded into PCT directly. This approach is particularly useful in the case of using dictionaries or lexica as "corpora." (Note that PCT can simply set all frequencies for words to "1" if token frequencies are unavailable.) Additional information can be included in such a file (e.g., parts of speech, morphological breakdown); such columns are readable in PCT, but they are not required for the basic algorithms to work.

Second, PCT can create a corpus file from a single file or directory of files containing running text (e.g., transcriptions of fieldwork sessions). PCT supports any consistently formatted file structure, including interlinear glosses with multiple lines (e.g., separate lines for orthography, morphological structure, phonetic transcription, and gloss). When reading in such files, the user is prompted to give PCT information about the basic parsing parameters of the data, such as what type

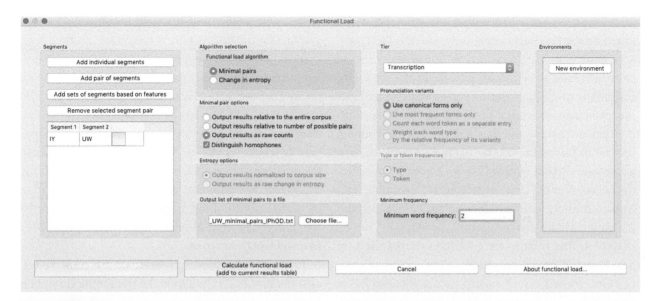

Figure 51.5a
Phonological analysis specification for the functional load of [i] versus [u] in the IPhoD corpus.

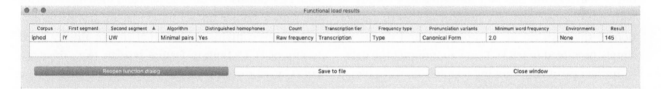

Figure 51.5b
Summary results from the analysis.

	A	B	C	D	E	F
1	First segment	Second segment	First word	First word transcription	Second word	Second word transcription
2	IY	UW	feeds	F.IY.D.Z	foods	F.UW.D.Z
3	IY	UW	beats	B.IY.T.S	boots	B.UW.T.S
4	IY	UW	mi	M.IY	Moo	M.UW
5	IY	UW	me	M.IY	Moo	M.UW
6	IY	UW	beast	B.IY.S.T	boost	B.UW.S.T
7	IY	UW	tea	T.IY	tu	T.UW
8	IY	UW	tea	T.IY	two	T.UW
9	IY	UW	tea	T.IY	too	T.UW
10	IY	UW	means	M.IY.N.Z	moons	M.UW.N.Z
11	IY	UW	steel	S.T.IY.L	stool	S.T.UW.L
12	IY	UW	scene	S.IY.N	soon	S.UW.N
13	IY	UW	key	K.IY	coup	K.UW
14	IY	UW	key	K.IY	Qu	K.UW
15	IY	UW	keep	K.IY.P	Coop	K.UW.P

Figure 51.5c
First part of the individual minimal pairs found in the analysis.

of information each line represents, what delimiters might be used between segments/syllables/morphemes, how particular characters such as punctuation should be treated, and so on. Upon reading in the data, PCT converts it to the standard corpus format and includes the token frequencies it calculated across the file(s). Both the standard corpus columns and the original running text are displayed in PCT (see figure 51.6, which shows a corpus of Gitksan created from a set of transcribed stories collected at the University of British Columbia from Barbara Sennott [née Harris]; see Hall, Pine, & Schwan [2018] for details, and see Holton, Leonard, & Pulsifer, chapter 4, this volume, for guidelines on the usage of data from Indigenous people).

Third, corpora can be created from a TextGrid file or set of TextGrid files created in Praat (Boersma & Weenink 1992–2021). Thus, if audio recordings have been made and then annotated/segmented, the text can be pulled out of the TextGrid files and converted to a corpus. As with running text files, any number of tiers of annotation in the TextGrid file is supported, and the user is simply prompted to tell PCT how to interpret the data.

In the case of both running text and TextGrid files, it should be noted that PCT supports what we call *pronunciation variants*, in other words, different pronunciations of the same word. Thus, if a word is represented orthographically on one tier in a consistent fashion (e.g., <probably> on an orthography tier), but has multiple different transcriptions for different instances of the word on another tier (e.g., [pɹɑbəbli] and [pɹɑli] on a pronunciation tier), PCT can associate those different pronunciations with the single lexical item. This information is used by certain analysis algorithms, allowing a user to choose how to treat such variable data, for example, by using only the canonical pronunciation (if labeled), or by using only the most frequent pronunciation, or by weighting the various pronunciations according to their frequency of occurrence.

In all cases, a transcription/feature file must be created to allow PCT to interpret the transcription symbols used, but as mentioned in section 3.1, such a file can be created with any symbols and features, allowing maximal flexibility. Any of the pre-existing files that come with PCT can also be downloaded and then modified for use with a similar transcription system. If a user's custom corpus contains symbols that are not already listed in any of PCT's built-in feature systems (e.g., the symbol /ƛ/ used for some Pacific Northwest languages), the corpus can still be loaded, and PCT will automatically assign each of those symbols a feature value of "n" for

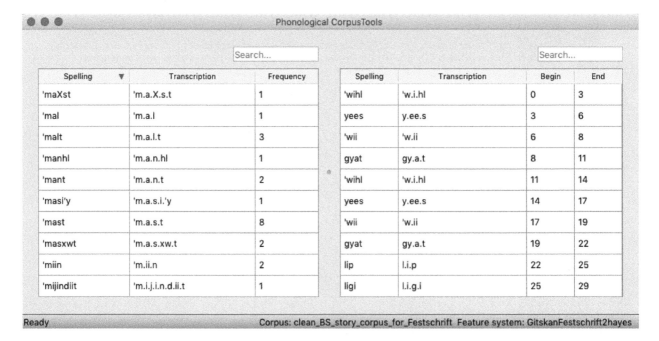

Figure 51.6
Example of a corpus created from running text. See Hall, Pine, and Schwan (2018) for further discussion. The standard alphabetized corpus is on the left, with token frequencies calculated across all of the stories in the collection; the original text in order is shown on the right.

all features. These values can be edited manually from within PCT, and the user is notified about feature-less symbols before corpus loading completes.

By default, PCT assumes that a corpus lacks any multi-character sequences. If a corpus contains any such characters, such as diphthongs or affricates, then the user must specify them in PCT before or while loading their corpus. This can be done manually by including a delimiter within the transcriptions themselves (e.g., using a period to delimit the individual segments in [tʃ. aɪ.m] "chime"). Alternatively, a list of the characters that should be treated as multi-character sequences can be given to PCT (e.g., [tʃ], [aɪ]), and the delimitation can be done automatically.

Once the corpus has been created and a feature file associated with it, then corpus analysis can proceed in exactly the same ways as described in section 3.3.

5 Conclusion

In conclusion, PCT is a software tool that is designed to facilitate phonological analysis of transcribed corpora. By being open source, clearly documented, and freely available, we hope that it contributes to transparent, replicable corpus analysis. Users are encouraged to become familiar with the software through the use of pre-existing corpora and then to expand their studies to their own fieldwork data.

More broadly, we hope that PCT encourages good data management practices, both in itself and as a model for other similar projects. In particular, we would like to see other analysis algorithms being shared in similar fashion rather than being individualized, stand-alone scripts designed for use in particular projects. For example, we would personally be delighted to have other researchers write or collaborate on an analysis script that could be incorporated into the PCT framework and thus shared with the field as a whole. Even if that particular route is not suitable for a project, we would like to see it become common practice for researchers to think about how their scripts might be used by other scholars with other data sets, and make such scripts fully re-usable by, for example, including documentation and a clear explanation of how data must be formatted to apply the algorithms in question. These practices take time and commitment and are not commonly recognized as accomplishments in the wider world of academia, but we hope that this mindset

can change. Being able to point to volumes such as this Handbook as a call to arms for best practices is an important first step in changing the status quo.

Notes

1. PCT is primarily designed to work with transcriptions from spoken languages. Our research team also has a piece of software, Sign Language Phonetic Annotator+Analyzer (SLP-AA; see Lo & Hall 2019), which is designed to facilitate the transcription of signed languages (primarily using the system developed in Johnson & Liddell 2010, 2011a, 2011b, 2012), and we are currently working on adapting the phonological analysis algorithms provided in PCT to work with these transcriptions. All examples in this chapter, however, are from spoken languages.

2. It is also possible that the user is interested in answering questions that can be addressed with pre-existing corpora, in which case there is less concern about data management of the corpus itself.

3. Note that this example phonological search is done on the English CELEX corpus (Baayen, Piepenbrock, & Gulikers 1995) simply to demonstrate PCT's ability to do syllable-based searches. Syllables are not encoded in the IPhOD corpus, so only segmental searches can be performed on it.

4. Note that the PCT documentation for each algorithm is quite extensive and includes information about how and why each measure has been used for linguistic inquiry.

5. However, care should be taken to make sure that comparable analyses are also being done with the same versions of PCT, in case the details of the analysis algorithms have changed from one version to the next in light of advances in the field. That said, because PCT is stored and released publicly on GitHub, it is possible to pull any previous version of the software to exactly replicate a previous analysis.

6. It should be kept in mind that researchers must adhere to the usage guidelines that accompany the corpora they access; see also discussion in Holton, Leonard, and Pulsifer, chapter 4, this volume; Collister, chapter 9, this volume; and Conzett and De Smedt, chapter 11, this volume.

References

Baayen, R. Harald, Richard Piepenbrock, and Leon Gulikers. 1995. *The CELEX Lexical Database*. Philadelphia: Linguistic Data Consortium, University of Pennsylvania.

Boersma, Paul, and David Weenink. 1992–2021. Praat: A system for doing phonetics by computer [computer program]. www.praat .org.

Brent, Michael R. 1999. An efficient, probabilistically sound algorithm for segmentation and word discovery. *Machine Learning* 34 (1–3): 71–105. https://doi.org/10.1023/A:1007541817488.

Brysbaert, Marc, and Boris New. 2009. Moving beyond Kučera and Francis: A critical evaluation of current word frequency norms and the introduction of a new and improved word frequency measure for American English. *Behavior Research Methods* 41 (4): 977–990. https://doi.org/10.3758/BRM.41.4.977.

Bybee, Joan L. 2001. *Phonology and Language Use*. Cambridge: Cambridge University Press.

Cedergren, Henrietta J., and David Sankoff. 1974. Variable rules: Performance as a statistical reflection of competence. *Language* 50:333–355. https://doi.org/10.2307/412441.

Chomsky, Noam, and Morris Halle. 1968. *The Sound Pattern of English*. New York: Harper and Row.

Cohen Priva, Uriel. 2008. Using information content to predict phone deletion. In *Proceedings of the 27th West Coast Conference on Formal Linguistics*, ed. Natasha Abner and Jason Bishop, 90–98. Somerville, MA: Cascadilla Proceedings Project.

Cohen Priva, Uriel. 2015. Informativity affects consonant duration and deletion rates. *Laboratory Phonology* 6 (2): 243–278. https://doi.org/10.1515/lp-2015-0008.

Durand, Jacques. 2014. Corpora, variation, and phonology: An illustration from French liaison. In *The Oxford Handbook of Corpus Phonology*, ed. Jacques Durand, Ulrike Gut, and Gjert Kristoffersen, 240–264. Oxford: Oxford University Press.

Durand, Jacques, Ulrike Gut, and Gjert Kristoffersen, eds. 2014. *The Oxford Handbook of Corpus Phonology*. Oxford: Oxford University Press.

Fosler-Lussier, Eric, and Nelson Morgan. 1999. Effects of speaking rate and word frequency on pronunciations. *Speech Communication* 29 (2–4): 137–158. https://doi.org/10.1016/S0167-6393(99)00035-7.

Frisch, Stefan. 2012. Phonotactic patterns in lexical corpora. In *The Oxford Handbook of Laboratory Phonology*, ed. Abigail C. Cohn, Cécile Fougeron, and Marie K. Huffman, 458–470. Oxford: Oxford University Press.

Frisch, Stefan, Janet B. Pierrehumbert, and Michael B. Broe. 2004. Similarity avoidance and the OCP. *Natural Language and Linguistic Theory* 22 (1): 179–228. https://doi.org/10.1023/B:NALA.0000005557.78535.3c.

Gahl, Susanne, Yao Yao, and Keith Johnson. 2012. Why reduce? Phonological neighborhood density and phonetic reduction in spontaneous speech. *Journal of Memory and Language* 66 (4): 789–806. https://doi.org/10.1016/j.jml.2011.11.006.

Garofolo, John S., Lori F. Lamel, William M. Fisher, Jonathan G. Fiscus, David S. Pallett, Nancy L. Dahlgren, and Victor Zue. 1993. *TIMIT Acoustic-Phonetic Continuous Speech Corpus LDC93S1*. Philadelphia: Linguistic Data Consortium, University of Pennsylvania.

Goldsmith, John, and Jason Riggle. 2012. Information theoretic approaches to phonological structure: The case of Finnish vowel harmony. *Natural Language and Linguistic Theory* 30 (3): 859–896. https://doi.org/10.1007/s11049-012-9169-1.

Greenberg, Joseph H., and James J. Jenkins. 1964. Studies in the psychological correlates of the sound system of American English. *Word* 20 (2): 157–177. https://doi.org/10.1080/00437956.1964.11659816.

Hall, Daniel Currie, and Kathleen Currie Hall. 2016. Marginal contrasts and the Contrastivist Hypothesis. *Glossa: A Journal of General Linguistics* 1 (1): 1–23. https://doi.org/10.5334/gjgl.245.

Hall, Kathleen Currie. 2009. A probabilistic model of phonological relationships from contrast to allophony. PhD dissertation, The Ohio State University.

Hall, Kathleen Currie. 2012. Phonological relationships: A probabilistic model. *McGill Working Papers in Linguistics* 22 (1): 1–14.

Hall, Kathleen Currie. Forthcoming. Corpora and phonological analysis. In *The Oxford Handbook on the History of Phonology*, ed. B. Elan Dresher and Harry van der Hulst. Oxford: Oxford University Press.

Hall, Kathleen Currie, Blake Allen, Michael Fry, Khia Johnson, Roger Yu-Hsiang Lo, J. Scott Mackie, Michael McAuliffe, and Stanley Nam. 2018. Phonological CorpusTools, version 1.4 [computer program]. https://github.com/PhonologicalCorpusTools/CorpusTools/releases.

Hall, Kathleen Currie, J. Scott Mackie, and Roger Yu-Hsiang Lo. 2019. Phonological CorpusTools: Software for doing phonological analysis on transcribed corpora. *International Journal of Corpus Linguistics* 24 (4): 522–535. https://doi.org/10.1075/ijcl.18009.hal.

Hall, Kathleen Currie, Aidan Pine, and Michael David Schwan. 2018. Doing phonological corpus analysis in a fieldwork context. In *Wa7 xweysás i nqwal'utteníha i ucwalmícwa: He Loves the People's Languages: Essays in Honour of Henry Davis*, ed. Lisa Matthewson, Erin A. Guntly, and Michael Rochemont, 615–630. Vancouver: UBC Occasional Papers in Linguistics.

Hayes, Bruce. 2009. *Introductory Phonology*. Hoboken, NJ: Wiley/Blackwell.

Hockett, Charles Francis. 1966. The quantification of functional load: A linguistic problem. RM-5168-PR. Santa Monica, CA: RAND Corporation. Available from https://eric.ed.gov/?id=ED011649.

Jakobson, Roman. (1941) 1968. *Child Language Aphasia and Phonological Universals*. The Hague, the Netherlands: Mouton Publishers.

John, Tina, and Lasse Bombien. 2014. EMU. In *The Oxford Handbook of Corpus Phonology*, ed. Jacques Durand, Ulrike Gut, and Gjert Kristoffersen, 321–341. Oxford: Oxford University Press.

Johnson, Robert E., and Scott K. Liddell. 2010. Toward a phonetic representation of signs: Sequentiality and contrast. *Sign Language Studies* 11 (2): 241–274. https://doi.org/10.1353/sls.2010.0008.

Johnson, Robert E., and Scott K. Liddell. 2011a. A segmental framework for representing signs phonetically. *Sign Language Studies* 11 (3): 408–463. https://doi.org/10.1353/sls.2011.0002.

Johnson, Robert E., and Scott K. Liddell. 2011b. Toward a phonetic representation of hand configuration: The fingers. *Sign Language Studies* 12 (1): 5–45. https://doi.org/10.1353/sls.2011.0013.

Johnson, Robert E., and Scott K. Liddell. 2012. Toward a phonetic representation of hand configuration: The thumb. *Sign Language Studies* 12 (2): 316–333. https://doi.org/10.1353/sls .2011.0020.

Khorsi, Ahmed. 2012. On morphological relatedness. *Natural Language Engineering* 19 (4): 1–19. https://doi.org/10.1017/S1351 324912000071.

Kullback, Solomon, and Richard A. Leibler. 1951. On information and sufficiency. *Annals of Mathematical Statistics* 22:79–86. https://doi.org/10.1214/aoms/1177729694.

Lo, Roger Yu-Hsiang, and Kathleen Currie Hall. 2019. SLP-AA: Tools for sign language phonetic and phonological research. *Interspeech*, 3679–3680. Available from https://www.isca-speech .org/archive/Interspeech_2019/pdfs/8028.pdf.

Luce, Paul A., and David B. Pisoni. 1998. Recognizing spoken words: The neighborhood activation model. *Ear and Hearing* 19 (1): 1–36. https://doi.org/10.1097/00003446-199802000-00001.

Peperkamp, Sharon, Rozenn Le Calvez, Jean-Pierre Nadal, and Emmanuel Dupoux. 2006. The acquisition of allophonic rules: Statistical learning with linguistic constraints. *Cognition* 101:B31–B41. https://doi.org/10.1016/j.cognition.2005.10.006.

Phillips, Betty. 2006. *Word Frequency and Lexical Diffusion*. Basingstoke, UK: Palgrave Macmillan.

Piantadosi, Steven T., Harry Tily, and Edward Gibson. 2011. Word lengths are optimized for efficient communication. *Proceedings of the National Academy of Sciences* 108 (9): 3526–3529. https://doi.org/10.1073/pnas.1012551108.

Pinnow, Eleni, and Cynthia M. Connine. 2014. Phonological variant recognition: Representations and rules. *Language and Speech* 57 (1): 42–67. https://doi.org/10.1177/0023830913479105.

Pitt, Mark A., Laura Dilley, Keith Johnson, Scott Kiesling, William Raymond, Elizabeth Hume, and Eric Fosler-Lussier. 2007. Buckeye Corpus of Conversational Speech. 2nd release. Columbus: Department of Psychology, Ohio State University. www .buckeyecorpus.osu.edu.

Rose, Yvan. 2014. Corpus-based investigations of child phonological development: Formal and practical considerations. In *The Oxford Handbook of Corpus Phonology*, ed. Jacques Durand, Ulrike Gut, and Gjert Kristoffersen, 265–285. Oxford: Oxford University Press.

Rose, Yvan, and Brian MacWhinney. 2014. The Phonbank project: Data and software-assisted methods for the study of phonology and phonological development. In *The Oxford Handbook of Corpus Phonology*, ed. Jacques Durand, Ulrike Gut, and Gjert Kristoffersen, 380–401. Oxford: Oxford University Press.

Ryan, Kevin. 2014. Onsets contribute to syllable weight: Statistical evidence from stress and meter. *Language* 90 (2): 309–341. https://doi.org/10.1353/lan.2014.0029.

Saffran, Jenny R., Elisa L. Newport, and Richard N. Aslin. (1996). Word segmentation: The role of distributional cues. *Journal of Memory and Language*, 35:606–621. https://doi.org /10.1006/jmla.1996.0032.

Sloetjes, Han. 2014. ELAN: Multimedia annotation application. In *The Oxford Handbook of Corpus Phonology*, ed. Jacques Durand, Ulrike Gut, and Gjert Kristoffersen, 305–320. Oxford: Oxford University Press.

Surendran, Dinoj, and Partha Niyogi. 2003. Measuring the functional load of phonological contrasts. In Technical Report TR-2003-12. Chicago: Department of Computer Science, University of Chicago. https://arxiv.org/pdf/cs.CL/0311036.

Vaden, K. I., H. R. Halpin, and G. S. Hickok. 2009. Irvine Phonotactic Online Dictionary, version 2.0. www.iphod.com.

Vitevitch, Michael S., and Paul A. Luce. 2004. A web-based interface to calculate phonotactic probability for words and nonwords in English. *Behavior Research Methods, Instruments, and Computers* 36 (3): 481–487. https://doi.org/10.3758/BF03195594.

Wedel, Andrew, Scott Jackson, and Abby Kaplan. 2013. Functional load and the lexicon: Evidence that syntactic category and frequency relationships in minimal lemma pairs predict the loss of phoneme contrasts in language change. *Language and Speech* 56 (3): 395–417. https://doi.org/10.1177 /0023830913489096.

Wedel, Andrew, Abby Kaplan, and Scott Jackson. 2013. High functional load inhibits phonological contrast loss: A corpus study. *Cognition* 128 (2): 179–186. https://doi.org/10.1016/j .cognition.2013.03.002.

Weide, Robert L. 1994. CMU Pronouncing Dictionary. Available from http://www.speech.cs.cmu.edu/cgi-bin/cmudict.

Yao, Yao. 2011. The effects of phonological neighborhoods on pronunciation variation in conversational speech. PhD dissertation, University of California, Berkeley.

Steven Moran

1   Introduction

This data management use case describes PHOIBLE Online, a typological database of phonological inventory data from spoken languages developed in Moran (2012) and made publicly available online by Moran, McCloy, and Wright (2014).[1] The aim of this chapter is twofold. First, for developers of typological databases, we provide an overview of our data management workflow. We illustrate how we collect, curate, and disseminate the phonological inventory data in light of the issues raised by the contributions in Berez-Kroeker et al. (chapter 1, this volume). Second, for users and data consumers, we describe how to access the data, and we provide a brief overview of use cases and research questions that have been asked with PHOIBLE.

2   For developers: Data management workflow

Kung (chapter 8, this volume) discusses how to develop a data management plan (DMP). DMPs are now a standard requirement for many grant applications. The requirements of the DMP will differ from funding agency to funding agency and the topics of the DMP will differ from research project to research project. However, DMPs generally revolve around data collection and handling, documentation and metadata, data storage and preservation, data sharing, and ethical considerations. The data management workflow for PHOIBLE involves three steps:

1. Data collection and documentation
2. Data storage and preservation
3. Data sharing and reuse

Moran (2012) provides a detailed overview of PHOIBLE and its initial development. Herein we discuss in detail our current data management workflow, which has been applied successfully to similar typological data

sets, for example, a database of reconstructed phonological inventories (BDPROTO; Marsico et al. 2018; Moran, Grossman, and Verkerk 2020) and a database of borrowed speech sounds (SegBo; Grossman et al. 2020). Our hope is that the issues discussed here are beneficial to other projects developing typological databases.

2.1   Data collection and documentation

PHOIBLE is a repository of cross-linguistic phonological inventory data from spoken languages, or in other words, the description of consonants, vowels, and tones in a large sample of the world's languages. These data have been extracted from primary source documents, such as grammars, and from existing databases, such as the UCLA Phonological Segment Inventory Database (UPSID; Maddieson 1984; Maddieson & Precoda 1990). We have compiled these different sources into a single interoperable resource through a data aggregation pipeline illustrated in figure 52.1.

The basic setup includes two metadata files (InventoryID-Bibtex.csv and InventoryID-LanguageCodes.csv), which index each inventory's bibliographic reference(s) and its unique language name identifier (colloquially called language code). Along with the raw data sources (e.g., spreadsheets containing phonological inventory data, database dumps from other segment inventory databases in various digital formats), we aggregate the different data sets and their metadata into a single aggregated table. An example is given in table 52.1. We make these data available via a web application (discussed in section 3) and as raw text in CSV format. All index files, raw data sources, the aggregation script, and aggregated data are openly available in our GitHub repository online.[2]

Regarding our data collection and source documentation, we provide a bibliographic record for each source, that is, its *doculect* (Cysouw & Good 2013), from which we extract information about a language's phonological

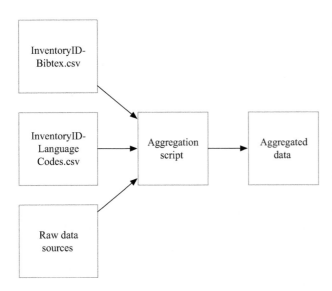

Figure 52.1
PHOIBLE aggregation pipeline.

inventory. We keep track of our references using BibTeX, a bibliography management software. BibTeX is stored in a plain text UTF-8 file.[3] An example of a BibTeX entry is:

```
@book{Cho1967,
Address={Uppsala},
Author={Cho, Seung-Bog},
Publisher={Almqvist and Wiksells},
Series={Acta Universitatis Upsaliensis, Studia
Uralica et Altaica Upsaliensia},
Title={A Phonological Study of Korean},
Volume={2},
Year={1967}}
```

Each bibliographic reference is given a unique identifier (here "Cho1967"), which we map to a particular PHOIBLE InventoryID in the CSV file InventoryID-Bibtex.csv that tracks which references belong to which data points, as illustrated in table 52.2.[4] We also keep track of the original source document from which the phonological inventory was extracted. Original sources

are available online as PDF or as URLs to their original databases as listed in the Filename field.

The InventoryID-Bibtex.csv file is cross-referenced via the InventoryIDs to the file InventoryID-LanguageCodes.csv.[5] An example is given in table 52.3. This file contains inventory level metadata in terms of language name identifiers from the Glottolog (Hammarström, Forkel, & Haspelmath 2018) and from ISO 639-3.[6] This file also indicates the source from which the inventory came, for example, the Stanford Phonology Archive (SPA) or UPSID databases.

Mapping each inventory to a standard language code allows us to uniquely identify languages and dialects, and it also allows us to incorporate additional metadata from other linguistic and non-linguistic databases. For example, with Glottocodes we can merge into the PHOIBLE aggregated phonological inventory data information about a language's genealogical classification (e.g., language family, language genus), its geographic location (e.g., the macroarea in which its spoken, latitude and longitude coordinates), as provided by the Glottolog[7] and other resources. This additional information about languages and their speakers allows us to extend the PHOIBLE data to undertake quantitative analyses (see section 3), and it also provides additional information for displaying PHOIBLE's contents online in worldwide map formats (see figure 52.2).[8]

Good (chapter 3, this volume) discusses the scope of linguistic data in terms of the field's unusual position as a discipline that intersects humanities and science. In the development of PHOIBLE, data collection was initially a qualitative endeavor (independent of our database): a linguist went to the field to document and analyze the phonemic contrasts in a language. Given the different linguistic training and theoretical backgrounds of different linguists, phonological descriptions of the same language almost always differ in their

Table 52.1
Example of PHOIBLE aggregated data

InventoryID	Glottocode	LanguageCode	LanguageName	Phoneme	Source
1	kore1280	kor	Korean	m	spa
1	kore1280	kor	Korean	k	spa
1	kore1280	kor	Korean	i	spa
1	kore1280	kor	Korean	a	spa
1	kore1280	kor	Korean	p	spa

Table 52.2

Example from InventoryID-Bibtex.csv

InventoryID	BibtexKey	Filename
1	Cho1967	kor_SPA1979_phon.pdf
423	Martin1957	http://web.phonetik.uni-frankfurt.de/L/L2170.html

Table 52.3

Example from InventoryID-LanguageCodes.csv

InventoryID	Language Code	Glotto code	Language Name	Source
1	kor	kore1280	Korean	spa
423	kor	kore1280	Korean	upsid

number and composition of phonemes. To address this issue, we include multiple phonological inventories of the same language (or dialect) by different researchers and we leave it to users to decide which phonological description(s) they want to use in their analysis.[9]

The aggregation of the different sources in PHOIBLE is a quantitative product, which can be used for cross-linguistic comparison and statistical analysis. Different input sources come with different types of annotation (e.g., different transcription practices, different ways of describing phonological features). To make generalizations across all sources, we have typologized the data extracted from grammars into a uniform annotation using the International Phonetic Alphabet (IPA; International Phonetic Association 2015) encoded in the Unicode Standard (Unicode Consortium 2018). We discuss these decisions in detail in Moran and Cysouw (2018), a practical guide aimed at language scientists working in multilingual computational environments, in which we explicitly define a "strict" IPA that normalizes transcription practices across language descriptions from thousands of languages. For PHOIBLE users, we document our decisions regarding phonetic annotations in a set of notational conventions available online.[10]

2.2 Data storage and preservation

Mattern (chapter 5, this volume) discusses sustainability of linguistic data, its life cycle, and principles of data management in terms of sustainable data formats, version control, documentation, and archiving (see also Buszard-Welcher, chapter 10, this volume, regarding archiving and time-depths). For PHOIBLE, we collect the extracted

data from grammars in easy-to-use working formats, such as Microsoft Excel and Google spreadsheets. These software tools allow us to quickly collect data and to share it with each other, so that we can compare and discuss our interpretations of the original source grammar. These working formats are not meant for long-term storage or archival preservation. Instead, we convert these spreadsheets into Unicode UTF-8 plain text CSV files, which we store in an online and publicly available GitHub repository.[11] GitHub lets us track changes over time and helps us manage our data and aggregation script through an issue tracker,[12] where each issue describes one clearly identified task (e.g., inventory ID 5 is missing a phoneme, correct it; update the aggregation script to include a new resource). Tasks can be assigned to the various contributors and we can set deadlines in order to manage the creation of new data releases, for example, version 2.0.

Han (chapter 6, this volume) gives an overview of data transformation in terms of data format and conversion, cleaning and reorganization, merging and processing. In our repository, we maintain our input data, metadata, and the scripts we wrote to aggregate the various sources together into a version that we release publicly. Once we are settled on a particular state of the data and feel they are ready for release, we create a version number that adheres to Semantic Versioning[13] and we release the data and our code together on GitHub.[14] This includes transforming the data into the Cross-Linguistic Data Format (CLDF) specification, which defines entities for languages, parameters (entities for comparative concepts), values (the measurements of these concepts), and sources (where the data come from). For details see Forkel et al. (2018) and the CLDF website.[15] Our CLDF data are encoded in four Unicode UTF-8 plain text CSV files that can be linked via primary keys into a relational database (Moran & McCloy 2019a). These tables provide the input format to update our web interface that is in the Cross-Linguistic Linked Data (CLLD) project,[16] which hosts many other typological data sets, such as the World Atlas of Language Structures (WALS; Dryer & Haspelmath 2013), the Automated Similarity Judgment Program (ASJP; Wichmann et al. 2019), and Tsammalex (Naumann et al. 2015).

Once we release a version of PHOIBLE on GitHub, we then archive that release on Zenodo (see Andreassen, chapter 7, this volume, who discusses issues of data archiving).[17] Zenodo adheres to FAIR (Findable, Accessible,

Interoperable, and Reusable) principles (Wilkinson 2016) and provides a new digital object identifier (DOI) for each new release along with a bibliographic citation that users can use when citing a particular release of the data in their research papers.

2.3 Data sharing and reuse

The data from PHOIBLE are shared via our GitHub repository, through Zenodo archived releases, and via the online web application. Ongoing development work on GitHub contains the most-up-to-date data and code.

It is not only pertinent to share data, but also the code that is used to transform and generate it (Barnes 2010). The necessity of reproducibility and replicability is particularly important in light of large quantitative data sets, including typological databases, on which statistical analyses are undertaken (Moran 2016). When these sources are made publicly available, it is pertinent that reproducibility and replicability are transparent, as noted by Gawne and Styles (chapter 2, this volume). This is not only important for the data publishers, but for data consumers. Consider, for example, how the reuse of data in linguistic studies leads to findings that may change from one analysis to another because of different language sample sizes (e.g., Everett, Blasi, & Roberts 2015 vs. Roberts 2018) or use of different statistical methods (e.g., Hay & Bauer 2007 vs. Moran, McCloy, & Wright 2012).[18]

Champieux and Coates (chapter 12, this volume) describe metrics for evaluating the impact of data sets. Metrics are obviously useful for relaying to funding agencies the impact of a data set, whether through scientific citations or use. For PHOIBLE, we track citations through Google Scholar, and to increase exposure and discovery, we list PHOIBLE in the Open Language Archives Community (OLAC).[19] OLAC tracks and evaluates metadata quality through data integrity checking (e.g., whether ISO 639-3 codes are valid in light of the fact that they are periodically updated). Due to our rigorous adherence to identifying data sources with language codes, OLAC gives PHOIBLE an overall five out of five star rating for metadata quality. This means users know which languages or dialects are present in our worldwide sample.

3 For users: Overview and use cases

The 2019 edition of PHOIBLE Online includes 3,020 inventories that contain 3,183 distinct phonemes found in 2,186 languages (Moran & McCloy 2019b). As such, PHOIBLE represents the largest database of sound systems about the world's languages as it builds on and brings together the SPA (Crothers et al. 1979), the UPSID (Maddieson 1984; Maddieson & Precoda 1990), the South American Phonological Inventory Database (SAPHON; Michael, Stark, & Chang 2012), Alphabets of Africa (Hartell 1993), Systèmes alphabétiques des langues africaines (Chanard 2006), the database of Eurasian phonologies (Nikolayev, Nikulin, & Kukhto 2015), Australian phonemic inventories (Round 2019), and hundreds of individual data points extracted from grammars by the PHOIBLE editors.

PHOIBLE Online is a web application that provides access to the phonological inventory data for browsing and searching by language, inventory, phoneme, and source. Languages are displayed on a worldwide map and each data point is color-coded for language family, as illustrated in figure 52.2. Each point can be clicked on and the user is taken to the phonological inventory—available both in a table format and as an IPA chart.

PHOIBLE Online allows users to explore the sound systems of the world's languages. We have received many reports that it is a useful tool in linguistic courses on phonology, typology, and languages of the world. We also make the PHOIBLE data available via one large aggregated CSV file (in tabular format; described in section 2.1). In linguistic courses with a quantitative focus, the phoneme inventory data and associated metadata (e.g., language family, geo-coordinates) are a powerful resource for learning descriptive statistics (e.g., what is the frequency distribution of sounds in the world's languages? how many data points belong to each language family?) and also for learning how to plot data with software such as R (e.g., plot the frequency distribution of sounds; plot the languages on a worldwide map).

There has also been a broad range of published research that uses the PHOIBLE data, including studies on linguistic and genetic diversity (Creanza et al. 2015), phonetics (Dediu & Moisik 2019), phonology (Cohen Priva 2017), typology (Nikolaev & Grossman 2018), historical linguistics (Barrack, McCloy, & Wright 2014), and computational linguistics (Johny, Gutkin, & Jansche 2019).[20]

Some of my own research has involved testing whether there is a correlation between the population size of speech communities and the number of sounds in their languages (Moran, McCloy, & Wright 2012), investigating whether there are compensations

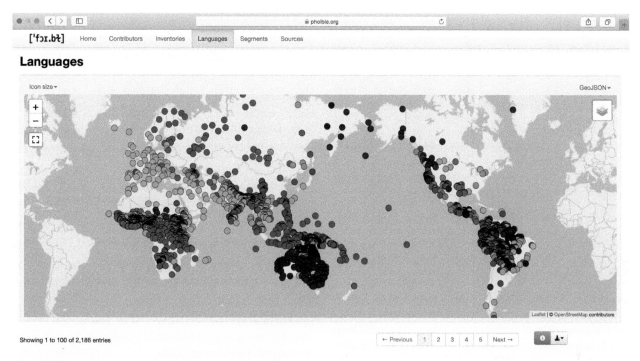

Figure 52.2
PHOIBLE Online.

in phonological system complexity cross-linguistically (Moran & Blasi 2014), and showing that labiodental sounds (such as "f" and "v") were innovated after the Neolithic period due to changes in food processing technology and its effect on human bite configuration (Blasi et al. 2019). In each of these studies, we were able to extend the PHOIBLE data with information about linguistic and non-linguistic variables, such as language family phylogenies, demography, and subsistence type, via our use of standardized language codes and the ability to use them to link together different databases, such as the Glottolog (Hammarström, Forkel, & Haspelmath 2019) and D-PLACE (Kirby et al. 2016). This illustrates the power of using linguistic metadata, beyond just uniquely identifying data points, so that we can undertake interdisciplinary research.

Notes

1. https://phoible.org/.

2. https://github.com/phoible/dev.

3. https://github.com/phoible/dev/blob/master/data/phoible-references.bib.

4. https://github.com/phoible/dev/blob/master/mappings/InventoryID-Bibtex.csv.

5. https://github.com/phoible/dev/blob/master/mappings/InventoryID-LanguageCodes.csv.

6. https://iso639-3.sil.org/.

7. https://glottolog.org/meta/downloads.

8. https://phoible.org/languages.

9. For more information, see our comprehensive FAQ: http://phoible.github.io/faq/.

10. http://phoible.github.io/conventions/.

11. https://github.com/phoible/dev/tree/master/raw-data.

12. https://github.com/phoible/dev/issues.

13. https://semver.org/.

14. https://github.com/phoible/dev/releases.

15. https://cldf.clld.org/.

16. https://clld.org/.

17. https://zenodo.org/.

18. See also enlightening discussions by Hatton (1997), Roberts and Winters (2013), and Silberzahn et al. (2015).

19. http://www.language-archives.org/.

20. For the full list and access to these papers, see: https://scholar.google.com/scholar?hl=en&as_sdt=2005&cites=576981116309388928&scipsc=.

References

Barnes, Nick. 2010. Publish your computer code: It is good enough. *Nature* 467 (7317): 753–753. doi:10.1038/467753a.

Barrack, Charles M., Daniel R. McCloy, and Richard A. Wright. 2014. Did murmur spread in Pre-Proto-Indo-European? *Indogermanische Forschungen* 119 (1): 149–158.

Blasi, Damián E., Steven Moran, Scott R. Moisik, Paul Widmer, Dan Dediu, and Balthasar Bickel. 2019. Human sound systems are shaped by post-Neolithic changes in bite configuration. *Science* 363 (6432). doi:10.1126/science.aav3218.

Chanard, C. 2006. Systèmes alphabétiques des langues africaines. http://sumale.vjf.cnrs.fr/phono/.

Cohen Priva, Uriel. 2017. Informativity and the actuation of lenition. *Language* 93 (3): 569–597.

Creanza, Nicole, Merritt Ruhlen, Trevor J. Pemberton, Noah A. Rosenberg, Marcus W. Feldman, and Sohini Ramachandran. 2015. A comparison of worldwide phonemic and genetic variation in human populations. *Proceedings of the National Academy of Sciences* 112 (5): 1265–1272.

Crothers, John H., James P. Lorentz, Donald A. Sherman, and Marilyn M. Vihman. 1979. Handbook of phonological data from a sample of the world's languages: A report of the Stanford Phonology Archive. Department of Linguistics, Stanford University.

Cysouw, Michael, and Jeff Good. 2013. Languoid, doculect and glossonym: Formalizing the notion "language." *Language Documentation and Conservation* 7:331–359.

Dediu, Dan, and Scott R Moisik. 2019. Pushes and pulls from below: Anatomical variation, articulation and sound change. *Glossa* 4 (1): 1–33. https://www.glossa-journal.org/articles/10.5334/gjgl.646/.

Dryer, Matthew S., and Martin Haspelmath, eds. 2013. *WALS Online*. Leipzig, Germany: Max Planck Institute for Evolutionary Anthropology. https://wals.info/.

Everett, Caleb, Damián E. Blasi, and Seán G. Roberts. 2015. Climate, vocal folds, and tonal languages: Connecting the physiological and geographic dots. *Proceedings of the National Academy of Sciences* 112 (5): 1322–1327. doi:10.1073/pnas.1417413112.

Forkel, Robert, Johann-Mattis List, Simon J. Greenhill, Christoph Rzymski, Sebastian Bank, Michael Cysouw, Harald Hammarström, Martin Haspelmath, Gereon A. Kaiping, and Russell D. Gray. 2018. Cross-linguistic data formats, advancing data sharing and re-use in comparative linguistics. *Scientific Data* 5:180205.

Grossman, Eitan, Elad Eisen, Dmitry Nikolaev, and Steven Moran. 2020. SegBo: A database of borrowed sounds in the world's languages. In *Proceedings of the Twelfth International Conference on Language Resources and Evaluation (LREC 2020)*. http://www.lrec-conf.org/proceedings/lrec2020/pdf/2020.lrec-1.654.pdf.

Hammarström, Harald, Robert Forkel, and Martin Haspelmath. 2018. *Glottolog 3.3*. Jena, Germany: Max Planck Institute for the Science of Human History. https://glottolog.org/.

Hammarström, Harald, Robert Forkel, and Martin Haspelmath. 2019. *Glottolog 4.0*. Jena, Germany: Max Planck Institute for the Science of Human History. https://glottolog.org/. Accessed October 7, 2019.

Hartell, Rhonda L., ed. 1993. *Alphabets des langues africaines*. Dallas: UNESCO and Société Internationale de Linguistique.

Hatton, Les. 1997. The T experiments: Errors in scientific software. *IEEE Computational Science and Engineering* 4 (2): 27–38.

Hay, Jennifer, and Laurie Bauer. 2007. Phoneme inventory size and population size. *Language* 83 (2): 388–400. doi:10.1353/lan.2007.0071.

International Phonetic Association. 2015. *International Phonetic Alphabet*. International Phonetic Association. https://www.internationalphoneticassociation.org.

Johny, Cibu C., Alexander Gutkin, and Martin Jansche. 2019. Cross-lingual consistency of phonological features: An empirical study. *Interspeech* 2019 (September 15–19): 1741–1745.

Kirby, Kathryn R., Russell D. Gray, Simon J. Greenhill, Fiona M. Jordan, Stephanie Gomes-Ng, Hans-Jörg Bibiko, Damián E. Blasi, et al. 2016. D-PLACE: A global database of cultural, linguistic and environmental diversity. *PLoS One* 11 (7): e0158391.

Maddieson, Ian. 1984. *Pattern of Sounds*. Cambridge: Cambridge University Press.

Maddieson, Ian, and Kristin Precoda. 1990. Updating UPSID. *UCLA Working Papers in Phonetics* 74:104–111.

Marsico, Egidio, Sebastien Flavier, Annemarie Verkerk, and Steven Moran. 2018. BDPROTO: A database of phonological inventories from ancient and reconstructed languages. In *Proceedings of the Eleventh International Conference on Language Resources and Evaluation (LREC 2018)*, ed. Nicoletta Calzolari, Khalid Choukri, Christopher Cieri, Thierry Declerck, Sara Goggi, Koiti Hasida, Hitoshi Isahara, et al., 1654–1658. Paris: European Language Resources Association (ELRA).

Michael, Lev, Tammy Stark, and Will Chang. 2012. *South American Phonological Inventory Database*. http://linguistics.berkeley.edu/saphon/en/.

Moran, Steven. 2012. Phonetics information base and lexicon. PhD dissertation, University of Washington.

Moran, Steven. 2016. Commentary: Issues of time, tone, roots and replicability. *Journal of Language Evolution* 1 (1): 73. doi:10.1093/jole/lzv011.

Moran, Steven, and Damián Blasi. 2014. Cross-linguistic comparison of complexity measures in phonological systems. In *Measuring Grammatical Complexity*, ed. Frederick J. Newmeyer and Laurel Preston, 217–240. Oxford: Oxford University Press.

Moran, Steven, and Michael Cysouw. 2018. *The Unicode Cookbook for Linguists: Managing Writing Systems Using Orthography Profiles*. Berlin: Language Science Press. doi:10.5281/zenodo.1300528. http://langsci-press.org/catalog/view/176/889/1135-2.

Moran, Steven, Eitan Grossman, and Annemarie Verkerk. 2020. Investigating diachronic trends in phonological inventories using BDPROTO. *Language Resources and Evaluation*. https://doi .org/10.1007/s10579-019-09483-3.

Moran, Steven, and Daniel McCloy. 2019a. *cldf-datasets/phoible: PHOIBLE 2.0.1 as CLDF Dataset*. https://doi.org/10.5281 /zenodo.2677911.

Moran, Steven, and Daniel McCloy, eds. 2019b. *PHOIBLE 2.0*. Jena: Max Planck Institute for the Science of Human History. https://phoible.org/.

Moran, Steven, Daniel McCloy, and Richard Wright. 2012. Revisiting population size vs. phoneme inventory size. *Language* 88 (4): 877–893. doi:10.1353/lan.2012.0087.

Moran, Steven, Daniel McCloy, and Richard Wright, eds. 2014. *PHOIBLE Online*. Leipzig, Germany: Max Planck Institute for Evolutionary Anthropology. http://phoible.org/.

Naumann, Christfried, Tom Güldemann, Steven Moran, Guillaume Segerer, and Robert Forkel, eds. 2015. *Tsammalex*. Leipzig, Germany: Max Planck Institute for Evolutionary Anthropology. https://tsammalex.clld.org.

Nikolaev, Dmitry, and Eitan Grossman. 2018. Areal sound change and the distributional typology of affricate richness in Eurasia. *Studies in Language* 42 (3): 562–599.

Nikolayev, Dmitry, Andrey Nikulin, and Anton Kukhto. 2015. The database of Eurasian phonological inventories. http:// eurasianphonology.info.

Roberts, Seán G. 2018. Robust, causal, and incremental approaches to investigating linguistic adaptation. *Frontiers in Psychology* 9:1–22. doi:10.3389/fpsyg.2018.00166. https://www .frontiersin.org/article/10.3389/fpsyg.2018.00166.

Roberts, Seán, and James Winters. 2013. Linguistic diversity and traffic accidents: Lessons from statistical studies of cultural traits. *PLOS One* 8 (8): 1–13. https://doi.org/10.1371/journal .pone.0070902.

Round, Erich. 2019. Australian phonemic inventories contributed to PHOIBLE 2.0: Essential explanatory notes (Version 1.0). Zenodo. http://doi.org/10.5281/zenodo.3464333.

Silberzahn, Raphael, Eric L. Uhlmann, Daniel P. Martin, Pasquale Anselmi, Frederik Aust, Eli C. Awtrey, Štěpán Bahník, et al. 2015.

Many analysts, one dataset: Making transparent how variations in analytical choices affect results. https://osf.io/gvm2z.

Unicode Consortium. 2018. *The Unicode Standard*, version 11.0.0. Technical report. Mountain View, CA: Unicode Consortium. http://www.unicode.org/versions/Unicode11.0.0/.

Wichmann, Søren, Eric W. Holman, and Cecil H. Brown. 2019. The ASJP database, version 18. https://asjp.clld.org.

Wilkinson, Mark D. 2016. The FAIR guiding principles for scientific data management and stewardship. *Scientific Data* 3:160018. doi:10.1038/sdata.2016.18.

53 Managing Data in a Typological Study

Volker Gast and Łukasz Jędrzejowski

1 Introduction

Studies in linguistic typology may pursue various types of epistemological objectives. As the term *typology* suggests, early approaches, inspired by structuralist biology, aimed at taxonomizing languages—not in genealogical or geographical terms, but with respect to structural properties (e.g., Schlegel's 1808 morphological types), often with the idea of identifying the (holistic) "character" of a language (von der Gabelentz 1891).[1] In the twentieth century, the "Greenbergian" approach to typology became prevalent (Greenberg 1966; Comrie 1989; Croft 2003), seeking to identify correlations between properties of languages and, ultimately, finding "linguistic universals." Toward the end of the twentieth century, a "distributional" approach to linguistic typology established itself (Nichols 1992, 2007), seeking to determine—and explain—the distribution of linguistic features in time and space ("What's where why?," cf. Bickel 2007, 2015). This approach is also associated with the idea of focusing on more fine-grained properties of linguistic systems, making linguistic typology a multivariate endeavor (cf. Bickel 2010). What all major paradigms within linguistic typology have in common is that they deal with linguistic variation and the limits of that variation.

The approaches to linguistic typology mentioned have traditionally been based on generalizations made in grammatical descriptions and can thus be subsumed under the term *grammar-based typology* (though studies in lexical typology are based on dictionaries or word lists rather than grammars). More recently, attempts have been made to carry out typological studies on the basis of textual data, thus establishing *corpus-based typology* (cf. Goldhahn, Quasthoff, & Heyer 2014; Futrell, Mahowald, & Gibson 2015; Culbertson 2017; Alzetta et al. 2018). Corpus-based approaches mostly address the questions of Greenbergian typology, but the use of corpus data obviously opens up new possibilities in terms of statistical modeling.

The present chapter provides an overview of central matters of research data management for major approaches to linguistic typology as we have characterized. It focuses on grammar-based research, but the data model described in section 3 can, mutatis mutandis, be applied to corpus-based approaches as well. Following this brief introduction, section 2 addresses some general questions concerning empirical approaches to linguistic typology. Section 3 provides a description of one particular typological database, the Typological Database of Impersonals (ImproType). Section 4 contains some remarks on data storage and export, as well as examples of research questions addressed using data from ImproType. Some concluding remarks are made in section 5.

2 Empirical approaches to linguistic typology

As Chomskyan universalism is broadly rejected in linguistic typology, the question arises how the elements underlying crosslinguistic comparison—functional domains (e.g., future tense, impersonalization), linguistic categories (e.g., adjective, affix), and relations holding between members of these categories (e.g., subject, agreement)—can be defined in such a way that comparability can be assumed. The present chapter does not focus on this question, which has been widely debated without a general consensus being reached. Haspelmath (2010:664) introduced the term *comparative concept* as a solution to this problem: "concepts specifically designed for the purpose of comparison that are independent of descriptive categories" (664).[2] For example, typologists have long been aware that there is no crosslinguistically applicable notion of "subject" (e.g., Keenan 1976), so a statement such as "in language *L*, the subject *S* of a verbal predicate *V* generally precedes *V*" (i.e., "the language is SV") is impossible to verify or falsify. According to Haspelmath's approach, linguists can define a comparative concept "subject," for example, using criteria like the ones discussed by Keenan.

As comparative concepts are theoretical concepts and thus not directly observable, they can only be defined intensionally. To be used in a crosslinguistic study, they consequently have to be operationalized. Operationalization is "the construction of actual, concrete measurement techniques" for theoretical constructs (Babbie 1989:5). Consequently, a procedure has to be devised that allows researchers to identify the (theoretical, intensionally defined) comparative concept "subject" in any given (clause or predication of a) language. How this is done is a central design feature of any typological study, and the specific operationalizations used in any given study are a matter of "construct validity" (Cronbach & Meehl 1955).

A second important quality criterion of empirical research is reliability. In the case of typological studies, reliability most importantly concerns the consistency of classification: given some property *P* assigned to some entity *x*, would different researchers, or even the same researcher at different times, classify *x* in the same way (with respect to *P*)? Anyone who has participated in a typological project will be familiar with the sometimes-unexpected difficulties that one encounters when classifying data, even for major variables and well-known languages. Reliability can be tested by running interrater reliability tests, when several researchers annotate the same data set independently, and the degree of (dis)agreement on the coding decisions is determined. While interrater reliability testing is (still) often neglected in linguistic typology, it is regarded as an essential component of studies in psychology and other fields (see for instance Hallgren 2012).

As validity and reliability are primarily a matter of research design, not of research data management, we will not go into any further detail at this point. What matters from the point of view of research data management is transparency in three respects: (i) the comparative concepts have to be defined explicitly, (ii) the operationalizations used have to be precisely described, and (iii) the data analyzed, and the software/scripts used for the analysis, should be made available to the readers (cf. also Holton, Leonard, & Pulsifer, chapter 4, this volume). If conditions (i) and (ii) are met, a study can be said to be *reproducible*; if, in addition, condition (iii) is met, the study can be said to be *replicable* (cf. Plesser 2018; cf. also Gawne & Styles, this volume).

Crosslinguistic variation manifests itself in properties of linguistic systems. Typological studies traditionally refer to such systems as "languages," but there are nontrivial problems with this term. First, what we traditionally call a *language* is a social construct; from a cognitive point of view, linguistic systems are stored in individual minds, as a part of a language user's linguistic repertoire. Related to this problem is the question of delimitation between levels of classification such as idiolects, varieties, languages, genealogical groupings, and so on. Moreover, there is no objectivity in describing linguistic data, and any description of any linguistic system implies a fair amount of subjective analytical decisions. Rather than referring to "languages," typologists have therefore started to use the term *doculect* for "a linguistic variety as it is documented in a given resource" (Cysouw & Good 2013:342). In practice, typological studies standardly use information from different sources, however, thus effectively subsuming doculects under abstract entities mostly (still) labeled "languages." As this is not the place to solve the fundamental problem of what entities underlie or constitute the observations in typological research, we will adhere to this established practice in the following. It should be borne in mind, however, that *language* will be used as meaning "linguistic system as perceived by some (group of) analyst(s)."

Simplifying somewhat, linguistic systems can be regarded as comprising sets of elements (e.g., words) classified into categories (e.g., adjective, feminine, singular), and relations holding between the elements of specific categories (e.g., agreement between an adjective and a noun modified by that adjective; cf. Corbett 2006). In a grammar-based approach, the basic properties underlying crosslinguistic studies are typically generalizations or existential quantifications over elements of the categories constituting the linguistic systems in question (cf. Dryer & Haspelmath 2013 for various examples). For instance, the property of being isolating is a generalization over the form (non-segmentability) of the words of a language (cf. Bickel & Nichols 2013); the property of being a verb-object language is a generalization over the order of constituents of specific categories, and with specific functions, in a language (cf. Dryer 2013); and the property of having a velar nasal is an existential quantification over the sound inventory of a language (cf. Anderson 2013). In such studies, properties are thus attributed to languages, and we can make statements such as "English has a velar nasal."

Typological studies dealing with the realization of functional domains such as the future tense are often based on existential quantifications as well, such as when they determine whether or not a language has an inflectionally realized category expressing the domain in question (cf. Dahl & Velupillai 2013). Such studies often assume a one-to-one relationship between languages and (the existence of) grammatical subsystems expressing the relevant functional domains ("language *L* has/does not have a future tense").[3] In other functional domains, such one-to-one relationships cannot be assumed. For example, languages may have various types of impersonals, the phenomenon documented in the ImproType database described in section 3 of this chapter. French uses *on* as an impersonal pronoun, cf. (1) (see for instance van der Auwera, Gast, & Vanderbiesen 2012; Gast & van der Auwera 2013; Gast 2015 on impersonals).

(1) French *on*

On	*ne*	*vit*	*qu'*	*une*	*fois.*
IMP	NEG	lives	but	one	time

"One/you only live(s) once."

Some languages use verbal strategies to describe actions or events without specifying the participants, cf. the Estonian examples in (2).

(2) Estonian

a. *Tullakse* *ja* *minnakse.*
   come.PRES.IMP and go.PRES.IMP

   "They (people) come and go."

b. *Siin* *ehitatakse* *uut* *maja.*
   here build.PRES.IMP new.PART house.PART

   "Here they are building a new house."

   (Blevins 2006:238, referring to Tuldava 1994:372)

Polish often uses the reflexive pronoun *się* (cf. (3)), but it also has other means, such as the impersonalizing suffix *-no*, cf. (4).

(3) Polish

SIĘ

Żyje	*się*	*tylko*	*raz.*
live.3SG	REFL	only	once

"One only lives once."

(4) -NO

Znowu	*podniesio-no*	*podatki.*
again	raise-NO	taxes

"They've raised taxes again."

As the Polish examples illustrate, there is no one-to-one relationship between languages and "expression strategies" for a given domain or category. Consequently, properties can only be attributed to expression strategies, not to languages. Note also that typological studies may be interested primarily in correlations between formal and functional properties of expression strategies, or the division of labor between the strategies available in a given language (cf. section 4). While it is relevant that a given linguistic expression strategy *S* is an element (or combination of elements) of some language *L*, the typologically relevant properties are primarily attributed to *S* in such cases, not to *L*. The data structure needed for this type of study can thus be illustrated as shown in figure 53.1.[4]

Properties can be stored in the form of attribute-value pairs, represented as "ATTRIBUTE: value" in the following. For example, if the main exponent of an impersonalization strategy is a verbal affix, it can be said to have the property "CATEGORYOFEXPONENT: verbal.affix."

3 Managing typological data in databases: The Typological Database of Impersonals (ImproType)

3.1 The structure of the database

The ImproType database[5] grew out of a project jointly carried out by research groups from the Friedrich Schiller University of Jena and the Université de Paris VIII. This database is an instance of the Extensible Linguistic Database (XLD) system developed by Dimitriadis and van Vugt. Impersonals were introduced with examples from French, Estonian, and Polish in (1)–(4). Given that the notion of "impersonal" covers a broad range of

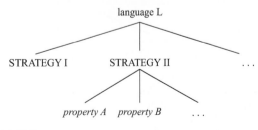

Figure 53.1
Basic data structure for strategy-based typological studies.

expression strategies (e.g., pronouns, non-finite forms), it is defined in functional terms as an operation on argument structure, cf. (5).

(5) IMPERSONALIZATION is the process of filling an argument position of a predicate with a variable ranging over sets of human participants without establishing a referential link to any entity from the universe of discourse. (Gast & van der Auwera 2013:136)

The definition in (5) can be regarded as a comparative concept. This comparative concept was operationalized using translation equivalence with a set of trigger sentences that were administered in five major European languages (English, French, German, Russian, Spanish). The set of trigger sentences included (inter alia) the examples in (6)–(8), as well as their translations into the other major European languages.

(6) You/one only live(s) once.

(7) They have raised taxes again.

(8) One/you should not drink and drive.

Each language is assumed to have a repertoire of expression strategies, in other words, ways of expressing impersonalization as defined in (5). A database used as a repository for a (grammar-based, functional) typological project of this type minimally thus requires ways of associating expression strategies with a given language and attributing properties to these expression strategies. Moreover, we need to store metadata (cf. also Good, chapter 3, this volume) and examples illustrating the properties attributed to the expression strategies. The basic data model of the ImproType database is shown in figure 53.2, which extends figure 53.1. The arrow between properties (of strategies) and examples indicates that these entities can be linked to each other in the database (cf. section 3.3).

Given that the creation of typological databases has increasingly become a cooperative endeavor, with researchers contributing from all parts of the world, there are a few technical requirements on such databases. Trivially, a typological database should be accessible online. Less trivially, ways have to be found to ensure consistency, in the sense that different contributors should use identical terms for the properties that they assign to observations. One way of ensuring consistency is by restricting the possible values available for some attribute. If a database allows users only to select from predefined values, the database should be extensible, in the sense that new properties (both attributes and values) can be added if need be. As modifications of the database structure should only be carried out by specific users (e.g., from the core project team), a typological database moreover needs appropriate user management facilities. Even though it was mentioned in section 3 that reliability is not primarily a matter of research data management, a typological database can moreover be designed in such a way that it aids enhancing the reliability of the data, for example, by providing instructions and examples.

3.2 Properties stored in the ImproType database

The domain of impersonalization has been studied in quite some detail from a theoretical point of view, based on well-known European languages (e.g., van der Auwera, Gast, & Vanderbiesen 2012; Gast & van der Auwera 2013; Gast 2015). Impersonals vary in terms of specific structural and distributional properties. As illustrated in (1)–(4), the expression strategies may belong to different syntactic categories, and they may have different morphological realizations. More fine-grained distinctions can be made, for example, relating to morphosyntactic

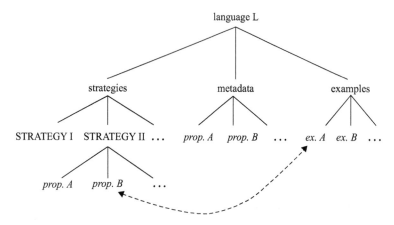

Figure 53.2
Basic data structure of the ImproType database.

properties (such as agreement), and the syntactic functions that can be impersonalized. Moreover, strategies of impersonalization vary in terms of their distribution relative to semantic contexts. For instance, some impersonals (such as English *one*) are mostly found in generic or modal sentences (cf. (9)), whereas others are also used in (non-modal) episodic sentences, for example, German *man* (cf. (10)).

(9) English *one*

    a. Generic/modal

       One shouldn't drink and drive.

    b. Episodic

       *One has stolen my bike.

(10) German *man*

    a. Generic/modal

       Man sollte nicht betrunken Auto fahren.

       IMP should not drunk car drive

       "You/one should not drink and drive."

    b. Episodic

       Man hat mein Fahrrad gestohlen.

       IMP has my bike stolen

       "Someone stole my bike."

The range of distributional properties investigated for each expression strategy cannot be explained in detail here (cf. van der Auwera, Gast, & Vanderbiesen 2012; Gast & van der Auwera 2013). Suffice it to say that three dimensions of classification (i.e., attributes) figure centrally in the distribution of impersonals: (i) event quantification (episodic, habitual, generic), (ii) quantification over participants (existential/singular, existential/plural, collective, universal), and (iii) referential restrictions (exclusive/unrestricted, exclusive/restricted/ external, exclusive/restrictive/internal, inclusive). These properties can be cross-classified, yielding a feature grid with $3 \times 4 \times 4 = 48$ cells or nodes as shown in figure 53.3. The gray shades distinguish feature combinations that

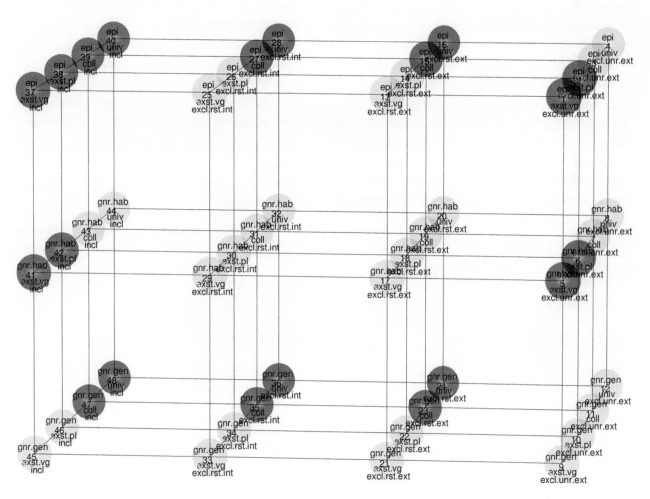

Figure 53.3

Feature grid underlying the Typological Database of Impersonals (ImproType).

are represented in the database (dark gray) from those that are excluded (light gray), either because they are logically impossible or because they are not sufficiently distinct from neighboring nodes (i.e., the distinction cannot be operationalized).

For a selection of the nodes shown in figure 53.3, diagnostic sentences were identified, operationalizing the feature combinations in question. For example, node 48 is associated with the features "generic," "universal," and "inclusive" and thus represents sentences of the type *One only lives once* (6), as this is a generalization over all human beings including both interlocutors.

3.1   An example: Entering Polish data into ImproType

In this section the workflow for data input into ImproType will be illustrated in a simplified form, using data from Polish provided by the second author of this chapter. The database has an input mode and an output mode. In input mode, it has the form of a questionnaire, and the attribute-value pairs are, for the most part, phrased as questions, sometimes providing some context or exemplification. Any answers given can be corrected at any time of the input process, with the exception of the unique identifier of the *answerset*.

3.3.1 Add user   A user with a user identifier and a password was added by a project member with "account management" rights, mostly one of few administrators. Users providing data will normally have rights for "simple property management" (the other options are "entity management" and "all property management").

3.3.2 Add answerset   Answersets (corresponding to a language or doculect) can be added by users with "entity management" rights. These users will mostly be project members familiar with the structure of the database. The top of the section with information on the answerset is shown in figure 53.4. The answerset in question is here called "poli1260LJ," using the Glottocode for Polish (poli1260, cf. Hammarström, Forkel, & Haspelmath 2019) with an identifier for the expert (the data were provided by Łukasz Jędrzejowski).

3.3.3 Provide metadata   The following metadata was gathered:

- Language: variety, Glottolog code, ISO 639-3 code (cf. Eberhard, Simons, & Fennig 2019), any transliteration conventions, consulted sources
- Type of analysis: single consultant analysis, analyst working with a consultant, consultant-analyst (plus a second analyst), based on written sources only
- Analyst conducting session: name, analyst's familiarity with the language
- Interview sessions: dates, interview languages
- Consultant: name, date of birth, gender, occupation, level of education, level of proficiency in the analyzed language, language biography, age of acquisition, familiarity with the grammar of the language

As a point of reference for the impersonals, the most important existential and universal indefinite pronouns were moreover elicited (e.g., Polish *ktoś* "someone," *wszyscy* "everyone").

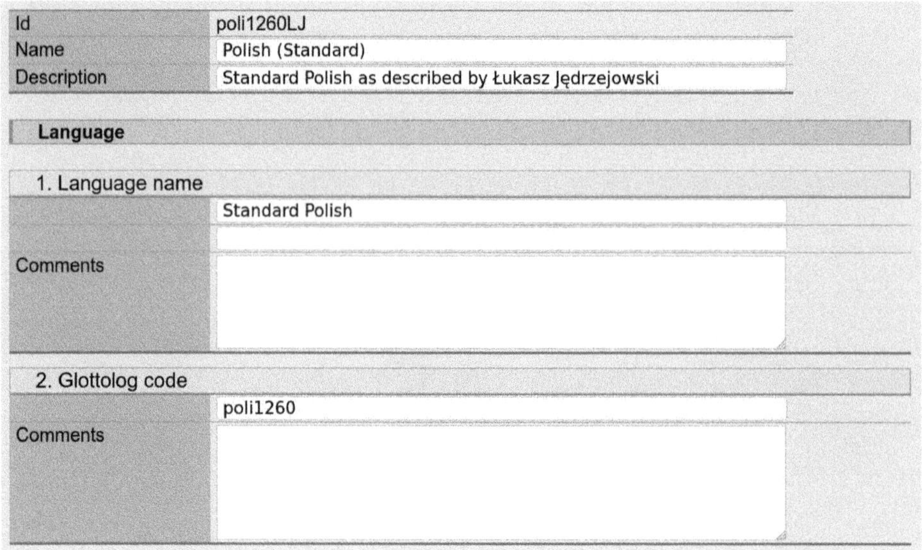

Id	poli1260LJ
Name	Polish (Standard)
Description	Standard Polish as described by Łukasz Jędrzejowski

Language

1. Language name

| Comments | Standard Polish |

2. Glottolog code

| Comments | poli1260 |

Figure 53.4
Input screen for properties of the answerset (doculect).

3.3.4 Identify the impersonalization strategies of the language under analysis

To identify the most important impersonalization strategies of the language in question, trigger sentences such as those in (6)–(8) were administered. Moreover, consultants were asked specifically if a form of the second-person singular, or the third-person plural, could be used impersonally. For Polish, six expression strategies for impersonalization were identified in this way. They are illustrated in (3), (4), and (11)–(14).

(11) TO

Przebi-to   mu   opony.

puncture-TO   him.DAT   tires

"They punctured his tires."

(12) NO+SIĘ

Nie   powin-no   się   kłamać.

NEG   should-NO   REFL   lie.INF

"One should not lie."

(13) 3PL

Znowu   podnieśli   podatki.

again   raise.3PL.L-PTCP.VIR   taxes

"They've raised taxes again."

(14) 2SG

Bilet   kupujesz   w   autobusie.

ticket   buy.2SG.IND   in   bus.LOC

"You/one (can) buy(s) a ticket in the bus."

Each of the strategies was then added to the answerset. For each strategy, a typical example is required. The input screen for examples is shown in figure 53.5. Examples are associated with one strategy/marker, and they are classified in terms of grammaticality. The range of values for the variable "grammaticality" can be customized (like any other value for a given attribute) by users with "all property management." There is also a comments field for prose comments (not shown in figure 53.5).

Examples can (but do not have to) be linked to coding decisions. In terms of the data model, this means that each example will be associated with a set of attributes corresponding to properties of the strategy in question, for example, GENUNIVINCL for "generic, universal, inclusive." Because examples are uniquely linked to expression strategies (such as SIE) from answersets (such as poli1260LJ), such attributes can uniquely identify coding decisions.

The following basic properties were determined for each strategy (mainly properties of the exponent[s]):

- Name and description of the strategy
- Main exponent(s) (e.g., *się*)
- Lexical gloss or likely historical source of the exponent (e.g., reflexive pronoun)
- Locus of encoding (e.g., auxiliary, in argument position, on predicate)
- Any specific properties of the verbal predicate (e.g., non-finiteness)
- Obligatoriness of the exponent
- Phonological properties of the exponent (possible stress)
- Possibility of anaphoric reference of the impersonalized argument position

3.3.5 Determine morphosyntactic and distributional properties of the expression strategies

Having described the formal makeup of the expression strategies, we can determine their distributional properties. ImproType divides these properties into two major sections, morphosyntactic properties and semantic properties. The section on morphosyntax requires a complete paradigm of the exponent(s) and contains questions relating to the following:

- Categories of gender, number and case
- Syntactic functions that can be impersonalized

Sentence Id	1053
Marker used	SIE ⌄
Grammaticality	(ok) ⌄
Original text	Żyje się tylko raz
Morphemic tier	
Gloss	live.3SG REFL only once
Translation	One only lives once.
Answerset	poli1260LJ

Figure 53.5
Input screen for examples.

• Binding properties (possessive determiners, reflexives and reciprocals, binding across clauses, binding into a purpose clause)

As has been pointed out, for each coding decision, examples should be provided, using the input screen shown in figure 53.5. For instance, the questionnaire contains the question "Can the impersonalized argument bind possessive determiners in the same clause (e.g., *One/you$_i$ should not waste one$_i$'s/your$_i$ time*)?" If this is possible, as in English, the answer will be "yes" (TRUE), and a grammatical example should be provided; otherwise the answer is "no" (FALSE), and an ungrammatical example should be given.

The section on semantic properties is subdivided into questions about universal readings and questions about existential readings. This is only a matter of exposition (configurable in the database), and from the point of view of data structure, all properties are simply attributed to the expression strategy in question. This section is organized around sentences that are defined in terms

of the semantic features introduced and summarized in figure 53.3. Figure 53.6 shows the input screen for node 16, which stands for the features "exclusive/restricted/external," "episodic," and "universal."

Figure 53.7 illustrates the structure of the ImproType data, adding some examples to the diagram in figure 53.2.

4   Retrieving and analyzing the data

The database has a search mode, which allows users to search answersets, strategies, and examples, using all the properties stored in the database as filters. The search form is generated dynamically; that means that if a new attribute is added, or a new value for an attribute, these attributes and values will also be displayed in the search form. Figure 53.8 shows a part of the section for "Impersonal strategies" from the database.

To carry out quantitative studies, the data can be exported (cf. also Han, chapter 6, this volume). While the database itself does not have an export function,

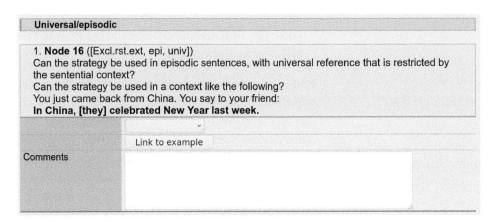

Figure 53.6
Input screen for distributional questions.

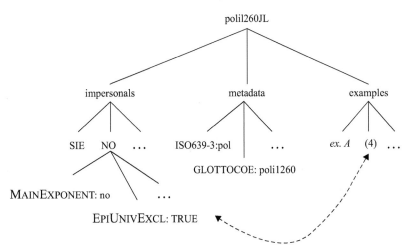

Figure 53.7
Data structure of ImproType (simplified).

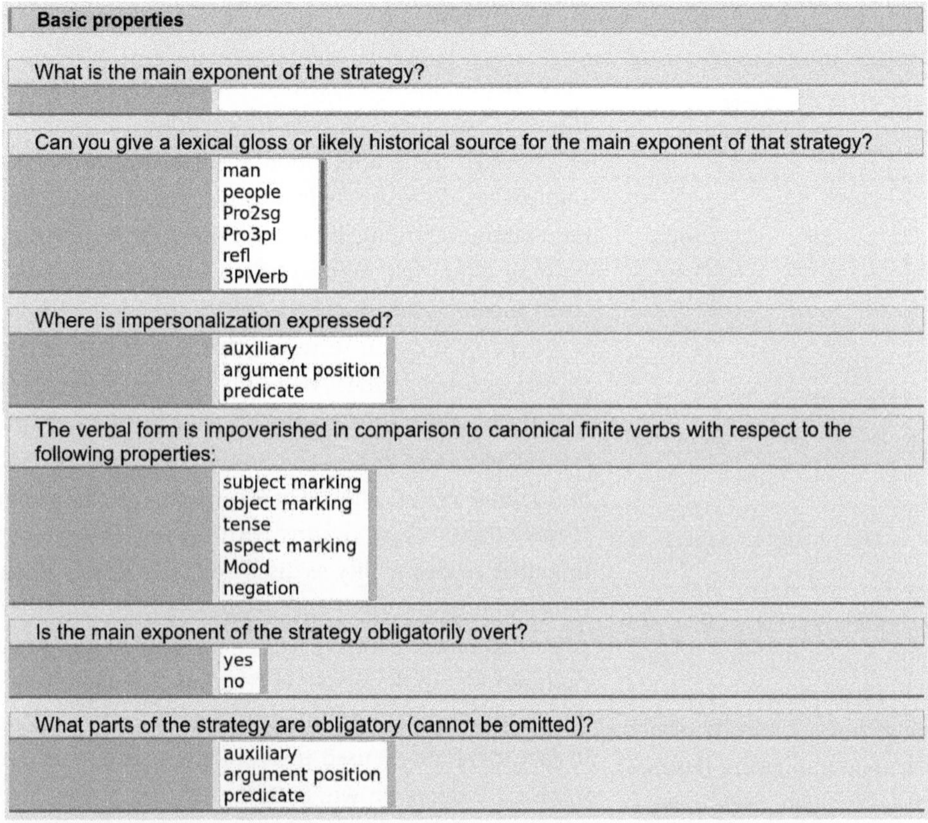

Basic properties

What is the main exponent of the strategy?

Can you give a lexical gloss or likely historical source for the main exponent of that strategy?

man
people
Pro2sg
Pro3pl
refl
3PlVerb

Where is impersonalization expressed?

auxiliary
argument position
predicate

The verbal form is impoverished in comparison to canonical finite verbs with respect to the following properties:

subject marking
object marking
tense
aspect marking
Mood
negation

Is the main exponent of the strategy obligatorily overt?

yes
no

What parts of the strategy are obligatory (cannot be omitted)?

auxiliary
argument position
predicate

Figure 53.8
The search form.

a Python script for the export of data from any XLD database is available on GitHub.[6] So far the data have been described in an abstract format, in the form of tree diagrams with attribute-value pairs as their leaves. Such attributions of properties can be stored in various ways. The XLD system underlying the ImproType database uses a relational database system (MySQL) for that purpose, where the data are distributed over various tables. As the database is fully extensible—new attributes and values can be defined for the entities "answerset" and "strategy"—these attributes and values are also stored in the database (and recovered dynamically for any operation, either input or output). The export script for XLD databases returns the data in the form of JavaScript Object Notation (JSON) objects (cf. Han, chapter 6, this volume). JSON objects can be regarded as sets of attribute-value pairs. They have the form shown in (15).

(15) {ATTRIBUTE-1: value-1, ATTRIBUTE-2: value-2 . . . }

Given that JSON objects may have other JSON objects as their values, a treelike structure underlying the data of the ImproType database can be stored in the JSON format as shown in (16).

(16) {ANSWERSET:
  {STRATEGIES:
    {STRATEGY-1:
      {ATTRIBUTE-S1: value-1, ATTRIBUTE-S2: value-2 . . . },
      STRATEGY-2:
      {ATTRIBUTE-S1: value-2, ATTRIBUTE-S2: value-4 . . . }
      . . . }
  METADATA:
    {ATTTRIBUTE-M1: value-5, ATTRIBUTE-M2: value-6 . . . }
  EXAMPLES:
    {EXAMPLE-1:
        {ATTTRIBUTE-E1: value-7, . . . }
    }
  }}

Once the data have been exported, they can be analyzed using quantitative methods. Given the relatively low coverage of lesser-described languages in the database, robust quantitative statements cannot yet be made. We will therefore restrict ourselves to illustrating the type of question that can be addressed with the data from Impro-Type in the following.

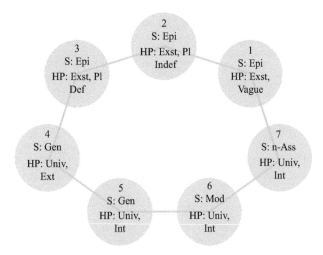

Figure 53.9

The semantic map proposed by Gast and van der Auwera (2013).

One of the central topics in semantic typology is the mapping from form to function. We assume that linguistic markers are semantically homogeneous in the sense that they cover a set of meanings that are directly related to each other. In the semantic map framework (Haspelmath 1997; van der Auwera & Plungian 1998; Gast & van der Auwera 2013), meanings are assumed to form a network, and markers are hypothesized to cover a contiguous region in that network (the "contiguity requirement"). Gast and van der Auwera (2013) have proposed the semantic map shown in figure 53.9.

The nodes of figure 53.9 correspond to sentences of the following type (the number category of the verb depends on the number category of the relevant impersonal):

1. IMPRS has/have stolen my car.
2. IMPRS has/have surrounded us.
3. IMPRS has/have raised taxes again.
4. IMPRS eat(s) dragonflies in Bali.
5. IMPRS only live(s) once.
6. IMPRS should not drink and drive.
7. What happens if IMPRS drink(s) sour milk?

The data in the ImproType database can be used to test the semantic map shown in figure 53.9. If a language has a strategy that violates the contiguity requirement, the hypothesized semantic map can be regarded as falsified. While no such cases have come to our attention yet, the database still contains relatively few non-European languages, as the process of data gathering is time-consuming and mostly requires native linguists.

5 Conclusions

This chapter has intended to provide an overview of the ways in which the data of a typological study can be managed using a relational database system such as ImproType. While we believe that typological databases are extremely useful, in various ways, it should have become clear that many challenges remain, some of them theoretical or methodological, others technical.

We pointed out in section 2 that, in general, empirical research has to meet two important quality criteria, validity and reliability. Finding clear definitions and precise operationalizations is a question of research design, and a database can only be of limited use for these tasks. Note that our way of dealing with the problem of cross-linguistic comparability as discussed in section 2—using translation equivalence with sentences from major languages as operationalizations of the variant properties captured in the database—is certainly not ideal. Obviously, multimodal stimuli would be helpful and are in fact increasingly used in typological studies (cf., for instance, Fedden, Brown, & Corbett 2010).

While validity is essentially a question of research design, not research data management, a database can help researchers to ensure a certain level of consistency and reliability. For example, it can provide explanations and examples, as a part of a protocol (cf. Holton, Leonard, & Pulsifer, chapter 4, this volume) built into the software as it were, and it can restrict the range of values available for a given attribute. Still, the reliability of the coding decisions would have to be checked with interannotator agreement tests, to see to what extent the operationalizations are robust. While the database provides an infrastructure for this—different answersets could be filled in by various specialists—we have not been able to carry out such tests, partly because financial or time resources were lacking. The problem is of an even more general nature, however: in linguistic typology, data from specific languages can often only be provided by very few specialists, sometimes just a single scholar. In such cases no interannotator reliability testing is possible. The distributed nature of the data collection process, with contributions made by various colleagues from all parts of the world, makes it difficult to gather sufficient amounts of data even for languages with a high number of language users or specialists. One way of dealing with this problem in our project was by having data sets double-checked by core team members and getting back to the informants in case of doubt with respect to specific coding decisions, but we cannot rule out that the database may contain inconsistencies. The fact that we have not been able to quantify interannotator reliability for the data is a serious drawback when it comes to publishing results based on the database, as interannotator reliability testing is more and more becoming a standard in international publishing. Given the general nature of this problem, formulating standards of empirical research specifically for typological studies would be a welcome step in turning linguistic typology into a full-fledged empirical paradigm (cf. also Gawne & Styles, chapter 2, this volume).

Notes

1. "But what an achievement it would be were we able to confront a language and say to it: 'you have such and such a specific property and hence, also such and such further properties and such and such an overall character'—were we able, as daring botanists have indeed tried, to construct the entire lime tree from its leaf. If an unborn child could be baptized, I would choose the name typology" (von der Gabelentz 1891:481, translation quoted from Ramat 2011:21).

2. "Unlike descriptive categories, [comparative concepts] are not part of particular language systems and are not needed by descriptive linguists or by speakers. They are not psychologically real, and they cannot be right or wrong. They can only be more or less well suited to the task of permitting crosslinguistic comparison" (Haspelmath 2010:664).

3. The Typological Database of Intensifiers and Reflexives is an example of an early database implementing this type of data model; cf. Gast et al. (2007), Gast (2009).

4. In corpus-based approaches, properties of the type described in section 3 are not attributed to languages or strategies, but to markables, i.e., (sequences of) tokens of linguistic output as recorded in a corpus.

5. URL: https://linktype.iaa.uni-jena.de/ImproType. Guest login: "guest", password: "ImproGuest."

6. https://github.com/VolkerGast/ExportXLD.

References

Alzetta, Chiara, Felice Dell'Orletta, Simonetta Montemagni, and Giulia Venturi. 2018. Universal Dependencies and quantitative typological trends: A case study on word order. In *Proceedings of the 11th Language Resources and Evaluation Conference (LREC 2018), 7–12 May, 2018, Miyazaki*, 4540–4549. Paris: European Language Resources Association (ELRA). http://www.lrec-conf.org/proceedings/lrec2018/pdf/1109.pdf.

Anderson, Gregory D. S. 2013. The velar nasal. In *The World Atlas of Language Structures Online*, ed. Matthew Dryer and Martin Haspelmath, chapter 9. Leipzig, Germany: Max Planck Institute for Evolutionary Anthropology.

Auwera, Johan van der, and Vladimir Plungian. 1998. Modality's semantic map. *Linguistic Typology* 2:79–124. https://doi.org/10.1515/lity.1998.2.1.79.

Auwera, Johan van der, Volker Gast, and Jeroen Vanderbiesen. 2012. Human impersonal pronouns in English, Dutch and German. *Leuvense Bijdragen* 98:4–26.

Babbie, Earl B. 1989. *The Practice of Social Research*. 5th ed. Belmont, CA: Wadsworth.

Bickel, Balthasar. 2007. Typology in the 21st century: Major current developments. *Linguistic Typology* 11:239–251. https://doi.org/10.1515/lingty.2007.018.

Bickel, Balthasar. 2010. Capturing particulars and universals in clause linkage: A multivariate analysis. In *Clause-Hierarchy and Clause-Linking: The Syntax and Pragmatics Interface*, ed. Isabelle Bril, 51–101. Amsterdam: Benjamins. https://doi.org/10.1075/slcs.121.03bic.

Bickel, Balthasar. 2015. Distributional typology: Statistical inquiries into the dynamics of linguistic diversity. In *The Oxford Handbook of Linguistic Analysis*, 2nd ed., ed. Bern Heine and Heiko Narrog, 901–923. Oxford: Oxford University Press. https://doi.org/10.1093/oxfordhb/9780199677078.013.0046.

Bickel, Balthasar, and Johanna Nichols. 2013. Fusion of selected inflectional formatives. In *The World Atlas of Language Structures Online*, ed. Matthew Dryer and Martin Haspelmath, chapter 20. Leipzig, Germany: Max Planck Institute for Evolutionary Anthropology.

Blevins, James P. 2006. Passive and impersonal constructions. In *Elsevier Encyclopedia of Language and Linguistics*, 2nd ed., ed. E. K. Brown, 236–239. Amsterdam: Elsevier.

Comrie, Bernard. 1981. *Language Universals and Linguistic Typology: Syntax and Morphology*. 2nd ed. Chicago: Chicago University Press.

Corbett, Greville. 2006. *Agreement*. Cambridge: Cambridge University Press.

Croft, William. 2003. *Typology and Universals*. Cambridge: Cambridge University Press.

Cronbach, Lee J., and Paul E. Meehl. 1955. Construct validity in psychological tests. *Psychological Bulletin* 52:281–302. https://doi.org/10.1037/h0040957.

Culbertson, Jennifer. 2017. New approaches to Greenbergian word order dependencies. In *Dependencies in Languages*, ed. N. Enfield, 23–38. Berlin: Language Science Press.

Cysouw, Michael, and Jeff Good. 2013. Languoid, doculect, glossonym: Formalizing the notion "language." *Language Documentation and Conservation* 7:331–359.

Dahl, Östen, and Vivikai Velupillai. 2013. The future tense. In *The World Atlas of Language Structures Online*, ed. Matthew Dryer and Martin Haspelmath, chapter 67. Leipzig, Germany: Max Planck Institute for Evolutionary Anthropology.

Dryer, Matthew. 2013. Order of object and verb. In *The World Atlas of Language Structures Online*, ed. Matthew Dryer and Martin Haspelmath, chapter 83. Leipzig, Germany: Max Planck Institute for Evolutionary Anthropology.

Dryer, Matthew, and Martin Haspelmath. 2013. *The World Atlas of Language Structures Online*. Leipzig, Germany: Max Planck Institute for Evolutionary Anthropology.

Eberhard, David M., Gary F. Simons, and Charles D. Fennig, eds. 2019. *Ethnologue: Languages of the World*. 22nd ed. Dallas: SIL International. http://www.ethnologue.com.

Fedden, Sebastian, Dunstan Brown, and Greville G. Corbett. 2010. Conditions on pronominal marking: A set of 42 video stimuli for field elicitation. University of Surrey. http://dx.doi.org/10.15126/SMG.25/1.

Futrell, Richard, Kyle Mahowald, and Edward Gibson. 2015. Large-scale evidence of dependency length minimization in 37 languages. *Proceeding of the National Academy of Science* 112 (33): 10336–10341. https://doi.org/10.1073/pnas.1516565112.

Gabelentz, Georg von der. 1891. *Die Sprachwissenschaft. Ihre Aufgaben, Methoden und bisherigen Ergebnisse*. Leipzig, Germany: Weigel.

Gast, Volker. 2009. A contribution to two-dimensional language description: The typological database of intensifiers and reflexives. In *The Use of Databases in Cross-Linguistic Research*, ed. Martin Everaert, Simon Musgrave, and Alexis Dimitriadis, 209–234. Berlin: De Gruyter Mouton. https://doi.org/10.1515/9783110198744.209.

Gast, Volker. 2015. On the use of translation corpora in contrastive linguistics: A case study of impersonalization in English and German. *Languages in Contrast* 15:4–33. https://doi.org/10.1075/lic.15.1.02gas.

Gast, Volker, and Johan van der Auwera. 2013. Towards a distributional typology of human impersonal pronouns, based on data from European languages. In *Languages across Boundaries. Studies in Memory of Anna Siewierska*, ed. Dik Bakker and Martin Haspelmath, 31–56. Berlin: De Gruyter Mouton. https://doi.org/10.1515/9783110331127.119.

Gast, Volker, Daniel Hole, Ekkehard König, Peter Siemund, and Stephan Töpper. 2007. *The Typological Database of Intensifiers and Reflexives*. http://www.tdir.org.

Goldhahn, Dirk, Uwe Quasthoff, and Gerhard Heyer. 2014. Corpus-based linguistic typology: A comprehensive approach.

In *Proceedings of the 12th KONVENS Conference*, ed. Josef Ruppenhofer and Gertrud Faß, 215–221. Hildesheim, Germany: Universitätsbibliothek. http://nbn-resolving.de/urn:nbn:de:gbv:hil2-opus-2846.

Greenberg, Joseph. 1966. Some universals of grammar with particular reference to the order of meaningful elements. In *Universals of Language*, ed. Joseph Greenberg, 73–113. Cambridge, MA: MIT Press.

Hallgren, Kevin A. 2012. Computing inter-rater reliability for observational data: An overview and tutorial. *Tutorials in Quantitative Methods for Psychology* 8 (1): 23–34. https://doi.org/10.20982/tqmp.08.1.p023.

Hammarström, Harald, Robert Forkel, and Martin Haspelmath. 2019. *Glottolog 3.4*. Jena, Germany: Max Planck Institute for the Science of Human History. https://glottolog.org.

Haspelmath, Martin. 1997. *Indefinite Pronouns*. Oxford: Oxford University Press.

Haspelmath, Martin. 2010. Comparative concepts and descriptive categories in crosslinguistic studies. *Language* 86:663–687. https://doi.org/10.1353/lan.2010.0021.

Keenan, Edward L. 1976. Towards a universal definition of subject. In *Subject and Topic*, ed. Charles N. Li, 303–333. New York: Academic Press.

Nichols, Johanna. 1992. *Linguistic Diversity in Space and Time*. Chicago: University of Chicago Press. https://doi.org/10.7208/chicago/9780226580593.001.0001.

Nichols, Johanna. 2007. What, if anything, is typology? *Linguistic Typology* 11:231–238. https://doi.org/10.1515/LINGTY.2007.017.

Plesser H. E. 2018. Reproducibility vs. replicability: A brief history of a confused terminology. *Frontiers in Neuroinformatics* 11:76. https://doi.org/10.3389/fninf.2017.00076.

Ramat, Paolo. 2011. The (early) history of linguistic typology. In *The Oxford Handbook of Linguistic Typology*, ed. J. J. Song, 9–24. Oxford: Oxford University Press. https://doi.org/10.1093/oxfordhb/9780199281251.013.0002.

Schlegel, August Wilhelm von. 1808. *Über die Sprache und Weisheit der Inder: Ein Beitrag zur Begründung der Alterthumskunde; Nebst metrischen Übersetzungen Indischer Gedichte*. Heidelberg, Germany: Mohr und Zimmer.

Tuldava, Juhan. 1994. *Estonian Textbook*. Bloomington: Indiana University Press.

Malin Petzell and Caspar Jordan

1 Introduction

This case study evaluates methods of data processing used in a linguistic research project on the semantics of verbal morphology in Bantu languages.[1] The project involves language data collected during fieldwork on six language varieties, all of which are under-described. Early on it became clear that combining a relatively complex research subject with a multitude of languages, together with the fact that there is little previous information on them, would lead to some specific requirements on managing the language data, and on the way the researchers could interact with them. After having dismissed traditional approaches such as detailed manual interlinearization and computational corpora for reasons to be explained herein, we experimented with two different methods. The first involved a qualitative data analysis software and the second a fairly uncomplicated database setup. The software used for data processing included Toolbox (https://software.sil.org/toolbox/), NVivo (https://www.qsrinternational.com/nvivo/home), and a combination of Microsoft Excel 2016 (http://products.office.com/excel/) and OpenRefine (http://openrefine.org); the latter being the one we opted for in the end.

This chapter will start by briefly describing the research project, the requirements we had for the data management and the data collection. Then we will mention the different methods we dismissed and examine the two we tried including the work of coding, preparing for filtering, and tidying up the language data. After a note on metadata, we will evaluate and explain why we opted for the more straightforward database setup in the end.

2 The project and its background

The purpose of the research project, "The semantics of verbal morphology in central Tanzanian Bantu languages: a comparative study," is to describe and analyze the semantic construal of (universal) tense, aspect, and mood (TAM) notions and their grammatical encoding on the verb in the East Ruvu Bantu language varieties (Kagulu, Kami, Kwere, Kutu, Luguru, and Zaramo). These varieties show a significant degree of diversity in terms of their TAM systems, despite an otherwise close relationship (Petzell & Hammarström 2013). In the project, we examine the TAM systems of these languages by studying the verb forms, their basic meanings, extended functions and distribution, and how the TAM markers interact with the lexical semantics (aspectual classification) of the verb stem. To do this we needed to gather language data involving different verbs in a number of different frames as well as single sentences. Data collection was carried out by the principle investigator, Malin Petzell, in the Morogoro region in central Tanzania. Because of the complexity of the language data, some project funds were used to hire a dedicated data manager, Caspar Jordan, to work on structuring the data and making them accessible.

The Bantu language varieties in the East Ruvu group are under-described in general, and there is little information about their grammatical structure and TAM systems. There are three comparative analyses (Petzell 2012; Petzell & Hammarström 2013; Bar-el & Petzell, forthcoming), and there are published grammatical descriptions in three of the language varieties in which TAM and the verb are described, namely in Luguru (the dated Seidel 1898; the somewhat newer Mkude 1974), Kagulu (Petzell 2008), and Kami (Petzell & Aunio 2019). For the other language varieties, only outdated or short linguistic documentations can be found, such as an account of Kami written more than a hundred years ago (Velten 1900). Additionally, a comparison of TAM in Kami, Kagulu, and Luguru is being produced (Petzell & Edelsten, in prep.).

As mentioned, the aim of the research project was to answer questions on the semantics of TAM and their interaction with the verb stem. How this was done will be explored herein, starting with the requirements we had on the data from the six language varieties.

3   Requirements on the data

First of all, TAM is a rather broad field covering all sorts of semantic and morphological intricacies, implying that an extensive amount of language data is needed to map TAM in general. Covering six language varieties further expands the need for data. Furthermore, the comparative nature of the project entails that each language can be studied from a typological angle, rather than forming the basis for an in-depth analysis of TAM in a single language. The very fact that the language varieties are closely related is the motivation for studying them together. Variations within and between languages may give clues that lead to further insights into the whole system, but this requires comparisons of morphemes and semantics between language varieties; in other words, the data need to be comparable. The complexity of the subject (TAM) and the need for comparability together give rise to a central requirement of the data management for this project: the researcher needs to be able to perform advanced filtering and search operations on the data, using categories such as the semantics of the sentence, interesting morphemes, specific language(s) as well as language user(s) (to be able to identify idiosyncrasies). For instance, the project needed a tool that enabled searches for a specific morpheme in a specific semantic frame, for example, in the vicinity of a temporal adverbial, or where a phrase in the affirmative carries the habitual marker but is not tagged for past.

3.1   (Un)Structured data and data collection

At the beginning of the project it was not clear to what level the data we included would be structured (i.e., comparable). In the collected data there were both stories and elicited sentences; the former were assumed to be less predictably structured than the latter. By *unstructured data*, we mean data that do not follow a predefined data model, such as a relational database. To a linguist, describing text as unstructured may seem counterintuitive, but in a context where computers are used to sift through data, the quantity of which makes a close reading less feasible, it makes sense, because the methods of searching for and retrieving information differ between structured and unstructured data. In this specific case,

both the stories and the elicited sentences may be viewed as unstructured, even though the sentences were elicited to be comparable, and thus to contain more or less the same semantic structure, across languages. In the end, we decided not to include the stories in the data set, as they were not semantically comparable enough to benefit from being coded along the same principles as the elicited sentences. The stories will still be used in the final grammatical analysis, although not coded and processed in the same way as the single sentences in the database.

It should also be mentioned that the coding functions primarily as a facilitator for searching and filtering and does not constitute a comprehensive analysis on its own, even though we do consider coding to be an analytical process, which naturally involves a certain amount of interpretation.

The language data were collected during field trips to central Tanzania in 2016 and 2017 (for more on data collection, see Good, chapter 3, this volume). The elicited sentences were collected in the following way: language users were given questionnaires to take home consisting of a set of sentences in Swahili, which is their second language, to be translated into their respective first languages. The language users and the principal investigator would then meet for an elicitation session where they would discuss the sentences and their translation to make sure that the Swahili was understood as intended. This is a necessary step, given that the sentences were not situated in a broader context. There was also an English translation of every sentence to further clarify the intended meaning. Most language users wrote their translations by hand and these were later typed on a computer and put into Microsoft Word tables. A few language users wrote their translations directly into Word tables. In addition to the source sentences and translated sentences, the tables also contain an index number (sometimes a letter as well, e.g., 126A) and, in some cases, comments or alternative translations by the language users. These index numbers combined with the language user abbreviation and the questionnaire number subsequently made up the unique *identifier*, as described in the metadata discussion (section 6). For storage, we decided to use our university's cloud storage solution, GUbox (https://www.box.com), given that we wanted to keep our emerging data files safe and accessible for both Petzell and Jordan. This gave us the safety of automated backup and version handling, while allowing both of us easy access to the files at all times.

The language data and metadata will be archived with the Swedish National Data Service (www.snd.gu.se) once the project is finished. The Swedish National Data Service will keep the data safe and accessible for a foreseeable future (for a discussion about archiving, see Andreassen, chapter 7, this volume).

4 Dismissed methods

Had the project focused on one of the major languages of the world, with documented texts and other written data, it would have been relatively easy to build a corpus suitable for computational analysis that could then be queried using a corpus querying tool such as Korp (Borin, Forsberg, & Roxendal 2012). However, we decided not to do that for several reasons: (1) Corpus building is greatly supported by the existence of language materials such as grammars and lexica, but for our languages, these do not generally exist. (2) A discussion with the Korp development team revealed that Korp (and several other corpus tools) does not support multilinguality very well. Because we are working with six languages, we would thus have had to go through six separate corpus-building processes, still ending up with a setup that would not have been ideal for comparative research. (3) Corpora tend to be large, containing millions or hundreds of millions of words. Though this does not seem to be necessary for a corpus to be useful (cf. Ross 2018), it would not be worth the endeavor in this project to build a relatively minute corpus.

The traditional alternative to building a computational corpus would be to build a corpus in Toolbox or some other tool for linguistic annotation that requires meticulous manual annotation (interlinearization) by the researcher—a laborious process. Having built Toolbox corpora for two of the language varieties (Kami and Kagulu) for previous research projects, it was decided that the level of detailed annotations that Toolbox and similar programs offer was not necessary for our purposes in the current project. In addition, Toolbox does not accommodate comparative work on several languages very well, as every language would have to be put in its own Toolbox project, making it impossible to search simultaneously over multiple languages. The same goes for other relevant software such as Fieldworks (FLEx; http://software.sil.org/fieldworks).

Seeing that neither computational corpora nor traditional annotation-based work seemed to be the solution, we searched for a system and/or workflow and/or data structure that would allow us to smoothly code a fairly large amount of textual data and that would allow complex filtering and search operations. Section 5 discusses the two methods we tested, namely NVivo and OpenRefine.

5 Two tested methods

As there was no obvious best way to approach the data-related processes in this project and as we did not have any methodological role model, we did a fair bit of experimenting before trying NVivo. NVivo is a Computer-Assisted Qualitative Data Analysis Software (CAQDAS) application designed for qualitative analysis of text, audio, video, and other kinds of data. The NVivo program gives the user the possibility of selecting parts of the textual data and assigning to them one or more user-defined codes called *nodes*. These nodes can then be used to filter through the data to find elements relevant to a specific theme or category, but also to build a hierarchy of nodes or to relate nodes to each other in other ways. The right half of figure 54.1 shows a list of parts of text assigned to the node "PFV" (perfective aspect). The left half shows the hierarchy of nodes, where PFV is one of several nodes grouped together under the top node "TAM English." NVivo also provides visualization tools that support the user in finding structure in the data.

After discarding NVivo for reasons discussed in section 5.1, we moved on to trying a second method, which involved using a combination of Microsoft Excel and OpenRefine to build a fairly straightforward database. This approach ended up being our solution of choice. OpenRefine is a tool that allows its users to perform a broad selection of data-cleaning operations on tabular data, both numerical and textual. It supports regular expressions (see Han, chapter 6, this volume) and has its own syntax, called GREL (General Refine Expression Language), which can express complex processing tasks. Together, these features make it possible to perform complicated text processing operations, both searching and transforming (disorganized) data into useful, well-organized tables. OpenRefine works well with Excel spreadsheets, which turned out to be advantageous because Excel has some functions that are missing from OpenRefine. A combination of the two provided a powerful tool for cleaning and indexing untidy textual data.

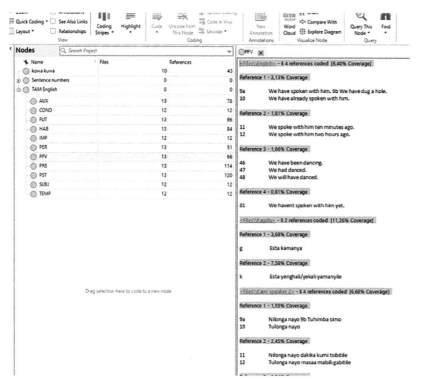

Figure 54.1
Screenshot from NVivo 12.

5.1 The first approach—coding in NVivo

Seeing that we wanted to describe, analyze, and compare the TAM markers in these six language varieties, we needed a way to compile concordances both for specific morphemes and for specific semantics across six language varieties. Additionally, it would also be helpful to be able to search for temporal adverbials (as a string of characters) or for specific realizations of morphemes. This multitude of categorizations, together with the fact that our data are of a "qualitative nature,"[2] led us to believe that it would be to our advantage to use a piece of CAQDAS software, and because there was some experience in our department with using NVivo, we opted for that. The first nodes (i.e., codes) we decided to use were typical TAM categories such as past, present, and future tense and perfective, habitual, and persistive aspects. The coding for these categories was mostly based on the English-language elicitation sentences. Cues used were the tense and aspect of the English sentences and adverbs denoting temporal and/or aspectual semantics. For two categories, Swahili was used to code for the Swahili morphemes *-me-* (perfect and/or perfective) and *-li-* (past), because the distinction between the two is not always overtly present in English. A document explaining the coding procedure for each code was created and stored together with the data.

It very quickly became clear that NVivo was not ideal for the coding necessary in this project. One reason for this is that we wanted the same coding for the same sentence in the target languages, and we wanted to code the sentence in the six language varieties at the same time—something that NVivo only allows using a workaround. By coding every sentence to a node for its index number, it becomes possible to write a "coding query" to get a list of all sentences with a specific number. This list could then be coded to a TAM node. For example, if sentence 126A was in the present tense, a coding query for sentence number "126A" would give a list of all the translations of sentence number 126A in every one of the six language varieties. This list could then easily be coded to the node "PRS" (present tense). This method worked, but required a lot of additional data cleaning, such as creating lines for every case of missing data, that is, where a language user had not given a particular sentence, merging two lines when the language user offered two alternative translations, and other similar tasks. This extra work was necessary because coding sentences to their index number automatically required each sentence to be exactly one line, as the coding was based on the number of the line.

Another reason for abandoning NVivo in our project was the difficulty of coding on the morpheme level instead of on the word or even sentence level. A sentence would usually be coded to more than one node (e.g., past tense, persistent aspect, and the Swahili morpheme -*li*-), but in the list of results only one coding could be seen at a time.

What is more, the search function in NVivo was insufficient for our needs. In a search, the result list would not show the sentence surrounding the word that matched the search criteria, nor the translation, which was in another file ("source" in NVivo lingo). This rendered a smooth analysis impossible because it required switching between the different tabs. Another problem was that searching in NVivo does not allow truncation at the beginning of search expressions, making it impossible to search for morphemes in the middle of words, which is a serious shortcoming for Bantu linguistics given that Bantu languages are agglutinative and that Bantu words usually are concatenations of multiple morphemes. Finally, the program inexplicably crashed on a few occasions.

When we began coding in NVivo, we realized that we would get a better overview of the coding and also be able to work faster if we first collected our coding in a spreadsheet. Therefore, we created a spreadsheet with one row per elicitation sentence and one column per code, which was then used to code every single elicitation sentence by marking the appropriate cell. This left us with a spreadsheet of all the coding, which would soon turn out to be highly useful.

5.2 The second approach—coding in OpenRefine combined with Excel

After realizing that NVivo was not ideal for our purposes, it was practical to try using the spreadsheet as the primary tool for the entire data management, including the first steps of analysis. To be able to do these first steps of analysis, however, we needed to be able to filter out lists of sentences based on various combinations of coding. Given that we did not consider that Excel alone provided us with the search and filtering options we required, we then turned to OpenRefine.

The codes were transferred from the sheet with the elicitation sentences (a few hundred) to another sheet containing all the translated sentences (just over 8,700) using the Excel function =VLOOKUP, and matching by sentence ID, so that every translation of, for instance, sentence 126A received the same coding. Excel was also useful in filling in blank rows in the coding columns so that every cell in a column contained a 1 or 0 value rather than a 1 value or no value. In this way, it became

possible to filter not only for positive coding but also for negative coding, which is a very useful functionality that allows for double-checking.

As mentioned, our coding thus far had been based on the English language, and in one case Swahili. As the work progressed, we needed to extend our methods of coding to include searching for a morpheme (string of characters) that only existed in the target languages and that did not necessarily translate consistently into English or Swahili. One such morpheme may appear as -*tsa*- or as the allomorph -*tso*- and is a future marker. We used OpenRefine to create a code for this by using the regular expression .*ts[ao]\B* to filter through all the sentences in the six language varieties examined. This generated a list with all the sentences where the strings *tsa* or *tso* appear within a word, that is, not word-initially and not word-finally (*tsa* in the beginning of a word is a different morpheme altogether [see section 5.3] and *tsa* at the end is the verb "come"). Based on this list, we created a new coding column by means of the GREL expression *if(or(contains(value, "tsa"), contains(value, "tso")), "tsa tso", "")*. This generated a column containing the value "tsa tso" for all sentences in the list created with the regular expression. All other sentences had no value in that column. In another step, Excel was used to replace the coding with 1 for "tsa tso" and 0 for no value, because, by then, we realized that it was favorable to have a code for no value as well. The gain here was clear: creating the coding by means of a regular expression may give some faulty coding but it saves the researcher the trouble of going through all sentences by hand. The coding was verified by spot checks but also by cross-referencing with the coding for non-future tense, as *tsa/tso* was not expected to turn up in sentences that are, for instance, in the past tense. What is more, searching for sentences in the future but excluding the *tsa/tso* future marking generated a small number of sentences where there were interesting morphological realizations of the future tense in the target languages.

Because we worked in Excel spreadsheets, we had to take precautions always to work in copies of the data set when changing anything, to avoid the danger of involuntarily changing the original data. For a while, we considered using a SQLite database that offers stricter content control, in other words, it makes it harder to involuntarily change the original data files. However, SQLite does not come with support for regular expressions, and finding information on how to add such support was harder than expected; consequently, the idea was discarded.

Having decided on the software, we then proceeded to perform advanced filtering operations.

5.3 Filtering in OpenRefine

In OpenRefine, the filtering function (i.e., search) would always display the whole sentence, because the results list is row based and every sentence has its own row. In addition to displaying the context of a word, this also means that all the other coding for that sentence is visible as well, and even the translation in a separate column. One drawback here is that the coding can only be done on sentence level, not word level, but in this specific case, sentence level was sufficient as it was easy to identify the relevant morphemes within the sentences.

There are two main filtering options that we used in OpenRefine: text facet and text filter. The *text facet function* provides a list of all the unique values in a column, and by clicking on one of the values, all the rows that have another value will be hidden. It is also possible to reverse the effect so that all rows except the ones with the selected value are shown. As mentioned, generating a list where certain codes or strings of characters (such as a morpheme) are *not* present turned out to be decidedly constructive. The *text filter function* allowed us to search for a string of characters within a column, displaying all the rows that contained the string. This function understands regular expressions, which means that we could do very complex text string searches. An example is the regular expression \b(tsa|dza|za|nz'a), which returns all

rows where any of the strings *dza, tsa, za* or *nz'a*[3] is found word-initially or as an independent word. This way of searching and filtering formed the basis for an article about the unique particle *tsa*[4] that has no equivalent in English or Swahili (Petzell 2020) and that would have been hard to analyze otherwise. A further filtering operation performed on the particle *tsa* was to combine it with the code for the Swahili perfect -*me*-, which should not find any results because the particle uncommonly co-occurs with a perfect reading—and indeed, this filter did not generate any hits.

A final example of filtering is when we wanted to find out how the future perfect is expressed in these languages. We filtered for the code "FUT" (for future tense) combined with the code for the Swahili perfect -*me*-, which generated a list of thirty-seven sentences; see figure 54.2.

5.4 Tidying up the data

The Excel–OpenRefine method required a tidier data set than NVivo would as both Excel and OpenRefine give advantageous filtering functionality provided that the information is well organized. Sentence numbers, translated sentences, and original Swahili and English sentences all needed to be placed in separate columns, while language users' comments and the researcher's comments were moved out of the spreadsheet and stored elsewhere. Fortunately, OpenRefine provides a range of tools to solve these kinds of problems, for example, to standardize sentence numbers that were sometimes found in a column of their own, sometimes in front of the sentence itself, sometimes demarcated by a full stop and

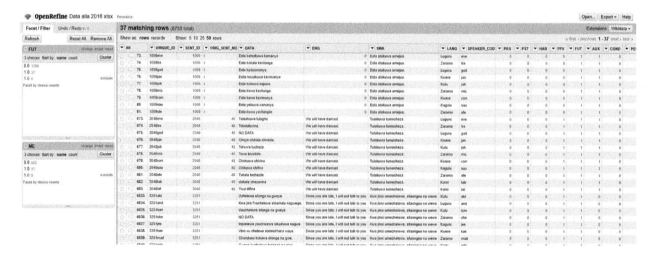

Figure 54.2
Screenshot from OpenRefine.

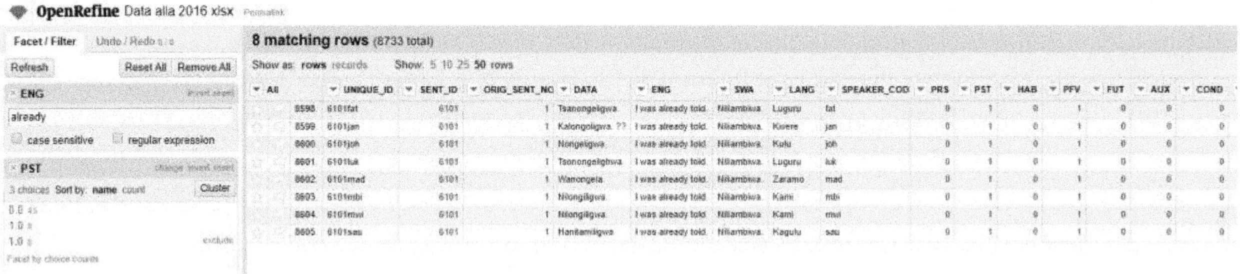

Figure 54.3
OpenRefine filters and the results of the filtering.

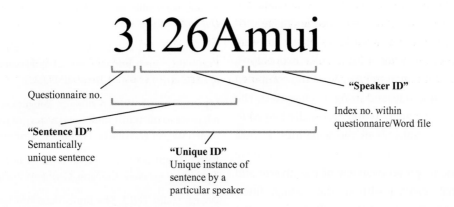

Figure 54.4
This figure shows an ID that refers to a specific translation of an elicitation sentence (sentence 3126A) by a specific language user (mui). By removing the first number, the remaining numbers (126A) point to the exact location of the data in the original questionnaire. A few sentence numbers are followed by a capital letter, which is part of the sentence number. The questionnaire number refers not to the filled-in questionnaire but to the template questionnaire. This is because data from several different questionnaires were used. The questionnaire number is arbitrary.

sometimes not, and so on. Once this standardization was completed, it became possible to filter the 8,700+ sentences to get all instances of one specific sentence, something that otherwise would only have been possible by manually going through all the Word files separately. Figure 54.3 shows two filters, a text filter for the word *already* and a text facet where the user has chosen the value 1 for PST, applied to the data set of 8,733 sentences. Together the filters result in a list of 8 sentences which are in the past tense (value 1 for the PST column) and where the English elicitation sentence contains the word *already*.

Keeping Swahili, English, and the target-language data in separate columns allowed us to search efficiently for morphemes and words in a specific language. Other important columns included sentence ID, unique ID (see section 6), language user ID, language ID, and columns for all the codes we used.

6 Metadata

Each language user was coded with a three-letter abbreviation, and the *metadata* (i.e., data on the data; see Good, chapter 3, this volume; Kung, chapter 8, this volume) on the language user, such as their place of birth, age, level of education, occupation, family situation, and so forth, were kept in a separate file. The metadata also noted when, where, how, and by whom the data were collected.

Excel was used to create unique identifiers for every instance of a sentence by combining the sentence ID (derived from the index numbers found in the Microsoft Word tables preceded by the number of the questionnaire) and the three-letter code for the language user. In this way, it became possible to refer to every single sentence in the collection (see figure 54.4), which can also be done when citing the data in various publications. It also made it possible to cross-reference every sentence with the language user's metadata to check for variables such as education, parents' background, spouse from another language group, and such, as well as with the original Microsoft Word file where the language users' and the principal investigator's comments and alternative translations are kept. This can also be useful if a language user were to wish to be withdrawn from the study, as the data supplied by that person would be easy to locate and delete.

7   Conclusions

We have shared our experience building a small database containing data from six under-described language varieties using OpenRefine. The advantages of the software were the possibility to filter using regular expressions, the easy tidying of disorganized data, and the combined searches (filters) using codes and strings of characters. The software facilitated the analysis and eventually helped to answer research questions about the semantics of TAM and the verb in these language varieties. It would have been problematic to get an overview of the diverse and rather substantial material without the coding, filtering, and search functionality that OpenRefine or similar software offers. Had we had more time and resources, we would have liked to fully annotate all the language data for future purposes in software such as FLEx or Toolbox, but for this project it was neither necessary nor feasible.

NVivo did not serve our purposes, but for even more unstructured data it is most likely a useful tool. The two main reasons we ended up not using NVivo were that the language translations ended up in different tabs, making it difficult to compare between languages, and that cross-referencing and searching generated lists that did not contain the amount of information we needed.

Given the quantity of our textual material, our research objectives, and the resources at hand, we are very satisfied with the results these methods of data processing generated. Consequently, we recommend using a combination of a spreadsheet and a data cleaning and filtering software such as OpenRefine.

Notes

1. We are grateful to two anonymous reviewers for valuable comments and to Riksbankens Jubileumsfond for providing the funding for the research project.

2. It may be argued that qualitative and quantitative are features of the analysis method rather than of the data. However, text is usually thought of as qualitative data in the data management discourse.

3. The target languages are not standardized; thus there is considerable variation in pronunciation and spelling of the same morpheme.

4. The particle encodes some type of shared knowledge or shared reference and conveys different meanings similar to "at a specific time," a locative reference "at that place," or even "for a reason."

References

Bar-el, Leora, and Malin Petzell. Forthcoming. (Im)perfectivity and actionality in East Ruvu Bantu. *Language Typology and Universals* 74 (3).

Borin, Lars, Markus Forsberg, and Johan Roxendal. 2012. Korp—the corpus infrastructure of Språkbanken. In *Proceedings of LREC 2012*, 474–478. Istanbul: ELRA.

Mkude, Daniel J. 1974. A study of Kiluguru syntax with special reference to the transformational history of sentences with permuted subject and object. PhD thesis, University of London.

Petzell, Malin. 2008. *The Kagulu Language of Tanzania: Grammar, Texts and Vocabulary*. Cologne, Germany: Rüdiger Köppe Verlag.

Petzell, Malin. 2012. The under-described languages of Morogoro: A sociolinguistic survey. *South African Journal of African Languages* 32 (1): 17–26.

Petzell, Malin. 2020. An analysis of the verbal marker *tsa* in Luguru. In *The Semantics of Verbal Morphology in Under-Described Languages*, ed. M. Petzell, L. Bar-el, and L. Aunio. Special issue, *Studia Orientalia Electronica* 8 (3): 119–133.

Petzell, Malin, and Lotta Aunio. 2019. Kami G36. In *The Bantu Languages*, 2nd ed., ed. M. van de Velde, K. Bostoen, D. Nurse, and G. Philippson, 563–590. London: Routledge.

Petzell, Malin, and Peter Edelsten. In preparation. TAM marking in Bantu languages of Morogoro region, Tanzania. Unpublished manuscript.

Petzell, Malin, and Harald Hammarström. 2013. Grammatical and lexical comparison of the Greater Ruvu Bantu Languages. *Nordic Journal of African Studies* 22 (3): 129–157.

Ross, Daniel. 2018. Small corpora and low-frequency phenomena: *try and* beyond contemporary, standard English. *Corpus* 18. https://journals.openedition.org/corpus/3574.

Seidel, August. 1898. Grundriss der Wa-Ruguru-Sprache. In *Die mittleren Hochländer des nördlichen Deutsch-Ostafrika*, ed. C. Waldeman Werther, 436–455. Berlin: Verlag von Hermann Paetel.

Velten, Carl. 1900. Kikami, die Sprache der Wakami in Deutsch-Ostafrika. *Mitteilungen des Seminars für orientalische Sprachen* 3:1–56.

55 Managing Data in TerraLing, a Large-Scale Cross-Linguistic Database of Morphological, Syntactic, and Semantic Patterns

Hilda Koopman and Cristina Guardiano

1 Introduction

TerraLing (https://www.terraling.com) is a database-backed web application set up to collect, store, and explore data for comparative research in the linguistic sciences. TerraLing is publicly accessible and open-ended: new languages, contributors, properties, and databases can be added so as to allow the database to grow over time. Its basic setup allows working with linguists who are native speakers or signers as language experts providing the data. This gives researchers the opportunity to use the tools of theoretical linguistics to access the implicit knowledge of native speakers/signers to probe crosslinguistic variation. The basic database schema is flexible, which means it can be adapted to the research needs of individual researchers. TerraLing aims (i) to make linguistic data widely available on a group of sister databases, whether the data come from well-studied or understudied languages, from spoken or signed languages, or from endangered, extinct, or emerging languages; (ii) to provide a common set of powerful queries and analytical tools on the web application to explore the data in each database, and (iii) to enable language researchers to easily set up additional sister databases. The long-term goal is to turn TerraLing into a ready-made community tool that linguistic projects can use to gather and store their data for comparative research purposes.

1.1 Brief history of TerraLing

TerraLing is the result of a collaboration of linguists and computer scientists from NYU and UCLA over the past decade. It is currently led by Hilda Koopman (UCLA, Linguistics) and is based on original ideas of Chris Collins and Richard Kayne (NYU, Linguistics), who envisioned a publicly accessible, open-ended, language expert–oriented internet database (described in Collins & Kayne

2007). This vision defined the basic functionality of the database (as described in section 2), designed by Dennis Shasha (NYU, Computer Science).

TerraLing was built from scratch. An NSF-funded[1] pilot web application was launched in 2009 around the language-expert SSWL (Syntactic and Semantic Structures of the World's Languages) database.[2] Based on the lessons learned from the original prototype, it was reprogrammed as TerraLing, with Marco Liberati and Hannan Butt at the backend.[3] As it failed to secure further NSF funding, the overall project slowed down, but programming continued on a volunteer basis, supervised by Dennis Shasha,[4] and linguistic development continued in the background.

In July 2017, TerraLing was sufficiently developed for migration of the original SSWL database and for hosting new databases. In August 2020, outdated tools and dependencies were updated by Shailesh Vasandani and Hannan Butt. Further work on the backend, search tools, user interface, and administrative interface is in progress.

With Nina Haslinger, Ethan Poole, and Viola Schmitt joining Hilda Koopman and Cristina Guardiano on the general board, initiatives to keep the community of project developers and language experts engaged have included a biannual newsletter, annual workshops, and monthly community meetings.

As of June 14, 2021, TerraLing hosts six databases:

1. SSWL
2. Conjunction and Disjunction
3. Anaphora
4. Cinque's Universal 20 database[5]
5. Passive-like constructions
6. Quantification and Plurality

1.2 Rationale

The idea of an open-ended,[6] language expert–oriented online database was borne out of a general need for a tool that can support theoretically guided research.

Formal syntacticians and semanticists consider data about the properties of individual languages. However, it is necessary for the field to progress further to find out what generalizations hold across languages and why they hold, what properties can vary and why, what properties are invariant across languages, what properties correlate, and what gaps there are: this will invariably help narrow down the set of hypotheses that we entertain about the Language Faculty.[7]

Future theoretical progress in formal syntax/semantics thus demands that we move toward theory-oriented thinking to make precise empirical predictions of different proposals that can be tested on comparative data for as many languages/dialects possible. This enterprise requires that we make inventories about what is found (at the necessary level of granularity), a task that not only serves theoretical linguistics, but also linguistics in general, as well as related fields.

This method of investigation crucially requires novel tools and novel ways of collecting the data. To do so successfully, we have to import a basic methodological tool of formal linguistics, which is the use of introspection, that has driven most results in formal syntax and semantics so far.

Work in the description and analysis of the structure and distribution of linguistic diversity across time and space, as well as on the internal structure and nature of human language, has produced a huge amount of empirical/typological data from different types of languages. These data should be made available in some repository form and be accessible to the general public to be useful.

Within the typological and documentary linguistics tradition, new data have been made available through many new reference grammars of individual languages (many previously undescribed), as well as through publicly available databases such as the famous online global database WALS (Dryer & Haspelmath 2013), which collects the research results of many authors and is based on research spanning many decades. Yet, for all their virtues, descriptive grammars, WALS, or *corpora* for that matter, are not sufficient to answer the questions for theoretically guided research, access to native speakers/signers' intuitions is crucially required as well.[8] To probe the structure of some sentence, we need to apply a battery of diagnostic tests to it. Such tests produce constructed examples, which require judgments as to whether these are acceptable or not (with a certain meaning and given a particular environment). These will have to include intuitions on constructed examples that control for a number of variables.

The data coming from the formal linguistic tradition that have been made available in some repository form accessible to the general public are mainly: (i) new descriptive grammars (based to a large extent on introspective judgments), and (ii) databases that document microvariation, that is, variation found in closely related varieties of languages/dialects.[9] The research on languages that are widely and intensely studied continues to yield an astounding amount of new knowledge (and the end is nowhere in sight). This can be measured by the new descriptive grammars that resulted almost exclusively from the generative syntax tool kit,[10] for example, the two thousand pages of Huddleston and Pullum (2005) on English, the five thousand pages on Bosque and Demonte's (1999) Spanish grammar, or the eight (open-access) volumes of new description of Dutch syntax written by Hans Broekhuis and collaborators (e.g., Broekhuis & den Dikken 2012; Broekhuis 2013; Broekhuis & Corver 2016). Furthermore, native speakers seem to agree on the vast majority of these data. As we stress, these descriptions mostly result from introspective data guided by the ever larger number of diagnostic tools and methods that formal linguistic theory provides[11] (and these descriptions build on previous grammars, general literature, corpora, any data that exist, as well). This raises the question how reliable introspective data are. Though introspective methods are often considered to be unreliable, it is important to point out that this is not confirmed by experimental research. Quite the contrary, Sprouse, Schütze, and Almeida (2013), Sprouse and Almeida (2012), and Schütze and Sprouse (2014) have experimentally tested the data in journal publications or textbooks discovered by these methods and proven they are highly replicable (between 95% and 98% depending on the data sets). Thus, to enable theoretical progress on the basis of cross-linguistic data, we should be able to access the intuitions of native speakers or signers: TerraLing allows doing so (though nothing forces us to gather data in this way).

Against this background, we now turn to section 2, which discusses the database functionality and describes the flexible database schema, the search interface, and the basic management setup. Section 3 is written as a guide for the reader who would want to develop content for one of the existing databases, set up their own database within TerraLing for a cross-linguistic project, or would otherwise want to be involved in the general project. Section 4 discusses data collection, various issues related to glosses, and academic credit. Section 5 provides a short summary of the chapter.

2 Basic database functionality and description

To fulfill its goals, TerraLing and its database(s) must meet the following four types of functionality:

1. They must persist and expand over time and be openly accessible worldwide.

2. They must allow flexible additions to data as new properties and new languages are added, without any need for reprogramming.

3. The web application must allow disciplined and secure curation of data by multiple linguists.

4. The data stored in the database(s) must be easily extractable and usable for exploration and research purposes.

We briefly discuss how this is achieved and present a basic description of the (flexible) database schema.

2.1 Durability and accessibility

TerraLing and its databases must be able to last over time and be openly accessible worldwide.[12] TerraLing is currently hosted on the highly secure industrial site ACS (Amazon Cloud Services) and is accessible worldwide. Regular automated backups further protect the data.[13] While the default option is to be openly accessible, it is also possible to restrict access to a database, if so required. Each individual database has a toggle for a *private* or *public* setting. A private setting restricts access to a group of researchers for a specific duration (e.g., for the duration of a funded project). A simple switch to a public setting will make the database publicly accessible.

2.2 Basic design

The project builds on a simple but flexible property-as-value model, which Professor Dennis Shasha has used successfully in his work in plant genomics.[14] This model ensures that new content can be added over time. Linguistic data are characterized by data linked to *objects of*

description (typically languages or dialects). Each such object can be characterized by a set of *property-value* pairs.[15]

The information stored in the database is represented through four types of tables:

1. Languages (*languagename, propertyname, value, contributorname, date, time*)

2. Properties (*propertyname, description, contributorname, date, time*)

3. Examples (*languagename, sentenceid, type, propertyname, value, comment, contributorname, date, time*)

4. Contributors (*contributorname, affiliation, username, password, e-mail, date, time*)

The *Languages* table gives the values for each property. For example, there is an SSWL property for *Predicative adjective agreement (Pred_Adj_Agr)*.[16] The value of this property can be *Yes, No,* NA (not applicable).[17] For French and Icelandic, the value is *Yes,* and for Dutch it is *No.* A complete listing of properties with their values and accompanying examples for a language is equivalent to a rough grammatical sketch for the areas the properties cover.

In the *Properties* table, each property is associated to a description. *Property Descriptions* have a specific format (as discussed in detail in section 3.4) that provides the definitions of the values of the property and presents a concrete example of a property development.

Evidence for a property setting is given in the form of examples, stored in the *Examples* table. Each example consists of a line of text, a gloss (we recommend using Leipzig glossing conventions whenever possible, but see section 4.2 for further comments), a translation, and a comment field. The comment field allows contributors to provide further information, which can include further information about the distribution, or the source of the information, for example.

The *Contributors* table contains information about who contributes data to the database (where *data* means the *Property Description*, property-value pairs, or examples). This information is displayed in the example from Basaá

malaŋ	má	yé	ma-kéŋí
6.onions	6.SM	BE.PRES	AGR-big

The onions are big
Space for any comment or reference.

Paul Roger Bassong   (SSWL: example_1480)

on page 619.[18] Users interact with a web interface to add or explore data.[19]

2.3 Experts

TerraLing allows for a completely new take on typological research: as opposed to all other linguistic databases, it works with native linguists who are native speakers or signers (or have a deep knowledge of a language) as language experts. This means that it lets us access the implicit knowledge of native speakers and signers directly on a broad typological scale.

TerraLing is set up so as to enable linguists who are native speakers or signers to sign up as an expert contributor for their language. They may do so individually or as a group.[20] Experts must be approved before they can provide data, that is, before they are allowed to set property values and provide examples that illustrate the values. Data are tagged by the name of the expert contributor and remain under their sole control: experts (but no one else, except an administrator) can change values, examples, or comments. Experts do not have the power to delete their language.[21]

To further ensure the quality and reliability of the data, experts are sometimes paired up with a "mentor" who provides them with explanations about the *Property Descriptions*, checks the property values and the examples, and provides feedback. We would like to generalize this system in the future as it allows an organized check on the data, in addition to familiarizing the community with the database. Further ways to control data reliability are discussed in section 3.4.4.

To allow for disciplined and secure curation of data by multiple linguists, TerraLing has a role module, which defines the following roles: *Administrator* (site administrator, group administrator), *Language Expert*, *Property Author*, and *Member*. Administrators control access to the site or group module. Site and group administrators can assign roles to members and make members into experts for a specific language, for example, or demote experts into members. They have full control over the site or their group's database, except for the ability to delete the group. Access levels thus depend on a specific role assigned to contributors.

2.4 Usability for research purposes

To ensure maximal usability, TerraLing has built-in search functionality, implemented by a JavaScript API that queries the existing rails service. The search interface can be accessed from the masthead and consists of an *Advanced Search* page and a *History* page, where saved searches can be stored.

The *Advanced Search* page allows thousands of simple and complex queries, including universal implications and similarity trees. Any field is searchable, and searches can be combined. Searches can be constrained by (all, or any subset of) *languages*, by (all or any subset of) *properties*, by specific combinations of *values*, and so on. Up to six properties can be crossed so as to extract all the relevant data patterns in the database. *Compare* allows comparing up to eight languages for all properties that are entered.

All data or search results can be downloaded in .csv format from the *Advanced Search* page, or saved on the application, to be later accessed or rerun. Examples can be downloaded from the *Languages* page in .json format.

At the time of writing, the search functionality is being improved and further developed, depending on available means and opportunities. This holds as well as for the user interface, *Property Descriptions*, and how-to document videos. The database is slowly but constantly being developed: the entry page of each database provides a snapshot of the overall data in that database. Because data entry is continuing, this snapshot changes with time. The total percentage of properties set for each language can be found on the *Languages* page; the number of languages set for each property can be found on the *Properties* page. Our ultimate goal is to code up over time as many languages or dialects as possible from all contients (thus, the family skew is irrelevant). As far as the examples are concerned, it is difficult to calculate the exact number of missing ones: as a matter of fact, not all properties need to be exemplified, because one single example can serve to exemplify many properties.

3 Managing data in the databases of TerraLing

This section addresses readers who may want to develop their own (hypothesis-driven) comparative research project and use TerraLing to do so. We start out with a general overview of the workflow in section 3.1. In section 3.2, we discuss the details of the different aspects of the development.

3.1 General workflow

The TerraLing database is different from existing databases in the following ways.

(i) Requests for proposals to set up a new database, or develop new properties to an existing database, can be submitted at any time to the board for review. The board asks experts to review and, if necessary, help to improve the submission. If approved, the new properties are fed into the system and data collection can start. The set of linguistic questions for which relevant data can be collected is thus unrestricted.

(ii) New language experts and new languages (including extinct languages) can be added at any time.

(iii) The search engine allows for simple and complex searches (properties of languages, which can be combined and constrained as necessary) and correlated searches (property or language correlations), as well as for more complex tasks such as searching for implications and typological gaps. It also includes visualization tools such as maps and similarity trees (see section 2.4). Hence, the system is fine-tuned for cross-linguistic research on theoretical questions.

To ensure interoperability between the databases on TerraLing, properties should (preferably) have a particular format (see section 3.4.3). Possible answers are restricted to *Yes*, *No* and NA. Phenomena under consideration must be properly described and illustrated by examples that support the property value to ensure data reliability. Each *Property Description* has to specify precise criteria for a *Yes* and *No* answer, without technical jargon (and perhaps provide an example of how to set the two values), so experts from different backgrounds can understand how to apply them to their language. Notions that are often required in properties, such as *neutral context*, are pre-specified in the system and connected via links to the actual queries via a *Glossary*. All these requirements must be met so as to make the task doable and to generate comparable data (on this topic, see also section 4, and Gast and Jędrzejowski, chapter 53, this volume).

Much of the empirical work in any project consists of formulating research questions and plausible properties that fit the requirements of the database, as we see in section 3.2.

3.2 Development of a project

With the description of the database and the general workflow as a background, this section will guide readers who may want to develop their own comparative research project, contribute to an existing one, and use TerraLing to do so. We start with some examples of existing projects in section 3.3 and discuss the steps in the development of a new project up to the collection stage with some real examples in section 3.4.

The resulting project, whether in syntax, semantics, or morphology, or their interfaces, could aim to:

1. Add further content to one of the existing databases, for example, to SSWL, Conjunction and Disjunction, or Anaphora.

2. Convert some existing data set into a TerraLing database allowing it to grow further (as, e.g., Universal 20, Cinque's database).

3. Set up a new database on TerraLing to meet the specific goals of a particular research project.

3.3 Examples of hypotheses-driven research currently in TerraLing

We start with a small sample of the various theoretically inspired research projects that can be found in the databases on TerraLing. These projects are at the stage where data are being collected, stored, and explored.

The Conjunction and Disjunction database (https://www.terraling.com/groups/8) explores the semantics of conjunction and disjunction by investigating the cross-linguistic realization of such elements. The research is guided by theoretical hypotheses in semantics concerning the meaning of these elements and explores how these hypotheses can be tested on typological data. The project already generated important results.[22]

Within the general large-scale SSWL database, we mention the following three theoretically inspired projects:

1. Anders Holmberg and Craig Sailor explore the syntax of *yes* and *no* and gather data on SSWL to determine how affirmative and negative questions can be answered. Different types of elliptical answers are collected. This is the first-time systematic investigation on answers.[23]

2. Cristina Guardiano and Hilda Koopman are engaged in a systematic documentation project of the determiner region of noun phrases. This is an area where we find much cross-linguistic variation, both synchronic and diachronic, with formal properties touching on bare nouns versus determined nouns, and issues related to case, adpositions, demonstratives, classifiers, noun classes, quantifiers, and numerals. There is no other database that systematically records this variation for comparative purposes. This project is ongoing (current data for between 55 and 97 languages depending on

the property).[24] The properties are organized around the following variables:

a. An indefinite, definite (or generic) reading of (unmodified) noun phrases, depending on whether the noun is:

b. i. A mass noun, a singular or plural count noun

ii. A noun with (intrinsically) unique reference

iii. A proper name, or a proper name modified by an adjective

c. What syntactic position the noun phrase occupies (object, subject)

d. How determiners (when present) are ordered with respect to the noun

e. Whether the noun is a vocative.

3. Cinque's Universal 20 database[25] is a conversion into TerraLing format of Guglielmo Cinque's private database (in Word format), of Greenberg's Universal 20 (Greenberg 1963). Universal 20 concerns the attested cross-linguistic word order patterns of *Dem(onstrative) Num(eral) Adj(ective) N(oun)* in the world's languages. In his influential article, Cinque (2005) tallies the patterns that are attested and unattested cross-linguistically. These turn out to be partially different from Greenberg's original universal: only 14 of the 4! = 24 possible patterns appear to occur. The reason why this is so, Cinque proposes, should be found in the Language Faculty: the unattested patterns cannot emerge from the rules of the grammar. Because the absence of such patterns is crucial, it is imperative to continue to gather all available comparative evidence and explore potential counterexamples. This database compiles the available information from many heterogeneous sources (previous databases from various sources, data from grammars, articles, native speaker linguists) supplemented by Cinque's own continued research since his article. All data sources are indicated. There are currently data from 1,687 languages in this database.

3.4 Getting to the collection stage: from research questions to a table of variation and property descriptions

In this section we guide readers who may want to develop their own hypothesis-driven comparative research project through the various different stages and aspects of content development of a new project, with specific focus on how to get from a research question to the collection stage.

Because the novelty of the database is to explore theory-driven questions with comparative data, we focus here on the development of a specific research question and the lessons we have learned from setting up such projects. The main challenges lie in developing research questions and translating these into queries that can generate comparable linguistic data in a reliable fashion to seed the database and—ideally—that allow testing theoretical hypotheses. The database is well-suited for the development of a microcomparative project, as variation found in closely related languages/dialects provides an important window in the principles of the Language Faculty. Given the fact that a great many properties are shared by closely related varieties, these conditions may approximate those of a controlled experiment.

Development of a project is best done through collaborations or in a seminar or workshop-like environment.[26]

The concrete project we build in section 3.4.2 concerns aspects of the distribution and interpretation of adnominal adjectives. It builds on the substantial body of knowledge accumulated over the years in the general typological and formal linguistic literature (in particular, Dixon 1982; Dixon & Aikhenvald 2004; Cinque 2010, and the references cited therein). A partial questionnaire[27] develops this domain in a TerraLing format.

At the most general level, linguists start with the quite general research question *how to define an adjective cross-linguistically?*, and given a definition, ask the following question:

Q1: How is an adjective ordered w.r.t the noun?

Leading to questions why, and what the comparative picture can tell us about Universal Grammar.

This led to a multitude of sub-questions, for example, this small subsample:

Q2: Are adjectives always ordered on one side of the noun?

Q3: If a language allows stacking adjectives, is there a universal order of different adjectival classes, and if so, how do we explore this question with comparative linguistic data?

Developing answers to these questions will show how to set up a table of variation, which in turn will lead to the formulations of *Property Descriptions*. These must be formulated in such a way as to generate reliable comparative data.

3.4.1 Development of a table of variation and corresponding properties

The development of a set of properties is based on a table of variation, which must capture all relevant differences between languages in the specific domain of inquiry. These have binary values, encoded as *Yes/No*.[28]

A single binary property can define at most two types of languages. Adding a second property yields four types of languages (see table 55.1), adding a third yields eight types of languages (table 55.2), and so forth. Thus, n properties yield a typology of 2^n potentially different languages.

Data collection is based on the notion of *property*. A property can be described as the smallest visible phenomenon able to capture cross-linguistic structural diversity. Properties are conceived as available, in principle, in any language; thus, they must be defined in theory-neutral terms, in other words, avoiding notions (and related terminology) too strictly connected to a specific theoretical vision/background. Properties are conceived as the empirical manifestations of precise structural phenomena. They must be able, in principle, to represent all possible aspects of diversity manifested by a given phenomenon and at the same time make any language comparable with any other. Thus, they combine requirements of descriptive cross-linguistic adequacy with the need of in-depth explanation of the structure of individual grammars. One lesson we have learned from developing properties so far is that "binning," that is, collapsing different properties, must be avoided (as much as possible). Decomposition into ever finer smaller (sub)properties is necessary both to ensure generating comparative data and to allow their theoretical exploration. To attain typological exhaustiveness, as many properties must be formulated as needed to capture the observed space of variation. This is a challenging task.

3.4.2 A concrete example of a coding schema

We can illustrate this procedure with a concrete example, namely the properties for A(djective) N(oun) orders, which allow comparing the way this is done in SSWL with WALS (Dryer 2013b). This will serve to make the following points: (i) known variation must come out as a result of the coding (hiding known and easily observable variation is not acceptable), and (ii) coding must be based on easily observable criteria so as to ensure reliability and feasibility. We also demonstrate how to use the TerraLing data schema to capture further variation, in effect developing part of the project mentioned in section 3.4.1.

On the most general level, adjectives can either follow the noun, precede the noun, or do either. In WALS, this translates into one feature, *Order of Adj N*, that has four values: *N Adj*, *Adj N*, *no dominant order*, and *only internally headed relative clause (RC)*. In SSWL, there are two separate (independent) properties, *Adj N* and *N Adj*, each with two possible values (*Yes/No*).

Comparison between WALS and SSWL yields different results. For instance, as shown in table 55.3, French is classified as *N Adj* in WALS but as *Adj N: Yes* and *N Adj: Yes* in SSWL.[29]

Because French clearly has prenominal and postnominal adjectives (*une jolie petite fleur rouge*, lit: 'a nice little flower red'), the *N Adj* value in WALS is very surprising. This is because WALS utilizes the notion *dominant order*:[30] in French *N Adj* is considered dominant because many more types of adjectives follow the noun than can precede it. This now raises various problems. The first problem with this classification is that in WALS French and Swahili are in the same set of languages. But that is

Table 55.1

Abstract typology, two properties

	Property 1	Property 2	Language?
I	Yes	No	
II	No	Yes	
III	Yes	Yes	
IV	No	No	

Table 55.2

Abstract typology, three properties

	Property 1	Property 2	Property 3	Language?
I	Yes	No	Yes	
II	Yes	No	No	
III	No	Yes	Yes	
IV	No	Yes	No	
V	Yes	Yes	Yes	
VI	Yes	Yes	No	
VII	No	No	Yes	
VIII	No	No	No	

Table 55.3

A comparison of Adj N orders in WALS and SSWL

WALS		SSWL		
Order of Adj N	Language?	*Adj N*	*N Adj*	Count? Language?
Adj N	. . . Bengali . . .	Yes	No	59 . . . Bengali . . .
N Adj	. . . *French*, Swahili, . . .	No	Yes	98 . . . Swahili . . .
No dominant order	. . . Tagalog . . .	Yes	Yes	86 . . . *French*, Tagalog
Internally headed RC	. . .	No	No	3 . . . lacks Adjs

incorrect, because all adjectives follow the noun in Swahili, but not all adjectives follow the noun in French. Thus, the first fault of the dominant order criterion is that it fails to capture typological diversity. The second problem is that it is impossible to give instructions so as to get reliable comparative data. Assume for example we have a hypothetical un(der)described language that is just like French. How would one code such a language? Moreover, it prevents exploring further questions, for instance, about possible regularities of which classes of adjectives precede the noun and why. Finally, the notion of dominant order reveals (and corroborates) the hidden assumption that a language should be uniform in terms of word order (e.g., all modifiers should precede, or follow, the noun). This assumption is in fact not warranted, because languages are quite generally mixed. Coding the variation is therefore important for gaining further understanding in principles underlying linear orders.

The structure of the two relevant properties in SSWL does not need to assume any notion of dominant order: all logical possibilities are represented. In fact, all the four language types generated from the two properties are currently attested in the database (see table 55.3; the fourth type, at the bottom of the table, instantiates a language with no adjectives). Thus, Swahili and French come out as different, as desired. However, French and Tagalog come out as belonging to the same type, namely to the set of languages that allow both *Adj N* and *N Adj* order. This is in fact all the information that these two basic properties in SSWL can provide (though additional information can be found in comments). To further explore whether there is variation between French and Tagalog (or for that matter for the other languages with these property values), and how it is manifested, further finer-grained properties must be formulated, for instance, about the relative order of different classes of adjectives (say *color* or *size* adjectives) with respect to the noun. This is plausible given

widespread agreement in the literature that the different classes of adjectives line up according to a universal hierarchy *(subj. comment > size > age > shape > color > gender > nationality > material*; see for example Sproat & Shih 1991; Cinque 1994; Dixon & Aikhenvald 2004).

Suppose we add two pairs of new properties in the database: (1a) *Adj*$_{color}$ *N: Yes/No*, (1b) *N Adj*$_{color}$: *Yes/No*, (2a) *Adj*$_{size}$ *N: Yes/No*, (2b) *N Adj*$_{size}$: *Yes/No*. This allows us to capture (i) the fact that French *color* adjectives must always follow the noun: *une fleur rouge* (lit. 'a flower red') leads to the values *Adj*$_{color}$ *N: No, N Adj*$_{color}$: *Yes*, and (ii) the fact that basic *size* adjectives such as *petit, grand* ('small,' 'big') precede the noun in French with the values *Adj*$_{size}$ *N: Yes, N Adj*$_{size}$: *No*. Tagalog, on the other hand, allows both orders for *color* and *size* adjectives (Schachter & Otanes 1983), which leads to the values *Adj*$_{color}$ *N: Yes, N Adj*$_{color}$: *Yes*.

This yields table 55.4 on page 625, where the differences between Tagalog and French come out correctly, as well as a difference between French and Italian with respect to the order of the basic *size* adjectives.[31]

In principle, the additional two properties generate sixteen possible combinations of values: a combination of four *No* defines a language with no (*size* and *color*) adjectives, the combination labeled as "V" in the table defines a language without *color* adjectives, but with prenominal *size* adjectives, and so on. Which patterns are not attested cross-linguistically will fall out from this data schema.

A fine-grained collection of data such as the one we propose reflects the comparative landscape and can support theoretical explorations and predictions through the sophisticated search interface.

3.4.3 *Property Authors* **and** *Property Descriptions* Once a table of variation, or a hypothesis about the data that allow supporting or refuting a theoretical hypothesis, has been developed, the next step is how to translate these into *Property Descriptions*.

Table 55.4

A more fine-grained SSWL typology

	Adj_{size} N	N Adj_{size}	Adj_{color} N	N Adj_{color}	Language?
I	No	Yes	No	Yes	Swahili
II	Yes	No	No	Yes	French
III	Yes	Yes	No	Yes	Italian
IV	Yes	Yes	Yes	Yes	Tagalog
V	Yes	No	No	No	Lacks color A
VI	No	No	No	Yes	Lacks size A
VII	. . .				

Property Descriptions are formulated by *Property Authors* and are submitted to the editors. *Property Descriptions* (or queries) define and explain the property, provide restrictions about what (not) to consider, define an elicitation task with clear contexts and scenarios that serve to generate the examples on which the property values are assigned. To help the contributor, *Property Descriptions* must show how the property will be set for English and must present examples of languages that represent the combination of different values.

3.4.4 Feasibility testing   Once an initial set of properties has been developed, the properties are sent out to a group of contributor volunteers that test them on feasibility and provide feedback. Can the task be done on their language? Are definitions clear? If they are unclear or ambiguous can the definitions be improved? Depending on feedback, *Property Descriptions* are further refined or adjusted.

4   Data collection

After approval, the new properties are pushed on the database, and the collection stage can start. Contributors read the *Property Descriptions* on the *Edit Language* page, produce examples on the basis of the elicitation tasks, and determine the value. To save the property value, contributors must indicate their level of confidence in the setting of the value. There are three levels of confidence: (i) *certain* (many properties are completely uncontroversial), (ii) *revisit* (some cases are more questionable, require more thought either because the language does not provide an easy answer, or the property may be ill-defined or not refined enough), and (iii) *need help*, which will send a message to the *Administrator* and *Property Author*.

We are currently developing an off-line guided questionnaire format to help streamline the task for the contributors. It really requires two separate skills: an *elicitation*

task and a *classification* task (applying criteria to assign values).

Values are illustrated with glossed examples that illustrate the set values with examples from individual languages and give further information when relevant.

4.1   Data reliability

There are multiple sources for possible errors in the database. So far, there is no central control mechanism: the data are controlled by hand (by the *Administrators*). New data go in a queue to be checked. Reliability of the data is ensured through the adoption of the following measures.

Language Experts must be approved by the *Administrators*, and each property value and example are tagged by a contributor: therefore, it is always possible, when checking the data and values provided, to interact with the contributor, ask for explanations, further examples, corrections, and so forth. Errors can be corrected at any point, and comments can be added to explain specific value settings.

Each *Property Description* must also be approved by the *Administrators* to make sure that the descriptions conform to the general guidelines. The main strategy is to lower the chances different types of mistakes can be made at the entry level. Measures include (at present) (i) making the task easy and small (breaking down questions in small parts); (ii) avoiding "binning" (causes cognitive overload); (iii) giving clear instructions, providing illustrations in the form of examples, and so on; (iv) presenting all relevant information on one page to minimize the chance shortcuts or guesses are made; (v) making a contributor reflect on their confidence in the value (contributors must indicate their level of confidence to save the value). Avoiding technical jargon is also crucial to make the *Property Descriptions* accessible to contributors. Confusion happens in particular when standard terminology (e.g., *case, agreement, clitics, bare nouns*) is used and not defined. As a matter of fact, these terms cover different phenomena in different linguistic communities and traditions, and contributors will be biased according to the uses they have in their respective communities. Consequently, it is crucial that all technical terms are defined with no ambiguity. Obviously, contributors must read and use these definitions of technical terms and not take shortcuts (i.e., make sure that they understand the meaning of the terms used in the *Property Description*). Overall, it becomes clear quite quickly (from general low confidence scores and problems around terminology or low number of answers) which properties are prone to present problems and need extra attention. Another very useful guide for contributors comes from the *Examples* that illustrate each property value: properties not illustrated with examples are potentially problematic; properties usually not problematic are those that can be easily verified because they are part of the general knowledge base.

Because for the contributors of underdescribed or low-density languages the task is inherently more difficult (there are less possibilities for independent control), we have the "mentor" system mentioned in section 2.3.

Once data are entered, the strategy is to make corrections easy: it is common for contributors to autocorrect their values or examples. Properties that are answered *Yes* are easy to judge: it is in general sufficient to present a (productive) example to earn a *Yes* value. Properties that have a *No* value are more problematic. Further strategies include (i) checking examples to see whether they illustrate the value; (ii) having a feedback system to identify possible errors and weed them out (originally, SSWL had a forum feature that was set up for that purpose, but because it got little use, we have not reprogrammed it in TerraLing); (iii) enlisting the community (property contributors, administrators, mentors, local community with a common research or areal interest, and such) to explore the data: this invariably brings up questions, and errors; and (iv) finally, we find that search functions are very useful to identify potential outliers, which could turn out to be mistakes or reflect genuine differences. For example, the search function *Compare* is a useful tool to identify potential outliers.

4.2   Examples and glossing

Our guidelines are that for languages with written orthographies: examples are entered into the standard orthography of the language; if there is no standard orthography, examples are entered in the orthography that has been adopted in the linguistic community for the language (or related languages).

As for glossing, our guidelines recommend using the Leipzig glossing conventions,[32] but we have not systematically enforced this. This is in part because there are problems with the glossing and naming conventions, where linguists have a strong tendency to (mis) take glosses for analyses. Furthermore, different local communities have developed their own glossing dialects and descriptive terminology.

4.3   Citation guidelines

In this section we provide some practical information about citation guidelines for academic credit, CV, and personal statement.[33] A cite key on the welcome page of each data set in TerraLing is currently in development, closely following the model in WALS.

Our citation recommendations can currently be downloaded from Hilda Koopman's website (https://linguistics.ucla.edu/person/hilda-koopman). They will soon be available on the main TerraLing website. We list them here:

a. The general work

    Koopman, Hilda, Dennis Shasha, Hannan Butt and Shailesh Apas Vasandani (eds.), TerraLing, 2017—, https://www.terraling.com, Accessed on [DATE].

b. Each individual database

    [TEAM LEADERS/EDITORS],[34] [DATE STARTED—], [*NAME OF DATABASE*], [URL], Accessed on [DATE].

    Examples:

    SSWL

    Koopman, Hilda (ed.) (2012—), SSWL, The Syntactic and Semantic Structures of the World's Languages, https://www.terraling.com/groups/7, Accessed on [DATE].

    Conjunction and Disjunction

    Schmitt, Viola, Enrico Flor, Nina Haslinger, Eva Rosina, Magdalena Roskowski, and Valery Wurm (eds.) (2017—), *Conjunction and Disjunction*, https://www.terraling.com/groups/8, Accessed on [DATE].

c. Property Authors

    A considerable amount of research goes into the development of *Property Descriptions*, queries, glossary entries: *Property Authors* must be cited when you use their definitions and schemas of variation.

    Examples:

    A single Property Definition

    Cattaneo, Andrea, Chris Collins, Jim Wood (2011), Predicative Agreement. In: *SSWL*, https://www.terraling.com/groups/7. Accessed on [DATE].

A glossary entry

Flor, Enrico, Nina Haslinger, Eva Rosina, Madalena Roszkowski, Viola Schmitt, and Valerie Wurm (2017—), Coordination. TerraLing glossary entry, https://github.com/terraling -glossary/glossary/wiki/Coordination. Accessed on [DATE]

A subgroup of properties

Guardiano, Cristina, and Hilda Koopman (2015—), 33 Article properties for objects, from https://terraling.com/groups/7/properties/467 to https://terraling.com/groups/7/properties/500. In: SSWL. Accessed on [DATE]

d. Language Experts and Examples

We recommend that if you use datasets in presentations or written work, you minimally use footnotes to acknowledge all the language experts who contributed the data in the datasets.

We encourage generous and inclusive citations for language data, and sending a contributor a note to this effect. If language data ultimately comes from some source other than TerraLing (e.g., theses, published papers, monographs, websites), that source should be cited.

As for citing examples, we suggest either acknowledging the language expert in the text and adding a footnote with a link to the example, or alternatively providing the language expert's name and the link in a footnote added to the language name.

e. Curriculum vitae, web page, and research statement

Contributors should record the details of their contributions on their CV, Webpage/Project Webpage, and Research Statement.[35] For *Property Authors, Language Experts*, and *Administrators*, we recommend the following:

i. Property Authors

Property Authors should put links on their CV, personal webpage, and project webpage to *Property Descriptions* and glossary entries as illustrated earlier in this section. This could be done for instance under a heading *Web publications*. These should also be submitted in their dossiers for the purposes of hiring, promotions, and referred to in research statements stating the nature of the work involved.

ii. Language Experts

We recommend Language Experts list their contributions on their CV. This could be done for example under a suitable heading like *Web publications*. In addition, language experts can download their datasets and transform them in a PDF form, and make them available on their personal webpage.

Here are some examples of different ways this could be recorded:

Paul Roger Bassong (2014—), Language expert for Baasá for the TerraLing group: SSWL (https://www.terraling.com/groups/7) and Conjunction and Disjunction (https://www.terraling.com/groups/8).

Or:

Contributions to TerraLing:

Paul Roger Bassong (2014—) Basaá. Dataset, examples, and comments for TerraLing group SSWL (*Property Values*: 150, examples: 151, as of August 18, 2020).

Paul Roger Bassong (2017—), Basaá. Dataset, examples, and comments for TerraLing group Conjunction and Disjunction (*Property Values*: 40, examples: 42, as of August 18, 2020).

iii. Administrators

List your administrative functions under *Service to the Field* or *Reviewing/Editing*

Name, [DATE], The TerraLing group [NAME OF DATASET].

5 Summary

In this chapter, we provided a general description of the goals, design, structure, and potential of TerraLing (https://www.terraling.com), as well as a snapshot of its current state in terms of contents. TerraLing is a collection of databases, which is, virtually by definition, constantly in progress and constantly capable of being enriched and developed according to the most updated advances in theoretical and comparative linguistics, as well as in digital technologies.

The main purpose of TerraLing is to build a linguistic database of cross-linguistic properties that can support theoretical research. Its basic setup allows working with linguists who are native speakers or signers as language experts providing the data. This provides researchers with the opportunity to use the tools of theoretical linguistics to access the implicit knowledge of native speakers/signers to probe the cross-linguistic situation. The basic database schema is flexible, which means it can be adapted to the research needs of individual researchers. Because the database codes observable fine-grained variation, the database can in fact support a broad community of scientists. The long-term goal is to turn TerraLing into a ready-made community tool that linguistic projects can use to gather and store their data for comparative research purposes.

Notes

1. NSF SGER: Prototype and Specifications for a Web-based Database of the Syntactic Structures of the World's Languages (SSWL). BCS 0817202, $68,133 with supplement, Chris Collins, PI.

2. With "Semantic" added to the original name.

3. With the help of many programmers over the years as listed on the website.

4. With some financial support of various UCLA Faculty Research Grants and a grant of the Truus and Gerrit van Riemsdijk Foundation, hereby gratefully acknowledged.

5. SSWL (https://www.terraling.com/groups/7) is managed by Hilda Koopman, UCLA, Linguistics; Conjunction and Disjunction (https://www.terraling.com/groups/8) is a semantic typology database, led by Viola Schmitt and her project members, University of Vienna, Linguistics; Anaphora (https://www.terraling.com/groups/9) is led by Dominique Sportiche, UCLA, Linguistics; Cinque's Universal 20 database (https://www.terraling.com/groups/15) is managed by Guglielmo Cinque (University Ca' Foscari, Linguistics) and Hilda Koopman, UCLA, Linguistics.

6. See Gawne and Styles, chapter 2, this volume.

7. See for example Kayne (2013) and Cinque (2005) and references cited there.

8. See for example Davis, Gillon, and Matthewson (2014).

9. http://www.dialectsyntax.org/wiki/Projects_on_dialect_syntax.

10. Acceptability judgments in fact do require detailed contextual information (cf. Good, chapter 3, this volume): examples should always be considered in context (see the Coordination and Disjunction Database for detailed examples: https://www.terraling.com/groups/8).

11. See in particular Sportiche, Koopman, and Stabler (2013: chapters 3, 6, 7, 11, 12).

12. See Kung, chapter 8, this volume.

13. See Han, chapter 6, this volume.

14. TerraLing is built on Ruby on Rails, one of several web development frameworks that support database-backed cross-browser web applications and enjoy strong open-source community support. Because Ruby on Rails embodies a model-view-controller paradigm, changes can be quickly deployed on a browser, first on the programmer's laptop and then on the web using Capistrano. The model-view-controller design pattern allows different sites to share the same data model (same database schema) but different user-visible names (different views). Ruby on Rails and the backend database we have chosen MySQL are open source and free, thus lowering the barriers to entry. The search interface is implemented with a JavaScript API that queries the existing rails service. The database software is freely available on GitHub.

15. In our system, all properties can be reduced to binary values. This will be shown in more detail in section 3, where we also illustrate the effects of this choice in terms of accuracy of the typological variation that underlies any analysis.

16. https://www.terraling.com/groups/7/properties/407.

17. NA means that the language provides no insight into a phenomenon because it lacks a certain property (i.e., if a language has no subject-verb agreement, any property that follows up on subject-verb agreement is irrelevant). The system also contains blanks, namely no answer is given to a certain property: this usually happens when a contributor has not yet answered a property or, in the case of ancient languages, when the corpus used does not contain the relevant data.

18. Basaá is spoken in Cameroon. SSWL registers the ISO or Glottolog code for each language, as well as geo-coordinates for mapping purposes. SSWL does not record genetic affiliations (Bantu, A40), which are based primarily on lexical relatedness, while Cinque's Universal 20 database does.

19. The interested reader can find further information on how to navigate TerraLing here: https://linguistics.ucla.edu/wp-content/uploads/2017/04/Navigating-Terraling-1.pdf.

20. As we link languages to individual speakers/signers (and to locations, via geo-coordinates), we expect that data provided by a contributor might not correspond exactly to those provided by a different contributor (of the "same" language). If two contributors disagree in assigning property values (and there is no misunderstanding in assigning values), two variants of the language, representing the two contributors' judgments, can be added, in consultation with the administrators. If disagreement only concerns one or few properties, then a comment is sufficient to describe variation.

21. A language or dialect in SSWL can therefore be defined as the set of forms and property values that characterize the grammar of a specific individual: the contributor. This notion

is similar to but more restricted that the notion of doculect (see Gast and Jędrzejowski, chapter 53, this volume). *Doculect* can be used to refer to a specific set of corpora, for example, or an analysis "this language/dialect is classified as VSO by linguist1, but as VOS by linguist2."

22. See https://www.univie.ac.at/konjunktion/texts.html for results and further information.

23. See the twenty-two *Property Descriptions* starting from Q01_Initial polar Q-marker (https://www.terraling.com/groups/7/properties/445) and Holmberg (2015), which explores the results.

24. At the time of writing, there are seventy properties, starting (for object properties) with O 01_Indef Mass_1_Can be bare (https://www.terraling.com/groups/7/properties/467).

25. https://www.terraling.com/groups/15.

26. We welcome researchers who would like to get involved in helping to push the many projects in advanced stages of development to the collection stage and become one of the *Property Authors*. Interested readers are encouraged to get in touch with the TerraLing board (Hilda Koopman, Cristina Guardiano, Nina Haslinger, Ethan Poole, and Viola Schmitt) at linguistic-explorer@gmail.com.

27. https://linguistics.ucla.edu/wp-content/uploads/2017/04/Adjectival-Questionnaire.pdf.

28. In this section, we leave NA out of consideration.

29. Count in the SSWL table refers to the number of languages with these values setting at the time of writing.

30. In Matthew Dryers's online supplement on WALS (Dryer 2013a) a number of statements are given as to how dominant order is determined for the word order properties and why it is adopted. It should be clear from these statements that these are not scientific criteria, nor were they meant to be. The goal is clear: to find some measure (however crude it may be) that allows comparing languages, regardless of the extent or quality of their documentation. Notice that this type of ambiguities/inaccuracies in coding the data might produce unforeseen consequences when data are used for broader purposes, for instance, to infer phylogenetic hypotheses about language evolution that are immediately and widely discussed in the general press.

31. Finer distinctions among *petit*, *grand*, and *gigantesque* ('gigantic') can be built in by further refining the properties.

32. https://www.eva.mpg.de/lingua/resources/glossing-rules.

33. See Conzett and De Smedt, chapter 11, this volume.

34. We leave it open to the managers of each database whether this is the name of the project leader/editor, the names of the team, or community, or "et al."

35. See Champieux and Coates, chapter 12, this volume and Alperin et al., chapter 13, this volume.

References

Bosque, Ignacio, and Violeta Demonte. 1999. *Gramática descriptiva de la lengua española*. Madrid: Colección Nebrija y Bello, Espasa.

Broekhuis, Hans. 2013. *Syntax of Dutch: Adjectives and Adjective Phrases*, vol. 2. Amsterdam: Amsterdam University Press. doi:10.26530/OAPEN_431435.

Broekhuis, Hans, and Norbert Corver. 2016. *Syntax of Dutch: Verbs and Verb Phrases—Volume 3*. Amsterdam: Amsterdam University Press.

Broekhuis, Hans, and Marcel den Dikken. 2012. *Syntax of Dutch: Nouns and Noun Phrases—Volume 2*. Amsterdam: Amsterdam University Press. doi:10.26530/OAPEN_431435.

Cinque, Guglielmo. 1994. On the evidence for partial N-movement in the romance DP. In *Paths towards Universal Grammar*, ed. Luigi Rizzi, Raffaella Zanuttini, Jan Koster, and Jean-Yves Pollock, 85–110. Washington, DC: Georgetown University Press.

Cinque, Guglielmo. 2005. Deriving Greenberg's Universal 20 and its exceptions. *Linguistic Inquiry* 36 (3): 315–332.

Cinque, Guglielmo. 2010. *The Syntax of Adjectives: A Comparative Study*. Cambridge, MA: MIT Press. https://doi.org/10.7551/mitpress/9780262014168.001.0001.

Collins, Chris, and Richard Kayne. 2007. A proposal for a database of the syntactic structures of the world's languages. http://ling.auf.net/lingbuzz/003404.

Davis, Henry, Carrie Gillon, and Lisa Matthewson. 2014. How to investigate linguistic diversity: Lessons from the Pacific Northwest. *Language* 90 (4): e180–e226.

Dixon, Robert M. W. 1982. *Where Have All the Adjectives Gone?* Berlin: Walter de Gruyter.

Dixon, Robert M. W., and Alexandra Y. Aikhenvald, eds. 2004. *Adjective Classes: A Cross-linguistic Typology*. Vol. 1. Oxford: Oxford University Press.

Dryer, Matthew S. 2013a. Determining dominant word order. In *The World Atlas of Language Structures Online*, ed. Matthew S. Dryer and Martin Haspelmath. Leipzig, Germany: Max Planck Institute for Evolutionary Anthropology. https://wals.info/chapter/s6. Accessed May 19, 2019.

Dryer, Matthew S. 2013b. Order of adjective and noun. In *The World Atlas of Language Structures Online*, ed. Matthew S. Dryer and Martin Haspelmath. Leipzig, Germany: Max Planck Institute for Evolutionary Anthropology. https://wals.info/chapter/87. Accessed May 1, 2019.

Dryer, Matthew S., and Martin Haspelmath, eds. 2013. *The World Atlas of Language Structures Online*. Leipzig, Germany: Max Planck Institute for Evolutionary Anthropology. http://wals.info/. Accessed September 28, 2015.

Greenberg, Joseph H. 1963. Some universals of grammar with particular reference to the order of meaningful element. In *Universals of Language*, ed. Joseph Greenberg, 73–113. Cambridge, MA: MIT Press.

Holmberg, Anders. 2015. *The Syntax of Yes and No*. Oxford: Oxford University Press. doi:10.1093/acprof:oso/9780198701859 .001.0001.

Huddleston, Rodney, and Geoffrey Pullum. 2005. *The Cambridge Grammar of the English Language*. Cambridge: Cambridge University Press.

Kayne, Richard S. 2013. Comparative syntax. *Lingua* 130:132–151. https://doi.org/10.1016/j.lingua.2012.10.008.

Schachter, Paul, and Fe T. Otanes. 1983. *Tagalog Reference Grammar*. Berkeley: University of California Press.

Schütze, Carson T., and Jon Sprouse. 2014. Judgment data. In *Research Methods in Linguistics*, ed. Robert J. Podesva and Devyani Sharma, 27–50. Cambridge: Cambridge University Press. https://doi.org/10.1017/CBO9781139013734.004.

Sportiche, Dominique, Hilda Koopman, and Edward Stabler. 2013. *An Introduction to Syntactic Analysis and Theory*. Hoboken, NJ: John Wiley & Sons.

Sproat, Richard, and Chilin Shih. 1991. The cross-linguistic distribution of adjectival ordering restrictions. In *Interdisciplinary Approaches to Language: Essays in Honor of S.-Y. Kuroda*, ed. C. Georgopoulos and R. Ishihara, 565–593. Dordrecht, the Netherlands: Kluwer. doi:10.1007/978-94-011-3818-5_30.

Sprouse, Jon, and Diogo Almeida. 2012. Assessing the reliability of textbook data in syntax: Adger's Core Syntax. *Journal of Linguistics* 48 (3): 609–652. https://doi.org/10.1017 /S0022226712000011.

Sprouse, Jon, Carson T. Schütze, and Diogo Almeida. 2013. A comparison of informal and formal acceptability judgments using a random sample from linguistic inquiry 2001–2010. *Lingua* 134:219–248. https://doi.org/10.1016/j.lingua.2013.07.002.

Alena Witzlack-Makarevich, Johanna Nichols, Kristine A. Hildebrandt, Taras Zakharko, and Balthasar Bickel

1 Introduction

This data management use case describes AUTOTYP, a large-scale research program with goals in both quantitative and qualitative typology.[1] It was launched in 1996 by Balthasar Bickel and Johanna Nichols; however, individual data collection began much earlier. The theoretical framework was adopted in early 2001 and has been refined and elaborated on since then. The technological framework was adopted in 2001 as well and has experienced multiple updates since.

AUTOTYP is one of the oldest typological databases still in use and continuously developed for almost twenty-five years. Although the growth of the database proceeded uninterruptedly, several bursts of intensive data collection are associated with a number of research projects (see section 4).

The goals and principles of AUTOTYP follow from our understanding of the goals of linguistic typology more generally. They were originally formulated by Johanna Nichols in *Linguistic Diversity in Space and Time* (Nichols 1992). As such, we aim at identifying patterns in structural features among the world's languages—whether they are universal preferences or patterns with skewed distribution due to geographical or genealogical factors—and discovering principles governing their distribution. These goals are often phrased as searching for answers to the questions of "what's where why?" (Bickel 2007).

AUTOTYP is a typological database; that is, the kind of data it contains are generalizations about phonological and morphosyntactic structure of languages. The primary source of these generalizations is our interpretation of the analysis of annotated or structured forms of data collected from language use found in reference grammars or field-work (cf. Good's [chapter 3, this volume] discussion of the kinds of data used in the study of language in general, as well as more specifically in areal-typological studies).

The aim of this chapter is twofold. First, in section 2 we outline some fundamental design principles of AUTOTYP. Section 3 illustrates the implementation of these principles with one module of the AUTOTYP database, namely the grammatical relations module. This section will be of use to readers who plan to start their own typological database or who are already working on one. Section 4 is aimed at users and data consumers. It describes how to access the data and provides a brief overview of several use cases and research questions that have been asked with AUTOTYP.

2 The principles of AUTOTYP

Several other typological databases are comparable to AUTOTYP due to the nature of their goals and the type of data collected. However, from its first days, AUTOTYP followed a radically different design philosophy than the one adopted by many traditional typological databases, such as WALS (Dryer & Haspelmath 2013) or more recently Grambank (Grambank Consortium 2019). Whereas some of these principles are occasionally used by other databases, others remain truly unique to AUTOTYP. In what follows, we will first outline the five major principles of AUTOTYP: namely, modularity and connectivity (section 2.1), Autotypology (section 2.2), the division of labor between definition files and data files (section 2.3), the principle of late aggregation (section 2.4), and the exemplar-based method (section 2.5). Section 3 illustrates how these principles are implemented in practice using the example of the AUTOTYP module on grammatical relations.

2.1 Modularity and connectivity
AUTOTYP is not a single database but rather a network of thematically defined databases or modules on a wide variety of topics that all share the same infrastructure

and design principles. Each module can function as a stand-alone database, and it can easily be linked to other, already existing or future databases. This gives AUTOTYP databases the potential to grow in any possible direction without necessitating revisions of their basic design structures.

Most modules were developed by one or two researchers, often within the framework of a specific research grant. A data module typically covers a clearly defined typological domain with varying internal complexity ranging from relatively narrow ones with just a few variables in one or two tables (e.g., clusivity[2] or inflectional synthesis of the verb[3]) to broader and more complex ones with several dozen variables (e.g., noun phrase structure, clause linkage, word domains, grammatical markers). Structurally and conceptually, the most complex module is dedicated to grammatical relations: it encompasses several tables and over a hundred variables (see section 3).

We furthermore distinguish between service modules and data modules. The primary service module `Register`[4] contains an inventory of languages and their genealogical classifications and locations, as well as tables with linguistic areas, subsistence types, and sampling options. Initially, it also contained a bibliography module; however, now we keep track of our references using a BibTeX file.

All AUTOTYP modules (and the bibliography file) are linked together in a relational network via numerical language IDs, which are also mapped to other common language name IDs, such as Glottocodes from Glottolog (Hammarström, Forkel, & Haspelmath 2019), ISO 639-3 codes for the representation of names of languages, as well as WALS codes (Dryer & Haspelmath 2013). When developing a new module, we emphasize connectivity with existing modules and data reuse by different projects. The data module most other modules are connected to is the `Grammatical_markers` module. It contains information on over five thousand grammatical formatives (e.g., case and agreement markers, TAM affixes, and other grammatical markers) with details about their position, locus, degree of fusion, and exponence. Any other module—and these are the majority—that includes structures characterized by a specific grammatical formative is linked to this module.

2.2 Autotypology

Typological databases use categorical generalization as an abstraction tool. A closed, a priori determined list of possible values (i.e., an etic grid) is used to capture differing observations. Such lists can be motivated by tradition, for example, traditionally, case systems are classified as showing either accusative or ergative or neutral or tripartite or horizontal alignment (Comrie 1989:125–128). Idealized intuitions can also play a role; for example, a verb agreement system is classified as representing one of the five common alignment types or it is classified as a hierarchical agreement system, which is often represented as any system of agreement where a person hierarchy matters (e.g., Mallinson & Blake 1981). Theoretical considerations might as well be responsible. For instance, prior to the 1980s, in descriptive and theoretical accounts, clause linkage was believed to be either coordination or subordination. Later, another type—cosubordination—was added to this typology and became an integral part of some theoretical frameworks (Olson 1981; Foley & Van Valin 1984). Consequently, these three discrete categories show up in some typological surveys (e.g., Schmidtke-Bode 2009:150). However, as Bickel (2010) demonstrates, cross-linguistic variation in clause linkage is higher than what is allowed by these three categories, which entail sets of strictly correlated properties. Finally, in many cases, plain convenience is a crucial factor in categorical generalization. For instance, typologists who classify whole languages as belonging to one of the five morphological alignment types mentioned above are well aware of different types of splits and differential marking patterns (see, e.g., Comrie 2013a, 2013b on case alignment). However, it is simply easier to both code and process one-type-per-language data sets that do not require any further aggregations, as well as to do statistical analysis on one data point per language.

From its beginning, AUTOTYP chose a different approach, which we call the *autotypologizing method* in Bickel and Nichols (2002) or just *autotypology*. The idea is to prioritize coding adequacy and compatibility of the data with a wide range of theoretical frameworks over easy encoding with a list of predefined values. What does this shift in priorities mean in practice? Instead of sticking to an a priori defined etic grid, developers of AUTOTYP modules dynamically expand lists of possible values during data input (this characteristic is discussed in more detail in Bickel & Nichols 2002). In practice, it looks as follows: Many modules indeed start with lists of possible values motivated by theoretical research and typological studies. However, we do not stop here: when coding a new language, we first check whether the previously established notions are sufficient for this language. If not, we postulate new possible values and carefully define them in a definition file (see section 2.3). This often means that, particularly at the beginning of a project, database entries are constantly revised, and the initial coding is replaced by more fine-grained values or even several variables, thus constantly reflecting the emerging typology of the phenomenon of interest (see section 3). This procedure is time-consuming in the beginning because the introduction of most new types requires a review and often a revision of all previous entries, but after about forty to fifty entries, new types become less likely to emerge and the typology stabilizes. The advantage of this procedure is data accuracy on a level that is impossible in databases with predefined typologies.

Occasionally, descriptive needs go beyond the mere revision of definition files. In this case, entire new variables (fields) or even tables are added to the respective module and all the data points entered to that point are reviewed and revised. As a general design principle, AUTOTYP favors the increase in the size and complexity of the database rather than in the complexity of coding decisions. For example, a database on clause linkage mentioned earlier does not adhere to the traditional distinction between coordination and (co)subordination and does not force each phenomenon in each coded language into one of these types; instead, it has gradually evolved into a set of specific variables that capture the full diversity of the phenomenon at hand.

2.3 Definition files versus data files

The Autotypology principles outlined in section 2.2 require differentiation between *data files* and *definition files*. Data files contain actual data on individual languages or constructions in individual languages. Definition files are essentially lists of possible values for each variable coded. In addition to category labels, they contain detailed linguistic definitions of each possible value, as well as a description of the coding procedure. As definition files are created dynamically and are updated throughout the whole process of data collection (see section 2.2), they thus reflect an empirically well-supported

and detailed typology of the phenomenon at hand at any time. The two file types allow for dual use of the database in research: the data files allow quantitative typological inquiry into statistical correlations between structural, genealogical, or geographical features, while the definition files produce contributions to qualitative typology because they contain all and only notions that are cross-linguistically relevant and viable.

The binary distinction between data and definition files does not always work in practice. Some files have a dual status. For instance, the `Predicate_class_def` file serves as a definition file for the purposes of defining grammatical relations: it codes language-specific minor verb classes that have deviating coding patterns (see section 3). However, due to its language-specific character and the type of information coded (lists of predicates, type and token frequency of predicate classes, semantic domains, and so on) it can also be regarded as a data file and indeed it was used in Bickel et al. (2014) to answer the question whether there is cross-linguistic evidence for postulating clusters of predicate-specific semantic roles, such as experiencer, cognizer, or possessor.

2.4 Late aggregation

As we outlined in section 2.2, during data encoding, we choose the lowest-level, most exhaustive model that is appropriate to the data domain and the purpose of data collection. However, to answer specific research questions, the available data are typically filtered and aggregated. *Data aggregation* is any process in which information distributed over multiple values of a data set (or a subset of it) is grouped together and expressed in one single value, such as for purposes of statistical analysis. In linguistic typology, the most common variable for aggregation is probably aggregation by language. Data aggregation can apply simple mathematical functions. For instance, to calculate the degree of inflectional synthesis per language, every entry coding an inflectional category (e.g., polarity, evidentiality, argument role) that can be expressed in a synthetic word is counted as one and then all entries are added up. This yields one number per language that represents its degree of inflectional synthesis (see Bickel & Nichols 2013c for further details on this aggregation procedure). Other research questions require more elaborate aggregations and grouping by multiple variables.

In AUTOTYP, we systematically and explicitly adopt the principle of *late aggregation*. Late aggregation means that no aggregation takes place at the stage of data collection. All aggregations are defined by algorithms applied to the data as collected and stored, outside the database. That is, the categories used during coding are not necessarily identical to the aggregated categories used in analyses. For instance, in the inflectional synthesis example we coded detailed information about every individual inflectional category. However, we did not code the degree of synthesis per se. This number was calculated outside the database.

One advantage of the late aggregation approach is sustainability: the same data can be reused to answer different research questions or to comply with different theoretical frameworks (see Buszard-Welcher, chapter 10, this volume). It also allows one to evaluate different but related generalizations simultaneously without the necessity for additional dedicated coding. Thus, a wide range of different and competing aggregations can be supported by the same data. The researcher—and not the data—controls the depth and the scope of aggregation. Furthermore, the late aggregation approach also provides for empirical responsibility: as the data encoding model is exhaustive (that is, no special cases or exceptions are left behind), it reduces chances of opaque mapping of language facts to possible values of a variable and the algorithmic form of aggregations allows tracing aggregated data points back to their original empirical basis. Finally, this design principle is durable: it ages well because the fine-grained underlying coding is typically less susceptible to shifts in theory and research questions than aggregated data points are.

2.5 Exemplar-based method

As we outline in section 2.2, during data encoding, we choose the lowest-level, most exhaustive model that is appropriate to the domain in question. While AUTOTYP allows one to record all this variation, for many typological surveys it is still desirable and more efficient to have one data point per language only. This can be achieved without early aggregation and without predefined lists of gross language types by following what we call the *exemplar-based method*: we select one particular exemplar of paradigms or structural domains as representative for the whole range of possible values or variables a language has to offer.

This exemplar is identified following a standard algorithmic definition. To answer many research questions,

we aim at selecting a high-frequency or well-understood exemplar: for example, as exemplars for tense (in `Inflectional_synthesis`), we use tense morphology in general if all tense categories and markers have the same position and other properties; otherwise, we pick a synthetic basic present and non-imperfective past. As the exemplar for case marking alignment, we choose arguments of frequent verbs and independent clauses. Importantly, the choice of the exemplar is made not during the phase of data encoding but first at the stage of data aggregation. If desired, any other algorithmic definition for the identification of the exemplar can be adopted without having to recode the data. Also the exemplar-based method allows free addition of further data points when the need arises (or resources become available): one can simply add information of non-exemplar variants in each language, without any redesign of the database and its coding principles.

3 For developers: AUTOTYP principles at work

One of the most recent and most elaborate AUTOTYP modules is `Grammatical_relations`. In this section—primarily meant for developers of typological databases—we provide an overview of this module and highlight how the design principles outlined in section 2 were implemented in it.

The term *grammatical relations* (GRs) traditionally denotes the relations between a clause or a predicate and its arguments. The two traditional major types of GRs are subject and direct object. These categories are among the most basic concepts of many models. However, in response to many challenges with the way traditional GRs were identified and characterized (for a recent overview, see Witzlack-Makarevich 2019), recent, typologically supported research on GRs takes a construction-specific and language-specific view of GRs. That is, instead of adopting universal atomic notions of subject and object, one considers all relevant language-specific morphosyntactic properties of arguments (i.e., all relevant constructions) without prioritizing among them and without cherry-picking the ones that support the linguist's intuition. The general principles of this approach, as well as major variables were first outlined in Bickel (2011). The manuscript of that paper served as the starting point for the development of the AUTOTYP module on grammatical relations in 2006.

GRs are defined as equivalence sets of arguments, treated the same way by some construction (or *argument selector*) in a language (Bickel 2011). Cross-linguistically common argument selectors are, for example, case marking, agreement on the verb, or passivization. Languages vary in terms of how many argument selectors they have (see, e.g., the collection of papers in Witzlack-Makarevich & Bickel 2019).

The data in the module on GRs are extracted from primary source documents (grammars and articles), and only occasionally are they obtained via personal communication from speakers and specialists. The extraction of the necessary data is first recorded in a language report: a text document that apart from the decision on the assignment of values and motivation behind it has multiple examples, paradigms, and citations from the primary sources. The language reports are particularly useful at the initial stages of module development when new values are identified and added to the value lists and coding decisions need to be revised (see section 2.2). They also prove to be useful when further variables are added. For instance, the GRs report often contains full paradigms of verb agreement. Originally, we only coded for a high-level agreement variable (i.e., which argument the verb agrees with), at a later point we wanted to expand the data set with details about overt and zero agreement markers, as well as portmanteau markers. In this case, we relied on the paradigm in the language reports and only occasionally had to consult primary sources.

Being a relational database, the Grammatical_ relations module can be understood as a collection of relations, which are perceived by the user as related tables (for an introduction to relational databases, see, e.g., Harrington 2016 or Kroenke et al. 2019). Each table is a set of data elements (or values) in the form of rows and columns. Each row (or record) corresponds to some object (e.g., a selected argument, a grammatical relation, or a language). Each column (also called field or attribute) represents a property of this object. The linking between individual files is realized by means of a common field (an identifier). To relate any two files, they simply need to have such a common field.

In line with the definition given in the beginning of this section, the major entity of the Grammatical_relations module is a single GR coded in the Grammatical_relation table illustrated in table 56.1. Every record in the Grammatical_relation table contains information about the language in question (linked to the Language table of the Register module via a unique language identifier [LID]), the argument selector (e.g., a specific case) that forms the subset, and the selected arguments. Thus, each GR of a language as defined above forms one record in the database. For every language there are as many records as there are GRs established by various argument selectors. For instance, in the example from Hindi in table 56.1, there are separate entries for individual cases, as well as entries for agreement and syntactic constructions, such as raising to object. This aspect differentiates the module from those typological databases that have individual languages as central entities. As of February 2020, the module contains data on 4,400 argument selectors in 779 languages.

The data entry is done via various layouts in File-Maker Pro specifically developed for the purposes of data entry. One of the layouts is shown in figure 56.1. Many similar layouts for data entry are developed on the fly to make individual data entry tasks easier.

The field SourceID contains BibTeX keys that link this database to our bibliography database. We keep track of our references using BibTeX, a reference management software.

Table 56.1

An example of the Grammatical_relation table with a selection of entries for Hindi (LID 99)

GRID	LID	SelectorID	Traditional_term	Grammatical_markerID	Selected_itemID	SourceID
63	99	2	Genitive case	32	214, 215, 551, 552, . . .	Mohanan1994Argument
92	99	2	Ergative case	29	201, 202, 205, 209, . . .	Montaut2004Grammar
94	99	2	Nominative case	28	195, 196, 197, 198, . . .	Montaut2004Grammar
93	99	2	Dative case	30	126, 178, 312, 311, . . .	Montaut2004Grammar
2881	99	2	Locative case	33	21636, 21637	Montaut2004Grammar
97	99	3	Agreement (trigger potential)	31	125, 461, 462, 464, . . .	Montaut2004Grammar
56	99	7	Raising to object	NA	543, 544, 455, 546, . . .	Bickeletal2000Fresh

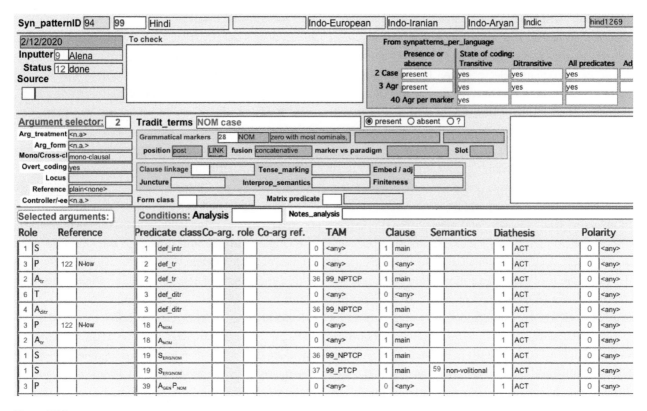

Figure 56.1

One of the FileMaker Pro interfaces of the AUTOTYP `Grammatical_relations` module.

BibTeX is stored in a plain text UTF-8 file. An example of the BibTeX entry for the first line in table 56.1 follows:

```
@book{Mohanan1994Argument,
    Address={Stanford, CA},
    Author={Mohanan, Tara},
    Publisher={Center for the Study of Language and
    Information},
    Title={Argument structure in Hindi},
    Year={1994}}
```

The `Grammatical_relation` table is linked to a number of tables, schematically represented in figure 56.2. First, it is linked to the `Language` table from the `Register` module via `LID`. This table provides the language name as used in AUTOTYP (e.g., Hindi) and alternative names, the genealogical affiliation, the area where the language is used, as well as language IDs from Glottolog (Hammarström, Forkel, & Haspelmath 2019, `ind1269` for Hindi) and ISO 639-3 (`hin`) for easy mapping to other databases.

The implementation of the AUTOTYP principle of modularity (section 2.1) can be illustrated with the modules `Grammatical_relations` and `Register`. The general information about individual languages (3,012 entries as

of February 2020) is stored in the `Language` table of the `Register` module. It contains the information on the genealogy (e.g., branch and stock names) and geographic distribution (e.g., areas and coordinates) of individual languages. The primary key is a numerical language ID (`LID`). `LID`s are used to link the general information about languages to files on various aspects of grammar, among them to the `Grammatical_relations` module. In turn, as we have mentioned, `LID`s are associated with other codes, for instance, Glottolog (Hammarström, Forkel, & Haspelmath 2019) and ISO 639-3. This allows for a straightforward compatibility of the AUTOTYP databases with other databases following one of these standards.

As figure 56.2 shows, the `Grammatical_relation` table is in a many-to-one relationship with the `Selector` table, which specifies the precise nature of the argument selector and contains such variables as whether the selector is a coding construction (e.g., agreement) or a behavior construction (e.g., control of reference), whether it is a mono-clausal or cross-clausal construction, whether it involves head or dependent marking, and so forth (see Witzlack-Makarevich 2011 for details on the typology of argument selectors).

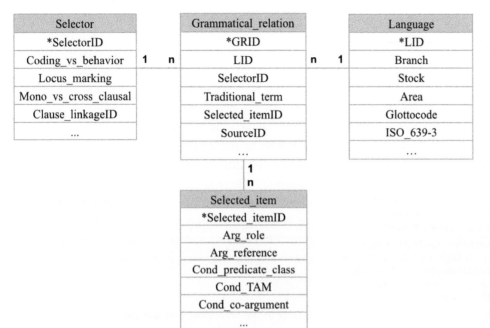

Figure 56.2
`Grammatical_relations`
module in AUTOTYP.

Table 56.2

An example of the `Selected_item` table in AUTOTYP listing a selection of entries for the nominative case in Hindi

Selected_itemID	Arg_roleID	Arg_referenceID	Cond_predicate_classID	Cond_TAMID	Cond_clauseID
195	1 (=S)	0 (=any)	1 (=default_mono)	0 (=any)	1 (=main)
196	2 (=A)	0 (=any)	2 (=default_bi)	36 (=99_NPTCP)	1 (=main)
198	3 (=P)	122 (=N-low)	2 (=default_bi)	0 (=any)	1 (=main)
197	4 (=A$_\text{ditr}$)	0 (=any)	3 (=default_tri)	36 (=99_NPTCP)	1 (=main)
203	6 (=T)	0 (=any)	3 (=default_tri)	0 (=any)	1 (=main)
237	2 (=A)	0 (=any)	18 (=A$_\text{NOM}$)	0 (=any)	1 (=main)
4172	3 (=P)	122 (=N-low)	18 (=A$_\text{NOM}$)	0 (=any)	1 (=main)
13804	3 (=P)	0 (=any)	39 (=A$_\text{GEN}$ P$_\text{NOM}$)	0 (=any)	1 (=main)

Following the principle of the differentiation between data files and definition files (see section 2.3), for each argument selector, `Selected_item` lists only the IDs for role and reference of selected arguments and all relevant conditions on argument selection (e.g., predicate class, TAM, type of clause). The exact specifications of the values behind these IDs are stored in the respective definition files. However, for friendliness to human readers, table 56.2 includes in parentheses the labels of the individual values from the respective definition files. (For our definition of the argument roles S, A, P, A$_\text{ditr}$, T, and G, see Bickel 2011 and Witzlack-Makarevich 2019; NPTCP stands for a non-participle verb form.)

A typical definition file is illustrated with a few entries in table 56.3. For instance, it spells out what is behind the `Arg_referenceID` 122 from table 56.2.

A less typical and more complex definition file is illustrated in table 56.4. This is the `Predicate_class` table, which captures predicate classes as condition on argument selection, in other words, the situation where a specific case marking or construction is available only to arguments of a specific group of predicates. For instance, the majority of Hindi A arguments vary between nominative and ergative case marking as conditioned by the morphological form of the predicate, such as whether it involve a participle or not—a situation often confused with TAM-based split in marking. However, a few Hindi predicates (`Predicate_classID` 18) do not participate in this alternation: their A argument is always in the nominative no matter what the shape of the predicate is. The definition files represent a taxonomy of encountered typological types and thus feed qualitative typology.

Table 56.3

An example of the Reference definition table in AUTOTYP

ReferenceID	Label	Description
0	Any	
5	Pro	Free pronouns that head NPs, not pronominal agreement markers
105	1sgPro	First-person singular pronoun
123	3duPro	Third-person dual pronoun
34	N-anim	Animate noun
121	N-high	Noun with a higher discourse rank than "N-low" (where rank is determined by discourse factors with language-specific weights)
122	N-low	Noun with a lower discourse rank than "N-high" (where rank is determined by discourse factors with language-specific weights)

Neither table 56.1 nor table 56.2 contains any explicit information on the alignment of the case marking (e.g., "S=A≠P" or "nominative-accusative alignment"); however, this is often the kind of information researchers are interested in when studying grammatical relations. AUTOTYP differs from traditional typological databases in that in most cases, data are entered in a fairly raw format, as in table 56.1. It is comparable to reference grammar descriptions that list how e.g. individual cases, such as the nominative case, are used, i.e. which argument roles they cover and under which conditions they occur. For most analytical purposes, these data will be filtered, aggregated, and reshaped.

Thus, we systematically follow the principle of late aggregation (see section 2.4) and avoid any data aggregation at the stage of data collection. All aggregations are defined algorithmically in R (or occasionally Python) scripts outside the database. For instance, for the analysis presented in Bickel, Witzlack-Makarevich, Choudhary, et al. (2015) we only needed the data on the degree of ergativity of case marking. For this purpose, we first filtered from the Grammatical_relation table (table 56.1) only the entries on case marking and ignored all other argument selectors. Then, only a subset of entries with the relevant selected_itemIDs was filtered from the Selected_item table (table 56.2). A range of further filtering conditions were imposed to select the desired exemplar (see section 2.5 on the exemplar-based method), for example, we were only interested in the case marking of the arguments of the default mono- and

bivalent predicate classes and only in active clauses. After the data were filtered properly, we proceeded with the aggregation and specifically considered whether the A argument is marked differently from the S argument (the case marking of the P argument was irrelevant for this research question). As some languages have split case marking, so that parts of the system align S and A and parts of the system do not, some languages have multiple entries. The aggregated results for Hindi are shown in table 56.5, and they can be further aggregated to one quantified alignment statement per language, for example, Hindi is to 25% ergative (S≠A). A range of other filter options and aggregations was performed on the same data (the relevant references can be found in section 4).

4   For users: Overview and use cases

There has been a broad range of published research based on the AUTOTYP data. A number of early data sets from AUTOTYP were integrated into WALS (Haspelmath et al. 2005) and are accessible via the WALS website (https://wals.info/; Dryer & Haspelmath 2013). These data sets are aggregations from the modules on the locus of marking (i.e., head vs. dependent marking, Nichols & Bickel 2013a, 2013b, 2013c), exponence and fusion of selected inflectional formatives from the module on grammatical markers (Bickel & Nichols 2013a, 2013b), and inflectional synthesis of the verb (Bickel & Nichols 2013c) from the module on verb synthesis. The noun phrase structure module provided the data for two further aggregated WALS chapters, Bickel and Nichols (2013d) on obligatory possessive inflection and Nichols and Bickel (2013d) on possessive classification, as well as for a PhD thesis by Rießler (2011). Another early data set comprises data on clusivity and is analyzed in Bickel and Nichols (2005). Data sets from the module on word domains served as the empirical base for aggregations in Bickel, Hildebrandt, and Schiering (2009) and Schiering, Bickel, and Hildebrandt (2010, 2012). The data set used to develop the module on clause linkage is aggregated and analyzed in Bickel (2010).

In recent years our own research has produced a number of publications based on various subsets of the data from the module on grammatical relations. The theoretical foundation behind this module was outlined in Bickel (2011). Its structure is described in detail

Table 56.4

An example of the `Predicate_class` definition table in AUTOTYP with some default and Hindi predicate classes

Predicate_classID	Label	Description	Translation_equivalent	Class_size	LID
1	Default monovalent	Monovalent predicate class with the default (or canonical) marking pattern of behavior	(Open class)	Large	0 (=any)
2	Default bivalent	Bivalent predicate class with the default (or canonical) marking pattern of behavior	(Open class)	Large	0 (=any)
3	Default trivalent	Trivalent predicate class with the default (or canonical) marking pattern of behavior	(Open class)	Large	0 (=any)
18	A_{NOM}	Bivalent Hindi-specific predicate class whose A argument is always in the nominative case and never in the ergative case	116 (=bring), 117 (=forget)	Very small (<5)	99 (=Hindi)
39	$A_{GEN} P_{NOM}$	Bivalent Hindi-specific predicate class whose A argument is in the genitive case and P argument in the nominative case	136 (=have)	Very small (<5)	99 (=Hindi)

Table 56.5

An example of data aggregation on the basis of the data in the `Grammatical_relations` module of AUTOTYP

LID	S_A_alignment	Clause_type	Structural_condition
99 (=Hindi)	S = A	Dependent	99_NPTCP
99 (=Hindi)	S = A	Main	99_NPTCP
99 (=Hindi)	S = A	Dependent	99_PTCP
99 (=Hindi)	S ≠ A	Main	99_PTCP

in Witzlack-Makarevich (2011). A subset of the database capturing the proportion of ergative alignment of case marking in some six hundred languages was used as the basis for our claim that languages tend to avoid ergatives when they evolve over time (Bickel, Witzlack-Makarevich, Choudhary, et al. 2015). A different subset of the data on case marking was used to test the hypothesis that if a language has differential subject or differential object marking the distribution of cases results from a universal effect of referential scales (first tested in Bickel & Witzlack-Makarevich 2008 and then on a larger data set in Bickel, Witzlack-Makarevich, & Zakharko 2015). Various hypotheses related to the principles underlying the subject and object agreement systems on the verb were tested using the agreement subset of the data in Bickel et al. (2013), Bickel, Witzlack-Makarevich, Zakharko, and Iemmolo (2015), and Witzlack-Makarevich et al. (2016). In each case a slightly different aggregation of the data was performed. In contrast to other publications based on the subset of case and agreement marking with major verb classes, Bickel et al. (2014) considers the subset of the data dedicated to case marking in minor verb classes in over 140 languages.

Starting with the very first AUTOTYP publications we prioritized openness, both in terms of transparency of methodology, as well as in terms of data accessibility (see Gawne & Styles, chapter 2, this volume, on open research in the social sciences). For many of the papers listed herein, the aggregation scripts, aggregated data, as well as scripts used to perform the statistical analysis are available via the publishers' websites, whenever the publishers provided this option. For instance, the data used in Bickel et al. (2014) are available as an online appendix at https://doi.org/10.1075/sl.38.3.03bic.additional. The data used in Bickel, Witzlack-Makarevich, Choudhary, et al. (2015) include the database of case-marking patterns (a `.csv` file, https://doi.org/10.1371/journal.pone.0132819.s001), bibliographical references of the sources

used (a BibTeX file, https://doi.org/10.1371/journal.pone
.0132819.s002), as well as an R script with step-by-step
results of the language evolution analysis (https://doi.org
/10.1371/journal.pone.0132819.s003). Small data sets
were occasionally added directly as tables in an appendix,
as in Bickel (2010) or Schiering, Bickel, and Hildebrandt
(2012). The data sets mentioned above as well as other
data sets have been made available via AUTOTYP website
at https://github.com/autotyp/autotyp-data.

In addition to the many data sets made available
on various platforms over the course of the last twenty
years, Bickel et al. (2017) is the first major release of over
thirty AUTOTYP data sets (in over fifty tables) accompanied by metadata files. This release includes over
one thousand variables with a total of about 4.5 million typological data points. We use `.csv` format for the
data, `.yaml` format for metadata, and `.bib` format for
bibliographical references. In addition, the geographical
data is available in `.kml` format (see Mattern [chapter
5, this volume] on sustainable data formats and Han
[chapter 6, this volume] on data formats and conversion). Finally, we also provide the entire data set as a
list in R's `.rds` format. We have archived this release
on Zenodo (see Andreassen [chapter 7, this volume] for
a discussion of issues of data archiving). Zenodo provides a new digital object identifier (DOI) for each new
release along with a bibliographic citation that users
can use when citing a particular release of the data in
their research papers.

In general, AUTOTYP data sets have rarely been
used by researchers who were not part of the project.
We believe that the major hurdle is that typologists
still almost universally operate under the premise that
whole languages are the proper level on which to code
data. In our experience, the importance of this premise declines to the extent that researchers learn how to
write algorithms for data aggregation. The current move
toward training linguists in methods of modern data
science, including basic scripting techniques and statistics, makes us confident that future generations will
overcome the traditional hurdle of adopting AUTOTYP
principles and using AUTOTYP data. An example of this
is the recent use of AUTOTYP data by Schmidtke-Bode
and Levshina (2018), who challenge the results of Bickel,
Witzlack-Makarevich, and Zakharko (2015) by performing alternative statistical analyses.

Notes

1. We are grateful to Andrea L. Berez-Kroeker, Steven Moran,
and an anonymous reviewer for quick and helpful comments
on an earlier version of this chapter.

2. The data set is available as part of Bickel et al. (2017) under
https://github.com/autotyp/autotyp-data/blob/master/data
/Clusivity.csv.

3. The data set is available as part of Bickel et al. (2017) under
https://github.com/autotyp/autotyp-data/blob/master/data
/Synthesis.csv.

4. We use the monospaced font to refer to AUTOTYP's modules, tables, or fields, as well as to file extensions. Starting from
Bickel et al. (2017), we consistently use upper camel case for
variable names. We capitalize the first letter and use underscore
in table and module names. For data entry, we used FileMaker
Pro—a cross-platform relational database application from
Claris International, a subsidiary of Apple Inc. It integrates
a database engine with a graphical user interface (GUI). File-
Maker Pro databases, which correspond to our modules, have
the extension `.fmp12`. Individual tables correspond to files in
these databases and as such are not individual files, for this
reason no extension is given when we refer to them in the rest
of the chapter. They can be exported in various formats (e.g.,
`.csv` or `.tab`), as discussed in section 4.

References

Bickel, Balthasar. 2007. Typology in the 21st century: Major
current developments. *Linguistic Typology* 11 (1): 239–251.

Bickel, Balthasar. 2010. Capturing particulars and universals in
clause linkage: A multivariate analysis. In *Clause-Hierarchy and
Clause-Linking: The Syntax and Pragmatics Interface*, ed. Isabelle
Bril, 51–102. Amsterdam: John Benjamins.

Bickel, Balthasar. 2011. Grammatical relations typology. In *The
Oxford Handbook of Language Typology*, ed. Jae Jung Song, 399–
444. Oxford: Oxford University Press.

Bickel, Balthasar, Kristine A. Hildebrandt, and René Schiering. 2009. The distribution of phonological word domains:
A probabilistic typology. In *Phonological Domains: Universals
and Deviations*, ed. Janet Grijzenhout and Kabak Barış, 47–75.
Berlin: Mouton de Gruyter.

Bickel, Balthasar, Giorgio Iemmolo, Taras Zakharko, and Alena
Witzlack-Makarevich. 2013. Patterns of alignment in verb
agreement. In *Languages across Boundaries: Studies in the Memory
of Anna Siewierska*, ed. Dik Bakker and Martin Haspelmath, 15–36.
Berlin: Mouton de Gruyter. https://doi.org/10.1515/978311033
1127.15.

Bickel, Balthasar, and Johanna Nichols. 2002. Autotypologizing databases and their use in fieldwork. In *Proceedings of the*

International LREC Workshop on Resources and Tools in Field Linguistics, Las Palmas, 26–27 May 2002, ed. Austin, Peter, Helen Dry, and Peter Witternburg. Nijmegen: ISLE and DOBES.

Bickel, Balthasar, and Johanna Nichols. 2005. Inclusive-exclusive as person vs. number categories worldwide. In *Clusivity: Typology and Case Studies of the Inclusive–Exclusive Distinction*, ed. Elena Filimonova, 49–72. Amsterdam: John Benjamins.

Bickel, Balthasar, and Johanna Nichols. 2013a. Exponence of selected inflectional formatives. In *The World Atlas of Language Structures Online*, ed. Matthew S. Dryer and Martin Haspelmath. Leipzig: Max Planck Institute for Evolutionary Anthropology. http://wals.info/chapter/21.

Bickel, Balthasar, and Johanna Nichols. 2013b. Fusion of selected inflectional formatives. In *The World Atlas of Language Structures Online*, ed. Matthew S. Dryer and Martin Haspelmath. Leipzig: Max Planck Institute for Evolutionary Anthropology. http://wals.info/chapter/20.

Bickel, Balthasar, and Johanna Nichols. 2013c. Inflectional synthesis of the verb. In *The World Atlas of Language Structures Online*, ed. Matthew S. Dryer and Martin Haspelmath. Leipzig: Max Planck Institute for Evolutionary Anthropology. http://wals.info/chapter/22.

Bickel, Balthasar, and Johanna Nichols. 2013d. Obligatory possessive inflection. In *The World Atlas of Language Structures Online*, ed. Matthew S. Dryer and Martin Haspelmath. Leipzig: Max Planck Institute for Evolutionary Anthropology. http://wals.info/chapter/58.

Bickel, Balthasar, Johanna Nichols, Taras Zakharko, Alena Witzlack-Makarevich, Kristine Hildebrandt, Michael Rießler, Lennart Bierkandt, Fernando Zúñiga, and John B. Lowe. 2017. *The AUTOTYP Typological Databases*. Version 0.1.0 https://github.com/autotyp/autotyp-data/tree/0.1.0. http://doi.org/10.5281/zenodo.3667562.

Bickel, Balthasar, and Alena Witzlack-Makarevich. 2008. Referential scales and case alignment: Reviewing the typological evidence. In *Scales*, ed. Andrej Malchukov and Marc Richards (=Band 86 der Linguistischen ArbeitsBerichte). Leipzig: Institut für Linguistik.

Bickel, Balthasar, Alena Witzlack-Makarevich, Kamal K. Choudhary, Matthias Schlesewsky, and Ina Bornkessel-Schlesewsky. 2015. The neurophysiology of language processing shapes the evolution of grammar: Evidence from case marking. *PLOS ONE* 10 (8): e0132819. doi:10.1371/journal.pone.0132819.

Bickel, Balthasar, Alena Witzlack-Makarevich, and Taras Zakharko. 2015. Typological evidence against universal effects of referential scales on case alignment. In *Scales: A Cross-Disciplinary Perspective on Referential Hierarchies*, ed. Ina Bornkessel-Schlesewsky, Andrej Malchukov, and Marc Richards, 7–44. Berlin: De Gruyter Mouton.

Bickel, Balthasar, Alena Witzlack-Makarevich, Taras Zakharko, and Giorgio Iemmolo. 2015. Exploring diachronic universals of agreement: Alignment patterns and zero marking across person categories. In *Agreement from a Diachronic Perspective*, ed. Jürg Fleischer, Elisabeth Rieken, and Paul Widmer, 29–52. Berlin: De Gruyter Mouton.

Bickel, Balthasar, Taras Zakharko, Lennart Bierkandt, and Alena Witzlack-Makarevich. 2014. Semantic role clustering: An empirical assessment of semantic role types. *Studies in Language* 38 (3): 485–511.

Comrie, Bernard. 1989. *Language Universals and Linguistic Typology: Syntax and Morphology*. 2nd ed. Chicago: University of Chicago Press.

Comrie, Bernard. 2013a. Alignment of case marking of full noun phrases. In *The World Atlas of Language Structures Online*, ed. Matthew S. Dryer and Martin Haspelmath. Leipzig: Max Planck Institute for Evolutionary Anthropology. http://wals.info/chapter/98.

Comrie, Bernard. 2013b. Alignment of case marking of pronouns. In *The World Atlas of Language Structures Online*, ed. Matthew S. Dryer and Martin Haspelmath. Leipzig: Max Planck Institute for Evolutionary Anthropology. http://wals.info/chapter/99.

Dryer, Matthew S., and Martin Haspelmath, eds. 2013. *The World Atlas of Language Structures Online*. Leipzig: Max Planck Institute for Evolutionary Anthropology. https://wals.info/.

Foley, William A., and Robert D. Van Valin Jr. 1984. *Functional Syntax and Universal Grammar*. Cambridge: Cambridge University Press.

Grambank Consortium, eds. 2019. *Grambank*. Jena: Max Planck Institute for the Science of Human History. http://grambank.clld.org.

Hammarström, Harald, Robert Forkel, and Martin Haspelmath. 2019. *Glottolog 4.1*. Jena, Germany: Max Planck Institute for the Science of Human History. http://glottolog.org.

Harrington, Jan L. 2016. *Relational Database Design and Implementation*. 4th ed. Burlington, MA: Morgan Kaufmann.

Haspelmath, Martin, Matthew S. Dryer, David Gil, and Bernard Comrie. 2005. *The World Atlas of Language Structures*. Oxford: Oxford University Press.

Kroenke, David M., David Auer, Scott L. Vandenberg, and Robert C. Yoder. 2019. *Database Concepts*. 9th ed. New York: Pearson.

Mallinson, Graham, and Barry Blake. 1981. *Language Typology. Cross-Linguistic Studies in Syntax*. Amsterdam: North-Holland.

Nichols, Johanna. 1992. *Linguistic Diversity in Space and Time*. Chicago: University of Chicago Press.

Nichols, Johanna, and Balthasar Bickel. 2013a. Locus of marking in possessive noun phrases. In *The World Atlas of Language Structures Online*, ed. Matthew S. Dryer and Martin Haspelmath. Leipzig: Max Planck Institute for Evolutionary Anthropology. http://wals.info/chapter/24.

Nichols, Johanna, and Balthasar Bickel. 2013b. Locus of marking in the clause. In *The World Atlas of Language Structures Online*, ed. Matthew S. Dryer and Martin Haspelmath. Leipzig: Max Planck Institute for Evolutionary Anthropology. http://wals.info/chapter/23.

Nichols, Johanna, and Balthasar Bickel. 2013c. Locus of marking: Whole-language typology. In *The World Atlas of Language Structures Online*, ed. Matthew S. Dryer and Martin Haspelmath. Leipzig: Max Planck Institute for Evolutionary Anthropology. http://wals.info/chapter/25.

Nichols, Johanna, and Balthasar Bickel. 2013d. Possessive classification. In *The World Atlas of Language Structures Online*, ed. Matthew S. Dryer and Martin Haspelmath. Leipzig: Max Planck Institute for Evolutionary Anthropology. http://wals.info/chapter/59.

Olson, Michael L. 1981. Barai clause juncture: Toward a functional theory of inter-clausal relations. PhD dissertation, Australian National University.

Rießler, Michael. 2011. Typology and evolution of adjective attribution marking in the languages of Northern Eurasia. PhD dissertation, University of Leipzig.

Schiering, René, Balthasar Bickel, and Kristine A. Hildebrandt. 2010. The prosodic word is not universal, but emergent. *Journal of Linguistics* 46 (3): 657–709.

Schiering, René, Balthasar Bickel, and Kristine A. Hildebrandt. 2012. Stress-timed=word-based? Testing a hypothesis in prosodic typology. *STUF—Language Typology and Universals* 65 (2): 157–168.

Schmidtke-Bode, Karsten. 2009. *A Typology of Purpose Clauses*. Amsterdam: John Benjamins.

Schmidtke-Bode, Karsten, and Natalia Levshina. 2018. Reassessing scale effects on differential case marking: Methodological, conceptual and theoretical issues in the quest for a universal. In *Diachrony of Differential Argument Marking*, ed. Ilja A. Seržant and Alena Witzlack-Makarevich, 509–537. Berlin: Language Science Press.

Witzlack-Makarevich, Alena. 2011. Typological variations in grammatical relations. PhD dissertation, University of Leipzig.

Witzlack-Makarevich, Alena. 2019. Argument selectors. A new perspective on grammatical relations: An introduction. In *Argument Selectors: A New Perspective on Grammatical Relations*, ed. Alena Witzlack-Makarevich and Balthasar Bickel, 1–38. Amsterdam: John Benjamins.

Witzlack-Makarevich, Alena, and Balthasar Bickel, eds. 2019. *Argument Selectors: A New Perspective on Grammatical Relations*. Amsterdam: John Benjamins.

Witzlack-Makarevich, Alena, Taras Zakharko, Lennart Bierkandt, Fernando Zúñiga, and Balthasar Bickel. 2016. Decomposing hierarchical alignment: Co-arguments as conditions on alignment and the limits of referential hierarchies as explanations in verb agreement. *Linguistics* 54 (3): 531–561. https://doi.org/10.1515/ling-2016-0011.

Contributors

Hiroyuki Akama is an Associate Professor at the Institute of Liberal Arts and the School of Life Science and Technology, Tokyo Institute of Technology. With a philosophical background in language and cognitive science, he has been encompassing various areas of linguistics and interdisciplinary technologies with a focus on "semantic networks."

Juan Pablo Alperin is an Assistant Professor at the School of Publishing, an Associate Director of Research of the Public Knowledge Project, and the Co-director of the Scholarly Communications Lab, all at Simon Fraser University. He is a multidisciplinary scholar, with training in computer science, geography, and education who believes that research, especially when it is made freely available, has the potential to make meaningful and direct contributions to society.

Helene N. Andreassen is a Senior Research Librarian at University of Tromsø – The Arctic University of Norway (UiT), where she primarily works with education and research data management. She co-chairs the RDA Linguistics Data Interest Group and is one of the managers of the Tromsø Repository of Language and Linguistics (TROLLing). Helene holds a PhD in French Linguistics and her current research concentrates on L1 and L2 phonology.

Lynnette Arnold is an Assistant Professor in the Department of Anthropology at the University of Massachusetts, Amherst. She teaches classes in linguistic anthropology. Her ethnographic work focuses on language and migration in the Americas, and she also participates in activist efforts with the Language and Social Justice Committee of the Society for Linguistic Anthropology.

Christine Beier is an Assistant Adjunct Professor in the Department of Linguistics at the University of California, Berkeley, and co-founder of Cabeceras Aid Project. Her work focuses on the documentation, description, revitalization, and revalorization of endangered languages primarily in Peruvian Amazonia, linked to humanitarian work promoting the well-being of local participants.

Philippa Bell is an Associate Professor of Second Language Education at the Université du Québec à Montréal. Her research interests focus on the development of grammar through corpus research and the effects of different teaching approaches on the development of implicit and explicit knowledge in second language classrooms.

Andrea Berez-Kroeker is a Professor in the Department of Linguistics at the University of Hawai'i at Mānoa, where she teaches classes primarily in language documentation. She is active in the field of endangered language archiving and her research interests include morphology, discourse, and data sustainability for linguistics.

Balthasar Bickel is a Professor in the Department of Comparative Language Science at the University of Zurich and is the Director of the National Research Center Evolving Language. He uses experimental and data-science methods across languages and species to uncover the cultural and biological forces that shape language and vocal communication.

Claire Bowern is a Professor of Linguistics at Yale. Her research focus is historical linguistics and language documentation, especially of the Indigenous languages of Australia. Her work combines fieldwork with archival research. She is currently editor of the journal *Diachronica*.

Julie Brittain is a Professor of Linguistics at Memorial University of Newfoundland (Canada). Her work focuses on the syntax of Algonquian languages and on the acquisition of Cree as a first language. Since 2004 she has been director of the Chisasibi (Cree) Child Language Acquisition Study (https://www.mun.ca/cclas/).

Laura Buszard-Welcher is Director of Operations and The Long Now Library at The Long Now Foundation. Her research interests include endangered language documentation and description, language revitalization, language archiving, the future of human communication, and how it will be mediated by technology.

Robin Champieux is the Director of Digital Scholarship and Research Engagement at the Oregon Health and Science University, where she leads the library's scholarly communication and research data services. Her work and research are focused on enabling the creation, reproducibility, accessibility, and impact of digital scientific materials. She is the co-founder of the Metrics Toolkit and Awesome Libraries.

Heather L. Coates is the Digital Scholarship and Data Management Librarian at the Indiana University–Purdue University Indianapolis University Library Center for Digital Scholarship and the Indiana University Data Steward for Research Data. Her work in the library centers on supporting faculty success in research and career advancement. As an open research advocate, she cares deeply about the integrity, accessibility, and sustainability of the scholarly record as a public good. She is a co-founder of the Metrics Toolkit.

Laura Collins is Professor Emeritus of Applied Linguistics at Concordia University, Montreal (Canada). Her previous corpora projects, in collaboration with Concordia colleagues, examined spoken teacher input and pair-work interaction in foreign language classrooms. She is the Past President of the American Association for Applied Linguistics.

Lauren B. Collister is the Director of the Office of Scholarly Communication and Publishing at the University Library System, University of Pittsburgh. She holds a PhD in Sociolinguistics from her time researching language change in online discourse. Her current work covers publishing, copyright, author rights, and advocacy for open research.

Philipp Conzett is a Senior Research Librarian at UiT The Arctic University of Norway working with Digital Scholarship, especially Open Science and research data management. He is one of the managers of the Tromsø Repository of Language and Linguistics (TROLLing) and is currently doing research on word-formation and grammatical gender in Norwegian.

Rolando Coto-Solano is an Assistant Professor at Dartmouth College. His research includes Natural Language Processing for underresourced and Indigenous languages, language revitalization, and tonal phonetics. He has worked on revitalization projects in the Cook Islands, Mexico, Bolivia, and has also carried out research in languages from Costa Rica and Vietnam.

Christopher Cox is an Associate Professor in the School of Linguistics and Language Studies at Carleton University. His research centers on issues in language documentation, description, and revitalization, with particular focus on the development and application of language technology and linguistic corpora in these contexts.

Onno Crasborn is a Professor of Sign Language of the Netherlands (NGT) at Radboud University (the Netherlands). He works on the linguistic structure and use of this language and is the co-author of both an adult corpus of NGT and a longitudinal data set of sign language acquisition in the Netherlands.

Scott A. Crossley is a Professor of Applied Linguistics and Learning Sciences at Georgia State University. His primary research focus is on natural language processing and the application of computational tools and machine learning algorithms in language learning, writing, and text comprehensibility. His main interest area is the development and use of natural language processing tools in assessing writing quality and text difficulty.

Anne Cutler is a Distinguished Professor at the MARCS Institute, Western Sydney University (Australia); previously she was Director at the Max Planck Institute for Psycholinguistics

in Nijmegen (the Netherlands), where she headed the Comprehension Group to which her co-authors here also belonged. Her research concerns how language-specific structure constrains speech decoding processes.

Don Daniels is an Assistant Professor of Linguistics at the University of Oregon. His research focuses on historical linguistics and morphosyntax, and he conducts fieldwork in Papua New Guinea.

Kelsey Daniels is an English as Second Language instructor at Lane Community College and a doctoral student in Higher Education Leadership and Policy at Vanderbilt University. Her professional interests include college students' academic preparation, enrollment, persistence, and attainment, and she conducts linguistic fieldwork in Papua New Guinea.

Judith Degen is an Assistant Professor of Linguistics at Stanford University. Her research interests lie in the cognitive science of meaning: she works in experimental and computational semantics and pragmatics on phenomena that include implicature and reference.

Katherine Demuth is a Distinguished Professor of Linguistics and Director of the Child Language Lab at Macquarie University in Sydney (Australia). Her work has focused on children's language development (phonology, morphology, syntax) and language processing abilities using a wide range of methods (corpus analysis, behavioral, and neural experiments such as production, perception/comprehension/eye tracking, electroencephalograph).

Koenraad De Smedt is a Professor of Computational Linguistics at the University of Bergen (Norway), where he teaches natural language processing. His current research interests are in corpus linguistics and grammar. Since 2008 he has been National Coordinator for Norway in CLARIN (the European Research Infrastructure for Language Resources and Technology).

Philip T. Duncan is an Assistant Teaching Professor in Linguistics at the University of Kansas. His research focuses on syntax and its interfaces with semantics and morphology, specifically working with languages of the Americas (Me'phaa, Kaqchikel, Kiksht) and West Africa (Ibibio, Ikpana).

Mirjam Ernestus is a Professor of Psycholinguistics and Director of the Centre for Language Studies at Radboud University (the Netherlands). Her research focuses on how speakers produce and listeners understand informal conversational speech, where reduced pronunciation variants contain fewer phonemes and even syllables than are postulated in canonical forms.

Charlie Farrington is a Digital Specialist in the Department of English at North Carolina State University and a Courtesy Research Associate in the Department of Linguistics at the University of Oregon. His current research focuses on the regional development of African American Language varieties, focusing on consonantal features.

Ben Foley is Project Manager of the Centre of Excellence for the Dynamics of Language's Transcription Acceleration Project, bringing cutting-edge language technology within reach of people working with some of the world's oldest languages. Ben's previous experience with Aboriginal language resource development has resulted in apps and websites galore, including Iltyem-Iltyem sign site and Gambay First Languages Map.

Robert Forkel is a Scientific Programmer at the Max Planck Institute for Evolutionary Anthropology in Leipzig (Germany). Since putting the World Atlas of Language Structures online in 2008, he has been tasked with curating a number of cross-linguistic databases. This background provided motivation and expertise for leading the Cross-Linguistic Data Formats (CLDF) initiative for the standardization of crosslinguistic data.

Valerie Fridland is a Professor of Linguistics in the English Department at University of Nevada, Reno, specializing in sociolinguistics. Her recent research investigates variation in vowel production and vowel perception across dialects in the Northern, Southern, and Western United States, exploring links between social factors and speech processing.

Volker Gast is a Professor of English Linguistics at the University of Jena. His current research interests are mainly in linguistic typology and language documentation. He has been involved in several typological database projects and is working on the multilevel annotation of texts from typologically diverse languages.

Lauren Gawne is a Senior Lecturer at La Trobe University. Her research focuses on the documentation of Tibeto-Burman languages, with specialization in evidentiality, gesture, and critical approaches to language documentation.

Jeff Good is a Professor in the Department of Linguistics at the University at Buffalo. His research interests include morpho-syntactic typology, language documentation, and comparative Niger-Congo linguistics. His documentary work focuses on endangered languages of the Lower Fungom region of Cameroon and includes significant interdisciplinary data collection components.

James Grama is a Postdoctoral Fellow in the Sociolinguistics Lab in the Department of Anglophone Studies at the University of Duisburg-Essen, specializing in sociophonetics. His research focuses on variation and change in English dialects, English-based creoles, as well as underdocumented languages.

Russell D. Gray is the Director of the Department of Linguistic and Cultural Evolution at the Max Planck Institute for Evolutionary Anthropology in Leipzig (Germany) and holds adjunct positions in the School of Psychology at the University of Auckland and the Department of Philosophy at the Australian National University. He helped pioneer the application of computational evolutionary methods to linguistic and cultural evolution, focusing on Southeast Asia and the Pacific.

Simon J. Greenhill is a Senior Scientist in the Department of Linguistic and Cultural Evolution at the Max Planck Institute for Evolutionary Anthropology in Leipzig (Germany)

and the Australian Research Council Centre of Excellence for the Dynamics of Language at Australian National University. His research focuses on language diversity and what it tells us about human prehistory, mainly using Bayesian phylogenetic methods.

Vera Gribanova is an Associate Professor in the Linguistics Department at Stanford University. Her research in theoretical syntax and morphosyntax focuses on ellipsis and the mapping between phonological and morphosyntactic structures. Her empirical focus is on Russian (Slavic) and Uzbek (Turkic), an underinvestigated language of Central Asia.

Stefan Th. Gries is a Professor of Linguistics at University of California, Santa Barbara and a 25% Chair of English Corpus Linguistics at the Justus Liebig University Giessen. His research is on quantitative corpus linguistics, cognitive linguistics/construction grammar, and psycholinguistics.

Cristina Guardiano is a Professor of Linguistics at the Università di Modena e Reggio Emilia. She works in the fields of historical linguistics, formal comparative syntax, Romance and Greek dialectology, with research reaching into Indo-European historical syntax, parametric comparison, and the morphosyntactic structure of the nominal domain.

Kathleen Currie Hall is an Associate Professor in the Department of Linguistics at the University of British Columbia. Her research focuses on answering questions in theoretical phonology, especially about phonological relationships, using techniques from a wide variety of areas, including experimental phonetics, psycholinguistics, corpus linguistics, sociolinguistics, and information theory.

Na-Rae Han is a Senior Lecturer in the Department of Linguistics at the University of Pittsburgh, where she teaches computational linguistics and data science methods. She participated in multiple linguistic data and annotation projects throughout her career, many of which were published by the Linguistic Data Consortium.

Kristine A. Hildebrandt is a Professor in the Department of English Language and Literature at Southern Illinois University, Edwardsville. She is also the co-founder and Co-director of the Interdisciplinary Research and Informatics Scholarship Center there. She works on language documentation, typology, and phonetics and phonological analysis of Tibeto-Burman languages.

Brittany Hoback is a Linguistics Doctoral Candidate at Victoria University of Wellington. Her research focuses on community language maintenance and documentation in Southeast Malekula, Vanuatu. This includes a Denggan grammar sketch and documentation of sociolinguistic language use and attitude change during the creation of a Denggan writing system.

Julie A. Hochgesang is an Associate Professor in the Department of Linguistics at Gallaudet University. Her research interests include phonetics and phonology of signed languages and language documentation/corpus linguistics of signed languages, particularly American Sign Language. She is primarily responsible for the maintenance of the ASL Signbank.

Elliott M. Hoey is an Assistant Professor at Vrije Universiteit Amterdam. He uses conversation analysis to examine how language and other conduct are used in real social interactions.

Gary Holton is a Professor of Linguistics at the University of Hawai'i at Mānoa, where he teaches courses in documentary linguistics and biocultural diversity. His research focuses on the diversity of linguistic and cultural knowledge systems, employing interdisciplinary, community-based approaches to language maintenance and language documentation.

Lynn Hou is an Assistant Professor in the Department of Linguistics at University of California, Santa Barbara. Her research interests encompass documentary and descriptive linguistics with an emphasis on usage-based linguistics and child language acquisition of sign languages.

Laura A. Janda is a Professor of Russian Linguistics at UiT The Arctic University of Norway. She is a member of the Norwegian Academy of Science and Letters and past President of the International Cognitive Linguistics Association.

Łukasz Jędrzejowski is a Postdoctoral Researcher at the University of Cologne (Department of German Language and Literature I–Linguistics). His research interests include comparative syntax, semantics, and the syntax-semantics interface. The linguistic phenomena he has recently worked on include subordinate clauses and habituality.

Caspar Jordan is a linguistics PhD student at Uppsala University and former Research Data Advisor at the Swedish National Data Service. He holds an MA in Language Documentation and Description from the School of Oriental and African Studies in London.

Jason Kandybowicz is an Associate Professor of Linguistics at the Graduate Center, City University of New York. He specializes in syntactic theory, syntactic documentation, and the syntax-phonology interface. His fieldwork focuses on the Niger-Congo languages of West Africa, in particular, those spoken in Nigeria and Ghana.

Tyler Kendall is a Professor of Linguistics at the University of Oregon. He works on the corpus-based and sociophonetic study of language variation and change and has developed several software programs for archiving and analyzing sociolinguistic data.

Eve Koller is an Assistant Professor at Brigham Young University Hawai'i. She holds a PhD in Linguistics from the University of Hawai'i at Mānoa. Her research interests include historical linguistics, language typology, morphology, writing systems, and language documentation and reclamation.

Hilda Koopman is a Distinguished Professor at the Department of Linguistics at University of California, Los Angeles. Her theoretical interests include theoretical syntax and morphology and comparative syntax. She has published on a wide range of topics covering many diverse languages.

Susan Smythe Kung, PhD, is the Manager of the Archive of the Indigenous Languages of Latin America at the University of Texas at Austin, as well as a documentary linguist. She is internationally engaged in the formulation of best practices for organizing, archiving, sharing, and citing language documentation data.

Kristopher Kyle is an Assistant Professor in the Department of Linguistics at the University of Oregon. His research interests include corpus linguistics, second language writing, computational linguistics, second language assessment, and second language development.

Michelle La is a graduate student in the Department of Sociology and Anthropology and a Research Assistant with the Scholarly Communications Lab at Simon Fraser University. She is an advocate for untraditional forms of research communication. Her research interests include economic anthropology and open scholarship.

Nala H. Lee is an Assistant Professor of Linguistics at the National University of Singapore. Her research focuses on the structural and sociological features of creoles and language endangerment, especially with regard to how levels of endangerment are assessed.

Wesley Y. Leonard is an Associate Professor in the Department of Ethnic Studies at the University of California, Riverside. As a linguist and activist in language reclamation efforts, he works to build capacity for Native American communities engaged in language continuance.

Ryan Lepic is an Assistant Professor in the Department of Linguistics at Gallaudet University. He is interested in how languages change as a result of how they are used and in ideologies about the relationship between sign language and co-speech gesture.

Johann-Mattis List is a Senior Scientist at the Department of Linguistics and Cultural Evolution of the Max Planck Institute for the Science of Human History. His research is devoted to computer-assisted approaches in historical linguistics, which help to bridge the gap between classical and computational approaches.

Roger Yu-Hsiang Lo is a PhD Candidate in the Department of Linguistics at the University of British Columbia. His research focuses on the link between speech production and perception, primarily using corpus data and experimental approaches.

Matthew Lou-Magnuson is a Software Engineer with Base2 Solutions, Bellevue, Washington. He holds a PhD in Linguistics and Multilingual Studies from Nanyang Technological University (Singapore). His research focuses on computational methods in language learning and historical linguistics, specifically on morphological and typological language change.

Megan Lukaniec is an Assistant Professor of Indigenous Language Revitalization in the Indigenous Studies Program at the

University of Victoria. She is active in community-based Wendat language reclamation, and her research interests include Iroquoian linguistics, morphology, discourse, language contact, and language change.

Rachel Macdonald is a Postdoctoral Researcher in the Department of English Language and Linguistics at the University of Glasgow. Her current research focuses on using speech corpora to examine sociophonetics and sound change across dialects of English.

J. Scott Mackie holds a PhD from the University of British Columbia, where he was also a Postdoctoral Fellow working on the development of computational tools for linguistic research. He now works in industry, in the area of natural language understanding and voice assistants.

Travis Major is a PhD Candidate in the Department of Linguistics at the University of California, Los Angeles. His research involves developing a symbiotic relationship between careful linguistic description and advancing linguistic theory. His theoretical interests are centered on syntax and its interfaces with semantics/pragmatics and prosody/intonation.

Emma Marsden is a Professor of Applied Linguistics at the University of York (United Kingdom). Her research interests include the learning and teaching of grammar in a second language, language processing, measuring language knowledge, and classroom interventions. She has led several open science initiatives in the field for sharing materials and data (Instruments for Research into Second Languages [IRIS]), findings (Open Accessible Summaries in Language Studies [OASIS]), and research-informed educational resources (The National Centre for Excellence for Language Pedagogy [NCELP]). She is currently the journal editor of *Language Learning*.

Eleanor "Nora" Mattern is a Teaching Assistant Professor at the University of Pittsburgh's School of Computing and Information. Her research interests are in the areas of information policy, archives, government information practices and systems, and digital curation.

Michael McAuliffe has a PhD from University of British Columbia and was a Postdoctoral Fellow in Linguistics at McGill University (Canada), where he developed software tools for phonetic research and large speech corpora. He now works in industry on natural language understanding for voice assistants.

Bradley McDonnell is an Assistant Professor in the Department of Linguistics at the University of Hawai'i at Mānoa. His specializations include documentary linguistics, Austronesian languages, interactional linguistics, and usage-based linguistics. He is also interested in improving data management workflows for reproducible research in linguistics.

Erin C. McKiernan is a Professor in the Department of Physics, Biomedical Physics program at the National Autonomous University of Mexico in Mexico City. She is a researcher in experimental and computational biophysics and neurophysiology,

and an advocate for open access, open data, and open research. She is the founder of the "Why Open Research?" project (http://whyopenresearch.org/), an educational site for researchers to learn how to share their work.

Lev Michael is a Professor in the Department of Linguistics at the University of California, Berkeley. His research explores the ways that social and cultural processes shape language and is methodologically grounded in language documentation and description, language typology, and historical and contact linguistics.

Steven Moran is an Assistant Professor in the Institute of Biology at the University of Neuchâtel. His research focuses on the evolution of human speech and the phonological system, quantitative approaches to linguistic diversity, and aspects of language ontogeny from a crosslinguistic perspective.

Sally Akevai Nicholas is a lecturer in Linguistics at Massey University (New Zealand). Her research focuses on the description, documentation, and revitalization of her ancestral language: Cook Islands Māori. To that end, she is working on a range of NLP projects aimed at enhancing the description of endangered languages.

Johanna Nichols is a Professor Emeritus in the Department of Slavic Languages, University of California, Berkeley, and currently a Research Supervisor in the Higher School of Economics, Moscow, and a recent Helsinki University Humanities Visiting Professor, University of Helsinki. She works on typology, historical linguistics, linguistic geography, Slavic, and Nakh-Daghestanian.

Meredith T. Niles is an Assistant Professor of Food Systems and Policy at The University of Vermont. She studies food systems and the environment from the perspective of people, behaviors, and policies. She is an advocate for open research and science through her work on the board of the Public Library of Science and through research exploring faculty perceptions and behaviors related to open science. She is passionate about making research more publicly available to maximize the benefits of science for society.

Luca Onnis is Co-founder of the Laboratory of Social and Language Psychology at the Università degli Studi di Genova (Italy). He studies basic mechanisms of human learning, with a view to explaining how language emerges both in individuals and societies. He combines experimental methods including behavioral, computational, and brain imaging.

Nick Palfreyman is a Reader in Sign Languages and Deaf Studies and Co-director of the International Institute for Sign Languages and Deaf Studies at the University of Central Lancashire. He has worked with the Indonesian deaf community since 2007 and conducts research on sociolinguistics and cross-modal language typology.

Malin Petzell is a Senior Lecturer in African Languages at the Department of Languages and Literatures, University of

Gothenburg. Her research interests include language description (documentation and analysis), Bantu languages, nominal and verbal morphology, aspectual classification, and field methods.

Shana Poplack is Distinguished University Professor and Canada Research Chair in Linguistics at the University of Ottawa. She founded and continues to direct the Sociolinguistics Laboratory, repository of numerous spoken-language corpora, all constructed by her and her team. These have served as the basis for a wide variety of influential studies on language contact, variation, and change.

Peter L. Pulsifer is a Research Scientist at the National Snow and Ice Data Center. His interests include data management and sharing protocols, traditional and community-based knowledge, and web-based mapping technologies.

Chase Wesley Raymond is an Associate Professor of Linguistics at the University of Colorado, Boulder. His interests lie at the intersection of language and social identity, in both ordinary and institutional interaction, with an emphasis on grammar. Recent publications include articles in Language in Society and the Journal of Sociolinguistics.

Yvan Rose is a Professor of Linguistics at Memorial University (Canada). He focuses on the integration of perceptual, acoustic, and articulatory factors within models of phonology and acquisition. Spearheading the development of Phon (https://www.phon.ca), he is Co-director of PhonBank, a web-accessible database documenting phonological development and speech disorders across different languages and speaker populations (https://phonbank.talkbank.org).

Victoria Rosén is an Associate Professor of Linguistics at the University of Bergen (Norway). She has worked on syntax, Vietnamese, Lexical-Functional Grammar, treebanks, multiword expressions, and language technology. From 2010 she has led the treebanking infrastructure INESS (Infrastructure for the Exploration of Syntax and Semantics).

Christoph Rzymski is a Scientific Programmer at the Max Planck Institute for Evolutionary Anthropology in Leipzig (Germany). He is interested in research infrastructure and the development of tools for scientific projects.

Nay San is a PhD candidate in Linguistics at Stanford University and is interested in leveraging computational methods for the documentation and linguistic analysis of endangered languages, particularly of those in Australia. Before Stanford, he worked on describing vowel variation in Kaytetye and automating data processing tasks for producing a dictionary of Warlpiri.

Kevin P. Scannell is a Professor in the Department of Computer Science at Saint Louis University. His main interest is the development of technology that helps speakers of Indigenous and minority languages use their language online, with a particular focus on Irish and the other Celtic languages.

Lesley A. Schimanski is a Psychology Instructor and Research Associate in the Scholarly Communications Lab at Simon Fraser University. She enjoys applying her research methodology expertise to interdisciplinary fields of study and is passionate about helping others to access and understand scholarly works that can have a positive real-world impact.

Morgan Sonderegger is an Associate Professor of Linguistics at McGill University (Canada). He works on variation and change, phonology, and phonetics, primarily using corpus data and quantitative methods, as well as software for speech database management and automated speech analysis.

Jane Stuart-Smith is a Professor of Phonetics and Sociolinguistics at the University of Glasgow. Her research interests include sociophonetics, especially relating to sound change and social identities, working with a range of spoken sociolinguistic data sets of different sizes, from small (specific socio-dialects) to current large-scale work across English dialects.

Suzy Styles is a Developmental Psycholinguist trained in Linguistics, Asian Studies, and Experimental Psychology. She researches sensory systems in language processing and bilingualism at Nanyang Technological University in multilingual Singapore, where she established the BLIP Lab to investigate Brain, Language and Intersensory Processing.

Gregorio Tiburcio Cano is a Supervisor of Bilingual Indigenous Education in the Office of the Secretary of Education of Guerrero, Mexico. He has a Master's degree from the Center for Research and Higher Studies in Social Anthropology, where he worked on the verbal morphology of his language, Me'phaa Vátháá.

Judith Tonhauser is a Professor in the Department of Linguistics at the University of Stuttgart. She conducts research in semantics and pragmatics with an empirical focus on Paraguayan Guaraní and English.

Harold Torrence is an Associate Professor of Linguistics at the University of California, Los Angeles. His research focuses on the morphosyntax of complementation, interrogatives, and relative clauses in West African and Meso-American languages.

Tiago Tresoldi is a Postdoctoral Researcher at the Max Planck Institute for Evolutionary Anthropology in Leipzig (Germany). His main research interest is the human language, from its aesthetic uses to computational methods of investigation of its history.

Rory Turnbull is a Lecturer in Phonetics and Phonology at Newcastle University. His research interests lie at the intersection of phonetics, phonology, and psycholinguistics and involve a variety of methodologies.

Daan van Esch is a Technical Program Manager with Google in Amsterdam, the Netherlands. His research interests include speech processing, natural-language processing, and developing scalable ways to bring language technology to as many languages as possible. He is also interested in how machine learning can help accelerate language documentation work.

Matthew Wagers is a Professor of Linguistics at the University of California, Santa Cruz. His research focus is language processing, especially the processing of syntactic information and its representation in memory.

Natasha Warner is a Professor in the Department of Linguistics at the University of Arizona. Her research focuses on the phonetics of reduced, conversational speech, and on revitalization of the Mutsun language (a Costanoan language of California).

Andrea Weber is a Professor of English Linguistics and Chair of Psycholinguistics and Applied Language Sciences at the University of Tübingen (Germany). Her research focuses on how our experience with languages shapes our perception of language, in particular how we learn the sounds and words of our native and non-native languages and store and access them when needed for language use.

Erin Wilkinson is an Associate Professor in the Department of Linguistics at the University of New Mexico. Her research interests include bilingualism in signing populations, language change and variation in signed languages, and signed language typology.

Bodo Winter is a Senior Lecturer in Cognitive Linguistics at the University of Birmingham (United Kingdom) and a UK Research and Innovation Future Leaders Fellow. His work combines corpus linguistics with experiments to study iconicity, gesture, metaphor, and perceptual language.

Alena Witzlack-Makarevich is a Senior Lecturer in the Department of Linguistics at the Hebrew University of Jerusalem. Her research focuses on linguistic typology and morphosyntax. She has also been working on language documentation and description of Khoekhoe (Khow-Kwadi), Nǁng (Tuu), as well as Ruuli (East Bantu).

Taras Zakharko is a Scientific Programmer at the Department of Comparative Language Science, University of Zurich. He develops methods and tools for linguistic databases.

Index